T0408770

WORKS ISSUED BY
THE HAKLUYT SOCIETY

THE VOYAGE OF CAPTAIN JOHN NARBROUGH TO THE STRAIT OF MAGELLAN AND THE SOUTH SEA IN HIS MAJESTY'S SHIP *SWEEPSTAKES*, 1669–1671

THIRD SERIES
NO. 33

INTERNATIONAL REPRESENTATIVES OF THE HAKLUYT SOCIETY

The *Sweepstakes* off El Morrión in the Strait of Magellan, 13 November 1670,
by Mark Myers.

THE VOYAGE
OF
CAPTAIN JOHN NARBROUGH

TO THE STRAIT OF MAGELLAN AND THE SOUTH SEA IN HIS MAJESTY'S SHIP *SWEEPSTAKES* 1669–1671

Edited by
RICHARD J. CAMPBELL
with
PETER T. BRADLEY
and
JOYCE LORIMER

Published by
Routledge
for
THE HAKLUYT SOCIETY
LONDON
2018

First published 2018 for the Hakluyt Society by
Routledge
2 Park Square, Milton Park, Abingdon, Oxon OX14 4RN

and by Routledge
711 Third Avenue, New York, NY 10017

Routledge is an imprint of the Taylor & Francis Group, an informa business

British Library Cataloguing-in-Publication Data
A catalogue record for this book is available from the British Library

Library of Congress Cataloging-in-Publication Data
A catalog record for this book has been requested

ISBN: 978-1-908145-20-8 (hbk)
ISBN: 978-1-351-16856-4 (ebk)

Typeset in Garamond Premier Pro
by Waveney Typesetters, Wymondham, Norfolk

Routledge website: http://www.routledge.com
Hakuyt Society website: http://www.hakluyt.com

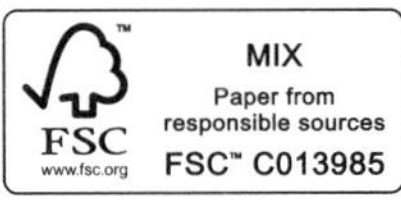

Printed in the United Kingdom
by Henry Ling Limited

For Alec

CONTENTS

LIST OF MAPS AND ILLUSTRATIONS

Maps

Colour Plates

Figures

PREFACE AND ACKNOWLEDGEMENTS

I wish to express my gratitude to a number of libraries and archives who have facilitated my access to manuscripts which appear in this volume. The Trustees of the British Library allowed me to publish the manuscripts of Captain Narbrough's and Lieutenant Peckett's journals, as well as images from Narbrough's charts and extracts from Captain John Wood's journal. The Bodleian Library permitted the publication of their version of Narbrough's journal. The Royal Society's archives fursished me with Richard Williams's 'short accompt', and the Beinecke Rare Book and Manuscript Library, Yale University, provided me with a copy of William Chambers's journal from the James Marshall and Marie-Louise Collection. The United Kingdom Hydrographic Office has allowed me to publish extracts from the Sailing Directions for South America, and the extracts from the journals of the First Earl of Sandwich are printed here with the permission of the present Earl of Sandwich. I would also like to thank the staff at the British Library, the National Archive, the Somerset Heritage Centre, the Taunton Public Library, and the United Kingdom Hydrographic Office, all of whom have been most helpful.

I am also grateful to David Davies, Richard Dunn, Peter Barber and Glyndwr Williams who all read through sections of the Introduction and saved me from a number of errors and inadequacies. The Hakluyt Society provided an editorial committee comprised of Gloria Clifton, Joyce Lorimer, Peter Barber, Margaret Deacon, Anthony Payne, Catherine Scheybeler and Glyndwr Williams whose members advised me on various matters for which I am duly grateful. In particular I would like to recognize Peter Barber for his assistance with Narbrough's original manuscript and charts, and Catherine Scheybeler for doing some research in the Spanish Archives for me. In addition I have had help from Bruce Barker-Benfield, Michael Barritt, Patricia Buckingham, Michael Carter, Andrew David, Phillipa Grimstone, John Hudson, Frank Reed, Adrian Webb and Peter Whithead, to all of whom I extend my gratitude.

Peter Bradley has generously shared his expert knowledge on the Spanish documentary record and secondary sources of Narbrough's enterprise. He has contributed two sections to the Introduction: on the fate of the detainees in Valdivia, and on the Spanish reaction to Narbrough's voyage.

I am particularly appreciative of the help I have had from Joyce Lorimer, who has made a major contribution to this volume as assigned series editor for the Hakluyt Society. In addition to that responsibility, she has located and translated various Spanish documents; checked the translation of others; provided me with the sections in the Introduction on the comparison of British Library Add. MS. 88980 A with the Bodleian Library MS. Rawl. A 318, Narbrough's interaction with the Indigenous Peoples, and on new material relating to the identity of Don Carlos; as well as patiently helping me in numerous other ways.

I would add my apologies to anyone whom I ought to have mentioned, but have failed to do so, and add that I am no less grateful for their help.

Richard J. Campbell

Published with financial assistance from the
American Friends of the Hakluyt Society

LIST OF ABBREVIATIONS

AGI	Archivo General de Indias (Seville)
BAE	Biblioteca de Autores Españoles
BL	British Library
BN	Biblioteca Nacional
CSPD	Calendar of State Papers Domestic
JHSE	Jewish Historical Society of England
ODNB	*Oxford Dictionary of National Biography*
NOED	*New Oxford English Dictionary*
TNA	The National Archives

NOTE ON MEASUREMENT OF LENGTH AND ON CURRENCY

Lengths

In the sixteenth century the only distance-measuring instrument available to mariners was the log line, calibrated using a rule, in fathoms of 6 feet, and used for measuring the depth of water. All other offshore distances were estimated by eye, at which mariners became quite adept. It was possible to obtain a reasonably accurate distance to the horizon, and this could be used to judge distances offshore.

Cable's Length

The cables required by a Busse (a 70 ton fishing vessel), in 1615, were 100 fathoms long.[1] Samuel Pepys's *White Book* for 8 March 1664/5 concerning Boatswains' practices in abuse of cables records 'few that go out 100 or 110 fathoms coming home more than 70 or 80', and under 24 May (1669) makes mention of a cable of 10 inches and 120 fathoms.[2] The entry in Falconer's *Universal Dictionary*, 1769, states that 'All cables ought to be 120 fathoms in length'.[3] In *The Sailor's Word-book*, 1867, that a 'measure of about 100 fathoms [600 feet], by which the distances of ships in a fleet are frequently estimated. ... In all marine charts a cable is deemed 607.56 feet, or one-tenth of a sea mile. In rope-making the cable varies from 100 to 115 fathoms.'[4] While it is not possible to give a definite figure for the length Narbrough used, it would seem that it was probably of the order of 600 feet.

Mile, League, Degree

The modern accepted international length of a sea mile is 1,852 metres (about 6,076 feet). In the sixteenth and seventeenth centuries the degree was considered to contain 60 miles or 20 leagues (the English league being 3 miles). William Bourne (1535–82), considered the English league to be 2,500 fathom in 1574, or 5,000 feet to the mile.[5] Richard Norwood (1590–1675) gives the same figure as the accepted length,[6] but goes on to say that he conducted experiments, 1633 to 1635, by observing the sun's altitude in York and London[7] and measuring the distance between and found that the length

[1] E.S., *Britaines Busse*, 7th page (pages not numbered).

[2] Latham, *Samuel Pepys*, pp. 113 and 9.218.

[3] Falconer, *Universal Marine Dictionary*.

[4] Smyth, *Sailor's Word-book*, p. 151.

[5] Taylor, *A Regiment*, p. 238.

[6] Norwood, *Seaman's Practice*, pp. 1, 2, 7, 48.

[7] Depending on the figure of the earth used, the modern value in the mean latitude between London and York is about 365,075 feet.

of a degree was 367,200 feet (lacking 4 feet which he regarded not). He confessed the experiment was not as exact as was requisite[1] and, having shown that the correct distance between the marks on the logline for a half-minute glass was therefore 51 feet, went on to advocate using 360,000 feet to the degree, since the ship's way was commonly greater than the log indicated, and 'every Man desires to have his Reckoning something before his ship, that he fall not with a Place unexpected',[2] reaching land before he anticipated. This would mean that the log should be marked every 50 feet so that the passage of a knot in half a minute would indicate a speed of one knot. (The sixteenth-century logline had been knotted every 42 feet.[3]) Phipps, in 1773 in his voyage towards the North Pole, was still vexed by the problem, and says that in 1570 the log was invariably marked at 42 feet intervals to 30 seconds and in the reign of Charles II seamen having found the old log not to answer had shortened the glass to 25 seconds, which was equal to a line marked at 50 feet intervals with a 30 second glass.[4] Narbrough makes no mention of the log he used; it may have been knotted at 42 feet intervals with a 25 second glass or 50 feet intervals with a 30 second glass, both of which would have given similar results. Narbrough does not state what length of degree he used, but in view of the general agreement between his astronomical latitude determinations and those obtained by account it would seem he was probably using Norwood's figure of 360,000 feet to the degree. It is also possible that he was, like Captain James on his voyage to discover the North West Passage in 1631, using Snellius's figure. The latter stated 'I caus'd many small Glasses to be made, whose Part of Time I knew to a most insensible Thing, and so divided and appropriated the Log-line to them; making use of *Wilibrodus's* and *Snellius's* Numbers of Feet answering to a Degree, and approv'd by Master Gunter.'[5]

Bow Shot

In October 2002 a trial was carried out to assess the effectiveness of the longbow as a weapon of war. The trial used a replica of a long bow from the *Mary Rose* and arrows of various weights. The mean range of fifteen shots was 293½ yards, with the six shots from light arrows averaging over 330 yards. The spread was from 357½ to 249 yards. It would seem therefore that about 300 yards would be a reasonable figure to accept for the distance intended by Narbrough.

Musket Shot

Reckoned to be a distance of 400 yards but the effective range of a smooth bore musket firing a one ounce ball with good effect was about 250 yards.[6]

[1] Ibid., p. 7.

[2] Ibid., p. 48.

[3] Taylor, *Regiment*, p. 128.

[4] Phipps conducted experiments using lines marked every 45 feet, 49 feet and 51 feet, together with a Log by Bouguer and mechanical logs by Russell and Foxon. See Phipps, *Voyage*, pp. 87–98.

[5] James, *Dangerous Voyage*, p. 129. Willibrod Snellius (1580–1626) measured the length of a degree between Alkmar and Bergeb op Zoom and Alkmar and Leiden by triangulation, starting in 1615, and came up with a mean value of 28,500 Rhynland perches (also known as Rhynland roods), which approximates to 107,370 metres or 352,263 feet. Smith, *From Plane*, pp. 64–6.

[6] Smyth, *Sailor's Word-book*, p. 489.

Gun Shot
In *The Sailor's Word-book*, 1867, Smyth states that 'Formerly the distance up to which a gun would throw a shot direct to its mark, without added elevation, ... was about 800 yards.'[1]

Currency

English
In 1670 the money of account in use in England was pounds (£), shillings (s) and pence (d), halfpennies and farthings. 4 farthings or 2 halfpennies = 1d, 12d = 1s, 20s = £1 (modern currency 100p = £1). A farm labourer's wage in 1670 was about 10½d per day or 5s 3d per six-day week (26·25p), which is approximately equal to £47·75 per week at the present day.

Groat — worth 4d.
Guinea — worth 20s. The gold guinea was first introduced in 1663. The value fluctuated reaching 30s in 1695. It was fixed at 21s in 1717.
Jacobus: — a gold coin issued by James I in 1603, initially called a Sovereign and valued at 20s. In 1604 a second issue, slightly lighter, was produced called a Unite. In 1604 the value of the Sovereign rose to 22s and in 1612 to 24s when the value of the Unite was fixed at 22s.

Spain and the Spanish Empire in the Americas
maravedi: — the least monetary unit of account. 34 *maravedi* = 1 *real.*
real: — a silver coin.
peso: — a silver coin, 8 *reales* = 1 *peso de ocho* or piece of eight was valued at 4s 8d in English currency. 4 *pesos* = 1 *doblon*

Portugal and Brazil, Madeira, the Açores and Cape Verde Islands
real, pl. réis — the smallest coin minted in this period was the copper 1½ *réis*. The 1 *milréis* = 1,000 *réis*, written 1$000. In the 1670s the *milréis* was worth about 81s 85d.

[1] Ibid., p. 358.

INTRODUCTION

In 2009, the British Library launched a successful public appeal for donations to enable it to purchase a manuscript volume written by Captain John Narbrough.[1] A note on the first page of the manuscript indicates that he acquired the blank volume on 7 April 1666, and states it is 'his Booke'. It contains the logs of his naval service in the Caribbean 1666–8 and his voyage through the Strait of Magellan to Chile, which was carried out as a result of a proposal made by one Don Carlos Enriques to the King, as well as copies of his commissions, instructions and correspondence relating to them, together with his instructions to the commander appointed to accompany him on his 1669 voyage.[2] His record of his 1669–71 voyage, here transcribed and made available in print for the first time, records Narbrough's careful survey and delineation of part of the coast of Patagonia and the Strait of Magellan, and of his voyage along the Chilean coast as far north as Valdivia, accompanied by three manuscript charts and one printed chart. Printed with it here are the full transcript of a previous partially published fair copy of a portion of the journal running from 13 October 1669 to 9 January 1671,[3] and three journals of men who served in the expedition. Also included are Portuguese and Spanish State Papers and Colonial Office documents recently discovered in The National Archive, Kew which clarify when and how Don Carlos Enriquez arrived at the court of Charles II and provide the sequence of proposals which he made to the King and his ministers.[4] Entries in the journal of Edward Montague, 1st Earl of Sandwich cast further light on these interchanges.[5] Spanish State Papers held by the British Library reveal that a copy of Don Carlos's testimony to authorities in Chile in January 1671 was subsequently forwarded to James Duke of York by an informant in Spain.[6] All of these accounts, together with the images of Narbrough's manuscript charts and those subsequently published from them, and with the information from the journal and Sailing Directions of John Wood which were subsequently partially published,[7] and which are referred to, constitute the fullest known account, written and cartographical, of the venture and allow for a clearer appreciation of Narbrough's abilities as a commander, navigator and hydrographic surveyor. Previously characterized by nineteenth- and twentieth-century scholars as 'weak'

[1] Later Sir John Narbrough (Narborough). The purchase was made in 2010.

[2] Now BL, Add MS 88980 A.

[3] Narborough, 'Voyage to the South-Sea', published in *An Account of Several Late Voyages and Discoveries to the South and North ...*, 1694 and 1711. See below, p. 14.

[4] TNA, CO1/33, No. 103c, ff. 245r–252v, 253r–264v; No. 103d, ff. 265–268v; No. 103f, ff. 271r–272v. SP89/10, ff. 94r–v, 96r–v; SP94/54, ff. 184r–191v; SP94/55, ff. 13r–47v, 50r–51v.

[5] Journal of 1st Earl of Sandwich, vol. 9, pp. 265–6; vol. 10, p. 262; currently in the archive of the 11th Earl of Sandwich at Mapperton in Dorset.

[6] BL, Add MS 21539, ff. 16r–23v; 28457, ff. 2r–22r.

[7] Published by William Hack[e], 1699, *A Collection.*

and 'inexperienced'[1] and his voyage as 'discreditable'[2] and having 'failed miserably',[3] the fuller record here provided shows him to have been an efficient and distinguished officer, charged with an ambiguous and difficult mission, overtly directed to explore the Patagonian coastline and ascertain the practicalities of peaceful trade with the natives, but undoubtedly also expected to ascertain the Spanish strength in the area and the potential for the incursion of the English into the Spanish gold trade in the southern limits of the viceroyalty of Peru. Given these objectives he carried out his instructions to the letter and provided a written and cartographic record of where he sailed, what he saw and those he encountered. Those who were subsequently to rely on it for passage through the same difficult waters found that record to be 'so just and exact, that we think it impossible for any living to mend his Works'[4] and that 'His voyage, more than any other, may be regarded as a directory for the navigation to the coast of *Patagonia* and the *Strait of Magalhanes*'.[5]

1. The Manuscript and Printed Records of the Voyage Included in this Volume

a: British Library, BL, Add 88980A, Narbrough's 'Booke' Containing the Journal and BL, Add 88980B, C and D, Accompanying Charts of the Voyage of the Sweepstakes

Narbrough's copy of his journal is written in a paper 'Booke', bound in the original vellum, with one surviving ribbon and the stub of a second.[6] This document, together with the accompanying charts, was owned by successive Earls of Romney. Sir Robert Marsham, 5th Baronet and 1st Baron of Romney married Elizabeth, eldest daughter and coheir of Sir Cloudesley Shovell and Elizabeth, widow of Sir John Narbrough in 1708.[7] Both Narbrough's sons were drowned with Sir Cloudesley Shovell when the *Association* was wrecked off the Isles of Scilly in 1707, and it is assumed, although it cannot be proved, that Narbrough's notebook and maps passed from Narbrough's widow into the Marsham family and remained there until its sale.

The paper 'Booke' was clearly bought and used by Narbrough for keeping a record of a variety of matters. Inside the front cover are notations of loans to Colonel Drakes and Mr Samuel and a death notice. On the facing page is the inscription 'John Narbrough his Booke Aprill the 7: 1666' written in the same hand as the rest of the 'Booke'; the initial letter with a great flourish.

The 'Booke', which has no continuous pagination, contains a journal of Narbrough's time in the *Victory*, from 1 May 1666, to 10 June, when he received his Commission to command the *Assurance*, which he joined in Harwich on 11 June 1666; then a journal until 15 October 1666, when the *Assurance* was in Woolwich.[8] This is followed by a few

[1] Burney, *Chronological History*, III, p. 374.

[2] Markham, *Threshold*, p. 35.

[3] Hack[e], *A Collection*, reprint 1993, Introduction, p. 12.

[4] Bulkeley and Cummins, *Voyage*, p. 148.

[5] Burney, *Chronological History*, III, p. 373.

[6] The dimensions of the book, 31·7 × 21 × 4·5 cm, are given in the form of height followed by width and where appropriate thickness.

[7] *Burke's Peerage*, III, p. 3386.

[8] No reason is given for this stay in harbour.

notes and then his journal of his voyage in the *Assurance* to the West Indies, from 8 April 1667 until 29 October 1667, in Suriname River, Guiana, when he was ordered to transfer to the *Bonaventure*, where he remained in the West Indies until his return to Chatham in November 1668. The journal of his voyage in the *Sweepstakes* follows. Narbrough entered notes and copies of his correspondence and documents relating to his voyages at the end of his 'Booke' after turning it upside down and writing forwards, each entry progressing from left to right. He recorded navigational information on star altitudes in southern latitudes on the inside cover, followed by an undated list of ships 'Goeing with Prince Rupert',[1] correspondence dated between 1666 and 1667 during his time in the West Indies, together with his Commissions for command of HMS *Assurance* and *Bonaventure*. The most recent correspondence relating to the *Sweepstakes* voyage, together with his Commission and his orders for the same, follows at the end of these entries towards the middle of the 'Booke'.

The 'Booke' is accompanied by three manuscript charts: 'Draught of Porte San Julyan', 58 × 44·8 cm, BL, Add MS 88980B; 'Port of Baldavia on the Coast of Chile &c.', 44 × 57 cm, BL, Add MS 88980D; and 'Port Dissier Harbower', 56·5 × 43·8 cm, BL, Add MS 88980C – all of which are annotated in the same hand as the journal. There is also a printed chart of 'Magellan Streights' with inset of Patagonia, dedicated to the Earl of Oxford and Mortimer, BL, Add MS 88980E.[2]

The British Library manuscript is apparently written in the same hand as that which wrote the two Narbrough manuscripts in the Pepys Library, Magdalene College, Oxford, MS 2555 and MS 2556, covering Narbrough's service in the *Prince*, 7 January 1672 to 18 September 1672, and in the *Fairfax*, 18 September 1672, to 1 July 1673, respectively. These were edited for the Navy Records Society by R. C. Anderson in 1946.[3] In his introduction he states these [Narbrough's journals] were 'fair copies written continuously. At the same time, they appear to be in Narbrough's own writing and they contain a large number of sketches of pieces of coast, landmarks and occasionally ships ... little sketches of a hand holding a lead-line, a conventional representation of the sun, or an anchor inserted in the margin where there is mention of soundings, observations or anchoring.' Similar little sketches appear in the British Library manuscript, together with two elaborate coloured plans of anchorages, 'Punta del Gada' and 'Roade of Angria'. It would seem extremely unlikely that Narbrough had the same clerk with him in all his ships from 1 May 1666, when the journal starts with his service in the *Victory*, until 1 July 1673, when Pepys Library MS 2556 ends, so that it can be confidently asserted that these manuscripts and charts accompanying them are in Narbrough's own hand.

b: Bodleian Library, Rawl. MS A. 318

The manuscript is bound in brown leather with blind tooling in panel designs of the late seventeenth or early eighteenth century. Richard Rawlinson's bookplate is on the inside

[1] It contains the names of the commanding officers and the signals to be used 'when the Prince would speake with any on[e] of them'. The ships are those of Prince Rupert's squadron at the Four Days' Battle, June 1666, and so the list would appear to have been entered before that date, while Narbrough was serving in the *Victory*.

[2] This appears to be a copy of the chart reproduced in the second edition of the voyage, dated 1711. It has the same dedication, 'Pag:' above the border in the top right-hand corner and the name of Puerto San Julián in the wrong place. See remarks on these charts below, pp. 16–17.

[3] Anderson, *Journals and Narratives of the Third Dutch War*, pp. 56–154, 187–296.

of the front cover. The volume was rebacked in the nineteenth century and the spine carries a red leather label, inscribed, in gilt lettering, 'SIR J. NARBROUGH'S VOYAGE TO THE STRAITS OF MAGELLAN 1669–70'. The leaf-measurements are approximately 41·6 × 24·9 cm.

The manuscript starts with one unnumbered flyleaf of thinner paper, on the recto of which is the statement, in Richard Rawlinson's hand,[1] 'This is part of Sr John Narbrough's[2] voyage, somewhat different from the print.' The verso is blank. The text of the journal, which is paginated on both recto and verso from 1 through 226, runs from 13 October 1669, off the Island of Porto Santo,[3] to 9 January 1671, 'before Batchellors River' in the Strait of Magellan. This is followed by several unnumbered pages, blank but still with frame-ruling throughout. It is well written as a fair copy in a small round hand, presumably that of a clerk.

c: The Relationship of the Sweepstakes Journal in BL, Add 88980A to Rawl. MS A. 318[4]

As required of the captain of a commissioned ship, John Narbrough maintained a continuous, daily, manuscript log recording the course and position of the vessel, the weather encountered, and the activities of the ship's company during each day of the voyage. Narbrough refers to 'my day account which I Keept in my voiage' in his entry for 21 February 1670 in BL, Add 88980A.[5] That daily log does not appear to have survived, but the *Sweepstakes* journal copied into his 'Booke' (BL, Add 88980A)[6] was almost certainly based on it. Although Narbrough's spelling and grammar are so eccentric as to make his use of verb tenses an unreliable guide, the inconsistencies in the physical configuration of the *Sweepstakes* journal are sufficient to indicate that it was not kept up on a regular daily basis. Each page is numbered in the left-hand top corner and carries a ruled-off running head giving the month, the situation of the ship and the year of the voyage. Pages 1 to 63 are ruled vertically into four columns, with the first and second narrow columns from the left generally used for the day's date and marginalia respectively, the third broad central column reserved for the text of the daily entry, and the fourth narrow column on the right used to note compass direction or coordinates. From page 63 to page 159 Narbrough ruled his pages in three columns, using that on the left for the day's date and marginalia, with right-hand column varying in width sometimes too narrow to carry any information. From page 160 to page 253 he adopted a three-column system, sometimes ruling two narrow columns on the left for day and marginalia respectively, sometimes allotting a single narrow column to each side of the central text and using that on the right for marginalia. Sometimes Narbrough divided and subdivided his daily entries by horizontal rulings, while at other times they are distinguished only by date and the beginning of a new line.

The journal would appear not to have been written continuously as entries tend to alter their style and ink from time to time and there are additions and a few corrections, together

[1] The description of the manuscript and identification of Rawlinson's hand was provided by Dr Bruce Barker-Benfield, Senior Assistant Librarian, Department of Special Collections and Western Manuscripts at the Bodleian Library.

[2] There is a false start for the next word 'voyage' here, which is crossed through.

[3] Ilha do Porto Santo, 33°03′N, 16°20′W.

[4] Contributed by Joyce Lorimer.

[5] See below, p. 203.

[6] See above, p. 2.

with gaps where it might be thought additional information, possibly plans of anchorages or further descriptive text, was to have been added. The Islotes Evangelistas, at the west end of the Strait of Magellan, are referred to as 'Norresses Ilands' in this journal but on Narbrough's charts[1] and in Rawl. MS A. 318 as the 'Iles of Derection'. Bearing in mind that the original would have been written up from the log kept of the ship's movements each watch and on return from expeditions ashore, it seems quite possible that this is a contemporaneous document kept by Narbrough and from which his official version for the Duke of York was to be compiled. It has the appearance of having been prepared for presentation (although writing it in the same volume as his previous journals and the inclusion of letters and other material would seem to contradict this), and it may be that this document was the journal referred to below which Narbrough took to show the King.

Narbrough states that, on 28 June 1671, he took his draughts [charts] and journal to Mr Wren who viewed them and took him to see the King and Duke of York who viewed his draughts and discussed the voyage.[2] There is no further mention of the journal, but on 12 January 1672 he states 'I went to whitehall & Delivered my Large Draughts of the Straights of Magellan: & of the South Sea and of the Coast of Chile & Patagonia:[3] & a draught of Porte Disier & Porte Saint Julyan: & the Porte of Baldivia in the South Sea[4] to Mist*er* Secretary Wrenn: to be keept for his R*oyal* Highness.'[5]

Written up later than the daily events described, in one case Narbrough appears to pick up his journal account by using a daily entry as a place for summative notes which may have served an aide memoire for subsequent entries. His journal entry for 21 February 1670 is unusually long.[6] First it provides an organized and detailed description of the landmarks, distances, and soundings for the coastline southward from a first sighting of Cabo Blanco to Puerto Deseado. This form of organized presentation at first gives the modern reader the misleading impression that Narbrough is tidying up his record to present a more certain knowledge of where he was and where he went than he had at the actual time when he kept his log. For example, his journal entry for 21 February 1670 asserts that he set his 'Course By my Compas WBN to hale in to the land to make Cap St George Ales Cap Blanco Brancas Blanca: which I did make at 8 aclocke this morninge' and then gives an orderly description of the coastline south to the bay containing the port of San Julián.[7] John Wood's journal (BL, Sloane MS 3833) records far more uncertainty as to their position:

> The Land which we Made was Cape Blanco so Caled by the Spanards butt by the English Cape St George butt then one att the Top Mast head Saw an Island to Beare of us S*outh* & by

[1] Narbrough's 'Royal Map' and 'Sloane Map'.

[2] See below, p. 360.

[3] These could be BL, Add MS 5414 Art 29A, and BL, Maps K.Top 124.84. It is interesting to note Pepys's remark on the standard of drawing in Narbrough's journal and charts. He records that 'Mr. Evelyn, from the rudeness of Sir John Narbrough's drawings extant in the Book of Voyages I sent him observes to me the expectation he has of the effects of our mathematical boys' education in Christ's Hospital upon that head, and gives me a very proper hint towards illustrating the usefulness of drawing in a navigator from the scandalous instances of the want of it visible in Sir John Narbrough's original draught he gave me of the Magellan Straits, and the drawings therein of men and beasts done by his own hand.' Tanner, *Samuel Pepys's Naval Minutes*, p. 391.

[4] These would appear to be copies of the charts purchased with the journal.

[5] Pepys Library MS 2555, f. 10.

[6] See below, pp. 201–14.

[7] See below, p. 211.

> *East,* which we Imaigen to be the Cape because Mr Hackluite in his Relation of Fulers Voyage[1] sayed thatt the Cape did Make Like an Island soo we Toke This Island for the Cape and Sayled by itt to the Southward ... The Island which we Made for the Cape was Pinguin Island.

Wood indicates that Narbrough made Penguin Island first and, mistaking it for Cabo Blanco, sailed south the next day before turning back to Penguin Island, then northwards to Cabo Blanco and then south to Puerto Deseado.[2]

The remainder of the entry for 21 February, however, makes it clear that the navigational information in it is only the first part of a set of notes which pulled together a description of the salient facts about the coastline from Cabo Blanco to Puerto San Julián and reminded him of events which had occurred and what he had seen during his first extended stay ashore. The sailing directions are followed by short references to travels inland, topography, the land and marine fauna seen, as well as the signs that indigenous people were thereabouts. He had opened some of their graves and his men had encountered four of them. The entries which follow resume their more usual daily form, with more expanded commentary on the matters noted on 21 February occurring at the appropriate day.[3]

As discussed above, the *Sweepstakes* journal, like the rest of the content of the 'Booke' (BL, Add 88980A), is written in Narbrough's hand. The engaging, erratic, phonetic spelling of his journal allows the reader to pick up his regional pronunciation, to appreciate his garbled attempts at Spanish, and enjoy his blistering assessments of his 'distracted' passenger, Don Carlos, and of the 'could, vile base' or 'vile, and filthy fowel' weather encountered in the Strait. The version preserved in the Bodleian, Rawl. MS A. 318 is, as Richard Rawlinson endorsed it, 'part of S*ir* John Narbrough's voyage, somewhat different from the print'. It also differs considerably from the journal. It was obviously written up for Narbrough by an educated clerk, possibly someone in the employ of the Admiralty, but under his oversight and direction. Although the spelling, grammar, rendition of numerals and calculations of position and distance travelled, longitude and meridian distance, are all regularized, it is still Narbrough's personal account, written in his voice, most noticeable in the many reflective passages giving his opinions on a variety of issues and his considered reaction to events. Portions of the text read as if they were directly dictated.

Comparison of BL, Add 88980A to Rawl. MS A. 318 allows the reader to see which portions of the journal record were omitted from Rawl. MS A. 318 and which were expanded upon. The first entry in Rawl. MS A. 318 is dated 13 October 1669 when Narbrough reached the Canary Islands.[4] There are no daily entries for 14–16 and 31October, or for 1–4 November. Continuous daily records follow through until March of 1670, when no entries are given for 8–10, 15, 16, 18, 19 and 29 of that month. Nothing is recorded for 10, 11, 23–27 and 29–30 April; 1, 4, 8–12, 15–21, 23–25 and 27–29 May; or 2–5, 8–11, 13–14, 16–19, 21 and 24–30 of June. There are no entries made for

[1] See below, p. 210, n. 4.

[2] Wood, BL, Sloane MS 3833, ff. 13v–14r.

[3] See, for example, the subsequent entries in BL, Add 88980A for 4, 7, 13, 20 March; 21, 22 April; 7, 13 May; 20, 22 June; 16 Aug.

[4] It is possible the first page of this journal may be missing since the published account starts on 15 May 1669, with further entries for 26 and 29 Sept. and then records the arrival at Madeira on 17 Oct. 1669; Narbrough, 'Voyage to the South-Sea', pp. 1–2.

2–11, 13, 16, 17 and 19–30 of July; 1, 3–7, 9, 10 and 12–15 of August; 2, 3, 6, 8, 9, 11–14 and 27–29 of September; 4–10 October; and 9, 12 and 30 of November. There are daily entries for December 1670 and up to 9 January 1671, when the manuscript account ends.

Rawl. MS A. 318 is a longer and in several ways a fuller account of Narbrough's voyage, but it is, therefore, a selective one. It is useful to consider when it might have been written before analysing what may have influenced the selection of its content. There is no indication in any of the surviving records that a clerk formed part of Narbrough's company for the voyage in the *Sweepstakes*; which indicates composition after the return to England. The *Sweepstakes* came to anchor off The Downs on 13 June 1671. On the 18th, George Digby, 2nd Earl of Bristol, came aboard 'to see my Draughts and discoursed with mee Concerninge Magallan Straits'. They met again in the evening two days later 'to Discourse of My voiage'. Narbrough generally uses 'Draughts' to mean charts, as he does in his journal entry for 28 June. Anchored below Gravesend by then, Narbrough went 'to white hall & to Sainte Jameses. I went to Mr Wrenn I showed him my Draughts and Journal: Mr Wrenn Carried me to His Majesty & R*oyal* Highness at Barke Shire House. I had the Honnor to Kise His Majestys & Royal Highnesses hands: it was his Maj*esties* & R*oyal* Highnesses Pleasuer to vew my draughts and to Discours of my voyage: For two houers time.'[1] The writing of Rawl. MS A. 318 could hardly have been begun, let alone completed, by 28 June. While there is no further mention of the development of another account, Narbrough did note in his journal of his service in the *Prince* that, on 12 January 1672, he 'went to whitehall & Delivered my Large Draughts of the Straights of Magellan: & of the South Sea and of the Coast of Chile & Patagonia: & a draught of Porte Disier & Porte Saint Julyan: & the Porte of Baldivia in the South Sea to Mist*er* Secretary Wrenn: to be keept for his R*oyal* Highness'.[2] Narbrough had been appointed First Lieutenant of the *Prince* on 5 January and joined the ship on 15 January 1672. It may well be the case that a written account of his voyage, which now survives as Rawl. MS A. 318, was also delivered for perusal by 'his R*oyal* Highness' (James, Duke of York), at the same time. This surmise has some support from what is known about the acquisition of Rawlinson papers by the Bodleian Library. At the sale following his death a large number of the books and manuscripts belonging to Thomas Rawlinson (1681–1725) were bought by his younger brother Richard Rawlinson (1690–1755). He was also a great collector and developed considerable skill in locating papers thought to have been lost, notably the State Papers of John Thurloe and the Admiralty papers of Samuel Pepys. Richard Rawlinson bequeathed all of his manuscripts, among other things, to the Bodleian Library at Oxford. It is not clear whether Rawl. MS A. 318 was among Pepys's papers or if it had been collected by Thomas or Richard Rawlinson from some other source, but the former seems most likely.

Is Rawl. MS A. 318 complete as it was composed or is what survives an edited version of an original version containing records for all the omitted daily entries? While there is no firm evidence to allow for a definitive answer to this question, a comparison of its contents to those of the *Sweepstakes* journal in BL, Add 88980A gives the reader some important clues, by permitting analysis of the nature of the material which was omitted as opposed to that which was included.

[1] See below, p. 360.

[2] Narbrough's journal of service in the *Prince*, Jan.–Sept. 1672, is found in Pepys Library, MS 2555, f. 10.

The daily entries found in BL, Add 88980A but omitted from Rawl. MS A. 318 fall into four broad general categories. The most obvious is the exclusion of the record of the period between Narbrough's receipt of his commission and his arrival at the Canaries, 5 May–12 October 1669 outward, and of his return voyage after 9 January 1671, two days subsequent to his anchorage off Río Batchelor in the Strait. The second category of omissions are the brief journal entries which contained little other than a description of the weather, which was either so foul or contrary as to make it impossible to get under way, or to undertake any onshore activities. The third grouping of omissions might be loosely categorized as 'ship housekeeping'. For example, the daily journal entries for Narbrough's sojourn in the Canaries 13–16 October, which recount his visit to the governor in Funchal, meetings with the English consul and merchants resident there, and the taking on of supplies, are not found in Rawl. MS A. 318, which subsumes all four days into one entry for the 13th, retaining only a commentary on the behaviour of Don Carlos and a description of the appearance of the island of Madeira. Many of the other daily journal entries omitted from Rawl. MS A. 318 relate to the state of supplies, the repair and maintenance of the *Sweepstakes*, punishments of crew members, and ordinary occupations of his party during the wintering over at Port San Julián. A fourth, more specific category is that of the marginal drawings of people, animals, birds and coastal elevations which add such interest to the journal are missing from Rawl. MS A. 318, although comments relating to them are often carried over. If Rawl. MS A. 318 was created around the time when Narbrough was preparing charts then this material was carried over to them and not required.

Whether Rawl. MS A. 318 in its present form reflects what Narbrough produced after his return to England, or what remains after the editing of his account by someone else, the rationale for excluding the types of material found in the journal from it can be explained. The drawings in the journal, were transferred to Narbrough's maps, although Pepys was to find the 'rudeness' of them 'scandalous instances' of the lack of training in drawing for navigators.[1] The detail of the uneventful outward voyage to the Canaries might well be seen as of no particular interest. The return through the Strait and homewards might be considered to have no further significant information, particularly since, as will be discussed below, some of the more detailed navigational information for the outward passage through the Straits found in Rawlinson clearly incorporates the more accurate understanding acquired on the return and not found in the *Sweepstakes* journal

Although Rawl. MSA. 318 retains the journal form, it has a coherent narrative structure. Here copies of instructions and letters which Narbrough wrote and received and which he copied in the back of the reversed 'Booke' (BL, Add 88980A) are woven into the narrative. The content of some of the daily entries common to both the copy of the *Sweepstakes* journal and Rawl. MS A. 318 is substantially the same, except for slight differences in grammar, spelling and phraseology. Generally, even where the common Rawlinson entries are brief, those in the journal are always shorter. They also tend to be more to the point, offering direct narrative statements, rather than extended descriptions or observations, about what had been seen or done on the day. As can be seen below, the manuscript provides a consistently fuller description of the elevations and landmarks of the shorelines, the winds, tides, currents, soundings, channels, shoals, rocks and other

[1] See above, p. 5, n. 3.

hazards, and of the topography, vegetation, flora and fauna of the islands and mainland. Many entries contain advice for navigators who might follow Narbrough to those waters.

Concern to provide the most comprehensive guide for other seafarers probably explains differences in identification of landmarks between the journal and Rawl. MS A. 318. The greater part of the information about the naming of islands, capes and other landmarks noted in the outward passage through the Strait is confined to Rawl. MS A. 318. Sometimes the information in the two records differs. In the *Sweepstakes* journal entry for 14 November 1670 Narbrough writes that 'I have sailed this all day' and had Cape Deseado to 'the SW of me dist*ance* one League'. Thereafter Cape Deseado is the feature identified as marking the entrance point from the Pacific into the Strait on the south side. In Rawl. MS A. 318, Narbrough claims to have noted and named Cape Pillar on the 14th, which is the actual western entrance to the Strait on the south side and is the feature which Narbrough navigates by when re-entering it.[1] Similarly, on 19 November in the *Sweepstakes* journal Narbrough noted that he named the islands, now known as the Islotes Evangelistas, as 'Norresses ilands' after the seaman who first sighted them. In Rawl. MS A. 318 and on both Narbrough's manuscript charts they are renamed the 'Islands of Directions' or 'Iles of Derection',[2] no doubt reflecting Narbrough's confirmed understanding of their importance as landmarks for the approach to the Strait.

The Royal Society had issued 'Directions for Sea-men, bound for far Voyages' in 1666 and expanded further in April 1667 on the types of observations which should be taken during them.[3] However, as can be seen and will be discussed further below, in addition to being subject to the general expectations of journal keeping, Narbrough had sailed with very specific orders, given to him on 29 August by King Charles II, in the presence of the Duke of York, Prince Rupert, Lords Sandwich, Arlington and Ossory, Mr Middleton and the Duke's secretary, Mr Wren.[4] These made it clear what portion of the South American coastline he was to 'discover', and directed him to make exact observations of the sailing conditions and topography of the region. He was to sail in company with Captain Fleming in a pink, named *Batchelour*, whose vessel would undertake close inshore reconnaissance. He was to attempt to make contact with the indigenous inhabitants, treating them with the utmost respect and assessing the possibilities for friendly trade, taking the advice of his mysterious supernumary Don Carlos, 'Especially if you find he hase Really any former accquainttance with the Place, you are allso to Permitt him to goe ashore if he dissier it'. Don Carlos was to be treated 'with all Possible Respecte and Cevellity as a Person of quallity',[5] as were any Spanish subjects who might be encountered. It also appears that Narbrough was given verbal instructions to inquire about the size, condition and military forces of the Spanish settlements in Chile and to make diligent searches and inquiries after gold deposits whenever he had the opportunity.

These orders would seem to provide a further insight into why the daily entries common to both the *Sweepstakes* journal in BL, Add 88980A and Rawl. MS A. 318 differ in terms of the detail they contain and form. In all likelihood BL, Add 88980A, the copy of the daily log, had been substantively completed during the voyage.

[1] See below, p. 485.

[2] See below, p. 592, n. 4, Plate 5 and Foldout.

[3] See below, p. 26, n. 1.

[4] See below, p. 139.

[5] See below, p. 122.

Narbrough had been summoned to give a verbal account of his voyage to Charles II, the Duke of York and other leading ministers immediately on his return. By then Don Carlos had disappeared near Valdivia and four members of Narbrough's company had been detained by the Spanish authorities there. The copy of the *Sweepstakes* journal, indicates that the original daily journal or log of the voyage would have provided a clear record of the daily observations and experiences of the voyage. The two-hour long 'Discours' with the king and the lord high admiral would have allowed Narbrough to offer his first retrospective reflections on its outcome. The account in Rawl. MS A. 318, it can be argued, represents his further considered knowledge, opinions and conclusions under the headings set out in his orders. The rendition of the navigational information would have been influenced by his work on the charts. The daily housekeeping details of ship life are replaced by advisory passages about the efficacy of vinegar, fresh greens, penguin and seal meat and daily exercise for counteracting scurvy, and on the method used to keep his company healthy in the tropics or during the cold winter months at Puerto San Julián. Greater space is devoted to efforts to describe the form and vegetation of the coastline and the birds and animals he had seen, again depicted on his charts. as are the indigenous people he encountered in the Straits. In Rawl. MS A. 318 the longer narrative of the encounters with groups of hunter-gatherers in the Strait give a better sense of his interest in and curiosity about them than can be gleaned from the shorter entries in the *Sweepstakes* journal; as do Narbrough's sympathetic accounts of the maltreatment of Indians in service at Valdivia who would, he opines, welcome an English attempt to drive the Spaniards out. More information is provided about the coastal defences of Valdivia, about the organized Indian resistance which made it difficult to establish permanent Spanish settlements further in the interior, and the opportunities for trade with the enclaves on the coast.

Writing after his return to England freed Narbrough from the constraints of the directive to treat Don Carlos 'with all Possible Respecte and Cevellity as a Person of quallity', which clearly restricts his commentary in the *Sweepstakes* Journal. There, in the entry for 16 October 1669 made in Funchal harbour, Narbrough carefully logged Don Carlos's bitter complaints against Charles II and the Duke of York, citing the names of officers on the quarterdeck who could testify to what had been said.[1] Most of his other journal entries about his dealings with his passenger are restricted to short statements. Obviously frustrated by Don Carlos's total ignorance of the coast of Patagonia and Chile, Narbrough did note that he 'Clearely Perceived he never was in these Parts nor in any Parte of amarica to the South of Panama: but all was lies which hereerto he had related of his Beinge here: for he Could not tell where to Goe nor what to doe neither did he know where the Spanards were Satled'.[2] In Rawl. MS A. 318, the story of his passenger's increasing unhappiness and reclusiveness, his unfamiliarity with the entire passage from the River Plate to Chile, and his final disappearance ashore, is fully rehearsed, as are Narbrough's iterations of his own assurances to Don Carlos that he stood ready to help him wherever possible. Narbrough's final summative statement about his passenger, written on 21 December 1670, if it was read by the Duke of York, cannot have given him any satisfaction, but it doubtless relieved Narbrough's feelings.

[1] See below, p. 154.

[2] See below, p. 280.

Finally, the composition of Rawl. MS A. 318 gave Narbrough an opportunity to present his own orderly account of his most difficult attention to orders, after the treacherous detention of four of his men by the Spanish governor at Valdivia. The seizure of the men is fully reported, as is the alleged unhappiness of other Spanish officers with the governor's dishonourable disregard for proper conduct under a flag of truce. The exchange of letters by which he attempted to recover the prisoners is documented, as are his communications to the detainees. His decision to leave them behind is set in the context of his explanation to his ships' company that he was grieved not to have a 'com*m*ission to take Satisfaction for the wrong the Spaniards had done mee in detaining my officers, but my Commission charged mee not to molest any Spaniards at Sea or on land, So I durst not proceed in any hostile manner against them but according to the tenour of my Instructions, which was ever my resolution to preform [*sic*], as I would advise all persons to do the Same'.[1]

Comparison with the copy of the *Sweepstakes* journal in BL, Add 88980A allows the reader to gain a very clear sense of Narbrough's purpose in writing Rawl. MS A 318. Whether the early and closing months of the *Sweepstakes* voyage were originally part of it or not, the focus of the manuscript was to give as complete a report as possible on the each of the stated objectives of the voyage, and explanations of the extent to which they had been achieved.[2]

d: British Library, Add MS 5414,29, The 'Sloane Map'[3]

The chart is drawn on paper, 84 × 99 cm. It is graduated in degrees of latitude from 50°S to 54°30′S, subdivided at 10′ intervals, and there is no longitude scale. North is at the top and there is a scale of 20 English Leagues. It shows none of the characteristics of Narbrough's own hand, and is a typical product of the Thames School, possibly from the workshop of either John Thornton or William Hack[e].[4] The hand that drew this chart has been identified as the same hand that drew Maps 16 (Maryland), 17 (Virginia) and 20 (Carolina from Cape Henry to Saint Augustine) in the Blathwayt Atlas.[5] It could be that this chart was prepared for the Committee of Plantations, or was one of a small number of copies prepared for presentation to important people, of whom Christopher Monck, 2nd Duke of Albemarle might well have been one. A large number of the latter's manuscripts were acquired by Sir Hans Sloane (1660–1753) on his death in 1688, and on Sloane's death his collection was acquired by parliament for the nation which, together with the collections of the Harleys (1st and 2nd Earls of Oxford), and of Sir Robert Cotton founded the collection of the British Museum.[6]

[1] See below, p. 529.

[2] Rawl. MS A. 318 also contains a proposal for a trading voyage to this coast and round the world with an offer by Narbrough to lead such a voyage, which does not appear in the British Library journal.

[3] See Plate 5. For William Hack or Hacke, see Kelly, 'Hack, William', *ODNB*.

[4] I am grateful to Peter Barber, Head of Map Collections at the British Library, for this information.

[5] This atlas, called after William Blathwayt, the secretary of the Committee of the Lords of Trade and Plantations, in whose library it survived, is now in the John Carter Brown Library. It consists of 13 manuscript and 35 printed maps used by the committee (of which Nabrough's chart of the Strait of Magellan is No. 42). Black, *Blathwayt Atlas,* pp. 4–5, 211.

[6] MacGregor, 'Sloane, Sir Hans', *ODNB*.

e: British Library, Maps K. Top 124.84. The 'Royal Map'[1]
The chart is drawn on vellum, 79 × 183 cm, and the body of it is also typical of the Thames School, but of a higher standard of workmanship than the 'Sloane Map'. It is graduated in degrees of latitude, from 52°5′S to 54°15′S, subdivided at 5′ intervals, with a scale of ten English Leagues. There is no longitude scale shown. North is at the bottom. The colouring and execution, particularly of the physical relief (the mountains and suggestions of blue haze for the distant peaks), and the superb depiction of the ships, suggest that this is the work of the head of the workshop. The Title 'THE LAND OF PATAGONA &c.' (with its revealing use of the first person 'as I passed and repassed the Straits') and the long texts on the natives and the tides are in Narbrough's own hand, while the drawings of people and animals and some of the place names also appear to be by Narbrough.[2] It was formerly in the royal collection and may have been prepared for presentation to the Duke of York, or possibly even the King.

f: British Library, Sloane MS 819. Lieutenant Peckett's[3] *Journal of the Sweepstakes*
The Manuscript (external measurements 31·5 × 21·8 cm) is bound in orange buckram with leather spine and corners. It is inscribed on the front cover with crest 'BIBLIOTHECA MANUSCRIPT SLOANEIANA' and on the spine: 'SLOANE MS 819: BRITISH LIBRARY: PECKETT'S VOYAGE TO MAGELLANS STRAITS'. Folios are inserted individually between guards, average size 30·5 × 19 cm, numbered on the recto only.[4]

g: Royal Society CI.P/7i/32. Richard Williams's 'short accompt'
The manuscript, which is now bound in a larger volume, is headed 'A Voyage of the Sweepstakes to the Straites of Magellan', with 'Captain Narbrow Commander' in the margin. It is signed 'Your Hon*o*rs humble Servant Richard Williams', and dated 'From a Board their Ma*je*sties *Sweepstakes* June 13, 1671, in the downes'. It should be noted that the date of this document, 13 June 1671, is the date that the *Sweepstakes* anchored in The Downs, so this was sent off before Narbrough had had a chance to report to the Duke of York which was a highly irregular proceeding. It was presented to the Royal Society on 13 July 1681. The manuscript is 11 pages long. Thomas Birch, in his *History of the Royal Society*, states 'Mr Houghton brought on the relation of Sir John Narborough's voyage through the Straits of Magellan to Baldivia, which relation being pretty long, the Society desired that Mr Hooke would peruse it; and that if it contained anything very considerable, it might be transcribed.'[5]

h: Beinecke Library, Osborn b394. William Chambers's Journal of the Batchelour
The manuscript is bound in original limp vellum, 20 × 15·5 cm. The folios are unnumbered. It consists of 104 pages written on recto only covering the period

[1] See Foldout.

[2] I am grateful to Peter Barber, Head of Map Collections at the British Library, for this information.

[3] See below, pp. 590–623.

[4] The arrangement of the manuscript is as follows: f. 1r title, verso blank, ff. 2r–17r text, f. 17v blank, ff. 18r–22v tables from log of ship's distances run etc., f. 23r table of bearings and distances between ports, headlands etc., f. 23v blank.

[5] Birch, *History of the Royal Society*, IV, p. 94. John Houghton (1645–1705) was elected FRS on 1680, proposed by Robert Hooke. He was a dealer in tea, coffee and chocolate, and interested in trade with the Americas. McConnell, 'Houghton, Sir John', *ODNB*.

1 November 1669, at São Tiago, to 2 April 1670, to departure from Río Santa Cruz. There is a note on the front endpaper in the hand of Edward Montagu, 1st Earl of Sandwich. This appears to be the only record from the voyage of the *Batchelour*, and was preserved by the Earl of Sandwich.

The *Batchelour* returned to Penzance on 26 October, 1670.[1] On 28 February 1671, the Navy Commissioners were informed that the 'original journal of Captain Humphrey Fleming, late master and commander of the *Batchelour* pink', had been examined and compared 'with the copy delivered by him into the office, and find that from 29 Oct, 1669, when the pink was off Sancta Diago [São Tiago], to 1 April 1670, when she arrived at [actually departed from] de la Cruz, they differ in wind, course, distance &c., but that it was occasioned by the original journal allowing 31 days to February'. Two days later the captain's journal was compared 'with that of Wm. Chambers the mate, and that although they do not agree, they conceive it was not done out of design, but was the fault of the transcriber'.[2] This would appear to be the occasion when the transcript was made. William Chambers 'late mate of the Batchelor pink' is last recorded on 23 May 1671, writing to the Navy Commissioners 'praying a bill for his wages according to the Duke of York's order'.[3]

2. Captain John Wood's Account

Captain John Wood's record of the voyage has not been included in this volume since it is readily available in contemporary printed versions[4] and repeats much information that is in the manuscripts printed here. The manuscript and contemporary printed versions of it are listed below. Commentary on significant information additional to that in the other documents, has been included in footnotes. The manuscripts can be found as follows.

a: British Library, Sloane MS 3833. Mr (Captain) John Wood's Journal of the Sweepstakes
The Manuscript (external measurements 50·6 × 36 cm) is bound in beige buckram with leather spine and corners. It is inscribed on the spine: VOYAGE OF THE SWEEPSTAKES TO AMERICA: BRITISH LIBRARY SLOANE 3833. The folios are bound in with new end papers and are numbered on the recto only. After a list of ships and a ruled page, the text begins on f. 3r and runs through to f. 25v. It is followed by the beginning of an uncompleted entry for 26 September 1669, duplicating (but not exactly) the beginning of the entry on f. 3r, and a number of pages of miscellaneous notes and diagrams. Folios are approximately 49·7 × 34 cm. There are a number of drawings and charts included in the text, which runs from 26 September 1669 to 30 November 1670.

b: British Library, Sloane MS 46A. Mr (Captain) John Wood's Sailing Directions for Strait of Magellan
The Manuscript (external measurements 41·5 × 30 cm) is bound in red buckram with leather spine and corners. It is inscribed on the front with the crest BIBLIOTHECA

[1] *CSPD, 1670*, p. 496.
[2] *CSPD, 1671*, p. 108.
[3] Ibid., p. 365.
[4] See below, pp. 684–5. Hack[e], *A Collection*, pp. 59–100. A modern reprint by the John Carter Brown Library was published in 1993.

MANUSCRIPT SLOANEIANA and on spine SHARP'S SOUTH SEA VOYAGE ETC: BRITISH MUSEUM: SLOANE MS 46A. The folios' internal measurements are 40·5 × 26·7 cm. Folios 1–138 comprise the journal, distance tables etc. of Captain Bartholomew Sharp. John Wood's Sailing Directions are found in ff. 139–168.

c: British Library, Sloane MS 46B
The Manuscript (external measurements 41 × 28·5 cm) is bound in black leather with Royal Arms on front and red labels on spine. The spine is inscribed *SHARP'S SOUTH SEA VOYAGE: WOOD'S STRAIGHTS OF MAGELLAN: SLOANE MS 46B: PL.LXXXIVII.* The title page is coloured and inscribed to the Duke of Albemarls by Guilielmus Hack, Anno 1683. John Wood's Sailing Directions are found in ff. 144–148.

3. Contemporary Records and Published Accounts of the Voyage Made after Narbrough's Return

a: Francisco de Seyxas y Lovera, Piratas y contrabandistas de ambas indias, y estado presente de ellas
Written in 1693 but never published, now rediscovered and made available in an edition by Clayton McCarl, published in 2011. This work includes some intriguing commentary on the identity and career of Don Carlos Enriques.[1] Seyxas y Lovera is better known for his *Theatro Naval Hidrographico de los Fluxos, y Refluxos, y de las Corrientes de los Mares, Estrechos, Archipielagos, y Passages Aquales del Mundo* (Madrid, 1688), and his *Descripcion Geographica, y Derrotero de la Region Austral Magallanica* (Madrid, 1690).

b: Samuel Smith and Benjamin Walford's, An Account of Several Late Voyages &c., 1694
The first English account of Narbrough's voyage appeared in 1694 in *An Account of Several Late Voyages and Discoveries to the South and North Towards the Streights of Magellan, the South Seas, and the vast Tracts of Land beyond Hollandia Nova &c. Also Towards Nova Zembla, Greenland or Spitsberg, Groynland or Engrondland, &c.* by Sir John Narborough, Captain Jasmen Tasman, Captain John Wood and Frederick Marten of Hamburgh. London: Printed for Sam Smith and Benj. Walford, Printers to the Royal Society, at the Prince's Arms in S. Paul's Churchyard, 1694.[2] A second edition appeared in 1711.[3]

[1] For a discussion of the life of Francisco Seyxas y Lovera (1646–1705), and his commentary on Don Carlos Henriquez, see below, pp. 56–7.

[2] See Plate 11. The reason for the delay in publication is not known. It could have been that the King was not keen to publicize the route through the Strait of Magellan in order to retain a later option of establishing trade, or wished to discourage the activities of the freebooters operating off the South American coast. Possibly the project was shelved because of the Third Anglo-Dutch War, and not revived. It might also have been due to a lack of a financial incentive and general apathy as a result of difficulty trading in the area, or because Narbrough himself was fully employed on other matters and just did not get round to it.

[3] *An ACCOUNT of several Late Voyages and Discoveries: I. Sir John Narbrough's Voyage to the SOUTH-SEA by the command of King Charles the Second: And his Instructions for Setling a Commerce in those Parts. With a Description of the Capes, Harbours, Rivers, Custom of the Inhabitants, and Commodities in which they Trade. II. Captain J Tasman's Discoveries on the Coast of the South Terra Incognita. III. Captain J Wood's Attempt to Discover a North-East Passage to CHINA. IV. F. Marten's Observations made in Greenland, and other Northern Countries.* London: Printed for D. Brown without Temple-Bar, J. Round in Exchange-Ally, W. Innys in St. Paul's Churchyard, and T. Ward in the Temple-Lane, 1711. See Plate 12.

The first edition contains an Epistle Dedicatory, 'To the Honourable Samuel Pepys, Esq. Secretary of the Admiralty of England, to K. Charles and K. James II,' signed by the printers, Samuel Smith and Benjamin Walford, which is not included in the second edition. Both editions contain an Introduction,[1] referred to in the first edition as 'The Bookseller's Preface, or Introduction', and in the second simply as 'The Introduction'. The second edition contains an extra chart titled 'A Chart of the Western and Southern Oceans Describing the course of Sr John Narbrough's Voyage to the South Sea'. The text in the two editions appears to be the same with a few minor differences in spelling and in use of italic print.[2]

The basis for these two editions is Rawl. MS A. 318. There is no indication who edited it. The latter account runs from Wednesday 13 October 1669, when Porto Santo was sighted, to Monday 9 January 1670/1, when the *Sweepstakes* was anchored before the 'Batchelors River' in the Strait of Magellan on the return journey. The published account is only about one-third of the length of the manuscript, and runs from 15 May 1669, when Narbrough received his commission from the secretary to the Duke of York, to Saturday 10 June 1671, when the Scilly Islands were sighted on the return to England. The account then states, on p. 121, 'we shall continue home to *England*, from the *MS Diary*, taken by Sir *John's* ingenious *Lieutenant, Nathaniel Pecket*'.[3] It is not clear where the initial part from 15 May to 13 October 1669, comes from. It is reduced to take up one and a half pages (about 400 words), with entries for 15 May, 26 and 29 September, and 17 October. This would equate to slightly less than one page of Rawl. MS A.318, which starts with the date and text for 13 October about one-third the way down a recto page, without any preamble or title, or indeed any running head which subsequent pages carry. Bearing in mind that the publishers, Smith and Walford,[4] signed the Epistle Dedicatory and refer to themselves as 'we' in the remark about the continuation, it can only be presumed that they were responsible for the editing. This appears to be confirmed by Admiral James Burney who published extracts from the 1694 edition with additions from Captain John Wood's published account and Lieutenant Peckett's journal in his *Chronological History of the Voyages and Discoveries in the South Sea or Pacific Ocean*, Part III, in 1813, pp. 316–76, with remarks on the Charts of the Strait of Magellan, pp. 376–82. Burney states that Smith and Walford 'received the original journal of Captain Narbrough from the then Secretary to the Admiralty, the Hon. Samuel Pepys. Some want in skill in drawing up the abridgement

[1] The introduction was written by Sir Tancred Robinson (1657/8–1748), physician and naturalist, who, in 'A letter sent to Mr William Wotton, *BD* Chaplain to the Right Honourable the Earl of Nottingham concerning *Some Late Remarks*, &c. Written by *John Harris*', states: 'As for Mr Harris his unkind Animadversions ... I confess to you that I am the *Author* of that *Introduction to Sir* John Narborough's *Voyage*, as also of the *Epistle Dedicatory* before *the* English *Translation of Father* Le Compte's China, and of all the *Extracts* of the *Hortus Malabaricus* in the *Philosophical Transactions*.' British Library 816.m.19 (24).

[2] Peckett's name is spelled Nathaniel in the 1694 edn, Nathanael in the 1711. Cape Blanco is in most places Blancho, pp. 126–8, 1711 edition. Days are in italic in 1711 edition. Degrees and minutes are abbreviated to d and m in 1711. Directions in some cases are reduced to initial capitals, e.g. South-west to S.W. in 1711. Pagination is identical up to p. 97, thereafter differences occur.

[3] BL, Sloane MS 819.

[4] Smith (bap. 1658, d. 1707) was a bookseller who spoke French and Latin and imported large numbers of foreign books. His catalogue of 1695 lists over 3,000 titles. From the beginning of his career he had published the *Philosophical Transactions of the Royal Society*. He went into partnership with Benjamin Walford, a book auctioneer, in 1692 and they were officially sworn 'printers to the Royal Society' in 1693. See, Smolenaars, 'Smith, Samuel', *ODNB*.

has occasioned breaks in the narrative; but the parts deficient can be supplied from other sources, of which the principal is the manuscript journal of one of Narbrough's Lieutenants, Nathaniel Pecket, which has been preserved in the British Museum.'[1]

c: The Published Chart of the Strait of Magellan, 1673[2]

This is titled '*A New Mapp of MAGELLANS STRAIGHTS Discovered by Capt: John Narbrough (Commander then of his Majeste's Ship the Sweepstakes) as he sailed through the sade Straights* Made and sold by John Thornton Hydrographer at the signe of England Scotland & Ireland in the Minories & by James Atkinson Mathematical Instrument Maker on the East side of S. Saveris Dock over against the Griffin and at his shop at Cherry Garden stairs.' Published in 1673,[3] this chart was reproduced c. 1680 with the imprint changed to read 'By John Thornton John Seller William Fisher James Atkinson John Colson' and again with the imprint reading 'By John Thornton Hydrographer at the Platt in the Minories London'.[4] The chart appears to have been drawn from the 'Sloane Map'.[5] It is on a 'Flat Earth' projection with its latitude of origin in 52°30′S, i.e. it approximates to a Mercator projection in that latitude.[6] All the names on the Sloane map were included[7] but a large number of descriptive remarks were omitted. There is an inset showing 'Patagonum Regio' from 39°10′S just north of Valdivia[8] to just south of Cape Horn, which is not on the 'Sloane Map'.

A version of this chart was published with the narrative in 1694. It was re-engraved by John Sturt apparently direct from the 'Sloane Map'. It is slightly smaller than the Thornton chart, with the insert of 'Patagonum Regio' and the same geographical limits. It has a number of additional legends from the 'Sloane Map'.[9]

[1] Burney, *Chronological History*, III, p. 316.

[2] See Plate 9.

[3] The chart was advertised in the *London Gazette*, 31 March to 3 April 1673; see, Tyacke, *London Map-Sellers*, p. 8. It was reproduced in *Atlas Maritimus or a Sea Atlas &c.* by John Seller, London, 1675, in which the previous chart, 'The Sea Coast of Brazil', is dedicated to 'John Narbrough who passed and repassed the Streights of Magellan in the year 1670'.

[4] Black, *Blathwayt Atlas*, II, pp. 212–13.

[5] BL, Add MS 5414,29.

[6] 'Flat Earth' Projection: Over a small area (about 12 miles from the point of origin) the earth may be assumed to be flat. Thus there is no need to introduce any alterations to measurements made on the earth's surface to make it orthomorphic. Errors at 50 miles from the point of origin may amount to about one part in 12,000, so that in the seventeenth century errors in measurement are likely to have exceeded charting errors by a considerable margin, and therefore this projection would appear perfectly satisfactory up to about one to two degrees from the latitude of origin. Hatfield, *Admiralty Manual*, pp. 27–30. The latitude and longitude divisions are in the ratio 97:59, which is the proportion to be expected in 52°30′ (the latitude of the eastern entrance of the Strait of Magellan) on a Mercatorial projection. It is not a true Mercator projection, since the divisions are all equal, but it would have been reasonably orthomorphic in that limited area with relatively little change of latitude. The border is graduated in Degrees, with latitude divided into 5-minute intervals and longitude into 10-minute intervals, from 50°35′ to 54°20′ South and from 286°20′ to 295°10′ East of the Lizard.

[7] C. Quad and Royall road were omitted on the original plate, but inserted later, certainly by 1676. Black, *Blathwayt Atlas*, II, p. 212.

[8] Valdivia entrance, 39°51′S, 73°23′W.

[9] Río Santa Cruz 50°08′S, 68°20′W; variants de Crews, Cruss, Cruze, is not named but is shown in the same place as on the Sloane map. On the insert the name of 'Entreada de S. Sabastina' (Bahía San Sebastián, 53°12′S, 68°18′W) is shown as 'Entreada de Sabastina and R Cruss'. Río Santa Cruz is incorrectly labelled P. S. Julian. The indentation on the coast labelled Po. S Julian on the Thornton chart has no name.

It is titled 'To the Honble Sam: Pepys Esqr. This Mapp of the STREIGHTS of MAGELLAN Drawn by S[r] Jo[n] Narbrough is humbly Dedicated by Sam: Smith and Benj: Wallford'.[1] In the second edition, 1711, the dedication and coat of arms of Samuel Pepys (who had died in 1703) is replaced with one to 'To the Hon.[ble] Robert Earl of Oxford and Mortimer.[2] Baron Wigmore. L.[d] High Treasurer of Great Britain. L.[d] Lieuten[t] of the County of Radnor & one of her Maj.[ties] most Hon:[ble] privy Council' with his arms surmounted by an earl's coronet superimposed. The remainder of the cartouche and supporting angels are unchanged.

d: William Hack[e]'s publication of John Wood's Voyage thro' the Streights of Magellan
William Hack was primarily a cartographer[3] who adopted the title of Captain in about 1695, although there is no evidence that he ever went to sea. He published the atlas of charts seized by Captain Bartholomew Sharp off Cape Pasado in June1681. He also published atlases of the coastlines of Africa and the Orient, and obtained and published the journals of Sharpe and Basil Ringrose.[4] His *A Collection of Original Voyages: containing: I Capt. Cowley's Voyage round the GLOBE II Captain Sharp's Journey over the Isthmus of Darien, and the expedition into the South Seas, Written by himself. III Capt. Wood's Voyage thro' the Streights of Magellan. IV Mr Roberts's Adventures among the Corsairs of the Levant: his Account of their Way of Living; Description of the Archipelago Islands, Taking Scio, &c.* was printed for James Knapton, at the Crown in St. Paul's Church-Yard in 1699.[5] Captain Wood's account in this volume is based on extracts from his journal[6] and Sailing Directions[7] which take the voyage as far as the west end of the Strait of Magellan. Thereafter it is based on Lieutenant Peckett's journal.[8]

4. The Context of Narbrough's Voyage

In 1669 Narbrough was instructed that 'The Designe of this Voiage one [on] which you are sent beinge to make a discovery Boath of the Seas and Coasts in that parte of the world and if it be possible to lay the foundation of a Tread'.[9] In the time of Elizabeth I there had been considerable English interest in the Strait of Magellan and the area of South America adjacent to it. Sir Richard Grenville had petitioned the Queen, in 1574, for permission to colonize lands in the southern hemisphere not already occupied. This was granted but

[1] In the Amsterdam 1969 reprint, I Digo Ramiras (Islas Diego Ramírez, 56°30′S, 68°43′W) appears as Digo mirez.

[2] Robert Harley was created Earl of Oxford and Mortimer in 1711.

[3] This is the same man whose workshop may have been responsible for the 'Sloane Map', BL, Add MS 5414,29. See Plate 5.

[4] Kelly, 'Hack, William', *ODNB*.

[5] This was reprinted for the Carter Brown Library, with an introduction by Glyndwr Williams, Delmar, NY, 1993.

[6] BL, Sloane MS 3833.

[7] BL, Sloane MS 46A, and MS 46B. There are copies of this in the Admiralty Library, Portsmouth, in the Pierpoint Morgan Library, NY, and another, formerly the property of the Marquis of Bute, in private hands.

[8] BL, Sloane MS 819.

[9] See p. 121.

subsequently withdrawn for fear of antagonizing Spain. Drake's voyage round the world of 1577, when the situation had changed, was ostensibly to investigate the prospects of settlements in a similar area.[1] Richard Hakluyt produced his pamphlet advocating taking and settling the Strait in 1579–80.[2] Thomas Cavendish (Candish) sailed round the world through the Strait of Magellan in 1586–8 and tried again in 1591–3.[3] Richard Hawkins had sailed in 1593 intending to make for Japan by way of the Strait of Magellan, but was captured by the Spaniards while raiding the west coast of South America, in 1594, and did not return to England until 1603.[4] After James I made peace with Spain subsequent English endeavours in the Americas were directed to areas not effectively occupied by the Spanish Crown, on the islands of the Caribbean and the rivers of the Atlantic coastline of South America stretching south from the Orinoco to the Amazon. By the outbreak of the Civil War English plantations had been established in the Windward and Leeward Islands and in Suriname. During the Interregnum, Cromwell's ill-considered and incompetently executed Western Design against Spanish holdings in the Caribbean resulted in a fiasco at Hispaniola but did achieve the capture of Jamaica.[5] Interest in the Strait of Magellan revived again in 1655 when Simón de Cáceres put a proposal to Cromwell for an expedition to the South Sea to seize Valdivia, which came to nothing.[6] News about English intentions in this area, possibly reflecting discussions in London, reached Peru in 1656–60 and again in 1662–3.[7] Nevertheless, the Interregnum marked a watershed in state policy both in terms of the defence of its colonies and the regulation of trade with them.

During the Civil War, the navy, led by its Admiral, Sir Robert Rich, 2nd Earl of Warwick, sided with the Parliamentarians and took relatively little part in the war in England.[8] At the start of 1649 the Rump Parliament had only fifty warships plus a few light vessels. Between 1649 and 1660 some 216 ships were added to the navy, of which 110 were former prizes. The officers were selected with ideological criteria playing a major role in order to ensure the fleet's political reliability. Not all the vessels survived into the Restoration; however, Pepys lists 161 ships owned by the state, 135 of which were first to sixth rates. The government failed to find a practicable means of financing the fleet, which, together with the expense of their building programme and the First Anglo-Dutch War (1652–4), resulted, by the end of the Interregnum, in empty store-rooms, massive debts

[1] Andrews, *Trade, Plunder and Settlement*, pp. 116–66; Appleby, 'War, Politics and Colonization', in Canny, *Origins of Empire*, pp. 61.

[2] Quinn and Quinn, eds, *Particuler Discourse*, 1993.

[3] Hakluyt, *Principal Navigations*, III, pp. 30–53, 803–37, 842–52.

[4] Williamson, *Observations*, pp. lxxxiii, 7.

[5] Capp, *Cromwell's Navy*, pp. 88–9.

[6] Simón (Jacob) de Cáceres was a Jewish merchant, born in Amsterdam and resident in London, who advised Cromwell during the capture of Jamaica. Williams, *Great South Sea*, p. 77; Bradley, *Lure of Peru*, p. 98; Capp, *Cromwell's Navy*, pp. 87–91.

[7] Bradley, *Lure of Peru*, pp. 88, 96.

[8] It did, however, play a substantial part in the Irish side of the war, and assisted the land campaigns in England by transporting supplies and reinforcements, and, by protecting commerce, maintaining customs revenues to help with finances, and acting as a deterrent preventing foreign powers from sending help to the royalists. Part of the Channel Fleet, anchored at The Downs, sailed for the Netherlands to join the Prince of Wales in 1648. Capp, *Cromwell's Navy*, pp. 2–6, 53.

to contractors and wages of personnel unpaid. It was estimated that the debt was £1,200,000 when Charles II returned to the throne in 1660.[1]

Whatever the failures of Cromwell's Western Design, the Penn and Venables expedition to the Caribbean in 1655 signalled the entry of the state into the direction and control of its interests in the area.[2] The Navigation Ordinance of 1651,[3] on which the subsequent acts of the Restoration Parliament were based, applied to Englishmen and aliens alike and established the principle that merchandise be brought directly from its country of production, or from the port whence it was usually first shipped, in ships either of the country of origin or of usual first shipment, or in English ships.[4] In 1655, Oliver Cromwell set up the 'Committee and Standing Council for the advancing and regulating the Trade and Navigation of the Commonwealth', and among its over 70 members was Edward Montagu, subsequently 1st Earl of Sandwich,[5] who was also a member of the Protector's Council. Its principal aim was to consider by what means the traffic and navigation of the Republic might best be promoted. It appears to have come to an end in May 1657. During the period between 1654 and 1660 the welfare of the overseas plantations seems to have been dealt with chiefly by the Protector's Council delegating some of the work to committees specially set up.[6]

At the Restoration the majority of the officers in the fleet had served during the Interregnum. Some were purged but most were reemployed during the Second Anglo-Dutch War (1665–7) when they did their duty loyally. Some survived to play an important role in the Third Anglo-Dutch War (1672–4) but by that time most of the officers were products of the Restoration era.[7] During the Interregnum the administration of the Navy was carried out by various committees. At the Restoration an Admiralty commission of twenty-eight with a Navy commission of seven experts under it was in place.[8] Charles II himself took a considerable interest in naval affairs,[9] and one of his first acts in 1660, was to appoint his brother, James, Duke of York, to the post of Lord High Admiral,[10] with executive control of the Navy, while the administrative organization temporarily remained in place.[11] On 2 July it was ordered by the King in Council that the

[1] Ibid., p. 10. See also Tedder, *Navy of the Restoration*, pp. 1–6. Tedder also lists the ships of the fleet and the number of months they were unpaid, the longest period being 52 months. Among the first acts of the Restoration Parliament was the establishment of a committee to disband and pay off the army and deal with the navy's debts. Although considerable sums were dedicated to this task, Parliament was never able to provide sufficient finance to run the navy properly and shortage of cash presented a continual problem.

[2] Capp, *Cromwell's Navy*, pp. 87–91.

[3] Ordinance of 1651, Cap. 22, Goods from Foreign parts by whom to be imported.

[4] Andrews, *British Committees*, p. 24; Harper, *English Navigation Laws*, pp. 38–49.

[5] See below, p. 138, n. 5.

[6] Andrews, *British Committees*, pp. 39–40.

[7] Capp, *Cromwell's Navy*, pp. 372–91.

[8] Tanner, *Administration*, p. 21.

[9] See, for example Davies, *Lover of the Sea*, in which he comments extensively on the King's interest in, and knowledge of, naval affairs including the naming of ships, the naming of the *Sweepstakes* being one of his choices. Ibid., p. 2.

[10] James Stuart, the second son of Charles I, was proclaimed Duke of York at his birth in 1633. In 1659 he was created Earl of Ulster and in 1660 Duke of Albany. Pinches, *Royal Heraldry*, pp. 185–6. He acted as Lord High Admiral from the Restoration, presumably by virtue of the grant made in about 1649. His appointment by letters patent is dated 29 Jan. 1661/2. Sainty, *Admiralty*, p. 20.

[11] Orders in Council dated 31 May and 2 June 1660.

existing commissions be dissolved and the ancient form be restored with a Navy Board, consisting of the Principal Officers of the Navy, namely the Treasurer, Controller, Surveyor, and Clerk of the Acts together with three Commissioners, under the direction of the Lord High Admiral.[1] In 1669, when Narbrough sailed, these offices were filled by Sir Thomas Osborne and Sir Thomas Littleton, joint Treasurer; Sir John Mennes, Controller; in 1667 the offices of Controller of Treasurer's accounts, William Brouncker, Viscount Brouncker, and Controller of Victualling Accounts, Sir Jeremy Smith, were created to assist the Controller; Thomas Middleton, Surveyor; and Samuel Pepys Clerk of the Acts.[2]

During the Second Anglo-Dutch War of 1665–7, fleets were once again despatched to the Caribbean to respond to French assaults on the Lesser Antilles and the Dutch capture of Suriname. Narbrough was given his first command in *Assurance* on 9 June 1666 and sailed for the West Indies as part of Sir John Harman's squadron where he took part in the recapture of Suriname on 7 October, 1667. In general, trade suffered a setback in the Civil War and Anglo-Dutch wars; however, after the Restoration a real effort was made to enhance foreign trade. The Navigation Ordinance of 1651 was revised and re-enacted in the Navigation Act of 1660 and further enhanced in 1663.[3] Charles II appointed a committee for Trade and Plantations, amongst whose members was Edward Montagu (now Earl of Sandwich); their task being 'to review ... and deliberate upon any petitions, proposals, memorials, or other addresses ... concerning the plantations, as well in the Continent as the Islands of America'.[4] A second commission for the Council of Trade was issued dated 13 April 1669, on which were forty-six members, including the Duke of York, Prince Rupert, the Earl of Ossory, Lord Arlington and the Earl of Sandwich. Their duties included 'further encouragement of yo*ur* Maj*estyes* Subjects in their Trade and Commerce both at home and abroad'.[5] Prince Rupert (1619–82), Count Palatine of the Rhine, Duke of Bavaria, K.G., was the third son of Fredrick V, Elector Palatine of the Rhine and Duke of Bavaria and Elizabeth, daughter of James I. He was a founder of the Royal Society and a first Governor of the Hudson's Bay Company. Prince Rupert played a leading role in persuading Charles II and a group of merchants to back a project for fur trading in the Hudson Bay region. After a first successful voyage the Hudson Bay Company was set up on 2 May 1670.[6]

[1] Tanner, *Administration*, p. 21; Collinge, *Navy Board*, p. 1; Capp, *Cromwell's Navy*, p. 371.

[2] Tanner, *Catalogue*, I, p. 12; Sainty, *Navy Board*, pp. 21–2.

[3] Essentially these required specified commodities from the colonies to be shipped to English ports in English- or colonial-built ships of which the masters and at least three-quarters of the crews were to be English or colonial subjects. Davis, *Rise of the English Shipping*, pp. 12, 306–9; Unger, *Shipping*, pp. 39, 120–21; Harper, *English Navigation Laws*, pp. 408–10.

[4] Andrews, *British Committees*, pp. 62–7. The commission for the Council of Trade was dated 7 Nov. 1660 and that for the Council for Foreign Plantations 1 Dec. 1660. The commission for the Council of Trade was revoked and a new patent issued in Oct. 1668.

[5] Ibid., p. 93.

[6] For this venture, see Rich, *History*, pp. 36–42; Beckles, *The Great Company*, pp. 23–34. The initiative to send the first English trading voyage of 1668–9 into Hudson Bay followed upon approaches from two French fur traders, Médard Chouart, Sieur des Groseilliers (1618–96) and his brother-in-law Pierre-Esprit Radisson (1636–1710). They had applied to a group of Boston merchants in 1662 for financial backing for fur trading in the Hudson's Bay region. When this was denied they embarked for Europe and, after a similar application to Louis XIV failed, obtained a letter of introduction to Prince Rupert from the English ambassador at the French court, and crossed to England. The Royal Charter of the Hudson Bay Company Charter, granted 1670,

Narbrough's voyage took place in the delicate context of Charles II's overt and covert foreign policy. The treaty 'for the composing of differences restraining of depredations and establishing peace in America: between the crowns of Great Britain and Spain', was reached in 1667 and officially signed as the Treaty of Madrid in 1670.[1] In that same year, in an effort to secure his financial independence from parliament Charles II entered into the secret Treaty of Dover, whereby he would receive considerable financial support from Louis XIV, in return for which he undertook to support French policy in Europe.[2]

5. The 'Proposition' of Narbrough's Voyage

In 1669 two proposals were submitted to King Charles II, by a gentleman who was apparently Spanish, calling himself Don Carlos Henriques.[3] The first reference to him is found in a letter, dated 1/10 June 1669, from Sir Robert Southwell,[4] who was on the point of returning from Portugal, to Joseph Williamson,[5] secretary to Lord Arlington. Southwell reported 'Here lately come from Madrid to this Place, a single Person, who calls himselfe Carlos Henriques, he is the son of an English man borne in Cadiz, and has lived long in the West Indies', going on to say that he was involved in an insurrection and sent home a prisoner and, having been released, wished to offer his services to the King.

---

lists those who at their own cost and charge undertook the expedition. These included Prince Rupert, the Duke of Albemarls, the Earl of Craven, and Lords Arlington and Ashley as well as seven baronets and knights, five esquires and one John Portman, a Citizen and Goldsmith of London. Pinches, *Royal Heraldry*, p. 171.

[1] 'A treaty for the composing of differences restraining of depredations and establishing peace in America: between the crowns of Great Britain and Spain' was concluded at Madrid on 8/18 July 1670, by Sir William Godolphin. By this treaty Spain agreed that England was to hold all territories in the Western Hemisphere it had already settled. English shipping had freedom of movement in the Caribbean.

[2] Jones, *Charles II Royal Politician*, p. 47. The formal treaty, the heart of which was to be an aggressive war against the Dutch, was concluded through the normal diplomatic channels and was signed on 21 Dec. the same year,; ibid., pp. 89–90.

[3] During his period in England Don Carlos spelled his surname as Enriques. Those who had dealings with him referred to him as either Enriques or Henriques, see below, pp. 52–7.

[4] TNA, SP 89/10 ff. 94r–v. Sir Robert Southwell (1635–1702) came from Kinsale in Ireland. His family had supported Charles I during the Civil War. After the Restoration he entered public life in 1664, first as Secretary to the Commission of Prizes and then, in the same year, purchasing 1 of the 4 clerkships to the Privy Council. He was appointed Emissary to Portugal in 1665, and went to Lisbon early in 1666 where he helped bring about the Peace Treaty between Spain and Portugal (signed 13 Feb. 1668). He subsequently negotiated a trade agreement with Portugal. In Oct. 1671 he was appointed ambassador in Brussels and held numerous subsequent public offices. He supported William of Orange in 1668 and became Principal Secretary for Ireland. He was President of the Royal Society 1690–95; Bernard, 'Sir Robert', *ODNB*.

[5] Sir Joseph Williamson (1633–1701), entered public life at the Restoration as Under Secretary to the Secretary of State for the South, Sir Edward Nicholas, holding the same post under the latter's successor, Sir Henry Bennet (Lord Arlington from 1663). He became in effect the de facto head of the Restoration Government's Intelligence Service. He was knighted in 1672 and became Secretary of State in 1674, until he was replaced after falling from grace in 1679 as a result of the 'Popish Plot'. Subsequently, he regained the trust of William III and was one of the plenipotentiaries at the Peace of Rijswijk (Ryswick) 1697 and ambassador at The Hague; Marshall, 'Williamson, Sir Joseph', *ODNB*.

He had letters from Mr Werden[1] to Lord Arlington and Lord Sandwich.[2] Southwell arranged Don Carlos's passage to England in the company of his own household servants. There he presented his first proposal,[3] dated 29 June 1669, asking Charles II to provide a vessel of about 100 tons with a crew of 100 men for an expedition to South America, promising 'an undertakeing from whence will Redowne unto Y*ou*r Ma*jest*ie great Glory with general increase of all Trade & Comerce of your Kingdome'. This communication was followed by a second, dated 14 July.[4] In this he described his proposed undertaking as 'a buisnesse of great wieght and importance ... the like as I beleeve not having been propounded to any Monarch since the first Conquerors of America and of partes of Asia'. The design was for a voyage to the Strait of Magellan to found an English colony and subsequently to proceed on up to Lima, with the apparent, if not expressly stated, aim of joining and inciting the local indigenous people in rebellion against their Spanish overlords, and bringing them under the protection of the British Crown.

Charles II apparently referred the matter to the Earl of Sandwich,[5] who interviewed Don Carlos Enriques (who in that meeting gave his name as Henríques) on 21 July. Sandwich recorded in his journal that a 'Spaniard that sayes he is the Henrique of the family of the Conde de Alba de lista'.[6] According to Sandwich, Charles II refused to consider any venture which would breach the peace process with Spain by intervening in Chile or Peru, but was willing to listen to something which would 'helpe us to discover Considerable trade and advantages upon the Coasts of America doune from Baldivia (the last Spanish Towne in Chili[7]) to the Streights of Magellan and Thence againe up as farr as the Rio de Plata in which Tract noe treaty of State intervenes. To This Proposal the K*in*g my m*aste*r Hearkens and send a shippe of 26 gunns with him under an able English Captain and a Pincke also, for discovery.'[8] It is probable that Sandwich made this entry in his diary sometime after the meeting had taken place, since he would have had to report to the king. Clearly no such decision had yet been communicated to Don Carlos who continued to complain of the lack of a response and his desperate need for financial assistance as late as 19 August.[9] Charles II may well have ordered Don Carlos's proposals to be discussed by the Council of Trade, which could have accounted for the delay until

[1] The father of Sir John Werden (1640–1716) had close contacts with James, Duke of York, and through his influence his son was appointed as a volunteer in Lord Sandwich's flagship in 1665. He then accompanied Sandwich's embassy to Madrid in 1666 and, when the latter returned home in 1668, he remained as Chargé d'Affaires. He subsequently held various diplomatic posts, transferring his allegiance to William III after the Glorious Revolution. Venning, 'Werden, Sir John', *ODNB*.

[2] These do not appear to have survived.

[3] TNA, SP 94/54 ff 184r–194v. See below, pp. 89–98.

[4] I am particularly grateful to Joyce Lorimer who located and obtained copies of these documents and checked the contemporary translations. The Spanish version is at TNA, CO1/33, No. 103c, ff. 245r–252v, and the English translation at TNA, CO1/33, No. 103c, ff. 253r–264v. See below, pp. 98–111, for a full transcription of the English version of this proposal from which the quotations are taken.

[5] Lord Sandwich was recently returned from his ambassadorship in Madrid, and so would be an ideal person to investigate the proposal.

[6] For a review of Don Carlos's various claims about his identity, see below, pp. 52–7.

[7] This was not in fact the southernmost Spanish settlement, since there was an establishment at Castro on Isla Chiloé.

[8] Journal of 1st Earl of Sandwich, Vol. 9, pp. 265–6, currently in the archive of the 11th Earl of Sandwich at Mapperton in Dorset.

[9] See below, pp. 116–17.

mid-August before any final decision was made. On 3 August Narbrough was ordered to sail in the *Sweepstakes* for The Downs and to await further instructions, so it would appear the voyage was under active consideration at that time.

It is possible that a lengthy missive in Spanish, submitted by Don Carlos on 16 August and endorsed in English by the person who received it, as a 'Relac*io*n of the Kingdo[me] of Peru and other parts of the West Indyes', helped settle the matter.[1] At least it appeared to substantiate his knowledge of the Spanish empire in the Americas. Writing on fourteen sheets of paper folded folio-wise to form two leaves or four pages, Don Carlos carefully numbered the top left-hand corner of the first recto of each group of two leaves.[2] After a short introduction he began his *Relación* on the recto of the second leaf of his complete document, excusing himself for not describing 'the climate, and latitude or longitude of the seat of this empire, its coastlines, ports, lakes and rivers, since these details can be seen on a globe and can be learned in the various chronicles written about this. I will largely pass over the particulars of what others have seen and described and learned.' Instead, he declared, he would focus on things of which he had learned from 'experience and information' gained 'during the time that I have spent in the West exploring the extended and vast empire of America'. Careful reading of his cramped text provides little to substantiate his claims to special inside knowledge, although he did note specific places or events which he stated that he had seen or witnessed. It is clear that his objective was both to enhance his own credibility by demonstrating the breadth of his knowledge and to encourage support for his proposition by showing the returns as well as the cost, inefficiency and instability of the Spanish Empire in general, and the viceroyalty of Peru in particular. The document has some logical order although he apologized for its deficiencies in his conclusion, noting that he had set things down in the order in which he remembered them.

Beginning with an account of the Consejo de Indias and Casa de la Contratación, which he described as 'the columns on which this edifice is built', he then moved on to the official structure of the two viceroyalties of New Spain and Peru. He paid particular attention to the social tensions which wracked the viceroyalties, noting conflicts between the secular and clerical authorities; between the Spanish-born grandees appointed to the viceroyalties and other high office, Spanish '*criollos*', and the '*mestizos*' of mixed Spanish and Indian blood born in the Americas.[3] His detailed information on the routes of the New Spain, Tierra Firme, Manila and *Mar del Sur* fleets would not have offered much that was new to his intended readers. Neither would his comments on the expense of the system and the rampant corruption which reduced the potential returns to the Spanish Treasury, for which he provided estimates. His criticism of the damage caused by the

[1] The documents found in TNA, SP94/55 are not bound in chronological order. This document, which was not dated by Don Carlos, is preceded by a document endorsed as received on 14 Aug. 1669, but followed, ff. 39r–47v, by Spanish original of the paper submitted by Don Carlos on 29 June, See below, pp. 52, 89–98. The endorsement for TNA, SP94/55, ff. 13r–40v, should, it appears, be the small square of paper bound and enumerated as f. 49/f. 51, which reads 'Relac*io*n of the Kingdo[me] of Peru and other parts of the West Indyes delliuer'd in by D*o*n Carlos Enriques this 16. of Aug*u*st 1669'. This precedes Don Carlos's letter of 19 Aug.; see below, pp. 24, 116–17.

[2] In the process of binding TNA, SP94/55, ff. 13r–40v, Don Carlos's carefully numbered sets of two leaves (starting ff. 13r) were miscollated. His set 7 has been collated as a second set 2. To make sense of his document that should be read after set 6.

[3] *Criollos*, creoles, here referred to those people classified as Spaniards of American origin.

asiento (monopoly licence to import slaves) granted to the Genoese merchant Domingo Grillo in 1662 suggests that he was fully aware that the subject was of interest to the English Crown, given that the Royal African Company, which had subcontracted to supply slaves to Domingo Grillo in 1663, had lost all but one of its supply bases in Africa as a result of the Second Anglo-Dutch War.[1] A subsequent, long and wearingly miscellaneous list of what he alleged to be the cost of stipends and perquisites of multiple officeholders in multiple levels of secular, religious and military administration in the two viceroyalties continued his theme of the inefficiency, expense and waste of the imperial system. This was countered by his account of the magnificence of its cities. Referring to his own time spent in Peru, he extolled the architectural beauty of Lima, the forces and weaponry which could be assembled for its defence, and the agricultural productivity of the provinces served by a magnificent, but now neglected, Inca road system. He then listed the rich mineral resources of both viceroyalties. He contrasted the wealth of the mine engineers in Peru, and the profits made by local *Curacas* who supplied bands of forced labourers with the sufferings of the Indians who worked the mines. His representation of upheavals in La Paz in December 1661 as an Indian revolt is belied by both contemporary accounts and recent historical studies, and makes it doubtful that he had, as he claimed, been a witness to them. He concluded his *Relación*, with information about the cargos of the Manila galleons, and miscellaneous notes about the other natural resources and manufactures produced in various parts of the Spanish empire, promising that he could speak more about the military and political operation of the government of the Indies on another occasion.

Whether in response to the *Relación* or not, on 18 August Mr Wren wrote to Narbrough, now anchored at The Downs, to inform him that something had come up concerning his voyage which required his presence in Whitehall. This would indicate that the decision to go ahead with the voyage had now been taken, although Don Carlos had yet to be informed, since he wrote again on 19 August indicating his intention to go to Jamaica if his proposal was not accepted. By 25 August, however, he was seeking funds to purchase necessities for the voyage, which was now going ahead.

6. The Commissioning of John Narbrough

On 15 May 1669, while the *Sweepstakes* was at Deptford, being fitted out by Jonas Shish, the master shipwright, for a voyage to the West Indies,[2] Narbrough received his commission to command the same, from the Duke of York, which he copied into his journal.[3]

[1] For a discussion of the operation of the *asiento* system under Domingo Grillo, see Klooster, *Illicit Riches*, pp. 108–12.

[2] On 9 May 1669, Wren had written to Pepys 'When the board attends his Royal Highness tomorrow, they are to be prepared to give an opinion which 5th Rate Frigate will be most fitting to be sent to the West Indies', *CSPD, 1669*, p. 319. On 13 May, Thomas Middleton had informed the Navy Commissioners 'I think the *Fountain* will be the most proper ship for the voyage to the West Indies, if his Royal Highness does not appoint the *Sweepstakes*, ibid., p. 325. See also p. 131, n. 1 and p. 120, n. 14.

[3] BL, Add MS 88980A, 24th unnumbered page from the back of the 'Booke' reading forwards. See below, p. 87, n. 1.

On 3 August he was ordered to sail for The Downs and await further instructions. He took his leave of the King that day and of the Duke of York the next day and finally got away on the 10th, anchoring in The Downs the next day, where he waited for his orders to sail. On 19 August he received a letter, written the day before, from Mr Wren, secretary to the Duke of York, to come up to London, 'There havinge somethinge lately fallen out which will have soe much influence upon your instructions that it will be requisite you should be here present'.[1] Narbrough travelled up to London the next day and called on Mr Wren 'concerning my voyage to the southward', and met the Duke of York two days later who 'moved me the same'. He was ordered to wait in town and on 27 August to attend at Lord Arlington's lodging,[2] where he met with Prince Rupert, Lords Sandwich and Arlington, and Mr Middleton, who laid the proposals for the voyage before him. On 29 August he was in attendance before the King, the Duke of York, Prince Rupert, Lords Sandwich, Arlington and Ossory, Mr Middleton and the Duke's secretary, Mr Wren, 'where his Maj*es*ty was pleassed to Give hereinge to the vojage and ordered mee what I should acte in my vojage and to what plased'.[3] The next day the King and Duke of York left town for Southampton and Narbrough called on Mr Wren when he no doubt received his orders and instructions to reduce his complement to 80 men. He spent the evening with Lords Sandwich and Arlington at Goring House. On 31 August Narbrough saw the Principal Officers[4] and received all his arrears of pay as well as £200 contingency money. Finally, before returning to his ship on 3 September, he spent some time purchasing necessaries for the voyage – no doubt including charts – and obtaining permission for Lieutenant Peckett to take the place of Lieutenant Touckin, who, for an unspecified reason, could not go on the voyage. The *Batchelour* of London, with Humphrey Fleming as Master, was hired to attend him on the voyage and to be used for inshore work where it would not be safe to venture in the larger ship. Back in The Downs he had to wait for the *Batchelour* to arrive and for Peckett and Don Carlos to join the company, and then for fair weather, before he could sail on 26 September.

There appear to be no minutes or record of what passed at Narbrough's meetings with the King and his ministers. Bearing in mind that Sandwich was comparatively recently returned from his post as ambassador in Madrid where he had conducted the initial negotiations for the Madrid treaty, relations with Spain are likely to have been high on the agenda. Given the remarks he made in his journal about the King remaining 'fast to his faith passed to the Spaniard', it would appear likely that the peace between the two nations was discussed and the requirement to keep clear of the places where they were settled and not to do them 'any Injurie' was emphasized and reiterated. Narbrough was to examine the South American coast from south of Río de la Plata, through the Strait of Magellan and northward up the west coast as far as Valdivia and, if possible, lay the foundation for trade. The nature of that trade was not stated, but there can be little doubt the intention was to investigate sources of gold and silver which the Spaniards regularly obtained from

[1] See below, p. 116.

[2] Presumably Goring House , now demolished. Buckingham Palace was built on the site. See below, p. 118..

[3] It is worth noting that the Duke of York, Prince Rupert, the Earl of Sandwich and the Earl of Ossory were all members of the Council of Trade (which had 46 members all told), established 'for Keeping a control and super-inspection of his Majesty's Trade and Commerce'. Andrews, *British Committees*, p. 93. Colonel Middleton had been a member of the former Council for Foreign Plantations in 1660, ibid., p. 68.

[4] See above, p. 149.

the area. He was ordered to make contact with the native inhabitants, treating them with the greatest respect, and to try to gather information about mineral deposits and other prospects of commerce with them. He was to examine the coast, anchorages and ports, fixing their positions and those of all prominent headlands, making charts and reporting on their suitability for shipping, the trade winds, tides and hinterland. Although not stated, he would certainly have been expected to report on the fortifications and strength of all the places he visited.[1] He was to take advice from Don Carlos, if he found him to have any knowledge of the area. Although the King and his ministers had accepted Don Carlos's proposal for a voyage to South America, they apparently did not entirely trust him. Narbrough was directed 'for the Seafety of your Shipp and men and the main end of your vojage you are not to Relie upon him But upon your own Prudence and Vigilence'. As Lord Sandwich later noted in his journal, it was 'sent ... onely upon discovery of new Ports and Com*m*erce in Those parts; The motive whereunto was the report of a Spaniard that Pretended the Knowledge of the Coast and interest amongst the Spaniards and Indians too that live in and neere Chili'.[2]

7. Narbrough's Ships

a: The Sweepstakes

The *Sweepstakes*[3] was built in 1666 by Mr Edgarr, at Yarmouth as a 5th rate, and reclassified as a 4th rate in 1668. She carried 36 guns.[4] She was sold on 24 May 1698.[5]

Narbrough's detailed description of the ship can be found in his journal, as follows:

> The Shipp drawes now abaft 13 foote & a half & afore 12 foote & one inch
> The Sweepstakes is a 11 foot 3½ inches from the seeleinge in the hould to the lower side of the Plancke on the gundecke at the main mast.
> The Sweepstakes is a 12 foot and 6 inches deepe from the Boattom Plancke to the Plancke on the gunDecke at the mainmas [*sic*]:
> The Sweepstakes is a 6 foot wantinge an inch from Plainke to Plainke betwen the deeckes at the mainmast;
> Maine yard is 66 feet longe and [*blank*] inches through

[1] It should be noted that the Royal Society had issued 'Directions for Sea-men, bound for far Voyages' in 1666 and expanded on them in April 1667 which recommended the observations which should be taken during the voyage. *Philosophical Transactions*, Royal Society, vol. 1, pt 8, pp. 140–43; vol. 2, pt 24, pp. 433–48. Directions of this sort were not uncommon and had, for example, been given to Arthur Pet and Charles Jackman for their intended voyage to China through the North-east Passage in 1580; Hakluyt, *Principal Navigations*, I, pp. 435–9. These called for all the normal navigational observations, making charts, observing the winds and tides etc., as well as to 'understand or perceive of the manner of the soil, or fruitfulness of every place or countrey you shall come in, and of the manner, shape, attire and disposition of the people, and of the commodities they have, and what they most covet and desire of the commodities you carry with you. It behoveth you to give trifling things unto such people as you shall happen to see, and to offer them all courtesie and friendship you may or can, to win their love or favour towards you, not doing or offering them any wrong or hurt', ibid., p. 436. Observations were to be taken of the 'force by sea and land' of their destination: 'the wals and bulwarks of their cities, their ordinance, and whether they have any calivers, and what powder and shot', ibid., p. 439.

[2] See below, p, 128.

[3] This was not the first royal vessel of this name. The *Swypstake* was included in the navy of Henry VIII. Knighton and Loades, *Anthony Roll*, p. 55.

[4] Tanner, *Catalogue*, I, p. 275

[5] Lyon, *Sailing Navy List ... 1688–1860*, p. 13; Tanner, *Catalogue*, I, p. 278.

to looke For though this voyage Beinge intended only for
Discovery noe Profitt is lost for from them yo from
hence the observation is to be made what Commodities
those Countries Can afoard and what they Can take
from us

The Proposition of this voyage haveinge Ben made By
to his Majes By Don Carlos Enriques who Pretends
to have lived longe and to have Born Command in
those Parts he willbe sent with you upon the Shipp
and you are to treat him with all Possible Respecte
and Civillity as a Person of quallity you are allso to
be advised By him in Sendinge a Shore and Endeavour-
inge a Corrispondencie with the Natives Especially if
you find he hase Really any former acquaintance
with the Place or People you are allso to Permitt him
to goe a Shore if he desire it But for the Saufety of
your Shipp and men and the maine end of yor voyage
you are not to Relie upon him But upon yor own
Prudence & Vigilence

The Batcheller of London Humphrey Flemminge
Master beinge hired to attend you in this voyage you
are from time to time to give her Such orders as you shall
think necessary and to send her upon discoveries into
Baies & Rivers & Such places as it is not reasonable to
venture the Kings Shipp and if you see Reason for
it you are to take the men out of that Vessell & give
her Some of yor owne in Stead of them

You are to keep an Exacte Journall of yor Proseedings
a true Coppy whereof you are to deliver to My Secretry
at yor Returne into England: Given under My hand at St
James this: 29th: August 1669:

James

Vera: Copia: —— recd it :30: instant:

By Comand of his R: Highness
M. Wren:

Figure 1. The final page of Narbrough's copy of his Instructions for the voyage from James Duke of York. Journal (BL, Add MS 88980A), unpaginated. Courtesy of the Trustees of the British Library.

Fore yard is 59 feet longe and [*blank*] inches through
Mizon yard is [*blank*] feet longe and [*blank*] inches through
Maine top mast is 46 feet long and [*blank*]:
The Boulspret is 39 feet ½ without Board:
MainSaile is 56 feet squar [*sic*] at the head; 28 Cloathes in it.[1]

It is not known how long the main mast was; however, based on the tables of proportions of mast spars and rigging, and a comparison with similar vessels of the period,[2] it would seem reasonable to accept 75 feet for the main mast and 66 feet for the fore mast. From this, using the relevant formulae for the proportional sizes between the various spars,[3] and Narbrough's figures above, the following table gives the probable dimensions of the masts and yards.

Mast/Spar	Length		Diameter	Mast/Spar	Length		Diameter
Feet	Inches	Inches		Feet	Inches	Inches	
Main mast	75		23½	Sprit top mast	13		4
Fore mast	66		20½	Main yard	66		16
Mizzen mast	50	3	15¾	Fore yard	59		14¾
Bowsprit	49	6	15½	Spritsail yard	59		12¼
Main top mast	46		12¾	Mizzen yard	59		9¾
Fore top mast	39	7	12½	Crossjack yard	39	7	8

Narbrough started recruiting for a complement of 115, the normal peace-time number, and on 13 August, 1669, noted that at the muster he had 119 belonging. He was then instructed to reduce his complement to 80 and discharged 35 men on 4 September when he states 'my complement is now 80 men all a board'. Later, on 22 December, he records that he sailed with 86 men onboard. This must represent the complement of 80 with 6 supernumeraries.

b: The Batchelour

The hiring of the *Batchelour* for the voyage resulted in considerable delay while she was got ready and embarked stores. The vessel is described by Narbrough in his journal as 'a pinke Englesh Built of about Eighty tunes: She draws about 9 foot water: of forse fower Small ordinance of Iron & sume small Shoot and Eighten men'.[4] In Narbrough's published work 'Voyage to the South-Sea', she is described as 'the *Batchelour Pink*, burthen 70 Tuns, with four great Ordnance, and all other Munition proportionable; mann'd with nineteen Men, one Boy'.[5] Pinks were small vessels with the hull form of a ketch. They were noted for having narrow sterns.[6] No dimensions are given; however, the *Chestnut*,[7] of similar tonnage, listed by Pepys as a pink built in 1656, was 45ft long by the keel, 18ft 6in beam,

[1] Narbrough journal, BL, Add MS 88980A, verso of first page. The cloths in the main sail refer to the number of breadths of canvas.

[2] Lees, *Masting*, pp. 183–4, 192–50.

[3] Ibid., pp. 183–4.

[4] See below, p. 128.

[5] Narborough, 'Voyage to the South-Sea', p. 2. This is not in Rawl. MS A. 318, upon which this published version is based, neither is it in Lieutenant Peckett's nor John Wood's journals, so it must be presumed to have been added by the editor, unless it was on a missing page, See above, p. 15.

[6] Falconer, *Universal Dictionary*.

[7] Tanner, *Catalogue*, I, pp. 292–3.

draught 8ft 4in and 81 tons burden, carrying 8 guns and with a peace-time complement of 26,[1] so that it would be reasonable to assume similar measurements for the *Batchelour*.

The *Sweepstakes* was not an ideal vessel for coastal exploration in the region to which she was bound. She was square rigged and could therefore only sail six points (67½°) off the wind, with consequent leeway, so that working close off a lee shore, such as the south-west coast of Latin America, where the prevailing winds are strong and westerly would be extremely hazardous. Her draught of nearly 14 feet (4·27 metres) would make close inshore work impracticable, and might preclude her from entering some of the anchorages or harbours. On the other hand she carried boats and the materials to construct a shallop which could be used for inshore work and to investigate harbours before the ship entered and the *Batchelour* was to accompany her to assist with the inshore work. Her size and reduced complement would mean she had a considerably increased endurance (and would cost the crown less in wages) and could remain without dockyard support for a prolonged period. As a 4th rate her allowance was six anchors and seven cables,[2] and she may have carried more. Bearing in mind the wear cables suffered from rubbing on a hard seabed while the ship was at anchor, and the difficulty of getting to sea if an onshore wind should get up, the number and length of the cables was of paramount importance. Finally, her appearance and fire-power were sufficient to impress the local inhabitants of the places visited, so that on the whole *Sweepstakes* was probably as suitable a vessel as any available at the time.

8. Captain John Narbrough and His Officers

Captains and Lieutenants in the fleet held their authority by virtue of commissions from the Lord High Admiral, who appointed them to a specific ship for as long as that ship remained in service, unless subsequently reappointed.

a: John Narbrough

John Narbrough was baptized in the parish church at Cockthorpe, Norfolk, on 14 October 1640, the fifth son of Gregory Narbrough.[3] He is reputed to have gone to sea as the cabin boy of his kinsman Sir Christopher Myngs and gone from ship to ship with him.[4] He records in his journal that he had been two years in the Mediterranean and made two voyages to St Helena and one to Guinea. His first appointment as Lieutenant was to the *Portland* (50), under Christopher Myngs, in 1664, although it is probable that he served with Myngs in the *Marston Moor* (52) in 1657 in the West Indies and may have been involved with him in the attacks on Cumaná, Puerto Bello and Coro (where the treasure seized 'disappeared' on the way back to Jamaica). Myngs retained his command after the Restoration, when his ship was renamed *York*. Narbrough went on to serve as Lieutenant in the *Royall Oak*, *Tryumph*, *Royall James*, *Fairfax* and *Victory*, in the last of which Myngs was then flying his flag. That ship took part in the Four Days' Battle (1–4 June 1666)[5] in

[1] Tanner, *Catalogue*, I, pp. 292–3.

[2] Sir Anthony Deane, *Doctrine of Naval Architecture*, 1670; see Lavery, ed., *Deane's Doctrine*, pp. 110–11.

[3] Dyer, *Life*, p. 1.

[4] Ibid., p. 8.

[5] The battle took place during the Second Anglo-Dutch War off the Thames estuary in the southern North Sea, and was won by the Dutch. The fleets were commanded by the Duke of Albemarle and Prince Rupert on the English side and Michiel de Ruyter on the Dutch side. See, Fox, *Four Days Battle*.

which Myngs was mortally wounded and Narbrough assumed the command. He was promoted and given his first command, in the *Assurance*, on 9 June 1666. He sailed for the West Indies as part of Sir John Harman's squadron and took part in the recapture of Suriname (7 October 1667). Three naval captains, Hammond of the *Bonadventure*, Carteret and Narbrough led the naval party ashore and cast lots to see who should be senior captain, which fell to Narbrough.[1] Captain Hammond was killed in the action and Narbrough, although wounded with a 'musket bullet' in his right thigh 'which is not probable to be repaired by time and age',[2] was promoted to the command of the *Bonadventure*,[3] where he remained until October 1668. On 15 May 1669, he was appointed to command the *Sweepstakes* and made the voyage covered in this publication.

On his return he remained in command until 4 January 1672.[4] On 7 January he was personally appointed by the Duke of York, as First Lieutenant and second in command of the *Prince* (100) under Captain Sir John Cox. This was the Duke of York's flagship, and when her captain was killed at the Battle of Sole Bay during the Third Anglo-Dutch War, Narbrough became her commanding officer. He commanded the *Fairfax* in 1672. He then became Flag Captain to Admiral the Earl of Ossory in the *St Michael* at the Battle of Texel (11 August 1673). He was promoted Rear Admiral of the Red, flying his flag in the *Henrietta*, 17 September 1673 and knighted later the same month. He sailed for the Mediterranean where, after blockading the port of Tripoli, taking action against shipping in the harbour and against Tripolitine warships at sea, he managed to enforce peace, signing a treaty with them on 5 March 1676. He became a Commissioner of the Navy in 1676, a post he held for the rest of his life. He served again in the Mediterranean in the *Plymouth* in 1677 with 35 vessels against the Algerian forces but with little success, returning to England in 1679.

He married Elizabeth Calmady, in 1677, who died in 1678. His second wife, was Elizabeth Hill by whom he had five children. Narbrough died in the West Indies on 26 May 1688, and his body was buried at sea.[5] There is no known portrait of him.[6]

[1] Ibid., p. 42.

[2] Ibid., pp. 55–6.

[3] Narbrough's service in both the *Assurance* and *Bonadventure* journals are recorded in BL, Add MS 88980A.

[4] TNA, ADM 33/121.

[5] Having heard of the wreck of the *Nuestra Señora de la Concepción*, lost in 1641 with a fabulous treasure onboard, he became involved, from 1682, in attempts to salvage it. The first effort by William Phips in Jan. 1687 resulted in Narbrough receiving £21,766. He then took charge of a subsequent expedition, which was far less successful, and on which he died of a fever. His bowels were brought home and his body buried from a pinnace over the wreck with great ceremony, the *Foresight* and all the other ships and vessels firing salutes, and the pinnace striking its flag as his body was lowered into the sea; Earle, *Wreck*, pp. 215–16. His bowels were buried in St Clement's Church, Knowlton in Kent, together with the bodies of his daughter Ann (1683) and son Isack (1686/7), in a large tomb-chest on the south side of the chancel, which is surmounted by a memorial to Lady Elizabeth D'Aeth, his daughter. The monument to his two sons, John and James, who were drowned with Sir Cloudesley Shovell when the *Association* was wrecked off the Scilly Islands in 1707, is situated opposite Narbrough's tomb-chest; see Plates 13 and 14. Six weeks before King James II fled London in 1688 he had conferred a baronetcy on Narbrough's eldest son, John, who was then still a child. Cloudesley Shovell had sailed with Narbrough in the *Sweepstakes* and married Lady Narbrough after his death; Davies, 'Narbrough, Sir John', *ODNB*.

[6] The picture illustrated in his biography and in various other volumes is a copy of the portrait of Sir Christopher Myngs by Sir Peter Lely in the National Maritime Museum.

b: Lieutenant Thomas Armiger

Thomas Armiger was a relative of Christopher Myngs and presumably obtained his place in the *Sweepstakes* through this connection.[1] He was one of the party detained by the Spaniards in Valdivia in December, 1670, when he informed the Spanish authorities that he was forty-seven years of age. According to Narbrough he was 'aged forty years and born in Norfolk', which, bearing in mind his relationship to Myngs, seems likely. He died, still in Spanish detention, in 1674, 'unfortunately still professing the Anglian heresies'.[2]

c: Lieutenant Nathaniell Peckett

Nathaniell Peckett was recommended for his lieutenancy in the *Sweepstakes* by Narbrough, in place of Lieutenant Anthony Touckin, who could not make the voyage,[3] and so was presumably known to him beforehand. In his will, dated 11 February 1692, Peckett appointed his brothers-in-law Jonas Shish and Fisher Harding as his executors.[4] The former, Jonas Shish the younger, appears to have been the son of Jonas Shish the elder, the Master shipwright of Deptford from 1668 to 1680 (d. 1680). The latter, Fisher Harding, was a prosperous builder of Deptford, who named his sons Fisher, Jonas and Shish. From these names it would seem that his wife, Elizabeth, was a daughter of the elder Jonas Shish. Since Peckett identified both his executors as his brothers-in-law it follows that Peckett's first wife must also have been a daughter of Jonas Shish the elder.[5] The latter was the Master Shipwright who prepared the *Sweepstakes* for her voyage, so this may be the connection.[6] Peckett was a man of some substance, who sold the *Providence* of London, of which he was also then Master, 'now Rideing in the River of Thames, London', to the Navy Commissioners, on 26 April 1672, for £670.[7] He later went on to command a merchant vessel, the *Unity Merchant*, which was in part owned by Cloudesly Shovell, and had shares in other merchant vessels.[8]

d: Abraham Hyatt

Abraham Hyatt is named in the Muster List with '*Ma*' for Master after his name[9] and referred to by name in Narbrough's journal on 16 October 1669. He was promoted Captain of the *Dove*, a dogger (Dutch fishing vessel) on 13 May 1673 and was drowned

[1] Davies, *Gentlemen*, p. 25.

[2] Bradley, *Pirates*, pp. 97, nn. 19, 100. See below, p. 50.

[3] See below, p. 140.

[4] TNA, PROB 11/414/93. There is no direct evidence that this Peckett was the same man who served with Narbrough, but in view of the somewhat unusual name, his nautical interest and place of residence it seems highly likely.

[5] TNA, PROB 11/488/196, 483/275.

[6] See below, p. 131, n. 1.

[7] TNA, TS 21/3, No. 59. The *Providence*, 67 feet on the keel, 180 tons, was commissioned 1 May 1672, under Captain William Andrews, as a fireship and used as such and expended in service at the first Battle of Schooneveld, 28 May 1673; Winfield, *British Warships*, p. 242.

[8] Davies, *Gentlemen*, p. 24. He had two children, Nathaniell and Mary, and left each of them a house, in Rotherhithe and Stepney respectively. His second wife was Lady Katherine Wyborne, widow of Sir John Wyborne (Governor of Bombay for the East India Company 1686–90, d. 1691). In Peckett's will, she was left £1,500 together with the plate which carried his coat of arms and various other items, including all the belongings she had brought to their marriage, and the right to reside rent-free in the house in which he was dwelling at the time of his death. His will was proved on 16 March 1693, TNA, PROB 11/414/93.

[9] TNA, ADM 39/2510.

on 24 February 1674 when his ship was wrecked at Bulmer.[1] Burney's *Chronological History* states that Greenvile Collins was on board the *Sweepstakes*, which is followed by most subsequent accounts. Baigent goes further and states that he was 'master of the *Sweepstakes*' and 'in sole charge of the navigation on this voyage'.[2] Burney's assertion is based on a letter which Collins wrote to Nicolaes Witsen, dated 10 June 1691, in response to a request for Collins's opinion regarding a passage to Japan via the North from Europe either by the Northwest or Northeast passages:

> In the year 1669 I had the honour to be wit[h] Sir John Narborough in the Southsea, whose noble design was most unfortunately frustrated by the Cowardise of our Consort, who most Basely left us in a storm, before we got to the Straits of Maggalenna, and Return'd back for England; reporting, that we were lost in a storm. This ship was loaden with stores and provisions, and all manner of Necessaries for such a Voyage; with materials for Building a small sloop in the South Sea, being more Convenient for Discovery. And had not this misfortune happen'd our design was to have sailed to California, and from thence to have search'd the North Coast. But to our great grief, we were forc'd to return from Baldivia in the South Sea to England.[3]

e: Mr John Wood

John Wood appears to have been the same John Wood who commanded the *Sophia* (4th rate, captured from the Dutch in 1652) from 14 November 1660 to 2 October 1661, the *Providence*, fireship, from 29 July 1665 to 7 February 1666, the *Unicorn*, fireship, from 29 August 1666 to 20 September1666, and the *John*, fireship, from 15 June1667 to 18 September 1667. Wood's subsequent career is well documented.[4] His position in the *Sweepstakes* is not clear, but it seems most likely that he was a gentleman volunteer, or

[1] Winfield, *British Warships*, p. 220. Tanner, *Catalogue,* I, p. 369, states that it was named the *Dover*, and that he was dead by the end of 1688.

[2] Baigent, 'Collins, Greenvile', *ODNB*.

[3] Witsen, *Noord en Oost*, p. 911. The letter is in English and followed by a translation into Dutch, pp. 911–12. Burney, *A Chronological History*, III, pp. 319–20, reprints this letter, quoting *Nord & Oost Tartarye*, 1692, vol. II, p. 566. Collins does not appear on the Muster List (TNA, ADM 39/2510), but since this is dated July 1669 and more men were recruited after it was forwarded, with 5 men discharged before sailing, this is not conclusive. The pay list for this voyage has not survived, but that for the next has (TNA, ADM 33/121) which shows that Narbrough himself remained on board until 4 Jan., and a number of others, including the gunner, purser and Cloudesley Shovell, much longer. Collins is not mentioned by name in any of the journals. He joined the *Triumph*, 15 Jan. 1672, as Master's Mate (TNA, ADM 33/113). It is possible that Collins, who served as master in the *Speedwell*, Captain John Wood, in 1676, and as Narbrough's master in the *Plymouth*, in 1677, when Narbrough was in the Mediterranean, may well not have served on the *Sweepstakes*'s voyage but learned of it at a later date. His letter to Witsen contains incorrect information about the objects of the voyage and the dependence on the stores and provisions carried in the *Batchelour* (excepting the shallop).

[4] He subsequently served as 2nd Lieutenant in the *St Andrew* 1671, commanded the *Kent* (4th rate) 1 Aug.–15 Oct. 1672, when the ship ran aground on the Lemon and Ower sandbank off Yarmouth and broke up. He served as Lieutenant in *Assistance*, *Princess*, *Lyon*, *Sovereign* all in 1673 then commanded the *Bonadventure* (4th rate), 17 Aug. 1673–23 Dec.1674. He commanded the *Speedwell* (5th rate), 15 Mar. 1676 for a voyage of Arctic exploration in search of the Northeast passage to China, and was wrecked on Novaya Zemla 29 June 1676. He then commanded the *Diamond* (4th rate) 4 April 1677–31 Dec.1679 and finally the *Constant Warrick* (4th rate) 16 July 1681, on which he died 25 April 1682. See, Tanner, *Catalogue*, I, pp. 425–6; Winfield, *British Warships,* pp. 99, 100, 102, 110, 157, 237–9; Charnock, *Biographia*, I, p. 380. Falmouth burial records show that he was buried on 28 April 1682, in Falmouth. In his will he is represented as of the parish of St Margaret, Westminster, and he left his 'whole personell Estate' to his wife, Elizabeth. No children are mentioned in the will, but one of the witnesses was William Wood, possibly a brother or cousin, TNA, PROB 11/370/385.

'king's letter boy',[1] since his name is not included in the Muster List that has survived. He is always referred to by Narbrough as 'Mr John Wood' which would be appropriate for a gentleman. Admiral Burney would appear to be responsible for the myth that he was the Master's Mate;[2] this position was in fact held by Giles Wood,[3] whose similar name no doubt gave rise to the confusion.

In about 1676 a map of the world was published in two sheets. Beneath Captain Wood's arms (argent a wolf passant sable, a chief gules; crest on a mural crown a wolf's head sable, collard argent[4]) is the inscription 'To Capt: John Wood this Map of the World Drawn according to Mercators Projection is humbly Dedicated by Robt. Morden & Willm. Berry, Sold at the Atlas in Cornhil & at the Globe in the Strand, London'. Another map, 'A New Mapp of Jamaica. According to the last Survey, London, printed by James Moxon and sold at his Shop in the Strand neer Cherincros at the Sign of the three Herings,1677', was also inscribed 'To Cap. John Wood Gent. This Mapp is Humbly Dedicated by James Moxon'. This document has the same arms above the dedication cartouche as the world map.

f: Mr John Fortescue

John Fortescue is described by Narbrough as 'Gentleman, aged twenty seven Years, and born in Kent'. He was presumably serving as a volunteer in a similar capacity to John Wood. He was one of the party detained by the Spaniards in Valdivia in December 1670, and described himself to the Spaniards as 'a soldier, cosmographer and mathematician on the expedition'.[5] At this time his father was still living, as Fortescue wrote to Narbrough from captivity asking for the ship's small pinnace and stating that the latter would pay him for it. His father may have been Captain John Fortescue.[6]

g: Captain Humphrey Fleming

Humphrey Fleming is described by Narbrough as 'a man about 45 yeares of age'. After the voyage he obtained a certificate for master of a 5th rate, dated 13 January, 1671,[7] but it has not been possible to find out anything about his subsequent career.

[1] The 'volunteer' system was instituted in 1661 and was originally intended to get young gentlemen to learn navigation and seamanship to qualify them for a commission. It entailed service on several voyages by authority of a royal letter to the ship's captain, at a midshipman's rate of pay.

[2] Burney, *Chronological History*, III. p. 316. Burney's assumption is probably the result of a statement by Narbrough on 4 Nov. 1670, that he sent his boat sounding along the coast and 'called this Wood's Bay by my mate's name that was in the Boate'. Captain Wood's published account says 'called by our Captain Wood's Bay, according to my Name', Hack[e], *A Collection*, p. 89; although this is not in Wood's manuscript account.

[3] John Wood states in his journal 'the 22th day of June [1670] I Borowed a boate of the Cap*tain* & did intend to goe 8 or 10 Miles SW. I had gott to goe with me Gyles Wood, Mrs Mate, John Sedgeck quarter Mr & John Lowes fore Mast Man', BL, Sloane MS 3833, f. 20r. Giles Wood's name appears on the Muster List, having joined on 18 June 1669, directly after that of Richard Haddock (who was transferred to the *Batchelour* as a mate), but his position is not stated. TNA, ADM 39/2510.

[4] These arms are shown for Wood, in the first quarter of the arms of Sir Robert Wood of Islington and Kingston, in the county of Middlesex, pensioner of King James and King Charles, with the same crest. See Armitage, *Middlesex*, pp, 174, 186; Berry, *Encyclopœdia*, II, includes Wood [Middlesex, 1606] ar. A wolf passant, sa. A chief gu. – Crest, out of a mural coronet gu. A wolf's head sa. Collared ar.

[5] Bradley, *Pirates*, p. 97, n. 19.

[6] See below, p. 556, n. 1.

[7] TNA, ADM 106/2908.

h: Supernumeraries: Don Carlos Henriquez and Solomon Franco

What little can be known with any certainty about Don Carlos Henriquez Clerque, his frequently changing representation of himself according to his present circumstances, and speculation about what may have been his true identity, will be addressed further below.[1] Narbrough thought that he was Jewish.

A small, number of *Marranos* settled in England during the reign of Elizabeth I, but most of these were expelled in 1609.[2] In 1656, following a petition by Menasseh ben Israel and statements (by the Chief Justice of the upper bench, Sir John Glynne, and the Chief Baron of the Exchequer, William Steele) that there was no legal impediment,[3] Lord Protector Oliver Cromwell agreed to the return of the Jews and allowed them to meet in their houses for public prayer. It has been argued that this action was not only a result of religious toleration but was also part of Cromwell's mercantile policy.[4] At the Restoration, despite various attempts to have the Jews expelled again, their position was strengthened – the Jews of Amsterdam having provided Charles II with considerable assistance during the Interregnum.[5] The numbers of Jews living in London in 1660 has been estimated to have been thirty-five heads of households, or a total of about 150 people.[6] A similar estimate for 1660 gives a total of 188 people, rising to 219 in 1669 and 414 in 1684 (the latter figure taken from Abraham Israel Zagache's census).[7]

Although a number of references have been found to individuals bearing the name Solomon Franco, or Frankhes at this time, there can be no certainty as to whether they all refer to the same man. In 1660, an informer's list of Jews living in Fenchurch Street, London included Sin. [Señor] Solomon Frankhes.[8] Since this is the only individual of this name recorded at that time, and bearing in mind the small size of the Jewish community, it is quite possible they do all refer to the same person.

A Solomon Franco Baixela was living in London and gave Hebrew lessons to Elias Ashmole in 1652. He was born in Vila Nova in 1625, and married his cousin Sarah Franco (b. Amsterdam 1635) in Amsterdam in 1661.[9] This was probably the same Solomon Franco who has been identified as being among members of the community in the period when Rabbi Jacob Sasportas was Chief Rabbi, who was appointed on 19 April 1664, fled the country during the Great Plague in about August 1665 and refused to return thereafter. Solomon Franco and other members of the community had come into conflict with the Chief Rabbi because they refused circumcision, possibly because they wished to preserve their capacity to move between the Christian and Jewish worlds.

[1] See below, pp. 52–7.

[2] Samuel, 'Portuguese Jews in Jacobean London', pp. 171–87.

[3] Roth, 'Resettlement of the Jews', p. 10; Lipman, *Three Centuries of Anglo-Jewish History*, pp. 1–25.

[4] Samuel, 'The readmission of the Jews', pp. 164–6.

[5] Wolf, 'Jewry of the Restoration', pp. 12–16, 24–5.

[6] Ibid., p. 12.

[7] Diamond, 'Cemetery of the Resettlement', p. 182.

[8] Wolf, 'Jewry of the Restoration', p. 7. It is interesting to note the first name on this list is that of Duarte Henriques, so there just might be a connection between Don Carlos and this family.

[9] I am grateful to Peter Barber who forwarded this information, which was kindly provided to him by Edgar Samuel, from the record found in Verdouner and Snel, *Trouwen in Mokum: Jewish Marriage in Amsterdam, 1598–1811*, The Hague, 1991.

In 1664 the accounts of the London community show a payment to Solomon Franco of £12 11s 0d in settlement of claims and a further payment in 1670 for further claims. These payments would indicate that he was employed in some minor capacity in the first years of the Congregation. In 1668, by then as Rabbi Solomon Franco, he converted to Christianity, and published the pamphlet *Truth springing out of the earth*,[1] republished in 1670.

A Solomon Franco is also recorded as a London Merchant aged about 42 years in October 1658. He, together with Duarte Enriquez Alvarez,[2] London merchant said to be about 40 years old, and Simon de Souza, London merchant aged about 55 years, gave evidence in a legal case brought by Manuel Martinez Dormido[3] who traded with Brazil and was owed large sums of money by 'diverse persons dwelling in Pernambuco'.[4]

A merchant called Solomon Franco arrived in Boston nine years earlier, in 1649, in the capacity of supercargo with a shipment of freight originating in the Netherlands. He was then said to be aged about forty. He was the agent for the Dutch merchant Immanuel Perrada and the freight was imported under the authority of Major-General Edward Gibbons. When the goods were offloaded Franco sought payment for his services, setting off a dispute as to whether the this was owed to him by Gibbons or Perada. Gibbons denied any obligation to pay him and the ship departed leaving Franco in Boston. He was unsuccessful in filing suit but did receive an allowance from the court of six shillings per week for ten weeks' subsistence until he could find passage out. Returning to Holland he then made his way to London settling among the Sephardim community. Recent scholarship places him in the broad, network of Jewish merchants who traded to the West Indies, Africa and South and North American colonies, operating within a cultural threshold between the Christian and Jewish worlds, with some practising Catholicism and some reclaiming Judaism.[5] Recent studies also identify the Solomon Franco who arrived at Boston in 1649 as the same man who announced his conversion to Christianity and left his family to the care of the synagogue in London in 1668.[6]

[1] This was a royalist panegyric dedicated to Charles II. In it he announced his conversion to Christianity, which he credited to the miraculous nature of the Restoration and to the arguments of his Christian friends that the Cabal proved that Jesus was the Messiah. Schuchard, *Restoring the Temple of Vision*, p. 676.

[2] Duarte Enriques Alvarez had come to London from the Canaries where he had been head of the revenue. He had been burned in effigy by the Inquisition on his departure. Diamond, 'Community of the Resettlement', pp. 143, 146.

[3] Manuel (or Emmanuell) Martinez Dormido (also known as David Abrabanell and David Abarbanel Dormido) was one of the key figures in arranging the Resettlement of the Jews in England under Cromwell. He was born in Andalucía and had a distinguished career in Spain before being arrested by the Inquisition and spending 5 years in prison. On his release in 1632 he went to Bordeaux and in 1640 to Amsterdam. He lost most of his wealth on leaving Spain and had further severe losses when two of ships were lost in Pernambuco in 1654. He arranged with Cromwell to live in London where he arrived in 1654. He is included in the informer's list of 1660. He was a leading figure in the small Jewish community in Restoration London. Wolf, 'Jewry of the Restoration', pp. 7, 10; Diamond, 'Community of the Resettlement', p. 135.

[4] Woolf, 'Foreign Trade of London Jews', pp. 46–7, 53–4.

[5] Smith, 'Strangers and Sojourners', pp. 21–2; Hoberman, *New Israel/New England*, pp. 32–4. For further reading on the diaspora of Jewish settlement in the Americas, see Mordecai Arbell, *Spanish and Portuguese Jews in the Caribbean*, 1981; *Portuguese Jews of Jamaica*, 2000; *The Jewish Nation of the Caribbean: The Spanish-Portuguese Jewish Settlements in the Caribbean and the Guianas*, 2002.

[6] Sarna et al., *Jews of Boston*, p. 21; Hoberman, *New Israel/New England*, pp. 32–4.

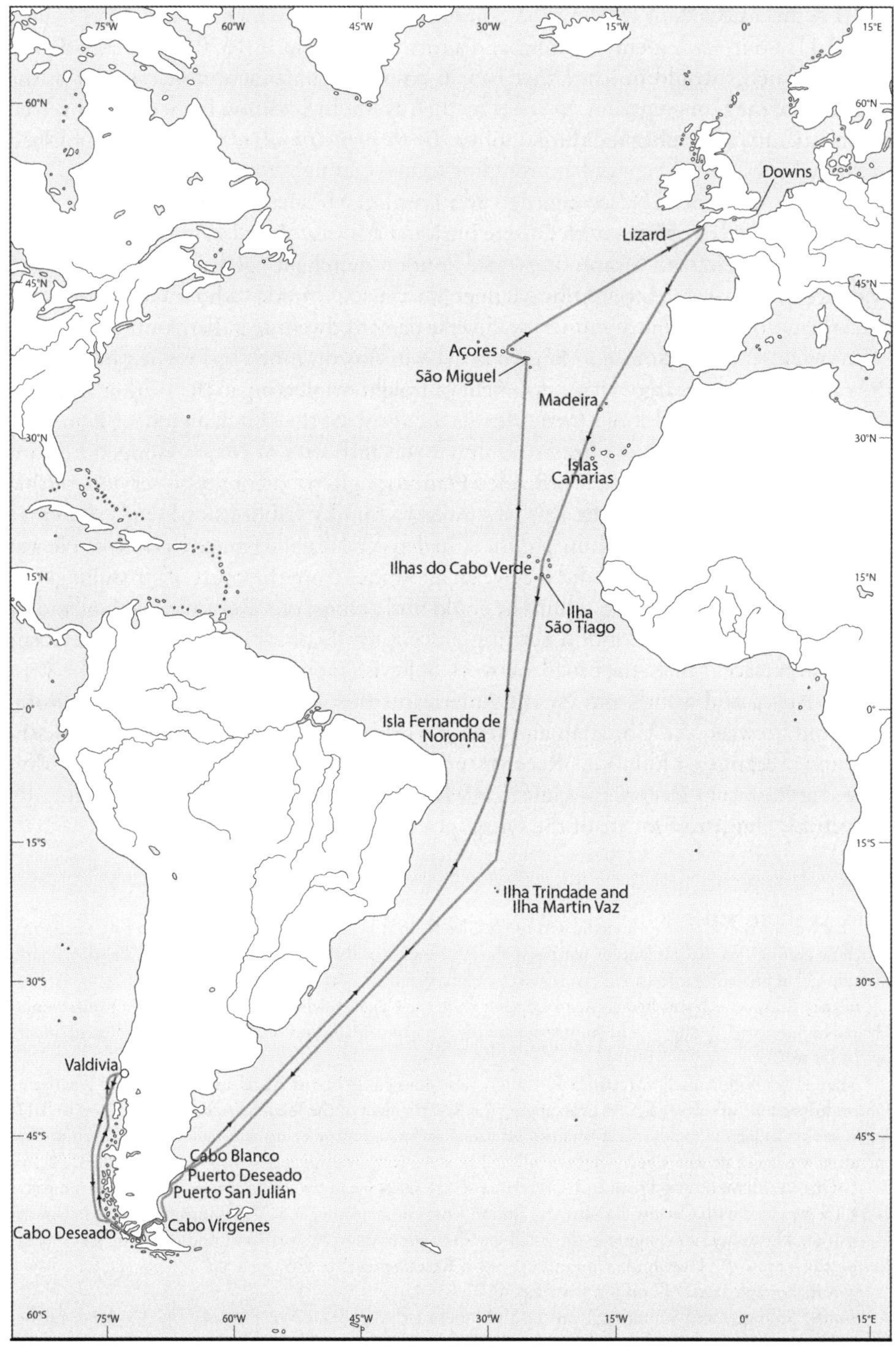

Map 1. Track of the *Sweepstakes*, Captain John Narbrough, 29 September 1669 to 10 June 1671.

9. The Events of the Voyage

The expedition sailed from The Downs on 26 September 1669, with the *Batchelour* pink, Captain Fleming, in company and all store and personnel embarked. Narbrough issued orders to Captain Fleming for keeping company with him,[1] and they took their departure from the Lizard on 29 September intending to make straight for the island of São Tiago in the Cape Verdes, but Narbrough agreed to put in to Madeira to embark wine at Don Carlos's request. The ships arrived there on 14 October and sailed two days later. Don Carlos came back from conducting business ashore in what Narbrough describes as a 'rageing passion', and expressed himself in no uncertain terms on the quarter deck in front of all the officers.[2] At that point the real destination of the voyage had not been publicly given out, and Don Carlos, hearing ashore discussion that she was bound for the West Indies, may have feared that the expedition was really bound there. After a short call at the Island of Maio to embark salt they arrived on 30 October at Praia on the island of São Tiago, in the Cape Verde Islands, where they encountered the Portuguese fleet bound for Brazil. Having embarked water and a little wood, together with eight cows and fodder, they departed on 5 November to cross the Atlantic. Narbrough did not inform his officers of their true destination until the ships had sailed from São Tiago at which time he also gave Captain Fleming his orders.[3]

On passage they had quite a lot of calm weather in the doldrums and Narbrough took the pink in tow on a number of occasions to ensure they kept up with each other and did not get separated. On one occasion they did indeed become separated but encountered each other again shortly thereafter. On 5 January 1670, they were in the vicinity of the islands of Trindade and Martin Vaz, which were shown on charts as Ascensaon, Trinidade, St Maria d'Agosta and Martin Vaz, covering a spread of 10° of longitude.[4] They took soundings and kept a careful look out, but did not sight them. Towards the end of the month they began to encounter signs that they were approaching land and started sounding again and, on 1 February had ground in 70 fathoms, in about 39°S.

Narbrough's instructions stated 'You are not to medle with the Coast of America nor Send on Shore, unles in the Case of great nessety, till you are got to the Southward of Rio de Plata and you are not to doe any Injurie to such Spaniards as you shall happon to meett nor meddle with any Place where they are Planted.' In poor visibility, Narbrough worked his way south, in and out of soundings, in compliance with this order. On 19 February, in thick fog, the two ships lost contact with each other. The *Batchelour* failed to find the

[1] See below, pp. 126–8, 146, 373–5.

[2] See below, p. 154.

[3] See below, pp. 159, 373.

[4] These were shown from the middle of the 16th century on Portuguese world charts; see charts for 1545, 1632, 1640 in Cortesão, *Portugalia*, plates 79, 533, 497. 'Ascençaon' and 'I.de Trindad' are shown on the chart of 'Brasilia' in Doncker's *Sea Atlas*, which terminates about 50 leagues east of the latter so that St Maria d'Agosta and Martin Vaz are not shown. Their positions were also listed in tables in manuals and almanacs, e.g. Tapp *Sea-Mans Kalender*, pp. 165, 171, 178 (St Maria d'Agosta not included), Sturmy, *Mariners* (1683), p. 187. 'Ascençaon' was searched for by Pérouse in 1785, who was informed by the Brazilians that they had searched for it in 1764 and having failed to find it, had expunged it from their charts. The editor of the account of Pérouse's voyage, Milet-Mureau, disapproved of this action since he continued to believe in the islands' existence; see *Voyage*, pp. 279, 283. Island 'Ascensao' was still included in Norie, *Directions* (1819), p. 4, where its existence was stated to be doubtful.

rendezvous at Puerto San Julián, and after a short period in Río de Cruz returned home.[1] On 21 February, Narbrough records making Cabo Blanco. Both Lieutenant Peckett and Mr John Wood state that the first landfall was Isla Pengüino[2] (Penguin Island) and it seems probable that this was indeed the case and that Narbrough's description was inserted after he had subsequently visited the cape, as at this stage in his journal he inserted a long description of the coast, harbours and flora and fauna.[3]

Following his orders Narbrough sailed south noting the features of the coast. He anchored in a bay south of Punta Mercedes, overnight on 22 February, where he went ashore, before turning north again and after identifying Isla Pengüino, and inspecting Puerto Deseado (Port Desire) at low water, entered the harbour on 27 February to refit and embark fresh water, and to refresh his men. On 25 March, having claimed the harbour and surrounding country for King Charles II, Narbrough sailed north to Cabo Blanco to look for the *Batchelour*, and then south again. The ship arrived off Puerto San Julián, the appointed rendezvous, on 2 April, which was inspected by boat without finding the pink. Narbrough then continued south, but was forced by bad weather to return and to anchor off Puerto San Julián on 6 April, entering the harbour the next day. Since the season was too far advanced for entering the Strait of Magellan, and in hope that the pink might yet arrive, it was determined to winter where they were despite the need for fresh provisions. Narbrough himself went on and sent out other expeditions in all directions, inspecting the natural resources of the land and regularly remarking on any minerals found and the search for gold. Plans were produced of Puerto Deseado, and Puerto San Julián[4] with full details of the tidal streams, and sailing directions for entering both harbours were included in his journal and details and positions of coast features were meticulously recorded. Throughout the time in Puerto Deseado and Puerto San Julián Narbrough had made every effort to make contact with the indigenous inhabitants, but the latter had done their best to avoid all contact. There were frequent signs of their presence.

By July, scurvy was beginning to take its toll of the ship's company, but it was not until 16 September[5] that he was able to get to sea again and make for Isla Pengüino and Puerto Deseado to obtain fresh victuals, arriving there two days later. Here the access to fresh meat and eggs helped the men sick of the scurvy to recover. Narbrough sailed for the Strait on 14 October off which he anchored on the 22nd.[6]

[1] A report from Thomas Maynard, English Consul in Lisbon, dated 17 Sept. 1670, TNA, SP 89/10, ff. 306r–307r, states that he was informed by some Englishmen that came to Lisbon in the Brazil fleet that they had encountered an English Flyboat, that had sailed with the *Sweepstakes*, and been separated from her in fog. Having failed to find the appointed rendezvous in 'River St Julian' it was returning home and had put in to Brazil to refresh the crew, and intended to make for the Barbados. The seamen reported 'that their Master used noe diligence to finde the River St. Julian; and in all probability they speake truth; for the Bay of St Julian is not difficult to be fownd'. I am grateful to Joyce Lorimer for this information. On 26 Oct. 1670, it was reported from Falmouth, that the *Batchelour* was 'Put into Penzance with much difficulty' and the *Sweepstakes* 'is supposed to be lost', *CSPD, 1670*, p. 496.

[2] See below, p. 658.

[3] See below, pp. 203, n. 2, 579.

[4] Plates 1 and 3.

[5] By which time 8 men had died, 1 of a flux and 3 of scurvy; no cause is given for the others although it was presumably scurvy.

[6] Magellan had found and entered the Strait on 21 Oct. 1520.

The passage through the Strait was accomplished in good order.[1] Time was spent anchored in the vicinity of Isla Isabel (Elizabeth Island), close west of the second narrow, at Puerto del Hambre (Port Famine) and at various other locations. Generally the ship sailed by day with the boat examining the shore, and anchored at night, but on occasion, when the weather was good, they sailed all night. They arrived off Cabo Pilar on 15 November but were forced by bad weather to anchor in Puerto Misericordia (called by Narbrough Tuesday Bay) and so did not enter the Pacific Ocean until 19 November.

They called at Isla Guamblín (I. de Nuestra Senora del Socorro)[2] where Don Carlos expected to be able to 'despatch his business', but which proved to be devoid of inhabitants. Narbrough comments that Don Carlos appeared to be totally unacquainted with the coast and that he believed he had never been in the area before and 'all was lies which heerrto he had related of his Beinge here'.[3]

Narbrough hoped to land on Isla Guafo but they were unable to do so due to the weather, nor was he able to investigate Castro, which he was very keen to do. In the event, due to the persistent westerly gales they sailed for Valdivia, off which the ship arrived on 15 December.[4] At his request Don Carlos was landed in a small bay on the south side in the approaches to Bahía Corral, into which flows the Río Valdivia. The town of the same name lay eight miles upriver. Narbrough subsequently discovered that his passenger had taken all of his possessions with him and clearly, despite his request for a boat to re-embark him the next night, had never intended to return. He did not set eyes on him again.

Narbrough stood off all night and next day sent a boat ashore to the Spanish fort with a flag of truce, to seek permission to wood and water,[5] and to buy fresh provisions. The initial interchanges between the English and Spanish were friendly. On 18 December, however, the Governor detained Lieutenant Armiger, Mr Fortescue and two other men, and refused to release them. Narbrough sent a number of letters requesting that they be set free, but bearing in mind that there was peace between England and Spain, and that he had strict orders not to take any offensive action against the Spanish, he was unable to do anything. Anticipating that his men would be sent to Spain and then returned to England, Narbrough sailed on 21 December to commence his return journey home. The journal contains relatively few remarks about the stay at Valdivia, but the Rawlinson manuscript has copies of all the letters exchanged and detailed conversations Narbrough had with the Spaniards who visited the ship and with the natives who came on board.[6]

Narbrough went to great pains to investigate the nature of the country passed through and the willingness of the people to trade. His passage home was dominated by his concern

[1] See below, pp. 255–73, 314–485, 585–92, 614–15.

[2] See below, pp. 278, 492, 580, 615.

[3] See below, p. 280.

[4] See below, pp. 285, 503, 594, 616.

[5] This was a common practice accepted generally between nations not at war. Gentili, *De Jure*, p. 91, was of the opinion that nations at peace could not keep anyone from running water or kindling a fire: 'These duties of humanity I do not lay down as laws for foemen. I am now speaking of those who are not enemies.' Vitoria, *Political Writings*, p. 279, held that 'By natural law running water and the open sea, rivers and ports are the common property of all'.

[6] See below, pp. 510–28, 536–52, 555–8.

for his ship. The main mast was in a very poor condition and had to be mended with splints secured along it. While working his way south it was found to be broken in the partners and not safe to bear a full spread of canvas. Narbrough reluctantly had to give up any hope of examining the southern coast of Chile due to the state of his mast and the constant westerly winds blowing in on the coast. He made the entrance of the Strait on 6 January 1671, anchoring again overnight and examining the shore as he went. He reached Puerto del Hambre on 11 January. Here they undertook a proper repair of the main mast. Narbrough had to rig sheer legs, using the main top mast with a spare top mast he had onboard, and lift the main mast, cut a section off the lower end, reshape it and fit it back in the step. This was a very tricky operation and required skilled seamanship, but is covered in the journal in only a few sentences. You can almost hear the relief in Narbrough's voice as he wrote that the weather was calm and the work was completed successfully.

The *Sweepstakes* left Puerto del Hambre on 4 February and the Strait ten days later, and proceeded north to Puerto Deseado where Narbrough stocked up with fresh provisions before crossing the Atlantic. He took his departure from Cabo Blanco on 26 February, and although he had hoped to land further north he was forced off shore by the weather and thus set out for home. The ship arrived off Ponta Delgada, on São Miguel in the Açores, on 19 May, where men were sent ashore to buy salad and fruit and to get news off the political situation in Europe. Narbrough called again at Terceira to embark bread and water and, having arrived off the Scilly Islands on 10 July, anchored in The Downs on the 13th. He was ordered to proceed to the Hope anchorage and thence to Deptford, arriving on 28 July, whereupon the ship went into the dockyard and was paid off on 1 August, 1671.

The *Sweepstakes* was refitted in Deptford. Jonas Shish, the master shipwright, sent the Navy Commissioners an estimate for the cost of repairs on 1 August 1671, and reported on 16 November that she was near ready for launch. On 18 January she was reported ready to take in victuals.[1] On 3 October 1671, Secretary Wren informed the Navy Commissioners that Captains Narbrough and Perry were to command the two ships selected to be sent to the West Indies.[2] Finding the assigned ships unsuitable due to their draught, Narbrough recommended the *Sweepstakes* and *Francis*; however, by the time they were ready the need was over.[3] He actually remained in command of the *Sweepstakes* in Deptford until 4 January 1672.[4]

10. Interactions with Indigenous Peoples[5]

Narbrough's instructions explicitly required him:

> to remarquie the temper and inclination of the inhabitancets and where you can gaine any Correspondency with them you are to make them sensible of the great Power and wealth of

[1] *CSPD, 1671*, pp. 410, 514, 558, 570; *1671–1672*, p. 90.

[2] *CSPD, 1671*, p. 512. Captain Walter Perry was appointed to command the sloop *Emsworth* in 1667 and transferred, with many of his men to the *Royall James* in January/February 1671, having been granted a Trinity House Certificate of Competence as a Master dated 27 January 1671. He was killed at the battle of Sole Bay, 28 May 1672. *CSPD, 1671–72*, pp. 121, 608; Tanner *Catalogue*, p. 392.

[3] Dyer, *Life*, p. 91; *CSPD, 1671*, p. 514.

[4] TNA, ADM 33/121.

[5] Contributed by Joyce Lorimer.

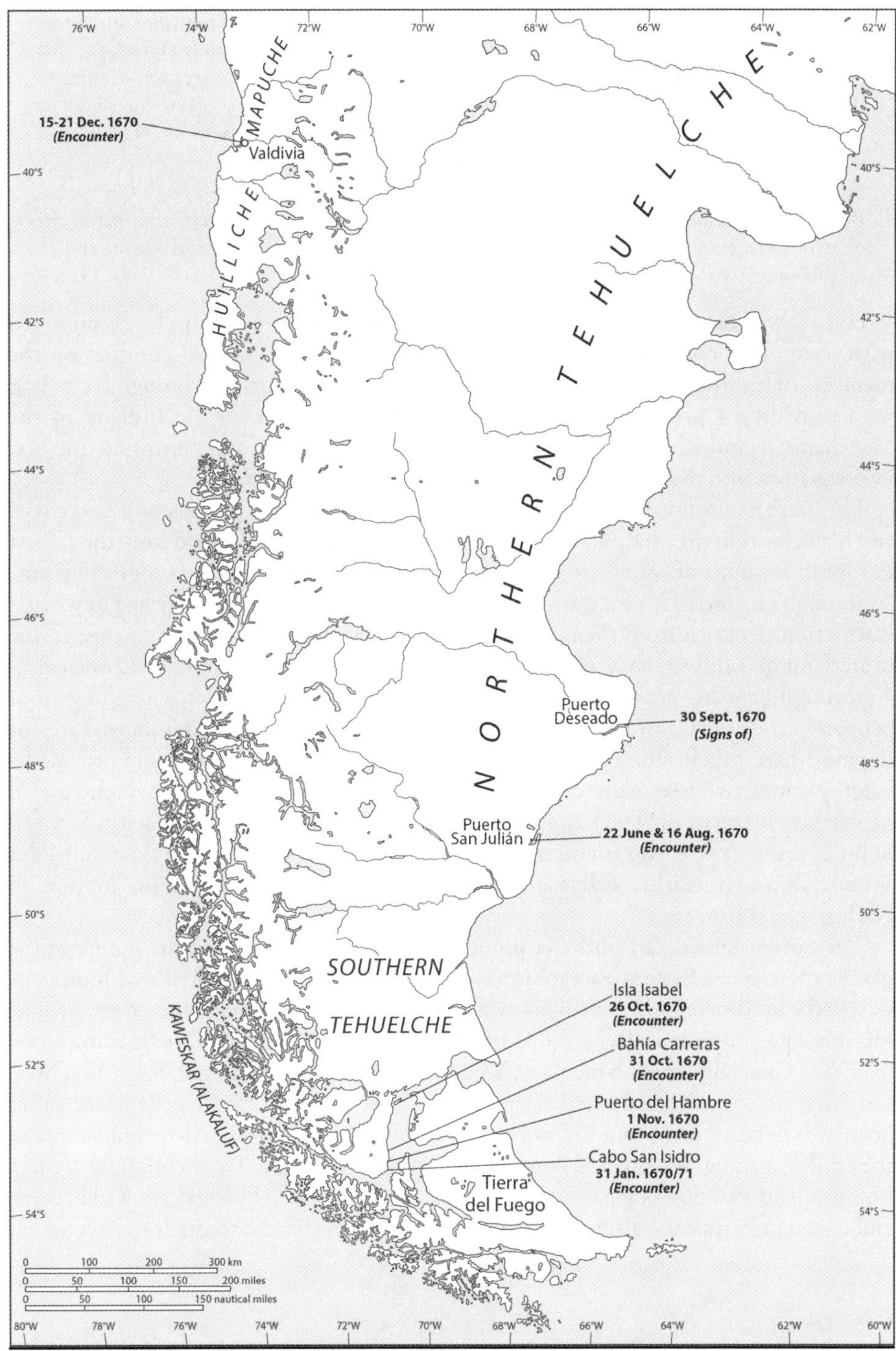

Map 2. Narbrough's contacts with Indigenous people.

> the Prince and Nation to whom you belonge and that you are one [on] porposs to set one [on] fote a trade and make frendshipp with them. But above all you are to take Care that your men doe not By any injuris or rude beheaviour to them Create an Avertion in them to the English Nation but that one [on] the other side they endeviour to gaine their love By kind & Cevill Eusage. For your easeier gaineinge a Correspondencce with the Natives their will be put on Board you an Asortement of goods proper as nere as Can be Conjectured for those People. To the Prudent disspossal of which you are To looke. For though this vojage, Beinge intended only for Discovery noe Proffit is lokt for from them yett from hence the observation is to be made what Commoditis those Countries Can afoard and what they Can take from us.[1]

He followed these orders to the letter, treating the indigenous groups he encountered with scrupulous courtesy and imposing the same standards of civil conduct on the members of his ship's company. Mateo Martinic Beros states that 'Narbrough is credited with providing a promising start to the new relationship with the Indians' of the Magellanic region which was followed up by later expeditions and permitted 'the first investigations into their ethnic and cultural traits'.[2]

The harsh environment in which the peoples of the east coast of Patagonia and coasts and islands within the Strait of Magellan subsisted was clearly established from the earliest European accounts of voyages to the region. While 'noe Proffit' was 'lokt for from them', Narbrough's record of his inquiries among them strongly suggests that he had unwritten instructions to learn from them whether gold deposits, already known to exist in the hinterland of Valdivia, were also to be found in the extreme south of the continent.[3] Narbrough kept his most consistent and detailed record of contact with indigenous peoples in the now incomplete Rawlinson manuscript. His entries in his journal are, for the most part, much shorter and less informative. He also drew images and provided a lengthy summative assessment of 'The Natives oF this Land as they Apeared unto me' in a legend on his chart of 'The Land Of Patagona &c. The Draught Of Magellan Straits'.[4] Some commentary is also found in the journals kept by Nathaniell Peckett and John Wood, although neither offers any significant additional information to that in Narbrough's accounts.

The earliest remarks by both Narbrough and John Wood relate to the stature of the people they saw in Eastern Patagonia and the Straits. Narbrough noted that footprints seen in the mud were smaller than his own before he had actually encountered any people. His subsequent opinion, after several meetings, was that 'they are oF a Medle Stature, noe taler then Generally Englesh men are'. Wood judged them, on first sight, to be 'Very Well sett Men of noe such Exterordenary Stature as is reported by Magellanes & other Spaniards to be 10 or 11 foot hie, none of these being above 6 at the Most, but I soppose they did Inmaging none would come here to disprove them'.[5] Their comments reflect how deeply the notion of gigantic Patagonians, first circulated by Pigafetta, had become embedded in European culture so that scientific observers like Narbrough and Wood felt

[1] See below, p. 122.
[2] Martinic Beros, 'Meeting of Two Cultures', pp. 111–12.
[3] See above, pp. 121510–28, 536–52, 555–83.
[4] See below, Plate 5, Foldout and Appendix 1.
[5] See below, p. 227.

the need to rebut it.[1] Recent work in physical anthropology provides a more kindly explanation for the origin of the myth than that supplied by Wood. Measurement of Aónikénk postcranial remains preserved at the Instituto de la Patagonia indicate that their stature ranged from 6 feet 8 inches to 6 feet 10 inches (174–8 cm), greater than that of other peoples of South and Meso-America and some 4 inches (10 cm) greater than that of sixteenth-century Spaniards.[2] Although there cannot be any absolute certainty, the evidence found in the reports of Narbrough and his men suggests that they encountered Aónikénk on the coast of eastern Patagonia, Kawésqar (Alakaluf) in the western half of the Strait of Magellan, and peoples now known as Reche-Mapuche in the vicinity of Valdivia.

Anthropologists draw two broad distinctions between the cultural adaptation of the peoples neighbouring the Strait of Magellan, characterizing them as either 'terrestrial' or 'maritime/canoe' peoples.[3] The Aónikenk were terrestrial hunter-gatherers who inhabited the Eastern Patagonia south of the Río Santa Cruz as indicated on Map 2. The territorial boundaries attributed here are not definitive since they were highly mobile and frequently travelled long distances for trading exchanges.[4] Narbrough's party had little direct contact with them, although they found numerous traces of their presence in their shore excursions at Puerto San Julián. Those they did encounter were almost certainly part of the small family bands typical of Aónikénk social organization. Narbrough saw bushes laid in 'halfe moones to Shelter the wind & weather off them', 'some Bushsey thrash to Windward of them & there they Lye downe & this is all they houses', as well as guanaco skins sewn together with gut, carried by one woman he encountered with a 'grate Bundle' on her back.[5] These brushwood windbreaks and rough skin tents, he rightly observed, were their only shelters from the bitter climate. Like other European mariners who touched on the coast, Narbrough's party marvelled at the ability of the Aónikénk to endure the cold, noting that they went naked except for a loose cloak, cap and foot coverings made of guanaco skin.[6] The square cloaks, which Narbrough described as 'Loose Garments of Beasts Skines Sewed to Gethers', Peckett as a 'fashon of a Blankett' and Wood as 'a skin of a Deare or sheep thrown Losely over there Shoulders' were made by the

[1] 'But one day (without anyone expecting it) we saw a giant who was on the shore, quite naked, who danced, leaped, and sang, and while he sang he threw sand and dust on his head. Our captain sent one of his men toward him, charging him to leap and sing like the other in order to reassure him and show him friendship. Which he did. Immediately the man of the ship, dancing, led this giant to a small island where the captain awaited him. And when he was before us, he began to marvel and to be afraid, and he raised one finger upward, believing that we came from heaven. And he was so tall that the tallest of us only came up to his waist. Withal he was well proportioned. ... The captain named the people of this sort *Patagoni*', Skelton, *Magellan's Voyage*, pp. 46–7, 50.

[2] Hernandez, García-Moro, Lalueza-Fox, 'Brief Communication', pp. 545–51.

[3] The Selk'nam of northern Tierra del Fuego and the Haush of south-eastern Tierra del Fuego are also classified as terrestrial hunter-gatherers. The Yamana of the Canal Beagle and Cabo de Hornos, the Kawésqar of the western channels, and the Chonos of the Chonos and Guaitecas archipelagos are classified as maritime canoe peoples. Borrero, 'Origins of Ethnographic', pp. 64–77.

[4] The designation and classification as southern Tehuelche was given to them by Spanish Jesuit missionaries in the mid-18th century. Although this name is still found, anthropologists now tend to use the name Aónikénk, which comes from the Aónikénk word 'tsoneca', meaning 'people of the south' and is closer to their own self-identification.

[5] See below, p. 235, n. 3.

[6] See below, p. 245.

women. They were, in fact, skilled productions, stretched, scraped, painted with complex designs, and cut and sewn together to make the best use of the material.[1]

Aónikénk bands tracked the seasonal migrations of the guanaco and rhea by foot. Since guanaco are strongly territorial in behaviour and will range over no more than 20 kilometres in difficult terrain, Aónikénk hunters could predict their most likely location and intercept them in places where the land form or ground cover made it easy to surprise them.[2] Narbrough noted brushwood and stone outcrops used as hides in ambushing game.[3] The primary hunting weapons were bows and arrows. Lieutenant Peckett found two of their arrows 'headed with flint-Stones very artificially, and feathered. The arrows are made of wood and are but Small, and about two foot 4 inches Long. They are 3 peeces of Sticks put into a hole at the ends of each other, and fastened with a Small green gut, and So the heads of Stone are put on.'[4] The Aónikénk also used bolas.[5] Their subsistence patterns depended heavily but not exclusively on land mammals and birds. Those near the coast also gathered mussels and other shell-fish at low tide, speared fish in tidal pools and took advantage of beached whales if the opportunity arose.[6]

In addition to local migrations required by seasonal hunting and gathering activities, Aónikénk also regularly undertook long-distance expeditions to trade with groups on the Pampas north of the Río Negro and in the southern cordillera. Narbrough's statement that he 'saw where people had made earthen pots, and had glazed them, for there lay some of their Stuffe run together' does not make clear whether he came across the leavings of ceramic production or shards of pottery. Pottery had certainly been acquired by the exchanges noted above from prehistoric times, but may have been made locally, supplementing the baskets and skin bags and armadillo shells also used as containers.[7] The three small pieces of hammered 'Goold wier' which John Wood found carefully 'tide up in a mussel Shell with a Gut Stringe' on the shore of 'the Iland of true justice',[8] was probably acquired by long-distance trade rather than produced locally.[9] Contact with Europeans had brought access to metal goods either by exchange or salvaged from wrecks and abandoned coastal settlements. Aónikénk adaptation of such acquisitions is demonstrated by a tool made from a 'Smal point of a naile in a Stick for a bodkin' found in the bundle brought in by two of Narbrough's company. The groups encountered by Narbrough's company, however, showed no willingness to trade, avoiding his shore parties wherever possible and signalling to those they did meet that their presence was unwelcome.

[1] See below, p. 532; Prieto, 'Patagonian Painted Cloaks', pp. 173–85.

[2] Borrero, 'Origins of Ethnographic', p. 76.

[3] See below, p. 451.

[4] See below, p. 439.

[5] Archaeological investigations indicate that this hunting weapon appeared in Patagonia at least as early as 4,500 BP. (BP, meaning 'before present', is used mainly in geology and other scientific disciplines to specify when events in the past occurred. Because the 'present' time changes, standard is 1 January 1950 for commencement date of the age scale, since radiocarbon dating became practical in the decade following.) The Aónikénk began to use horses for hunting with bolas in the 18th century. See, Borrero, 'Origins of Ethnographic', p. 60; Martinic Beros, 'The meeting of Two Cultures', p. 124; Mena, 'Middle to Late Holocene', p. 58.

[6] Borrero, 'Origins of Ethnographic', pp. 76–7.

[7] Mena, 'Middle to Late Holocene', pp. 57–8.

[8] The easternmost of Islas Cormorán.

[9] Recorded in the journal and Rawlinson for 13 May, 1670.

The Kawéskar whom Narbrough encountered in the complex western channels of the Strait of Magellan were clearly well accustomed to interchanges with Europeans attempting to sail through to the Pacific. Although commonly designated Alakaluf, surviving members of the people use Kawésqar as their authentic name.[1] Like the Yamana of the Canal Beagle and Cabo de Homos, and the groups collectively referred to as Chono of the Chonos and Guaitecas archipelagos, the Kawésqar are classified as maritime hunter-gatherers or 'canoe peoples'.[2] The residence of all these peoples was determined by the extent of the southern beech forest which provided them with essential resources for the construction of canoes, as well as for weapons, tools and household utensils. The Kawésqar occupied the western archipelagos of Southern Chile from approximately the Golfo de Peñas to the Penínsulãr Brecknock and the western channels of the Strait of Magellan as far east as Isla Isabel where Narbrough first encountered them.[3] Family groups depended for movement and subsistence on wood-framed, bark canoes, often carrying permanently burning fires in the same. Narbrough had an opportunity to inspect two of their canoes at Bahía Carreras and 'saw they were made of the rind of the trees, and Sewed together and Splinted with Sticks Split on the inside they were doubled with peeces of rind, and ballast lay in their bottoms. These Boats were built very well, and much like the Canoas in New England, peeked up at each end like a norway yaule [yawl], they have Small padles to padle them, these boats would Carry eight or ten people in each, they were eighteen foot Long and neare four foot broad, and thirty inches deep.'[4] Their canoes gave them mastery of the tortuous channels of the western Strait and Pacific littoral in ferocious weather, although they also constructed log portages across islands and peninsulas to give them more direct routes through their maze-like environment.[5] As Narbrough noted, they also constructed 'arbours' or dome-shaped huts on the shoreline, often leaving behind the wooden frames, which they covered with skins, when they moved on.[6] Narbrough made detailed notes of the appearance of a Kawésqar family group encountered at Isla Isabela. He also tried valiantly to record some words of their language, noting that they pronounced 'the word ursah often, but what it meant I could not understand, nor one word they Spake. If they did not like any thing they would rattle in their throats and cry ur urah.'[7] Given the eccentricity of his own spelling of English it is unsafe to conclude anything from his phonetics.[8]

Although they were largely maritime hunters Kawésqar subsistence was, as Narbrough remarks 'what they Can gett either of fish or flesh by industry'.[9] Sea mammals including

[1] They were called Pecheray/ais by Louis Antoine de Bouganville who seemingly mistook a word which was a form of greeting in their language for their proper self-ascription. Variant spellings are Alekaluf, Alacaluf, Alcaloof, Alakaluf, Alkaluf and Halakwulup. For Kawésqar, variant spellings are Kaueska, Ḳawasḳar, Kaweskar, Qawashqar. See MacKaye Chapman, *European Encounters*, pp. 1–51; Martinic Beros, 'Meeting of Two Cultures', p. 113.

[2] Borrero, 'Origins of Ethnographic', pp. 64–77. The ethnic distinctions between these groups remain a matter of debate.

[3] Ibid., pp. 66–7; Chacon, Mendoza, eds, *Latin American Indigenous*, p. 213.

[4] See below, p. 471. See Campbell, 'Journal of HMS *Beagle*', pp. 245–6, for a detailed description of the construction of these canoes.

[5] Borrero, 'Origins of Ethnographic', p. 66 and fig. 21.

[6] See below, p. 247.

[7] See below, p. 466.

[8] Kawésqar language still survives among elders of their people in Chile.

[9] See below, p. 466.

seals, sea lions, otters, dolphins, fish and seabirds were hunted, and seabird eggs and shellfish (particularly mussels) gathered. Like the Aónikénk, however, they also hunted guanaco ashore, using both sea-lion and guanaco skins for their capes and covering of their shelters. Berries and wild plants were also part of their diet. Narbrough decribed their bows as 'about an ell Long, and their arrows near eighteen inches Long, and neatly made of wood, and headed with peeces of flint Stones, neatly made broad arrow fashion and well fastened to the arrow, the other end is feathered with two feathers, and tied on with a gutt of some beast, when it is green and moist, the bow-string is a twisted gutt'.[1] Barbed harpoon tips were made from sea-mammal bone. Bone wedges were used to strip tree bark, but stone, sea mammal and guanaco bone, and mussel shells provided the edges of cutting tools. Narbrough also noted their accuracy in hitting targets with sling stones.[2]

Over a century and a half of sporadic encounters with Europeans had made Kawésqar hunters 'very desirous of Iron trade and very Covetous', eager to trade for hatchets and knives and even attempting 'to break the boat's Iron Grapnel with Stones, and would have Carried it away'. Probably the glass in the mirrors given to the women was subsequently broken and used for cutting or projectile points.[3] Narbrough's inquiries after gold aroused little interest and brought no results except in an interchange at Puerto del Hambre at the beginning of November 1670. While one man wished to keep Narbrough's gold ring he readily exchanged it for a knife. Narbrough believed that:

> at last they understood my meaning and spake very earnestly one to the other a small time, and them spoke to mee, and pointed to my ring several times, and weafed his hand up on the mountains which lies north over Port famin, and are high Craggy tops & barren with Snow on them. They Lye on the back of these hills which are next to the water Side and are growne all over with woods very thick. I was in hopes now to find some grains of gold amongst them if opportunity would permit, by reason they understood my meaning and that I desired such things in exchange for hatchets and knives. I made signs to them to look for Such as they wafted was in the hills and bring it to mee. They spake one to the other, but what they said or intended I cannot tell.[4]

Deposits of alluvial placer gold are to be found on the northern and southern shores of Strait Magellan, particularly in the area of Punta Arenas. Washings do occur on the beaches.[5] However, the modern reader has no more clues than Narbrough as to what his informants meant to communicate to him.

Narbrough's stay off Valdivia brought him into only limited contact with Indians who were either enslaved or in labour service to the Spaniards of the fort or the settlements near it. His descriptions of his interactions with them stress their cruel subjection to Spanish masters and their accounts of warlike peoples inland who fiercely resisted the Spaniards and controlled access to known gold deposits. Narbrough's reports could, at best, confirm the general understanding of the embattled state of Indigenous–Spanish relations in the marginal colonies of Chile, but gave no new, more specific, political intelligence.

[1] See below, p. 467.

[2] See below, p. 472.

[3] See Borrero, 'Origins of Ethnographic', p. 74, and below, pp. 420, 438, 448, 465, 473–4, 504, 525, 528, 540–41, 544–5, 552.

[4] See below, p. 473.

[5] See Penrose, 'Gold Regions', pp. 686–8, 692–6. The gold mining industry reached its peak in southern Tierra del Fuego in 1893, with some 800 men employed. Bridges, *Uttermost*, pp. 173–4.

Narbrough's informants may well have been from the Pecunche or Huilliche. The prehistoric and historical evolution of the ethnicity of the peoples commonly referred to as 'Araucanians', but now known as Reche-Mapuche, is a matter of scholarly debate.[1] Several mapagungudun-speaking communities inhabited the greater part of southern Chile in the pre-Hispanic period. The Pecunche 'people of the north' inhabited the region from just north of the Maipó south to the Río Bio Bio. The Pehuenche 'people of the pine' resided in the cordillera. The territories of the Huilliche, 'people of the south' extended from the Rio Bueno south to Estero Reloncavi and possibly extended to the Chiloé archipelago. Operating normally as relatively small communities which regulated their own affairs but came together in larger groups when necessary, the southward expansion of the Inca state in the late fifteenth century led to the intensification of networks between the northern and southern peoples. The arrival of the Spaniards extended rather than initiated these developing relationships. 'True people' (*Che*),[2] as recorded by Spanish missionaries and soldiers in the first fifty years of contact, continued to have a strong social structure of totemic clans and kin-groups (*lef*) with complex terminology for systems of clans, moieties and tribes. Resistance to the Spaniards led to broader alliances (*vutanmapus*) under warleaders (*toquis*) such as that led by the warrior Capolicán against Pedro de Valdivia's disastrous move to establish settlements south of the Río Bio Bio in 1552–3.[3] During the remainder of the sixteenth century the southern margins of Spanish settlement operated as an 'open frontier' with isolated forts and cities dependent on mining, agriculture and ranching worked by a restive Indian population. The decision of Governor Martin Garda Oñez de Loyola to establish a fort south of the Río Bio Bio led to a widespread and bloody uprising beginning in 1598 which wiped out thousands of Spanish settlers and settled the river as the effective southern boundary of Spanish holdings for two centuries. The fort and city of Valdivia was not repopulated until 1645, under the direct administration of the viceroyalty of Peru.

In the seventy years preceding Narbrough's appearance off Valdivia the Spanish policy towards the indigenous peoples south of the Bio Bio oscillated between extremes of conciliation and excessive violence, reflecting the conflicting approaches and interests of the Jesuits on the one hand and the military and *encomenderos*[4] on the other. Historians have generally characterized the period as one of constant war of 'blood and fire' punctuated by sporadic peace. Jesuit efforts to restrict Spanish forays to the defence of the Bio Bío frontier, broke down in the face of indigenous resistance to raids designed to secure supplies of labour, particularly after the Crown reinstituted slavery by a Real Cédula of 13 April 1625.[5] A second major general uprising occurred 1654–62 against

[1] Boccara, 'Poder colonial e etnicidade', *passim*, sees the process of identity reconstruction, known as ethnogenesis, which formed the Reche-Mapuche people, as a product of their reaction to the Spaniards which culminated in the mid-18th century. Sauer, *Archaeology and Ethnohistory*, argues for a much longer period of development, reflecting the fluid nature of *Che* socio-political organization and dating back to the prehistoric period.

[2] See Sauer, *Archaeology and Ethnohistory*, pp. 47–8.

[3] See Jones, 'Warfare, Reorganization', p. 146.

[4] The *encomienda* system in the Spanish New World assigned to the *encomendero* the right to receive tribute and labour services from Indian peoples in a particular district, in return, theoretically, for serving as their protector, and fulfilling the crown's military and civil needs in that area.

[5] The crown did not repress slavery until 1683.

the excesses of such incursions. Nevertheless, from the turn of the seventeenth century periodic parleys or *parlamentos* between Spanish and indigenous leaders established peace or periods of coexistence, using formal indigenous rituals and language. Both parties found it in their interest to participate and compromise. Spanish administrators could see that the improvement of relations with the Reche-Mapuche could deter them from forming alliances with the Dutch and other European intruders on the coast. The leaders of the Reche-Mapuche had, by the middle of the mid-seventeenth century, learned to differentiate and shrewdly negotiate between different Spanish interest groups and thus move from constant conflict to periodic policy agreements.[1]

Narbrough's conversations with Indians who came aboard the *Sweepstakes* gleaned information that 'there is much gold, and that the Indians and Spaniards have much oroe [ore] ... I give each of the Indians a knife and thankfull. I bid them speak to the Indians of the Mountains that I would give them knives & glases if they would come to mee. I was in great hopes all this time I should have the opportunity to Speak with my golden friends ... these Indians Said that the Indians of the Countrey have much gold, and they sell it the Spaniards for knives, hatchets, beads, glasses &c. They Say that the Indians of the Countrey fight with the Spaniards and kill them, and cut off their heads, and that they burn the Spaniards houses and Corn, and get their horses and ride on them, and fight on horsback.' He was confident that 'what nation soever come into this part of the world with four saile of Ships and five hundred men with power to take, will make themselves masters of all this Countrey of Chili a pleasure, and bee well paid with gold & silver for their pains. And also enjoy the fountains of gold & Silver which the whole world thirst after, for the Indians will bee their friends and help them to destroy the Spaniards through the whole land.'[2] The Dutchman Hendrick Brouwer's failed expedition to Isla Chiloé and Valdivia in 1643 had been based on similar ill-based assumptions.[3] The long history of independent and successful resistance to Spanish colonization made the Reche-Mapuche equally unwelcoming to other Europeans offering settlement and support in return for access to their gold.

11. The Fate of the Detainees[4]

The four members of the *Sweepstakes* crew detained by the Spanish authorities were joined on the next day by Don Carlos, who arrived naked at the fort. He immediately sought to establish his distinct identity, with declarations to his captors both in Valdivia in January 1671 and to the governor of Chile at Concepción a month later, which persuaded them to believe he was the *director* of their ship. Narbrough had referred to him as Don Carlos.

Given the seriousness and perplexing nature of the information gathered, it was vital that the viceroy, the Conde de Lemos[5] be advised of the presence of English intruders in the South Sea so that he could not only take appropriate action, but also undertake their

[1] See Goicovich, 'On the Mechanisms of Power', *passim*.

[2] See below, p. 530.

[3] Schmidt, *Innocence Abroad*, pp. 205–10.

[4] Contributed by Peter T. Bradley.

[5] See below, p. 543, n. 2.

interrogation personally in Lima. They sailed from Chile in February 1671 and were imprisoned in the court jail. The origins and background of Don Carlos were a puzzle from the start. His story was that he was born in Alsace (Germany), although 'in inclination and religion' he claimed to be Spanish and the viceroy was led to believe he was from San Lúcar de Barrameda.[1] Because of his loyalty to the 'true church', he explained his behaviour in Valdivia as being motivated by his wish to reveal the aims of the 'heretics'. However, he claimed to have been as a child continuously under the protection of the Queen Mother of England,[2] until as a teenager he began to travel widely through kingdoms and provinces in Europe. His signature on early documents appeared as Carlos Henríquez Clerque. His fellow prisoners seemed to reinforce his more elevated role and status in their statements and the letters they wrote.[3] For example, Fortescue and Armiger proclaimed that it was only after they had sailed 1,000 leagues after their departure that Don Carlos opened and read secret orders known only to himself and the Duke of York. They further suggested that the source of such instructions was the Earl of Sandwich,[4] former English ambassador in Spain, who had supported his inclusion in the present venture. Furthermore, Don Carlos claimed to have visited Chile before, had personal knowledge of the region, and not only had many friends there, but, according to Armiger, a sister married to a person of authority. One assumes with a degree of amusement, Armiger further added that Don Carlos went around saying that he was the illegitimate son of Prince Rupert, Count Palatinate of the Rhine and cousin of Charles II.[5]

As the months passed, Lemos must have begun to feel overwhelmed by the complexity and variety of information disclosed by his English prisoners, and especially by Don Carlos. At the same time, he was troubled by the latter's detailed disclosure of what he purported to be future hostile English aims in the South Sea, at a time which coincided with news of the capture of the fort of Chagres and the sack of Panama by Henry Morgan. Lemos must have been further bewildered when he noted of Don Carlos that 'he says he knows me and the governor of Chile'.[6] Astutely, the viceroy promptly decided that such a profusion of dilemmas could perhaps best be attended to in Spain. Therefore, he reported his decision to dispatch Don Carlos Henríquez Clerque, '*director*' of the English ship, and his shipmates, together with the transcripts of interrogations in Lima and Chile and the letters the detainees had written, in the galleons due to leave for the Isthmus of Panama. From thence they could be sent for further interrogation in the Casa de Contratación (House of Trade) in Seville.[7] However, on landing the *president* of Panama refused to allow them to embark in the galleons at Portobelo, claiming that he had not been sent copies of proceedings taken against Don Carlos in Lima and that they were not properly registered for the passage to Spain. The following year saw the arrival in Peru of responses to the documentation sent by Lemos to Spain.

[1] 36°46′N, 6°21′W, down river from Seville. Bradley, 'Narborough's Don Carlos', pp. 465–70.

[2] Henrietta Maria (1609–66), youngest daughter of Henri IV, King of France and Navarre, married to Charles I (while Prince of Wales) 1625.

[3] AGI, Lima 72, Letters of Armiger and Fortescue, 28 and 29 April, 18 and 29 Sept. 1671.

[4] See below, p. 138, n. 3.

[5] AGI, Lima 72, John Fortescue's letter of 29 Sept. 1671 also reported that Don Carlos was claiming that Prince Rupert was his father.

[6] AGI, Lima, 72, Lemos to Queen Regent, 28 March 1671.

[7] AGI, Lima, 72, Lemos to Queen Regent, 15 May 1671, 29 May 1672.

In January 1673, the analysis of documents in the Casa de la Contratación was that not only should an example be made of Don Carlos, but also of the other prisoners. Their expedition had gathered valuable information detrimental to Spain about the route into the South Sea, and also about ports and settlements there. Furthermore, Don Carlos had revealed in Valdivia an acquaintance with the discredited and recently dismissed governor of Chile, Francisco de Meneses Brito, whom he had intended to help by removing him from Chile, thereby saving him from the doubtlessly critical results of the enquiry into the many unacceptable actions of his controversial administration.[1] On the basis of this proposal alone, the Queen Regent, Mariana de Austria was to be informed that Don Carlos and his companions deserved the death penalty, since his action could have provoked a revolt in Chile and disturbances amongst the supporters and opponents of Meneses. The issue relating to Meneses would also figure in the final judicial procedures taken against Don Carlos in Lima in 1682. In a decree issued on 25 April, the Queen Regent affirmed that he was known to be untrustworthy, unscrupulous, a vagabond who had spent his life wandering from country to country and settling in none, and generally disturbing the peace. Furthermore, it ordered that the prisoners should be returned from Panama to Lima, where appropriate punishment could be meted out to them following the proper judicial processes. Lemos's future involvement in their case, however, had already ceased with his death in December 1672.

Unfortunately, from the Spanish perspective, matters in Peru failed to advance satisfactorily for many years despite repeated crown instructions to act. At first the delay occurred due to the death of Lemos, and the fact that government of the realm had passed into the hands of the Real Audiencia, as was the usual practice in such instances. This body recorded that the English prisoners were back in Lima in mid-April 1673, and then appointed an official to draw up a list of the charges against them. At the end of their term in office, the *audiencia* recorded that one of them had died late in July 1674, shortly before the new viceroy, the Count of Castellar,[2] was officially received in Lima.[3] His attention was soon diverted by rumours of ships in the southern waters of the viceroyalty in 1675, and in November 1681 the outcome of fresh legal proceedings initiated by his successor was still pending. By then, however, the cases of more prisoners, seized in January 1681 as a result of the buccaneer attack led by John Watling on the port of Arica, were also under scrutiny.[4] The combination of a new wave of hostile intrusions into the South Sea via the Isthmus of Panama, and the swearing in of a diligent and energetic viceroy in

[1] Francisco de Meneses Brito (1615–72), Governor of Chile 1664–7. He was dismissed by the Queen Regent, imprisoned and put on trial for misconduct during his time as Governor. He died before the trial was concluded. Bradley, 'Narborough's Don Carlos', p. 467.

[2] Baltasar de la Cueva y Enríquez de Cabrera (1640–86), Conde de Castellar in right of his wife Teresa María Arias de Saavedera, 7th Condesa del Castellar and 5th Marquesa de Malagón. He was a younger son of the 7th Duque de Alberquerque: Viceroy of Peru 15 Aug. 1674–7 July 1678.

[3] Hanke, *BAE*, vol. 284, pp. 32–3. A later viceroy identifies the death as that of Tomás Inglés (i.e. Armiger), ibid., p. 231, and AGI, Lima, 78, 27 Aug. 1678, who died still 'sadly professing Anglican heresies'. Richard Simson's account of the voyage of John Strong, BL, Sloane, 86, f. 23, believes that Armiger lived in Valdivia, helped them build fortifications, and died there later. Perhaps there was a mix-up between Tomás Inglés and Tomás de la Iglesia (Highway); see below, pp. 289, 560.

[4] Bradley, *Pirates*, pp. 124–5.

November 1681, the Duque de La Palata,[1] would at last unmistakably seal the fate of Don Carlos, if not that of his companions.

What irked the new viceroy was the failure of his predecessors to take punitive action for eleven years, during which it was allegedly impractical to lock the detainees in prison cells all the time, even recently whilst buccaneers roamed the South Sea. Consequently, they had virtually occupied their own dwelling, communicated with the local population, and in one instance had formed a family. This seemed so wrong, Palata commented, 'that I ordered them to be locked up, their cases to be proceeded with, and justice fulfilled'.[2]

On 22 April 1682, Juan Luis López,[3] alcalde del crimen in Lima, declared that Don Carlos Clerque, *director principal* of the expedition to Valdivia had been condemned to death. He was accused of being a traitor, pirate, and unlawful explorer in the South Sea, on an expedition for the King of England with aims contrary to the interests of the Spanish crown, and bearing gifts intended to attract malcontents, including indigenous people, to the English cause. However, there were still further details to add to Don Carlos's story. Firstly, on receiving news of his sentence he now confessed that he was a priest, who had entered holy orders in Cuzco under the name Joseph de Lizarazu, although his true name was Carlos Clerque. Given the discord this statement provoked amongst his judges, about whether it was still legitimate to carry out the sentence, or whether proof should be sought concerning the veracity of the claim, Palata decreed on 4 May that an enquiry should be initiated to examine whether a prisoner taken into custody under the laws of war and wearing secular clothing, but now claiming to be a priest, could be executed, or whether he should be allowed time to produce evidence of this assertion. A minority of the judges were minded to grant him that concession, but the majority were opposed, as López sets out in detail. Their opinion rested on the fact that he had worn secular clothing in Chile and Peru for eleven years, and they felt his new claim was contrived only to avoid or at least delay the sentence. Moreover, Don Carlos did not offer to present evidence nor did he excuse why he did not. The conclusion, therefore, was that his allegation was false. As a result, there existed no well-founded reason for relaxing the sentence, since it was issued according to the laws of war and could be fulfilled in conformity with them, as López painstakingly elaborates.[4]

As far as Don Carlos was concerned, the end of the decade-long saga loomed during his interrogation under torture on 5 May 1682. His confessions were now laden with withdrawals of past statements. He was not a priest, but had used his knowledge about the missing priest Lizarazu as an opportunity to fabricate a defence. Nor was he Carlos Clerque, or the illegitimate son of Prince Rupert and Madame Clerque, nor was he born in Brisac (Alsace) which he had previously used to hide his true origin. The truth was that he was French, from St Malo, and his real name was Oliveros, son of Oliveros Belin. On 8 May, the diarist Mugaburu recorded that he was garrotted in the court prison and then taken out into the *Plaza Mayor* as public evidence of the fulfilment of justice, and

[1] Melchor Navarra y Rocafull (1626–91), Duque de Palata in right of his wife, Francisca Toralto de Aragón, 2nd Duquesa de la Palata, 2nd Principessa di Massalbrense: Viceroy of Peru, 20 Nov. 1681–5 Aug. 1689.

[2] Hanke, *BAE*, vol. 285, p. 307.

[3] Juan Luis López, 1st Marqués del Rico (c. 1644–1703). He came to Peru in the train of the new viceroy.

[4] López, *Decission*, pp. 2–8, 14–16, 24. 'Tractatus de Fori privilegio', BN (Lima), MS B.283, damaged original in Latin.

as a warning to others, as was another unnamed Englishman captured at Arica.[1] Mugaburu makes no mention of the fate of Don Carlos's former companions of eleven years.

12. Further Information about Don Carlos Found in Recently Located Materials[2]

Recently located primary sources do not contain any evidence which provides any greater certainty as to the real identity of the so-called Don Carlos, but they do clearly indicate his remarkable facility for inventing different accounts of himself depending on his circumstances. What Don Carlos told the authorities in Valdivia on his first arrival, and his subsequent re-creations of himself in his last years spent in Chile and Peru, now stand as only the lattermost personae created by his fertile imagination, which continued to be embroidered after his death. It may well be that the name extracted from him by torture before his execution was his true one.

Materials in the Colonial Office records and State Papers Spanish and Portuguese, preserved in The National Archive at Kew, give a clear picture of when and how he arrived at the court of Charles II in June 1669 and who he then claimed to be. In Portugal, at the beginning of that month, he had told Sir Robert Southwell that he was 'the son of an English man borne in Cadiz, and has lived long in the West Indies, and is very well verst in the Spanish affaires of the South Sea. He was then found in some Insurrection and sent home a Prisoner, and having got off, he is going for England to offer his service to the King.'[3] Southwell felt it worthwhile to provide means for his passage to England, but only in the company of his returning household servants. His own missives, and the reports of observers who encountered him, indicate that Don Carlos arrived in London in a needy and ragged condition.[4] Nevertheless, despite his appearance, he immediately made sweeping claims to have high-ranking patrons and to have had a distinguished and wide-ranging service in the Spanish Indies. In his first written proposition to Charles II, dated 29 June[5] he asserted that he had gone out to Peru as a page in the entourage of Don Pedro Álvarez de Toledo, 1st Marquis of Mancera, who had held the office of viceroy from 18 December 1639 to 20 September 1648. He further stated that, since 1651, he had been recognized as the adopted son of Pedro Bohorques who, by Don Carlos's account, was not a common adventurer but rather a knight of the order of Calatrava; king of 'two of the greatest Provinces in Perue'; husband of an Inca princess; Capitán General of the Armada of the South sea; Governor of the province of Tucumán and of Buenos Ayres; Capitán General of Chile and latterly Colonel and General of Callao, which he had ultimately surrendered to a brother named Don Francisco de Victorias.[6] As for himself, Don Carlos

[1] Ryal Miller, *Chronicle*, pp. 267–8.

[2] Contributed by Joyce Lorimer.

[3] See below, pp. 21, n. 4, 88.

[4] See below, pp. 88, 111, 115.

[5] See below, p. 112.

[6] For the life of Pedro Bohorques, often referred to as the 'fake Inca of Tucuman', see Ryal Miller, 'Fake Inca', *passim*; Lorandi, *Spanish King of the Incas*, *passim*. Bohorques, born in Andalucia in 1602 into a common labouring family, had gone out to Peru at the age of 18. He had married into a *mestizo* family and lived with them for some 15 years before beginning to travel and live among the indigenous peoples, studying their culture and learning Quechua. He made a series of jungle forays between 1630 and 1637 searching for the mythical kingdom of Paytiti, supposed to lie near the source of the Huallaga river. Although successive viceroys were at

claimed to have served, in 1661, as almirante of the armada of the South Sea, and to have made an extensive survey 'of all the Sea Ports and garrisons and Sea Coasts from the Californias to the Straight of Magalanes on the South Syde, and from the s*ay*d Straights to the River of Buenase Ayres on the North', as well the first discovery of the Solomon Islands. For this service he was, he said, accepted into the military order of Calatrava under the patronage of Don Luis Enriques de Guzmán, 9th Conde de Alba de Liste, viceroy of New Spain 1650–53, and of Peru, 1655–61. By 1665, according to this account, Don Carlos was serving in Chile as Lieutenant General to Don Francisco de Meneses Brito, the Governor and military commander, and explained his arrival back in Europe as a consequence of their prosecution by the current viceroy, Don Pedro Antonio Fernández de Castro, 10th Conde de Lemos.[1] During his meeting with the earl of Sandwich, on 21 July, he further claimed to be 'of the Henriques of the Family of the Conde de Alba de Lista'.[2] In his paper delivered for King Charles II, four days later, he stressed that he had great experience in the naval and military arts and that his advice had been 'followed in many committees of State as well as of War'. In his 'Relacion of the Kingdo[me] of Peru and other parts of the West Indyes', delivered on 16 August,[3] he claimed to have witnessed upheavals which occurred in La Paz in 1661, during the viceroyalty of Don Diego de Benavides de La Cueva y Bazán, 1st Marquis of Solera and 8th Conde de Santisteban.[4] He also stated that he had been in Havana in 1668 and, from his comments, appears to have returned to Spain on one of the vessels of the carrera de Indias. Finally, on 19 August, he wrote to an unnamed recipient at court that he could no longer maintain himself in England, but was considering going to Jamaica 'because in Jamayca and Barbada there are many [men] who were under my command in Cartaxena'.[5] It was after he had surrendered himself to the Spanish authorities in Valdivia, as Peter Bradley has described above, that Don Carlos presented a very different, but no less pretentious, autobiography to the bewildered Spanish officials there. At that point he began to call himself Carlos Enrique Clerque and asserted his connections to the English royal family, although retaining his claims to have previously spent time in Chile, to have family there, and to be acquainted with Francisco de Meneses Brito and the Conde de Lemos, the current viceroy.[6] To add to the confusion the Queen Regent wrote to the viceroy at the end of December 1671 to warn him that the so-called Don Carlos Enrique Clerque was really the interpreter Thomas Highway, in disguise, and that he should be arrested and punished properly.[7]

---

first disposed to sponsor his expeditions, he was jailed when they proved to be fiascos. He was eventually exiled and imprisoned in the *presidio* at Valdivia in 1651, where it is reported that he again managed to win the confidence of the authorities. He made his getaway with a *mestiza* companion about 1656–7 and established himself in Peru in the province of Tucumán in the Calchaquí valley. There he was acclaimed by the Calchaquí peoples, who maintained a strong resistance to Spanish colonization, and welcomed his claims to be the Huallpa-Inca, which were also initially recognized by the local Spanish authorities. Subsequently, he was arrested for leading a revolt against the crown in 1659, imprisoned in Lima and finally executed in 1672.

[1] Viceroy of Peru 21 Nov. 1667–6 Dec. 1672.

[2] See below, p. 112.

[3] For a summary of the same, see above, pp. 23–4, 116, n. 2.

[4] Viceroy of Peru from 31 Dec. 1661 to his death on 16 Mar. 1666.

[5] See below, p. 117.

[6] See below, pp. 49–50, 53, 55, 89.

[7] AGI, Lima 72, Queen Regent to Lemos, 29 Dec. 1671.

The two entirely different versions of himself which Don Carlos presented to English and Spanish authorities indicate that both must be taken with a large pinch of salt. The materials stemming from his presence in London in the summer of 1669 show that it was his knowledge of the Spanish Indies, as well as the letters from Southwell and Werden, which got him a hearing with the Duke of York and other royal ministers, not any connection to the royal family. The persona he presented to them in 1669, under the name of Enriques, was a selective fusion of biographical elements of two distinct Spanish noble families. He claimed kinship with Don Luís Henriquez de Guzman, Marquis of Villaflor and 9th Conde de Alba de Liste, but stated that he had gone out to Peru in the household of the Marquis de Mancera. His account of his naval service in the Pacific seems to have been built from elements of the career of Baltasar Pardo de Figueroa y Lopidana, born in Galicia in 1619, son of Ares Pardo de Figueroa, Governor of Galicia. Baltasar Pardo de Figueroa had gone out to Peru in 1639 in the company of the Marquis de Mancera. The latter had appointed him Governor of Tucumán in 1642. He subsequently held the position of Capitán General of the *Flota de la Mar del Sur* and had been found to be attempting to smuggle a large amount of contraband silver out of Peru in 1653. He was commander of the garrison of Callao in 1667. He was killed in Lima in 1674.[1]

As Peter Bradley has written elsewhere, an individual identifying himself as Balthazar Pardo de Figueroa had appeared at the court of Louis XIV, seemingly about 1665 or 1666.[2] The discovery of Don Carlos's written presentations to the English court in 1669, make for some interesting comparisons to Pardo de Figueroa's communications about himself. He had apparently first managed to gain an audience with the controller general of finance, Jean Baptiste Colbert, and had received sufficient encouragement to address a memorial to the King. A Spanish and French version of what he wrote can be found among the Colbert Papers in the Bibliothèque Nationale.[3] Neither document bears a date but were received and annotated as '*Biblioteque 1665 Relation des Indes Occidentales par Balthazar Pardo de Figueroa*'. The writer claimed to have been a member of the city council and municipal official[4] of the city of Cuzco, lord of the valley and towns of Urubamba,[5] Commander-in-chief of the town and mine of Huancabelica,[6] Governor of the company of 500 gentlemen of Peru, Protector general of the Indians of Chile and member of the royal Council of War. He was, he said, the grandson of Henry

[1] Lohmann Villena, 'Los Americanos en las Ordenes Nobiliarias', tomo 1, pp. 313–16; Ryal Miller, *Chronicle*, pp. 31–41, 83, 108, 110–11, 118–19, 165, 209. This diary, maintained by Josephe and Francisco Mugaburu from 1640 to 1697, confirms that Baltazar Pardo de Figueroa held numerous offices in Peru, but it has not been possible to identify him with all those claimed by the individual who appeared at the French court.

[2] Bradley, 'Narbrough's Don Carlos', p. 471.

[3] The Spanish version is found in BN, Melange Colbert, 31, ff. 526–556, followed immediately by the French translation. The French translation was published by Henri Ternaux-Compans, in *Archives de Voyages ou Collection d'Anciennes Relations*, Tome II, Paris, pp. 241–96, with the title 'MEMOIRE *Presenté à Louis XIV par D. Balthasar Pardo de Figueroa, pour l'engager à entreprendre la conquête du Pérou*. (tire des manuscrits de Colbert)'.

[4] Regidor and Alferez.

[5] Spelled in the Spanish version as Urutamba and in the French translation as Urutamballe. This refers to the valley of Urubamba, known as the 'sacred valley' of the Incas, north of Cuzco.

[6] Spelled as Guincabelica in the Spanish and Huancabelica in the French translation. Huancavelica was a Spanish settlement in Peru. Mercury mines had been discovered in the area in 1564.

Vitambergue,[1] Colonel of a German regiment, and of Anne Clerque. His own mother had married Don Balthazar Pardo de Figueroa and given birth to him in 1625. His father, who had died in 1643, had served as Governor of Santo Domingo, of Guatemala, and as perpetual Governor of Callao[2]and Maestre de Campo general of the kingdom of Peru. The writer had then returned to Spain where he had served as cuatralbo[3] of the galleys until 1649 and had travelled to Flanders, Germany, Italy and other parts of Europe. In 1650 he had taken up service as captain of the guard to the Conde de Alba de Liste when the latter took up the post of viceroy of New Spain. He had subsequently accompanied him to Peru in 1656 when the latter transferred to the viceroyalty. The similarities between the autobiographical account of the so-called Balthazar Pardo de Figueroa, presented to Louis XIV, and that of Carlos Enriques, presented to Charles II four years later, are noted in more specific detail below.[4] Both claimed connections to an Inca princess, to have made survey of the coasts of America and discovered the Solomon Islands, and to have held a senior military position under Francisco de Meneses Brito in Chile. Both claimed to have lost that position when the latter was removed from the governorship (according to Pardo de Figueroa, for suspicion of supporting the imprisoned Pedro Bohorques) and had returned to Spain. Pardo de Figueroa claimed that the Governor of Havana had stolen all his money and papers and shipped him off to Tenerife for passage to Sevilla. It was by divine mercy that he had arrived at the feet of Louis XIV but he did not explain how that had occurred. His proposal to Louis XIV required a substantial fleet of ships. That which Enriques presented to Charles II is substantially the same. An island (non-existent but allegedly at the eastern end of the Strait) would be fortified, a colony would be settled within the Strait, providing a base for intelligence gathering and assaults on Pacific shipping. It is possible that Balthazar Pardo de Figueroa and Carlos Enriquez were one and the same person, an imposter who tried his luck first at the French and then at the English court. It is equally possible that that they were separate individuals and that they had conspired together. Alternatively, if Don Carlos really was Oliveros or Olivier Beilin, he could have acquired a copy of Balthazar Pardo de Figueroa's account.[5] Whether it is a case of one or two men who had served under Francisco de Meneses Brito in Chile, it is possible that the stories about Pedro Bohorques had been picked up there. The latter had been banished from Peru and committed to prison at the fort in Valdivia for some years about 1651. It should also be noted that Pedro Bohorques had taken numerous wives, one of them, whom he married in 1658, was the daughter of a mestizo of Calchaquí named Luis Enriquez who assumed the position of second-in-command of his army. As Peter Bradley has noted elsewhere, whatever may be

[1] The French version gives this as 'Vuitemberg'.

[2] French version gives this as 'Caillas'.

[3] A commander of 4 galleys.

[4] See below, p. 93, n. 10.

[5] It appears that some French soldiers did serve in the troops that Francisco de Meneses Brito took to Chile, taking the overland route from Buenos Aires. On 12 June 1667 the Queen Regent signed a general directive informing all governors in the Americas that war had broken out with France and ordering them to register all foreigners who had entered Spanish territories without a licence, and to embargo of their goods. The interim governor of Chile, who replaced Francisco de Meneses Brito, reported 'that since in this government there are no French other than a poor soldier who came from Spain in the troop which the Governor Francisco de Meneses brought by Buenos Aires it has not been necessary to undertake the actions which Your Majesty orders', Barros Arana, *Historia General de Chile*, V, p. 89.

the case, the motive could well have been to raise an expedition, possibly to free and support the violent and insubordinate Francisco de Meneses Brito. It might, alternatively, have been intended to either free the 'fake Inca' Pedro Bohorques once again, or try to assume his mantle and set up a separate kingdom in Chile and Tucumán.

Narbrough, who had Don Carlos in his ship's company for over a year, thought that he was a Jew. Don Carlos also claimed associates in Jamaica. One Jacob Jeosua Bueno Enriques, 'de nasion ebrea', had lived there for two years and had learned of the existence of a copper mine and made proposals to King Charles II for its development in 1661.[1] Peter Bradley first explored Don Carlos's possible connections to London Jewish merchants in 1986.[2] Clayton McCarl's recent edition of Francisco de Seyxas y Lovera's *Piratas y contrabandistas* (written in 1693 but not rediscovered until 2007 and published in 2011) offers a late seventeenth-century explanation of Don Carlos's origins and career. Seyxas y Lovera claimed to have been in possession of an account of Narbrough's voyage given to him by 'Thomas Ricardo', allegedly a lieutenant on the *Sweepstakes* and later a pilot on Seyxas y Lovera's own ship when he was licensed by Spain to privateer against French shipping. By Seyxas y Lovera's account, Don Carlos, whom he called 'Carlos Henrriquez Ckrelck', was a crypto-Jew, born in Spain in a community of the same. His father had maintained him in England and the Netherlands from 1640 to 1656, giving him an education which allowed him to present himself as either a Catholic or a Jew. He had left the Netherlands in 1656 and spent more than a decade in Peru and Chile. He had appeared in Europe again in 1667 and subsequently attempted, unsuccessfully, to persuade the English, Dutch and French courts to provide him with the shipping and forces to pass through the Strait and conquer and assume government of Chile. Seyxas de Lovera alleged that wealthy Jews had lobbied on Don Carlos's behalf, and that he had returned to the court of Charles II supplied with letters of credit to fund one-third of the cost of the proposed expedition. Plans for a larger expedition, secretly supported by the Duke of York and Charles II, had come to the notice of London merchants.[3] These had protested that Don Carlos was both known to be a Jew, and untrustworthy, and that his project would damage their own commercial interests now that peace had been made with Spain. Don Carlos had sailed with Narbrough as pilot and guide, proving incompetent to perform these duties, and had left the ship in Valdivia because he feared repercussions, either from his shipmates or when he returned to England. Seyxas y Lovera also claimed that, after Narbrough's return, members of London's Jewish community had tried to defend Don Carlos's actions to the King, and that a further English expedition was sent to the Strait in 1675.[4]

Seyxas y Lovera, a Galician, was himself a picaresque character who had, as he recorded in his *Descripcion Geographica*, travelled widely in the Far East and the Spanish Indies, in

[1] TNA, CO1/15, no. 74, Proposalls from a Jew Concerning a Copper Mine in Jamaica, 24 July 1661.

[2] Bradley, 'Narbrough's Don Carlos', *passim*.

[3] No record of any such plans had been found.

[4] See McCarl, ed., *Piratas*, pp. 144–51, and 'Carlos Enriques Clerque as crypto-Jewish confidence man', *passim*. No record of any approach by London Jewish merchants to King Charles II about Don Carlos after Narbrough's return has yet been found. Seyxas de Lovera may be making a confused reference to a petition about the right to practise their religion, which leaders of the London Jewish community had made to Charles II in 1674. Fraser, 'Cromwell, Charles II and the Jews', pp. 23–4. Apart from privateering ventures from Jamaica, no officially sanctioned expedition sailed into the Pacific until that of Captain Strong in the *Farewell* (also known as the *Welfare*) in 1689–91, when 10 sailors were also captured and detained by the Spaniards.

Dutch, French and Spanish shipping, and engaged in slave trading to Brazil and privateering. At the time when he completed *Piratas y Contrabandistas*, in 1693, he held a minor municipal appointment in New Spain. There he came into conflict with the viceroy and spent much of his appointment in prison. He subsequently left for France where he lived until his death in 1705. As Clayton McCarl notes, there is no record of Thomas Ricardo or of his account of the Narbrough voyage which Seyxas y Lovera claimed to possess. In the absence of any reference to him in the muster list of the *Sweepstakes*, or of a lieutenant of that name in any of the contemporary naval records, it must be presumed that Seyxas de Lovera invented him to give versimilitude to his narrative. Seyxas y Lovera, did, however, move among the same maritime and merchant communities in Europe and the New World, where he might well have picked up fragments of real information, as well as exaggerated tales, circulating about the Narbrough expedition and Don Carlos's subsequent activities in Peru. Don Carlos's 'relación', written in August 1669, demonstrates a fairly detailed knowledge of the Caribbean and the trade routes of the galleons and *flota* and *navios de permission* of the *Carrera de Indias*, although he clearly had never been south of Buenos Aires and knew nothing of the Strait of Magellan or the Pacific coast. His complaints about the transfer of the *asiento* licence to the Genoan merchants Domingo Grillo and Ambrosio Lomelino, may well reflect the resulting losses suffered by his crypto-Jewish relatives, or indeed by himself, after being shut out of that trade.[1]

In the end we are left with what Narbrough wrote about Don Carlos. He thought Don Carlos was Jewish and about forty years old. He noted that Don Carlos spoke and wrote both French and English, that he seemed to know more about the English nobility than Narbrough did, that he was no seaman, and that he did not think he had military experience either. He also took all his possessions with him when he left the *Sweepstakes*, obviously not planning to return. Amongst these were four seals, undoubtedly intended to authenticate whatever enterprise was intended.[2] At best, the recently uncovered English and Spanish materials demonstrate that the so-called Don Carlos, was an accomplished confidence trickster. They support Peter T. Bradley's assessment that he was a Jew and had connections to the Jewish community in London. Finally, they suggest that, whether he had actually been in Chile before or not, his real objective was in some way to resurrect and profit from the activities of Pedro Bohorques, the 'fake Inca of Tucumán'.

13. The Spanish Reaction to Narbrough's Voyage[3]

When on 23 January 1671 news was received in Lima of Narbrough's presence on the coast of southern Chile, it immediately provoked anxious reactions concerning its possible impact on vital maritime contacts with Chile and Panama. Hostile foreign intrusion into the South Sea had ceased after the withdrawal from Valdivia of Hendrick Brouwer's expedition in 1645.[4] However, viceroys remained aware of the mechanisms that needed

[1] See above, p. 24, n. 1, and below, p. 673.

[2] See below, p. 522.

[3] Contributed by Peter T. Bradley.

[4] Bradley, *Pirates*, pp. 71–86.

to be enacted in order to counteract such threats, the outlines of which had been drawn after Francis Drake had entered the Bay of Callao in February 1579. Since then they had been regularly updated during the succeeding years of Dutch intervention in the Sea.[1] Now, in 1671, the hasty reactions of the Conde de Lemos were inspired by the fact that the news had originally referred to twelve vessels.[2] Local governors of ports between Arica and Guayaquil were ordered to call up their militias, and warnings were delivered to the viceroy of New Spain (Mexico), and the *presidentes* of Quito, Santa Fe de Bogotá, Guatemala and Panama. On 24 January Callao's permanent *presidio* of armed men was placed in a state of readiness, some of them in bays south of the port, whilst in Lima men who had served in wars in Europe were called up to reinforce the capital's thirteen militia companies. Cavalry companies were paraded, and companies of free Black and Mulatto militia were called up. Three weeks later, on 14 February, the viceroy received the welcome news that only one English ship had entered the South Sea and the costly emergency measures were rescinded.[3]

Nevertheless, one feature of these customary precautions in response to foreign intrusions did have an impact for Chile. This was the immediate closing of the port of Callao until accurate news about the location of the intruders was available. This action prevented the dispatch of the important annual shipment of the *situado*[4] upon which Chile, including the remote Valdivia especially, depended. Even when news of Narbrough's departure reached Lima, a second treasury council meeting decided that aid would still have to be delayed until the following spring. The best that could be risked, was the dispatch of a single ship to transport 10,000 *pesos* in silver (rather than an average cargo usually valued at 250,000 *pesos*) plus gunpowder and munitions. It was instructed to proceed no further south than Valparaíso, in the (very unlikely) hope that some of the cargo could be carried overland to Valdivia despite the winter rains, swollen rivers and attacks by Araucanian warriors.[5]

Valdivia between 1599 and 1645 had been unoccupied since the massacre of its inhabitants by Araucanian warriors. As a result of the expedition of Hendrick Brouwer in 1643, which reached the head of the bay unchallenged and anchored at the mouth of the river, rudimentary forts were constructed and a new settlement established between 1645 and 1647. In the 1650s, when it was clear the Dutch were not going to return, voices were raised in Lima for the abandonment of Valdivia once more, and both the viceroy and the Governor of the port agreed. However, this was not done and the reaction to Narbrough's unopposed but unthreatening visit was a fresh incentive for strengthening its defences. Existing forts downriver from the town were remote from one another and accessible only by boat or canoe, and each in turn might be overcome, perhaps without the garrison at Valdivia itself upriver being immediately aware of the threat. Consequently, in the early 1670s, the defences dating from the late 1640s on the island of Mancera at the mouth of the river, and at Corral across the bay on its southern side, were strengthened by the completion of a fort at Punta de Amargos on the southern coast, begun in 1658 but

[1] Bradley, *Pirates*, pp. 4–70.

[2] AGI, Lima, 72, Lemos to Queen Regent, 28 March 1671.

[3] AHN, Diversos, Cartas de Indias, 392, items 1–11; Bradley, *Defence of Peru*, pp. 142–3; AGI, Lima 72, Lemos to Queen Regent, 14 Feb. 1671; Ryal Miller, *Chronicle*, pp. 171–2.

[4] Support, silver, supplies etc.

[5] AGI, Lima 72, Lemos to Queen Regent, 2 May 1671.

still uncompleted, and most significantly by a second fortification across the bay on the mainland at Niebla. The latter had been proposed thirty years previously, but only now, after Narbrough's unopposed passage to the head of the bay, was entrance into the River Valdivia defended by the crossfire of forty-eight guns from three directions: the island, the mainland to the north, and the forts on the southern coast of the bay. Finally, to provide an early warning of the approach of enemy ships, a battery was placed on the western headland at the entrance to the bay below Morro Gonzalo.[1]

However, in the post-Narbrough era Valdivia remained an unpopular location. Then, in the 1670s, Viceroy Castellar had begun to attend not only to its military needs and the grievances of convicts and delinquents exiled from Peru who manned the forts, but with some success to the alleviating of conditions under which they and settlers existed. He ensured that shipments of food, arms and everyday necessities were more regular, and stored securely in crown warehouses. Separate quarters were constructed to house married and unmarried residents, a church was rebuilt, a new school was provided, and a new hospital was staffed by a doctor and a surgeon. Expanded facilities were also created for the repair of ships in three new yards. Therefore, after Narbrough's departure, Valdivia was consolidated as a significant, occupied, and permanent southern frontier of Spanish settlement on the South Sea coast. The legacy of the viceroy's work post-Narbrough at Valdivia had secured the port from any potential risks posed by buccaneers in the South Sea from the 1680s, or by John Strong in 1690.[2]

Nevertheless, Castellar was still confronted until 1675 with the worrying question of the legitimacy of the intelligence he received from Chile about Don Carlos, specifically his confessions concerning England's long-term interests in the region. Previously in the 1660s, information had been sent to Lima about discussions in England relating to commercial prospects for embarking on a South Sea route, via Peru to the East Indies. It later transpired that there was a direct link between Don Carlos and this proposal. For example, during his first declarations in Chile he mentioned some of those involved, such as councillors of state with whom he claimed to be acquainted, the issues they discussed, and the aspirations they harboured in the South Sea.[3] Significantly, though, whereas in England he had sympathetically endorsed the proposals, he now revealed them in a manner to enhance his own personal stature, and to the detriment of the English crown. Therefore, when after Narbrough's departure Castellar was informed that foreign ships had been seen off the coast of southern Chile, undoubtedly at the back of his mind and influencing his actions were the warnings first expressed there by Don Carlos.

[1] Bradley, *Defence of Peru*, pp. 183–90. See Map 9, p. 288.

[2] Bradley, *Pirates*, pp. 108–84, and *Last Buccaneers*, pp. 6–29.

[3] *Information given in Valdivia*: BN (Lima), MS F.160 (damaged), copy BL, Add MS 28457, 'Avisos generales en raçon de las proposiciones que se hizieron a Carlos 2° de la Gran Bretaña'. AGI, Lima 73, 'Testimonio de los autos sobre averiguar los designios del enemigo'. BN (Madrid), MS 1871929, Carta escrita por Carlos Henríquez Clerque alemán [al] gobernador de Chile, 16 Jan. 1671. BN (Madrid), MS 2341, f. 143, and BL, Add MS 21539, f.16. 'Copia de carta de Carlos Henríquez Clerque al Conde de Lemos', 28 Jan. 1671. *Information given in Concepción*: AGI, Lima 73 'Autos continuados'. BN (Madrid), MS 18719[28], 'Papel de Carlos Enrique Clerque al gobernador de Chile', 11 Feb. 1671. AGI, Lima 72, 'Copia del papel que escriuio en esta ciudad ... Carlos Henriquez Clerque'. Seyxas y Lovera, in 1693, records that he believed Don Carlos had been in Chile/Peru from 1656 until 1667 and then made fruitless efforts to persuade the English, Dutch and French to send fleets to take over Chile, details of which, together with more background information, are given in McCarl, *Piratas*, pp. xlv, 144–54.

Keen to inspire confidence in the veracity of his information, Don Carlos authenticated his background by claiming seventeen years of service to the English crown. This enabled him to reveal the dangers to the Spanish empire from England, France and Holland, all jealous of its power and wealth. The evidence was said to be derived from his acquaintance with authors of a memorial concerning trade, presented to the crown in London in 1663 by what was recorded in Spanish documents as the *Real Compañía de Comercio* (presumably the Council of Trade). Their motives derived from growing competition by Dutch merchants with English trade, and it was hoped they would also gain support in Denmark and Sweden. However, according to Don Carlos, Charles II was not yet prepared to back the project, that is until 1669 when the King recalled him from a mission to Sweden to offer his assessment of it. Basically, the challenge to Dutch commerce would derive from exploring the viability of a western route for English merchants into the South Sea, from there continuing onwards to the East Indies. In essence, he argued, this was transposed into the work of exploration embarked upon by Narbrough, on whose expedition he claimed to have been appointed as *Director general.* The plan was to reconnoitre unoccupied locations in the vicinity of the Straits of Magellan, both in the Atlantic and in the South Sea as far as 40°S, which might be considered viable for fortification and population. If such sites were found, an English fleet would soon return with weapons and families to settle.

Therefore, a new period of unrest in Peru and Chile was aroused, when Viceroy Castellar was alerted from Spain that it was likely that three English ships were soon to head for the South Sea. In practice, no remedial action was immediately taken in Spain, nor on behalf of Viceroy Castellar in Peru, but a warning was sent to the Governor of Chile which reached him in December 1673. In the coming years, the governors of Chile, Juan Henríquez, and of Chiloé, Francisco Gallardo, were to play key roles in responding to reports, initially of foreigners from Europe on the coasts and islands of southern Chile, but later unsurprisingly of Englishmen after the recent events in Valdivia, and in the context of continuing reports from Spain about English aspirations in the South Sea. At first, a vessel was sent by Governor Henríquez to Chiloé, with instructions to explore southern coasts in January or February 1674. It failed to execute its mission. A second one from Chiloé was tasked with searching as far as the Strait of Magellan, but returned in February or March 1674 without success. No journal was written and no latitudes recorded. However, the most incredible feature of this second venture was the fact that it returned with several native Chonos Indians. Most notable on this and on later occasions, was one of them named Talcapillán, who claimed that there were already populated forts on a mainland and insular site. This information was passed on to Governor Henríquez and to Lima. Then in October 1674, the Governor of Chiloé sent out another expedition in seven *piraguas* under the command of his son Bartolomé, with Talcapillán as their guide.[1] They returned at the end of January 1675 without any sightings of foreign vessels. But again they were amply armed with detailed descriptions by Talcapillán and others, sent

[1] Urbina, 'Talcapillán'. Castellar to Queen Regent, 28 April 1675, named the supposed sites as Ayauta and Callanac, 160 leagues from Chiloé. Various declarations of Talcapillán and other Chonos, letters of Juan Henríquez in Concepción, Francisco Gallardo in Chiloé, and the report of Bartolomé Gallardo in Lima, 8 May 1675, are found in AGI, Lima 73.

to Lima to inform Viceroy Castellar personally of the events in Chile. Mugaburu reported in Lima that one of them bore the news that 'the enemy was laying siege to islands near the Strait of Magellan at 51°S'.[1] Viceroy Lemos had previously counselled without response, in March 1671, that the Spanish crown should send six armed ships to defend the Strait, since if an enemy were to occupy a port there, it could result in the occupation of Valdivia.[2]

In mid-April 1675, some of those who had participated in the reports arrived in Lima, elaborating their stories with further detailed descriptions of the populated sites, their defences, their weapons, and their occupants unrecognizable as Spaniards. Viceroy Castellar might have been forgiven for wondering whether this could still be a sequel to Narbrough's expedition, bearing in its wake some of the repercussions outlined by Don Carlos. They also now mentioned that the foreigners had brought gifts for them, a statement that preceded one of the charges later laid against Don Carlos at his trial.[3] By now, however, the governors in Chile no longer seemed to believe that foreign settlements thrived in such inhospitable southern zones as those described, and they believed that the Strait of Magellan was more likely to attract foreigners bent on undermining Spanish supremacy in the region. Castellar, faced with Talcapillán and his companions, now seems to have become sceptical of the often repeated, unlikely tales from southern Chile, and turned against the first principal source of them, who finally confessed his errors. A contribution to this process may have been the fact that when Castellar asked Narbrough's detainees, who had been in prison now for four years in Lima, whether during their voyage to Valdivia they had seen any of the settlements alleged by Talcapillán and his companions, they denied it.[4]

Having resolved that worrying dilemma, Castellar's principal anxiety had become the pressing need to dispatch crown and private silver to Panama. He had distributed the usual warnings along the coasts, reviewed his troops and even organized mock battles in Lima. Given the vital importance of Peruvian silver for the Spanish economy, it was an obligation that viceroys were always fearful of not fulfilling on time, thereby failing to synchronize its arrival in Panama with that of the galleons at Portobelo to carry it to Spain. For six months he was baulked by the refusal of merchants to put their own silver at risk, whilst news of intruders continued to circulate amongst them. Some of them, in fact, argued that crown silver should first be used to dispatch a fleet to Chile to dislodge the English enemy reported to be there. They relented only when informed that they would be held responsible for all additional costs caused by further delays. As a result, it was finally resolved in Lima that increasingly unreliable tales did not merit the cost of sending armed ships to Chile.[5] Therefore, the spin placed upon the activities and objectives of the Narbrough expedition by the revelations of Don Carlos brought no actual danger to the viceroyalty of Peru. On the other hand, Castellar's decision to assuage his lingering unease

[1] Ryal Miller, *Chronicle*, p. 223.

[2] AGI, Lima 72, Lemos to Queen Regent, 28 March 1671.

[3] Ryal Miller, p. 226. AGI, Lima 73, Declarations of Indians, 29 Oct. 1674, 25 Feb. and 19 April 1675; letters of Governor of Chile, 6 Dec.1674 and 12 March 1675.

[4] AGI, Lima, 73, Declarations in Lima by the English detainees, 25 Feb. 1675.

[5] AGI, Lima 73, 'Resolución en la Junta General en Lima [2 May 1675] sobre poblaciones de Ingleses'; Ryal Miller, *Chronicle*, p. 229.

did bring rewards of a maritime and cartographical nature, not only for Peru and Chile but also for Spain.

In September 1675, he agreed to dispatch two vessels to southern Chile to resolve remaining fears raised by the reports of English settlements there, provided this did not require financial contributions by the crown. Two vessels left Callao under the command of the Capitán de Mar y Guerra Antonio de Vea and Capitán Pascual de Iriarte, with a mission to begin a search from Chiloé towards the Straits of Magellan.[1] Vea's vessel was damaged in the Chacao Channel[2] on the north coast of the island, with Vea resuming the exploration of archipelagos in boats at least as far as 47°S in the Golfo de Peñas.[3] Iriarte was reported to have explored islands beyond the western entrance to the Straits of Magellan. Tragically, seventeen of his men, including his son, who had previously been sent ashore in a boat near the Islotes Evangelistas,[4] had perished in a storm whilst attempting to leave a plaque commemorating their visit. No trace was found anywhere, of course, of the supposed English settlements. Importantly, however, Vea's journal, including his *Carta idrográfica*, filled significant gaps in Spain's outdated geographical knowledge of the region, gathered hands-on experience of the southernmost coastal regions of the viceroyalty of Peru, and later contributed to Spain's reuse of the southern route into the South Sea in the early eighteenth century.[5]

14. Navigation

a: Narbrough's Navigation

At the time of Narbrough's voyage coastal navigation was based on charts showing the coastline, but not necessarily to scale and with relatively little offshore detail, together with knowledge of the passage handed down the generations and recorded in sailing directions known as 'rutters'. On an unknown coast and close inshore the mariner had to feel his way with lead and line.[6] Narbrough refers to Hakluyt's work, probably using the second edition of *Principal Navigations*[7] which contained the voyages of previous English navigators round South America with their descriptions of the coast, as well as the account of Sir Francis Drake,[8] both of which he used for their respective sailing directions.[9]

[1] Vea, 'Relación diaria'.

[2] Canal Chacao 41°50′S,73°29′W.

[3] 47°20′S,75°10′W.

[4] 52°38′S, 75°08′W.

[5] Bradley, *Defence of Peru*, pp. 206–7, briefly notes the departure of the first small squadron commanded by Jean Nicolas Martinet, to head directly for Peru in 1716 to reinforce the *Armada del Mar del Sur*, the first to do so directly from Spain to the South Sea since the early 16th century.

[6] First mentioned by Herodotus c. 450 BC, bk 2.5.

[7] Hakluyt, *Principal Navigations, Voiages, Traffiques and Discoveries of the English Nation &c*, London 1598–1600.

[8] Drake, Sir Francis, *World Encompassed*, London, 1628.

[9] In Hakluyt, *Principal Navigations*, vol. III, rutters are found at pp. 724–6, 825–35. The principal voyages are those of Francis Drake, pp. 730–42; Nuno da Silva, pp. 742–8; John Winter, pp. 748–53; Thomas Candish [Cavendish], pp. 803–25, all of which contain navigational information. Drake, *World Encompassed*, pp. 17–46.

The lead at this time was generally of six or seven pounds weight,[1] shaped like a rod or narrow cone with the apex attached to a marked line and an indentation in the bottom for arming it with tallow. When a sounding was taken the depth of the water was measured by the marks on the line and the tallow brought up a sample of the seabed.[2] This was of inestimable value to the mariner who recorded in great detail the nature of the seabed and used it in conjunction with the depth to help him locate his position.[3] The size of the sample was generally less than 2 inches in diameter and only relatively small pieces of sediment, gravel, sand, small shells, mud and clay, adhered to it; weed, rock, shingle, pebbles and stones[4] were determined by the shape of the indentations left behind in the tallow. Narbrough frequently records 'ooze' (which is spelled in various ways) and refers to a fine mud, through which an anchor might well drag and which was therefore poor holding ground.

By the second half of the seventeenth century oceanic navigation consisted basically of the ancient simple method of trying to determine in what direction and how far a ship had travelled, i.e. dead reckoning (see below), augmented by astronomical observations for latitude, and this remained the principal method for many years to come.

Direction was found by the magnetic compass.[5] Variation,[6] the difference between the point indicated by a magnetic compass and true north, was appreciated as early as 1451,[7] and the fact that it changed with time was confirmed by Henry Gellibrand in 1634 by comparing observations taken in 1580, 1622 and by himself in London.[8]

The variation of the compass could be observed by taking a bearing of the sun and its altitude in the morning and again in the afternoon when the sun was at the same altitude. Taking the mean of the bearings gave a true north–south line, which, by comparison with the magnetic bearing gave the variation.[9] For a single observation the true bearing could also be calculated which was then compared with the bearing from the magnetic compass,[10]

[1] Goell, *Sea Grammer*, p.56.

[2] The normal length of the lead-line was 20 fathoms marked at intervals of 2, 3, 5, 7, 10 and 15 fathoms, while the deep-sea-line was 100 or even 200 fathoms long marked at 10-fathom intervals, starting at 20 fathoms.

[3] *The General Instructions for Hydrographic Surveyors*, Admiralty, 1884, p. 8, still stress this point as in the remarks on 'nearing the English Channel on the usual and best parallel of 49°20′N, the same depth of 73 fathoms occurs at spots 125 miles apart; but at the outer depth the bottom is "fine sand", and at the inner it is "ooze", which distinction, in foggy weather is therefore the mariner's only guide'.

[4] Pebbles and shingle are essentially water-rounded pieces of rock, while stones are pieces recently broken off and not yet rounded. What exactly Narbrough intended by 'Pepble stones' is not clear but would probably have been small water rounded pieces of rock, from about the size of a pea to that of a walnut.

[5] The compass is first recorded in Europe in the late 12th century by Alexander Neckham (1157–1217), although it may well have been in use earlier. Taylor, *Haven-finding*, pp. 95–6.

[6] This is known to scientists as declination.

[7] Taylor, *Haven-finding*, p. 173.

[8] Gellibrand, *Discourse Mathematical*, p.19.

[9] This ignores the change in the sun's declination and change of the vessel's position, which, due to the inherent inaccuracies in the compass and difficulties with an accurate observation, was unlikely to make any difference. It does not appear to have been used by Narbrough.

[10] The bearings were taken with an azimuth compass: a compass mounted in gimbals in a box used for observing the magnetic bearing of the sun for comparison with its calculated bearing to obtain the variation. It was fitted on top with a ring engraved in degrees round its circumference, mounted on this was a rotating alidade with a pointer at one end and a vertical arm with a slit in it at the other. From the top of this a thread ran across

the difference being the variation. The calculation of this was much easier when the sun's zenith distance was 90°, i.e. at sunrise or sunset, which was called an amplitude and involved only the declination of the body and the observer's latitude. When the sun was above the horizon it was called an azimuth, and involved the altitude as well as the declination and latitude.[1]

That metal near the compass affected the direction in which it pointed was appreciated in the sixteenth century, but the theory behind this and how the effect changed with the direction in which the ship was pointing was not. That had to wait for a proper explanation until the nineteenth century.

Distance offshore was measured by eye and experience; distance through the water by the mariner's log, which was first described by William Bourne in 1574, although it was in use before that date.[2] It consisted of a float, weighted on one side so that it would stand vertically in the water, on the end of a marked line, which could be paid out over the stern of a vessel. The length of line that ran out in a given time, measured by a sand glass or recitation of an incantation, gave the vessel's speed. The relative positions of ports were provided either in the form of a table of co-ordinates (latitude and longitude) or shown graphically on a chart or globe. Tables of positions were provided in most navigation manuals and ephemerides.[3]

Astronomers had been able to define latitude on shore relative to the sun and stars since antiquity, so that the first co-ordinate of the port was reasonably well established in terms of angular measure on the earth's surface. Longitude, which was not shown on early charts, was initially estimated from direction and distances travelled between ports, although it was recognized that this could be provided by time difference. (The principle

---

the instrument. The box was rotated until zero of the ring was aligned with the north point of the compass card and the alidade then rotated (with the vertical arm away from the sun) until the shadow of the thread fell on the slit. The bearing of the sun could then be read off the pointer.

[1] For an amplitude, the Sine of the angle between the heavenly body and east or west is equal to the Sine of its declination divided by the Sine of the co-latitude (90° latitude) (i.e. Log. Sine angle is equal to log. Sine declination minus Log.Sine co-latitude). If the sun's declination is northerly, then the angle is north of east or west, and if southerly, south of east or west. For an azimuth, Sellar, *Practical Navigation*, p. 51, explains how to solve the spherical triangle involved: 'Add the three Sides together, and from their half Sum subtract the Side opposite to the angle required. Then to the Complements Arithmetical of the Logarithm-Sines of the containing Sides, add the Logarithm-Sines of the half Sum and the Remainder: Half the total of these four Logarithms is the Sine-Complement of half the Angle required.' He gives examples at pp. 94–7. The three sides are the co-latitude, the co-declination and the co-altitude, of which the co-declination is the side opposite. The 'Complements Arithmetical of the Logarithm-Sines of the containing sides' are 1 minus Log. Sine co-latitude and 1 minus Log. Sine co-altitude: the 'Remainder' is the co-declination subtracted from half the sum of the co-latitude, co-altitude and co-declination. These four logarithms added together and divided by 2 give the logarithm of the cosine of half the azimuth measured from the elevated pole. No wonder the mariner preferred taking equal altitude azimuths or an amplitude when he could!

[2] Taylor, *Regiment*, pp. 126–8, 237–8, 297–9. Among the finds from the *Mary Rose* (sunk 1545) there was a log reel, indicating that it was in use long before its description by Bourne. Marsden, *Mary Rose*, II, p. 346. I am grateful to Richard Dunn for drawing this to my attention.

[3] It is not known what books Narbrough had with him but John Tapp's *Sea-mans Kalendar*, first published in 1602, regularly updated and republished, edited by Henry Phillipes, London, 1669, would seem a likely candidate. The list of longitudes and latitude is given at pp. 165–79, with the longitudes listed, following Mr Emery Mollineux, from the west end of São Miguel in the Açores.

of using lunar distances to establish time was first published in 1514.[1]) It was later established ashore in some places by the timed observation of eclipses.[2]

One of the additional problems was the physical length of a degree on the earth's surface, which was required to relate distance travelled in terrestrial units (nautical miles, kilometres etc.) to angular measure. By the sixteenth century mariners in England, according to William Bourne, were generally accepting that the nautical mile (the sixtieth part of a degree) was 5,000 feet, with three nautical miles to a league.[3] Richard Norwood gives the same figure for the accepted length,[4] but goes on to say that, having conducted experiments, he found the length of a degree to be 367,200 feet[5] and, having shown that the correct distance for a half-minute glass was therefore 51 feet, went on to advocate using 360,000 feet to the degree,[6] which seems to have been generally accepted.[7]

By 1473 European mariners were using quadrants[8] to measure the altitude of the pole star and marking them with the elevation of various ports etc., making due allowance for the fact that the star was not actually at the pole. The pole star cannot, of course, be seen in the southern hemisphere and since any heavenly body, provided its position can be predicted, can be used, the sun was the obvious choice.[9] From the quadrant the next step was the mariner's astrolabe (a stripped-down version of the astronomer's astrolabe)[10]and then the cross staff,[11] which became the mariner's preferred instrument. In 1585 John

[1] By Johann Werner (1468–1522), Andrews, *Quest*, pp. 27, 151.

[2] Philipp Eckebrecht (1594–1667) produced a world map using difference of time to establish longitude based on lunar eclipses in 1630, ibid., *Quest*, p. 55. James notes '*Master Gellibrand's Observations touching Longitude* in 1633, But the Longitude of a Meridian is that which hath, and still wearieth, the greatest Masters of Geography: Nevertheless, hath not the wise Creator left Man unfurnish'd of many excellent Helps to attain his Desire: For, Eclipses, especially of the Moon, (whose Leisure we must often wait, and perhaps go without, if the Heavens be not propitious to us) we have the Concourse of quick pac'd inferior Planets, with superior ones, or their Appulses with some fix'd Star of known Place, or else some other Artifice deriv'd from their Motions and Positions.' James, *Dangerous Voyage*, pp. 134–5.

[3] Taylor, *Regiment*, p. 237.

[4] Norwood, *Seaman's Practice*, pp. 1–2, first published in 1637.

[5] Ibid., p. 7.

[6] Ibid., p. 48.

[7] See above, pp. xviii–xix.

[8] An instrument for measuring the altitude of a heavenly body. A quadrant was a quarter of a circle plate of wood or brass, graduated in degrees round the circumference, with two pinhole sights along one side and a plumb line falling from the apex. The observation was taken by holding the instrument vertical pointing at a star, rotating it until the star was visible through the two pinholes and then clamping the plumb line on the scale with the thumb, and reading it. For the sun, the instrument was pointed at the sun and aligned so that the light fell through the two pinholes and again the plumb line was clamped and read.

[9] The first set of tables for the sun's declination appeared in Portugal in 1485.

[10] The mariner's astrolabe was an instrument for observing the altitude of heavenly bodies. It consisted of a heavy brass ring about 6 in (15 cm) in diameter inscribed round the circumference in degrees with a rotating arm pivoted in the middle. This arm had two sights on it each with a pinhole in it. The action was to hold the instrument, suspended from a small swivelled ring at the top so that it hung vertically, and sight a star through the pinholes. At the end of the arm a pointer indicated the elevation on the inscribed circle, which it was possible to read to about the nearest ¼°. To observe the sun, its rays were allowed to fall on one pinhole and, when the arm was aligned so that the light coming through fell on the second pinhole, the arm was read as before.

[11] An instrument for measuring the altitude of a heavenly body; see Figure 2. A cross staff consisted of a wooden rod with one or more sliding cross pieces. The operation was to place one end of the rod on the cheekbone and slide the cross piece in or out until one end of it appeared to rest on the horizon while the other bisected the heavenly body being observed. The angular distance was then read on a scale inscribed on the rod. When

Davis described his back-staff[1] (also known as Davis's Quadrant). A refined version of this instrument[2] would have been the one used by Narbrough and his officers for observing the altitude of the sun, while the astrolabe, quadrant or cross staff would have been used for the stars. The altitudes of all heavenly bodies were normally observed when they were on the meridian, i.e. due north or south, when their altitude would be a maximum (or for circumpolar stars either a maximum or a minimum). The method was to start observing before the body reached the meridian while it was still rising (or possibly falling in the case of circumpolar stars) and to continue observing until the maximum (or minimum) altitude was reached.[3] The back-staff could only be used for observations of the sun. The accuracy of these instruments depended on the accuracy of their construction as well as the skill of the observer. The cross staff at this time was graduated at ten-minute intervals while the back-staff could be read to the nearest minute of arc. With a well-made back-staff it has been estimated that an accuracy of between 6 and 12 minutes of arc should be possible.[4] Narbrough normally records his observations to the nearest minute of arc, and sometimes indicates when he was using the back-staff.[5]

Longitude was another matter. Bourne stated, 'I woulde not that any Sea men shoulde be of the opinion that they mighte get anye Longitude with instruments. Therefore let no Sea men trouble themselves with anye such rule, but (according to their accustomed manner) let them keepe a perfite accompt and reckening of the way of their shippe, whether the shippe goeth to leewards or makith hir way good, considering alwayes what things be against them or with them: as tides, currents, winds, or such like.'[6] Immediately

---

observing the sun, a smoked glass could be used attached to the upper end of the cross piece. This instrument normally had two or possibly three cross pieces, of differing lengths and with their own scales, the appropriate one being used depending on the altitude to be measured. To find the correct position to hold the rod on the cheek two cross pieces were used, set to the same angle (but since they were different lengths at different positions on the rod) and by holding the rod to the cheek the correct position could be determined where the eye saw the ends of both bars in line with each other.

[1] Markham, *Voyages and Works*, pp. 330–34.

[2] By the time of Narbrough this instrument (see Figure 3) consisted of a rod, AD, with two arcs mounted on it, ABGC and ADFE, at the front end of which was a slit, A, through which the horizon was viewed. The 60° arc, ABGC, was mounted on top of the rod and was the smaller of the two and situated behind the horizon vane. It carried a movable vane, G, and was calibrated in 5° intervals. This vane, which had a pin-hole in it, was set at an appropriate value and not moved during the observation. The lower arc, ADFE, carried a movable sighting vane, F. This arc carried a transversal scale calibrated from 0° to 30° in 5′ or 10′ intervals, which could be read to 1′ along the fiducial edge of the sight vane. The operation was to stand with the observer's back to the sun so that the bright spot of light from the vane on the 60° arc fell on the horizon vane. The observer moved the instrument and the sighting vane up and down keeping the horizon visible through the sighting and horizon vanes, until the spot of sun-light from the 60° vane fell directly on the slit in the horizon vane. The altitude was then the sum of the readings on both arcs.

[3] The calculation was relatively simple. Rules were provided in navigation manuals. Sellar, *Practical Navigation*, pp.168–73, gives 'Rule 1. If the Sun come to the Meridian of the South, and have South-Declination, subtract the Declination from the Complement of the Meridian-Altitude, the remainder is the latitude of the place of Observation Northerly: but if the Declination exceed the Zenith-distance, then subtract the Zenith-distance from the Declination, the remainder is the Latitude Southerly.' The other rules deal with every other combination of north and south latitude and declination and all were accompanied by examples. The accuracy of the observation was such that corrections for height of eye and refraction were normally ignored.

[4] May, *History of Marine Navigation*, p. 23.

[5] For the accuracy Narbrough achieved, see below, pp. 71–3.

[6] Taylor, *Regiment*, pp. 239–40.

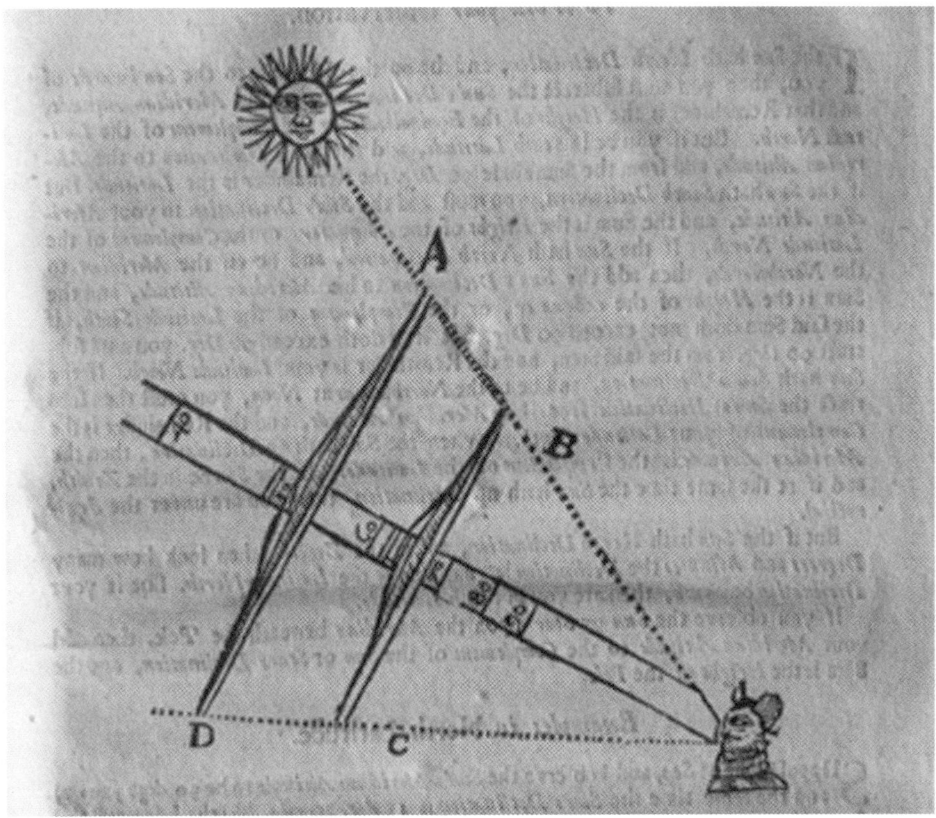

Figure 2. Illustration of the use of a cross staff, from Samuel Sturmy, *The Mariners Magazine; or, Sturmy's Mathematicall and Practicall Arts.* Photograph courtesy of Richard J. Campbell.

the problems of lee-way, the amount a ship drifts off her steered course, due to the wind and unknown currents and tidal streams, appear. The former could be judged by looking astern and noting the angle of the wake to the course steered or by experience: the latter could be measured, if it was possible to anchor the measuring vessel. Otherwise it was estimated from a boat using a sea-anchor (a large cauldron or similar object lowered as far down as practicable) and noting the direction and speed of a float – usually the log and line – released from the boat.[1] It was also possible to determine the difference in the calculated and observed latitudes over 24 hours and deduce the current from it. This, of course, gave a retrospective value, in a north/south direction only, while any east/west component had to be estimated from experience, which might be used for future calculations.

The general method of calculating the ship's position was by dead reckoning. That is to say using the course (corrected for variation) and speed, with due allowance for currents tide and lee-way, to calculate the direction and distance the vessel had moved from noon one day until noon the next day. The day was divided into watches of four hours, with the

[1] This at best gave the speed and direction of the surface current relative to that at the depth of the sea-anchor.

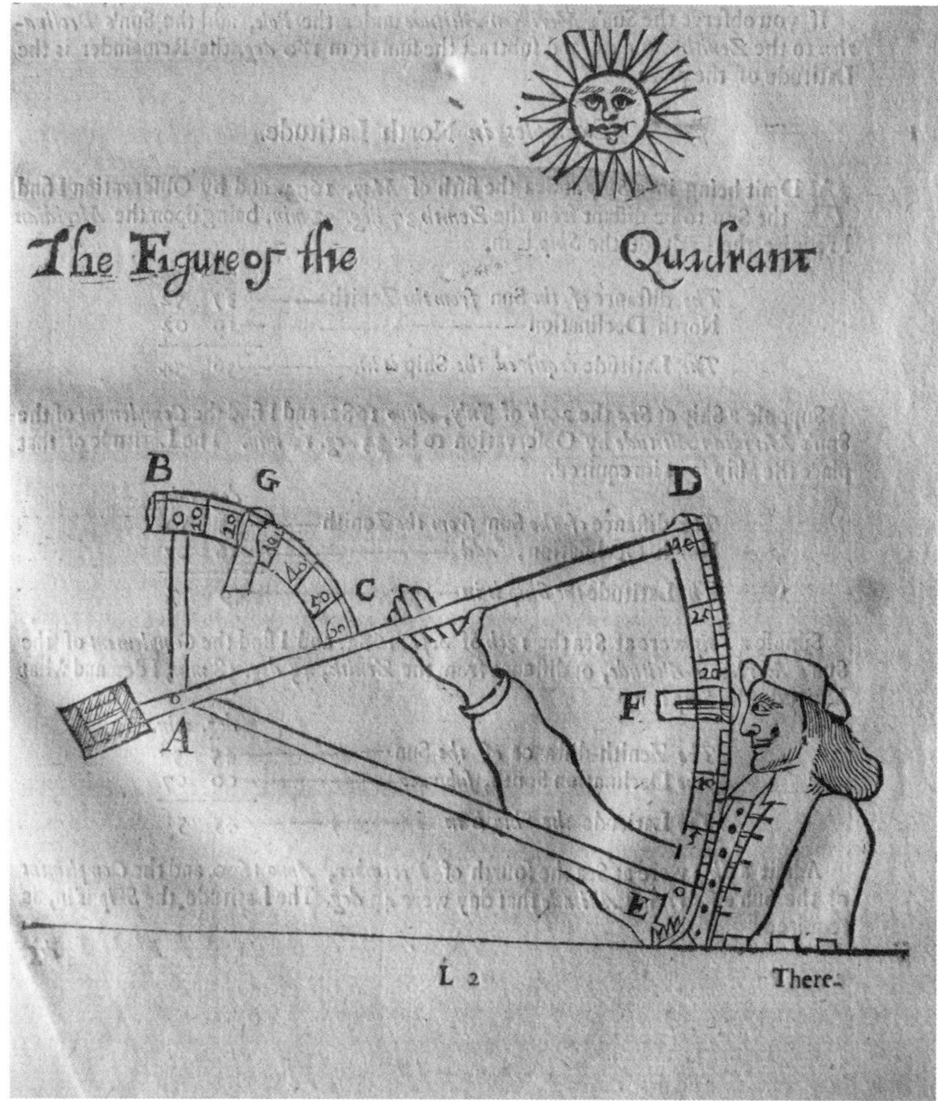

Figure 3. Illustration of the use of a back-staff from Samuel Sturmy, *The Mariners Magazine; or, Sturmy's Mathematicall and Practicall Arts*. Photograph courtesy of Richard J. Campbell.

period between 4 pm and 8 pm in two-hour watches. The log was streamed at regular intervals and the speed recorded. A board was kept with the ship's course and speed noted at intervals and at the end of the watch the ship's Master would ascertain the distance travelled and the course made good during the watch: these would then be used at noon to produce the course and distance made good since noon the previous day. These were then converted into difference of latitude and departure using a set of tables.[1] Since one

[1] Today called a traverse table, and available in the navigation manuals of the day, such as Seller, *Practical Navigation*.

mile equalled one minute of latitude the distance made good north or south (sometimes referred to as 'northing' or 'southing') converted directly into difference of latitude. The departure, the distance travelled east or west (again sometimes referred to as 'easting' or 'westing'), could be used directly to produce the Meridian Distance, or converted into difference of longitude. This was called the Account: using the meridian distance for the account was referred to as 'plain sailing', and using the longitude as 'Mercator sailing'. The problem with plain sailing is that on a sphere the physical length of a minute of longitude is dependent on its distance from the equator. On the equator a mile of departure is equal to one minute of longitude but at 60°, N or S, it is two minutes and thereafter rapidly increases to infinity at the pole in proportion to the secant of the latitude. Thus, using 'plain sailing', if a ship sails east or west in one latitude and returns in another she will not get back to the place from whence she started. This problem was fully explained by Edward Wright.[1] In Mercator's charts the latitude scale is expanded away from the equator so that a line cutting all meridians in the same angle appears as a straight line on the chart. Using longitude to produce the noon position ensures that, no matter what latitude travelled, it should always be possible to know one's location and hence position relative to the known positions of ports and dangers. Narbrough wrote:

> I do not make any Account of plain Sailing[2] to be fit for Seamen to observe; but the best Navigation is by *Mercator*, sailing according to the Circle of the Globe, which I ever sailed by, and keep my Account of Easting and Westing by Longitude, which is the best and most certain Sailing, to give the true description of the Globe. I have noted down the Meridian distance I made daily, whereby such Navigators and Seamen as know better, may have that to give them the knowledge of the distances of Places, according to their Understanding. Most of our Navigators in this age sail by the Plain Chart, and keep their Accounts of the Ships way accordingly, although they sail near the Poles; which is the greatest Error that can be committed; for they cannot tell how to find the way home again, by reason of their mistake.[3]

In his various journals the noon position is obtained from the point of departure or previous day's noon position by a table using the distance run and the course made good. This gives the difference of latitude and the Departure.[4] Then, either by converting the starting and final latitudes to meridian parts using a table[5] which gives the difference of latitude in meridional miles (i.e. units of one minute of longitude on the equator) and by similar triangles the departure was converted into difference of longitude, or possibly more simply by multiplying the departure by the secant of the mean latitude. From the difference of latitude and longitude the current day's noon position could then be calculated. This was the position by account or dead reckoning. If it was possible to

[1] Wright, *Certain Errors*, first published in 1599.

[2] It is in effect treating the earth as flat and using only difference of latitude and Departure to calculate the account.

[3] Narborough, 'Voyage to the South-Sea', p. 85.

[4] The table is based on difference of latitude equals distance run multiplied by cosine course and departure equals distance run multiplied by sine course.

[5] Again included in navigation manuals and based on the table produced by Edward Wright, *Certaine Errors in Navigation &c.* London, 1599, and improved in the 2nd edn, 1660.

obtain an altitude of the sun at noon the latitude could be calculated using the sun's declination[1] (it is not clear if Narbrough made allowance for refraction and height of eye).[2] The difference between calculated and observed latitudes had then to be accounted for, either by the assumption of a current or an error in the course or speed made good and the longitude adjusted accordingly. This gave the observed position.

The calculations involved in this were relatively straightforward, and greatly facilitated by the use of logarithms, invented by John Napier (1550–1617) and generally available by the 1630s.[3]

Narbrough records his course made good and distance run, daily, together with the differences of latitude and longitude and the final accepted latitude, and the longitude relative to a specified point of departure, usually the Lizard. There is no indication of any adjustment made for disagreement between observed latitude and latitude by account, although on occasion he states they did not agree and blames a current for the difference. He appears to have accepted a final position and then calculated his accepted course and distance run to agree with it. His calculations are generally very accurate.

Narbrough's latitudes are normally based on observations of the sun on the meridian, which depend on a knowledge of the sun's declination (which varies throughout the year), and on occasion the Pole Star, tables for both of which were supplied in the navigation manuals available at the time. He also used the stars of the Southern Cross on the meridian, the declinations of which were not generally available and for which Narbrough had inscribed values in the end of his journal (together with a value for Canopus which he did not use). It is not stated where he obtained these values. The latest Star Catalogue available appears to have been that of Fredrick de Houtman (1571–1627), published in Amsterdam, 1603, as an appendix to a *Dictionary of the Malaysian and Madasgaskar languages*.[4] This gives the following values for Crusis, p. 241; α Carinæ Canopus, p. 237; and α and β Centauri p. 240, probably for 1600:

Star	Assenti*on*	Decl*ination*	Mag*nitude*	Name in table
δ Crusis	179°35′	56°26′	3	De Westerlijckste Narm vande Cruzero
Crusis	180°20′	58°27′	5	Een onder dese
α Crusis	182°25′	60°40′	2	De onder este ofte voet vande Cruzero
γ Crusis	183°	54°48′	3	De bovenste vande Cruzero
β Crusis	186°	57°08′	3	De ostelijckste Narm vande selbe
Canobis	93°40′	52°15′	1	Canobis de lichste int Koer vant Schip
β Centauri	204°10′	58°08′	2	Eeninde flincher been Centauri
α Centauri	213°48′	58°48′	1	Eeninde rechter voet Centauri

[1] Obtained from an ephemeris, such as Tapp, *Sea-mans Kalender*, London, 1602 and subsequent editions. Declination was also generally given in navigation manuals.

[2] These had been tabulated by Wright, *Certaine Errors in Navigation*, but in view of their small size and the inaccuracy of instruments used at sea, he recommended mariners not to be over-scrupulous in their application. Waters, *Art of Navigation*, pp. 225–7.

[3] Ibid., pp. 402–15.

[4] Observations of the southern constellations had been taken by Pieter Dirkszoon Keyser (c. 1540–96) and Frederick de Houtman (1571–1629) and published in 1603 as de Houtman, *Spaekende Woordboek*. These had been amended and published again by Johannes Kepler in 1627, Kepler, *Tabulæ Rudolphinæ*, both of which were based on an epoch of about 1600. Kepler, p. 117, lists Canopus in Argo Navis, and, p. 114, the stars of the

Edmond Halley's *Catalogus Stelarum Australium*, 1678, based on his observations on St. Helena in 1677, gives the following positions for the end of 1677:

Star	Ascensio. Recta	Distan a Polo	Differ. Asc. Rect.	Dif. Dist. a Polo	Mag
δ Crusis (Brachium præcedens Crusis)	179°39′	33°06′	1°16′	33′	3
α Crusis (Pes Crusis)	182°20′	28°45′	1°19′	33′	2
γ Crusis (Caput Crusis)	183°27′	34°45′	1°20′	33′	2
β Crusis (Brachium sequens crusis)	187°24′	32°10′	1°24′ 33′	2	
α Carinæ (Canobus)	94°13′	37°34′	0°33′¼	2′	1

Differences are for 100 years. If the Right Ascension (RA) is less than 90° and greater than 270°, distance from the pole must be increased for years to come and decreased for years past, and vice versa.

Comparison of Polar Distances from the de Houtman table with Narbrough's and Halley's values, all adjusted to 1669, using Halley's rate of change of Polar Distance are as follows:

Star	de Houtman	Narbrough	Halley
δ Crusis	33°11′	33°10′	33°09′
α Crusis	28°57′	28°44′	28°48′
γ Crusis	34°49′	34°50′	34°48′
β Crusis	32°29′	31°50′	32°13′
Canopus	37°43′	33°46°	37°34′

From this it is apparent that de Houtman's values were remarkably accurate (bearing in mind that he was probably observing with a cross staff or an astrolabe), and that Narbrough's values may have been updated from de Houtman's table with an error of 4° in Canopus.[1]

The only way to assess the accuracy of Narbrough's navigation is by a comparison of his quoted values for places with their modern accepted positions. These of course suffer

---

Southern Cross in Centaurus by latitude and longitude from the eliptic. These stars were not in Tycho Brahe's original catalogue but added by Kepler in the *Secunda classis* and *Tertia classis*. The former were stated to be derived from Hipparchus, retrieved and amended by Ptolemy and converted to the end of 1600, while the latter were from Keyser. An appendix (unpaginated) titled *Tabulæ Canonicæ Stellarum* gives the following slightly different values with names and updated values to 1677 added:

Star No.	Name	Dec.	R.A.	Dec. 1677	Polar Dist. 1677
300	δ Crusis	57°41′	178°36′	58°06′	31°54′
301	α Crusis	60°06′	183°02′	60°31′	29°29′
302	β Crusis	57°52′	185°24′	58°17′	31°43′
287	Canopus	51°34′	93°30′	51°36′	38°24′

[1] Timothy and John Gadbury recalculated and updated George Hartgill's *Astronomical Tables* in 1656, for the epoch of 1670, and although these include values for some of the stars of the Southern Cross they do not appear to have been used since the values for declination do not correspond. Tapp, *Sea-mans Kalendar*, 1631, also gives values for some of the south polar stars, including 'The Southermost of the Crosiers', but again the values do not correspond.

from the problem of not knowing the actual point whose coordinates Narbrough gives to compare them with their current values. There are one or two places where this problem does not arise, as in the anchorage in Royal Road where he gives his anchor bearings and his position can be accurately determined. Here his latitude is within 2′ of the modern position. His position for Cabo Froward is likewise within 2′. In general his more indeterminate positions are within 10′, with the exception of Cabo Deseado and the features in the western entrance to the Magellan Strait where he is 20′ or more in error. In one place he advocates entering the Strait in latitude 53°S and in another in 52°50′S. Cabo Deseado, the southern entrance point lies in 52°45′S. The reason for this error is not apparent, but it was probably due to the weather conditions and the difficulty in obtaining an accurate observation with the instruments available to him.[1] Narbrough's longitudes are all based on his calculations of his distance run from the Lizard and considering the difficulties involved their accuracy is exceptional. For example, he places Cabo Blanco in 61°56′W and Puerto Deseado in 62°00′W, both from the Lizard, i.e. 67°08′W and 67°12′W from Greenwich, the modern values being 65°45′W and 65°53′W from Greenwich. This works out at errors of 56 and 53 nautical miles respectively. The mouth of the harbour of Valdivia he places 70°19′W of the Lizard or 75°31′W from Greenwich, while its true value is 73°26′W, an error of 96 nautical miles.

Attempts were made to try to obtain an accurate position for the harbour of San Julián. The latitude was observed in the normal way (taking account of refraction) and observations were taken of the moon in conjunction with Mars, and again of the time the moon was on the meridian, for longitude. The result was latitude 49°14′S, longitude 75°W of London, compared with modern values of 49°19′S,[2] 67°43′W of Greenwich. These observations were taken by Mr John Wood and the calculations are given in his journal (pages 22v and 23r). John Wood also observed the eclipse of the moon in Puerto Deseado on 18 September 1670 and obtained a longitude of 73′W of London. Wood's observations are based on his determination of local time and the ephemeris predictions available to him at that date. It is not entirely clear how he determined local time. Possibly working from the local time of meridian observations carried forward by a mechanical timepiece or hourglass. He states in one case that he used the altitude of Mars at 68°52′, which was on the meridian, with a resultant error of the order of one hour. The predictions of the lunar eclipses at this time might be in error up to an hour, so that his results were not very accurate. The principal problem, however, appears to have been the lack of appreciation of the importance of an accurate local time, without which no reasonably accurate determination of longitude was possible.[3]

[1] Narbrough states 'The mouth of Magellan's Straits on the west end next the South Sea lies in the Latitude of fifty three degrees South as I observed by the Quadrant of Mr John Davis'es invention'; see below, p. 485. It appears that this was the only actual observation taken to determine this position.

[2] The modern position of Puerto San Julián is the position of the town and it is highly unlikely that Narbrough's observations were taken in the same place. The entrance to the harbour lies in 49°15′S, which is very close indeed to the value obtained.

[3] The local time can be obtained from the latitude, Declination and Altitude of the heavenly body. The calculation was explained in the navigation manuals of the time, e.g. Tapp, *Sea-mans Kalender*, pp. 133–4; Sturmy, *Mariners Magazine*, Book VI, pp. 123–4. Tapp also gives the Declination and Right Ascension of 65 stars (excluding those round the southern pole) and a table of the Complement of the Sun's Right Ascension from which the time of a star coming to its meridian can be calculated by simple addition, Tapp, *Sea-mans Kalender*, pp. 88–99.

Narbrough observed a partial eclipse of the moon on 26 March 1670 from which, together with his latitude observation, he deduced Cape Blanco to lie in latitude 47°20′S, longitude 69°16′W of London, modern position latitude 47°12′S, 65°45′W of Greenwich.Had both Narbrough's and Wood's observations been based on an accurate local time and matched by corresponding observations at a known locality, possibly London, very much better results might have been expected.[1]

b: Charts

It is not clear what charts Narbrough carried: he mentions a book called the 'Sea Atlas'. This would appear to be *The Sea Atlas or Watter World &c.* by Henry (Hendrik) Doncker, a translation of *Zee-Atlas oft Water-Waerelt*, Amsterdam, 1660. The English version has this date on the title page, but the chart of Spitsbergen is dated 1663, so it would appear the date should be 1663. The penultimate chart is of South America (Plate 2) and shows a large number of names and details mentioned by Narbrough. He also refers to a 'Mercator's map'. He is unlikely to have had one of the Mercator/Hondius/Jansson atlases since these were large, and increasingly multi-volume, and dealt almost exclusively with terrestrial cartography. The probability is that this was a manuscript chart on vellum based on a Dutch original, which has not survived.

Chambers mentions that they were looking for a 'sunken rock that the draught specifies to lye in the Lat*itude* of 49°10′ some 6 leagues off shore'.[2] This was the rock Narbrough called the Eddystone[3] and it is not shown on the Doncker chart so they must have had some other chart in addition to this.

c: Chambers's Navigation

Chambers's journal starts with the *Batchelour* anchored off Praia (2 November 1669) and ends when the ship left Puerto Santa Cruz (1 April 1670). His latitudes are based on observation and dead reckoning. Of the 53 occasions when both Chambers and Narbrough obtained latitude by observation of the sun, 34 are within 0′ to 9′, 14 within 10′ to 19′, and 5 within 20′ to 30′ of each other, which are very creditable results, considering that, when not under tow, the two ships may have been some distance apart. Unlike Narbrough he made no attempt to observe the stars when the sun was too high to observe. He does not make it clear whence he took his departure.[4] His positions have

[1] The observations taken by Captain James in Charlton (Charleston), 29 October 1631, of the lunar eclipse, which was, by arrangement, also observed by Henry Gellibrand at Gresham College, London, and the moon's culmination (i.e. bearing due south) on 23 June 1632, gave longitudes of 79°30′ and 78°30′W of London. Charleston is 79°45′W of Gresham College; James, *Dangerous Voyage*, pp. 135–42. Gellibrand commented 'The Difference between that of the Eclipse and this latter Observation is only four Minutes of Time, or one Degree, a Difference easily pardon'd, especially if we shall compare the same with some other Places which lie in the Heart of *Europe, Rome* and *Norimburg*; Their difference of Longitude *Rigiomontanus* makes 36; *Werner* 32; *Appian* 34; *Mæstlin* and *Origan* 33; *Stofler* 18; *Maginus* 26; *Schoner* 12; *Mercator* and *Hondius* as much; *Stadius* 13; *Jansonius* 10; *Longomontanus* 16; *Lansberg* 10; *Kepler* by two observations on two Lunar Eclipses, but four Minutes of Time', ibid., p. 142.

[2] See below, p. 645.

[3] See below, p. 210.

[4] On leaving Praia he refers to taking 'our' departure from São Tiago. His first two days' run, 6 and 7 Nov. 1669, and estimated position would indicate that he put Praia in 0°15′W. However, on 14 Jan. 1669/70 he recorded his longitude as 5°49′W, or 6°01′W of São Tiago, the former presumably from Praia, and on 29 Jan. he records his longitude as 21°53′W, 23° from São Tiago.

been calculated using the accepted course and distance run to give a difference of northing/southing and easting/westing in miles. Sometimes he calculates his course and distance run using his midday observation, without giving the dead reckoning values. Latitudes are either dead reckoning values or adjusted to conform to the observed values. Longitudes appear to be a direct addition of easting/westing, (what Narbrough called 'plainsailing') taking no account of the convergence of the meridians. The result was that, when the ships parted company in the night of 19/20 February 1669/70, Narbrough's longitude from Praia was 43°23′.5W, while Chambers recorded 30°53′W. Subsequently, Chambers placed Cabo Blanco in longitude 44°10′ while Narbrough made it 61°56′W of the Lizard.[1] It is also worth noting that Chambers made a number of what appear to be mathematical errors in his calculation, some of which are noted in the transcription of his journal. His assessments of course made good and distance run are frequently very different from those accepted by Narbrough.[2] Narbrough's values appear, from his estimate of the distance between Cabo Blanco and the Lizard, and the difference in his dead reckoning between leaving Cabo Deseado for Valdivia and return to Cabo Deseado again, to have been remarkably accurate. The conclusion must be that, while Chambers's observations of the sun were reasonably accurate, his overall navigational skill was poor.

15. Narbrough's Surveying

Narbrough's instructions required him 'to Take observations with as much accouracy as you Can of all head lands Islands Bayes havens Roads and mouthes of Riveers where you come Boath in the North and South Sea and to Cause Draughts or designes to be made of them'. He was also required 'to take exact Notice of all Currants and trade winds you meet with'.[3]

The 'Royal Map' (which has north at the bottom) and the 'Sloane Map' are both graduated in latitude and have a compass rose and a scale on them. There are no longitude graduations on the 'Royal Map'. The 'Sloane Map' has vertical lines ruled on it, which have no indication of longitude on them and do not match those on the published chart.

The method Narbrough used to construct his charts can only be suggested by an examination of them together with the journals, since he does not tell us himself how he set about it. His charts of the coast were probably made by using his observed latitude and dead reckoning longitude to give him a starting position, from which the ship's track could be laid down to the next observed position. The initial blank sheet, to judge from the 'Sloane Map' and published chart, appears to have been inscribed with a latitude scale of equal divisions. He probably started by plotting his known latitude on this, and from there plotted his subsequent positions as he went, by dead reckoning. Then knowing the longitude of his dead reckoning positions, calculated according to 'Mercator sailing',[4] a longitude scale could be inserted on the chart later. This would have produced a chart for the Strait of Magellan, which would be orthomorphic over a limited range of latitude,

[1] The actual position is 60°40′W of the Lizard.

[2] For example, see below, pp. 622, nn. 1, 4; 631, n. 2.

[3] See p. 122.

[4] See above, p. 69.

i.e. a 'flat earth projection'with its latitude of origin (i.e. where it touches the earth) in about latitude 52°30′S; which is the latitude of the eastern entrance of the Strait.

In preparing his draughts Narbrough would have plotted his position, on a chart as described above, as he passed through the Strait using the compass rose and scale, correcting his course for the variation, which he frequently records observing, and the position from any latitudes he was able to observe. Soundings, if taken, would be inserted in the appropriate place along the track. He did not prepare sailing directions as such for the Strait: he did, however, describe the best method for making the western entrance of the Strait and his journal is full of descriptions of the coastline[1] and natures of the seabed, together with details of the weather.

The journal does not contain navigational information in the same form as that in which it is given on passage in the open sea, in the form of days' runs. Instead we have descriptions of the passage in the form

> I weighed and Steered South & B*y* East by my Compasse five leagues, So the Strait Lyes in this reach to point Low,[2] which is a point on the north Shore which is seen as you ride in Port famin. The Compasse hath Sixteen degrees variation here, Easterly, so that my South B*y* East is South four degrees forty five minutes westerly by the true compasse. The Strait here at Port famin is neare five leagues broad to the South east, and at point Low about four leagues broad, the South land rounds up to the westward, and Shuts in with the north Land at the end of every reach, so as if there [were] no passage. But as you Saile along it opens more and more unto you. The Land is of a great height on both sides rounding up the Sides of the hills & woods growing green on them, but snow lyes on the tops. The Channel is very deep water and no ground at two hundred faddom, but under the north Shore there is anchoring in the Low Bayes,[3]

and

> From the pitch of Cape Froward to the pitch of Cape Holland, the Strait lyes in the Channel west and by North, nearest; and is distant full five Leagues; And, from the pitch of Cape Holland to the pitch of Cape Gallant the Strait Lyes in the Channel West and by North a litle northerly and is distant eight Leagues. From the pitch of the Strait Lyes in the Channel, North-west and by west a litle northerly.[4]

He would have inserted the salient features relative to his track and then sketched in the coastal detail by eye and from the information collected by his boat, which he used to examine the inshore water, taking soundings as she sailed along searching for anchorages. He also records on occasion firing a saker and noting the fall of the shot to help him judge distance.[5] The track is shown on the 'Royal Map' with soundings and anchors to indicate where the ship anchored. Additional soundings are included, presumably taken from the boat, which would have been positioned by eye relative to the land features. There are very few soundings west of the anchorage in York Road, presumably because of the depth

[1] See, for example, his descriptions of Cabo Virgenes, pp. 225, 314, 300, and Cabo Deseado, p. 485.

[2] Cabo San Isidro (53°47′S,70°58′W), shown on Narbrough's 'RoyalMap' as 'Pt Low'.

[3] See below, p. 474–5.

[4] See below, p. 460..

[5] See below, p. 462, n. 1. Since he does not give the elevation it is not practicable to tell the range he used for his gunshot.

of water and the fact that part of the passage was made in the dark. The track is not shown on the 'Sloane Map', but it can generally be followed from the line of soundings. The soundings are similar on the two charts but not always identical, more being shown in places on the 'Royal Map' than the 'Sloane Map'.

From his original draughts prepared on board, which have not survived, the 'Sloane' and then the 'Royal' Maps would have been drawn by professional cartographers in London after his return home.[1] The 'Royal Map' includes, at the bottom, a very long description of the native peoples, with drawings of them, their huts and boats, all apparently in Narbrough's own hand, together with a second paragraph on the currents and tidal streams in the western part of the Strait and a note that it is 'much better', or easier, to pass eastward through the Strait than westward. At the left-hand edge of the map is another legend (written at a right angle to the map) which details the currents and tidal streams at the eastern end of the Strait where he says that:

> The Tide of Flod Comes from the South wards and Sets Strong into the Straits at the First Narrow: it keeps it Course as one [on] other Coasts, and Sets in Six houres & the Ebb Set out Six houres: The Flood Rise Perpendiculer in the first Narrow Better then three Fatham: & It is A high water In the Narrow at Eleven oF the Clock one [on] the Change day of the Moone: as I observed. The Tide Run boath Ebb & Flood Stronger then at Gravesend.[2]

The plans of the various harbours would have been made in a similar way. They are also on the 'flat earth projection' with the point of origin (i.e. point of contact with the earth) in the middle and hence also orthomorphic over the very limited area covered. All three charts have plain ungraduated borders. On 23 March 1670, in Puerto Deseado he recorded, 'I fitted my boat and went up the river, having 13 armed men with mee, as also Lieu*tenan*t Pecket and M[r] John Wood. I draughted out the river as I rowed up, and Sounded it all along.' The three harbour plans appear to have been drawn by Narbrough himself[3] and, as can be seen from them, he was not a skilled cartographer. The plan of 'Port Dissier' (Plate 1) shows the harbour itself with a large area outside stretching beyond 'Penquiens Ile'. The title includes the latitude. Salient land features and all the positions where the ship anchored are shown, together with the offshore dangers and rocks and there is a much greater number of soundings than one might have expected, no doubt taken from the boats going to and fro and positioned by eye with the assistance of the compass. There is a scale, a compass rose and no further information. The islands in the harbour are all named and the positions of two fresh water springs are shown. The plan of 'Porte San Julyan'[4] contains considerably more information. The coastline, fresh water pond,[5] islands and offshore dangers are all delineated together with a scale and compass rose. The entrance to the port is full of shoals with numerous soundings round them. The anchorages used are also noted. All this information would appear to have been inserted by eye, although no doubt the compass was used to assist in positioning the ship and boats. There are also legends detailing the indigenous people and wildlife together

[1] See above, pp. 11–12.

[2] See below, p. 677.

[3] The plan of 'Porte San Julyan', Plate 3, is annotated 'John Narbrough fecit 1670'. On the plan of the 'Port oF Baldavia', Plate 4, he places his name at the end of the principal legend.

[4] Plate 3.

[5] The salt pond is also mentioned, but it is 7 miles from the entrance of the harbour and not shown on the plan.

with drawings of three of the former and a hare, a 'guianaco', a polecat a duck and a goose, while mention is also made of the fish that could be caught. A note gives the position of the port and the variation and a final note gives the tidal information, range, time of high water and tidal streams. The plan of the 'Port oF Baldavia'[1] is again replete with information. The coastline, islands and forts are shown, together with a scale and compass rose. There are somewhat fewer soundings reflecting the length of stay and restricted travel of the ship and boats. The legends are more copious detailing the normal positional and tidal information. The latter, however, includes comments on the streams running out of the rivers, and the diminished salinity of the water. There are pictures of two natives, and of Narbrough's and Spanish boats. The guns in each fort are specified. There is also a note prominently placed under the scale at the top which states 'I Am in Formed that here is much Gold in this Land'. The note goes on to comment on the relations of the Spaniards with the natives.

Narbrough recorded in his journal the position and variation of each port and full details of the currents, tidal heights and tidal streams, together with the time of high water at the full and change of the moon.[2] There are also copious directions for entering the various ports,[3] noting the danger to be avoided and the best anchorages.

His instructions also required him 'in all places to observe the Nature of the Soyle what fruts Cattle or mineralls it Produceth and what fish the Sea and rivers aBount with'. The journal includes copious information on the native inhabitants, flora and fauna, and soil and minerals. He examined the country wherever he went and searched for people and minerals.[4]

From his charts and the descriptions in his journal it is apparent that Narbrough provided very comprehensive details of everything he was required to do in his instructions, consistent with the methods available to him at the time. In general the positions of his land features are good: their latitudes, with the exception of the western entrance to the Strait are excellent[5] and his estimation of distance travelled and hence longitude, bearing in mind the slow speed of his vessel and the difficulty of obtaining a

[1] Plate 4.

[2] On the plans of 'Porte San Julyan' and 'Port oF Baldavia' these are also recorded. On the 'Draught of Port Dissier' he only gave the latitude of the port. For details of the legends on the plans, see Appendix 1.

[3] That for Puerto Diseado, describes the entrance and dangers in considerable detail and then reads: 'The best Cominge in is at the Last quat*er* Ebb: for then you may See all the danger and be Sur keep the medle of the Chanell: and you may Gooe Safe. You will See up the River white Clifes and above them in the hills is a Round hill or hommake which is whitesh: keep that in the midle of the Chanell after you are with in the narow: one [on] the South Side there is Sum Rockes: and the water Comes over that Pointe at halfe floode which makes a great Eady: and Just with in one [on] the north Side their Lyes a pinte [point] of Rockes which are all Sene till the first quarter flood. I Rode above them Two Cables Lengths: nerer the North Side then the South.'

[4] See below for example, pp. 207, 214, 220, 243.

[5] Comparison of Narbrough's and modern latitudes:

	Narbrough	Modern
Puerto Deseado	47°48′S	47°45′S
Puerto San Julián, entrance	49°10′S	49°14′S
Cabo Vírgenes	52°26′S	52°20′S
Cabo Froward	53°52′S	53°54′S
Cabo Deseado	53°05′S	52°45′S
Bahía Corral	39°55′S	39°51′S

reliable current measurement, are quite exceptional.[1] He made the distance from 'Cape Virgin Mary, to Cape Dessiade with every Reach and turning to bee one hundred and Sixteen Leagues' while a modern estimate for the track between positions south of Cabo Vírgenes and north of Cabo Deseado would be about 104 leagues. Narbrough may, of course, have started east of Cabo Vírgenes and included some diversions which would not be used today, i.e. passing north and west of Isla Isabel, so that a correct modern value might be even closer to his figure.

16. The Outcome of the Voyage

The voyage was not followed up, presumably because the political situation was such that trade in the area could only be established by direct conflict with Spain, as Narbrough had found out. This was neither desirable nor financially practicable and the country was soon to be involved in the Third Anglo-Dutch War. Narbrough's report of his voyage was not published until 1694 when it appeared as 'Sir John Narbrough's voyage to the South-Sea' in *An Account of Several Late Voyages & Discoveries to the South and North Towards The Streight of Magellan, the South Sea, the vast Tracts of Land beyond Hollandia Nova &c*, with a second edition in 1711. It was translated into French and German and abbreviations of it were included in various compendia of voyages.[2] Narbrough's chart of the Strait of Magellan was published in 1673[3] and remained in use for many years as the 'foundation for all subsequent Charts'.[4]

On 30 October 1672, a memorial was given to the Spanish ambassador, the Marquis del Fresno,[5] by royal command, which, after explaining the actions taken to satisfy Spanish complaints concerning depredations by Englishmen in the West Indies, stated:

> His Ma*jes*ty having on his part so fully complied with his obligation in pursuance of the Article of the late peace,[6] hopes that the Queen of Spaine has or will likewise give order for the redresse of severall injuries his subjects have sustained from hers, & particularly his Ma*jes*ty com*m*ands mee to recom*m*end to his Ex*cellen*cy the case of the Lieu*tenan*t & several seamen belonging to his Ma*jes*ties Ship the Sweepstakes, who were made prisoners about two years since at Baldivia in the West Indies, Where they Were sent on shore by their Captaine, & have been since detained by the Governor of that place. Hereof I informed the Conde de Molina,[7] then Ambass*ado*r, Who promised to represent the same effectually to the Queen his Mistress, and obtaine her Orders for their liberty; Which not being (as his Ma*jes*ty is informed) yet done, his Ex*cellen*cy is desired to employ his good offices to that purpose.[8]

Judged against his orders (and the unwritten implication that he was to investigate the possibility of siphoning off some of the Spanish South American gold trade), Narbrough

[1] See above, p. 72.
[2] See Appendix 4.
[3] See Plate 9.
[4] Burney, *Chronological History*, III, p. 376.
[5] Pedro Fernández de Velasco Ayala, 2nd Marqués del Fresno.
[6] The Treaty of Madrid.
[7] Antonio Francisco Mexía de Tovar y Paz, Knight of Santiago, 3rd Conde de Molina de Herrera (c. 1620–74). He was appointed ambassador in 1662, and remained in London until 1672. He sent a detailed report on Narbrough's expedition to Spain in Aug. 1671. See Urbina, 'La Sospecha de Ingleses', pp. 24–6.
[8] TNA, CO 1/29, No. 39.

carried out his mission to the letter. He produced charts of the ports he visited,[1] as well as the Strait of Magellan.[2] He made contact with the native inhabitants wherever and whenever he could,[3] and discovered that the natives of Patagonia and the Strait of Magellan did not have access to supplies of gold or indeed have anything with which to trade. He reported that there was no prospect for a new port south of Valdivia.[4] He established that gold was only available in the areas already occupied by the Spaniards, and that it would only be possible to trade in those areas by force. It is true he did not examine the south-west coast of Chile, as instructed, but in view of the state of his main mast and the prevailing weather conditions this was an act of prudence and not a failure of duty. The subsequent longevity of use to which Narbrough's account and his chart[5] were put, together with the esteem in which he was held by his contemporaries, both senior officers and the sailors who followed him from ship to ship, stand witness to his leadership and the achievements made during this voyage.

Nothing in Narbrough's orders indicates that the crown expected him to take any serious action against the Spaniards; indeed this was expressly forbidden and precluded by the reduced size of his complement. In Valdivia, bearing in mind that he had fewer than 70 men and the garrison ashore was of the order of 600,[6] it would have been extremely foolish for him to have attempted to recover his detained men by force. In view of the treaty between England and Spain it was not unreasonable to expect them to be returned home from Spain.[7]

From Narbrough's original orders, the journal and the other accounts of the voyage, together with the published results, it is apparent that Narbrough did exactly as he was instructed and, despite the captives taken by the Spaniards and the negative trading prospects, it would therefore seem reasonable to regard the objectives of the expedition as having been successfully accomplished, and, as Dyer put it, 'his reputation greatly enhanced'.[8]

17. Use of the Published Version of Narbrough's Voyage by Other Navigators

William Dampier was familiar with Narbrough's 'Voyage to the South-Sea', but cannot have had it with him in his first voyage round the world, since he left England in 1679 and did not return until 1691, three years before it was published. He did, however, in his record

[1] Puerto Deseado, Plate 1, Puerto San Julián, Plate 3 and Bahía Corral (Valdivia), Plate 4.

[2] Plate5 and Foldout.

[3] See above, pp. 40–48 and Map 2.

[4] The only significant ports in the area today are Puerto Montt (41°30′S, 72°55′W) on the west coast of Chile inside Isla Chiloé in Golfo de Ancud, and Punta Arenas (53°10′S, 70°54′W) in the Strait of Magellan.

[5] See below, pp. 79–82, and Appendix 1.

[6] Bradley, *Pirates*, p. 96, says the nominal complement was 600 to 700, comprised of one company of cavalry to the north of Valdivia, seven companies of infantry manning the town and forts, and one company of artillery men manning 35 guns. Lemos mentions an actual complement of 586 in March 1671, and Castellar lists 728 in Sept. 1677.

[7] Narbrough was not to know that Henry Morgan's sack of Panama had taken place on 28 Jan. 1671, a month after he had sailed from Valdivia. This would render any prospect of his crew members being freed less likely (although prisoners of Morgan's company were ransomed by the Spanish at 120 pesos (£30) per head). Zahedieh, 'Morgan, Sir Henry', *ODNB*.

[8] Dyer, *Life*, p. 90.

of his own voyage (published in 1697) remark that 'In Sir *John Narborough*'s *Voyage* also to *Baldivia* (a City on this Coast) mention is made of very high Land seen near *Baldivia*'.[1] Again, discussing the Spanish trade between Acapulco and Manila, which he says was carried out by two vessels, he notes that 'Sir *John Narborough* therefore was imposed on by the *Spaniards*, who told him that there were eight Sail, or more, that used that Trade'.[2]

Edmond Halley, writing about the longitudes used on his variation chart ('as observed in 1700') in reply to a criticism of Monsieur de Lisle, stated:

> I do not pretend that I had all the observations made with all the Precision requisite, to lay down incontestably the *Magellan* Streights in their true Geographical site; but yet it has not been without good grounds that I have placed them as I have done. For when Sir *John Narborough*, in the year 1670 wintered in Port St. *Julian*, on the Coast of *Patagonia*, Capt. *John Wood*, then his Lieutenant, and an approved Artist in Sea Affairs, did observe the beginning of an Eclipse of the Moon, *Sept* 18 *Stil. vet.* at just 8 at night: And the same beginning was observ'd by M. *Hevelins* at *Dantzick* at 14^h 22′; whence Port St. *Julian* is more Westerly than *Danzick* 6^h 22′, or than *London* 5^h 6′, that is 76½ Gr.[3]

Numerous seamen relied on Narbrough's published work for circumnavigation voyages via the Strait of Magellan. Commodore Anson,[4] who made that voyage 1740–44, made frequent reference to it. He appointed Port St Julián as the first rendezvous for his squadron, relying on Narbrough's description of it, with the next rendezvous at the Island of Nostra Senora del Socoro, 45°S.[5] Anson noted 'the many and valuable improvements he furnished to geography and navigation' which Narbrough had made, comparing his longitudes obtained for Cape *Virgin Mary* (Cabo Virgenes) favourably with those obtained by his ships to the detriment of those given in Frezier.[6]

Callender reprinted Narbrough's 'Voyage to the South-Sea' from Smith and Walford's *An Account of Several Late Voyages* verbatim,[7] in his 1768 collection of voyages. In his subsequent 'Remarks', he writes 'This Journal has always been reckoned the best drawn up, and the most useful of any wrote by the navigators to *Magellanica*, and accordingly we find it often appealed to by *Frezier, Anson* and other seamen in their accounts of those coasts.'[8]

[1] Dampier, *New Voyage*, p. 95.

[2] Ibid., p. 246.

[3] Halley, 'Some Remarks', p. 168.

[4] George Anson (1725–60) made his voyage round the world in HMS *Centurion*, 60, in 1740–44, after which he was appointed to the Board of Admiralty. Promoted Rear Admiral in 1745 and Vice Admiral in 1746, he commanded the Western Squadron and after his victory off Cape Ortegal in 1747 he was raised to the peerage as Baron Anson of Soberton. He became First Lord of the Admiralty in 1751. He returned to sea in command of the Western Squadron again in 1758 for the summer and then back to the Admiralty again. He died at his home in June 1762 at the height of a victorious war. He was responsible for many lasting and effective reforms to the Royal Navy. See Rodger, 'Anson, George, Baron Anson', *ODNB*.

[5] Walter, *Voyage*, p. 54.

[6] Ibid., pp. 90, 92.

[7] Callender, *Terra Australis Cognita*, vol. II. pp. 422–519. There are a few minor typographic changes and the diagram of 'The *Crosers Stars*' (Southern Cross) on p. 15 has been omitted.

[8] No mention of Narbrough's published work has been found in Frézier, *Voyage*. There is a reference to 'gathering Memoirs for drawing of the chart [the Strait of Magellan]', p. 285 but this, while showing a number of tracks of French vessels starting in 1706, has no reference to Narbrough, nor indeed would his chart appear to have contributed to its production. He does mention on p. 287 that Monsieur de Lisle showed him '*English* Memoirs' and this might be a reference to Narbrough's 'Voyage to the South-Sea'. The account of Commodore Anson's voyage contains a number of references to Narbrough. Walter, *Anson's Voyage*, pp. 58, 61, 64–5, 88–90, 92.

Some of the survivors of the *Wager*, a former East Indiaman purchased for Commodore Anson's expedition to sail under Captain David Cheap and wrecked on the Chilean coast north of the western entrance to the Strait of Magellan in 1741, built a small vessel and sailed through the Strait (with considerable loss of life on the way). They used Narbrough's account as their guide, and were full of praise for it, remarking 'As for every other part of the *Streights* of *Magellan*, from Cape *Victory* to Cape *Virgin Mary*, we recommend Sir *John Narborough*, who in his Account is so just and exact, that we think it is impossible for any Man living to mend his Works.'[1] They visited Port Desire and returned to England via Rio de Janeiro and Lisbon.

In his voyage in the *Wager* and *Tamar*, 1764–6, Commodore the Hon. John Byron (who had served as a Midshipman under Captain Cheap in the *Wager*), makes frequent mention of Sir John Narborough's descriptions of Port Desire,[2] and his passage through the Strait of Magellan. He also quotes Bulkeley and Cummins[3] so that he must have had their account with him as well.

In his voyage of 1766–9, Captain Philip Carteret[4] had Narborough's charts and 'Voyage to the South-Sea' with him, as did the expedition commander Captain Wallis in the *Dolphin*. Carteret made full use of them on at least one occasion, to find a safe anchorage when he was unable to get clear of the Strait in April 1767.[5]

Louis de Bougainville, writing of his 1766–9 voyage, stated 'Upon the whole, how often have we regretted that we had not got the Journals of Narborough and ..., such as they came from their own hands, and that we were obliged to consult disfigured extracts of them: besides the affectation of the authors of such extracts, or curtailing everything which is useful merely in navigation; likewise, when some details escape them that have a relation to that science, their ignorance of sea-phrases makes them mistake necessary and useful expressions for vicious words, and they replace them by absurdities.'[6]

Others, such as Captain MacBride, returning from establishing a colony on the Falkland Islands, mentioned Narborough on his chart of Puerto Deseado forwarded to the Admiralty on 21 March 1767.[7] Joseph Banks, discussing the oceanic birds encountered off New Zealand in his *Endeavour* journal of 1770, refers to 'a few birds calld by S[r] J[no] Narbourough Penguins',[8] which would indicate a familiarity with Narbrough's account[9] if not the presence of it on board *Endeavour*. Antonio de Córdoba carried Narbrough's 'Voyage to the South-Sea' and quoted from it[10] in his surveys of the Strait of Magellan, 1785–6 and 1788–9, as did Captain P. Parker King and Captain

[1] Bulkeley and Cummins, *Voyage* (2nd edn), p. 148.

[2] Gallagher, *Byron's Journal*, p. 33.

[3] Ibid., p.45.

[4] He had sailed with Byron in 1764.

[5] Wallis, *Carteret's Voyage*, p. 41.

[6] Bougainville, *Voyage*, p. 196.

[7] UKHO A List c.80. Captain John MacBride (c. 1735–1800), sailed in HMS *Jason*.

[8] Beaglehole, ed., *Endeavour Journal*, II, p. 5.

[9] There is a copy of the 1694 edition in the British Library with the stamp 'Jos Banks' in the front.

[10] Vargas y Ponce, *Relacion*, p. 5, 'Lastly as every information that could be collected respecting the object of the voyage must be useful, either as furnishing advice to be followed, or as pointing out what was to be avoided, the same officers collected accounts of all expeditions to the Strait of Magellan and the Pacific which had been published by all nations'; *Apéndice a la Relacion*, p. 75, 'Cape Pilar ... which with reason Narborough called the desolation of the South'.

Robert Fitz-Roy, in their respective surveying voyages to the Strait of Magellan, in 1826–30 in the *Adventure* and in 1831–6 in the *Beagle*.[1]

18. Historical Opinion on Narbrough's Conduct of the Voyage

Narbrough was well received on his return home, but subsequent historical assessments of his achievement have been very mixed. Commodore Anson was of the opinion that:

> The discovery of this coast hath formerly been thought of such consequence, by reason of its neighbourhood to the *Araucos* and other *Chilian Indians*, who are generally at war, or at least on ill terms with their *Spanish* neighbours, that *Sir John Narborough* was purposely fitted out in the reign of King *Charles* II, to survey the Straits of *Magellan*, the neighbouring coast of *Patagonia*, and the *Spanish* ports on that frontier, with directions if possible, to procure some intercourse with the *Chilian Indians*, and to establish a commerce and a lasting correspondence with them. His Majesty's views in employing *Sir John Narborough* in this expedition, were not solely the advantage he might hope to receive from the alliance of those savages, in restraining and intimidating the Crown of *Spain*; but he conceived, that, independent of those motives, the immediate traffic with the *Indians* might prove extremely beneficial to the *English* nation ... It is true, that *Sir John Narborough* did not succeed in opening this commerce, which in appearance promised so many advantages to this Nation. However, his disappointment was merely accidental, and his transactions upon that coast (besides the many valuable improvements he furnished to geography and navigation) are rather an encouragement for future trials of this kind, than any objection to them; his principal misfortune being the losing company of a small bark which attended him, and having some of his people trapanned at *Baldivia*. However, it appeared, by the precautions and fears of the *Spaniards*, that they were fully convinced of the practicability of the scheme he was sent to execute, and extremely alarmed with the apprehension of its consequences.[2]

Another instance of the high regard in which Narbrough was held by seamen at this time is afforded by the buccaneer William Ambrose Cowley, who, in the *Bachelor's Delight*, surveyed the Archipiélago de Colón or Islas Galapágos in 1684 and named some of them after famous people – King Charles's Isle, King James' Isle, Norfolk Isle, Albemarls Isle and so on – amongst which he included Sir John Narbrough's Isle in compliment to him. William Hacke included a depiction of the island (Plate 10) in the manuscript atlas presented to Lord Somers in 1698 and afterwards owned by Robert Walpole, before being acquired by George III from John, 2nd Viscount Sydney, the grandson of Colonel Delwyn.

On the other side, Admiral Burney, who included Narbrough's voyage in his *Chronological History of Voyages*, 1813,[3] scathingly dismissed Narbrough as 'Weak, inexperienced and seduced by an ambition to shew himself an expert and crafty statesman'.[4] He went on to say 'It might ironically have been said, that the business of Narbrough's voyage was to set four men ashore at *Baldivia*. The persons landed were left to their fate without interference being made on their behalf by the British

[1] King and Fitz-Roy, *Narrative*, I, pp. 4–5, 25, 76, 99, 123, 192; II, pp. 365–6, 374–5.

[2] Walter, *Voyage*, pp. 88–9.

[3] Burney, *Chronological History*, III, pp. 316–82.

[4] Ibid., p. 374.

Government'.[1] In fairness to Admiral Burney, it must be added that he also held that 'The Chart made by Captain Narbrough of the *Strait of Magelhanes* may be esteemed the foundation of all subsequent Charts, although in their construction, this of Narborough's has not been sufficiently consulted'.[2] Burney was unaware of Narbrough's orders and based his assessment on the orders that Narbrough had given to Captain Fleming and a letter Greenvile Collins sent to Nicolaes Witsen, in 1691, which the latter had published.[3] Clements Markham, in 1873 shared Burney's unfavourable opinion. When referring to John Wood, Markham states that he had served 'under Sir John Narbrough during that officer's discreditable voyage to Patagonia and Chili in 1669'.[4]

Florence Dyer, in her biography of Narbrough written in 1931, held that 'The voyage greatly enhanced his reputation. He had already shown in the campaigns of the Anglo-Dutch War that he was a man of unflinching bravery and courage. Now he had proved himself to be, in addition, a capable leader of men. He had persuaded his sailors to follow him on a lone and hazardous journey, and he brought back his ship and men in safety after they had been given up for lost.'[5] He had achieved the main objectives of the voyage, and did not have what might be termed as a 'spectacular career' but 'he was one of the many admirals who, besides fighting for England, devoted all their energies to increasing the efficiency of the Navy' and 'was invaluable in forming the traditions of the new class of professional seamen which were then in the making'.[6]

Peter T. Bradley gives a comprehensive account of the voyage[7] and concludes that the abandonment of the captured shore party 'was not gallant and in another age, that of Drake and Hawkins might well have been different. The only other possible alternative might have been to have sailed the coasts of the viceroyalty in the hope of taking a Spanish ship off the Peruvian coast and arranging an exchange of hostages [an action expressly forbidden in his orders!]. Where Narborough failed was in trying to deceive the Spanish without realising that they had the same intentions, and perhaps with greater justification.'[8] Narbrough's enthusiastic commentary on the opportunities for trade and settlement offered nothing radically new but had 'provided the precise information that might make such an enterprise just a little easier and surer of success. The work of Narborough and Wood was to become the standard English guide to the region for decades.'[9]

Glyndwr Williams argues that 'Unlike the proposed venture of the Cromwellian period, the Narborough expedition was not openly hostile to Spain; but in Spanish eyes

[1] Ibid., p. 375. Admiral Burney (1750–1821) had sailed with Captain Cook on his second and third voyages returning from the latter (on the death of Captain Charles Clarke) in command of the *Discovery*. In June 1782 he was appointed to the command of the *Bristol* (50) sailing to India, but fell seriously ill in 1784 and returned to England. Due to an act of direct disobedience to his orders in 1782, he was never employed again, despite repeated applications, and was only promoted to Rear Admiral on the retired list at the age of 71, in 1821, as a direct result of the intervention of the Duke of Clarence, Lord High Admiral and future King William IV. Troide, 'Burney, James', *ODNB*.

[2] Burney, Chronological History, III, p. 376.

[3] See above, p. 32, n. 3.

[4] Markham, *Threshold*, p. 35. I am grateful to David Brittain for drawing my attention to this.

[5] Dyer, *Life*, pp. 90–91.

[6] Ibid., pp. 235–6.

[7] Bradley, *Lure*, pp. 86–102; *Pirates*, pp. 87–107.

[8] Bradley, *Lure*, p. 95; *Pirates*, p. 97.

[9] Bradley, *Lure*, p. 99; *Pirates*, pp. 103–4.

its motives were just as suspect as if Narborough was intent on a plundering raid.'[1] In his expressed opinion, sending a party of eighteen men ashore at Valdivia was 'folly' and that, when four of his men had been taken prisoner, to then send an open letter to the captive Lieutenant Armiger instructing him to report on the fortifications and strength of the defending forts was 'a fatally nonsensical move'. In comparison to other English seamen who had entered the South Pacific, 'neither as a successor of Drake nor as a forerunner of Cook does Narborough inspire confidence'.[2] In his opinion, Narbrough was 'ineffective' and fortunate to escape from an ill-considered mission with the loss of so few men'.[3] He judges Narborough's chart, published in 1673, to be 'most useful and remained the standard authority for decades to come'.[4]

In his recent entry in the *Dictionary of National Biography*, J. D. Davies, makes use of Narbrough's journal and presents a more favourable, although brief, all round picture of the voyage, stating that 'His journal for the voyage bears witness to his high degree of technical competence, his concern for his crew's welfare, and his genuine interest in the lands and peoples he saw'. He notes that, although Narbrough was subsequently criticized for leaving his men behind as captives, he nevertheless was a popular senior officer.[5]

Perhaps the last word should be left with John Campbell, who, in his remarks on Sir Cloudesley Shovell in 1744, wrote that the latter owed his preferment to 'the Favour of the famous Sir *John Narborough*, a Man who having raised himself to the highest Honours of his Profession, by mere dint of Capacity, was a generous Patron of all who discovered any Degree of Worth'.[6]

19. Editorial Conventions Adopted in the Transcription of the Manuscripts.

In 1582, by Papal Bull, Pope Gregory XIII replaced the Julian Calendar then in use throughout Christendom with the Gregorian Calendar. Most Catholic countries, including Spain and Portugal and their overseas territories, changed in accordance with this instruction, while most Protestant countries, including England, retained the Julian Calendar, with the New Year starting on 25 March. During the seventeenth century the difference between the two calendars was ten days; the Gregorian date being later than the Julian.[7] Since the records and communications contained within this edition are largely addressed to others operating with the same calendar, the dates have been retained as given in the transcriptions of the original texts, with no annotation of the difference between Old Style and New Style except in the case where a communication or event brings the differing usage into direct juxtaposition. Dates for January in the English nautical journals are given as 1669/70 or 1670/71. Editorial commentary on the history of events is given in Gregorian dates.

In so far as practicable, wording of all the English texts has been reproduced as they were written. Following the guidelines of the Hakluyt Society, contractions have been

[1] Williams, *Great South Sea*, pp. 77–82.
[2] Ibid., p. 79.
[3] Ibid., p. 80.
[4] Ibid., pp. 80–82.
[5] Davies, 'Narbrough, Sir John', *ODNB*.
[6] Campbell, *Lives of the Admirals,* IV, p. 300.
[7] Thus 1 June in Julian reckoning would be 11 June in the Gregorian calendar.

expanded (with the exception of those in current use today) using the spelling normally adopted by the particular author with the additional letters italicized. Initial and medial u and v, i and j have been changed to modern usage. Older forms such as y^e, y^n, y^t have been silently changed to 'the', 'then' and 'that', as have, w^{ch}, w^t and wth to 'which', 'what' and 'with'. The ampersand, '&', has been retained, where used in the original. Narbrough also uses an older symbol for the same which has been expanded to 'and' without comment.

Following Hakluyt Society Guidelines, proper names of persons and places are given as spelled in the editing of the original texts, with accepted modern forms in the Introduction. At the first occurrence in the edited texts, all subsequent variants of the spelling are listed, with the accepted modern spelling and further identification provided in a footnote. For place names, the modern version adopted is, by convention, that used by the authority having recognized sovereignty over the territory in question. Country names and those of internationally recognised features are given in their accepted English form. Names are indexed by their modern form with the variant older forms indexed and cross-referenced to the modern usage.

The daily records of Chambers, Narbrough and Peckett were kept in simple journal form. Peckett's log is presented as he configured it. Narbrough's journal in BL, Add MS 88980 A. presents some particular challenges. It was not kept up on a daily basis and its varying form has been noted above.[1] Given the inconsistency of the column rulings, only the structure of the page divisions, with the left-hand top corner numbering and a ruled-off running head, giving the month, the situation of the ship and the year of the voyage, has been retained with entries set within normal margins. Narbrough's journal, in both Add MS 88980 A. and the Rawl. A. 18, has numerous marginalia consisting of symbols, drawings and brief notations. These have been noted within square brackets inserted into the text at the place where they occur. These most commonly occur in the left-hand margins. Where pages were ruled with right- and left-hand margins the marginalia sometimes occur in the right-hand margin; this has been noted. Richard Williams's surviving manuscript is not a journal but rather a 'short accompt', or summary overview, highlighting what he considered to be the significant events or observations of the voyage.

In BL, Add MS 88980 A. Narbrough's own spelling is to a large extent phonetic and far from regular, as can be seen by the multiple renditions of the name of the *Sweepstakes* in his journal. As far as possible, his spelling has been reproduced exactly since it gives the reader a vivid sense of his regional accent and voice. When the word intended is not readily obvious the modern spelling has been inserted immediately afterwards in square brackets. Explanatory footnotes have been added where the meaning of a word or phrase is not clear, particularly if nautical terms are in use. Capitalization follows the original. The spelling of Rawl. A. 18, a clerk's copy of Narbrough's journal, is fairly regular and understandable, as is the punctuation. The text is written in a neat, cursive hand, but the writer did not have a consistent cursive or joined form for the lower-case letters at the beginning of words. Since the clerk's upper-case hand is quite distinct, capitals have only been retained where clearly intended, with the exception for compass points and directions which have all been capitalized for sake of consistency.

The punctuation of BL, Add MS 88980 A. is exceptionally erratic. Narbrough tends to use only a colon and a dash and these at irregular intervals and sometimes in unexpected

[1] See above, pp. 6–11.

places. If a sentence ends before the end of a line he may either fill in the space with dashes, or if the text reaches to the end of the line, leave it without any form of stop. He also uses a dash in the text generally to denote a change of subject matter. The original punctuation suggests he wrote as he spoke, in short, plain statements. Dashes and colons have been removed and periods inserted where necessary to make the text understandable for the modern reader. Don Carlos's missives follow the composition patterns of early modern Spanish sentences, where 'and' substitutes for punctuation breaks. Some of the sentences take up as much as a paragraph with little or no intervening punctuation. Fortunately Don Carlos does express himself clearly. The translations attempt to give an impression of his voice but commas and semi-colons have been inserted where necessary to make sense of his various representations.

In all the accounts, latitudes, longitudes and other mentions of angular measure are also given in the manuscripts in a variety of forms. Narbrough uses 4=5-2 (4°5′·2) as a general rule and sometimes the = and - are transposed or omitted. He also uses 21=50, with a small cross above each figure, 36 deg:27-5 (36°27′·5), 36=deg:13-5 (36°13′·5) and various other combinations. Peckett uses 49^{d} 39^{m}: Chambers uses various forms e.g. 49 degres = 20^{m} in the text, but generally 49:20. 23:15 in the marginal notes meaning latitude 49°20′, longitude 23°15′. The tenths of a minute are also given in various different forms, e.g. 5 tents, 5 t, 5/10 etc. All these different forms have been rationalized to modern degree and minute symbols with the tenths in decimal notation, e.g. 4°5′·2. Directions are given in points of the compass, i.e. N, SW, NNE etc. For the most part Narbrough gives the cardinal points in the abbreviated form above. Occasionally he uses the abbreviation N° and S° for N and S. These have been rendered as N and S. The capital B occurring between points of the compass, e.g. NEBE, should be read as NEbyE.

PART I

The Prelude to Narbrough's Voyage

1. Narbrough's commission to take command of the *Sweepstakes*, 15 May 1669.[1]

James Duke of Yorke & Albany,[2] Earle of Ulster, Lord High Admirall of England and Ireland, Constable of Dover[3] Castle, Lord Warden of the Cinque[4] Ports and Governor of Portsmouth &c.

To Captaine John Narbrough Captaine of His Majest*ie*s Shipp *Sweepstakes* for this Expedition:

Whereas I have appointed you to be Captaine of the Shipp above named, These are therefore to will & require you forthwith to goe onboard the said ship and to take the Charge and Command of Captaine in her accordingly. Hereby Chargeinge and requiering all the Officers and Company of the said shipp joyntly and severally to behave themselves in the said imployments with all due respects and obedience to you their said Captaine. And you likewise to observe and follow such orders and directions you shall from tyme to tyme receive from my Selfe or any other your Superiors for His Majest*ie*s Service. Hereof nor you nor any of you may faile as you will answere the contrary at their perills, for which this shall be your warrant. Given under my hand and Seale at S^t^. James the 15 of May 1669.

James

By Command of His R*oyal* Highness

M. Wren[5]

These is a true coppy of my Commission which I received to Comand the *Sweepestakes* at S^t^. James the same day beareinge the date being Satturday. The Shipp being at Deptford.[6]

[1] BL, Add MS 88980A, 24th unnumbered page reading from the back of the 'Booke' forwards.

[2] The title of Duke of York was conferred by King Charles I on his son James in late 1633, shortly after his baptism. He was created Duke of Albany by Charles II in 1660 after the Restoration; variant Allbany.

[3] Dover; variants Dovier, Doviour.

[4] Variant Chinque.

[5] Mathew Wren, Secretary to James, Duke of York.

[6] Deptford; variant Deptforde.

2. Robert Southwell to Joseph Williamson, about Don Carlos Enriques 1/10 June 1669[1]

[f. 94r] Aldea Gallega[2] 3 league from Lisbone June1/10 1669

Deare Brother.[3]

I have at last made a shift to gett my face towards home, which is noe small consolation unto me.[4] All I can say of this place you will find in what I write to my L*o*rd nothing being very new Since the packett I sent you of May19/29.

Heir [*sic*] is comeing out a manifesto of all the Princes Proceedings in a few dayes it will be free of the Presse, and then Mr. Parry[5] will [store] you.

Here lately come from Madrid to this Place, a single Person, who calls himselfe Carlos Henriques, he is the son of an English man borne in Cadiz, and has lived long in the West Indies, and is very well verst in the Spanish affaires of the South Sea. He was then found in some Insurrection and sent home [f. 94v] a Prisoner, and having got off, he is going for England to offer his service to the King. He came here to me in some want and shewed me letters from Mr Werden[6] to My Lord Arlington, & Lord Sandwich,[7] and after writt to me, the inclosed. I have here given him some helpe and procured his passage, with my servants that I now send home. I suppose Mr. Werden gives a full account of the man. I can only say of him that he seemes very well verst in things relating to that part of the world and his demeanour here has beene very regular and with good breeding. I have noe other reason to suspect that he may be employed by Spaine to discover our Intentions uppon them in those parts then that he says in discourse how he would give the Capt*ain* of the ship some gratuity at his comeing to London where he had some creditt. This is but a hint towards the generall rule of suspecting the worst but if he be really bent agen the Spaniards, & he should be slighted their; I doe presume he would be a shrewd toole in the hands of the French. I have nothing more to add knowing you will say something hereof to my L*o*rd. I kisse y*ou*r hands and for ever Deare Brother y*ou*r most affect friend & servant.
Robert Southwell.

[1] TNA, SP89/10, f. 94r–v. This English diplomatic correspondence is dated according to both the Old Style (Julian) still in use in England and the New Style (Gregorian) calendar used in Portugal and Spain.

[2] Also known as Aldea Gallega de Marceana, situated on the estuary of the Tagus, 11 miles north of Setubal.

[3] Williamson was at this time Keeper of the king's library at Whitehall and of the State Paper Office. He is said to have introduced more methodical approaches to document management and to have been a key figure in the bureaucacy, as well as in gathering intelligence relevant to domestic security and foreign policy issues. Marshall, 'Williamson, Sir Joseph', *ODNB*.

[4] Southwell had been engaged in the negotiation of a commercial treaty between England and Portugal in 1668. He had just taken leave to depart for England. See, Barnard, 'Southwell, Sir Robert', *ODNB*.

[5] It has not been possible to identify this person.

[6] See above, p. 22, n. 1.

[7] See below, p. 138, n. 1.

My letters to my L*o*rd I send in another vessell going in Company, bec[a]use in the ketch theire is already the Princes letter about Antonio de Sousa and I alsoe enclose his L*o*rd[ship] an other.

3. Translac*i*on of the Paper dellivere*d* in Spanish by Don Carlos Enriques, 29 June 1669[1]

[f. 184r] Sir

Fortune gives mee occasion to bee a petic*i*oner unto Y*ou*r Ma*jes*tie at whose Royall ffeete I lay myselfe with the humillitye and dutye of a Loyall Subject, the memory of which Could never bee worne out of my thoughts though the absence of thirtye years might devert it, yet considering the love of my Contry I could not seeke that generosity in any other Prince that might prove of greater effect to me than what I know in my owne Naturall King and Lord under whose Protection I hope to deserve Ease and Comfort in my troubles.

And Because it seems neccessarye to give a derect account unto Y*ou*r Ma*jes*tie of the Causes which have brought mee to this Extremitye, I will relate them unto Y*ou*r Ma*jes*tie as followeth.

Finding myselfe in the yeare Sixty five in the Kingdome of Chile[2] Executing the office of Gove*rn*or of the Armey of the s*ay*d Kingdome as Liu*tenan*t Generall[3] to Don Francisco of Meneses my Gener*a*ll,[4] It happene*d* that a tumult did arise in all the places within his Juri*s*dic*ti*on, People Crying out Long Live the King and D*o*n Fran*cis*co of Menezes and lett the bad Government dye, all which was fomented by the s*ay*d Don Francisco of Menezes who alsoe would in[cite][5] mee to take possession of the Government of two other bordering Provinces to Chile [f.184v] of which my Father (as I shall shew hereafter) had made himself King, though I would by no meanes understand what hee[6] meant because I did not soe well understand what hee aymed at, though he allwayse proffessed as great ffriendship to mee as any body [*sic*] Could doe, and soe at last spoake plaine, that himselfe and I should Joyne hands in the matter and helpe one another that soe wee might preserve

[1] TNA, SP 94/54, ff 184r–191v. The title of this document is taken from the endorsement of the same on f. 191v. The Spanish original, found in TNA, SP 94/55, ff. 39r–47v, is endorsed 'June 29 1669 Don Carlos Enriques his storye of severall passages hapene*d* in the West Indyes together w*i*th his propos*icio*n for discouerye of the Passage through the Straights of Magelanes & the Coast of the South Sea &ca. 29th June 1669.' The folios of this latter document have been collated, numbered and bound in the wrong order. Folio 42 is missing. To achieve the correct order the folios need to read f. 39, [42 missing], 44, 40, 41, 45, 43, 46, 47. In TNA, SP 94/54, ff. 184r–191v, the English translator captured both the information and meaning of the proposal. Any minor differences have been noted below.

[2] Variants Celee, Chele, Cheli, Chely, Chila, Chili, Chilli.

[3] Tiniente General in TNA, SP 94/55, f. 39r.

[4] TNA, SP 94/55, f. 39r reads Cappitan General, the rank of the territorial governor and military commander. For the career of Don Francisco de Meneses Brito, see above, pp. 50, 53, 55–6 and below, p. 91, n. 9.

[5] The end of the word is illegible. TNA, SP 94/55, f. 39r reads '*insitava*', for '*incitava*', meaning 'incited'.

[6] The translator made a valiant effort to make sense of the 13 lines of Don Carlos's sentence. In both the original Spanish and the translation it is clear that the 'he' here refers to Don Francisco de Meneses Brito, not to Don Pedro de Bohorques whom Don Carlos claims further below to have earlier adopted him as his son. See above, p. 52, and below, pp. 93–5.

our selves till wee might have succour from the Govern*o*r of Brassill,[1] but for as much as I could never perswade myselfe that such a thing Could bee caryed on, and that though really it might, the thing would never prove of Advantage or Securitye to mee, for manye Inconveniencyes that represented themselves to my reason. The first becoase I saw him who I esteemed and looked upon as a father a Prisoner,[2] the Second having seen and knowne D*o*n Francisco de Menezes to be very Industrious and Cunning and that hee would call to his helpe his Contrymen, the third The not having in those Provinces which I was to Governe any Conveniencyes whereof I might preserve myselfe, and that the Kingdome of Chile had all neccessaryes not onely to deffend itselfe, but alsoe to take from mee my Scepter upon any occasiones of difference that should happen betweene us, which of necesssitye would fall out some time or another betweene two soe neer Neighbours. And therefore to prevent the afforsa*i*d Inconveniencyes I deverted the occasion the best I could having allwayse an Eye to preserve the Armeys in their obedience to the King, [185r] though w*i*th no small trouble for they were People very fond of Changes. But It being soe that D*o*n Fran*cis*co would doe nothing without my advise and I representing to him the Hazards that atended his design hee Judged it the best way to make shew of faithfulnesse and to Retyre to the Armey which I had upon the frontiers for feare that at the Court of the sayd Kingdome Called St Iago they would force him to accept the Crowne.

Thus having Come to the Armey & taken advise It was resolved as the best course to quiett and Pacifye the Kingdome by some slight or another Promissing in the Kings name a Generall pardon and imediatly to send a way a Courrier to the Roy*a*ll Acuerdo[3] who Govern*e*d then at Lima by reason of the Death of the Vice-Roy called the Earle of St Estevan,[4] giving notice of all that happen*e*d, And to make himselfe the more Creditted faithfull, hee alsoe made it his request that hee might bee admited[5] to surrender his Employment and that they would send another to Governe in his Place. The Roy*a*ll Accuerdo (in Pollicye) deffer*e*d his answer at that time but in the yeare sixty six hee provided for both o*u*r Employment in the Carying to Chile aboute a thousand five hundred foote as a Recruite and some new Govern*o*rs for severall Guarisons and in mony three hundred Thousand peeces of Eight to pay off the Armey, and a Generall pardon to all the Kingdome which was proclaimed in September of the same yeare. And soe Don Fran*cis*co & I having delivered up our [f. 185v] Com*m*ands to our successours wee Come to Lima to give an account of o*u*r Charge as it *i*s usuall, but that would not be admitted off until that the Vice-Roy the Earle of Lemos[6] should Come, who arrived there about the Later end of the last yeare sixtye seven, and like a new Come Minister and poore did before wee were any wayse aware Com*m*and to have Don Fran*cis*co & myselfe aprehended and our goods & effects seized, and having examined us upon severall unproubable[7]

[1] Brazil; variants Brasil, Brasile, Brasilia, Brassell, Brassill, Brazeel, Brazeele, Brazila, Brazilia.

[2] Here Don Carlos appears to refer to Don Pedro de Bohorques, who was imprisoned by the Spanish authorities in 1659.

[3] Bernado de Iturriaza y Mansilla, Dean of the Audienca of Lima, acting Viceroy of Peru March 1666–Nov. 1667.

[4] Diego de Benavides de La Cueva y Bazán, 1st Marquis of Solera, 8th Conde Santisteban del Puerto, Viceroy of Peru 31 Dec.1661–16 March 1666.

[5] Permitted.

[6] Pedro Antonio Fernández de Castro, 10th Conde de Lemos, Viceroy of Peru 21 Nov.1667–6 Dec. 1672.

[7] The word in TNA, SP 94/55, f. 44r is '*improbable*', meaning unlikely or improbable.

Articles a Processe was drawne up against us to which wee made *our* deffence, but Judgment passing against us It was decreed that my Generalls goods should bee Confiscated and aplyed to the expence of *Camara* and that himselfe should serve *with* a Pike in his hand three yeares in Oran.[1] And that I should bee banished for ever ffrom the Indyes and my goods Confiscate and to bee applied to the Expence of the wars. Butt when wee apealed our apeal was rece[ved][2] and *our*selves sett free to passe into Europe, and soe it falling out that at this time the Galleons and fleete of Terra ffirma were in the harbour of Portovelo under the com*m*and of the Prince of Montesarcho[3] I passed to[4] Cartagena[5] by land, having Power from my Generall to sollicitt his buisinesse seeing wee were both Comprehended under the same Articles and that hee was himselfe faine[6] to remaine at Lima very ill of the Goute and other infirmityes which come from ould age.

Having arived at Madrid in Spaine and presented myselfe before the Councell of [f. 186r] Indyes the Earle of Peñaranda[7] was pleased to take notice of *our* buisnesse but no resolution was taken there upon in three months at the end of which a more favorable Sentence was passed moderateing the first one, It being order*ed* that the monyes and movable goods of us both should continue Confiscated as the same was derected by the sentence passed at Lima, but that *our* other estates[8] should bee restored to us againe in the same Plight that the same was when first siezed on. That my Gen*era*ll might continue at Lima during the three yeares which hee was to spend at Oran discharged of all Employments, and that my banishment should onely bee for foure yeares to bee spent wherever I should think fitt in Europe.[9]

[1] Oran, Algeria, taken by the Spaniards in 1509.

[2] The English translation gives a clearer statement of process, than the involved sentence of the Spanish original (TNA, SP 94/55, f. 44r). However, Don Carlos's use of Spanish legal terminology, such as '*descargo*' (meaning 'defence') and '*en grado de apelacion*' (meaning 'appelate court', or 'on appeals'), together with his handwriting and general compositional skills, suggest that he may have had training as a clerk or notary. The Camara was the Treasury.

[3] Puerto Bello; variants Port Bel, Portobelo, Porto Bello, Portovelo, Portvelo. TNA, SP 94/55, f. 44 reads 'Principe Montes Harcho'. Andrea d'Avalos d'Aquino d'Aragona, Príncipe de Montesarchio (1618–1709), served as Captain General of the *Armada de la Guarda de la Carrera de Las Indias*, which left Cádiz on 3 March 1667. This would seem to indicate that Don Carlos was at Porto Bello in that year; see San Pio and Zamaron, *Catálogo de las Colección*, pp. 162, 164.

[4] The verb *pasar*, can be read as meaning 'to travel, pass by, happen, and spend time'. Here it is clearly used in the first sense.

[5] Cartagena; variant Cartaxena.

[6] Obliged or well pleased, *NOED.*

[7] Gaspar de Bracamonte y Guzmán, 3rd Conde de Peñaranda (c. 1595–14 Dec.1676), Spanish statesman and diplomat, serving in that period as advisor to the queen mother, Mariana of Austria, then holding the regency for her son Carlos II (1665–1700).

[8] TNA, SP 94/55, f. 44r reads 'bienes rayzes', the legal term for land or real estate.

[9] Don Carlos correctly states that the Conde de Lemos removed Francisco de Meneses Brito as Governor of Chile and instigated the normal inquiry (*residencia*) into the complaints about his tenure of office. The remainder of Don Carlos's commentary misrepresents what actually happened. The new Viceroy left Cadiz on 3 March 1667 in the *Armada de la Guarda de la Carrera de Las Indias*, under Andrea d'Avalos d'Aquino d'Aragona, Príncipe de Montesarchio. The inquiry into Meneses Brito's period of office, did not begin until 1668 and continued for 2 years during which time he was held, first in the city of Córdoba in Tucumán, then transferred to Arica in Chile. he died in Trujillo in 1672. The report of the inquiry reached the Consejo de Indias in 1672 and was still under consideration some 10 years later.

This is Great S*ir* a shortt account of my storye since my going into the Kingdome of Chile untill this p*re*sent time and therefore[1] it *is* now fitt to relate some thing of an Elder date which Concernes my p*re*sent pretenc*io*ns and that is as followeth.

In the yeare 1661 being then Cap*tai*n of the Admirall of the Fleete in the South Sea[2] there fell to mee the honnor of the *habbito* of *Calatrava* which the Earle of Alva de Liste had provided for mee[3] in Recompence of a Generall visitac*io*n which I made by order of the s*ay*d Vice-Roy (to whome the Roy*a*ll Councell of the Indyes had Comitted that Care) of all the Sea Ports and guarisons and Sea Coasts from the Californias to the Straight of Magalanes[4] on the South Syde, and from [f. 186v] the s*ay*d Straights to the River of Buenase Ayres[5] on the North Syde,[6] with one Gally and two *Cosmografos*[7] which for this purpose were apointed by the s*ay*d Vice-Roy. In which Voyage I did not onely fullfill my Comiss*io*n but alsoe discover*ed* the Isles of Solomon of which I tooke possess*io*n and there fixed a Pillar with an Inscripc*io*n containeing his Chatoli*que* Ma*jes*ties name thereon.[8] In Recompence of which Service the s*ay*d hon*n*or of Knighthood or *habitto* was Conferred on mee with a perpetual pay of a Cap*tai*n of ffoote to be payd allwayse out of any of his Ma*jes*ties treasuryes wherever I should live, and to that Effect was sent an order from the Roy*a*ll Councell of the Indyes by the hands of the Earle of St Estevan[9] w*i*th power alsoe to the s*ay*d Earle to appoint the persons who should make tryall of my progeny as in such Cases is usuall,[10] which ceremony was performed accordingly. I all wayes passing for the

[1] This portion of the sentence was inserted by the translator. The remainder of the sentence follows Don Carlos's original in TNA, SP 94/55, f. 40r.

[2] TNA, SP 94/55, f. 40r clarifies the translation. Don Carlos claims to have been 'Cappitan de mar y guerra de la *Almiranta* de la *armada del mar del Sur*', that is 'captain of the men of sea and war in the *almiranta*' – the second ship in the chain of command of the armada.

[3] The Spanish military religious Order of Calatrava was founded by a group of Cistercian monks in 1158 and dedicated to the reconquest of Spain. The knight brethren, or *freires*, were originally obliged to obey the Cistercian rule and the use of the word 'habit' here continues that tradition, although by the late 15th century the Order, now closely tied to the noble families of Spain, had been secularized and brought under the Council of Military Orders of the royal government. Luis Enriques de Guzmán, 9th Conde de Alba de Liste, was Viceroy of Peru 24 Feb. 1655–31 Dec. 1661. The English translator uses the verb to provide in the sense of to procure which is used in the Spanish original.

[4] Strait of Magellan; variants Straight, Streights, Strieghts; Magalan, Magalanes, Magallan, Magelanes, Maggalan, Maggellam, Maggellan, Magilan, Magilaine, Magiline, Magillane, Magillaine, Magllan.

[5] Buenos Aires; variants Buenos Ayres, Buenos-ayres, Buenase Ayres.

[6] 'South Syde' and 'North Syde', 'por la banda del zur' and 'por la banda del Norte' in TNA, SP 94/55, f. 40r, refer to the Pacific and the Atlantic oceans, known as the *Mar del Sur* and the *Mar del Norte* respectively.

[7] Cosmographers or map-makers.

[8] Alvaro de Mendaña was the first Spaniard to reach the Solomon Islands in 1568, the name he gave to them reflecting his expectation that he would find riches there. A second expedition, led by Mendaña and Pedro de Quiros, did not take place until 1595. It was unsuccessful and narratives of the two voyages were kept secret by the Spanish Crown for fear that other nations would take possession of the islands. Their exact location remained uncertain until Philip Carteret reached them in 1767; see Wallis, *Carteret's Voyage*. Don Carlos claims to have rediscovered them 116 years earlier. The English translator does not include Don Carlos's further claim to have left 15/75 '*forcados*' (prisoners condemned to the galleys) behind, as well as a column marking the ceremony of possession.

[9] Don Diego de Benavides de La Cueva y Bazán, 1st Marquis of Solera and 8th Conde de Santisteban del Puerto, Viceroy of Peru 31 Dec. 1661–16 March 1666. TNA, SP 94/55, f. 40r notes that the latter was the successor to Luis Enriques de Guzmán, 9th Conde de Alba de Liste.

[10] The Spanish reads '*mis pruebas*', the term for the investigation to prove descent from nobility, required of any aspirant to the military orders in the 17th century. The English translator uses 'progeny' for 'progenitors'.

sonn[1] of Co[*rone*]ll Peter Boxorques[2] a knight of the same order of Calatrava, who was at that time a Prisioner in one of the Towers of the Pallace for having Crowned himselfe King of two of the greatest Provinces in Perue Called Paraguay and Patagones[3] bordering upon Chile which Provinces hee himselfe had Conquered at his one [own] Charges (though it *is* true that hee did it more by Slight and Cunning then Strenght [*sic*] of Armes and then maryed himselfe to a Colla[4] which in Spanish signifyes a Princese daughter to an Emperrour (as in Effect shee is being Grand Childe [f. 187r] to Ataballiba, Ynga of the Perue whose Predessesours retyred themselves to those Provinces,[5] the Inhabitants being the most Ingenious, Active, and warrlike men that are to bee found in all America,[6] hopeing ffrom them (in time) to Recover their former Libertye & power./

The afforsayd Don ~~ffrancisco~~ Pedro[7] Baxorques in the yeare 1651 Adopted mee his sonne, having often in his will being at point of death declared mee as such and his Lawfull hier [*sic*], meerly out of a naturall affection which hee had for mee ever since the time that Don ffrancisco de Toledo Marquis of Mancera[8] went to Perue to Governe there, with whome the sayd Don Pedro Boxorques went as Cap*tai*n of his Guards,[9] and I at the same time as the *sayd* Marquises Page, after which my sayd reputed ffather[10] exercised severall Employments as Generall of the Armada of the South sea,[11] Gover*no*r of Tucaman and

[1] TNA, SP 94/55, f. 40r reads *hijo natural*. Spanish law recognized the natural child born to a couple as legitimated by the subsequent marriage of the parents under Church law. See Frye, *First Chronicle*, p. 5, n. 10.

[2] See above, p. 52. In TNA, SP 94/55, f. 40r Don Carlos gives his rank as Maestre de Campo (campmaster), a military position with administrative and judicial powers over infantry forces. As can be seen above, Bohorques had never held any such rank.

[3] In 1656 Bohorques had established himself among the indigenous peoples of the Calchaquí valley in the Province of Tucumán, a region which encompassed parts of Peru, Argentina and Paraguay. For a more detailed history of his escapades, see, Ryal Miller, 'Fake Inca of Tucumán', *passim*; Lorandi, *Spanish King of the Incas*, *passim*.

[4] Both the English and Spanish texts give the word as *colla*, properly *coya*, referring to a woman of the highest Inca rank.

[5] Ataballiba is one of the Spanish variant spellings which frequently occur in 16th- and 17th-century literature for Atahualpa/Atawalpa Inca, executed by Francisco Pizarro in 1532. In both the Spanish text and English translation '*cuyos antepassados*' or 'whose Predessesours', clearly refers to the predecessors of Bohorques's wife, these having retreated to form the neo-Inca state in Vilcabamba, where Tupac Amaru, the last Inca ruler, was captured and executed in 1571.

[6] Variant, Amarica.

[7] Francisco is struck through and Pedro written above.

[8] Pedro Álvarez de Toledo, 1st Marquis of Mancera (c. 1585–1654), Viceroy of Peru 18 Dec. 1639–20 Sept. 1648.

[9] In TNA, SP 94/55, f. 41r Don Carlos also adds that Bohorques held the position of Corregidor (chief magistrate) of a district. The name is abbreviated but may be Sanara.

[10] TNA, SP 94/55, f. 41r reads '*despues dicho mi Padre puttativo exercio differentes puestos de la armada del zur*', translated 'after the said my presumed father held various posts in the armada of the South Sea'. Here, in the list of appointments which follow, the individual calling himself Don Carlos presents the first version of his paternity, combining elements of the biography of Pedro de Bohorques with those of Baltasar Pardo de Figueroa de Lopidana. The latter had been in military service in Flanders and Spain, was appointed Gobernador y Capitán General del Tucumán en 1642, and Capitán general de la Flota de la Mar del Sur in the 1650s, dying in Lima 1674. See above, p. 54. For the individual of the same name who appeared at the court of Louis XIV about 1665–66, see above, p. 55.

[11] The *Armada del Mar del Sur* was created in 1578 to protect the convoys carrying silver from the mines of Upper Peru to Panama, and to defend the entire coastline of the viceroyalty of Peru. Callao, variants Calao, Calleo, was the principal port for Spanish commerce in the Pacific.

Buenase Ayres, Gover*no*r and Cap*tai*n Gen*era*ll of the Kingdome of Chile, and afterwards [Colon*e*ll] and Gen*era*ll of the Porte of Callao which last Com*m*ande hee surrender*ed* w*i*th the approbation of the Councell of Indyes unto his Brother Don ffrancisco de Victorias[1] who was then Constable of the Circuite and towne of Potosi and Generall of the Province of Cacharcas,[2] but my s*ay*d ffather through his great Zeale and Confidence found himselfe at last in the Power of his enemyes,[3] who out of envey and mallice faining that they had a designe to treate with him touching [f. 187v] some thing of the Roy*a*ll Service, sent a Lawyer[4] of *Chuquisaca* del Plata[5] called Don Pedro Retuerto[6] under the Caracter of an [~~Ambassador~~] Amuoy[7] but w*i*th secrett instru/der/c*i*ons to gett together in Tucaman all the Horsse that hee Could and to lay them in an Ambush round aboute the place where the Conference was to bee held which was upon the frontiers of both Jurisdic*i*ons.[8] The s*ay*d Lawyer gott together of the Militia of Tucaman about 300[9] horse besydes 300 more which hee brought from Chuquisaca & besydes 10,000[10] foote, and soe having devided them into severall convenient stac*i*ons hee sent notice to sayd my father of his arrivall who (trusting in the Roy*a*ll faith) went to the meeting with onely 300 Indians on horsse with Lances & Arrows and some few a foot w*i*th baggage, all which beleeved themselves very safe going with my father who they knew had before sent a Religious Person a Jesuite[11] as his Ambassadour to give account of his mariage and Colonac*i*on[12] to the Vice-Roy and of the reasons that moved him soe to doe, promissing withall to Acknowledge allwayse his Catholiq*ue* Ma*jes*tie for his King and Naturall Lord and to pay his Ma*jes*tie Every yeare a Certaine Tribute and other Circumstances, Praying that the s*ay*d Vice-Roy would send him Churchmen to Administer the Holly [*sic*] Sacraments to the Christians that were in his Company and to Cathaquise the Infidells, and that the Answer made there unto was very sivill with a promisse that there should bee sent to him a Minister of the Councell to agree to all hee desired and Conferr with him upon other things [f. 188r] of Convenienceyes, but in the end hee was made a Prissioner though they used him with reverence all along till hee dyed, aboute which time

[1] Victoria in TNA, SP 94/55, f. 41r.

[2] Charcas; variants, Cacharcas, Las Charcas. The Audiencia of Charcas was established in 1559 under the viceroyalty of Peru. It was based in La Plata, see below, n. 5.

[3] Don Carlos's account glosses over the frustrating and unsuccessful efforts of the Spanish authorities to contain and suppress Bohorques's activities during the years 1656–59, see above, pp. 52–7.

[4] Oidor or Oydor, a judge on the bench of the Audiencias or high appellate courts of the viceroyalties. The viceroyalty of Peru was divided into 6 Audiencias at this period.

[5] Chuquisaca, founded in 1538 as Ciudad de la Plata de la Nueva Toledo and generally known as La Plata; now Sucre, the constitutional capital of Bolivia and of the Department of Chuquisaca. Variants, Chuquisaca del Plata , Chuquissaca alias Platta.

[6] Judge Juan Retuerta was selected as the emissary for the Audiencia de Charcas in which he served.

[7] '*Enviado*' (envoy) in TNA, SP 94/55, f. 41r.

[8] Judge Retuerta met Bohorques at Escoipé Pass near Salta,Tucumán in April 1659.

[9] 800 in TNA, SP 94/55, f. 41r.

[10] 10,500 in TNA, SP 94/55, f. 41r .

[11] '*Religioso de la Compañia*' in TNA, SP 94/55, f. 41r, referring to the Company or Society of Jesus or Jesuits. Don Carlos is correct in stating that the Jesuits working in the region did work with Bohorques, recognizing that his control over the peoples of the Calchaquí valley would allow them to carry out their mission which had, before his arrival, been entirely unsuccessful.

[12] Clearly a scribal error for '*coronacion*' found in TNA, SP 94/55, f. 45r.

hee declared mee his Lawfull hier [*sic*] as it was his Custome to doe upon other occasions of Danger. Hee was above six yeares Kept Prision*n*er in a Tower without Ever Examining or having any question putt to him or giving him any reason for his Restric*i*on but onely that hee was kept there by derec*i*ons from the King and must continue soe untill new order from his Ma*jes*tie. As soone as hee dyed the Indians made great inroads into Tucaman & Chile burning severall townes and taking away much Cattle and many Prisioners. I being then in Chile, My Mother- in-Law[1] and the Principale Cosiques[2] of the Provinces sent severall of the Jesuits to offer mee the Government promising to shew mee the same obedience as to my father and that they would informe themselves soe in Millitarye affayres as to bee able to sett mye father at Libertye or att least to revenge the wrong done him, And they not onely promissed this but alsoe severall other Provinces who onely watched occasion to see some one Province begin that soe they might themselves follow the same Example and thereby free themselves from the heavy yoake of Spain. To the affores*ay*d offerrs I made answer w*i*th great shew of gratefullnesse Esteeming in much the hon*n*ors and fav*o*rs which they did mee [f. 188v] but that as to the matter of taking upon mee the Government It would first doe well to Consult many things of Safetye without which all our indeavours would Come to nothing And that to accept of a Jewell which I could not preserve or keepe from my Enemyes it would not doe well besydes being Every Day oblidged to bee on horseback and subiect to suffer Tyranye.[3] That therefore I was Resolved to watch opertuntye to passe into Europe to seeke the protec*i*on of some Powerfull Prince or Monarke under whose wings[4] what was designed might bee obtained, but that as for that present Conjunture of time it would bee but in vaine to trye to swim against the streame,[5] our Enemyes being in all things strong and wee in want of shipping & other Conveniencyes by which wee might send notice into Europe in cases of neccessitye or to pray succour before the Catholique King could send to his one [own] partye, besyds the want of Coyne (which was never then used amongest them) and the want of men disiplyned in millitarye affairs. The want of knowledge in the use of fyre Armes, the want of Armes, Ammunic*i*on, and other neccessaryes for the warr and in Effect all things for which reason I could admitt of none of thier offerrs Though, notwithstanding they still promisd to acknowledge mee upon all occasions.

My ffather left a daughter behinde him, and now the affors*ay*d Provinces are [f. 189r] much Peopled with Spaniards and many convert Indians who were brought to the knowledge of the truth by the dilligence and care of the Jesuites who alsoe Govern my mother and sister and takes soe much paynes that it *is* believed that in lesse then a yeare, eight thousand Spaniards have betaken themselves to inhabitt in the sayd Provinces, ffor

[1] '*Madrasta*' meaning 'stepmother' in TNA, SP 94/55, f. 45r, presumably referring here to Bohorques's wife who was, he claimed, an Inca *Coya*. See above, p. 52.

[2] *Casiqui* or *cacique*, meaning indigenous lord or chief, originating in the circum-Caribbean region but used by the Spaniards to describe other indigenous leaders within the Spanish empire in Latin America.

[3] The translator clearly had some difficulty in understanding Don Carlos's metaphor here. TNA, SP 94/55, f. 45r reads '*estando cada dia obligado a estar con el pie en el estivo y sujetto yr a padecer tiranias*' meaning 'forced every day to keep one foot in the stirrup [be ready to flee] and to be subject to tyranny'.

[4] The word in TNA, SP 94/55, f. 45r is *sombra* meaning 'shade' or 'protection'.

[5] Here the translator substitutes 'to trye to swim against the streame' for '*tirar cozes contra el aguijon*', meaning 'kick against the goad'.

that it is a Co*u*ntrye full of gould miens, silver miens and Copper, And through the industrye of the s*ay*d Religious there is now there above thirtye thousand men that understands the use of fyre Armes.

These Provinces have many good Ports both to the South and to the North, and towards the aforemenc*i*oned straights of Magalanes from whence the Inhabitants have Comunicac*i*on and some time warr with the Indians that Inhabitt Terra del fuego[1] Crossing the Straights in boats that rowe with 24 oars./

This is in Shortt Great S*i*r the cause of my care beseeching y*ou*r Ma*jes*tie to bee pleased to Com*m*and my request to bee heard recieving mee under y*ou*r Roy*a*ll Protec*i*on with the assurerance of an humble & faithfull subject./

And to the end this truth may appeare and whatsoever Else I have Related, I beseech Y*ou*r Ma*jes*tie that if it stands with your Roy*a*ll service y*o*u will give mee a vessel of about one hundred Tunns more or lesse and one hundred Armed [f. 189v] men and Provition for tenn months with which I may bee inabled to enter into the South Sea with requissitt secrisye to secure and settle the mindes of my ffriends and to order matters w*i*th my uncle Don Francisco de Victoria Governour of Calao[2] soe as shall be thought fitting and alsoe to cary off my owne goods to satisfy the expences of pay of the s*ay*d Frigatt[3] and the Charges of the voyage, and to shew Y*ou*r Ma*jes*ties Pilotts and other officers whome y*o*u shall thinke fitt to send w*i*th mee the Severall Intrances of the s*ay*d sea, The Ports and Contryes that may bee planted and what else of Conveniency to Y*ou*r Ma*jes*tie shall offer in the sayd voyage./

For the performance of all which I now offer unto Y*ou*r Ma*jes*tie as an ingagement for all the bennefitt I expect, my hon*n*or and my life the most pretious Jewells which (with the Devine assistance) I could preserve from more dangers and troubles then I can now expresse, not being able at present to injoye any other Comfort by reason of the great Expenses & Charges which I have been att to cast up my buisinesses and Cleer myselfe well of them, Itt being well knowne that the ministers that now Governe the Monarchy of Spaine are easily leade w*i*th such weaknesse.[4]

What I can assure is that god[5] preserving my life and Y*ou*r Ma*jes*tie affordeing mee the fav*o*r of Y*ou*r Roy*a*ll Protec*i*on and helpe to cary on what is propounded, [f. 190r] I Trust in my knowledge and experience of things that there shall bee sett on foot an undertakeing from whence will Redowne unto Y*ou*r Ma*jes*tie great Glory with a generall increase of all Trade & Comerce of y*ou*r Kingdomes, provided that this matter bee putt in execution with that expedition and secresye that the case requires Leving to my care to shew in time that the insuing particullars shall be fulfilled and Compleated./

1st. That whatsoever shall bee undertaken in this matter shall prove easy in the Comencing and ffinishing./

2. That it shall bee performed w*i*th smale Charge and great securitye./

3. Without breaking or Contradicting any Treaty of Peace or ffriendship now in fforce./

[1] Tierra del Fuego; variants Terra del Fogo, del Fugo, Terra Foggo.

[2] See above.

[3] *Fragatta* (*fragata*) in TNA, SP 94/55, f. 43r, referring in this English translation to an English ship, generally meaning a small three-masted warship.

[4] Neither the Spanish (TNA, SP 94/55, f. 46r) nor the English wording is very clear but presumably Don Carlos means that they are subject to bribery.

[5] Not capitalized in TNA, SP 94/55, as would usually be the case.

4. Of great advantage now in times of Peace and much more in times of warre./
5. That what shall bee obtained will be easily mantained with small danger of the losse of men or mony./
6. That what sea Ports are inhabitted shall bee found secure and ease in the going in and Coming out with any winds and are very sound in the bottome and safe./
7. And lastlye that the sayd Provinces shall be found very Comodious for Inhabitting and furnished with all man*n*er of necessaryes for Living, for they are very fertill, full of fruites, Phisicall earbes,[1] Timber for building, Graine of severall kinds, Pumgranads[2] and good ffish along the sea Coasts, all man*n*er of mettalls [f. 190v] in miens [mines] (except onely Steele and Iron) Pearle and many miens of Divers pretious stones, and Inhabitants naturallye very Ingenius and of most generous and Loyall humo*u*r and of a very good aspect, as being bread under a very wholsome Climate & of good Ayre and a Contry very well waterd with wholesome Springs. The people are much inclined to Armes and are of a bigg Stature and very dexterous on Horseback, the Country alsoe abounding in great man*n*er of Horses of the like shape and nature with those of Andaluzia in Spaine./

These Provinces have still maintain*e*d thier libertyes and defended themselves against the Spanish Tyrany, never admitting them to deale among them in thier Country, admitting onely the Jesuites who by thier good example and Pollicye have not onely preserved themselves among the[3] Inhabitants but are now become owners of thier soules & bodyes. It was they that first aproved of my fathers takeing to wyfe the afforsa*y*d Princes and taking upon him the Crowne without comitting Crime, since hee tooke not away the right of any body else and that what he recieved from her was nothing else but the propertye and right of the giver.

The severall Vice-Royes doe use all dilligence to reduce the mindes of the Inhabitants of the s*ay*d Provinces to the Kings [f. 191r] will that soe they might send Bishops and Govern*o*rs, but the natives and alsoe the Religious and Spaniards that live there doe keepe themselves very firme from admitting that designe to take Effect, of which design I gave them notice from Lima by my Uncles dere*ci*ons before my parting thence, and desired them withall they should not forgett mee since I Continued them and thier Concernes very firme in my hart, And was going into Europe with fervent design to returne againe in a Condition to helpe my mother and sister.

Royall and Sacred Ma*jes*tie seeing good Luck Com*m*only depends on great dilligence in the affayres and the Hazard Consists in dellayes, I doe once more beseech Y*ou*r Ma*jes*tie (If it may bee) that you grant mee this fav*o*r which I hope to deserve of Y*ou*r bountye, God preserve Y*ou*r Ma*jes*tie as I wish with many and happye yeares for the welfare of Y*ou*r Ma*jes*ties Loyall Subjects./

Y*ou*r Ma*jes*ties most Loyall and Humble Subject

Don Carlos Enriques

[1] The translator omitted the word 'vegetables' [*legumbres*] after fruits. His rendering of '*yerbas medicinales*' would appear to mean herbs for use in physic.

[2] The translator also appears to have had difficulty deciphering Don Carlos's wording at the end of this line. TNA, SP 94/55, f. 46r, appears to read '*ganados y aves*' meaning 'livestock, and birds'.

[3] This word is repeated in the text.

[f. 191v] [*Endorsed:*] June the 29 1669.[1]

Translac*i*on of the Paper dellivere*d* in Spanish by Don Carlos Enriques

4. Narbrough's copy of his orders to proceed to Long Reach[2]

James Duke of Yorke & Albany, Earle of Ulster, Lord High Admirall of England and Ireland, Constable of Dover Castle, Lord Warden of the Cinque Ports and Governour of Portsmouth &c.

You are, with the first opportunity of wind and weather, to saile with his Maj*esty*'s Shipp under your Command to Long Reach where you are to Continue untill further order. Given under My hand at S[t] James the 5 July 1669.

James

To Captaine Narbrough Commander of his Maj*esties* Shipp *Sweepstakes*

Vera Copia

5. Don Carlos Enriques Second proposs*itio*n in order to a voyage to the West Indyes. Rec*eive*d Jully the 14 1669[3]

[f. 253r] May it please *you*r Ma*jes*tie

Notwithstanding that new things are Com*m*only looked upon as difficult, and especially that this which I pretend to give a beginning unto, may seeme soe, Yett in a buisnesse [*sic*] of great wieght [*sic*] and importance as this (being carefully looked into) shall bee found, The like as I beleeve not having been propounded to any Monarch since the first Conquerors of America and of the partes of Assia [*sic*], who undertooke things that had not surety or promisse of good successe that I have, atained by practise & speculac*i*on whereby to labour with neccessary insight without runing myselfe in the darke depending onely upon fortune, as was done in the time of the Serene Princes Queene Elizabeth by S*ir* ffrancis Drake, though with different designe, for hee went onely as the huntsmen to try what they can finde, and though hee hath been indeavored to bee imitated by severall

[1] The Spanish original, TNA,SP94/55 ff. 39r–47v, is endorsed '*Para su Magestad Britanica que Guarde Dios*' in Don Carlos's hand. 'June 29. 1669 Don Carlos Henriques his storye of severall passages happen'd in the West Indyes together w*i*th his proposs*icio*n for discoverye of the passage through the Streights of Magelanes & the Coast of the South Sea &a. 29th June 1669' in a different hand.

[2] BL, Add MS 88980A, 27th unnumbered page reading from the back of the 'Booke' forwards.

[3] TNA, CO1/33, No. 103c, ff. 252v–264v. The Spanish original is found on ff. 245–252v. The English translation follows on ff. 253r–264v. This present transcription begins with the endorsement on f. 252v of the preceding Spanish document. The contemporary translation is generally sound as to meaning but the word selection and style reflects English usage of the time. Any significant differences are noted below.

other navigators as well of Engl*and* as of ffrance & Holland, they have not mett with the same good luck because of thier [*sic*] Temeritye and rashnesse but quite contrary had soe ill successe that of severall that ventured few ever returned to thier Contrye to give account of thier [ffellows].

This my pretenc*i*on Sacred & Roy*a*ll Ma*jes*tie being on its way to greater ends and assured (that God Lending mee life and y*ou*r Ma*jes*tie y*ou*r Roy*a*ll favor and Prottec*i*on with necessary Power for its preservac*i*on I hope in time to returne to kisse y*ou*r Ma*jes*ties Roy*a*ll ffeete and to offer you in Effect the fruites of my now Promisses./ [f. 253v] And because it is ffitt to informe y*ou*r Ma*jes*tie of some of the Convenencys necessary for the Carying on of the Voyage to which having respect, I am of oppinions (with Submission allwase to a better) That the ffollowing Convenencyes shall bee provided.

[*margin:* 1st] That it being intended imediatly to make a Colony planting at the Strieght [*sic*] and that Convenent [*sic*] Places for that purpose bee inspected, It will be neccessay [*sic*] to provide two vessells, the one of two hundred tunns built Pinkewyse,[1] and well fitted with all Equipage & victualls for the s*ai*d voyage and Conveniencyes for one hundred & fiftye men who shall bee imployed in the offices and Capasityes [~~following~~] which shall bee hereafter menc*i*oned.

[*margin:* 2.] One other Vessell of fiftye Tunn built Frigattwayse [*sic*], which shall bee fitted alsoe with all neccessaryes, and mand with fifty men that soe she may returne with notice what shall offerr upon fitting occasions unto y*ou*r Ma*jes*tie to acquaint you with what shall happen.

[*margin:* 3.] The s*ai*d vessells may bee fitted out under pretext of being bound for Jamaica or any other Island of those of Barlovento and the Comissions may runn accordingly, but alsoe to Carye secrett Comissions which may not bee oppend or touched untill being gone out of the River de la Plata[2] the same shall (in presence of the Derectors & other officers of the s*ai*d vessells bee oppen*e*d & read, or at some other place more Southwards of the s*ai*d River which Comiss*i*on or Instruc*i*ons y*ou*r Ma*jes*tie may however bee first pleased to cause to bee Comunicated to mee for my better Satisfac*i*on and Securitye. [f. 254r]

[*margin:* 4.] That the vessells doe cary not onely the fflaggs of Coulors of England[3] but alsoe those of Severall other Contryes to serve as a disguise when occasion shall offerr and alsoe Colours with the *Braço fuerte [*marginal note with right-hand brace:* Braço fuerte, is an arme houlding a sworde in a redd field being an ensign that is Generall and to be used by any nacion] Seeing they are Colours that any nac*i*on may use, And each vessel to Carye alsoe one other fflagg all white which may serve upon other occasions likewyse.

[*margin:* 5.] That the officers and persons insuing may bee prouided for the s*ai*d voyage viz:

[1] See above, p. 28.

[2] Río de la Plata; variants de, de la, del; Plat, Plate, Platta, Platte, Platto.

[3] TNA, CO1/33, No. 103c, f. 246v, reads V. M , '*de Vuestra Magestad*', meaning 'of Your Majesty'.

4. Priests of a middle age who shall understand the Spanish and ffrench Languages & goe disguised in secullar habbitt with a Reserve of Spanish apparell, Hatt, sworde, band,[1] & sute,[2] and alsoe all necessarye vestements for saying of masse.
4. Derectors who (if it may bee) shall bee men that doe speake and write the afforsa*i*d Languages and to Cary alsoe a Reserve of Spanish aparell, and shall understand (at least two of them) the exercyse of Armes and millitarye affayres, and that the other two have Skill in Maritime affayres.
4. Pylots who shall understand Cosmographye and speake one of the afforsa*i*d two Languages or the Lattin and every one of them Carying with him double Instruments of his Arte and a Reserve of Spanish Cloaths.
4. Surgions that shall speake the sa*i*d Languages every one Carying his box well furnished with saves [salves][3] and the Instruments of his trade, and Spanish Cloaths as afforsayd
4. Carpenters and Caulkers with double Instruments of their trade.
4. Coupers with double Instruments of thier trade.
4. Smiths with singles Instruments of their trade which smiths shall alsoe understand locksmiths worke.
4. Armourers two of which (if it may bee) shall understand ffounders worke as Casting of Artillerye [f. 254v] and Bells, with the instruments of thier [*sic*] Arte
2. Inginiers and Architects
2. Master builders or Surveyors who shall understand Geometrye well:
4. Stone Mason Masters
4. Master Bricklayers
2. that shall under[stand] laying Tyle[4]
2. Plasterers[5]
2. Charcole makers
2. Saddle makers & makers of furniture for Horsses
2. Kettle makers[6]
2. Lanthorne makers[7]
2. Ship Candlers[8]
2. Sculpters
2. Trompetts[9]
2. Drummers[10]

[1] TNA, CO1/33, No. 103c, f. 254r reads '*cuello*' meaning 'collar'.

[2] TNA, CO1/33, No. 103c, f. 254r. reads '*calsado*' meaning 'shod'.

[3] TNA, CO1/33, No. 103c, f. 254r reads '*medicinas*'.

[4] TNA, CO1/33, No. 103c, f. 247r reads 'laying of tile and brickwork'.

[5] TNA, CO1/33, No. 103c, f. 247r the word is '*caleras*', '*cal*' meaning 'lime' or 'whitewash'.

[6] TNA, CO1/33, No. 103c, f. 247r the word is '*calderero*' also meaning 'boilermaker'.

[7] TNA, CO1/33, No. 103c, f. 247r the word is '*faroleros*' meaning 'lanternmakers'.

[8] TNA, CO1/33, No. 103c, f. 247r reads '*maestros de velas de navio*'. '*Vela*' can mean candle or sail. Since sail-makers would seem to be the intended meaning, this may be either a translation or spelling error.

[9] Presumably trumpeters as in the Spanish.

[10] TNA, CO1/33, No. 103c, f. 247r reads '*tambores por caxas de guerra*', meaning 'drummers for sounding to arms'.

2. Apothegaryes & herbalists
3. Corne Millers who shall understand winde mills
3. Refiners of Gunnpowder
4. Master Turnners[1]
80. Markes men that shall understand Artillirye and officers of all kinde[2] both of sea and Artillirye
40. Millitarye persons which shall bee soldiers well season'd
28 or thereabouts officers, as sarjants of foote and Cornnetts[3] of Horsse
200. Which in all makes two hundred men and is the number I desire, and which I pry (it being soe requissitt in the beginning) that soe many as can bee found of them maybee RomanCatholiq*ues*, and such as shall understand one of the affors*ai*d Languages ffrench or Spanish for soe it will bee of great importance to prevent many inconvenencyes that may happen.

Over & above what the s*ai*d vessells shall Carye for the use of the voyage it will bee neccessarye that they cary alsoe the following things., viz: [f. 255r]
30. *quintalls* [4] of Cannon Powder
12. *quintalls* of good[5] muskett powder
4. quintalls of refined powder for fowling
8. Peeces of Artillirye with thier field Cariages and all neccessary Instruments 4 whereof to bee of a foure pound bullett & 4 of an eight pound bullett,[6]
2 demi-Coulverins of a 12 ponde [*sic*] bullett
8. morter-Peeces of Iron or brasse[7] Chamber'd
30. quintalls of musquett Ball, some plaine & some with [Chaines][8]
100. Chaine Bulletts for the two biggest gunns
50. Barr shott of bigg & middle sieze[9]
1000. round & foursquared Bulletts for all the three siezes of Gunns
20. quintalls of Match
one Barrell of fflints[10]
4. Bells of foure Severall sorts smaler & greater
1000. hand *Granados*[11]

[1] TNA, CO1/33, No. 103c, f. 247r reads '*Maestros de poleas y torneros*', meaning 'tackle/ pulley makers and turners'.

[2] TNA, CO1/33, No. 103c, f. 247r reads '*mayores y menores*', meaning 'greater and lesser'.

[3] TNA, CO1/33, No. 103c, f. 247r reads '*cornetas de caballos*', meaning 'cavalry buglers'.

[4] The Spanish *quintal* was a cwt or 100 Castilian *libras*, amounting to 101.47 lbs.

[5] TNA, CO1/33, No. 103c, f. 247r reads '*fino*' meaning 'of high quality'.

[6] TNA, CO1/33, No. 103c, f. 247r has '*calibre*' or 'caliber' instead of 'bullet' here and the next entry.

[7] TNA, CO1/33, No. 103c, f. 247v has '*bronze* (*bronce*)', meaning 'bronze'.

[8] TNA, CO1/33, No. 103c, f. 247r reads '*rassa y ramadas*'. Muskets did not fire chain shot. The Spanish word 'ramada' may mean a 'shelter' or 'arbour' made from branches. Here it could refer to musket cartridges comprising powder and ball wrapped in paper tubes twisted at both ends to close. These were in common use by the 17th century.

[9] TNA, CO1/33, No. 103c, f. 247v has '*palenquetas*' which means 'iron artillery bar-shot' used against the rigging and masts of enemy ships.

[10] TNA, CO1/33, No. 103c, f. 247v reads 'shotgun flints'.

[11] Grenades.

300. * Alcancias of glasse or earthenware [*marginal note with right-hand brace: Alcancias* are glasse or earthen round potts full of Combustible stuffe used upon occasion to fyre an enemyes ship when they come to boarde. /][1]
50. ffowling Peeces
100. Pykes
50. Lances or halfe Pikes
100. Case of Pistolls for the Girdle
200. Semiters or Hangers with scabards & belts[2]
100. baggs or great pursses for amunition
100. Complete bandoleers
100. quintalls of Leaden piggs[3]
100. quintalls of unwrought Iron in barrs
20. quintalls of steele
100. quintalls of Stone Coale or Sea Coale
200. Sheetes of Tinn
20. quintalls of a man*n*er of nayles Spykes & tacks
50. quintalls of hartea/harsea[4] for a Reserve
[f. 255v]
2000. Yardes of Canvas for a Reserve to make Tints [*sic*], Barakes[5] and other Convenencyes to keepe of the weather
3. quintalls of Candleing treed[6] or packtreed
4. Great Ancors of 600$^{l.}$ wieght and of 300$^{l.}$ wieght to bee kept for a Reserve
4. Cables of 10 & of 13 Inches forty same
4. Smale Ancors of 150$^{l.}$ wieght apeece
4. Smale but long Cables of six & seven Inches[7]
12. quintalls of Tallow Candles for a reserve
12. quintalls of Tallow unwrought
12. quintalls of Rosen[8]
20. greate Netts for ffish, with quintalls of Tarre for a Reserve
20. Barrills of Alquitran or stuffe to Corrien[9] with
50. Lanthornes of Tinn

[1] Two entries were omitted in the translation of the TNA, CO1/33, No. 103d, f. 247v, the first for 1,000 lanterns for artillery and stone ball guns; the second for 50 flintlock and 50 matchlock muskets.

[2] TNA, CO1/33, No. 103c, f. 247v reads '*Alfanges Con baynas y tiros*' meaning 'Scimitars with sheaths and straps'.

[3] An oblong mass of iron or lead from a smelting furnace, *NOED*.

[4] TNA, CO1/33, No. 103c, f. 247v reads 'harsia', which it has not been possible to identify. It would seem that the contemporary translator did not know its meaning either, since no English equivalent was given.

[5] TNA, CO1/33, No. 103c, f. 247v reads '*de lona de reserva para barracas: toldos y lo demas necessario*', meaning canvas for barracks and awnings or canopies. The contemporary translator grasped the intent of Don Carlos's entry.

[6] TNA, CO1/33, No. 103c, f. 247v reads '*hilo de vela*', translated here as 'coarse thread'.

[7] This comes before the preceding entry in TNA, CO1/33, No. 103c, f. 247v.

[8] Rosin. TNA, CO1/33, No. 103c, f. 247v reads '20 quintals of pitch as a reserve' but does not mention fishing nets.

[9] TNA, CO1/33, No. 103c, f. 247v refers only to tar. The contemporary translator added the explanation that the tar, or some other such substance, was needed for careening.

100. Shuffles[1] shood with Iron
100. Hatchetts for cutting of wood[2]
100. Pickaxes
12. Pitchforkes
12. Iron Sledges of 15$^{l.}$ wieght
24. Iron Crows[3] of 30$^{l.}$ wieght each
12. Grinding Stones with thier Co[a]riages shood[4]
13. quintalls of Sulpher unrefined
3. quintalls of Cotton tread [thread] for tallow or wax Candles
24. Smale Boxes of Lamb[lamp]-black
4. Netts to ffish for pearles[5]
6. greate Netts for ffish, with Corks & leads
12. Shortt nett with poles to bee used in ffresh water Rivers for ffishing[6]
200. Pounds of ffishing Line
2000. Fishing hookes of all kinds <u>12</u> of them to bee with Chaines
12. Speares for ffish and 12. great harping Irons
150. Ores [oars] 30. of 24. foot long, 40. of 18. foot long, and the rest of 15. foot long

[f. 256r] One Long Boate Cover'd such as the Piratts use, with all its neccessaryes as I shall (if neede bee shew unto the makers of it) soe as that it may bee taken asunder and caryed in severall peeces in the Pinke./

Besydes what is above sett downe y*ou*r Ma*jes*tie may bee pleased to order the payment of the sum*m*es of mony hereafter menc*i*oned which sum*m*es to bee Layd out as I shall sett downe viz:

1st[7] Two hundred pounds ster*ling* to bee employed in buing [*sic*] the things following which shall bee given to gaine ffriendship and Comerrce with the Indians of the Strieghts which things they esteame much Viz:[8]

Tobaco in the Rowle
Tobaco pipes
ordinary knifes
ordinary middle sieze sissors
Tinsell leafes[9]

[1] Shovels.

[2] TNA, CO1/33, No. 103c, f. 247v. The Spanish original indicates that these were intended for clearing wood or brush.

[3] TNA, CO1/33, No. 103c, f. 247v reads '*barretas*', meaning 'crowbar'.

[4] TNA, CO1/33, No. 103c, f. 247v reads '*piedras de amolar calsadas*'. It could mean that the millstones should have iron rims.

[5] In TNA, CO1/33, No. 103c, f. 248r '*v ostiones*' is added, presumably ' viz: oysters'.

[6] TNA, CO1/33, No. 103c, f. 248r reads '*atarrayas*', meaning 'casting net'.

[7] TNA, CO1/33, No. 103c, f. 248r has '200^{l}' in the margin.

[8] TNA, CO1/33, No. 103c, f. 248r presents the following items in a numbered list of 13 items. As noted below, the translation omits the 7th entry in the original.

[9] TNA, CO1/33, No. 103c, f. 248r reads 'sheets'.

Smale Bells such as the morish dancers were[1]
ordinary fflagiletts[2] or whistles
[*marginal note with right-hand brace:*] *Matchettes are kinde of great broade knifes that the Indians use to hang at thier sydes * Matchettes with handles[3]
ordinary needles & quilting needles
middle sieze pinns & bigg pinns
Smale ordinary looking-glases
Conterfiete Amatists, Rubyes or the like[4]
Conterfiett pearles.

2. That wee may bee able to Refresh in the Islands and to take some things with us to Present unto the Casiques[5] and Govern*o*rs and others with whome wee shall deale in those parte[s] as alsoe provision for the use of the Like neccessitated persons of the Company,[6] y*our* [*margin:* 100l.] Ma*jes*tie may bee pleased to com*m*and one hundred pounds money to bee payd which shall bee layd out in Ribbons and silke & worsted stokins which shall bee give[n] att [f. 256v] the Canaryes[7] (where wee must rest) in exchange for the afors*ai*d neccessaryes & Regalos.[8]

3. For feare of what may happen having arrived upon the Coasts of America It will be neccessarye to Cary along with us some money in Spanish Coyne, and soe y*ou*r Ma*jes*tie may bee pleased to order [*margin:* 50l.] the payment of fiftye pounds more in halfe peeces of Eight & quarter peeces all of Mexico and of Perue of those that have the pillars in the stamp.[9]

4. That Neccessary Regalo and other things for the voyage may not bee wanting and to prevent the inconvenencyes that time may bring upon us, as well in respect of my one particullar as of those which y*ou*r Ma*jes*tie shall thinke fitt to send as Comarads along with mee, y*ou*r Ma*jes*tie may bee likewyse pleased to order the payment of 300l. [*margin:* 300l.] more, which sum*me* may bee putt into the Custody of any such person as y*ou*r Ma*jes*tie shall thinke ffitt to bee disposed of as wee shall want it.

5. And because at pr*e*sent I want myselfe many necessaryes, and shall want more for the voyage [*margin:* 300l] I must be fforced to pray y*ou*r Ma*jes*tie that together with the rest, y*o*u will alsoe order the payment of 300l. for my one use, either by way of succour, helpe for my Jorney, or by way of loane (as y*ou*r Ma*jes*tie shall thinke fitt) the sayd sum*me* alsoe to be putt into the Custodye of such a person as y*ou*r Ma*jes*tie thinke convenent soe that

[1] TNA, CO1/33, No. 103c, f. 248r only reads 'bells'. The translation omits the immediately following entry which reads 'ordinary flutes'.

[2] A small flute.

[3] Presumably machetes.

[4] TNA, CO1/33, No. 103c, f. 248r. The Spanish original reads '*Granetes Vaccalorios*'. The second word should be possibly have been '*arbolorios*' which would mean deep red beads, or the same in necklaces, of little value.

[5] See above, p. 95, n. 2.

[6] TNA, CO1/33, No. 103c, f. 248r. The Spanish reads 'sick and needy persons'.

[7] The Canary Islands; variants Canarias, Canaries, Canaryes.

[8] Gifts.

[9] Spanish colonial silver coins struck in Mexico, Santo Domingo and Lima mints 1536–72, and at Bogotá, Potosi, Cartagena and Lima mints 1651–1773, had two pillars stamped on one side.

upon my desire from time to time hee furnisheth mee out of it with neccessaryes for the decencye[1] of my person.

Having the afforsaid things and your Majesties Royall commands, going out of the Channell wee shall steere our Course as ffolloweth viz:

From the Channell wee shall sayle towards [f. 357r] the Island of Teneriffe[2] in the harbour of which Island wee will stay untill wee have taken in ffresh water and bought what shall bee wanting. And from thence wee will sayle to the Isle of St Tiago of Caboverde[3] or else to the Porte itselfe and there refresh our men againe, and take in water & wood, for these restings[4] before passing the Line, will bee very necessary for the recreacion of our people and to avoyd many Infermityes.

From Cabo Verde wee shall sayle towards the River de La Plata and the weather favouring shal Ancor under the Shelter of the Island of Flores which is upon the sayd River to the westwards,[5] there wee will take in water and fitt out the Long boate, and then myselfe, one of the best Cosmographers, and one of the Derectors going into the same will Rowe on Coasting along by the Land, Leaving derecions with our two ships to keepe in sight of us still, and that in case they shall bee separated from us by weather, to Rondevous[6] at a certaine place (the first that shall Come thither being to stay for the rest) betweene the Bay of St Peter (which is a very Cleer Bay & of good sande and very good Ancorage),[7] and the Barr[8] of the Strieghts and there to putt up thier Lanthornes[9] and in case the weather shall oblidge them to Ancor, they may goe into the said Bay and Ancor there; The said Bay is from the mouth of the Strieghts [*sic*] aboute twentye Leagues, and if necessitye shall oblidge them to goe to the Strieghts they may Ancor [f. 257v] on the north syde of the Island of Buena-vista[10] which lyes at the mouth of the said Strieghtes and if the winde bee high and north they may goe to the south syde of the said Islande for it hath securie Ancorage all round besydes that the sayd Coasts are but seldom entroubled with any great windes, and those that happen houlds but for a short time, they are for the most part South & Southwest windes and for [reamedie] againe[st] them the harbours on all sydes of the Island are very good.[11]

[1] The Spanish original '*apresto y dessencia de mi persona*'. '*Apresto*' can mean 'size', but may equally be intended as 'appearance' or 'presentation'.

[2] Tenerife, the largest of the Canary Islands; variants Tenerif, Tenariffe, Teneriffe.

[3] São Tiago de Cabo Verde; variants Caboverde, Cap do Verde, Cape Verde Islands, Islands of Deverde.

[4] TNA, CO1/33, No. 103c, f. 248v reads '*escalas*', meaning 'stop-over'.

[5] TNA, CO1/33, No. 103c, f. 248v reads 'on the West side'.

[6] TNA, CO1/33, No. 103c, f. 248v reads '*rande vous*', the French for '*encuentro*'.

[7] TNA, CO1/33, No. 103c, f. 248v reads '*Baya de San Pedro*'. The ports or anchorages north of the eastern entrance to the Strait are: Puerto San Julián (60 leagues N); Río Santa Cruz (45 leagues N); Puerto Coig (30 leagues N); Río Gallegos (20 leagues N). Don Carlos might have meant the latter, given the distance, or Puerto San Julián given that it was named after a saint, but it is equally likely merely a reflection of his total ignorance of the region and his fertile imagination.

[8] TNA, CO1/33, No. 103c, f. 248v reads '*boca*', 'mouth' or 'entrance'.

[9] The translation does not follow the order in which the information is given but is generally sound as to meaning and content, except that in TNA, CO1/33, No. 103c, f. 249r the Spanish reads '*haziendo ve[o]rdos a la mar y a la terra y con faralones*', meaning 'keeping watch at sea and on land and with lanterns'.

[10] There is no such island in the mouth of the Strait, indication that Don Carlos had never been there.

[11] TNA, CO1/33, No. 103c, f. 249r reads '*para cuyo reparo ay a barlovento y sotavento = muy buenos y seguros puertos*', meaning 'for shelter from which there are very good and safe anchorages to the windward and leeward'.

Having arrived at the s*ai*d Strieghts we shall Come to Ancor and then take possession of Elizabeths Island[1] and of the Spaniards call'd the Isle of Santa-Clara which hath in Circumference about six and thirtye miles and in Latitude Little more than three Leagues, Its a verye plaine con*n*try full of hearbage and Trees with many Cleer and sweete streemes of water, It hath a Harbour to the South in ffigure of a halfe moone, the points of which are distant aboute two miles and are a Rockey ground but such a Kinde of Rockes as may bee wrought for the building theron neccessary forts for the deffence of the s*ai*d Harbour, and other the plantac*i*ons that shall bee made under the Shelter thereof. The s*ai*d Harbour is Capable to Containe fortye[2] sayles of High built or great ships; It hath very safe Ancorage and many good Landing places,[3] The s*ai*d Island is distant from the Continent to the South aboute fortye miles, and to the North aboute foure or fiue miles. the Contryes about it are peopled with Indians some inhabitting two and some three Leagues within the Con*n*try, except onely some few ffishermen that [f. 258r] that in ffishing time use to dwell upon the Coasts; In this Island as soone as wee arrive shall bee agreed the forme that may bee taken for erecting of buildings and makeing of fortificac*i*ons, and gaining Correspondencye and Comunicac*i*on with the Indians, and soe leaving all things in good order I will fitt out the Long boate and with the people & Derectors that shall bee neccessarye I will goe into the South Sea and soe Coast along Inspecting the severall harbours & Creekes neccessary in which wee may without any danger take all Convenent refreshments untill wee come to the Sallinas de Guara[4] which are some fortye miles distant by sea from Calao and by Land from Lima aboute eighteen miles, It's a very safe Coast and free from any rack of seas,[5] there being no rocks or stones thereabouts,[6] then three of us[7] will lande and in the night goe to Lima leaving derec*i*on with our boate to keepe thereabouts allwayse makeing to the Sea in day time but soe as not to loose the sight of the land and in the night to keepe under the shoare, There's no feare of danger in those seas from the Equinoctiall unto fiftye degrees to the South for no other windes blows there but South windes and at thirtye degrees it blows soe soe temperately that it never rayseth the sea soe as to hinder a squiffe[8] bee it never soe smale from sayling; There shall bee derec*i*on left withe our boatemen that after the first two nights they doe every night after at every turning of the glasse shew a smale light as the burning a little powder or soe, that when wee are returned with our dispatch [f. 258v] wee may percieve [*sic*] where they are being come to the same place where they sett us on shoare where wee will alsoe answer them with the like signe that they may know us.

[1] Isla Isabel (52°52′38″S, 70°42′46″W), or Elizabeth Is; variants Elesabeths, Elezabeth, Elezabeths, Queen Elizabeth, Queen Elizabeths. The principal Spanish voyages through the Strait of Magellan do not mention Isla Santa Clara as a name for Isla Isabela. Sir Francis Drake (1578) named the three neighbouring islands, Elizabeth, Bartholomew and St George. Pedro Sarmiento de Gamboa (1580) named the Islas Marta and Madalena, but apparently thought Isla Isabela was part of the mainland. This would appear to be another of Don Carlos's inventions. The island is actually 7½ miles long, 2miles wide, about 16½ miles in circumference.

[2] TNA, CO1/33, No. 103c, f. 249r reads '*sinquenta*', fifty.

[3] TNA, CO1/33, No. 103c, f. 249r reads 'safe and clean anchorage and beautiful landing places'.

[4] TNA, CO1/33, No. 103c, f. 249r reads '*Salinas de guaura*', most likely the Bahía Salinas (11°11′S, 77°43′W), approximately 50 miles north of Callao.

[5] TNA, CO1/33, No. 103c, f. 249r reads '*ressaca de mar*', meaning 'surf'.

[6] TNA, CO1/33, No. 103c, f. 249r reads 'the beaches being very flat and without any rocks'.

[7] TNA, CO1/33, No. 103c, f. 249r reads '*tres camaradas*'. This is the second time the word 'comrade' appears raising the question of whether he hoped to take other men he already knew on the voyage with him.

[8] TNA, CO1/33, No. 103c, f. 249r reads '*esquife*', meaning a light rowing boat.

Having arrived at Lima wee shall negotiate what is neccessary in order to understand how to Governe our affaires upon all occasions, and I will gett of my uncle three or foure Chile men to take along with mee which will serve to teach the Priests and to bee our Interpreters to the Indians with whome wee shall have occasion to deale, and to returne to the Strieghts to see and give dere*ci*on in what shall bee requisitt.

And seing niether [*sic*] humane reason or understanding can reach soe farr as to finde out sufficient proven*ci*ons for future [acci]dents that may happen upon occasions in time, since experience shews us daylye the neccessitye of makeing new Laws & Constu*ci*ons to prevent Inconvencyes and in them to to observe what untill then is Come to our Knowledge, soe that for me to treate by way of discourse of what shall fall out in this voyage alltogether were to Ingulfe myselfe in a deepe sea writinge things perhaps which will signifye little or nothing afterwards[1] for that things may fall out soe as that the best Capatitye shal have neede to seeke out new inven*ci*ons reamidyes for them, never thought of till then,[2] And therefore I will passe by the useing any more preambles in the case since I am no historian,[3] though a deplorable experimenter[4] who sollicitts [f. 259r] to serve *you*r Ma*jes*tie with hopes to bee rewarded with the *mercedes* and hon*n*ors that *you*r Ma*jes*tie greatnesse and accustomed libralitye Conferrs upon *you*r subjects.

And seeing *you*r Ma*jes*tie will[5] appoint Derectors of that sufficencye and Capatity that is requissitt [in][6] the Ministers of soe great a Monarch,[7] that soe they atend with zeale the hon*n*or of thier Prince and the saftey of his state[8] & the lives & libertyes of his subjects with whome [I] must alsoe bee forced of neccestye to Confer and determine all things that shall offerr upon all occasions I beseech *you*r Ma*jes*tie with all humillitye,[9] that all things may bee disposed soe as that my hon*n*or & life may runn no Hazard in the Company of those whome I thus voluntarilye Choose, For as I have allready sayd, future accidents can onely bee prevented by god, And in long Voyages many difficultyes doe often offer to those who never had experence [*sic*] of them before, And it would not bee for mee to venture myselfe with such as at the first seeming danger would imagen themselves presently drownd or killed and soe fall into dispayre (though no reall danger were neer) and then make make mee suffer for all, with false testimonyes or Informacons, or perhaps with daring actions; soe that I doe not intend to venture or expose myselfe to such hazards unlesse *you*r Ma*jes*tie shall bee pleased to grant mee the following requests, without the Authority of which, it will bee impossible to ataine anything in

[1] A fingerpost symbol is drawn in the Spanish text at this point.

[2] TNA, CO1/33, No. 103c, f. 249v reads 'never up to that point known or invented'.

[3] TNA, CO1/33, No. 103c, f. 249v reads '*coronista*'which has more the sense of chronicler.

[4] TNA, CO1/33, No. 103c, f. 249v reads '*explorador experimentado*', or 'experienced explorer'. The contemporary translation of Don Carlos's paper provides a cruder and less polite version of Don Carlos's Spanish prose.

[5] TNA, CO1/33, No. 103c, f. 249v reads '*Y pues que Vuestra Magestad ha de nombrar*', which should be read as 'And further that Your Majesty may be pleased ...'.

[6] The word is overwritten and difficult to decipher.

[7] Here the Spanish word '*ministros*' has the sense of 'representatives' or 'agents', referring to the other directors whom Don Carlos envisioned would serve on the Council of his projected colony.

[8] TNA, CO1/33, No. 103c, f. 249v reads '*Real hazienda*' which here means 'royal treasury 'or 'estate' in the sense of income or property.

[9] TNA, CO1/33, No. 103c, f. 249v reads '*con la humilidad y rendimiento que devo*', meaning 'with the humility and submission which I owe'.

our designe for it will bee often neccessary to take Resolutions that will seeme impossible [f. 259v] bee effected, and to loose the occasion wherein [as] neccessarye to labour incontenently for such may some times bee layed asyde by repugning Councell and all *ou*r good luck consist in the execution or not and then the lossess of us all insue, And soe not to precipatate myselfe, flying[1] all risque[s], I say that to ataine our ends in this undertaking of soe great importance, It will bee neccessary that who ever hath in Charge the Carying it on shall alsoe have Authoritye and plenitude Power, to dispose & Governe, Derect, and determin, all manner of things that shall offer, and have an absolute Dominion and facultye over the subjects, as well to Rewarde as to Chastyse, according as the neccessitye of times shall require for if y*ou*r Ma*jes*tie shall intrust a subject and designes to doe him hon*n*or it must not bee by tying his hands from doing the worke Comitted to him, nor Constayning [*sic*] or Controaling his will in the determina*ci*on of things, nor by nameing derectors in this Case that may prove rather my judges then advisers, for then I shall not bee able to complye what otherwyse I shall doe going assured of y*ou*r Ma*jes*ties helpe and protection and with y*ou*r Roy*a*ll Comission wherein I may bee Naturalised as a subject unto y*ou*r Ma*jes*tie and alsoe granted the hon*n*or of making mee free and priviledged as nobles with the same fav*o*rs Priviledges and exemptions that Englishmen injoye. [f. 260r]

[*margin:* 1st] Before wee begin our voyage I desire that in the secrett Commiss*io*n or Instruct*io*ns which shall bee sent sealed up, y*ou*r Ma*jes*tie may bee pleased to name mee as Chiefe Com*m*anding therein, alsoe that together with the Derectors, I may Conferr, Resolve and determin what shall seeme best and most convenent for the service of God and the good of y*ou*r Ma*jes*tie s Crowne, without the Contradic*io*n of any other, but that what Wee shall soe in Councell doe, bee aproved of and admitted as good and vallid and that all things else done to the Contrarye shall bee of no force.

[*margin:* 2.] That no body shall in pubblique or in secrett, or must upon any pretence whatsoever fained or Reall, indeavour to hinder the prosecition of the sayd voyage in which all things must bee caryed on at the discretion of the sayd Councell without being Contradicted in what shall relate to the Roy*a*ll Service.

[*margin:* 3.] That the s*ai*d Derectors and the rest that shall have vote in the s*ai*d Councell doe take care to keepe the Peace and submitt to mee as to thier Superiour helpeing and assisting mee upon all occasions.

[*margin:* 4.] That whatever shall bee done or executed on the progresse of the voyage or in America or in any parte of Europe, nobody shall have power to call mee to account for it in any kinde of way, bee hee of what degree or quallitye soever.

[*margin:* 5.] That y*ou*r Ma*jes*tie doe Revoke as from this present time all Comissions whatsoever which are Contrary to the affors*ai*d articles, declaring such Comissions as null and invallid forever; I doe not propound these things [f. 260v] out of Ambittion or greedinesse of gaining hon*n*or to myselfe but meerly for the hon*n*or of y*ou*r Ma*jes*tie and

[1] Fleeing.

to secure what I soe much desire to goe through with in *your* Ma*jes*ties service, and without them it will bee very difficult for me soe to doe.

For being watchfull that *your* Ma*jes*ties hon*n*or doe suffer noe detriment at any time preventing the accidents that maye happen in things that neccessitye shall force us too, not being able to passe them by, and alsoe the better to gaine the good will of the Confederates and ffriends that wee shall make, it's neccessary that when all things are to bee made pubbliq*ue* (though what may bee shall still bee kept secrett) Though it may not bee soe kept for a long time, Wee must bee forced to use some Industry and Skill, and because there will bee a neccessitye that I declare myselfe head of those (who I hope will shew thier fface when I shall have neede of them) and that they may not suspect that *your* Ma*jes*tie is hee that assists mee, and that those of America may not be startled at the Religion, the protestants must desemble some times and bee present at the Roman Ceremonyes and I will upon occasions give out that they are Irish and that I came out of Europe at my one Charge, for the Irish is a People that the Spaniards love very well for they beleeve themselves to have been the first that planted in Ireland after the Flood and besydes they looke [f. 261r] upon them as great Catholiques, and seeing that of neccessitye severall ships of America will come and goe from Europe, some with advise and some with Merchandise in which may passe secrettly many men, Armes and Amunition, and though in time that some may Chance bee discover'd, yett I hope it may happen in such a Conjuncture of time as that Spaine may bee neccessitated to keepe in friendship *your* Ma*jes*ties Crowne, As alsoe I hope I shall myselfe soe labour in the thing that in a short time I shall Reduce the Indians (or most of them)[1] to Come under *your* Ma*jes*ties protec*io*n and preserve themselves allwayse there and will oppen unto *your* Ma*jes*tie the doores of Trade and Comerce with Buenos ayres, Puerto Bello, and Panama and shutt them against all other nac*io*ns.

I begg *your* Ma*jes*ties pardon if I speake with too much Confidence for I am oblidged thereunto by the fervour of my hart which can*n*ot desimble what it containes, and if here be confidence it's not occasioned by distrac*io*n but by the assurance of the evident and firme ffondation which is allready lay'd to ffacilitate this undertaking which is much firmer then I can well expresse Butt as all things requiring fitting time and occasion, nothing hath been stirr'd in this matter untill now, my friends not having heard of my good or ill fortune of which they still expect the news, (and that) (if *your* Ma*jes*tie is pleased to grant mee the grace and fav*o*r which I desire as of my naturall King [f. 261v] and Lord) I hope to cary to them myselfe in person, For which fav*o*r I will not onely acknowledge myselfe *your* Ma*jes*ties subject but the humblest of *your* slaves, ffor I doe protest before god and man to sollicitt and procure all the dayes of my life in what Contry or quallitye soever I am, the hon*n*or and service of *your* Ma*jes*tie and the increase of *your* Roy*a*ll Comerce preserving myselfe allwayse under the proteccion of *your* Ma*jes*ties imperiall Crowne, without which it were impossible to preserve mee, whereas having it (though secrettly) those partes of America shall bee made more impugnable[2] then can bee imagined. For as

[1] TNA, CO1/33, No. 103, f. 251r reads '*Las Indias o la mayor parte a estar y conservarse debajo de la Real Proteccion de V.M. a quien abrire puertas para el comercio* ...', which would suggest that it is the Indies not the Indians which Don Carlos hopes to bring under the English crown and open up trade to the same.

[2] 'Open to assault' or 'to be taken by storm'. TNA, CO1/33, No. 103d, f. 251r reads '*in*expugnables' meaning 'impregnable'.

I know what it is that hath not hitherto been experienced there by reason of the Spaniards ill government & Tyrany, occasion'd by thier Idlenesse and Covetousnesse which are Vices that occasion even among themselves soe much contenc*io*n & disorder that there is not a nac*io*n amongst them which doe not indeavour to Consume and drinke one anothers blood being every day in Armes, one against another soe that some times five thousand Spaniards have been violently kill'd and murther'd in the Kingdome of Perue alone, without regard to ViceRoy or Governours butt killing them alsoe, for if they can not doe it with the sworde they doe it with poyson, and all this done that none may have incouragement to bee zealous in the service of the King or Contrye [f. 262r] but to strive who can steale most and thereby gett the more.

Were there a Gov*ernou*r in whome concurr'd the vertues of zeale, Prudence and Experience uninterested[1] and who would seeke no more then the hon*n*or of god and the welfare and preservac*io*nof the Pubbliq*ue*,[2] its most evident that there would not bee a spann of ground in all the Provinces and Contryes of America but what would bee full of People & Riches and would soe abounde of all things that it would bee nothing Inferior to any other parts of the world nor neede to covett any thing from them but should rather inrich all places else with thier Treasure, For if att present there wants of those Treasures that formerly were found there, or that Trade is decayed, It is not that Treasure is not to bee found but because there wants People to worke in the miens [*sic*] and to discover them, for they were the Indians whome nature indowed with the supernaturall parts for the ministrye of those things and without them other nac*io*ns are worth nothing for the purpose, but the poore People by reason of the opression of the Spaniards choose to runn away further into the Contrye where when any Spaniard comes they eate him by mouthfulls soe much is the naturall hate they beare him; And soe the smale parte of the Con*n*trye (in Comparic*io*n of the rest) which the Spaniards doe injoye is like a Disert peopled by a few Indians who many wayse sufferr the inconvenencyes [f. 262v] that are occasioned them by labouring in such Miens [*sic*] as are allready discover'd, bring to supplye the places of themselfes and thier absent ffriends.

And to Conclude there wants nothing in the Empire but a Protector or Leader under whose wings they might take off thier intolerable yoake, which they could not yett doe for want of such a one and for want of Armes and Amunition which the Spaniards doe with great care watch to keepe from them, not permitting them to Cloath themselves after the Spanish way nor to goe shoo'd nor to ryde on horseback, and much lesse to have or use any man*n*er of Armes though but a staffe with an Iron head,[3] and all to keepe the poore natives still under and repressed;

In fine it is a Contrye from whence with much ease Comerce and Trade may bee held with the parts of Afrique viz: <u>Cabo Verde</u>, <u>Guinye</u>,[4] and <u>Angola</u>, from <u>Buenos-ayres</u>, with <u>Assia</u> on the parts of <u>Phillipina</u>[5] and the <u>East Indyes</u>, from the Porte of <u>Acapulco</u>,[6] with Europe by those wayse that are knowne to all, And yett this soe obscure and

[1] TNA, CO1/33, No. 103c, f. 251v reads '*desinteressado*', meaning 'selfless' or 'disinterested'.

[2] TNA, CO1/33, No. 103c, f. 251v reads '*de la republica*'.

[3] TNA, CO1/33, No. 103c, f. 251v reads '*baston con punta*', which may mean a club or a spear.

[4] Guinea.

[5] The Filipinas or Phillipines; variants Phillipina, Phillipine.

[6] Variant Aquatulco.

incomunicable as if it had never been seen through the ill management & ordering of Spaine, which would cause pittye even in the worst of enemies.

It will bee very Convenent to Cary along with us three Comissions,[1] the first as is allready [f. 263r] sayd with pretence of going for Jamaica[2] or some other island, The second to bee used when wee are passed the Canaryes, as if designed for some of *you*r Ma*jes*ties factoryes in parte of the Indyes, and the third (as I have allready sayd), for the preservac*io*n of my owne Authoritye and the securitye of my person that being Come to the Strieghts the s*ai*d Comiss*io*n may bee oppen'd and read in publiq*ue* in presence of all the Company.

Once more I returne to beseech *you*r Ma*jes*tie that my sayd propossistion being seen, reade, premeditated and consulted, *you*r Ma*jes*tie doe derect what shall bee most for *you*r Roy*a*ll service Com*m*anding mee to bee examined upon all points wherein y*o*u shall finde difficultye without deffering it to the time that I must bee necessitated to goe into Flanders to sollicitt my Stypende there, for it it can*n*ot bee done otherwyse then by being personally upon the place, and I finde myselfe with smale fforce to subsist in this Court any longe time; God preserve *you*r Ma*jes*tie the many happye yeares that I wish &c.[3]

Your Ma*jes*ties most affection*a*tt Most Loyall and most Obedient subiect
D*o*n Carlos Enriques.

[f. 263v and f. 264r *blank*]

[f. 264v] [*Endorsed:*] 1669 Jully 14 Translac*io*n of Don Carlos Enriques second paper or propossistion in order to a voyage for the West Indyes.

6. Entry in the Journal of Edward Montagu, 1st Earl of Sandwich, 21 July 1669[4]

[p. 264] *This Spaniard comes hither discontented & poore & pretends to know every Thing of the Spanish management of the Indias, & Theier faults and weakenesse & would faine the K*in*g my m*aste*r to some animatinge a rebellion in the Indias wherin he pretends to helpe us to greate riches & possessions, Principally he boasts of his Interest in Chili & Peru. But to This he findinge noe eare but (my m*aste*r being fast to his faith passed to the Spaniard) he pretends to helpe us to discover Considerable trade & advantages upon the Coasts of America downe from Baldivia[5] (the last Spanish Towne in Chili) to the Streights of Magellan & Thence againe as farr as the Rio del Plata in which Tract noe treaty of State intervenes. To this Proposition the K*in*g my m*aste*r Hearkens & send [*sic*] a shippe of 26 Gunns w*i*th him under an able English Captain & a Pincke also, for discovery.

[1] TNA, CO1/33, No. 103c, f. 251v reads '3 patentes', meaning 'licence', 'commission' or 'patent', although here the sense might also seem to be orders.

[2] Variant Jamayca.

[3] TNA, CO1/33, 103c, f. 252r reads 'for the protection and comfort of your loyal and devoted subjects'.

[4] Mapperton, Journal of Edward Montague, 1st Earl of Sandwich, vol. 9, pp. 265–6.

[5] Valdivia; variants Baldava, Baldavia, Baldiava, Baldivia, Baldva, Balldava.

[p. 265] [*margin:* July 1669 21] * A Spaniard that sayes he is of the Henriques of the Family of the Conde de Alba de Lista gave mee the follewinge account:[1]

7. D*o*n Carlos Enriques Paper dellivere*red* In Jully the 25th 1669[2]

[f. 265r] I have presented to Your Royal Majesty the management of the venture which I have proposed in two different forms – the first at little cost, being a ship, and going and coming without intent to do more than discover the ways which can be followed thereafter; and also, by my concern, to raise the spirits of those who hope to pursue their aims; as well as being able to bring back sufficient goods to meet the expenses of the voyage and return with the necessary preparation.

The second is proposing to go with the intent to immediately settle a colony in order to carry out the business in more peace and security and without loss of time, though the the voyage is seemingly more costly, requiring risk and trust to good fortune, even though is is very safe, apart from the usual perils and risks of the sea and that I might lose my life.

As to the first design, it appears to me that its execution does not require much State resources but a vessel and cost and risk. It is only to explore, without interference, whatever comes in its way. If something should happen as is usual for a traveller – if attacked by someone one defends oneself which is not held to be a crime, but previously to be worthy of an honour — and the sea, like the land, has pathways on which it is not possible to put any door and which each one travels at their own risk, because, in all honesty, in the event of being encountered and recognized, there will be no party involved but a ship, and no discovery of any secret by which Royal Authority will suffer any harm.

As to the second I am not unaware that it is necessary, so as not to fail in one's duty, to look into and examine many factors as is customary for the heads of state, preparing for all the accidents which might occur in the present and strike in the future [f. 265v] in order thus to achieve a good decision about that which it is hoped to gain and to preserve it in times of peace and war against the calamities which strike all republics at times – And how it is necessary to consult wise and experienced ministers which I do not doubt exist in Your Majesty's kingdom, so great and so zealous of your Royal service. So I am silent. It is better better that it falls to [them] since my voice will lack terms to explain it.

But since every day new lights and difficulties about costs present themselves, which even though information and account may be had of them, [they are more like those of] explorers who consider from a distance; others [are like] the conjectures of Mathematicians who write about everything, as they do about the planets and stars, explaining their qualities and forms and influences without having seen either the shadow or the substance of any one of them. Although they only exist in their minds, in order to

[1] The Earl of Sandwich added a number of pages of notes under the heading 'Of the Government of the Spanish West Indias'. These might be his notes of information which Don Carlos gave him or his own information based on his own period of residence in Spain. In his letter dated 25 July 1669 Don Carlos claimed that he could give a 'very full acc*oun*tt of the man*n*er of govnm*ent* & all things elce in the Indyes'. He did deliver a 'Relac*i*on of the Kingdo[me] of Perue and other parts of the West Indyes' on 16 Aug. 1669. His conversation with the Earl of Sandwich may reflect that he was already working on it.

[2] Translation, TNA, CO1/33, No. 103d, ff. 265r–268v.

differentiate and distinguish themselves and add to the worth of their science, they[1] contradict the man of experience. Against whom they usually form and propose such subtle arguments in which, at times the knowledge and reasoning is so obscure that no response remains to be found, even though in fact he[2] is not lacking either science or experience to perform with complete perfection and more skill in everything than those who look at the atlases every day and read the pilot-books and practice pole star elevations and observations. And when they have to ride out a storm and find themselves blind and powerless, it is, at times, the work of a simple sailor, which conducts a ship between precipices and takes her out of them and brings her in a safe port without having ever studied any argument.

I say this not because it may be understood what will happen in the venture which I propose and when it might occur. I trust in divine aid that I will not be lacking intelligence, accompanied by the experience which I have acquired over many years in the military and naval arts which I have studied since my tender years [f. 266r] and, in many circumstances, given my opinion which has been followed in many committees of State as well as of War . Even if all is said to be extinguished so that nothing more than ash preserving some heat, it lives and survives with hopes of being brought back to life.

With regard to the second proposition Your Royal Majesty I can give information about how to build a fortification and protect ourselves within it on arrival; about exchange and dealings with the [*native*] inhabitants; about means of getting help in case of need, and the finances and growth which will pour into the Royal Treasury, and the other particulars which are required in similar circumstances. But I see myself, in this Your Majesty's court, like a body without a soul, in great despair, finding myself committed by my word and without power to turn to other protection and having to suffer such indecency and so little respect that I grumble indiscreetly in order to be permitted to speak. I am only left to complain to whoever I went to see and whoever ordered me to come. But I do not so much complain for the sake of complaint as by these sighs, to relieve the pain which afflicts me, to see myself idle and in a place where I need to accredit myself properly, lacking decency, without a sign of light in anything and without means to act; all are terrible afflictions for which I find no remedy.

That which I humbly beseech Your Majesty is that, that if you should be pleased to order consideration of the proposed business, note be taken that the most best time to go to cross the line is November so as to reach the strait in good time for the crops which the Indians in the Strait bring in in March and April, being *mays* [maize] which is the wheat of the Indies and *papas*, a fruit like the potatos of Malaga and other very substantial grains which keep all year. Which they bury in secret caves because of the wars which they usually have with one another in such times and it is very difficult [f. 266v] to find them [the caves] when they do not wish to reveal them and finding [the crops] still in place it is very easy to trade them for whichever of the things which they commonly trade for, which I have spoken of already.

Also if one arrives in Summer time, [it is] a time convenient for cutting and drying wood for the buildings and for firing lime, tiles and brick which may be needed and other such things. And as Summer ends in the Strait and the Kingdom of Chile, it begins in

[1] That is the inexperienced travellers and opinionated scientists.

[2] That is the experienced traveller.

Peru, even though there is no more difference between Winter and Summer than that for five months of the yea, from October to February inclusive, the Sun cannot be seen because of a mist which exudes a fine drizzle which creates a very agreeable and healthy coolness over four hundred leagues longitude and fourteen latitude. Elsewhere there are downpours, cold and hot spells at [their appointed] times as in Europe, even though with variations of temperature according to place – valleys, mountains and plains – the altitude of the sun having no effect on the climates. This comes from experience as I have crossed the Equinoctial line many times – sometimes to the west and other times to the East, by sea and by land, and in some in extreme cold and others heat and others in temperate [climate], all being so variable as to amaze the most subtle astrologer.

It has never been my intention to write about what is not the subject of the business but only to bring that precise understanding of what can be done for the service and increase of your Royal Crown so that it may be looked into and seen if it is advisable to pay attention to it. As for the rest I excuse myself that although I would be able speak very well from personal knowledge of the politics and spiritual and temporal government of those parts; of the finances and from whence they are drawn; of their minerals, fisheries, shipping, business, fruits and other things in general and particular; of their ports settlements and defences – their conquests and how to conquer them; of rebellious Cassiques, governors and individuals and the disposition and mood of the creoles. [f. 267r] All of which I leave to the necessary time when I may demonstrate my experience of each thing.

As to me,[1] Sacred, Royal Majesty, fortune has not left me with more strength to present to Your Majesty that which I have referred to, the which I am forced to leave to Divine Will and be patient, it being an assured business and for which nothing more has to be worked out for Your Majesty than particular increases. Even though on those also the interests of a vassal who begs that Your Majesty may be pleased not to permit his detention in this Court, acquitting him of the the obligation to spend more time in it in the case where no part of the proposition has been settled. And if, in the interest of Your Royal Service, I should be ordered to remain in it, may you be pleased to order that I be assisted with necessities free of charge.

May God grant Your Majesty the many and happy years which I desire and have need of.

Your most humble , obedient and loyal vassal kisses the royal feet of Your Majesty,

Don Carlos Enriques

[f. 268v] D*on* Carlos Enriques Paper delliver*ered* In Jully the 25th 1669.[2]

Setting forth viz.

[1] The sentence begains with '*Yo*' meaning 'I', but the disconnect with the remainder of the sentence suggests that this should be translated in the self-referential form I have used here.

[2] In this case the English summary of Don Carlos's letter is written on the outer wrapper of the packet together with the endorsement of when it was received.

That hee hath in his late propossi*cio*ns to *you*r Ma*jest*ie offer'd two things, the one easy & without haszard, as his going the intended voyage w*i*th one vessell to discover the Coasts & the passage of the Straight of Magalanes, the other more chargeable and requiring greater circumspection as the carying more shipping & going w*i*th intenc*i*on to settle neer the Straight a Colony of Eng*lis*h without delay.

That the time of the yeare to passe the Line is [*word or words obliterated*] soe neer that it will bee necessary to goe from hence in Nove*m*bre [that] soe they may comme to the straights in March or Ap*r*ill about which time the Indians use to gather thier harvest, being mayes or Indian wheat and *papas* which is a kinde a *patata*, soe the subsistance may bee easily had, but afterwards very dificult to bee come at by strangers because the natives hurd it up in caves [*edge of page*]

That hee can when requissitt give a very full acc*oun*tt of the man*n*er of govnm*en*t & all things elce in the Indyes &ca[1]

That hee is not in Condition at pr*e*sent to subsist here & therfore prayes a dispatch in [*sai*d], a dismisse, or some reliefe which hee shall atende –

8. Narbrough's copy of his orders to proceed to The Downs,[2] 1 August 1669[3]

By Command of his R*oyal* Highness M. Wren

James Duke of Yorke & Albany, Earle of Ulster, Lord High Admirall of England & Ireland, Constable of Dovier Castle, Lord warden of the Chinque [Cinque Ports] and Govennour of Portsmouth &c.

You are with the first oppertunity of wind and weather: after you have received in your provissions, and that the Shipp: under your Command is ready to saile to Carry her into the Downes where you are to stay untill you receive forther order. Given under my hand at whitehall: the first day of August 1669.

James

To Captain Narbrough Commander of his Maj*esty*'s Shipp Sweepstakes

By Command of his R*oyal* Highness

M. Wren

received this the 2 day of august,1669, at 3 oclock in the afternoon. London.

[1] See above, pp. 21–4.
[2] The Downs; variants Dowenes, Downes, Downse, Dowens, las Duenas.
[3] BL, Add MS 88980A, 27th unnumbered page reading from the back of the 'Booke' forwards.

9. Narbrough's copy of the letter requiring his attendance in London, 18 August 1669[1]

Captaine Narbrough

There havinge somethinge lately fallen out[2] which will have soe much influence upon your instructions that it will be requissite you should be here present, To that purpose his R.H. has Commanded Mee to dissier you to make what hast you Can up to London and that you take Care for leaveinge the ship under your Command Safe in the hands of your Lieutenant.

I am Your faithfull servant

St James 18th of Aug*us*t 1669 M. Wren

This is a coppy of a letter received By mee in the Downes The 19 of Au*gus*t 69.

10. Don Carlos Enriques to an unnamed recipient, 19 August 1669[3]

[f. 51r] Being determined not to come back to bother Your Excellency any more with my writings, nevertheless courtesy and due attention obliges me to break that said intention – a document usually allows for greater explanation and finds an opportunity to be read, which the owner [writer] does not, whose presence tends to be seen as an annoyance when it is thought that he goes to make a request. Even if it may be for only one single instant of attention, it is enough and experience has taught me that I must not make a solicitation again, and that the promises and word of lords most times turn into feathers which the wind carries away. For which reason, and having discovered many persons to be absent from this court that I came from Madrid to find, to the which I many times did favours and lent money in friendship moved by the affection which I have always had for their nation and in hopes to be able to see them again in these parts. But my shortlived luck[4] has deprived me of this pleasure forcing me to turn to His Majesty, from whom, since he is engaged in the proposed business, I have ventured to beg assistance for means to present myself decently until it should be time to leave. What is more, I have learned, all of which I do not doubt, that this petition, together with another joined with it in which I asked for the favours and honours that were to be given to me in the case that I might suddenly go with a direct order to make a settlement, has reduced support for it.[5]

[1] BL, Add MS 88980A, 26th unnumbered page reading from the back of the 'Booke' forwards.

[2] Don Carlos had delivered a lengthy and rambling compendium, written in Spanish, on aspects of the administration of the Spanish Empire which was endorsed by a secretary as a 'Relac*i*on of the Kingdo[me] of Perue and other parts of the West Indyes delliuered by Don Carlos Enriques the 16. Of August 1669'. For a summary of the latter see above, pp. 21–4. The receipt of it may have prompted the summoning of Narbrough to London.

[3] Translation, TNA, SP94/55, ff. 50–51.There is no indication as to whom this letter is addressed.

[4] TNA, SP94/55, f. 50r reads '*corta suerte*'.

[5] The word in the Spanish original is *dessaconar*, which most likely should be read as *desazonar* which means to make tasteless. Presumably there had been criticism of the demands relating to his position, authority and rank which Don Carlos had made in his second proposition, see above, pp. 98–111.

Further since the proposals of men move forward only by the permission or will of the Divine Spirit, as frequently happens, while I have no ulterior motive I cannot prevent the suspicions which may come from those who are hostile in contrast to my own straightforwardness, which your Excellency may believe is why I have reached this extremity =

Furthermore Your Excellency may trust that I did not come to the court because of necessity, or to reside or subsist at royal expense and that had I known, before presenting my credentials, of the absence of the said lords I would have taken another more certain way and in this same court I would not lack credit at present if my modesty did not deter me. And although even if in many days I might be able to be where I might have more peace and consolation I could not absent myself without affording [you] all the due civility and attention of my customary [good] faith and word, for the preservation of my own honour and so as not to thought to be dealing falsely not in the way of truth.

And because I judge that my proposals must not be of any convenience to His Majesty my stay and delay in this court does not seem to be of any use either, for which reason I must depart from it, by Your Excellency's leave, who I beg will be pleased to pardon my faults and in whose presence I hope to appear some day in another light, not to be so slighted as up to now, because I will have warned of the said upheavals even if the crown of the American Empire might be allowed to drop, which might be of very faint consolation to me in comparison to the embarassment of being slighted, because although I may appear poor and proud I am able to say that by the mercy of God nobody has seen me beg for alms. And if present clothes do not make a man neither does a title make a nobleman, time which changes everything will change it also in its course. ... From the inn[1] today Monday 19 of August 1669.

I was determined to go to Jamayca from whence I might be able to serve the interests of this crown as I might do by the straights – but have not wished to settle on anything before going first to furbish what is needed for whatever voyage I may decide; because in Jamayca and Barbada there are many [men] who were under my command in Cartaxena and rather than offending them it would do them much good.

Don Carlos Enriquez [*Endorsed:*] August 1669: D*on* Carlos Henriques[2]

11. Narbrough's copies of the order to reduce the complement of the *Sweepstakes*, 24 August 1669, and the certification that he had not been able to undertake it until after 2 September 1669.[3]

James Duke of Yorke & Albany, Earle of Ulster, Lord High Adm*ira*ll of England & Ireland, Constable of Doviour [Dover] Castle, Lord Warrden of the Chinque [Cinque] Ports & Govennour of Portsmouth &c.

[1] TNA, SP94/55, ff. 51r reads '*posadas*', the plural of the the word for 'inn'. It could also be read as 'lodgings'.

[2] Pencilled date by curator 9/19 August.

[3] BL, Add MS 88980A, 26th unnumbered page reading from the back of the 'Booke' forwards.

Where as I have thought fitt that the Complement of his Maj*esty's* Shipp under your Command be lessened, These are to will and requier you forthwith to discharge all such men as you have in the said Shipp above the Number of Eighty, which is the Complement appointed for her in here present vojage to the west indis: for which this shall be your warrant.

Given under My hand at S[t] James this 24 of Aug*us*t 1669.

James

To Capt*ain* Narbrough Captaine of his Maj*esty's* Shipp Sweepstakes.

A treue coppy of a letter to me By Command of His R*oyal* Highness

M. Wren

Recevied this letter at S[t] James the 26 of Aug*us*t 1669.

I doe Certifie that Captaine Narbrough staidd in London by Express order till September the second 1669 to attend Sum Command which were given him By his R*oyal* Highness and for that reason Could not goe downe to his Shipp to Discharge his Men.

M. Wren

A true Copy of Mr wrens Certificate one [on] the Back of the order.

12. Narbrough's copy of a letter requiring his attendance on Lord Arlington, 25 August 1669[1]

Capt*ai*n Narbrough

There is some Bussiness to be Tranceaccted this afternoon which will require your attendance: I doe theirfore dissier that you will be at my Lord Arlingtons Lodginge at Whitehall between three and fower aclocke: I am your faithfull servant

S[t] James 25 of Aug*us*t 1669. M Wren

a copy of a letter

[1] BL, Add MS 88980A, 28th unnumbered page reading from the back of the 'Booke' forwards, Mathew Wren to John Narbrough, St James's Palace, 25 Aug. 1669.

13. Don Carlos Enriques's Memorandum of absolutely necessary things beyond what is customary[1]

	12:	shotguns
	12:	spears for hunting game[2]
X[3]	3:	quintals[4] of fine gunpowder
	2:	fishing nets with cork floats and lead sinkers
	100:	lines and 100 hooks of the 4 kinds
	4:	harpoons with five spikes
	4:	harpoons
X	12:	quarrymens' picks
	12:	wooden mallets
X	12:	crowbars
X	12:	spits
	12:	spades shod [with iron]
X	300:	metal hoops for barrels
	20:	quintals of sheet lead
	100:	sheets of tin
	24:	axes
	100:	[Candles] of ordinary wax for lanterns[5]
	20:	lbs of cotton thread =
	5:	quintals of tallow candles
	5:	quintals of musket cord
	[1C][6]	shotgun flints

All that is necessary, as I have said, for the cheer and cure of the sick –

250 pounds sterling, [or] more, in the goods which I have stated for the strait.

200 pounds in merchandise for acquiring goods in Madera:[7] or Canarias and Cabo Verde for the refreshment of the company and for gifts to those of the strait and south sea.

Item 50 pounds in money of the Castile mint in 4 and 8 real coins.[8]

Item those things necessary for the said voyage which I have beseeched Your Majesty to provide me with ==

[1] Translation, TNA, CO 1/33, No. 103f, ff. 271r–272v. The title here is taken from the English endorsement on the document. No contemporary translation has been found.

[2] TNA. CO 1/33, No. 103f, f. 271r, reads '*lansas de monte*'. '*Monte*' means 'scrub' or 'woodland'. '*Batir el monte*' means 'beating for game'.

[3] The X indicates a marginal mark against an item. The marks may indicate that not all the items requested were actually supplied.

[4] See above, p. 101, n. 4.

[5] TNA, CO 1/33, No. 103f, f. 271r, reads '*hachiotes de sera ordinaria Para faroles*'. Presumably '*hachiote*' refers to some form of candle.

[6] 100.

[7] Madeira; variants Madera, Maderas, Maderia, Medera, Mederea, Mederia. Medreia.

[8] Spanish silver coins.

All at very little cost and very necessary and important for the said voyage, the which I trust in God will be very happy and whose beginnings will afterwards follow the ends which are hoped for to the honour and glory of Your Majesty and the common good of those concerned.

[ff. 271v–272r *blank*]

[f. 272v] [*Endorsed:*]

Aug*u*ste 25. 1669.

D*o*n Carlos Enriques note of severall neccessaryes for the voyage to the west Indyes

D*o*n. Carlos Enriques.

14. Narbrough's copy of the order to reduce the present complement of the *Sweepstakes*, 26 August 1669[1]

Capt*ain* Narbrough

These are to accquainte you that, By an order from his R. Highness Come to our hand this day, the Complement of men for the *Sweepstakes* in her present voiage to the west Indis is to be reduced to Eighty: wee doe therefore here by direct that upon receipt hereof you doe accordingly reduce the said Shipps Company now under your Command unto the aforesaid Number of Eighty by dischargeinge all above that Number: Giving unto Each person thuse discharged a printed tickett for the time he hath servied. To which purpose wee herewith send you some printed Blankes & remain,

Navy Office   your very loving friends

26 Aug[st] 69

Jo Menns, T. Middleton, Jere Smith.[2]

A true Coppy of a letter to mee with the order which I received 27 Aug*us*t 69 at London.

The number I reduced to 80 the 4 of S*eptem*ber 69 in the Downes

[1] BL, Add MS 88980A, 29th unnumbered page reading from the back of the 'Booke' forwards, Mathew Wren to John Narbrough, St James's Palace, 25 Aug. 1669.

[2] All three signatories were officials of the Navy Board. Sir John Mennes, held the office of Controller 28 Nov. 1661–18 Feb. 1671; Thomas Middleton (Medellton, Meddleton, Medleton, Midleton), that of Surveyor 25 Nov.1667–21 June 1672; Sir Jeremy Smith, that of Controller of Victualling Accounts, 17 June 1669–3 Nov. 1675; see Collinge, *Navy Board Officials*, pp. 122, 132, 139.

15. Narbrough's copy of a letter requiring his attendance on Lord Arlington, 28 August 1669[1]

To Captaine *Joh*n Narbrough Command*er* of his Maj*estys* Shipp the *Sweepstakes* in the Downes,

These.

Capt*ain* Narbrough

My Mast*er* Commanded mee to write to you to dessier you to be at My Lord Arlingtons Lodginge at whithall prossisely by five oclock this afternoon.

I am your Most affectionate Servant Tho*mas* Billope[2]

Saturday morning. 28 of Aug*ust* *1*669.

16. Narbrough's instructions for the voyage of the *Sweepstakes*, issued 29 August 1669[3]

Instructions for Capt*ain* John Narbrough

You are with his Maj*es*tis Shipp *Sweepstakes* under your Command with the first opportunity of wind & and weather, to saile to the Coast of Amarica, to the Southward of Rio de Plata.

In your way you are to touch at St Iago: one of the Cap*e* Isles of Cabo Verde where you are to fill all your Emty [*sic*] Caske with fresh watter & furnish your selfe with fresh provissions. But for doeinge this you are to stay at Porto Pray[4] and not goe to the Towne Because of the great Danger of leaveinge their a Cable & an Anchor Behind you.

You are not to medle with the Coast of America nor Send on Shore, unles in the Case of great nessety, till you are got to the Southward of Rio de Plata and you are not to doe any Injurie to such Spaniards as you shall happon to meett nor meddle with any Place where they are Planted.

The Designe of this Voiage one [*sic*] which you are sent beinge to make a discovery Boath of the Seas and Coasts in that parte of the world and if it be possible to lay the foundation of a Tread [trade] their in order thereunto: you are from the southward of Rio de la Plata to pass all alonge the Coast of America: untill you Come to the Straights of Magellan.

[1] BL, Add MS 88980A, 28th unnumbered page reading from the back of the 'Booke' forwards.

[2] Thomas Billop, was Mathew Wren's clerk, Latham and Mathews, *Pepys' Diary*, X, p. 30.

[3] BL, Add MS 88980A, 36th, 37th and 39th unnumbered pages reading from the back of the 'Booke' forwards. The 38th page is blank.

[4] Praia, capital of Cabo Verde; variants Porto, Puerto Praim, Pram, Pray, Praya, Praye,Praym, Priam.

Through which you are to Pass wind and weather permiting into the South Seas, and saile alonge the Coast northwardly till you Come as high as Baldivia, which Lies about fowerty degres of Southern Lattitud: and from thence you are to indeavior to return againe into the North sea & make the Best of your way for the Dowens. But you are not so strictly to understand this Clause of your Instruction as to think your selfe indispensably obliged by it to goe as fare as Baldivia for in Case you happen Before upon any Place where the Convenence of the Porte the aboundance of Commoditys or the dispossitions of the People make you judge it is a place proper to establis a Traffique in & that the discovery of it does in a good degre ansewer the Intent of your Beinge sent out you may without Proseedinge any farther return to give an account of what you have found.

You are to Take observations with as much accouracy as you Can of all head lands Islands Bayes havens Roads and mouthes of Riveers where you come Boath in the North and South Sea and to Cause Draughts or designes to be made of them. Also you are to take exact Notice of all Currants and trade winds you meet with.

You are in all places to observe the Nature of the Soyle what fruts Cattle or mineralls it Produceth and what fish the Sea and rivers aBount with.

You are allso to remarquie the temper and inclination of the inhabitancets [*sic*] and where you can gaine any Correspondency with them you are to make them sensible of the great Power and wealth of the Prince and Nation to whom you belonge and that you are one [on] porposs to set one [on] fote a trade and make frendshipp with them. But above all you are to take Care that your men doe not By any injuris or rude beheaviour to them Create an Avertion in them to the English Nation but that one [on] the other side they endeviour to gaine their love By kind & Cevill Eusage. For your easeier gaineinge a Correspondencce with the Natives their will be put on Board you an Asortement of goods proper as nere as Can be Conjectured for those People. To the Prudent disspossal of which you are To looke. For though this vojage, Beinge intended only for Discovery noe Proffit is lokt for from them yett from hence the observation is to be made what Commoditis those Countries Can afoard and what they Can take from us.

The Proposition of this vojage haveing Ben made By to his Ma*jes*tie By Don Carlos Enrigus who Pretends to have lived longe and to have Born Command in those Parts he will be sent with you upon the Shipp and you are to treat him with all Possible Respecte and Cevellity as a Person of quallity you are allso to be advised By him in Sendinge aShore ore Endeaviouringe a Corrispondencie with the Natives Especially if you find he hase Really any former accquainttance with the Place or People you are allso to Permitt him to goe ashore if he dissier it. But for the Seafety of your Shipp and men and the main end of your vojage you are not to Relie upon him But upon your own Prudence and Vigilence.

The *Batcheller* of London Humphery Fleminge Master beinge hiered to attend you in this vojage you are from time to time to give her such orders as you shall Thinke neassecary and to send her upon discoveris into Baies & Rivers & such places wher [*sic*] it is not reasonable to ventur the Kings Shipp and if you see Reason for it you are to Take the men out of that Vessel & give her some of your owne in Stead of them.

You are to Keep an Exacte Journall of your Proseedings and a trew Coppey where of you are to deliver to My Secretary at your Return into England. Given under My hand at S[t] James this 29th August 1669.

James

Vera Copia: recidit 30 instant.

By Command of his *Royal* Highness M Wren

17. Note and copies of Narbrough's correspondence with officials of the Navy Board, 6–9 September, 1669[1]

(i) *Septem*ber 7 1669 Beinge Thursday I wrot up to Collonell Meddleton, Servaier [Surveyor] of the Nayvie, to Send mee downe a haurser for Boy [buoy] roaps, for I have but three in all. I am now with the *Sweepstakes* in the downes: and Sum tared lines. He recevied my letter.

(ii) Capt*ain* Narbrough

In answer to yours of the 6, wee shall exspecte a muster booke from you, as you theirin prommise it beinge very convenient that it should be with us before the men discharged bringe their Ticketts to be examined. We have ordered you another monthes provissions for your spendinge in the Chanell that soe it may be the latter one you begin to eate of that as was laid in for your voiage, and soe it may last the longer. The pinke, that is to Come to you, is now at Gravesend and therefore a haurser Cannot be sent you for buoy rops as you dessire but in Cause nessecity require it you must Cut one of your own store hawzers: wherein wee dout not but you will be Cearefull to see all good huzbandre used. Wee wish you a Good vojage and remaine,

Your very lovinge friends,

Bronker,[2] Jo. Mennes, Middleton, Jer Smith.

Na*v*y office

9 September. 69

veary Copia. I received 11 *Septem*ber. Downes.

[1] BL, Add MS 88980A, 28th unnumbered page reading from the back of the 'Booke' forwards.

[2] William Brouncker, 2nd Viscount Broncker of Lyon (1620–84). He had been the first president of the Royal Society (1663–7) and was appointed an Extra Commissioner 7 Dec. 1664–16 Jan. 1667 and Controller of Treasurer's Accounts 16 Jan. 1667–28 Feb. 1680. See, Collinge, *Navy Board*, pp. 88–9; McIntyre, 'Brouncker, William', *ODNB*.

18. Narbrough's copy of a letter directing him to await the provision of some necessities requested by Don Carlos[1]

Capt*ain* Narbrough

I have received your last letter and at the same time Cam one from Don Carloss to his R*oyal* H*ighness* with a dissier theirin of sume ot*her* things, which he Sayes will be very Nessesary towards the Good Sucksess of this Buissness. His R*oya*L H*ighness* has communicated it to sum of the Lords whoe have ben Concerned in this affaiers whoe have All Concluded that you shall stay untill those things Cane be sent Downe on Board to which porpose you will receive his R H orders for goeinge to Portsmouth & stayeinge their untill forther directions be Given you about which such dispatch shall be made that you shall lose noe time for prosedinge on your vojage. I am your faithful servant

Whitehall[2] M Wren

21 September 1669

very Copy Rec*eive*d 23

19. Narbrough's copy of his orders to proceed to Portsmouth, 21 September 1669[3]

James Duke of Yorke & Allbany, Earle of Ulster, Lord Hige [*sic*] admirall of England & Ireland, Consta*ble* of Doviour Castle, Lord Warden of the Chinque Ports~~mouth~~ and Govenour of Portsmouth &c.

You are with the first opportunity of wind and weather to saile to Portsmouth where [you] are to stay till you receive forthor orders. Given under my hand at whitehall the 21 of September 1669.

James

To Capt*ain* Narbrough Commander of his Maj*esty*'s Shipp *Sweepstakes*

By Command of his R*oyal* H*ighness*

M Wren. a trew coppy 23[4]

[1] BL, Add MS 88980A, 31st unnumbered page reading from the back of the 'Booke' forwards.
[2] The palace of Whitehall, London; variants White Hall, Whithall.
[3] BL, Add MS 88980A, 31st unnumbered page reading from the back of the 'Booke' forwards.
[4] Made on 23 Sept. 1669.

20. Narbrough's copy of a letter directing him to depart as soon as the provisions for Don Carlos are received[1]

Capt*ain* Narbrough

By my last one [on] Tusday you received his R*oyal* H*ighness* orders for Sailinge to Portsmouth, which was occationed by a letter from Don Carlos to his R*oyal* H*ighness* disieringe a further Supply of sum provissions which were Neassecary for the vojage, for which there is order given, and the Servey*or* has taken Care that they be sent to you with all speed, boath to the Downes & to Portsmouth soe that ife the wind hangs out of the way that you Cannot saile out of the Downes they will be with you there in 24 howers: as sone as you have received the Provissions I desier you will make all possible hast of your vojage which I wish may be very Prosperus.

I am Your faithfull servant M Wren

Whithall 23 September 1669

In Case you received the Provissions & stores from the Sorvyor [surveyor] before you goe out of the Downes you are not then to thinke your selfe obledged for all your order to that purpose to goe to portsmouth.

M. Wren

a trew copy

21. Narbrough's copy of Thomas Middleton's letter prior to his departure, 23 September 1669[2]

Capt*ain* Narbrough

I have sent you by the *Bzan*[3] the Provisions & Stores that were demanded by Don Carlos, to whome pray Present My kind respects & likewise to my Couzen Midleton & Soloman.[4] I have received your 2 letters and thanke you for them. I pray take Care to Charge your Boatswain & Carpenter with all stores sent them downe since their departure from Deptford & be sure you rescerve one of your Iron Buts to fill with Gould for a good vojage to you. your assured lovinge friend

23 September 1669 Thos Middleton

a true Copy Rec*eived* 24 day.

[1] BL, Add MS 88980A, 30th unnumbered page reading from the back of the 'Booke' forwards.

[2] BL, Add MS 88980A, 30th unnumbered page reading from the back of the 'Booke' forwards.

[3] The pink named *Bazan*.

[4] It is not clear who Couzen Midleton was, although presumably related to the writer. There is no Middleton on the extant muster list. Solomon was presumably Solomon Franco, see above, pp. 34–5.

22. Narbrough's copy of his letter and Instructions to Captain Fleming, 26 September 1669[1]

Capt*ain* Fleminge

Sir, I have sent you sailmornige[2] instructions By My Leut*ant* Pecket which I dessier you will indeviour to keepe me Company all this vojage for I shall deo [do] it to you: & if this wind stands or any other as will carry us out of the Cannell [Channel], I will not touch any where in England: & if a ccontrary [*sic*] wind forses mee back & I be to the westward falmouth is the Porte: if I cannot reach falmouth then Plymouth: if not Plymouth then the Ile of White. Exspectinge the wind hange at west or their abouts & a liklelyhood of faier weather wee may stop at tore bay [Torbay]: which if we should miss of each other By badness of weather in England I pray at that Porte you come to write up emeadiatly that we may know of each other. If I gett Cleare of England my Next Porte is at Mederia at Fonchall,[3] to water & refresh But I shall not stay ther more than one Day: for our Randivos [rendezvous] are at S[t] Iago, one of the Cap Do Verde Iles at Port Praim where wee must sertainely stay and speeke with each other God willinge for their wee shall have forther Instructions. I pray doe not lose any time in Gittinge theather if wee be seaparrated. So Good [God] prosper us Boath.

I am, from on Board the *Sweepstakes*,

Sir, your very houmble Servant

September 26 day 1669 John Narbrough

This is a trew Coppy to Capt*ain* fleminge.

Saileinge Instructions for Captaine Humphry Fleminge Commander of the *Batcheler* Pinke, for the Better Keepinge Company with his Ma*jes*ties Ship the *Sweepstakes* at Sea &c.[4]

1. As sone as I lose [loose][5] my fore Top Saile and fire a Gun Being at an Anchor you are to make Ready and way and follow mee. And for the Better knowing mee in the Night Notice is to be taken that I have one Light on my Poope and in the Case of fowle weather and darke nights two: and you are to carry one.

[1] BL, Add MS 88980A, 32nd unnumbered page reading from the back of the 'Booke' forwards.

[2] It is not clear what this word should be. Possibly Narbrough started to write 'sailing instructions' and changed his mind to 'this morning', and failed to correct his text. Possibly it could have been meant to be understood as 'sailing/mooring'.

[3] Funchal, Madeira; variants Fanshaall, Fantiall, Fonchall, Fonchiyall, Foneiall, Fonliall.

[4] BL, Add MS 88980A, 40th· 42nd ,43rd, and 45th unnumbered pages reading from the back of the 'Booke' forwards. Page 44 is blank.

[5] Narbrough signalled by loosening or letting fly the sail so that it would flap in the wind.

2. If I waighe in the night I wile fire one Gun: and Change a Light one [on] the Maine topmaste Shrouds: which is to Be ansewered By you with a Light on your Miz*ze*n Shrouds and you are not to take it in tile[1] I take in mine.

3. In Case of Springeinge a Laecke [Leak] By day or any disaster under Saile where By Eighter [either] Shipp is disabled of keepeinge Company: then Such a Shipp as Shall have any disaster is to Make a Signe their of By fireinge two Guns distinctly one after the other and hale up his low Sailes and make a waft with his Ensign where it May Be Seene Best and if it Be in the Night Notice is to be Given by fireinge of Gunns and hangeinge out Lights in the Shrouds of Equal height where they may be Best sene.

4. If it ever Blow that wee Shorten Saile in the Night: Then I wil Put one Light over the other Light on the Pope and Eighthere Shipp is to Ansewer with one other Light Be Sids that they formerly Carried it Beinge understood in fowle weather & in darke Nights Eighther Shipp is to Carry a Light.

5. If I alter my Course in the Night I will fier one Gun without alterration of Lights.

6. In Case I Tacke in the Night I will show Two Lights one one [on] the fore Shrowds and another one the Mizon Shrouds halfe Shroude up which you are to Ansewer with one Light one [on] your fore shrouds: and to keepe it out till I take in mine and not till Then.

7. In Case of Separration by weather in the Night: wee meete the one with the other he that first discerns shall Put abroade two Lights one over the other in the Mane Shrouds and the other shall ansewer in the same place. The first signe beinge made and not Ansewered Accordingely it is to be understood that they are note of our fleete.

8. I[n] Case of Separration we Should meet again in the day at a distance the Signe shal be to Know to each other By haileing up our maine Sails and Loweringe our Maine Top Saile and layinge oure fore Saile a Backe Stayes: which is to be Ansewered accordingely and makeing a waft with your Ensigne at the Stafe which is to be Answered again by the same Signall.

9. I[n] Case you have dissire to Speake with mee you shall Spread your Ensigne from the head of your Maine Topmast downe the Shroud: Loweringe your Maine Top Saile that it may be the Better discovered: and fier a gune.

10. In Case I would speake with you I will put out a pendant [pennant] at my fore Top mast head at the sight of that Signall you are to Speake with me. If in Case eighther of us see land in the Night or any danger he that first see it is to fire a gun and show as many lights as he can: and tack or beare away from it.

11. If By Reason of fowele weather in the Night it Be thought meete to hand our heade

[1] 'Til' for 'until'.

Sailes and lye a Try[1] then wee shall show fower Lights of Eaquall height and you are to ansewer with the Like: and not to take them in till we take in ours.

12. In Case of thicke and foggy weather Great Care is to be takin to Keepe Company the one with the other: which you are to Keepe as nere mee as you Can Conveniently and if I Continy Saileinge: I will fire muskequets and Sound Trumpets and make what noies I can: which you are to ansewer with the Like: that we may here each other. But if it be so thicke that it is impossible to keepe Company then upon fireing three Gunns from mee you are to Lye by.

13. In Case wee should thinke fit to lye shorte at any time or a hull in Regrade of fowle weather then wee Shall Show three Lights the one over the other in the maine Shrouds or were that they may Best be seene or if you should have occation to Try or hull when I Bere away you are to fire a peece of ordinance and show the same number off Lights after the manner herein Exspresed. When wee shal see Cause in the night to make Saile after Blowinge weather: wee shall Shoote of two Peece of ordinance and Put out three Lights one over the other as was the Signe when we Shorten Saile: which upon Ansewer from you wee shal take in ouers [ours].

14. In Case of anchor in the Night I will fire one Gun and Show two Lights one upon the Poope and one on the fore Castle which you are to ansewer with the same.

15. In Case wee be seperrated And meet in the night Soe as to haile each other: he that haileth first Shall Say what Shipp is that he that is hailed Shall say Kinge Charles: He that first hailed Shall Say Prosper So by this we may know each other the Better and to Prevent the Danger of Sally men of war and &c.

Given on Board his Maj*es*ty Shipp the *Sweepstakes* this 26 day of September 1669.

John Narbrough

To Captaine Hump*hry* Fleminge, Command*er* of the *Batcheler* Pinke, These

23. Entry in the Journal of Edward Montague, 1st Earl of Sandwich, 19 October 1669[2]

[*margin:* October 1669 19] About a fortnight agoe sailed out of the Downes bound for the Streights of Magellan a shipp of 40 Gunns & a Pincke, sent Thither by the Kinge onely upon discove*r*ye of new Ports & com*m*erce in Those parts; The motive wherunto was the report of a Spaniard that Pretended the Knowledge of that Coast & interest amongst the Spaniards & Indians too that live in and neere chili. Valdivia is the last place to the Southward wher[e]in the Spaniards have any Guarrison in the South Sea & the Rio de Plata in the Ocean, wherefore to keepe faire w*i*th the Spaniard the shippe is ordered not to goe further towards the North Then Those 2 places.

[1] See below, p. 148, n. 7.

[2] Mapperton, Journal of Edward Montague, 1st Earl of Sandwich, vol. 10, p. 262.

PART II

Narbrough's Journal

a:

[1] **1669. A Jornall Be Gan with his M*a*jest*ie*s Shipp the *Sweepstakes* the 15: Day of may 1669. The Shipp at deptford[1] which Beinge then ordered to fitt.[2] And Keept By Captaine John Narbrough: then Commander of her one [on] her Vojage through the Straits of Magallan: into the South Sea to Baldavia[3] and from thence Back againe unto England to Deptford[4]**

Sweepstakes Frigatt: . ~ // Re[5]

15 MAY:

Beinge Satterday in the yeare 1669: I received my Commission for to Command the *Sweepstakes* at S[t] Jameis:[6] the Shipp at Deptford.

16

Beinge Sunday: I was at my Loodginge at London.

17

Beinge munday I went aBoard her then she began to fit by the Carpenters of the dockeyarde at Deptford.

18 June.

Beinge Friday in the yeare 1669: I Entered men aBoard the *Sweepstakes* at deptford[7]

[1] Deptford dockyard (51°29′N, 0°01′W), was one of the naval bases where the smaller naval ships were laid up 'in ordinary', in reserve with minimal crews.

[2] Get ready for sea.

[3] Valdivia in Chile (39°50′S, 73°13′W). Described, in 1662, as 'the most noted Town of all these parts [the country of the *Auracans* in Chile] situate in the Valley of *Guadallanguen*, in the Latitude of 40 degrees, or thereabouts; adorned with a safe and capacious *Haven*, and neighboured by *Mines* of Gold of such infinite riches, that *Baldivia* [Pedro Gutiérrez de Valdivia, c. 1500–53] (by whom built for defence of those mines) received thence daily by the labour of each single work-man, 25000 Crowns a man and sometimes more. Sacked by the *Salvages*, An. 1599, since repaired by the *Spaniards*.' Heylyn, *Cosmographie*, p. 1074.

[4] The words 'and from thence Back againe unto England to Deptford' added in a different style probably at a later date.

[5] The words and symbols following the name of the ship are in red ink.

[6] St James's Palace was built by Henry VIII, on the site of the former leper hospital dedicated to Saint James the Less, between 1531 and 1536. It was used by Cromwell as a barracks and restored by Charles II, whose main residence was the Palace of Whitehall. This was largely destroyed by fire in 1698, when Saint James's Palace became the principal residence of the monarch.

[7] 'Entered men' means started to embark the crew and entered them on the ship's muster list.

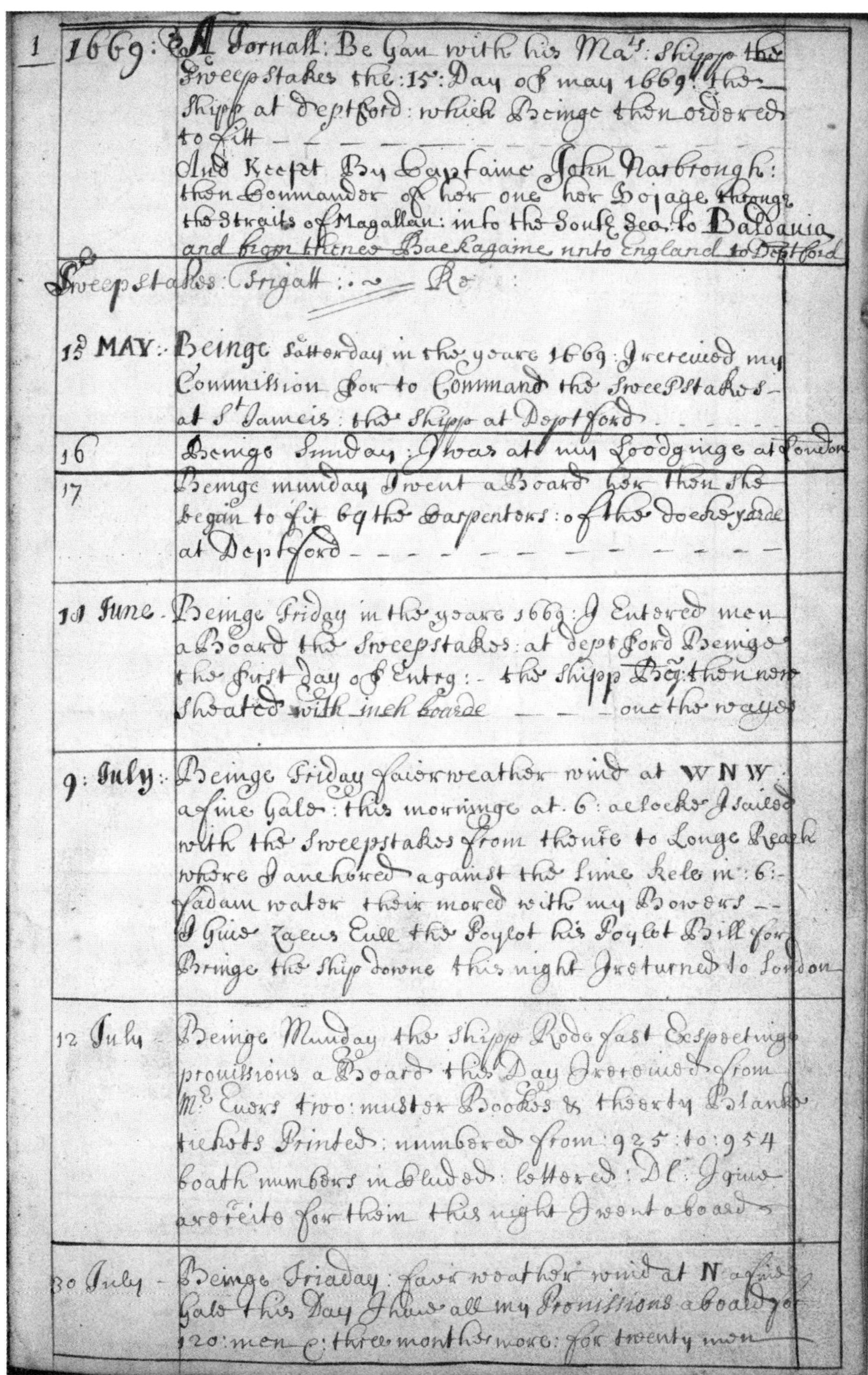

1 1669: A Jornall: Be Gan with his Maᵗˢ: Shipp the Sweepstakes the: 15: Day of may 1669: the Shipp at deptford: which Beinge then ordered to fitt — — —
And Keept By Captaine John Narbrough: then Commander of her one her Voiage through the Straits of Magallan: into the South Sea: to Baldavia and from thence Backagaine unto England to Deptford

Sweepstakes: Frigatt: Ro:

15 MAY: Beinge Satterday in the yeare 1669: I receiued my Commission for to Command the SweePstakes at St Jameis: the Shipp at Deptford — — —

16 Beinge Sunday: I was att my Loodginge at London

17 Beinge munday I went aBoard her then she began to fit by the Carpenters: of the dockeyarde at Deptford — — — — — — —

11 June. Beinge Friday in the yeare 1669: I Entered men aBoard the Sweepstakes: at deptford Beinge the first day of Entry: the Shipp Beinge then new Sheated with inch boarde — — one the ways

9: July: Beinge Friday fair weather wind at WNW. a fine Gale: this morninge at 6: aclocke I sailed with the Sweepstakes from thence to Longe Reach where I anchored against the Lime kele in: 6: fadam water their moored with my Bowers — I Give Zacus Cull the Poylot his Poylot Bill for Bringe the Ship downe this night I returned to London

12 July Beinge Munday the Shipp Rode fast Expectinge provisions aBoard this Day I receiued from Mr Evers two: muster Books & thierty Blank tickets Printed: numbered from: 925: to: 954 boath numbers included: lettered: Dl: I give a receite for them this night I went aboard

30 July Beinge Friday: fair weather wind at N a fine Gale this Day I have all my Provisions aboard for 120: men: three months more: for twenty men

Figure 4. The first page of Narbrough's *Sweepstakes* Journal (BL, Add MS 88980A). Courtesy of the Trustees of the British Library.

Beinge the first day of Entry: the Shipp B*einge* then new sheated with inch boarde[1] – one [on] the wayes.[2]

9 July:
Beinge Friday faier weather wind WNW a fine Gale:[3] This morninge at 6 aclocke I sailed with the *Sweepstakes* from thence to Longe Reach[4] where I anchored against the Lime Kele [kiln] in 6: fadam water their mored with my Bowers.[5] I Give Zacus Eull the Poylot his Poylot Bill for Bringe the Ship downe[6] this night I returned to London.

12 July
Beinge Munday the Shipp Rode fast[7] Exspectinge provissions a Board. This day I received from Mr Evers two: muster Bookes & theerty Blanke tickets Printed: numbered from 925 to 954 boath numbers included: lettered Dl: I give a receite for them.[8] This night I went aboard.

30 July
Beinge Friaday faer weather wind at N a fine Gale. This day I have all my Provissions aboard for 120: men & three monthes more: for twenty men.

[2] **July *Sweepstakes* Ridinge in Longe Reach:**
30
Beinge Friday Good weather. This day I had 114 men aboard & all things Ready for the sea: Sixten tunn of water aboard: This day I Saluted the Kinge as he passed By with one

[1] Jonas Shish in Deptford dockyard applied to the Navy Commissions on 18 May 'having received a warrant for fitting the *Sweepstakes* for the West Indies I judge it convenient to sheathe her, and require for this a supply of board or fir-timber'. *CSPD*, 1669, p. 332. He applied again on 25 May, 'I want a supply of sheathing board for the *Sweepstakes* ordered on a voyage to the West Indies.' Ibid., p. 343. On 12 June he reported 'We are sheathing the *Sweepstakes*, which will be ready to take her provisions next week.' Ibid., p. 361.

[2] 'On the ways'. The ways were two parallel platforms of timber on which the ship's cradle slid when launching. Now referred to as a slip-way.

[3] 'Gale' did not have the same meaning in the 17th century as it does today. 'Manwayring, *Sea-mans Dictionary*, p. 44 describes a gale as 'When the wind doth not blow too hard, but reasonably, so that a ship may beare her top-sailes, a-tripp [fully hoisted], we call it (according to the strength of it) either an easy or loome-gale, which is when it is little wind; a fresh, stiffe strong gale when it is much wind.'

[4] Long Reach extends from Crayford Ness (51°28′·9N, 0°12′·8E), to Greenhithe (51°27′N, 0°17′E), about 13 miles downriver from Deptford.

[5] Bower anchors.

[6] To enable him to collect payment for piloting the ship.

[7] Remained at anchor.

[8] The *General Instructions to Captains* of 1663, article 13, called for them to muster the ship's company once per week and for the despatch of two complete muster books listing all members of the ship's company, to the Navy Board every two months. Davies, *Gentlemen*, p. 46; Tedder, *The Navy*, pp. 67–8. These were intended to give Admirals 'a true account of the Condition of the Fleet, as to Number and Ability of Men and likewise to prevent the wasting of His Majesty's Treasure, by the Abuse of Pursers, or any others complying with them, or neglecting to keep the due Checque upon their books and accounts; whereby many times the King allows Victuals and Wages to Men who serve not on the Ships, or for longer time than they have served'. Musters were also carried out by the Clerks of the Checque in the royal dockyards and by Muster Masters who were appointed to the fleet. The duties of the latter included examination of the muster book and mustering the ship's company to ensure that it contained a correct account. James, *Memoirs*, pp. 141–5, gives the instructions for Thomas Woodgate, Muster Master of the Division of the Rear-Admiral of the White. The tickets refer to the system of payment, see above, p. 681.

& twenty Gunnes:[1] 16: Saker[2] & five twelfe pound*ers*.[3] This Day the Clarke of the Cheque[4] mustered the men & had: 114 aboard.[5] The 28 of this instant I received the Dukes[6] instructions to keep Cheque over all my officers: & I received a press warrant.[7] Then I put up the Lawes of warr in the Stearage.[8]

31

Beinge Satterday faier weather wind at NE. This day I put 5: trouncers[9] ashore I have now: 112 men Belonge to the Shipp: this Eveinge [*sic*] the Kinge passed up to London. I disch*arged* the stewards mate John Groviour & Give a Certificat. I demanded of the Clarke of the Cheqe [cheque] at woollwich[10] a must*er* book.

[1] The standard number of guns for a Royal Salute. Guns were fired to salute the king and royal family as well as noblemen and admirals, castles and cities both British and foreign. A table of salutes was laid down by the Duke of York in 1663 (James, *Memoirs*, p. 81), which specified 'That no commander of a ship of the second rank, (being neither Admiral, Vice-Admiral or Rear-Admiral) at the first coming, and saluting his Admiral, shall give to his Admiral above eleven Pieces, his Vice-Admiral nine, his Rear-Admiral seven, and the rest proportionately less by two, according to their ranks.' Details were also included on responding to salutes by foreign vessels, the boarding and disembarking of ambassadors, noblemen etc. When entering foreign ports commanding officers, before saluting, were required to send ashore to ensure that any salute would be answered gun for gun, and without this assurance no salutes were to be fired. Ibid. p. 170. The instructions given to Robert, Earl of Sunderland, Ambassador Extraordinary to the King of Spain, dated Nov. 1671, require him, among other things, to represent to the Queen Regent the 'Personall Indigneties' practised by the 'States Generall' against King Charles II '& that lately they refuse to strike sayle to Our Flagg, as was practiced in former times and conditioned for in the late Treaty' of Westminster at the end of the First Anglo-Dutch War. He was to request the Queen Regent to use her 'utmost Authority & Credit' to oblige them to conform to the treaty. TNA, SP 95/58, ff. 74r–75v. This preoccupation with protocol at sea was not an English obsession only, the King of Spain issued an order on 27 May 1664, which was reissued and enlarged by the Queen Regent on 30 August 1671, to regulate salutes between Spanish vessels and between them and the chief towns which were all listed. TNA, SP 94/58, ff. 179r–182r. Monson's *Naval Tracts* includes a section on the occasions on which ships should salute castles or one another at sea with their ordnance, in which he comments 'the vain drinking of healths is another means to waste powder which a General must likewise forbid, except it be the health of a free prince or men of that rank and condition, and then not to exceed one piece when the health shall be begun. The King's, the Queen's, or their issues, is exempted of this strictness.' Oppenheim, *Naval Tracts*, IV, pp. 132–7. Thus the salutes fired on drinking toasts in Valdivia were quite in accordance with current practice. See below, p. 681.

[2] A saker was about 8 or 9 feet long and about 5 lb calibre. The normal complement required to man a saker was 3 men. Smyth, *Sailor's Word-Book*; Tanner, *Catalogue*, I. p. 239.

[3] The normal complement required to man a 12 lb gun was 4 men.

[4] The Clerk of the Cheque, William Sheldon, was the dockyard official responsible for mustering the crews of ships in the dockyard.

[5] This is presumably the Muster List, TNA ADM 39/2510, now in The National Archives at Kew, which contains 114 names, the last of whom was entered on 8 July.

[6] James, Duke of York, Lord High Admiral, and subsequently King James II.

[7] A warrant allowing him to make use of a press gang to complete his crew.

[8] The Articles of War, 13° Car. 11 St.1 c. 9 (1661), *An Act for establishing Articles and Orders for the regulating and better Government of His Majesty's Navies, Ships of War, and Forces by Sea*, consisted of 35 articles and a *Proviso touching the powers of the Lord Admiral*, and dealt with 'The Publick Worship of God' and the conduct expected of 'Every Captain and all other Officers, Mariners, and Soldiers of every Ship, Frigot, or Vessel of War'.

[9] Trouncers are defined in Smyth, *Sailor's Word-Book* as 'wasters'. The shore-based press gangs were notoriously corrupt and tended on occasion to collect totally unsuitable men who were not seamen. Captains sometimes refused to accept such men. Fox, *The Four Days' Battle*, pp. 22–3. It is presumably a group of such men that Narbrough discharged.

[10] William Sheldon. The ships anchored in Long Reach would have came under the authority of Woolwich Dockyard for mustering.

1 August
Beinge Sunday faier weather wind at NE a fine Gale. This day I went up to London.

2
Beinge munday: the Shipp Ride fast: The Boats*wain*[1] had his small sails Changed at Deptford I was att London: The Boatswain had Canvas to put a Cloath[2] into his fore topsaile: which he did put in the next day aboard – Wind at NW.

3
Beinge tusday faier weather wind at E by S. This day I received my order to Saile the Shipp into the downs:[3] I had it Brought to mee By Mr John Wood[4] in London at my Lodgeinge. I had Sailed But Stayed for a fortenights provissions more. This day I tooke my Leave of the Kinge. I demande of Mister Shelldon a muster Booke of Entrie & discharge of my men and showed him my Enstructions. Lettle wind this day at E.

4
Beinge wedensday faier weather wind E. This day I toke leave of his R*oyal* H*ighness*: I did disspatch my provissions aboard. This day My Leiut*enant*[5] went to Mr Sheldon for a muster Boke But Could not have it of him.

[3] **August: *Sweepstakes* in Longe Reach 1669:**
5
Beinge thursday faier weather & a fresh gale at E: This day I was at the Navy Office to Get the Provissions abord: this day was a muster aBoard & had 118 men Entered & 117 aboard.

6
Beinge Friday faier weather wind at E a gale. This day I tooke leave of London and went aboard: this night at 12 aclocke I Came a Board. This day I Enterd fower men more in longreach.

7
Being Satterday Blew fresh at E: I losed my fore topSaile and Haled home the Sheets but could not Saile a hige [high] watter here at 6: aclocke this fore none the hige with a fortnights pr*ovisions* Came aboard I tooke it in:[6] wee had nowe Spent Eight days of our

[1] William Holloway is recorded as boatswain in the Muster List, TNA ADM 39/2510.

[2] Canvas was supplied in bolts or rolls which were sewn together to make the sails. In the19th century bolts were about 39 yards long and from 22 to 30 inches wide (Smyth, *Sailor's Word-Book*) but dimensions varied in earlier years.

[3] Anchorage off Deal (51°13′N, 1°24′E), on the east coast of Kent.

[4] John Wood does not appear in the Muster List, TNA ADM 39/2510. See pp. 32–3.

[5] This was probably Lieutenant Thomas Armiger who is shown in the Muster List of 9 July, although it might possibly have been Lieutenant Touckin who gave up his Commission on 1 September. He is not on the Muster List and quite probably never joined.

[6] This statement is confused, but presumably means that the high water was at 6 o'clock and that during the forenoon a fortnight's provisions were embarked.

Bread & three Buts of Sea Beare[1] – A fresh Gale at E: This Eveinge we Ride fast the Shipp drawes now: abaft 13: foote & a half & afore: 12: foote & one inch.

8

Day Beinge Sunday Blowinge weather wind at S: all day Raine this morninge. This morninge I sent a letter to *Maste*r Sheldon to demand a muster Booke [*margin: fingerpost*] & my Leuetenat allso But he would not deliver me any I know not his Reason*ing*. Lettle wind this Eveinge wee lay Ready to Saile But Could not: Reainey weather to night.

9

Beinge munday Rainey Clowdy weather wind veareinge Rownd the Compass:[2] This moreninge wee onemored [unmored] and sailed Downe past Greenehive[3] – the wind Came to the E: and much Raine: I Came [*margin: right fingerpost*] into Longe[4] againe: at 4 aclocke in the aforenone I [*margin: left fingerpost*]wayed the wind at west a fine Gale: & halfe flod and stood Downe: at 8 aclocke I anchored at [*margin: right fingerpost*] houle havenen[5] & mored in 6: fadam at ¼: Ebb: theere Rood [rode] all night wind at W: a gale.

[4] **10 August *Sweepstakes* at hole heaven one moreinge[6] 1669**

Beinge Tusday faier weather wind at W: Gale. This morninge wee one mored & Sett Saile Downe for the Boy of the Red Seand: a tid of Eb in hand. This morninge I spake wite my Brother Loads[7] he came from Burdux:[8] At 12 aclocke I anchord nere the Boy of the Red Sand: it bore South E of me: I Stayed there till halfe flod wind at South W a fresh gale: at 3 aclocke I waied & Stood fore [*margin: drawing of a buoy*] the narrow: We pased the Boy of the Red Sand[9] to South of us: and[10] Steared South E: over the flats we had 3: fadam and a halfe and fower fadam we pased By to the Norward of us a Boy over the warke [wreck]:[11] at 5 aclocke I passed throwe the Narrow[12] you leafe the Boy of the wollepacker to the N E:ward of you & the Boy of the Spell to the South W of you: I had just 3 fadam water in the Narrowit was nere a high watter dead neap tide: Rainey Gusty [*margin:*

[1] Three butts of the sea allowance of beer.

[2] The wind was said to veer when it altered its direction, rotating round specifically in the direction of the sun's course. Veering round the compass is to rotate through 360°, or to vary its direction all over the place.

[3] Greenhithe (51°27′N, 0°17′E), at the east end of Long Reach.

[4] Long Reach.

[5] Hole Haven (51°30′·6N, 0°33′·0E), south of Canvey Island; variants hoe, houle havenen, heaven.

[6] See above, p. 135, n. 9.

[7] This is probably Narbrough's brother-in-law, Robert Loades who was married to his sister Anne (bap. 1633) and the father of Edmund Loades (bap. 29 Aug. 1699) who entered the Royal Navy and, after a distinguished career, was Captain of the *Association*, Admiral Sir Cloudeseley Shovell, when she was lost with all hands, including both Narbrough's sons, John and James, in 1707. Harris, *Sir Cloudesley Shovel*, pp. 30, 121–2, 284, 362; Charnock, *Biographia Navalis*, III, pp, 45–8; *England Selected Births and Christenings, 1538–1975,* 1526327. I am grateful to Steven Narbrough for this information.

[8] Bordeaux (44°51′N, 0°34′W); variant Burdux.

[9] Red Sand about 11 miles east of Sheerness (51°26′N, 0°44′E); variant Red Seand. The buoy was at the east end of the shoal.

[10] The word 'and' repeated in the original.

[11] This buoy is not shown on contemporary charts.

[12] The Narrow was a passage between two shoals off Reculver (51°22′·7N, 1°12′·1E) and about 7 miles west of Birchington (51°22′·5N, 1°18′·5E), marked by the Woolpack buoy on the NE side and the Spell buoy on the SW side.

drawing of 2 buoys] weather: To stere for the Boyes of the Narrow Keepe Burchinton Stepple[1] Shett with the west End of the white Clefe.[2] We passed the Boy of the Searne[3] to the E:ward of us So we Steared for marget Road[4] and anchored in 6 fadam water & ½. I fired a Saker for to Salute a vessell which fired 3 Gunes to Salute the Shipp.

11

Beinge weddensday faier weather wind at W this morninge: we waied and stood into the Downes[5] and the wind toke us Shorte[6] it was 6 aclocke in the afternone before I anchored in the downes. [*margin: fingerpost*] This Day I have Exspended of my sea provissions [*margin: drawing of 2 casks, and 2 biscuits*] seaven days Bread and two days fresh and fower days Beare [beer] to morrow I begine holly one [wholly on] my sea provisions: By reason this pett [press?] warrant is out. Sea Bere drunke 7 Buts: Bread 4 Baggs: flesh 138 peeces. [*margin: drawing of a hand pointing, two barrels and two discs*] This day I anchored in 7 fadam water the mill and the Castle[7] in one:[8] I mored:[9] the Raw Bucke Admiral.[10] I give Zecke Eull poylot Extr*a* a bill for poylotinge the Kings Shipp Swepatakes in to downes.[11]

[5] **12 August 1669 *Sweepstakes* at anchore in the Downes.**

Beinge Thursday faier weather wind at SE a fine Gale. This mored[12] and Gott our Boy it was sunke[13] at Eveinge mored againe: Seaven fadom at a low watter. I mustered and had 115 men belonge to[14] the Shipp: and all a Board Exseptinge three. Today the Boatswain Began to new fitt his rigen.[15] Today I sent By the Post a letter to Seacertary wren: and another to the Commissioners of the navy & one to M*iste*r Billop.[16] The *Raw Bucke* [Roebuck] kings firgott [frigate] Rids admirall:[17] and setts the watch with a gunn: and

[1] Birchington church spire (51°22′·4N, 1°18′·5E).

[2] Keep Birchington steeple in line with the west end of the white cliff.

[3] This marked the SW end of Searn Shoal which extends eastwards to Margate Sand.

[4] The road (51°24′N,1°22′E), off Margate.

[5] The anchorage off Deal, in (51°13′N, 1°27′E).

[6] They had to make short tacks into the wind.

[7] Dover Castle (51°08′N, 1°19′E).

[8] In transit or in line with each other.

[9] To lay out two anchors for the ship to ride to. This was either done with both anchors laid out in a similar direction and separate from each other and so that the weight of the ship was taken on both anchors at the same time, or one into the tide and the other down tide so that the ship rode first to one anchor and then, when the tide turned, to the other thus restricting the swinging room.

[10] The King's frigate *Roebuck* (16), Captain George Liddell, was the senior officer in the anchorage.

[11] Ticket, see below, p. 681..

[12] Possibly this should read 'this day unmoored', meaning weighed one of the two anchors used for mooring, since the ship was already moored and moored again later.

[13] The anchor was normally marked with a buoy secured to the crown. In this case the buoy had sunk and would have been recovered when the anchor was weighed.

[14] The word 'to' repeated in the original.

[15] Renew the rigging.

[16] Thomas Billop, clerk to Mathew Wren. He was secretary to the Earl of Clarendon, 1660–67, then to the Duke of York, 1667–72, and became clerk to Sir John Werden Bart, extra Commissioner of the Navy, 1673–7. Latham and Mathews, *Diary*, IX, p. 287, where he is called Billup. Collinge, *Navy Board Officials*, pp. 22, 51, 86 and 148.

[17] This would appear to be 'Road admiral' or senior officer of the ships riding at The Downs, since the commanding officer of the *Roebuck*, Captain George Liddell, was not an Admiral.

releive it with the same.[1] My pinnice[2] went ashore: at night Came aboard – This Eveingen the wind[3] came to the South East and Blew a fresh gale Cloudy & raine & much litghinge into the wester Board. Raine and wind to Night.

13

[*margin:* Mustr:] Beinge Friday faier weather wind at SSW a Stife gale. This day Capt*ain* Lidall[4] Came aboard me & M*aste*r Balt St Mitchell:[5] Muster Master here [*margin:* must] Cam aboard and mustered the Shippes Company and found 119 Belongeinge to the Shipp: and most aboard. This day in the Eveinge I receve*d* By the Post a muster Booke from M*iste*r William Sheldon Clarke of the Cheque at woolwich at tested [attested] By his hand: This day wee proved our flesh in the hould & found it very Good: Boath Beefe and porke: very sweet: of the first we tooke in: and Bread Drie and Good. Faier weather today our Ship Sid[e]s scraped and tared and all things fitted for sea: Raine this Night.

14

Beinge Satterday Blowinge weather wind SWBS. This day Captaine Liddle waied and Stood to the North foreland[6] and there Anchored. I made fitte the shipp in all things.

[6]

15

Beinge Sunday Blowing weather wind at SWBS and Cloudy: with Showers of raine and wind. This afternone Came into Downes two E*ast* india Ships from india: on [one] anchored the other went through. This night it Blew fresh and rained wind at SSW.

16

Beinge mundy faier weather this day w*ind* at SW. This day Came two East India ships more into downes: I rode fast and sent the Longe Boat ashore for watter they filled six hougsheads and Came aboard againe by none [noon]: I ro[a]d faste. I vewed the hould and other plases and saw all things well our men imployed in fittinge our riginge. Calme weather this Eveinge and so Continued all night noe gun fired to sett the watch as I heard.

[1] The standard practice in an anchorage is for all the naval ships present to follow the senior officer's motions, striking top masts etc., so this would be to ensure that all the ships anchored in The Downs kept the same time.

[2] Pinnace.

[3] 'the wind' repeated in original.

[4] Captain George Liddell, appointed to the *Roebuck* in 1666. He had been a Lieutenant in the *Assurance* and *Monck* in 1661 and commanded the *Hare*, fireship, in 1665. Tanner, *Catalogue*, I, p. 379.

[5] Mr Balthazar St Michel, the son of Alexander St Michel, and the brother-in-law of Samuel Pepys. After service in the Dutch army and the Guards he was made Muster-Master of the fleet, 1666–8, and then Muster-Master at Deal (where he was also a sub-commissioner of the sick and wounded during the Third Anglo-Dutch War), and at Tangier from where he returned home in 1680. Subsequently he was appointed to the Special Commission of 1686 (with Sir John Narbrough) as resident commissioner for Deptford and Woolwich, losing this office in the Revolution of 1688. Latham and Matthews, *Diary*, X, pp. 375–6; Tanner, *Catalogue*, I, pp. 73–4 and 85.

[6] The North Foreland (51°22′N, 1°27′E), is the north-east corner of the Isle of Thanet, about 10 miles north of the anchorage at The Downs.

17
Beinge tusday faier weather But Cloudy this morninge the wind Came up at N a fine gale. All the fleet waied and went out of the downs to the Southward Save my Selfe and one Shipp more inward Bownd. A fresh gale towards Eveinge. This day I fettched one Boate of Ballase [ballast] aboute three tunnes and toke itt into the ship: this day I discharged ashore Jo*h*n Beets an able seaman sicke: this day I fired two saker to two seaverall Ships to answer their saluts. Faier weather this afternone and all night.

18
Beinge wedensday faier weather wind at N a fine gale. This day I had another Boate of Ballas: Rod fast all day. This day the East india Ship went out of the Downs: I ame all alone: this day I discharged Gore west and Jo*h*n Stafe able seamen ashore for preferment: I wrote M*aste*r Wren. Wind this Eveinge at South and faier weather.

[7] **August: *Sweepstakes* in the Downes att Anchor 1669.**
19 Day
Beinge Thursday Cloudy weather: wind at SW a fine gale: this morninge I sent my Longe [boat] and master in her to the Goodin Sand[1] to Gitt a vessell of[f] which was ashore: and did it She Came into the Downes: the masters name is [*blank*] Southend the Ships name is the *Edward* a pinke Belongs to London: Bound for London: Came from verginne.[2] The Sergant of Dovier [Dover] Came aboard the *Sweepstakes* to mee to detaine the vessell for the Groundedge: So he returned againe.[3] Faier weather this Eveinge: this Eveinge I received a letter from M*aste*r wren to Come up to white hall:[4] faier weather all night.

20
Beinge Friday faier weather wind at NW. This moringe I went ashor at deale[5] and so to London.

21
Beinge Saterday faier weather wind at W. This morninge I went to London: and to S[t] James and Spake with Seacretary Wren[6] & discoursed Concerninge my voiage to the Southward.

22
Beinge Sonnday faier weather. I was London this morninge I spake with his R*oyal* H*ighness*[7] at S[t] James and he moved the same to mee.

[1] Goodwin Sands, (51°12′N, 1°34′E).
[2] Virginia.
[3] Presumably this means Narbrough declined to detain the master of the pink.
[4] The Palace of Whitehall, situated between Northumberland Avenue and Downing Street, extending from the River Thames west to Horse Guards Road, had been the main London residence of the King since 1049. Only the Banqueting Hall, built in 1622, survives.
[5] Deal (51°13′N, 1°24′E), the town adjacent to The Downs anchorage.
[6] Secretary to James, Duke of York.
[7] James, Duke of York, Lord High Admiral.

23
Beinge munday faier weather: I had order to wate. [*margin:* 23 day a man died Ro Dale.]

24
Beinge tueday faier weather I wated at white hall.

25
Beinge wedensday faier hote weather.

26
Beinge thursday faier weather.

27
Beinge Friday faier weather. This afternone I was befor his R*oya*l H*ighnes*s at my Lord arelintons Lodgine[1] wher was allso Prince Rupert[2] & my Lord Sandwich[3] my Lord arlinton and Commissioner Medleton which Laid the Propostialls of the voiage to mee which semmed a mater of honnourable Consiqunce wherin I was very willinge to prosseed.

[8] **August *Sweepstaks* at Anchor in the Downes: 1669.**
28
Beinge Satterday faier weather. I was to the Navy Office[4] and the[r] passed an order for more provissions for fowerteen Dayes for one hounder and Twenty men[5] for the *Sweepstakes*.

[1] Presumably Goring House, the residence of Lord Arlington. The house is no longer extant. Buckingham Palace was built on its site.

[2] Prince Rupert (1619–82), Count Palatine of the Rhine, Duke of Bavaria, K.G., 4th son of Frederick, King of Bohemia and Elizabeth eldest daughter of King James I of England. He had been a General of Horse under Charles I during the Civil War and a Royalist Admiral. He commanded at sea during the Second Anglo-Dutch War (1664–7), and was a founder of the Royal Society. Roy, 'Prince Rupert', *ODNB*.

[3] Sir Edward Montagu (1625–72), 1st Earl of Sandwich. He served as a Parliamentarian during the Civil War and was appointed General at Sea by Cromwell in January 1652. He supported Richard Cromwell after his father's death in 1658. He was with the fleet off Sweden and Denmark when the latter fell from power and returned with the fleet to England to await events. He was suspected of involvement in a royalist rising in 1659 and ceased to command the fleet. The next year in March he was re-appointed General at Sea and in May brought the fleet over to Charles II. At the Restoration in 1660, he was created Earl of Sandwich, and was one of the Garter Knights who bore the canopy over the King's head at the coronation. He was elected to the Royal Society in 1661. Appointed Admiral of the Blue in Feb.1665, he served under the Duke of York in the Second Anglo-Dutch War and commanded the rear squadron at the Battle of Lowestoft. In Oct. 1665 he was appointed Ambassador to Spain and returned to England in Sept. 1668. With the advent of the Third Anglo-Dutch War he was again appointed Admiral of the Blue hoisting his flag in the *Royal James*, and died when his ship was burnt down to the water line on 28 May, in action against the Dutch Fleet at the Battle of Solebay. Davies, 'Montague [Mountagu], Edward', *ODNB*.

[4] The Navy Office was at the house which formerly belonged to Sir John Wolstenholme in Seething Lane. It had been purchased for £2,400 in 1654 and continued in use until about 1780. Tanner, *Catalogue*, I. p. 23n; Oppenheim, *Administration*, p. 349.

[5] The peace-time complement for the *Sweepstakes*, as a 4th rate, was 115 men, so this must have been increased for this voyage to allow for the extra men, Don Carlos and his party, that he was required to carry.

29

Beinge Sunday faier weather. This afternone I was Before his Maj*estie* and his R*oyal* Highness and Prince Rubert & the Earle of Sandwich and my Lord arlington and my Lord Osserie[1] and Mr wernn [Wren] and Comissioner midleton and where his Maj*es*ty was pleassed to Give hereinge to the vojage and ordered mee what I should acte in my vojage and to what plased.[2] Soe I tooke leave of the Kinge and Duke and all the rest of the Lords. I lay this Nighte at My Lord Willoughbyes.[3]

30

Beinge munday faier weather. This morninge I was with Seacretary wernn [Wren] at St James: The Kinge and Duk[e][4] went to South hamton: I had order from his Royall Highness to reduce my Complement of men a Board to 80:[5] which he Certified one [on] that order what occation my Stay and how longtime. This day I had my Instructions Concerninge My vojage in the *Sweepstakes* from Mr wrenn and what Company is to Goe with mee & an order for all my Pay as was formerly due and an order for two hundered pounds Contengent mony. This Eveinge I was Befor My Lord Sandwich and my Lord arlington at Goereinge house.[6] This Eveinge I tooke leave of Mr Wrenn. He goes out of towne in the morininge.

31

Being Tusday faier weather. This Day I was with the Principall Officers and had order for all my arrears and 200: pounds Contengent mony which I received this afternone all at

[1] Thomas Butler (1634–80), Earl of Ossory, son of James Butler, 12th Earl and 1st Duke of Ormond and 5th Earl of Ossory. He was a personal friend of Charles II and had been in exile with him. He fought in the Dutch Wars in 1665 at the battle of Lowestoft and in 1672 at the Battle of Solebay. In 1673 he was appointed Rear Admiral of the Blue in the *St Michael* with Captain Narbrough as his flag captain, where he fought in the Battle of the Texel. He went on to be Vice Admiral of the Red and subsequently Commander in Chief of the Fleet in the absence of Prince Rupert. In 1675 he became Master of Trinity House and a member of the Admiralty board. He was appointed governor of Tangier in 1680, but died at Lord Arlington's house in London on 30 July. Davies, 'Butler, Thomas sixth earl of Ossory', *ODNB*.

[2] It is worth noting that the Duke of York, Prince Rupert, the Earl of Sandwich and the Earl of Ossory were all members of the Council of Trade (which had 46 members all told), established 'for Keeping a control and super-inspection of his Majesty's Trade and Commerce'. Andrews *British Committees*. p. 93. Colonel Middleton had been a member of the former Council for Foreign Plantations in 1660. Ibid., p. 68.

[3] William Willoughby (bap. 1615, d. 1673), 6th Baron Willoughby of Parham. He was appointed Captain-general and Governor of the Caribbean Islands and Vice Admiral of Barbados for the remainder of the term of office of his brother, Lord Francis Willoughby (d. 23 June 1666 in a hurricane off Guadeloupe) as Governor of Barbados. It was during his term of office that Cayenne and Suriname were recaptured from the Dutch, by an expedition under Rear Admiral Sir John Harman and Lieutenant General Sir Henry Willoughby, in which Narbrough took part and was wounded. Narbrough was at this time in command of the *Assurance* having sailed from England in Sir John Harman's squadron, and presumably knew Lord Willaboughby, and was probably an old friend of his. Lacombe, 'Willoughby, Francis, 5th Baron of Parham'. *ODNB*, Dyer, *Life*, pp. 36–56.

[4] The Duke of York.

[5] Although at this time the *Sweepstakes* had been reclassified as a 4th rate, her peace-time complement as a 5th rate had been 95 men so this would mean that, while there was unlikely to be any problem working the ship, it would not be practicable to man all the guns at the same time.

[6] See above, p. 138, n. 1.

The treassuerry offices of M*aste*r Lettleton[1] which I give my hand for and ame to account for it at my Returne: This day I dined at Commissioner Midletons.

[9] **September *Sweepstakes* at Anchor in the Downes 1669.**

1

Beinge wedensday faier weather. I was this day disspatchinge to Gitt away from London. I was Byinge [buying] of meteralls [materials] for the voiage: my Leiut*enant* Tucken[2] Give up[3] his Commission and Could not Goe the voiage: this day I Carried Nath*anyell* Peckett to Commissioners Coll*onell* Medleton to have his Consent to have him my Leiut*enant* which he did doe.

2

Beinge Thursday faither Thursday.[4] I was at Commissioner midletons talkeinge Conc[e]rninge the voiage and I went to depford and fetched the Stores aded to the Shipp and put them aboard the Pinke Called the *Batcheller* and to*ok* a receite for them.

3

Beinge Friday faier weather. This morninge I Came from London: and Came Downe to Gravsend[5] at a 1: aclocke I tooke horse for the downse: at 9 aclocke I Came aboard the Shipp in my Penness:[6] faier weather wind at NW: a fine Gale.

4

Beinge Satterday faier weather wind at SW a fine Gale. This morninge I saw But two vessells more in the Downes Besids my selfe: this moringe I Called all hands up and mustered: and this day Discharged 35: of my men and Give them their printed Ticketts[7] for their tim and so sett them ashore. My Complement is now 80: men all a Board: I received a foretnights provissions for 120: men: from London of all sorts.[8]

[10] **September *Sweep* at Anchor in the Downes 1669.**

5

Beinge Sunday faier weather wind at W a fine Gale. Wee Rod faste & sett my discharged

[1] Sir Thomas Littleton (c. 1620–1681), 2nd. Bart. He was appointed joint treasurer of the navy with Sir Thomas Osborne in 1668 until 1671, when he had to resign (after his brother misused the funds at his disposal in the navy pay office to finance Thomas Blood's attempt to steal the crown jewels), and Osborne became the sole treasurer. He was appointed to the Admiralty Commission in Feb. 1681 shortly before his death on 12 April that year. Ferris, 'Littleton, Sir Thomas',*ODNB*; Tanner, *Catalogue*, I, pp. 12 and 58.

[2] This would appear to be Anthony Touckin, commissioned Lieutenant in the *Sweepstakes*, July 1669, by the Duke of York. Tanner, *Catalogue*, I, p. 415.

[3] The word 'my' crossed through in original.

[4] This may have been meant to read 'faier weather Thursday'.

[5] Gravesend.

[6] Pinnace. The commanding officer's boat, 25 feet long and fitted with oars and sails.

[7] For their pay, see p. 681.

[8] Narbrough reported to Col. Thos. Middleton 'I have discharged my men to 80, and shall send the muster-books next post. I expect my provisions from Dover, and have room to take a month's more bread and flesh, having little or nothing between decks. I want a hawser and 6 tarred lines, and will charge my boatswain with them.' *CSPD, 1669*, 6 Sept., p. 476.

men ashore beinge in all 35: I gave them all Prented ticketts: this day camm a shipp Called the *Duke of yorke*[1] and sum others – I give tickets to 35.

6
Beinge Monday faier weather wind at WNW a Gale. We Rod fast and fitted such things as were to fitt. This Eveinge I tooke in a monthes provissions more for 80 men as Came from Doviour[2] from that victuler: faier weather all Night. Here is Severall Ships in the Downes outward bound.

7
Beinge Tusday faier weather wind at N: a fine gale. This morninge all the Shipps in the Downes waied and Stood to the Southward Exseptinge the *Sweepstake* shee Rood fast: the afternone wind E faier weather all night.

8
Beinge Wedensday faier *weather* wind at EBS and fine Gale: noe Ships in the Downes But the *Sweepstakes*: This morneinge I sent my Long Boat[3] ashore fore watter. She Came aboard againe at none all filled.

9
Beinge Thursday faier weather wind at SE a fine Gale[4] we rod fast. This Day Came in one Shipp Bound fro [for] franch Belongs to new Castle.[5]

10
Beinge friday faier weather wind at E. a fine gale wee rode fast. This forenone the new Castle Shipp Sailed to the So*uth*ward. This day I received a Letter from the Commissioners of the Nayie [Navy] Concernige my not sendinge up a muster Booke: and it mentioned another monthes Provissions for mee aComeinge aboard.

[11] **September the *Sweepstaks* at Anchor in the Downes 1669.**
11
Beinge Satterday Good weather wind at EBS a fresh galle [gale]. This day the Boatswaine spent Good store of his Junke[6] in makeinge plats[7] and spunjarne[8] and sinnet[9] and strands

[1] There was no King's ship of this name at this time so presumably it was a merchant vessel.
[2] Dover (51°07′N, 1°20′E).
[3] The largest boat in the ship, fitted with mast and sails and normally used for embarking wood and water and carrying stores.
[4] A wind which did not blow too hard, but reasonably so that ship could carry topsails fully hoisted, probably about 13–19 knots, unlike a gale force 8 today which is defined as 37 knots.
[5] France; variant Franch. Newcastle.
[6] Junk: pieces of old cable and condemned cordage.
[7] Platts: flat rope mats made by weaving rope yarns together, used for preventing the cable wearing in the hawse hole, or more generally for preventing wear elsewhere.
[8] Spunyarn: a small line made by twisting together two or three strands of old rope and used for various purposes such as seizing and serving ropes, weaving mats, making strops etc.
[9] Sennet or sinnet: a flat cordage made by plaiting 5, 7 or more strands of old rope together, and beaten flat with a mallet, used for serving ropes, twisting round a rope to prevent it chafing.

to laie on the shrouds for service a Loft[1] and Catharpan plats[2] wee spent sum store of spunjarne and yorpjarne[3] in Seaseinge[4] our riginge and ratlens[5] and in Blockes and Serveinge[6] rops and Strops[7] and in many such things as allso in Seasinge oure Gerge Blockes[8] into their strops and in fleetinge our shrouds fore and afte[9] spent 3 tared lines. This afternone I sent up two Perfecte muster Bookes of my Shipp to the prinscipall officers of the Navy mustered one [on] the 10: of this monthe with the letter [*margin:* – a] and noe Closs Essued [no clothes issued] to any man at this time:[10] tickets: deliver in that Booke 35. I have now aboard 78 men and Boyes. This afternone towards Eveinge it began to Blowe at E: wee lowered our maine yard and fore yard aporte Longe.[11] A frese Gale all the Night.

12

Being Sunday faier weather but a fresh gale wind at ENE: I rod fast: yards downe. Faier weather all night.

[1] Serving to prevent chafing.

[2] Catharpings: small ropes passing through blocks on the shrouds near the deck, running from side to side to haul the shroudes taut. They were only used on the main and fore shrouds. They were also used at the upper ends of the shrouds, near the tops, but in this case blocks were not used.

[3] Yorpjarne does not appear in any of the available nautical dictionaries. It seems likely this is Rope yarn, a standard term for any form of yarn untwisted from a larger rope and used for making mats, serving ropes and a number of other purposes.

[4] Seizing is to secure two ropes together with some form of small rope yarn, also the fastening of a block into the end of its pendant. In general it means binding things together.

[5] Ratlins, also ratlines: the lines which go across the shrouds to make steps to enable the men to climb aloft.

[6] Serving is when a piece of rope has a mat, sennet or canvas tied round it to prevent it chafing or fretting.

[7] Strop: a piece of rope spliced into a circular form used to surround the body of a block. It is also used to describe any circular rope used for hoisting cargo or twisting round a large rope to secure a tackle to it, as for example when setting up the shrouds.

[8] A block is a flat piece of wood with the centre cut out called the shell, and fitted with one or more sheaves, which rotated on a pin, which passed through the sheaves and the shell, allowing a rope to run over them. Blocks might have more than one sheave, e.g. a double block had two sheaves and a treble block three sheaves etc. The block was fitted with a strop, a length of rope round the outside of it with an eye above the block and sometimes another below it. The upper eye is used to secure the block in its location. The lower eye takes the end of a rope or fall when two blocks are being used to form a tackle to increase the mechanical power. Blocks came in different sizes and were named and distinguished by the ropes that passed through them. There is no mention of 'Gerge' in any of the available nautical dictionaries and it seems likely that these are the blocks for the gears, or jeers, an assemblage of blocks and tackles by means of which the lower yards were hoisted and lowered. A tackle consisted of two blocks, one of which was secured (the standing block) to which a rope was made fast and passed down through the other block and back through the standing block, running over sheaves. It might go round two or three times. The action was to haul on the free end and thereby bring the two blocks towards each other. Tackles were used for all sorts of purposes, from running the guns out to hoisting in stores and hauling up the masts and sails.

[9] The shrouds are the upper and lower standing rigging used to support the masts. They were fitted in pairs i.e. a single rope was used with a loop in the middle fitted over the masthead. The lower end was attached to a dead-eye (a flat piece of wood with three holes in it), which was secured to a second dead-eye by a lanyard passed through the holes. The lower dead-eye, in the case of the upper masts was secured to the tops of the lower masts, and in the case of the lower masts to the chain-plate and the hull. Fleeting the shrouds is to correct their tension by adjusting the distance between the dead-eyes which was done by hauling on, or slackening off, the lanyard. See Harland, *Seamanship*, pp. 19–25.

[10] Clothes, normally referred to as 'slops', were sold to the ship's company by the purser who charged the cost against each man's pay in the pay list.

[11] 'Aporte Long: Down a portlast' was a term used in the 17th century to mean lowering of the yard right down to the gunwale, with the yardarms projecting outboard.

13
Beinge munday faier weather wind at ENE a fine Galle. This day wee mended the service of our Cables as was with the horses.[1] A great sea went one [on] the shore side. Faier weather all night.

14
Beinge Tusday faier weather wind at ENE a fine gale. This day I sent a letter to Coll*onell* medleton.

15
Beinge Wedensday faier weather wind at EBN a fine gale. This day my Leitt*enant* Nath*anyel* Peckett Came aboard.[2] I sent a letter to Mr Wrenn to St James.

[12] ***Sweepstakes* September 16 Day 1669 in the Downes.**
16
Beinge Thursday faier weather wind at EBN a gale. This Eveinge my Purser Allex*ander* Curtis Cam aboard.[3] I sent a letter to the victuler of Doviour to dissp[a]ch away the Provissions by my steward. This day Came throwge the Downes a small vessell from bantam[4] about 25: tunns belonginge to the E*ast* Indian Comp*any*.

17
Beinge friday faier weather wind at E: a fine gale. This day I tooke in a monthes provissions for 80 men which Cam from Doviour By [*blank*] master.

18
Beinge Satterday faier weather wind at E a fine Gale. This Day I wrote a letter to Mr Wren and on [one] to Coll*onell* Medleton.

19
Beinge Sunday faier weather wind at E in the morninge but small winde: at 7 aclocke in the morninge the wind Came up to the SW and Blew a fresh gale. This fore noe [noon] the *Batcheler* Pinke Capt*ai*n fleminge Master and anchored in the Dowenes. This day the Spanish Gentl*eman* Sinor Don Carlos Henrecus Cam aboard mee and Brought all his things aboard and two men that waited one [on] him which I had order to victuall all three and did Give order to my Stuward to Esue [issue] to them Provissions which he did. I allso received my stores from the Pinke which shee tooke in at deptford. I allso Received a packet of instruction from Coll*onell* medleton and allso letters. Fresh gale at South west this Eveinge and Cloudy: wind SBW all night. I stroke my low yards.[5]

[1] Mended the servings on the cables where they passed through the hawse holes.

[2] Presumably he brought his servant, Austen Dusney, with him bringing the complement up to 80. Alex Curtis, the Purser, who came aboard the next day was already on the Muster List.

[3] The purser customarily left one eighth part of the allowance of victualls ashore, and received the value for that part in money. The purser therefore joined his ship at the last possible moment in order to be able to collect this money. Tanner, *Catalogue*, I, pp. 160–61.

[4] Bantam now Banten, Jawa Barat, Indonesia (6°01′S, 106°08′E).

[5] Lowered the lower yards. A seamanlike precaution in times of strong wind or heavy weather to reduce the top-weight.

20

Beinge munday faier weather wind at SW a Stife Gale. I rod lose with my for topsaile to be gone: But Could not for it Blew fresh this afternone: I got up my yards. I sent a letter to M*aste*r wrenn of the arrivall of that and Don Carlos & the Pinke and I allso wrot to Collonell medleton. Wind SBW alnight. The *Amity*[1] Cam through.

[13] **September *Swepstakes* in the Downes Bound out 1669**

21

Being Tusday faier weather wind at SSW: a Stife Gale all Day so as I Could not saile. This Eveinge I Rec*eive*d a letter from m[r] wrenn to hasten my saileinge.Wind at SSW al night a fine gale. This day m*iste*r Brewerton[2] Came aboard. It Blew fresh all Night.

22

Beinge wedensday Hassy [hazy] weather this morninge wind at WSW a stife Gale all day. This Eveinge I received a letter from m*iste*r wren & his R*oyal* H*ighness* instructions for saileinge to Portsmouth. Wind at WSW a Stife gale all night I rod fast.

23

Beinge Thursday hassy weather wind at WSW or thereabo*ut* a stife gale all day & night I rode fast.

24

Beinge friday hassy Gusty weather wind at WSW a Stife Gale I lowered my yards. This afternone I had severall stors Came to mee from deptford Store house in the *Bzan*: will*iam* write Commander[3] I tooke them in they are to build a Shallop.[4] I had a letter from Coll*onell* Medleton and a bill of ladinge of the things.

I had this Eveinge a letter from Mr wrenn to Count*er*mand my Portsmouth order.

I sent a letter to Coll*onell* Medleton this afternone by M*aste*r write Capt*ain* [of the] *Bizan*: faier weather all this Night wind at WSW.

[1] *Amity* (38), 4th rate, Captain Stephen Pyend, appointed 1666. Tanner, *Catalogue*, I, p. 396.

[2] It is not clear who Mister Brewerton was, or if he remained on board. He is not included when Narbrough mentions the 'Gentlemen' or indeed mentioned again in any of the journals of the voyage, so he probably went ashore again. He might have been a volunteer 'per order', an officer under training. This method of entry was established in 1661 and entailed serving several voyages as a volunteer with the pay of a midshipman, by the authority of a royal letter to the ship's captain. Davies, *Gentlemen*, p. 16. Thomas Brewerton was appointed Lieutenant to the *William and Thomas* in 1672, and this may have been the same officer. Tanner, *Catalogue*, I, p. 329.

[3] *Bezan*, yacht, Captain William Wright, appointed 1666. Captain Wright went on to command the *Kitchin*, yacht, 1671; the *Portsmouth*, yacht, 1678 and 1686; and the *Monmouth*, yacht, 1687. Tanner, *Catalogue*, I, p. 428.

[4] Described in Lightbody, *Mariner's Jewel*, p. 83, as 'small boats belonging to Great Ships'. They were taken by larger vessels shaken down, in pieces, so that they could be carried below and assembled when required. Size varied and this one was probably equipped with a mast and sail.

25

Beinge Saterday wind at SW: hassy weather this morninge a stife gale I Could not doe any thinge to Gitto [get to] windward. This morninge I gott up my topmast.[1] I sent[2] the deales[3] aboard[4] the *Battheller* Pinke[5] the M*aste*r Fleminge master. I Charged all my officers with the stores they received from Deptford. Hassy weather to night. This Day one of my men named John Narbrough,[6] Boatswa[i]ns mat[e] Brake his Legge.

[14] **September *Sweepstakes* in the Downes waieinge[7] 1669**

26

Beinge[8] Sunday foggy Rainey weather the morninge the wind veared about to the NNE. [*margin:* Waied out of the Downes][9]At 6 aclocke a fine Gale I hailed home my for top saile sheets[10] and waid as fast as I Could. At 10 of the Clocke I got under saile and Got my Boats Boath aboard[11] and all my men and I sett all the Saile I Could make and stood away to the Southward in Company with the *Batcheller* a pinke Englesh Built of about Eighty tunes: She draws about 9 foot water: of forse fower Small ordinance of Iron & sume small Shoot and Eighten men: the Captaine name Humpry Fleminge: a man about 45 yeares of age: Shee is fitted for 10 monthes Comepleat of all things as to hole [whole] alowance.

I have 80 men aboard and Provissions at hole [whole] alowance for 14 monthes of all sorts – wood 8000: watter 22 tunes: Beare 40: tuns: Brandy: 4½ tunns in lew [lieu] of Beare. Shipp fitted with all stores for 18: Monthes: Great ordinance of Iron 36: fire armes

[1] The lower part of the mast was stepped on the keel and then passed up through the decks. The portion above the lower mast was the topmast and above that the topgallant-mast. The upper masts were set up by hoisting them through a square hole between crosstrees and trestletrees (which formed the top) and then through a hole in the fore part of the cap (a piece of wood fitted over the top of the lower mast), and securing them in place with a fid. See Harland, *Seamanship*, pp. 19–20, and 114–15.

[2] The word 'sent' repeated in the original.

[3] Planks from which the shallop was to be constructed.

[4] 'aboard' repeated in the original.

[5] 'aboard' struck through in the original.

[6] This John Narbrough is shown on the Muster List, TNA ADM 39/2510, as having joined on 18 June 1669, and is not mentioned again. He may have been a relation of the Captain, possibly the son of an elder brother, but there appear to have been a number of other John Narbroughs living in Norfolk at this time.

[7] Weighing.

[8] In red ink.

[9] In red ink.

[10] Hauled in the fore topsail sheet to set the sail.

[11] Boat hoisting: the boats were stowed on the booms amidships between the fore and main masts. They were hoisted in and out by means of tackles secured to the bow and stern of the boat, and rigged from the masts and yards. (The system was similar to the 'union purchase' method used for handling cargo today.) Pendants were secured to the top of the fore and main masts which were joined by a triatic stay, forming a continuous line between the tops and hanging down appreciably over the boats: from two points over the boat (where the pendants joined the triatic stay), the fore stay tackle and main stay tackle went down to the bow and stern of the boat. A second set of tackles (the fore yard tackle and the main yard tackle) went from the ends of the boat to the ends of the fore and main yards, which were in their turn supported by extra tackles. To hoist the boat out, it was lifted from its stowage position amidships by means of the main stay and fore stay tackles, with the yard tackles slack; the fore and main yard tackles were then hove in and the weight of the boat transferred to them. As the stay tackles were slackened off the boat moved out board over the ship's side; then, keeping the latter slack, the boat was lowered into the water by the yard tackles. The operation was carried out in reverse to hoist the boat in board. Harland, *Seamanship*, pp. 282–5.

50: Picke and Bills and all other Munition for 18: monthes. Shipp Draw: 13 feet water and one halfe abaft and 12: feet 4: inches afore – Burden two hundered and seaventy tunns or therabouts. This afternone at 4 of the Clocke I was of[f] foulston.[1] I sent Captaine fleminge his Saileinge instruction to keepe me Company and a letter allso wher wee are to Radivo [Rendezvous] B*y* Leiut*enant* Peckett[2] – Faier weather this Eveinge at 6 aclocke – wind at E a fine gale: Course SWBW. Wee have 40 or feivty Saile of marchants Shipp in Comp*any*.

[15] **Seeptember the *Sweepstakes* at Sea of [off] the white[3] 1669**
27

Beinge faier weather all last night and a fine fresh gale wind at EBS: a light mone [moon]. Wee steared away with all the Saile we could make WSW half a pointe Southerly. This morninge we were tharwht of Chischester:[4] at 12 aclocke at none we had Donenose:[5] N: of us about 5 leagus Distance. This day at none wee tried our new quadrons[6] and find them to be very Good instruments for truthe wee made donenoz to ly in 50°30′ observied By the ☼ at none.[7] The *Batcheler* Pinke and *Sweepstakes* now Sailes much as one.[8] This Afternone at 4 of the Clocke the midle Body of the Ile of White Bore NE of me sum 6 leagus dista*nce*. A fresh gale at E this Eveinge: Course WBS: we saile about 7 leagus a watch:[9] at least a Brave light mone and faier weather all night. This day my master[10] Beinge by mee ordered to vew my Provissions finds one hogshead of the Ships Brandy to be two thirds out By reasson the Badness of the Caske: it was well Stowed in the Brandy Roume with the Rest so as noe man Could ever Come to draw of it.[11] This Day I put [*margin: fingerpost in red ink*] all my Shipp Company in Gennerall to [*margin:* short Alowance] six men to fower mens alowance of all Sorts of Provissions:[12] Beganit this day Binge Munday morning the 27 day of september 1669. Faier weather all night and a fresh gall at EBS: Course WSW: halfe a pointe southerly.

[16] **September *Sweepstakes* at Sae [sea] of[f] the Boult[13] 1669**
28

Beinge Tusday this morninge faier weather wind at E: a fresh gale Course W: By Cause wee would make the Land Plaine to take our departure.[14] At 12 aclocke wee oBservid the ☼ and was in the Latt*itud* of 49°45′: we steeared W & Sumtime WNW to make the land.

[1] Folkestone (51°05′N, 1°12′E).

[2] See above, p. 31.

[3] Isle of Wight.

[4] Athwart or abreast of Chichester (50°50′N, 0°46′W).

[5] Dunnose (50°36′N, 1°11′W), on the Isle of Wight.

[6] Quadrant. Probably a Davis's back-staff, which was also known as a quadrant. See above, p. 96 and Figure 3.

[7] Dunnose Head lies in 50°36′N. Bearing in mind that the distance offshore had to be estimated by eye this is a very respectable observation. John Wood, BL, MS 3833, f. 3r, made it 50°28′N.

[8] At similar speeds.

[9] That is 21 nautical miles in 4 hours, or 5¼ knots.

[10] Abraham Hyatt, see above, p. 31.

[11] So that no one could get at it to steal the brandy.

[12] This was a not uncommon practice and the men were compensated by a monetary payment. See below, p. 682.

[13] Bolt Head (50°13′, 3°47′W).

[14] See the land properly to take their departure, the final fixed position from which the account and meridian distances would be calculated. See above, pp. 62–73. For P:oint of Departure, see p. 69.

At 4 of the Clocke wee saw the Lizard: it Bare WNW of mee Distanece 7 Leagus wind at SEBE a fine eassy gale wee Steared away WSW hasy Glume [gloomy] weather. At 6 aclocke it Bare NW of mee about 8 leagus of[f] mee: lettle wind veareinge to the south: we stered SW: at 8 of the Clocke the wind Came up to the SW a fresh gale: we plyed to windward. Little wind all night we stood to & fro.

29

Beinge[1] weddensday faier weather Sumtime hassy wind at SW and at W: at none it Came to the NWBW a fresh gale: I stood to the Southward as nere as I Could ly. This Day at none the Lizard bar North of mee Somethinge to the E: Distance about tuelfe lagus [twelve leagues]: I saw the Pointe of it. At 2: aclocke the wind Cam to the NNW a fine galle Course SWBW: at 6 aclocke it Provid lettle wind and so Continued all night. This day I spake with a french Banker Bound home far deep.[2] The Lizard Beinge in the Lattitude of 50°10′ N and in Longitud 18°30′E[3] of the meridian of the west Parts of S[t] Michalls Island one of the Azores where M[r] Emeny Mullinex[4] Begines Longitud. Latt*itud* I sailed from is 49°35′ & Long*itud* 18°30′E.

30

Beinge Thursday Cloudy hassy weather wind vear all betwen the WNW & the SWBW a stife Gale faier weather last 24 howers. Course made good from yesterday at none till today at noe [noon] SWBW 1°25′ southerly: dist*ance* [*margin:* 37′ L.] Rune 29·4 mills: depart 24 mills: deff*erence* Lat*itud* 17 mills. Lat*itud* by observation ☼ 49°18′: Long*itud* 17°53′: def*erence* 37′ west.

[17] **1669 October: the *Seepstakes* at Sea in the Chaps Chanel**[5]

1

Beinge[6] Fraiday Blowinge weather winds Betwen the west and the South & be [by] west. Course mad good from thursday none till to day at none west 4°15′ northerly: Distance Sailed 54 mills: departur 53·8 mills: defference of Latt*itud* 4 mills: Latt*itud* By observation of the ☼ one [on] the meridian [*right margin:* 49°22′]: Longit*ud* 16°32′: deff*erence* 1°21′ west: Long*itud* from the Liz*ard* 1°58′: meridian distance from the Lizard 77·8 mills west. Their Came a great sea this 24 howers out of the WSW: the shipp labars very much in the sea. We sumtimes keep out our maine top saile & sumtimes the fore top saile: and plyed to windward wind at SBW. This Evinge Calme at 12 aclocke at night.

[1] Date and first word in red ink in the original.

[2] A French fishing vessel bound home from the Grand Banks for Dieppe; variant Deep. Wood, BL, MS 3833, f. 3r: notes that 'she had lost her Main Top Mast Tre Days before by Stress of Weather.'

[3] This position is the same as that given in Tapp, *Sea-Mans Kalender*, p. 172.

[4] Emery Molyneux (fl. 1587–1605), best known for his large terrestrial and celestial globes. Taylor, *Mathematical Practitioners*, p. 188. Edward Wright's world map in Hakluyt, *Principal Navigations* uses St Michaels for the origin of its longitudes as well. The *Seamans Kalender* John Tapp, newly calculated and corrected by Henry Phillipes, London, 1669, p. 66, states: 'I following Mr. *Emery Mollineux*, according to his great Globes, do account the *Long.* from the Westermost parts of *S. Michaels*, another Isle of the *Azores*, the midst of which Isle is 50 *min.* in *Longit.*' The position of the western end of São Miguel (St Michael) is 37°51′N, 25°51′W of Greenwich.

[5] Chaps Channel: Chops of the Channel the entrance to the English Channel.

[6] First word in red ink.

2
Beinge[1] Satterday Cloudy hassey weather all this day and little wind: a great Rowellinge [rolling] sea Came out of the NW. Course mad from friday at none till today at no*ne* W: distance Sailed 48 mills: departur 48 mills: [*margin:* :49=22[2]] Def*erence* Latta*tud* 00: Lat*itud* by accounte 49°22′: Longit*ud* 15°18′: Def*erence* Long*itud* 1°14′: Long*itud* Li*zard* 3°12′: Meridian distance from the Lizard 125·8 mills. Little wind this after none at NNW & Cloudy weather this eveinge: Little wind all the first parte of the night.

3
Beinge[3] Sunday Cloudy hassy weather wind at N at 2 of the Clocke & came to the NNE a Small gale: Calme this afternone. Course mad Goode from Satterday at none till to day at none SWBW: distance Sailed 19·9 mills: dep*artu*r 16·5 mills: Def*erence* Latt*itud* 11′ [*margin:* 49=11[4]]: Lat*itude* By observat*ion* of the ☼[5] at none 49°11′: Def*erence* Longit*ud* 24′: Long*itud* 14°54′: Long*itud* from the Lizard 3°36′: meridian distance from the Lizard 142·3 mills west. [*margin: fingerpost*] Much wind this Eveinge at West & at North.

[18] **1669 October: *Sweepstakes* at Sea in the Lat*itud* 48°36′ N**
4
Beinge Munday[6] Blowinge weather and Raine wind at WNW and a great sea: wee lay atry[7] under my mainsaile and handed[8] my head sailes. Course made Good from Sunday none till today at none By Judgment SBW 4°45′ west: Distance Sailed 36·5 mills: departure 10 mills: Def*erence* of Lat*itud* 35′: Lat*itud* by accounte 48°36′: Long*itud* 14°39′·6: defe*rence* 15′·4: Lo*ngitud* Li*zard* 3°51′·4: meridian dist*ance* from the Lizard 152·3 mills west. Last night I had one of my fore shrouds Broke & Splet my fore topsaile and store [tore] severall Ropes apeeces for they weer ould: it Blow hard this afternone: I had cout op [cut up] seavrall fadams a bad[9] Ropes for uses as for Strops and takells. At Six aclocke this after none I set my Courses & refed[10] my fore Course: wind at NW: Cours SW: a stout gale and a great sea I had sum water between deckes wee towed[1] our shipp much. This night at 12 aclo*cke* a great Shipp pased By mee to the E*ast*wards.

5
Beinge Tusday hassy Gusty weather wind at NW and at 10 aclocke SW: I plyed to the southward with all inde*vor*: Gusty weather to night. Course made Good last 24 howers

[1] Date and first word in red ink.

[2] In red ink.

[3] Date and first word in red ink.

[4] In red ink.

[5] In red ink.

[6] Headline and '4 Being Munday' in red ink.

[7] Try: to lie-to in a gale and by a balance of the sails keep the ship's head to the sea, with as much sail as could safely be carried, to prevent the ship rolling to windward. While trying a ship was said to be atry.

[8] To hand a sail is to furl it, i.e. secure it to the yard arm.

[9] When ropes were worn in places where they rubbed it was the practice to cut them up and use the good parts for tackles, strops etc.

[10] Reefing is the act of reducing the sail area by hauling it up to the yard and securing it with reef points, or alternatively by taking up a portion of the sail from the bottom and again securing it with reef points. The courses are the sails hanging from the lower yards of the ship, i.e. the main-sail the fore-sail and the mizen.

[11] Tew: to beat, flog, thrash, belabour; the ship took a pounding from the sea. *NOED.*

from munday none till to day at none South: distance sailed 40 mills: dep*artur* nots [nothing]: Def*erence* Latt*itud* 40′: Latt*itud* By Judgment 47°56′: and Longittud west 14°39′·6: Def*erence* 00°00′: Long*itud* west from the Lizard 3°51′·4: meridian distance west 152·3 mills. Hassy Cloudy weather all night and gusty we tacked[1] 4 times this night.

6

Beinge Wedensday Gusty weather this 24 howers wind betwen the SW and NW vearable: we handed Boathes topsailes. I Cut out more new riginge to day: a greate sea Com out of the NW. Course made from tusday at none till today at none SWBS 4°45′ west: distance sailed 22·1 mills: dep*artu*r 13·8 mills: Def*erence* Latt*itud* 17′·3: Lat*itud* By Judg*ment* 47°39′: Long*itud* 14°18′·9: Def*erence* 20′·7: Longit*ud* from the Lizard 4°12′·1: meredian dist*ance* 166·1 mil.

[19] **October the *Seepstakes* at Sea outward B*ound* in N Lat*itud* 46°29′N**

7

Beinge Thursday Blowinge hassy weather wind at NW a great sea Cam out of the NW: the Shipp Rowled very much as put mee dout Sumthinge would give way: I lay By from 12 at night till 6 this morninge then Stered away SW. Master mosely[2] tooke his leave of mee and steared a nore westerly Course:[3] the Pinke keeps mee [company][4] But Carries an eassy Saile She lost her two Courses and fore Topsaile the other night By a gust. Wee shipped seaverall seas to day. Course made Good By Judgment from wedensday none till to day at none South: distance Sailed 70 mills: Departur nots [nothing]: Def*erence* Lat*itud* 1°10′: Latt*itud* By Judg*ment* 46°29′: Long*itud* 14°18′·9: Def*erence* 00°00′: Long*itud* from the Lizard 4°12′·1: Meridian Dist*ance* 166·1 mills. Wind this afternone Came to the NNW a Stife gale: wee stered SW Southerly.

8

Beinge friday hassy Gusty weather & raine. Course made from Thursday none till to day at none SWBS 5° westerly: distance Sailed 106 mills: depart*ur* 66·5 mills: Def*erence* Latt*itud* 1°22′·2: Lat*itud* By Judg*men*t 45°07′: Long*itud* 12°44′·9: Def*erence* 1°34′: Long*itud* from the Lizard 5°46′·1: meridian dist*ance* 232·6. Course SBW halfe westherly all night.

[1] To tack is to alter course changing the wind from one side to the other with the ship's head passing through the wind. The tack is the rope used to haul down the clew (lower corner) of the sail. The tacks were said to be close aboard when the clew was hauled down tight in a forward position and at the same time the sheets (on the other lower corner) were hauled tight aft, so that the ship could head as close to the wind as possible: with the starboard tacks aboard meant the clew was hauled down on the starboard side thus the wind was on the starboard side and the ship was said to be on the starboard tack.

[2] Presumably this refers to a vessel that had been keeping company with Narbrough in *Sweepstakes*.

[3] Wood, BL, MS 3833, f. 3v: 'Bound for Jamaco.' Jamaica had been an English colony since its capture from the Spanish by the expedition led by William Penn, General at Sea, and Colonel Robert Venables, sent out as part of Oliver Cromwell's Western Design. The expedition failed in its main objective, which was to take Santo Domingo.

[4] Original has an extension mark over the final 'e' of 'mee' to indicate something should be inserted. 'Company' seems appropriate, but it might mean 'with mee'.

9

Beinge Satterday hassy weather wind at NNE a Stife Gale & a great sea. From friday at none till to day at none I made my Course SBW 6° westerly: Distance sailed 140 mills: Departuer 41·2 mills: Def*erence* Lat*itud* 2°13′: Latt*itud* by Observation ☼ 42°54′: Longit*ud* 11°47′·5: Def*erence* 57′·4: Longit*ud* from the Lizard 6°43′·5: meridian distance Wind this Even*ing* at NE 273·8 mills] a stif gale I stere SBW: the [ship] Rowle much.
I Punesht my Coppers mate [*blank*][1] at the mainGeres.[2]

[20] **October 1669 *Sweepstakes* at Sea Bound out 40° 23′ N**

10

Beinge Sunday hassey weather: wind at NE a Stife gale. Cours mad from Satterday at none till to day at none SBW: Distane Sailed 154 mills: Departure 30: def*erence* Lat*itud* 2°31′: Latt*itud* By Judgment 40°23′: Long*itud* 11°17′·3: Def*erence* 40′·2: Long*itud* from the Lizard 7°26′·7: meridian Dist*ance* 303·8 mills. Wee Steere SBW Be [by] the Compass. I loss a great deale of time By the pinke for She sailes heavie:[3] I goe away with only my fore saile and main topsaile and Sprite Saile.

11

Beinge munday Cloudy weather wind at NE. From Sunday non till to day at none I made my Course SBW: Dist*ance* Sailed 140 mills: Depar*tur* 27·2 mills: D*efference*[4] Latt*itud*

[1] Cooper's mate? Space left blank in original for the man's name.

[2] The Manger is a framework of planks built either round the hawse hole or across the ship directly abaft it, before or abaft the foremast, to prevent the water which comes in at the hawse hole (the holes cut in this side of the ship on either side of the stem through which the cables pass when the ship is at anchor) in heavy weather running along the deck and down into the hold. The water is returned to the sea through the manger scuppers. The punishment is not specified, it is unlikely to have been corporal punishment, flogging, in view of the head-room and space between decks but was probably either confinement in the manger, a spell in the stocks or some other form of exemplary punishment. Punishment in the Restoration navy was not as harsh as it later became. It was regulated by The Articles of War. Among other things they called for: Art. XVII death for desertion; various other crimes and sentences were specified ending with Art. XXXIII 'All other Faults, Misdeameanors, and disorders committed at sea, not mentioned in this Act shall be punished according to the Laws and Customs in such cases used at Sea.' This act was later augmented by ten additional orders in 1663, which provided punishments for lesser crimes and gave captains more discretion. A general background to traditional punishment at sea with specific crimes and punishments is given in Twiss, *Black Book*, I, pp. 67, 105 129; II, pp. 225–6, 447, 457; III, pp. 19, 433–59, 511; IV, pp. 57, 317, 431. See also, Davies, *Gentlemen*, pp. 95–8; Davies, *Pepys's Navy*, pp. 160–61. Nathaniel Butler in *Dialogues*, c. 1634, lists the punishments then in use. They might be one of the following. Punishment at the capstan (secured to the capstan with arms outstretched and weights hung round the neck) or in the bilboes, irons or stocks Ducking at the main yard arm secured the malefactor by 'a rope fastened under his arms and about his middle and under his breech' and then had him hoisted 'to the end of yard and from thence is violently let fall into the sea, sometimes several times one after another'. Butler further noted 'drawing under the keel of the ship which is termed keel raking. And while he is thus underwater a great gun is fired right over his head' and in the case of murders, mutinies and the like the penalty was 'hanging to death' at the yard. See Perrin, *Boteler's Dialogues*, pp. 17–19. Sir Thomas Allen recorded in his journals for 1661–78 the punishements of 2 hours clapped in the stocks for striking a Lieutenant; 20 lashes for theft; ducking and towing ashore for seditious and mutinous words. A rogue 'that stole my salmon' was whipped, and, of three men who committed theft ashore, one received 5 lashes alongside three ships, another was ducked three times, and the last (who also struck a midshipman) given 10 lashes alongside three ships. Anderson, *Journals*, I, pp. 6, 69, 121, 241; II, p. 206.

[3] The pink could not keep up with the *Sweepstakes*.

[4] Original has 'Dep:'

2°17′: Latt*itud* 38°06′: Longitud 10°31′·9: Def*erence* 00°35′·4: Longit*ud* from the Lizard 08°02′·1: Mer*idian* D*istance* 331 mills. My Purser Essued [issued] Cloathes to the Seamen for their occations.[1] Faier weather all night: Course SBW: a stife gale at NE.

12
Being Tusday faier weather wind at NE a stife gale this morninge I spake with a London pinke Bond for Cannary.[2] Cours mad from munday none till to day at none SBW: Distance Run 141 mills: Depart*ur* 27·5 mills: Def*erence* Latt*itud* 2°18′: Latt*itud* at none By observation of the Sunn 35°48′: Long*itud* 09°56′·4: Def*erence* 35′·5: Long*itud* from the Lizard 8°37′·6: merid*ian* Dist*ance* 358·5 mills. Faier weather this afternone wind at N a fresh gale. The London pinke keeps mee Company: Course Beinge now South and Soe Steared all night. This day Done Carolus Asked mee If I had any wine for him I answered him I know noe wine to be in the Ship but Brandy: he said the Shipp must goe to Medera.

[21] **October *Sweepstakes* at Sea in the Latt*itud* of 33°35′ N Lat*itud***
13
Beinge Weddensday hassy weather wind at N & Came NNW: this morninge at 6 aclocke I steared away SBW: Smoath water and a fresh gale. Course mad this last 24 howers South 6°30′ westerly: Distance Sailed 134 mills: Departuer 15·5 mills: Latt*itud* at none By Judgment 33°35′: def*erence* 2°13′: Long*itud* 9°38′: Def*erence* 18′·5: Longit*ud* west from the Lizard at none 08°56′: Meridian distance in mills 374: and in Leagus 124 [and] 2 mills. Course By Compass South a lettle westerly. Hassy weather at none I Could not observe nor at night the starr.[3]
This day at 12 aclocke at none I saw Porto Santo:[4] it Bare South of mee: I judge about ten Leagus Distance: wind at NNW a stife gale. Course By Compase at that time was SBW But I alltered it & steared SSW to Goe aweather of P*orto San*to for mederia Iseland.[5] Don Carlous desiered me by all means to Put into Mederea. Porte to Santo makes wen it is South of you 10 leagus in this forme[6] & 4 leagus SSE.[7] At 1 aclocke I saw mederiea about 12 leagus SW from mee it makes in this maner[8]
I steared SW till I Came in fower leagus of it at 5 a Clocke: the Southernmost Point Beares S of mee: I tacked and stood of[f] and handed Boath my topsailes and laid my fore saile to the mast:[9] faier weather all night wind at NW. Att 5 aclocke in the morninge I Bore away to Goe in Betwen the Deserts[10] and the Island.

[1] *Issued* is hardly the right word here since ready-made clothes, slops, were sold to the ship's company by the Purser. The sale was regulated by the Lord High Admiral who laid down the prices that might be charged for them against the man's pay while the Purser got 12d in the pound for issuing them and keeping the accounts. James *Memoirs*, pp. 75–9. The order requiring men to have been onboard for two months before slops could be sold to them had been rescinded in November 1664. Ibid., pp. 114–15.
[2] Canary Islands (28°N, 15°30′W). Wood, MS 3833, f. 3v: 'Laden with corne'.
[3] This would be the Pole Star from which Latitude could be obtained. See Navigation, pp. pp. 62–73. For the Pole Star, see pp. 65, 70
[4] Ilha do Porto Santo (33°03′N, 16°20′W).
[5] Ilha da Madeira (32°45′N, 17°00′W).
[6] Small view of the coast inserted at this point.
[7] Small view of the coast inserted at this point.
[8] Small view of the coast inserted at this point.
[9] Furled both topsails and backed the fore sail, to hold the ship still in the water during the hours of darkness.
[10] Ilhas Desertas, northern island, Ilhéu Chão (32°35′N, 16°33′W).

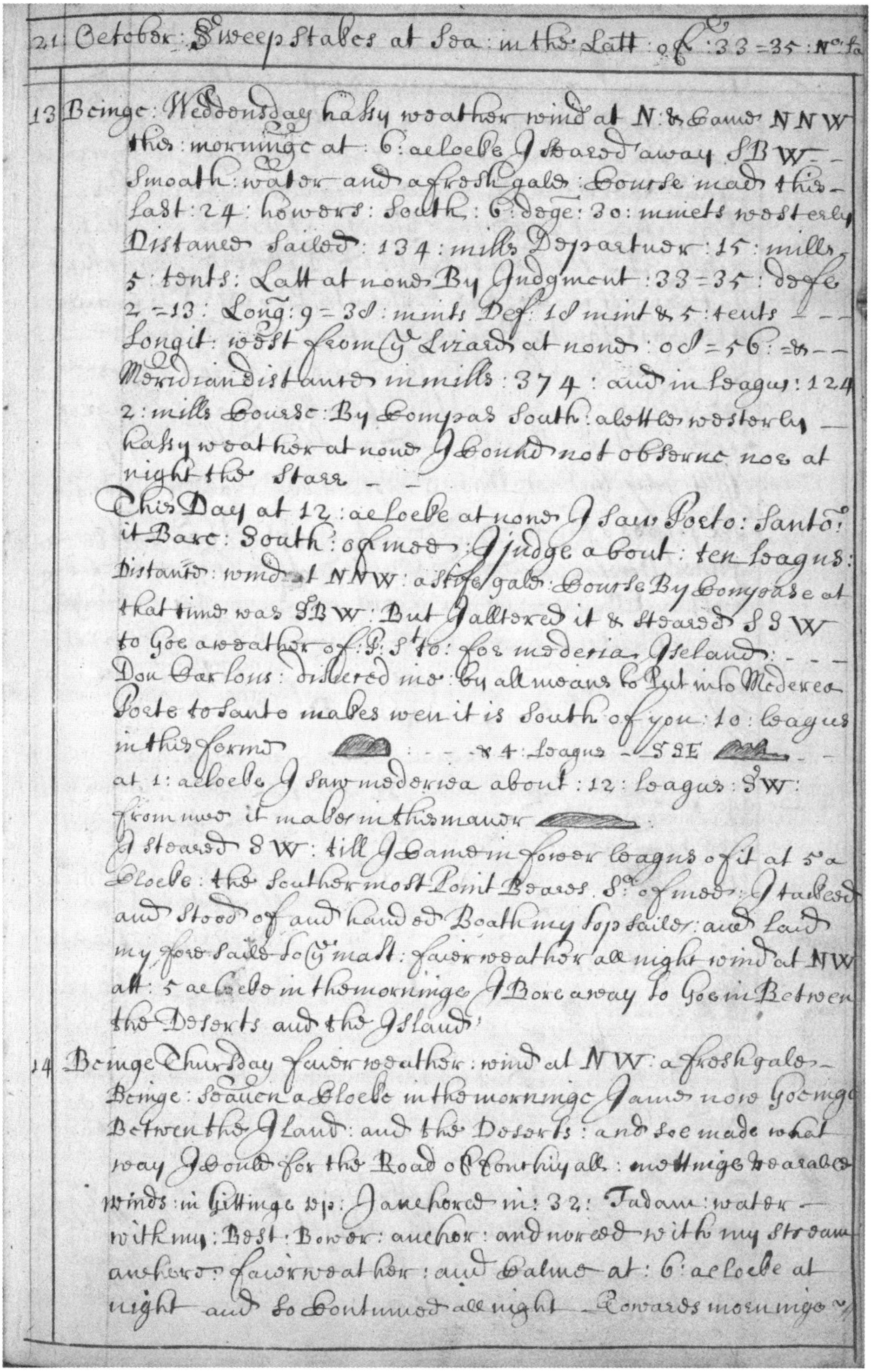

Figure 5. Narbrough's *Sweepstakes* Journal (BL, Add MS 88980A), p. 21. Courtesy of the Trustees of the British Library.

14

Beinge Thursday faier weather wind at NW a fresh gale. Beinge Seaven a Clocke in the morninge I ame now Goeinge Betwen the Iland and the Deserts: and soe made what way I Could for the Road of fonchiyall:[1] mettnige [meeting] vearable winds in Gittinge up:[2] I anchored in 32 Fadam water with my Best Bower anchor and mored with my stream anchore.[3] Faier weather and Calme at 6 aclocke at night and so Continued all night. Towards morninge [22][4] at my Comeinge to anchor [*margin: anchor symbol*] I sent my Boat ashor to aquainte the Govinour of what I was: and when I anchored I fired nine Gunes: the towne saluted me with seaven: I give five more at my moreinge. I had the Counsill Came aboard of mee: at his Departur I fired five Gunes: at seaven aclock at night: [*margin:* Island Medera] his Name is Richard Pickford.[5] I anchord to the westward: the E Pointe Beares EBS and the west Pointe Beares west: in 32 Fadam. Latt*itud* 32°10′: Longit*ud* from the Liz*ard* 10°01′ wes*t*: Mere*dian* d*istance* 143 Leagus: the Road.[6]

15

Beinge friday faier weather. I gott a Boat ladinge of fresh water a Board and on stowed [unstowed] the Shipp to Gitt my Gunnes Downe in the hould:[7] and sent to gitt six pipes of wine filled. At night I had gott fower gunes Dowen and had Calked the Starboard sid with out Board. Befor night at Eveinge the English marchants Came aboard mee at their departur I fired 5 gunnes. Faier *wea*ther all night: I left worke Beinge night and Darke.

16

Beinge Satterday faier weather. I stroke Gunns into the hould[8] and Calked the larboard sid with out Board. This afternone I had Six pips of wine [*margin:*18 milray a pipe] Came

[1] Funchal (32°39′N,16°54′W).

[2] Wood, BL, MS 3833, f. 4v: 'at 11 wee was Becalmed The High Land Takeing away our Wind. Then we hoysed out our Boates and Towed the Ship.'

[3] The anchors normally used were referred to as Best Bower and Small Bower, the former normally stowed on the starboard side. The stream anchor was smaller, about one third the size of the bower anchors.

[4] There is no running header at the top of the page in original. Narbrough entered the next line of the continuing entry into the ruled-off header space.

[5] Pickford; variant Picford.

[6] The position refers to that of the Road or anchorage. Wood, BL, MS 3833, f. 4v: noted 'There is Thre Castles Belongeth to The Towne one is Seated att the East end of the Towne haveing 6 Small guns and one at the West End which is of the gratest forse haveing 14 guns wherof 4 are Culverin The Rest Minions the Third is Seated on a Rock a Musquett Shott from the Shore haveing 5 guns. The Landing Place is under The Grate Castle wher allso is the fresh Watter. There is in the Towne 5 Churches 2 Nuneryes a Collidge of Jesueits and one friery: a frotnight Before we came There was a Generall Muster made of all the Men in the Island & There was found 2400 fighting Men. There is in the Towne and Island 12 famellyes of English. The fiute [fruit] of This Island is Swete and Soure Oringes Leamons Dates figes Wallnutts Chesnuts Pomgarnets Plantons Bannanus Oynones but The Chefe is the Grapes where with The [they] make 20,000 Pipes of Wine a yeare: which the [they] Vent [sell] in the West India whereof Barbados hath 10000 pipes a yeare: On the Disards is Some few famellyes of Portogauls which Live By fishing and a Little Cotton. The Island of Porta Sancto is Inhabeted allsoe by Portugauls But Live in grate feare of The Salle Men of War [Moroccan pirate vessels out of Sallee, now Rabat].' The pipe is generally reckoned as 2 hogsheads or 105 imperial gallons, *NOED.*

[7] This would make more room for the sailors on the main deck and improve the stability of the ship by lowering the centre of gravity. Also, but probably not fully appreciated at the time, by taking a large portion of the iron onboard further from the compasses it would improve their reliability.

[8] Eleven guns were struck down according to Richard Williams, see below, p. 612.

a Board: Cost 18 mill Raye[1] the Pipe two of them Beinge in quarter Caske Cost 800 Rayes more: Laid out more for Refreshments 12: [*margin: fingerpost*] Mills & Eighty Rayes in orangis & lemons and onjon[2] to M^r R Picford: the wine Comes to 116:720 Ra:
And the other things Comes to 12:080
128:800

This Eveinge at 8 aclocke I waied [*margin*: anchor symbol] and Stood away SW: lettle wind all night. I wrote a letter to Mr Wren to accquainte him of my Beinge here and Saileinge: I left it with the Connsell: at his going of[f] I fired five Gunes and so fared well.

[23] **October 16 *Sweepstakes* in Maderia Roads awayinge**
This Eveinge Don Carlos was Eleuiated with hereinge made ashore that Put him into a Rageinge Passion at his Comeing a Board that he wished the Shipp and men all at the Devell and that the Kinge had Trappaned him to Be sould at Barbados and sevrall other Exspressions hee Euse one [on] the quarter de*ck* that he would be hanged Before ever he would serve the Kinge or Duke for they were not of that honor he toake them to Be of: this was in the hereinge of Leuet*enant* Armiger & Master hiett[3] & Mr Wood[4] and others of the officers – as mats [mates]. Also he Said he would Spoile the voiage in heareinge of Mr Solomon franco.[5]

17
Beinge Sunday faier weather wind at NW a Small Gale.
Course By Compass SW: I made all the Saile I could. This Day at none the west Pointe of the Island of mederia Bare N of mee Distance about Eight Leagus or 24 mills. That Place is in Latt*itud* 31°56′ and in Longitud 08°19′[6]and in Long*itud* from the Lizard 10°15′ and Def*erence* of Meridians 441 mills or 147 leagus. This day at 12 aclocke I was

[1] This is a 'milréis' see above, p. xx. Thus the pipe cost £6 2s 9d. One price for claret in England in 1669 was £4 3s 4d per tierce (one third of a pipe) making it £12 10s 0d per pipe, which seems to be reasonably representative of prices at the time. Thorold Rogers, *History of Agriculture*, p. 448.

[2] Onions. It was well known at this time that oranges and lemons were a very effective antiscorbutic, and that fresh vegetables were good to refresh the crew. Onions, when eaten raw, are an antiscorbutic as well, but it is probable that they were taken on board as fresh vegetables, with a reasonable hope that they would keep, rather than for their antiscorbutic effect. Vasco da Gama, on 7 Jan. 1499, having received a message of welcome and a present of sheep from the King of Malindi, states in his journal: 'The Captain in turn sent a man back to shore with these messengers who had come out, to return the following day with oranges, that were much desired by the sick that we carried' who were suffering from scurvy. Drake had used thyme, marjoram, alexander and scurvy grass to refresh his men in the Strait of Magellan. In 1601 Sir James Lankaster had taken bottles of lemon juice to sea with him on a voyage to the East Indies to prevent scurvy, and there were many other instances of the use of anti-scorbutics but it was not until the first 35 years of the 20th century that lack of vitamin C, ascorbutic acid, was identified as the cause of the problem. See, Carpenter, *History of Scurvy*, pp. 1, 2, 13, 17, 173–97; Glenn, *En Nomes de Deus*, p. 108.

[3] Abraham Hyatt, the Master; see, TNA ADM 39/2510.

[4] This is probably Mr. John Wood, who would appear to have been a volunteer, as opposed to Giles Wood the Master's mate, since the mates are referred to next.

[5] Solomon Franco was the Jewish merchant embarked in the *Batchelour*, who was presumably visiting the *Sweepstakes* at the time.

[6] This is from west end of São Miguel; variant St Michell in the Açores; variant Asores. Tapp, *Seaman's Kalender*, p. 173, gives Madera Islands (31°29′N, 8°11′W); Funchal is not included in the table.

in the Lattitud of 31°38′: By Judgment and in Longet*ud* from the west Parte of Sainte Michells Iland one of the Asores 8°19′: and in Long*itud* from the Lizard 10°15′: merid*ian* distance 441 mills or 147 leagus west. Faier weather this afternone: Course By Compase SW: Calm to night.

18
Beinge Munday faier weather this morninge Lettle wind at WNW: Course By Compas SW. From yesterday at non till to Day at [noon] my Course is SW: Distance Sailed 24 mills: 17 mills Departur: Def*erence* Latt*itud* 17′: Lat*itud* By oBservation of the Sune 31°21′: Long*itud* 8°00′: Def*erence* 0°19′: Long*itud* from the Lizard 10°34′: Meridian Distance from the [Lizard] 458 mills or one hundered feivety two leagus 2 mills. Capt*ain* Fleminge & Sinor franco Came aboard the Spanard[1] was reconceilled with hiem selfe. A fresh gale at N this night and sume Raine.

[24] **October 19 the *Sweepstakes* at Seas Lat*itud* 29°46′N**
19
Beinge Tusday faier weather: wind at NBE a Stife Gale: Course By Compass SSW. Cours mad from Munday none till today at noe South 19°45′ west: Distance Sailed 101 mille: Departure 34 mills: Def*erence* of Latt*itud* 1°35′: Latt*itud* at none By observation of the ☼ 29°46′: Long*itud* 7°20′: Def*erence* 40′: Depart*ur* from the west parte of mederia 51 mills or 17 Leagus: and Longitud from Mederia 59′. The Pinke in Company and fresh gale NBE.
This day I meded [mended] my sailes as the Rats had eaten in the[2] Store Roume [room]: I had all the Doogs in the Shipp wormed. This day in the Eveinge I pased By the Island of Palme[3] faier weather & a fresh gale at N.

20
Beinge Weddensday faier weather wind at NBE a fine Gale Course By Compase SSW. This morninge tooke an amplytud:[4] But lettle or no variations.[5] Cours this last 24 houers SSW: Distance Sailed 124 mills: Departur 48 mills: Deference of Lat*itud* 1°55′: Latt*itud* By observinge the ☼ 27°51′: Longit*ud* 6°25′: Def*erence* 55′: Departur from mederia 99 mills or 33 leagus: and Long*itud* 1°54. This morninge I muster men & have 80 in my ships Company and Six Spare which are not entered:[6] I Read all the artickells ovier to them.[7] Faier weather a fresh gale: Course alltered at none to the SBW: the Ile of Fera[8] Beares E distance 9 leagus.

[1] Don Carlos.
[2] The word 'the' repeated in the original.
[3] La Palma, Islas Canarias (28°40′N, 17°50′W); variant Palme.
[4] See above, p. 64.
[5] Wood, BL, MS 3833, f. 5r: 'This Morning I saw allsoe the Peack of Tenerif The Highest Mountane in the World: it Bore East from us Aboute 50 Leagues.'
[6] Those not entered would be Don Carlos and his two servants and probably the volunteers.
[7] These are the *Articles of War* of Charles II (13° Car. 11 St.1 c. 9 (1661), which were required to be read to ship's companies; see above p. 132, n. 2; p. 150, n. 2.
[8] This was El Hierro (27°45′N, 18°00′W); variant Fera;. It is called Fierro in Tapp, *Sea-Mans Kalender*, p. 169, and shown on charts as Ferro or Fierro.

21
Beinge Thursday faier weather wind at NBE a fine gal. This moringe I tooke an Azamuth ☼ at 17°50′ All*titude* E in the Latt*itud* 26°16′N Declination ☼ 14°20′ S: I find my true Az*imuth* to Be 116°40′ from the N meridian and my Magnett Az*imuth* ☼ By my Compass to Be 114°58′ from the N meridian: By which I find my variation of my Compass to Be 1°42′ E.

[25] October 21 *Sweepstakes* at Sea in Latt*itud* 25°58′N Lo*ngitud* 6°11′
21[1]
Beinge Thursday faier wind at[2] NBE a fine gale: Course By Compas SBW southerly. Cours made from weden*sday* None till to day at none 8° S 6° west: distance Rune 114 mills: Depart*ur* 12 mills: Def*erence* Latt*itud* 1°53′: Latt*itud* By account 25°58′: & Long*itud* 6°11′: Def*erence* 14′: Long*itud* from mederia 2°08′: Meridian dist*ance* from the west Ende of mederia 111 mills or 37 Leagus. Hassy weather this after none: Course By Compass SBW all night. Latt*itud* at 12 aclocke at night Observed By the N ☆ 25°10′.

22
Beinge Friday Good weather wind at NBE a fine gale: Course By Compase¸ SBW. From Thursday none till Today at none Course madSBW: distance saielled 90 mills: Departuer 17·5: Def*erence* Latt*itud* By obser*vation* 1°28′: Latt*itud* Per OB*servation* ☼ 24°30′: Long*itud* 5°51′·5: Def*erence* 19′·5: Long*itud* from mederia 2°27′·5: Meridian distance 128·5 mills: & in Leag*us* 42 and 2·5 mills. No Ammpl*itude* nor Az*imuth* of the ☼ this morninge Beinge hassy Horzion. Little wind this afternone: a great homeinge sea[3] come out of the NNW. I Brought my ould sailes to the yards[4] faier weather all night.

23
Beinge Satterday faier weather wind at NBE a fine gale: Coures By Compass SBW: distane sailed from friday none till to Day non 86 mills: departur 17 mills: Def*erence* Latt*itud* 1°24′: Latt*itud* By observations of the sun 23°06′: Def*erence* Long*itud* 18′·5: Long*itud* 5°33′: Longitud from mederia 2°46′: Merid*ian* distane 145·5 mills and in leags 48 & 1 mill ½. Faier weather the wind vears to the NE. I Crosed the Tropicke of Cancer at 7 aclocke this morninge with all my men in health: I Bless the Allmighty God for it.

24
Beinge Sunday faier weather wind NEBE a fine gale. Course mak from [Satterday] till [to] day at none by Compas SbW westerly: true Course mad S 19° west: distance Sailed 120 mills: departur 39 mills: Def*erence* of Latt*itud* 1°53′: Latt*itud* by observation of the ☼ 21°13′: Long*itud* 4°51′: Def*erence* 00°42′: Long*itud* from Mederia 3°30′: meridian distance 184·5 and in leagus 61 [and] 1·5 mill. Faier weather this after[none] wind at NEBE a Stife gale: Cours SBW.

[1] Narbrough inserted the days's date again here, presumably to make it clear that the entry carried over on to the beginning of f. 25.
[2] 'at' repeated in the original.
[3] The meaning of this is not clear but it probably means a steep or tumbling sea.
[4] Changed the sails for the old ones.

[26] **October *Sweepstakes* at Sea in the Latt*itud* N18°51′.**
25
Beinge Munday faier weather wind at NEBE a fine gale: Course by Compass SBW: But Course mad good last 24 howers S 15° west: distance Sailed 147 Mills: departur 38·5: Def*erence* Latt*itud* 2°22′: Latt*itud* per observation ☼ 18°51′: Longit*ud* 4°10′·5: Def*erence* Longitud 40′·5: Longitud from the west End of mederia 4°10′·5: Meridian distance 222·5 Mills or leagus 74·5. I tooke an amplitud at ☼ risinge But no variation of the Compass a fresh gale this afternone at NNE and ENE. This day I cast a but of beare haveinge had Complant by my seamen: and servaied by My Mast*er* and found it Stunke and judg itt one fitt [unfit] to Drinke.[1] This day I saw flieing fis[h] beinge the first fish sene since our Comeinge out of the downes. Att 4 aclocke this after[noon] I stered South.

26
Being Tusday faier weather this forenone a fresh gale at NEBE: Course By Compas from munday at none till 4 aclocke SBW: and from fower till 6 in the moring South: from Six to 8 South west & from 8 to 12 west be South: wind all this time at NE. These severall Courses was Because I would fale with the Island of Salt or Sall.[2] Course made true from Mounday none till to day at none S 21°20′ west: distance Sailed 140 mills: Departur 50 mills: Def*erence* Latt*itud* 2°09′: Latt*itud* Per observation of the ☼ 16°42′ Longitud 3°17′·5: Def*erence* 53′: Longitud from Mederia 5°03′·5: Meridian distance 272·5 mills: or in Leagus 90 le*agus* & 2·5 mills. Faier weather this afternone: Course West till 4 aclocke then Lay By to Stay for the Pinke: I furled my main Saile and fore Topsaile: I Lay By with my head to the N ward till five aclocke next morninge.

[27] **October *Sweepstakes* at Sea neare the Island of Sall.**
27
Beinge Weddes*day* hassy weather this morninge at 6 aclocke I bore away west with all the saile I Could make wind at NE a fresh gale: att 9 aclocke I made the Island of Sall: it Bare west of mee distance about 5 leagus: then I steared SW for the Island of Bonavest.[3] I make the Island of Sall to ly in the Latt*itud* of 16°40′ N and in Longegutud from the west part of St Michell 1°48′: Longitud from Mederia 6°35′·5: Meridian distance from mederia the west Parte of it [*margin: fingerpost*] to the East Parte of Sall 361 Mills or leagus 120 and 1 m*ill*: Longitud from the Lizard 16°45′·5 and Meridian dis*tance* 802 Mills or 267 Leagus 1 Mille: As I make. W Sall Makes went it Beare west of you in one Round homack [*margin: fingerpost*] as thus[4] but when you Com neare it it Shows it sellfe in three homacckes and Low land to the Southward of it. [*margin: fingerpost*] Course made from Tusday at none till to day at none WSW 7°37′ west: distance Sailed 88 mills: dep*artur* 84·6: Def*erence* Lat*itud* 22′: Lat*itud* By account at none 16°20′: Long*itud* 1°32′.
[*margin*: Long. 1°45′ meridia*n* dis 357 : or leagus 119. Lzard 798 or in leagus 266[5]].This day at 2 aclocke Bonavest Bare South of me distance about 5 leagus: the westermost Pointe

[1] A foul butt of beer was cast overboard.
[2] Sal (16°46′N, 22°53′W), in the Cape Verde Islands.
[3] Boa Vista (16°05′N, 22°50′W).
[4] Small view of the coast inserted at this point.
[5] 357 and 798 distance figures are in miles.

bare SWBS distance about[1] seaven leagus.[2] The Eveinge I passed By itt to the Southward of it and Stood for May. Cours S & SBW this night and I Sum times I lay By for their lye a rock in the way: wind at ENE a fine gale

28
Beinge Thursday faier weather wind at ENE a stife gale. This morninge I Swaw [saw] the Island of may[3] it Bare [*margin:* Lat 14°40′, Long.1°25] South Be [by] West of mee. I halled in for the Road and anchored in a 11 fadam water Sandy [*margin: anchor symbol*] ground about halfe a mille from the shore: the [*margin:* Fro lizard is in Longitud 17°05′, merid: 376 , in lea*gus*: 125, Lizard: 817 or leagus 272: 1/3] northarmost [pointe] of the Road bore NNW ½ a ponte weserly: the Southermost Pointe bear from me SE. I wanted Salt which occasioned my Comeinge here this day I goot Sum aboard with a great deale of deffeculty[4] and goot Good Store of fish with my Saine:[5] as Mullett and Cavalles and Silver fish and Petter fish.

[28] **October the *Sweepstakes* in Isle may Roade.**
29
Beinge Friday faier weather this Morninge wind at NE a fine Gale. This morninge I Sent my Boat ashore and Goot more fish and Bought Sum goats of the Islanders: They are all Black People my men Killed Sum with their Doogs:[6] my Seamen refreshed them selvfe finely here. This day att none a Shipp Passed by in Sight to the South*ward*: at 2 aclocke we saw to the nor*th*ward a fleet of Shipps about twenty Six Saile: They steared for St Jago:[7] I mad[8] them to Be the Portygall Brasell fleet. I fired a gun & goot my Boat of[f] which was ashore a fishinge. Noe fresh water here nor wood which I was informed was to Be had here. This Eveinge I gott Eight Cowes aboard which of the Govonor Cost Six Peeces of Eight apeece:[9] Exelent fat Beast and seaven goats this Govonour is a Blackman & so are all the Rest. This night twelf aclocke I waied and went for St Jagoe: at 12 at none next day I anchored: faier weather all ni*ght*.

[1] The word 'about' repeated in the original.

[2] Wood, BL, MS 3833, f. 5v: 'Att 2 we Sayled Betwene Sall and Bonevest: att the West Side of Bonevest is good Rideing for Ships Betwixt a Little Rockye Island and The Shore in 10 fadam Water. The Inhabatants are Portegauls and Live by Breading of Cattle and Cotton which they Send To the West India. Ther is alsoe good fresh Watter but not Easylye gott on.'

[3] Maio (15°08′N, 23°12′W), in the Cape Verde Islands.

[4] Wood, BL, MS 3833, f. 5v: 'There gooeth all Wayes a grate Suff a Shore. The Longe Boatt was to fetch Salt which is Their in gratte Aboundance. Their is a Salt Pond 4 Miles Longe. The Heate of the Sun drying The Watter to Salt. The Pond is Close to the Sea Side ... Some of our Men Went into the Country To hunt Wild goatts which is Their 2000 in a flock. This Island is not the Kinges But Some Privett Mans in Portugall. The Inhaba*tants* are all Black: But Speak Portugues.'

[5] Seine fishing net.

[6] Presumably goats not islanders.

[7] São Tiago (15°05′N, 23°35′W), in the Cape Verde Islands.

[8] There is a word crossed out here and 'mad' inserted over it.

[9] The piece of eight, the Spanish *peso* or *piastra*, was the universal currency of Europe and the Western Hemisphere. It was worth 4s 6d (22·5p). McCusker, *Money*, pp. 7–8. The price of a cow was therefore £1 7s 0d. In England at this time the price of beef animals varied, average costs in harvest years 1669, 1670 and 1671 were: Oxen £6 14s 4d, £6 2s 11d, £6 5s 9d, Bullocks, £3 5s 8d, £4 18s 11d, £3 13s 4d, and runts (smaller animals of breeds) £3 16s 3d, £3 6s 1d and £3 12s 0d. Thirsk, *Agrarian History*, pp. 836–7, 893.

30
Beinge Satterday faier weather wind at NEBN a fresh gale. This day at 12 aclocke I anchored at Po*rt* Pram[1] with my Best Bower in tenn fadam water: the E Pointe Bare E and the west Pointe WSW about halfe a mill of[f]. [*margin: drawing of a larger and smaller vessel at anchor*] This Bay Semes to be a good Road but open for any Ennemy: and of Small force two forts about 10 Gunns a Peece and they Stand one [on] the top of two hills which Cannot doe much harme in the Road:[2] her is a fine Revelett [rivulet] of fresh water Clos to the sea sid in the Sandy Bay Good fillinge of Caskes: Lettle wood to be had here. I mored to the westward with my small Bower in a 11 fadam water. When I Cam in I found here a fleet of Portesegalls [Portugals] of 36 Saile bound for Brassell [Brasil]:[3] the Admirall Salluted mee with 5 Gunns I ansewered him with 5:[4] here was Capt*ain* Francis Willkesheir[5] in the *Jeruserlem*:[6] he saluted me with five I ansewered him with three: the vice Admiral gave mee three I ansewered him with three: I saluted the fort with five guns: he gave three I gave one. I sent to aske to watter & wood which was granted mee. I goott aboats ladinge of fresh water aboard to night.[7]

[1] Praia (14°55′N, 23°31′W).

[2] Their guns were too far off to command the roadstead.

[3] As a result of the war with the Dutch and shipping losses in 1647–8, the *Companhia Geral do Comércio de Brasil*, was formed in 1649 with considerable monopolies and other trading advantages in return for an agreement to provide 36 warships to convoy merchant vessels to Brazil. Due to lack of finance and other difficulties, this was formally incorporated in the crown in 1664, and convoys were provided on a reduced scale. In general the fleet sailed annually and took about two to three months to reach Brazil. Boxer, *Portuguese*, pp. 220–27.

[4] Wood, BL, MS 3833, f. 5v, 29 October: 'The Admiral Called *The Father Eternall Being* The Bigest Ship in the Woorld Being in Burden 25 hundred Tun.'

[5] Ibid., f. 6v, has Wiltshire, and Williams Wilshire, see p. 612. He was in fact Francis Wilshaw (see note following), Lieutenant in *Old James* and *Royal James*, 1665; Captain of *Antelope*, 1666, *Concord Merchant*, 1673, and *Forsight*, 1677. He also commanded the East India Ship *Resolution*, 1681–2 and 1683–4. He is recorded as being dead by 1688. Tanner, *Catalogue*, I, p. 425; Farrington, *Biographical Index*, p. 859.

[6] The *Jerusalem* carried stores to Lisbon for Sir Edward Spragg's squadron. 'John Brooks and Edw. Homewood to the Navy Commissioners. The *Golden Hand* became so leaky ... we have been constrained to lighten her to make her tight. The provisions for Sir Edw. Spragg's division I have directed the master of the hoy to put on board the *Jerusalem*.' *CSPD, 1669*, 24 June, Chatham, p. 380. 'Captain Tinker and 2 others to the Navy Commissioners. We estimate the tonnage of anchors, cables, sails etc put on board the *Jerusalem* to be transported to Lisbon for the ships under Sir Edw. Spragg at 50 tons.' Ibid., 8 July, p. 401. 'Thos. Maynard, Consul to the Navy Commissioners. The *Jerusalem* arrived 5 days since, and I have an order from the Prince to get the provisions ashore for the use of the fleet; ... The bill of lading and invoice came not enclosed, as intended, but Capt. Willshire has a bill, which must govern me in giving an acquittance.' *CSPD, 1669*, p. 439, 4/14 Aug. Lisbon. 'Captain Fras Willshaw, of the *Jerusalem*, to the Navy Commissioner. In the absence of Sir Robert Southwell I delivered the letters and stores to Consul Maynard.' Ibid., From Lisbon, 16 Sept, p. 494.

[7] Wood, BL, MS 3833, f. 6v: 'They have 2 Little fortts In This Harbour of 4 Small guns Apeace. The Towne of S[t] Jago is distance from This Harbour 10 Miles. I went from Pryea Thether. The way is all Rockye Mountanus and Barran Land Except one Vallye in which is Seated Some few houses and a Litle Chaple and Heare They Plant Indian Corne Choco Nuts Plantanes Bannanus & This parrish is Called S[t] Martins it is distant from the Towne 3 miles. This Valley is Wattered with a fine Rivelett of Sweet Watter one Mile from the Towne is a Plaine. The Towne is Incompased Rownd with a Rockye Mounttaine. Upon the Mounttane as you goe into the Towne Standeth a faire Castle. But hath Nott more Then 3 guns & They Butt very Small. The Goeing downe from The Castle into the Towne is Very Stepe: Before you Come into the Towne Standeth the Governors house with a forte of Small force Likewise. There is in the Towne Some 300 houses and hath with Portugalls & There Neagros aboute 600 fighting Men. There is a good Rivelet of Watter Runeth Through The Towne. The Harbour before the Towne is nott Safe for any Ship by Reson of the Rocks & foule Ground. I Lay one Night in The Towne: in The Night I went out to See the flames of the Burning Island of fouge [Fogo, 14°54′N, 24°28′W] which is heare Plainly Seane.'

[29] **October *Sweepstakes* att anchor in Port Pray: St Jago.**
31
Beinge Sunday faier weather wind at NNE a fine gale. This morninge I goot a boat of fresh water aboard but Could not fetch any more for the Portegis Boats. Faier wea*ther* all night. This day my men have fresh Befe for alowance.

1 November 1669:
Beinge Munday faier weather wind ENE. This morninge I Rumegd my hould[1] and found 12 Buts of London Beare leaked out wood Bound:[2] I Stayed my foremast & Sett up my Shrouds and Calked my Starbad Sid with out Board[3] & trimed my water Caske. This day Capt*ain* willksheier wayed and Saluted mee with five gunns I answerd him with three: this day a great Parte of the Porttegall fleet wayed they Saluted me with Severall gunns: I ansewered them accordingly. All this day I was fittinge my Shipp for sea with all Exp*e*dition. My men Bought here a great many Coaker nuts [coco-nuts] & such Kind of Refreshinge.

2
Beinge Tusday faier weather: the Rest of the Portegall fleet Sailed. I Sett up my mane Shrouds and Callked my Larboard Side & Stowed my Shipp: one of the Portegall Shipps left an anchor in my Longe Boate about a Thousand waite[4] & three fadam of 8 inch Callble [cable] which I tooke aboard he sailed without takinge notice to fetch itt. Mey boat fetched watter to day.

3
Beinge weddenesday faier weather wind at ENE. I Got most of my Caskes trimed: I fettched mor water. To day I tooke all the Goods out of the *Batcheller* Pinke and Put aboard the *Sweepstakes* and there [three] Caske of salte. My men eat fresh beafe Every day for their allowance.

4
Beinge Thursday faier weather wind at ENE. This Morninge I losed my for top Saile and fired a gun to Saile: I sent my Penas [pinnace] to St Jago town to by oyle [oil] and wood for the Pinke: I Servaied the Pinks Provissions & find it well Cond*ition*: I to [took] a drafte of the Bay:[5] I gott two Boats ladinge of fresh water aboard and had my Shipp well stowed: I sent a letter to M^r wren by the way of Lizbon by a Portegall Mast*er*. This night my Pennas Came aboard againe: Lettle or noe Sugar to be bought in this Island now. I Stayed to gitt a boat of wood which was bought Cost 12 Pecces of Eight and allso I Stayed for Sinor Carrolos.

[1] Rummaged my hold, searched or examined the contents of the hold, probably with a view to restowing and securing it better for sea.

[2] Beer barrels are normally bound with iron hoops, but at this time wood (presumably withy) was also used. The implication is that the leakage was due to the wooden binding, but see below on 30 Nov. (p. 160) where iron-bound casks leaked as well.

[3] Set up the fore stay and the shrouds by taking up any slack with the lanyards through the dead-eyes, and caulked the starboard side out board.

[4] 10 cwt.

[5] Made a chart of the bay. This does not appear to have survived.

[30] **November the *Sweepstakes* at Anchor in Porte Praya**

5

Beinge Friday faier weather wind at ENE a fine gale. This morninge I losed my fore top saile and haled home the seats[1] and gott my Small Bower aboard: I Sent my Penace a shore & Leut*enant* in her to take leave of the Goveuernour and to Breinge of[f] Sen*or* Carrolus: I Sent my Longe Boat ashor and Brought of[f] the wood which Cost 12 Peeces of Eight it is Extreame deare Sinor Carrolus Came of[f] in her: it was about 2 aclocke in the afternone: the People are most Blacke Portegeses & much given to thefeinge [thieving].[2] I would advise all People to be well furneshed with wood befor they come here: for here is none to be had but at great Reats: here is very good fresh water.

At 4 of the Clocke this Afternone I waied: I saluted the Govinore with five Gunns: He Gave mee Three. I Sett my Sailes after my Boats wher in & all things Stowed and Steared away SBE: wind at ENE a fine gale: the *Batcheler* in Company with mee. I Gave the Commander of her Instructions to Keepe mee Company all alonge in this voiage and allso to Mr Solomon franco on Board her and a Booke Called the Sea Attlas[3] which has all drafts & Charts in it thes I delivered to Boath of them in the *Sweepstaks* Great Caben: in Sight of boath my leiuetenants and Mast*er*. [*margin:* A mate to the] So thye went aboard their owne Shipp about Six aclock in the afternone: & one of my Meds men [Midshipmen] Rich*ard* Hadocke[4] By name to be a mate theire.

The Southermost Parte of the Island of St Jago lies in about 14°30′ N Lattitud and Long*itud* 1°11′ E. At Six aclocke this Eveinge the South E Pointe of St Jago Bare N of mee distance a Bout 9 mills. At 8 aclocke I made what Saile I Could wind at ENE a fine gale: Course By Compass SBE. Course mad from the Southeastermost Pointe of the Ile Land of St Jago till Satterday at none S 7°01′ East: dist*ance* Sailed 69 ½ mills: depart*ur* E 8 mills ½: Lat*itud* by acco*unt* 13°21′. The Isle of St Jago the South E End is in Latt*itud* 14°30′ N & in Long*itud* from St Michell 01°11′ E: Long*itud* from the Lizard 17°19′ W: Meridian distance from Lizard 830·3 mills or in Leagus 277: [*blank*] Longitud from med.[5] [*blank*] mer*idi*an

[1] Sheets: ropes fastened to the lower corners of the sail, used to set the sail. To haul home the sheet is to pull it closer to the stern to trim the sail nearer the wind.

[2] Francis Rogers had a similar experience here on 23 Jan. 1701/2, which he described in his journal: 'St. Iago ... a fine fruitful, plentiful island, but hot, most of whose inhabitants are a sort of Banditti (or banished, transported for crimes) or thieves, as an abundance of our Countrymen can witness when they touched there for water or fresh provisions, it being very common with the black Portuguese (they being mostly so here) to whip a gentleman's sword from his side, or hat or wig off his head and show how fast they can run, which healthful gift of theirs proves very beneficial for the saving of many of their bones.' Ingram, *Three Sea Journals*, pp. 147–8.

[3] This was almost certainly *The Sea Atlas or the Water-World, Shewing all the Sea Coasts of ye Known parts of ye Earth &c.*, Henry Doncker, Amsterdam, 1660, which contains a chart of South America from *Cabo St Anthony* to *Caep de Hoorn* and up the west coast to *B.de Tongoy*, showing virtually all the names of features mentioned by Narbrough apart from those to which he himself gave names.

[4] Richard Haddock was most probably the son of Andrew Haddock, brother of Sir Richard Haddock. He was appointed, in 1672, to command the *Thomas and Ann*, fireship, and fought at the Battle of Solebay, and in 1673 to command the *Ann and Christopher*, fireship. In 1677 he commanded the *Quaker*, yacht, and in Pepys's List died in 1678. Charnock, however, says that he went on to command the *Charlotte*, yacht, the *Grafton* and the *Saint Andrew*, in 1690. Tanner, *Catalogue*, I, p. 358; Charnock, *Biographia Navalis*, I, pp. 334–5. The Haddock family had strong maritime connections from the 14th century which continued until the time of the Hanoverian monarchy, providing two Admirals. Davis, *Gentlemen*, pp. 28, 59; *Pepys's Navy*, p. 281.

[5] This could be an abbreviation for Madeira.

[31] **November *Sweepstakes* at Sea Bound to the South**

6

Beinge Satterday hassy weather wind at ENE a fine gale this morninge & all day Course By Compass SBE: I made alle the saile I Could all night and day. Cours made frome Ile St Jago till to day at none South 7°01′ E: distance Run 69½ mills: departur east 8 mills ½: defference Latt*itud* 01°09′: Lat*itud* By account 13°20′. It was hassy & Cloudy all day & night so As I Could nott take any observation neither Azimuth nor Amplitud at ☼ Risinge or Settinge. Longitud from the E Parte of the Ise Land of St Jagoo 00°08′·8 E: Merid*ian* distance E from St Jago 08·5 mills: 2 leagus 2·5 mills: Longit*ud* from St Michells E 1°19′·8 E: Longit*ud* from the Lizard west 17°10′·2 & Meridian Distance from Lizard 821·8 mills or 274 lea*gus*.

7

Beinge Sunday hassy weather wind at ENE a fine gale: this night I had a Popeinge Sea[1] Came out of the South. [*margin:* a tow] This morninge at 8 of the Clocke Captaine flemge Cam aboard me for Canvas But had none.[2] This forenone I toke the *Batcheller* in Towe by his Small bower [cable] and made all the Saile I Could Course by Compas SBE. Course made from Satterday none till to day at none South seaven degres East: distance sailed 106 mills: depart*ur* 13 mills east: Def*erence* Latt*itud* 1°45′: Latt*itud* by account 11°36′: [*margin:* 22′·2] Longit*ud* from St Jago: Longitud from the Lizard 16°56′·8: Meridian distance west 808·8 mills or 269: [*margin:* 'Lo: 1°33′·2] Meridian distance from the Roade of Port Praya in the Iseland St Jago 21·5 mills: or Seaven Leagus ·5 E: and from the Lizard of England 808·8 mills or 269 l*eagus*. My men Eat fresh befe and Broath every day at none.

8

Beinge Munday hassy Cloudy weather this morninge wee had a great Shower of Raine and it Proved Calme it Cast the *Batcheller* Lose:[3] the wind Came to the E and to the ESE and SE this forenone. Course made from Sunday at none till to day at none South 1°2′ west: distan[c]e Sailed 68·5 mills: departur 1·2 mill west: Def*erence* Latt*itud* 01°08′: [*margin:* Long. 1°31′·8] Lat*itud* by account 10°28′: Longitud fro St Jago 20′·8 E: Long*itud* from the Lizard 16°59′·2: Meridian dist*ance* from St Jago 20·3 mills and or leagus 6 & 2·3 mills: Lizard 810 m*ills*.

[32] **D:[4] November 1669 the *Sweepstakes* at Sea in the Latt*itud* 10°03′N**

9

Beinge Tusday hassy Rainey weather wind last 24 houers veareable Betwen the South E and South with Raine and Cailmes: Sumtimes we handed our top Sailes in: Course was

[1] This is probably a 'Poppling sea: Waves in irregular agitation'. Smyth, *Sailors Word-Book*, p. 538. A pooping sea is a sea in which the waves come up from astern and break over the poop, which, since Narbrough was steering SBE with the wind at ENE seems unlikely, and in any event, on that course, a wave from the south would not have broken over the poop.

[2] This would be for canvas to repair his sails.

[3] This will have been because without a wind the two ships would be likely to collide if kept too close together.

[4] On pp. 32–7, Narbrough ruled 2 columns in the left-hand margin and inserted 'D:' in the the outermost as a header for the daily dates entered below. No use was made of the inner column except as a place to write the first 2 or 3 letters of the word 'Beinge'.

to the Southward as neare as I Could ly. Course Made from Munday at none till to day at none South 28°30′ west: distance Sailed 28·5 mills: departur west 13·6 mills: Latt*itud* By observation ☼ 10°03′: Def*erence* 25′: Longit*ud* from St Jago 0°06′·6 E: Longit*ud* west from the Lizard 17°12′·4 west: Meridiane distance from the Lizard 823·6 m*ills* or 274 ½ [leagus]: Meridian dist*ance* from St Jago 6·7 mills East or 2 leagus ·7 [mills]. Wind to day at E a fresh gale Course by Compass SBE: Raine this afternone and much Raine to Night. Longit*ud* from St Michells E 1°17′·6.

10

Beinge wedenssday Cloudy hassy Rainey weather wind veareable Betwen the EBN & ESE: Sumtimes a gale much Thunder and Lightininge. Cours Made from tus*day* none till to day at none South: Distance Sailed 85 Mills: Def*erence* Latt*itud* 1°25′: Latt*itud* By account 8°38′ North: Longit*ud* from St Jago 00°06′·6: Longit*ud* from St Michell 1°17′·6: Long*itud* from the Lizard 17°12′·4 west: Merid*ian* dist*ance* from St Jago 6·7 mills E or 2 leag*us* 0·7 of a mill: Merid*ian* from the Lizard west 823·6 Mills or 274 L*eagus* ½. [*margin: fingerpost*] I tooke an Amplitud at Sun Settinge and found 1°40′ variation to be west: faier weather all night: Cours S°S°E by Compas.

11

Being Thursday hassy Cloudy Rainey to day: wind at E: Course by Compass SSE when I could ly Soe. Course made from none yest*erday* till none to day South 7° East: dist*ance* Sailed 70 mills: depart*ur* 8·5 mills: Def*erence* Lat*itud* 1°09′: Latt*itud* By account 07°29′: Long*itud* from St Jago 15′·3: Def*erence* 8′·7: Long*itud* from St Michells 1°26′·3: Long*itud* west from the Lizard 17°03′·7: Merid*ian* dist*ance* from the Lizard west 815·1 mills: Merid*ian* [distance] from Saint Jago East 15·2 mills or 5 leag*us* 0·2 mills.

[33] **November the *Sweepstakes* at Sea in Latt*itud* 07°07′N 1669**

12

Beinge friday hassy Cloudy weather with Raine winde this 24 howers veareable Betwen the SSE & E a small Gale. Course made Last 24 howers SW: distance Runn 31 mills: depart*ur* 22 mills: Def*erence* Latt*itud* 22′: Lat*itud* By observation of the ☼ 7°07′ N: Meridian distance west from St Jago 6·8 mills or leagus 2 & 0·8 of mill: Long*itud* from St Jago 00°06′·9 west: and Long*itud* from St Michells 01°04′·1 & Longitud from the Lizard 17°25′·9: Meridian dis*tance* west 837·3 Mills.

13

Beinge Satterday faier weather wind at ENE a Small Gale Course By Compase SSE: a great sea Cam out of the South. Course made Good Last 24 houers South: Distance Sailed 60 mills: Def*erence* Latt*itud* 1°00′: Lat*itud* Per Ob*servation* ☼ 6°07′: Meridian dist*ance* from St Jago west 6·8 m*ills* or 2 leagus & 0·8 of a mill: Longit*ud* from St Michells 1°04′·1: Longit*ud* from St Jago 6′·9: Longit*ud* from Lizard west 17°25′·9: Meridian dist*ance* from the Lizard west 837·3 Mills. [*margin:* Azim] This day I tooke an azimuth in the forenone But found [*margin: fingerpost*] noe variation at all: I tooke an Amplytud att Sun [*margin:* Amp] Settinge and had noe variation. Rainey Gusty weather found [*margin: fingerpost*] this night.

14
Beinge Sunday Cloudy weather wind Betwen the EBN & ESE: Sumtimes a Gale and Sumtimes little wind much Raine and Gust to day: a great sea Cam out of the South: Course By Cumpase South SE and Sumtimes South. Course made Good last 24 howers South: distance Sailed 67 mills: dep*artur* 00: Def*erence* Latt*itud* 1°07′: Lat*itud* By ob*servation* ☼ at none 05°00′: Meridian dist*ance* from S[t] Jago 6·8 [mills] or 2 leagus 0·8 of a mill: Longit*ud* from S[t] Miells [Michells] 1°04′·1: Longit*ud* from S[t] Jago 06′·9 west: Longit*ud* from the Lizard 17°25′·9: Meridian distance from the Lizard 837·3 Mills.
This morninge at 7 aclocke I tooke the *Batcheller* in a tow: much Raine & Gusts to Night winds vearable Betwen the ESE and SSE: I lay as neare as I Could.

[34] **November 1669 *Sweepstakes* at Sea Lat*itud* 4°01′:N Long*itud* 18°25′**
15
Beinge Munday Gusty Rainey Cloudy weather wind at SE and at SSE. Course made from Sunday at none till to day at none SW: distance Sailed 83 mills: departur 59 mills: Def*erence* Lat*itud* 00°59′: Lat*itud* P*er* ob*servation* 04°01′: Meridian distance from S[t] Jago west 65·8 mills: or legus 22: Longit*ud* from S[t] Jago 01°06′ west: Long*itud* from S[t] Michells 00°05′ & Longit*ud* from the Lizard 18°25′: Meridiain distance from the Lizard 896·4 Mills: or 299 Leagus west. [*margin: fingerpost* ☼] At 12 aclocke to day I tacked and Stood to the Eward: I lay up EBN: wind at SWBS a Stife gale: at fower of the Clocke the wind veared about to the Southward with a Turnado and Came to the ESE: I Steared away S: at 6 aclocked Cleared up the wind Came to the SE: Course By Compas SBW all night. This Eveinge I Cast of[f] the *Batcheler* from my Stearne.

16
Beinge Tusday Gusty Cloudy weather and Raine wind at SEBE: a Stife gale Sumtimes made me hand[1] my top Sailes seaverall times. This day I Caused to be made three new tar Pawlens for the gratings[2] for the ould ones were nought. I have not one man Sicke aboard. Course made from Munday none till to day att none South 27°30′ west: distance Sailed 46·2 mills: depat*ur* 21·4 [mills]: Def*erence* Lat*itud* 41′: Lat*itud* P*er* obser*vation* ☼ 3°20′ N: Meridian Distance to the westward of S[t] Jago 87·2 mills: or Leagus 29: Long*itud* from S[t] Jago 1°27′·5 west: and in Longit*ud* to day at none 359°43′·5[3] from S[t] Michells: Longitud west from the Lizard 18°46′·5: Meridian distance west from the Lizard 917·9 Mills or 306 leagus.

[*margin: fingerpost* tacke] Wind at SE: at none I Tacked & Stood to the Eward with my Starboard tacke aboard:[4] Course By Compas EBN & ENE. This day wee Caute a Sharke.

[1] Take in or furl the top sails.
[2] Tarpaulin: canvas well covered with paint to make it waterproof, to cover the gratings and prevent the sea entering the lower deck.
[3] This is measured east so that the ship is actually 0°16′·5 west of St Michaels (São Miguel).
[4] See above, p. 149, n. 1. The tack tackle was used for hauling down the tack.

[35] **November 1669 *Sweepstakes* at Sea Latt*itud* 04°00′N**

17

Beinge wedensday Cloudy Gusty Raney weather wind at SE: a Stife gale Sumtimes. I stood all this 24 howers to the Eastward with my Starboard Stacks [tacks] aboard Close haled:[1] Course by Compase EBN & ENE: with the *Batcheler* in Company.

Course Made Last 24 howers N 51°15′ E: distance Sailed By My Loge 64 Mills: departur E 50 Mills: Def*erence* Latt*itud* 40′: Latt*itud* By account at none 04°00′ N: Meridian Distance to the westward of St Jago 37·2 Mills: Longit*ud* west from St Jago 37′: Longitud from St Michells Iseland E 34′. Longit*ud* from the Lizard West 17°56′.

Meridian Distance from the Lizard west 867·9 Mils. Wind at SE: Gusty Rainey weather to night I handed My Top Sailes 3 times to night. Course by Co*mpas* ENE.

18

Beinge Thursday Rainey Cloudy weather wind at SE & at SEBS & at SSE & Sumtimes Calme: Cours By Compas EBN & E. Cours made this Last 24 houers N 63°30′ Ea*ster*ly: distance Sailed 62 Mills: depart*ure* 55·6 mills: Def*erence* Lat*itud* 00°28′·7: Lat*itud* by account 4°28′·7 at none: Meridian Distance from St Jago 18·4 M*ills* E: Longit*ud* from St Jago Eas*t* 19′: Longit*ud* fro St Miells [Michells] E 1°30′ And Long*itud* from the Lzard West 17°: Meridian distance west 812·3 Mills. A Turnado this afternone and much Raine.

19

Beinge friday Raine weather and vearable winds: Course by Compase E & EBN. Course made By judg*ment* from Thursday at none till to day at none ENE: distance Sailed 31 Mills: departur E 28·7 Mills: Def*erence* Latt*itud* 12′: Latt*itud* by account at non 4°41′ N: Meridian distance from St Jago 47·1 Mils E: Longit*ud* from St Jago 48′: Longit*ud* from St Miclls E 1°59′ and Longitud west from the Lizard 16°31′: Meridian distance from the Lizard west 783·6 Mills. I judge here is a Currant [*margin: fingerpost*] Setts to the norward. I saw two Sail to day SE of mee.

[36] **November 1669 the *Sweepstakes* at Sea in N Latt*itud* 4°30′.**

20

Beinge Satterday Raine Gusty weather wind at EBN & at SE & at S: I tacked seaverall times this last 24 houers and handed my top sailes five time: this night at 12 aclocke I lost Company with the *Batcheller* Pinke in Mat [Mate] woods[2] watch. This day I saw a feleet [*sic*] of Shipps of 13 Saile to the Southward of mee: I Plyed to the Southward what I Could they Plyed to the Southward allso. Much Raine today: I filed a tun of fresh water:[3] Course By Compase SSE & SW and sumtims S: Sumtimes winde & sumtimes Calme: I stry[4] much of my Rigeinge & Sailes this weather and Rote all things aboard.[5] Cours made By judgement S 25°5′ west: distance Sailed a 11·8 mills: departur west 5 Mills: def*erence* of Latt*itud* 10′·7: Latt*itud* By account at none 4°30′·3: Meridian distance from St Jago E

[1] Close hauled, as close to the wind as possible.

[2] Giles Wood, the masters mate. He went on to be Second Lieutenant in the *Prince*, 1672, and in the *Royal Charles*, 1673, and was dead by the end of 1688. Tanner. *Catalogue*, I, p. 425.

[3] Collected a tun of rain water to supplement the ship's supply of drinking water.

[4] Stry is an old form of Stroy, to destroy, *NOED*.

[5] This weather destroys the rigging and sails and rots all things on board.

42·1 Mills and Longitud from St Jago 43′: Longitud from St Milles Iseland 01°54′ E: Longitud from the Lizard 16°36′ west: Meridian distance from the Lizard west 788·6 Mills.
I judge a Currante Comes out of the South by reason my Def*erence* of Lat*itud* By observation of the ☼ is much more than the way of the Shipp Can make it. This night much Rain.

21
Beinge Sunday Showerry weather wind vearable at SE & at S and SW: Course By Compase to the Southward as neare as I could ly: lettle wind moust Part of the day and night befor. This morninge I say [saw] a Saile: I fired 2 gunnes to give her notice Shie ansewered mee it was the Pinke which Lost my Company the night before. I Stood to the Eward. This day I Came Close By the Portegall fleet they gave me Chase I bore of[f] to leward of them so they gave over. Cours made N 14°55′ E: distance Sailed 33·8 mils: dep*artur* E 8·7 mils: Def*erence* Lat*itud* 32′·7: Lat*itud* 5°03′ N: Meridian dist*ance* from St Jago 50·8 Mils E & Long*itud* 53′8 E: Long*itud* from St Mis*ells* 2°02′·8 E & Lo*ngitud* from Lzard 16°27′·2: meridian distance from the Lizard 779·9 Mill west.

[37] **November 1669 the *Sweepstakes* at Sea Lat*itud* 5°03′N**
22
Beinge Munday Cloudy Rainey weather wind betwen the SSE & ESE: I tacked & Stood to Southward: I have had noe opportunity this five dayes to take an Amplitud or Azimo*th*. Course made from Sunday at none till to day at none West: distance Sailed 18 Mills: departur 18 Mils: Def*erence* [Latitud] 00′: Lat*itud* by judgement 5°03′: Calme most Parte this last 24 houers. I judge a currant Sett to the Norward 15 mills in 24 howers for I find it Soe By my observation which Cause of a Currant Settinge is occationed by the Southerly winds.[1]
Meridian Distance from St Jago 32·8 Mills & Longitud from St Jago E 33′·8: Longit*ud* from St Mille 1°44′·8: Longitud from the Lizard 16°45′·2 west & Meridian Distance from the Lizard 797·9 Mils. Wind vearable this afternone: much Raine to night. This day I made an End of all my Cowes as I Brought from Porte Praya.

23
Beinge Tusday Cloudy Rainey weather wind SE & SSW: Smoath water & whit Clouds hangeinge their heads to the Southward the Light Couds Comes out of the SE very Swift: Sum thunder to day: Course By Compas to day SSE. Course made from munday at none till to day at none S 4°43′ E: distance Sailed 24·5 mills: departur E 2 mills: Def*erence* Lat*itud* 24′·3: Lat*itud* By acco*unt* 4°39′.
Meridian Distance E from St Jago: the S E Pointe: 34·8 mils And Longit*ud* from St Jago 35′·8. Longit*ud* from the west Parte of St Mills 1°46′·8 E. Longit*ud* west from the Lizard 16°43′·2. Meridian Distance from the Lizard W 795·9. Much Raine to day: at 10 aclocke the wind Came to the NE: Course SSE: Calme this afternone and much Raine to Night and lettle winde. I judge a Currant sett 12 or 14 mills in 24 howers to the Nward.

[1] A wind from the south would indeed cause a surface current to set to the north.

[38] **November 1669 *Sweepstakes* at Sea in Latt*itud* 4°33′N**
24
Beinge wedensday Cloudy Raine winds variable and Calmes: here Setts a ccurrant Stronge to the NW*est*ward at least 12 or 14 mills in 24 howers: I Eused all Endeviours to gitt to the Southward But Could not the winds Came allwayes to the SEBS & SSE as Sone as the Raine was over. I made my Course SW By what I alowed for the Currant: distance Sailed inine [nine] mills: Departur west 6·3 mills: Def*erence* Lat*itud* 6′·3: Lat*itud* By judgement 04°33′ N. No oBservation. Meridian Distance E from Port Praya 28·5 mils E. Longit*ud* from S[t] Jago that is Port Praya 29′·5 E. Long*itud* from S[t] Mic[he]ls Ile 1°40′·5 E. Longit*ud* from the Lizard 16°49′·5 W. Meridian distant from the Lizard 802·2 mils. Captaine fle[m]inge came a Board of mee and left one of his men with mee named Gilbert Elles.[1] Much Rain to n*ight*.

25
Beinge Thursday Rainey weather winde veareable and Ca*lme*: I Tacked Severall times to night and this forenone. Course made from weddensday at none till to day at none NW: distance 14·1 mils: departur 10 mills W: Def*erence* of Lat*itud* 10′: Lat*itud* By observation at none 4°43′ N.
Meridian distant from Porte Praya 18·5 mils E
Longit*ud* from Port Praya 19′·5 E. Longit*ud* from S[t] Mi[ch]ells 1°30′·5 E
Longit*ud* from the Lizard 16°59′·5 W. Meridian Distant 812·3 miles W
[*margin: fingerpost*] This day we Caute two Bonnetos:[2] Captaine fleminge Came aboard of mee and Sino*r* franco: I tryed the Currant and found it to Set to the Nwest 12 or 14 mils in 24 howers: much Raine this afternone and this night. I give Charge to Captaine fle[m]inge to fill fresh watter when it Rain & to B*e* Carefull of his Provissions.

[39] **November 1669 *Sweepstakes* at Sea in N Lat*itud* 4°51′**
26
Beinge Friday Rainey Cloudy weather wind veareable Betwen the ESE and the South. Course made this 24 hower NBW: distance Proves 8 mils: departur W 1·6 mil: Def*erence* Latt*itud* 7′·8 N: Lat*itud* By judgment 4°51′. This night at Sun Set I tooke an Amplytud But found [*margin: fingerpost*] noe variation at all.
Meridian Distance from Porte Praya 16·9 mils E
Longitud from Porte Praya 17′·9 E
Longitud from S[t] Miclles 1°28′·9 E
Longitud from the Lizard 17°01′·1 W
Meridian distant from the Lizard 813·8 m*ills* W

27
Beinge Satterday faier Calme weather all day. I judge I drove to the NW 8 mils: departur 5·7 mile: Def*erence* Lat*itud* By account 5′·7: Latt*itud* by acc*ount* 4°57′: Lat*itud* By

[1] No reason is given for this. It might have been for a medical reason or possibly that he was a troublemaker who could not be properly handled in such a small vessel.

[2] The Atlantic bonito (*Sarda sarda*), the striped tunny growing up to 3 ft long, 18 lb (8·3 kg) and common in tropical waters. *NOED*; Pepperell, *Fishes*, pp. 100–101.

observation of the ☼ at none 4°56′. I tooke an Amplitud at Sun Set and had 15° [*margin: fingerpost*] veariation westerly.
Meridian distant from Port Pray is 11·2 mils E
Longitud Port Praya is 12′·2 E
Longitud from S[t] Michells is 1°23′·2 E
Longitud from the Lizard is 17°06′·8 W
Meridian distant from the Liz*ard* is 819·5 m*ils*

28
Beinge Sunday faier weather Smoath water wind at SEBE and SSE: at 2 aclocke in the moringe I tack and Stod to the Eward. Course mad Last 24 houers ESE 9°40′ E: distance Sailed 12·6 mils: depart*ur* E 12·3 mills: Def*erence* Latt*itud* S 2′·8: Latt*itud* By Observation ☼ 04°54′. Noe veariation as I Could find By my azimuth to day.
Meridian distan[c]e from Porte Praya 23·5 mils E
Longitud from S[t] Jago: or Port Praya 24′·5 E
Longitud from the Ile S[t] Miels 1°35′·5 E
Longitud from the Lizard 16°54′·5 W
Meridian dist*ance* from Lizard 807·2 Mil W
Wee tooke 4 Bonetos to day.

[40] **November 1669 *Sweepstakes* at Sea Latt*itud* 5°6′N**
29
Beinge Munday faier weather Smoath water wind betwen the SBE and SE a smale gale: I Stod to the Eward. After divers Courses I Made My Cours Last 24 howers N 74°30′ E: distance Sailed 45 mils: Departur E 43·4 mils: Def*erence* Lat*itud* 12 mils: Lat*itud* By observation ☼ 5°06′ N.
Meridian distance from Porte Pray E 66·9 mils
Longitud from Porte Praya 1°08′ E
Longitud from St Miells 2°19′ E
Longitud from the Lizard 16°11′ W.
Meridian distant from the Liz*ard* 763·8 mil W

30
Being Tusday faier weather Lettle wind Betwen the SSE and the E: Smoath water:[1] here sett a currant to the NNE-warde about 8 mils in 24 howers. After divers Courses this 24 houers I made my true Course N 61°30′ E: distance Sailed 19 miles: departur 16·7 mils: Def*erence* Lat*itud* 9 mils: Lat*itud* By Observation of the Sun at none 05°15′ N. I never Could have any observation of a Star. Here Sets a Currant to the NNE-ward 8 or nine miles [*margin:* ☽] in 24 houers: I judge it Sett NNW at the [*margin: fingerpost*] mones [moon's] in Crease: and NNE at the mones Decrease.
Meridian distance from S[t] Jago Por*t Praya* 83·6 mils E
Longitud from Port Praya 1°24′·7 E
Longitud from S[t] Miells 02°35′·7 E

[1] Wood, BL, MS 3833, f. 8v: 'This Morning we Chacht 4 Sharkes one haveing 5 young ones in her of 2 fotte Longe apeace. (All The Shipes Company are in health.)'.

Longitud from the Lizard 15°54′·3 W
Meridian distant from the Lizard 747·5 W
Much Raine to night and Calme. All the Possible indeviours I Can make I Canott Gitt to the Southward: the wind hang at the SE quart*er*. This day wee found 4 Buts of our Iron Bound bere leacked out the Case Proveinge Nought.[1]

[41] **December 1669 *Sweepstakes* at Sea Lat*itud* 5°15′**

1

Beinge Wedensday Raineny weather most Parte of the day and Calmes. After severall Courses and what the Currant Set mee I make my true Course to Be West: distant Sailed five mils: departur west 5 mils: Latt*itud* By judgment at none 5°15′ N.
I tryed the Currant with my Boat it Beinge Calme:[2] I find it Sett NNE in the Runeinge of halfe a minut Glase thre fadame.[3]
Meridian distance from Porte Praya 78·6 Mils E
Longitud from Port Praya 1°19′·7
Longitud from St Miells 2°30′·7
Longitud from the Lizard 15°59′·3 W
Meridian distance from the Lizard 752·5 mils
We Caute Sum Bonnetos today & Teberons.[4]

2

Beinge Thursday Rainey weather wind at N: Cours by Compase SSE: then the wind Came to SSE. After Severall Courses I make my Course South 16°34′ E: distane Sailed 38·4 mils: departur 11 mils E: Def*erence* Lat*itud* 37′·3: Lat*itud* By account at none 4°38′ N.
Meridian distance from Porte Praya 89·6 Mils E
Longitud from Porte Praya 1°30′·7 E
Longitud from St Miels 2°41′·7 E
Longitud from the Lizard 15°48′·3 W
Meridian distance 741·5

3

Beinge friday faier weather wind at SSE & at SEBE. Course mad NNE: distant Sailed 24 mils: departur 9 mils: Def*erence* Lat*itud* 22 mils: Lat*itud* By obs*ervation* ☼ 5°00′.
Meridian distant from Port Praya 98·6 Mils E

[1] See above, 1 Nov., p. 160. The point being that iron-bound butts were no better than wooden-bound butts.

[2] In calm conditions done from a boat, which had to be hoisted out and moved clear of the ship. The current was then measured by lowering a sea-anchor, either a large kettle, cauldron or some similar object as far as possible below the boat to moor it, and then streaming the log. The direction in which the float went and the speed at which it ran out gave the direction and rate of the current. At best this would only give the current relative to any that might be flowing at the level of the sea-anchor, and since the boat might drift to and fro above the sea-anchor it could be quite difficult to obtain a realistic result even for that.

[3] 0·36 knots to the NNE.

[4] Tiburon: A name given by 16th- and 17th-century navigators to one or more large species of shark, applied specifically to the bonnet-headed shark (*Reniceps tiburo*). *NOED*.

Longitud from P*orte*[1] Praya 1°39′·7 E
Longit*ud* from St Mile 2°50′·7 E
Longitud from the Lizard 15°39′·3 W
Meridian distance 739·5 W

[42] **December 1669 *Sweepstakes* at Sea in Lat*itud* 05°00′.**
4
Beinge Satterday faier weather wind veareable betwen the S & the ESE and Calme. Course mad west: distance Sailed Six miles: departur W 6 [mils]: Lat*itud* Per observation of the ☼ 5°00′.
Meridian distance from Porte Praya 92 Mils 6 E
Longitud from Porte Praya 1°33′·7 E
Longitud from St Miels 2°44′·7 E
Longitud from the Lizard 15°45′·3 W
Meridian distance from the Lizard 745·5 W
Much Bonetos and Albycors[2] and Sharkes[3] in these seas and flieinge fish.

5
Beinge Sunday faier weather Lettle wind at SSE and at S and SE: Smoath water and Calme: after Severall Courses I make my True Cours NEBN: aloweinge the Current to it which Sett at Least 14 Mils in 24 howers NE: now it is lettle wind I tryed it and fond it Soe as well as By my observation Showes it. For last 24 howers My Course would have Ben E Southerly: But at none I find by obser*vation* of the Sun I ame 16′ more northerly then I was the day Before & had Boath dayes very Good obser*vation*. [*margin: fingerpost*] I also tryed with my Boateh [boat] and found it to Set NE: the Same as before.[4] My way was by vearinge downe a greate Loge Board made one [on] Purpose for that office one hundered and fivety fadam under water which Cause my Boate to Ride till I tryed the Strenght of it. Course NEBN: distane Sailed & drove 19·2 mils: dep*artur* 10·7 mills E: Def*erence* Lat*itud* 16′: Lat*itud* P*er* ob*servation* ☼ 5°16′ N.
Meridian distans from Porete [Port] Pray 102·8 Mils E
Longitud from Porte Praye 1°44′ E
Longitud from St Miles 2°55′·8 E
Longitud from the Lizard 15°35′ W
Meridian distans from the Lizard 735·3 W

[1] 'St Mils' originally written here and corrected.

[2] Albacore (*Thunnus alalunga*), a large species of tunny growing up to 66–88 lb (30–40 kg). *NOED*; Pepperell, *Fishes*, pp. 78–80.

[3] There are a large number of sharks found in the Atlantic, the most common of which are probably the blue shark (*Prionace glauca*), the thresher shark (*Alopias vulpinus*) and the mako shark (*Isurus oxyrhinchus*). See Pepperell, *Fishes*, pp. 173–218, which covers all likely varieties. For the oceanic species of flying fish (Exocoetidae), ibid., pp. 227–9.

[4] The current was measured which agreed with the astronomical observations. Wood, MS 3833, 5. 9r: 'This day the Master of the Ship went out in the Boatt to try the Currant and Sayed itt Sett to the NE & by N but I went out and found itt to sett but ENE.'

[43] **December 1669 the *Sweepstakes* at Sea in Lat*itud* 5°12′.**

6

Beinge Munday faier weather But Lettle wind at S and Smoath water: I Stood to the E*ast*ward.

Cours mad this 24 houers after divers Courses EBS: distance Sailed 22 mils: departur E 21·5 Mils: Def*erence* Lat*itud* 4′·3: Lat*itud* By account 5°12′.

Meridian distane from Porte Praya 123·3 Mils E

Longitud from Porte Praya 2°05′·5

Longitud from S[t] Mils 3°16′·5

Longitud from the Lizard 15°13′·5 W

Meridian distane from the Lizard 713·8 Mils W

The Currunt Set Northerly.

7

Beinge faier weather Lettle wind and Sumtimes Calme Somath [smooth] water. After divers Courses By Compas I made my Course from Munday none til today at none South 60° E: distance Sailed 32 Mils: depart*ur* E 27·7 mils: Def*erence* Lat*itud* 16′: Lat*itud* By obser*vation* of the ☼ 4°56′.

Meridian distance from S[t] Jago 151 Mils

Longitud from S[t] Jago 2°33′·2

Longitud from the Lizard 14°45′·8 W

Meridian distance from the Lizard 686·1

This day we all dranke water in the shipp for we Could not Come at any Beare: Two Buts of Beare found leacked out. seaverall sea fowles Senne which we Calle men of warr.[1]

[44] **December 1669 *Swepstake* at Sea Latt*itud* 4°54′.**

8

Being Weddensday faier weather winde vearable betwen the S and SW: letle winde: I Stood to the E*ast*ward. After divers Courses I made my True Cours SE: distance Sailed 5·6 miles: Departur 4 miles E: Def*erence* Lat*itud* 4′: Lat*itud* By observation ☼ 4°52′ N.

Meridian Distance from Port Pray 155 Mils E

Longitud from Porte Praya 2°37′·2 E

Longitud from the Lizard 14°41′·8 W

Meridian Distance from the Lizard 682·1 mils.

9

Being Thursday Blowinge Gusty weather wwinds vearable betwen the SE and SW: Rainey weather and Calme to night.

After Divers Courses my true Course from weddensday at none till to day at none is S 74° E: Distance Sailed 28 mils: departur 27 mils E: Def*erence* Lat*itud* 7′·7: Lat*itud* By account 4°44′.

Meridian distant from Porte Praya 182 mils E

Longitud from Porte Praya 3°04′·5 E

Longitud from the Lizard 14°14′·6 W

Meridian distans from the Lizard 655·1 mile W

[1] Frigatebird. Probably the magnificent frigatebird (*Fregata magnificans*), as the Ascension frigatebird (*F. aquila*) is not normally found as far north as this. Harrison, *Seabirds*, pp. 308–13.

10
Being friday Rainey weather this morninge and Calme: at 8 aClocke the wind Came to the SW a fine gale and Soe to the W: I stered S. After divers Courses this 24 houer I make my true Course to Be SSE: distance Sailed 22 mile: Departur 8·4 mils: Def*erence* Lat*itud* at none 20′·2: Lat*itud* By account at none 4°24′ N
Meridian Distance from Porte Praya 190·4 mils E
Longitud from Port Praya 3°12′·9 E
Longitud from Lizard 14°06′·2 W
Meridian Distance from the Liz*ard* 646·7 W

[45] **December 1669 *Sweepstakes* at Sea in Latt*itud* 3°57′ N.**
11
Beinge Satterday this 24 howers the wind have ben Rounde the Compase: and Raine and Sum Calmes. Course made SSE: distance Sailed 29 mils: dep*artur* E 11·1 miles: Def*erence* Latt*itud* 26′·8: Lat*itud* By account at none 3°57′.
[*margin: fingerpost*] I tooke an amplitud at Sun Settinge But found noe veariation.
Merid*ian* Distance from Porte Praya 201·5 M*ils*
Longitud from Porte Praya 3°24′ E
Longitud from the Lizard 13°55′·1 W
Meridian distant from the Lizard 635·6 Mi*ls*.

12
Beinge Sunday faier weather wind Betwen the SW and S a fine gale: and at SE. After divers Courses I made my Course SBE: distance Sailed 38 miles: departur E 7·4 miles: Def*erence* Lat*itud* 37′: Lat*itud* by observation ☼ 3°20′. I judge a Current Sett to the SE-ward. I tooke an Amplitud at ☼ Seteninge [setting] and had 34′ veariation E.
Meridian distance from Porte Porte P*ray* 208·9 M*ils* E
Longitud from Porte Pray 3°31′·5 E
Longitud from the Lizard 13°47′·6 W
Meridian distane Lizard 628·2 Mils W

13
Beinge Munday Sum Raine winds Beten the SWBS and the SE. After Several Courses I made my Course South 53°18′ E: distanet Saild 33·2 Miles: departur 27 mils E: Def*erence* Latt*itud* 20′·1: Lat*itud* By account at none 3°00′.
Meridian distant from Porte Praya 235·9 Mils E
Longitud from Porte Praya 3°58′·5 E
Longitud from the Lizard 13°20′·6 W
Merid*ian* Dist*ance* from the Lizard 601·2 Mils W

[46] **December 1669 *Swepstakes* at Sea Lat*itud* 2°47′ N.**
14
Beinge Tusday faier weather wind at S and SBE & at SSE. Ater Severall Courses these 24 houers I make my true Course S 54°40′ W: distance Sailed 22·5 mils: Departur W: 18·4 Mils: Def*erence* Lat*itud* 13′·4: Lat*itud* By Observation of the ☼ 2°47′.
Meridian distant from Porte Praya 217·5 M*ils* E

Longitud from Port Praya 3°40′ E
Longitud from the Lizard 13°39′·1 W
Meridian dist*ance* from the Lizard 619·6 M*ils* W

15
Beinge Weddensday faier weather wind at SSE & at S. After Severall [courses] I make my true Course to Be South 32°58′ W: distance Sailed 17·9 mils: departur 9·7 Miles W: Def*erence* Lat*itud* 15′: Lat*itud* By obser*vation* ☼ 2°32′.
Meridian distanc from Porte Port 207·8 Mils E
Longitud from Porte Praya 3°30′·3 E
Longitud from the Lizard 13°48′·8 W
Meridian distant from the Lizard 629·3 Mils W

16
Beinge Thursday faier weather wind at SSE and at S. Course made Good S 45°10′ West: distance Sailed 11·3 Miles: departur 8·0 Mils West: Def*erence* Lat*itud* 8′: Latitud P*er* observation ☼ 2°24′ N.
[*margin: fingerpost*] At 4 aclocke Past none I tooke the Pinke in Toow.
Meridian distant from Porte Praya 199·8 M*ils* E
Longitud from Porte Praya 3°22′ E
Longitud fro the Lizard 13°56′·8.
Meridian distant from the Lizard 637·3 Mils
Much Bonnetos in these seas: Severall taken.

[47] **December 1669 *Sweepstakes* at Sea Latt*itud* 1°57′ N**
17
Beinge friday faier weather wind at SSE and South and at SSW a fine gale. Course mad made this 24 houers South 58°42′ West: distanc Sailed 52 mils: departur 44·3 Mils West: Def*erence* Lat*itud* 27′: Lat*itud* By obser*vation* of the ☼ at none 1°57′.
Meridian distant from Porte Praya 155·5 M*ils* E
Longitud from Porte Praya 2°38′·0 E
Longitud from the Lizard 14°41′·1 W
Meridian distant from the Lizard 681·6 M*ils*.
[*Margin: fingerpost and symbol for securing the mast*] This day I found a defective Place in my Maine Mast alowe Betwene Decks: one [on] which I Put a twenty foote fish – and would it it well.[1]

18
Beinge Satterday faier weather wind att SBE and at SSE and SE: this 24 houers it hold a fresh gale: I stered By my Compase SW & SWBS and SSW was as nere as I Could ly. From friday at none till to day at none I made my Course good alowinge all falts to it: SW

[1] Possibly meaning 'Would [woold] it well', wooded. Narbrough found a defective place in the main mast below decks and put in a 20 ft long 'fish'. This was a long piece of hard wood convex on one side and concave on the other bound to a mast or spar to strengthen it. They were well secured with bolts and hoops and bound over with rope. This last action was called woolding. The symbol in the margin appears to represent wooden splints bound with crossed rope.

3°15′ westerly: distance Sailed 54 Miles: departur west 40·4 miles: deference of Lattitud 36′: Latt*itud* By observation at none ☼ 1°21′ N
Meridian Distanc from St Jago 115·1 Mils E
Longitud from Port Pray or S^t Ja*go* 1°57′·6 E
Longitud from the Lizard 15°21′·5 W
Meridian Distane from the Lizard 722 Mils W
My men are al in Reassonabble Good health: I have Causeid the Chyrurgion[1] to have Bloded most Parte of my men within the Tropicke and Line. I find leackeage in my Brandy By Reason of a Sappy Stafe[2] have leacked out one half hogshead.

[48] **December 1669 *Sweepstakes* at Sea Lat*itud* 0°44′ N**
19
Beinge Sunday faier weather and a fresh gale this 24 houers wind at SEBS & SSE & SE: I Stered By my Compas SWBS and SW & SSW. I made my True Course this 24 houers SW 5°22′ westerly: Distance Sailed 58 Mils: departure west 44·7 Mils: Def*erence* Lat*itud* 37′: Lat*itud* By observation of the ☼ at none 44′ N.
I judge here is very Little Current the first quarter of the Mone: I find noe variation.
[*margin*: fingerpost] I Catched 40 Bonets & olbyCores[3] to daye with hookes and Lines.
Meridian distant from Porte Praya 70·4 Mils E
Long*itud* from Porte Praya 1°12′·8 E
Long*itud* from the Lizard 16°06′·3 W
Meridian distant from the Lizard 766·7 Mils W
A fine Gale at SEBS: I ly as nere as I Cane and Keepe my Larboard Tacke a Board: Course By Compas SSW and SWBS° sumtimes: Smoath water.

20
Beinge Munday[4] faier weather from Sunday at none til to day none wind at SEBS and SE & SSE a fresh gale: Course By Compase SSW and SWBS and SBW. Course made this 24 hou*ers* SWBW: Distance Sailed 63 Miles: Departur W 52·6 Mils: Def*erence* Lat*itud* 35′ Lat*itud* P*er* oBservation Sun ☼ 00°09′ N
Meridian Distante from Port Praya 17·8 Mil E
Longit*ud* from Porte Praya 00°20′ E
Longit*ud* from the Lizard 16°59′·1 W
Meridian Dist*ance* from the Lizard 819·7 Mils.

[1] The Chirurgeon, surgeon. Keevil, *Medicine*, II, p.162, remarks 'Captains had not changed in outlook since the time of Lord Wimbledon's expedition [Ibid., I, p. 165] "sickness was incident to all sea voyages" and they like their predecessors of 1625 "could by observation give some good judgement" on medical matters: a surgeon was a surgeon and not a physician.'

[2] Sappy stave: a stave which was not properly seasoned and still had sap in it.

[3] Bonitos and albacores.

[4] Narbrough's record becomes difficult to follow on p. 49. Monday is given as 20 Dec. on p. 48. Most of the entry on p. 49 concerns Tuesday 21 Dec. but the entry is interrupted mid-page by a lengthy undated paragraph about Wednesday under that date. He concludes the page by recording his estimates of his position for Tuesday at noon, followed by commentary on the winds and his course in that Tuesday afternoon. A separate entry for Wednesday 22 Dec. is made on p. 50. The confusion may reflect that the journal was suspended for a time around 20–22 Dec. and regular entries resumed later from the daily log.

[49] **December 1669** ***Sewpstakes*** **at Sea Lat*itud* 17′S**
21
Being Tusday hassy Cloudy weather ther wind at SEBS and at SSE and S: Smale winds: I Stood Cloase haled with my Larboard takes aboard to the Southward. I made my Cours this 24 houers SW: distance Sailed 36·7 miles: Departur West 26 Mils: Def*erence* Lat*itud* 26′: Lat*itud* By observation of the Sun at none 00°17′ South.
[*margin:2 fingerposts*] Wedensday:[1] at 6 aclocke in the Afternone I Crosed the Equinoctiall [*margin:* Crosed the Eq:] East of the Meridian of Porte Praya of the Island of St Jago one of the Cap Verde Ils 8·8 mils E and in Longitud E from St Jago 11′: Longitud West from the Lizard 17°08′·1: Meridian Distantce frome the Lizard 828·3 Mils. The wind was then at SEBS a stife Gale: Smoath wather [water]: I had then the *Batcheler* Pinke at my Stern in A Towe. This night at Sun Set I tooke an Amplytud and found But theerty minuts variation E*ast*erly.
True Amplytud 23°11′ } variation 00°30′ E.
Magnetic Amplytud 23°41′ }
Wee tooke 20 Bonnetos and albecors to day. seaveral sea fowles flyinge to and froe.
This time my Men are al in Good health: Being 86 in Number – all that I Brought out of Eng*land*.[2]
Tusday at none: I make my Meridian Distance From Porte Praya 8·2 Mils W
And Lon*gitud* from P*orte* Paraya 00°06′ W
Longitud from the Lizard 17°25′·1 W
Meridian Distanc from the Lizad 845·3 Mils W
This Afternone at 6 aClocke I tacked and Stood to the E:ward: wind Came to the SBE: at 12 aClo*cke* night the wind Came to the SE: I tacked and sto*od* to the Southward: Course by Compas SSW.

[50] **December 1669** ***Sweepstakes*** **at Sea Lat*itud* 0°40′ S**
22
Beinge Wedensday Cloudy weather: wind at SEBS and S and SSE and SE a fresh gale. Atfter divers Courses this 24 houers I make my true Cours to Be South 21°22′ west: distance Sailed 24·7 Mils: Departuer West 9 Miles: Def*erence* Lat*itud* 23 mils: Lat*itud* By obser*vation* of the ☼ 00°40′ S.
Meridian Distanc from Porte Praya 17·2 Mils W
Longitud from Porte Praya 15′·5 W
Longitud from the Lizard 17°34′·6 W
Meridian Dist from Lizard 854·3 Mils W

23
Beinge Thursday faier weather: wind at SEBS and SE. I make my True Course this 24 houers to be SWBS: and my distance Sailed 43·2 mils: Departur West 24·2 Miles: Def*erence* Lat*itud* 00°36′: Lat*itud* P*er* obser*vation* ☼ 01°16′ S.

[1] This would appear to be an error, since the line had been crossed the day before, the noon position on the Tuesday being south of the equator. Rawlinson, MS A318, f. 22, records crossing the equator on Monday 20 Dec., which agrees with John Wood's journal, MS 3833, f. 9v.

[2] The 80 on the Muster List and 6 additional who were not mustered. Richard Haddock had been transfered to the *Batchelour* on 5 Nov. and Gilbert Elles from the *Batchelour* to the *Sweepstakes* on 24 Nov.

Meridian distance from Porte Praya 41·4 Mils W
Longitud from Porte Praya 00°41′ W
Longitud from the Lizard west 17°59′·1 W
Meridian distance Lizard west 878·5 Mils W
Faier weather all night: wind at SE & SEBS.

24
Beinge friday faier weather wind at SSE and SEBE & at ESE a fine ordinary Gale: Smoath water:
Course By my Compase the 24 houers SW & SSW and SWBS & South. I make my true Course to Be SWBS: Distance Sailed 53 miles: Departur west 29·6 miles: def*erence* Lat*itud* 44′: Lat*itud* By obser*vation* of the Sun at none 02°00′ South.
Meridian distance from Porte Praya 71 Mils W
Longitud from Porte Praya 01°10′·8 W
Longitud from the Lizard 18°28′·9 W
Meridian distance from Lizard 908·1 Mils W
I judge a Currant Sets to the Southward.
[*margin: Drawing of fish*] Wee Catched 40 or 50 fish Caled Olbycors to day.

[51] **December 1669 *Swepstakes* at Sea Latt*itude* 03°09′S.**
25
Beinge Satterday Cloudy weather wind at SEBE a Stife gale:
Course By Compase SBW. Course mad this 24 houers SBW: distance Sailed 70·5 miles: Departur West 13·8 miles: Def*erence* of Lat*itud* 01°09′: Lat*itud* Per observat*ion* ☼ 03°09′ S
Meridian Distance from Porte Praya 84·8 Mils W
Longit*ud* from Porte Praya 01°24′·8 W
Longit*ud* from the Lizard 18°42′·9 W
Meridian dist*ance* from the Lizard 921·9 Mils W
I judge a Currant Sett nere 20 miles in 24 houers to the SE:ward as I have found it By my obser*vation* of the Sun this two days: Beinge Boath very Good: I judge a Currant Sets more Stronger By reason it Beinge nere a full moone.[1] I have Run by my loge this 24 houers But 54 miles SBW: wind at SEBE: and have differed 69 miles in Latitud. The water indeferant Smoath this 24 houres.
I have Spared 6 tunn of Emty Iron Bound Cask the Pinke to file with water to keepe her Stife:[2] it Beinge Capt*ain* flemings disier: their Beinge Iron hoops.

26
Beinge Sunday faier weather wind at SE and SEBS and SSE a Stife gale and Came to the ESE. After divers Courses thes 24 houers I make my true Course to Be SSW: Distance

[1] Near the time of spring tides. The main cause of the surface currents in the oceans is the wind, thus the trade winds are the mainspring of the mid-latitude surface current circulation. There are of course other currents, both sub-surface and with vertical components, with differing cause, but the action of the moon is not deemed one of them.

[2] The casks would be filled with water (probably salt but possibly rain water) and stowed low in the hold to lower the centre of gravity of the pink, and make her more stable, decreasing the amount she rolled and heeled to the wind and thus increasing her speed.

Sailed 62·5 mils: departur west 24 Miles: Def*erence* Lat*itud* 58′: Lat*itude* Per observation ☼ at the meridian 04°07′ S.
Meridian distance from Porte Praya 108·8 Mils W
Longitud from Porte Praya 01°49′·0 W
Longitud from the Lizard 19°07′·1 W
Meridian distance from the Lizard 945·9 Mils W
[*margin: drawing of bird*] Many sea fowle sene to day flyinge to and frowe. I have the Pinke in a Towe.

[52] **December 1669 *Sweepstakes* at Sea Latt*itud* 05°25′ S**
27
Beinge Munday faier weather wind at ESE A fine Stife Gale: Cours By Compass South. I make my true Course this 24 houers to Be SBW: distane Sailed 80 miles: Departur west 15·6 mils: Def*erence* Lat*itud* 01°18′: Lattitud Per obs*ervation* ☼ one [on] the meridian 05°25′ S
Meridian distans from Porte Praya 124·4 Mils W
Longitud from Porte Praya 02°04′·6 W
Longitude from the Lizard 19°22′·7 W
Meridian distance from the Lizard 961·5 Mils W
I find three degres E variation here E
By an Amplitud taken at Sun Settinge.

28
Beinge Tusday hassy weather: wind at E and at ESE Stife Gale and Sumthinge Rufe Sea: Cors By Compase SBE and S all this 24 houers. Course made Good from yesterday at None till to day at none South: distance Sailed By my obser*vation* ☼ 95 miles: But By my Loge But 86 miles and so it have difered this 4 dayes which Gives mee to beleive that a Stronge Currant Sett to the Southward: Departur:[1] Def*erence* Latt*itud* 01°35′: Lat*itud* Per obs*ervation* of the ☼ one [on] the Meridian 07°00′ South. I have the Pinke Stile in a Tow.
Meridian distance from Porte Praya 124·4 Mils W
Longitud from Porte Praya 02°04′·6 W
Longitud from the Lizard 19°22′·7 W
Meridian dist*ance* from the Lizard 961·5 Miles W
Here is 5° variation E.
Mity [mighty] Temparrate weather: and healthey with a fine Gale: and Coole in the Eveinges.

[53] **December 1669 *Sweepstakes* at Sea in the Lat*itud* of 8°30′ S**
29
Beinge weddensday hassy Cloudy weather: wind at ESE & at E: Sumtimes a good Stife gale: Course By Compase SBE & S. This morninge the Pinke Brooke Lose here Towe. Cours made from Tusday at none till to day at none South 6° west: distance Saild 91 miles: Departur West 9·5 miles: Def*erence* of Lat*itud* 01°30′. Lat*itud* By account at none 08°30′ S. I Could not take Eighter [either] Azim*uth* or Amply*tud* to day.

[1] There was no departure since the course was south.

Meridian distance from Porte Pray 133·9 Mils W
Longitud from Porte Pray 02°14′·3 W
Longitud from the Lizard 19°32′·4 W
Meridian distance from the Lizard 971 Miles W.

30
Beinge Thursday hassy Cloudy weather: wind this 24 houers at ESE and at E a Stife Gale: Course By Compase SBE and S and S ½ E. I make my True Course to Be S 15° west: Distanc Sailed 72·5 Miles: Departur West 18·8 Miles: Def*erence* Lat*itud* 01°10′ S: Lat*itud* Pre obser*vation* ☼ one [on] the meridion 09°40′ South.
This forenone I tooke the Pink in a Toowe with my Stream Cable. I have a Leacke Stronnge in my Bowes: it makes about 16 inches a watch wat*er*.[1]
Meridian distance from Porte Praya 152·7 M*ils* W
Longitud from Port Praya 02°33′·3 W
Longitud from the Lizard 19°51′·4 W
Meridian distance from the Lizard 989·8 Mils W
[*margin: 2 fingerposts*]This afternone I tooke an Azimuth and finde 6°10′ variation E*ast*erly fair weather al Night. This Eveinge at 9 aclocke Nebelus Major was very aparant in the heavens: he makes like Parte of the Milky way: in Largnes as Bigg as a Sheet.[2]

[54] **December 1669 *Sweepstakes* in the Lat*itud* 10°56′ S**
31
Beinge friday faier weather wind at EBS and at ESE: a fine Gale al this last 24 houres: Course By my Compasse SBE and S: But I make my True Course to Be SBW: distanc Sailed 77·5 Miles: Departur west 15·2 mils: Def*erence* of Lat*itud* 01°16′: Lat*itud* Per observation ☼ one [on] the meridion 10°56′ S
Meridian distane from Porte Praya 167·9 Mils W
Longitud from Porte Praya 02°48′·8 W Longitud from the Lizard 20°06′·9 W.
Meridian dist*ance* from the Lizard 1005 Miles W
I found here By an Azamath takeine in the forenone 7°28′ E variation.

The 1 day of January: 1669.[3] I tooke an Amplytud at Sun Settinge and By my Comp*asse* the Sun Set 27° to the South of the west But my true amplitud at that time in this Latt*itud* of 12°00′ South Lat*itud* is But 22°15′: which Being Subtracted from 27°00′ leaves 4°45′ the variation E: that is the North Pointe varies of the Compas 4°45′ Easterly and Soe al the Rest of the Points: Consequ[e]ntly thes Afternone I had nere the Same variation By an Azimuth: which I tooke with my Azimuth Compass:[4] Beinge varie Cleare weather.
I find dayly a Stronge Currant which Set mee to the Southward: which I find betwen my Logg and observation Every 24 houers: foor I have Ben very Cearefull in takeinge Care of Boath and Every 24 howers I find ten of twelfe miles deference: that is I ame more to the South by my observation than By my Logg 10 or 12 mile Every 24 houers.

[1] The depth of water in the bilge rises 16 inches in 4 hours (a watch), which would have to be pumped out.
[2] Nebulus Major was an early name for the Large Magellanic Cloud. Bayer, *Uranometria*, 1661, pl. Aaa (49), shows the Magellanic clouds as Nebecula major and Nebecula minor.
[3] 1669/70.
[4] See above, p. 63, n. 10.

[55] **January 1669 the *Sweepstaks* Latt*itud* 11°48′ S**

1

Beinge Satterday faier weather wind all this Last 24 houers at SE and SEBE and ESE: A fine Smale gale:
Course By Compass SSW and South as nere as Conveniently I Could ly. Course mad Good SBW: Distance Sailed 53·2 miles: Departur west 10·4 mils: def*erence* Lat*itud* 00°52′: Lat*itud* Per ob*servation* ☼ 11°48′ South.
[*margin:* Azi: Comp] Capt*ain* Fleminge had an Azimuth Compas of mee.
Meridin [*sic*] distance from Porte Pray 178·3 Mils W
Longitud from Porte Praya 03°00′·1 W
Longitud from the Lizard 20°18′·2 W
Meridian dist*ance* from the Lizard 1015·4 Mils W
A Currant Set here to the Southward.
Variation here 05°00′ E.

2

Beinge Sunday a fine gale at EBS and E faier weather and Smoath water: Cours by my Compase SBE But aLowe my True Cours to be South: Distance Sailed 74 Miles: departure:[1] Def*erence* Latt*itud* 01°14′: Lat*itud* by obser*vation* of the ☼ 13°02′ S.
Here is nere 6° E variation and a Stronge Current Set to the Southward.
Meridian dist*ance* from Porte Praya 178·3 Miles W
Longitud from Porte Praya 03°00′·1 W
Longitud from the Lizard 20°18′·2 W
Meridian dist*ance* from the Lizard 1015·4 Miles W
I find here 6°40′ E variation By an Azimath taken in the afternone.
My men are all in Good health: God by Prayesed: Beinge 87[2] in Number the Same as I Cam out with from England. Sum Bonnetos Taken to day. I have had all aLonge in the voiage fine Temprate weather.

[56] **January 1669 *Sweepstakes* in Lat*itud* 14°10′ S**

3

Beinge munday faier weather wind at ESE a fine Gale al this 24 houers:
Course by Compase SBE But haveinge the toow at my Sterne and findeinge 7°15′ E variation I make my tru Cours to be SBW: distance Sailed 79·7 Mils: departur west 13·6 mils: def*erence* Lat*itud* 1°08′: Lat*itud* by observation of the ☼ in the Merd*ian* 14°10′ S
Meridian distane from Porte Praya 191·9 Mils W
Longitud from Port Praya 03°14′ W
Long*itud* from the Lizard 20°32′·1 W
Meridian dist*ance* from the Lizard 1029 Miles W
Variation in the afternone at Sun Set 5°48′ E
Lat*itud* By account 14°25′ S

[1] The departure is zero since the course is due south and has been left out in the original.

[2] This would appear to be an error since the previous remarks give 86 as the total of the men on board, and no further transfers had taken place.

4

Beinge Tusday faier weather this 24 houer wind at ESE and at E a fine Gale: Smoath water: my Course by the Compase is South be [by] E But I make my True Course South by alowanec of the variat*ion*: distance Sailed by my Looge But 76 miles: dist*ance* Sailed by my Latt*itud* 83 miles.[1] I judge A curante Set to the Southward. Departur west–: defference of Lat*itud* 01°23′: Lat*itud* By Good observation of the ☼ one [on] the Merid*ian* 15°33′ So*uth*.

Meridian distance from Porte Praya 191·9 Mils W

Longitud from Porte Praya 03°14′ W

Longitud from the Lizard 20°32′·1 W

Meridian dist*ance* from the Lizard 1029 Miles W

At 12 acclocke I Stered So*uth* by my Compase the wind at E a fine Gale. This day one of my [*margin: fingerpost* mort] Ships Company Died: named John Mahew: Aged [*margin:* A man Died] 18 yeares: borne at Epswched [Ipswich] in Suffolke.[2]

Variation at Sun Set 6°25′ E by an Amplyt*ud*.[3]

[57] **January 1669 the *Sweepstakes* in Lat*itud* 16°56′ S**

5

Beinge Wedensday faier weather Smoath water wind at EBN: a fine Gale al this 24 houers. Cour*se* [by] my Compass So*uth*: But I make my true Course aloweinge the variation to it to be SBW: distanc Sailed 85 miles by observation & Cours: But by my Loge But 74 miles: a ccurrant Set to [*margin: drawing of a lead and line*] the Southward: Departur West 16·7 mils: def*erence* Lat*itud* 1°23′: Lat*itud* by obs*ervation* ☼ 16°56′ So*uth*.

Variation 6°46′ E by obser*vation* in the morninge.

[*margin: fingerpost*] I Sounded at 184 faddam of Line and noe Ground.

Meridian distaunce from Port Praya 208·6 Mils W

Longitud from Porte Praya 3°31′·3.

Longitud from the Lizard 20°49′·4.

Meridian distance from the Lizard 1045·7 Mils.

Variation of my Compase By an Amplytud which I tooke at Sun Set was 6°48′ E

Little wind this afternone: I Sett my top Saile Stertinge Sailes:[4] wind at EBN Cours Stered S.[5]

6

Beinge Thursday faier weather wind at ENE and at E and at NE: a fine Smale gale this 24 ho*uers*. I Stered by my Compase South but alowinge variation I make my Course So*uth*

[1] By observation of the Latitude.

[2] Wood, BL, MS 3833, f. 10v, says he was one of the captain's servants.

[3] Wood, BL, MS 3833, f. 10v: 'This Nigh[t] I observed By the Bright Starr in Auriga Caled the She Goate [Capella, α Aurigæ] whose Long*etude* is ♊ 17°09′ & Latt*itude* 22°51′ N*orth* Declynation 45°37′ N*orth* & found my Selfe by her Meridian Altitude To Be in the Latt*itude* of 16°10′. By the Suns Ampletude This Night I found the Varation of the Compas To Be 6°00′ E*ast*.'

[4] Probably studding sails.

[5] Wood, BL, MS 3833, Wood, BL, MS 3833, f. 10v: 'This Morning att 3 of the Clock I Observed Jupeter To Bee in a Straight Line with 3 of his Companyons beinge the 3 farthest from his Body the 4th beinge hid from my Sight by his Beames. They Poynted from him SW by W; he was 20°00′ Hye Setting in Long*etude* 8°25′ ♋ & in Latt*itude* from the Ecliptick 7° N*orth*.'

8° *West*: distance Sailed 67 miles: departur west 9·3 miles: def*erence* Lat*itud* 01°06′: Lat*itud* Per ob*servation* 18°02′. Variation in the morninge 6°58′ E
Meridian distane from Porte Praya 217·9 M*ils*.
Longitud from Porte Praya 03°41′.
Longitud from the Lizard 20°59′·1 W
Meridian distance from the Lizard 1055 Mils W
Wind Came to the NE this forenon: faier weather all night & lettle wind: I Sounded at 193 faddam: noe Ground. Noe Amplytude to night.[1]

[58] **January 1669 *Sweepstakes* in the Lat*itud* 18°30′**
7
Beinge friday faier weather wind at NNE a Small Gale: a great Shouer of Raine to night very Smoath water Severall Sea fowles flyeinge to and froe. I Expecte to be nere the Latt*itud* of the Island of Assention ore [or] to See it before night accordinge to my Reckeinginge and Draft.[2] I have Stered So*uth* till 6 aclocke this morninge and then South be West: –Lat*itud* at 6 aclocke this morninge 18°30′ So*uth*: variatione at Sun Riseinge 7°48′ E: havinge a Good amplitud.
Course made from Thursday none till to day at none South ten degres west: distance Sailed 49 Mils: Departur west 8·4 Miles: def*erence* Lat*itud* 48′: Lat*itud* By account at none 18°50′ South.
Meridian Dist*ance* from Porte Praya 226·3 Miles W
Longitud from Port Praya 03°50′.
Longitud from the Lizard 21°08′·1.
Meridian distance from the Lizard 1063·4 Miles W
Variation at Sun Set 8°06′ E
I Sunded at 6 aclock at night noe Ground at 140 fad*am*[3] the Line Brake and I Lost my Lead. I Cast of[f] the Pinke from my Sterne By reason of lookenige out to night[4] Reckeing

[1] Wood, BL, MS 3833, f.10v,'This Last Night I Observed by The Starr Caled CASTOR or APOLLO [α Geminorum]: beinge In Longetude ♋ 15°34′ & Latt*itude* 10°02′ N*orth*: DECLINATION 32°30′ N*orth*: & found My Self in the Latt*itude* of 17°28′ S*outh*. Now the Sunn Beinge Almost in our ZENETH I could nott Observe the Sun att his Meredian Altitude. I find by the ☼ Ampletude That HEARE is 7°00′ VARATION East.

[2] Assention; variant Aseneam. These are Trindade and Martin Vaz Islands which lie in 20°30′S, 29°19′W and 20°28′S, 28°51′W respectively. Assention does not exist. The position of Trinidad is given in Tapp, *Sea-mans Kalender*, p. 178, as 19°10′S, 355°20′E, which is 4°40′ west of St Michaels or 23°10′ west of the Lizard (given as 18°30′E), ibid. p. 172. The position of Ascension is given as 18°50′S, 353°20′E, which is 6°40′W of St Michaels or 25°10′W of the Lizard. Ibid. p. 165. On the chart of 'Brasilia' in Doncker's *Sea Atlas* 'Ascençaon' is shown about 240 leagues off the coast of Brazil, in about 20°S, with 'I de Trindad' about 70 leagues further E by N, in about 19°S. Narbrough's position, 21°08′W of the Lizard, was thus about 4° of longitude from Ascension and his noon latitude 18°50′S corresponded exactly with it. He would have known that while latitudes were reasonably accurate longitudes were liable to considerable error (Captain Sturmy places Ascension in 17°19′S, 17°01′W from the Lizard. He also lists Trinidada, 19°50′S, 14°24′W, St Maria Dagasta 19°38′S, 12°14′W, and Island de Martin 19°00′S, 08°03′W, all of which formed a line of islands and were shown on charts at the time, Sturmey, *Mariners Magazine*, p. 187. Hence Narbrough's concern that as he approached the latitude given for these islands he might encounter them. Furthermore he refers to his 'draft', chart, which may have placed the islands in a slightly different position. See also below, p. 392. [Voyage]

[3] The lead did not reach the seabed with 140 fathoms of line out.

[4] The pink was cast off since if they came upon breakers or shoal water in the night taking avoiding action quickly would be difficult, and possibly dangerous, with the pink in tow astern. Furthermore with the ships

my Selfe nere the Island of Assention in Lat*itud* of 19°10′ South: But Saw none of those Islands: I judge I went to the westward of them.
[*margin: fingerpost*] Many Sea fowles flyeninge to an froe: Course SBW By my Compase: I made all the Saile [*margin: fingerpost*] I Could to the Southward: a fine Gale al night at NNE and Smoath watter: much fish about the Shipp But Could not tak any.
All my men are in Good health. I Brought a new fore Saile to the yard to mend the ould one.

[59] **Jannary 1669 *Sweepstakes* Latt*itud* 19°48′ S**
8
Beinge Satterday faier weather wind at NNE a fine fresh Gale:
the Course By my Compas was SBW: I had 8°40′ variation E this morninige by an Amplytud: I Sounded but noe Ground. My true Course from yesterday at none tile to day at none is *South* 19°35′ west: distance sailed 61·3 Miles: depart*ur* 20·6 miles West: def*erence* Latt*itud* 58′: Latt*itud* by account and By my Loge at none 19°48′ South.
Meridian distanc from Porte Praya 246·9 Mils W
Longitud from Porte Praya 04°11′·7 W
Longitud from The Lizard 21°29′·8 W
Meridian distancc from the Liz*ard* 1084 Miles W
Variation at Sun Sett by an Amplytud 10°06′ E
Lat*itud* at two acclock in the moringe by observations of the Great Beares Side[1] 20°28′ South.
The Sun in my zeneth[2] at 2 aclock in the morneinge the 9 day. [*margin:* ☼ Zeneth] Misty Temprate weather we had under the Sunn.[3]

9
Beinge Sunday faier weather: I tooke the Pinke in a Towe this morninge wind at NBE a fine Gale:
Course By my Compass SSW all this last 24 houers: variation at Sun Rising 11°08′ E True Course made was S*outh* 30°30′ west: dist*ance* Sailed 56·7 miles: def*erence* Lat*itud* 00°49′: depart*ur* west 28·9 miles: Lat*itud* By account at none 20°37′ South Lat*itud*.
Meri*dian* distance from Porte Praya 275·8 Mile.
Longitud from Porte Praya 04°42′·9.
Longitud from the Lizard 22°01′ W
Meridian dist*ance* from the Lizard 1112·9 W
I have 11°26′ variation E By an amplytud taken at Sun Sett: Lat*itud* 20°50′ *South* and Longitud 22°04′ from the Lizard.

---

sufficiently separated if one ran aground she could warn the other to stand off (by firing a gun or other signal) and the safe vessel could then give assistance or if necessary rescue the crew of the grounded vessel.

[1] Great Bear's side: β Ursæ Major.

[2] Directly overhead.

[3] Wood, BL, MS 3833, ff. 10v–11r: 'All This Day Wee Expected to See one of The Islands Eather TRINADADE [Ilha da Trindade] or Acention but Could See Neather. By My Reaconing I Sayled by A Duch Draught Printed [no date given] (10 Leagues To the Eastward of ASCENTION & By an ENGLISH Draught 30 Leagues Made by one Welch [see above, p. 183, n. 2] But By One of MERCATERS [*blank*] Leagues. THE HOLLANDS Draught Maketh the Land Lye 100 Leagues More To the Westward Then our English doe.'

[60] **January 1669 *Sweepstakes* in the Lat*itud* 21°44′ S**
10
Beinge faier weather this 24 hower wind at NNE fine gale:
By my Compas SSW or nere it: Variation this morninge 11°25′ East. [*margin: drawing of a compass*] My Course made this 24 houers aloweinge al faults to is SWBS: distance Sailed 80·5 mils: Departur 44·8 mils west: def*erence* Lat*itud* 01°07′: Latt*itud* By judgement 21°44′ S*outh*. Variation at ☼ Sett 11°52′ E [*margin: 2 fingerposts and 5 ☆ for the southern cross*] This night I tooke Seaverall Observations of the Southerne Constellations of the heavens.
Meridian distance from Port Praya 320·6 Mils W
Longitud from Porte Praya 05°30′·4 W
Longitud the Lizard 22°48′·5 W
Meridian distan*ce* from the Lizard 1157·7 Mils W

11
Beinge Tusday faier weather wind at N*orth* a fine fresh gale this 24 houers: Smoath water and Temporate healthey weather.
Variation of the Compase 11°50′ E
True Course made is SWBS: distance Sailed 90 Miles: departur west 50 miles: def*erence* Latt*itud* S*outh* 1°15′: Lat*itud* by Judgment at the ☼ one [on] the meridian 22°59′ S
Variation at Sun Set 11°52′ E
The Cause of my keepinge So Southerly a Cours is to make my Passage the Shorter to the Porte of St Julyan[1] Lyinge in the Latt*itud* of 49°16′ South and Long*itud* from the Liz*ard*.[2]
Meridian distance from Port Praya 370·6 Mils W
Longit*ud* from Porte Praya 06°24′·9 W
Longit*ud* from the Lizard 23°43′ W
Meridian dist*ance* from the Lizard 1207·7 Mils W
This day I Rumaged[3] my hould and Stowed al Lumber downe and filed Eight tun of Salt water:[4] I have fresh water for Six weekes.

[61] **January 1669 *Sweepstakes* at Sea Bound out 24°49′.**
12
Beinge Weddensday faier weather from Tusday att none till to day at none: wind at NNW a Stife gale:
Course by my Compass SSW But my True Course I make to Be SWBS & distance Sailed

[1] Puerto San Julián (49°19′S, 67°43′W); variants Port, Porte, St Julian, Julians, Julyan, Narbrough is trying to approximate his course to a great circle which is the shortest distance between two points on a sphere. Wood, BL, MS 46A, p. 146, notes 'This Port was named by Ferdinando Magellan a Portugall who for some difference or discontent against Emanuell his Prince left his Countrey and Went for Spaine where he was entertained by Charles the 5th for the discovery of a Passage this way for the Molluco Iselands which he did Pforme through this straights which bears his name and was killed by the Natives of Molluco Iselands.' This information is repeated in BL, MS 3833, f. 20r.

[2] No figure is given.

[3] See above, p. 160.

[4] Tun: large cask or barrel. *NOED*. The tun was filled with salt water to replace the fresh and maintain the vessel's stability. See above, p. 176, n. 2.

132 miles & Departure west 73·4 miles: def*erence* Latt*itud* 01°50′: Latt*itud* By account at none by my Looge 24°49′ South.
Merid*ian* distance from Porte Praya 444 Miles W
Longitud from Porte Pray 07°45′·2.
Longitud from the Lizard 25°03′·3.
Meridian dist*ance* from the Lizard 1281·1 Mils.
No Amplitud or Azimuth to day: it is Cloudy. This Afternone at 1 acclocke wee had a Stoute gale of wind at West: and much Raine: all the Afternone I handed[1] Boath my Top Sailes But set them in an hower after.
I keept the Pinke yet in a Toowe.
I Brought my mended fore Saile to the yarde:[2] itt tooke up 19 yards of Canvas to Repaier it.[3] Much Raine to night and a fine gale to night at NW.

13
Beinge Thursday Cloudy weather this morninge the wind Came to the NNE: a fine gale: Course by my Compass SWBS: a greate Sea Came oute of the SE. My True Course made is SW: dist*ance* Sailed 69·5 miles: departuer 49 miles west: def*erence* Latt*itud* S*outh* 49′: Lat*itud* by account 25°38′ S*outh*.
Meridian distance from Porte Pray 493 Mils W
Longitud from Porte Pray 08°39′·2 W
Longitud from the Lizard 25°57′·3 W
Meridian distance from the Lizard 1330·1 Mils W
This morninge I Cast the Pinke Lose: Beinge a greate Sea.[4] Variation 13°04′ E at Sunset.

[62] **January 1669 *Sweepstakes* at Sea Latt*itud* 26°40′ S**
14
Beinge friday Cloudy Gusty Rainey weather wind at NNW: a great Rowleinge [rolling] Sea Cam out of the South:
Course By my Compass SWBS: But My True Cours made this Last 24 howers is SW 7° westerly: dist*ance* Sailed 101 Miles: departur west 79·4 miles: def*erence* Lat*itud* S*outh* 1°02′: Lat*itud* by obser*vation* ☼ 26°40′ South.
Meridian dist*ance* from Porte Praya 572·4 Mils W
Longitud from Porte Praya 10°07′·2 W
Longitud from the Lizard 27°25′·3 W
Meridian distantce from the Lizard 1409·4 Mils W
Variation by my Amplytud at ☼ Set 13°51′ East.

[1] Furled.

[2] He replaced the foresail which had been changed on 7 January, with the mended one.

[3] The amount of canvas needed was 19 yards from one bolt the widths of which varied between 24 and 30 inches.

[4] Towing in heavy weather is difficult and can be dangerous as the towed vessel rides forward in the sea and then falling back brings the towrope suddenly tight with consequent danger of parting it or damaging the towing points. If the towrope is short the towed vessel may ride forward and collide with the towing vessel. If the towed vessel sheers away from the course there is also the possibility of girding (a sideways pull which can capsize a vessel).

But few fish Seene now and then a small bonneto taken by harpeinge Irons:[1] Sum Sea fowle flyeinge to and frow [*margin: drawing of a bird*] which wee Calle Black Boebyes.[2] Two Corlews[3] I sawe flyeinge to the Eastward.

15

Beinge Satterday Cloudy Rainey weather wind at NNW A gale: Seaverall Claps of Thunder and Lightinge this morninge:
Course by my Compass SWBS: But my True Course this 24 houers is SW 5°10′ westerly: distance Sailed 81 miles: departur west 62·4 mils: def*erence* Lat*itud* So*uth* 52′: Lat*itud* by accounte at none 27°32′ South.
Meridian distance from Porte Praya 634·8 Mils W
Longitud from Porte Praya 11°16′·8 W
Longitud from the Lizard 28°34′·9 W
Meridian distance from the Lizard 1471·9 Mils W
Rane to night and gusty weather wind at NNW.

[63] **January 1669 *Sweepstakes* at Sea Lat*itud* 29°00′ S**

16

Beinge Cloudy Rainey weather and gusty and a stoute [gale] of winde at NNW: with much Raine to day:
Course By my Compase SWBS: I went away [with] only my fore Course:[4] this Eveinge I Sounded and noe Ground at [*margin: fingerpost and drawing of a lead and line*] 130 fatham. My True Course made this 24 houres is SW: and distance Sailed 124 miles: departur west 88 miles: def*erence* of Latt*itud* 01°28′: Lat*itud* by account at none 29°00′ So*uth*.
Variation I judge to be 14° E: noe amplytud.
Meridian distance from Porte Pray 722·8 Miles W
Longitud from Porte Praya 12°56′·6 W
Longitud from the Lizard 30°14′·7 W
Meridian distance from the Lizard 1559·9 Mils W

17

Beinge Munday Cloudy Gusty weather and Raine wind at NNW till 6 aclocke this morninge then it Cam to the SSW a gale: I Plyed to windward.
Course made this 24 howers is SW 5° So*uth*: distance Sailed 89 miles: departur west 57·1 mils: def*erence* Latt*itud* 01°08′: Lat*itud* by obser*vation* ☼ 30°08′ South.
Meridian distance from Porte Praya 779·9 Miles W
Longitud from Porte Praya 14°02′·1.

[1] Harping iron: a barbed spear or javelin used for spearing whales and large fish, a harpoon. *NOED*.

[2] The brown booby (*Sula leucogaster*), masked booby (*S.dactylatra*) and red-footed booby (S. *sula*, are all found in this area, but the brown booby seems the most likely bird as having the largest area of dark colouring. Harrison, *Seabirds*, pp. 291–2, 389–90. In Rawl. MS A. 318, Narbrough identified these birds as Black Noddies; see below, p. 394.

[3] This is presumably curlew (*Numenius arquata*) but since they are not normally found at sea this is probably a misidentification.

[4] With only the fore course (the lowest square sail on the fore mast) set.

Longitud from the Lizard 31°20′·2.
Meridian distance from the Lizard 1617 Miles.

18
Beinge Tusday Cloudy weather wind at SEBE a gale.
True Course made this 24 houer South 71° west: distance sailed 43 mils: dep*artur* 40·7 mils: def*erence* Lat*itud* 14′: Lat*itud* 30°22′ S
Meridian distance from Prot Praya 820·6 Mils.
Longitud from Porte Praya 14°48′·9.
Longitud from the Lizard 32°07′·0.
Meridian distance from the Lizard 1657·7 Mils.

[64] **January 1669 *Sweepstakes* at Sea Latt*itud* 31°08′ S**
19
Beinge wedensday Cloudy Gusty weather wind at SE this 24 houers: a Stoute gale: and a great Sea out of the Southerboard:
Course By my Compass SWBS: But I make my True Course to be South 60° west: distance Sailed 92 miles: departur west 79·2 miles: def*erence* Lat*itud* 46′: Lat*itud* By account at none 31°08′ S
Meridian distance from Porte Praya 899·8 Mils W
Longitud from Porte Praya 16°21′·4.
Longitud from the Lizard 33°39′·5.
Meridian distance from the Lizard 1736·9 Mils.
This day I Brought my new Sailes to the yards douteinge I Should have a Storme[1] for it had an il aspect: this night it Blew a Stout [gale] of wind at E
[*margin: fingerpost*] Variation is nere as I Could finde is 15°00′ E

20
Beinge Thursday faier weather wind at ESE a St*out* Gale.
Course By my Compass SWBS: But I make my True Course to be South 60° west: dista*nce* Sailed 108 miles: departure west 93·5 miles: deff*erence* Latt*itud* 00°54′: Lat*itud* by ob*servation* ☼ 32°02′ S
Meridian distance from Porte Praya 993·3 Mils W
Longitud from Porte[2] Praya 18°10′·9.
Longitud from the Lizard 35°29′·0 W
Meridian distance from the Lizard 1830·4 Mils.
I ame forced to Lose a greate deale of time in Stayeinge for the Pinke: She Sailes Soe heaveey: I ame unwilinge to Leave her by reason of discover*ing* the Coast with her when I ame in the Cuntry.[3]
Variation at ☼ set 18°16′ E

[1] Expecting a storm.
[2] The word 'Porte' repeated in the original.
[3] The pink, with its much lesser draught than the *Sweepstakes*, would be able to go safely closer inshore and therefore provide more information about depths inshore and nature of the seabed as well as seeing any harbours, rivers or bays that might not be obvious from further out.

[65] **January 1669 *Sweepstakes* at Sea Latt*itud* 32°50′ S**

21

Beinge friday faier weather: wind at SE and SSE a fine gale: and Smoath water: my Course Stereed by my Compass was SWBS: a fine gale this 24 houers. My True Course made is South 60° west: distan*ce* Sailed 74·5 miles: departur west 64·5 mils: def*erence* Latt*itud* 48′: Latt*itud* By ob*servation* Sun 32°50′ *South*.
Meridian distance from Porte Praya 1057·8 Mils W
Longitud from Porte Praya 19°27′·7.
Longitud from the Lizard 36°45′·8.
Meridian distance from the Lizard 1894·9 Mils.
Variation By an Amplytud at Sun Sett 17°10′ E
This day I ordered Seaverall new Ropes to be Reived[1] and the ould ons to be Layd up for other offices.[2]
My men are all in Good health: Blessed be God.
It Proved Calme this afternone: Smoath water.

22

Beinge Satterday faier Calme weather I drove to the N:ward this 24 houers 6 miles: departur 00: def*erence* Latt*itud* 6′: Latt*itud* by accounte at none 32°44′ S*outh*.
Meridian distance from Porte Praya 1057·8 Mils W
Longitud from Porte Praya 19°27′·7.
Longitud from the Lizard 36°45′·8.
Meridian distance from the Lizard 1894·9 Mils.
This day I Sent my boate aboard the Pinke and mad here Cleane under water: it Beinge quite Calme all day and Smoath water.[3] Temprat weather and houle Sume [wholesome] aier. This afternone I Saw Severall Smale whales[4] and a great many Sea foules flyinge to and froe: [*margin: drawing of a hand holding a lead and line*] I Sounded But had noe ground at 140 fadams.

Magn*etic* Amplytud	38°30′
True Amp*lytud*	20°11′
Variation By an Amplytud at Sun Sett*ing* is	18°19′ E

[66] **January 1669 *Sweepstakes* in the Latt*itud* 33°18′ S**

23

Beinge Sunday faier weather and a fine gale at NE:
Course by my Compase SWBS: But I make my True Course to Be SWBW: distance

[1] To reeve is to pass the end of a rope through a block. This means that some of the running rigging was replaced.

[2] They would probably have been used for spun yarn or oakum (for caulking the planks).

[3] The boat would lie alongside the pink, which would be heeled over by moving weights on board, and the weed and barnacles scrapped off the side with blades attached to the ends of poles. This way it would be possible to reach some way below the waterline. The object of this is to reduce the drag caused by the growth on the side and increase the ship's speed.

[4] The small whales that might be seen in this area include Cuvier's beaked whale (*Ziphius cavirostris*) 20–28 ft (6–7·5 m); southern bottlenose whale (*Hyperoodon planifrons*) 23–32 ft (7–9·8 m); Arnoux's beaked whale (*Berardius arnuxii*) 33–42 ft (10–12·8 m); killer whale (*Orcinus orca*) 21–27 ft (7–9 m). Harris, *Guide*, pp. 137–9.

Sailed 61 miles: departur west 50·8 miles: deferen of Latt*itud* 00°34′: Lat*itud* By observation of the ☼ 33°18′.
Meridian distance from the Porte Praya 1108·6 Mils W
Longitud from Porte Praya 20°28′·7.
Longitud from the Lizard 37°46′·8.
Meridian distance from the Lizard 1945·7 Mils.
Variation of my Compase is now 18°04′ E
Variation of the Comp*ase* By an Amp*lytud* at ☼ Set 17°36′ E

24
Beinge Munday hassy weather: wind at NE a fine Gale:
Course By my Compas SWBS: But By Reasson of varia*tion* I make my True Course to be this 24 houers SW: distance Sailed 90·5 miles: departur west 64 miles: def*erence* Latt*itud* 01°04′: Latt*itud* by account at none 34°22′ South.
Meridian distance from Porte Praya 1172·6 Miles W
Longitud from Porte Praya 21°45′·7.
Longitud from the Lizard 39°03′·8.
Meridian distance from the Lizard 2009·7 Miles.
I judge a curant Sets out of the River of Plat to the South Eastward: for I have fond that I have Gone [*margin: fingerpost*] more to the Southward then I ded exspecte: I ame nowe open with the mouth of the River [*margin: fingerpost*] as I judge.[1] I Sounded this Eveinge at [*margin: drawing of ripple or outflow*] 140 fathams But noe Ground fresh gale But hassy weather wind at NBE: Course by the Compas SWBS. Variation By an Amplytud at Sunset 17°36′ E
This Eveinge my Castellean Lost his memmory in Practice of Gusmond: which he dose indeffer*ent*.[2]

[67] **Jaunary 1669 the *Sweepstakes* at Sea Latt*itud* 35°47′ S*outh*.**
25 Beinge Tusday hassy weather wind at NNE and No*rth* and NNW a fine Gale: and a Light mone [moon] nere her full:
my Course By my Compas SWBS: But alowinge for the variation Beinge 17° E and a Currunt which Setts out of the River of Plate to the Southward I find to day By my observation of the Sun at None To make my True Course SW: distance Sailed 120 Miles: departure west 85 miles: def*erence* Latt*itud* 01°25′ S*outh*: Latt*itud* By Good obser*vation* of the ☼ at non [noon] 35°47′ S*outh*.
Meridian distance from Porte Praya 1257·6 Mils W
Longitud from Porte Praya 23°29′ W
Longitud from the Lizard 40°47′·1 W
Meridian distance from the Lizard 2094·7 W
I Could not have any amplytud to day Beinge hassy.
This Eveinge one of my fore Shrouds Brooke: this night Sum Showers of Raine: and a Stout gale of wind at west.

[1] Abreast the mouth of Río de la Plata (River Plate).

[2] The meaning of this is not clear. 'Castellean' is 'Castilian' and almost certainly refers to Don Carlos. Narbrough's comment is deliberately allusive, but it most likely means Don Carlos was drunk or sick from overeating and that this was often the case.

26

Beinge Wedensday Cloudy hassy weather wind at SE and at SSE: a Stoute gale of winde it Came from the west to the South*ward* to the SE this moringe and Blow hard: I lay atry 2 howers.
Course by my Compas SWBS this 24 houers: But I make my True Course to be South 61°20′ west: distance Sailed 90 miles: departur west 78·6 mils: def*erence* Latt*itud* 00°43′: Latt*itud* By A Good observation at none of the Sun 36°30′ South Lat*itud.*
Meridian distance from Porte Praya 1336·2 Mils W
Longitud from Porte Praya 25°06′·0.
Longitud from the Lizard 42°24′·1.
Meridian dist*ance* from the Lizard 2173·3 Mils.
This morninge one of my maine Shrouds Brooke.[1]

[68] **Janary 1669 the *Seepstakes* at Sea Latt*itud* 36°10′ S**

27

Beinge Thursday faier weather: wind this 24 houers at S*outh* and SBW a fine Gale:
Course By my Compass SWBW and WBS and W*est*: But findinge 20° variation of the Compase E*ast*arly and By my obser*vation* at none I make my True Course to Be No*rth* 70° West: distance Sailed 52·6 miles: departur weste 49·6 mils: def*erence* Latt*itud* 00°18′: Lat*itud* By ob*servation* ☼ 36°12′ S
Meridian distance from Porte Praya 1385·8 Miles W
Longitud from Porte Praya 26°06′·6.
Longitud from the Lizard 43°24′·7.
Meridian distance from the Lizard 2222·9 Miles.
Variation at Sun Settinge By Amplytud is 19°59′ E
My Magniticall Amplytud was 38°11′ S*outh* from the W

28

Beinge friday faier weather this moreninge the winde Came to the E and to the NE: a fine gale and Smoath water:
Course By my Compas SW and W*est* and SWBW. After Severall Courses I make my true Cours to Be North 75° W: distance Sailed 35 miles: dep*artu*r west 33·8 miles: def*erence* Latt*itud* 00°09′: Lat*itud* By observa*tion* of the Sun one [on] the Meridian 36°03′ South.
Meridian distance from Porte Praya 1419·6 Mils W
Longitud from Porte Praya 26°49′·6.
Longitud from the Lizard 44°07′·7.
Meridian distance from the Lizard 2256·7 Mils W
Variation found By amplytud at ☼ Risinge 19°53′ E
This day the Shipps Company dranke Beare: very Good.
The Aier Coole and Temporate and healthey.
I Sounded to day But noe Ground at 120 fadams.

[1] Wood, BL, MS 3833, f. 12r: 'Heare I Judge My Self To be a 130 Leagues To the East of CAPE St ANTONY By a Duch Chard in Plano & by Mercators Chard 82 Leagues.' Cabo San Antonio lies on the south side of the entrance to Río de la Plata, 36°27′S, 56°42′W. Wood's reference to a plane chart means one which did not allow for the changing width of the meridians.

[69] **January 1669 the *Sweepstakes* in the Lat*itud* 37°21′ S**
29
Beinge Satterday hassy weather wind at N*orth* and at NW A Stife Gale al this 24 howers: Course By my Compass SW: But I make my True Course to be SWBW: distance Sailed 140 mils: departur west 117 Miles: def*erence* Latt*itud* By obser*vation* 01°18′: Lat*itud* at none 37°21′ S
Meridian distance from Porte Praya 1536·6 Mils W
Longitud from Porte Praya 29°14′·6.
Longitud from the Lizard 46°32′·7.
Meridian distance from the Lizard 2373·7 Mils.
Variation By an Amplytud at ☼ Riz is 19°10′ E
Foggie weather this Eveinge with Sum Raine: the wind Came to the WSW a Stife gale: this night I Sounded But had noe ground at 100 fadams: it is Coole weather.[1]

30
Beinge Sunday hassy weather: wind at South a Sti*fe* Gale and a tumbleinge Sea: Course By my Compass So*uth* and S°W and WSW. Course mad this 24 houers SSW: distance Sailed 92 miles: departure west 35·4 mils: def*erence* Latt*itud* 01°25′: Latt*itud* By obs*ervation* ☼ 38°46′ S*outh*.
Meridian distance from Porte Praya 1572·0 Miles W
Longitud from Porte Praya 29°59′·6.
Longitud from the Lizard 47°17′·7.
Meridian distance from the Lizard 2409·1 Mils.
I find a Stronge Currunt Setts to the Southward which I judge Coms out of the River of Plate: this day at 12 aclocke I observed the water of the Sea to be of a more whiteer Couler than is Euseall [usual]: I Sounded But noe Ground at 100 fadoms: few fish to be sene about the Shipp: Sum Greate Sea foules sene flyinge to and fro. Wind this afternone at S: Cours SWBW.
Variation of the Compas at Sun Settinge is 19°00′ E
Magnetticall Amplytud at Sun Settinge 37°30′ W*est* S*outhe*rly.[2]
True Amplytud then was west Southerly 18°30′.

[70] **January 1669 the *Sweepstakes* at Sea 39°27′ S**
31
Beinge Munday Calme this morninge then the wind Came to NW a fine gale: at 11 aclocke the wind went Round the Compas to the westward: and Cam to the No*rth* with much Thunder and Lighteninge and Sum Raine: very darke Clouds: Could aier and hassy. Severall spots of weeds drave Past the Shipp and a Great many Sea fowles of a Blacke couler seene: Smoath water. My men all in Good health: wee drink Bere. This day one of my maine Shrouds Brooke and one fore Shroud Brooke and the Stroope [strop] of the maine jeare Blocke.[3] Variation By an Amplytud at the ☼Riz is 19°43′ E Severall Gobs

[1] Wood, BL, MS 3833, f. 12r: 'This day att Noon Cape S[t] ANTONY the Cape to the Southward of ROE DE LA PLATO Bare WNW of Mee 70 Leagues by a duch plane Chard Butt by Mercators Chart itt Bare from Mee NW 20 Leagues.'

[2] The sun set to the south of the western cardinal point.

[3] The main jeer block was the block used for hoisting the main yard up the mast into its normal sailing position.

[jobs] of Carpenters woorke done to day to the Shipp: Sids alofte and to the deakes. My top Saile Sheets and Riginge Groues [grows] ould.
After divers Courses made this 24 houers I make my True Course to Be SW: distance Sailed 58 Miles: departur west 41 miles: def*erence* Lat*itud* 00°41′: Lat*itud* By account at none aloweinge a current to Sett to the Southward Latt*itud* 39°27′ South.
Meridian distance from Porte Praya 1613 Miles W
Longitud from Porte Praya 30°52′·1 W
Meridian distance from the Lizard 2450·1 Miles W
Longitud from the Lizard 48°10′·2 W
This Eveinge at 7 aclocke I Sounded But noe Ground at 130 fadams: Very many Riplins Sene as if their were Severall Setts of Tids:[1] But noe Ground.
Very Could weather and Shearp aier wind at SSE. Severall whales Seene nere the Shipp of an ordinary Biggness: The flyeinge fish and Bonnetos have quiet Left the Shipp.
This night it was Could: Sharpe aiere.

[71] **February 1669 the *Sweepstakes* at Sea Lat*itud* 39°15′ S**
1
Beinge Tusday Cloudy foggie weather this mor*ninge* and Little [wind] at SE: I Stood to the SW: this forenone I [*margin: drawing of a bird*] saw a Bondance [abundance] of Sea fowles flyeinge and Swiminge: it Proved Calme: here wee saw a great many Small Shrimps about the Shipp and Eight younge Seals [margin: *drawing of a seal*] Close By the Shipp of a Blacke Couler as Bigg as an ordinary Spanell dooge each of them:[2] they did not Stay Longe by the Shipp: I Sounded but had noe gound at 140 [*margin: drawing of a hand holding a lead and line*] fadam. About 12 aclocke the wind Came to the SSE: I stered SWBW By my Compas: I Alowe 19° variation Easterly that is the north Pointe is 19° to the Eastward: Noe observation this two dayes it Being Cloudy. Afternone a fresh gale at SSE:
Course By my Compas SWBW. The Aier is mighty Could as is in England in September:[3] these Seas are very apte to veayable [variable] and Changeable winds: for this three or fower dayes followinge the winds have Rund Round the Compass two or three times in twenty fower houers: the water very Changable: of a whitis Collour which Gives mee to beleve wee are in Soundinge[4] for the Coast here is Sandy and Should [shoal] a great way of[f] as what I have from others.[5] After divers Courses this 24 houers I make my True Course to Be WBN: distance Sailed 61·5 miles: departur west 60 miles: def*erence* Latt*itud* 00°12′: Latt*itud* by accou*nt* at 39°15′.
Meridian distance from Porte Pray 1673·00 Miles W
Longitud from Porte Praya 32°12′·7 W

[1] Rippling on the surface of the sea, like the meeting of tidal streams.

[2] Possibly the South American fur seal (*Arctocephalus australis*) or the South American sea lion (*Otaria flavescens*), both of which might appear black and vary in size up to about 6½ ft (2 m) and 9 ft (2·8 m) in length respectively. Shirihai, *Complete Guide*, pp. 334–6, 344–5.

[3] This was the time of the Little Ice Age (c. 1550–1850). The Thames froze over in 1655, 1663, 1666, 1667, 1683 and many other years, so that temperatures were colder than today.

[4] A ship was said to be in soundings when the depth of water was such that it could be measured by the lead line.

[5] From the reports of other mariners.

Longitud from the Lizard 49°30′·8 W
Meridian distance from the Lizard 2510·1 Mils W
This Eveinge I Sounded But noe Ground at 130 fada*ms*: wind at South a fine fresh gale: I Stered by my Compas WSW. At 10 aclocke at night I observed the water to [*margin: drawing of a ripple or outflow*] Riple: I Sounded And had Ground at 70 fadams: [*margin:drawing of a hand holding a lead and line*]. Grisly[1] Red fine Sand: I hove the Lead againe immediatly and had the Same Soundings: I tacked and Stood to the E:ward: I fired a Gun for the Pinke to tacke which dide.

[72] **February 1669 the *Sweepstakes* in the Latt*itud* 39°15′ S**
2
Beinge wedensday Cloudy weather this morninge wind att SBE and So*uth* and SW: I Plyed to the Southward: little wind this 24 howers. I make make my True Course west: distance Sailed 10 miles: departur west 10 miles: def*erence* Latt*itud* 00°00′: Latt*itud* By observation of the Sun on the meridian 39°15′ South.
Meridian distance from Porte Praya 1683·0 Mils W
Longitud from Porte Praya 32°25′·6 W
Meridian distance from the Lizard 2520·1 Mils W
Longitud from the Lizard 49°43′·7 W
Variation of the Compas by a Good Amp*lytud* is 17°05′ E
Here is many Riplinge of the water and Sevearall Spots [*margin: drawing of weed*] of weeds as Sea ore Senne:[2] But I doe not find any Currant or tide Sett any way in this offinge.[3] Today [*Margin: drawings of a fish, seal, bird at beginning of next 3 lines*] I Saw many Great whales and fower Small Seales and aBounddance [abundance] of Pyed fowles as bigg as Sea Guls[4] flyinge to and frow and Swimminge: it Proved Calme. I this afternone I hoisted out my Boate and Sounded[5] [*margin: drawing of hand holding a lead and line*] But had noe Ground at 140 fadams: I judge the Banke Rizeth Steep.
I Shoot 16 of those fowles they Beinge veary tame and [*margin: drawing of a bird*] would not Rise when I Shoot amongst them and killed their Consorts Close By them till I dissterbd [disturbed] them with the boate: they are wery Good meate.
I judge I am not Past fowerty Leagus of the Land of Cape Das Aranas Gordas.[6] My Entent is to hale in with the Land at Cape Blancos[7] for the Coast is Should al aLonge here and never a Good harbower: as is Reported By Mr Harkcluts Bookes of Mr Cavandish Vojage

[1] Grizzly: greyish. *NOED*. Wood, BL, MS 3833, f. 12v, 2 February: 'Last Night at 10 of the Clock we Sounded & found ground being 70 fadtham Deape Black Sand Mingled with Some Red.'

[2] See below, p. 399, where Narbrough explains that they are over beds of seaweed.

[3] Meaning to seaward: to get an offing is to get well off the land.

[4] This sounds like the Cape or pintado petrel (*Daption capense*), length 15–16 in (38–40 cm) wingspan 32–6 in (81–91 cm), slightly smaller than the common gull (*Laurus canus*), which is common in these latitudes and is essentially dappled black and white. Harrison, *Seabirds*, pp. 236–7, 336–7.

[5] It is easier to sound from the bow of a boat as it can be kept head to wind and held up to the lead line (to keep it vertical) by the oars.

[6] This is shown on the Doncker chart (Plate 2) as C. das Arenas Gardas in 38°20′S.

[7] Cabo Blanco (47°12′S, 65°45′W); variants, Balanccoo, Blancas, Blancco, Blankeo, Bllanco, Brancae, Brancas. Also known as Cape St George, Gorge, and Cape of Good Hope.

this way:[1] And alsoe this Country is apte to Sunden [sudden] Gusts of winds out of the Sea.

[73] **February 1669 the *Sweepstakes* at Sea in Latt*itud* 39°22′ S**

3

Beinge Thursday faier weather and Little wind betwen the SWBW and S all this 24 howers. True Course mad this 24 [howers] is SE: distance Sailed 9·9 miles: depar*tur* E 7 mils: def*erence* of Latt*itud* 00°07′: Latt*itud* by ob*servation* of the ☼ 39°22′ S
Meridian distance from Porte Praya 1676·0 Miles W
Longitud from Porte Praya 32°17′·1
Longitud from the Lizard 49°35′·2
Meridian distance from the Lizard 2513·1 Mils W
Variation of the Compas By an Amplitud at ☼ Set 20°30′ E
Could weather and Great dues [dews] in the Night
Noe Small fish Sen about the Shipp or in the Sea.

4

Beinge friday faier weather the wind Came to the No*rth* a fine Gale and ware[2] weather: Course by my Compase SWBW: But I make my true Course this 24 howers WSW: distance Sailed 62·5 miles: departur wes*t* 58 mils: def*erence* of Latt*itud* 00°24′: Lat*itud* by ob*servation* ☼ 39°46′ S
Meridian distance from Porte Praya 1734 Mils W
Longitud from Porte Praya 33°34′·1 W
Longitud from the Lizard 50°52′·2 W
Meridian distance from the Lizard 2571·1 Mils W
Variation of the Compas at Sun Rize 20°16′ E
Variation of the Compas at Sun Sett 20°51′ E
[*margin: drawing of a hand holding a lead and line*] I Sounded at 7 aclocke But noe Ground at 140 fadam*s*
This afternone I Consulted with my officers whether it would be Best for me to Stay for the Pinke and take her alonge with me or to make the Best of my way towards the Straights: that I myght not lose this oppertunity of this wind: it Beinge at No*rth*: they all Concluded to keepe her Company: which I deede.

[74] **February 1669 the *Sweepstakes* att Sea Lat*itud* 40°42′ S**

5

Beinge Satterday foggie hassy weather wind at No*rth*: a fine gale this 24 houers and Smoath watter warem temprate Aier:
Course By my Compase from friday at none tile today at none SWBS: But I make my True Course to be SWBW: distance Sailed 101 mils: Departur west 84 mils: def*erence* Latt*itud* 00°56′: Latt*itud* By account at 12 aclocke 40°42′.

[1] Francis Petty, 'The prosperous voyage of M. Thomas Candis esquire', Hakluyt, *Principal Navigations*, III, pp. 803–25. 'The 16 day of December [1586] we fell with the coast of America in 47 degrees ⅓ the land bearing West from us about 6 leagues off: from which place we ran along the shore, untill we came into 48 degrees. It is steepe beach all along.'

[2] See below, p. 400, where the word is given as 'warm'.

Meridian distance from Porte Praya 1818 Mils W
Longitud from Porte Praya 35°24′·5 W
Longitud from the Lizard 52°42′·6 W
Meridian distance from the Lizard 2655·1 Mils W
Variation at Sun Riseinge to day is 19°18′ E
[*margin :drawing of weed and a bird*] Severall SPots of Rockeweeds Seene and Sea foules as Bigg as Gesse of blacke and white Couler.[1] At 7 aclocke this afternone I was in the Latt*itud* of 41°00′ So*uth* and in Longitud from the Lizard of England West 52°50′: and meridiane distance from the the Lizard 895 Leagus: And in Longitud West from the Island of St Jago 35°34′ And Meridian distance 616 Leg*us*. [*margin: drawing of a hand holding a lead and line* 50] Then I Sounded and had Ground at feviety [fifty] fadams: the Soundinges is fine Red Sande with Sum blacke: the water is of a deep willow Grenne. I judge I ame twenty Leagus of the Land: I Stered away from thence SBW by my Compase which is SWBS for the Compase have here 21° [*margin: drawing of a compass*] variation Easterly. At 12 aclocke at night I Sound*ed* [*margin: drawing of a hand holding a lead and line* 70] a Gaine and had 70 fadams: the Same Ground as before: rather finer Sand.[2] I had then Sailed from 7 aclocke to 12 aclocke 5 Leagus SWBS: it Beinge but SBW by the Compas: which thou must take heed to know the variation here: it Beinge ner two Points.
Advice with Don Carolus wher it would be Best to Land.

[75] **February 1669 the *Sweepstakes* in the Latt*itud* 41°48′ S**
6
Beinge Sunday hasy foggy weather: wind at N*orth* a fine Ga*le*: this morninge at 6 aclocke I Sounded and hade Ground [*margin: drawing of a hand holding a lead and line* 75] at Seaventy five fadams: fine white Sand and one S*um* great in it.[3] My Course from the first Soundinge at 7 aclo*cke* at night till this time was SBW by my Compas and I had sailed 14 leagus.
Course by my Compase this 24 houers was SWBW and SBW: But I make my True Cours to be So*uth* 48°30′ west: distance Sailed 100 miles: departur west 74·5 Miles: deference of Latt*itud* 01°06′: Latt*itud* by Obser*vation* of the ☼ one [on] the meridian 41°48′ South.
Meridian distance from Porte Praya 1892·5 Miles W
Longitud from Porte Praya 37°03′·8.
Longitud from the Lizard 54°21′·9.
Meridian distance from the Lizard 2729·6 Miles W
Noe Amplytud taken by Reasson of foggie weather this day But I judge here is 21° East variation. [*margin: drawing of a hand holding a lead and line*] I Sounded this Eveinge But noe Ground at 100 fadams: The Pinke in Company with mee: Calme in the

[1] These might be albatrosses which are generally black, dark brown or grey and white and have body of a similar size to a goose but an appreciably greater wingspan. The wandering albatross (*Diomedea exultans*), royal albatross (*D. epomophora*), black-browed albatross (*D. melanophris*), yellow-nosed albatross (*D. chlororhynchos*), grey-headed albatross (*D. chrysostoma*), sooty albatross (*Phoebetria fusca*), and light-mantled sooty albatross (*P. palpebrata*) might all be encountered in this position. The first two are larger than the others and are therefore more likely to have been the birds sighted. Harrison, *Seabirds*, pp. 221–32.

[2] Wood, MS 3883, f. 12v: 'Att 12 we Sounded againe and found 55 fatham Somewhat Smaller Sand the Water heare was of a Wilow greane Coulour.' Presumably one of these soundings has been incorrectly transcribed.

[3] This probably means that some of the grains of sand were of a greater size than those termed fine.

Eveinge mightty fooggy weather: at 8 aclocke at night the wind Came to the SW a fresh gale and Extrme thicke of fogg and Lighteninge Round the heavens: I Stood to the SE:ward. This night I fired Severall Muskeets to Give the Pinke notice in Keepinge Company.

7

Beinge Munday Bloweinge foggy weather wind at SW:
Course By my Compase SE: alowinge al falts and variation I make my True Cours this 24 houers to Be S 40°00′ E: distance sailed 60 mils: departur E 38·8 miles: def*erence* Latt*itud* 46′: Lat*itud* 42°34′ S.
Meridian distance from Porte Praya 1853·7 Mils W
Longitud from Port Praya 36°12′·2
Longitud from the Lizard west 53°30′·3
Meridian distance from the Lizard 2690·8 Mils W
Coulde weather to day and hassy fogge. I judge here is 20° E variation of the Compas.

[76] **Ferauary 1669 the *Seepstakes* [*sic*] at Sea in 43°09′ S**
8
Beinge Tusday hassy Cloudy weather with Sum Raine: wind at 8 aclocke to the WNW a Stife gale:
Course By my Compass SSW: But my True Cours this 24 houers South 30°11′ East: distance Sailed 40·4 miles: departure East ~~def Latt~~ 20·4 mils: def*erence* Latt*itud* 00°35′: Latt*itud* by accou*nt* at none 43°09′ South.
Meridian distance from Praya 1833·3 Mils W
Longitud from Porte Praya 35°44′·2 W
Longitud from the Lizard 53°02′·3 W
Meridian distance from the Lizard 2670·4 Mils W
Variation By an Amplytud at Sun Rise is 18°00′ E
Variation By A Good Amplytud at Sun Set is 19°48′ E
At 7 aclocke this afternone the wind Cam to the WSW a Stife Gale: I Stood to the SE:ward: much [*margin: drawing of weed*] Rockeweed past by mee to day: very Could Aier and So Continued all Night: Severall Sea foules Sene.

9
Beinge Weddensday faier weather this morninge But hassy Cloudy in the Afternone it Proved Calme:
Co*urse* By my Compase this 24 houers was SSW & SSE. I make my True Course to Be South 09° E distance sailed 66·5 mils: def*erence* Lat*itud* 01°06′: Departur E 10·4 mils: Latt*itud* by acc*ount* 44°15′
Meridian distance from Porte Praya 1822·9 Mils W
Longitud from Porte Praya 35°29′·8 W
Longitud from the Lizard 52°47′·9 W
Meridian distance from the Lizard 2660·0 Mils W
Variation By a Good Amplytud at Sun Riz is 19°30′ E
I am at halfe Lowance of Beere: my Beere in the Ship that is the Kings Alowance is as Good as Can be dranke and All the Rest of the Provissions Proves very Good.

[77] **Febrauary 1669 the *Sweepstakes* in the *Latitud* 44°56′ S**
10
Beinge Thursday hassy Cloudy Coald weather wind att SW and at South: I Stood to the South E:ward. At 12 aclocke to day I tacked and Stood to the W:ward: wind at SBE a Stife gale: A greate Sea Com out of the South. Course made Good this Last 24 ho*uers* is SW: distance Sailed 58 miles: departur west 41 miles: def*erence* Latt*itud* 00°41′: Latt*itud* by ob*servation* 44°56′ S*outh*.
Meridian distance from Porte Praya 1863·9 Mils W
Longitud from Porte Praya 36°27′·5
Longitud from the Lizard 53°45′·6
Meridian distance from the Lizard 2701 Mile W
I judge here is 19° variation E. At 12 aclocke to day I stood to the SW:ward.

11
Beinge friday Cloudy hasy weather wind at SSE a Stife gale: after divers Courses I make my True Cour*se* this 24 houers to Be No*rth* 72°38′ west: distance Sailed [*margin:* An Azimuth] 33·5 Miles: departur West 32 miles: def*erence* of Lat*itud* No*rth* 00°10′: Latt*itud* By Good ob*servation* of the ☼ 44°46′ S*outh*. Captaine fleminge had a new Cap for his fore mast.[1]
Meridian distance from Porte Praya 1895·9 Mils W
Longitud from Porte Praya 37°13′·5 W
Longitud from the Lizard 54°31′·6 W
Meridian distance from the Lizard 2733·0 Mils W.

12
Beinge Satterday Cloudy hassy weather and much winde this morninge at SW: Caused me to hand my fore saile and Try to the NW:ward: at 10 aclocke it Proved Lese wind: I Sett my Courses at 10 aclocke and Stood to the W:ward: Sum Raine and Slaty Snow to day. After divers Courses I make my True Cours to Be NWBN: distance Sailed 44·5 Miles: departur west 24 miles: def*erence* Latt*itud* No*rth* 00°37′: Lat*itud* at no*ne* 44°09′.
Meridian distance from Porte Praya 1920·7 Mils W
Longitud from Porte Praya 37°48′·1
Longitud from the Lizard 55°06′·2
Meridian distance from the Lizard 2757·8 Mils W.

[78] **Febrauary 1669 the *Seepstakes* at Sea Latt*itud* 44°20′ S**
13
Beinge Sunday Blowinge weather wind at SW it Put me To Try twice this 24 houers: about an houer at a time By Rainey Gusts: a Great Sea Cam out of the South: Rockeweds[2] drave Past mee to day: I So*unded* But noe Ground at 100 fadam: this afternone it Proved a fine Gale the wind Came to the WNW: I Stood to the westward as nere as I Could ly:

[1] The cap is a strong block of wood, with two holes in it, fitted to the top of the lower mast through which the topmast can be hoisted and lowered. A damaged cap would make the topmast unsafe.
[2] This word has a small cross above and below the letter c and the last syllable 'weds' has been inserted above the line in the original.

very Coald this Last 24 houers Consideringe the time of yeare: as alowinge here as you doe August in England: one Seale Sene to day & Severall Sea foules.
After Sev*erall* Courseis made I make my True Cours this 24 houers to be South 75° Easterly: distance sailed 42·3 miles: departur East 41 Mils: def*erence* Lat*itud* 00°11′ S: Latt*itud* By obs*ervation* of the ☼ 44°20′ South.
Meridian distance from Porte Praya 1879·7 Mils W
Longitud from Porte Praya 36°51′·5 W
Longitud from the Lizard 54°09′·6 W
Meridian distance from the Lizard 2716·8 Mils W
Variation of my Comp*as* by Good Ampl*ytud* 19°40′ E.

14
Beinge Munday hassy weather: wind at NNW A stife Gale:
Course By my Compase Last 24 houers was SE a 11 miles and SW 60 miles: haveinge Contrary winds. But I make my True Course to Be SWBW 01°05′ westerly: distance Sailed 61 miles: departure west 51·4 miles: def*erence* Latt*itud* 33′ South: Latt*itud* By observation of the ☼ one [on] the meridian 44°53′.
Meridian distance from Porte Praya 1931·1 Mils W
Longitud from Porte Praya 38°04′·1 W
Longitud from the Lizard 55°22′·2 W
Meridian distance from the Lizard 2768·2 Mils W
Variation by a good Amplitud occident is 20°40′ E.

[79] **Febrauary 1669 the *Sweepstakes* at Sea Lat*itud* 45°40′ S**
15
Beinge Tusday faier weather of wind but much fooge: all this forenone wind at ESE: Course by my Co*mpas* SW. After Severall Courses this 24 houers I m*ake* my True Course to be South 18°20′ west: distan*ce* Sailed 49·4 miles: departur west 15·5 mils: def*erence* Latt*itud* 00°47′: Latt*itud* by account 45°40′ S.
Meridian dist*ance* at non from Port Praya 1946·6 Mils W
And Longitud at none from Porte Praya 38°26′·1 W
Longitud at none from the Lizard 55°44′·2 W
Meridian distance from the Lizard 2783·7 Mils W
Smoath water and Cleare weather this afternone a fine gale at East: I stered SWB by my Compase which is nere WSW for here is 20° variation E This afternone Severall Small Seales Came Swimeing Close to the Shipp: I Shoot haile Shott[1] at one and [*margin:* al well in the Pinke] they went away. This night I Stered by my Com*pas* SWBW: the wind at north a fresh gale.
Variation of the Comp*as* By a good Ampl*itud* is 21°50′ E

16
Beinge wedensday fooggie weather wind at N – A fine gale:
Course By my Compas SWBW: I Sunded this morninge But noe Ground at 100 fathd*am*. I make my True Cours to be South 85°45′ west: and distance Sailed 108: *departur* west

[1] This is described as small shot.

107 miles: def*erence* Latt*itud* 00°08′: Latt*itud* by ob*servation* of the Sun at the meridian is 45°48′ So*uth*.
Meridian dist*ance* at no[o]n from Port Praya 2053·6 Mils W
Longitud from Port Praya 40°53′·1
Longitud from the Lizard 58°11′·2
Meridian dist*ance* from the Lizard 2890·7 Mile W
[*margin: drawing of a hand holding a lead and line* 55] At 12 aclocke today I Sounded and had Ground at 55[1] fadams: Graye Sand fine in Clyneinge to an oase [ooze].[2]
[*margin: drawing of a hand holding a lead and line* 53] I Steered away SSW by my Compas: at Six aclocke I Sounded and had Sandy Ground at 53 fadam. Variation of the Comp*as* by a Good Ampl*itud* is 19°00′ E

[80] **Feruary 1669 the *Sweepstakes* at Sea Latt*itud* 46°18′ S**
17
Beinge Thursday hassy weather and Small wind at NW: I Stered By my Compas SWBS. I make my T*rue* Course this 24 houers to be SWBW: distance Sailed 54 miles: departur west 45 mils: def*erence* Lat*itud* 00°30′: Latt*itud* by Good obs*ervation* of the ☼ is 46°18′ S.
Meridian distance from Porte Praya 2098·6 Mils W
Longitud from Porte Praya 41°59′·1 W
Longitud from the Lizard 59°17′·2 W
Meridian distance from the Lizard 2935·7 Mils W
Here is very faier Soundinge al a Longe this Coaste from the River of Plat to Cap S[t] George:[3] for I hav hade 56 fadams and 53 fadams: Rede Sande and I judge my Selfe By my accounte and my drafte to be 40 Leagus of[f] the Land that Bere west of mee which is Cap De matas.[4] Severall Sposts of Rockeweed seen al a Longe this Coast. This morninge I saw a deade whale which Stanike [stank] much: and Severall Sea fowles By her which eat of her flesh:[5] three Seales Seen to day. At 8 aclocke I Sounded and had fivety five fadam*s* water Red fine Sand inclineinge to oase [ooze]. Foggy weather this Eveinge: I judge 18° the Compase varies East. Mighty thicke foogs to night and the wind veareinge Round the Compase.

18
Beinge friday mighty fooggy weather this morninge the wi*nd* Came to the SSE: I Steerd SW By my Compase. Cours made Good this 24 houers is WSW: distance sailed 44·4 mils: departur west is 41 mils: def*erence* Latt*itud* 00°17′: Latt*itud* By Judgement at none is 46°35′S.

[1] Figure '55' is repeated in the original.

[2] Wood, BL, MS 3833, f. 13v: 'Att Noone we Sounded & found 55 fatham a Sandy Ozey ground not much unlike our former Soundings beinge Black & Red Mingled.'

[3] Río de la Plata (35°30′S, 56°00′W), to Cabo Blanco (47°12′S, 65°45′W).

[4] C de S. Elena, C de Matas is shown on Doncker's chart of South America (Plate 2) in about 45°30′S, and would appear to be either Cabo San Jorge or Cabo Aristizábal.

[5] Wood, BL, MS 3833, f. 13v: 'This Morning we Saw to Leeward about 2 Miles a Rock as we Imagened wheare upon we hozysed [hoisted] out our Pinnice & the Captaine and I went to See what itt might bee soe when we Came to itt we found att to bee A dead Whale whith some Thousands of foules aboute him which weare So fatt they Could not Rise out of the Watter.'

Meridian distance from Porte Praya 2139·6 Mils W
Longitud from Porte Praya 42°57′·1 W
Longitud from the Lizard 60°15′·2 W
Meridian dist*ance* from the Lizard 2976·7 Mile W
Wind at none was at ESE and began to Raine and Blowe: I Stood to the Southward till 2 aclocke then Tacked and Stood to the NE:ward for feare of Beinge in Bayed:[1] it Blew hard at ESE and at SE.

[81] **February 1669 the *Sweepstakes* at Sea Lat*itud* 46°24′ S**
19
Beinge Satterday Blowinge fooggy weather wind at SE and al over Cast: this morninge I had my main Saile Splet the Boult Rope Brake:[2] But Saved al the Canvas:[3] Sum times I Could Cary a Par [pair] of Courses and sumtimes Put to try. True Course made this 24 houers is N 30°15′ Easterly: distance Sailed 12·8 miles: departure E 6·4 mils: defe*rence* Latt*itud* 00°11′ N: Latt*itud* By account is 46°24′ S.
Meridian dist*ance* from St Jago that is P[4] Praya 2133·2 Mils W
Longitud from St Jago 42°49′·1 W
Longitud from the Lizard 60°07′·2 W
Meridian dist*ance* from the Lizard 2970·3 Mils W
I judge here is 18° variation of the Compas East.
Soundinges to day Severall times at 50 fadams and 53 fadams drake [dark] Saund with sum Brite [specks]. Severall whight Spoots [white spots] seene in the Sea to night which I belevie are Small fish or Shrimps. This Sea abounds much with Seals: But few other fish seene here Exsepte Sum whales and Sum Purposes: Many Sea fowles sene and Beeds of Rockeweeds. I have Continuall tryed to Catch fish in thes Seas But Could never take any in all my Saileinge Betwen the River of PLate and Cap*e* Blanckeo: I have sene Sum willackes[5] here which is like our fowles in the Europian Seas.
Temprate Coule Aier But mighty foogy this fower dayes. This Afternone three of my maine Shrouds Brake at once and Severall of my other Riginge Give way[6] this weet Blowinge weather: which I ordered new in their Places: the Shipp Complanes much in her [*margin:* fine gray sand] Bowes which the want of Ironwoorke all over.
This night it Proved lese wind at ESE: I Steered [*right margin:* lost the Pink] S By my Compas and Sett my top Sails. This night I Lost Sight of the Pinke at 10 aclocke: Shee not makeinge Saile: for next morninge I Could not See her.

[1] Embayed: being stuck inside a bay with an onshore wind, and unable to get out of it by tacking. This was in Golfo de San Jorge. See below, p. 426, n. 2.

[2] The boltrope is a rope sewn round the edge of a sail to prevent the canvas splitting.

[3] Wood, BL, MS 3833, f. 13v: 'Att 12 this Night our Maine Sale gave Way and Splitt & we Brought another to the yard by 3 in the Morn*ing*.'

[4] Port, Porte or Porto Praia. Narbrough uses all three forms.

[5] Willock: Guillemot, razorbill or puffin. *NOED*. (Guillimot, Smyth, *Sailor's Word-Book*.) None of these birds are normally found in this area. It might have been a shearwater, possibly the greater shearwater (*Puffinus gravis*), which is not too dissimilar and common in this area and ranges to Europe. Harrison, *Seabirds*, pp. 258–9.

[6] Wood, BL, MS 3833, f. 13v: 'which did much Indanger the Loseing of our Maine Mast.'

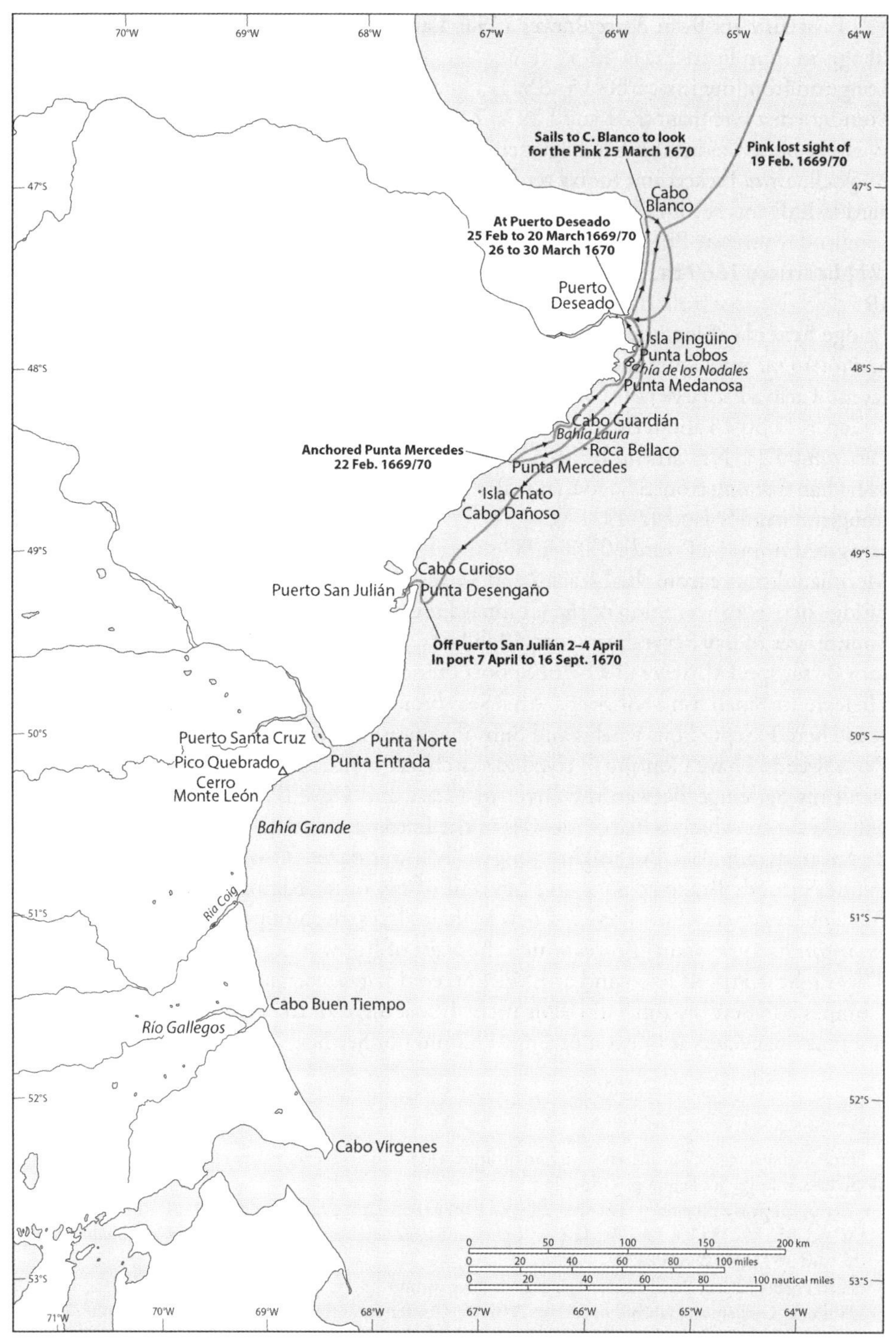

Map 3. Track of the *Sweepstakes* off the coast of Argentina, 19 February 1669/70 to 7 April 1670.

[82] **February 1669 the *Sweepstakes* at Sea Lat*itud* 47°20′ S**
20
Beinge Sunday foggie weather wind at E a fine Gale:
Course by my Compas SSW: and SW at 12 aclocke: But I make my True Course this 24 houers to be SSW: dist*ance* Sailed 60·5 miles: depart*ur* West 23·3 miles: def*erence* Latt*itud* 00°56′: Lat*itud* By account to day att none for it is foggy is 47°20′ S.
Merid*ian* dist*ance* from Porto Praya at none 2156·5 Mils W
Longitud from Port Praya at none 43°23′·5 W
Longitud from Lizart at none 60°41′·6 W
Merid*ian* dist*ance* from the Lizard at none 2993·6 Mils W
I judge here is 18° variation of the Compas E for the Last observation was 19° in the Lat*itud* 46°00′ and never Since I Could take any it hav ben So foogy. Mighty foogiy al this day: at 2 aclocke I judge my Selfe to be in the Latt*itud* of the Cap Blanco Brancae Blancas or Cap St George:[1] and it Be[a]rs west of mee By my Reckeninge 18 Leagus of[f]: I Stere SW by my Compas: wind at north a fine gale and Smoath water. Many Seals Sene to day and many Great Pyed Gules[2] and Sum Scules [shoals] of Smale fish Like Smelts which the Seals followes.
The Pinke is out of Sight for I have not sene here this day. At 4 aclocke I Sounded and had Ground at fevety fadam: Black Sand and Small Peavell [Pebble] Stones as Bigge as Pease and Beanes – or their abouts of Black and R*ed* Colloar and Gray. At 4 aclocke the wind Came to the No*rth* a fine gale: I Stereed WBN by my Compase. At 8 aclocke I Sounded and had Ground at 45 fad*ams*: Small Peable Stones and Blacke Sand as befor. At 10 of the Clocke at night I Sounded and had Ground at 38 fadams: Small Stones of white and Blacke Col*loar*: then I layd my head Sailes to the mast and drove[3] till Two aclocke: 2 mils SW: then I tacked and Stood to the NE:ward fower mils: the wind at No*rth* a fine Gale: then I Sounded and had Ground at 42 fad*oms*: Great Stones as Bigg as heasell nuts [hazel nuts]: at 6 aclocke in the morninge I tackeed and Stered in WNW for the Land: it was mighty fooggy.

[83] **Feberuary 1669 the *Sweepstakes* at Sea of[f] Cap St George 47°20′ S**
21
Beinge Munday Cloudy hassy weather: foggy: this morninge wind at NBE a fine fresh gale: Course By my Compas WBN to hale in to the Land to make Cap St George Ales [alias] Cap Blanco Brancas Blancas:[4] which I did make at 8 aclocke this morninge: I not Beinge But

[1] Cabo Blanco (47°12′S, 65°45′W). On Doncker's chart of S America (Plate 2) this cape is referred to as C.S. Jorge, C. Blanco, Barrancas, Blancas.

[2] Probably the Cape or pintado petrel (*Daption capense*). Harrison, *Seabirds*, 236–7.

[3] Backed the head sails and hove to.

[4] Cabo Blanco is described as 'composed of three distinct masses of rugged rock 42 m high, whitened by guano, which appear as islets when first sighted. These masses of rock form a small peninsula extending 6 cables S and joined to the mainland by a low isthmus with a cove on each side.' *South America Pilot*, II, para. 3.22. Wood, BL, MS 46A, p. 139, states: 'Cape Saint George. This Cape lyes in the Lat of 47°10′ So*uth* And is distant from Straights of Magellan 160 Leagues. Sr Francis Drake in the yeare 1577 gave this Place the Name of Cape Saint George But by the Spaniards called Cape Blanco from its whiteness for when the Sunne Shineth in the morning on it it appears white but in the Evening it sheweth Black with 4 hamocks – seeming to be Islands and I doe beleive them to be soe. This Cape lyeth in the Longitude of 297°00′ beginning at the Lizard neare the Lands end of England in the County of Cornewall difference of Longitude 63°00′ W.'

fower Leags of[f] the Land Bar west of mee: it was just Clea*r* up from Beinge fooggy: the No*rth*armost pointe Bare NW of mee about two Leagus of[f], the Southermost Land then in Sight of mee Bere South westerly about two Leagus. I Stood in west till nine of the Clocke to vew the Land: then the west Land was two leagus from me and I had seaventen fadam water: Rockey Ground or heard [hard] Shelly Rocke:[1] then the Eastermost Pointe of all Cap S[t] George Bere South of mee about six miles: it Semes to Be an ILand which I Could make noe otherwise as I Sailed a Longe By it about a mile from the maine: it is Rockey Sheles [shelves] ne[a]r it nere the main: it is of an ordinary heaight and makes with two Round homakes and a Sadlle Backe and ereguler in form: it Semes to be Barran: it was in Couler Red and Blacke. Their is a Rocke or two to the Southward of it and one table Smal Rocke to the N:ward of it: it makes a great water with in it and the maine.[2] I Sailed al A longe the Shore with in five Miles or nerer in Sum Places and had twenty five fadam warter: and Sum times 28. I saw no danger at all But what Show then Selfes nere the maine. The Land makes of an ordinary haight and Semes to be all dowines and no woods: Several Round hommackes and table Lands Show them Selfes in the Country: and noe mountaines the Land Lookes al of a Redish Couler: and seme to Bee Good Sheep Paster [Pasture] and Proffitable for our Country Greausers[3] and Shepards. The Sea Side all a Longe maks in Bayes and Red Beaches and Ereguler Rockes: the Bays are very Low Land. After divers Courses from Sunday at none till to day at 9 aclocke I make my True Cours to Be W 6°50′ North: and dist*ance* Sailed 50·7 mils: dep*artur* west 50 mils: def*erence* Lat*itud* 6′: Lat*itud* [*margin:* 47°14′] by a*ccount* 47°14′ S: for I have had no observation this three dayes.
Meri*dian* distance from Port Pray or S[t] Jago is 2206·5 Mils W
Longitud from Port Praya 44°38′·5
Longitud from the Lizard 61°56′·6
Meridian distance from the Lizard 3043·6 Mils W

[84] The Lyinge of the Coast from Cap S[t] George to Port desier.[4]
I make the E most Pointe or Pitch of the middle of Cap*e* S[t] George ailes [alias] Cap Barrancas Blancas[5] to Ly in the Latt*itud* of 47°20′ South Latt*itud*: and in Longitud from

[1] This would be identified from the indentations in the tallow at the bottom of the lead.

[2] Wood, BL, MS 3833, ff. 13v–14r: The Land which we Made was Cape Planco So Caled by the Spanards butt by the English Cape S[t] George butt then one att the Top Mast head Saw an Island to Beare of us *South* & by *East*, which we Imaigen to be the Cape because Mr Hacklute in his Relation of Fulers Voyage sayed thatt the Cape did Make Like an Island soo we Toke This Island for the Cape and Sayled by itt to the Southward … The Island which we Made for the Cape was Pinguin Island [Isla Pingüino (47°55′S, 65°43′W)] so Called from the Mulltetude of Them foules which are on itt.' Wood refers here to the translated 'Ruttier from the said river of *Plate* to the Streight of *Magelane*', included in Hakluyt, *Principal Navigations*, III, pp. 724–6, which states: 'From this Cape [Cabo Blanco] the coast lyeth towards the North side Northwest about 3 leagues all full of white cliffes steep up: and the last cliffe is the biggest both in length and height, and sheweth to be the saile of a ship when it is under saile. These white cliffes are 6 in number, And this Cape hath in the face thereof a certaine round land that sheweth to bee an Island afarre off: and it hath certaine poyntes of rockes hard by it.'

[3] This probably comes from Grease an obsolete form of Graze, hence a Greaser was one who greased (grazed) sheep. *NOED*.

[4] Pages 84–92 of the journal are devoted to a lengthy set of notes on the coastline from Cabo Blanco to Puerto San Julián and the events during his first period ashore. The first sentence here serves as Narbrough's subject heading for the next few pages. Page 93 is blank. The daily journal for the stopover at Puerto Deseado resumes on p. 94.

[5] See above, p. 201, nn. 1, 4.

the Lizard of England West 61°56′:[1] and meridian distance in Leagus 1014 and 1·6 miles: By my day account which I Keept in my voiage.

From Cap S[t] George their is Pecked Rockes Licke towers[2] and Castles aBout 2 Leags SSW: they are one [on] the maine and by the Sea Side: and from them Pecked Rockes SSW 2 Leagus more ther is aparchall [a parcel] of Rockes a good haith [height] a Bove water: halfe a mile in Lenth and a mile from the Shor they Stand of[f] the Southern fale [fall] of the Cap: you may Goe in [within] a League of them and no danger. Halfe a mile about those Rockes their is a Rockey Pointe to the SSW: And that Pointe is the Eastermost Pointe of the Begininge of a Good deepe Bay about 2 Leagues [wide]: the land Lyes in from that Pointe WBS: it is a Good Road:[3] in the Bay it have severall Rockey Islands in itt: at the Boatom it makes Low Land and So it dos all a Long the Shore. Their is 20 fadam Rockey Ground at the Goeinge in: But what there is at the Boatom I Know not for I did not Goe quite in: from this Bay to the N Pointe of Porte Diser[4] the Land Ly SBW and is Distance 7 Leagus. It is al Low land by the Sea Side and in Small Bayes and here and their a Singill Rocke: halfe way their Lis ner the Shore a Small Rockey Iland. The Land Makes with seeaverall table hills in the Country but not high:[5] you have all a longe this Shore about a Leage of[f] 20 fadam or 25 fadam: Rockey Ground: I Sailed So al a Longe. Ner the Pointe of Port Disier you will have Shoule water for their Lyes Rockes of[f] it which Sum Show them Selves: you may Know Port dissier as you Come alonge the Shore from the Norward By a Shoule or Legde of Rocks which Show them Selfe:[6] a good heaight and are about a league of[f] the Shore:[7] and their are three Bra[n]ches of Rocks more one [on] the north Side as you Coime in to the Bay:[8] for Porte dessier Lies in the North Parte

Variation of the Comp*as* By a Good Ampl*ytud* is 17°30′ E

Variation of the Compas By a Good Amp*lytud* ☼ Set 16°50′ E

[85][9] or Bite of the Bay. Their is a Large tablle Land ov[e]r Porte dissier in the Country:[10] which hath a gape [gap] in the North Ende of it: at the South Parte or Pointe of the Bay their is a Preity Bigge Rocckey Island: and five more Islands a Bout it and

[1] The actual position is 47°12′S, 65°45′W, or 60°33′W of the Lizard. Narbrough's position was therefore remarkably good considering the difficulties involved in carrying his longitude from the Lizard.

[2] Peaked rocks like towers.

[3] This is Caletta Sur (47°13′S, 65°45′W).

[4] Puerto Deseado (47°45′S, 65°53′W). Wood, BL, MS 3833, f. 15v: 'M[r] THOMAS CANDISH gave the Name of PORT DESIRE to This Harbor In his Voyage Round The Woorld 1586.' This is recorded in 'The prosperous Voyage of the worshipfull Master Thomas Candish Esquire ', see above, p. 62, n. 9. On p. 805, Pretty states 'The 17 day of December [1586] in the afternoone we entred into an harborough, where our Admirall went in first: wherefore our Generall named the said harborough Port Desire.' The Admiral, the flag ship, was the *Desire*.

[5] Behind this coastline lie Falso Pico de los Rios, Cerros Escola and Pico de los Rios with heights up to 355 ft (108 m).

[6] Roca Sorrell (47°43′S, 65°48′W).

[7] Actually about 1½ miles off shore.

[8] Roca Foca.

[9] The text, on p. 85, follows on from the remarks preceding the record of variation at the end of the previous page.

[10] In the land behind Port Desire. On the north side of the port, Cerro Bal 250 ft (76 m) and Cerro Alonso 217 ft (66 m) rise to Cerros Dirección 490 ft (149 m) 5 miles NW of the entrance.

three or fower Rockes: and this Island is of an indeferente height. It is Called Penguin Island[1] for the mulltitud of those fowles as are one [on] it:[2] it is about a mile from the Pointe of the maine:[3] it Lyes SE from Porte dissier three Leagus and Better. The Islands which are about it ar a greate deale Smaller then it and lyes betwen theat and the maine Pointe: which is Preyty high Land.[4] Alsoe if you be nere that Parte of the Bay you will See a Rock or Small Island nere the maine which make flate a loft Licke a table: and more Larger a loft then a low:[5] that Island or Rocke is steep dowine the Sids: it is Black: in the Bay ther is thre[e] white Clifes and a Black Spoot in the midlemost and a Ledge of Rockes in the Boatam of the South Parte of the Bay. In the Lowe Land you will See a Single Spireed Rocke Stand Perpendiculer one [on] a Round hommake: it make Exactly Like a Steepell or watch tower[6] as if it had ben Placed one [on] Porpose: it is a very faier marke for to know the [*margin: small view of El Torreon inserted at this point*] harbrough. It is one [on] the South Side of the Goeinge in of the harbrough halfe a mile from the water Side either from the Shore of the Bay or from the River with in. When you are in the offin[g][7] and have Penguin Island one [on] the S[8] or SBE and 2 Leagus from it you may Easly See this tower. It will com oppen to the Southward of a table Land which is in the Country and then you will have 16 fadan water: Good oasy Ground:[9] their I anchored till I discovered the harbrow:[10] the wind at West. Their is a point of Rockes Runes from the South Pointe of the Land at the Entry of the harbr*ow* mouth ner a mile SEBE into the Sea which are dry at a Low water:[11] you may be bould to Borrow nere them[12] and have theree fower five and Six fadam from them. But bee Suer keep nerer that Legde then the north Sid al the way in: which is the Best Side: for one [on] the North Side you will have 12 and 14 fadam: fowle Ground:[13] and a ledge of Rockes which Comes from a Blake Pointe of Rockes one [on] the North Side. In the midle you may Ride here and have Six fadam at [86] A Low water and Chingly Ground [Shingley ground]: here I rode two days for to Gitt in the wind Beinge a Stife Gale westerly.[14] At the Goeinge in of this harbor their Lyes two Rockes nere to Getther in the mid way which are above water at halfe Ebb and halfe flood:[15] they ly Sumwhat with out the mouth of the narrow. One [on] the South Sid is Blacke Steep Rockes Lowe to

[1] Isla Pingüino (47°55′ S, 65°43′ W) is 148 ft (45 m) high.

[2] Today the island is home to a colony of rockhopper penguins (*Eudyptes chrysocome*). Harris, *Guide*, pp. 33–4. At this time the penguins were Magellanic penguins (*Spheniscus magellanicus*), see below, p. 208, n. 13.

[3] Punta Norte (47°55′S, 65°47′W).

[4] The point rises to Cerro Mirador, 282 ft (86 m).

[5] Larger in the higher than the lower reaches.

[6] It is now known as El Torreón, and is 'a remarkable rocky knoll which resembles an isolated tower; a very useful mark for approaching the port'. *South America Pilot*, II, para. 3.42. It stands 92 ft (28 m) high.

[7] Out in the open sea.

[8] Bearing South.

[9] Good oosey ground, mud, good holding ground for anchoring.

[10] Examined the harbour.

[11] Restinga Chaffers extend about one mile from the south point of the harbour, with Isla Chaffers on them close off the shore.

[12] Sail close to them.

[13] Unsuitable for anchoring.

[14] Waiting to enter the harbour since the wind was in the west and blowing directly out of the harbour.

[15] Rocas de la Guardia.

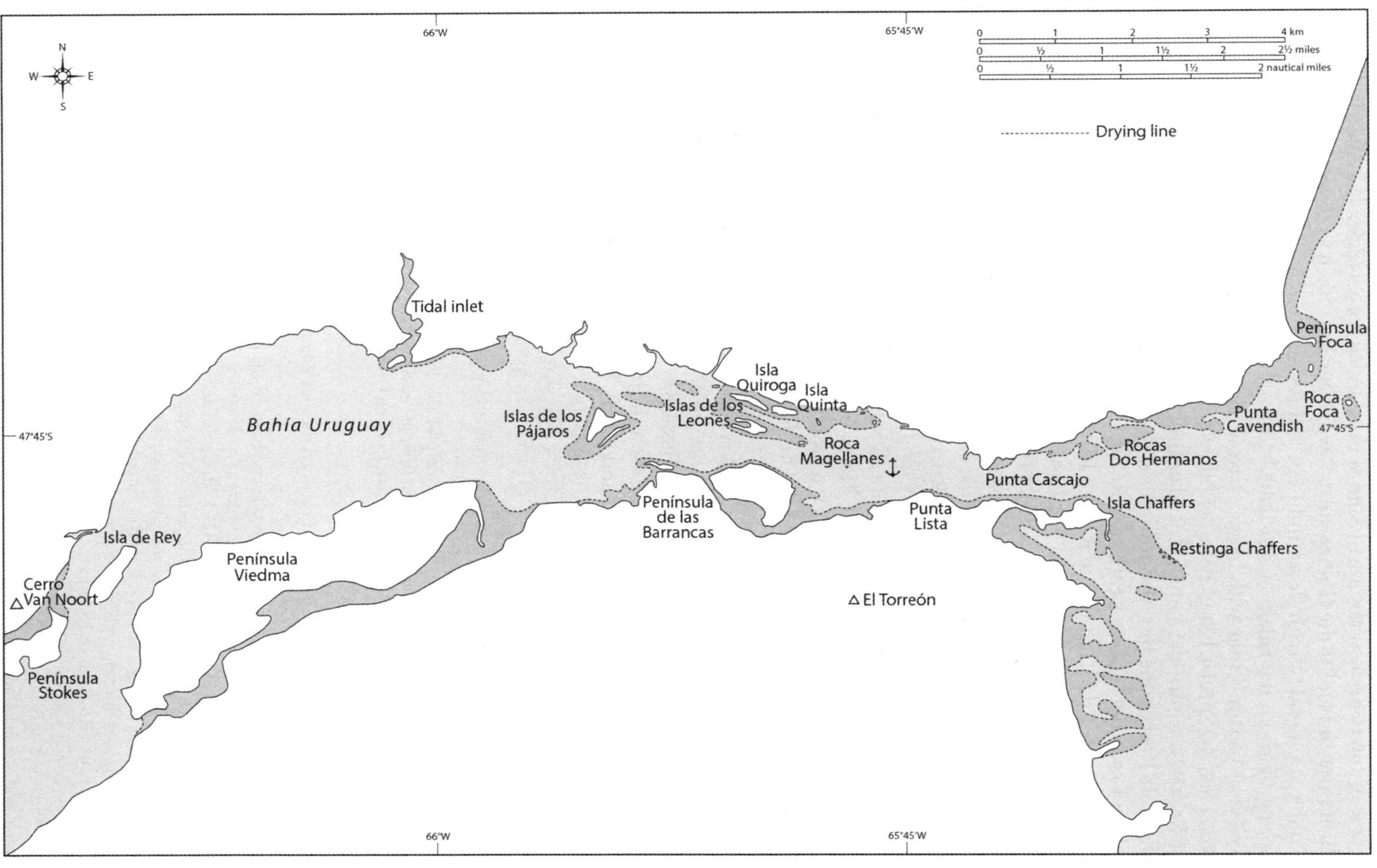

Map 4. Puerto Deseado (Port Desire).

the water and one [on] the north Side of the narrow is a Steep Stooney Beach.[1] It is in the norrowest Place at the Goeinge in, a Bow Shoot over:[2] then itt Comes Broader. Here Runs a Strong tide Boath flood and Ebb: and floweth north and South: and Riseth at Springe Tids theree fadam and A halfe.[3] Chingly osay Ground with in you may Ride well after you are a mile with in the Narrow and more as you Please: the Place where I Rod I had the Speeired Rocke one [on] the South Sid SE of mee Sheat with a Blufe Parte of Rockes[4] one [on] the Same Sid: and against a Beach one [on] the north Shore[5] above the blofe Rockes one [on] the north Side: their I hade Six fadam at a Low water. Above where I rode two Cables Lenth[6] is a Rocke in the midle of the Chanel which is above water at halfe tide:[7] and theree Rockey Islands which are allmost under water at a full Sea.[8] The best Cominge in is at the Last qua[r]*ter* Ebb: for then you may See all the danger and be Sur[e] keep the medle of the Chanell: and you may Gooe Safe. You will See up the River white Clifes and above them in the hills is a Round hill or hommake which is whitesh:[9] keep that in the midle of the Chanell after you are with in the narow: one [on] the South Side there is Sum Rockes: and the water Comes over that Pointe at halfe floode which makes a great Eady: and Just with in one [on] the north Side their Lyes a pinte [point] of Rockes which are all Sene till the first quarter flood. I Rode above them Two Cables Lengths: nerer the North Side then the South: all the Rockes ar full of Good Musells and Limpitts. This is a Good Place to Lay Ships a Shore to Grave one [on] A Chingly beach [87] To Grave.[10] This River Runs up But two or theer and twenty mils and their it Comes to a Small Creeck: and Drys at a Low watter, it is all Salt water, for I went up to discover it. It is very Rockey a Loft and the Cunt*ry* mighty Barran: noe wood at al in the hole Cuntry But Bushes: in the River their is Six or Seaven Small Islands[11] one of them have a Great many Bushess which is Good for fewell and an other have a Great number of Seales frequents it and Burds of the Sea: and the other Islands have Sea fowles one [on] them. The Land is very Barran all the hole Country over very

[1] Rocas Dos Hermanas.

[2] About 300 yards across. See above, p. xix.

[3] Mean High Water Spring Tide is 5.3 m, and the stream today runs at 5–6 knots at spring tides and 3–4 knots at neap tides. *South America Pilot*, II, paras, 3.33, 3.40.

[4] In line with bluff part of the rocks. This bluff was probably Punta Listra, 33 ft (10 m).

[5] Wood, BL, MS 46A, p. 140: 'You will have on Brest of you a small Bay which we called Coopers Bay.' This beach has now gone and been replaced by the wharf fronting Puerto Deseado.

[6] About 400 yards. See above, p. xviii.

[7] Roca Magallanes.

[8] Isla Quiroga, Isla Quinta and Isla de los Leones off the north shore of the harbour.

[9] Cerro Van Noort 177 ft (54 m).

[10] Graving is to lie a vessel ashore at high tide and burn off the impurities on the bottom at low tide, then paying it (recaulking between the planks as necessary and pouring in hot pitch or tar) before she floats off at the next high water. Wood, BL, MS 46A, pp. 142–3: 'In Case of necessity that one should be forced ... to Hall ashore to stopp a Leake or to grave there is on the South side 2 miles and a halfe up from the harbours mouth betwixt the Iseland and the maine a very good and Convenient Oozey Creeke where a shipp may lye ashore very well [143] without any Danger: or if you should be forced with Easterly windes with a Tyde of Flood and that you Cannot bring your shipp up with your anchors you must of necessity runne into this Creeke: but you must have a great Care of a Rock which lyeth in the faire way as [you] goeth into the Creeke. at halfe tide the Rock is covered: you may sayle on either side without any danger.'

[11] These include Isla do los Pájaros, 2 islands in mid channel about 3 miles within the narrow, and Isla del Rey also in mid channel 3 miles further up river.

Scarce of fresh water in the Sumer: and noe frute or erbs [herbs] at all or timber trees – but all like Barran downes: it is of a Sandy Gravelly Sile [soil] and Rockes in the Cuntry. A mile or two from the Sea Side I found Severall Red flent [flint] stones and white flents and Peeces of Green flent But no kind of minerall any where: for I travelled Severall miles one [on] the Land to Looke and discover the Land. I Could not See any of the men of the Cuntry in all my marches: But I saw where they had ben in Severall Places: they had made fiers: and I found Severall Graves which I opened and Saw dead men in them: they Bury their dead one [on] the tops of the hils and Cover them over with Rockes: they Lay them one their Backes with thir heads to the Westward:[1] they Seeme to be But of an ordinary Stature.[2] I saw severall Great Beasts much like Stakes [stags] But I Suppose they are those beasts which are Called the Perrvian Sheep:[3] for I found one dead which was very woolly: like the Red Spanish woolle. Here is many Large Easteredges [ostriches][4] and hares of a Great Biggnes:[5] I Caute Severall of them with my doggs:[6] they hole in the Ground Like Connis.[7] Heere is Armidillos[8] and Land Rats[9] and

[1] Thomas Cavendish, who visited and named Port Desire in 1586, commented: 'Their use is when any of them dye, to bring him or them to the cliffes by the sea-side, and upon the toppe of them they burie them, and in their graves are buryed with them their bowes and arrowes, and all their jewels which they have in their life time, which are fine shelles which they finde by the sea-side, which they cut and square after an artificiall manner; and all is layed under their heads. The grave is made all with great stones of great length and bignesse, being set all along full of the dead mans darts which he used when he was living. And they colour both their darts and their graves with a red colour which they use in colouring of themselves.' Hakluyt, *Principal Navigations*, III, p. 805.

[2] This is a reference to the reports of giants in this region. 'The people very tall and warlike, some of them of a *Gigantine* stature, affirmed (but I believe it not) to be eleven foot high; and by the *Spaniards* for that reason called *Patagons*.' Heylyn, *Cosmographie*, p. 1073. See above, pp. 42–3, n. 11, and below, p. 427.

[3] Guanaco (*lama guanicoe*) are camelids (camel-like animals) standing 6 ft (1·8 m) high, covered with fine hair, the upper parts reddish with white beneath, and capable of running at 37 mph (60 kph). Harris, *Guide*, pp. 162–7. Wood, BL, MS 46A, p. 150: 'Upon the Land are many Deere or Sheep which the Spaniards call Yanaques. They are a large Beast about 12 handfulls high: they have a long head and neck like to a camell: their Bodyes and hinder parts are much like a horse: they are very watchfull and shy: wee killed 7 of them the time wee lay there: their wooll is the finest in the world: in the countrey you may see in a Drove above 6 or 700 of them at a time: when they see you they will make a snort and kney like a horse.'

[4] This is Darwin's rhea (*Pterocnemia pennata*), a large flightless bird, much like an ostrich in appearance, but smaller standing about 4 ft (1·2 m), and capable of running at 30 mph (50 kph). Harris, *Guide*, pp. 23–5.

[5] This is probably the mara or Patagonian hare (*Dolichotis patagonum*), which is up to 32 in (80 cm) long and has a curious bouncing, antelope-like run attaining bursts of speed up to 30 mph (45 kph). The mara does not actually live in a hole in the ground, generally sleeping under a bush, but the females produce their young in burrows where they live and are fed by their mother until weaned. The European hare (*Leptus europaeus*), was not introduced into South America until 1888. Harris, *Guide*, pp. 126, 132–3.

[6] Wood, BL, MS 46A, p. 141: 'Wee killed 9 of them in one day which were very good meate and much bigger then our English hares some of them weigher 20 Lb a p*iece*.'

[7] Conies/coneys, rabbits.

[8] There are two types of armadillo found in Patagonia, the larger hairy armadillo (*Chaetophractus villosus*) and the pichi (*Zaedyus pichiy*). The former has a body up to 14 in (36 cm) long with tail 5¾ in (15 cm) and is principally a nocturnal animal though often active by day, while the latter has a body which is up to 9 in (23 cm) long with tail 4 in (10 cm) and is active by day. Harris, *Guide*, pp. 124–5. Wood, BL, MS 46A, p. 150: 'Here is a little Creature Something like to a Land Turtle with a joynted Shell On his Back the Spaniards calls them hoggs in Armour: they are Excellent good meate.'

[9] The only rat likely to have been seen by Narbrough is the rabbit rat (*Reithrodon physodes (auritus)*), which is nocturnal, secretive and indigenous. The brown rat (*Rattus norvegicus*) and the roof rat (*R. rattus*) were introduced from the Old World and would probably not have been common here at this time. Harris, *Guide*, pp. 129–30.

small Poull Cats[1] and wild doogs[2] and Catts.[3] Heree is kits[4] and Sum Parterages[5] and Small birds: very Good Duckes[6] and Small Cerlew[7] and sea Pickes[8] and other Sea fowelle in Great quantitis by the Shore Side – as for fish I ded not See much here is in the River mulletts[9] and smellts:[10] Great quantitis of Good musells and Limpeets one [on] the Rockes.[11]

Here are multituds of Seales[12] everywhere one [on] the Coast: the younge ones are very Good meat either fresh or Salte. I Sallted up teen hogsheads full of Sealle and it Proved very Good meate and the Penguns[13] Eate very well – salted. [88] One [on] the north

[1] There is no polecat known in Patagonia; this might be the Patagonian weasel (*Lyncodon patagonicus*) which is rare today. Harris, *Guide*, p. 153. In Rawl. MS 318, see below, n. 11 and p. 427, Narbrough refers to polecats and from the description they were Patagonian skunks (*Conepatus humboldti*). Ibid., p. 154.

[2] These are probably either the culpeo fox (*Dusicyon culpaeus magellanicus*) which is a wolf-like animal, or the Argentine gray fox (*D. griseus*) which is appreciably smaller than the former animal. Both come from the family *Canidae* to which domestic dogs also belong. Ibid., pp. 152–3.

[3] This is probably either the pampas cat (*Felis colocolo*) or Geoffroy's cat (*F. geoffroyi*), both of which are uncommon in Patagonia today. Ibid., p. 155.

[4] These are probably kites. The kites, hawks and harriers found in this area are the white-tailed kite (*Elanus leucurus*), red-backed hawk (*Buteo polyosoma*), cinereus harrier (*Circus cinereus*), long-winged harrier (*C. buffoni*). Of these the red-backed hawk and cinereus harrier breed in the area and are therefore the most likely to have been seen, while the white-tailed kite and the long-winged harrier are generally found further north. Ibid., pp. 66–8. Kite has many meanings in the *NOED* and this could conceivably be a 'flight of doves ... A school of pigeons'. The doves found in this area are the eared dove (*Zenaida auriculata*) and the rock dove (*Columba livia*). The picui ground dove (*Columbina picui*) is found in northern Patagonia and might have been sighted as far south as this. Ibid., pp. 91–2.

[5] The partridge (*Perdix perdix*) is not found in South America. It is possible these may have been tinamous which are about the same size and not too dissimilar in colouring. The Patagonian tinamu (*Tinamotis ingoufi*) is found in this area. Ibid., pp. 27–8.

[6] There are about a dozen varieties of duck which might be found in this area: the flying steamer-duck (*Tachyeres patachonicus*), crested duck (*Lophonetta specularioides*) spectacled duck (*Anas specularis*), white-cheeked pintail (*A. bahamensis*), common teal (*A. cyanoptera*), red shoveler (*A. platalea*), southern widgeon (*A. sibilatrix*), speckled teal (*A. flavirostris*), silver teal (*A. versicolor*), brown pintail (*A. georgica*), rosy-billed pochard (*Netta peposaca*) and lake duck (*Oxyura vittata*). Ibid., pp. 59–64.

[7] This may have been the Eskimo curlew (*Numenius borealis*), which was found in South America (now virtually extinct), but generally further north than this. Peña and Rumboll, *Birds*, plate 34.9. It might have been a whimbrel (*N. phaeopus*), or Hudsonian godwit (*Limosa haemastica*), which are a little smaller than the curlew but otherwise similar, and visit the area. Harris, *Guide*, pp. 77, 80–81. The snipes are generally too small and in all probabilty Narbrough would have recognized them since they are found in Europe (as is the whimbrel).

[8] These are probably sea pies – oystercatchers. The American oystercatcher (*Haematopus palliatus (ostralegus)*), Magellanic oystercatcher (*H. leucopodus*) and blackish oystercatcher (*H. ater*) are found in this area. Ibid., pp. 72–4.

[9] A name applied to any member of the *Mullidæ* (red mullet) or *Mugilidæ* (grey mullet) families. *NOED.*

[10] Southern smelts, family *Retropinnidae.*

[11] Wood, BL, MS 46A, p. 150 adds to this list: 'a little Creature with a Bushy Tayle which wee Called a huffer because when he seeth you he will stand Vapouring and putting with his Fore Feet upon the ground and yet hath noe defence for himselfe but With his Breech and that when one cometh near him he turneth his Breech toward you and squirteth at you which stincketh worse then any thing in the world.' This is the Patagonian skunk (*Conepatus humboldyi*). Its body is 15½ in (40 cm), tail 7¾in (20 cm), black or brown with 2 white lines extending back from the forehead on either side. Harris, *Guide*, p. 154.

[12] Southern elephant seal (*Mirounga leonina*), South American sea lion (*Otaria flavescens*), and South American fur seal (*Arctocephalus australis*) are commonly found in this area. Ibid., pp. 156–62

[13] Magellanic penguin (*Spheniscus magellanicus*), rockhopper penguin (*Eudyptes chrysocome*) and king penguin (*Aptenodytes patagonicus*) are found in this area. Magellanic penguins breed in burrows up to 6ft (2m) deep on

shore within the harbower North North West [*margin: small view of a hummock and tower-like rock hill with tower inserted at this point*] on it from the Pecked Rocke one [on] the South Side, up in the No*rth* sid in a Gulely [gully] of Rockes about theere quarters of an Englesh mile from the Salt water up a valy there is a fine Smale Springe of fresh water: and more a mile to the westward nere the Salt water Side of the river is an other Small Springe of fresh water: which Boath I diged & made a faier warteringe Placses out of which I tooke more than fowerty tunn[1] of water the twenty dayes I stayed their. This is a faier harbower for many Ships to Ride in and they will finde 4 and five fadam water at a Low water to Ride in: But the tides Runes very Strong that is they run Stronger then at Gravesend.[2] People must be Cearefull to vew the Place at a Low wat*er* [*margin:* tids Rise] for their is Sum Scartered Rockes wich then may be sen.[3] It Rises nere fower fadams one [on] high Springe tids: and [*margin:* High wat*er*]it is a full Sea in the harbower at halfe an hower Past a Leaven aclocke one [on] the full mone or Change:[4] the flood Comes from the Southward and it flows nere tide and halfe tide with out in the Roade to that in the harbower:[5] it houlds its Course Six howers Ebb and Six flod. The harbower of Port dissier is in the NW Parte of this Bay: and So is the Pecked Rocke. Porte disier Lyes in nere East and West.[6] You Ride Land Lockte within: a westerly wind is the worst wind to Ride their if it blowes for it Comes Right down the River and Commonly Blowes a Stout gale: and much one [on] that Pointe.[7] I found all the Coast much given to westerly winds.
The Compas have Seaventen degres theerty minuts Variation Easterly: the north fly or hand in Clines Soe much Easterly from its true Place: as By Offen Experiens made By Amplytuds and also when the Sun was one [on] the Merid*ian*.[8]
Porte Disier Lyes in the Latt*itud* of Fowerty Seaven degres fowerty Eight minuts By Good observation of the Sun which I tooke with Davises quardron[9] and other Instu*ments*: South Lattitud. And in Longitud from the Lizard of England West Sixty two Degres.[10]

---

open beaches, sand dunes and grassy slopes throughout the South American offshore islands; rockhopper penguins breed on tumbling scree, lava slopes and with tussock grass, on the islands of Cape Horn; king penguins breed on flat areas and sometimes among tussock grass, formerly in southern Chile and Argentina, it is unlikely they would have been found as far north as Puerto Deseado. Ibid., pp. 28–34. Shirihai, *Complete Guide*, pp. 44–9, 62–5, 80–81.

[1] Barrel or cask. *NOED*.

[2] Today the tide at Gravesend runs at up to 2·7 knots at spring tides. The rate was probably similar at this time.

[3] The ship would normally expect to enter an anchorage or harbour at, or approaching, high water, so that examining it by boat at low water to see what dangers were visible, should be a standard seaman-like practice.

[4] See below, p. 216, n. 6.

[5] In the harbour the tidal stream changes direction at high and low water, but outside the harbour it changes at half tide.

[6] The line of the harbour lies nearly east–west.

[7] Wood, BL, MS 46A, p. 142: 'The Tide in this Harbour runneth very strong and therefore must Consequently be a Badd Port in Winter when the Ice cometh downe the River which is Narrow and a storme Blowes at West which is very Comon in this Place and a Tyde of Ebb under foote Anchor and Cables Cannot hold.'

[8] Wood, BL, MS 46A, p. 152: 'I find the Variac*io*n by Severall Amplitudes and Azimuths 16° as I observed the North point being drawne Soe much to the Eastward. But in the yeare 1591 Mr John Davies observed at London was 10° Easterly but at this time is one Degree, at which time the Varia*t*ion Westerly: therefore it hath decreased or varyed at London a 11° Westward but in this Port Contrary Increased Easterly 11°.'

[9] Davis's Quadrant or back-staff.

[10] The position of Port Desire (Puerto Deseado) is 47°45′S, 65°53′W, which is 60°41′W of the Lizard. Narbrough's position was thus remarkably accurate for this date. Wood, BL, MS 46A, p. 139: 'Port Desire lyeth

And Meridian distance one thousand & feveten leagus 2·6 mils. [89] Penguins Ils Lyes in the Lattitud of fourty Seaven degres feveety five Minuts: And in Longitud from the Lizard of En*gland* Sixty one degrees feviety Seaven minuts[1] and Meridian dist*ance* one thousand and theerten leags two miles it is SE from Port Dissier a Bout three Leagus:[2] then the Land Lyes SSW wester*ly* to the South Pointe of a deep bay Called Spirings bay:[3] it is three Leagus ther is a Smale Rockey Iland or two wher many Seales frequnts [*sic*]. The Land inward is of an indefrent haight the Shore Lyes SSW by the Compas which it makes Sumwhat a bay which is Called Seals Bay.[4] Their is a Smale Rockey Iland at the South Pointe of that bay and many Seales Eus [use] it: it is distance from the Pointe of Spirings bay Seaven Leagus.[5] East from this Iland or Pointe[6] ther Lyes a Rocke five leagus of[f] the Land [*margin:* E a ston Rock] in the sea it makes Like the Edy Stone[7] you shale have twenty fadam water halfe a mile with in it for their I Sailed.[8] Thir is an other Smale bay Caled S[t] diones bay wher is the smal River of S[t] diones. Ther is Severall Rocks lyes before

in the Lat of 47°40′ South difference of Long*itude* from the Lizard 63°10′ W*est* and Meridian dist*ance* 3096 Miles. Ibid., p. 153: 'The 18th day of September 1670 at night I observed the beginning and end of the Eclips of the Moone in this harbour of Port Desire whereby I finde that the Difference of Long*itude* between London and this Place to be 73° which in time 4 ho*urs* and 52 minutes.' This is followed in the original by the calculation.

[1] See above, n. 1, p. 204.

[2] Distance about 10 miles, just over 3 leagues.

[3] Spiering Bay is shown on the Doncker chart (Plate 2) and is now known as Bahía de los Nodales (48°00′S, 65°52′W). Wood, BL, MS 46A, p. 144: 'To the Southward just above the Iseland lyeth a Deepe Bay and Called by Sr Francis Drake the Bay of troublesome for that it hath a Fall of Foule ground and severall Raggy Iselands. From Penguinne Iseland which is on the north part of this Bay Cross to the South point it is 3 Leagues S by W[t] By Compass but the true Course allowing varia*t*ion is So*uth* 27° W At the So*uth* point of this Bay are 5 Small Iselands which are much frequented by Seales and lye in the Lat of 47°57′ So*uth*.' I can find no reference in the accounts of Drake's voyage of Troublesome Bay. Islas Schwarz, Liebres and Shag all lie in the bay.

[4] This would appear to be Bahía Desvelos (48°18′S, 66°17′W). Wood, BL, MS 46A. p. 145 notes 'Called by Mr Thomas Candish Seales Bay'. See 'Certeine Rare and Special Notes most properly belonging to the voyage of *M. Thomas Candish* &c. written by *M. Thomas Fuller* &c.', Hakluyt, *Principal Navigations*, III, pp. 825–37. Fuller places the bay 'Southwards of Port Desire 12 leagues Southsouthwest'.

[5] The southern point of Bahía de los Nodales (Spirings Bay), is Punta Medanosa (48°06′S, 65°55′W). Southward from this point there is a shallow indentation in the coast about 22 miles long with Bahía Desvelos at its southern end. Cabo Guardián lies at its southern point, with Isla Rasa Chica off it.

[6] Cabo Guardián (48°21′S, 66°21′W).

[7] This is Roca Bellaco (48°30′S, 66°11′W), described as 'a blackish pointed and steep-to rock which dries 6 m (20 ft). No kelp is visible in the vicinity, and in calm weather the sea does not break over the rock at H[igh] W[ater]; at L[ow] W[ater] the rock can be seen from a distance of 6 to 10 miles. Overfalls extend SE from the rock; during strong winds they also extend NW to join those off the dangers fronting Cabo Guardián.' *South America Pilot*, II, para. 3.79. This rock is described by Thomas Candish as being 'about 5 leagues from the land, much like unto Ediestone, which lieth off the sound of Plimouth. This rocke standeth in 48 degrees ½ to the Southward of the line.' Hakluyt, *Principal Navigations*, III, p. 805. The Eddystone Rock off the entrance to Plymouth Sound lies in 50°11′N, 4°16′W.

[8] Wood, BL, MS 46A p.145: 'Note that from these Iselands lyeth the most danger that is on all the Coast of Patagonia for from these Iselands lyeth a Ledge of Rocks a League in the Sea and in fair weather you may see the Sea Breake on them: but this is not all the Danger for 4 Leagues from the shore lyeth a Rock much like the Edystone neare Plymouth in England and hath much foule ground about it and in the fairest weather the Sea may be Seene to breake on them. ... This Rock lyeth in the Lat*itude* of 48°14′ So*uth* and Long*itude* from the Lizard 63°30′ W The Course from Penguinne Iselands to this Rock is SW[r] 6°30′ So*uth* about 11 or 12 Leag*ues* but the true Course is SSW[t].'

this bay:[1] and the tids Run very Stronge it is a hige water here at a Leaven a Clocke one [on] the C*h*ange of the mone the flood Comes from the Southwarde al along this Coast. This Eady Stone Rocke Lyes in the Latit*ude* of fouerty Eight [degres] and twenty Minuts: one [on] the maine Land to the South ward of this is a longe steep Beach with Sum Round Smal hiles [hills] and flat table lands: the Shore Lyes SSW alonge after you are to the Southward of this beach the Land begin to Rise of indeferent height and great Plaines their you will See a Small flat Iland [*margin:* flat Ile][2] which Lyes a Bout fower miles from the maine. I Saw it but was not at it it is in Bigness a bove twenty Acare*s* of Ground: it Lyes in the Lattitud of fowerty Eight degr*ees* and fowerty Minuts by daviss quadrant.[3] More to the Southward of this Iland is a Low Plaine with a Beach: it Makes a Longe Bay: nere fower Leags Longe: in this Plaine is A Mighty Great Salt Pond: which in the Sum*mer* time have hundereds of Tuns of Excellent Salte: this Pond is twoo mils from the Sea: it Lyes in the Latt*itud* of fowerty Eight degres feivety feive Minuts. The Land Lyes from Pointe to Pointe SSW and NNE. To the South Pointe of this Bay is white Clifes about the height of the north forland and Sumwhat like them. [90] And the Land one [on] the Cuntry is in Severall high Round Coplen hils in the fore [form] of the tops of Moule [mole] hils[4] one higer than the Rest which is the only Marke to Know the Harbower of St Julyan[5] for it Lyes Just a Bout those white Clife in A Bite[6] of A Bay which is Beten [between] those white Clifes and the white Clifes to the Southward.[7] Those Coplen hils Lyes Right over the Harbower of St Julyan W*est* into the Land about five or Six mils. This Bay before St Julyan theer is three Rockes lyes of[f] the South Pointe[8] and in the Bay you may Anchor in tenn fadams: oasy Sand. The Harbower Lyes in the SW Parte of the Bay

[1] Probably Bahía Laura (48°24′S, 66°28′W), between Cabo Guardián and Punta Mercedes. Arrecife Guardián lies 3 miles SE of Cabo Guardián with another drying reef surrounded by kelp 3 miles ESE of Punta Mercedes, in the mouth of the bay. Modern charts do not show a river running into this bay, however the Doncker chart (Plate 2) shows I. de S. Dionisio with a river or estury in a bay close west of it.

[2] This is Islote Chato (48°45′S, 67°03′W), described as 'a dark sheer-sided islet 4 m [13 ft] high which forms a prominent mark'. *South America Pilot*, II, para 3.97. It is almost exactly 4 miles offshore. Wood, BL, MS 46A, pp. 145–6: 'near this Iseland [146] the Plaine Mercators Charts make a harbour called St Dnonitions: whether there be any Suche I know not'. Possibly this is the origin of Narbrough's St diones bay, above.

[3] Observation taken by back-staff.

[4] Coplen Hills, *Cople, Copple. NOED.* A little summit or eminence. This word was used by Narbrough in various ways and appears to indicate a small hill with relatively steep sides. He likens them to mole-hills in one place and refers to an island as copling up like a sugar loaf. He also used it to mean a summit or crest.

[5] Wood, BL, MS 46A, p. 151 notes the 'Markes to finde Port St Julians. When you are to the Southward of Cape St George or Port desire the first high Land that you shall see will be in the Lat*itude* of 48°40′ S*outh*, which is the Lat*itude* of this harbour and here the high Land endeth and Between the high Land and Lowe Land goeth into the harbour: but if you fall with the Land to the Southward of the harbour you will finde the Land to be Lowe from the harbour to the Lat*itude* of 50°20′ the Land being flatt without hamocks or woods being all steep white Cliffes to the Seaward.' This high land, now known as Monte Wood, 948 ft (289 m) (49°14′·5S, 67°45′W), lies 3 miles within the harbour of Puerto San Julián, while Monte Sholl, 1,004 ft (306 m) lies 2 miles farther in. 'Monte Wood ... and Monte Sholl ..., hills with flat summits, stand out well from the lower ground in their vicinity.' *South America Pilot*, II, para. 3.102.

[6] Bight: The corner or recess of a bay. *NOED*.

[7] Puerto San Julián lies at the back of a bay entered between Cabo Curioso (49°11′S, 67°37′W), and Punta Desengaño, 4 miles south. Wood, BL, MS 46A, p. 151, gives the distance from Puerto Deseado to Puerto San Julián as 'Distance 34 Leagues. Lat. 49°34′ S. 'Meridian Dist*ance* 39 Miles W....The varia*t*ion I finde, by Severall Amplitudes and Azimuts, to be 17° on the No*rth* point being drawne Soe much Easterly.'

[8] These rocks, which dry up to 13 ft (4 m), lie 6½ cables NNW of Punta Desengaño.

and have But an Narrow Enterence which a Stranger Cannot Perceive till he have discovered it with his boat. It is at the first Enterry a bout the Bredth of Portsmouth harbower in England at its Enterance[1] then it is Broader. Ther is in it two Ilands of a Pretty Bigness in the Harbower one [on] the west Side of the Chanell they have Bushess one [on] them: the one we Called true justice[2] the other hogg Iland: their is five Ilands in all at a Low water but of noe account. This Harbower have a Bare [bar] at the first Enterrance which have But fower foote water at a Low water. The first Goeinge in Lyes Southwest till you Come to the narrow then the River Lyes in SSW:[3] with in about a mile up the River one [on] the E*ast* Side lyes a Rocke[4] which you must have a care of for it is But just dry at a Low water: I Rod a bove it: and I Rod be Low it: ther is five fadam be low it at a Low water Clere Ground. One [on] the E*ast* Side at the Enter of this harbower is a Beachey Pointe Steep to:[5] and Sum Brooken Rockes with out it of an indeferent height But they are yust [just] Covered at a High water the tids Rise here one [on] the Springs [*margin:* Hig wa] three fadam and a halfe: it is a hige water here one [on] the full and Change[6] days of the mone at halfe an hower Past a Leaven of the Clocke: the tids Runes as Stronge as at Gravesend.[7] This River is al Salt water: it Runs up a Bout five mile and their Ends in Marshess: ther is whit Clefs at the uper End of the harbower Like fulers

[1] The entrance to Portsmouth Harbour at this date was much the same width as it is today, about 250 yards. The distance between Punta Peña, on the north side, and Punta Guijarro on the south side of the entrance, is about 4 cables, but the channel is about half that width between the off-lying rocks.

[2] Islas Justicia; variants Island of Justice, True Justice, Yustis. The 3 islands now known as the Islas Justicia lie on the east side of the channel with the 4 Islas Cormorán, on the west side. Narbrough's Island of True Justice, shown on his chart, is actually the easternmost of Islas Cormorán, adjacent to the main channel, while Hogg Island is the westernmost of Islas Cormoran. On this island, Magellan had executed the masters of the four ships that had conspired against him, Pigafetta, *Magellan's Voyage*, I, p. 50. Likewise Drake had executed Thomas Doughtie; Hakluyt, *Principal Navigations*, III, p. 733. Wood, BL, MS 46A, p. 146, notes that these excutions took place there, that Doughty was buried there, together with '2 of his men Slayne by the natives himselfe narrowly Escaped they were buried on the Iseland of true Justice whose Graves and Boanes wee found'.

[3] Wood, BL, MS 3833, f. 21r, states 'The Marks wee had to Run in & out by was the Rockey Poynt, Noted with a ┼ [shown on Wood's chart which is not included here] & the White Spots in the hill notted with the same Marke: when these are one in another [in line] you may Run in & for thawrt Markes to Know when you are on the Bar ther is to the Northward of the harbors Mouth serttane [certain] whitetish Clifes, which seem to be an Island: when the Midle of these Clifes & a Vally or Sadle in the Land Behind them are one in the other, then you are on the Bar: But the Best way Before you are to Bould to Run in, is to sound the Bar with your Boate & to Boy it: for I sopose the Bar Altereth with Easterly Winds the Rageing of the Sea Makeing the Beach to shoote & Remufe [remove].'

[4] Piedras Rodríguez, kelp-covered rocks which dry (are the same level as chart datum, approximately the level of the lowest tide), lying 1·9 miles SSE of Punta Peña the northern entrance point of the harbour.

[5] The eastern entrance point is Punta Guijarro and between it and Punta Desengaño (about 2¼ miles E) lie rocks along the shore with a channel between them and Banco Ferreyra the seaward end of which is 5 cables north of Punta Desengaño. The channel used by Narbrough was north of Banco Ferreyra, now known as Canal Norte. In 1969 the least depth in this channel was 7 ft (2·1 m) over a width over 109 ft (100 m) and 4 ft (1·2 m) over 219 ft (200 m). *South America Pilot*, II, para. 3.106.

[6] Full moon and change of the moon. The rise and fall of the tides are governed principally by the moon, although the sun and other factors play a part. The time of high water was therefore related to the day on which the moon was full or when it was not visible, or changed from waning to waxing. It was either given as a local time or the bearing of the moon at high water. This was sometimes known as the establishment of the port. Spring tides normally occur about two days after the full moon.

[7] Mean High Water Spring Tide is 24·6 ft (7·5 m) and the tide runs at rates of between 3 and 6 knots in the narrows and 1 to 3 knots inside the harbour. *South America Pilot*, II, para. 3.108, 3.116. The tidal stream at Gravesend today runs at up to 2·7 knots.

Earth and Sum vaines in it Like iseingglas [isinglass]. Its Steep Rockes at the Enterence one [on] the west Side with out is a longe Steep Beach.[1] You must Borrow one [on][2] the West to goe in for that is the faierest Channell. It ou*gh*t to be well discovred at a Low water By any Stranger.[3] [91] THe Harbowers mouth of Port St Julyan Lyes in the Lattitud of Fowerty Nine degres & tenn Minuts and in Longitud from the Lizard Sixty three degrs ten minuts[4] & meridian distance west one thousand and theerty leags. All the Shore to the South ward of St Julyan for tennty Leagus distance is Steep white Clifes and Plaine Land aloft with out any hills at all: you may Saile with in three Leagus of the shor and have twenty fadam Black oassy sand: the Shore Lyes SBW westerly. From Penguens Iland to Port St Julyan is theerty one Leagus SSW nerest by the Compas:[5] the Compas have Sixten degres theerty Minuts variation Easterly:[6] here is anchoringe in Severall Places A Longe the Coast & Cleare Ground. In Porte St Julyan their is fresh water in a Pond one [on] the East Side halfe a mile from the River: And Great Bushess which you may Git fire wood out of them But noe timber at all in the hole Cuntry[7] nor any kind of frute But all a dry Graise[8] Ground with out water. Fresh water is very Scarse here in the Sumer time But her is the Best wood for fireinge as I have sene heather to one [on] the Coast.[9] Here is in the Land Great Beasts Like Dere which are Called ynacos[10] they Bere the Red wolle: I killed five of them with my Gray hound as I had with mee. Here are many osterages and hares and foxes and Poulcats and armidillos:[11] I killed Severall of all those with my Grayhound and Gunn. Here are Sum Parterages and Green Plover[12] and Ducks and teall:[13] and Severall Sorts of Sea fowles which are all very Good Meate. Here is very Good fish in this harbower Like Codlens but Biger Severall of them as Bige as a Mans Legg: here ar Excellent Smelts: Good Mussells: I tooke one day with my fishinge Neet Seaven hundered and twenty five very faier and Good fish. Here is in the Monthes of december Jeanuary & Febreuary Excellent Salt in a Pond five miles to the No*rth*ward of this harbower by

[1] Rocks and dry banks extend a mile from the shore on the north side of the channel.

[2] Borrow on: Keep close to.

[3] See above, p. 209, n. 3.

[4] The harbour mouth is in 49°14′S, 67°45′W, which is 62°33′W of the Lizard.

[5] The distance is about 110 miles.

[6] Wood, BL, MS 3833, f. 22v: found the variation to be '17°02' ... the 17th day of August I found an Exact Meredian Line by the 3 shadowes of a Perpendiculer Erected on a true Horrozantall plane & there by found the Varation to be 17°00. ... Heare I found the Needle to Incline or Dip to an Angle of 70°30′, the South poynt under the Horozan.'

[7] Timber in this context refers to wood suitable for making masts or spars or other carpenter's work.

[8] 'Graise' is an alternative spelling for graze, and it may be Narbrough is using it in the sense of grazing land, or possibly rubbed or abraded: it can also be used to mean 'take off the grass close to the ground'. *NOED*.

[9] Wood, BL, MS 46A, p. 151: 'In the Sumer time here is noe Fresh water to be had but in the winter you may finde Snow water in many places the most Convenient place for a Boate to fetch water is at a Rock which lyes in this harbour.'Wood you have more here than at Port desire yet if 3 ships were to winter here there would hardly be enough to Supply their necessary occasions. It groweth near the water side in little Bushes.'

[10] Guanaco or wild llama with reddish-brown wool, see above, p. 207, n. 3.

[11] See above, p. 207, n. 8.

[12] The plovers found in this area are: golden plover (*Pluvialis dominica*), Magellanic plover (*P. sociallis*), semipalmated plover (*Charadrius semipalmatus*), two-banded plover (*C. falklandicus*). The last two of these breed in the area while the first two are visitors. None of them is green, although the Magellanic plover, a generally grey dove-like bird, would seem the most likely one to have been seen. Harris, *Guide*, pp. 74–6.

[13] See above, p. 208, n. 6.

Land my Selfe & Men fetche in Baggs a Bouve Six tuns of it. Shipps may Lad of it in time of the yare But in the winter it all disovles [dissolves].

Here are Sum families of People in this Land: one day fower of my Men Mett with Seaven of them & Called to them and Gave them a Knife and a Neckcloath and a bottle of Brandy which they Put up: and so went away: they Seme to be very fearefull they are Clad with beasts Skines [92] And are of Rude behaveour they Loge one [on] the Ground like Beasts they are But of a midlen Statuer[1] they keepe dogs which are much Like our Mungerell Mastefs in England I Suppose ther dogs of the Spannish race which they have Got by Sume meanse or other from them. I Cannot any way Conceive that those People have any thinge to trade with or have the knowledge of any thinge that is Good. I laid and Put up Knifes and Beads and other thinke one [things on] the Land in Severall Places: But never Could Perceive that ever they Cam nere them. I Eused all the Indeviour I Could to Trade with them that I Could But all was in vaine for they never would Com nere any of us.

I went theerty or fowerty mils with twelfe men with mee but Could not See any People. I Saw a Small Revellet of fresh water which runes into the uper End of the Great Salt Pond: and Severall Ponds of Salt water their is in the Cuntry. I was in the Cuntry five dayes and saw Nothinge but dere [deer][2] and osterages:[3] the osterages are nothinge Soe Large as those oster*ages* which are in Barbary:[4] the Bigest as Ever we Caute wayed But Sixty three Pounds: Guts and feathers and all things as he was. A hare have waied Eightenn Pound & a halfe Severall above Seaventen Pounds. The Land inwards is very Barren downs with hills and dales not Soe much as a bush to be sene any where [*margin: fingerpost*] nor any kind of Minerall or Metle: it is of a Sandy Gravelly Sile and Rockes in many Placess. Allwayes wher Soever I went I ever Looked for Mineralls but never Could find any. I once found a Pece of Cristell of an inch Longe as big as the Stem of a tobaccoe Pipe: I have found Severall Peces of white and Red flints and Gren flents which will Strike very Good fire: the Indians make ther arrow heads of them very fashonable: we found Sum of them in their arrows which they had lost. Their Arroes are made of a Sticke But they are not two foot Longe I saw five of them: they are feathered and headed with those flints very artificially: and ar made Broad Arrow fashion and very Sharpe Pointed and neatly fitted for their use.

[93] [*page blank*]

[94] **February 1669 the *Sweepstakes* at Sea of[f] Peng*uine* Ile. 47°59′.**
22

Beinge Tusday this morninge I Stood into the westward for I Stood of[f] Last night to See if I could See the Pinke But Could not the wind Beinge at No*rth* a fresh gale: the

[1] Pigafetta had described one of these people, called by Magellan the Pathagoni (dogs with large paws), as a giant 'so tall that the tallest of us only came up to his waist'. Pigafetta, *Magellan's Voyage*, I, p. 46.

[2] Narbrough desribes guanacos as large animals like deer above, so he is probably referring to guanacos here. There are deer in South America, most of which prefer forested areas, e.g. the Patagonian huemul (*Hippocamelus antisensis*), a deer of the southern Andes, found on steep rocky slopes with dense shrub and forest clearings. The only deer which might have been seen here is the Pampas deer (*Ozotoceros bezoarticus*), which is found in open flat land and rolling hills in Argentina today; however, it stands 38 in (95 cm) at the shoulder, weight about 75 lb (34 kg). Lord, *Mammals*, pp. 131, 134.

[3] See above, p. 207.

[4] Darwin's rhea, see above, p. 207, n. 4, stands about 4 ft (1·2 m) tall while the ostrich found in Africa (*Struthio camelus*) is 6½ ft (2 m) high.

winds at 12 Clock veareinge to the NW:ward I tacked and Stood in WSW: faier weather and a fine gale: I Could not See the Pinke any where and allwase keept men aloft to Looke out. This day at none I observed and was in the Latt*itud* of 48°20′. Lettle wind this after none: I Sounded and had Seaventen fadam oasey Sand. This Eveinge I got into the Shore and anchored in a beachey Bay[1] in twenty fadam water Sandy Ground: faier weather this Eveinge wind at W: the aier Could. I went ashore but Could not See any People Barran ground:[2] I made a fier for the Pinke to See it if Shee were one [on] the Coast: I Came aboard againe. The Shipp Rod in a League of the Shore.[3]

23

Beinge Wedensday wind at NW a fresh gale: this morninge I waied and Stood to the Northward to See for the Pinke – my Boate Sailed a longe the Shore. I Passed by a bay which have many Rockes befor it and an Iland at the No*rth* Pointe of it:[4] it is in the Lat*itud* of 48°12′.[5] I Stood to the N:ward till night then anchored in twenty five fadam oasey Ground a boute five miles from the Shore: this Bay is Called Seals Bay where I anchored.[6] It Blew to night about a leaven of the Clocke at West a mighty Storme and Sum haile and Slat: it Continued till fower the next morninge which forced me to Lower my yards a Port longs:[7] I fear this Storme Put the Pinke of[f] the Shore if she be not anchored.

24

Beinge Thursday wind at WNW a fresh gale. I waied [*margin:* 'Hump*rey* Smith Died in the ni*gh*t'] this morninge and stood to the N:ward my Boat went a longe the Shore.[8] I Passed by Spirings Bay which have an Iland at the South Pointe of it and Rockes in it: at the North Parte of it Stands a Pointe of Rockes which makes like a Castle and a tower in it of an indeferant height.[9] This afternone I Pased by Penguine Iland which lies to the Northward of Spirings Bay:[10] I Stood in to the Bay Before Port dissier ther anchored in

[1] A bay with a beach round it. This would appear to be the bay SW of Punta Mercedes (48°24′S, 66°28′W), which terminates in Morro Campana, a reddish bluff with a natural stone tower resembling a beacon.

[2] Wood, BL, MS 3833, f. 14r: 'As Sone as we was att an Anker the Cap*tain* & my Self went a shore'.

[3] Within a league of the shore.

[4] Wood, BL, MS 3833, f. 14r: 'The Cap*tain* and Leut*enant* went in the Pinnice all a Longe the Shore to find PORT DESIRE but found itt nott. The Island which we thought was Pinguin Island was nott itt. This Island Lyeth in the Latt*itude* of 48°12′ & hath 4 small Islands aboute itt & is att the So*uth* End of a Bay which I Called SWEEPSTAKS Bay.' Sweepstakes Bay would appear to be Bahía Desvelos (48°18′S, 66°17′W).

[5] This is probably Punta Medanosa off which Isla Shag lies.

[6] See above, p. 210, n. 6.

[7] Lowering the yard right down to the gunwale, with the yardarms projecting outboard.

[8] Wood, BL, MS 3833, f. 14r: 'There is an Island att the No*rth* end of This Bay which was the 3[d] Island wee tooke for Pinguin Island. Soe the Cap*tain* and I went in The Pinnice to this Island butt found itt not to be itt butt a Small Island with many Seales upon itt some of which we Slew.'

[9] Punta Lobos, 'composed of remarkable pillars of rock, the highest of which appears to be formed of large superimposed blocks'. *South America Pilot*, II, para. 3.70.

[10] Wood, BL, MS 3833, f. 14r: 'When wee Came to this Island we made a Fire that our Men in the Shipe Might See where wee was: on these Islands we found Millions of Seales one of Which I Slew as Bigg as any Horse in Ingland. Heare we found Many Hundereds of Pinguins which is a foulle as gratte as Some Gease the[y] goe upright & have noe feathers butt Downe: they are Indeferant good Meatte. Se we departed & sayled to the Ship who then had saw the harbour of Porte desire.'

Sixtenn fadam oasey Sand about a league from the maine: wind at *West* to night a fine gale: I keept a Light al night in Cas the Pinke Should Come alonge She might See it. Faier weather to night and lettle wind at *West* and SW.

[95] **February 1669 the *Sweepstakes* in the Bay of Port dissier.**

25

Beinge friday faier weather this morninge wind at west a fine gale. I haveinge But Little warter a Board nor wood and the Ship wanted a new Gain[1] of Shrouds for her maine Mast and Ballas:[2] I thought it fitt to Goe into Porte Dissier and ther fitt my Selfe with what I wanted Judginge allso the Pinke would Come ther for Shee was not Past by it. I vewed the harbow*er* with my Boat and found it a Safe harbower to fitt my Selfe.[3] I waied this forenone and went before the harbower with the Shipp and Anchored in Six fadam warter at a low warter. Faier weather all this day and night: I keept a light out al night.

26

Beinge Satterday faier weather wind at *West*. This morninge a fresh gale noe Pinke to be Seen: I Rod fast and mored with my Stream anchor: I sent men up the hills to looke for her but all in vaine. This day my Self and Master went into the harbower and vewed it well: it Blow hard this afternone at *West*: Cloudy weather to night: I keept a Light out. Wee eat Seale and Penguins: they are very Good and holse Sum [wholesome] food.

27

Beinge Sunday faier weather wind at west a fresh gale this morninge: I waied with the Shipp and Plyed in at the first of the flood to the narrow then Keeaged [kedged] in with my Two top Sails[4] and anchored and mored with my Two Bowers in Six fadam. Wee got Sum Buss wood [bush wood] aboard today for fewell: faier weather this Eveinge But Could wind at west. I got upon an Iland as many younge Shags[5] which were Ready to fly as Served all my Shipps Company for a dais diet Beinge Eighty five Persons.

28

Beinge Munday faier weather wind at NW a fresh gale: this morninge I one Bent[6] my Sailes and Put my maine Saile ashor to mend: and Set my Saile makers to worke: and the

[1] Probably used in the sense of an advantage, help or benefit; the main mast needed the help of a new set of shrouds.

[2] With the expenditure of stores, food etc. the ship was in need of more ballast.

[3] Wood, BL, MS 3833, f. 14v: 'The Cap*tain* & my Self went in with the Pinice and our Yalle [yawl] to sound the Harbour & found Watter suffishant for our ship. We went aboute 4 Miles up in the River & found a strong tide to sett from poynt to Poynt.'

[4] When the wind and tide were in opposition, as in this case, it was the practice to kedge with the assistance of some of the sails. Kedging with the top sails is to allow the ship to drift through the narrow on the tide using the top-sails to prevent her going too close to either shore. The kedge anchor, the smallest of the ships anchors used for steadying the ship in harbour, might also be taken ahead by boat and let go to haul the ship round by the capstan and thus keep her off the shores, being weighed again as the ship passed over it.

[5] These were probably either rock shag (*Phalacrocorax magellanicus*) or imperial shag (*P. atriceps atriceps*), both of which breed in this area and are common. The neotropic cormorant (*P. olivaceus*) is found throughout South America; the red-legged cormorant (*P. gaimardi*) is also a common resident and there is a colony opposite the town of Puerto Deseado today. Shirihai, *Complete Guide*, pp. 222–5; Harris, *Guide*, pp. 46–50.

[6] Unbent the sails, unlaced them from their yards and running tackle, so that they could be taken ashore.

Seamen to one Rige [unrig] the Shipp and to fit the Maine Shrouds: I went one [on] the North Shore and found out two Springs of fresh warter.

March 1669 the *Sweepstakes* in Porte dissier Latt*itud* 47°45′.

1

Beinge Tusday faier weather wind at No*rth* a fine gale this afternon the wind Came to the East a fine gale. To day I filled fower hogsheads of fresh warter and diged the Springs deeper: the Carpenters Calked the Ships Sids: the Seamen fitted the Rigen [rigging]. Close weather to night wind at E.

[96] **March 1669 the *Sweepstakes* in Porte Disier.**

2

Beinge Weedensday Cloudy Rainey weather wind at SE and Blows hard al day and Raines So as wee Could doe little worke: only mored the Ship fast: blew hard to night.

3

Beinge Thursday Blowinge Rainey Gusty weather this foreno[n]e wind Came to the SSE: this Eveinge the wind Cam to the Ea*st* a fine gale al night.

4

Beinge Friday faier weather wind at E a fine gale: went all hands and fitted the Rigginge and filled Sum fresh water. This day at twelfe aclocke I went with my Boats and fowerty Men with Stafes and handspikes to Seale Iland in the harbower in halfe an houer we killed fower hundered Seals Boath young and ould:[1] I laded my Boats and Brought them downe against the Ship and their Landed them. Faier weather to night.

5

Beinge Satterday faier weather wind at SW a fine gale. This morninge we went and flaed the and Salted the flesh in Bulke one [on] Boards to draine out the Blod: faier weat*her* al night the wind Came to the west and Blew hard to night.

6

Beinge Sunday Blowinge weather wind at W*est*. This day I went ashore one [on] the South Side and traviled Eight mile in the Land: But Could not Se any thinge But a dry Barran Land: at night Cam aboard againe wind at W*est* a fresh gale.

7

Beinge Munday Cloudy weather the wind veared to the So*uth* and to the E and to the NE and blow fresh al day. Today wee Packed up our Seals flesh in Caske: and had five Punsons and fower hogsheads full: the meat Eats very well Salted: of the fat of the Great ones we mad oyle [oil] for Lamps. The Great ones are much Like a Lyon and Roars Like a Lyon

[1] These were probably South American sea lions (*Otaria flavescens*), which prefer level sandy beaches for breeding, the pups being born mid-December to early February. Narbrough records below, 7 March, 'the Great ones are much Like a Lyon and Roars Like a Lyon But much Biger than a Lyon'. The male seal lion grows to 9 ft (2·8 m) and weighs up to 770 lb (350 kg). They produce a barking directional call to establish dominence within their group. Shirihai, *Complete Guide*, pp. 344–5; Harris, *Guide*, pp. 156–9.

But much Biger then a Lyon: they are full as Big as a horse: it is as much as three men can kill one with hand Spikes the Bast are Soe Stronge. The Best way to Kill is to Beat them one [on] the nose End: they will Run full Mouth at a Man to Bite him:[1] theirs noe killing them with a gun for they Beinge shoot through the head with a brase of bullets will goe away into the Sea.[2]

[97] **March 1669 the *Sweepstakes* in Porte Disire.**

8

Beinge Tusday wind at SE and Blowe hard with Sum raine and foogg: wee Got sum Ballas [ballast] aboard to day and filled fresh water.

9

Beinge wedensday Close weather wind at So*uth*: we followed our Riginge[3] and Put fower Par [pairs] of new Shrouds to the main mast and ourhaled the ould ones: wind veareynge to the W*est*.

10

Beinge Wedensday wind at W*est* and Blew hard one [on] the flood tide. This day wee followed one [on] our Riginge and one Stowed [unstowed] our hould: and Got up our Ground tear of Caske[4] and Put them A Shore for the Coppers to trim: I filled fresh water to day.

11

Beinge friday wind at West a fresh gale: wee filled water and Riginge and fetched Ballas. I went Eight miles one [on] the No*rth* Shore Right into the Land: Saw no People: all Barran Land Like new markett heath [Newmarket heath]: this night Cam aboard againe.

12

Beinge Satterday blowinge weather wind at NW: wee filled what fresh water we Could and fetched Ballas.

13

Beinge Sunday wind at W*est* the aier very Could and Clear. I went up the River with my boat about tenn mils from the Shipp and went a Shore one [on] an ILand: wher I Saw a Post Put up an End and Nailes drove in one [on] the Ground Lay a Pece of Sheet Lead about a foote Squar with a Super Scription [Margin: *fingerpost*] Staped one [on] it in Dutch: Left By Captain Jacob Lamar the tenth day of January one thousand Six hundered and Sixtenn: their was also a Paper writen and Put in a tin Cas wich was Rusted to Peeces

[1] With mouth wide open.

[2] Wood, BL, MS 46A, p. 144, noted that 'The way to kill Penguinnes and Seeles is with a good shorte Truncheion but the great Seeles are not easily kill'd for haveing shott them through the head with a Musquett they will finde 2 men ½ an houres labour to kill them: you may goe as neare to them as you please haveing noe defence for themselves'.

[3] This probably means 'surveyed the rigging' in the sense of following along the length of each rope to examine it for signs of wear, and hence the requirement to replace some of the shrouds.

[4] The lowest tier of casks.

that it Could not be Read: he Left theis here when he went one [on] his Southorn voiage through the Straits Lamar:[1] here Lys one [on] the Sam Iland Severall Peces of tember and Boards of the wrake of a ship which have ben Burned.[2] Wind at SW to night a fresh gale. I went into another Iland which Lys one [on] the South Shore: it is dry ovr at a low water[3] for their I Saw Severall har[e]s: my Gray hound Caute fower of them: I Called it har Iland:[4] it is the bigest in the River But very barran Land and noe fresh water on it nor on any of the Rest: Sum Small Bushes for fewell.

14
Beinge Munday faier weather wind at West the aier very Could: this day I Got my water aboard and fetched ballas and Cut downe Such Bushess as I Could find for fire wood.

[98] **March 1669 the *Seepstakes* in Porte Disier.**
15
Beinge Tusday faier weather wind at No*rth* a fine Gale: wee fetched Ballas and water & fitted out Riginge: Cloudy to Night.

16
Beinge wedensday faier weather wind at E a fine gale. Sum went and Cut fuell the Rest fetched Ballas and warter. We made fiers to night one [on] the hills for to show the Pinke if She Coms this way: noe Sign of her yet.

17
Beinge Thursday wee Cut more fewell and fetched warter. Faier weather to day wind at NW a fresh gale.

18
Beinge friday faier weather wind at W*est* a Stife gale: we fetched Ballas and fresh warter.

[1] Estrecho de Le Maire (54°45′S, 65°00′W).

[2] This is Isla del Rey which lies 7 miles within the entrance to the harbour. For Narbrough's fuller description of this incident in Bodleian, Rawl. MS A 318, see below, p. 426, n. 1. Wood, BL, MS 46A, pp. 141–2, records the discovery on 'another Iseland almost in the middle of the River which wee called Lemaires Iseland for in the middle thereof wee found a Post erected whereon was nailed a sheete of Lead and in a hole of the Post wee found a Tinne Box with writeing in it but it was soe much decayed that wee could not read it. On the Lead was stampt in great Letters these following words in Dutch: "Een Schip inde een iach: genaemt eendracht en horne gearriveert den viii Decembre veart Rocken meteen Shipd dracht den January MDCXVIII [Sloane MS 46B has MDCXVI which is the same as that given in Narborough *Voyages*, p. 36] Jacques Lemaire Wilcorius: Schouts. Ares Elæssen Jancornt Schouts." [142] This Lemaire was a Dutchman sett forth from Horne with a ship named the Endraught of horne and a Yatch: he arived at this Harbour the 2[d] of December 1615 and departed the 10th of January following with the Endraught onely as the Lead makes menc*i*on of: what he did with the Yatch I know not but I suppose he broke her up for wee found some sheating Boards here on the Iseland. he fell in with the streight of Magellan the 20th of January 10 dayes after his Departure from the Harbour and the 24th day he fell in with that which now beares his name. He was the first that ever discovered Terra del Fugo to be an Iseland.'

[3] This would appear to mean that the island is connected to the shore at low water.

[4] This is Península Viedma, which is connected to the mainland at low water. It is generally low and flat rising to an elevation of 130 ft (40 m) towards the western end.

19
Beinge Satterday faier weather wind at W*est* a fine gale: wee rige our fore mast and Cut more fewell.

20
Beinge Sunday faier weather wind at W*est* a fine gale. I went ashore this morninge one [on] the South Side and Travelled into the Land Sum tenn Mils But Saw noe People nor freh water nor any kind of wood: I Saw where the People had ben in Severall Places they Eus [use] fiers. I Saw Severall Companies of deare and oasterages and Sum hars & Parterages:[1] the Land a Barran downes of a Gravelly Soile dry Grays [grass] Growinge in Nots. I got aboard this night.

21
Beinge Munday faier weather wind at W*est* a fine gale: I riged the fore topmast and fetched Ballas and water.

22
Beinge Tusday faier weather wind at NW: wee fetched fewell.

23
Beinge wedensday faier weather wind at W*est* a fresh gale. I went up the River with my Boate this morninge: and found the River to Run up to the WSW:ward: I went to the head of it & found it Goe up but twenty two mills at the most:[2] their is Severall Small Ils in it But all good for little the hils are very Rockey up the River it Ends in a mudy Salt Lake: at the head noe Bushes or wood or fresh water to be sene up aloft[3] nor mineralls nore any thinge that is Good: the Land very dry and in Barran hills. I drue a draft of the River.[4] I went aboard next day morninge.

[99] **March 1669:70 the *Sweepstakes* in Porte Dissier.**
24
Beinge Thursday wind at W*est* Blowinge weather. This day we fetch fireringe and water and Got all things of[f] the Shore and had the Ship in a readiness to Saile in the morninge. The Best wood in all this harbower is in Sum Bushes like our white thorne in England these bears Small Nut gales and a Seed like in teast to bad Pepper: all the wood as Ever I saw Growinge here will not make a helfe for a Smal hand hatchet.

25
Beinge friday faier weather wind at WBN a Stife gale. [*margin:* Possetion taken of Port disier] I one mored [unmored] the Shipp. The hole Ships Company dranke the Kings health in his Good English Ship beare which wee had very Good at that time and Good

[1] See above, pp. 208, n. 5; 213.
[2] Wood, BL, MS 3833, f. 14v: 'The Cap*tain* [Wood, BL, MS 46A adds 'Leiut*ant*' here] & I went up the River to see how far it Ran & we found that farther then 20 Miles we Could not goe in the Boate the Country all the way up beinge Barran Rockey ground, there beinge no Signe of Ether Wood fresh Watter or of any Inhabitants.'
[3] Further up.
[4] Made a chart of the river. See Plate 1.

whises after.[1] This day I went one [on] Land one [on] Boath Shorse in the harbowr of Porte disier and their tooke Posestion of that land and Porte for His Majestis Euse.[2]
I waied at tenn aclocke and Cam to Sea: I left a Peece of Board one [on] a poast Put in the Ground one [on] the South Pointe to Signife my Beinge their and which way I was Bound in Cas the Pinke Should Come to this Porte. I was Cleare into the Sea by twelfe of the Clocke wind at NW: I got in my Boats and Stood to the Norward to See ife the Pinke Should Ride in any Bay ther abouts. This afternone it blew hard at WNW: the Clew of my Maine Saile give waie & Spllit the Saile through thart under the Refe:[3] I was forced to anchor in twelfe fadam warter Stonny Gravelly Ground: I brought another Saile to the yarde.[4] I anchored about fower Leagus to the Norward of the harbower: at tenn of the Clocke the Ebb Beinge done I waied and Plyed to the nor*thward* Soe far as Cape of Good hope or ales Cap San Gorge[5] but Could not Se any thinge of the Pinke. The Land Lies SSW from the Cape to Porte Dissier: and it is about Eight Leagus distance and noe more from the Cap to Porte Disier:[6] the Land of an indeferent height in Land: but the Sea Shore is all along a Steep Beach and you Shall See a Great Low Plaine or vally fower leagus from the Cape to the Southward. The North Parte of the Bay of Port Dissier is a leage [ledge] of Rocks which the Sea makes a Breach uppon: they ley about fower mils from the maine and three Leagus from Porte dissier.[7] The Petch of the Cape is But ordinary hight of Land and sheus like an Iland at the very Pitch:[8] it Lys in the Latt*itud* of 47°20′ S. Thir

[1] It is not clear if this was in celebration of the New Year or to mark the ceremony of Claiming the Land for the King. Bodleian Library Rawl. MS A 318, see below, pp. 208, n. 5; 213, records drinking the health after the ceremony so it was probably the latter.

[2] The right to claim undiscovered lands was based on the Roman law of *res nullius*, as encoded by Justinian, in 533 CE. This stated that 'What presently belongs to no one becomes by natural reason the property of the first taker', that 'If a thing be treated as abandoned, it ceases forthwith to be ours and will at once belong to the first taker because things cease to be ours by the same means they are acquired', and 'Without possession, there can be no usucapion'. Watson, *Digest of Justinian*, 41.1.3, 41.3.25, 41.7.1. Francisco de Vitoria (c. 1485–1546) concluded that the Indians did indeed possess true dominion of their lands, and that discovery was no just claim to possession unless the lands had no owner. Alberico Gentili (1552–1608) stated that ownership of un-owned things (*res nullius*) through occupation seemed valid. Hugo Grotius (1583–1645), held that 'the act of discovery is sufficient to give a clear title of sovereignty only when it is accompanied by actual possession' and 'discovery per se gives no legal rights over things unless before the alleged discovery they were *res nullius*'. He further stated 'This occupation or possession, however in the case of things which resist seizure, like wild animals for example must be uninterrupted or perpetually maintained, but in the case of other things it is sufficient if after physical possession is once taken the intention to possess is maintained. Possession of movables implies seizure, and possession of immovables either the erection of buildings or some determination of boundaries, such as fencing in.' Narbrough's claims were therefore based on the belief that hunter-gatherers did not own their land, not having worked it, and hence was *res nullius* and available to the first discoverer who took possession of it. Although Narbrough did plant some vegetables no real occupation took place, so that once he had departed, abandoning it, the land was, according to prevailing European legal opinion, available again for the autochthonous inhabitants or for the next comers. See, Benton and Straumann, *Acquiring Empire by Law*; Kingsbury and Straumann, *Roman Foundations*, p. 114; Scott and Deman Magoffin, *Freedom*, pp. 12, 13, 25, 26, 264, 265. For further information on this ceremony, see below, p. 430.

[3] The clue of the sail is either of the lower corners where the tack and sheets are made fast. This means the sail split across, horizontally along the line of the reef points.

[4] Changed the sail.

[5] Cabo Blanco (47°12′S, 65°45′W).

[6] The distance is about 35 miles.

[7] Roca Sorrell. See above, p. 203, n. 6.

[8] This was Cabo Blanco, the height of which is 138 ft (42 m).

is But tenn fadam water ESE from the Cap two leags and the Sundings are Small Peavell Stones Blackee Colored: their is a great Riplinge ouver thes. [*right margin:* Should][1]

[100] **March 1670 the *Sweepstaks* of[f] Porte Disier.**

26

Beinge Satterday wind at W*est* and Blows hard: this morninge the mone St one [set on] the west horizon just as the Sun Rose one the East [*margin:* ☽ eclips] orizon: the mone Being Eclipsed: at a 11 of the Clock 10 minuts at London or in that meridian in the forenone but here it was Eclipsed at 6 of the Clocke 3 minuts Past: which give 4 houers 40 minuts dif*erence* of time betwen the two meridians. I Could not See any Signe of the Pinke: the Cap Bar NWBW from mee about three Leagus from mee: I tacked & stood to the Southward. This afternone at two aclocke the wind Came to the SW a fresh gale & Cloudy weather: this Eveinge I anchored in Porte Disier Bay: EBS from the Port in Seaventen fadam warter: Black oasey Sand. I Could not Goe to the Southward: the wind Came to the South to night.

27

Beinge Sunday wind at SSW: it blew hard & hasey Cloudy Could weather: this day at none I observed the Sun and find Port disier to Ly in the Latt*itud* of 47°48′. I Rod fast all day this night Proved Lettle wind.

28

Beinge Munday Calme this morninge. I sent my Boats to Penguns Iland: it Beinge two Leagus from mee: to fetch fresh Penguns:[2] their Beinge Multituds of them. This forenone I way*ed* & I Stood to the Southward: the wind at WNW a small gale. My Boats Came a Board by tenn a Clocke Laden with Penguns haveinge about Sixtenn hundered in Boath

[1] This is in the vicinity of Banco Byron and Banco Ana which lie 5 miles E and 9 miles ESE of Cape Blanco. Banco Susana lies 2½ miles offshore about 7 miles SSE of the Cape. The least depth on Banco Byron is 3 ft (0·9 m), while a bank with depths of less than 60 ft (18 m) extends N for 10 miles covered with overfalls, and there are breakers 1¼ miles E and 4 miles NE. Banco Ana is also marked by overfalls and eddies and has breakers 1½ miles W of its S end.

[2] Wood, BL, MS 46A, p. 143, noted the multitudes of penguins giving it as his opinion, 'They are about the Biggness of Geese: to call them Fowles I think it improper because they have no Feathers nor wings: they have 2 Finns or Flapps that be very usefull for them in Swimming in which they be very nimble and active getting their Foode in the Sea when they are on the shore they will walke upright: theire breeding time is in the end of Septemb*er* and the beginning of October Att which time you may take as many on the shore as will Victuall a Navie Royall. Theire Eggs are Something less then goose Eggs Some laying one others two and Some three but none more: theire nests are ready made for them by nature on the Rocks and Sands laying 3 Eggs [which] are good to Eate.' Wood's description is insufficient to positively identify the species, but Magellanic penguins (*Spheniscus magellanicus*) and rockhopper penguins (*Eudyptes chrysocome*) which are about the same size, 16–17 in (40–44 cm) tall, are found in this vicinity. They inhabit burrows up to 6 ft (2 m) deep and also scrape out a nest beneath a bush. From a subsequent visit to this island when the birds were laying on 20 Sept. 1670, and their eggs were described, it is clear they were in fact Magellanic penguins. See below, p. 246. There is a rockhopper colony on this island at present (Harris, *Guide*, p. 34) so it is perfectly possibly there was one here in the 17th century. However, the rockhopper has a distinctive black hood with golden eyebrows ending in long swept-back golden plumes, which it might be supposed would have been mentioned had they been sighted by Narbrough or Wood. Wood, BL, MS 3833, f. 15v, records taking 'Aboard 14 Hundred Penguins & might have had a Hundred times as Many More'.

Boats. At three aclocke this afternone the wind Cam to the South and Blow hard a great Sea Cam out of the SE. This Eveinge I Bore Back againe and anchored in Port disier Bay in Sixten fadam: oasey Sand the Port beareinge WNW of mee about two leagus distance. It Blew hard to night at S*outh* and Sum Rain. You may Ride here with a SSE wind very well: for you may Bringe Pinguns Ils ESE of you.

29
Beinge Tusday Blowinge hasey Cloudy Could weather wind at SBE: I Rod fast: Smale Raine to day: this day wee Eat Penguns & Porrage. This Eveinge I wayed to See my anchor and anchored angaine:[1] wind att SSE to night and Blow fresh.

30
Beinge weddensday hasey weather and Calme this morninge.[2] This day the wind veared Round the Compas I wayed but forcd to anchor againe wind at S*outh*: at twelf a clocke to night the wind Came to the NW a fine gale I waied and Stood to the Southward.

[101] **March 1670 the *Seeepstakes* at Sea of[f] Sealls Bay Lat*itud* 48°04′ S**
31
Beinge Thursday wind at WBN a fine gale. This fore none I Steered a way SSW by my Compas with all the Saile I Could make. This day at none I was in the Lat*itud* of 48°04′ S*outh* by Good observation with davis quardrant. It Proved Calm the tide of flood beinge Come I anchored in twenty Seaven fadam warter Gretty black Sand: I was about five leagus from the Land. At Six aclocke this afternone I waied and Plyed to the Southward wind at SE a fine gale.

1
Aprill 1670: Beinge Friday faier weather wind at N*orth* a fine gale I Steered SSW. This Eveinge at Six aclocke I was up with the Eadie Stone rocke: which [is] in the Latt*itud* of 48°20′ S*outh* and about five leagus from the Land: you may just see the Breach of it at a high warter:[3] I Saw it and went about A mile with in it: I had twenty Six fadam Rockey Ground when it Bear E of mee: I had the wind at NW a fine gale: I Steared away SSW from it till twelfe aclocke at night then I lay by till Breake of day: faier weather all night.

[1] This was to check for chafing of the cable and to make sure the anchor had not got stuck.

[2] Wood, BL, MS 3833, f. 15v, adds 'The Leut*enant* & I went in to the Southermost part of the Bay to Seek if wee Could [find] the River of fresh Water which S[r] Francis Drack Sayed He found heare But we Could find Not any. Only Signes that in the Winter when freshes [freshets] Come downe the [they] Make Gulles as if Rivers had Been there.' Drake, *World Encompassed*, p. 24, records that 'Within, in the Southernmost part of this bay, there is a river of fresh water, with a great many profitable ilands; of which some have alwaies such store of Seales or sea-wolves as were able to maintaine a huge army of men. Other Ilands being many and great, are so replenished with birds and foule, as if there were no other victuals, a wonderful multitude of people might be nourished ...' The Latitude of the bay is given as 47°30′. No mention is made of the entrance to Puerto Deseado (Port Desire) 47°45′ S: Isla Pingüino (Penguin Island) is in 47°55′ S. The description would fit the Bay of Port Desire, but it may not be the same bay.

[3] It can just be seen, breaking at high water. See above, p. 210, n. 7.

2

Beinge Satterday faier weather this morninge wind at NNW a fine gale. I filled at day Light and Stered away SSW and SBW as the Coast lyes in twenty fadam warter black Sand Be*ing* about two Leagus of[f] the Land. This fore none I Saw a Small flat Iland to the westward of mee: it lye about a League of[f] the Land: it is in the Latt*itud* of 48°40′:[1] the Land against is indeferent hige. From this Iland it is But nine Leagus to S[t] Julyan harbower:[2] the Shore is steep Beach al a longe in a Plaine vally in Land thill yust [till just] you Com to the Bay before the harbower of S[t] Julyan: their is a pointe of white Clifes and the Land is in Round Copplen hills the highest land I saw in all the Coast are those hills over Port S[t] Julyan the tops maks Round lyke the tops of Blunt Suger loafes:[3] ther is not any Such hills any wher but thes. This afternone it Proved Calme I anchored in the Bay before S[t] Julyan harbower in twelf fadam water Blacke oasey Sand the harbower bearinge WSW of mee about two Leagus from mee. I Sent in my boate to discover the harbower and to See if the Pinke were their at night Came aboard againe and tould mee ther was a Saf harbower But noe Signe of the Pinke. Calme all night I Rod fast. This harbower Lyes in the Lattitud of fowerty nine degres and tenn minuts South of the Equinoctiall and in Longitud west from the Lizard of England Sixty three degres tenn Minuts:[4] And Meridian distance W*est* one thousand and theerty Leagus.

[102] **Aprill 1670 the *Sweepstakes* of [off] Port S[t] Julyan Latt*itud* 49°10′ S**

3

Beinge Sunday and Ester day: Calme faier weather all day. I rode fast I went into the harbower with my Boate and vewed it & Saw it a good Safe harbower to Ride in: this night I went a board Calme all night.[5]

4

Beinge Munday Calme this morninge: I waied and stood to the Southward: I Sailed with in two leagus of the Shore and had [*margin:* 25] twenty five fadam Blacke oasey Sand all alonge: wind at No*rth* a fine gale. This day at none I was in the Latt*itud* of 49°23′ By [*margin:* 25] Good observation of the Sun. I steered alonge SBW So the Shor lyes by the Compas: here the Compas have Sixten degres E [*margin:* vari: 17] variation.[6] The Shore is Steep whit Clefs al a longe to the Southward of St Julyan for twenty Leagus and Plaine

[1] Islote Chato, see above, p. 211, n. 2.

[2] Puerto San Julián.

[3] These are Monte Wood and Monte Sholl. See above, p. 211, n. 5.

[4] For the coordinates of Puerto San Julián, see above, p. 213.

[5] Wood, MS 3833, f. 15v: 'The Cap*tain* went this Morning in to see the Harbor & Returned att 5 att Night Butt Could not Beleve it was St Julian for four Reasons: First Because Mr Flecher who was S[r] francis Dracks Chaplin sayeth that on the South Side of the Harbor was Pecked Rocks Like Towers and hear is None: 2[ly] that it was in the Latt*itude* of 49°30′ & this But in the Latt*itude* of 49°08′: 3[ly] Because one Nunva De Silva a Portugall sayeth that hear was Hills that Made Like Towers: & 4[ly] M Fuller sayeth that it Lay in the Latt*itude* of 50°00′. Soe wee Sopposeing itt still to be to the Southward att 9 att Night we Wayed with the tide of Ebb itt being Calme all Night.' Wood explains that Narbrough was relying here on Drake, *World Encompassed*, p. 25; 'The voyage of John Winter', Hakluyt, *Principal Navigations*, III, p.751; 'Certain Rare and Special notes most properly belonging to the voyage of M. Thomas Candish', ibid., pp. 825–37; 'A ruttier from the river of Plate to the Streights of Magellan', ibid., pp. 724–5. The original of the latter is found in BL, Sloane 2292, which Wood thought to have been written by Nuno da Silva.

[6] It is not clear why the marginal figure differs from that in the text.

Land aloft with out Ever a hill. This night at Six aclocke I was in the Latt*itud* of 49°50′: Clos Cloudy weather & darke. I brought too and [*margin:* 27] Lay by all night: Sound 27: black fine Sand: 3 leagus of[f].

5

Beinge Tusday Cloudy hasey weather this mor*n*inge the wind Cam to the SBE a fine gale I Plyed to the Southward: at Eight a Clock this morninge the wind began to Blow and Proved hasey and foggy. I Stood into the Shore and had theerty fadam oasy Sande in a League and halfe of the Shore. I was in favety [fifty] degres Lattitud at nine of the Clocke this fore none: the Clife are steep and gray. I Adviced with my two Leiutenats and Master what I had best to doe:[1] the wind Beinge at South and very Cloudy and Lightned: I thought it Best to Stand of[f] into the Sea: But they all judg it more Safe to Bear up for Port S[t] Julyan and to goe into that harbower and See what the weather would Prove for if it Should Blow and we at Sea it will indanger the forsinge us of[f] the Land[2] and allsoe our Boates are not fitted to Cruse with the Shipp in the Streights till they ar Raised a Strake higher[3] allso if wee Stay at S[t] Julyan the Place appointed for Randivose [rendezvous] we may happily fall with the Pinke. The Sea began to Run high and it began to raine: I thought fit to looke Still for the Pinke: I Bar up for S[t] Julyan.[4] Much Raine this afternone and the wind Came to the SSW and Blew fresh. This Eveing I lay by till morninge.[5]

6

Beinge Wedensday wind at W*est*: I Stood into the Shore and anchored in Eight fadam water before the harbower: my Master Boyed the Bare at the Goeinge in.[6] Faier weather to day.

7

Beinge Thursday Cloudy weather wind at NBW this morninge very Could & a frost. I wayed one [on] the tid of flod and went in with the Shipp: I went over the Bar at three quarters flood and had twenty foote water: I anchored two mills with in the Narrow and mored and had fower fadam at a Low water.[7]

[1] Conferred with the two Lieutenants and the Master what it would be best to do. This was a common practice at this time.

[2] If it should blow while they were at sea it would put them in danger of being forced off the land (the prevailing wind being westerly).

[3] The boats were not suitable for the weather anticipated in the Strait until the gunwales had been raised a strake (plank) higher.

[4] For Wood's comments BL, Add MS 46A, p. 146; MS 3833, f. 20r, on the executions carried out by Magellan and Drake in this port see above, p. 212, n. 2.

[5] Wood, BL, MS 3833, f. 16v: 'We then Being Allmost in the Latt*itude* of 50°00′ & saw no Other Harbor wee Judged that Must be S[t] Julian which wee Had Passed By soe Wee Sayled Back to Northward Againe. This Night wee Lay By Because we would not Over Shoote our Port.'

[6] The Master laid buoys to mark the passage over the bar for the ship to go into the harbour.

[7] Wood, BL, MS 3833, f. 20r, notes 'Into this Porte wee Entered the 7th day of Aprill 1670 and heare Wintered, we finding the temper of the Weather to be neare that of ours in Ingland, or not soe Could; the Couldest Weather we had was aboute the Midle of June. Wood, BL, MS 46A, p. 152 gives 'Markes to Sayle over the Barr into the Harbour: Keep Rockey point on the No*rth* W*es*t Side ... and certaine white Spotts on an Inland hill ... and when these 2 are one in another [in line] you may runne in and out and for a Thwart marke to know when you are on the Barr there is at NE[t] about a Mile and ½ from the harbours mouth in the Bay Certaine white Cliffes that Seemeth to be Severall Iselands: when the middle of these Cliffes and a Saddle in the Land behinde them are in one then are you on the Barr.'

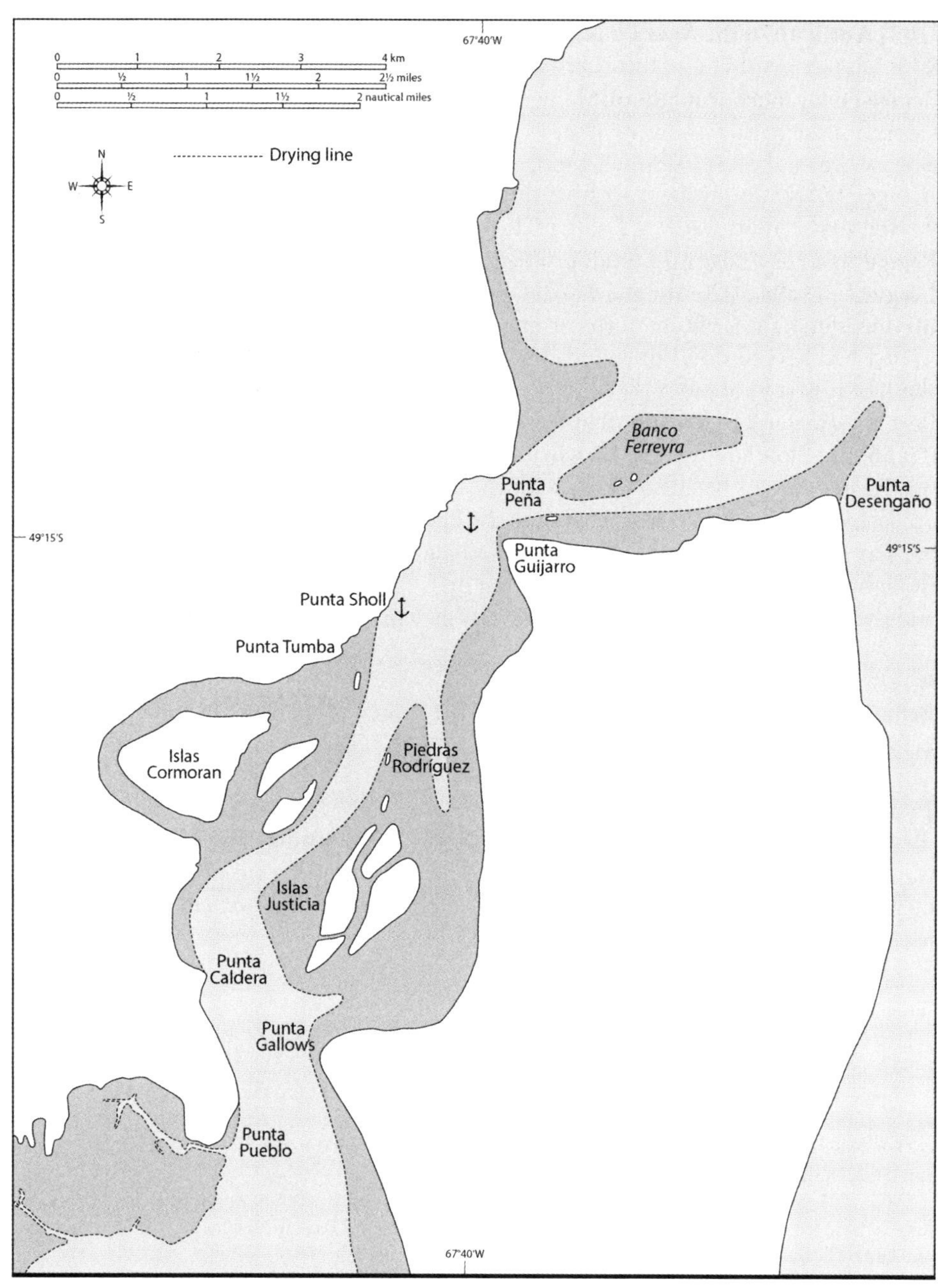

Map 5. Puerto San Julián (Port St Julian).

[103] **April 1670 the *Sweepstakes* in Port St Julyan.**

8

Beinge Friday much wind this morninge at NE: this forenone fair weather wind at No*rth*. I went up the harbower in my Boate:[1] it Gos [goes] up But Six mils and ther Ends in white Clifes and marshes. Much wind to night at SW and Snow.

9

Beinge Satterday Blowinge weather wind at SW and Exstreame Could the Land is all Covered with Snow. I went and Looked for fresh water but Could not find any to day it Blew hard to night at SW.

10

Beinge Sunday wind at SW and Blowes hard and Slatty Snow most Part all this day very Could: Blew hard to night at SW.

11

Beinge Munday wind at SW Blew hard Cloudy weather and very Could: blos hard to night.

12

Beinge Tusday wind at WSW a hard gale to day: I went ashor to Looke for warter and found a Swash of Snow warter[2] which wee made Eus [use] of all the winter. Les wind to night a great frost.[3]

13

Beinge wedensday faier weather wind at W*est*: lettle wind this morninge: I went and hailed my Saine and Caute five hunderd Brave fish as Bigg as a mans Legg and Like unto a Mullett.[4]

[1] Wood, BL, MS 3833, f. 16v, notes that he went with Narbrough in the pinnace.

[2] A swash is watery condition of land, ground under water. *NOED.* This is therefore a pool of melt water.

[3] Wood, BL, MS 46A, pp. 146–7: '12th of Aprill. My Selfe the Boateswaine and 2 men more went up to the Topp of a hill at East which is the [147] highest hill between Cape S[t] George and the Straights of Magellan on the Topp hereof I Engraved my name and called it mount Wood. From the Topp of this hill I saw to the Northward a great Lake seemeing to be a harbour which made me desirous of goeing to see it. The Boateswaine and 2 men more went with me about 2 miles towards it and then returned Back towards our ship leaveing me alone I being allmost come to the S*ai*d Lake made a stand to see which way it runne and lookeing about me I perceived Something to have a mo*t*ion behinde a Bush which I supposed to be one of the Countrey sheepe or Deere. I made towards it to shoote it but I founde it to be a man Native of the Countrey he seeing that I had discovered him he stood up and went a little further behinde a hill where mett him 6 more with Bowes and Arrowes: then I thought it not fitt to goe any further Soe I returned back toward the ship and the Natives followed mee at a distance about 2 miles and then left me at which time the Sunne was sett and I had 6 miles to the ship. Wood BL Sloane MS 3833, f. 20r: 'They were Very Well sett Men of noe such Exterordenary Stature as is reported by Magellanes & other Spaniards to be 10 or 11 foot hie, none of these being above 6 at the Most, but I soppose they did Inmaging none would come here to disprove them.' See above, pp. ?42–3.

[4] Wood, BL, MS 3833, f. 16v: 'This Day I Being on Shoare on the East Side I found a Pond of fresh Watter one Mile from the Watter Side.'

14
Beinge Thursday wind at W*est* and Blew hard. I Caute two hundered and fivety fish today and filled Sum fresh Watter. Very Could to night and freses hard.

15
Beinge friday Cloudy Blowinge weather wind at WBS: les wind to night. My Grayhound Caut a young deare[1] to day.

16
Beinge Satterday very Could this morninge Wind at WSW and blowes hard: and Raines this forenone Slatty Snow this afternone: much wind to night at SSW.

17
Beinge Sunday wind at SW a stife gale: Exstreame Could all the hills are Covered with Snow fres [freeze] much to night.

18
Beinge Munday wind at SW a Stife gale and Could weather Sum Snow this morninge: the winter is Come here Stronge: no Endureinge the Sea for any man on this Coast the aier is So Could in the winter. This day I Servid Brandy for a Lowance [allowance] at a quart a weke for a Man: I Goot a Long Boats Ladinge of wood aboard to day blew hard to night at SW.

[104] **APrill 1670 the *Sweepstakes* in Port S[t] Julyan.**
19
Beinge Tusday wind at WSW and blows hard. I went on the NW Shore to Looke for wood to Burn and found a Great deale of very Good wood for fireinge: hard by the warter Side: it Grous Crooked much like our whit thorne[2] in England: noe timber for any Euse but for fewell. Blew hard to night and very Could – fres [freeze] hard.

20
Beinge wedensday blowinge weather wind at WSW. I went and got a boats Ladinge of fresh water aboard: my Leiuetenat went and tenn men with him[3] Eight mils into the Land to See [*margin:* Indian sene] for People or mineralls But Could not Se any. Lettle wind tonight.

21
Beinge Thursday wind at W*est* a Stife gale it Blew hard at none to day. This day my Leiuetenant[4] found a very Large Salt Pond with a Bondance of Good Salt in it:[5] it was

[1] Probably a guanaco.
[2] Whitethorn, the common hawthorn (*Cratægus oxyacantha*).
[3] This may refer to the sighting by John Wood on 12 April. Wood, BL, MS 3833, f. 20r, 'Boath our Leff*tenants* & my self, with 10 Men more went to the same place where I saw the Pattagones, but we could not see any of them. This Lake we found to be a Salt Lake with many Thousand tuns of Salt therin. Upon the sand by the Lake we found the foot steps of Men Weemen & Children soe we Returned A board. From the Lake we fecthed neare 10 tun of Salt, att severall times.' Also mentioned in Wood, MS 46A, p. 147.
[4] Lieutenant Peckett records this find on 20 April in his journal, see below, p. 583.
[5] Salitral de Cabo Curioso.

about five mils from the Shipp: he Brought Sum aboard in his hankeachev [handkerchief] to Show mee. It blew very hard to night at SW and fresed.

22
Beinge friday wind at SW a Stife gale and Could aier. I went ashore to day and twenty men with mee to the Salt Pond and gat Salt out of the Pond and Brought as much a board as filled a Punshon: very Good Salt and Great quantitis of it and very whit much whiter than frensh Salt: and a nough [enough] to lade 1000 ship.

23
Beinge Satterday very Could this morninge a mighty Storm to day at WSW: lis [less] wind in the night.

24
Beinge Sunday faier weather but Coald the wind went Rond the Compas to day: it blew a fresh gale at WSW to night.

25
Beinge Munday faier weather wind at SW a fine gale. I fetched to day as much Salt aboard as filled Seaven hogsheads.

26
Beinge Tusday wind at SW: Close weather and Coald a great frost to night.

27
Beinge wedendensday [*sic*] Close weather and lettle wind to day: the Ise [ice] Beares very Stornge freses hard all day.

28
Beinge Thursday wind at WBS a fine gale Could frosty weather. I Strooke all Snuge aboard for I Saw their was noe Goeinge to Sea this winter to Pas the Streight the weather Beinge Soe Stormmy: I Cam to Latte [too late] into these Coasts by three Monthes. The wind Cam to the NNE this Eveinge and Rained. It Blew a mighty Storme to night and Sunke my Boate at my Stern and lost Sum of my oares: les wind toward day.

[105] **Aprill 1670 the *Sweepstakes* at Port St Julyan.**
29
Beinge Friday Blowinge weather and Raine: wind at W*est* all day: much wind at Eight aclocke to night at SW: and blew and Rained al night.

30
Beinge Satterday blowinge weather and Rainey this forenone: It blew at SW al night. My Best bower anchor Cam home.[1]

[1] It dragged along the seabed.

1
May 1670 Beinge Sunday wind at SW a fresh gale and Could weather to night.

2
Beinge Munday wind at N*orth* a fresh gale Cloudy Could weather. I fetched wood to burn to day.

3
Beinge Tusday faier weather wind at SW a fresh gale. This day I observed with the asterlobe[1] and find this harbower to Ly in the Latt*itud* 49°08′ South.[2]

4
Beinge wedensday wind at N*orth* a fresh gale & Could.

5
Beinge Thursday faier weather wind at SW all day and night a fresh gale very Could and frosty weather: we fetched wod E*ast* sid.[3]

6
Beinge friday wind at WNW a fine gale. I fetched Salte.

7
Beinge Satterday faier weather wind vearable: my Guner[4] Saw two of the Country People to day at a distance. They weafed him to Come to them But they went away pre*sen*tly.[5] Blew hard to night at W

8
Beinge Sunday faier weather wind at SW a fine gale.

9
Beinge Munday faier Sun Shine weather wind at SW a fine gale. Wee fetched Salt to day and wood.

10
Beinge Tusday Clear weather wind at SW a hard gale and very Could much snow fell to night.

11
Beinge wedensday blowinge Could weather much Snow one [on] the hils wind at SW this Eveinge.

[1] Astrolabe, see above, p. 65, n. 10.
[2] See above, p. 213.
[3] From the east side of the harbour.
[4] TNA, ADM 39/2510, Phillip White.
[5] Presently, in the sense of promptly.

12
Beinge Thursday much wind to day at WSW and very Could. Very Stormey weather this Eveinge and Slatty Snow.

13
Beinge friday indeferent weather wind at WSW a fine gale. This day wee fetched Salt.[1] One [on] M[r] John Wood walkeinge one [on] the Iland of true justice[2] found three Small Peeces of Goold wier tide up in a mussel Shell with a Gut Stringe: it was to the vallue of two shill*ings*.

[106] May 1670 the *Sweepstakes* in Puerto San Julian.
14
Beinge Satterday faier weather wind at WSW a fine gale. Wee fetched a boate load of warter. Blew fresh to night.

15
Beinge Sunday Dry Blowinge weather wind at WSW: it blew hard to night.

16
Beinge Munday wind at SW a Stout gale wee fetched warter.[3]

17
Beinge Tusday wind at W*est* a fresh gale this afternon it Cam to the SW and Blew hard Could and Cloudy weather.

18
Beinge weddensday Blowing weather wind at SSW Could Aier. This day wee new Pickled our Befe and Porke and mad a rume in the hould to Put our Salt in.

19
Beinge Thursday wind at S*outh* a Stout gale: very Could much Snow to day: much wind to night at NW: and Exstream Could.

20
Beinge friday Close Could weather the wind veared to the SE: and rained much wind to night at No*rth*: dark weather.

[1] Wood, BL, MS 3833, f. 20r: 'We went some 50 of us & Layed a grate deale of salt on a heap, the Water being then Run all away but which way I know not & there was Noething but salt Remaining and which was as firme as any free stone pavement; & as Even & as white as Snow. I paced the Lake over & found it to be foure Thousand Paces; which of my paces is 2 English Miles & a half; it being all the way over 3 or 4 Inches thick of Salt. The Length of this Lake is Very Nere 10 Miles, (for afterward we was at the head of it), soe that this day I Judge there Might be a Hundred Theusand Tunn of Salt in the Lake.'

[2] See p. 212, n. 2.

[3] Wood, BL, MS 3833, f. 20r: 'We went againe [to the salt lake] it being but the 3 day after, a thing Very strange & Worthie of Memory & to be Admired for there was not soe Much Salt Left as would fill an Egg Shell (there being in the Intrem noe Raine). From the time that I saw the Pattagones till June we Could never see any signe of them though wee dayly weare a Shore.'

21
Beinge Satterday Cloudy Coald weather wind at SW: a Stout gale it Rained most Part of the day much wind to night at SW: and Raine in terable gusts.

22
Beinge Sunday Much raine this morninge wind at SW a Stife gale. This forenone I Advised with my two Leiut*enants* and Master to Goe with the Shipp for Porte Dissier and winter ther: for wee Saw it Impossible for us to Past the Streights till the winter was over: the Aier Beinge So Exstreame Could: and the Contry Given to Such violent SW Stormes. Wheich after Seaverall Considerations wee all Concluded to winter here: and not to Put to Sea Beinge doutfull wee Should be forced of[f] the Land in Goeinge to Penguns Ile by Port Disier: and Porte dissier Beinge a bad winter harbower.[1] Fine weather this Eveinge.

23
Beinge Munday faier weather wind at SW a fine gale. Wee fetched water and wood before the winter Com one [on]. Much wind to night at *South*: and Raine and Snow.

24
Beinge Tusday much wind all this day att SSW and Snow noe Steeringe[2] aShore.

[107] **May 1670 the *Sweepstakes* in Port San Julian.**
25
Beinge wedensday wind at SW a Stoute gale: much Snow one [on] the Ground and a Great frost. I Could not gitt fresh warter.

26
Beinge Thursday wind at SW a Stife gale and very Could frosty weather. This day I haled one of my Boats ashore to trim.[3]

27
Beinge friday wind at SW a fine gale Sum Snow to Night.

28
Beinge Satterday wind at SW: Sum Snow to day and a great frost to night.

29
Beinge Sunday wind att SSW a fresh gale and frosty weather. To day I ordered Every man

[1] As Narbrough had remarked earlier (pp. 204–9), the wind blows largely from the west and straight down the harbour at Puerto Deseado, making it a dangerous anchorage in winter.

[2] Stirring or going ashore.

[3] This could have been to clean the boat, but since on 17 July (p. 238 below) Narbrough records that he launched the long boat having had a strake added fore and aft above the gunwale, it must have been to do the work required to make her suitable for work in the bad weather anticipated in the Straits.

[*blank*][1] Powder to Goun[2] with their Beinge much fowle in the river as duckes and brant Goose.[3]

30
Beinge Munday Coald weather wind at SW a Stife gale much frost and Snow one [on] the Ground. This day I one Riged [unrigged] my Topmast and mak all Snuge: the Ratts doe mee much mischef in my Sailes and Brad [bread]: doeing what wee Can to Prevent them yet they doe Eat the Sailes Lay them where I Can their Beinge Such nombers of them aboard: yet every night we kill nere a score of them with traps yet they inCreas mightily.

31
Beinge Tusday faier weather wind at SSW very Could. This day wee Got Good Store of fire wood aboard: faier Coald frosty weather to night: my men kill good Store of duckes with Guns.

1
June 1670: Beinge wedensday wind at SSW and faier weather. This day I mored the Shipp in a Good birth: in twenty foot warter at a Lowarter in Gravelly oasey Ground and in noe Great tide: in the Chanell betwen two Ilands.[4]

2
Beinge Thursday wind at SSW a Stife gale Snow and frost. We Began this day to Serve Bread out of the Bread roame.

3
Beinge friday Could frosty weather wind at SW a gale.

4
Beinge Satterday Could weather and frost wind at SW: Sum Small Brooken Eise [ice] drives downe with the Ebb.

5
Beinge Sunday Could frosty weather wind at SW: Sum Eise drivinge in the River.

[1] 'Man' is followed by a space as if Narbrough had intended later to insert the amount of powder and had not done so.

[2] This is presumably 'to gun with' to enable them to go fowling.

[3] The brent goose (*Branta bernicla*) is not normally found in this area. This is probably the upland goose (*Chloephaga picta*), which are not dissimilar, the male being largely white, or head white with lower breast and under parts barred black and white, flanks barred in both forms, while the female has a sandy to brick red head, breast barred brown and black turning to black, barred white and black on the flanks, grey back with tail and rump black, or kelp geese (*C. hybrida*), the male being white while the female is dark on top and boldly barred black and white on breast and flanks. They are common at the southern tip of South America. Peña, *Birds*, plates 15.9 and 16.1; Shirihai, *Complete Guide*, pp. 277–8.

[4] This was between the Islas Justicia and Islas Cormorán as shown on Narbrough's plan of Port San Julyan (Plate 3).

[108] **Jun 1670 the *Seepstakes* in Port San Julian.**

6

Beinge Munday Cloudy Coald weather wind at SW: and Snow this night the wind Cam to the ENE: it thoughed [thawed] to night, a great deale [*margin:* Weth*er* mild] of Broken Ise Cam drveinge downe the River: but did noe harm.

7

Beinge Tusday Close darke weather wind at NEBE a fine gale. Wee had a new mone this afternone: faier weather to night.

8

Beinge Wedensday faier weather wind at SW a fine gale we fetched wood for fireinge: noe fresh warter to be had for Ise.

9

Beinge Thursday faier weather wind at SW a fine gale we fetched more wood: a Cloudy frosty Eveinge.

10

Beinge friday Close weather with Small Raine wind at NNE a hard gale all day and night and foggy weather.

11

Beinge Satterday wind at NNE a hard gale and darke foggy weat*her* with Small Raine: I filled twenty two hogsheads of fresh warter. This day we opned our Bread Rume and Served Bread out ther Beinge opnen: the Second day of Jun Beinge the first bigininge in it. Sum Raine to night the wind Cam to the North.

12

Beinge Sunday wind at WNW a Stife gale Close weather.

13

Beinge Munday wind at W*est* but Lettle wind: vearable this Eveinge.

14

Beinge Tusday wind at No*rth* and Small Raine a stout gale.

15

Beinge weddensday wind at NW Gusty weather we fetched Salte.

16

Beinge Thursday wind at W*est* and at WSW: Gusty weather.

17

Beinge friday wind at W*est* very Gusty weather and raine: very Stormey all day: and night.

18
Beinge Satterday wind vearable Round the Compas in Gusts and violent Gust as much as anchors and Cabls Could hould.

19
Beinge Sunday wind at SW a fresh gale it Cam to the W*est* and Blew hard this afternone.

[109] **Jun 1670 the *Sweepstakes* in Port San Julian.**
20
Being Munday Close weather wind at WBS a fine gale. This day I wint into the Land to See for Indians: But Could not meet any I Put up Knifes and Beads in Seaverell Places wher they had Eused but Could wee Perceive they ever Cam ner them at any time or wer disierus to Come ner us: wee Saw wher they Lie a nights behind Bushess Like Brut beasts: they kill deare[1] and Easteragis [ostriches] and mak firs to roast musshells and Limpets: ther Liveinge is Ceartenly most miserable in the Could winter for we Saw wher they had Loged in Places within a mile of the Shipp: but every night thy had a new Loginge: the heavens is their Cannope and the Could Ground ther Bed*in*g: I would willinge have had Conference with them if possible to have Know what ther Country aforded. [*margin:* 49^{d} 14:] I killed with my Grayhound two Easterages and one hare as I was Travilen in the Cuntry.

21
Beinge Tusday wind at W*est* a hard gale: and so Continued all day.

22
Beinge weddensday wind at WNW a Stoute gale. This day fower of my men Goeinge in the Land mett with Seaven Indians: which Came downe the hill to my men: and weafed them to Goe to the Ship[2] and mad a Great noise: my men went up to them but them would not Shake hands with them but looked very fearfully Every way Continually keepinge their motion towards the Ship. They are Clad with beasts Skines losely over ther Shoulders: and Painte them Selfes Red and white with Earth and Grease: they are But of a midle Statur of men: they had every one his Bow and two arrows apeece: and two or three dogs with them. My men would have had them Come downe to the Shipp but they would not: So at ther departur they Gave them a knife and a longe neccloath [neck cloth] and a bottle of Brandy wine: Beinge all they had about them. So tooke their leaves of Each other: and Came aboard the Indians went into the Country and made a fier that night in Sight of the Shipp: and wee never Saw any after all the time of our abidinge in that Porte.[3]

[1] Presumably these are guanacos.

[2] Made a sign by waving that they should go to the ship.

[3] Wood, BL, MS 3833, ff. 20r–v: 'I Borowed a boate of the Cap*tain* & did intend to goe 8 or 10 Miles SW. I had gott to goe with me Gyles Wood, M*aste*rs Mate, John Sedgeck quarter M*aste*r & John Lowes fore Mast Man: we had not gone above 2 Miles & a half but wee Mett with 7 of theas Pattagones before they weare a Warre of us, or else wee should not have seen them, they were 3 Men, 3 Woemen & a Boy some 10 yeares of age. When they saw they could not shun us the 3 Men came toward us & Weaved us to be gone away but wee haveing noe Mind to doe them any Iniurye went towards them tell wee came within 2 pikes Length of them but the would suffer us to come no nearer. I gave them a East India Neck cloath, a Knive & a Bottle of Brandy, but all the while they Weaved us to be gone. Wood, MS 46A, p.148: 'One of them which was an old man Came near to us and

23

Beinge Thursday wind at west a fresh gale. I went ashore this morning to Looke for the Indians with the Same men as Saw them the day before. I went all over the hills wher they had Sene them But I Could not meet with them ore See any Signe of them Soe I Cam aboare.

24

Beinge friday wind at W*est* a Stoute gale much Snow this after none and to night and a great frost very Could.

25

Beinge Satterday wind at W*est* a fresh gale: and faier weather.

[110] **Jun 1670 the *Sweepstakes* in Porte San Julian.**

26

Beinge much wind at NW: and Snow a great frost to night.

27

Beinge Munday much wind at No*rth*: & very Could.

28

Beinge Tusday Clear weather But a hard Gale at WNW.

29

Beinge wedensday Clear weather wind at NW a fresh gale.

30

Beinge thursday Blowinge weather wind at WNW & Gusty.

1

July 1670: Beinge Friday Gusty Stormy weather wind at WSW.[1]

---

made Signes for us to be gone. I threw him a knife and a Bottle of Brandy and a NeckeCloth as he tooke up and kept yet nothing Could Pacify him but wee must be gone. The Woemen & the Boy satt behind a bush one of the Woemen haveing a grate Bundle of skins on her Back. They bee Well sett people and fatt of a Meane Stature & Naturally of a Broune Tawney Couller, but they paynt there bodyes all over with Red Oker which they have heare Very plentyfull; there faces are painted Very Rudely & horred to Behould with Red, white & Black. They have every one a skin of a Deare or sheep thrown Losely over there Shoulders Hardly comeing soe Low as to Cover there privet Members: on there heads they have a peace of skin for a Cap & on there feet they have skins tyed & Very White: there Bodyes being Elswhere Naked; there Weapons are Bows & Arrowes every one haveing a Bow not above 3 foot & a half Long & seem to bee very Slight: there Arowes are not 3 foot Long but they are Very Cuningly headed with flints of divers Colours & are Very Sharp. As for Habetation or place of aboade they have noe More than wild Beast for I sopose they Live Mightely in feare one of Another for where they come at Night they Lay some Bushsey thrash to Windward of them & there they Lye downe & this is all they houses they have & they Make Very small fires & certainely it is for fear they should be discovered; but how they gett fire I cannot Tell. There food is Deare, Seales & Muskels but I doe not know whether they eat it Raw or noe. They have doges ondefarant Large Wherewith they hunt.'

[1] The Bodleian Library Rawl. MS A 318 version gives the wind as WNW, see below p. 45.

2
Beinge Satterday wind at W*est*: this morninge and lettle wind my men went one [on] the East Shore and Cut wood: they Carried my Graihound with them and killed a Great deare: blew hard to Night at W

3
Beinge Sunday wind at S*outh*: Close weather and a Small gale.

4
Beinge Munday wind at W*est* and a Stife gale: all att west tonight.

5
Beinge Tusday wind at W*est* a Stife gale.

6
Beinge wedensday wind at W*est* and at N*orth* a Small gale and foggy Cleare to night and Gusty weather wind at NW & a frost allso.

7
Beinge Thursday Cloase weather wind at No*rth* a Small gale.

8
Beinge friday wind at W*est* a Small gale we fetched water.

9
Beinge Satterday Cloudy weather wind att SW with Gusts and Raine.

10
Beinge Sunday Close Cloudy darke weather wind at SW and Rain.

11
Beinge Munday Calme this morninge wee went awoodinge it blew a fine galle this after[none] at N by W. Sin*o*r Carrolus Setts in A mes by him Selfe.[1]

12
Beinge Tusday Close weather and lettle wind at NBW.

13
Beinge wedensday Close Cloudy weather wind at NBW a fresh gale all day it blew hard tonight.

[1] Mess is the normal name for the place where a company of officers or sailors eat together. This therefore means that he either sits alone in his cabin or the gunroom.

[111] **July 1670 the *Sweepstakes* in Porte San Julian.**

14
Beinge Thursday wind att NNW: blew hard all day. This day wee halled up our Sailes out of the Store rumes: and found them to be much Eaten againe with the Rats for all wee had Put them downe but a fortnight before: I had them aShore one [on] the Iland of yustis:[1] in our tent and mended them.[2]

15
Beinge friday lettle wind at W*est*: and at SE in the Eveinge.

16
Beinge Satterday faier weather wind at W*est* a fine galle but Could. This day I killed three hares two with my dogg: one I Shoot.

17
Beinge Sunday faier weather this morninge wind at W*est*: very Could and fres [freeze] hard all day this night at 8 aclocke the wind Came to the South and blew a mighty Storme and Snowed much: very Could. This day I Lauched my Longe boate of[f] the Shore: Shee Beinge Rebilt a Strake fore and afte and new timberd.[3]

18
Beinge Munday much wind all day at SBW and Sum Snow with much frost. This morninge william Cristian died of the [*margin:* A man died] Scarvie: he was one of the *Trumpeter*s Crew: aged fivety years.[4]

19
Beinge Tusday wind at SW a fine gale frosty Could weather the Ground Covered with Snow.[5]

20
Beinge wedensday Cloase weather wind at W*est* a Small gale.

21
Beinge Thursday faier weather wind at SW a Small gale Could frost weat*her*.

22
Beinge friday Close Cloudy weather wind at SBW a Small gale.

23
Beinge Satterday blowinge weather wind at SSW and Snowed to day Slatty Snow all night.

[1] See above p. 212, n. 2.
[2] The tent is shown on Narbrough's plan of the harbour, Plate 3.
[3] Having had a strake added above the gunwale fore and aft, and new timber added to the hull where required.
[4] Wood, BL, MS 3833, f. 18v: 'aboute 60 yeares ould'.
[5] Ibid., f.18v: 'We Bueryed Will*iam* Cris*tian* much snow on the ground.'

24
Beinge Sunday wind at SW and blew hard and Snowed wind Cam to the SSW: this Eveinge it Snowed most Parte to night.

25
Beinge Munday wind at S*outh* a Small gale and fooggy all day. Wee fetched wood: we Sould Will*iam* Christians Close at the mast.[1] A frost tonight.

26
Beinge Tusday winde at S*outh* a Small gale. I Cout[2] up Seaven fadam of[f] my Best bower it Beinge worne: to make Spunyarne.[3]

27
Beinge weddensday Close foogey weather wind at No*rth* a Small Gale. This day I had my Topmast up and Riged.

[112] **July 1670 the *Sweepstakes* at Port San Julian.**
28
Beinge Thursday Rainey Slatty Snow wind at W*est* a fresh gale.

29
Beinge friday much Snow to day: wind at S*outh* a fresh gale.

30
Beinge Satterd wind at So*uth* a fine gale Sum Raine this morninge foggy weather most Parte to day.

31
Beinge Sunday faier weather wind at SW a Stife gale.

1
August 1670: Beinge Munday Close weather wind at SW.

2
Beinge Tusday Close weather very Could wind at SW a gale.

3
Beinge weddensday wind at SW a fine gale Could weather.

[1] Sold William Christian's clothes at the mast. This was in accordance with the Duke of York's *Instructions to be observed in the Impresting or Vending of Cloaths on board any of his Majesty's Ships*, Art XI, dated 26 March 1663. James, *Memoirs*. pp. 76–9. The proceeds went to the deceased's executors. The practice of auctioning dead men's clothes on board is still continued today.

[2] This word is not clear in the original, but the sense makes it 'cut'.

[3] This would presumably be cut off from the outer end of the cable where it was worn with rubbing on the sea bed.

4
Beinge Thursday wind at W*est* & this afternone at No*rth* a Small gale.

5
Beinge friday Could weather wind at N*orth*: much wind to night and Snow.

6
Beinge Satturday Close weather wind at SW we filled fresh water.

7
Beinge Sunday wind at W*est* a Stife gale and Could. Wee got our topmast aded.[1]

8
Beinge Munday Close weather wind at WSW a fine gale. I helded [*margin:* A M[an] Died] the ship and washed her:[2] this Afternone John Rigner Died of a flux:[3] he was a Seaman[4] of twenty five yeares of age.

9
Beinge Tusday wind at SW a Stoute gale. Wee buried Jo*h*n Rigner. It blew hard to night & very Could.

10
Beinge weddensday wind at SW: Blew hard all day.

11
Beinge Thursday wind at SW and Could blew hard all day. This day [*margin:* A M[an] Died] Edward weeb Died of the Scurvie:[5] I have now ten men Sicke of the Scuervy: this day I Brought my Sailes to the yards[6] very Could to night.

12
Beinge Friday wind at SW: very Coald much wind to night at WSW.

13
Beinge Satterday Coald blowinge weather wind at SW: Coald to night.

[1] This word is not clear. It might be 'added' or possibly 'fidded' (to fix the mast in position by passing a fid or pin through its lower end which takes the weight of the mast), but the meaning would appear to be that the topmast was hoisted and set up.

[2] Narbrough heeled the ship over and cleaned the side as low as possible to take off the winter growth.

[3] Flux: an abnormally copious flowing of blood or excrement etc. from the bowels or other organs, *NOED*. In this case probably a form of dysentery.

[4] Wood, BL, MS 3833, f. 19r: 'a fore Mast Man'.

[5] Ibid., f. 19r, the name is written 'Edward Webb'. In Bodleian, Rawl. MS A. 318 (see below, p. 447), he is called Edward Web and described as a man about 30 years old and as having been a Lieutenant in the Navy. He was presumably Lieutenant Edward Webb who was appointed to the *Revenge*, 1666 and *Anne*, 1668. Tanner, *Catalogue*, I, p. 421.

[6] Secured the sails to the yards ready for use.

14
Beinge Sunday a Great Storme to day at SW and Continued al night.

15
Beinge Munday Could Sharp weather wind at SW a Stoute gale the hills are Covered with Snow it freseth [freezeth] much to night little wind at west.

16
Beinge Tusday Close weather wind at west and NW a fine gale. This day I filled fresh warter one [on] the East Sid. John Sedgwicke[1] and andrew Cotton Saw tow Indians and went to their Bundls which were skines of dear or wianacos [guanacos]: they Brought them aboard and two doogs:[2] which I Carred to the Same Place the next day and left them and Beads and Bills & knives: one [on] sticks in the same Place

[113] **August 1670 the *Sweepstakes* at Port San Julyan.**
Stukinge in the Ground and Standinge up: and I tied Strings of Beads a Bout their doogs neckes when I let them goe which dogs I suppos went dierectly to their masters for wee saw them no more. I Punnished the men for meddleinge with the Peoples things for it was my disier to have Conference with them ar to treat them kindly that whoe Soever Came after might have Conference with them for they are only fearfull that wee Should doe them harme which I beleve Sum Nation formerly have done them injueriye.

17
Beinge weddensday a small gale this morninge But this afternone it blew hard at SW and Continued So all night.

18
Beinge Thursday faier weather wind at north. I was Read*y* to Saile.

19
Beinge friday fogey weather with Sum Snow this morninge wind at N°E: I Rod fast this day My Master of the Shipp Boyed the Bare with two Can boys mored with two Grapnells.[3]

20
Beinge Satterday wind at NE and Blow a storme a great Sea Rane one [on] the Bar. This day John Satton[4] the Stuards mat [steward's mate] died of the scuervie.[5] A Man died

[1] John Wood says he was a Quarter Master. Wood, BL, MS 3833, f. 20r, 22 June.

[2] Wood, BL, MS 3833, f. 20v: 'Our Men Being on the East side filling of Watter, 2 of them went a fowleng, there names John Segeck & Andrew Cotton, & as they was goeing they saw two Pattagones Behind a Bush, soe they Went towards them but thay Ran away & Left all there bagage behind them, which was Many deare skins sowed together with gutts & in these there was severall Bags of flints & Little bages of Red, white & Black paynt & a grate Many simple things not all worth 6 pence, & 2 dogs they Left tyed, which with the Bundle of things they brought Aboard, for which the Cap*tain* was Very Angery with them.' This incident is recorded under 10 Aug. in Wood, BL, MS 46A, p. 149.

[3] Small anchors.

[4] In Wood, BL, MS 3833, f. 19r, the name is given as 'John Stanten'.

[5] The words 'A Man died' appear to be a note at the end of the text for the day.

21

Beinge Sunday wind at South. My Boats went for wood and warter: a Sudden Storme Rose at west and Sunke them Boath one [on] the Shore: this night I went ashore and Got them of[f] in my yoale[1] [yawl] they received lettle harme. Close weather to night.

22

Beinge Munday Close weather wind at No*rth* a fine gale. My Master went to the Bar in the Boat and Boath the Boys were Suncke.

23

Beinge Tusday Close weather wind at NW a fine gale. I went to the Bare in my Boats and my Master with me: But I found he had layd them he Could not tell where for he had noe markes for them:[2] I Sweepedd all the Chanell over[3] But Could not find them. The tid Beinge Com and it blow hard I went aboard wind at W

24

Beinge weddensday Close weather this morninge but this afternone much wind at W*est* so as I Could not Saile with the Ship. I went againe to the Barr But Could not see my Boyes. I judge they are Buried under the Beach of the Barr.

[114] **August 1670 the *Sweepstakes* in Port San Julian**

25

Beinge Thursday Cloudy Coald weather wind at SW a strong gale. This morninge I went to the Barr and had three very Good Sweeps but Could not find my Grapnells: I tak marks one [on] the Land to Saile out in the Best of the Chanell.[4] I went aboard But it was So much wind one [on] the flood as I Could Not lose to Saile[5] wind at SWBW all night and blow hard.

26

Beinge Friday Cloudy Coald weather wind at SWBW much wind one [on] the flood tide So as I Could not Saile. I toke Posseton.[6]

27

Beinge Satterday Cloudy Coald weather wind at SBW: much wind today. I Could not

[1] Yawl: the smallest boat in the ship.

[2] It might have been expected that the Master would have noted transit marks on the shore in the positions where the anchors for the buoys had been laid to enable him to return to them, but he had not done this.

[3] The buoys would probably have been moored with rope lines attached to the grapnels, and had they sunk they would have been lying on the sea bed down tide from them, at the end of their respective mooring lines. Sweeping the channel would have been done by dragging a creeper (four-clawed hook on a line) along the sea bed to try to pick up the moorings. If the buoys were still attached to their moorings there was a real chance of catching them with the creeper; however, had the lines parted, unless the anchor itself was caught, there was very little likelihood of recovering anything.

[4] Identified marks on the land to act as a leading line for the best track over the bar.

[5] There was so much wind when the tide began to flood that the sails could not be set to sail out of the harbour.

[6] Took possession of Puerto San Julián in the name of King Charles II.

Saile: I onemored [unmoored] But had much adoe to keep my Shipp of[f] the Shore: So I got mored againe. Much wind at West to night.

28
Beinge Sunday faier weather this morninge & Sun Shine. I waied and it Proved much wind So as I was forced to anc*hor* a mile below wher I rod before a hard gale at West al night.

29
Beinge Munday Cloase Cloudy weather wind at SW and rain & Gusty weather the wind Came to the north. This day I went with twelfe men armed[1] into the Cuntry due west North west: tenn miles to night ther logded [*sic*] in a vally.

30
Beinge Tusday fogey weather wind at North. I travilled to day theerty miles into the land and Could not goe any forther for hills and dales: all a Barran Land in the Cuntry not Soe much as a Bush to be seene a lettle gras and the land is of a graveelly Soile and Rockes: the land all over is of a Salt Peeter natur[2] So as nothinge Can grow many Salt warter Ponds in the Cuntry in Sandy vallies: lettle fresh water any wher: I fell with a small Rivellet of Fresh warter which Came out of the Cuntry and Ran into the Great Salt Pond: noe mineralls or any kind of ore to be Senne nor any timber any wher noe People to be senne: But Severall Places wher they had ben. This day it was very fogey weather & weet much: we lost our way in the hills: for ther is noe remarkable Place: noe woods nor tree: I had a Compas. We lay tonight under a bush.

31
Beinge wedensday wind at N a fine gale. This day Polliecarpus [*margin:* A m Died] Ingham died: Chy*rurgeons* mate.[3] This Eveinge I Cam aboard the Ship Beinge out three days and two Nights in the Cuntry.

[115] **September 1670 the *Sweepstakes* in Porte San Julian**
1
Beinge Thursday Cloas hasey weather wind at north a Small gale. This [*margin:* A ma Died] day Christopher Tucke Died Steward of the Ship: they wer buried one [on] the Iland of true justice. Much wind at north to night.[4]

[1] Wood, BL, MS 3833, f. 19r: 'The Cap*tain* and my self with 11 Men More went into the Country.' This is presumably the expedition recounted for 1 Sept. below.

[2] Saltpetre, potasium nitrate, white crystalline substance. *NOED*. Presumably Narbrough means the ground is salty.

[3] Surgeon's mate.

[4] Wood, BL, MS 3833, f. 20v: 'The first day of September the Cap*tain* & my self with 11 Men went up into the Country & the farther wee went the More Baran was the ground. We went aboute 25 Miles Right up into the Land & Lay out two Nights & returned Aboard the 3[d] day: without seeing of any People or any thing worth taking Notice of only some foules aboute the Bignes of a swan which was of a pure Scarlet Coulour & 10 Miles up we found a Rivelet of fresh Water.' This was probably a Chilean flamingo (*Phoenicopterus chilensis*), Harris, *Guide*, pp. 55–6.

2
Beinge Friday Cloudy Blowinge weather wind at NNE and Could. I Could not Git to Sea wind still Contrary.

3
Beinge Satterday Cloase weather wind at north a fresh gale.

4
Beinge Sunday faier weather wind at SW. I got under Saile but it fell Calme all the flood So I anchored againe: it Proved fogey weather this afternone the wind Came to the NW and blew.

5
Beinge Munday Cloudy weather wind at West this morninge then Came to the NW and Blew a Mighty Storme: I got downe my yards and topmast it Continued Stormey all night.

6
Beinge Tusday Cloudy Coald weather the wind Came to the WBN and blew a hard Gall all day and much wind to night.

7
Beinge wedensday Cloudy Snowey weather and haile very Coald the wind Came to the SW. I got up my yards and topmast But the wind veared to the SSW and Blow a mighty Storme. I let fall my Sheat anchor[1] and got down my yards and topmast. It Proved a mighty Storme to night I was in Great danger of driveinge ashore it Blew So vehemently.

8
Beinge Thursday Snowey weather and Coaald much wind all day at SSW but it Proved indeferent weather to night.

9
Beinge Friday faier weather wind at north. I got my Sheat anchor aboard and new mored with my Bowers and got up my yards and top*mast*.

10
Beinge Satterday indeferent weather wind at NBE a fine gale: this afternone the wind Came to the NW and blew hard. This after none [*margin:* A man Died] Nathanell Nash died: a Seaman.

11
Beinge Sunday Cloudy weather wind at WSW a fine Gale Sum Rane. This forenone I got onemored [unmored] the wind Came to the East then went Round the Compas twice to day: much wind at west to night.

[1] The sheet anchor was the largest anchor in the ship, normally stowed abaft the bower anchors and used in emergency.

[116] **September 1670 the *Sweepstakes* in Porte San Julian**

12

Beinge Munday wind at WBS a hard gale all day and Gusty weather much wind to night at SW: at twelfe of the Clocke I was doutfull of my anchor and Cables to hould.

13

Beinge Tusday wind at W a Stout gale this forenone the after none the wind Came to the ENE a fresh gale: the winds are very vearable this month and mighty Boisterus Runinge Round the Compas two or three times in twenty fower houers: wind at N and at NW to night.

14

Beinge weddensday faier weather wind at NNE all day. I Could not Saile. Faier weather to night wind Cam to the west.

15

Beinge Thursday faier weather this morninge wind at w*e*st Sumtims Lettle wind and Calme. I waied one [on] the flood and got downe a harquebus Shot Lower[1] But anchored againe it fall flat Calme till halfe Ebb: the wind Cam to the South west with haile and Snow and blow vehemently in Gusts. This Eveinge [*margin:* A: M Died] Zecias Bynon died: a Seaman. Gusty weather to night.

16

Beinge friday wind at w*e*st and B*y* South a fresh gale. This morn*inge* I waied and Got to Sea: I had a quarter les then fower fadam water one [on] the Bar[2] it was nere a high water. The Chanell lies in South west be South: by my Compas: over the Bar and in to the narrow: till you Come to bringe the harbower open: then SSW: the Chanell is two Cables lenth broad one [on] the bare: the midle Grounds are Covered at halfe flood and the beach one [on] the west Side: its ful Sea at halfe an hower Past a Leaven of the Clocke one [on] the Change of the mone: the tids Rise nere fower fadam and runs as Strong as in the hope or at Gravesend.[3] The mouth of Port San Julyan Lies in the Latt*itud* of fowerty nine degres & ten minuts: as I observed by the quadrant which M[r] John Davis invented & in Longitud from the Lizard of England Sixty three degres & tenn minuts west:[4] and meridian distance one thousand and theerty leagus.

From San Julyan I Steered NNE: the wind Came to the South west and Blew fresh. My men Beinge very weeak and mettinge a Contrayrie wind: My Selfe and officers judge it most fitt to goe for Port dissier: and their to refresh our men for ther is Penguns and Seals anough which are Good Provissions.[5]

[1] Harquebus, an early form of portable gun with a long barrel, generally longer than a rifle but smaller than a musket, which may have made this shorter than the distance of a musket shot, which was about 400 yards. See above, p. xix.

[2] Just over 22 ft of water on the bar.

[3] The Mean High Water Spring tide today rises to 24·6 ft (7·5 m) and the stream in The Narrows runs at 3–6 knots. *South America Pilot*, II, paras. 3.108, 3.116. The stream at Gravesend and at the Hope runs at up to 2·7 knots.

[4] Puerto San Julián lies in 49°14′S, 67°37′W, which is 62°25′W of the Lizard.

[5] The fresh food would act as an antiscorbutic.

[117] **September 1670 the *Seepstaks* at Sea one the Coast of Amarica**
17
Beinge Satterday wind at West this morninge a fresh gale: I was tharte[1] of the Eadistone Rocke:[2] the wind Came to the South I Stered north be [by] East and then north westerly and haled in for Penguens Iland:[3] it blew much wind to day: I Spleet my for top Saile.[4] At twelfe aclock to day I went into the Bay of Port disier[5] and Anchored in twelfe fadam warter in the midle of the Bay two mils of[f] the shore. Faier weather to night wind at west South west.

18
Beinge Sunday very Gusty weather wind at WBS this morninge and looked very windy: much wind to day at ten aclock and Snow and haile & Slatey Coald weather: handsum weather this Eveinge. I waied and Stood into Port disier and turned into the harbower and anchored in the Birth wher I rod before and mored[6] faier wea*ther*. Tonight their was a pertiall Ecleips of the mone.[7]
[*blank space*]

19
Beinge Munday wind vearable Round the Compas. We fetched fresh warter for ther is Good Stoor now wher wee had diged our wells befor.

20
Beinge Tusday wind vearable round the Compas. We went and Killed sum seales one [on] an Iland which lies in the harbower this afternone we Salted them up. I went to Penguen Iland with my boats and laded them with Seals and Penguens: the Penguens were numberless one [on] the Ilands for ther was a great many Eggs it was just laieinge thim [laying time] with them: their Eggs are very Good and houls Sum [wholesome] to Eat as any Egg what Soever they are Sumwhat bigger then ducks Eggs and whit Shelled.[8] The Iland whas all Covered with them and Birds and Seals boath younge and ould Seales. This after none I went aboard againe for in two howers time Eight men might Lad a Barke of tenn tuns with Seales and Penguens ther is Such quantitis: the Penguens

[1] Athwart, or abreast of the rock.
[2] Roca Bellaco, see above, p. 210, n. 7.
[3] Isla Pingüino, see above, p. 204.
[4] Wood, BL, MS 3833, f. 19v: 'at 3 the wind blowing fresh our Maine Topsale split in 3 places'.
[5] Puerto Deseado, see above, p. 204.
[6] Wood, BL, MS 3833, f. 19v: 'at half past 6 we weare in the Narrow of the harbors mouth, it being dead Low water, the Wind came to the SW soe we Kedged in & came to an Ancker in the same place that we Roade in before'.
[7] A large blank space, approximating to 8 lines follows, possibly for details of the eclipse to be inserted later. Wood, BL, MS 3833, f. 24r, estimated 'it Appeirs That the Eclipse Began at London September the 18th at 13h37m58s or at 17 Min 58 Seconds past One on Monday Morn*ing* being the 19th day. But I found the Beginning in This Harbor of Porte Desire to be on Sunday September the 18th att 5 Minutes & 58 Seconds past 9 of the Clock att night by Observation of the Scorpions Heart [Antares or α Scorpii]. Now The Difference Betwixt These 2 Times is 4 houres 52 Min*uts* which Converted into Degres Gives 73 Deg*res* which is Diff*erence* of Longitude Betwixt London and Porte Desire.'
[8] See above, p. 222, n. 2. These would have been Magellanic penguins, which lay white eggs in mid-Oct. to mid-Nov. The rockhopper lays greenish-blue eggs, from mid-Nov. Shirihai, *Complete Guide*, pp. 65 and 81.

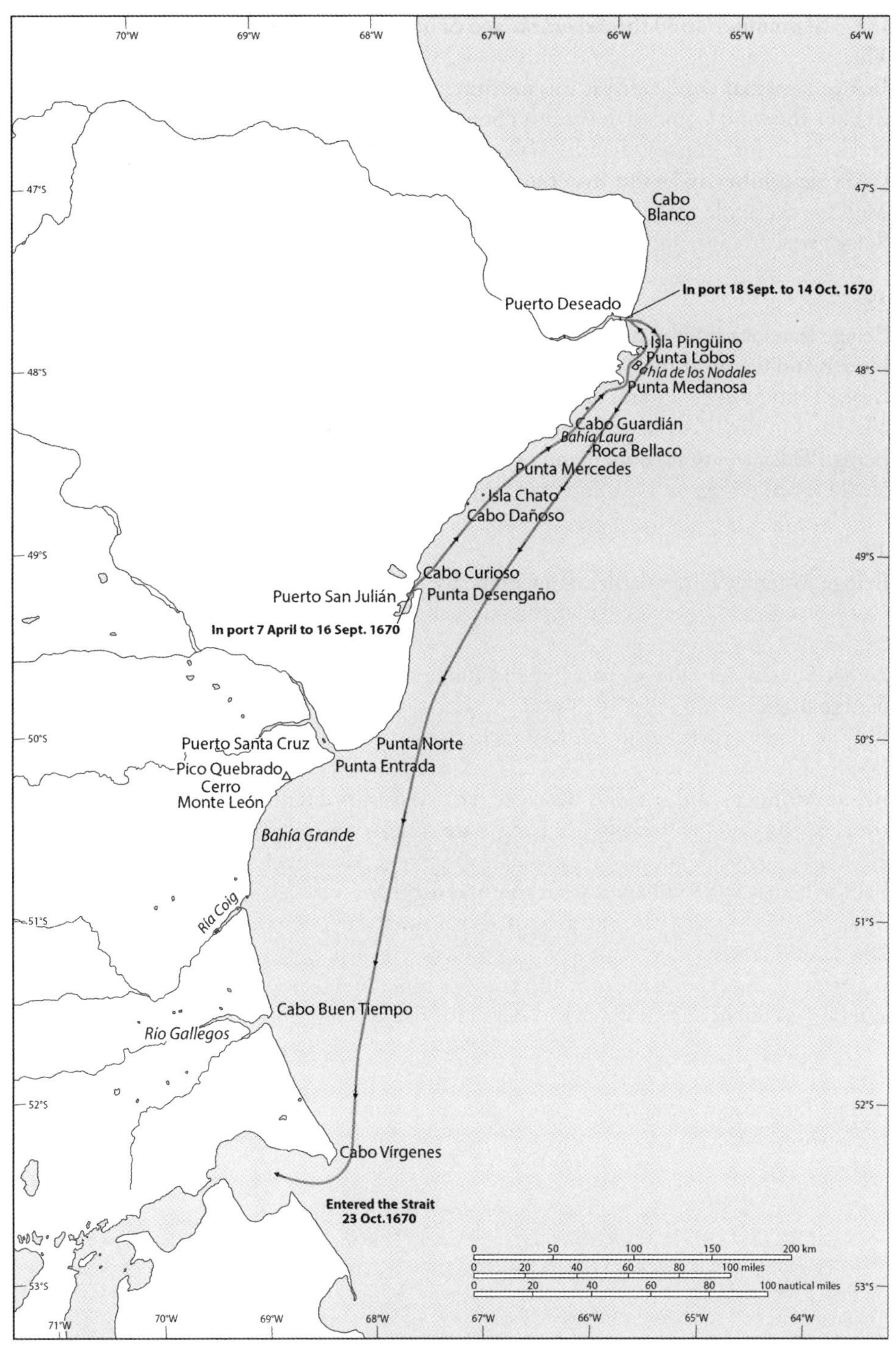

Map 6. Track of the *Sweepstakes* off the coast of Argentina, 7 April 1670 to 23 October 1670.

and Seales ar Good food Boath fresh and Salt. We were all in ten days time as lusty as when wee Came out of England: and when I Cam in here I had above twenty men Sicke and Severall had the Scuervie: for the time wee were at Port dissier wee Fared Mighty well for food.

[118] **September 1670 the *Sweepstakes* in Port Dissier**

21
Beinge wedensday wind veareable Round the Compas faier weather.[1]

22
Beinge thursday faier weather we skined: Salted our Seals flesh in Packe the[y] Beinge Bluded and Guted at the Iland and the Penguens allsoe.

23
Beinge friday we went to the Iland againe & Laded boath my boats with Penguens and Smal Seals and Eggs and Came aboard that day.[2]

24
Beinge Satterday faier weather and Calme: we Salted our flesh.

25
Beinge Sunday very foogey weather and Raine to day wind Cam to the north and blow hard to night.[3]

26
Beinge Munday wind at north west wee fetched fresh warter.

27
Beinge Tusday wind at NW a stout gale and foggey.

28
Beinge wedensday wind at no*rth* and vearable round the Compas and base weather fogey and rain we fetched fresh water and fewell for the fier.

29
Beinge Thursday wind at north a Stout gale all day and night and raine a foog we fetched frseh [fresh] water.

[1] Wood, BL, MS 3833, f. 23v: 'This Morning the Cap*tain* Came aboard from Pinguin Island with 500 Seales & 300 Pingquins. This day we flea Them Ashore.'

[2] Ibid., f. 23v: 'the Cap*tain* went to Pen*guin* Island with The Long Boate and Pines & Returned at 4 in the Afternoon with 600 Seales & many Ping*uins* Eggs'.

[3] Ibid., f. 23v: 'The 25 day of September at Night they [the Pattagons] Came downe to the Spring where our men had Bin a Washing & Toke away a Grate Iron Pott & all the Linnen; at this Spring Mr Tho*mas* Candish had a Man & a Boy Shott with there Arrowes as they was a Washing.' This incident is described in Hakluyt, *Principal Navigations*, III, p. 805.

30
Beinge friday wind at West and Came to the SE and blew hard and rained. This night the People of the Cuntry Came to one of our wells in the vally half a mile from the water Side and Carred away an Iron Pot of my Pursers and Severall Cloas [clothes] of my mens which they had Left Beinge their the day before a washinge.[1] We heard noe more of them nor never Could Se any in that Port. Thay had made in a valy a moddle of the Shipp: in a Banck of Earth and Sticked Bushes in for the hull of the Shipp: and Set up Stickes for mast: as for fore mast and main mast and mizon mast and Ensigne Stafe and bould Sprit.[2] They had mad it much like a Boat one [on] the Stockes[3] and at Lest as bigg as my Pinass: a boat twenty five foot longe and had Reded it all over with ther red Earth. I Suppos they mad it in memory of our Beinge their before for they have noe other way to record but by Emitation: wee Left it a lone one touched [untouched] at our Cominge away I left beads and other Small trifefels [trifles] at it hanginge to the Ensigne Stafe.

[119] [*blank page*]

[120] **October 1670 the *Sweepstakes* in Port disier**
1
Beinge Satterday Gusty Cloudy weather wind at So*uth*: Sum Thunder this afternone. I was up in the Land but saw no People.

2
Beinge Sunday faier weather wind at WBS a fine gale. This afternone I went to Penguin Iland with Boath my Boats. This Eveinge it thundered much and Lightneed & Rained much in a Great Gust wind at W: I lay at the Iland all night with my Boats at an anchor in a Small Bay in the NW Parte of the Iland: the bay is indeferent for boats to Ride in but ther Commonly Gose a Great Sea all about the Ile which makes it bad to Land.

3
Beinge Munday wind at NW a Stoute gale. I Came from the Ile laden today with Pengu*i*ns: this night I Got aboard. I left Leiuet*enant*[4] at the Ile with Eight men to make Blubber for oile for our Lamps. The wind at west to night a gale.

4
Beinge Tusday wind at W a Stout gale. Wee Salted our Penguens into Caske: after twenty fower howers: after they ar Salted – draine ther Blood from them Clen & Put Clere Pickle to them: they keep variwell:[5] the like wee doe to our Seales flesh but we Salt that first in Bulke: three or fower days & then Re Pack it.

[1] This incident is described by John Wood as having taken place on 25 Sept.; see above, p. 248, n. 3.

[2] Bowsprit: a large spar, ranking with a lower mast projecting forward from the bow of the ship from which the spritsail was carried on the spritsail yard, and from the sprit top-mast, rising from the forward end of the bowsprit, the sprit topsail on the sprit topsail yard.

[3] Stocks: a frame of blocks on which ships were built.

[4] This was probably Lieutenant Armiger since Peckett makes no mention of the trip in his journal.

[5] The penguins were salted and stowed in casks. Twenty-four hours after they had been salted the blood was drained from them and they were cleaned and pickled. Thus they kept very well.

5
Beinge wedensday Rainey weather wind Round the Compas.

6
Beinge Thursday wind Round the Compas twice today.

7
Beinge friday wind at W a Stoute Gale all day.

8
Beinge Satterday wind at NW a stout gale wee fetched more Peng*uens*.

9
Beinge Sunday a mighty Storme to day at W: I Strok my topmast.

10
Beinge Munday Cloudy weather wind at W: I mead Ready to Saile.

11
Beinge Tusday wind at WSW with Slatty hail and snow to day.

12
Beinge wedensday Cleare weather wind at W a hard gale all day. This day I got all my things of[f] the Shore and had Eightein Cask of Seals and Penguins as to Say Punshions. I waite only the Almighties Pleasuer to Saile the first faier winds for the Straits of Magallan.[1]

13
Beinge veary Stormy weather wind at W.

14
Beinge friday faier weather wind at W a Stife gale. At Six a Clocke this morninge the tid Served I waied and went to Sea: at tenn of the Clocke the wind Came to the SSW a fresh gale. I[2] Stood into the Bay and anchored in 14 fadam oasey Sand. A fresh gale all night at S. I made halfe a Tun of Seal oyle for my Lamps.

[121] **October 1670 the *Sweepstakes* at Sea of[f] Penguen Iland**
15
Beinge Satterday the wind Came to the N a fresh gale. This morninge at three aClocke I waied and Stood out of the Bay: at Seaven I Passed Penguens Ile:[3] then I Steered from

[1] Wood, BL, MS 46A, p. 154: 'Before wee departed hence we Sewed Severall English Seeds Viz[t]. Turnips Carrotts Colworts Redishes Beanes Peas and Onions which at our Returne Back we found Some of each that the Patagonianes had left. The Turnips was very good the Redishes Peas and Beanes were gon to Seed. Wee could not peceive that the Indians had used any of them but puld them out of the Earth and left them there to Decay.'

[2] 'wayed and' crossed through in the original.

[3] Wood, BL, MS 3833, f. 25r: 'our Boates went to the Island & Returned A board Laden with Pinguins & Eggs. att 12 we departed from Ping*uin* Island'.

Penguns Ile SSW & this afternone I Pased by the EadyStone Rocke in halfe a mile to the E*ast*ward of it. When you are thart[1] of the Rocke the Sadle table Land one [on] the maine beres west North west of you: then you are to the Southward of it. Lettle wind to night at WBN: I Steered South South west.

16
Beinge Sunday wind at NW a fine gale but hasey: I Steered SWBS by my Compas. This day at none I was by Good observation of the ☼ in the Latt*itud* of 49°08′ but Could not See the Shor: wind veared to the E a fine gal: I Steered SWBS till Six aclocke: then I Sounded and had ground at Ten fadam: oasey Sand: a very Thick foog. I haled of[f] SE: at twelfe aclock at night I Sounded and had fowerty fadam black oazay Sand: I judge I ame Seaven Leagus of[f] the Land and to the Southward of San Julian: a very thicke weet fogg. I handed my TopSailes and Stood of[f] EBS: the wind at N a fresh gale and a great Sea Came out of the NE.

17
Beinge Munday a mighty thick fooge all day wind at NNE a fresh gale and a great Sea: the Shipp Labored vary much: I lay by with my head to the E*ast*ward till tenn of the Clock then Sounded and had 45 fadam. I Stood of[f] ESE: very Thick and foogey: I Could not See the Land. I reackein my Selfe nine Leagus of[f] at twelfe aclock today and in the Latt*itud* of 49°40′. I lay of[f] and one [on] all night betwen therty fadam and fevety fadam[2] oasey Sand: the foge Beinge Soe thicke as I dare not ventur to Saile.

18
Beinge Tusday very foogey and Coald wind at NNE but Came to the SBE and Blow hard: at Six aclocke this afternone it Cleared & I saw the Land: I was about Seaven Leagus of[f] it. I Sounded and had theerty Six fadam: blackesh Sand: I was in the Latt*itude* of 49°50′: the Land is all Plaine a loft Soe far as I Could See boath to the Northward and Southward it is white Clefes to the Sea Steep up and of a good height.[3] I lay of[f] and in all night: very thicke weet fooge and a great Sea out of the E.

[122] **October 1670 the *Sweepstakes* of[f] the hill of St Yves Lat*titud* 50°18′ S**
19
Beinge wedensday this morninge I Sounded and had Ground at fevety Six fadams: at fower of the Clock I judge my Selfe tenn leagus of[f] the Land: the wind Came to the North a fresh [gale] I Steered in WSW: at Eight a Clocke it Cleared up: I Stood within fower Laegus of the Land and I had theerty fadam black Sand: the Land lies alonge Southwest & be [by] South and North East & be North: in the Latt*itud* of fevety degres the Land is low in a longe low beachey Bay: which bay begings [*sic*] at the South Parte of

[1] Athwart or abreast.

[2] They sailed towards the land until the depth was 30 fathoms and then to seaward, until it was 50 fathoms, and then inshore again, all night.

[3] Wood, BL, MS 46A, p. 154: 'Southward of Port St Julians the Land is allsoe Lowe and even without hills or woodish: steep white Cliffs till you come in the Lat of 50° and then it begineth to be high Land with a point lying out to the Northward.'

the white Clifes which are in the Latt*itude* of 49°50′.[1] This beachey Bay hath at the South End Good high Land with white Clifes to Seaward: it maketh a Cap as you Come from the Nortward: this Cap I Called Beachey head for this like Beachey in England. This high land is Called the hill of Sant ives: it maketh a flat table land aloft and a Round Cople hill at the North End of it: its yust [just] Even with the table Land and ther is Sum Cople Round hills by the Sea Side to the Southward of San Ives about a League.[2] I had a Good obser*vation* to day of the ☼. I find the hill of St Ives to Ly in the Latt*itud* of 50°18′[3] and Beachey head in 50°10′. I Stered away SSW as the Lande lies by my Compas: But here is 16°37′ variation E. Here is faier Soundinge all alonge this Coast black Sandy Grond in fower leagus of the Shore is twenty five fadam. This night at Seaven aclocke the wind Came to the South and Blow hard: I handed my Top Saile and Stood of[f] to the Eastwards all night a great Sea Cam out of the South East which made me Try under my Maine Saile.

20

Beinge Thursday faier weather this morninge the wind Came to the N a fine gale I Sett my Top Sailes at Breake aday & Stood into the Shore SW: at Seaven a Clocke I was in three Lea*gus* of the Land: I had Nineten fadam Black oasy Sand. The Sea Shore is white Steep Clifes and lies SW & NE. I had a fine gale at N: I Steered all alonge the Shore in 19 and twenty fadam SWBS. This day at none I had a Good observation and was in the

[1] Beachy Head in England, is a range of undulating sheer white chalk cliffs with heights up to 534 ft (163 m). See below, p. 456. *South America Pilot,* II, para. 3.135 notes 'Southward from about 49°25′S the coast consists of sheer white cliffs about 295 ft (90 m) high for 29 miles. From about 49°58′S they become darker and gradually decrease in height to Punta Norte.' Cabo San Francisco de Paula, 49°44′S, 67°43′W, which is not a prominent headland, lies in this stretch of coast and from it the coast bends round SW to Punta Norte, 72 ft (22 m) high, at the entrance to Río Santa Cruz (which Narbrough missed). In appearance this part of the coast would appear to be distinctly similar to that round Beachey Head in England. Narbrough's Beachy Head can thus be confidently located between these two points. The bay, Bahía Grande, lies to the SW of Río Santa Cruz. Cerro Monte León, 50°19′S, 68°53′W, lies close to the coast in the bight of this bay 22 miles from the entrance to Río Santa Cruz. It appears conical from NE, and rises to 1,106 ft (337 m) and is the highest peak in the area. This is probably the hill Narbrough took to be the hill of St Ives, which he states (p. 456) was the highest hill on this coast. Cerro Observacíon, 1,043 ft (318 m), lies 2 miles south of Cerro Monte León and terminates in a headland with high dark cliffs. Wood puts the hill in 50°22′S and Peckett puts it in 50°S with Beachy Head in the same Latitude (p. 585). The inset of South America on Narbrough's published chart (Plate 9) shows Beachy Head north of Río Santa Cruz, which on the above identification it is, and 'hills St Ives' on the coast further north still which is contrary to the latitudes Narbrough gives for them. The probability is therefore that 'hills St Ives' has been incorrectly positioned on this chart. The Doncker chart shows Río de la Cruz in approximately 51°S, with Morro de S Yves north of it, but it is not clear if the hill is on the coast or not. Wood, MS 46A, p. 155 states: 'Eight Leagues to the Southward of the hill Ives lyeth a harbour Called by Ferdinando Magellan St Crus but wee did not see it Therefore I can say nothing of it and M^r hacklewt in his voyage Saith that from St Ives to Rio de Cruz it is 8 Lea*gues*', Hakluyt, *Principal Navigations*, III, p. 725; see below p. 457, n. 2). Cerro Pan de Azúcar Grande, 518 ft (158 m), 49°38′S, 68°33′W, stands about 30 miles north of the entrance to Río Santa Cruz and a similar distance inland. It is possible that this is the Hill of Saint Ives of both Hakluyt and the Doncker chart.

[2] Wood, BL, MS 46A, p. 154: 'This hill is the hill of St Ives which lyes in the Lat of 50°22′ S*outh* the Course By Compass is S*outh* 28° W*es*t But the true Course is S by W^t dist*ance* 23 Lea*gues*. Betwixt the point of St Julians and the hill of St Ives you shall have 20 25 and 30 Fathom good ground a League from the Shore. The Tyde runneth Strong: the flood Setteth N by E^t and Ebb S by W^t.'

[3] Wood, BL, MS 3833, f. 25r: 'This day I had a good Observation & found my Self in the Latt*itude* S 50°18′. The hill of St Ives Bareing W by S.'

Latt*itud* of 50°33′. I Steered SSW all night in twenty fadam oasey Sand: the Shore is white Steep Clefs in Severall Places and Plaine Barran downes aloft. Faier weather to night I Saw the Shore all alonge as I sailed: to night I Steered allonge SWBS and South South West with an Easey Saile: the wind at N a fine gale. Noe fire to be Seene one [on] the Land any where: Sum whalls Seene to night Spoutinge nere the Shipp.

[123] **October 1670 the *Sweepstakes* on the South Cost Amarica**
21
Beinge friday faier weather and Lettle wind at NBE. This morninge I was in fower leagus of the Shore Steringe away SWBS as the Land Lies: the Land is steep white Clefes in doackes[1] and Black Steps: it is of an indeferent height and Plane downes without any wood: I went in 19 fadam oasey Sand all this forenone. At twelfe aclock to day I had a Good observation of the ☼ and was in the Latt*itud* of feviety one and twenty one minuts and in 19 fadam [*right margin:* 51°21] Black oasey Sand: the Land of a Good height heigher then the land to the No*rth*ward of it and low flatt Land to the Southward of it in a low long bay. This Cap is Steep up as you Come frome the Norwards by the Sea Side in Steep white Clefes. I Caled [*right margin:* C Fai wea] this cap faier weather[2] be Reason of a faier day. From this Petch of the Cap SSE fower leagus the Shoulds [shoals] ly ofe [off] which Comes out of the Bay: I had but ten fadam water for two miles Runnige SEBS: we Saw breachers is with in us.[3] Five or Six Leagus SE from this Cap you will have twenty Six fadam warter black Sand. To the Southward of this Cape the land is low and their is Seaven or Eight hills apers one [on] the low land like Ilands of a Prety height:[4] you must have a care to keep out of this Bay for the Shore is flat fower leagus of[f]. To the South of these Coplen hills the land apears in white Clefes of an indiferent height & Plane aloft: the Coast from Cap faier weather to the Southward Lies SSE for nine leagus distance. Calme this Eveinge and the tide of flood Beinge Come at Eight aclocke I anchored with my small bower in twenty Eight fadam Blacke oasey Sand. I was five leagus from the Land: the Coplen hills barr WBS of mee: the tids Runnes of an indeferent Strenght and flowes at a high warter here one [on] the Chang & full mon at ten aclocke: the flood setts NW & the Ebb SE. This day I observed the ☼ Amplituds at Rizinge and Setinge and find my Compasses to have Seaventen degres variation Easterly. Faier weather all night & letle wind. I find the tide to Rize three Fadams:[5] heer is good Anchoringe all a longe this Coaste. I try for to Catch fish but Can not take any: many Large Whalls Sen and Purposes and Seales: Severall Pied.

[1] Dokes, small depressions or hollows. *NOED*.

[2] This is probably Cabo Buen Tiempo (51°33′S, 68°57′W), the north entrance point to Río Gallegos; variant Gallogue. Narbrough does not give a latitude for this headland, but states that shoals extend seaward from it, which indeed they do off the river mouth. In Rawl. MS A. 318, he states 'goes in the river of Gallegos', p. 458. Wood, BL, MS 3833, f. 25r, places the Cape at 51°24′.' In BL, MS 46A, p. 155, he notes 'In the Lat of 51°30′ there lyeth a Cape which is all white steepe Cliffes: the Cape haveing noe name I called it Cape Blanckford. From the Cape lyeth a Banck of Sand SE[t] into the Sea: about 3 Leag*ues* off wee had 11 Fathom water: on it the Flood setteth N by E[t] the Ebb S by W[t].'

[3] Saw breakers inshore of the ship.

[4] These are probably Colinas Los Frailes (51°50′S 69°10′W).

[5] This will have been obtained by taking one sounding at low water and another at high water. Since the ship is unlikely to have been in exactly the same place, indeed it probably moved twice the length of cable in use, the accuracy cannot be good.

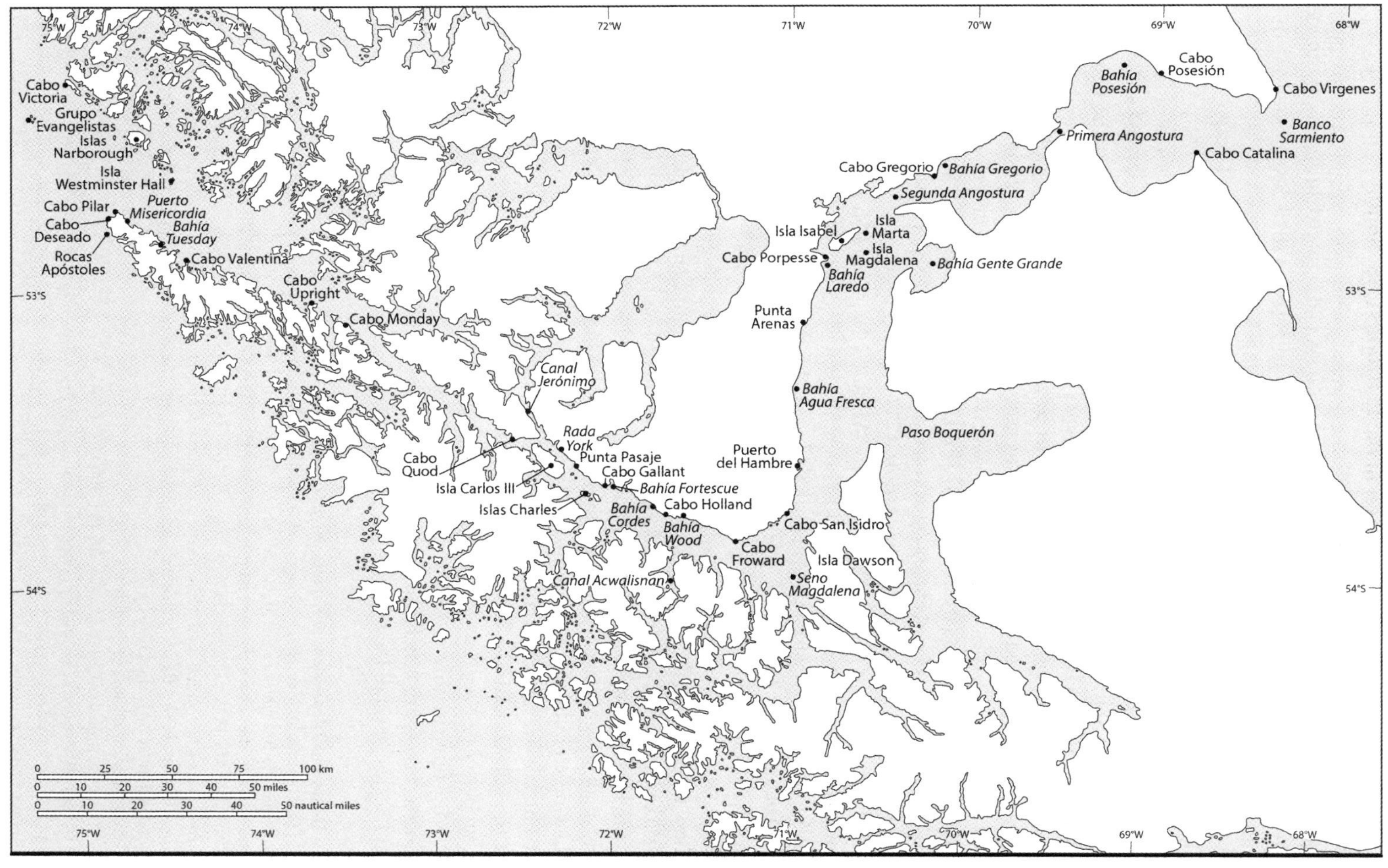

Map 7. Strait of Magellan (Estrecho de Magallanes).

[124] **October 1670 the *Sweepstakes* in the Latt*itud* 51°58′ South**

22

Beinge Satterday faier weather and letle wind at N. I waied at one a Clocke this morninge and Stood to the SE:ward: Calme this forenone. At Eight of the Clocke I anchored in theerty fower fadam warter at a low warter and at a hige warter I had theerty Seaven fadam: the warter Rizeth But three fadam[1] as I Can Perceive: I was But 4 Leagus of[f] the Land: the Shore is Plaine Land aloft of an indeferent height with white Steep Clefs and lies SSE and NNW. To day none I was in the Latt*itud* by Good observation of 51°58′. At one aclocke this afternone the wind[2] Cam to the NEBE: a fresh gale. I waied and Stood away SE and SSE and had theerty fadam warter all alonge in fower leagus of the land: the Land is white Clefs: Steep up of an indeferent hight and Plaine alofte. The Cap vergen mary[3] is Reather higher land then any of that Shore in fower leagus:[4] it is Steep up: Exsept at the foote ther Rounes a low Pointe out to the SW:ward with Sum Bushes on it: which Pointe is a Bache [beach] of a leage longe by the Sea Shore which Comes from the low land as falles from the Cap as you Come from the NW: and Bringe the Cap W of you you will See the westerd land appere out of the Cap in a Round Coplen hill:[5] their is a longe Black Spoot in the Clife a Cables lenght to the N:ward of the Cap & a lettle fall of the Plaine land aloft over that Spoot. This Evenige at Seaven of the Clocke I anchored in twenty Six fadam warter blacke Sand: the Cap Vergen Mary Bare WBS about fower leagus of[f] wher I rod at anchor. I saw the land of the South Shore of the Streits of Maggellan trent away to the SE:ward.[6] Faier weather al night wind at N a fine gale Smoath warter.

23

Beinge Sunday faier weather all day: wind at North a fine gale. At fower aclocke in the morneinge I wayed and Stodd away to the Southward till I Brought Cap Vergen Mary WNW of me. I haled in SW and Came over A Sand Bancke which had But Seaven fadam warter one [on] it: and about it I had Eighten and twenty fadam: it Bar ESE from the Cap nere fower leagus of[f]:[7] their was a Replein [rippling] over it.[8] The tide of flood

[1] See above, p. 253, n. 5.

[2] The words 'the wind' repeated in the original.

[3] Cabo Vírgenes (52°20′S, 68°2′W); variants Cap Vergen Mary, Marry, Virgin Mary, Virginmary. Called the Cape of Eleven Thousand Virgins by Magellan for the 11,000 virgins who, according to legend, accompanied Saint Ursula from Britain to Rome and were martyred with her on their return journey at Cologne; their feast day fell on 21 Oct. Skelton, *Magellan's Voyage*, I, p. 51. Pedro Sarmiento de Gambóa, tried to change the name to Cabo de la Virgen Maria. Markham, *Narratives*, p. 151. It is referred to as Cape Joy by Thomas Candish (Cavendish). Hakluyt, *Principal Navigations*, III, pp. 825 and 828–9.

[4] Cabo Vírgenes is 135 ft (41 m) high. Wood, BL, MS 46A, p. 155, states from Cabo Buen Tiempo 'to Cape Virgin Mary the true Compass is S by W[t] about 20 Leag*ues* but the Course by Compass is So*uth* 29° W*est*. The Land all that way is lowe with white Cliffes: the Sounding all the way is 28 and 30 Fathom Good Sandy ground: the flood setteth betw*een* the 2 Capes NNE[t] and the Ebb SSW[t]: it is high water at full and Change at 10 of the Clock and riseth ab*out* 4 Fathom.'

[5] When the cape is to the west of the observer the land to the west will appear from behind it as a small round hill.

[6] Punta Catalina (52°32′S, 68°46′W), is the northern point of the coast on the south side of the entrance to the Strait of Magellan, from which the coast of Isla Grande de la Tierra del Fuego leads away SE.

[7] Banco Sarmiento extends 20 miles SE from Cabo Vírgenes. The bank is unstable and liable to vary in extent and depth. It consists of shingle and inside the bank coarse sand and shingle mixed; the shallower the water the coarser the bottom. *South America Pilot*, II, para. 7.41.

[8] The tidal stream in the entrance to the Strait runs at 2–5 knots.

wher I Rod Sett WSW: it Runs but Small it Rize nere three fadam: it flows here nere nine aclocke one [on] the Change of the mone. I tryed to Catch fish in all Placis in this Coast with hookes But never Could take any. From the Sand Bancke of[f] the Cap I Steered WSW till I brought the Cap N of me then steered in W: the Cap Beinge three leagus of[f] mee.[1] I went West & WBS & WBN within two leagus of the N Shore: I had theerty Eight and fowerty fadam warter blacke Sand: nere Eight leagus to the W:ward from the Cap all along as I sailed. When you have the Cap North of you you may Se the land of terra foggo[2] ly out SSE in white Clefs of a Preety hight:[3] that Land is distance from the Cap about Eight leagus[4]

[125] **October 1670 the *Sweepstakes* Enteringe the Streights of Magellan** and trents up to the NW:ward that it Comes Soe nere the north Shore that it make But a Passage of about a League Broad which is the first narrow[5] of the Streights of Maggallan. This day I Sailed from the Cap when it was N of me W into the first Enterance which makes Like a deep Bay: nere ten leagus all alonge the Shore within a leage or five miles and had 30 and 36 fadams: the North Shore is the Safe est Saileinge. When you are nine leagus in the bay one [on] the north Shore ther you See Steep Clefes a letle west of a whit Sandhill: those Clefes at the Pointe is Called Point Possession:[6] from there the land lies Roundinge in a bay[7] to the W:ward and to the South W:ward a low shore by the water side and flat ofe [off]: it makes in hills one [on] the NW Land in the Bay their is fower Pecked up Rockes ner together which stands a good waie up the land.[8] The narrow Entranc[9] is SW Southerly from Ponte Possession: distance about Six leagus. Thou maiest keep in the midway & Goe Safe and have 24 fadam warter till thou Comest ner the narrowist Part of all which is But one League Broad and three leagus longe.[10] Their is flats Boath one [on] the north Sid and one [on] the South Side till thou Comest to the narrow which is Steep Beach and Sum Rockes

[1] Wood, BL, MS 46A, p. 156: 'When you sale in or out [of the Strait] you must be sure to give this Cape a good bearth for within the Cape lyeth a long Beach the East point whereof beares from the Cape SSW^{t} by Compas. this beach seemeth to make a harbour between it and the Cape.'

[2] Tierra del Fuego.

[3] Wood, BL, MS 46A, p. 156: 'The Land on the South Side of the Streights mouth is all white Cliffes about the height of the Isle of weight and is about 8 Leagues over from Cape Virgin Mary (but by me Called Cape joy). This South Land haveing Noe name I called it Queene Katherines foreland.'

[4] The width of the entrance to the Strait is about 15 miles.

[5] Primera Angostura (52°30′S, 69°35′W).

[6] Cabo Posesión (52°18′S, 68°58′W). Wood MS 3833, f. 25r: 'This day at 12 we was a Brest of Poynt Position, I being in the Latt*itude* of 52°20′.' Wood, BL, MS 46A, pp. 156–7: 'From Cape joy the Land lyeth in by Compas w*est* 9 Leag*ues* unto a point which the Spaniard Called point poss*ess*ion.' Woods adds a paragraph paraphrasing information from 'A discourse of the West Indies and South Sea written by Lopez Vaz' (in Hakluyt, Principal Navigations, III, pp. 793–6), which describes the actions taken by the Spanish crown to reconnoitre and settle the Strait of Magellan in response to Sir Francis Drake's raids in the Pacific. See Phillips, *Struggle for the South Atlantic*, passim.

[7] Bahía Posesión (52°15′S, 69°12′W).

[8] Orejas de Burro (Ass's Ears); these stand on the hill 2 miles WNW of the summit of Monte Aymond (52°09′S, 69°30′W), 856 ft (261 m).

[9] The entrance to the Narrows. The entrance to Primera Angustora (52°30′S, 69°35′W), lies between Punta Delgada on the north side (from which Banco Dirección extends 5 miles NE with Banco Plumper and Banco Narrow extending a further 6 miles NE), and Punta Anegada on the south side (from which Banco Orange extends ENE 8 miles).

[10] Primera Angostura (First Narrow) is 2 miles wide and 10 miles long.

on the north Side and one [on] the South Side Rise up Clefs of a llettle hight: the land is low one [on] Boath Sides in lettle hommackes. The tide Runs very Stronge in the narrow[1] Boath Ebb and flood and Rizeth fower fadams: it Floweth one [on] the Change day here at Eleven of the Clocke: the Ebb Runeth out of the Streights.[2] This afternone I Gote yust [got just] up to the narrow but the tide Runinge So Stronge out that I Could not Enter into it haveinge a fresh gale of wind at NNE: the wind veared[3] to the SW and Put mee out: three Leagus from the narrow NNE: I anchored in the faierway in twenty five fadam: Peavell Stones and oase: I Rod fast all night: faier weather and lettle wind to night: wher I rode the narrow Bar SSW from mee and the fower Pecked Rocks NW.

Cap Vergen Mary at the N Pointe of the Enterance of the Streights of Maggalan from the North Sea Lies in the Latt*itud* of fivety two degres and twenty Six minuts South of the Line and In Longitud west from the Lizard of England sixty five degres fowerty two m*inuts*[4] and Meridian distance one thousand and [*margin:* va– 17° E] Sixty two leagus. The Land is Plaine and Barran one [on] Boath Sids here without wood: the Land Lies west in from the Cap nere ten leagus: of an indeferent height it have a fale of a low land down to the warters Sid: which low land joine to the beach which Comes from the Cap: their is Shoulds lies from the Pointe of this Beach.

24

Beinge Munday faier weather & lettle wind at SSW. I waied this fore none But findinge my Selfe not able to gitt through the narrow I anchored againe in the faierway in nientenn fadam warter: Smale Stones and oase. Hasey weather to night.

[126] **October 1670 the *Sweepstakes* in the Streights of Magellan**

25

Beinge tusday fooggy weather this morninge wind at NE a fine fresh gale. At fower of the Clocke this morninge I waied and Stood in for the first narrow SSW: the Compas here have Eighten degres variation Easterly: the fooge Comeinge very thicke as I Could not See the Shore and was just Entered in the Narrow I was forced to anchor in the Midle of the Chanell in theerty Eight fadam Peavell Stones: the Eb Sett out of the Streights here very Stronge and Runs out Eight howers: and the flod Seets in But fower howers: the warter Riseth about fower or five fadam. At Seaven this fore none it Cleared up & I waied: wind at NE a fine gale I Steered South South West through the first Narrow: at twelfe aclocke I was throwghet [through it]: then I Steered SW ½ a Pointe westerly for the Second Narrow[5] which is distance from the first narrow nere nine Leagus.[6] The first Narrow is nere one Leage Broad and three Leagus longe:[7] Streight

[1] *South America Pilot*, II, para. 7.29, states that the tidal stream in Primera Angostura (First Narrow) reaches 6–8 knots.

[2] Wood, BL, MS 46A, p. 158: 'The Tyde runneth very strong the Tyde of flood setteth in, the Ebb [out] but the Tyde riseth and falls about 6 or 7 Feet: it is high water at full and change.'

[3] The word 'veared' repeated in the original and struck through.

[4] Cabo Vírgenes is 63°09′W of the Lizard.

[5] Segunda Angostura (Second Narrow) (52°43′S, 70°20′W).

[6] The distance between the two Narrows is 20 miles.

[7] Wood, BL, MS 46A. p. 159: 'The Course by Compas through the Narrow is W^t^SW^t^ and ENE^t^ but the varia*tion* being 17° or 18° the true Course is W*est* 5° S*outh*. The length of the Narrow from E*ast* to W*est* is 3 Leag*ues* which maketh the Disstance from Cape joy or Virginmary to this place 17 Leag*ues*.'

through and deepe warter for I had no Ground at fowerty fadams Soundinge: the land one [on] Boathe Sids of an ordinary height: a lettle Steep up and a Beach at the foot next the warter: the land is low above two leagus in land one [on] Boathe Sids and Barran drie Ground without wood or fresh warter: it is Should Boath Sids at the first Enterance a mile into the Chanell and you will See a Great many Beds of weeds which are driveinge:[1] they are noe danger. But of[f] the Points wher you See Growinge weeds there is Shoule warter have a Care of them for their ar Rockes.[2] Your Best way is to keep the mid way in the Chanell which I did. After you are through the first narrow one [on] the Points to the west are Should a Good way of[f] Espeacially one [on] the Pointe of the north Shore there is a Pointe of Rockes lias a mile of[f] and have weed one [on] them: Give them a berth.[3] After the first Narrow the warter Groues Broad like a Great Bay: it is low land one [on] the Shore one [on] Boath Sids But Rizinge inwards of Preaty high downes: the Shores trents Roundinge till they Come to the Second Narrow like Bayes one [on] Boath Sids: it is from Side to Sid in this warter Six leagus Broad and nere nine Longe.[4] I Sounded as I Sailed through the midle to the Second Narrow and had twenty five fadam: and twenty fadam at an other Soundinge nere the Second Narrow Soe I judge ther is Good Soundinge all through it it[5] was Smale Peavle Stones with Sandy oase. I had a fresh gale and Could not take tim to Sound here all alonge as I Sailed: nere the Second narrow one [on] the north Shor is a Good Bay their is white Clefe and a Cap which is Called Cap Gregoria[6] it is at the Enterance of the Narrow. The land is of an indeferent height toward the warter Side but one [on] the South Side it is Steep up in Clfes all the narrow throwgh and Barran Land aloft and Plaine: and one [on] the North Shore it is in a Bay Roundinge. This narrow is Nere three leagus Longe and two Leagus Broad:[7] I Sounded at the westermost End of this narrow in the faierway & had theerty fadam Rufe Ground:[8] the Points one [on] Boath Sids are Steep up & theer turnes in deepe Bay Boath to the Nortward of the Pointe of the North Shore: & to the South [ward of the] Po[inte of the] S Shore.[9]

[1] The beds of seaweed are floating free.

[2] This sign of danger was well recognized. It is mentioned in a 'Ruttier for the sayd river of *Plate* to the Streight of *Magelane*', in Hakluyt, *Principal Navigations*, III, p. 726, and is commented on in most voyages through the Strait.

[3] This is Bajo Satélite which extends SW from Punta Satélite, the point on the northern side of the narrow at its western end.

[4] The width between the shores of the Second Narrows is 15 miles.

[5] The word 'it' is written three times in the original.

[6] Bahía Gregorio east of Cabo Gregorio (52°40′S, 70°13′W), which is the entrance point on the north side of Segunda Angostura.

[7] 'The S shore of Segunda Angostura is cliffy and higher than the north shore.' *South America Pilot*, II, para. 7.116. The Second Narrow is about 12 miles long and 4 miles wide at its west end. Wood, BL, MS 46A, p. 159: 'The second narrow is in Bredth from one Side to the other about 5 Miles at the East end but at the West end it is something less. The Course by Compas through this narrow is SW by S but the Course is W*es*t 17° So*uth*. The length of this narrow from one end to the other is 3 Leag*ues* which maketh the dist*ance* from Cape joy 28 Leag*ues*.'

[8] This will be from the indentations in the tallow at the bottom of the lead, probably what would be called 'hard' today.

[9] The Point on the north shore is Punta Gracia (52°44′S, 70°32′W), and on the south shore Cabo San Vicente (52°47′S, 70°26′W), with Promontorio Sweepstakes, a prominent headland, 2 miles ENE of it.

[127] October 1670 the *Sweepstakes* in the Streight of Magellan
When you are all most Shoot through this narrow you will See thre Ilands: one is Called Elezabeath Ile[1] which is the Bigest: the other Bigest is Called San Georges Ile:[2] the Le[a]st is Called San Bartlemes Ile:[3] they lie tryanglwis and ar distance the one from the other fower Miles:[4] they are South West from the Narrow & distance fower leagus.[5] The Streights here have a Great Roundinge hooke and turneth away to the S:ward: the Land is one [on] the maine of a Great height and have Snow one [on] the tops of them.[6] Here is a should which lies from the Pointe of the narrow of the South Side towards San Bartlemess Ile: nere a leage of[f] it lie rocks SW from the Pointe. Their is a Great Bay[7] in to the So*uth*ward about this Po*int*: and Shoulds in it and a Smale flat Ile.[8] I had little flatteringe winds for an hower at the west*ern* one [end] of the narrow then the wind Came to the South a fine gale: I stod in to the north Part of Elezabeth Ile in two miles of the Shore and Anchored in Eight fadam and a halfe: Black fine Sand: the E Pointe of the Iland Bar SBE of mee. Faier weather to night: wind at SBW.

26
Beinge Weedensday Cloudy hassey weather wind at SBW a fresh gale. I Could not way the wind Contrary. This morninge I went in my Boate to S[t] Bartholmes Ile and Sounded in the Chanell betwen that Ile & Elezabeths Ile:[9] had noe Ground at theerty fadam: & I Sounded one [on] the North Sid of Elezabeth Ile & had But five and Six fadam Blacke Sand for a league of[f].[10] This day I Saw Ninetenn Indian Men and Eight women and two Chillderin: I went a Shore to them and they traded with us for nives & Beads &c: But I Could not finde that they have any Gould or Silver or any thinge that is God [good]: they are a Miserable Pore People their weomen were Shelles about their Neckes and leather thongs instead of Breaslets: their Cloathinge is

[1] Isla Isabel (52°53′S, 70°44′W). The island was named by Sir Francis Drake for Queen Elizabeth I. Wood, BL, MS 46A, p. 159, advises mariners not to anchor in the broad area between the two Narrows since there is no shelter there. If their cables should part they will certainly be driven ashore, since they can hardly discern the entrance of the Narrow from a distance, due to the low level of the land, and if the visibility should be poor it is almost impossible to find it steering by the compass in the daytime, much less in the night.

[2] Isla Magdalena (52°55′S, 70°35′W).

[3] Isla Marta (52°51′S, 70°35′W).

[4] Isla Isabel is by far the largest of the group, being 7½ miles long, while Isla Magdalena is under 1 mile and Isla Marta smaller still.

[5] Wood, BL, MS 46A, p. 160: 'From the Second narrow to Queen Elizabeth Island the Course by Compas is SW[t] But the true cours is W[t] 28°40′ S[o] Dist*ance* 4 Leag*ues* which maketh 32 from Cape Joy. All the Land from the Second Narrow to the head of Queen Elizabeth Island is very high shewing to be dry & Baren in Some places But in Some valleys the soyle is fertile and Beareth good gras: in the Low Land groweth little Berries which are Excellent good fruite which wee called Magellan Grapes: they are of a Purple Colour Seeded tasting like our European Grapes: they grow single on Small Bushes like Berries. there is allso another Sort of Berry like a Small Cherry of a Red Colour wee called them harts.'

[6] Cordillera Gregorio rise to 1,180 ft (360 m) north of Segunda Angostura with Cerro Centinela, 879 ft (268 m) and Monte Garcia 646 ft (197 m) west of it.

[7] Bahía Lee lies directly south of Cabo San Vicente with the entrance to Bahía Gente Grande (52°57′S,70°12′W), 10 miles south of the point

[8] Isla Contramaestre (52°57′S, 70°22′W), which lies in the entrance to Bahía Gente Grande.

[9] Paso Reina (52°54′S, 70°39′W).

[10] Paso Real (52°51′S, 70°44′W).

Nothinge But a lose Skine hangine Mentle [mantle] fassion: al the other Part of their body is naked: they are But of a Midle Stature and tawny Coullor. The thinge wee had of them were Bowes and arrows & their Coats Skins of dear: they are of a Rud behaviour: to Catck at every thinge they See But Part from Nothinge: I left them quikly & whent aboard.

[128] **October 1670 the *Sweepstakes* in the Streights of Magallan**
27
Beinge Thursday wind still at SW a fresh gale. I Rod fast. The hills one [on] the North Shore Begin to Show them Selfes of a Great height & Covered with Snow: the Land is a Great height one [on] the South Side with Snow one [on] the hills: this is a very Good Road with the wind at South and to the westward & Northerly to the NNE.[1] The Strights Rounds here of a Great Breadth and turnes away to the Southward: Elezabeaths Ile is nere thre leags in Lenght and one leag over:[2] it is a Gren Grassey Iland without wood or fresh warter: as wee Could Perceve: their is Small beris Groues thir of Couller Red much like a hurt:[3] the other two Ilands ar Green Gras aloft[4] & full of holes where the Penguins Breeds.[5] This day my Boat went Round Elezabeths Iland[6] and found a Chanell about half a mile Broad of fower fadam warter betwen the Ile & the maine at the West End.[7] Their Grows Great Bushey woods one [on] the maine & very thick up the Side of the high hill. My Boat went to St Geor[g]es Ile which is that Sum Call Penguns Ile for the quantity of fowles: it is the Southermost Ile. At night Shee Cam aboard with a hundered Penguns: they are in holes & must be Pulled out with gafes: they are hard to Gitt. Here gose great Riplens [ripplings] about this Ile & thou must have a Care of thy Boate.[8] It Blow hard to night. I Rod fast.

28
Beinge Friday wind at SW and Blew hard all day. I Rod fast. We have Senn Seaverall firs as we have Sailed in the Streights one [on] the South Side & this day their was two very Great ones. The Endians as were one [on] Elezabeths Ile are of[f] unto the maine. Here Runes But a Small tide and Rizeth not Past two fadam: it Runes Soe unCertain as I Could not under Stand it in observinge the time of full Sea one [on] the Change of the mone But as much as I Could Perceve the flood Comes from the Southward. Here is whales: But I Could never as yet Catch any fish: But one Marey[9] here are wild Goose & Duckes: But Small Stoore of other fowles.

[1] The anchorage is sheltered from the winds listed.
[2] It is 7½ miles long and 2 miles wide.
[3] Hurtleberry, whortelberry. This might be *Rubus geoides*, which grows up to 2½ ft (72 cm) high and has orange or red berries that are eaten by the native peoples. Moore, *Flora*, pp. 127–9, 369.
[4] On top.
[5] See above p. 208, n. 13.
[6] Wood, BL, MS 3833, f. 25r: 'This day I went Round Q E Island in the pinis with the Leff*tenant* & we went to St George^s^ Island & Brought aboard 100 pinguins.'
[7] Paso Real, on the NW side of Isla Isabel leads to Paso Pelicano, between the west end of the island and Cabo Porpesse on the mainland.
[8] The tidal streams run at 2–5 knots in the vicinity of the island with overfalls over the rocks off its east side.
[9] This is presumably the flatfish Mary-sole or sail-fluke (*Rhombus megastoma*), or smear-dab (*Pleuronectes microcephalus*). *NOED*.

29

Beinge Satterday wind at WBS a fresh gale. I wayed & Stood Betwen Elezabeths Ile and San Bartholumes Ile and turned up to the maine one [on] the North Side: at the Southwest End of Elezabeth Ile and their anchored in a lettle Bay:[1] about a mile & halfe of[f] the Shore & had feivtene fadam: Black Sand: San Georges Ile Bear NE of mee: this Bay is yust [just] to the Southward of a whitte Steep Clefe which is one [on] the maine at the South End of the Passagge betwen Elezabeths Ile and the maine.[2] I Could not Perceve much tide to Run here: this Bay is Steep to the Shore for I had much troble to Gitt to an anchor: it Blew soe hard at SW. The Chanell Come betwen Elezabeths and San Bartlmes Ile & Runs up alonge By the South Side of Elezabeths Ile to this Bay: and then to the Southward: ner the Shore.

[129] **October 1670 the Sweepstaks in the Streights of Magallan**

It is deep warter all alonge nere the Iland: ther lies a Great Should from the west End of San Georges Iland: at least a league longe to the westward:[3] their Groues weeds one [on] it as ther dos uppon all the Shoulds in this Streights for wher thou Seest Groueinge weeds ther is Shoald warter: this Should lies untoward in the way: my Boat Souned over it & on it ther was fower fadam warter Sea By Ground: just over to the Southward tenn fadams:[4] a Great Riplen [rippling] Runs over it. The Streights here is Seaven Leagus Broad E & W from Side to Sid But Grous narrow & narrower to the Southward: the Land here one [on] Boath Sids is a good height: in land the hills are high one [on] boath Sids and Covered all white with Snow the lower land next the warrter Side is Geenesh: and on the NW Side full of Great Busshey woods very thick. Faier weather to night. I Rod fast.

30

Beinge Sunday hasey foogey weather this morninge wind at West a fine gale. I waied and Stood to the Southward Close by the Shore: I had oasey Sand where I rode: the Land lies South alonge here the hills are indeferent high But trend down low to the warter Side and are full of Gren Busshes very thicke:[5] and a letle more Southerly it is woods of indeferent Good timber But not very tall: the wood Groues much like Elmes and Allders.[6] Here are Bayes one [on] the nort Shore: Betwen Elezabeths Ile & Port fammine where a man may Anchore & Ride well with a westerly wind: if he be benighted in a mile or halfe

[1] Bahía Laredo (52°58′S, 70°48′W).

[2] Cabo Porpesse (52°56′S, 70°47′W).

[3] There is a shoal, Banco Walker, 3 miles to the westward of Isla Magdalena (St George or Penguin Island), which is 3 miles long in a NNE–SSW direction, with a least depth of 20 ft (6 m) on it, but it is not connected to the island. Wood, BL, MS 46A, p. 162: 'At S[t] Georges there lyeth a Bank about a Mile Long on which is about 3 or 4 Fethom and may be in some places less but this Bank may bee seene a great way off for there groweth a great many weeds on it.'

[4] The meaning of this is obscure. It probably means there was 4 fathoms of water over the shoal, with seaweed all over the ground, and just to the southward of it 10 fathoms.

[5] This could be *Chiliophyllum fuegianum*, an erect evergreen shrub growing to 3–4 ft (90–120 cm) high, or *Berberis buxifolia*, an erect shrub up to 13 ft (4 m) high, both of which are common in this area. Moore, *Flora*, pp. 27, 66, 225.

[6] The dominant species in the deciduous forest in this area and further west are *Nothofagus pumilo* and *N. Antarctica*, the former growing to 100 ft (30 m) while the latter only reaches 50 ft (15 m). They are of the family *Fagaceae* to which beech trees belong. Moore, *Flora*, pp. 26, 81.

a mile of the Shore. As thou Saile alonge betwen Elezabeths Ile & Port famen ther is faier Sandy Soundings at 15 and Sixten fadam deep in Severall Placess But in the Chanell two or three miles of[f] ther is noe Ground at a hundered fadam.[1] Gusty weather today: I keet [kept] as nere the north Shore as I Could make what way Possible to the Southward: the wind at SW and Gusty in flaws of[f] the hills & night Groueinge I Goot into the Shore and anchored in a Smal bay in a Leaven fadam warter: Gravelly Ground. In this Bay [*margin:* Fresh warter] their is two Rivelets of fresh warter wherfore I Called it fresh warter Bay:[2] alsoe it is Convenient to fill: and here is Good Wood: the wood very thick and Grow down to the Sea Side and the trees ar one foot & half through: here is allsoe Bushes much like Currant Busshes: this Bay is one [on] the north Shore and it is tenn leagus from the west End of Elesabeths Iland to the Southward. The Streights here is about five leages Broad from Shore Sid to Shore Side. I Rod fast all night: Calm Sum times and Sumtimes Gusty. This day Thomas Stone died a [*margin:* A man Died] Seaman.

[130] **October 1670 the *Sweepstakes* in the Streights of Magalan at Po*rt* Famin**
31
Beinge Munday faier weather this morninge and letle wind at West. I waied and Stood to the Southward:[3] it Blow hard to day in Gusts at WNW. The Shore liys South alonge to Port Famin[4] which is a Prety deep Sandy Bay and a Good Rod from the wind at N to the SBW: you will have Seaven & Eight fadam warter in a faier Birth in the Bay. As you Come from the northward with in fower leags of Port famin ther is Revellts of fresh warter Runs down in many Places in valles where their is Grenn Trees: the Shore have faier Shouldings ner it in a quarter of a mile of[f] is fowrten and fivt*en* fadam But forther out noe ground.[5] In a leage and half of Port famin to the N:ward ther is a fine Small Bay[6] with a faier Rivellet of fresh warter and Conveniet fillinge: and Good wood and Larg timber trees of two foot trow [through] and fowerty foot longe in the Spindle of Good wood much like to Chasnut trees or Beech[7] ar very Good Graine and Stife: here is faier and Good timber in many Places in the Streights. This Bay have Eight fadam warter in three Cables lenghts[8] of the Shoree: Gravelly Ground. One [on] the ENE northerly Pointe of this Bay is

[1] Wood, BL, MS 46A, p. 162: 'From Queen Elizabeths Iseland to Port Famine the Course by Compas is *South* ½ W*est* But the true Course is S by E[t] 13 Leag*ues*.'

[2] Bahía Agua Fresca (53°23′S 70°58′W).

[3] Wood, BL, MS 3833, f. 25v: 'The Cap*tain* with the Pinnis went in Close under the Shore & he found 2 of the Magelanicans Cannoes & Spake with the People.'

[4] Puerto San Juan de la Posesíon or Puerto del Hambre (53°38′S, 70°56′W). Sarmiento de Gamboa left 338 colonists, with soldiers and craftsmen, there in May 1581. It proved impossible to provide the colonists with regular supplies. Thomas Cavendish found 16 men and 3 women surviving in Ciudad del Rey Felipe in 1587, and evidence that most of the inhabitants had died of starvation. He named it Port Famine. He carried one soldier away with him. A ship from Bristol picked up another man in 1589. Hakluyt, *Principal Navigations*, III, p. 806; Phillips, *Struggle for the South Atlantic*, p. 51.

[5] The depth of water was too great for the length of the lead line.

[6] This is Bahía Carreras (53°36′S 70°55′W), which is actually 3 miles north of Puerto del Hambre. It is the only bay in the area with a shoal of rocks running out from the northern point. It is called Canoa Bay on Narbrough's 'Royal Map' (Foldout).

[7] Chestnut trees or beech. The last word is not clear and looks like 'beect' but beech trees are referred to below. See below, p. 264.

[8] The cable's length is about 200 yards. See above, p. xviii.

Should: in Rocks nere tow Cables lenth into the Sea. In this Bay wee Spacke with Indians and went aShore to them and were very kindly Eused By them: they Seme to Be a very quite People for they were very femilliar[1] with us Boath ther men and weomen: the wemen delighted much that we Should tie Beads & Reabends [ribbons] about their Neckes and armes: as wee dide: I Gave them Severall things as they dissiered: Beads and hatchets and Bills and Knives &c Set*era*. They all much Disser any things as is Red: as Red Cloath Boath wollen and linen. They Gave me ther Skin Coats which are dere Skines and Sealeskins dresed after ther maner and Sewed together like a keferline[2] which is all the Cloathing they have: they are of an ordinary Stature and indeferent handsum faces: the women much Better faced then the men: ther visage longes: all of a Red Culor and Euse Paints. They were Much Pleased with our Companis: they Gave us food as they Eat which is Musles and limpets and Sea Eggs Raw. They are Ever lafeinge [laughing] when they are Pleased: they have a great many Small Childerin: their levieing is hard: they had here two Canoas which were mad of the Bark of the tres Sewn togeter with thongs: and Splented with inSide Peeckeing up at Boath Ends a Good height[3] and Set out with Stickes aloft:[4] they had Sand lay in ther Boathams and a fier in Each Canoa: their Canoas ar much like the New England Indian Canoas But not So handsum: thes Canoas Might Carry Eight men apeece. I Could not Perceve they had any Gould or Silver or any thing that is Good: the Riches they wer [wear] is Musshells and other Small Shells in Braclets about their Necks and Juells of Shells at their Brests.

[131] **October 1670 the *Sweepstaks* in the Strights of Magalan: at Po*rt* Famin**
Their is another Small Bay & Cove just before you Com at the Pointe to Goe in to the Bay of Porte famin: this Northeasterly Pointe of Port famim[5] is of an indeferent height and Barran in Sum Places and Singele trees Grow on it: Especall one Singele tree Grows one [on] the Plaine hill which you will See after you Com about the Pointe.[6] The Bay is a fine Shold Sandy Bay: you may Ride in Nine or tenn fadams warter in the midle of the Bay: it flous[7] at twelfe aclock one [on] the Change Day and the flood Comes from the Southward: it Riseth about tenn foote. One [on] the South Pointe of this Bay is low and Sandy and much drift timber lies one [on] it. Ther is a fine River of fresh warter Runs into the Sea:[8] here I wooded and wartered. All the land is Mountainnus and full

[1] Familiar: affable, courteous, sociable, friendly. *NOED*.

[2] This could be a cameline, a kind of stuff made (or supposed to be made) of camel's hair, or a garment made of this material, *NOED*. Cameline was a recognized form of woollen material in the 14th and 15th centuries. Piponnier, *Cloth Merchants' Inventories*, pp. 237, 243 & 245. It might also be derived from Keffel: A horse, *NOED*, and mean a horse-blanket. In any case it signifies a single cloak-like garment as shown in the vignettes on the 'Royal Map' (Foldout). In Bodelian, Rawl. MS A. 318, Narbrough says that their garments were 'in forme of a Carpet of about five foot square', see below, p. 466.

[3] The meaning of this is not clear, but it probably means that there was split wood inside (forming the ribs, thwarts and gunwales) and that the boat rose to a peak at each end.

[4] Literally this should mean 'set out with sticks above', but it probably means the sticks were used for masts.

[5] Punta Santa Ana (53°38′S, 70°55′W).

[6] Wood, BL, MS 46A, p. 163: 'You may know Port Famine when you come from the Northward for on the North point Standeth a great tree along [alone] by it selfe.'

[7] The tide flows, or is high.

[8] Río San Juan enters the harbour on the west side close north of Punta Sedger. This river was named River Sedger by Narbrough after his carpenter. See below, p. 588, n. 7.

of thicke woods very Green: the timber much like Beech[1] the land of a Good Sile Sumwhat Sandy: the hills Boath one [on] the North Shore and South ar Covered with Snow one [on] their toop.[2] I Could not Perceive any Place wher the Spanard had Bulded their Citty here.[3] The Gras is longe one [on] the Ground wher ther is no woods: here are Small beris one [on] little Bushes like Billberis and wild Currant trees: the woods are of Severall Sorts of tres.[4]
This day I anchored here the wind at SSW a fresh gale Calme tonight: the wind from the South to the ENE Blowes Right into the Bay.

1
November 1670 Beinge Tusday wind at South to day a fresh gale. I rod fast. I fetched wood and warter: in this River are Gess [geese] and Duckes and teall. This day the Same Indians which I Saw the day before came to me wher I was Cuting wood and Eat and dranke with us: and Gave us Bows and arrows: they will Eat any Sort of our food: wee gave them Seale oyle they much dissiered it to oile them Selfes with it they were unwillinge to Part from us. Calme tonight: I filled fresh wart*er* in my Boats in the River.

2
Beinge Weddensday Calme. This fore none wee fetched wood and warter: one of the ould Indian Men Came aboard of the Ship in My Boate to See the Shipp: wee filled his Belly and Gave him Beads and Knivs and Red Caps and flaps for the woomen to cover their Privates for they are Naked But mightyly aShamed and Eus [use] all Means Possible to hid their fore Parts. The Weomen Came to the warter Side: I gave them Severall Sorts of Beads and Glases: they were Mighty Pleased.

[1] Trees of the beech family (*Fagaceae*) grow in this area, see above, p. 262. *Nothofagus betuloides*, a tree up to 100 ft (30 m) high with trunk up to 6½ ft (2 m) in diameter, is also found here and further west, on better drained sites and usually away from the coast. Moore, *Flora*, pp. 28, 82.

[2] Wood, BL, MS 46A, p. 163: 'As you are sayleing from the Iselands to Port Famine you will See on the East side a great opening, as if there were a passage through for to the South, and you will see all the Land shut up and [Wood, MS 46B inserts 'noe' here] opening to be seene therefore have a care that you Saile not in there for feare you chance not to come out againe Except it goes out into the East Sea as the Spaniard Calls it the Enterance of St Cebastian.' This great opening is Paso Boquerón (53°30′S, 70°25′W), which leads to Bahía Inútil and does not connect with Bahía San Sebastián on the east coast of Isla Grande Tierra del Fuego.

[3] Wood, BL, MS 46A, p. 163: 'Here it was the Spaniard builded a Fortificac*io*n and named it the Cittadell of Don Phillip [Ciudad del Rey Felipe] which place was to prevent the English from passing but in truth it was to little purpose as well Say Dover Castle Could hinder all ships from passing the Chanell for at the first place the Straights are 6 Leagues over. M[r] Candish [Cavendish] fired their unhabited houses and Digged 4 great Gunnes out of the ground which the Spaniards had hid there. Wee could not finde that ever there was ever such a place built.'

[4] See above, n. 1. *Maytenus magellanica*, a small tree up to 23 ft (7 m) high, may be found in this area together with *Pernettya mucronata*, a shrub growing up to 6½ ft (2 m) fringing the forest above the high-water mark. *Ribes magellanicum*, up to 13 ft (4 m) high bears fruit, as does *Empetrum rubrum*, a low bush, the berries of both of which were eaten by the indigenous inhabitants. *Chiliotrichum diffusum*, another low shrub, and *Berberis empetrifolia*, a prostrate shrub, or *Berberis buxifolia*, an erect shrub up to 13 ft (4 m), both of which have pruinose purplish berries eaten by the local people, and grow in this area. *Berberis ilicifolia* is a possibility but it is an erect shrub or small tree up to 23 ft (7 m) and so is unlikely to be described as a bush. Moore, *Flora*, pp. 26–7, 66, 68, 123, 140, 160, 225, 368–9.

[132] **November 1670 the *Sweepstakes* Sailinge from Porte famine**

3

Beinge thursday Calme this moringe. At Eight aclocke I waied the wind at NW: I Steered from Port famin SBE half a pointe E*aster*ly by my Compas: five leagus to a Point[1] which makes the Strights Shew as if it were Sheet up:[2] it Rounds to the South westward. From this Pointe I Steered SWBW and SW nere fower leagus the Land high one [on] Boath Sids and Cragey hills: the South Shore Rounds up to the westward in Bayes and Shew as if ther were Chanells or freets[3] into it in two or three Places hereabouts: the nort Shore have Bays and Covs all alonge here & Small Iles ner the Shore: the Streights here is about fower leagus over from the north Shore to the South Shore[4] and Makes as if ther were no Passage: the Lands Sheats in the one with the other and the Streights Rounds here by lettle and little to the westward and Growes narrower and narower: at Cap froward it is not more then three Leagus Broad[5] and then it makes away to the WBN Sumwhat Broader: it is three leagus from the Pointe before mentioned to Cap froward and I Steered SWBW from the P*ointe* to Cap froward: So it is Eight leagus from famin Bay to the Pitch of Cap froward[6] which is a high hill and Steep up:[7] noe Ground to be Goot in the Chanell. The South Shore is very Cragey one [on] the hills with Rockes and Sum woods one [on] them and much Snow: the Shor Sid Steep to and Rockey. Here is Severall Small Coves one Boath Shores for Boats and Ships if they were well discovered: here is a Cove one [on] the South Side yust over aginst Cap froward Sumwhat to the Southwestward. The South Sore [*sic*] is Ilands and Coves all alonge:[8] the South land to the westward of Cap froward is very Rockey & Cragey with little or noe wood Groweinge one [on] it But a kind of yeallowes [yellowish] Moss: in tufs: and So it Continus for Severall Leagus. Very Gusty to night and foggey. I layd Plyinge to & fro to the westward of Cap froward three leagus all night.

Cap Froward is the Southermost Land of Amarica and Lyes in the Latt*itud* of feivety three degrees feivty two Minuts So*uth* and in Longitud west from the Lizard Sixty Eight degr*ees* & Fowerty min*uts*:[9] Meridian distance one thousand and ninety nine Leagus 2 mils.

[1] Cabo San Isidro (53°47′S, 70°58′W).

[2] Shut up, there was no way out from a closed bay. Wood, BL, MS 46A, p. 165 'When you are off this Point you Cannot perceive which way the passage goeth and one that knowes it not would think that there were noe passage the Land being high seemeth as though the North Side joyned to the South soe that you would thinck it was to the Southward of you but as you Saile further you will see a passage open to the westward about Cape froward. From this Point to Cape Forward [Cabo Froward] 53°54′S, 71°18′W] the Course By compas is SSW[t] 3 Leagues but the true Course is So*uth* 3° [west] with this Cape is the Southermost Promontory of Land of all the Continent of America whose is 54°02′ So*uth* and difference of from the Lizard is 66°32′ W*est*.'

[3] Fret, a breach or passage made by the sea. *NOED*.

[4] South of Puerto del Hambre the Strait is 8 miles wide and off Cabo San Isidro it is 5 miles wide.

[5] It is actually 5 miles broad, a little under 2 leagues.

[6] Distance about 23 miles.

[7] Wood, BL, MS 46A, p. 166: 'This Cape is very high steep and Rockey and very much given to flawes of winde therefore was named Cape froward'. *South America Pilot*, II, para. 7.354, notes 'Cabo Froward, the S extremity of Península Brunswick and of the mainland of South America ... rises abruptly to an elevation of 359 m [1,155 ft]. The cape is backed by Morro Santa Agueda, and Monte Victoria lies 2¼ miles NNW.'

[8] Bougainville examined three bays in this area in 1767, Caleta Beaubasin (54°05′S, 71°02′W), Bahía Mazarredo (53°58′S, 71°30′W) and Caleta Cascade (53°58′S, 71°31′W), and confirmed them as excellent anchorages. Dunmore, *The Pacific Journal*, pp. 19–20.

[9] Cabo Froward lies in 53°54′S, 71°18′W which is 66°06′W of the Lizard.

Pointe Famin in the Streights of Magilan in which Bay the Spaniards Built the Citty of Don Philliph Lyes in the Latt*itud* of feivty three degrees theerty Minuts South of the Equator and in Longitud west from the Lizard of England Sxty Eight degr*ees* and nine minuts:[1] and Meridian distance one thousand and Ninty two Leagus west. At Port Famin and at Cap Froward and in the Streights of Magilan My Compases now have Seaventen degres tenn Minuts variation Easterly: that is the North Point varies Easterly so much.

[133] **November 1670 the *Sweepstakes* in the Streights of Magallan**

4

Beinge Friday Calme all day. I layd driveinge in the Streights a lettle to the westward of Cap Froward and Could not gett a Place to Anchor in: it is Steep to the Shore[2] here and there a Place is Sand where a man may Stoop for a night: the tids Runs here But ordinary and the flood Comes from the Northward:[3] and it is a high warter at Cap Froward at a quarter of an houer Past a Leaven one [on] the full and Change of the mone: it Riseth about three fadam by the Shore scarce that. I doe not Perceive any turnings or wochings[4] of the tids here as Sume writs of that have Sailed here formerly But the tids Runes as ordinarily as in other Coasts. I lay be Calmed all this Night in the Midle of the Chanell and drove But two Leagus to the Eastward with a hole tide of Flood. The Snow lies very thick one [on] the hills one [on] Boath Shores.

5

Beinge Satterday a fine gale this moringe at East. I Steered west north west by my Compas to Git under the north Shore for one [on] the South Shore is Small Iles and Cragey Rockes and Coves. This Reach lies from Cap Froward WNW nine Leagus or tenn there it Maks a Shoetinge up [shutting up]: the Streights Rounds to the Northwest. On the north Shore fower leags to the west of Cap Froward is a small Sandy bay:[5] and a fine fresh River:[6] their is feivten fadam two Cables lenth of the Shore: Six leagus west from Cap froward one [on] the north Shore to the westward of a Steep hill[7] the land trents low to the warter Sid: for three leagus west ther is another fine Sandy Bay[8] wher you may anchor in Eight nine or tenn fadam fower Cables lenght of[f] the Shore: here is a Rivelet of fresh warter. Oppposet to this Bay one [on] the South Side wee Saw a fier newly mad By the Indians at the Sight of our Shipp. The wind Came to the north west and blew in flaws: I Plied to the westward

[1] Port Famine (Puerto del Hambre) lies in 53°38′S, 70°56′W which is 65°44′W of the Lizard.

[2] Steep to, meaning that the depth of water increases rapidly away from the shore.

[3] The direction of the channel directly off Cape Froward is east–west but to the east of the Cape it turns to the north towards Port Famine. The flood tide therefore comes from the direction of Port Famine, and flows from the east round the Cape.

[4] Turnings or workings, swirls or whirlpools.

[5] Bahía Wood (53°49′S, 71°37′W), named by Narbrough for his mate, Giles Wood, who was in the boat which examined it. See below, pp. 476, 589. Hacke, 'Captain Wood's voyage', p. 89: 'Called by our Captain *Wood's*-Bay, according to my name.' This remark does not appear in either John Wood's Sailing Directions, BL, MS 46A, or his journal, BL, MS 3833.

[6] Río San José runs into the head of the bay.

[7] This is Cabo Holland (1,299 ft (396 m), 53°47′S, 71°41′W), which forms 'a remarkable bold ridge, 4 miles in length, lying paralell [*sic*] to the NE shore. The SW side of the ridge has precipitous cliffs with densely wooded ledges; the NE side slopes gradually to the valley of Río San José.' *South America Pilot*, II, para. 7.353.

[8] Bahía Cordes (53°43′S, 71°55′W).

what I Could and Anchored in a Bay one [on] the north Shore in nine fadam warter Sandy Ground: half a mile of[f] the Shore.[1] The wind at WNW to night. This Bay have a fine Sandy Cove in it were their is two fadam warter: the Bay is just to the Eastward of Cap Gallant:[2] Cap Gallant is theereten or fowerten Leagus to the westward of Cap froward:[3] it is one [on] the north Shore and it is the Cap which is at the Begin[in]g of the NW Streight.

[134] **November 1670 the *Sweepstakes* in the Streights of Magallan**

6

Beinge Sunday Calme this forenone I Rod fast. In this Bay Called Fortiscue Bay their is a Brav[4] Small harbower in it wher a ship may Secur her Selfe without anchor or Cable: it is Sandy one [on] Boath Sids and noe tide Runs here is Sixten foot warter at a Low warter: noe wind Can hurt you: the tids Rize about ten foot it is a hige warter at twelf aclocke one [on] the Change day here. This Harbower I Called Port Gallant[5] for it lies just to the Eastward of Cape gallant: heres two Streames of fresh warter Runs into it: and Much woods about it of Good timber. The land is low by the warters Sid to the Eastward and a bay about two miles to the Eastward with a lettle Ileland & Rockes in it it is Called Cordis Bay.[6] The Land to the west and north of Port Gallant is very high snow hills for this Port is just at the Foot of them.[7] The Streights is fower leagus Broad here from the north Shor to the South Shore:[8] But here lies twoo Great Iles[9] in the Chanell E & We lenthwise nere in the Midle of the Streights of[f] of Cap Gallant: their is Smal Iles about them five or Six these Ilands ar full of timber. Here the Streights Rounds to the Northwest ward and Makes Sheetinge [shutting] up So as a man would thinke ther were noe Pasage: their is Severall Small Iles lies all alonge the South Shore and one [on] the South Shore ther is a Great many Good harbowers But I had not time to discover them now. The Land one [on] Boath Sids is in Cragey hills and Rockes little wood one [on] the south Shore, that one [on] the north Shore is not so Good as that at Port famin. In Port Gallant wee Saw two Indians huts or Cabins and at the Great Iland of[f] of Cap Gallant I Saw one Indian Cabin netly Built like an arbor with Bowes [boughs]: In it I left Beads and rings &c: not touching any thinge belonging to it. I Suppos the People wer gone a fishinge or huntinge for their food. Noe Beasts in the woods or fowells or fish in the Sea as wee Can See here But a Great many whales all the Streights alonge as I have Sailed.

This after none I waied wind at SE a fine gale: I Steered west two leagus and then NW one leage and a halfe and went into a fine Sandy Bay which is Called Elezabeths Bay:[10] it

[1] Bahía Fortescue (53°42′S, 72°00′W).

[2] Cabo Gallant (53°42′S, 72°02′W). Cabo Gallant is a massive steep-to cape which rises to Monte Cross, 2,460 ft (750 m), 1½ miles N.

[3] The distance is 23 miles.

[4] This word is spelled 'brav' in the original and it would appear to be either 'braw' or 'brave', both of which have the same meaning – worthy, excellent, capital, fine. *NOED*.

[5] Caleta (Puerto) Gallant (53°41′S, 72°00′W).

[6] Bahía Cordes (53°43′S, 71°55′W).

[7] Monte Cross, see above, 2.

[8] It is 7–8 miles wide.

[9] Islas Charles (53°44′S, 72°06′W).

[10] Bahía Isabel (53°37′S, 72°12′W). Wood, MS 46A, p. 167: 'Four Leagues NW[t] by Compass from the Cape on the North side lyeth a Brave Sandy Bay which Mr Candish called Elizabeth Bay where you have very good Anchoring in 8 or 9 Fathome: on the East side of this Bay is a little Ledge of Rocks which you must give a Bearth.' See, Hakluyt, *Principal Navigations*, III, p. 806.

is one [on] the North Shore and at the first Begininge of the NW Rech [reach]: here the Streights is But five Miles Broad. I Rod in this Bay all night wind at West: I anchored in twelfe fadam Sandy Ground: the tids Runs indeferent Stronge and Rise two fadam and Better, at the Begininge of this Reach ther Runs a Riplinge of the tids Cros the Chanel: the flood Comes from the westward. Two leags to the westward of this Bay the Streights Makes Sheetings up.

[135] **November 1670 the *Sweepstakes* in the Streights of Magallan: in Elezabethes Bay**

7

Beinge Munday Cloudy foggey weather wind at W and at NW. I Rod fast all day: I went in my Boat over to the South Shore But Saw nothinge in the land worth observation: the land is full of Ereguler hills with Snow and of a Bogey Moassey quallety with trees and Rushey Grass noe Beasts or fowles Sene: Sum Gineper [juniper] tres[1] the other tres Such as are one [on] the north Shore: this afternone I went aboard againe. I Saw wher the Indians have Ben most Part wher I went in the woods: one [on] Boath Shores ther are trees Beare leaves like Bay trees or lemon trees whose Barke is very hoat of Strenght much like hoat Ginger:[2] and thicke the trees are in Good quantities: I garthered of the Barke to Carry a Longe with mee. The wind At west all night a fresh gale I rod fast though one a Lee Shore.[3]

8

Beinge Tusday Gusty Cloudy weather wind at WNW and raine to day. I Rod fast haveing boath my Bower anchors at Ground: very fogegy this Eveinge and Raine and gusty weather: I fitched a long boats Ladinge of fresh warter: much raine to night: But Snow on the hills.

9

Beinge wedensday Gusty Rainey weather all this day wind at West: al the hills are white with Snow which fell last night blew and rained all this day and night the wind Cam to the NNW.

10

Beinge thursday Rainey this morninge wind at NW and began to blow hard: at Eight aclock I let fall my Sheat anchor and Rod by my Sheat anchor and Best Bower. Much

[1] The only member of the family *Cupressaceae*, to which the Junipers belong, growing in this area is *Pilgerodendron uviferum*. It reaches up to 33 ft (10 m) high and is found in the coastal forest and on sheltered lowland bogs further inland. It was also referred to as *Libocedrus tetragona*, or *Thuja tetrogona*. Moore, *Flora*, pp. 63–5.

[2] The Winter's bark tree (*Drimys winteri*), called after Captain John Winter of the *Elizabeth*, who sailed with Drake to the South Seas in 1577. It is a tree growing up to 65 ft (20 m) high, trunk up to 3 ft (1 m) in diameter, with oblanceolate to elliptical leaves, shiny green above, glaucous or white punctate beneath (not unlike the leaves of the bay tree, *Laurus nobilis*), with small white flowers and a bluish-black shiny berry. It is found throughout the western part of the Strait and together with *Nothofagus betuloides* may become co-dominant or locally dominant. Moore, *Flora*, pp. 28, 65.

[3] Lee shore, with the wind blowing towards the shore, and therefore making departure difficult.

wind and Raine to day and Snow and haile filthy fowle weather all day and night wind at west.

11

Beinge friday wind betwen the SW and NW and blew and Rained and Snowed all day and very Could and vile and Base weather: the hils Covered with Snow. Gusty weather all this night.

12

Beinge Satterday Gusty weather wind at SW: and Snow Sumwhat less wind this forenone I waied my Sheat anchor and howe Short of my Best Bower and found the Cable much worne. To night faier weather: I fetched two Long boats ladinge of fresh water.

[136] **November 1670 the *Sweepstakes* in the Streights of Magallan C*ap* quad**

13

Beinge Sunday faier weather but Coald little wind at SE. I waied this morninge at Six a Clocke out of Elezabeth Bay and mad what Saile I Could to the west ward: it was But lettle wind all day and offen flatinge Everiway[1] by Reason of the high land. At twelfe aclocke I was of[f] San Jorems River[2] which is a Great Chanell or River one [on] the north Side and runes into the Land northwest then winds to the northward through high Snowey hills: a man would judge that River to be the Streights till he Come nere it to See the Streights open to the westward for the land Sheats one in with the other[3] a league to the westward of San Joroms Chanell or River. Two leagus from Elezabeth Bay to the westward one [on] the north Shore ther is a fresh water river[4] But Should within and about a musket Shot[5] broad: it runs into the Land I know not how far: I went into [it] with my Boate about a mile: the land trent low from the hills to boath Sids of it the land is full of woods one [on] Boath Sids the River the ground is of a boogey Mosey Soile: much like our Rotton heathi ground in England the timber but ordinary. In this River I Saw Gees all whit and Sum Black and white:[6] they ar as Big as Brant Gees: here is many

[1] Varying in every direction.

[2] Canal Jerónimo (53°33′S, 72°23′W); variants San, St, Jerom, Jorem, Jorum.

[3] Shuts one in with the other; the two sides appear to overlap so that it looks as if there is no channel through.

[4] Río Batchelor (53°34′S, 72°19′W), which flows into Rada York; variants, Battchellers. Wood, BL, MS 46A p. 167: 'Two Leagues NW by W[t] by Compass from Queen Elizabeths Bay lyeth another Sandy Bay which is a good Roade for ships that are bound either into the South or North Sea you may Anchor in 8 or 10 Fathoms good Ground. In this Bay is a Fresh water River into which you may Rowe 4 Miles up with your Boate. In this Place M[r] Candish killed Some of the Natives out of a humour. The Tyde Setteth indifferent strong the Flood setteth to the Eastward and the neape to the westward the Tyde riseth & falleth 10 Foote. I called this place Yoarke Roade when you are in the Roade all the Land to the westward is shutt up Soe that you would thinck there were noe passage that way.'

[5] About 400 yards.

[6] Probably the kelp goose (*Chloephaga hybrida*), the male of which is white, the female black with white barring below and white tail, which inhabits the area through the Strait of Magellan and up the Chilean coast. Jaramillo, *Birds*, p. 74.

duckes.[1] Here is Good anchoringe in the Bayes to the Eastward and westward of this River a mile or more or before the Rivers mouth: you may Ride in Seaven Eight or teen fadam warter: in Eighter [either] Places before Spoaken of and you will have Sandy Gravelly Ground: and be more then five Cables lenth from the Shore: the tids Runes indeferent and Rise about ten foot here but how it flows I know not, nor whether the flood Comes from the westward or not:[2] this River I Called Batchellers River: from this River it is about Six mils to San Jeroms River. The Streights is here about two leags Broad Scars [scarce] that:[3] the land one [on] the South Side Cragey Rockey hills of a Grat height Covered with Snow Steep to the Shore and Rockey in Bayes and Coves and many Small Islands lies alonge by the Shore.[4] Whether the high Land be Great Islands I know not but their runs Sounds in a great way in many Places I Saw as I Sailed by: I have Sen draughts has made them all Islands.[5] The Streights lies West north west from Elezabeth Bay to San Jeroms River: and is distance nere fower Leagus.

[137] **November 1670 the *Sweepstakes* in the Streights of Maggallan *Cap* quad**
Thou maiest See the North land or Pointe of San Jorems River when thou are in Elezabeth Bay: From San Jorems River the Strights lies west and be [by] South two leagus: then west one league or better to Cap dequad:[6] which Cap is one [on] the north Shore here the Strights rounds in a Ellboe and makes a Shetinge up at Cape dequad, about Cap dequad the Lannd Is Cragey hills one [on] Boath Shores and the Streig*hts* not more than five miles Broad:[7] from Cap dequad to the westward the Streights lies north West halfe a Pointe westerly by the true Compas fowertenn Leagus: my Compas varieth Seaventen degres Easterly. This reach the Streights is about five miles Broad and that is the most:[8] many Coves one [on] the South Shore and Small Iles:[9] half a mile to the west ward of Cap quad ther is two Small Iles and rockes and a bay ore Cove to the westward of the Cap one [on] the north Shore.[10] The land begin to Grow very bar [bare] Cragey Rockeys one [on] Boath Shors a Scarce of timber but fire wood anough: here is Sum Small gineper [juniper] trees.[11]

[1] The ducks that inhabit this region are: flightless steamer-duck (*Tachyeres pteneres*); flying steamer-duck (T. *patachonicus*); spectacled duck (*Speculanas specularis*); crested duck (*Lophonetta specularoides*); torrent duck (*Merganetta armata*); speckled teal (*Anas flavirostris*). Summer visitors are: yellow-billed pintail (*A. georgica*); silver teal (*A. versicolor*; Chiloe wigeon (*A. sibilatrix*); red shoveler (*A. platalea*); Andean duck (*Oxyura ferruginea*). Jaramillo, *Birds*, pp. 76–82.

[2] The flood tides generally enter the Strait from both the east and west ends and meet at Cabo Crosstide, the northern extremity of Isla Carlos III, opposite the mouth of Canal Jerónimo, so that it is not surprising the Narbrough found them confusing.

[3] The Strait is between 3 and 4½ miles wide and has a large island in the middle, Isla Carlos III. The channel is less than 2 miles across.

[4] This is Península Ulloa which rises to 2,533 ft (772 m).

[5] Charts that showed them all as islands.

[6] Cabo Quod (53°32′S, 72°33′W); variants Quad, Quade, dequad, de Quade, Quado. Cabo Quad stands out from the east, and projects well out into the Strait with a cleft in the summit, 800 ft (244 m) high. Wood, BL, MS 46A, p. 168: 'Three Leagues W*est* by Compas from St Jeromes Chanell lyeth a Cape which the Hollanders Call Cape Quad.'

[7] Actually less than 2 miles across.

[8] Generally the width here is 2–2½ miles wide.

[9] Narbrough does not mention El Morrión (53°34′S, 72°32′W), the eastern entrance point to Bahía Butler, a prominent granite promontory on the south shore SSE of Cabo Quod

[10] Bahía Barceló (53°31′S, 72°33′W).

[11] See above, p. 253, n. 1.

At fower aclocke I was a Brist [abreast] of Cap de quad: at Eight aclocke to night I was fower leagus to the westward of the Cap: the wind at SSE: a fine small gale. I Steered all night WBN halfe a Pointe northerly by my Compas: the mone Eleven dayes ould faier mone light: I Saw boath Shors very Plaine al night. This day I and my Master of the Shipp servaied the Best Bower Cable: and found it nere Straned in theree Places and Seaverall Places much Rubd:[1] I was loath to Cut any of it But Consideringe the danger of a Bad Cable in these Parts and how much wee were Presserved by it but twenty howers before: forceed my to Give order to Cut five and fivety fadam of Cable of[f]: my Boatswaine was forced to make Euse of Sum of it for Plats and nipers[2] Presently for the ould ones were Spent.
The Streights nine leags from Cap dequade lies NWBW: then it lies north west nere fower or five leags: the Streights Grows Broader and Broader after you are nine or tenn leagus to the westward of Cap de quade: it is nere there abouts fower leagus from Shore to Shore:[3] very Gray Rockey Cragey hills of Boath Shores not very high lands but barran a knoufe [enough] of all things Exsepinge Rocks and Snow fresh water Comes tumblen down in many Paces.

[138] **November 1670 the *Sweepstakes* in the Streeights of Magallan of[f] C*ap* quad 14**
Beinge Munday faier weather this morninge wind at SEBE a fine fresh gale. I Steered WNW northerly weth what Saile I Could make: I was at Eight aclock this morninge fowerten leags to the west ward of Cap de quade here is harbowers and Coves at Every leag distane one [on] the South Shore: Great Bayes and Sounds one [on] the north Shore.[4] Now I keep the South Shore far aboard for it is the Best Shore to Saile out By, I am nere two leags of[f] the South Shore and have Sailed So all this day: the north Shore maks in Great Bayes and Blufe head lands and Small Islands and Rockes Eight leagus within Cap victory[5] which Cap is the Pointe of the north Shore Enteringe into the South Sea. This Cap victory Maks like an Ileland till you Com ner it for the land lis in a Bay and Low with hilllocks or little hills to the Eastward of it and Raget with Snow. From Cap de quade to Cap Munday[6] the Streights lies Nor*th* West and be west: this Cap munday is a Cap one [on] the South Shore and is distance from Cap de quade fowerten Leagues: here the Streights is fower or five Leagues Broad[7] and Six leags to the westward of Cap Munday the Streights is nere Eight Leagus Broad and houlds full that Bread to the South Sea.[8] From

[1] This would be due to the wear at anchor in Elizabeth Bay (Bahía Isabel).

[2] Platts were flat ropes, made of rope yarns from condemned cable, platted together to form a mat which was used in the hawse hole to prevent the cable chafing. Nippers were short lengths of rope, made of the strands of condemned cordage, about a fathom and a half to two fathoms long, used to hold the cable off the capstan when the cable was too slimy to grip by hand.

[3] About 13 leagues from Cabo Quod the Strait opens out to a width of about 6 miles. Narbrough has probably made a mistake inserting 9 leagues here and meant 9 plus the additional 4 or 5 mentioned above.

[4] Golo Xaultegua, a large gulf, leads eastward off the Strait in this area. The name of this gulf is one of the few Fuegian indigenous names collected by Sarmiento de Gamboa, which are still in use today.

[5] Cabo Victoria (52°17′S, 74°55′W); variant Victory. 'So called from the name of the ship in which some of *Magellanes* Souldiers did first compass the world.' Heylyn, *Cosmographie*, p. 1074.

[6] Cabo Monday (53°11′S, 73°24′W); variants, Moonday, Munday.

[7] The distance is about 38 miles (just under 13 leagues) and the Strait is 6 miles wide at this point.

[8] Eight leagues to the west of Cabo Munday, past Isla Tamar, the Strait widens out to about 12–14 miles and continues at about that width to the ocean.

Cap Munday to Cap dissier or Cap disiado[1] which Cap is the out most Cap of the South Shore att the Enterens into the West Sea is distance theerden [*blank*] Leagus[2] and the Cours is from the one to the other west north west halfe a Pointe northerly and East South East halfe a Pointe Southerly: the Midle of the Chanell into the Streights is nerst NW and SE in and out in Breath from the north Shor to Cap disiado Six Leagus.[3] One [on] the north Shore their is a Great many Ilands and Brooken Ground So as you Can hardly See the maine Land: this Brooken Ground is N and NNE and NE from Cap disiado. This day at Seaven aclocke in the afternone Cap disiado Bare SW of me dist*ance* one League.[4] It Proved Calme to night and very foogey and Rained much, I drove Sumwhat to the North westward this night. Here Runs But little Currant and that runs out of the Streights As what I found by this nights Calme. I caannot Perceive Any Current to Sett in or out But a Small tide which Ebs and flowes about five foot.[5]

[139] **November 1670 the *Sweepstakes* Enteringe the South Sea**
15
Beinge Tusday very fogey Rainey weather the wind at at NW a fresh gale and looked very much Like fowle weather: Cap disiado bar South West South from mee by my Compas: distance three leagus. At fower aclock this morninge I Saw all the South Sea oppen but findinge I Could not Git into the Sea I bar into the Streights and Anchored in a Bay one [on] the South Shore: about three Leagus from Cap Dissiado: I anchored in ten fadam warter Sandy Ground in a Cables lenth of the Shor. In the west End of this Bay thir is a fine Close Cove land lockt: a Bow Shot[6] Broad and three longe:[7] this Bay have three Ilands at the nortwest Part of it ner the Shore and here is fair Soundings al over it: ten and fiveten fadam water: here Groues Severall weeds in the bay and at the mouth of it ther is not less than ten fadam & Eight fadam among the weeds: the Land is of a Good haight here in hills one higher than an other and barran rocks: here groues wood one [on] the hills Sids for fewell and fresh water Runs down in many Places. I Called this Bay Tusday Bay.[8] A hard

[1] Cabo Deseado (52°45′S, 74°43′W); variants, Disiade, Disado, Disiado, Disseada, Dissiado, Dissier. Narbrough's 'Royal Map' and 'Sloane Map' (Foldout, and Plate 5) show the western end of Isla Desolación (which he calls South Desolation) as Cape Disseada, with Cape Piller (Cabo Pilar 52°44′S, 74°40′W) about 2 miles NE of the western extremity.

[2] This must be 30 leagues as the distance is about 58 miles.

[3] The Strait is about 12 miles across opposite Cabo Pilar.

[4] This must refer to Cabo Pilar, as 1 league NE from Cabo Deseado would put him within a mile of Cabo Pilar and in a very dangerous situation.

[5] The current in this part of the Strait flows SE at a mean rate of ½ to 1 knot and a maximum rate of 1½ knots. The tidal streams are generally weak and appear to be regular with slack water occurring at high and low water by the shore. The combined effect is to increase the SE flow on the flood and to reduce or cancel it completely on the ebb. *South America Pilot*, II, paras 7.9–11, 7.320, 7.511–12.

[6] A bow shot was about 300 yards; see above, p. xix.

[7] Named on the 'Royal Map' (Foldout), as Sleepers cove. It is about 200 yards wide and 800 yards long on the Plan of the Harbour of Mercy, by Lieutenant Skyring, HMS *Beagle*, 1828.

[8] This was not the bay now called Bahía Tuesday (52°51′S, 74°27′W), but, as can be seen from Narbrough's 'Royal Map' (Foldout), and from the description, Puerto Misericordia (52°47′S, 74°35′W) (later known to the English as The Harbour of Mercy). The bay was named by Sarmiento, who entered the Strait in the *Nuestra Señora de Esperanza* in 1580 after a terrible storm and found refuge in this bay which he named Bahía Misericordia 'seeing that our Lord God had saved us from such dangers as we passed through during the storm'. Sarmiento, *Viage al Estrecho*, p. 176; Markham, *Narratives of the Voyages*, pp. 99–102.

Gale of wind this afternone at west and Blew hard and Rained all night. The warter riseth here about 8 foot and it is a high water one [on] the Change day at twelfe of the Clocke: litle tid Runes here. I rod fast all night. The flood Coumes out of the South Sea.

16
Beinge wedensday Cloudy foogey weather and Raine much wind at West to day and at north west and much Raine all day and night and foogey base weather and Coald.

17
Beinge Thursday foogey Rainey weather wind at NNW A hard gale this forenone les wind this Eveinge, But much raine Calm at ten aclocke to night: towards twelfe aclocke it Began to blow at NW and rain.

18
Beinge Friday Cloudy weather and raine and Snow much wind today in Gusts at North west: this Eveinge it blew Soe hard as I Caused my Sheat anchor to be let goe. This day one [*margin:* A m*an* Died] of my Company Died: by Nam John Richardson: of medstone in Kent: he was my[1] Servant. Wendy rainey weather to night.
The Ground one [on] these Rockey mountains is no natuerall Ground: but A boge for it is Rotton with Beinge Ever weete. I Run in my Lance with one hand to the Rockes which it Grow one [on].

[140] **November 1670 the *Sweepstakes* Pasinge Cap Dissiado the Second tim[e]**
19
Beinge Satterday very Rainey weather to day at twelfe aclocke the wind Came to the East a fine gale. I waied and Stood into the South Sea: much raine and foge one [on] the hils: at fower of the Clock this afternone the Nedle hill Pointe of Cap dissiado Bare South of mee: I was ner a league from it.[2] I Steered West north West by my Compas into the Sea wind at East north East a fine gale: I Saw at five of the Clock fower Small Ilands which lies towards the north Part of the mouth of the Streights in the Sea: distance from the north Shore about five or Six Leags to the westward and they Lie From Cap disiado by the tru Comp*as* North north West: and are distante nere Eight Leagus:[3] their is one of these Ilands Coplen up like a Suger Loafe[4] which lies in the midle and the westermost Iland is flatest and make a doake[5] in it: they ley Prety nere to gether: and are but of an indefrente height they may be Called Rockes: as well as Ilands for they be but great rockes where foules brede one [on] them never the Les I Caled them Norresses Ilands[6] for Norres was the first man of my compa*ny* that Saw them and had a disier they Should be Called after his nam. At Eight a Clocke to night these Ilands bar NNW of mee by my Compas and distance ner three Leagus: at ten aclocke to night it blew much wind at NNE and at north

[1] The word 'Chir,' short for Chirurgeon or Surgeon, struck through.
[2] This sounds like Cabo Pilar; see above, p. 272, n. 1.
[3] They are 9 miles from the north shore and 24 miles from Cabo Deseado.
[4] Sugar loaf: a molded conical mass of sugar. *NOED.* This is Islote Pan de Azúcar, which means sugar loaf.
[5] See above, p. 253, n. 1.
[6] Islotes (Grupo) Evangelistas (52°45'S, 75°06'W). In Rawlinson, MS A 318 and 'Voyage to the South-Sea', p. 79, Narbrough calls these the Islands of Direction.

and a very Great hollow Sea Runs here: Rained all this night: I Stood to the westward. I Could not See the Cap one [on] the north Shore which is Called Cap victory for Raine and fooge which hangh over the Land neither Could I See anny Land Lie out to the westward of the north of that Land as was next mee one [on] the maine.
The mouth of the Streeights here is nine or tenn Leagus Broad from Cap disiado to the north Shore.[1] I Sounded and had Ground at theerty Eight fadam: Rufe Rockey Ground: beinge Six leags WNW from Cap disiado: the Land one [on] the north Shore is high hilley land with Peeckinge tops[2] and Snow one [on] them. Cap Disiado is the wester most Land of the South Shore at the mouth of the Streights of Magallan Enteringe the South Sea: this Cap is very Remarkable Land it is high and Steep up with Peekes one [on] the hills and Shous ragett rockes one [on] the tops of the hills with a high Coplen Shewger Loafe [sugar loaf] hill at the north Parte: the Cap maks Blufe a leage and halfe north & South to a mans Site when he is fower or five leagus at Sea: at the north Corner of this Cap next the Streights ther Stands tow high Peeked Rockes: like the nedles at the Ile of Whit[3] but a great deal higher and Biger:[4] one the water Runs Round it the other is one [on] the Edge of the hill allso their is two

[141] **November 1670 the *Sweepstakes* in the South Sea**
Rockes which lies in the Sea two or three Cables Lenght from that nedle: from thence the Land Runs to the South Westward A leage or two the Lower Land trentinge to a low Pointe: wher ther lies in the Sea Many Cragey Pecked Rockes and Brooke*n* Ground ner two leags of[f] the Shore very dangerous: from this Pointe the Land trents to the South farther. I Called thes Rocks the Judges.[5]
Cap Disiado lies in the Latt*itud* of feivty three degres and feive minuts South and in Longitud West from the Lizard of Eng*land* Seaventy two degres feivety Six minuts.[6]
Meridian distance one thousand one hundered & fowerty nine Leagus.[7]
The Compas have 14°00′ variation Easterly at Cape Disseade.

20
Beinge Sundday very Stormey weather wind Came to the South west at Eight aclocke this forenone: I tacked and Stood to the WNW:ward Caringe my Courses:[8] a very Great Sea

[1] The distance between Cabo Deseado and Cabo Victoria is 28 miles, but the width of the Strait from Cabo Deseado to the north shore is about 12–14 miles; the north shore being all rocks and islands.

[2] The summits are in sharp peaks.

[3] The Needles, 50°40′N, 1°35′W, at the west end of the Isle of Wight.

[4] This is Cabo Pilar (52°44′S, 74°40′W). 'The sides of the cape are sheer and cliffy, and it is backed by two mountains which form a high and remarkable promontory. Seen from the E, the cape appears to have a double-peaked summit. The E peak, 1 mile SE of the cape, is 561 m (1,840 ft) high; the W peak shaped like a tower, rises to an elevation of 552 m [1,811 ft] from the shore W of the cape. The part of the cape facing the strait presents a low rounded hill; its W side, facing the Pacific Ocean, shows considerable erosion by the sea. Peñones Lanchas Españoles, several small but steep islets, lie close off the cape; the largest an enormous detached rock 93 m [305 ft] high, is prominent from E.' *South America Pilot*, II, para. 7.517.

[5] Rocas Apóstoles (52°46′S 74°45′W). 'Rocks from 1 to 15 m [3 to 49 ft] high, lying on a reef extending 2 miles from the coast and fringed with breakers.' *South America Pilot*, II, para. 5.350.

[6] Cabo Deseado (52°45′S, 74°43′W), which is 69°31′W of the Lizard.

[7] Wood, BL, MS 46A, p. 168: 'The Course from Cape Quad to Cape Desyer is NW[t] by W[t] the distance 16 Leagues which maketh the Length of the Straights from Cape Virgin Mary or Cape Joy to Cape Deseado or Desyer 113 Leagues.'

[8] Sailing under the lower sails only.

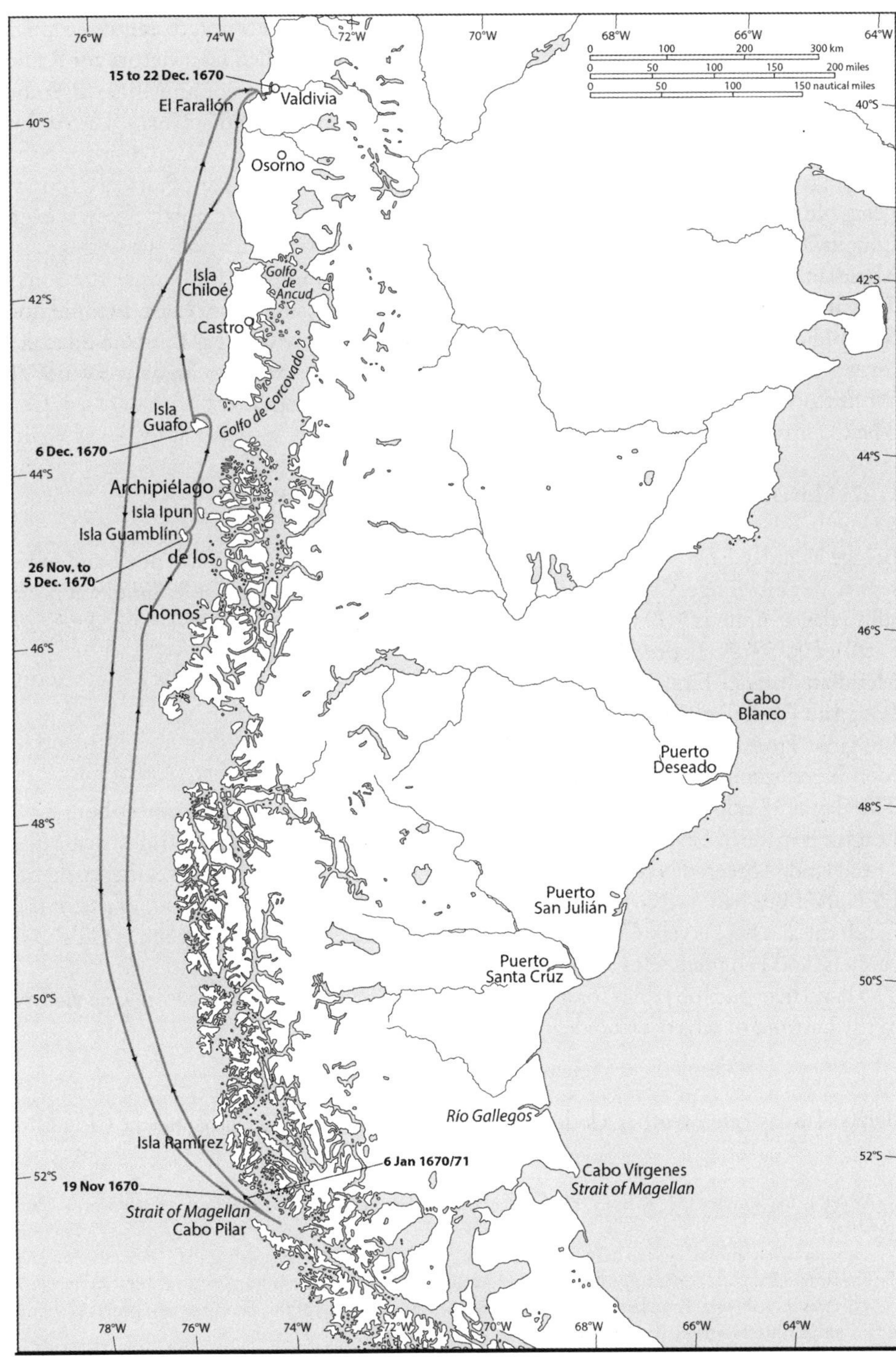

Map 8. Track of the *Sweepstakes* off the coast of Chile, 19 November 1670 to 6 January 1670/71.

Come out of the wester board which Causeth the Ship to labowr very Sorely. Noe Land to be Seen to day nor noe observation: the Sun is Clouded.
Cours made from fower aclocke yesterday till to day at twelf aclocke WBN: distance Sailed 36 mils: departur west 35·4 mils: def*erence* of Latt*itud* 00°07′ No*rth*: Lat*itud* by account 52°51′ S.
Meridian Distance From Cap Disiada West 35·4 mils
Longitud From Cap Disiada West 00°05′·6
Longitud From the Lizard of England West 73°52′
Meridian distance From the Lizard West 1160 L*eagus* 2·4 m*ils*
This afternone a very Great Sea So as I was in danger of losing of my Mast. I Could not Se any Land this Eveinge my Cours was west north west by my Compas But I Could make my way But north & by west the Sea runinnge So loftie: les wind to night at SWBW: I Set my top Sailes at 12 aclocke and Steered NW by my Compas.
The Compas have fowertenn degres variation Easterly.

[142] **Movember 1670 the *Sweepstakes* in the South Sea 51°52′ S**
21
Beinge Munday Faier weather wind at WSW the Sea indeferent Smoath noe Land to be sene to day morninge. Cours by my Compas NW: Cours made true from Sunday at none till to day at none is NBW: distance Sailed 60 mils: depar*tur* west 11·7 mils: def*erence* Latt*itud* 00°59′ N: Lat*itud* by obs*ervation* ☼ 51°52′ S.
Meridian distance From Cap Disieade west 47·1 mils
Longitud From Cap Disiade 01°14′·7 west
Longitud From the Lizard of England 74°10′·7 west
Meridian distance From the Lizard 1164 Leagus 2·1 mils
This day at 12 aclocke wee Saw the Land it bar EBN of mee and was distance about nine Leagus: it made in Severall hills with Snow one [on] them it was high Land & made like a head land.[1] I Steered NNW: wind at West a fine gale: Calme and faier weather to night. I Sounded But had noe Ground at Sixty fadam. At fower aclocke I was out of site of the Land: the aier here is very Cauld: the Sea of a blew Couler Sum Sea fouls Sen as Guls[2] and gannets[3] and Penguens[4] But noe fish.
The Land here one [on] this Coast lies northwesterly and South Easterly from Cap victory to the Latt*itud* of feivety twoo degres.

22
Beinge Tusday Faier weather a letle Shouer of raine this morninge darke blacke Clouds to

[1] Probably Isla Ramírez (51°50′S, 75°00′W), a large island 13 miles from north to south, which rises to 2,000 ft (610 m).

[2] The most likely gulls to be seen here are the dolphin gull (*Larus scoresbii*), the kelp gull (*L. dominicanus*) and the brown-hooded gull (*L. maculipennis*), all of which breed in the area. Jaramillo, *Birds*, pp. 126–8.

[3] This was probably the Peruvian booby (*Sula variegata*), as other birds of this family are not generally found as far south as this. Harrison, *Seabirds*, p. 290.

[4] These were probably Magellanic penguins, which are common in this area. They may, however, have been king penguins (*Aptenodytes patagonicus*) which, although not now found in this area, formerly bred along this coast, rockhopper penguins or macaroni penguins (*Eudyptes chrysolophus*) may also be found in this area. Shirihai, *Complete Guide*, pp. 42–81.

the Southward. This night I tore a hole in my fore Saile with beateinge[1] Beinge be Calmed. A fine gale Sprounge up this forenone at South: I Steered West north west by my Compas to Git an offinge.
Course made true from munday none till today at none is north distance Sailed 52 miles: def*erence* of Latt*itud* 00°52′ North: Latt*itud* by Good observation of the ☼ is 51°00′ S.
Meridian distance from Cap Deseade west is 47·1 mils
Longitud from Cap diseada is 01°14′·7 west
Longitud from the Lizard is 74°10′·7 wes*t*
Meridian distance is 1164 Leagus 2·1 mils
This afternone the wind Came to the Southwest: I Stereed west north west till 8 aclocke then north a fresh gale al night.
This afternone I Called my two Leiuetenants and Master into the Great Cabin and Sinor Carrolus: wee advice [*sic*] where it would be best to hale in for the Land which was Concluded to Goe in in the Latt*itud* of 45°30′.

[143] **November 1670 the *Sweepstakes* in the S*outh* Sea Latt*itud* 48°54′ S**
23
Beinge wedensday hassey weather wind at SW A fresh gale. At 8 aclocke this morninge I Steered North by my Compas: my Comp*as* varieth fowerten degres Easterly: I Saile now nere nine leagus in fower howers:[2] a fresh gale of wind at SW hasey weather: I had no observation to day. Cours made true from tusday at none till to day at none is North twenty five degres west: distance Sailed 140 mils: Departur west 59 mils: def*erence* of Latt*itud* by account 02°06′ N Latt*itud* by account att none is 48°54′ South.
Meridian distance from Cap disiade 106·1 mils
Longitud from Cap Diseade 02°46′·1 W
Longitud from the Lizard 75°42′·1 W
Meridian Distance from the Lizard 1184 Leagus 1·1 M*ils*
Today at 12 aclocke I Steered north by my Compas: which is north be East for the Compas have fowerten degres variati*on* Easterly: it blew hard thes afternone at WSW: and all night a great Sea runs: and Could Aier hasey weather with Sum Clouds of raine.

24
Beinge thursday hasey Coald weather wind at SW and Came to the SSW: a Stout gale all day a Great Sea runs.
Course made from yesterday at none till today at none is North 15° Easterly: distance Sailed 170 miles: departure East 44 miles: def*erence* Latt*itud* 02°43′ N: Latt*itud* 46°11′ By account.
Meridian distance from Cap disiado 62·1 mils
Longitud from Cap deseade 01°41′·5 West
Longitud from the Lizard 74°37′·5 West
Meridian distance from the Lizard 1169 Lea*gus* 2·2 Mils

[1] Since the ship was becalmed, this probably means that the sail was beating against the mast, rather than that the ship was tacking or turning to windward in a fresh wind, which is also known as beating.
[2] A speed of 6¾ knots.

To day at 12 aclocke I Steered North North East: wind at SSW a stout gale. I dar not ventur to hale in with the Land[1] the weather beinge So Stormey and the winds hanginge So much out one [on] the wester board till now[2] a great western Sea Constantly: hasey darke Could weather to night.

[144] **November 1670 the *Sweepstakes* in the So*uth* Sea Lat*itud* 45°31′S**
25
Beinge Friday hasey weather and Sumtis [sometimes] a thicke weet fog and blowinge weather wind at SW: at twelfe aClocke at night I lay by with my head to the north westward till three in the morninge then made Saile in ENE: a Stout gale at SW: hasy weather this forenone.
Course mad true from yeasterday at none till to day at non is North East be East 3°45′ Easterly: distance Sailed 80 mils: departur East 69·5 miles: def*erence* Lat*itud* north 00°40′: Lat*itud* by obser*vation* ☼ is 45°31′ S.
Meridian distance from Cap Disiade East is 7·4 mils
Longitud from Cap disiadie East 00°01′·1 Wes*t*[3]
Longitud from the Lizard 72°57′·1 west.
Meridian distance west from the Lizard 1146 Lea*gus* 1·8 Mil
It is hasey with S*h*ouers this afternone wind at SSW a stoute gale: I Steered in ENE By my Compas which is nere EBN. This Eveinge at Seaven aclocke I made the Land: it Bar NE from mee I judge it five leagus of[f], it is of an ordinarie height. I lay of[f] and in all night. This Place Sin*o*r Carrolus Adviceed mee to Goe to he Beinge in my Cabine: in Poublique advice with my two Leue*tenants* and Master he Said here, at this Iland he was accquainted and Should find a Readie way to disspatch his Buisnes in a Short time to the Purpose.

26
Beinge Satterday hasey Cloudy weather and fogey wind at SWBS a Stout gale. I Steered in with the Land it is the Iland which is Called Nesterra Sinoro dell Suckeoro[4] in the drafts.[5] At one aclocke this afternone I anchored at it one [on] the north East Side in ten fadam warter oasey Sande: about a mile from the Shore: the wester most Pointe of the Iland beras [bears] NWBW of me distance a league and the Eastermost Pointe bears SE distance two mils.

[145] **November 1670 the *Sweepstakes* at anchor under the Ile of Succoro**
This Iland is of an indeferent height and full of woods:[6]very thick of good Large

[1] To haul in with the land, to approach to the land.

[2] The winds were blowing so constantly from the west.

[3] The departure converted to difference of longitude gives a position west of Cape Deseado, despite the Meridian Distance placing it to the eastward of the Cape.

[4] This island is shown on the Doncker chart as I. de Nuestra Senora [Señora] del Socorro and is now know as Isla Guamblín (44°51′S, 75°05′W); variants Nesterra Sinoro dell Suckeoro, Nestria Seniora Sarraco.

[5] On the charts.

[6] 'Isla Guamblín ... is 217 m (712 ft) high, comparatively level, and thickly wooded. In general its coasts are sloping and covered with verdure, but there are some remarkable cliffy outcrops which show distinctly against the dark woodland.' *South America Pilot*, III, para. 3.119a.

timber trees like Eash:[1] and here is of those trees as are in the Streights of magellan which rine is hot like Ginger:[2] here is Good fresh warter: I fetched here boath wood and water. The Iland is about two leags longe from the north west Pointe to the South East Pointe and in broadth over to the Southwest one leage: it lies at least fower or five leagus of[f] the maine: you may Saile betwen that and the maine Safly. I rod one [on] the north East Part of it: which is a good road with the wind from the north west Southerly to the South South East: with fair Shouldings about it. The tow Points Show them Selfes with a breach of Sea. Here is People Come here Sumtimes for wee Saw an arbower or hunt [hut] of the Indians but Could not Perceive any Pepole to be one [on] it now: in this Iland wee Saw Severall Sea fowles and ducks brant Geese: boath whit and Pied:[3] and other Small birds in the woods: noe Beast Seen nor minerall: the Earth is a black mould.

This Iland Called the Lady of Succor: Lies in the Latt*itud* of 45°08′ S and in Longitud East from the meridian of Cap disiado 59′·9.

Meridian distance from Cap disiadio East 50·1 mile

Meridian distance from the Lizard west 1132 Lea*gus* 1·7 mile

Longitud from the meridian of the Lizard west 71°57′·9

27

Beinge Sunday wind at WSW and blew hard and raine most Parte of the day with fooge I rod fast. Wee fetched wood and fresh warter vile and filthy fowel weather to day and this night. This day I Caused the Bread to be taken out of the Bread roume [room] and found but fower days Brad for my Company: the Rats had made Such Spoile amonst the Bread as it is in Creadable to reporte: all the Seallinge in the boattom of the rome was Eatinge into holes: the Rome Beinge not tined but Paied over with roasoned Canvas:[4] the rats have disstroied Compleatly fowerten weekes bread for the hole Company: allso they have disstroied a hole Punshen full of Peas: not leaveing So much as one hole Pea in the Caske: wee ever eused all means to kill what wee Could yet they Increased much and Breed in the Bread like Mise in a bearne [barn] of Corne.

[146] **November 1670 the Sweepstaks at anchor in the So*uth* Sea 45°00′ S**

Beinge Sunday in the morninge I Sent my Pinas a Shore to the Iland to See what they Could discover: but when Shee returned which was at none toould [told] mee they Could not discover any thinge of People or any Signe of ther Beinge there this year. This morninge at nine aclocke in my Great Cabine Senor Carolus disiered to advice with mee and my Leiut*ants* and Mast*er* which I Called Presently to assemble: he declared thus that he thought it fit to land one [on] the maine opposet to the Iland in a harbower Called Sant

[1] This might be *Nothofagus nitida* which grows on this island today and is up to 115 ft (35 m) tall, diameter 6½ ft (2 m). It has hard glossy green lanceolate shaped leaves 1·2 in (3 cm) long, which are not too dissimilar to those of the common ash (*Fraxinus excelsior*).

[2] Winters bark trees; see above, p. 268, n. 2.

[3] These were presumably kelp geese.

[4] Covered with rosined canvas. Rosin is obtained as a residue of the distillation of oil or turpentine from crude turpentine. *NOED*.

domingo:[1] as the drafts mention ther to goe with our Ship and See to Speake with Such People as wee Could meet with. I Clearely Perceived he never was in these Parts nor in any Parte of Amarica to the South of Panama: but all was lies which hereerto he had related of his Beinge here: for he Could not tell where to Goe nor what to doe neither did he know where the Spanards were Satled [settled]. This Eveinge he had A disier to be Set a Shore ner the Iland of Castro:[2] I judge he Cannot tell where to Goe. Rainey fowle weather all this day and night wind at WSW.

28

Beinge Munday blowinge rainey weather wind at WSW and very thicke: I rod fast: wee fetched wood and Fresh water: wind and rained all night.

29

Beinge Tusday wind betewn the west and the South west blow hard and raine and foogey weather: wee Could not Sail. Wee fetched wood and Fresh water faier weather this afternone. This Eveinge Sinor Carolus Adviced mee that it woould be best for him to be landed a letle to the Southward of Castro[3] one [on] the Coast which is about 43° of Lat*itud* and thier he would Euse a meanes Posible for a trade: I Sattisfied him I was will*ing* to doe anythinge that would Serve to tend to the Good of our voiage & not to Come Soe far for nothinge.

30

Beinge wedensday faier weather this morninge wind at NW a Small gale. I waied and Stood to the maine but I Could not land one [on] it with my Boate for Shoulds and Broaken Ground. All alonge the maine it Is Ilands So far as wee Could See which lies within a quarter of a mile or les of the maine with brooken Ground about them.[4] The Land is very hilly and Mountainnus and full of woods: noe Sine of People here. It Proved very fowle weather to night so as I was forced to git over to the Iland from wence I Cam and anchor wind at WNW.

[1] P° de S. Domingo is shown on the Doncker chart (Plate 2) as an estuary due east of I. de Nuestra Señora del Socorro. It is probably a reference to the present Puerto Santo Domingo (43°58′S, 73°06′W), which lies on the mainland, in the northern part of Canal Moreleda, inside Archipiélago de los Chonos.

[2] Castro is shown on the Doncker chart and appears to refer to Isla Chiloé, on the east coast of which lies Ciudad de Castro. See next note below.

[3] Ciudad de Castro (42°29′S, 73°46′W), was founded in 1567, and is situated on the east side of Isla Chiloé on the west side of Golfo de Ancud. Described in 1662 as 'Castro, the most Southern Town of all this Province, in the *Latitude* of 44, built in a large and fruitful island of the Bay of *Ancud*'. Heylyn, *Cosmographie*, p. 1074. Basil Ringrose says in his *South Sea Waggoner*, 1682, 'The City of Castro which is Inhabitted by the Spaniards and a place of great trade, for to it the Indians bring Ambergrease, hides tallow, and ships from lima Come and bring them Cloathing for theire Comodityes. Now the Spaniards Can goe no further in theire Coasters because they trade no further and will not that theire owne people know the passage out of these seas.' Howes, *Buccaneer's Atlas*, p. 250.

[4] This is Archipiélago de los Chonos a generally barren rugged chain of islands, steep on the western side with summits up to 4,920 ft (1,500 m), lying off the main land of Chile from about 44°S–45°S. See also Peckett's journal, p. 593.

[147] **December 1670 the *Sweepstakes* in the South Sea Ile Socour**

1

Beinge Thursday Rainey blowinge weather wind at NWBN till fower aclocke this afternone then the wind Came to the South west. I waied and Stood to the northward: it Provied Calme: I anchored againe in 13 fadam blacke Sand and Rod all night beinge Calme and fogey. Here is very Good Sandy Ground all the way from this Iland over to the Ilands one [on] the maine Side and the most water is twenty five fadam deep: ther is Good riding under the Iland Adjaente to the maine with northerly winds. I Sawy noe fruts in any of thes Ilands nor herbs but Sum Smal berys un Sauvery [unsavoury] tast: the trees very Green and bears a Smal round leafe much like unto Box: the wood very heavey & not very large nor hard: no Beasts Se[e]n here nor fowles: Sum Small Birds lik linets[1] and Sum kits:[2] Smal Store of fish in these Seas as we Could perceive. This day all my ships Bread is Exspended: wee Eat Peas & oatmeall in*stead*.[3]

2

Beinge Friday faier weather this forenone wind at W a Stout Gale. I waied and Stood to the norward: but at twelfe a Clocke the wind Came to the norwest and blow hard with gusts and raine: I Could not Cary it Cleare of the Land to the nor*th*ward:[4] I tacked and Stood to the Southward: it blowed hard and rained So as it made mee hand my top Sailes: I was forced to beare to leward of the Iland from whence I Came and Anchored one [on] the East End in a Sandy bay: about a mile of[f] the shor in nine fadam water Sandy Ground. It blow hard this Eveinge at NW and Rained the Aier very Could Consideringe it is the height of Sumer here. I was today in the Latt*itud* of 44°34′ by Good observation of the Sun.
A hard *gale* all night at NNW and filthy rainey weather and a Great Sea: base Stormey weather towards morninge.

3

Beinge Saterday Gusty weather with haile and Raine wind at NNW & Sumtimes at NW: a Great Sea vile base weather all this day and to night. I rod fast.
The tids Rize here about Eight foot one [on] the Springe:[5] it is a high warter at this Iland at nine aclocke one [on] the Change day the Flood Comes from the Southward: here Rune But a Sm*all* tide. Two Great whales Senne today: Severall Porposes Sene today.

[148] **December 1670 the *Sweepstakes* in the South Sea Lat*itud* 44°55′ S**

4

Beinge Sunday Rainey Gusty weather: wind at WNW very rawe and Coald Aier: and a Rowleinge [rolling] Great Sea Comes out of the west: I rod fast: rainey weather all night

[1] The linnet (*Acanthis cannabina*) is not found in Chile. This might have been a Patagonian sierra-finch (*Phrygilus patagonicus*), which is not too dissimilar to a linnet and is common in this area and found at the forest edge, but it is not really practicable to suggest a very likely alternative. Jaramillo, *Birds*, pp. 210–11.

[2] The kites/hawks found in this area are the Chilean hawk (*Accipiter chilensis*), the cinereous harrier, the variable hawk (*Buteo polyosoma*) and the rufous-tailed hawk (*Buteo ventralis*). Jaramillo, *Birds*, pp. 86–9. Kite also means a flock of pigeons or doves, *NOED*; but these are unlikely to found here.

[3] This word is written 'in' with a tilde over the last letter to indicate it should be expanded. This might therefore be 'instead' or 'in lieu'.

[4] The ship could not sail to windward of the land and so had to tack.

[5] At Spring tide.

wind betwen the WNW & NBW. Their is Shoald water at the SE Pointe of this Iland more than a mile into the Sea to the SE:ward.

5

Beinge Munday Rainey darke weather: little wind at SE. I waied and Stod to the norward this morninge at Eight a Clocke: at ten aclocke the wind Came to the north west and raine and Gusty weather and haile: I Plied to Git of[f] the Shore: many Ilands within fower leagus to Leward of mee: which lies nere the maine. So far as I Could See to the norward and Southward the Coast is all Ilands: and Dangerus to Come nere it for the winds Generally blow right one [on] the Shore with Raine and Gusty weather and very thick that a man Cannot See a mile from him. This afternone at two a Clocke the wind Came to the WSW a fresh gale: I Stood of[f] NW: A great Sea Runes here. The Ship Complaines in her bowes: and makes water at the hooadinge.[1] This Eveinge at 8 aclocke the west Part of the Iland of Sucoro Bare South of mee distance about five Leagus. Blow hard to night at WBN.

6

Beinge Tusday Cleare weather this fore none. I observed the ☼ one the Meridian and was in the Lat*itud* of 43°47′. Rainey Gusty weather this afternone wind at NW.
Course mad from last night at 8 cl*ocke* till today at none is North 07°50′ East: distance Sailed 59 mils: departur East 8 miles: dif*erence* Lat*itud* 00°58′.
Meridian distance from Cap disiado East 58·1 mils
Longitud from Cap Disiado East 01°12′·4
Longitud from the Lizard west 71°45′·4
Meridian distance from the Lizard west 1129 Lea*gus* 2·7 mils
This morninge we Saw the Land out in the NBE: I Stod in with it and Plied under the South Part of it: it makes like an Iland.[2] We saw the Land all a Longe to the northward and Southward in Coplen hils and high land. I Sent my Boat to the Land But they Could not Goe a Shore the Sea Breaks so much: noe site of People the land woods. [*margin continuation:* It began to Raine and Blow I Stood of[f] much wind to night at NW]

[149] **December 1670 the *Sewpstakes* in the Coast of Chelie Lat*itud* 44°08′ S**
7
Beinge wedensday very Stormey weather wind Betwen the NNW and W with raine and haile and vile bas[e] wather: a great Sea Comes out of the wester board. I Stood of [off to] the Southward under my Courses sCars [scarce] able to Carry them: Still havinge a lee Shore in vew. This Coast is very dang*erous* for the winds Generally Blowes westerly Right one [on] the Coast and very Stormey: neither is their any Soundings till you are in two leagus of the Land[3] their is therty fadam Sandy Ground: in the Latt*itud* of 44°34′ South.

[1] The hoodings (whoodings) were the foremost planks of the ship, below the waterline, adjoining the stem.

[2] This is probably Isla Guafo (43°37′S, 74°44′W), a large island which is densely wooded and rises to 787 ft (240 m) with a noticeable depression in the middle. *South America Pilot*, III, paras 5.6, 5.7. It is shown on the Doncker chart (Plate 2) between P^{ta}. Sta. Clara, at the southern end of Castro (Isla Chiloé), and Cabo de Ilas, but not named.

[3] It is not possible to anchor and in poor visibility soundings would give little or no warning of the proximity of the land.

Course made from last night till to day at none is SW: distance Sailed 40 mils: departur west 28·4 mils: dif*erence* Latt*itud* 00°28′·4 South: Latt*itud* by accounte 44°08′ So*uth*. I judge my Selef Eight leagus of [f] the Land.
Meridian distance from Cap disiado East 29·7 mils
Longitud from Cap disiado East is 00°34′·4
Meridian distance from the Lizard west 1139 Lea*gus* 1·1 mil
Longitud from the Lizard west 72°23′·4
Blew hard all night and Showers: wind at WNW.

8
Beinge Thursday Cloudy Gusty rainey weather wind at WBS: this morninge at fower a Clocke I tacked and Stood to the northward.
Course mad from yesterday at none till to day at none is South be west: distance Saile 33 mils: departur 6 mils west: def*erence* Lat*itud* 00°30′ South: Lat*itud* by obser*ation* ☼ is 44°38′.
Meridian distance from Cap disiado East 23·7 Mils
Longitud from Cap disiado East 00°26′
Meridian distance from the Lizard west 1141 Lea*gus* 1·1 mil
Longitud from the Lizard west 72°31′·8

9
Beinge Friday wind at WSW and blows hard in Gusty Rainey weather and a Great Sea: I Ply what I Can to the northward all this last 24 howers. Cours made from yes*ter*day at none till today at none is NW: distance Sailed 11·3 miles: def*erence* Lat*itud* 00°08′ No*rth*: Latt*itud* by ob*servation* of the ☼ is 44°30′ South: dep*artur* west 8 miles.
[*2 lines blank*]
[*Note at the bottom of the page*] the remaining Part of this twenty fower howers is in the other sid

[150] **December 1670 the *Sweepstaks* in the South *Sea* Latt*itud* 44°20′ S**
9
Meridian distance From Cap Disseada East 15·7 miles
Longitud from Cap Disiada East 00°15′
Longitud from the Lizard west 72°42′·8
Meridian distance from the Lizard west 1144 Lea*gus* 0·1 mil

10
Beinge Saterday wind betwen the NW and WSW Gusty Stormey weather and a Great Sea: I Ply what I Can to the Norward: Every night the winds Comes to the NW which forse me to Stand to the SW ward: and in the day to the norward so as I Can make but lettle way to the norward. After divers Courses in this last 24 howers I make my true Cours to be NNW: distane Sailed 10·8 mils: departur west 4·1 mils: def*erence* Lat*itud* 00°10′ No*rth*: Lat*itud* by account is 44°20′.
Meridian distance from Cap Deseada East is 11·6 mils
Longitud from Cap Diseada East 00°09′
Longitud from the Lizard west 72°48′·8

Meridian distance from the Lizard west 1145 Lea*gus* 1·2 mils
I Stood to the northward all night havinge my top Sails abroad wind at WNW a fresh gale: Sum raine to night. I had my maine top Saile Splite in handinge: I Brought my other top Saile to the yard.[1]

11
Beinge Sunday Rainey Gusty weather wind veared to the NBW and Blow fresh: I tacked and Stood west at a 11 aclocke this fore none: a Great Sea Comes out of the NW. Cours mad true from yesterday none till to day at none is North: distance Sailed 70 miles: dep*artur* 00: def*erence* of Lat*itud* north is 01°10′: Lat*itud* By account is 43°10′ S.
Meridian distance from Cap Diseada East 11·6 mils
Longitud from Cap diseada East 00°09′
Longitud from the Lizard west 72°48′·8
Meridian distance from the Lizard west is 1145 Lea*gus* 1·2 mile
At twelfe aclocke the wind veared to the NW: I tacked and Stod to the westward: it Blow hard this afternone: at 12 A Clocke to night it Blow veri hard and Rained: a great Sea. The Compas have tenn degres variation Easterly.

[151] **December 1670 the *Sweepstakes* in the South Sea Lat*itud* 43°53′ S**
12
Beinge Munday at two aClocke the wind Blew So hard at NW as forced me to hand my head sails and try: here runes a mighty great Sea: it rained all this day and very Stormey: I laid my Ships head to the Southwestward.
Cours made true from Sunday at none till to day at none is SSW: distance Sailed 47 miles: departur west is 18 mils: def*erence* Lat*itud* is 00°43′ S Lat*itud* by account is 43°53′ South.
Meridian distance from Cap diseada west 6·4 mils
Longitud from Cap Deseada west 00°15′·5
Longitud from the Lizard west 73°13′·3
Meridian distance from the Lizard west 1151 Lea*gus* 1·2 mils
Much wind this Afternone: my maine Saile Spleet: I one Bent [unbent] it and Brought an other to the yard: and I brought a new meson [mizen] too from my Mison Split. This After none at two a Clocke I Brought the Ship one [on] the Starboard tack and tryed to the northward: wind veared to the SW. I have a Leacke Brooke out in the Larboard quarter alow which makes much warter: we are forced to Bale it out a Baft for it will not run forward to the Pomp.[2]

13
Beinge Tusday this morninge at two a Clocke the Storm Seased: I made Saile and Steered NW till twelfe acloacke – then NBE: wind at WSW a fresh gale: a great Sea Runs.
Cours made true from Munday at none till to day at none is North: distance Sailed 51 mils: departur 00: def*erence* Lat*itud* 51′: Lat*itud* By Good obs*ervation* of the ☼ is 43°02′ South.

[1] The main top sail was split while furling and replaced with another sail.

[2] The water would not run along through the bilge to the well under the pump, which was probably a fixed chain-pump. This might have been because there was a blockage or possibly due to the trim of the vessel, the bow being higher than the stern.

This Afternone I Caused a fish to be Put one [on] the mainmast: for wee found it much defective by Rotennes. [*right margin: fingerpost*]
Meridian distance from Cap Deseada west 6·4 mils
Longitud from Cap Diseada west 00°15′·5
Longitud from the Lizard west 73°13′·3
Meridian distance from the Lizard west is 1151 L*eagus* 1·2 mil
This day I Caused 8 fadam of my Sheat Cable to be [*right margin: fingerpost*] Cut of[f] as it was rubed one strand through. And I Cut 4 fadam of[f] my best Bower that Beinge much worne.

[152] **December 1670 the *Sweepstakes* in the South Sea Latt*itud* 41°55′**
14
Beinge wedensday faier weather wind at SW a fine gale. Now I Steered in north East for the Land: seeinge the weather Sumwhat Sattled: for before I dar not deale with the Land the winds blowinge Continually one [on] the Coast.
Course made true from yesterday none till to day none is north be East: distance Sailed 68 miles: departur East 13·4 mils: def*erence* Lat*itud* north 01°07′: Lat*itud* by ob*servation* 41°55′.
Meridian distance from Cap Disiada E 7·0 miles
Longitud from Cap diseada East 00°02′·8
Longitud from the Lizard west 72°55′·0
Meredian dist*ance* from the Lizard west 1146 Lea*gus* 2·8 mils
Faier weather to night wind at SSW a fresh gale: I Steered in ENE for the Land.

15
Beinge Thursday faier weather wind at SSW a stout gale. This morninge wee Saw the land it Bar East of me about 6 leagus: the Land is of a Good height in large hills trenting meanley to the Sea Sid and all Growne with woods. I Stood in a leage of the Shore: beinge in the Latt*itud* of 40°40′ and had noe ground: a faier Coast to Sail by the land lies NNE and SSW. In the Latt*itud* of 40°30′ I Saw a Gully of fresh water run into the Sea: and a Small Pecke Rock licke a Sugar loafe Stands nere the Shore:[1] it blew So hard as I Could not Send a Shore. I Steered all alonge the Shore to the northward for Baldava:[2] the land all woody of a faier height. Baldav [*sic*] is in the Latt*itud* of 39°56′ South: the harbower is in a Large Bay: just a Bout the Pitch of a Steep Rockey Gray Cap to the norward of the Said Cap Calld Cap Gallera.[3] The warter in the harbow makes two waies: one to the northestward the other to the Southward: the towne[4] Stands in a Pointe in the middle: of a mean heaight above the Serface of the water: with a mud wall about it. The mouth of the harbower lies in S*ou*East and out No*r*west with Rockes one [on] the South Shore

[1] This is possibly El Farallón (40°20′S, 73°49′W), an isolated conical rock, which lies at the southern end of Caleta Milagro, where Río Zehuilauquén enters the sea.

[2] Puerto de Valdivia is 8 miles up the Río Valdivia which flows into Bahía de Corral (39°49′S, 73°27′W).

[3] The point shown on Narbrough's plan of the 'Port oF Baldavia' (Plate 4), as Point Gally (Cap Gallera), is the point under Morro Gonzal (39°51′S, 73°28′W), a steep cliff slightly reddish in colour with a wooded summit. The point, known today as Punta Galera, lies in 39°59′S, 73°43′W, 15 miles SW of Morro Gonzalo.

[4] This is not the town of Baldivia, but Fuerte San Pedro and the buildings round it on Isla Mancera (39°53′S, 73°24′W).

and a Small Sandy bay:[1] the land one the South Shore lies out west to the Cap Gallerres from the harbowers mouth nere fower miles: here lies Sum Rockes above warter yust at the Pitch of the Cap or Pointe and one rock lies Singell a bout a Cables lenth within the Cap to the Eastward.[2]

[153] **December 1670 the *Sweepstakes* one [on] the Coast of Chelie**

Course made true from wedensday none till thursday none is[3] [*right margin:* 40°23′]
North 50° East: distance sailed 143 mils: departur East 109·4 mils: def*erence* Lat*itud* 1°32′
Meredean distance from Cap Deseada East is 116·4 mils
Longitud from Cap deseada East 02°25′·8
Longitud from Cap Lizard west 70°32′·0
Meredian distance from the Lizard west 1110 Le*agus* 1·4 m*ils*
This day at none I was in the Lat*itud* of 40°23′ by obser*vation* of the ☼ and in a leage of the Land: noe Soundinge: the Land all woody and a faier Good heaight: I Sterd NNE for Cap Galleres which is at the South Pointe of Balldava. At 4 aclocke this afternone I Stood into the Bay of Balldava: and adviced with Sin*or* Carlus as Concerninge Landinge: I Saw a Smoake a Shore in the bay or harbower: Sin*or* Carrolus would be landed here [*right margin:* Baldava] which was done as he disiered for I Set him a Shore in [*right margin:* Sinor Carolus landed] the Bay one the South Side[4] within the Pointe of Galler: I Saw noe body where he Landed: the Land high and all woodey he went all alonge by the waters Sid into the Porte he tould mee he would Give me an Ansere in the mor[n]i[n]ge. I Stood of[f] to Sea this night at Eveni[i]ge a Cannoe with Seaven men Cam Close to the Ship but would not Come aboard they went a Shore againe: they would not ansewer us: I judge one man was a Spanard the Rest Indians: I beleive they were afraid when they Saw wee were Strangers. Wee Eused all indeviours of Show of frendshipp unto to them never the less they Rowed a way with all Speed for the Shore. I tacked and Stood of[f] into the Sea all night wind at SSW and at SW a fresh gale to night: I Sounded fower leagus of[f] the Shore but noe Ground at 100 fadam: I Streched of[f] fieve leagus into the Sea WBN then tacked and Stood in at one of the Clocke: Soe I Plyed to and fro to keepe to windward: hasey weather to night: the mone nere her full. I Could not Perceive and tide or Current to Sett any way here: I beinge fower leags of[f] the Shore: noe Sine of fier to night one [on] the Shore.
This Eveinge I tooke an Amplitud and I find the Compas to have Eight degres variation Easterly: Beinge in [*right margin: fingerpost*] the Lat*itud* 40°00′ South: and ner the Shore of Baldavia.

[154] **December 1670 the *Sweepstakes* of][f] of Baldiva**

16

Beinge Friday faier weather wind at SSW a stout gale: I Plied in. I Sent my Boat a Shore with a flagg of tructhes [truce] at five aclocke Shee Came aboard againe with fower Spanards in her besids my men: my men were very Curtiusly treated at a forte: which the

[1] Caleta San Carlos.

[2] There are two offshore rocks in this area, Roca Peña Sola, an above water black rock, 6 cables ENE of Morro Gonzalo and about 1 cable offshore, and Roca Theben, 4 cables further ENE, over which the sea does not break. Narbrough is presumably refering to Roca Peña Sola which would be visible from the ship.

[3] 'is' is repeated in the original.

[4] Caleta San Carlos.

Spanards have of Seaven Gunns: the forte fired Severall gouns at drinkenge of healthes. I Salluted thes men with nine Gunns at ther Cominge A board.
I Could not here any newes of Sinor Carlolus My Gentleman.
I Stood of[f] to night wind at SW and SSW a fine gale.

17
Beinge Satterday hasey fogey wind at SW a stoute Gale. This day I Stood in to the Shore and anchored before the Harbower of Baldiva in 14 fadam water Sandy Ground in half a mile of the Shore:[1] the Cap Gallere bar WSW of mee about three quarters of a mile: it was nere twefe a Clocke when I anchored. I Saluted the forte with Seaven Gunns they Saluted mee with five. I Sett thes men A Shore this after none at two aclocke at the forte: they treated my men very Cevelly and fired Severall Guns. I Pres*e*nted the Govennour with a Cheshire Chese and half a dusen Bottles of medera wine and fower dusen of to Bacco pips[2] and a large case of Botles and Six drinkinge Glases: the Govennor of this forte Sent mee of[f] tow dussen [two dozen] Small loafe of Bread and two Gares of this Country mum made of Maies which is much like Smoakey beare[3] also he sent mee a Small Sallat [salad] this night my Boat Cam aboard againe: I Could not here any news of S*e*nor Carrolus. I had account how the Cuntry was of thes Spanard and the manner of their Leiveinge and what Natives was in Pease [peace] and what was in wares [wars] with them and how they Cam by their Gould: which is but Small Store yearly now for the Indians have but little & what they have Cumes out of the in Land mountaines and those Indians ar at wars with the Spanards. This harbower of Baldiava is keept by the Spanards as A Garrison with Six hundered Spanish Souldiers: also they have a great many Indians which ar their frinds that lives aboute them But they leives in a great deale of Sleaverry [slavery] for the Span*ards* makes them worke for them when they Please and Beat them most miserabley in my Site for nothinge at all but only to Show their Greatness: the Por miserable Indians Grones under their heavey burden.

[155] **December 1670 the *Sweepstakes* at Anchor before Baldava**
18
Beinge Sunday faier weather wind at SW: in the day time a fresh gale but every night the wind Comes of[f] the Shore and blowes a fine gale at ESE: thus it dos Continually while it is faier weather: the Aier here is very temprat neither too hot nor to Coald fine dues [dews] fale [fall] in the nights. This day at tenn a Clocke in the forenone I Sent my Small Boate with my Leiut*enant* in her and the Trumpeter with a flagg of truths [truce] flyinge: to the forte to know if I might Send for water as they had Promised mee before I might have water or wood which I Pretended I wanted which was my only disigne how I Should here from Sin*o*r Carrolus: for I Sett him a Shore at the wateringe Place which I rod [off] all the time I was here in Gun Shoot with my Shipp[4] judgeinge it the Best waie to Efecte my designe which might very Easelly have ben Efected if it had ben as what he realted [related] to mee what he Could doe with the Spanards and Indians. But I find them all

[1] Off Caleta San Carlos, the bay shown on Narbrough's plan of the 'Port oF Baldavia' (Plate 4) as English Bay.
[2] Tobacco pipes.
[3] 'Jars of this country's Mum', a drink made of maize much like a smoky beer.
[4] Probably about 800 yards. See above, pp. xx, 462, n. 1.

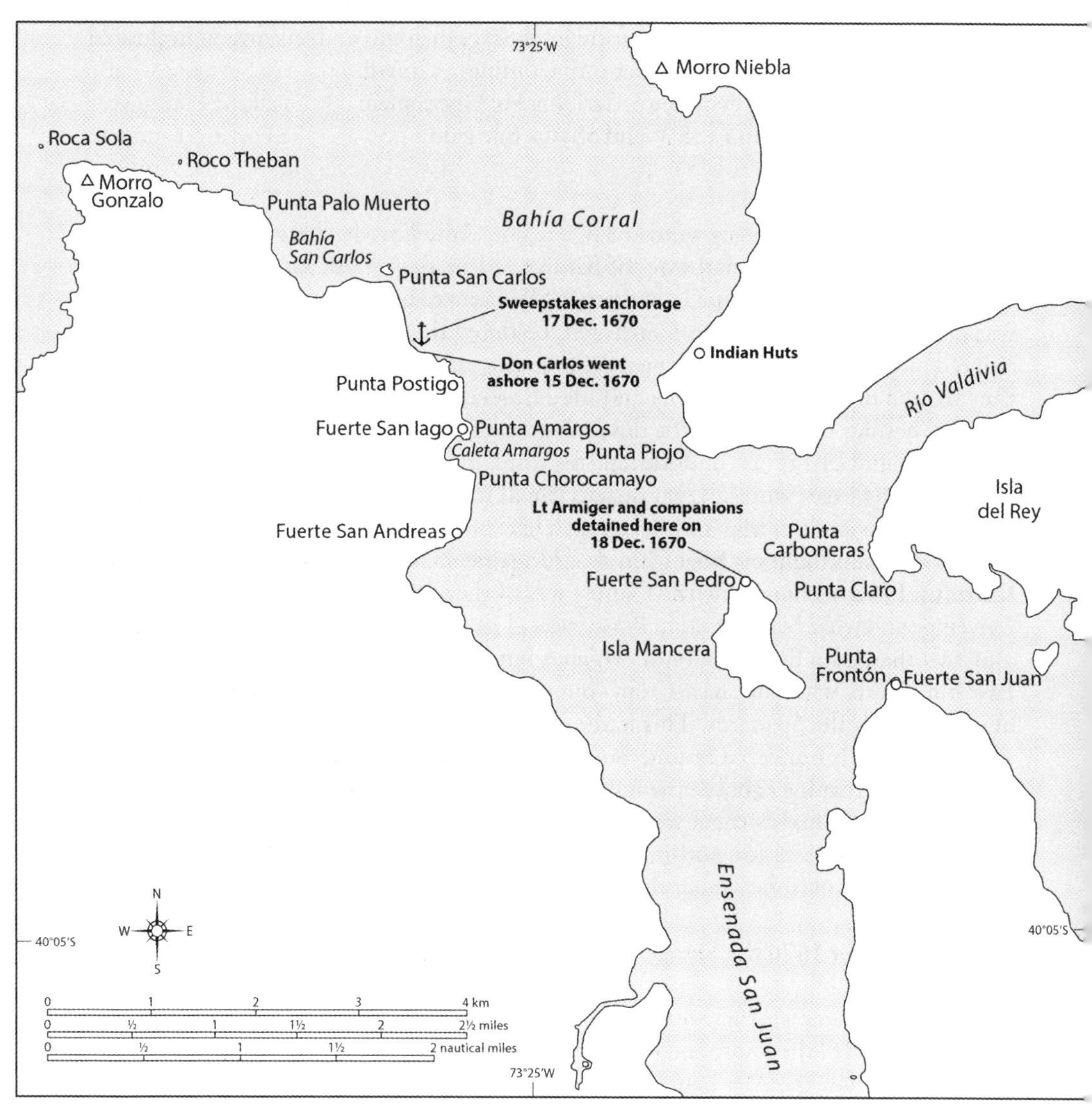

Map 9. Bahía Corral, Valdivia (Baldivia).

Lies what ever he Saide: and he wanted only A passage into this Cuntry: for it is Imposible to Settle a trad here with the Natives for they Selldom Come to the Sea Side and what I Could Perceive Either in this Place or any other alonge the Coast and all the Harbowers and Ports one [on] the Coast the Spanards are Sattled in only to take Possition and trie for a trade. This day the Govennour of Baldiva Stoped my Leiutenant Thomas Armiger and Mister John Fosticue [Fortiscue] and Hugh Cooe Trumpeter and Thomas Highway linguest: they haveinge a flage of truthe [truce]: his Ansewer why he keept them was that I Should Bringe the Shipp into his Harbower. I wrot to the Govennour to Send them of[f]: he Answered he would Send them for Spaine: the Govennour Sent mee of[f] 120 Small loafes of Bread and fower Gares of mum of Chely which they Called wine.[1] I Sent him A shore A Chesier Chese and a Box of Butter and Six Bottles of Mederia wine and a Paper of Nutmeggs: these I Sent in my owne Small boate with two Seamen which Came away Presntly after they had delivered their Message. They treated my Leiuetenant and men very Curtiusly. I received leters from them to Send all their things a Shore, which they had Sent to them the next day by a Canoa that Cam of[f] to me with one Span*ia*rd and Six Indians which I treated with much respecte. They Gave mee an account of the whole State of the Cuntry and would willingely have Come for England. I gave the Indians Knives and Beads and Glases &c.

[156] **December 1670 the *Sweepstakes* at Anchor before Baldiva**
19
Beinge Munday faier weather wind at SW a fresh gale I rode fast. This day I went ashore where I Set Sinor Carlous ashore to looke for him but Could not here any news of him nor See any Signe of People But Spanards: for he was landed within a mile of a forte of Six Gunes which Stood one [on] the South Side of the harbower of Baldava[2] behind a Pointe of Rockes in the Scurte of the woods[3] wher he went directly unto it at his first landinge not knowinge where he went for he was a Stranger in this Cuntry or otherwise very Polliticke.

This day I had five Indians Cam aboard in a Canoa which I made much of and gave them knives and beads. I inquired what they had in ther Cuntry they tould mee nothinge but maies & Pertatos [maize and potatoes]. I Showed them Silver and Gould:they tould mee the Indians of the mountaines had Gould and horses and vicongnes and vinacos[4] but they had nothinge. They were mightily tacken with what I gave unto them. They tould mee they were frinds unto the Spanards and lived one [on] this land: which was hard by the

[1] See above, p. 287, n. 3.

[2] This would be Fuerte San Iago [Santiago] on the lower slopes of Punta Amargos called F[t] S. IAGUA on Narbrough's plan of the 'Port oF Baldavia' (Plate 4).

[3] In the skirt of the woods, at the edge of the woods.

[4] Vicuña (*Vicugna vicugna*) and guanaco (*Lama guanicoe*). 'The *Vicugue* [Vicuña] resembleth a Goat, but greater and more profitable; of the *Fleece* whereof they make Rugs, Coverings, and Stuffs: and in the *Belly* find the *Bezoar*, sometimes two or three, a sovereign *Antidote* against Poisons and Venemous Diseases. ... They have in their Woods and Pastures infinite numbers of beasts somewhat like wild goats, (which they call *Vicagues*) and great store of a kind of Sheep, by them called *Pacos* [Lamas] profitable both for fleece and burden; as big as a small breed of Horses, but in taste as pleasing as our *Mutton*, and no less nourishing. A Creature so well acquainted with its own abilities, that when he findeth himself over-loaded, no blows, or violence shall make him move a foot forward, till his load be lessened; and of so cheap a dyet, that he is content with very little, and sometimes passeth three whole days without water.' Heylyn, *Cosmographie*, pp. 1018, 1063.

forte. Thes People are of a Small Statur and tawne Cullered and looke very ennocntly the Spanards keep them in might Subjection: they would be very Glad wee would Come and lieve with them and Beat the Spanards away. I Sent my Peness into the mouth of the harbower to ley their with a flagg of truhts [truce] to See if any woould Come to Parly with them but noe body Cam nere them. They had Seaven fadam water in the midle of the Porte and Sandy Ground: their is faier Soundings before the harbowers mouth: 20 fadams and 18 and 16 and 14 and 10 and 9 and 8 and 7 fadam Sandy Ground. I Could not Perceive any rub of my Cables received here by this ground wher I rod in 14 fadam. The Porte of Baldava Shoues it selfe to be a very faier Porte and a Good out let: it lies very faierly in a faier bay:[1] the mouth is nere a mile Broad from the South Shore to the north Shore: it lies in and out SE and NW at the first Enterence: about a mile one Arme or River turnes away to the Southward of a Good Breadth:[2] an other Arme or River turnes about A Pointe[3] to the NE:ward of a good breath which Runes up to the Citie of De Baldiva: which is nine miles up that River which Citie is a Garrison of Spanards.[4] In the Creack betwen the two Rivers[5] is a fine Small Iland ajacent to the East maine.[6] In this Iland is a towne and a Small Castle or fortifications[7] of twelf Gunns which are Placed in Severall Parts to Command these rivers and to Secure their Magusene[8] for they have most or all of their Provissions Brought by Small Shippinge from Lima. Here was one Small Ship in the harbower burden about fowerty tunes she Rod about two miles up in the South arem or River betwen two fortes:[9] one Seaven Guns the other five guns. Ther nature of ther Guns wer Sacker and demiculverings and hole Culvering. Their is another forte of fower Guns and nine Guns at Baldava.

[157] **December 1670 the *Sweepstakes* in at Anchor before Baldava**

Here is fresh water runs into the Sea in three Places: just a bout the Pointe of Gallerea to the Eastward I filled Severall tuns Good water and Good fillinge and great Plenty: the Shore Sid is rockey: but ther is Severall Small Sandy bayes:[10] here is Good Store of fish: Cavalles and breames and other Small fish I Saw them Swiminge by the Shore Side: here is whales and Purp*oses* and Seales in this Sea: woods grow downe to the Sea Sid: Sum ap[p]le tre[e]s.[11]

[1] Bahía de Corral.

[2] Ensenada San Juan.

[3] Río Valdivia is entered between Punta Niebla and Punta Carboneros after rounding Punta Piojo (39°52′S, 73°24′W).

[4] Ciudad de Valdivia lies on the south bank of the river 9 miles within the entrance.

[5] Narbrough's plan of the 'Port oF Baldavia' (Plate 4), shows three arms leading out of the harbour. These are Río Valdivia to the NE, Río Torna Galeones to the SE, which is the creek refered to, off which lies Isla Mancera, with Ensenada San Juan to the south.

[6] Isla Mancera.

[7] Shown on Narbrough's plan of the 'Port oF Baldavia' (Plate 4), as Fort St Peter, Fuerte San Pedro. This would appear to be the place Narbrough first thought was the town of Baldivia, see above, p. 285, n. 4.

[8] To guard or keep secure their magazine or store house.

[9] In the bay now known as Puerto Corral (39°53′S, 73°25′W), as shown on Narbrough's plan of the 'Port oF Baldavia' (Plate 4), within Fort St Andrew.

[10] This would appear to be in Caleta San Carlos where Narbrough shows Aqua del Oro flowing into the sea. The Chilean chart shows a small stream flowing out 3½ cables west of Punta San Carlos, the eastern extremity of the bay, and a number of sandy beaches between areas of rock and weed.

[11] See below, p. 505, n. 1.

The harbower with in at Baldava is fresh water: the tid Rise about Six foot[1] the Streame Runs all waies out: of a meane Sternght [strength]. The woods are Gren the land is Rockey the timber is but ordinary as what I Saw ther is Severall Apple trees Groues by the woods Side with Green Aples one [on] them but noe other frut as I Saw. Long notey [knotty] Canes[2] grow here where the water is. The Spanjards tould mee the Cuntry Inland is all woodey and large timber and many People which lives nere the Andies or Cordileros [Cordilleras] that houlds war with them: and ar very vallante. Allsoe they Saie [say] they have Good Store of Gould and that they were Armer [wear armour] of Gould to Secure them Selfe in the wares and they Say the Cuntry is very frutfull Inland: and the Indians never Com to the Seaside for fear of Beinge takin by them.
All Europian mannifactur is a Good Commoditie here with the Spanards: if ther wer a fre[e] trad Cloaths hats Stockings and K[n]ives &c. might be Sould at great Rates. K[n]ives which Coast three Shillings the Case were Sould for five Peeces of Eight the Case a Peece: Gunes are much Esstemed here and watches ar of great vallew [value] and all Such mannafactuer. Gun Pouder is very Scearse; it is worth Six Shillinge a pound: grapnells and anchors are wantinge here and I belevie Canvas for Sailes is wanteinge for ther boats Sailes are Cotten Cloath.

20
Beinge tusday indeferent faier weather wind at WSW a Stout gale. I Rode fast with the Ship: the Boats went a Shor and fetched fresh water iust against the Ship: noe Singe [sign] of indians or of Sin*or* Carlos all this day. This Afternone A Canoa Came A board with one Spaniard and five Indians: they Came from the Govennour with a leter from Leuit*enant* Armiger to Send him his Cloathes and Bedinge A shore and that the Govennour was Risouleved to keepe them. I mad the Mesenger well Com [welcome] and Sent him ashore Againe with the Cloathes and a letter to the Govennour in demandinge my men. I Rod fast all night Keepinge a good watch. This Spanjard would have Come away with me for he Said he had lived in this garrisson 14 yeares and had not A Peece of Eight.

[158] **December 1670 the *Sweepstakes* at Anchor Baldavia**
21
Beinge wedensday hasey weather wind at WSW A Stout gale all day. This morninge I Sent my Penass A Shore Right against the Ship at the Place where I landed Sin*or* Carrolus to See if they Could here anny News of him: they Stayed ther most Part of the day But Could not here any news of him. This Place where he was Landed is within a mile and halfe of the Spanish Forte. I judge he went thether directly for ther is noe traveellinge any other way for the hills and thicke woods.
This day at none the Canoa Came A board Againe and Brought the Same Spanard as was here yesterday and Six indians to Padle or Row him A board: he Came from the forte with leave frome the Govennour to bringe a letter from Leuit*enant* Armiger to Send him the Rest of his things and Sum Beads to give to the Indians all which I Sent to him. this

[1] The Mean Higher High Water is 4 ft (1·2 m).
[2] This appears to be bamboo. The only forms now growing in Chile are *Chusquea culeou* and *C. quila*. Both differ from other bamboos in having solid canes. The former grows to 20 ft (6 m) and was used by the indigenous people for the hafts of their spears, while the latter reaches 50 ft (15 m) and grows in dense climbing or decumbent clumps. These were probably the latter which prefers a lower wetter location.

Spaniard tould my the Govennor was Indeviouringe to take this Shipp. He Brought with him in the Canoa tenn Gares [jars] of wine of Chely to Sell and tobac*co* and Mallassos: I would not Suffer one drop of his wine to Com into the Shipp. He bought leeninge [linen] and woolings and Cases of Knives and severall things of the Shipps Company and Give a Good Price for that he bought. The mony which he laid out aboard the Shipp was nere fowerty Pound all in Piller Peeces of Eight: he Said the Mony was Severall Gentlemens aShore which sent him of[f] to by these things. He tould mee that the Souldiers would be glad that Sum Strangers would Come and take the Place: he saide that they lived in a Garrisson and Could not by any means Git away and that they never Got any mony for they were Paid in Goods which was Brought from Lemma [Lima]. He would faine have had mee to keept him. He tould mee that if this Place wer taken the in Land Indians would Side with us and turn the Spanards holey [wholly] out of Chili. At night he went away. My Boat Cam of[f] noe Singe [sign] of Sinorr Carrolos. It loak very Black to Sea. I waied and Got of[f] the Shore.

[159] **December 1670 the *Sweepstakes* of[f] Baldiva Returninge**
22
Beinge Thursday faier weather wind at SW a fresh Gale. I Plyed of[f] and one [on] a letle to the Southward of the Cap Gallere. I indevioured to git in to a Sandy bay to anchor but Could not fetchet this day noe Signe of Indians livinge nere the Sea Side nor no fier sene any where one the Shor the land all woody.

23
Beinge friday hasey fogey weather wind at SW: But Came to the west this After none and looked very Blacke to Seaward. This day at 10 aclocke I anchored in A Sandy Bay about fower leagus to the Southward of Baldiva.[1] I rod in twenty fad*am* water Black Sand in half a mile of the Shore: the Shore is rockey to the northward and Southward of the Bay. I had the South Point of Land Barr SWBW of me trentinge to a low Pointe which lies five leagus to the South of Baldiva.[2] I Sent my Boate a Shore here to See for Indians; they Staied till night lookinge to and fro and made fiers But Could not See any People or Signe of People. Ther was a faier vally the Land of a Good height and large hills all woody from the Sea Shore up to the tops of the hills. The wood is but of An ordinary Bigness and no very Good timber; the woods ar all Green, the land very Rockey, the Earth that is is of a Black Soile, noe signe of ore or minerall any where. Fresh water runs into the Sea in Severall Places. Noe frute Sene here or Beast; Sum fowles in the woods as Carron Crows[3]

[1] This was probably Caleta Chaihuín (39°55′S, 73°36′W), which lies about 10 miles SW along the coast from Morro Gonzalo. There is a sandy beach and the Islotes Loberia lie at its southern end, with Río Chaihuín flowing into the back of the bay at its northern end. Punta Galera lies a further 6 miles along the coast and is described as being low and wooded. *South America Pilot*, III, paras 7.50, 7.61.

[2] This was probably the point now known as Punta Galera (39°59′S, 73°43′W), which lies 15 miles from Morro Gonzalo.

[3] The carrion crow (*Corvus corone corone*) is not found in Chile. William Funnell, in his account of Dampier's voyage in 1703 (in Golfo de Nicoya, Costa Rica, far north of Narbrough), states: 'The carrion-crow is as big as a small turkey, and, in all respects, very like one; for I never saw any difference, either in colour or shape. The flesh of them both smells and tastes so strong of musk, that there is no eating it. These creatures commonly resort to places where any dead creature is, and feed upon it; for which reason they are called carrion: but the reason why they are called crows, I know not; for they are nothing like them.' Callander, *Terra Australis*, III, p. 167. The bird

and kits[1] and wood Pigions[2]and Small birds of divers Sorts. Few fish in these Seas, many Seals ner the Shore one [on] the Rockes, and Sea Guls. This Bay lies in the Latt*itud* of 40°06′ South And in:
Meridian distance from Cap Diseade East 125 miles
Longitud from from Cap Diseade East 02°38′·8
Longitud from the Lizard west 70°19′·0
Meridian distans from the Lizard west 1107 Lea*gus* 1·8 mile
The Coast all hereabouts is Steep to: you Can find noe Ground at 100 fadam in a mile of the Shore, Exsept it Being baies. Here is no Comeinge one [on] the Coast for the winds are Given to Blow So much out of the west with Storms and Raine neith[e]r Can A man find Bays to anchor in and all the Harbowers the Spanards have Setled: you Canot land one the Shore the Sea runes Soe high Exsept it be very faier weather which it is Sildom for now it is the best of the Sumer, and the weather Exstream fowle. My Intente is to Goe in at Castro[3] and See what Can be done their: if weather P[e]rmitt. This Eveinge I waied and Stood of[f] to Sea wind at SBW a Stout gale with foog and Raine: and at 12 aclock it Cam to the SW and Blow hard I handed my top Sailes.

[160] **December 1670 the *Sweepstakes* on the Coast of Celee**
24
Beinge Satterday Rainey Guesty fogey weather wind at the SSW and blew hard: I Stered of[f] west.
Course made true from the time I waied Anchor out of Sandy bay till to day at none is west be north: distance Sailed 46 mils: departur west 45 mils: def*erence* Lat*itud* 00°09′ north: dist*ance* Sailed 46 mils: Latt*itud* By account at none 39°57′ S.
Meridian distance From Cap Gallara 48 mils west
Longitud from Cap Galera west 01°04′·2
Longitud from the Lizard west 71°23′·2
Meridian distance from the Lizard west 1123 Leagus 1·8 mil
Fogey Bas weather all this night: I indevioured to git of[f] the Shor.

25
Beinge Sunday hasey Gusty weather wind at WNW a Stout gale and raine a great Sea Comes out of the west. Cours mad true after divers Courses is S 17°55′ west: distance

seen by Narbrough may have been a caracara, a falcon and largely a scavenger. It might have been the southern caracara (*Caracara plancus*), which has a black crown and largely brown and grey plumage, is slightly larger than the crow and is common in this area, or the striated caracara (*Phalcobaenus australis*) which is overall blackish brown and of a similar size, but is not usually found as far north as this. However, the most likely would seem to be the chimango caracara (*Milvago chimango*), smaller than the other varieties, of similar brownish colouring and described as an abundant counterpart of the northern hemisphere crow. Jaramillo, *Birds*, p. 90.

[1] The kites and hawks found in this area are: the Chilean hawk, the white-tailed kite (*Elanus leucurus*), the cinereous harrier, Harris's hawk (*Parabuteo unicinctus*), the variable hawk and the rufous-tailed hawk, while the white-throated hawk (*Buteo albigula*) is a summer visitor. Jaramillo, *Birds*, pp. 86–8. It is possible therefore that Narbrough meant doves (since wood pigeons are the next species mentioned). The following pigeons and doves are found in this area: the rock dove, the eared dove, the Chilean pigeon (*Patagioenas araucana*), the Picui ground-dove. Ibid., pp. 138–40.

[2] Possibly the Chilean pigeon.

[3] Puerto Castro (42°29′S, 73°46′W); see above, p. 280, n. 3.

Saile is 50·4 mils: departur west is 15·5 mils: def*erence* Lat*itud* S is 48′: Lat*itud* 40°43′ S.
Meridian distance from Po*int* Gallera west 63·5 mils
Longitud from Po*int* Gallera west 01°24′·7
Longitud from the Liz*ard* west 71°43′·7
Mer*idian* dist*ance* from the Liz*ard* west 1128 Le*agus* 2·3 mils
This night at nine aclock the wind Cam from the NW to the SE with raine and wind in Gust. I handed my top Sails and Stood to the westward to git of[f] the Shore: Bas[e] weather.

26
Beinge Munday hasey fogey Cloudy weather and raine wind at S a Stout gale: I keept my Courses abroad: a great Sea. Cours mad true from yesterday none till today none is South 56°40′ west: distance Sailed 60 miles: departur west is 50 mils: def*erence* Lat*itud* is 33′: Lat*itud* by account 41°16′ S.
Mer*idian* dist*ance* from Po*int* Galera west 113·5 mils.
Longitud from P*oint* Galera west 02°31′·7.
Longitud from the Liz*ard* west 72°50′·7.
Meridian dist*ance* Liz*ard* west 1145 Le*agus* 1·3 mile.
Gusty durty darke weather to night with raine the wind veareinge to the west: at 10 aclocke I tacked and Stood to the Southward and Steered SSW: noe Comeinge nere the Land the weather Soe Boystrus [boisterous].

[161] **December 1670 the *Sweepstakes* one [on] the Coast of Chely**
27
Beinge tusday fogey Cloudy windy weather wind at WNW.
Course mad true from yesterday none till today none is S 37°10′ west: distance Sailed 40 miles: depertur west 24·3 mils: def*erence* Lat*itud* S 32′: Lat*itud* by acc*ount* 41°48′ S.
Meridian dis*tance* from Po*int* Gallera west 137·8 mils
Longitud from Po*int* Gallera west 03°04′·02
Longitud from the Lizard west 73°23′·2
Meridian *distance* from the Lizard west 1153 leagus 1·6 mil
A hard gall at WNW this afternone and all night.

28
Beinge wedensday Cloudy hasey weather wind at West a Stout gale: Co*urs* SBW and SSW. Cours mad true from yes*terday* none till today at none is SBW: distance Sailed is 106 mils: depart*ur* west 20·7 mils: def*erence* Lat*itud* S*outh* 01°43′: Lat*itud* By observation of the ☼ is 43°31′ S
Merid*ian* dist*ance* from Po*int* Gallerea west 158·5 mils
Longitud from Po*int* Gallera west 03°32′·2
Longitud from the Lizard west 73°51′·2
Meridia*n* d*istance* from the Lizard west 1160 le*agus* 1·3 mile
Cloudi hasey weather this afternone: wind at west a stoute gale I Steere SBW westerly: Rainey and Gusty to night.

29
Beinge t[h]ursday Cloudy weather wind at West a stoute gale and a Goulteringe[1] Sea Come out of the SW. Cours made true from yesterday at none till today at none is South: distance Sailed 73 mils: dep*artur*:[2] def*erence* Lat*itud* S 01°13′. Lat*itud* by ob*servation* ☼ 44°44′.
Mer*idian* dist*ance* from Po*int* Gallera west 158·5 mils
Longitud from Po*int* Gallera west 03°32′·2
Longitud from the Lizard west 73°51′·2
Meredia*n* d*istance* from the Lizard west 1160 Le*agus* 1·3 mil
Cloudy weather this afternone & hasey the Skye full of durt and raine: the winde veared to the west north west and North west this evening and blow hard: durty weather to night.[3]

[162] **December 1670 the *Sweepstakes* one the Coast of Chele 46°16′**
30
Beinge friday Stormey Gusty weather wind at NNW this morninge: a mighty Storme I was forced to Bring the Shipp to a try the Sea run Soe deep:[4] much haile and raine this forenone: the wind Came to the west I Set my fore Saile and Stered SSW and SBW: much wind. Cours made from yesterday none till today none is SSW: distance Sailed 100 miles: departur west 38·2 mils: def*erence* Lat*itud* 01°32′ S: Lat*itud* ☼ 46°16′.
Mered*ian* dis*tance* from Pointe Galera west 196·7 mils
Longitud from Pointe Galera west 04°26′·8
Longitud from the Lizard west 74°45′·7
Mered*ian* dist*ance* from the Lizard west 1173 Le*agus* 0·5 mils
Wind Came to the west South west this day at twefe aclocke I Stered South: much wind and a great Sea I judge my Selfe to be about 38 leagus of[f] the Land.
This Afternone at 4 of the Clocke the Carpenter [*margin:* the maine mast Brook shorte] Came to mee and tould mee the maine mast Craked in the well and that he was a fraid it would Give way. I looked upon it & Saw it much defective: I have two fishes[5] one [on] him now: I was forced to bringe the Ship to trie I laid her head to the northward wind at WBS a hard gale and a great sea: I dar not bear Saile for fear of Rowleinge [rolling] my mast over Board it Beinge bad. I tryed all night: Base Gusty weather and haile. My mast is soe Bade as I dare not ventur ner the Shor.

31
Beinge Satterday Gusty rainey heailey weather wind at WBS and West and WBN: I mad Saile and Stered South West be South with my Courses abroad the Sea runs high: I Stered SW Southerly the wind Came to the NW. Cours mad true from yesterday at none till to day at none is South 62° East: distance Sailed 19·2 miles: departur East 17 miles: def*erence* 00°09′ S: Lat*itud* by account is 46°25′ S.

[1] This sounds like a word Narbrough invented. It could be joltering from to jolt, meaning to move with continuous jolting; or from gaustering, meaning noisy, boisterous, swaggering. *NOED*.
[2] There was no departure since the course was south.
[3] This sentence appears to have been added subsequently, written in a different, italic hand.
[4] The waves were so great and the troughs so deep.
[5] Fish; see above, p. 173, n. 1.

Mer*idian* dist*ance* from Po*int* Gallere west 179·7 mils
Longitud from Po*int* Gallere west 04°04′·8
Longitud from the Lizard west 74°23′·7
Mer*idian* dist*ance* from the Lizard west 1167 lea*gus* 1·5 m*il*
This afternone it blew hard at NW & Rained I Stered SW & be South to night.[1]

[163] **January 1670 the Sweepstakes in the So*uth* Sea Coast Cely 47°47′**
1
Beinge Sunday Cloudy Gusty rainey weather and Sum haile wind at NW: A Stout gale: a great *Sea* Comes out of the west: the weather is So foule and the wind blowes So Right one [on] the Land as I dar not Come ner it. Cours made from *yes*terday at none till to day at none is South 39° west: distance Sailed is 105 mils: Depart west is 66 miles: def*erence* Latt*itud* So*uth* 01°22′: Latt*itud* By account is 47°47′ S.
Merid*ian* Dist*ance* from Point Gallere west 245·7 mils
Longit*ud* from Point Galere west 05°42′·5
Longit*ud* from the Lizard west 76°01′·4
Merid*ian* Dist*ance* from the Lizard west 1189 le*agus* 1·5 mile
It blows A Stout gale at NW and Showers: now at twelf aClocke I Steere Away S. This Afternone at 6 aclock the wind Came to the north: very Stormey: I handed the maine Saile and Steered a longe with my fore Saile all night very Stormey weather this night the wind at N. This Evenige one of my men: Richard Earle by name [*right margin:* A man Dround] a Seaman: fell over Board and was drounded.

2
Beinge Munday Gusty Stormey weather wind veared this morninge from the N to the westward and to the SW and Blowes much wind: one of the maine Shrouds broke at Eight aclocke I handed my fore Saile and tried with the Ships head to the Southward: wind at WSW: a hard gale and a greate Sea Runs lofty here.
Course made true from yesterday at none till to day at none is S: distance Sailed 88 mils: def*erence* Lat*itud* 1°28′: Lat*itud* By account is 49°15′ S
Merid*ian* dist*ance* from Po*int* gallerre west 245·7 mils
Longit*ud* from Po*int* galere west 05°42′·5
Longit*ud* from the Lizard west 76°01′·4
Merid*ian* Dist*ance* from the Lizard west 1189 Le*agus* 1·5 mil
I lie a try. This afternone the tiller Brooke Shorte of[f] in the Ruther [rudder] head:[2] I Caused a new tiller which I had to be fitted. Stormey weather all night winde at WSW & raine.

[164] **January 1670 the *Sweepstakes* in the S Sea Returninge**
3
Beinge tusday Gusty rainey haileinge stormey weather wind at WSW: I lay atry with the Shipps head to the Southward till 4 aclock this morninge: then it Proved less wind I Set

[1] This note again appears to have been added subsequently in a different, italic hand.
[2] The ship was steered by a vertical staff, pivoting where it passed through the deck, and attached to the tiller below, which was a wooden bar from the top of the rudder, leading forward. With the tiller broken it would not be possible to steer the ship.

my Courses and Stered SSE: a great and loafty Sea. This morninge two of the maine Shrouds Brooke and the Sea Staved my Boats one [on] the deck:[1] my fore Saile gives way the riginge and Sailes are much tewed[2] with this weather: the Shipp Complaines much in her uper worke by rowling: mighty great Shours of haile this forenone. Cours mad from yesterday none till to day none is SEBS: distance Sailed 62·3 mils: departur East 34·7 mils: defer*ence* of Lat*itud* 00°52′: Lat*itud* ☼ 50°07′ S.
Mered*ian* dist*ance* from Point Gallere west 211 mils
Longitud from Point Galere west 04°49′·0
Longitud from the Lizard west 75°07′·9
Merid*ian* dist*ance* from the Lizard west 1177 le*agus* 2·8 mils
This Afternone the wind held at SW and WSW I Stered SSE and S as the winds served: this Eveinge the wind Cam to the WNW: a fresh gale and Continued all night.

4
Beinge weddensday indeferent faier weather wind at NW and somtims at WNW: a fine gale I Stered away S making the best of my way.
Cours made from yesterday at none till to day at none is South: distance Sailed is 84 mils: def*erence* Lat*itud* is 01°24′ S: Lat*itud* by A Good observation at none is 51°31′ South.
Mered*ian* distance from Po*int* Galere west 211·0 mils
Longitud from Po*int* Galere west 04°49′·0
Longitud from the Lizard west 75°07′·9
Meredian dist*ance* from the Lizard west 1177 le*agus* 2·8 mils
This morninge at ☼ Rizinge I tooke an Amplitud: I find the Compasses to have 10°28′ variation Easterly.
This afternoone I stered away South the winde att W and sometimes att WSW: and Soe continued to night in gusts and raine & slate a base Sea run here.[3]

[165] **January 1670 the *Sweepstakes* in the S Sea returne** [*right margin:* 52°50′]
5
Beinge Thursday fogey weather and Small Raine and gusty wind at WSW: I Steered SSE till Eight of the Clocke this forenone then I lay by [*margin:* lay by recon to be in the Latt*itud*] Judgeinge my Selfe in the Latt*itud* of the Streights mouth: and about twenty fower Leagus to the westward of it – the weather Beinge durty I dar not beare in for the Land: waiteinge Gods Pleaseuer &c.
Cours made true from wedensday at none till to day at none is South and be East: distance Sailed 82 miles: dep*artur* East 16 miles: def*erence* of Lat*itud* 01°20′: Lat*itud* by account 52°51′.
Mered*ian* dist*ance* from Po*int* Gallera west 195 mils
Longitud from Po*int* Gallera west 04°23′·3
Longitud from the Lizard west 74°42′·2
Mered*ian* dist*ance* from the Lizard west 1172 le*agus* 1·8 m*il*

[1] The sea broke some of the planks in the boats.
[2] The rigging was much worn by the constant beating it received from the weather.
[3] This sentence appears to have been added subsequently, written in an italic hand in different ink.

At 12 a Clocke I Bare away and Steered in for the Land [*margin:* Baraway brought too]
EBN 7 leag*us*: till Six aclock then I Brought too: it Proved fogey weather and Rainey wind at WBS: a fresh gale. At 10 aClocke to night it Proved Clearer weather: I filled and Steered for Cap Dissiada[1] ENE By my Compas: wind at WSW a fresh gale: a great Sea runs. [*margin:* Saw land. *small view of three islands drawn immediately below*] At 4 of the Clocke in the morninge wee Saw the Ilands we Called Norres Ils:[2] which lis 8 leags NNW [*margin:* L 52 °50′] from Cap Diseade they Bar NE from me 4 leags.

6

Beinge Friday Close Cloudy weather wind at WSW a fresh gale: this morninge I was Steeringe in ENE by my Compas for the Streights: at 4 aClock in the morninge I reckeinge my Selfe about nine leages of[f] of Cap Disseada: and in the Latt*itud* of 52°53′:[*margin:* Lat*itud* 52°53] at 4 of the Clocke this morninge lookinge abroad wee Saw [*margin:* Saw land. *small view of 4 islands inserted at this point*] the 4 Small Iles which lies at the north part of the mouth of the Streights: they were distance about 4 leags from mee and Bar NE: they are in the Lat*itud* of feivety two deg*rees* and fowerty minuts S: they are A very Good wishinge to fall with all to Steere for Cap Dissiada.[3] The Southermost and Eastermost of thes Ils is a mile distance from the other three: and it is Coplen Pecked up Ile like a Suger loafe[4] of a mean height and Stansd Singelly by it Selfe.

[166] **January 1670 the *Sweepstakes* Enteringe the Streights: Homew*ard***
Beinge friday wind at WSW: A stout Gale at 5 A clocke [*margin:* Ils oF hope sene] in the morninge: the Iles Bare north of mee:[5] I Steered in E: a letle Past five aClocke I Saw Cap dissiado: it Bar ESE of mee distanc about 9 leags the top of the hills Covered with fooge [fog]: I Steered in EBS: at nine A Clock the Cap of Disseada bar South of mee: I Saw the Land one [on] the north Side of the Streights it makes all like Ilands.[6] Cours Made from thursday at none till friday nine aClock the forenone is E: distance Sailed is 75 mils: departur E 75 mils: Latt*itud* By account is 52°52′ S.
Mered*ian* dist*ance* from Baldavia west 120 mils
Longitud from Baldavia west 02°25′·0
Longitud from the Lizard west 72°43′·9
Mered*ian* dist*ance* from the Lizard west 1147 le*agus* 1·8 m*ils*
This Morninge at Nine of the Clocke I was just Ent*ering* [*margin:* Cap Disiado Ber S Foge] into the Streights of Magillan: Comeinge out of Mare Del Zur or the South Sea: Returninge for England. Fogey Rainey weather all this day I Could Scarce See the Land many times.

[1] Cabo Deseado (52°45′S, 74°43′W).
[2] Islotes (Grupo) Evangelistas (52°24′S, 75°06′W).
[3] Wishing: desire, *NOED*. Narbrough means that a navigator should desire to sight them in order to be able to steer for Cabo Deseado.
[4] Islote Pan de Azúcar. See above, p. 273, n. 4.
[5] From the context these would appear to be Norres Islands (Islotes Evangelistas). See above, p. 273, n. 6.
[6] These islands are now known as Grupo Narborough (52°30′S, 74°30′W) and Grupo Westminster (52°35′S, 74°25′W).

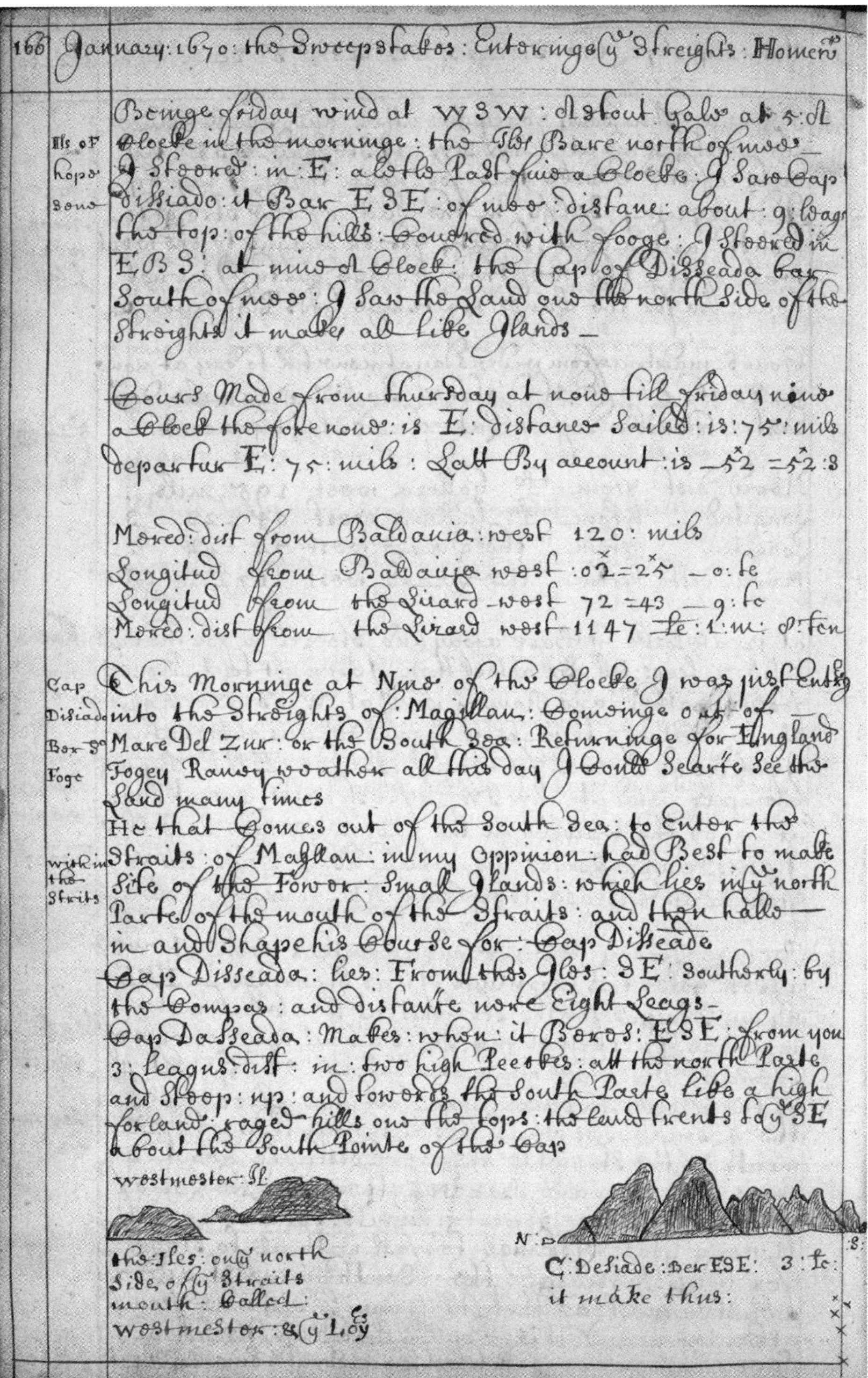

166 January: 1670: the Sweepstakes: Enteringe ye Streights: Homeward

Ils of hope Sone

Beinge friday wind at WSW: A Stout Gale at 5: A Clocke in the morninge: the Iles Bare north of mee_ I Steered: in E: a little Past fiue a Clocke: I Saw Cap Dissiado: it Bar E SE: of mee: distane about: 9: leag the top: of the hills: Couered with fooge: I Steered in E B S: at nine A Clocke: the Cap of Disseada bar South of mee: I saw the Land one the north Side of the Streights it makes all like Ilands_

Cours Made from thursday at none till friday nine a Clocke the fore none: is E: distanes Sailed: is: 75: mils departur E: 75: mils: Latt By account: is 52 = 52: 3

Mered: dist from Baldauia: west 120: mils
Longitud from Baldauia west: 02 = 25 _ 0: le
Longitud from the Liard west 72 = 43 _ 9: le
Mered: dist from the Lirard west 1147 Le: 1: m: & ten

Cap Disiad Bar Se Foge

This Morninge at Nine of the Clocke I was just Entrg into the Streights of: Magellan: Cominge out of Mare Del Zur: or the South Sea: Returninge for England Fogey Rainy weather all this day I Could Scarce See the Land many times

with in the Straits

He that Comes out of the South Sea: to Enter the Straits: of Magellan: in my Oppinion had Best to make Sike of the Fower: Small Ilands: which lies in ye north Parte of the mouth of the Straits: and then halle in and Shape his Course for: Cap Disseade

Cap Disseada: lies: From thes Iles: SE: Southerly: by the Compas: and distance none Eight Leags_

Cap Disseada: Makes: when: it Beres: ESE: from you 3: leagus dist: in: two high Peekes: all the north Parte and Steep: up: and towords the South Parte like a high forland: raged hills one the tops: the land trents to ye SE about the South Pointe of the Cap

Figure 6. Narbrough's *Sweepstakes* Journal (BL, Add MS 88980A), p. 166. Courtesy of the Trustees of the British Library.

He that Comes out of the South Sea to Enter the [*margin:* within the Strits] Straits of Mag[e]llan: in my Oppinion: had Best to make Site of the Fower Small Ilands which lies in the north Parte of the mouth of the Straits: and then halle in and Shape his Course for Cap Disseade. Cap Dissiada lies From thes Iles SE Southerly by the Compas and distance nere Eight Leags.[1] Cap Dasseada Makes when it Beres ESE from you 3 leagus dist*ance* in two high Peeckes att the north Parte and Steep up: and towerds the South Parte like a high foreland: raged hills one [on] the tops: the land trents to the SE about the South Pointe of the Cap.[2]

Westmester Il
[*small view*]
the Iles on the north
Side of the Straits mouth
Called Westmester & the Loy*ers*[3].

[*small view*]
C. Desiade Ber ESE: 3 le*agus*
it make thus.

[167] **January 1670 the *Sweepstakes* Enteringe the Strits in Return: W End**
He that Comes out of the South Sea to Pass the Streits [*margin:* Norris Iles in site: A great help to recover the Straits] of Magalan it is Best for him to make the Ilands and then he may directe his Course for the Cap: for Commonly the land have a Fogg one [on] it when the Iles are Cleare: and you will See the Ilands which lies with in the Straits when you are abrest of Norrises Iles when they Beare N of you. The Iles are to be knowne for three of them lies nere to gether and makes flatesh and ragit with a doake[4] in the wester most: the East ar most Stands Singly and Makes like a Great haie Coocke [hay cock] or Suger loafe. At 4 of the Cloacke this afternone it was very fogey and Rained I Could not keept Site of the Land to Saile alonge. I haled into an open Bay in the South Side and Anchored in 14 Fadam: Stoney Ground: thes Bay have two deep Coves in it and mighty dep water. I Anchored just about the W Pointe at the Goeinge in nere Beeds [Beds] of weeds: for in other Places I Could not find Ground Close to the shore: in this [*margin:* Anchord] Bay their is Severall Ilands. I Called it Iland Bay: [*margin:* Called Iland bay] it is about 7 leages with in the Straits Mouth: their is a Bay and A Sound[5] and the small bay which I Called Tusday Bay[6] wher I anchored outward bound betwen Cap Diseade And this Bay.[7] I went A Shore this Afternone the Land all Rockey in high mountaines and Scrubey bushes: Snow one [on] the hills noe Sine of People the Land unpasable for high Steep Cragey hills All

[1] The distance is 25 miles.

[2] The entrance point of the Straits on the south side is Cabo Pilar, 1½ miles ENE of Cabo Deseado the westernmost point of Isla Desolación from which the coasts leads SE. See above, p. 274, n. 4.

[3] Islas (Grupo) Westminster, which includes Isla Westminster Hall and Islas Lawyers; variants, Loyers.

[4] See above, p. 253, n. 1.

[5] There are actually three entrances between Puerto Misericordia (Tuesday Bay) and Narbrough's anchorage shown on 'Royal Map' and 'Sloane Map' (Foldout and Plate 5). These are labelled 'A Deepe Sound', Surgidero Skyring (52°48′S, 74°32′W); 'A Sound', Bahía Trujillo (52°52′S, 74°25′W), off which Bahía Tuesday leads; and 'A Cove', Bahía Vio (52°44′S, 74°20′W).

[6] Puerto Misericordia (52°47′S, 74°35′W). See above, p. 272, n. 8.

[7] From the 'Royal Map' this anchorage is close east of Cabo Valentina (52 ° 55′S, 74°17′W), the western entrance point of Bahía Valentina, which is nearly 6 leagues within the Strait. The anchorage, close inside the western point between kelp-covered rocks amidst a group of small islands, is mentioned in *South America Pilot*, II, para. 7.522.

this Parte of the Streight one [on] Boath Sids as far as Port famine till you Come into the South Sea: noe Sign of ore or Minerall or any thinge that is Good. Much raine to night and fogg: wind at WBS A Stoute gale.
This Parte of the Straits is Given much to westerly winds for I beleive it blows westerly theere [three] forths of the year And Stormes and Raines and foggs:[1] very Coald and Base vile wather.

[168] **January 70 the *Sweep* in the Straits: C Munday**
7
Beinge Satterday Cloudy Rainge Fogey weather wind at W a Stoute gale. At 4 A Clocke this morning I waied and Steered away EBS: vere base and Durty weather all this day: I keep in A mile of the South Shore. Here is at ever mile or two miles distance Coves or Round Bays or Sounds one [on] the South Side and one [on] the north Side many Sounds and Bays and Coves. At 9 a Clocke I Pased by Cap Munday:[2] at ten a Clocke I Came into the Narrow of the west Parts of the Streits: which narrow is not more than five miles Broad from Side to Side for 12 Leagus distance:[3] the Land high one [on] Boath Sids in Ereguler Cragey Rockey hills with Snow Continually one [on] them Scrubey woods towwards the foots of them and base bogey Ground: Soe lose that I trust a hal of Pike holey [wholly] into it with one hand till it Came to the Rocke.[4]
At 6 aclock this afternone I Pased by Cap quade:[5] at Cap Quad the Straits makes A Shootinge up [shutting up] to the Site [sight]: for ther the Straits turns like an Ellboe. At 8 aClocke I Anchored at the mouth of Batchellers River[6] which is Good Cleare Sandy Ground in Seaven or Eight or nine Fadam water: a faier Birth of[f] the Shore. This River is one [on] the north Shore five leags to the Eastward of Cap quad and two leags to the Eastward of St Joroms Canell or River[7] which runes into the north land: this Batchellers River lies in a valley and a fine Groves of trees at the mouth of it ther is the Best ridinge before of all this Parte of the Straits.[8] Calme weather to night But Small fogy Raine.

8
Beinge Sunday Calme faier and Cleare weather and Sun Shine today very hote. This morninge at 4 of the Clocke I manied my Piness and went into Batcheller River a bout

[1] The meteorological table for Islotes Evangelistas (Norris Islands) shows an average annual rainfall of 2,704 mm, with 275 days with 1 mm or more rainfall; mean wind speed is 17 knots with gales on 85 days of the year the direction predominantly westerly, fog on 5 days per year. *South America Pilot*, II, para. 1.167.

[2] Cabo Monday (53°11′S, 73°24′W).

[3] The actual width varies between 3 and 4 miles for 36 miles.

[4] I thrust a helve of a Pike wholly into it with one hand.

[5] Cabo Quod (53°32′S, 72°33′W).

[6] This is Rada York (53°34′S, 72°19′W), named York Road on the 'Royal Map' and 'Sloane Map', where Río Batchelor flows into the Strait.

[7] Canal Jerónimo (53°33′S, 72°23′W).

[8] *South America Pilot*, II, para. 7.384, states: 'the roadstead fronting the mouth of Río Batchelor, is not considered a safe anchorage; it is exposed to the prevailing W winds and is subject to violent squalls, Furthermore, due to the strength and variability of the tidal streams in the vicinity, a vessel at anchor would sheer most uncomfortably even during light winds.' It would appear therefore that Narbrough is referring to the holding ground of good sand, which was unlikely to damage a ship's cable.

fower miles with my Boate which is the fordest [furthest] that shee Could goe: their the river groues to a Creake for ½ a mile then it Groues to a great Broad water in a valey with severall Small Iles in it and in Compased with Cragey high hils: I travilled ner ten mils to discover the land which whas the fordest I Could goe for mountanes and barran Rock: noe Signe of Minerell Or any thinge that is good: noe Singe of man or Beast. At night I Cam aboard: ground Bogey.

[169] **January 1670 the *Sweepst* in the Straites at Anchor**

9

Beinge Munday Close fogey weather and Calme. This morninge I went with my Boate over to the South Shore and went into a very faier bay wher ther is two faier Coves in it which are Land lockte: and very Safe for Shipps, Rocks one [on] the Shores Side Steep up: 8 and 9 fadam water in the Cove, rufe Ground: A Ship may make fast to the trees: noe wind Can hurt thim. Heer is A many Good Musells in this Coves: about 5 or 6 inches longe: the tide Rise about Eight foote and it is a hige water at 2 aClocke one [on] the full and Change. Here the land is Bogeey one [on] the hills Sids as in other Places the woods Shrubey: much Jeneper trees[1] and thes Peper rine tres:[2] here I Saw Severall Indian huts But noe People: Noe Singe of metle or minerall. This Bay lies two leags from Point Passage: West: this Pointe Passage is opposet to Elezabeth Bay[3] one [on] the South Side: Elezabeth Bay one [on] the north Side.[4] I Called this Bay which I was in Mussell Bay[5] & Pease Cove. Much Raine this Afternone: the wind Came to the west at night.

10

Beinge tusday Cloudy fogey weather wind at west. I waied this morninge and in hallinge my Cat the Rop[e] Brake the Anchor Ran down and lost the Cat Blocke.[6] We hove the Anchor up and Sailed to the Eastward: at nine aClocke this fore none I Pased by Pointe Pasage and Elezabeth Bay and By Arlintons Ile[7] and Ruports Ile[8] and James Ile[9] and

[1] Probably *Pilgerodendron uviferum* which is referred to by Hooker as *Libocedrus tetragona* and *Thuja tetragon*, Moore, *Flora*, p. 65, and described in Cunningham, *Natural History*, p. 174, as resembling a thuja, which itself is not unlike juniper.

[2] Winter's bark tree.

[3] Bahía Isabel (53°37′S, 72°12′W).

[4] Point Passage is not shown on either the 'Sloane Map' or 'Royal Map'. It is, however, named at p. 479 below and described as a low point abreast Rupert's Island on the north shore, now known as Punta Pasaje. It is the southern extremity of Bahía Isabel and Bahía Mussel lies about 4 miles west of it.

[5] Bahía Mussel (53°37′S, 72°17′W), on the NE side of Isla Carlos III. The name Pease Cove has not been retained.

[6] The cat-head was a short beam in the bows of a vessel projecting over the side above the hawse hole (through which the anchor cable passed). It had two or three sheaves in it which together with a rope, a lower block and large hook formed the cat-tackle. When the anchor had been weighed the hook of the cat tackle was hooked into the anchor ring and, by hauling on the tackle, the anchor was hung from the cat-head. A second tackle, the fish tackle, which was hung from a davit abaft the cat-head, was then hooked round the fluke and the anchor hove up horizontal, the weight was transferred temporarily to a stopper and the cat tackle unhooked and secured to a strop round the shank so that the anchor could be hove up tight and lashed to the ship's side. When at sea and clear of soundings the cable would be unbent and the anchor hoisted inboard and stowed below.

[7] Isla James (53°42′S, 72°12′W).

[8] Isla Rupert (53°39′S, 72°12′W).

[9] The western of Islas Charles (53°44′S, 72°08′W).

Charles Ile[1] and Mountigus Ile[2] and Munmurths Ile[3] and wrenes Ile[4] and Cap galant:[5] at one a Clocke I was a Brist [abreast] of Cap Holland:[6] thes Ilands lies all nere to gether abrist of Cape Gallante. At five A Clocke I was a Brist of Cap Froward[7] which is the Southermost Cape of Amarica. I Pase a longe NNE 4 leagus to Pointe Low:[8] at Seaven a Clock I was a Brest of Pointe Low then I Saw Pointe Ann[9] which is the Pointe at the East Part of Porte famin Bay:[10] it Proved little wind at WNW: I Stered NBW: it fell Calme all night letle or noe tide Runs here. I lay in the Chanell driveinge under Saile for here is noe Anchoringe deep water.[11] Pointe Low so Called for it trents to a low Pointe from the hige hilles.[12]

[170] **January 1670 the *Sweep* in the Straits: Porte Famin**

11

Beinge wedensday indeferent faier weather wind at E and at NW: a Flateringe vearable wind today. At A 11 aClocke I anchored in Porte famin in 12 fadam Sandy Ground: Point St Ann Bar NEBN of mee By the Compas [*margin:* Anchor at Port: Famin] I rod in the medle of the Bay and mored with my tow Bower Anchors and Cables: one to the No*rth*ward the other to the Southward: Calme this afternon and to night. This day I made way to onerigg [unrig] the maine mast to flett the Shrouds[13] they giveinge way at the head of the mast. The Carpenter and his Crew went a Shor to fit a fish for the Boult Sprete[14] which they did: the Boult Spret Beinge Sprung and very weeake.[15] Sum of the Boats Crue Caut Severall Brant[16] gess younge and oldons [old ones]: noe Singe of Indians.

12

Beinge Thursday faier weather wind at NW a fine gale. We made way to Clere our hould and to trem the Caske for wat*er* [*margin:* Fish: Caut Po Famin] the Boat went a fishinge and Caute about A hundered faier fish with the Saine: the fish are much like a Mullet they are the same Sort as we Caut at Port St Julyan and here is much Anchoves. Rainey weather to night wind at WNW and Gusty weather. I Rod fast.

[1] The eastern of Islas Charles (53°45′S, 72°05′W).

[2] Isla Monmouth (53°42′S, 72°11′W). This is shown as Earl of Sandwich Ile on both the 'Sloane Map' and 'Royal Map' (Plate 5 and Foldout).

[3] Now Isla Wood (53°46′S, 72°03′W).

[4] Islote Wren (53°46′S, 72°05′W).

[5] Cabo Gallant (53°42′S, 72°02′W).

[6] Cabo Holland (53°47′S, 71°41′W).

[7] Cabo Froward (53°54′S, 71°18′W).

[8] Shown on Narbrough's 'Royal Map' (Foldout), now Cabo San Isidro (53°47′S, 70°58′W).

[9] Punta Santa Ana (53°38′S, 70°55′W).

[10] Puerto San Juan de la Posesión (Puerto del Hambre) (53°38′S, 70°56′W).

[11] The water is too deep to anchor.

[12] *South America Pilot*, II, para. 7.326, describes it as 'a low but prominent rounded hillock, 21 m [69 ft] high and covered with trees, the termination of a ridge extending from Monte Tarn'.

[13] See above p. 142, n. 9.

[14] To fit a fish to the bowsprit, to put a strengthening piece on it.

[15] Sprung is said of a mast or spar when it has a crack running obliquely through any part of it, rendering it unsafe to carry sail.

[16] Brent geese inhabit the northern hemisphere; these were probably upland geese, which are common in this area. Jaramillo, *Birds*, p. 74. See below also, p. 233, n. 3.

13

Beinge Friday Gustie Raine weather wind at WNW. This day I ordered my Master to Cleare the hould and to veew[1] all the Provisions (which might be Sone [soon] done in the Ship[2]). Rainey weath*er* all this day Calme and rain to night.

14

Beinge Saterday Calme all the forenone and raine. This morninge I took the boate and weent alonge the Shore to See for Indians but Could not See any nor Signe of them [*margin:* thicke woods] neither Could I travill in the land for Impenetrable thicke woods the ould trees and bushshes are Soe thicke one [on] the ground. The wind round the Compass this afternone Calme and raine to night and Snow one [on] the hills tops.

15

Beinge Sunday wind at north this morninge and raine. [*margin:* Fish Caute] My men went and haled the Saine and Caute about A hundered fish Much like Mullets: this afternone at 1 a Clocke the wind Came to the SW and Rained and Blow hard: very Coald weather for the time of year [*margin:* Snow] Sum Snow fald this Evenige wind at SW a Stout gale al night.

[171] **January 1670 the *Sweewp* at Port Famin in the Straits**

16

Beinge Munday Fogey weather and Cloudy Som Snow fell to night one [on] the tops of the hills: wind at WSW a fresh gal. Today I had a Fish Putt one [on] the Boule Spreet [bowsprit]: the Boatswain fitted the Riginge for Every thinge is much towed.[3] The Saile Maker is Mendinge the Sailes: Every Man is imPloied [employed] at one thinge or other in fittinge the Ship: this Eveinge the Carp*enter* Brought Another fish A board to Put one [on] the main Mast. Rainey Gusty weather to night.

17

Beinge Tusday Cloudy weather and rain wind at SW: a stoute gale. This morninge the Boult Spreet was Gamind,[4] and Set oup the fore Shrouds, and Put a Boats ladinge of water Caske Ashore. This day the Carpenter went to [*right margin:* Main Mast Found brook] Put the fish one the main Mast and found the Main Mast Brooke Shorte below the Partners one [on] the Gun decke.[5] God Beinge Mercifull to us, Not to let it Goe by the Board in the South Sea for if it had with out all doubt the Ship must have drove one [on] Shore. But Now wee Can find Meanes to Presserve it for here are trees to Make fishes: and in Caus of Nessessity A Man May Make a ordinary Maste. This day the Carpenter Put A fish one [on] the Mast of theerty foot longe: A tree of this Cuntry which wee find lieinge [lying] by the Shore Side Beinge brought out of the valies in the

[1] View the provisions, inspect them.

[2] Because there were not many provisions left.

[3] Tewed, worn with beating.

[4] The bowsprit was gammoned. The act of gammoning was to secure the bowsprit with a lashing passed over the bowsprit and through a hole in the cut-water below it so that it would withstand the upward pull of the stays to the foremast.

[5] Partners on the gun deck. The framework of planks fitted to the gundeck round the hole through which the main mast passed.

time of Great freshes:[1] here lies much drift timber one [on] the Shore and many Large trees Sum of five foot diamitor and Strait theerty foot: the Natur of the wood is like Beach nearest.[2] Cloudy weather to night and Sum Rain wind at W.

18

Beinge wedensday Cloudy Gusty weather wind at W. This morninge wee went A shore and found out A tree which Aforded a very Good fish for the mainmast of theerty Six foot longe the ttree was two foot diametor and forty foot Straite: a burnt Place at the Roote: this was a drift tree Allmost Covered all over in the dry Sand at a full Sea marke. This Eveinge I had it Aboard fitt to Clap one [on] the Mast which I Entend to have one [in] the morninge next for I find the mast Extream Bad But wantinge a better wee must make the Best of a Bad markitt. This day I had the water Caske ashore and washed and Aired to fill in the morninge. Cloudy weather to night wind at W a fresh gale.

[172] **January 1670 the *Sweepstakes* Ridinge at Porte Famin: Straits Ma*gallan***

19

Beinge Thursday Rainey Blowinge weather wind at NW wee Could [not] git any fresh water A board: it blew so hard. The Carpenter Put A fish one [on] the main Mast: and vewinge the mast found the mainmast brooke Shorte of[f] just at the Stepp:[3] and all moast quite of[f] of the Stepp: the hell [heel] of the mast is quite Cripelled in the Stepp with his owne waite it Beinge Rotton in the harte of the mast – night Comminge one [on] I Cause the topmast to be got downe and with a Spare topmast which I had aboard: Riged a Pare of Shears:[4] and left of[f] worke for to night. Lettle wind to night at W Sum Raine.

20

Beinge Friday Cloudy Rainey weather all day the wind round the Compas: this morninge I went to worke with the Maine Mast and Lashed the windinge tackell Blocks and hove up the mast by the Sheares three foot: and found the helle of the Mast Brooke Shorte of[f] by the upper Parte of the Steep: the Carpenter Cutinge a new hele found

[1] Freshet: flood of river from heavy rain or melted snow. *NOED*.

[2] Presumably *Nothofagus pumilo*, a deciduous tree of the Southern Beech family, which grows in this area, up to 100 ft (30 m) in height and 4·3 ft (1·3 m) in diameter. Moore, *Flora*, p. 81.

[3] The step was a large block of timber secured to the keelson (an internal keel laid immediately on top of the middle floor-timbers over the keel and through-bolted to it) with a hole cut in it to receive the tenoned heel of the mast.

[4] This means the two spars were lashed together near one end and then opened out to form an A frame. The spars would have been laid out on the deck and the winding tackle (the largest tackle in the ship) secured to the lashing, together with a topping lift and possibly guys. The topping lift was taken to the foretop and the A frame raised into position over the main mast. The lower ends of the spars would be spread out on either side of the ship (probably with pads underneath them to spread the load) and secured. The lower block of the winding tackle was then secured to the mast with a strop and the running end of the tackle taken through leading blocks to the capstan. The mast, which weighed of the order of 4½ tons, could then be hoisted, repaired and lowered back into the step. This operation was normally carried out in the dockyard using a dockside crane or derrick, or by a hulk permanently fitted with sheers.

Figure 7. Diagram illustrating possible method of lifting *Sweepstakes*'s main mast. Note that rigging has been largely omitted to make the salient features clearer.

the Mast So defective by Beinge Brooke Shorte of[f] and Rotton that wee Cut of[f] Sixten inches more to Com to Sound wood: Soe that in all wee Shortned the mast twenty Six inches at the heelle and feted him for the Steep[1] and Lowered it downe againe and got up the Shrouds: the Bay was very Smoath water all day. This mast was Brooke Soe Short of[f] as it is much to beleive how it stood the tumblinge and Rowleinge [rolling] of the Ship in the South Sea: and allsoe it beinge Brooke Short at the Partners. But Now I have three good a Substanctiall fishes one [on] it and well Secured: which I hope will Carry the Shipp for England: for nothinge more Cane be Done to it Now to make it more fearmer than what is. This mast to the outward appearrance in England and alonge time After Semed to Any Mans vew to be a fearme [firm] and Clear mast: But it Proves the Contrary.

21
Being Satterday Faier weather all this day day wind at WSW a fresh gale But at night it Rained and fogey. This day wee Riged the mainmast and got a boats Ladinge of water aboard. The Shipps Company are now all of indeferent good health.

[173] **January 1670 the *Sweepstakes* Ridinge at Porte Famin: St*rait***
22
Beinge Sunday wind at W and NE a fresh gale and Raine all this afternone Cloudy to night.

[1] Cut the bottom of the mast into a tenon to fit into the step.

23

Beinge Munday Gusty Cloudy weather. Wee fitted our Riging and fetched wood and water Aboard. Could Cloudy weater wind at WSW to night.

24

Beinge tusday wind at NW: A Stout gale this morninge this Afternone Much wind at W and Slaty Snow and Raine to night. We mad the Shipp fitt to helld Against the morninge.[1]

25

Beinge weddensday Cloudy weather and Gusty with Slaty Snow wind at NW. This morninge wee heled the Ship and washed the Starboard Side and laid one [on] Stufe betwen the wals.[2] Ther is A great deale of Snow one [on] the hills one [on] boath Shors: Rainey gusty weather to night wind at SWBW.

26

Beinge Thursday Rainey weather. This Morninge I helled the Ship and washed the Larboard Side but Could not laid one [on] Stufe the wind blowinge to [too] hard at W and gusty weather to day: wee Cut wood and fitted the riginge and Searched the Shipp in the Bowes.[3] Much Snow fell this afternone and very Could weather the wind at SW and blow in gusts: very hard Sumtimes this Eveinge and very durty darke weather to night.

27

Beinge Friday Gusty Stormey weather wind at NNW Sum times and at W and SSW in Gust flieinge to and frow: darke Cloudy weather all Night.

28

Beinge Satterday Calme this morninge. I Caused the Ship to be helded and Stufe Laid one [on] betwen and under the wales[4] and the Boate to fetch wood: by tenn a Clocke it began to Blow wind at NW: and blow hard in gusts all the Afternone and most Parte of the night with rain.

29

Beinge Sunday Cloudy weather but lettle wind all day at west. This morninge I went over in the Pinas to the South Shore and haled the Pinass drie one [on] land: beinge tenn of us in Company and went into the land five mils.[5] Wee Stayed ther all night: the land woody: wind at W.

[1] Ready to be heeled over in the morning.

[2] Heeled the ship over, washed and cleaned off the growth on the starboard side and recaulked between the planks (wales).

[3] Examined the ship in the bows, presumably to look for a leak, possibly the one mentioned on the way to Baldivia. See above, p. 282.

[4] To complete the work on the larboard (port) side.

[5] This will have been Isla Dawson which lies opposite Puerto del Hambre (Port Famin) across Paso del Hambre.

[174] **January 1670 the *Sweepstakes* at Anchor Po*r*t Famin in the Str*aits*S**
30
Beinge munday Windy weather wind at SW: much wind all day and Cloudy. This day I and my Company travelled to and fro in the Land and found it hilley and Rockey with woods and Barran Plaines: Sum Ground of a good Soile of Black earth others Rockey the woods of the Sam Sorte of trees as are one [on] the north Shore and the Land much like it. Severall Revellets of fresh water Com Runinge downe the hills.
Noe Signe of Beasts in the Land: or fowle in the woods Exsept kits[1] and Green Parrikeetos[2] which wee Saw Severall None of us beleiveinge that Parreketos Could have lived in Soe Coald a Climat if we had not Senn them in the woods: Brant Gees[3] and Duckes[4] by the Shore Side: noe frute in the woods nor herbs that are good: the gras long and Sogey: heath with beris one [on] it and Buseses with Red bereris[5] of a good tast and noe harem: Bushes [*margin:* Beris] with beres when Rip ar blacke like Small Slos tast like Graps: wee Called barrberes for the leaves of the bushes are green and tarte.[6] Noe venemous varrment Senn. Noe kind of Mettle nor mineralls any where. This night faier weather I Cam to the Boate and lay ther in a tent which we built: Severall Indian huts Sene by the Sea Side but noe People have ben ther lattly: the land have noe Signe of any thinge walkinge in it but by the Shore Sids, the Shore Side Rockey and Peavell Stones. Should wather lis of[f] the Shor and Rockes: this land Beres ESE from Port famin: distance five leagus: little tids Runs in this Part of the Straits as I can Perceive the water Rize by the Shore about Eight foot: it is a hige water here at one a Clock one [on] the Change day: the flod Come from the Southward.
I was at an Iland which lies a mile from the South Shore: in tim of year ther breeds fowles one [on] it and gulls and wite belled divers[7] and other berds of the Sea. This Iland Bers ESE from Porte famin it lies lowe and is not Sen at Port famin. I Called it Gull Ile for the Guls breedinge one [on] it.[8]
The Straits here is A Bout five Leagus Broad from the north Shore to the South Shore:[9] I Perceive but Small tids to Run in the midle of the Straits.

[1] The kites here are similar to those seen on Isla Guamblín, p. 281, n. 1, with the exception of the white-tailed kite (*Elanus leucurus*), and the addition of the cinereous harrier (Circus cenereus). Jaramillo, Birds, pp. 86–8.

[2] The only parakeet found in this area is the austral parakeet (*Enicognathus ferrugineus*). Jaramillo, *Birds*, p. 142.

[3] Probably upland geese, although kelp geese, ruddy geese (*Chloephaga rubidiceps*), and ashy-headed geese (*C. poliocephala*) are also found in this area. Jaramillo, *Birds*, p. 74.

[4] For species of ducks see above, p. 280, n. 1. The flightless steamer duck is the most likely, being a marine duck found along the coast in this region; the flying steamer duck is marine and fresh water, found mainly in ponds and lakes.

[5] Probably *Empetrum rubrum*, common in the *Nothofagus* forest and dwarf shrub heath in this area. Moore, *Flora*, pp. 123, 368, see above, p. 264, nn. 1, 4.

[6] See above, p. 264, n. 4.

[7] These might be shag which are referred to by Peckett as 'white breasts' (pp. 455, n. 1; 493; 580, n. 5 below), either the imperial shag, or the rock shag, Shirihai, *Complete Guide*, pp. 222–5; or possibly the Magellanic diving petrel (*Pelecanoides magellani*), which are common, white beneath, and breed in this area. The common diving petrel (*Pelecanoides urinatrix*) is a similar bird found in this area but is less common. Both species are inshore marine birds found in canals and fjords rather than the open ocean. Jaramillo, *Birds*, p. 52.

[8] Probably the Rocas San Pedro y San Pablo (53°42′S, 70°44′W), two above-water rocks which lie about 1 mile offshore, and are the only feature answering Narbrough's description.

[9] The Strait varies in width from 9 to15 miles. It runs north–south in this area, so Narbrough must be refering to the west side, part of the South American mainland, as the north side.

[175] **January 1670 the Sweepstakes at anchor in Port Famin in the Str** [corner damaged]

31

Beinge tusday Faier weather wind at SW a fresh gale. This morninge I Cam over in my Boat to the north Shor and landed at Point Low:[1] there Came an Indian Man to me and Beeged for victualls: I gave him three Gulls and two whit brist divers: he went to his fier and Singed of[f] the feathers and tere the Fowles a Peeces with his teeth and Eat them Rare[2] guts and all and Chawed the bones Rare like any dogg: this man Eat three gulls and two whit Breest fowles and two Skins of other fowles in less then halfe an houers time he Semed [*margin:* An Indian Man Came to me] to be almost Starved: He was all A lone: his liveinge was one [on] Musells and Limpets when he Could git them: he was but of Small Statur: Aged about theerty years: of a tawney Couler: Short Black heier Flagin down Round fated [featured] and lettle Eis and blacke: Flates nosed: he was Naked all over: here [hair] one [on] his uper lip and one [on] his Previtis. I gave him Beads and a knive: I learned him to Speake the word Englesh man and I Shawed him the union Coulers and Signified to him of our Country. He Stayed with me till night and then went his way lafinge [laughing] with fowles as I give him he had nighther [neither] bow nor arrow only a Stafe in his hand. He had Sene me before (for he made Signes that I give the Indi*ans* glases): he neither under Stode any kind of mettle, Eighter Gould or Silver, for I Showed him boath, he lafed when he Saw the Efiges of the kinge one [on] a five Shillinge Peece.

This day I Saw at Port famin in the woods the footeinge of [*margin:* Deres Footinge] deare in two Places and Parrickettos fleinge in those woods [*margin:* Green Perriketos] which I had not sene all the time I was ther before. Cloudy weather to night wind at W a fine gale.[3]

[175] **February 1670 the *Sweepstakes* at Anchor at Port Famin**

1

Beinge Wedensday Cloudy Gusty Blowinge weather wind at SSW and SW. This day wee Got wood a board and Sum water I rod fast darke weather to night and letle wind.

2

Beinge thursday wind at WBS: much wind all day so as I Could not way. This day I got a Spar fish aboard the Shipp. Less wind to night at NWBW.

3

Beinge Friday wind at W. This morninge I got the Small Bower anchor a board judginge to Saile to the Northward for the winds Blows at the SW in the after nonenes and have don Soe ever Sence I Came into the Straites out of the South Sea: which winds I believe ar generall this Part of the year. It below [blow] So hard at SW as I Rode fast faier weather to night wind at W a fine gale.

[1] Cabo San Isidro. See above, p. 303, n. 8.

[2] This would seem to mean raw, uncooked, rather than rare, underdone.

[3] The remainder of the page is blank. Narbrough also numbered the following page as 175.

4
Beinge Saterday this morninge at three acclock I wayed it Proved lettle wind at W: I Stood into the Chanell: noe ground at A hundered fadam halfe a mile of[f] the Point Sa*nta* Ann:[1] I made noe way Either to the northward or to the Southward it beinge little wind. I would faine have sene the South Sea onece more to have discovered the South Coast of Chely: but Seinge the winds hanging Continually westerly: I waiteinge the oppertunity three weekes and my Provissions growinge Short and the time of year Spendinge a pass I Concluded to Saile to the north Sea: though unwillinge by reason I had not discovered the Coast one [on] the South Sea: the weather beinge soe Stormey and the winds all wase [always] out of the Sea: that I dare not deal with the Coast and the mainmast Beinge Soe bad in the heele and at partners.[2]
At twelfe a Clocke to day I was a brist [abreast] of freshwater bay[3] the wind at W a fresh gale: I Saw Smakes one [on] the South Land which is a brist of freshwater bay: the wind blowinge So hard westerly that I dar not ventur the Boat over to that Shore the Straits Beinge A bout Eight leagus Broad their.[4] This Eveinge at Six aclocke I anchored ner the Shore two leagus to the northward of freshwater Bay in twelfe fadam water Sandy ground: ner a mile of[f] the Shore. A good Shore to anchor one [on] for fair Soundinge: the Land ner the water Sid of a fine Rizeinge height to the great hills in Land which ar about Eight miles from the Shore Side:[5] the land all woodey of good timber and A good Soile of Earth: fresh water Rune in Severall Revellets.

5
Beinge Sunday wind at WSW and blew hard all day. I rod fast with the Ship: I Sent the Penass alonge the Shore to See for People they Came to A fire but Could not See any People. Gusty weather to Night wind at W.

[176] **Feberuary 1670 the *Sweepstakes* at Anchor**
6
Beinge Munday very windy weather wind at W: I rod fast it Beinge So much wind in gusts as ther was noe Saileinge: letle wind to night.

7
Beinge tusday letle wind Sumtimes at N and at SW: I rod fast. I went a shore in the woods and went three miles up the Land in a Revellet of water for their is noe goeinge Ells [else] the woods ar Soe thicke. I Saw the footinge of deer[6] in the Sand but noe Signe of any other Creatur: noe fowles nor birds: the land of a Sandy Gravelly Soile: the trees indeferent Large and tall of the kind of Beech wood:[7] noe Signe of any mettle or Stones

[1] Punta Santa Ana (53°38′S, 70°55′W).
[2] Narbrough abandoned any attempt to return to survey the south coast of Chile, because of the lateness of the season, the adverse winds and the state of his provisions. The final reason, the poor state of his mast, is written in an italic hand in different ink and would appear to have been inserted subsequently.
[3] Bahía Agua Fresca, (53°23′S, 70°58′W).
[4] The Strait is about 20 miles wide here.
[5] The hills west of this area rise to 2,132 ft (650 m).
[6] See above, p. 214, n. 2.
[7] See above, p. 264, n. 4.

but Peavell Stones: noe frut: Severall Brookes of fresh water Come Runinge from the Snowey mountain with a raped Streame.[1]
I haled [hauled] the Net here and Caut two hundered fair fish. My Leiutenant Saw one Indian at a great distance by the Shore Side: but he went his way and was not Spake with. This Land one [on] the Shore from Point Famin to Elezabeth Iland[2] is the Best and likelest land in all the Straits to be Plantable.[3]

8
Beinge wedensday Cloudy weather the wind at west a fine gale. This morninge at three a Clocke I waied and Stood to the northward and faier a longe the Shore I Sounded all alonge as I Sailed and had Eighten and twenty fadam water fine Black Sand: Beter then halfe a Mile of[f] the Shore very Good Ridinge all a longe this Shore. My Leiuetenant went with the Pinass Close a longe the Shore and to Se if he Could Speake with any Indians: But Could not he Saw Severall Places wher they had ben lattly and Signs of many People and where they had made their Canoas. He Caute Severall fish with the net: many Mighty large Smelts of twenty one inches longe and nine inches aboute. [*margin:* large smelts] This day at one A Clocke I Pased betwen Elezabeth Ile and the little Ile Caled St Bartholomue:[4] at two of the Clocke I Anchord in Eight Fadam Black Sandy Ground: a mile of[f] the north Shore: the Iland St Bartlomee and the Ile St George wer Sheet in one:[5] they Bere SSE frome [mee] by the Compas and the E Point of Elezabeth Ile bere SBE of mee. This afternone it Blow and Rained and thick and durty weather I mored the Shipe with the two Bowers. It Proved Reasonable good weather to Night the wind Came to the NNW.
I Sent my Leiut*enant* one [on] Shore one [on] the north Side against wher the Shipp Rode to See If he Could Discry any People and to make A Smoake: he Returned but Saw noe People.

[177] **February 1670 the *Sweepstakes* at Anchor in the Str*ait* Ma*gallan* in Royall Road**
9
Beinge Thursday Darke Cloudy weather wind at WBN a fine gale this forenone. This morninge I Sent my Leiut*enant* and tenn Men one [on] Land one [on] the north Shore to discover the Land up to the NW:ward after you ar within the Second Narrow: I went one [on] Shore with Six men one [on] the North Shore to the westward of the Second Narrow to discrie the Cuntry: the Land is of a mean heaith ner the water Side but five Mile in the Land it is high Plaine downes: the Land is without wood or fresh water A Cleane grase land and a dry A Good Black Soile of Earth: very Good Land to Greas [graze] Cattle in the gras very Sweete: here is Good travellinge. Here are Exlent tasted beris wich growe nere the Ground they are as Bigg as Peas and of a Red Couller[6] these are in great quantity: here ar other Black Beries which growes one [on] Prickelly bushes: [*margin:* Frut in the Strait of Magallan] Like Barrbary Bushes:[7] the Beries are of a Good tast – noe Signe of other frut.

[1] The reference to the stream is written in an italic hand in different ink and appears to have been added subsequently.
[2] Isla Isabel (52°53′S, 70°44′W).
[3] Narbrough was anchored about 7 miles south of the present town of Punta Arenas.
[4] This channel is now called Paso Reina.
[5] Shut in one, the two islands were in line.
[6] Probably *Empetrum rubrum*; see above, p. 264, n. 4.
[7] Probably *Berberis empetrifolia*; see above, p. 264, n. 4.

This Land in my oppinion would bere and Produce Good Corne And be made a fine habbitable land the Aier temperate: Beast as I Saw were Ynacos [guanacos]: Fowles were Osterrages[1] [ostriches] and Pied Geese[2] and duckes[3] and Currlus[4] [curlews] and Blacbirds[5] and thresshes[6] and werens[7] and other Small birds: all thes feeds one these Beris: ther are of the Geese and Currlus ineumerable quanties. Noe People Seene but Seings where they had burned the grase. My Leiuetenant Saw the Same I Saw as to the Natur of the Cuntry and of Annimall he was at least fiveten miles distance from the Place wher I was. Noe signe of wood here Abouts. At Night I went A board: Much wind to night at W.

10

Beinge Friday wind at WSW and Blew hard all day soe as I Could not waie at Eveinge it was less wind. This day at none I observed the Sun and found this Place [*margin:* latitud: 52° 46′] to be in the Latt*itud* of 52°46′ by the quadrant of Davis.[8] This Place is a Good Road to Rid in for here is Should water and good Ground: an EBS wind is the worst wind for the narrow is open one [on] that Pointe. I haveing a disier to vew the South Shore Rode here till the weather Permitted the Pasinge with my Boat: I Saw a Great Smoake one [on] the South Land downe by the waters Side which had ben Continued for five dayes time. It blew hard to night at WSW: faier weather towards morninge.

11

Beinge Satterday faier weather wind at NBE this mor*ninge* [*margin:* Men sent ashore] but after it Cam to the west and Proved Calme: I rod fast. I Sent the Penass to the South Shore to discover the Land at the Second Narrow: I Sent Men one [on] Shore one the north Shore to See for People but Saw none.

[178] **February 1670 the *Sweepstakes* at Anchor in Ro*yall* Roade**

12

Beinge Sunday faier weather this Morninge wind at NNE a fine gale I Rod fast it Proved Calme all day. I Sent the long boat to San Georges Iland to Gitt Penguens: I Sent my yoale [yawl] ashor with tenn Men one [on] the north Shor to See if they Could mett with People they Returned A board and Saw none: the Penass is Coastinge one the South Shor down to the first narrow. One the north Shore at the west Part of the Second Narrow to the north ward of the Clefe in the Bite[9] there is a harbower or Broad Roundinge Lake:

[1] The greater rhea (*Rhea americana*) is not normally found as far south as this, so this must be Darwin's rhea; see above, p. 207, n. 4. Harris, *Guide*, pp. 23–4.

[2] See above, p. 308, n. 3. Upland geese or possibly kelp geese, both could be described as pied and eat, among other things, grasses and berries although the kelp goose feeds principally on algae on rocky coasts. Shirihai, *Complete Guide*, pp. 277–8.

[3] For the large number of duck in this area, see above, pp. 270, n. 1; 308, n. 4. The spectacled duck and torrent duck are normally found slightly further west. Jaramillo, *Birds*, pp.76–82.

[4] Possibly a whimbrel (*Numenius phaeopus hudsonicus*), or Hudsonian godwit (*Limosa haemastica*), which are found in this area. There are also a number of sandpipers which visit this area. Jaramillo, *Birds*, pp.106–11.

[5] The austral blackbird (*Curaeus curaeus*) is the only blackbird likely to be found here. Jaramillo, *Birds*, pp. 206–7.

[6] The austral thrush (*Turdus falklandii*) lives in this area. Jaramillo, *Birds*, pp. 194–5.

[7] The grass wren (*Cistothorus platensis*) and the southern house wren (*Troglodytes musculus*) inhabit this area. Jaramillo, *Birds*, pp. 194–5.

[8] From his anchor bearings Narbrough was anchored in 52°49′S.

[9] Bight, recess or curve in the coast.

three fadam water at the Goeinge in and fower fadam with in all flat Shores.[1] Five leags to the westward of this harbower their is another harbower or Lake one [on] the North Shore which Rune into the Northward Six Mils[2] but two fadam water at the [*margin:* lakes discouerd] Goeinge in: the tide Runes in here indeferent Strong: the water floutheth [floweth] a bout nine foot: it is a high water one [on] the Change day at 9 a Clocke. The Eastermost Lake I Called Crab Lake for Crabs which I Caute their and the westermost Lake I Called Duck Lake for the many Ducks Senn their.[3] It floweth halfe tid one [on] the Shore to [*margin:* tids obserued] that in the ofinge in the Bay: [in] this Bay it is a high water at twelfe a Clock one [on] the Change day and Soe it floweth in the Second Narrow and the flood Coms from the Eastwards and Runs into the Straits a good Stronge tide: the water Rise by the Shor about Nine foote. [*margin:* Cut of the ould Cable] I Cut of[f] the Best Bower Cable 47 fadam it Beinge ould.
This Eveinge My Selfe and Purser[4] with fower more went downe to the Clifs one [on] the north Shore to kill fowles with our Peecses[5] for thir is amany whit Brest foules[6] [of] divers breeds there under those Clefs. Wee Saw a Vinaco[7] [*margin:* A large vianaco taken] which wee beset and Shoot him in the Eies with Small Shoot and forced him to take the Sea: wee Caute him with our Boat: he waied two hundered & Sixty fower Pownds as he was a Live he was very Good Meate and much like A Large Stagg without hornes for Largness. He waied hole 264 Po*unds* neate. Faier weather to Night.

13
Beinge Munday Cloudy darke weather wind at NW A Stout gale all day. I wayed this forenone and Stood towards S[t] Gorges Iland for my Long Boate: at twelfe a Clocke I Saw her Plyinge up to mee: I Plyed to and fro S[o]unding the Bay one [on] the North Side of Elezabeth Iland and had very fair Soundings at 14: 12: 10: 9: 8: 7: fadam water braw Sandy ground[8] all the bay over. At Six I Anchored in 8 fadam the Ile S[t] Bartleme bore SEBS of mee. [*margin:* the long boat came aboard wth 700: pengu]

[179] **Februeary 1670 the *Sweepstakes* Saileinge out of the Straits of Mag*a*la*n***
14
Beinge Tusday faier weather wind at WSW A Stoute [gale]. This morninge I waied with the Shipp and Stood to the E:ward at Seaven of the Clocke I Passed the Second

[1] Called Oase Harbour on the 'Royal Map' and 'Sloane Map' (Foldout and Plate 5) and now called Ensenada Oazy (52°42′S, 70°33′W).

[2] Shown on the'Royal Map' and 'Sloane Map' (Foldout and Plate 5) as Peckits Harbour, now called Puerto Zenteno (52°46′S, 70°44′W).

[3] Wood BL, MS 46A, p. 160: 'Betwixt the west point of the 2[d] narrow and the head of Queen Elizabeths Iseland on the North shore there are 2 Small harbours which are good and safe for Small Ships one of which is near 2 Leagues from the narrow the other about 3 Leagues and a ½. The Eastward I called Crabb harbour from the Many Long legged Crabbs wee found there which are indifferent good provision in case of necessity: the other which is the westermost I called Port Vaughan and is the Best of the two.'

[4] Alex Curtis. TNA, ADM 39/2510.

[5] Fowling pieces.

[6] 'Foules' is written in different ink in an italic hand and appears to have been inserted subsequently.

[7] Narbrough's 'Royal Map' (Foldout) has a legend in the vicinity of the Punta Gracia, the NW entrance point of Segunda Angostura, stating 'Here I killed a Guianaco which waied Two Hundred Sixty Fower Pounds'.

[8] Braw sandy ground good holding ground for anchoring.

Narrow then I Stered ENE and NE and E for the First Narrow: at twelfe of the Clocke I Entered the narrow their I Swaw my Pinnas: which I had Sent to discover the South Shore in that Parte of the Straites: at two of the Clocke I was through the Narrow I Brought tow[1] and tooke up my Pinas and hoisted her in. My Leiutenant and men had benn in the South Land in Severall Places: and Saw Smok and fiers made in the Grase But when they Came at them the People were Gone they Could not Speake with any People. The Land one [on] the South Side in this Parte of the Straits is a dry Land And Gravevell Soile: Ereguler Land in Gullys and hillocks: very Barran noe Signe of wood or fresh water: the Gras in tufes Grews [tufts grows].[2] It is high Land in the Cuntry: But very Low towards the water Sid and in the first narrow one [on] Boath Shors low Plains. In [*margin:* Three larg Anchors sene A Shore] the the First Narrow at the West End one [on] the north Shor Above A full Sea Marke[3] their Lies three Large Anchors which are of the Spanish Built: the Bigest is twelf foot longe the other two A Leaven foot longe: they are sum what Eaten with Rust but they may doe a kindness ife An anchor should be wanted. I would not meddle with [them] to bringe them a way for that Reason: I judge they have Laid their a Longe time: And were warked their by Sum Spanish Shipp:[4] for here wee found An Iron Sledge of twenty Pounds waite the which I Suppose was A tope Commander:[5] Noe Signe of anythinge Ells belonginge to A Shipp to be sen one [on] the Shore: my leuetenant looked for gunns but found none.

From this narrow I Steered NE for the Clife one [on] the north Shor:[6] which Clife Bare north of mee at fower of the Clock [*margin:* Cap: Vergin Mary: 4: leags distance wen it Bar west] then I Stered EBS By my Compas: to Run downe to Cap Vergen marry.[7] At nine A Clock Cap Vergen Mary Bare W of mee and was distance about Two Leagus then I haled NE By my Compas: the wind at west south west A Stout gale: the mone [moon] Shineinge very Brite: at ten a Clocke I Steered NBE .

As you Steer up the Straits from Cap Virgen Mary you most have A Care and Give the Cap A league Birth for their li[e]s Rocks and Sands which doe Show them Selfe at A low water and their Lies within the Cap to the South A longe lowe Beach which trents SW from the Cap with a Showle Point [*margin:* sand Banks] tenn Leagus to the westward of the Cap up the Straits: one [on] the South Part of the Chanell th[w]art of the Clife of Point pos*sess*i*on* their Lies Should Banckes of Sands: the tid Riples over them: keep to the norward of these Shoulds a Good birth.[8]

[1] Hove to and stopped the ship.

[2] This would appear to be tussock grass (*Poa flabellata*), which covers a large part of this area. Moore, *Flora*, p. 3.

[3] Above the level of high tide.

[4] Hauled up to their present position by some Spanish ship.

[5] Top Commander. A commander is normally a wooden mallet used for driving the fid (a tapered wooden spike) between the strands of a rope to open them out when splicing. The name could also be applied to any form of hammer or sledgehammer. It seems unlikely that it was for use in the tops (at the tops of the masts), on account of its weight, so possibly it was deemed to be of a large or top size.

[6] This would be Cabo Posesión (52°18′S, 68°58′W).

[7] Cabo Vírgenes (52°00′S, 68°21′W).

[8] These shoals are off the eastern extremity of Banco Orange, which extends eastwards from Punta Anegada, the southern extremity of the eastern end of Primera Angostura (First Narrows).

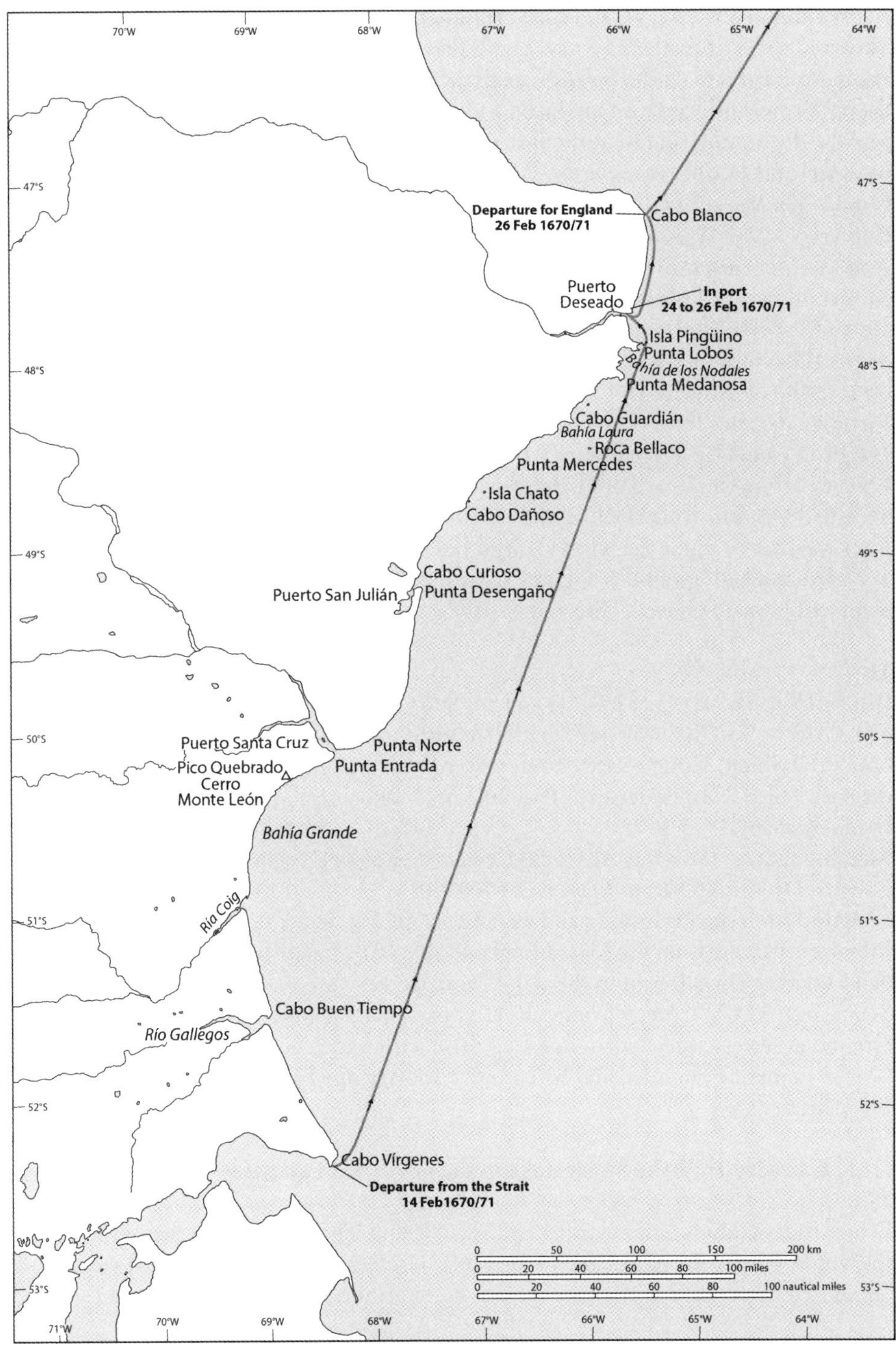

Map 10. Track of the *Sweepstakes* off the coast of Argentina, 14 February to 26 February 1670/71.

[180] **February 1670 the *Sweepstaks* Returninge into the North Sea**
15
Beinge Wedensday Cleare weather wind at WBS a Stoute gale [*margin:* In the North Sea:] this morninge at Fower of the Clocke I Steered N by the Compas: the Campas have Eighten degres variation Easterly: this morninge the fore topSaile Split I had it one Bent [unbent] and another Brought to.[1]
Cap Vergen Mary Lies in the Latt*itud* of 52°26′ South.
Cap Vergen Mary Lies in Long*itud* from the Lizard 65°42′ west.[2]
And Meridian distance in Leagus from the Liz*ard* 1062 west.
By account which I mad out from the Lizard of England.
Cours Mad true from nine of the Clocke last Night till to day at none is NE: distance Sailed 107·5 mils: departur E 76·0 Mils: deference of Latt*itud* 01°16′ north. Latt*itud* by observation of the ☼ is 51°10′ S
Meridian distance from Cap Vergin Mary E 29 le*agus* 1·0 mil
Longitud from Cap Vergen Mary E 02°03′
Longitud from the Lizard of England west 63°39′
Meridian Dist*ance* from the Lizard west 1032 lea*gus* 2·0 mils
Faier weather to night the wind Cam to the SW at 12 a [clock] to night a fine gale: I Sounded and had[3] ground at Eightey fadam: [*margin:* Soundings 80: Fad:] fadam: fine Sand with a Small Gravell. I Steered No*rth* by the Compas.

16
Beinge Thursday very faier weather and hot Sun Shine wind at WSW, in the morning, But a fine Aier at S all day after and smath [smooth] water, Many whales and Seales Seene a boute the Shipp. Course made from yesterday at none till today at none is N 28° E: distance Sailed 83 mils: departur East 39·2 mils: def*erence* Lat*itud* 01°17′ north: Lat*itud* by ob*servation* 49°53′ S.
Meridin dist*ance* from Cap Vergin Mary East 42 le*agus* 1·2 mils
Longitud from Cap Vergin Mary East 03°05′·0
Longitud from the Lizard England west 62°37′·0
Merid*ian* dist*ance* from the Lizard England we*st* 1019 lea*gus* 1·8 mils
Faier weather this afternone the wind came to the west a smale gale: [*margin:* Faire Soundings: 53:61:] I Steered N by the Compas. At 12 aclocke today I Sounded and had Ground at feivety three fadam fine Red Sand with Smale Gretty Stones: at tenn of the Clocke to night I Sounded and had ground at Sixty one Fadam: fine Reed Sand with a Black Mixter.[4]

[181] **February 1670 the Sweepstake in the north Sea Lat*itud* 49°22′ S**
17
Beinge friday Cloudy hasey weather and Small Raine. This morninge at five of the Clocke the wind Came to the North and to the NNE a fresh gale: at nine A Clocke I tacked and Stood to the westward as Nere the wind as I Could: at tenn A Clocke I Sounded and had

[1] Unbent (unlaced from the yard and removed) and another brought to the yard in its place.
[2] The actual position is 52°00′S, 68°21′W, which is 63°09′W of the Lizard.
[3] 'But' crossed through in the original.
[4] 'Fine red sand with a black mixture': this means black specks mixed in the red sand.

Ground at Sixty three fadam: fine Sand with letle gravell in it. I judge my Selfe A boute feivten Leagus of[f] the Shore. Course made true From yesterday none till today at none is NEBN: distance Sailed 36·7 miles: departur East 20·5 mils: def*erence* Latt*itud* 00°31′: Latt*itud* by Account is 49°22′ S.
Meredian dist*ance* From Cap Vergin Mary East 49 le*agus* 0·7 mils
Longitud From Cap Vergin Mary East 03°36′·5
Longitud From the Lizard west 62°05′·5
Meredian dist*ance* From the Lizard west 1012 le*agus* 2·3 mil
Faier weather to night wind at NNE: I Plyed to the northward in feivty and Sixty Fadam water.

18

Beinge Saterday Fogey weather all day wind at NNE and N a fine gale and Smoath water: I Sounded Every watch and had Sixty Fadam fine gravell Sand: and when I stood in to the westward and judged my Selfe ten leagus of[f] Shor I had feivety fadam watter a Shelly Rockey Ground with a mixtur of Sand: here is a very faier Soundings one [on] all this Coast from Cap Blanckeo to Cap Vergin Mary.[1]
Course true from yesterday at none till to day at none is No*rth* 12°25′ west: distance Sailed 15·4 mils: departur west 3·3 mils: def*erence* Lat*itud* 00°15′ No*rth*: Lat*itud* by Acco*unt* 49°07′.
Meredian dist*ance* From Cap Vergin Mary East 48 Lea*gus* 0·4 Mils
Longitud from Cap Vergin Mary East 03°30′·8
Longitud from the Lizard of England we*s*t 62°10′·7
Meredian dist*ance* From the Lizard west 1013 Lea*gus* 2·6 m*ils*

19

Beinge Sunday Fogey weather all day wind at NNE a fin gale this forenone Calme this afternone: I Plyed of[f] and in Betwen feivty and Sixty Fadam. Course made true from yesterday at none till today at none is N 45° E: dist*ance* Sailed 22·6 Mils: dep*artur* East 16·0 mils: def*erence* Lat*itud* N 00°16′: Lat*itud* by Acco*unt* 48°51′ N
Mered*ian* dist*ance* from Cap Vergin mary East 53 Le*agus* 1·4 Mil.
Longit*ud* from Cap Vergin Mary East 03°59′·8.
Longit*ud* from the Lizard west 61°41′·7.
Merd*ian* dist*ance* from the Lizard west 1008 le*agus* 1·2 mils.

[182] **February 1670 the Sweepstaks in the north Sea Latt*itud* 48°41′ S**
20

Beinge Munday fogey weather all day and letle wind at N in the fore none: at 12 A Clocke the wind Came to the SW a Smal gale: I Steered NWBN by the Compas: I Sounded at 12 aClocke and had Sixty fadam water fine Redes Sand in Clineinge [inclining] to A brightnes: Fogey weather towards Eveinge. Cours Made true from yesterday at none til today at none is ENE 3°30′ Easterly: distance sailed 30·6 Mils: departur East 29 Mils: def*erence* Lat*itud* 00°10′: Latitud by acc*ount* 48°41′.
Merd*ian* dist*ance* from Cap Vergin Mary East 63 le*agus* 0·4 mile.
Longitud from Cap Vergin Mary East 04°46′.

[1] From Cabo Blanco (47°12′S, 65°45′W) to Cabo Vírgenes.

Longitud from the Lizard west 60°55′·5.
Merdian dis*tance* from the Lizard west 998 le*agus* 2·2 mil.
Fogey weather all night and little wind at SSE: by the Compas I Steered in NNW: I Sounded Every watch and had ground at 58 Fadam fine Sand in Clineinge [inclining] to Redesh.

21
Beinge Tusday fogey weather this fore none and little wind Smoath water. A many large wales in the Sea Sene and many Seales about the Shipp and Sea fowles and beds of Rocke weeds driveinge.[1] I tryed to fish at Ground with hooks and lins but Could not Catch any Either great or Small: Severall Penguens in the Sea About the Shipp. Clear weather at none I had a very Good observation of the Sunn *Latitud* 48°12′ South.
Cours Made true from yesterday at none till today at none is NNW: distance Sailed 31·4 mils: departur west is 12 mils: def*erence* Latt*itud* 00°29′ N: Lat*itud* by Good ob*servation* of the ☼ 48°12′ S. Def*erence* of Longitud west is 00°17′·7.
Meredi*an* distance from Cap Virgin East 59 le*agus* 0·4 mil.
Longitud from Cap Virgin East 04°28′·3.
Longitud from the Lizard west 61°13′·02.
Meridea*n* distance from the Lizard west 1002 le*agus* 2·9 mils.
Faier weather this After none: But little wind at NNW: Smoth water. I tooke an Amplitud at the Sun Setinge and finde the Compas to have 15°43′ variation Easterly.
Tru Amplitud 09°47′ to the South.
Magnetic Amply*tud* 25°30′ to the South.
Hasey foogey weather this Afternone wind Cam to the north at 8 aClock: I tacked and Stood in West by the Compas.

[183] **February 1670 the Sweepstaks of[f] of Penguen Iland Lat*itud* 47°52′**
22
Beinge wedensday hasey weather wind at NBW a fresh gale I Stood to the westward: at 8 aclock this morninge I Sounded and had 50 Fadam: fine Bright Sand: fowertenn leagus of[f] the land in Latt*itud* 47°58′.
Cours Made true from yesterday at none till today at none is NW: dist*ance* Sailed 28·4 mils: depa*rtur* west 20 Mils: def*erence* Lat*itud* 00°20′: Lat*itud* by observation 47°52′.
Mered*ian* Dist*ance* from Cape Vergin Ma*ry* East 52 le*agus* 1·4 mil.
Longitud from Cape Vergin Ma*ry* East 03°58′·3.
Longitud from the Lizard West 61°43′·2.
Mered*ian* Dist*ance* from the Lizard West 1009 le*agus* 1·9 mil.
From twelfe to two of the Clocke I Sailed West 4 Leagus. At two of the Clocke the Afternone I Saw the Land: I was 4 Leagus from it, Penguen Iland[2] bore West of mee: I Sounded and *had* theerty five fadam Rockey Ground and as you Stand in to the land to the Southward of Pengune Ile it maks Ragitt. The tid of flood Beinge made I Streached into the Bay of Port disier: at Seaven A Clocke at night I tacked and Stood of[f] A great Sea here: at Eight of the Clock Penguen Iland Bar South of me distance one leage: wind at NBW A fresh gale I handed the fore top Saile: at two of the Clocke the wind Came to

[1] Drifting and not attached to the sea bed.
[2] Isla Pingüino (47°55′S, 65°43′W).

the NW and Blew fresh I handed the main top Saile there Run a Pitchinge Sea. I dar not ventur to Anchor in the Bay the wind beinge in [NW].

23
Beinge thursday Close hasey weather the wind vearinge betwen the NBW and NW A fresh gale. At 8 A Clock this morn*in*ge I Sounded and had ground at 42 fadam: Peavell Stones: nine leagus of[f] the Land: in the Latt*itud* of 47°30′: I made all the Saile I Could. At none today I had an observation and was in the Lat*itud* of 47°22′: I had 45 fadam Peavell Stones out of site of the land: I was ten leagus of[f] the land. The wind Cam to the NNW I tacked and Stood in West and WSW as nere I Could ly: the wind vearable. At 9 of the Clocke tonight I Anchored in twenty three fadam water: the ground Peavell Stons: About two leagus of[f] the Shore and five leagus to the N:ward of Port disier:[1] Calme to night and Smoath Sea.

24
Beinge friday faier weather the wind at NE a Small gale. I bore down to Porte Disier and Anchored in the Road in 13 fadam: the harb*ower* W.

[184] **February 1670 the Sweepstaks at Anchor of[f] Port Disier**
25
Beinge Saterday faier weather and Calme, this morninge I Sent into the harbower my Longe Boat and Pinas with Cask to fill water. At one of the Clocke this Afternone they Came Boath a board laden with fresh water the Pinas brought [*margin:* young foules] aboard two hundered young Shaggs[2] which they tooke out of their nessts [*sic*]: Allso they Brought A board very Good turnnups and Karrats and Redesses [*margin:* Turnups Carretts Reddishes] from the Place which I Sewe Seed in when wee were here before for in october I digged A Patch of ground and Put in those Seeds: and they therive very well: the Indians had Pulled Sum out of the Ground. This Land would Bere and Produce Any of our Europion Graine or Seeds: But fresh water is very Sceares: here Seaven Punsons was all I Could git and that Brackes [brackish]. Calme this after none, noe discrienige of Any of the Cuntry People for my Leiutenant went two miles into the Land: the Sumer have ben very dry here. This Eveinge the wind Came to the WSW: I waied: it fell quite Calme Againe I Anchored noe Soner Anchored but the wind Came to the SSE: and blew so hard all night as I Could not heave Ahead:[3] much wind and Raine to night at S.

26
Beinge Sunday A hard gale at S: this morninge at daylight we went to heaveinge with Boath Capsterns[4] to git up the anchor: at nine of the Clocke I waied and mad Saile and Steered NBE by the Compas alonge the Shore with in two leagus of it: at two of the Clocke this

[1] Puerto Deseado (47°45′S, 65°53′W).

[2] See above, pp. 216, n. 5; 580, n. 5.

[3] Could not heave the ship towards the anchor with the capstan.

[4] The two capstans can be used to back up each other weighing the anchor. In small ships such as the *Sweepstakes* the cable would have been brought directly to the capstan and hove in. 'When the anchor is in such stiffe ground that we cannot waigh it, or else that the sea goes so high, that the maine-capstane, cannot purchase in the cabell, then (for more help) we take a hawser [a Violl], and open one strand, and put in Nippers [short

Afternon the wind Came to the NNW A fresh gale: I had the [*margin:* Cape Blanco Shoald water] Pitch of Cap Blancco which Cap Makes like three Raget Rockey Ilands: if they be not Ilands:[1] I Could not well Perceive: they Bar WNW from me distance five miles. I Sounded and had ten fadam water Rockey Ground: I tacked and Stood of[f] East north East and Keept Sounding [*margin:* a Replin] and had but 9 and ten fadams for A miles dist*ance* Rocey Ground: then feivten fadam Peavell Stones and Blacke Gravell. Their Runes a Great Riplin and Race of a tid over it for at least a leage: Strechinge away NNE and SSW.[2] At fower a Clocke this Afternone the Cap Bar WBN ½ N by the Compas distance three Leagus from me: I had twenty fadam Peavell Stones: wind at NNW a fresh gale. I Stood of[f] NE northerly [*margin:* Departed From the Land:] faier weather to night the wind vered to the westward: I haled up to the westward to Gitt in to the Shore.

[185] **February 1670 the *Sweepstakes* to the Norward of Cap Blancco**
27
Day Beinge Munday faier weather to day wind at W and at WBS and at WNW: this Afternone I keept the wind as [*margin:* Stand in to the Shore] nere as I could ly with my Larbord tackes A board[3] to stand in for the Shore for it is my disier to vew all that Shore alonge to the northward and to indevier to Speeak with the natives: if winds and weather will Permitt me to Land about the Latt*itud* of fouerty fower degres or ther Abouts: for the land is not more then one hundered leagus Broad from the north Sea to the South Sea in these Lattituds[4] [*margin:* hops of Commerce] which gives Great hops of Commerce with the Chelis men one [on] this Side of the Cordeleros [Cordillera] or Mountains.
At 6 aclocke this afternone the wind Cam to the SW and [*margin:* a Storm Put me of the Coast] blew very hard: at Eight to night it Blew much wind at SSW and litened [lightninged] and thundered and Rained: Soe as I was forced to gett away before it NNE: at ten a Clocke the fore Saile Splitt: I Steered NE by the Compas: much lightninge to night and wind and Rained.
Cape Blancco in this Coast of Amarica lies in the Latt*itud* of 47°20′ South: And in Longitud west from the Lizard of England 61°56′:[5] And Meredian distance west from the Lizard 1014 leagus 1·6 mile by my Account from the Lizard theirther [thither].

---

lengths of rope] (from 6, or 8, a faddom distant from each other) and with these Nippers we bind fast the hawser to the cabell, and so bring this hawser to the Jeer-capstaine and heave upon it, and this will purchase more then the main capstaine can; The Voill is fastened together at both ends with an eye and a wall-knot, or else the two eyes seased together.' Manwayring, *Seamans Dictionary*, p. 112. The Voill was in effect a circular messenger with the ends joined, which was rotated round the jeer-capstan and forward to the hawse hole where the cable entered the ship. The nippers were attached by twisting them round the cable along the hauling part as the cable came in, and cast off as they approached the capstan while at the out board end more nippers were attached again in a continuous circular movement.

[1] Cabo Blanco; for description see above, p. 201, n. 4.

[2] Banco Byron lies 5 miles east of Cabo Blanco, a shoal area with depths of less than 10 fathoms (18·3 m) over it, extending north 10 miles and covered by overfalls, with patches of breakers at its northern end. Banco Ana lies 9 miles ESE of the Cape and is also marked by overfalls and eddies and patches of breakers. Further shoals lie 15 miles SSE of the Cape and 10 and 12½ miles further south with overfalls in heavy weather. *South America Pilot*, II, para. 3.21.

[3] Close hauled on the port tack.

[4] This is an accurate estimate of the distance between the East and West coasts of South America in the Latitude of about 46°S; in 44°S it is more like 120 leagues.

[5] The modern position of Cabo Blanco is 47°12′S, 65°45′W, which is 60°33′W of the Lizard.

After divers Courses mad from Sunday at fower of the Clocke in the afternone from my departur from the Cape For then it Bare WBN half a Pointe northerly by the Compas: distance three leagus from Mee: till today at none: My True Cours from the Cape is NE: distance 72 miles: departur E 51 miles: Def*erence* of Lat*itud* 00°51′ N: Lat*itud* by obs*ervation* of the ☼ is 46°29′ South. Def*erence* of Longitud from Cape Blancco is 01°14′·5.
Merid*ian* dist*ance* from Cape Blancco E is 17 Lea*gus* 0·0 m*ils*
Longit*ud* from Cape Blancco E 01°14′·5
Cap Blancco is the Land which I departed from in the South Coast of Amaricca: and at 12 aClocke to day I was so far distante from me as above mentioned. I Sounded at 12 of the Clocke But noe G*round* at 75 fadam.
The Compas have 17°00′ variation E here.

[186] **February 1670 the *Sweepstakes* homeward at Sea Lat*itud* 45°01′ S**
28
Beinge Tusday wind at SSE: much wind and Raine today: I Steered by the Compas NE. After divers Courses I make my true Cours from yesterday at none till today at non N 39°20′ E: distance Sailed 113·5 mils: Departur East 72 mils: Def*erence* Latt*itud* 01°28′: Lat*itud* By account 45°01′ S and Def*erence* of Longitud E is 01°43′.
Meredian Distance from Cape Blancco E 41 lea*gus* 0·0 m*ils*.
Longitud from Cape Blancco East 02°57′·5.
Course this Afternone and to night is NE by the Compas wind at SSE a hard gale: Gusty weather and haile to night.

1
March Beinge wedensday Gusty weather with Rain and hail wind at SSE: A Stout gale. Course made true from yesterday at none till today at none is NEBE: dista*nce* Sailed 168 mils: Departur East 140 mils: Def*erence* Lat*itud* No*rth* 1°33′: Lat*itud* By observat*ion* 43°28′: def*erence* Longit*ud* 03°17′ E.
Mered*ian* Dist*ance* from Cape Blancco E 87 Lea*gus* 2 mil*s*.
Longitud from Cape Blancco E 06°14′·5.
A fresh gale this afternone at SSE: at 4 of the Clocke I Steered NEBE by the Compas: faier weather.

2
Beinge Thursday Gusty weather with rain and haile to day wind at S and at SW: a hard Gale I Steer NEBE by the Compas: the Comp*as* have 19° variatio*n* E*ast*erly. True Course made from Yesterday none till today none is ENE 7° Easterly: distance Sailed 142·3 mils: Dep*artur* E 137·2 Mils: def*erence* Lat*itud* no*rth* 00°38′: Latt*itud* by obser*vation* 42°50′: Def*erence* Longitud East 03°06′.
Murede*an* Dist*ance* from Cap Blancco 133 Lea*gus* 1·2 mil.
Longitud from Cap Blancco E 09°20′·5.
The land of Cap Blancco is But of an indeferente height and low to the Sea one [on] the South Side: But one [on] the north Sid it Rizeth with whit Clifs and trent away to the NW:ward: Six leagus is as far as you Can well discry it at Sea: the Land is Barran without wood or fresh water.

[187] **March 1670 the *Sweepstakes* in the north Sea Home*ward* Lat*itud* 42°**

3

Beinge friday indeferent weather wind at SSE: A str*ong* gale all day: I Steered NEBE by the Compas. Course made true from yesterday at none till today at non is ENE 7° easterly: distance Sailed 187 mils: depart*ur* E 180·4 mils: def*erence* Lat*itud* 00°50′: Lat*itud* by ☼ 42°00′: Def*erence* of Longitud east 04°05′.
Mered*ian* Dist*ance* from Cape Blancco E 193 le*agus* 1·6 mil.
Longitud from Cape Blancco E 13°25′·5.
Gusty weather to night with rain and haile Course by the Compas is NEBE: the wind at S and at SW. This night the fore Saile Split.

4

Beinge Saterday Gusty weather and haile the wind betwen the S and the SW: A hard Gale of wind: Course by the Compase NEBE: But I make my true Course to by from yesterday at none till today none ENE 8°10′ Easterly: distance Sailed 175 mils: departur East 170 M*ils*: def*erence* Lat*itud* 00°43′: Lat*itud* by ob*servation* 41°17′: def*erence* Long*itud* 03°42′·6.
Mered*ian* Dist*ance* from Cap Blancco E 250 le*agus* 0·6 m*il*.
Longit*ud* from Cap Blancco East 17°08′·1.
Gusty weather this Afternone wind at SW: A hard gale the Ship Rowles much: the sea is lofty: Severall Sea fowles flyinge to and froe. Much haile to day and very large haile Stones: les wind to night.

5

Beinge Sunday indeferent faier weather wind at SW a fresh gale: Course by the Compas this 24 howers is NEBE. True Cours made from yesterday none till today at none is ENE 4°30′ Easterly: distance Sailed 165 mils: Departur East 157 mils: Def*erence* Latt*itud* 00°51′: Lat*itud* ☼ 40°26′.
Def*erence* Longitud East 03°32′.
Mered*ian* distance from Cape Blancco E 302 le*agus* 1·6 m*il*.
Longitud from Cape Blancco 20°40′·1.
A fresh gale at SW this Afternone I Steer NEBE by the Compas: the Compas varies 18° East. This day I ordered the fishes one [on] the mast to be new Spiked the Spikes Beinge Brooke.[1]

[188] **March 1670 the *Sweepstakes* at Sea homeward Lat*itud* 39°10′**

6

Beinge Munday Gusty Rainey weather wind at WSW: at one A Clocke to day the wind Came to SBE with Raine and thunder and lightninge: I Steered NEBE by the Compas all this last 24 howers. Course made tru from yesterday at none till today at none is ENE: distan*ce* Sailed 200 Mils: Depart*ur* East 185 miles: def*erence* Lat*itud* 01°16′: Def*erence* Longitud 04°01′ East: Latt*itud* by account 39°10′.
Mered*ean* dist*ance* from Cape Blancco East 364 le*agus* 0·6 m*il*.
Longitud from Cape Blancco East 24°41′·1.
Gusty weather this afternone wind at SSE: I Stered NEBE by my Compas all night. Sum Raine to night.

[1] For fishes (wooden splint-like pieces), see above, p. 173, n. 1.

7
Beinge tusday Close darke weather wind at SE a fresh gale. I Steered NE by the Compase But I make my tru Course to be EBN: dist*ance* Sailed 128 mils: Departur E 125 mils: def*erence* Lat*itud* 00°25′: Latt*itud* by account 38°45′ S: Deference of Long*itud* 02°44′ East.
Mered*ian* distance from Cape Blancco E 405 le*agus* 2·6 m*ils*.
Longitud from Cape Blancco East 27°25′·1.
This afternone at fower of the Clocke the wind Came to the East a fresh gale I Stered NNE by the Compas: Calme to night at twelfe of the Clocke.

8
Beinge wedensday Gusdy weather and raine the winde veareinge from the NNE to the WNW: at 6 aclocke this morninge I tacked and Stood to the Eastward. Course made true this twenty fower howers is East: dist*ance* Sailed 46 mils: Departur East 46 mils: def*erence* 00: Lat*itud* by accou*nt* is 38°45′ S: Def*erence* Longit*ud* 00°59′.
Mered*ian* dist*ance* from Cap Blancco East 421 le*agus* 0·6.
Longitud from Cap Blanc*co* East 28°24′·1.
Gusty weather this after none and all night a great Sea runs: the Ship labowers much: Cours by the Compas ENE.
This Eveinge at Sun Set I tooke An Amplitud and find the Compas to have twenty degres variation Easterly.

[189] **March 1670 the *Sweepstakes* in the north Sea homeward Bound**
9
Beinge Thursday Gusty Stormey weather this morninge and day wind at SSE: I Steerd NE by the Compas. Course made true from yesterday at none till today none is E: distance Sailed 110 mils: departur East 110 mils: def*erence* 00°00′: Lat*itud* by acco*unt* 38°45′: def*erence* Longit*ud* 02°21′.
Mered*ian* dist*ance* from Cap Blancco East 457 le*agus* 2·6 m*ils*.
Longitud from Cap Blancoo East 30°45′·1.
[*margin:* a new fish Put one the main Mast] This afternone at one a Clocke one of the maine Shrouds brooke: the mainmast Gives way much in the Place wher it is Sprunge.[1]
A fresh gale this afternone wind at SSE: I Steere NE by the Compas all night.

10
Beinge friday Cloase weather today wind at SSE a fine gale Course Steered by the Compas is NE: but my true Cours mad from yesterday at none till today at non is NEBE 08°45′ Easterly: distance Sailed 107 Mils: departur East 96·5 mils: def*erence* Latt*itud* 00°45′: Latt*itud* by ob*servation* ☼ 38°00′: Def*erence* Longitud 02°04′·4.
Mered*ian* distanc from Cap Blancco E 490 le*agus* 0·1 mils.
Longitud from Cap Blancco E 32°49′·5.
Faier weather this Afternone the wind Came to the S and SW.

11
Beinge Satterday Close weather wind at SW a fine Gale: I Steered NE by my Compas. I make my true Cours to be this 24 howers ENE: distance Sailed 59·5 mils: departur East

[1] Fractured.

55·0 Mils: def*erence* Lat*itud* 00°23′ north: Latt*itud* by account 37°37′: def*erence* Longitud 01°08′·5.
Meredian dist*ance* from Cape Blancco E 508 le*agus* 1·1 m*il.*
Longitud from Cape Blancco E 33°58′·0.
Close weather this afternone and a faier gale at SW: I Steer NE by the Compas: A fresh gale tonight.
Variation of the Compas is 14°20′ East by An Amplitud taken at Sunn Setinge.

[190] **March 1670 the *Sweepstakes* at Sea Latt*itud* 36°06′ S**
12
Beinge Sunday Cloudy weather wind at SSW: a fresh gale. Course made true from yesterday none till today none is N 59°30′ East: distance Sailed 180 mils: departur East 155 mils: def*erence* Latt*itud* 01°31′: Latt*itud* by ob*servation* ☼ is 36°06′: def*erence* Longitdud 03°15′.
Mered*ian* dist*ance* from Cap Blancco E 560 lea*gus* 0·1 mils.
Longitud from Cap Blancc*o* E 37°13′.
Faier weather this afternone and all night wind at S A fine gale: Course by the Compas NE.

13
Beinge Munday Cloudy weather and letle wind to day at S: Course Steered this 24 howers by the Compas is NE: But I[1] true Course is NEBE: distanc Sailed 140·5 mils: Departur East 117 mils: def*erence* Lat*itud* 1°18′: Lat*itud* by ob*servation* of the Sun 34°48′: Def*erence* Long*itud* 2°22′·2.
Mered*ian* dist*ance* from Cape Blancc*o* E 599 le*agus* 0·1 m*il.*
Longit*ud* from Cape Blancco E 39°35′·2.
Calme this afternone and to night: variation 15° E.

14
Beinge Tusday faier weather and little wind at NW and at E. True Course mad this 24 houers is NE: [*margin:* This day we went to hole alowance of al Prouis*sions*] distance Sailed 5·6 mils: Depart*ur* E 4 m*ils*: def*erence* Lat*itud* 00°4′: Lat*itud* by account 34°44′: def*erence* Longitud 00°05′·3.
Mered*ian* dist*ance* from Cap Blancco E 600 lea*gus* 2·4 M*ils.*
Longitud from Cap Blancco E 39°40′·5.
This afternone the wind Came to the N a fine gale. I Plied to and fro to the northward: this Eveinge I Split the fore Saile [*margin:* Fore Saile Splete] the Boult Rope Brooke:[2] I Brought the main top Saile to the fore yard the[3] other fore Saile was allsoe Amending.

15
Beinge wedensday hasey weather wind at NW a fresh gale. True Course made this 24 howers is NNW: dist*ance* 43 mils: dep*artur* W 6·5 mils: def*erence* Lat*itud* 0°40′: Lat*itud* by acc*ount* 34°04′: d*iference* Lo*ngitud* 0°10′·5 W.

[1] This should probably have been ‘my’.
[2] The bolt rope is a rope sewn round the sail to strengthen it.
[3] ‘the’ repeated in the original.

Mered*ian* dist*ance* from Cap Blancco E 598 le*agus* 1·9 mil.
Longitud from Cap Blancco E 39°30′.

[191] **March 1670 the *Sweepstakes* at Sea Latt*itud* 33°31′**
16
Beinge wedensday Cloudy weather wind at W with Sum raine it Came to the SSW a fine gale: Cou*rse* by my Compas NEBE. I make my true Course to be this 24 howers NEBE: dist*ance* 59 miles: depart*ur* East 49·2 mils: def*erence* Lat*itud* 00°33′: Lat*itud* by ac*count* 33°31′: def*erence* Longitud 00°58′·2.
Mered*ian* dist*ance* from Cap Blancco E 615 le*agus* 0·1 Mile.
Longitud from Cap Blanc*co* E 40°28′·2.
This afternone the wind Came to the NW a fine gale Sum Raine to night.

17
Beinge Friday Close weather wind at NBW a fine gale I Stood to the Eastward: after divers Courses I make my true Course to be ENE: dist*ance* Saild 83·3 mils: dep*artur* East 77 Mils: def*erence* Latt*itud* 00°32′: Latt*itud* by account 32°59′: def*erence* Longitud 01°43′·9.
Mered*ian* dist*ance* from Cap Bal*a*ncco E 640 Lea*gus* 2·1 M*il*.
Longitud from Cap Blanc*co* E 42°11′·9.
Close Cloudy weather wind at NNW: to night a fresh gale.

18
Beinge Satterday Close hasey weather and very hot: wind at NWBW & at SW a fresh gale. Cours mad true this 24 howers is NEBE: distance Sailed 106 Miles: departur East 80 Mils: def*erence* Lat*itud* 00°53′ N: Lat*itud* by account is 32°06′: def*erence* Longit*ud* 1°27′·6.
Mered*ian* dist*ance* from Cap Blanc*co* E 667 lea*gus* 1·1 M*il*
Longitud from Cap Blanc*co* E 43°39′·5

19
Beinge Sunday Cloudy rainey weather wind vearable betwne the SW & the NE: fresh gales. Course made true is North 24°30′ East: dist*ance* Sailed 76·8 Mils: dep*artur* East 31·5 Mils: def*erence* Lat*itud* 01°09′: Lat*itud* by Ac*count* 30°57′ S: def*erence* Longitud East 0°36′·8.
Mered*ian* distance from Cap Blanc*co* East 677 Le*agus* 2·6 M*ils*
Longitud from Cap Blanc*co* East 44°16′·3

[192] **March 1670 the *Sweepstakes* at Sea in the Lat*itud* 30°20′**
20
Beinge munday Cloudy hasey weather wind at NW & at SW and at No*rth*: fresh gales with raine. Course made true this 24 howers is NEBE: dist*ance* Sailed 67 Mils: depa*rtur* East 55·8 mils: def*erence* Lat*itud* 00°37′: Lat*itude* by ac*count* 30°20′: def*erence* Longitud is 01°05′ East.
Mered*ian* dist*ance* from Cap Blancco E 696 le*agus* 1·4 mil
Longitud from Cap Blancco E 45°21′·3

Much lightings and Raine this fore Parte of the night [*margin:* Guste raine] wind Came to the SW: a Stoute gale. Cours by the Comp*as* ENE: Sumtimes for to keep before the wind till a gust was over I Stered NNE by my Compas when the wind Served.

21
Beinge tusday Cloudy weather wind at SW a fresh gale. Course mad from yesterday none till today none is north East: distanc Sailed 96·5 mils: dep*artur* 68 mils: def*erence* Lat*itud* 01°08′: Lat*itud* by obs*ervation* of the ☼ 29°12′ South.
Mered*ian* dist*ance* from Cap Blanc*co* E 719 Le*agus* 0·4 Mil.
Longitud from Cap Blanc*co* E 46°39′·6.
Course Steered by the Compas today at none is NBE: wind veared to the South a fine gale darke the Evenige.

22
Beinge wednesday Close hasey weather wind at SSE a fresh gale Course by the Compase NBE. I make my true Course to be from yesterday none till today non north 26°30′ East: distance Sailed 134 Mils: departur west[1] 60 miles: def*erence* Latt*itud* 02°00′ north: Latt*itud* by account is 27°12′: def*erence* Long*itud* 01°08.
Meridian dist*ance* from Cap Blancco E 739 Lea*gus* 0·4 M*il*
Longitud from Cap Blancco E 47°47′·6
This afternone it Proved Shouery rainey weather the [wind] Came to the East and to the North to night [at] 10 a cloc*k*.
Variation of the Compas by an Amplitud takein in the west is 08°00′ E.

[193] **March 1670/1 the *Sweepstakes* at Sea home*ward* Latt*itud* 26°00′ S**
23
Beinge thursday faier weather today wind Cam to to the NWBN a fine gale. Cours mad Good from yesterday none till today at none is north 31° East: distance Sailed 84 mils: depart East 43·2 mils: def*erence* of Lattitud 01°12′: Latt*itud* by ☼ 26°00′ South: def*erence* of Longitud is 00°48′·7 East.
Meredian dist*ance* from Cap Blanc*co* E 753 le*agus* 1′6 M*il*
Longitud from the Cap Blanc*co* E 48°36′·3
Faier weather this Afternone. [*margin:* a man Punnished] At five of the Clocke this afternone I order one of my Ships Company to the mainegeers[2] for Robinge the Stewards Roume.

24
Beinge friday hasey Claldy weather wind at NNW a fine gale. After divers Courses I make my true Co*urs* to be this 24 houers North 39°15′ East: dist*ance* Sailed is 85 Mils: depart*ur* East 54 Mils: def*erence* of Latt*itud* 01°06′: def*erence* Longitude 00°59′·7: Latt*itud* by ☼ 24°54′.
Mered*ian* dist*ance* from the C*ap* Blanc*co* East 771 Le*agus* 1·6 mil
Longitud from Cap Blanc*co* E 49°36′·00

[1] This would appear to be an error for East.
[2] See above, p. 150, n. 2.

[*margin: drawing of 2 fish.* Flieing fish and dolph*in*] Cloudy weather this afternone and Gusty weat*her* wind at NWBW a fresh gale at night. This afternoen we Saw dolfins and olbycors about the Ship and flinge [fish]. My men all of indeferent good health.

25
Beinge Satterday faier weather the wind vearing betwen the north west and the north: this 24 houers a fine gale I Stood to the north Eastward with all the Sailed I Could make. I make my true Cours this last 24 houers to Be NEBE: distance Sailed 54 mils & departur East 45 mils: def*erence* of Latt*itud* 00°30′: def*erence* of Longitud East 00°:[1] Latt*itud* by ☼ 24°24′.
Merid*ian* distans from Cap Blanc*co* E 781 Le*agus* 1·6 m*il*
Longitud from Cape Blanco E 50°25′·4

[194] **March 1671 the *Sweepstakes* at Sea homward in Lat*itud* 24°12′ S**
26
Beinge Sunday faier weather wind at NBW a fine gale: I Stand to the Eastward with all thee Saile I Can. Course mad true this last 24 houers is north 72°30′ Easterly: distance Sailed 40 mils: depart*ur* East 38·2 mils: def*erence* Latt*itud* 00°12′: def*erence* Lon*gitud* 00°41′·3: Latt*itud* by Good observation of the Sun is 24°12′.
Meridian distance from Cap Blanc*co* E 794 le*agus* 0·8
Longitud from Cap Blanc*co* East 51°06′·7
Faier weather this afternone: Wind at NBW a fine Smale gale a good tempar*a*te Cleare Aier: Sum [*margin: drawing of fish* Fish sene] fish Senne about the Shipp. Today the Compas have 7°20′ variation by an amplytud obser*ved* at ☼ Settinge: Magnit*ic* Ampl*ytud* 15° Southward of the west: true amplytud 07°05′ north of the west.
Darke weather to night and Sume Raine wind at NW.

27
Beinge munday faier weather wind at NW a Smal *gale*. Course mad this 24 houers is NE: distance Sailed 56·5 mils: def*erence* Lat*itud* 00°40′: Latt*itud* by obser*vation* of the ☼ 23°32′: departur East 40 mils: def*erence* Long*itud* 43′·7.
Meridian dist*ance* from Cap Blanc*co* E 807 le*agus* 1·8 M*il*
Longitud from Cap Blanc*co* East 51°50′·4
This day at none I Crosed the tropicke of Capricorn with all my men in Good Health: Beinge Sixte nine [*margin:* men all in health] in number. The Compas have 7°34′ East variation by an Amplytud observed in the west: letle wind and far weather tonight Cours by the Compas NEBN and NNE.

28
Beinge tusday faier weather wind betwen the NW and N a Small gale. Cours mad true from yesterday none till to day non is NE: distance Saild 60·8 mils: dep*artu*r 43 mils: def*erence* Latt*itud* 43′: Latt*itud* by ☼ 22°49′: def*erence* Long*itud* E 00°46′·2.
Merid*ian* dist*ance* from Cap Blanc*co* East 821 le*agus* 2·8 m*ils*
Longitud from Cap Blanc*co* East 52°36′·6

[1] The minutes have not been filled in, from the Longitudes it should be 00°49′·4.

[195] **March 1671 the *Sweepstakes* at Sea homwards bo*und* Latt*itud* 22°18′**
29
Beinge wedensday faier weather wind at NNW a Small gale. Course made this 24 howers is No*rth* 53°30′ East: distance Sailed 52 mils: departure East 41·8 mils: def*erence* Latt*itud* 00°31′: Latt*itud* by obser*vation* ☼ is 22°18′ South: def*erence* Longitud East 00°46′.
[*margin:* variation 5°10′] Variation observide by an Amplytud is 5°10′ East.
Meridian dist*ance* from Cap B*lan*cco East 835 le*agus* 2·6 mils
Longitud forom Cap Blancco East 53°22′·6
Faier weather to night and lettle wind betwen the NW and north: Variation of the Compas by an Amplytud at ☼ steinge [setting] is 5°40′ East: noe fish nor fowle Sene. I keepe good Lookeinge today and tonight for Ilands which lies in these Lattituds and nere this Longitud but se none.[1]

30
Beinge thursday faier weather letle wind at north and at NNE. Tru Course made from yesterday at none till today at none is north: distance Sailed 22 mils: departur 00: def*erence* L*atitud* 00°22′: Latt*itud* by observation 21°56′ S: def*erence* Longitud. [*blank*][2]
Lettle wind and Smoath water hott wather and temperate.
Merid*ian* distanc from Cap Blanc*co* E 835 le*agus* 2·6 mils.
Longitud from Cap Blancco East 53°22′·6.
Lettle wind this After none at NEBE: Cours by Com*pas* NNW.

31
Beinge friday faier weather wind at NEBE a fine gale. Course made true from yesterday none till today at none is N 7° west: distance Sailed 72·8 Mils and departur west 8·9 Mils: def*erence* of Latt*itud* 01°12′ North: Lattitud by observation of the Sun ☼ is 20°44′ South: deference of Longitud this 24 houers is 00°09′·6 west.
Meridian dist*ance* from the[3] Blanc*co* East 832 Le*agus* 2·7 m*ils*
Longitud from Cap Blancco East 53°13′·0
[*margin:* variation 4°35′ East] Variation of the Compas is But 04°35′ East.
Faier weather: the Great bears Sid is 12° above the Horizon.[4]

[196] **Aprill 1671 the *Sweepstakes* at Sea homwards bound Lat*itud* 20°44′ S**
1
Satterday Beinge the first day of Aprill: 1671: faier weath*er* to day and a fine Small gale at ENE. Course from yesterday at none till to day at n*one* made true is NNW: distance Sailed 69·5 mils: departur west 26·7 mils: defer*ence* of Longitud west 00°28′·3: def*erence* of Latt*itud* 01°04′. Lattud By observation of the ☼ is 19°40′ S.
Meridian distance from the Cap Blanc*co* East 824 Le*agus*
Longitud from Cape Blanc*co* East 52°44′·7

[1] Presumably this is 'The Island of Assention' mentioned on the outward passage on 7 Jan. 1669/70, which was thought to lie in these Latitudes. See above, p. 181, n. 2.
[2] Space left blank. Since course made good was north there would be no difference of Longitude.
[3] The word 'Lizard' crossed through in original.
[4] The Great Bear's side is the star β Ursæ Majoris.

This day at none I looked out for the Ilse of Martine Vas:[1] and have keepte a man atopmast head this two days but noe Site of any thinge: noe Birds nor fesh to be Sene Eastward of these Iles nere 40 leagus. Faier weather to night and A fin gale at E.

2
Beinge Sunday faier weather wind all this 24 houers at ENE & NEBE: a fine fresh gale Course Steered by the Comp*as* is NBW & NNW. Course mad true from Satterday none till to day none is NBW 04°45′ westerly: distance sailed 100 Mils: departur west 27·4 Mils: def*erence* of Longitud W 00°29′·3: def*erence* of Latitud 01°36′ no*rth*: Latt*itud* by observat*ion* of the ☼ 18°04′ S.
Merid*ian* dist*ance* from Cap Blancco East 814 Le*agus* 2·6 Mils
Longitud from Cap Blancco East 52°15′·4
Faier weather this afternone wind at ENE a fine gale and at NEBE: Sumtimes I Steered NBW and Sumtims NNW.

3
Beinge Munday faier weather wind at ENE A fine gale. Cours mad tru is NBW: distance Sailed 102 Mils: depar*tur* west 20 mils: def*erence* of Longitud west: [*blank*][2] def*erence* of Latt*itud* By obs*ervation* 01°40′ no*rth*: Latt*itud* by obser*vation* ☼ 16°24′ S.
Meridian distance from Cape Blanc*co* 808 Lea*gus* 0·6
Longitud from Cap Blanc*co* East 51°54′·6
Faier weather this afternone wind at ENE a fine gale: Cours by Compas NBW: Variation 03°08′ E.

[197] **Aprill 1671 the *Swepstaks* att Sea in the Lat*itud* 14°56′**
4
Beinge tusday faier weather wind at ENE a fresh gale: Course by my Compas NBW & NNW Sumtims as the winds Shrinke.[3] I make my true Course to be NBW: distance Sailed 90·3 mils: Departur west 17·5 mils: Dif*erence* of Longitud we*st* 00°18′·3: Diference of Latt*itud* 01°28′ no*rth*: Latt*itud* by obser*vation* of the ☼ 14°56′ S.
Meridian Distance from Cap Blanc*co* E 802 Lea*gus* 1·1 m*il*
Longitud at none from Cap Blanco E 51°36′·3
Variation by an ampltud taken at ☼ Set 3° E.[4]

5
Beinge wendensday faier weather wind at ENE & NE: a fresh gale Cours by Compas NBW & NNW as the winds Served. I make my true Course to be from yesterday none till to day none NBW: distance Sailed 132 mils: Departur west 25·8 mils: def*erence* of Longitud west 00°26′·5: Dif*erence* of Latt*itud* 02°09′: Latt*itud* by observation 12°47′.
Merid*ian* dist*ance* from the Cap Blanc*co* E 793 Lea*gus* 2·3 m*ils*
Longitud from Cap Blanc*co* E 51°09′·8

[1] Ilhas Martin Vaz (20°28′S, 28°51′W). See above, p. 181, n. 2.
[2] Difference from the Longitudes is 0°20′·8.
[3] Presumably this means as the winds decrease.
[4] The figures '00' before 3° crossed through in original.

I doe not find any Curant Set to the Southward as I found outward in thes Lattituds, nor Soe much varia*tion* by three degres: I ame nowe a great deale to the Eastward more then I was when I went out one [on] this voiage and Crosed thes Parellells.

6

Beinge thursday faier weather wind at ENE a fresh gale. Course made true from yesterday none till to day at none is north 15° west: distance Sailed 114 mils: Departur west 29·4 mils: Dif*erence* of Long*itud* 00°30′·4: Dif*erence* of Latt*itud* 01°50′. Latt*itud* by ob*servation* of the ☼ 10°57′.
Meridian distance from Cap Blanc*co* E 783 Le*agus* 2·9
Longit*ud* at none from Cap Blanc*co* E 50°39′·4

[198] **Aprill 1671 the *Sweepstakes* at Sea Lat*itud* 09°26′ S**

7

Beinge Friday faier weather wind at EnE: a fine gale and Smoath wather: aier Clear. Sum fowles Sene A bout the Ship to day: agants and Small Petterells and tropicke birds.[1]
Variation of the Compas by an amplytud at Sun Rizinge 02°34′ E.
Course by Compas NBW and n*or*north west: the wind at NE: Sumtimes. Course mad true this 24 houers is NNW: distance Sailed 98·8 mils: dep*artur* W 37·8 mils: Dif*erence* Long*itud* 00°38′·2: Dif*erence* Lat*itud* 1°31′: Lat*itud* by good observation of the ☼ at the merid*ian* 09°26′.
Merid*ian* dist*ance* from the C*ap* Blanc*co* East 771 Lea*gus* 1·1 m*il*
Longit*ud* from the C*ap* Blanc*co* East 50°01′·2
Faier weather this afternone wind at NNE: a letle time it Came to the ENE a fine gale Course by Comp*as* NNW. My men all in good health Beinge 69 in number. Our alowance for a man for Seaven dayes time is three Pound and a halfe of flower & Eight Pound of Beefe and threten ounes of Chese & one Pinte & a halfe of Oatemeall: thes are at 14 ounces to the Pound: water what they will drinke: fireinge aknoufe [enough] for dressinge the Provi*sions*. I hope we Shalle have Provisions to least us into England at this Rate: if it be this tenn weekes Ere we gitt theither. Sum Sea fowles Sene to day noe fish. Variation of the Co*m*pas at night by ane Amplytude taken is 01°40′ East.

8

Beinge Satterday faier weather wind at E: fresh gale Cours by Compas NNW and NW. Cours mad true is NNW: distance Sailed 87 mils: Departur west 33 mils: Dif*erence* of Long*itud* 00°33′·2: Dif*erence* of Latt*itud* nor*th* 01°19′: Latt*itud* by observat*ion* of the Sun 08°07′ South.
Meridian distance from Cap Blanc*co* E 738 L*eagus* 1·1 m*il*

[1] Agant was probably a gannet. The northern gannet (*Sula bassana*) is not normally found as far south as this, but that is the only type of gannet it is likely to have been. Harrison, *Seabirds*, p. 288. The small petrels were probably storm-petrels, of which Wilson's storm-petrel (*Oceanites oceanicus*), the white-faced storm-petrel (*Pelagdroma marina*), the black-bellied storm-petrel (*Fregetta tropica*), the white-bellied storm-petrel (*F. grallaria*) and Leach's storm-petrel (*oceanodroma leucorhoa*) are the most likely to be seen in this area. Ibid., pp. 267–71, 274–5. The tropicbirds were probably either the red-billed tropicbird (*Phaethon aethereus*) or the white-tailled tropicbird (*P. lepturus*), both of which are found in this area. Ibid., pp. 281–3.

Long*itud* at none today from Cape Blanc*co* E 49°28′
Variation of the Compas is E 01°35′.

[199] **Aprill 1671 the *Sweep Stakes* at Sea Lat*itud* 06°30′ S**
8
Saterday night at 9 of the Clocke I observed the ☆ of the great Bears Back[1] one [on] the meridian About the Pole.

Altitud of the ☆ was	19°02′	90°00′
Declination of the ☆ is	63°35′ N°	82°37′
	82°37′	07°23′

By this ☆ of the Bears Backe I find my Lat*itud* 07°23′ S.
At the Same time I observed the ☆ of the great Bears Side.[2]

The ☆ Declination is 58°12′: Dist*ance* from the Pole	31°48′
The ☆ Altitud is	24°20′
By this ☆ of the Bers Side I find my Latt*itud*	07°28′

At a [*sic*] Eleven of the Clocke to night the Crosers[3] were one [on] their meridian above the Pole Antarcticke. I observed the ☆ one [on] the foot of the Cross[4] and found his Alltitud 36°14′.

His Decl*ination* is 61°16′ S: The ☆ Dist*ance* from the Pole	28°44′
By this ☆ one [on] the foot of the Crose I find the Lat*itud*	07°30′ S.

9
Beinge Sunday faier weather wind at E and ESE a Stife gale: Course Steered by the Compas NBW and NNW: for the winds would veary a Pointe or two: Smoath Sea. Course made true from yesterday none till to day at none is NNW: distance Sailed 105 mils: departur west 40·2 mils: dif*erence* of Long*itud* 00°40′·6: dif*erence* Lat*itud* 01°37′.
Latt*itud* by observation of the Sun is 06°30′ S.
Meridian distance from Cap Blanc*co* E 724 Le*agus* 2·9 M*ils*
Longitud at none from Cap Blanc*co* E 48°47′·4
Variation by an amplytud in the morn*ing* 01°19′ E.

10
Being Munday faier weather wind at East a fine gale. Course Steered NBW: distance sailed 106·5 mils: departur west 20·8 mils: dif*erence* of Longit*ud* 00°21′ we*st*: Dif*erence* of Latt*itud* 01°44′ N: Latt*itud* by account 04°46′ S.

[1] The upper pointer, Dubhe, α Ursæ Majoris. The declination quoted is the same as that given in Tapp, *Sea-Mans Kalender*, p. 90.

[2] The lower pointer, Merak, β Ursæ Majoris. The declination is the same as that given in Tapp, *Sea-Mans Kalender*, p. 90

[3] The Southern Cross, which is not included in Tapp, *Sea-Mans-Kalender*, since, as he states on p. 97, 'they are so far to the Southwards that they could not be observed by *Tycho* [Brahe], or any of the *European Mathematicians*, whose Observations are *Authentical*'. Narbrough has a note at the end of his 'Booke', which shows the form of the stars in the Southern Cross with details of their declinations and distances from the pole (together with that of Canopus), which he has used here. See above, pp. 70–71.

[4] Acrux, α Crucis.

Meridian distance from Cape Blanc*co* E 718 Leag*us* 0·1 m*il*
Longitud at noe [none] from Cap Blanc*co* E 48°26′·4
Variation at Sun Set by an amplitad 01°2′ East.

[200] **Aprill 1671 the Swep Stakes at Sea homwards Lat*itud* 2°46′ S**
11
Beinge tusday faier weather wind at ENE & at E and ESE a fresh gale as much as we Could Carey our top Saile Sturtinge Sails: Cours by Compas NBW. I make my true Cours to be this 24 houers is NNW: distance Sailed 130 mils: departur west 49·8 mils: Dif*erence* of Longitud west 00°50′: Dif*erence* of Latt*itud* 02°00′N: Latitud By observation of the ☼ 02°46′ S.
Meridian distance at non from *Cape* Blanc*co* E 701 *Leagus* 1·1
Longitud at none from Cape Blanc*co* East 47°36′·4
Faier weather this afternone at ESE the wind and a fresh gale: Course by Compas NBW all night.
Variation By an Amplytud at Sun Set 00°54′ E.

12
Wednsday faier weather wind at SE a fresh gale and Smoath Sea: Course this 24 houers by the Compas is N°bW. I make my tru Cours to be north 10° W and my distance Sailed 139 mils: Departur west 24·2 m*ils*: Dif*erence* of Long*itud* 00°24′·4: Dif*erence* Lat*itud* 02°17′ N: Latt*itud* by Good observation of the ☼ one [on] the Merid*ian* 00°29′ S.
Meridian dist*ance* from Cape Blanc*co* E 693 Leag*us* 0·9
Long*itud* at none from Cape Blanc*co* E 47°12′
Faier weather this afternone wind at SE a fine gale Course NbW: Clear Aier: noe foule nor fish Sene.
This Afternone a Bout five of the Clocke we were [*margin:* Cros the Equinoctial Line] under the Equinoctiall Line.
In Longitud from Cape Blanckeo E 47°06′·2 & in meridian dist*ance* from Cape Blanckeo E 691 Leag*us* 1·1.
Noe Amplitud to day the Horizon Beinge Cloudy: the variation by a nomon one [gnomon on] a Card when the ☼ was one [on] the meridian to day was But 00°36′ East.
At 10 of the Clocke to night I observed the ☆ of the Crosers: the ☆ one [on] the head †:[1]

His Merid*ian* Alt is	34°30′
Distance from the Pole antarticke	34°50′
Lattitude at the time is north	20′
The Crosers foot ☆[2] dist*ance* from the Pole	28°44′
Meridianall Altitude at the time	28°20′
Latt*itud* no*rth*	24′

[1] γ Crucis.
[2] α Crucis.

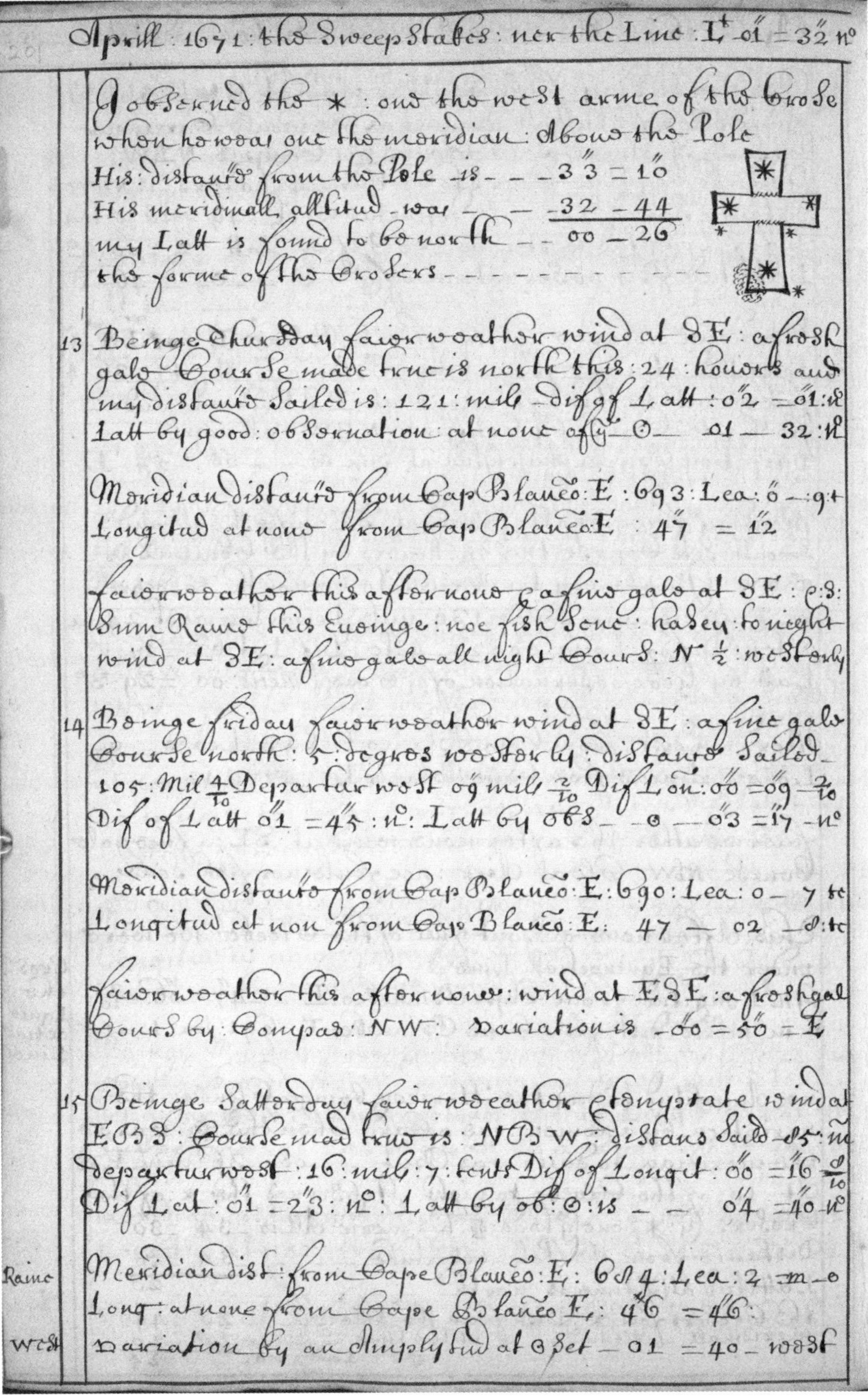

201

Aprill: 1671: the Sweepstakes: ner the Line: 1d – 01 = 32 no

I obserued the *: and the west arme of the Crose
when he was one the meridian: Aboue the Pole
His: distance from the Pole is — — 33 = 10
His meridinall allitud was — — 32 – 44
my Latt is found to be north — 00 – 26
the forme of the Crosers — — — — — —

13 Beinge Thursday faier weather wind at SE: a fresh
gale Course made true is north this: 24: houers and
my distance Sailed is: 121: mils dif of Latt: 02 = 01: no
latt by good: obseruation at none as — 0 — 01 — 32: no

Meridian distance from Cap Blanco: E: 693: Lea: 0 – 9 +
Longitud at none from Cap Blanco E: 47 = 12

faier weather this after none & a fine gale at SE: & S:
Sum Raine this Euninge: noe fish Sene: haden to night
wind at SE: a fine gale all night Cours: N ½: westerly

14 Beinge friday faier weather wind at SE: a fine gale
Course north: 5: degres westerly: distance Sailed
105: Mil 4/10 Departur west 09 mils 2/10 Dif Lon: 00 = 09 – 2/10
Dif of Latt 01 = 45: no: Latt by obs — 0 — 03 = 17 – no

Meridian distance from Cap Blanco: E: 690: Lea: 0 – 7 tt
Longitud at non from Cap Blanco: E: 47 — 02 — d: tt

faier weather this after none: wind at ESE: a fresh gal
Cours by: Compas: NW: variation is 00 = 50 = E

15 Beinge Satterday faier weather & steady state wind at
EBS: Course mad true is: NBW: distans Saild 85: m
departur west: 16: mils: 7: tents Dif of Longit: 00 = 16 6/10
Dif Lat: 01 = 23: no: Latt by ob: 0: is — — 04 = 40 no

Raine Meridian dist: from Cape Blanco: E: 684: Lea: 2 – m – 0
Long: at none from Cape Blanco E: 46 = 46:
West variation by an Amplitud at 0 Set — 01 = 40 — west

Figure 8. Narbrough's *Sweepstakes* Journal (BL, Add MS 88980A), p. 201. Courtesy of the Trustees of the British Library.

[201][1] **Aprill 1671 the *Sweep Stakes* ner the Line L*atitud* 01°32′ N**
I observed the ☆ one [on] the west arme of the Crose when he weas one [on] the meridian Above the Pole.[2]

His meridinall alltitude was	32°44′
My Latt*itud* is found to be north	00°26′
His distance from the Pole is	33°10′

The forme of the Crosers

13
Beinge Thursday faier weather wind at SE a fresh gale. Course made true is north this 24 houers and my distance Sailed is 121 mils: dif*erence* of Latt*itud* 02°01′ n*orth*.
Latt*itud* by good observation at none of the ☼ 01°32′ N
Meridian distance from Cap Blanc*co* E 693 Lea*gus* 0·9
Longitud at none from Cap Blanc*co* E 47°12′
Faier weather this afternone and a fine gale at SE and S*:* Sum Raine this Eveinge: noe fish Sene: hasey to night wind at SE a fine gale all night Course N ½ westerly.

14
Beinge friday faier weather wind at SE a fine gale. Course north 5° westerly: distance Sailed 105·4 Mil: Departur west 09·2 mils: Dif*erence* Lon*gitud* 00°09′·2: Dif*erence* of Latt*itud* 01°45′ N: Latt*itud* by obs*ervation* ☼ 03°17′ N.
Meridian distance from Cap Blanc*co* E 690 Lea*gus* 0·7
Longitud at non from Cap Blanc*co* E 47°02′·8
Faier weather this after none wind at ESE a fresh gal: Cours by Compas NW: Variation is 00°50′ E.

15
Beinge Satterday faier weather and temprate wind at EBS. Course mad true is NBW: distans Saild 85 m*ils*: departur west 16·7 mils: Dif*erence* of Longit*ud* 00°16′·8: Dif*erence* Lat*itud* 01°23′ N: Latt*itud* by ob*servation* ☼ is 04°40′ N.
[*margin:* Raine] Meridian dist*ance* from Cape Blanc*co* E 684 Lea*gus* 2·0 m*ils*
Long*itud* at none from Cape Blanc*co* E 46°46′
[*margin:* West] Variation by an Amplytud at ☼ Set 01°40′ west.

[*202*] **Aprill 1671 the *Sweep Stakes* at Sea Latt*itud* N 05°30′ N**
16
Beinge Sunday Sum Raine at two aclocke this morninge wind Came to the NE a fine gale Cours Steered NWBN by my Compas. This morninge at Sun Rizeinge I tooke an Amplytud with my Compas and find the magnet*ic* Amplytud to be 12°28′ to The

[1] Narbrough ceased to number the pages of his journal at this point. Page numbering from here onwards has been inserted on alternate pages in pencil by a curator. These pencilled numbers, with numbers inserted on all remaining pages to give a continuous sequence for ease of reference, are given in italics.

[2] See p. 333, Fig. 8. β Crucis. Narbrough's diagram occupies the right side of the page abreast of the 4 preceding lines of text. From the diagram it would appear that he refers to the Southern Cross as seen on the meridian with γ Crucis at the top, the north arm and α Crucis at the bottom, the south arm, making β Crucis the west arm. The star on the east arm, on this basis, is much less bright than the others and therefore less likely to have been observed.

northward of the East Poin*t* the true Amplytud is at the Sam time 13°38′ to the No*rth* of the E. Lat*itud* 05°30′ No*rth*. ☼ Declin*ation*13°34′ no*rth*. Mag*netic* Amp*lytud* 12°28′
I find the Compas to *have* west variation 01°10′. [*margin:* variation West]
Faier weather this forenone and a fine gale of wind at NE: Cours Steered NNW: affter Sum Courses this 24 hou*ers* I make my true Course to be NW: distance Sailed 69 mils: departur west 49 mils: Dif*erence* of Long*itdud* 00°49′·1: Dif*erence* of Latt*itud* 00°49′ N: Latt*itud* by ob*servation* of the ☼ 05°29′ N.
Meridian distance from the Cap Blanc*co* E 668 Le*agus* 1·0 mil
Long*itud* att none from Cap Blanco E 45°56′·9
Sum Shoures of Raine this after none and lettle wind at NNE: [*margin:* Rain] Smoath Sea & temprate weather. This day a Small [*margin:* a letle bird] Land bierd Cam and let[1] one [on] the Ship: noe [*margin:* men in health] Sea fouls Sene nor any fish Exseptinge Sum flyinge fishes: my men all in Good health: I Praise God. No Azimuth nor Allplitud to be taken the Sky all Clouded and over Cast: much littning [lightning] to night and Sum thunder and Raine: the wind Round the [*margin:* Raine] Compas to night. I Maced [maked] my way to the northwarde.

17
Beinge Munday Cloudy weather and little wind to day at NBE & NE Sumtimes: very hot weather: after divers Courses this 24 houers I make my true Course to be NW: distance Sailed 40·8 mils: Departur west 29 mils: Dif*erence* Long*itud* 00°29′: Dif*erence* Latt*itud* N 00°29′: Latt*itud* by the ☼ 5°58′.
Meridian distance from Cape Blanc*co* E 658 Lea*gus* 2·0 m*ils*
Longitud at none from Cape Blanc*co* E 45°27′·9
Variation of the Compas is west 01°40′.
Faier weather to night: wind at NNE a gale.

[*203*] **Aprill 1671 the *Sweep Stakes* att Sea Latt*itud* 06°27′ N**
18
Beinge Tusday faier hot weather wind at NNE a fine gale: after Severall Courses made from yesterday noone till today none i make my tru Course NWBW: Distance Sailed 52 mils: Departur west 43·4 mils: Dif*erence* of Longitud west 00°44′: Dif*erence* of Latt*itud* N 00°29′: Latt*itud* by observation of the ☼ one [on] the merid*ian* 06°27′.
[*margin:* variat 1°47′ W] Variation by an Amplitud in the morninge is W 01°47′.
Merid*ian* distance from Cap Blancco E 644 Lea*gus* 0·6
Longitud at none from Cap Blancco E 44°43′·9
Fair weather this Afternoon: wind at NNE a fine gale a homeinge Sea[2] Coms out of the N are Board: Sum Porposes Sene noe other fish. I tooke an Amply*tud* to day boath morninge & Eveinge and find the variation to be westerly 1°47′ in the morninge and 1°10′ in the Eveinge: much lightinge to night.

[1] Lit or landed.
[2] Home normally means the proper situation of an object, when it retains its full force of action, or when it is properly lodged for convenience. The meaning of this would therefore seem to be that the sea was as to be expected from the force of the wind.

19
Beinge Wednsday faier weather in the morning wind at NEBE a fine gale: Course by my Compas NWBN. After Sum Courses this 24 houers I make my true Cours to be NW: distance Sailed 86 mils: departur west 61 mils: Dif*erence* of Long*itud* west 01°02′: Dif*erence* of Latt*itud* 01°01′ north. Lattitud By Good obs*ervation* of the Sun 07°28′ north.
Meridian distance from Cap Blancco E 623 Lea*gus* 2·6 m*ils*
Longitud at none from Cape Blancco E 43°41′·9

20
Being Thursday faier weather wind at NBE and NNE A fresh gale Sumtimes. After Severall Courses I make the true Cours to be NWBW 5°45′ westerly: distance Sailed 78·5 mils: departur west 69·5 mils & Dif*erence* of Longitud west 01°11′·5: Dif*erence* of Latt*itud* 00°37′ N. Latt*itud* by observation of the Sunn one [on] the Mer*idian* 08°05′ N.
Meredian distance from Cap Blancco E 600 Lea*gus* 2·1 m*ils*
Longitud at noon from Cap Blan*cco* E 42°30′·4
[*margin:* varia 1°00′W*est*] Variation of the Compas is westerly 01°00′.

[*204*] **Aprill 1671 the *Sweepstakes* at Sea in Lat*itud* 08°53′ N**
21
Beinge friday hasey weather this morninge wind NNE a fresh gale: a Swell of a Sea Comes out of the north this two dayes. After Severall Courses this 24 houers I make my true Course to be NW 7° westerly: distance Sailed 77·8 mils: Departur west 61·5 mils: Dif*erence* Lo*ngitud* 01°02′ W: Dif*erence* of Lat*itud* 00°48′ N: Lat*itud* by observation of the ☼ 08°53′ N.
Meridian distance from Cap Blanc*co* E 579 Lea*gus* 0·6 m*il*
Longitud at noon from Cap Blanc*co* E 41°28′·4

22
Beinge Satterday faier weather wind at NNE a fine gale: [*margin:* Ould Saile Bent] this morninge I had the maine Saile one Bent [unbent] and the ould one Brought too: it Beinge mended: I have now all the ould Sailes to the yards: and the Sailmakers mendinge the others: I have ordered the Peece of Cable which [*margin:* Cable Splicd] was Cut of[f] of the outward ind of the Best Bower to be Spliced to the Enward ind of the Small bower to lenthinge it: for a moreinge Cable.[1]
After Severall Courses this 24 houers I make the tru Course to be NWBW: distance Sailed 75·5 miles: Departur west 62·8 mils: Dif*erence* of Long*itud* 01°03′·2: Dif*erence* of Lat*itud* by acc*ount* 00°42′ no*rth*: Lat*itud* at non 09°35′ no*rth*.
Faier weather to night & a Small gale at NNE.
Meridian distance from Cape Blanco E 558 Leagus 0·8 m*il*
Longitud at none from Cap Blanco Easte 40°25′·2

[1] The piece of cable cut off the outboard end of the best bower cable to be spliced to the inboard end of the small bower cable to lengthen it. The outboard end of the cable, as it is dragged over the seabed by the movement of the ship at anchor, gets the greatest wear. Its use at the inboard end of the small bower would mean that it was least likely to get any further wear, except possibly in the hawse hole where it could be well padded.

23
Beinge Sunday and the Kings Corronation day and San Gorges Day and Esterday: faier weather lettle wind at NBE. After Severall Courses from yesterday at none till to day at none I make my true Course to be NWBW: distance Sailed 64·5 mils: Departur west 54 Mils: Dif*erence* of Longitad west 00°54′·3: Dif*erence* Latt*itud* N 00°36′: Latt*itud* at none By Acc*ount* 10°11′N.
Meridian distance from Cape Blanco E 540 Le*gus* 0·8
Longitud at none from Cape Blanco E 39°30′·9

[*205*] **Aprill 1671 the *Sweep Stakes* at Sea homw*ard* *Latitud* 10°25′ N**
24
Beinge Munday faier weather wind vareinge betwen the NE and the north a Small gale. After Severall Courses from Sunday noon till to day noon I make my true Course to be WBN 08°45′ northerly: Distance Sailed 40·8 mils: Departur west 38·4 mils: Dif*erence* Lo*ngitud* 00°38′·6: Dif*erence* of Lat*itud* 00°14′ n: Lat*itud* by the ☼ on the me*ridian* 10°25′ N.
Merid*ian* distance from Cap Blanc*c*o E 527 Le*gus* 1·4 m*il*
Longitud at noon from Cap Blanc*c*o E 38°52′·3
Variation is found to be westerly 01°10′.

25
Beinge Tusday faier weather wind at N & at NNE: Smale winds and temprate weather not very hote: Sum Sea foules Sen to day and a tropick Bird:[1] noe fish. After divers Course from yesterday at none till today at noone I make my true Course to be NW and my distance Sailed 21·2 mils: Dep*artur* wes*t* 15 mils: Dif*erence* of Longitud west 00°15′·5: dif*erence* La*titud* 00°15′N.
Lat*itud* by observation of the ☼ at none 10°40′ N
Lat*itud* at Eight a Clock at night by the no*rth* ☆[2] 10°48′ N
Lat*itud* a letle Past 8 Clock at night by the ☆ *great* Ber Sid[3] 10°50′ N
Lat*itud* at the Same tim By the ☆ of the great bers back[4] 10°49′ N
Meridian dist*ance* from Cape Blanc*c*o E 522 L*eagus* 1·4 m*il*
Longitud at non from Cap Blanco E 38°36′·8

26
Beinge wedensday hasey weather letle wind at N & at NNE. After divers Courses from tusday none till to day non I make my true Course NW: distance sailed 58 mils: Departur west 41 mils: Dif*erence* of Longitud 00°41′·6: Dif*erence* of Latt*itud* 00°41′: La*titud* by account at none 11°21′ N.
Merid*ian* distance from Cape Blanc*c*o E 508 le*agus* 2·4
Longitud at none from Cap Blanc*c*o E 37°55′·2

[1] Probably the red-billed tropicbird, *Phaeton aethereus*.
[2] North star: Polaris, α Ursæ Minoris.
[3] Great Bear's side: Merak, β Ursæ Majoris.
[4] Great Bear's back: Dubhe, α Ursæ Majoris.

[*206*] **Aprill 1671 the *Sweep Staks* at Sea homw*ard* Lat*itud*[1]**
27
Beinge thursday faier weather wind att NNE and at NE a Fresh gale Course NW and NWBN: but I make my true Course is NW: distance Sailed 80·5 mils: Departur west 57 mils: Dif*erence* of Longitud 00°58′·5: Dif*erence* of Latt*itud* 00°57′N: Latt*itud* att noon by acco*unt* 12°18′ N.
Meridian dist*ance* from Cap Blanc*co* E 489 Lea*gus* 2·4 m*ils*
Longitud at noon from Cap Blanc*co* E 36°56′·7
Variation of the Compas is west 01°05′.

28
Beinge Friday faier weather wind at NEBN & NE and NNE: after Sum Courses from yesterday none till to day none I make my true Course to be NW: and distance Saild 89·4 mils: Departur west 63 m*ils*: Dif*erence* of Longitud West 01°04′: Dif*erence* of L*atitud* 01°03′. Lat*itud* at noone by account is 13°21′ north.
Merid*ian* distance from Cap Blanc*co* E 468 Lea*gus* 2·4
Longitud at non from Cap Blanc*co* E 35°52′·7

29
Beinge Satterday faier weather wind at NE a fresh gale. Course made true from yesterday at noone till to day at noone is NWBN: distance Sailed 102 mils: depart*ur* West 57 mils: Dif*erence* of Longitud W 00°58′·8: Dif*erence* of Lat*itud* N 01°25′: Lat*itud* by account 14°46′ N.
Meridian dist*ance* from Cape Blanc*co* E 499 Lea*gus* 2·4
Longitud at no*ne* from Cape Blanc*co* E 34°53′·9
The Reason I have had noe observation is the ☼ have ben Clouded nere and one [on] the Meridian and now I have the ☼ nere my zeneth.[2]

[*207*] **Aprill 1671 the *Sweep Stakes* at Sea Latt*itud* 16°41′ No*rth***
30
Beinge Sunday Sum Raine this Night this morninge wind at NEBN a Fresh gale: it Came to the ENE a fresh gale all day. My tru Course from yesterday at none till to day at none is NNW: distance Sailed 124·5 mils: Departur W 48 mils: Dif*erence* Long*itud* 00°49′·5: Dif*erence* of Lat*itud* 01°55′: Latt*itud* by account at none is 16°41′ N.
Meridian distance from Cape Blanc*co* E 433 Lea*gus* 2·4
Long*itud* at noon from Cape Blanc*co* E 34°04′·4
A fresh gale this afternone at ENE: Course by my Compas N: the aier temperat and Could to day. Variation of the Compas is But 00°40′ west.

May 1671: the *Sweepstakes* at Sea in the Lat*itud* 18°33′[3]
1
Beinge Munday faier weather wind at NEBE a fresh gale this day. Course made true from Sunday at noone till to day at noon is NBW: distance Sailed 114·5 mils: [*margin:* ☆

[1] No latitude given.
[2] The sun was too high to observe.
[3] This is an additional heading halfway down the page.

zenet] Departur west 22·3 mils: Dif*erence* of Long*itud* 00°23′·5: Dif*erence* of Lat*itud* 01°52′ no*rth*: Lat*itud* by account at noon 18°33′ N.
Meridian dist*ance* from Cape Blanco E 426 Lea*gus* 1·1 mil
Longitud at noon from Cape Blanco E 33°40′·9

2
Beinge tusday fair weather the wind at NEBE a fresh gal. Course made true from munday noone till to day at none is NNW: distance Sailed 115 mils: departur west 44 mils: Dif*erence* of Longitud west 00°46′·5: Dif*erence* Lat*itud* 01°46′: Latt*itud* by account at noone 20°19′.
Meridian dist*ance* from Cape Blanco E 411 Lea*gus* 2·1 m*il*
Longitud at non from Cape Blanco E 32°54′·4
A fresh gale this afternone at ENE: Cours north. Variation of the Compas is But 00°15′ west.
This Eveninge the SpritSail topmast Brake.[1]

[*208*] **May 1671 the *Sweep Stakes* at Sea Lat*itud* 21°42′ N**
3
Beinge Wednsday faier weather wind at NEBE a fresh gale. Course made true from tusday noone till to day none is NNW: distance Sailed 90·4 mils: depart*ur* West 34·7 mils: Dif*erence* of Long*itud* west 00°36′·6: Dif*erence* of Latt*itud* 01°23′ N: Latt*itud* by account 21°42′ N.
Meridian distance from Cape Blanc*c*o E 400 Le*agus* 0·4
Longitud at non from Cape Blanc*c*o E 32°17′·8
But lettle variation of the Comp*as* it is But 10′ we*st*.

4
Beinge thursday faier weather wind at NEBE at day lighte: this forenone at EBN a fresh gale. Course made true from yesterday at none till to day at none is NNW: distance Saild is 90·2 mils: departur west 34·5 mils: Dif*erence* of Longitud west 00°37′·2: Dif*erence* of Lat*itud* 01°23′ N: Lat*itud* by accounte to day att noon is 23°05′ N.
Meridian distance from Cap Blanco E 388 Lea*gus* 1·9 m*il*
Longitud at noon from Cap Blanco E 31°40′·6
At 12 aClocke today the wind Cam to the E a fresh gale: I Steered NBE: at 12 aClocke to night I Crosed the tropicke of Cancer in the meridian distance and Longitud that I was in at noone day before.

5
Beinge Friday faier temperat weather wind at EBN a fresh gale. Course made true from thursday none till to day noon is North: distance Sailed 68 mils: Dif*erence* of Lat*itud* 01°08′ N: Lat*itud* by account at non 24°13′ N.
Meridian distance from Cape Blanco E 388 Lea*gus* 1·9
Longitud at noon from Cap Blanco E 31°40′·6

[1] This was the vertical mast at the outer extremity of the bowsprit.

Fair weather this afternone wind at E: Cours NBE: noe observation of the ☆ the heaven Beinge Clouded.[1] Variation is But little wee finde 00°20′ west.

[*209*] **May 1671 the *Sweepstaks* at Sea homwards L*atitud* 25°38′ N**
6
Beinge Satterday fair temperrate weather wind at ESE a fresh gale. Course made true from yesterday at noone till to day at none is NNE: distance Sailed 92·2 m*ils*: Departur E 35·4 mils: Def*erence* Lo*ngitud* 00°39′: Dif*erence* of Lat*itud* 01°25′: Lat*itud* by observatio*n* of the ☼ 25°38′.
Mer*idian* Distance from Cap Blanco E 400 Lea*gus* 1·3 m*il*
Long*itud* at noon from Cape Blanco E 32°19′·6
Wind at South this afternoone a fresh gale Cours NNE.

7
Beinge Sunday fair weather wind at SE a fresh gale. Course NNE from yesterday at none till to day no*ne* and distance Sailed 113 mills: Departur E 43·2 mils: Dif*erence* of Longitud 00°48′: Dif*erence* of Lat*itud* 01°44′ N: Lat*itud* by observation of the ☼ at non 27°22′ N.
Meredian distance from Cap Bla*ncc*o E 414 Le*agus* 2′5 m*ils*
Longitud at none from Cap Blanc*c*o E 33°07′·6
[*margin:* A Saile Sene] This Afternoone I Saw a Saile Standinge South: I Spoke with him the Masters name John warwicke a dutch man and Shipp Bound to the Bermudus: haveinge the Duke of yorkes Pase: Captaine Robert Barber[2] is a Pasender in her: they are imployed to Git up Wraks which ar lost one [on] that Coast:[3] Barbar tells mee wee have Pease with all Christian Princes. They Reckon them Selfes to be 31°10′ in difierence of Longitud West from the Lizard of England: But I make my diference of Longitud according to my account out and what I have made homewards: to be 28°48′·4 to the westward of the Lizards Meridian: Soe they departed. Wind at SE a fine gale.

[*210*] **May 1671 the *Sweep Staks* at Sea in the Latt*itud* 28°12′ N**
8
Beinge Munday faier wather wind at SE a fine gal: noe variation that I Can observe. Course made true from yesterday at noon till to day at noone is NEBN: Distance Sailed 60 mils: departur East 33·5 mi*ls*: Dif*erence* of Longitud E is 00°38′: Dif*erence* of Lat*itud* 00°50′: Latt*itud* by observation of the ☼ 28°12′.
Meridian distance from Cap Blanco E 426 Le*agus* 0·0
Longitud at noone from Cape Blanco E 33°45′·6

[1] This could refer to all the stars in the heavens or it could be a reference to the Pole Star.

[2] Captain Robert Barber does not appear in any of the contemporary lists of Royal Naval officers and so may have been a merchant navy officer. It is unlikely that a boat was lowered for direct contact between the two vessels and more probable that they passed close to each other and conversed by shouting across the intervening sea. It may therefore be that Narbrough got the name wrong and that this should be Robert Butler who was employed by the Duke of York as master of the *Recovery*, fishing for wrecks in 1670. James, *Memoirs*, pp. 193–4.

[3] The Duke of York, as Lord High Admiral, was granted all wrecks by King Charles by Letters Patent dated 29 Jan. in the 12th year of his reign. James, *Memoirs*, p. 178. He gave instructions to Sir William Temple, Ambassador to the States of the United Provinces, dated Nov. 1669 and March 1670, to contract with Dutchmen who were acknowledged experts in salvage for the recovery of wrecks off the coasts of England and Ireland. Presumably this voyage was an extension of these arrangements. Ibid., pp. 179–8, 189–90.

Faier weather to day I mounted the Gunns as were in [*margin:* Guns mountd] the hould:[1] wind at SE a fine gale all night.

9

Beinge tusday fair weather wind at ESE a fine Small gale. Course made true from munday at noone till to day at noon is N 20° East: distance Sailed 70 mils: departur East 24·0 Mils: Dif*erence* Lo*ngitud* 00°27′·3: Dif*erence* of Lat*itud* 01°06′ N: Lat*itud* by account at noone 29°18′.
Meridian distance from Cap Blanco E 434 Le*agus* 0·0
Longitud at noone from Cap Blanco E 34°12′·9

10

Beinge Wednsday faier weather wind at SE a fine Gale. Course made true from yesterday at noon till to day at noon is north twenty degres East: distance Sai*le*d 76·5 mils: Departur East 26·6 mils: Dif*erence* of Longitud 00°30′·3: Dif*erence* of Lat*itud* 01°12′ N: Latitud today att noone By accounte 30°30′ N.
Meridian distance from Cap Blanco E 442 Le*agus* 2·6 m*ils*
Longitud at noone from Cap Blanco E 34°43′·2
Faier weather to night wind at South East a gale: Course north North East: my men all in good health Beinge Sixty Nine in Company.

[*211*] **May 1671 the *Sweepstakes* at Sea in the Lat*itud* 31°12′ N**

11

Beinge thursday faier weather wind at W and at WNW a fine gale. Course made true from yesterday noone till to day none is north E: distance Sailed 59·5 mils: Departur East 42 mils: Dif*erence* of Lo*ngitud* 00°49′: Dif*erence* of Lat*itud* 00°42′ N: Latt*itud* at none by account ☼ 31°12′.[2]
Meridian distance from Cap Blanco E 456 L*eagus* 2·6
Longitud from Cap Blanco E 35°32′·2
Lettle wind this afternoone at NW: Calme to night.

12

Beinge friday faier weather and letle wind at SW and Calme this forenone. Course mad true from yesterday at noon till to day at noon is NEBN: distance Saild 14·4 mils: Departur East 8 mils: Dif*erence* of Long*itud* 00°09′·3: Dif*erence* of Latt*itud* 00°12′: Lat*itud* ☼ 31°24′ N.
Meridian distance from Cap Blanco E 459 Le*agus* 2·6
Longitud from Cape Blanco E 35°41′·5
[*margin:* A sail senn] Lettle wind this aftern*one* at South: wee Saw a Saile at 12 of the Clocke to day: She Bar NE of mee: at five of the Clocke I Spake with her: it was the Nightingall Pinke from the Cannaris Bound for Boaston in New England: the masters name Robert Bristow, of London.[3] I Spared him one of my Maine Stertinge Saile

[1] The guns had been stowed below after leaving Madeira on the outward passage (see above, p. 153) and they were remounted so that the ship would be prepared in the event of meeting hostile vessels when approaching Europe.

[2] This could mean that the account agreed with the observed Latitude, but it may be a simple scribal error.

[3] Neither the *Nightingale* nor Robert Bristow are mentioned in Pepys's 'Register of Ships' or his list of 'Sea-officers of the Royal Navy'. Tanner, *Catalogue*, I, pp. 292, 329.

Bomes[1] to make him a yarde: he had a jurie maine Mast.[2] Faier weather to night I left him: [*margin:*A man Drownded] this night Andrew Floid the Carpenters mate fell over Board and was Drownded.
Wind at South tonight a fine gale: I Steered NEBN with all the Saile that I Could make: noe fish nor fowle to be Senn in these Seas. Beinge Calme I tried the Currant but found none: I veared downe the lead two hundered fadam But noe grounde.

[*212*] **May 1671 the *SweepStakes* at Sea in the Latt*itud* 31°51′ North**
13
Beinge Satterday fair weather wind at SouthBW a fine gale and Smoath water Course NEBN. True Course made from yesterday noone till to day at noone is NE: distance Sailed 38 mils: departur East 27 Mils: Dif*erence* of Longitud 00°31′·5: Dif*erence* Lat*itud* 00°27′ north: Latt*itud* by good observation of the ☼ at non 31°51′ N.
Meridian distance from Cape Blanco E 472 Lea*gus* 0·6
Longitud at noon from Cape Blanco E 36°13′·0
Faier weather to night wind at SSW a Stife gale Course NEBN: Smoath Sea.
Variation of the Compas is 00°15′ west. [*margin:* varia*tion*]

14
Beinge Sunday faier weather wind at SWBS a fine gale. Course from yesterday att noone till to day at noon is NEBN: distance Sailed 90·3 Mils: Departur East 50 mils: Dif*erence* of Longitud 00°59′·6: Dif*erence* Lat*itud* 01°15′ no*rth*: Latt*itud* by accounte to day at noone is 33°06′ no*rth*.
Meridian distance from Cap Blancco E 488 Le*agus* 2·6 m*ils*
Longitud at noone from Cap Blanco E 37°12′·6
Sum Raine to day and a fine gale at SW all night.

15
Beinge Munday faier weather wind at South a fine gale and Smoath Sea. Course made true from yester day at non till to day at noone is North 40° Easterly: distance Sailed 47 Mills: departur East 30·2 mils: Dif*erence* of Longitud 00°36′·2: Def*erence* Latt*itud* 00°36′: Latt*itud* ☼ 33°42′.
Meridian distance from Cape Blanco E 498 Lea*gus* 2·8 Mils
Longitud at noon from Cap Blanco E 37°48′·8
Faier weather to night and the wind at SE a fine gale and Smoath water. My men begin to droope and in Cline to have the Scurrvie: Seaven of my Compan ar Sicke.

[1] Sterting sail booms do not appear in any of the marine dictionaries of the period. it would appear to mean studding sail booms; small booms used to extend the yards and carry extra sails in light airs. The meaning of this is not clear. The term does not appear in any of the nautical dictionaries of the time. Narbrough states that on 12 May, 1671 he gave one of his main sterting sail booms to a pink to make a yard. The name would appear to be based on Old English *stort*, Middle English *stert, start*, which means a 'tail'. It may possibly come from the Dutch word *staart*, which again means a 'tail' It also was used to mean 'lengthening piece' or 'something that helps to join two parts', from which the Dutch *staarttouw*, 'stunsail boom lashing' comes. Based on this, and bearing in mind that the main sail would have had two studding sail booms, it would seem studding sail is the most probable meaning. See Sandahl, *Middle English*, III, pp. 98–9.

[2] A jury mast is one rigged temporarily to replace one lost in a gale or battle.

[*213*] **May 1671 the *Sweep Stakes* at Sea in the Latt*itud* of 34°54′ N**
16
Beinge tusday faier weather the wind at SEBE a fine gale and a Smoath Sea. Course made true from yesterday at noone till to day at noone is Course[1] North 40° Easterly: distance Sailed 94 mils: Departur E 60·3 mils: Dif*erence* of Longitude E 01°13′: Dif*erence* of Latt*itud* is 01°12′ N: Latt*itud* by Good observation of the Sun is 34°54′ N.
Meridian distance at non from Cape Blanco E 519 Le*agus* 0·1
Longitud at noone from Cape Blanco E 39°01′·8
[*margin: drawing of a fish*] Faier weather this after noone and Smoath Sea: wind at SE a fine gale. Sum olbyCor [albacore] fish Caute to day.

17
Beinge Wednsday faier weather wind at SE a fine gale. Course made true from yesterday noon till to day noon is North 40° Easterly: distance Sailed 106 miles: Departur E 67·8 miles: Dif*erence* of Longit*ud* 01°23′·5: Dif*erence* of Lat*itud* is 01°21′N: Latt*itude* by acco*unt* 36°15′ N.
Meridian Distance from Cape Blanc*co* E 541 Leagus 1·9
Longitud at noon from Cape Blanc*co* E 40°25′·3
[*margin:* Land] Fair weather this after noone wind at SE a fine gale. At Six a Clocke wee Saw the Ile of Saint Mary[2] one of the Iles of Azores: it Bar ENE From mee Distance by Estimation 17 Leagues. It made in this forme when it Bar ENE [*small view inserted at this point*]
[*margin:* A man Died] This morninge John Edwen Died of the Scurvie:[3] at Eveinge Buried with three vallies of Shoot:[4] hee hade ben a Captaine in former times. Faier weather to Night and lettle wind at SE: Course NEBE all night.

[*214*] **May 1671 the *SweepStakes* in Sight of St Michaells Ile: Azores**
18
Beinge Thursday faier weather and lettle wind at SE: this morninge St Michaells Ile[5] Bare NNE: Distance from mee about 14 leagues. It make in this forme: higer at Boath Ends then in the medle it Apeareth like two Iles. [*small view inserted at this point*]
St Marys Ile[6] Bar ESE from mee Dist*ance* about 8 leags: it Make thus
[*small view inserted at this point*]
I Steered By my Compas NBE at 8 of the Clocke to Stand up with the towne of St Michaells Ile: Caled Punte Dle Gada:[7] it is Seatted one [on] the SW Parte of the Ile. It was lettle wind moast Parte of this forenoone. Course made true from yesterday at non till today at noon is NEBN: Distance Sailed 75·5 miles: Departur East 42 miles: Dif*erence* of Longitude 00°52′·4: Dif*erence* of Latt*itud* 01°03′: Latt*itud* by Good observation ☼ is 37°18′ N.

[1] The x above the word may have indicated that it was marked to be deleted.
[2] Santa Maria (36°58′N, 25°06′W).
[3] This may be the John Edwin who is shown in Pepys's list of officers as having been appointed Lieutenant in *Royal Exchange* 1664, and being dead when the list was compiled in Dec. 1688.
[4] The appropriate salute for a commanding officer.
[5] São Miguel (37°45′N, 25°30′W); variants St Michalls, Michaells, Michells, Michiels.
[6] Santa Maria (36°59′N, 25°07′W); variants St Marys Ile, Island of St Maryes.
[7] Punte Del Gada (37°45′N, 25°40′W); variants Pantelege, Pounte Dle Gada, Punte Dle Gady, Punta del Gada.

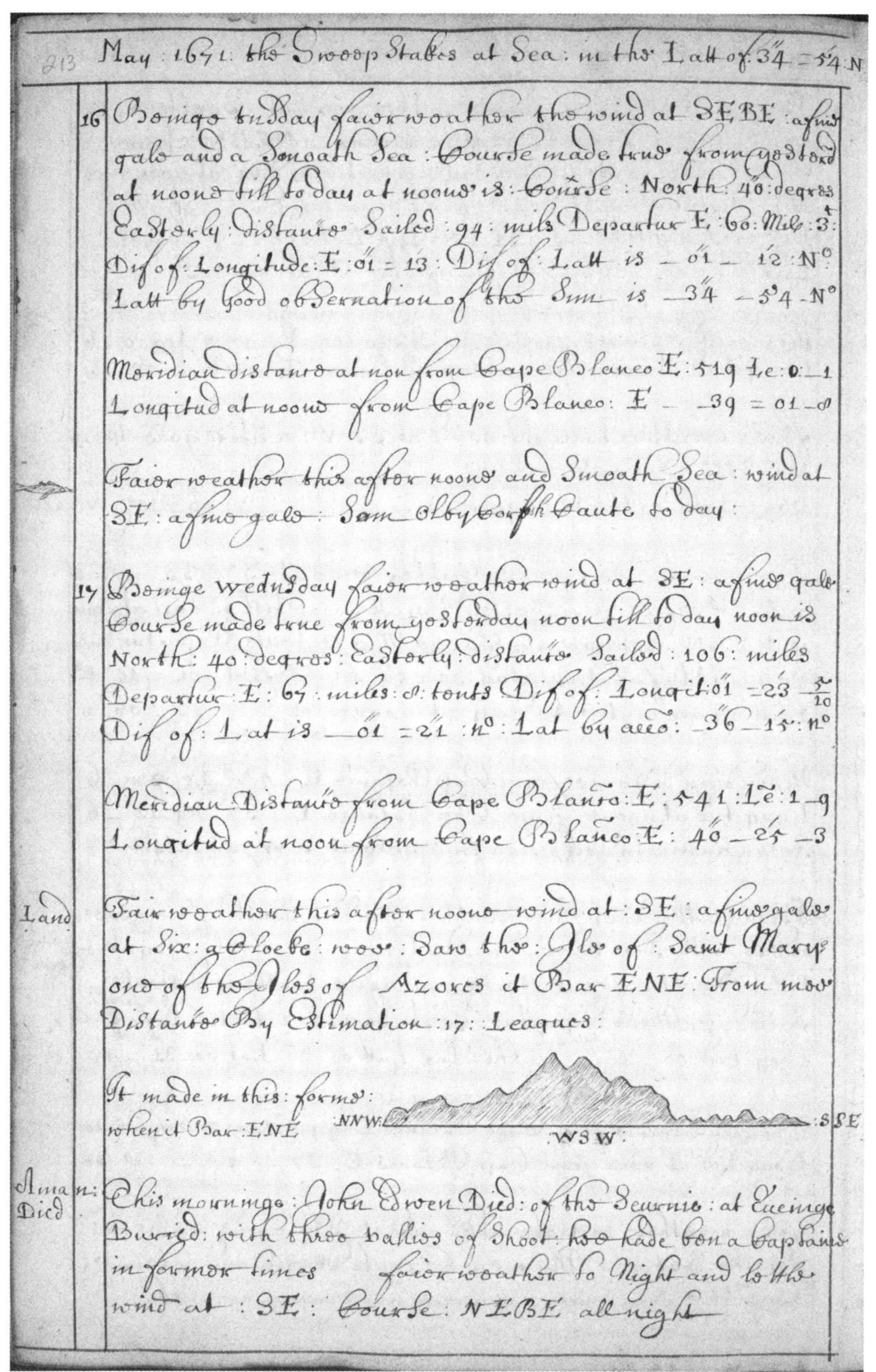

213 May : 1671: the Sweepstakes at Sea: in the Latt of 34 = 54 N

16 Beinge tuesday fair weather the wind at SEBE : a fine gale and a Smoath Sea : Course made true from yesterday at noone till to day at noone is: Course : North: 40: degrees Easterly: distance Sailed: 94: mils Departur E: 60: Mils: 3: Dif of: Longitude: E: 01 = 13 : Dif of: Latt is _ 01 _ 12 : No: Latt by Good observation of the Sun is _ 34 _ 54 . No

Meridian distance at noon from Cape Blanco E: 519 1e: 0 _ 1
Longitud at noone from Cape Blanco: E _ 39 = 01 _ 0

Fair weather this after noone and Smoath Sea : wind at SE: a fine gale: Sam Olby Corpll Caute to day:

17 Beinge wednsday fair weather wind at SE : a fine gale Course made true from yesterday noon till to day noon is North: 40: degrees: Easterly: distance Sailed: 106: miles Departur: E: 67: miles: 0: tents Dif of: Longit 01 = 23 5/10 Dif of: Lat is _ 01 = 21 : No: Lat by acco: _ 36 _ 15 : No

Meridian Distance from Cape Blanco: E: 541 : 1e: 1 _ 9
Longitud at noon from Cape Blanco E: 40 _ 25 _ 3

Land Fair weather this after noone wind at: SE : a fine gale at Six: a Clocke: wee: Saw the: Ile of: Saint Mary one of the Iles of Azores it Bar ENE: From mee Distance By Estimation: 17: Leagues:

It made in this: forme: when it Bar: ENE NNW : SSE : WSW :

A man Died n: This morninge: John Owen Died: of the Scurvie: at Eveinge Buried: with three vallies of Shoot: hee hade been a Captaine in former times fair weather to Night and little wind at : SE : Course: NEBE all night

Figure 9. Narbrough's *Sweepstakes* Journal (BL, Add MS 88980A), p. 213. Courtesy of the Trustees of the British Library.

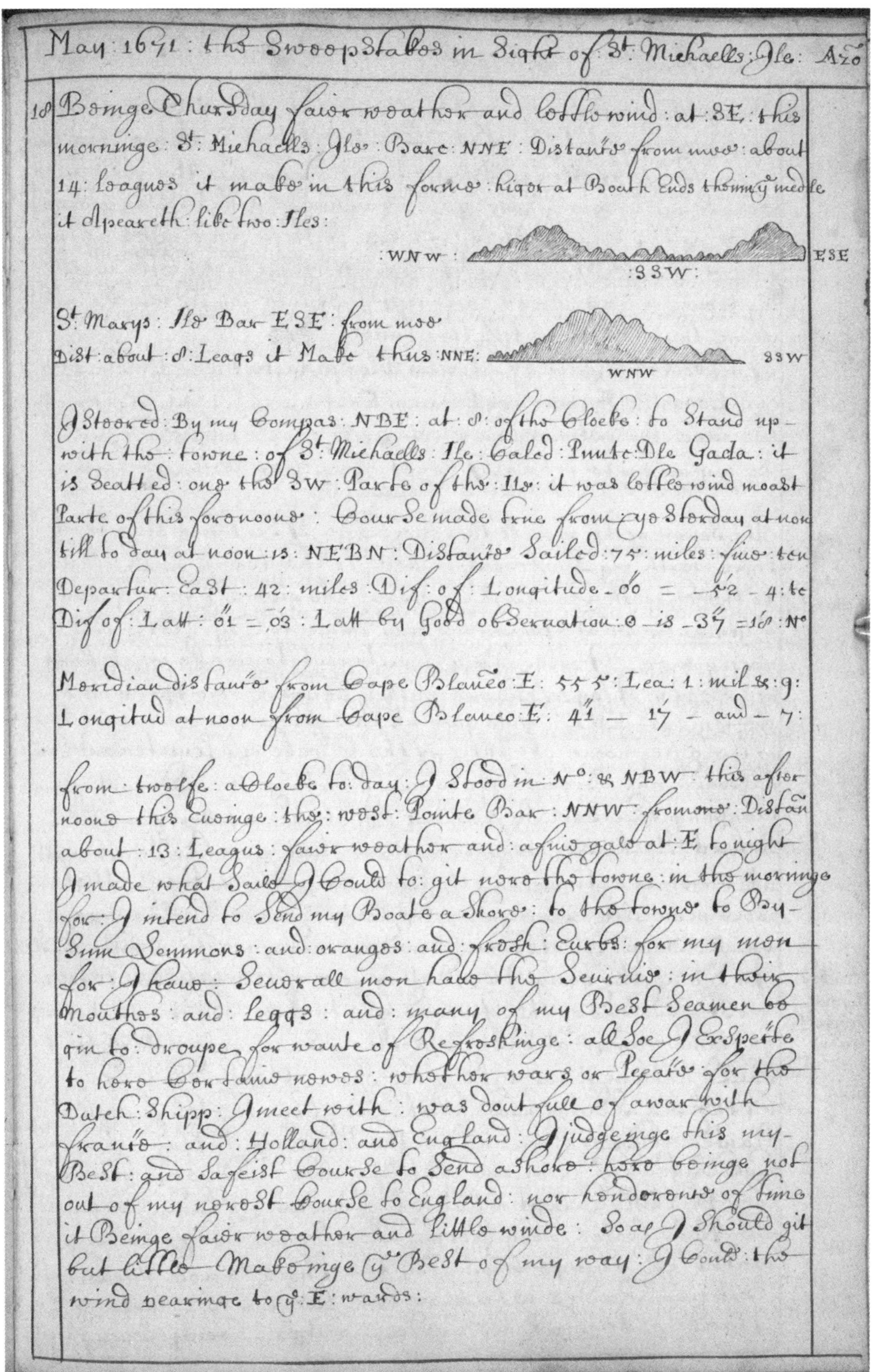

May : 1671 : the Sweepstakes in Sight of St. Michaells : Ile : Azo

10 Beinge Thursday faire weather and little wind : at : SE : this
morninge : St. Michaells : Ile : Bare : NNE : Distance from mee : about
14 : leagues it make in this forme : higer at Boath Ends then in ye medle
it Appeareth : like two : Iles :

St. Marys : Ile Bar ESE : from mee
Dist : about : 8 : Leags it Make thus NNE :

I Steered : By my Compas : NBE : at : 8 : of the Clocke : to Stand up-
with the : towne : of St. Michaells : Ile : Caled : Punte Dle Gada : it
is Seatted : one the SW : Parte of the : Ile : it was little wind moast
Parte of this forenoone : Course made true from ye Sterday at noon
till to day at noon is : NEBN : Distance Sailed : 75 : miles : true ten
Departure East : 42 : miles : Dif : of : Longitude 00 = 52 – 4 : te
Dif of : Latt : 01 = 03 : Latt by Good observation : ☉ is 37 = 18 : No

Meridian distance from Cape Blanco : E : 555 : Lea : 1 : mil & : 9 :
Longitud at noon from Cape Blanco : E : 41 — 17 – and – 7 :

from : twelfe : a Clocke to : day : I Stood in : No : & NBW : this after
noone this Eveninge : the : west : Pointe Bar : NNW : from mee : Distan
about : 13 : Leagus : faire weather and : a fine gale at : E to night
I made what Saile I Could to : git neere the towne : in the morninge
for : I intend to Send my Boate a Shore : to the towne to Buy-
Sum Lemmons : and : oranges : and : fresh : Earbs : for my men
for : I have : Severall men have the Scurvie : in their
Mouthes : and : leggs : and : many of my Best Seamen be
gin to : droupe for wante of Refreshinge : all Soe I Expecte
to here Certaine newes : whether warr or Peace for the
Dutch : Shipp : I meet with : was dout full of a war with
france : and : Holland : and England : I judgeinge this my-
Best : and Safeist Course to Send ashore : here beinge not
out of my neerest Course to England : nor hinderence of time
it Beinge faire weather and little winde : So as I Should git
but little Makeinge ye Best of my way : I Could : the
wind veeringe to ye : E : wards :

Figure 10. Narbrough's *Sweepstakes* Journal (BL, Add MS 88980A), p. 214. Courtesy of the Trustees of the British Library.

Meridian distance from Cape Blan*cc*o E 555 Lea*gus* 1·9 mil.
Longitud at noon from Cape Blanco E 41°17′·7
From twelfe aClocke to day I Stood in N & NBW this after noone: this Eveinge the west Pointe Bar NNW from me: Distan*ce* about 13 Leagus. Faier weather and a fine gale at E to night: I made what Saile I Could to git nere the towne in the morninge for I intend to Send my Boate a Shore to the towne to By Sum Lemmons and oranges and fresh Eurbs [herbs] for my men for I have Severall men have the Scurvie in their Mouthes and Leggs: and many of my Best Seamen begin to droupe for wante of Refreshinge: allsoe I Exspecte to here Certaine newes whether wars or Peace for the Dutch Shipp I meet with was doutfull of a war with France and Holland and England. I judgeinge this my Best and Safeist Course to Send ashore: here beinge not out of my nerest Course to England: nor henderence of time it Beinge faier weather and little wind: So as I Should git but little Makeinge the Best of my way I Could: the wind vearinge to the E:wards.

[*215*] **May 1671 the *Sweep Stakes* nere St Michealls Ile**
19
Beinge Friday faier weather wind at EBN a Small gale. This morninge at 6 of the Clocke I was with in two lea*gu*s of the towne of Punte Dle Gada: it Bar north from mee. Course made true from yesterday noone till to Day morninge at 7 of the Clocke then I was within two miles of the towne Pounte Dle Gaday: it Bar N from me a letle westerly: my Course was north and my Distance Sailed was 34 mils from thursday none till this time.
I make the Roade of Punte Dle Gada to Ly in L*atitud* 37°52′ N
and Longitud From Cape Blanco East 41°17′·7
And meridian distance from C*ape* Blan*cc*o E 555 *Leagus* 1·9 mil
By my accounte which I keept from Cape Blancco heether.
[*margin:* I sent the Boate a Shor] At Seven of the Clocke this morninge I Sent my Pinnase A Shore with my Leiutenant in her to the towne with a letter to the Englesh Counsell to disier the news and to accquainte the Govennor what I ame[1] and only disier to By a letle frute for my men: I orderd my Leiuetenant to maake what hast of he Could. I lay of[f] and one [on] with the Shipp before the towne the wind at ENE a fine gale all this fore none and most Part of the afternoone. At three of the Clocke my Leiuetenant Cam a Board and Brought frute and Sallettinge [salad] &c. and most of my Company hade Sum Refreshing: I Received a letter from Mr Richard Huchenson: Counsell their: that wee had Peeace with all Cristian nations: and that his Majestie & Ryall Highness were in health Seven weekes Scence. Here was Rideinge a Small Shipp of Absum:[2] Bound for mederia: Tho*mas* Smith Mast*er*. [*margin:* Parted From Punta Dle Gada] I made all the Saile I Could at fower of the Clocke to the westward End of the Ileland: for to Pas By it that way the wind Beinge at EBN: a Small gale. All night I Sailed within fower miles of the Shore: the Land is Clifey Rock by the Sea Side: of a good haith [height] and above the Clifs is all Planted fellds [fields] of Corn: and in the Medill of the Iland Runs a high Riged hill from one End to the other: and wood Growes all over this hill Exsept what is Cut downe: and the Land Mannuered: the Iland lookes very Greenn and is devied into fields. Deepe water all a longe Close By the Shore: & noe Anchoringe But in the Roades which are one [on] the SSW Parte of the Iland: and those Roades are deepe water: twenty Seven fadam

[1] To inform the Governor of the name and nationality of the ship.
[2] It has not been possible to locate a port of this name.

[*216*] May 1671 the *Sweepstakes* Before St Michells Ile

and twenty Eight and twenty five fadam: it is But a Banck that you Ride one [on]: and it is a mile and Better from the Shore Side: it is Right before the towne of Punte Dle gada which is the Best towne one [on] the Ile and Built one [on] the Shore Side: it is Plaine grenn land about it and Rocks one [on] the Shore Side: it is an unwalled towne and fortified to the Sea Side with a Castle: the gunns Stands open over the Castle wall. Their is a letle mould [mole] for to goe a Shore at the towne which is Smoath Landinge in it:[1] it is about the midlemost Parte of the town. Fresh water is Scearse here for Shipinge: here is noone in the town but what is Brought thether in Carts to Supply their occations. Villa Franca[2] is another towne which lies to the Eastwards of Punte Dle Gada.

This Iland of St Michalls is Plenty full of wheat and Beefe and Porke and other Provissions: a good Bullock is Sold for Seven Peeces of Eight:[3] all Provission for the Life of man is Plentifull.

The towne of Punte Dle Gada in the Island of Sainte Michiels and the Roade where the Shipps Doe Ride: and the Fadams of water noted by Figuers. The Road Lies in the Latitud oF 37°52′.[4]

[*217*] May 1671 the *SweepStakes* of[f] the West End of St Michalls Ile

20

Beinge Satterday faier weather: and lettle wind at NW. I was at the west End of St Michells Ile Standinge to the northward a Bout two leagus of[f] the Shore: and west from the town Punta Dle Gada 24 miles: at 12 of the Clocke I observid the Sun one [on] the meridian and was in the Lattitud of 38°00′ N. Course made true from Punta Dle Gada Road till to day at noone is west 18°30′ north: Distance Sailed 25·4 mils: Depart*ur* west 24 mils: Dif*erence* of Longitud 00°28′·2: Dif*erence* of Lat*itud* 00°08′.

Meridian dist*ance* from Cape Blanco E 547 Leags 1·9 mile.

Longitud from Cape Blanco E 40°49′·5.

Faier weather this after noone wind at north a Small gale: I Stood to the west to git an ofinge to Carit about the Iland to the northward.[5] At 12 aclocke to night I tacked and Stood to the E:ward: the winde at NWBN a Small gale: the Ile Bare NEBE from me.

21

Beinge Sunday at 4 aclocke this morninge the wind Came to the NE: a fresh gale. I was of[f] the west ind of the Ileland But Could not Carit a Bout:[6] I tacked and Stood to the westward. At 12 of the Clocke to day I was very nere the Place that I was in yesterday at noone: for I Saw that I Could gitt but little one [on] my Course for England: the winds Beinge Contrary.

Meridian Distance from Cape Blanco E 547 leagus 1·9.

Longitud at noon from Cape Bllanco E 40°49′·5.

[1] The landing is protected from the sea by the mole, giving smooth water in its lee.

[2] Vila Franca do Campo (37°43′N, 25°26′W).

[3] For prices of beef in England at this time, see above, p. 158, n. 9.

[4] See Plate 7.

[5] To make sufficient way to windward to pass to the northward of the island.

[6] Could not weather the island.

Hasey weather this afternone wind at NE a fresh gale. I Stood to the northward: the Ileland at 2 of the Clocke B[a]res ESE from me: distance fower leagus: I Stood to the N:ward all night.

22
Beinge Munday Faier weather wind at EBN a fine gale. Course mad true From yesterday at noon till to day at noone is NNW: Distance Sailed 9·7 mils: Departur west 3·7 mils: Def*erence* of Long*itud* 00°04′·9: Dif*erence* Lat*itud* 00°09′ N: Lat*itud* By accounte at noone 38°09′ north.
Meridian distance from Cape Blanco E 546 Lea*gus* 1·2 m*il*
Longitud at noone from Cape Blanco E 40°44′·6

[*218*] **May 1671 the *SweepStakes* betwen St Michalls & Tresceria**[1]
23
Beinge tusday faier weather: I Stood to the northward: wind at NE a fine gale the Iland of Trecera Bar WBS of mee at Eight of the Clocke in the forenoone: Distance about nine Leagus. At a Leven of the Clocke it Blew fresh at NEBE and like to hould in that quarter: I Doutinge wee might have a longe Pasage: I Bar for the Road of Trecera to Gitt fresh water and Bread. I find But Sixten Days water in the Shipp and But two Barrells of Flower Containeinge Seven hundered wate which we Eate in Lew of Bread: wee have had no Bread this five monthes but Eat flower in Stead of Bread: I find the flower which I have a Board will last But feivten dayes: which is two [too] lettle to Put to Sea with haveinge a Contrary wind for England. At St Michalls I might have had these Supplies But I was in hopes of a faire wind & loath to loose Soe much time now findinge the Contrary I judge it noe Discretion to Put my Selfe to Beate at Sea Beinge Soe Slenderly victualled.
Course made true from yesterday noone till to day at noon is NNW: Distance Sailed 60·5 mils: Departur west 23·3 miles: Dif*erence* of Long*itud* 00°29′·2: Dif*erence* of Lat*itud* 00°56′: Lat*itud* is 39°04′N.
Meridian distance from Cape Blanco E 538 Lea*gus* 1·9 mile
Longitud at noon from Cape Blanco E 40°15′·4
This afternoone at 6 of the Clocke I was of[f] the SE Parte of the Ile and Saw that I Could not git into the Roade: I Brought the Shipp to and Stood of[f] and in all night wind at NE a fresh gale.

24
Beinge Wednsday Hasey foogey weather the wind at NEBN a fresh gale: I Stood into the Roade. This morninge at nine of the Clock I Anchored in the Roade of Angria:[2] in Sixtenn fadam wat*er*. I Sent my Boate a Shore to accquaint the Govennor what I Am and to know if he will ansewer my Salute Gun for gun which he Promised to doe. I Saluted the Castle with nine Guns: they Ans*wer* nine: I gave three for thankes: they gave three againe. Mr William Scarifild: Consell: he Promised mee all Such things as I wanted which is Bread and fresh water. This afternoone I gott the Bread aboard which was theerten hundered and fourty Po*unds* and a Boats ladinge of fresh water.

[1] Terceira (38°39′N, 27°14′W); variants, Terceris, Trecera, Treceria, Tresceres.
[2] Angra do Heroísmo (38°39′N, 27°14′W).

[*219*] **May Ano 1671 the *SweepStakes* in the Road of Angria Treceria**
Course made true from yesterday at noone till to day that I anchored in the Road of Angria is WBS and distance Saild is 36 miles and Departur west 35·2 mils: Dif*erence* Lo*ngitud* 00°47′ W: Dif*erence* of Latt*itud* 00°07′: Latt*itud* by account is 38°57′ the Road Angria.
Meridian distance from Cape Blanco E 526 Lea*gus* 2·7 mils
Longitud I am in is from Cape Blanco E 39°28′·4
Fair weather this Eveinge and all night wind at NE a fine gale.
The Cety and Castle and Roade of Angria in the Iland of Trecera.[1]

[*220*] **May 1671 the *Sweepstakes* at Anchor in Angria Roade in Treceria**
25
Beinge thursday Cloase weather wind at north East a fresh gale. This day I gott water a Board and had Every thinge Ready to Saile: it Beinge lettle wind to night I rod fast.

26
Beinge Friday faier weather and little wind at north East. I got [*margin:* waied from Angria] the Shipp onemored [unmored] at nine of the Clocke in the morninge I waid and Stood out to Sea. I Saluted the Castle at my Goeinge away with nine Guns: they ansewered nine againe I gave five for thankes: they gave mee five againe. I made what Saile I Could to the west End of trescerea: at Six a Cloecke the west Pointe of the Ileland Bar NE of mee: Distance five leagus: wind at NE a fresh gale I Stood to the westward. I weathered St George Ile[2] fower leagus: I Saw Greatiotia[3] very Plaine it Bar NNW from mee. It Proved lettle wind to night sumtims at NNE: I Stood to the northward till tenn of the Clock at night then tacked and Stood to the E:ward.

27
Beinge Satterday faier weather and Lettle wind all day at NNE and at NE. I Plied to the northward Betwen the west Parte of Trescera and Grasiotia: But got very lettle all this day. I Saw the tope of the Peco[4] very Cleare and all the hig land of Trescera Clear & with out ever a Cloude. Course made tru from Angria Roade til to day at noone is NW: Distance from Angria ten leagus and departur west 21·2 miles: Dif*erence* of Longitud 00°27′ W: Dif*erence* of Latt*itud* 00°21′ no*rth*: Latt*itud* by accounte at noon 39°18′ N.
Meridian distance from Cape Blanc*c*o E 519 Lea*gus* 2·5 mils
Longitud at noon from Cape Blanc*c*o E 39°01′·4
Longitud at noon from Angria Road W 00°27′·0
Meridian distance from Angria Road W 7 lea*gus* 0·2 mile
This after noone it was But lettle wind at NNE: I Plied to the northward at tenn of the Clock to night the wind Came to the north I tacked and Stood to the Eastward: the [*margin:* drawing of a hand holding lead and line] Sea very Smoath: I Sounded But noe

[1] See Plate 8.
[2] São Jorge (38°40′N, 28°05′W).
[3] Graciosa (39°03′N, 28°01′W); variants, Grasiota, Grasiotia, Greatiotia.
[4] Pico (38°28′N, 28°52′W), height 7,713 ft, (2,351 m).

Ground at 130 Fadam: I was in three leagus of the west End of Tresceria. The Iland of Gratiotia is But a Small Ileland and not Soe High land as Trescera or St Georgs.[1]

[*221*] **May 1671 the *Sweepstakes* oF[F] the North Part of Tresceria**
28
Beinge Sunday Close Hasey weather the wind at NNW: I Stood to the E:ward. Course made true from yesterday noon till to day noone is NEBE: distance Sailed 46·6 mills: Departuer East 39 mills: Dif*erence* of Longitud 00°50′·4: Dif*erence* of Latt*itud* 00°26′: Latt*itud* By accounte att noone is 39°44′ north.
Meridian distance from Cape Blanco E 532 Lea*gus* 2·5 mils
Longitud at noon from Cape Blanco E 39°51′·8
Longitud at noon from Angria Road E 00°23′·4
Meridian distance from Angria Road E 5 Lea*gus* 2·8 mils
Lettle wind thes after noon at north: I Stand to the Eastward: the East End of the Ileland of Tresceres Bar nere South of me at noone to day and was Distance about Eight Leagus. Faier weather all night the wind at NBE a fine gale I Stand to the Eastward.

29
Beinge Munday faier weather the wind at NBE this forenon But a Small gale at none the wind Came to the West little wind. Cours made true from yesterday noone till to day at noone is EBS: Distance Sailed 56·2 mils: Departur East 55 Miles: Dif*erence* of Longitud 01°07′·9: Dif*erence* of Lat 00°11′ So. Latt*itud* by accounte at noone 39°33′ north.
Meridian distance from Cape Blanco E 551 Leags 0·5 mils
Longitud at noon from Cape Blanco E 40°59′·7
Longitud at noon from Angra Roade E 01°31′·3
Meridian distance from Angria Road E 24 Leags 0·8 mills
A fine fresh gale this afternoone at WBS: Course Steered is NE by the Compas a fresh gale all night at WSW and SW: Sum Raine to night.

[*222*] **May 1671 the *Sweepstakes* at Sea in the Latt*itud* of 40°44′.**
30
Beinge Tusday hasey weather wind at SWBW a fresh gale Course Steered NE. I make my true Course to be N 50° East: distance Sailed 110·5 mils: Departur East 84·5 mils: Diference of Lo*ngitud* 01°50′·2: Difrence of Latt*itud* 01°11′ N: Lattitud by account 40°44′ N.
Meridian distance from Cape Blanc*c*o E 579 Lea*gus* 1 mile
Longitud at noone from Cape Blanco E 42°49′·9
Longitud at noone from Angra Roade E 03°21′·5
Meridian distance from Angra Roade E 52 Lea*gus* 1·3 mile
A fresh gale at SWBS all this after noon and all night.

31
Beinge Wednsday Hasey weather wind at SWBW and West a fresh gale Course Steered is NE: But I make my True Cours to be north 50°E: distance Sailed 145 miles: Departur

[1] The heights of these islands are: Terceira 3,350 ft (1,021 m), Graciosa 1,320 ft (402 m) and São Jorge 3,455 ft (1,053 m).

East 111 miles: Dif*erence* of Longitud 02°29′·2: Dif*erence* of Lat*itud* 01°33′: Lattitud By accounte at noone is 42°17′ north.
Meridian distance from Cape Blanco E 616 Lea*gus* 1·0 mil
Longitud at noone from Cape Blanco E 45°19′·0
Longitud at noone from Angria Roade E 5°50′·7
Meridian distance from Angria Roade E 89 Lea*gus* 1·3 mile
The winde at West this after noone a fresh gale very hasey & fogey weather a fresh gale till ten of the Clocke to noight then it Proved Little wind: and much Raine the wind Cam to the South and to the South East and East Lettle winds. I made what way I Could to the NE:wards.

[*223*] **June 1671 the Sweepstaks at Sea in the Lat*itud* 43°21 N**
1
Beinge Thursday Fogey Rainey weather the wind vearable Round the Compas to day: Sumtimes Lettle wind and Sumtime a gale. After Severall Courses I make my true Course to be NE from yesterday noon till to day at noon: and distance Sailed 90·5 mils: Departur East 64 mils and Difference of Longitud 01°26′·3: Dif*erence* of Lattitud N 01°04′: Latitud by accounte at noon no obs*ervation* fogey wea*ther* 43°21′ north.
Meridian distance from Cape Blanco E 637 Lea*gus* 2·0 mils
Longitud at noon from Cape Blanco E 46°45′·4
Longitud at noon from Angria Road E 07°17′·0
Meridian distance from Angria Road E 110 Lea*gus* 2·3 mils
Fogey hasey weather this afternoo*n* the wind at SE: much Raine to night and Lettle wind at ESE.

2
Beinge Friday fogey wett weather the wind at NE a Stoute gale: I Stod to the northward. Course made tru from yesterday noon till to day none is NE: distance Sailed 50·8 Mils: departur East 36 mils: Def*erence* Lo*ngitud* 00°50′: Dif*erence* of Lat*itud* 00°36′: Latt*itud* by accounte at noon is 43°57′ N.
Meridian distance from Cape Blanco E 649 Lea*gus* 2·0 mils
Longitud at noon from Cape Blanco E 47°35′·4
Longitud at noon from Angria Road E 08°07′·0
Meridian Distance from Angria Road E 122 Lea*gus* 2·3 Mils
This afternoone the fore top Saile Split in Rags Beinge ould. It Blew hard this afternoon at NNE: I tacked and Stood to the E:ward.

3
Beinge Satterday faier weather win*d* at NNW: I Steer NE. After Severall Courses from yesterday noon till to day none I make my true Course to be E 15° Southerly: distance Sailed 23·2 mils: Departur East 22·4 mils: Dif*erence* of Longitud 00°31′·8: Dif*erence* of Lat*itud* 00°06′: Latt*itud* by observation of the ☼ 43°51′.
Meridian distance from Cape Blancco E 657 Lea*gus* 0·4 mil
Longitud at noon from Cape Blanco E 48°07′·2
Longitud at noon from Angria Roade E 08°38′·8
Meridian distance from Angria Road E 130 Lea*gus* 0·7 mil

[*224*] **Jun 1671 the *Sweepstaks* at Sea in the Lat*itud* oF 43°51′N**

4

Beinge Sunday faier weather: noe wind: from yesterday at none till to day at [none] a Sea Came out of the north west which Set me to the East 4 miles. Cours mad true From yesterday none till today noone is E: distance Sailed 4 miles: Departur East 4 mils: Dif*erence* of Longitud 00°05′·5: Lat*itud* ☼ 43°51′N
Meridian distance from Cape Blanco E 658 Lea*gus* 1·4 mile
Longitud at none from Cape Blanco E 48°12′·7
Longitud at none from Angria Roade E 08°44′·3
Meridian distance from Angria Roade E 131 Lea*gus* 1·7 mil
This afternoon the winde Came to the SSE a fine gale and Soe Continued all night with fog and Raine: I Steered NE.

5

Beinge Munday hasey fogey wet weather the wind at SSW: a fresh gale I Steere NE. Course made true from yesterday noone till to Day at noone NE: distance Sailed 87·8 miles: Depart*ur* East 62 mills: dif*erence* of Longitud 01°28′: Dif*erence* of Lat*itud* 01°02′N
Latitud at noone By accounte 44°53′ N.
Meridian distance from Cape Blanco E 679 Lea*gus* 0·4 m*il*
Longitud at noon from Cape Blanco E 49°40′·7
Longitud at noon from Angria Roade E 10°12′·3
Meridian distance from Angria Roade E 152 Lea*gus* 0·7 m*il*
Fogey hasey weather this afternoon: and Soe Continued to night the wind Cam to the East a Såmall[1] gale all night.

6

Beinge Tusday hasey weather the wind at NNW: a fine gale: this morninge at tenn of the Clock the wind Cam to the EBN a Small gall. Course made true From yesterday noon till today at noon is NE: distance Sailed 54 mils: departur west[2] 38 mils: Dif*erence* of Long*itud* 00°54′: Dif*erence* of Latt*itud* 00°38′: Lat*itud* by acco*unte* 45°31′ N.
Meridian distance from Cape Blanco E 691 Lea*gus* 2·4 mils
Longitud at noon from Cape Blanco E 50°34′·7
Longitud at noon from Angria Roade E 11°06′·3
Meridian distance From Angria Road E 164 Lea*gus* 2·7 mil
The wind Came to the South East this afternoone a fine gale and Soe Continued all night Course Steered NE.

[*225*] **June 1671 the *Sweepstaks* at Sea in the Latt*itud* of 46°46′N**

7

Beinge Wednsday very Fogey weather all day the wind at SW: a Stout gale: Course NE. Course made true from yesterday at noone till to day at noone is NE: distance Sailed 106 mills: departur East 75 Mils: diference of Long*itud* 01°47′·5: diference of Latt*itud* 01°15′: Latt*itud* by account at no*ne* 46°46′N.

[1] Presumably the x signals the letter to be deleted.
[2] This is an error. The departure should be east.

Meridian distance from Cape Blanco E 716 Lea*gus* 2·4 Mils
Longitud at noon from Cape Blancco E 52°22′·2
Longitud at noon from Angria Roade 12°53′·8
Meridian distance from Angria Roade 189 Lea*gus* 2·7 Mils
This day I had an other maine Saile Brought to the yard. Fogey weather all this afternoone and al night wind at the SW.

8
Beinge Thursday very foogey weather the wind at SW: A fresh gall: Course Steered is NE. Course made true from yesterday at noone till to day at noone is NE: distance Saild 128·5 mils: Departurur East 91 mils: dif*erence* of Lo*ngitud* 02°15′·5: Dif*erence* of Lat*itud* 01°31′ N: Latt*itud* By account at noon is 48°17′ north.
Meridian distance from Cape Blanco E 747 Lea*gus* 0·4 mils
Longitud at noon from Cape Blanco E 54°27′·7
Longitud at noon from Angria Road E 15°09′·3
Meridian distance from Angria Road E 220 Lea*gus* 0·7 mils
Fogey weather this day So as I Could not have any obser*vation* at twelfe of the Clocke to day: I alltered my Course and Steerd away NEBE by the Compase. I Reccon the Ile of Silly[1] to Bare NEBE of mee: and distance a Bout 70 Leagus. Hasey weather all night wind at SW a fresh gale.
I tried to Sound at Eight of the Clock But Could not git ground the Shipp Drove So fast to Le[e]ward: the wind Beinge fresh.[2] I was unwillinge to Sound againe to Loose time So filld and [*margin:* A Saile Seen] Keept one [on] my Course with all the Saile I Can make. I Saw a Saile out five Leagus to the Eastwarsds [*sic*] of mee Standinge to the northwards.

[*226*] **June 1671 the *Sweepstakes* in the Latt*itud* 49°18′N Soundings**[3]
9
Beinge Friday hasey weather the wind at WSW a Stoute gale: Course Stered by the Compas NEBE: But I make my true Course to be From yesterday at noone till to day at noon NEBE 3°45′ Easterly: distance Sailed 121·8 mils: Departur E 105 mills: Dif*erence* of Longitud 02°40′ East: Dif*erence* of Lat*itud* 01°01′ N: Latt*itud* by Good obs*ervation* ☼ 49°18′ north.
Meridian distance from Cape Blancco E 782 Le*agus* 0·4 mils
Longitud at noone from Cape Blanco E 57°07′·7
Longitud at noone from Angria Roade E 17°49′·3
Meridian distance from Angria Roade E 255 [Leagus] 0·7 mils
At 12 of the Clock I Sounded and had Sixty Eight fath*ams* Sand Redesh like Bran and Sum whitesh Sand[4] [*margin:* Sound 68: F] among it and two Small Scolup [scallop] Shells: white as Broad as a Groat[5] and Severall Peeces of Shells in the tallow: and lettle

[1] Isles of Scilly (49°55′N, 6°19′W).
[2] The lead did not reach the bottom since the ship was carried too fast to leeward by the wind.
[3] The ship was in a depth of water which could be measured by the lead.
[4] The word 'Sand' is repeated in the original with a small cross over it to indicate that it should be deleted.
[5] Groat, small silver coin, valued at four pennies, issued 1351–1662. *NOED*. The term was also used for the fourpenny coin at a later date. The size would appear to have been about 1 in (2·45 cm) in diameter.

Small Peeces of Red gravell: this I had thes Soundings,[1] com up in the tallow twice. At noon I Steered NE by my Compas the wind at WSW. I Sounded at Eight a Clocke this Eveinge and had Sixty Eight Fathams water: fine whiteis Sand and Sum Small Blacks[2] in [*margin:* Soundings 68:F] it and Small Lettle white mussell Shell and Sum Small heirs [hairs] Gliteringe Like herings Bones. I hove the Lead againe immediatly and had the Same depth of water: But fine Graies Sand and Sum Blackes amongst it and Small Peeces of Shell and Sum peeces of Shells with hollow Strakes in them of a Gray Couller and Crumbly Rotton: as Bigg as the naile of a Mans foore finger and Lettle betts of Redish Shells in the tallow and Small bets of Shells Like fish teeth.[3] From twelfe a Clocke till Eight a Clocke I have Sailed NE 34 mills: Lat*itud* 49°42′ I ame [*sic*] now in: I Steere away now ENE haveing the Chanell Faire open: the wind at WSW a fresh gale all night.

[*227*] **June 1671 the *Sweepstaks* in Sight of Silli Ilands**
10
Beinge Satterday hasey Fogey weather the wind at WSW a fresh gale. This morninge at 4 of the Clock I Brought too and Soun*d*ed and had Sixty onee fadam water and the Soundings which Cam up on the Lead was fine Redis Sand and a Great deale of Gravell boath blacke and white and Red amongst it: as Bige as Brooken Peper: and lettle yellow Gravle Sto*nes*. I hove the leade againe immediattly and the Soundings that Cam up on the Lead is fine Sand yellowes white and one Smale white Shell in it: the deepth of water as before: Sixty one fa*dams*. From Last night at Eight of the Clocke till to day at 4 of the Clocke I have Sailed 12 Leagues ENE by my Compas: my Latt*itud* now is 49°56′: I Steere now NE by my Compas. I reccon Silly to Bere NE of mee and distance of Seven or [*margin:* Made the Iland of Scilly] Eight Leagues. At Seven of the Clocke this morninge I made Silly one [on] the Deecke:[4] the Body Bar NE of mee a lettle northerly distance of Five Leagues: it made in Ragit Brooken Rockes to the NW Parte of it. I Saw after a lettle time Runninge, the Rocks Called the Bisshops[5] and the Clarkes: the Sea Brooke much one [on] them. The Bisshop is a Rocke Stand Coplen up of a Prety height Singly by him Selfe a Good way to the westwards of the Rest of his Companions. From to day at fower of the Clock till Seven of the Clocke that I made the Land: I Sailed NEBE nere a Eleven miles. I make my Latt*itud* to be now 50°02′. I Stood in with Silly north East till I made the two

[1] 'thes Soundings,' interpolated above the line.

[2] Some small black specks in the whitish sand.

[3] The nature of the seabed is recorded in detail so that mariners could judge their position off a coast. Tapp, *Sea-mans Kalender*, 1631, (not paginated) gives 'The soundings and grounds betweene *Ireland, England* and *Normandie*', and states 'Coming from Cape Finister, sayling N.N.E. if you have 80 fatham you are 80 leagues off the shore, and the ground is small blacke stones with great red sand: In the same course when you have 60 fatham, you are within 12 or 14 leagues of the shore, but shall not so soone kenne land as you think for: you shall a great while have 60 fatham: being at the N. Parts of the Channell about Silly: betweene Ushant and Silly, the Channell is 70 fatham: on the S. side of Silly, the ground is small red stones and fine white sand.' The *General Instructions for Hydrographic Surveyors*, 1884, p. 8, still stated 'In the approaches to the English Channel the same depths occur (73 fathoms), in 49°20′N, over a distance of 125 miles while the size of the sediment changes from fine sand at the western end to ooze at the eastern end.'

[4] It was visible from the deck.

[5] Bishop Rock (49°52′N, 6°27′W).

winde mills Plaine: which Stands one [on] St Maryes Iland:[1] and a mile and halfe from those two Mels Stands a tower to the westwards.[2] When the Mells Bar NNE of mee fower Leagus of[f] I Sounded and had fevity two Fadams: fine Sande a letle yellowish and Chafey.[3] I made Selly Plaine: I Steered away East for the Lizard.[4]

[*228*] **June 1671 the *Sweep Stakes* in the Chanell of England.**
10
At twelfe of the Clock to day the Easter most Parte of Silly Bar north of mee distance about three Leagues: thence I Stered East for the Lizarde. Course made true from yest*er*day at noone till to day at noone is NEBE: distance Sailed 80·8 miles: departur East is 68.8 miles:[5] Dif*erence* of Longitud East 01°48′·8: Dif*erence* of Latt*itud* 00°46′ north: Lat*itud* at noone by account 50°04′ north.
Meridian distance From Cape Blancco E 804 Lea*gus* 2·4 m*ils*
Longitud at noone from Cape Blancco E 58°56′·5
Longitud at noone from Angria Road E 19°38′·1
Meridian distanc from Angria Road E 277 L*eagus* 2·7 mils
A Fresh gale at SW this afternoone. To Day I Saw Eight Saile of great Shipps SE from Silly Eight Leagus of[f] they Stood to the Southwards. Att Seven of the Clock this afternoone the Lizard [*margin:* Lizard N] Bare north of mee: I was distante one League or 4 mils of[f] it. I Steere away EBN up the Chanell and E to night.
Meridian distance from Cape Blancco one [on] the Coast of Patagona to the Meridian of the Lizard is By my account made from thence East 819 Lea*gus* 2·4 mile & Longitud from Cape Blancco East 60°07′.[6]

[*small view inserted at this point*]

I make Meridian distance From Angri Roade to the Lizard:
Meridian distance From Angria Roade E 292 Lea*gus* 2·7 m*il.*
Longetud to the Lizard from Angria Roade E 20°48′·6.[7]

[*229*] **Jun the yere 1671 the *Sweep Staks* of[f] the Starte Pointe**
11
Beinge Sunday hasey weather wind at WSW a Fresh gale: I Steere EBN and ENE up in

[1] On Greenvile Collins's 1689 chart of the Scilly Islands, the two windmills are shown on the hill at the west end of St Mary's Island, south of Hugh Castle about a quarter of a mile SW of Hugh Town. Collins, *Great Britain's Coasting Pilot*, Chart 20. Subsequently they were shown on Admiralty charts, but by 1872 were designated round towers and had disappeared by 1899.

[2] There is no tower to the westward of the two mills. This probably refers to the lighthouse on St Agnes Island, shown on Collins's chart as about 1½ miles SW of the two windmills, of which he says 'On the Southernmost big Island there standeth an high *Light-house*, erected by the Corporation of the *Trinity-house* of *Deptford-Strond*, and is a most excellent good light, and may be seen six or seven Leagues off.' Ibid., p. 5.

[3] Chafey, chaffy: resembling chaff. *NOED*.

[4] Lizard (49°58′N, 5°12′W).

[5] The original reads '68: miles7/10Eight tenths:' The fraction appears to have been inserted subsequently to correct the original estimate.

[6] The modern value for this is 60°33′, so Narbrough's figure is remarkably accurate.

[7] The modern figure for this is 22°02′.

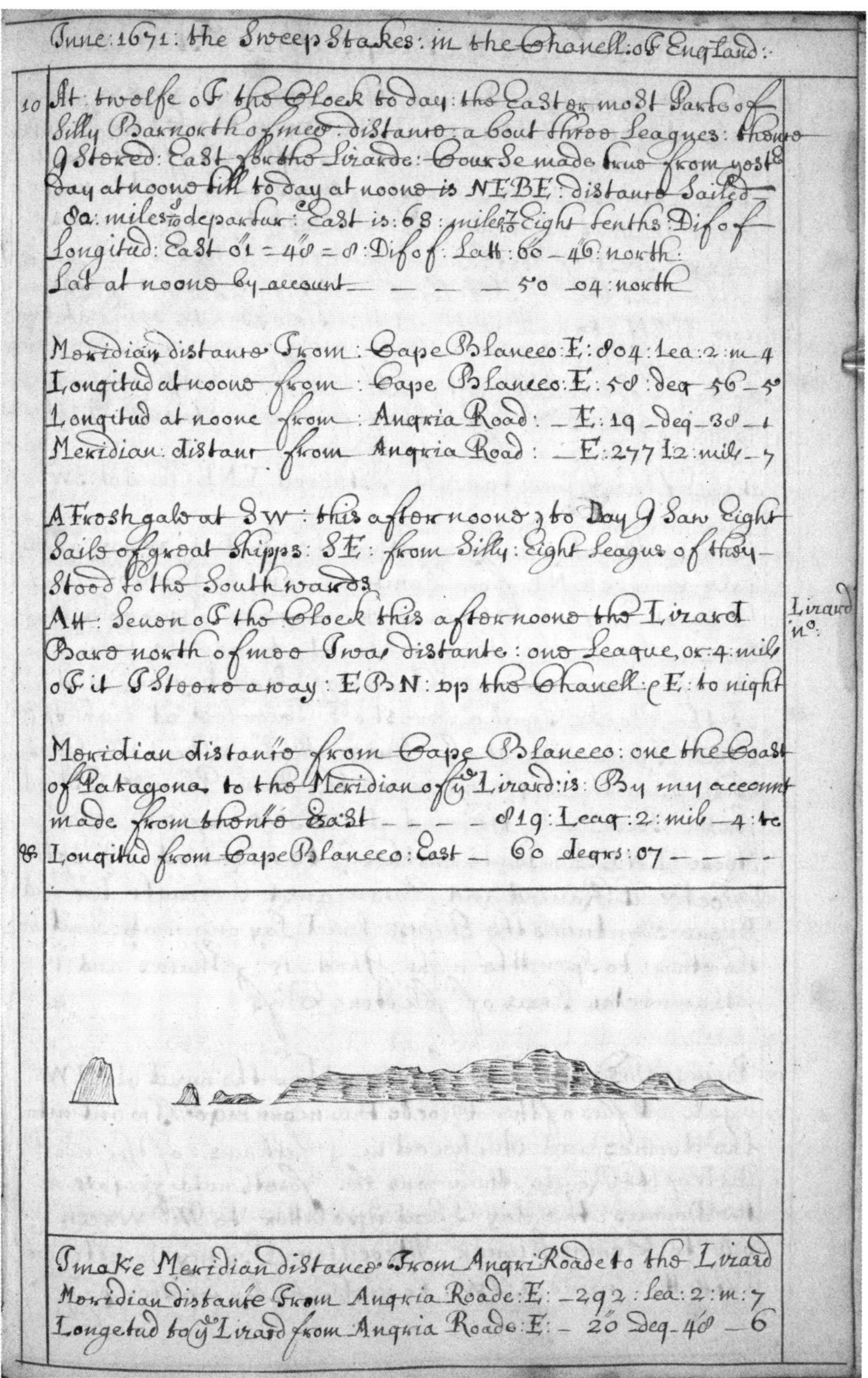

June: 1671: the Sweep Stakes: in the Chanell: of England:

10 At: twolfe of the Clock to day: the Eastermost Parte of Silly Bar north of mee: distance a bout three Leagues: then I Steered: East for the Lizarde: Course made true from yestarday at noone till to day at noone is NEBE: distance Sailed 90: miles departur: East is: 68: miles 7/10 Eight tenths Dif of Longitud: East 01 = 40 = 8: Dif of: Latt: 60 – 46: north:
Lat at noone by account — — — — 50 04: north

Meridian distance from: Cape Blanceo E: 804: lea: 2: m 4
Longitud at noone from: Cape Blanceo: E: 58: deg 56 – 5
Longitud at noone from: Angria Road: — E: 19 deg 38 – 1
Meridian: distanc from Angria Road: — E: 277 12: mils – 7

A Fresh gale at SW: this afternoone; to Day I Saw Eight Sails of great Shipps: SE: from Silly: Eight Leagues of they Stood to the Southwards
Att: Seven of the Clock this afternoone the Lizard Bare north of mee I was distante: one League, or: 4: mils of it I Steere away: EBN: up the Chanell E: to night — Lizard n°.

Meridian distance from Cape Blanceo: one the Coast of Patagona to the Meridian of ye Lizard: is: By my account made from thence East — — — 819: Leag: 2: mils – 4: tc
Longitud from Cape Blanceo: East — 60 degrs: 07 — — — —

I make Meridian distance from Angri Roade to the Lizard
Meridian distance from Angria Roade: E: – 292: lea: 2: m: 7
Longetud to ye Lizard from Angria Roade E: – 20 deg 40 – 6

Figure 11. Narbrough's *Sweepstakes* Journal (BL, Add MS 88980A), p. 228. Courtesy of the Trustees of the British Library.

the Chanell. This morninge at fower a Clocke I was a Brest of the Boult:[1] at 12 a Clocke I was a Brest of the Starte Pointe:[2] nere fower Leagues of[f] it: at 4 of the Clocke this afternoone I was a Brest of Portland:[3] at Eight of the Clock I was abrest of the hills Called St Aalbens:[4] about five leagues of[f]: I Steer now EBN to hall with out the Ile of White[5] wind at WSW a fresh gale. To day I ordereded that twenty fathams and a halfe of the best bower Cable Should be Cut of[f] for it was Straned at the Ile of Trecera in Rideinge their. At 12 of the Clock tonight I Steered ENE: wind at SW.

12
Beinge Munday hasey weather the wind at WSW a Fresh gale: Course ENE from Pointe of Land to Pointe of Land. To day at 4 of the Clocke in the morninge I was a Brest of Donsnoss[6] one [on] the Ile of White: at two of the Clock in the afternoone I was a Brest of Beachey heade:[7] at 4 of the Clocke I was a Brest of Faierlee:[8] at Eight of the Clock I was a Brest of Dungen Nase:[9] a Bout two leags of[f] it: I Saw the Light house one [on] the Nase Plaine: I Stood for the Fore Land:[10] the wind at WSW a fresh gale I Steere ENE ½ a Pointe northerly. To night at 12 of the Clocke it Rained and blew in gust: I brought too and Drove Sumtimes the Shipp head lay one way Sumtims the other: to Spend the night: I had 15 fathams and 17 fathams water: I was of[f] folcStone Clifs.[11]

13
Beinge Tusday hasey fogey weather the wind at NW a gale. At five of the Clocke this morninge I went into the downes[12] and Anchored in 9 fathams: of[f] the north Parte of the Roade: their was five foreth [fourth] rate frigates in the Downes. This day I Sent up a letter to Mr Wreen and one to Commissioner Medellton By my Leiuetenant Peckett. Wind at SW: tonight hasey weather and a gale.

[*230*] **June 1671 the *Sweepstakes* at Anchor in the Downes**
14
Beinge wedensday hasey weather: the wind at SSW a fresh gale: much Raniey foag this moringe: it Conti*nued* So all day faier weather to night.

15
Beinge Thursday hasey Fogey weather the wind at SW a Fresh gale all day and night.

[1] Bolt Head (50°13′N, 3°47′W).
[2] Start Point (50°13′N, 3°38′W).
[3] Portland Bill (50°31′N,2°27′W).
[4] St Alban's Head (50°35′N, 2°03′W).
[5] Isle of Wight (50°40′N, 1°20′W), 'To hall without the Ile' is to pass outside it, i.e. to pass to the south of it.
[6] Dunnose Head (50°36′N, 1°11′W).
[7] Beachy Head (50°44′N, 0°15′E).
[8] Fairlight (50°52′N, 0°39′E).
[9] Dungeness (50°55′N, 0°59′E).
[10] This is South Foreland (51°08′N, 1°23′E) just beyond Dover at the entrance to the anchorage at The Downs, not North Foreland beyond the anchorage between Ramsgate and Margate.
[11] Folkestone Cliffs (51°05′N, 1°12′E).
[12] The Downs (51°13′N, 1°27′E).

16

Beinge Friday Faier weather the wind at West a Small gale all day: I rod Fast. I received a Letter From M[r] Secretary wren.

17

Beinge Satterday Faier weather and Calme: the wind Cam to the ESE: this Eveinge a Fresh gale and So Continued all night. I Fired Seven gunns in Salutinge the Earle of Bristo.[1]

18

Beinge Sunday Faier weather the wind at E a fresh gale al day. I went a Shore to the Commander of the Castle at deale and their was my Lord digby the Earle of Bristo. He Came a Board the *Sweepstakes* to See my Draughts[2] and discoursed with mee Concerninge Magallan Straits at his Goeinge away I fired Eleven gunns to Salut him. The wind hold at East all night a fresh gale.

19

Beinge Munday hasey fogey weather the wind at East a fresh gale all day: and So it Continued all night.

20

Beinge Tusday hasey fogey flater*ing* weather the wind at NE a Fresh gale all day. This day I went a Shore to deale Castle and waited one [on] My Lord Digby: to Discourse of My voiage at Eveinge I Returned a Board. This Afternoone the Crowne[3] and the fleet waied and Sailed to the Southwards: wind at N to night a fresh gale. This Eveinge I Received orders to Saile out of the downs the first winds into the Hope:[4] of M[r] Wrenn.

21

Beinge wedensday hasey weather and the wind at NEBN a Fresh gale I Could not Saile. Three marchant Ships Salluted me to day I ansewerd them. Lettle wind to night I Rod fast.

[1] George Digby (1612–77), 2nd Earl of Bristol. Born in Spain (where his father was ambassador), he spent his first 11 years there. He supported Charles I during the Civil War and was appointed Secretary of State with a seat on the Privy Council in 1642. After defeat at the Battle of Sherburn in 1645, he escaped England and served in France where he entered the French Royal Army and commanded troops in Normandy. He remained in French service until 1656 when Charles II appointed him Secretary of State and Privy Councillor again. In Jan. 1659 he converted to Roman Catholicism and was dismissed from his offices. On the Restoration he was restored to his lands and titles but barred from office because of his religion. He opposed Clarendon and when the latter fell in 1667 returned to public life. He died in Chelsea on 20 March 1677. Hutton, 'Digby, George', *ODNB*.

[2] By 'Draughts' Narbrough usually means charts but in this case its might possibly have included draft journals also.

[3] The *Crown* (48), Captain William Finch, first commissioned as the *Taunton* in 1653 and renamed *Crown* in 1660. Winfield, *British Warships*, p. 105.

[4] The Hope anchorage in the River Thames stretches about 4 miles downriver from a mile below Gravesend (51°27′N, 0°23′E).

22
Beinge Thursday Faier weather and Lettle wind at E. To day I wayed and Plyed through the Gulls[1] at 11 of the Clock William Trevett Pillott: I had 8 Fatham through the dawke and the Litgh [light] house one [on] the Fore Land are the markes for that Chanell:[2] the tide Beinge Done I anchored of[f] the Pitch of the north foreland[3] in 9 Fathams: I rod here all night Lettle winde. I Salluted the Castle at deale at my Com*ing* away.[4]

[*231*] **June 1671 the *Sweepstakes* Saileinge over the Flatts into the River**
23
Beinge Friday Faier weather the wind at E a fine Small gale. I waied this morninge at daie Light and had a tide of flood. I Sailed through margat Roade[5] and through the gore[6] at 12 of the Clocke I Pased through betwen the Boyes of the Flats: it was just Ebb water I had three fathams and a quarter Large: Burchenton Steple[7] and the white Clife at the west End in one.[8] From the Boyes I Stered WBN & WNW For the Boy of the Red Sand: wind at East a fine gale: I had fower and five fadams as I Sailed over the Flats: I Pased to the Southwards of the Boy of the wrake [wreck] a Cables Lenth: the mast is Seen above water.
I Sailed for the Boy of the Red Sand I Pased a Cables Lenth to the northward of that Boy: I halled over for the Cant to thake [take] my Soundings from that I had Seven fathams water: I Pased by the Boy of the oase Edge to the Southward of it halfe a mile: I Steered up for the Boy of the nower:[9] I Passed by the Fregatts that Rod at the Boy of the nour: they were fower: they Saluted mee Each with five gunns I ansewered every one five: I Pased the Boy of the nower: this night I anchored in the Lower end of the hope:[10] the tide of Ebb Beinge Com. It was Calme all night.

[1] This is the English Channel between the Goodwin Sands (51°12′N, 1°34′E), and Ramsgate (51°20′N, 1°25′E).

[2] Narbrough had 8 fathoms in the Gull channel. The marks for steering through it were the doke, or dip, in the cliff and the South Foreland Light (51°08′N, 1°23′E), in line. John Seller gives the marks for sailing through the Gulls: 'You must keep St. Margets Church (which is near the South-Foreland) on a piece of wall that is built near the third cliff, (that is to the northward of the South-Foreland) or else to bring the Light-house on the South-Foreland in the southernmost Swamp, which Marks carry you through the Gulls'. Seller, *English Pilot*, Second Book, Pt 1, p. 3.

[3] North Foreland (51°22′N, 1°27′E).

[4] Deal (51°13′N, 1°24′E).

[5] Margate Road (51°24′N, 1°22′E).

[6] The Gore anchorage (51°24′N, 1°14′E), between the east end of Margate Sand and Reculver.

[7] Birchington church spire (51°22′·4N, 1°18′·5E).

[8] In line. This transit provided the leading line for the channel, in which Narbrough had 3¼ fathoms.

[9] The Nore buoy (51°29′N, 0°49′E), lies about 2½ miles NE of Sheerness. The channel passes between the banks of the Red Sand, on the south side, and the Oaze on the north side, and leads westwards to the Nore and the entrance to the Thames. Seller gives the following directions: 'From the Buoy of the Nower to the buoy of the Oze Edge the course is East one quarter northerly and West one quarter southerly distant about 5 miles: Betwixt the buoy of the Oze Edge and the buoy of the Red Sand lyeth a round shoal called the Spile, and bears south from the buoy of the Oze Edge on which shoal there is but 6 feet at low water – The buoy of the Red Sand bears from the buoy of the Oze Edge East a half northerly and West a half southerly.' Seller, *English Pilot*, Second Book, Pt 1, p.1.

[10] The lower end of the Hope anchorage about 4 miles below Gravesend (51°27′N, 0°23′E).

24
Beinge Satterday faier weather and lettle wind all day at West. This morninge I waied and went up the to the uper End of the hope[1] and their anchored and mored: I give the Pilott a Bill for his Pilottage.[2] I wrote a letter to the Commisioners and a letter to Secretary Wren to accquainte them of my arivall in the hope. Severall Marchants Ships and the Plesuer Boats Saluted mee to day I ansewered them. This night is was Calme [it was Calme].

25
Beinge Sunday faier weather the wind at west a fresh gale. To day Severall marchants Shipps Plied up one [on] the tide of flood three saluted with five gunns a Peece I ansewered them three Each. [*margin:* Leuiet Pecket] Faier weather to night the wind at west. Leiuetenant Pecket and his man Austen Dusney went From the Shipp.

26
Beinge Munday Faier weather the wind at west South west a fine gale the weather very warme: Severall marchants Shipps Came up the River to day and Saluted the Sweepstaks I ansewered them. The wind Blew Fresh at west to night.

[*232*] **June 1671 the *Sweepstaks* Rideinge at anchor in the Hope**
27
Beinge Tusday hasey weather the wind at SW a fresh gale & Raw and Cauld weather: three marchant Ships Saluted me to day. This night it Blow fresh at west.

28
Beinge weddnsday Fogey weather this morninge and Lettle winde at East. I received a letter From Mr Secretary wrenn to Com up to white hall: which I did & went from one [on] Board the Ship at five of the Clock this morninge in a wheary [wherry]: at a Elven I got up to white hall & to Sainte Jameses. I went to Mr Wrenn I Showed him my Draughts and Journall: Mr Wrenn Carried me to His Majesty & R*oyal* Highness at Barke Shire House.[3] I had the Honnor to Kise his Majestys & R*oyal* Highnesses hands: it was his Maj*esties* & R*oyal* Highnesses Pleasuer to vew my draughts and to Discours of my voyage: For two houers time: I tooke my Leave and Departed. Faier weather to night the wind at west a fine gale.

29
Beinge Thursday hasey Fogey weather this morning the wind at South a fine gale. I was at London.

30
Beinge Friday Sum Raine to day the wind at South west a fresh gale & Soe Continued all night.

[1] About one or two miles below Gravesend.

[2] This would enable the pilot to collect payment for his pilotage.

[3] This would appear to be the house at 14 Cleveland Row, Westminster, which had been called Berkshire House and at this time was the residence of Barbara Villiers the mistress of Charles II. When she was created Duchess of Cleveland in 1670 it was renamed Cleveland House.

July Ano 1671 The *Sweepstakes* Rideinge in the Hope

1
Beinge Satterday faier weather the wind at South west a fine gale and So Continued all night.

2
Beinge Sunday wind at Southwest to day a fresh gale & Sum Raine this night I Came A Board the Sweepstaks.

3
Beinge Munday faier weather the wind at west a fresh gale.

4
Beinge Tusday hasey weather the wind at west a fresh gale.

5
Beinge Wednsday Durty Cloudy Rainey all this day the wind at WSW a Stout gale and So Continued all night.

6
Beinge Thursday Cloudy weather the wind at West a Stout gale all day and all night.

7
Beinge Friday a stout gale all day at west and Cloudy weather Les wind at west to night: many Coller [collier] Ships ar Cuminge up.

8
Beinge Saterday Cloudy weather the wind at west a Stout gale.

[*233*] **July Ano 1671 the *Sweep Staks* Rideinge in the Hope**

9
Beinge Sunday Faier weather to day wind at SBE a Fine galle: this Eveinge it Lightned and thundered the wind Came to the E a fine gale it was very dark & Cloudy.

10
Beinge munday Cloudy weather the wind Cam to the west and Blew a Stout gale all day and Soe Continued to night.

11
Beinge Tusday Cloudy fogey weather the wind at SW & much Raine & Severall gusts of winde at west to night.

12
Beinge Weddensday hasey Cloudy weather and Raine the wind at West a Stout gale all night.

13
Beinge Thursday the wind at west a Stoute gale and much Raine this afternoone and to Night.

14
Beinge Friday the wind at west South west a Stout gale all day and much Raine & Base weather to night.

15
Beinge Satterday the wind at North west a Stout gale Sum Raine to day: a fresh gale & Cloudy weather to night.

16
Beinge Sunday hasey weather the wind at West Fresh gale all day and to night.

17
Beinge Munday faier weather Lettle wind to day at South East an Soe it Continued all night.

18
Beinge Tusday Cloudy Cold weather the wind at SE a fine gale all day and to night: Severall Marchant Ships Pased up and downe and Saluted the Sweepstaks.

19
Beinge Wednsday Cloudy Cold weather the wind at SE a fine gale all day and to night.

20
Beinge Thursday Cloudy Cold weather the wind at E a gale.

21
Beinge Friday Cloudy Cold weather the wind at E a fresh gale all day: Severall Marchant Ships Saluted the Sweepstaks.

[*234*] **July Ano 1671 the *Sweepstaks* at Anchor in the hope**
22
Beinge Saterday hasey Cold weather the wind at East & North East to day a fresh gale: two Ships Saluted us to day outward bound with three guns Eash. Faier weather to night.

23
Beinge Sunday haesey Cold weather the wind at NNE A fine gale: Lese wind to night at North: I Rode Fast.

24
Beinge Munday the wind vearable and Lettle wind to day Sum Raine to night: Saluted by marchant Shipps.

25
Beinge Tusday Lettle wind at East to day and Sum Raine to night: I Rode fast.

26
Beinge Wednsday the wind at East a Small gale to day & Raine Lettle wind all night: a marchant Shipp Saluted me.

27
Beinge Thursday hasey weather and Calm all the forenoon. This morninge at nine of the Clock I Received orders from the Commisioners to Bringe the Shipp up to deptford:[1] it was a quarter flood when I received the Letter of Mr Pen*eas* Pett.[2] I Sent a Shore to Gravsend for a Pylot but Could not git one in all the towne they Beinge not at home: I Could not Saile this day the tide would not Serve this Eveinge it Beinge to [too] late. I rod fast all night.

28
Beinge Friday the wind at East South East a fine gale hasey fogey weather and Rainey. This morninge the duke of Yoarke[3] Past By the Shipp in the Pleasuer Boate: I Saluted him with twenty one Guns. This morninge at nine of the Clocke I wayed wind at E a fresh gale. I Stood up to Gravesend with an Easey Saile: to Spend the time to Git water for the Ship:[4] I draw theirten fot water. I Saluted the forts at Gravesend with Seven Guns they ansewered mee with five: I answered three: I went up the River to Deptford: I fired Seven Guns to Salut Greenwich house. I mored at deptford to the hulke at a high water: about 5 of the Clock this afternoone: I gave the Pylott a Bill:[5] Rog*er* Yeoman By name of Gravesend. Lettle wind. I went & accquaint the Princip*all*

[*235*] **July Ano 1671 the *Sweepstaks* at Deptforde.**
officers Sir Jer*em*y Smith[6] & Coll*onel* Meddleton: & accquainted them of My arivall at Deptford with the Shipp & mored to the hulk.

29
Beinge Satterday faier weather the wind at West a Small gale all day. The men one Riged [unrigged] the Shipp[7] to day. I Could not have Litters [lighters] till night from the tower to Git out the Guns: allsoe the Guners Stores:[8] I ordered the Purser to have all his Book

[1] The Royal Dockyard at Deptford, 51°29′, 0°01′W.

[2] Probably meant to be Pheneas Pett. This might refer either to Phineas Pett, the Clerk of the Cheque at Chatham or to the man of the same name, the Master Shipwright at Chatham. In either case this would then mean that Mr Pett had brought the letter from the Commissioners.

[3] James, Duke of York.

[4] To allow time for the flood tide to make so that there would be sufficient water for the *Sweepstakes*.

[5] See above, p. 131, n. 6.

[6] See above, p. 120, n. 2.

[7] The company unrigged the ship, sending down all the upper masts and yards and preparing the ship to go into 'ordinary' (the normal reserve state with a much reduced company of ship keepers).

[8] These were returned to the ordnance depot at the Tower of London. The gun carriages, however, remained on board, since they were sometimes damaged and rotted ashore for want of a proper place to store them. James, *Memoirs*, p. 5.

& Papers Ready as Concerned the Shipp. I was to night with the Principall officers: They accquainted me they would have the Guns out one [on] Munday and Pay the Shipp one [on] Tusday.[1] Sum Raine to night and lettle wind at South.

30
Beinge Sunday the wind at South a fine gale: faier weather all day I was a Boarde the Ship: the wind at SW to night a Small Galle.

31
Beinge Munday Rainey weather all day the wind vearinge round the Compass in Gusts. This day I Got out all the Guns into a Liter [lighter] and Som of the Guners Stors. Much rain to night the wind at SW a fresh gale: a Great Spoute Seene to day at Limhouse Reach[2] much water fell from it: the wind at W. To night his Majesty & R*oyal* highness were a Board the Cleveland Pleasur Boate.

August 1
Beinge Tusday faieer weather the wind at west this Moringe a fresh gale. I went with all my Company to the Treasuerry office in Broad Street[3] and There Received our Pay for our Service in the *Sweepstaks*: Wee weere all Paide to a fardinge [farthing]: and Paide for Shorte a Lowance of Provission and for Eatinge of Seals flesh and for drinkeinge of water: wee received for our Short alowance &c. 05^{l}-09^{s}-06^{d}:[4] I never Saw better Payment in My days. This night wee Parted and went Every man his way with his mony in his Pocket. Sir Jerimiah Smith & Commissioner Medleton were at this Payment as Principall officers.[5] All the Seamen were mighty well Satisfied.

Fines.

[1] Payment was made ashore at the Treasury Pay Office. This had been arranged already. Colonel Middleton and Sir Jeremy Smith informed Lord Brounker, 'it was but yesterday we were informed by the Treasury of money being ready to pay off the *Sweepstakes*, which we intend to do Saturday'. Navy Office, 27 July, *CSPD, 1671*, p. 401.

[2] Presumably this was a waterspout seen at Limehouse Reach (51°30′N, 0°02′W).

[3] The Treasury Office was on the west side of Broad Street between Winchester Street and London Wall.

[4] When sailors did not get their due allowance of victuals they were paid an allowance in lieu. See above, p. 682.

[5] It was a requirement that ship's payments be witnessed by the Comptroller of his Majesty's Navy. This was relaxed in June 1672. James, *Memoirs*, p. 247.

b: 'This is a part of S[r] John Narbrough's voyages, somewhat different from the print.'[1]

[1] **On Wednesday October 13th. 1669**. At halfe an houre past twelve of the clock I saw the Island of Porto Santo,[2] it bare South of mee by my Compasse, and distance from mee by estimation neare ten leagues. It makes a high round Land with a fall in it at this distance.

Porto Sancto Isle make in this forme to mee when it bore South of mee ten leagues. } [*blank space for view*]

At the time when I saw the Island our Course was SBW. I altered it, and steared away SSW to go to the westward of it, wind at NNW a fine gale, the Pink being asterne of mee I stayed till Shee came up to mee, then made saile. Don Carolus desired mee to put into Madera Road,[3] for hee had things there at the Citty of Foneiall[4] that hee must needs have in the voyage. And also hee must furnish himselfe with wine and sweetmeats, or else not proceed on the voyage. I answered him I had no order to touch here, which he replyed hee must not go in this shipp no further then to S[t] Jago[5] if I did not get him these things here and was in great passion with mee, a small time of Consideration I concluded to go in for one night and a day, and to fill water, and also my Seamen would recruite themselves well with good drink for a cold Countrey, for they ever imagined wee were bound for Carolina, on the Coast of Florida, and to Virginia.
At one of the Clock wee saw Isle of Madera, it bore SW of mee, and by estimation twelve leagues off. It makes a high full land and long lyeing out NW & SE with foggs on the Land.

Madera Isle made in this forme to mee, when it bore Southwest of mee twelve leagues. } [*no drawing provided*]

Porto Santo Isle maketh in this forme to mee when it bore SSE of mee foure Leagues. } [*no drawing provided*]

[2] **October 1669 the *Sweepstakes* at the Isle of Madera**
Madera Isle is high land, and irregular in hills, with woods on the tops, and downes, the sides are planted with vines, there is some Sugar made in the Island. The inhabitants

[1] Bodleian Library, Rawl. MS A 318. This heading is the endorsement of the front cover of the manuscript by Richard Rawlinson endorsed 'This is a part of Sr John Narbrough's [*blotted illegible*] voyages, somewhat different from the print.' See above, pp. 4, 6.

[2] Ilha do Porto Santo (33°03′N, 16°20′W).

[3] The roadstead off Ilha do Madeira (32°45′N, 17°00′W).

[4] Funchal (32°39′N, 16°54′W).

[5] São Tiago (15°05′N, 23°35′W).

Portugals, the City of Fouliall is the metropolitan, and is scituated in a bay on the South part of the Island, close to the sea side, and walled next the Sea, & well fortified with ordinance, fresh water comes runing into the Sea, in the middle of the bay, in a faire rivulet from under an arch in the wall. The Shore side is great pe*avel [*margin:* Pibble*] Stones in the bay, and Rocks in other places, the Roade is foule ground, to the East part of it, the ships ride in shot of ordinance from the Citty. This Citty is about an English mile in length, and three quarters of a mile broad. The deserts[1] are barren rocky Isles of a good height, and lye at the SE Point of Madera Isle, Distant better then a mile from the Shore, and there's water enough between Madera and the deserts in the Midway, and no danger, the deserts trents to the South Eastwards.

Fouliall Bay in the Isle of Madera lyes in the Latitude of thirty two degrees and ten minutes north. And in Longitude, West from the Lizard of England 10°01′: And meridian distance in leagues 143. l*eagues.*

[*blank space for plan.*] [2]

Sunday being the seventeenth day, faire weather, and litle wind at northwest, Course by my Compasse Southwest. I make my true Course from Fouliall Bay till to day at noone South Southwest. Distance Sailed 34·6 mil. Depart*ure* West 13 miles. Diff*erence* Lat*itude* 00°32′. Lat*itude* by account 31°38′. Meridian distance from the Lizard West 147 Lea*gues* 1 mil.
Longitude from the Lizard West 10°17′.
Diff*erence* of Longitude from Fouliall West 00°16′.
To day at noone I saw the Island of Madera. It bore NBE the body of the Isle distant by estimation eleaven leagues. It makes in Blofe [bluff] body at the West end

[3] **October 1669 the *Sweepstakes* at Sea. Lat*itude* 31°38′N.**
And trents to the East. Course by the Compasse this afternoone SW, litle wind to night. I shape my nearest course for the Island of St Jago, with all the saile I can make the *Batchellour* Pink in Company. I give order to my master to make the best of his way to St Jago Isle, but not to leave the Company of the *Batchellour*,

Madera Isle made in this forme to mee when it bore NBE distant 11 leagues. } [*blank space for drawing*]

Munday being the 18, faire weather, & litle wind at WNW. Course made true [*margin* ^xx^] Fresh gale at N to night, & some rain, Course by the Compas SSW from Sunday noone til to day noone is SW. Distance Sailed 24 mile*s*. Departure West 17 miles. Diff*erence* of Lat*itude* 00°17′. Lat*itude* by observation of ☼ at noone is 31°21′N.
Diff*erence* of Longitude from yesterday at noone 00°19′W.
Meridian distance from the Lizard West 153 Lea*gues.*
Longitude from the Lizard West 10°36′·4.

[1] Ilhas Desertas, northern island, Ilhéu Chão (32°35′N, 16°33′W).
[2] The blank space approximates to 14 lines of text, presumably intended for a plan of the anchorage.

[*margin:* ××][1] **Tuesday being the 19th** day faire weather, wind at NBE a stiff gale, Course steared by the Compasse SSW. But my true course from yesterday at noone till to day at noone is South 19°45′ westerly distance sailed 101 miles. Departure West 34 miles. Difference of Latit*ude* 01°35′. Latitude by observation of ☼ 29°46′N.
Difference of Longitude to day at noone is 00°40′ West.
Meridian distance from the Lizard West 164 Leagues 1·1 mile.
Longitude from the Lizard West 11°16′·4.
Wind at NBE a fine gale I steared SSW by the Compasse this afternoone, And in the Evening passed by on the West side of the Isle of Palme,[2] as farre as wee could [x]well see it. And also the Peeke of Tenariffe[3] did show it self. Faire[x] weather all night and smooth water.

Wednesday being the 20, faire weather, wind at NBE a fresh gale. Course by the Compasse SSW and I make the true course to be SSW. Distance Sailed 124 miles. Departure West 48 miles. Difference of latitude 01°55′. Lat*itude* by observation ☼ 27°51′.
Difference of Longitude this 24 houres is West 00°55′.
Meridian distance from the Lizard West is 180 leagues 01 mile.
Longitude from the Lizard West 12°11′·4.
To day morning I observed the ☼'s ampl*itude* at riseing and find the compasse to vary but 01°08′E.
This afternoone I steered SBW by the compasse, and in the evening passed by the Isle of Fero,[4] to the westward of it as much as wee could well make it.
[x]It make in a round lumpe a good height.

Thursday the 21, faire weather, wind at NNE a fine gale, in the morning I tooke an azimuth ☼ at 17°50′ Altitude East in Latit*ude* 26°16′ North, the ☼'s declination 14°20′ South. I find my true azimuth to bee 116°40′ from the North meridian. And I find my magnet*ic* azimuth ☼ by my compasse to bee 114°58′ from the North meridian. By which I find the Compasse to have but 01°42′ variation easterly that is, my North Pole varieth 01°42′ from his true Pole easterly, & so all the other points Consequently.

[4] **Octob*er* 1669 the *Sweepstakes* at sea Latitude 25°58′.**
Thursday the 21th, faire weather, wind at North-North East , a fine gale. Course steered by the Compasse SBW southerly. But I make the true course to bee from yesterday noone till to day noone South 6° West. Distance Sailed 114 miles. Departure West 12 miles. Diff*erence* Lat*itude* 01°53′. Lat*itude* 25°58′.
Difference of Longitude this foure & twenty houres is West 00°14′.
Meridian distance from the Lizard West is 184 Leagues 1 mile.
Longitude from the Lizard West 12°25′·4.

[1] The clerk appears to have inserted superscript single or double x in the margin next to the beginning or end of the line as a mark for attention. Narbrough's journal contains more daily entries for the stopover in Madeira, but did not highlight the information marked here. It seems most likely that the symbols were intended to note missing information that should be added.

[2] La Palma, Islas Canarias (28°40′N, 17°50′W).

[3] Pico del Teide 12,200 ft (3,718 m) on Tenerife (28°17′N, 16°38′W).

[4] Now El Hierro (27°45′N, 18°00′W). See above, p. 158, n. 8.

Fryday the 22, good weather, wind at NBE a fine gale. Course by my Compasse SBW. But my true Course from yesterday noone till to day at noone is SBW. Distance Sailed 90 miles. Departure West 17·5 miles. Diff*erence* Lat*itude* 01°28′. Lat*itude* by observation of ☼ 24°30′.
Differ*ence* of Longitude West 19′·5.
Meridian distance from the Lizard West 190 Leagues 00·5 miles.
Longitude from the Lizard West 12°44′·9.

Saturday being the 23 day. Wind at NBE a gale. This day in the forenone I crossed the tropick of Cancer, all my men in good health, I bless the almighty for it. There have been many of my men which have blooded, as have been with mee in the Indies formerly, for I hold bleeding in these hot climats to bee a great preserver of health, and to divert Calentures.[1] I have had the experience of it in two voyages before to the Island of St Hellena, and also in one voyage on the coast of Guiana, where several of my men were much afflicted with that distemper, and blooding preserved them. In all these voyages I never was sick one day together, nor in two years time in the mediterranean sea, nor at the Canaries, for I ever breathe a veine as I goe neare the Equinoctial; This is but my opinion, others may bee of other opinions.
The wind begining to encline to the easter board. True course made from yesterday noone til to day noone, is SBW. Distance Sailed 86 miles. Departure West 17 miles. Diff*erence* Lat*itude* 01°24′. Diff*erence* Longit*ude* 00°18′·5. Latitude by observation of ☼ 23°06′.
Meridian distance from the Lizard West 195 leag*ues* 2·5 miles.
Longitude from the Lizard West 13°03′·4.

Sunday the 24, faire weather, wind at NEBE a fresh gale. Course by the compasse SBW westerly. True Course made is SBW 07°45′ westerly. Distance Sailed 120 miles. Departure West 39 miles. Difference of Latitude 01°43′. Diff*erence* of Longit*ude* 00°42′. Lat*itude* by obs*ervation* of the ☼ 21°13′.
Meridian distance from the Lizard West 208 Leag*ues* 2·5 miles.
Longitude from the Lizard West 13°45′·4.

Munday the 25th, faire weather, wind at NEBE, a fine gale. Course by the Compasse SBW. My true course made Last 24 houres is South 15° West. Distance Sailed 147 miles. And departure West is 38 miles. Diff*erence of Lat*itude 02°22′. Diff*erence* of Longit*ude* 00°40′. Latitude by observation of ☼ 18°51′.

[5] **October 1669. The *Sweepstakes* at Sea in Latitude of 18°51′ &ca.**
Meridian distance from the Lizard West 221 Leagues 1·5 mile.
Longitude from the Lizard West 14°25′·4.
This day wee saw severall flying fish, being the first fish seen since wee came from England. At foure of the clock I steered South.

Tuesday being the 26, faire weather, & a fine gale at NEBE. Course from munday noone till foure of clock this afternoone, is SBW And from 4 till 6 the next morning, South,

[1] Calenture: A feverish disease previously thought to be incident among sailors in the tropics. *NOED*.

EEPSTAKS AS I PASED AND REPASED THE STRAITS.

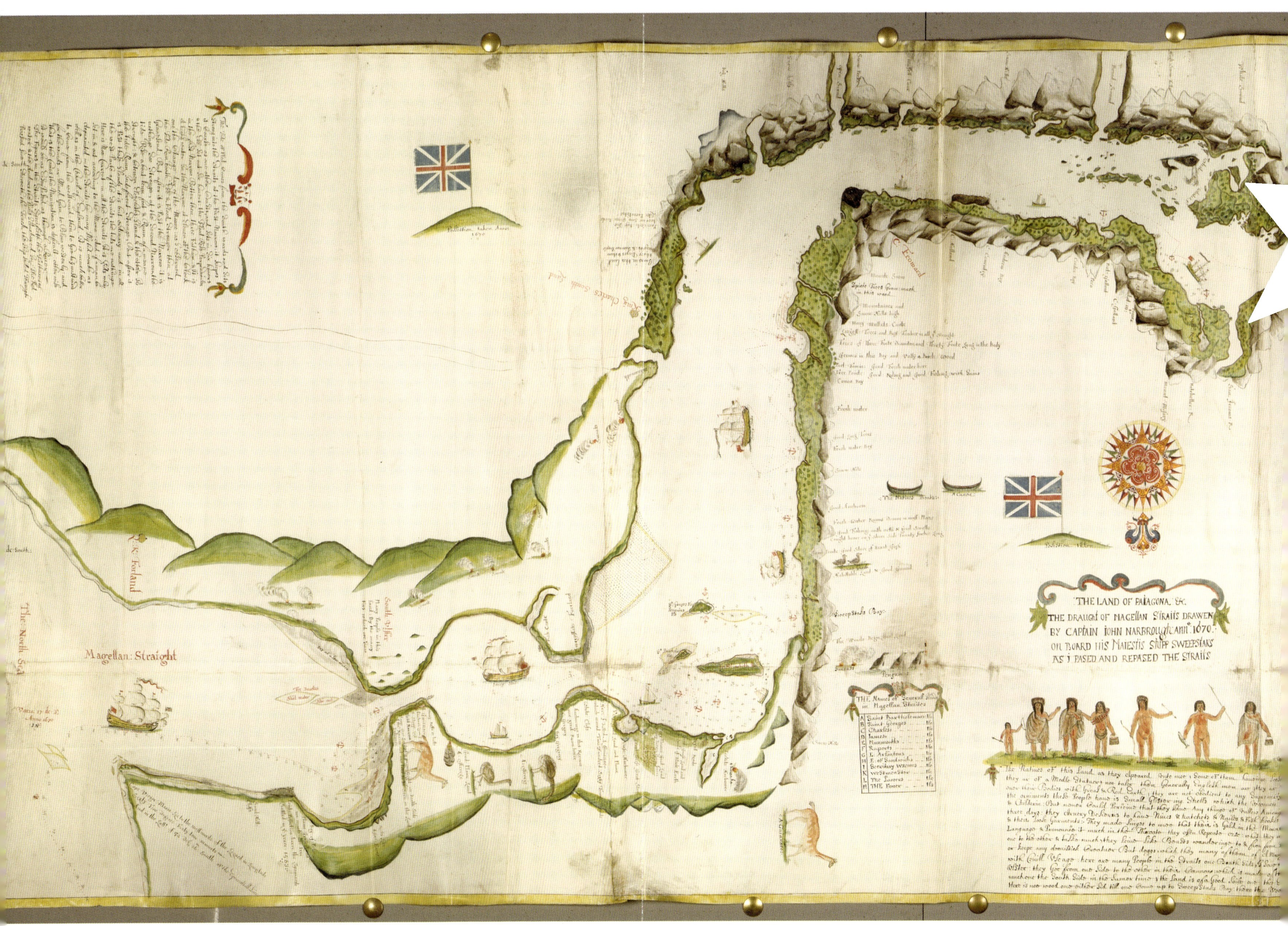

THE LAND OF PATAGONA &c THE DRAUGHT OF MAGELLAN STRAITS DRAWEN BY CAPTAIN JOHN NARBROugh ANN^O 1670 on BOARD HIS MAJESTIS S
(BL, Maps K Top 124.84), the 'Royal Map'. Courtesy of the Trustees of the British Library

and from six this morning til eight, West & by South. And from eight till twelve SWBW the wind all this time at North east. These several courses was because I would fall with the Island of Sale.[1] Course made true from yesterday noone till to day at noone is South 21°20′ west. Distance Sailed 140 miles. Departure west.[2] Diff*erence* of Latit*ude* 02°09′. Latit*ude* by observation of ☼ at noone 16°42′ N. Difference of Longitude from yesterday noone is West 00°53′.
Meridian distance from the Lizard West is 238 leagues 0·5 mil.
Longitude from the Lizard west, is 15°18′·4.
Course steered, West at 12 of clock to day, and so Continued all this afternoon. At night I lay by – I had sailed West 10 leagues.

Wednesday 27, faire weather, of wind, but hazy on the horizon. I lay by all night, sometimes to the Southward, and sometimes to the northward with the Shipp's head. The wind at ENE a fresh gale all night, I kept a light out for the Pink. At daylight I filled, and bore away, West, with all the saile I could make, wind at NE a fresh gale. At 9 of clock in the morning wee saw the Island of Sall, which made in a round forme and of a good height neare, when we first saw it. It might have been seen at a great deale farther distance, but now the horizon was very hazy. It bare West of mee distant about five leagues. I had sailed & drove from thursday at noone till that time I saw the Island – 74 miles.

[x]The Island of Sall make in this forme to mee when it was West of mee five Leagues. } [*blank space for view*]

[x]The Island of Sall when it beares northwest from you foure leagues, makes in this forme with 3 high hills & lowland to the South end, the roade is on the West side No fresh water on it. } [*blank space for view*]

The Island of Sall lyes in the Latitude of 16°42′ North of the equinoctial and in Longitude from the Lizard of England 16°45′·5. And in W meridian distance 267 Leagues 2 miles, west, by my account.

[6] **October 1669. The *Sweepstakes* at the Cape verde Isles.**
When I was in 4 leagues of Sall I steered away Southwest, to goe betweene Sall and the Island of Bonavast.[3] Course made true from tusday noone till to day at noone is WSW 07°37′ W. Distance Sailed 88 miles. Departure West 84·6 miles. Diff*erence* of Latitude 00°22′. Latitude by account at noone is 16°20′. Hazy weather. Diff*erence* of Long*itude* this 24 houres is 01°36′ west. Merid*ian* distance from the Lizard West 266 Leagues 1·1 mile. Longitude from the Lizard West at noone is 16°54′·4.
This afternoone Bonavast bore SBE off [of] mee, distant about foure leagues. I passed by to the Westward of Banavast. This Isle makes at a distance ragged, and full of hills, of a good height. His roade is on the northwest parte, here is Portugals liveing one [on] it. I steered SBW from the West point of Bonavast, for the Isle of May. I lay by to night

[1] Sal (16°46′N, 22°53′W). See above, p. 157.
[2] No departure is given, but it should be 51 miles West.
[3] Boa Vista, (16°05′N, 22°50′W). See above, p. 157.

sometimes, for there lyes a rock in the way.[1] The Island of Banavist lyes in the Latitude of 15°54′ N.
And in West Longitude from the Lizard of England 16°41′W.
And in West meridian distance from the Lizard 264 Leagues.
It lyes neare SBE from Sall. The rock which lyes in the way, lies off from the southwest part, Seaven leagues. It is as big as the Eady Stone above water, and the sea breaks over it.

Bonavist Isle made in this forme to mee when it bore South of mee dist*ance* 9 leagues. } [*blank space for view*]

Bonavist Roade where the Salt pond is is on the NW part, and it makes in this forme when you come in two leagues of it. } [*blank space for view*]

Thursday 28, faire weather, Wind at ENE a stiffe gale. This morning I saw the Isle of May,[2] the body bore SBW of mee, distance by estimation 8 leagues. It makes a high hill and Craggy to the East part of the Isle, and low land towards the water side, to the northwest part of the Island. May Isle lyes from Bonavist SBW distant neare 18 leagues. This day at 11 of clock I anchored in the Road, in 11 faddom water, sandy ground, about halfe a mile from the Shore, the northermost point of the Rode bore NNW ½ point to the West and the Southermost point of the Roade bore SE from mee, about a mile and a halfe distance. It is craggy rocks to the South of the roade, But on the N point it is a low sandy Shore. The road is on the NWBW part of the Island, in a small sandy Bay, and there is the salt pond a bow shoot from the sea, in the Low flat Land, fresh water is very scarce here. I went ashore presently after I anchored and found a heape of salt of about twenty tunns. I came aboard againe immediately, and had the long boat ashore, and got off about two tunns and a halfe of it. The suffe [surf] came in so much that wee could not gett more off. Wee halled a Saine here, and caught abundance of good mullets,

[7] **October 1669. The *Sweepstakes* at the Isle of May.**
And some small fish, and silver fish. One of the people of the Island came aboard, a negro, I sent him ashore, and bid him acquaint the people to bring downe Cattle, for I would buy some of them. I rode here all night, faire weather, the wind easterly, this Isle is dry land, without wood on this side, many goats & ginny hens.

Friday the 29, faire weather the wind at NE, a fine gale. This morning I sent my boate ashore, and bought some goats of the Islanders, and eight cows, excellent good meate, cost 6 peeces of eight a cow, the goates halfe a peece of eight a peece, giveing the skins againe.[3] My men caught a great many fish with the Saine to day, wee split them & layd them foure hours in Pickle, then dryed them to keep, which they will do very well for a long time into any Climate, if the mouth do not destroy them. I have the experience in other voyages, and they are very good victuals at Sea. I made what dispatch I could to be gone to St Jago Island. This day in the forenoon a shipp passed by to the westward, on the

[1] This is Leton Rock situated about 18 miles SW from Boa Vista.
[2] Maio (15°08′N, 23°12′W). See above, p. 158.
[3] Returning the skins to the Islanders. See above, p. 158, n. 9, for remarks on the exchange rate and prices.

South of the Isle. This afternoone wee saw severall Shipps come in sight from the northward, which were the Portugal fleet bound for Brazilia, they haled in to Porto Praya[1] in the Isle of St Iago to water. This night I weighed and stood away at twelve of clock SSW for Porto Praya, the Pinke in company with mee, my touching at the Isle of May was to get salt which I knew would bee a great helpe to get provision in the voyage.

The Island of May made in this forme to mee, when it bare southwest of mee distant 8 leagues. } [*blank space for view*]

The roade is in this forme on the NW part of the Island sandy ground. } [*blank space for view*]

Saturday the 30th, faire weather, wind at NEBN a fresh gale. This morning I steered SW for to go to the South side of St Iago Isle, for the roade of Porto Praya, the South part of the Island of St Iago lyes neare SW from the roade of the Isle of May, and distant 9 leagues. This day at 12 of the clock I anchored in Port Praya roade, with my best Bower anchor, in ten faddom water, rough ground. The East point bare East of mee, and the West Point West-Southwest, about halfe a mile off. I could not go into the best of the Roade for the Portugal fleet riding in it, being about thirty six Saile, the great *Pardee Eternal*[2]admiral bound for Brazil. The admirall is a very great ship, and well built, they say she is burden 17 hundred tuns, Shee hath ports for 3 tyre of gunns flush;[3] Shee had but eighty gunns, and was poorly mannd with Sea-men, and so were all the rest, Six well manned frigats might have taken most of that fleet. [As I came in to Anchor the Portugal Admiral saluted the Shipp with 7 guns, I fired 7 againe in thanks, then Capt*ain* Francis Wilkshier in the *Jerusalem*, & the other admirals saluted mee & I them &c.][4]
This Bay of Port Praya as they call it, is no port, but a fine round bay and high steep cliffy rocks on the East side, and in the bottom a steepe up-hill, where the Castle is, which hath but 4 guns, and is of no force; there is a small fort on the topp of the hill, on the East side, which hath 3 guns.

[8] **November 1669 the *Sweepstakes* at St Iago Isle at Praya roade.**
On the NW part of the Bay the Shore is gravelly sand, and there is a grove of Cocker nut [coco-nut] trees, there comes runing downe in the valley a rivulet of fresh water, which runs into the Strand, and soaks into the Sea, there is good filling of water, & a good quantity, the water is good and keeps well at Sea. To the West part of this Bay there is a small Island lyes close on the Shore, which hath grasse on it, that a man may cut for his cattle, which I did. [*Margin:* *Here runs a litle current to windward that is to the Eward, when it is litle wind in the night the water rises & falls two or 3 foot. But no certain account [can] bee given of the tides] This rode is of no safety for shipping, for a Ship of warre may take any ships out of this Bay, and receive no dammage from the forts ashore, and with fire Shipps a whole fleet might bee spoiled at pleasure, for it is a fresh gale every

[1] Praia (14°55′N, 23°31′W), at the SE extremity of São Tiago.
[2] The ship was the *Pai Eterno*, the admiral of the Portuguese Brazil fleet. See above, p. 159, n. 4.
[3] Three tiers or decks of guns.
[4] The square brackets are found in the original.

day, and the wind but two points off the Land, by which a man may fetch into any part of the Bay also the Bay lies open to the Sea, from the E southerly to the WSW*.
The Bay of Praya in the Island of S[t] Iago lyes in the latitude of 14°30′N.
And in Longitude West from the Lizard of England 17°21′.
And Meridian distance West of the Lizard 278 Leagues. By my account which I have kept of the Ship's way from the Lizard to this roade.

[*blank space*] [1]

Fryday the fifth of November. I ordered the hold to be locked up and no man to come into it but the Cooper and his mate to serve out drink at set times at morning noone and night. I had fifty tuns of Liquor aboard and at my Comeing away I had every mans Rundlets[2] and bottles filled. I ordered the allowance to bee 4 Cans of drink for 6 men a day, which at that allowance would last five months & better, and gave orders to all my officers in their respective places.

[9] **November 1669 the *Sweepstakes* at Sea off Port Praya.**
I called for my Lieutenats and master, and acquainted them that I had order to saile from hence to the coast of america, To the Southward of the river of Plate, & to the Straits of Magellan, through which wee were to passe into the South Sea, and that wee must shape our course to make the shortest way of it, and to be carefull to keep easterly enough to weather the shoulds of Brazil, called the Abroholls,[3] which lies in about eighteen degrees of southerly Latitude, for the winds blow for the most part thereabouts, between the Latitude of ten South, and the Latitude of twenty South at East B*y* South, and ESE fresh gales. Now in the time of this our discourse the mate came in and acquainted mee all things were stowed and the wind at EBN a fresh gale, I concluded with the Master that the best course at present would bee South and B*y* East and as wee gott southerly and the wind Large,[4] wee could alter our course as would seem most fitt. Wee steered a point or two from the wind, that the ship might have good fresh way through the Sea, I gave the master order to steere SBE by the compasse. I ordered my Lieutenant to call all hands to prayer, and I read Service, where with prayers to god almighty for a prosperous voyage, and to continue with health and love one to the other, and that we might prosper in this undertaking, to atchieve honour in our actions, and to the well likeing of his Ma*jest*ie.[5]

[1] The blank space approximates to 23 lines of text, presumably for a plan of the road.

[2] Runlet: A cask or vessel of varying capacity. Large runlets appear usually to have varied between 12 and 18½ gallons, small ones between a pint or quart and 3 or 4 gallons. *NOED*.

[3] Arquipélago dos Abrolhos (18°00′S, 38°50′W).

[4] Sailing 'large' is to sail with the wind on the quarter, meaning as the wind altered to blow from further abaft the beam.

[5] *Articles of War* state at the first article 'That all Commanders, Captains, and Officers at Sea shall cause the publick Worship of Almighty God according to the Liturgy of the Church of England, established by Law, to be solemnly, orderly and reverently performed in their respective Ships.' (An Act for establishing Articles and Orders for the regulating and better Government of His Majesty's Navies, Ships of War and Forces by Sea. 13° Car. 11 St.1 c.9, 1661.) For the full text, see Rodger, *Articles*, p. 13. The first instruction of the *General Instructions to Captains* of 1663 requires that 'Almighty God be duly served ... twice every day by the whole Ship's Company'. Tedder, *Navy*, p. 67. Narbrough does not mention holding prayers daily; however, he states that he called his company aft and gave thanks to Almighty God after particularly dangerous events and on one occasion, while

I commanded the head sails should be brased to the mast,[1] and lye to speak with the Pinke, which was done; I spoke to Capt*ain* Flem*m*ing, and Mr Solomon Franco with my Lieutenants, and master, & Don Carolus, to whom I declared the voyage & read my orders unto them, and never till now.
Also I signified to Capt*ain* Flem*m*ing how the navigation lay, by a draught[2] which I laid on the table before us, and how the winds are usually, and what course I would keepe till I got to the Southward of the river of Plate,[3] and then how I would hale along the Shore for the Port of San Julyan,[4] where I would water & fitt our Shipps, all this I shewed him on the draught, and so delivered the draught into Capt*ain* Humphrey Flem*m*ing's own hands, and bad him keep it and make use of it. Also at the same time I delivered one to the master of his Majestys Shipp the *Sweepstakes*, the draughts are of those which are called the Sea Atlas,[5] they are universal draughts, I provided them on purpose when I was at London, for this voyage, for I knew these people had none by reason they knew not the voyage till now, for I never mentioned the voyage to any Soule liveing till this day, and that then the Shipp was under saile before I declared it to any.
This evening at this time being in the *Sweepstakes* great Cabbin, before my Lieutenants & master, I read orders to them which I had drawne up before, I delivered them to Capt*ain* Fleming, and the same to Mr Solomon Franco, wherein I charged them to keep mee Company on this voyage. The order was as followeth.

Instructions for Mr Humphrey Flem*m*ing Comander of his Majesties hired Pink the *Batchellour*

By virtue of an order from his royall highness dated the 29th day of august 1669, to mee directed. You are hereby required to saile with his Majestyes hired

[10] **Instructions and orders for Capt*ain* Humphrey Flemming.**
Pink the *Batchellour*, which you are Commander of, and to keep company with his Ma*jes*ties Shipp the *Sweepstakes*, to the Coast of America, to the Southward of Rio de la Plata, and along the Coast of america to the Southward, till you come to the Straits of Magellan, lying in about fifty three degrees of South latitude, through which you are to passe into the South Sea, and saile along the West coast of America northerly, till you come as high as Baldivia, which lies in about fourty degrees Southern latitude, there you shall receive further order from mee or in my absence from the Com*m*ander in chiefe onboard his Ma*jes*ties Shipp the *Sweepstakes*, in case you keep company with her, whose

---

camping ashore with an exploring party, mentions that they set out after prayers. It would seem reasonable therefore to assume that prayers were held on board in accordance with the orders, and that this was such a standard practice that it was considered unworthy of comment.

[1] The head sails were braced to the mast, i.e. aback or turned so that the wind was against them, to take the way off the ship.

[2] A chart.

[3] Río de la Plata (35°30′S, 56°00′W).

[4] Puerto San Julián (49°19′S, 67°43′W).

[5] This appears to have been *The Sea Atlas or the Water World &c.* published by Henry Doncker at Amsterdam, 1660. See above, pp. 73; 161, n. 3.

company you are not to depart from nor leave upon any occasion whatsoever, as you will answer the Contrary at your peril, unlesse you have order from mee so to do, or in my ascence from the com*m*ander in chiefe in her. You are also to understand that you are to bee employed by mee, as I shall see occasion to employ you, to discover lands, bayes, havens, rivers or Straits &c[a].

The designe of this voyage on which you are employed being to make a discovery both of the Seas and Coast of that part of the world, and if possible to lay the foundation of a trade there. You are not to medle with the Coast of America nor send on Shore, unlesse in case of great necessity, till you are got to the Southward of Rio de la Plata, And you are not to do any injury to such Spanyards as you shall meet with, nor medle with any place where they are planted.

You are to take observations with as much accuracie as you can, and also to cause your mates and Company to do the Like, to observe all head-lands, Islands, Bays, havens, Roads, mouths of Rivers, rocks, and Shoulds, Soundings, Course of Tides and of flowings and Settings of Currants where you come, both in the North and South Seas, &c. And to cause draughts and designs to bee made of them. And also you are to take notice of all trade winds &c. you meet with, and of the weather, and especially to observe harbours in the Straits of Magellan.

You are in all places where you land to observe the nature of the soile, & what fruits, wood, graine & fowles & beasts it produceth, and what stones and minerals, and what fish the rivers and seas doth abound with. Of the mïneralls you are to use your utmost endeavour to procure them to Carry to England, and to deliver them to his Royal Highnesse's Secretary.

You are also to marke the temper and inclination of the Indians and inhabitants and where you can gaine any Correspondency with them, you are to make them sensible of the great power & wealth of the Prince and nation to whom you belong. And that you are sent on purpose to set on foot a trade, and to make friendship with them. But above all, for the honour of our Prince and nation, you are to take care, that your men do not (by any rude behaviour or injuries to them) Create an aversion in them to the English nation: But that on the other side they endeavour to gaine their love by kind and Civill usage, towards them, and whosoever shall Act otherwise you are to Correct him or them for so doing, which you are to acquaint your men with, that they bee not ignorant. You are to bee very Carefull of your provisions and Liquour, and husband it to the best advantage.

[11] **Instructions and orders for Capt*ain* Humphrey Flemming.**

That there bee no wastfull expence made of it, nor of your Ship's furniture, as sailes, anchors, Cables and rigging &c[a]., and that you endeavour at all places where you come, to get provisions, wood, and fresh water, so you do not endanger your Shipp nor men, which you are to bee very Carefull of, and in no cause to expose any one of your men to the hazard of their lives, but allwaies bee carefull that they go well guarded, and bee watchfull, for there have been many cutt off, by their own neglect.

You are to bee very carefull to keepe a good Command aboard, and over your men, And in case any mutinous practice happen under your Com*m*and, you are forthwith to make it knowne to mee. You are to bee carefull to have your Shipp kept sweet and cleane, for the preservation of your mens healths. And god prosper us. Given under my hand on

board his M*a*j*es*ties Ship the *Sweepstakes*, rideing at the Island of S[t] Iago, in Port Praya roade this 5th day of november 1669. John Narbrough.
To Capt*ain* Humphrey Flem*m*ing Comander of
the *Batchellour* Pink. These.

Instructions for the better finding each other after separation if it should Chance by foule weather or otherwise.

You are hereby required to saile with his M*a*j*es*ties hyred Pink the *Batchellour* under your com*m*and, and keep company with his M*a*j*es*ties Ship the *Sweepstakes*, along the coast of America to the Southward of Rio de la Plata, to Port San Julian, in that which lyes in about 49°20′ South lat*itutde* which your draughts mention. In case of separation at sea &c. in this voyage from each other, you are to use all endeavours to meet againe, that is to say, by looking well abroade at Sea, And to observe the order in your Sailing instructions to know each other at sight. The next Port of Rendevouz will bee at Port San Julian, which is on the Coast of America, as is said before, whither you are to make all the hast you can, & to stay for the *Sweepstakes* there two whole months, if you get thither before her, and Shee shall do the like for you. In your way thither after you have passed to the Southward of Rio de la Plata, it will bee best for you to saile along the coast of America, to see if you can fall with mee, and to make Cape Blanco,[1] which lies about 47°20′ South Latitude, and so to Port San Julyan, where you are to stay. You may also enquire for mee at Porte desire,[2] which lies in about 48° South Latitude. If I shall come to any place, & bee gone againe before you come there, I will leave a peece of board nailed to a Pole or tree engraven, mentioning the Shipps name, and the day of my departure, and the next port I am intended to. And I desire you will do the same at Port San Julian, I will do the same, and also leave an order for you tyed to a pole, being put in a glasse bottle, the pole shall bee placed on the Island

[12] **November 1669 the *Sweepstakes* at Sea in Lat*itude* 13° &c.**

which lyeth in the Harbour, at the West end thereof, where I shall build a tent. I pray bee carefull to Looke for it, and I shall do the same from you. It may bee I may have opportunity to touch on the Coast as I saile along, If I can find any trade with the natives. You may bee sure wherever I come to finde those memorials of my being there before you. So god prosper our intentions. Given under my hand on board his M*a*j*es*ties Shipp the *Sweepstakes*, rideing at Port Praya roade, at the Island of S[t] Jago, this 5th day of November 1669.
John Narbrough.
To Capt*ain* Humphrey Flemming
Com*m*ander of the *Batchellour* Pink.

I gave Capt*ain* Flem*m*ing orders (who had provisions & stores aboard for 16 months, & liquours for five, at good allowance) to put his men to two thirds, as the *Sweepstakes* men were. Evening comeing on, wee[3] made all the Saile wee could. Our men in as good health as when they came from England.

[1] Cabo Blanco (47°12′S, 65°45′W).
[2] Puerto Deseado (47°45′S, 65°53′W).
[3] A word is obliterated here, possibly 'weighed'.

At Six of clock this evening being fryday 5th November 1669, the East point of Port Praya Road, lyes in the latitude of 14°30′ North and in Longitude from the Lizard of England 17°19′ West. Meridian distance from the Lizard of England 277 leagues west. It bore North of mee, distant three Leagues, wind at ENE a fine gale, Course by the Compasse South B*y* East, so I steered all night, and had faire weather all night and a small Sea.

Saturday the 6th day hazy weather, wind at East North east, a fine gale. Course made this 18 houres from Port Praya, where I took my departure from is South 07°01′ East. Distance Sailed 69·5 miles: Departure East 8·5 miles: Diff*erence* of Lat*itude* 01°09′. Latitude by account 13°21′, at noone. Diff*erence* of Longit*ude* from Port Praya East 00°08′·8.
Meridian distance from the Lizard West 274 leagues 0·5 mil*es*.
Longitude from the Lizard West 17°10′·2.

Sunday the 7th, hazy weather, wind at East N East, a fine gale all night, I steered South B*y* East. Here comes a homeing Sea[1] out of the South and the Pink sailed very heavy. True Course made from Saturday at noone till to day at noone, is South 7° East. Distance Sailed 106 miles. Departure East 13 miles, Diff*erence* of Lat*itude* 01°45′. Latitude by account at noone 11°36′ N. Difference Longit*ude* East 00°13′·8.
Meridian distance from the Lizard West 269 leagues 2·5 miles.
Longitude from the Lizard West 16°56′·8.
My men eate fresh beefe and broth every day; from Port Praya I brought eight live oxen, to sea with mee, and grasse to feede them with all.

[13] **November 1669 the *Sweepstakes* at Sea in Lat*itude* of 8°38′ &c[a].**
This day at noone I took the Pink in a tow at my sterne, by his small Bower[2] and made all the saile I could make, getting Gies [guys] to windward from the head of my mast, to out Leagers to windward,[3] a fresh gale at East to night Course by the Compass S.

Munday the 8th, hazey weather, this morning wee had a great shower of raine and it fell Calm, I cast off the Pink for feare of her driveing aboard of mee,[4] the wind came to the East S East and SE this forenoone. Course made true from yestertday at noone till to day noone is South 1°02′ west. Distance Sailed 68·5 Miles. Departure 1·2 Mil. Diff*erence* of Latit*ude* 01°08′. Lat*itude* by account 10°28′N. Difference of Longit*ude*. West 00°02′·4
Meridian distance from the Lizard West 270 Leagues 0·7 mil.
Longitude from the Lizard West 16°59′·2.

Tuesday the 9th, hazy, rainy, Cloudy weather, wind varyable between the SE and the S small gales. Course made true this 24 houres is, South twenty eight degrees, thirty eight [minutes] west. Distance Sailed 28·5 miles: Departure West 13·6 miles. Diff*erence* of Lat*itude* 00°25′. Lat*itude* by ☼ 10°03′. Difference of Longitude 00°14′·2.

[1] 'homeing Sea'; see above, p. 335, n. 2. This is described as a 'Popeinge sea' in the BL Add MS 88980 A; see above, p. 162, n. 1.

[2] This is the cable for the small bower anchor.

[3] Rigging extra guys from the head of the mast to out-riggers on the windward side to provide extra support for the mast.

[4] For fear the two ships should collide in the calm conditions.

Meridian distance from the Lizard West 274 Leagues 2·3 miles.
Longitude from the Lizard West 17°13′·4.

Wednesday the 10th. Cloudy hazy weather, wind at EBN and ESE varyable, much [*margin:* Rain & thunder:] raine, and sometimes thunder, & Lightening. Course made true from yesterday at noone till to day noone is South, distance sailed 85 miles. Departure.[1] Difference of Latitude 01°25′. Lat*itude* by account 08°38′ N. Diff*erence* of Longitude 00°00′.
Meridian distance from the Lizard West 274 Lea*gues* 2·3 Mil.
Longitude from the Lizard West 17°13′·4.
I tooke an Amplitude of ☼ at setting, and find the Compasse to have 01°40′ [*margin:* variation 01°40′ west] variation west, it beeing more than I expected. Faire weather to night wind at EBN a fine gale. Course SSE by the Compasse.

Thursday the 11th. Cloudy rainy hazy weather, wind at East. Course by the compasse SSE when I could lye so. Course made true from yesterday at noone till to day noone is South 07° East. Distance Sailed 70 miles. Departure 8·5 miles. Diff*erence* of Lat*itude* 01°09′. Lat*itude* by account is 07°29′. Difference of Longitude 8′·7.
Meridian distance from the Lizard West 271 Lea*gues* 2·8 mil*es*.
Longitude from the Lizard West 17°04′·7.

Fryday the 12th day. Cloudy hazy weather with rain, wind variable between the East and the SSE, small gales. Course made true Southwest. Distance Sailed 31 miles. Departure 22 miles. Diff*erence* of Lat*itude* 00°22′. Latitude by observation of ☼ is 07°07′N. Diff*erence* of Longit*ude* this 24 houres West 00°22′·2
Meridian distance from the Lizard West is 279 Leagues 0·8 miles.
Longitude from the Lizard West is 17°26′·9.

Saturday the 13th, faire weather wind at ENE a small gale. Course steered by the Compasse SBE and South. A great Sea out of the South.

[14] **November 1669 the *Sweepstakes* at Sea Latitude of 05° &c. N.**
Course made true is South. Latitude by observation 06°07′ N.
Meridian distance from the Lizard West 279 Leagues 0·8 mil*es*.
Longitude from the Lizard West 17°26′·9.
[*margin:* no variation.] In the morning I tooke an azimuth and found no variation. At evening I tooke the ☼'s amplitude and found no variation.

Sunday the 14th. Cloudy weather, wind variable between the EBN and ESE sometimes a gale and sometimes litle wind, much raine to day, a great sea came out of the South. Course made true from Saturday at noone is South. Distance Sailed 67 miles. Diff*erence* of Latitude 01°07′. Latitude by obs*ervation* ☼ 05°00′ N.
Meridian distance from the Lizard West 279 leag*ues* 0·8 mil*es*.
Longitude from the Lizard West 17°26′·9.

[1] There was no departure since the course was South.

This morning at 7 a clock I took the *Batchellour* Pink in a towe, much raine & gusts tonight, wind variable between the ESE and the SSE. I lay as neare as I could lye.

Munday the 15th. Cloudy weather wind at SE and at SSE with gusts & raine. Course made true is SW. Distance Sailed 83 miles. Departure West 59 miles. Diff*erence* of Lat*itude* 00°59′ South. Lat*itude* by observat*ion* of ☼ 04°01′N. Difference of Longitude 00°59′·2.
Meridian distance from the Lizard West 299 Leag*ues* 0·6 mil.
Longitude from the Lizard West 18°26′·1.
At 12 of clock to night the wind came to the SSW. I tacked and stood to the Eastward, at 2 in the morning the wind came to the SSE with a turnado. I tacked and stood to the SW:ward. I cast off the Pink from my sterne the weather being gusty.

Tuesday the 16th, gusty cloudy weather with raine and gusts in whirlwinds for the most part of the day at South East & B*y* East. I handed my topsailes[1] several times to day. I caused 3 new tarpaulins to bee made for the grateings, the old ones being all to raggs. My men all in good health, god be praised. Course made true from munday at noone till today noone is South 27°30′ west. Distance Sailed 46·2 miles. Depart*ure* West 21·4 miles. Difference of Latitude 41′. Diff*erence* of Longit*utde* 00°21′·7. Latitude by obs*ervation* of the ☼ at noone is 03°20′ N.
Meridian distance from the Lizard West 307 Leag*ues* 0·0 mil*es*.
Longitude from the Lizard West 18°47′·7.
Wind at SE at 12 of the clock I tacked, and stood to the eastward. I lay up ENE with my starboard tacks aboard. No fish nor fowle seene to any of the Company as yet. Being now in the raines I give every man a dram in the night watch, to keep their stomacks warme, which is very apt to take cold in these Climates.

[*margin:* Rains] **Wednesday the 17th**. Cloudy, rayny, gusty weather, wind at SE a stiffe gale sometimes, I stood all this 24 houres to the Eastward, with my Starboard tacks aboard, the Pink in Company. Course made true this 24 houres NE 06°15′ easterly.

[15] **November 1669 the *Sweepstakes* at Sea in the Latitude of 04°00′N &c[a].**
Distance Sailed 64 miles by the Logg. Departure East 50 miles. Diff*erence* of Latit*ude* 00°40′. Lat*itude* by account at noone is 04°00′ N. Differ*ence* of Longit*ude* West 00°50′·2.
Meridian distance from the Lizard West 290 Leag*ues* 2·0 miles.
Longitude from the Lizard West 17°57′·5.
Wind at SE this afternoone and gusty, rainy weather to night, I hand the topsaile, three times. Course by the Compasse ENE.

Thursday the 18th. Cloudy rainy weather, wind at SE and SSE & sometimes calme. Course made true from yesterday noone till to day noone is NEBE 6°15′ easterly. Distance Sailed 62 miles. Departure East 55·6 miles. Diff*erence* of Long*itude* East 00°56′. Diff*erence* of Latit*ude* 00°29′ N. Lat*itude* by acco*un*t at noon 04°29′ N.
Meridian distance from the Lizard West 271 Leag*ues* 2·4 miles.

[1] Furled the topsails.

Longitude from the Lizard West 17°01′·5.
A turnado round the compasse this afternoone, & much raine to night. [*right margin:* turnado]

Fryday the 19th, raynie weather and variable winds. Course made according to judgment from thursday noone till to day noone, is East North east. Distance Sailed 31 miles. Departure East 28·7 miles. Difference of Longitude East 00°29′·4. Difference of Lat*itude* 00°12′ N. Latitude by account 04°41′. No azimuth or amplitude taken, the ☼ generally Clouded these five days.
Meridian distance from the Lizard West 267 Leag*ues* 0·7 mil*es*.
Longitude from the Lizard West 16°32′·1.
I saw two Saile to day in the South East of mee standing to and fro. I judge them to bee some of the Portugal fleet. This night the wind veered to the East. I [*right margin:* 2 ships seene] tacked and stood to the Southward. I handed and set my topsailes six times to night. At 12 aclock to night wee had a lost company of the *Batchellour* Pinke, yet wee carryed a light constantly on the Poope, in this dirty weather, and shewed our lights when wee tacked according to the orders in our Saileing order for keeping Company.

Saturday the 20th, rainy weather, wind variable between the EBN and the South. I tacked several times this 24 houres, and after divers courses made this 24 houres, I account my nearest course to bee South 25°05′ westerly. Distance Sailed 11·8 miles. Departure West 5 miles. Diff*erence* of Longit*ude* 00°05′·2. Difference of Lat*itude* 00°11′ S. Latitude by account 04°30′ North.
Meridian distance from the Lizard West 263 leag*ues* 2·7 mil*es*.
Longitude from the Lizard West 16°37′·3.

Sunday the 21th. Rainy weather, wind variable betweene the SE and SW. I plyed to the South East ward, what I could. After divers courses I make my true course this 24 houres N. 14°55′E. Distance Sailed 33·8 miles. Departure 8·7 miles. Diff*erence* of Longitude 00°09′ East. Difference of Latitude 00°33′. Latitude by account 05°03′N.
Meridian distance from the Lizard West 261 Leag*ues*.
Longitude from the Lizard West 16°28′·3.

Munday the 22d. Cloudy rainy weather, wind between the SSE vearing to the ESE. I stood to the Southward. No amplitude nor Azimuth can

[16] **November 1669 the *Sweepstakes* at Sea in Lat*itude* of 05°03′N.**
bee taken it is so Cloudy. After several Courses made from Sunday noone till to day noone, my true course is west. Distance Sailed 18 miles. Departure W 18 miles. Difference of Lon*itude* West 00°18′·7. Latitude by account 05°03′N.
Meridian distance from the Lizard West is 267 Leagues.
Longitude from the Lizard West 16°47′.
This day wee made an end of all the Cows, wee brought out.

Tuesday the 23d. Cloudy, rainy weather, wind at SE then Came to the SSW litle gales now and then, smooth water, the clouds are now white, and hang their heads to the Southwards,

the Lower cloudes come out of the South East very swift. Some thunder to day in the South, this rainy weather makes every thing mouldy, and rotten in the Shipp. Wee cannot find one dry place, for the gusts makes the Shipp lye along, and the raine beates in do what wee can, our provisions keeps very well, the rigging and sailes towes[1] very much, the top sailes are ever amending. Course made true from munday noone till to day at noone is South 04°43′ East. Distance Sailed 24·5 miles. Departure East 2 miles. Difference of Longit*ude* 00°02′·5E. Diff*erence* of Latit*ude* 00°24′. Lat*itude* by acc*ount* 04°39′N.
Meridian distance from the Lizard West 266 Leagues 01 mile.
Longitude from the Lizard West 16°44′·5.
Calme this afternoone, I hoisted out my boat and tryed the Currant,[2] by vearing downe a basket with weight in it, two hundred faddom downe and riding the boate by that Line, which will bring the boates head to ride at a point of the Compasse Constantly, then heave the Logg and trye how much it goes asterne in halfe a minute, so much wee judge the Currant to Sett in 24 houres, according to that proportion. But I do not trust to the truth of this way, when the foundation is so weake. If my boate could bee anchored to the ground then it would bee most Certaine, but since it cannot bee I trust to my observation, and there I find somewhat of a difference now and then. But I believe great Currents which are found so farre off Land as some write is the mis-steering, for hee that should Looke to the Connd[3] is negligent of his course,[4] and by that means other officers judge a currant, I ever observed so; But I conclude that a Currant Setts fourty or fifty leagues in the Sea, when a ship is before the mouth of a river &c[a].[5]

Wednesday the 24th, foggy weather & some raine, winds variable in turnadoes and showers. I use all endeavours to get to the Southwards, But could gaine but litle, for the winds were generally at SSE and SE and SWBS. I find a Currant according to the method as I tryed by my boate[6] to Sett to the NW twelve miles in 24 houres. Course made true this last 24 houres is SW. Distance Sailed 9 miles. Departure West 6·3 miles. Diff*erence* of Long*itude* 00°06′·4. Diff*erence* of Latit*ude* 00°06′·3. Latitude by account is 04°33′N.

[17] **November 1669. The *Sweepstakes* at Sea in the Lat*itude* of 4° &c[a].N.**
Meridian distance from the Lizard West 268 Leagues 1·6 mil*es*.
Longitude from the Lizard West 16°50′·9.

Thursday the 25th, rainy weather, wind variable and calmes. I tacked 8 times this last watch. Course made true this last 24 houres NW. Distance 14 miles. Departure 10 miles

[1] See above, p. 303. n. 3.

[2] See above, p. 169, n. 2.

[3] To Con, Conn, Connd, Cun, refers to the action of directing the man steering the ship how to steer. In action or confined waters it was normally done by the Captain or Master and at sea on passage by the Quartermaster. In the latter case the helmsman normally steered by a compass and direct conning was not necessary.

[4] Narbrough feels that the officer responsible for ensuring the helmsman steers the correct course is negligent.

[5] Narbrough states that he prefers to derive the current from the difference between his position by account (i.e. dead reckoning) and that by observation, rather than from direct current observation by boat. He does not believe in great ocean currents, the origin of which he attributes to bad steering on the part of the observer. However, he accepts that currents may be found 40 or 50 leagues to seaward of the mouths of great rivers.

[6] See above, 23 Nov.

west. Diff*erence* of Longitude 00°10′·2. Difference of Latit*ude* 00°10′N. Latitude by good observation of : at noone 04°43′N.
Meridian distance from the Lizard West 271 Leag*ues* 2·3 miles.
Longitude from the Lizard West 17°01′·1.
This day the men caught two Bonnitos with hookes.[1] These fish are larger then great mackrells, and much of that Shape & Colour, but nothing so good. If salted & dryed they are very feverish diet.[2] I tryed the Currant by vearing down the basket, then heaved the Logg, and found a Currant Sett to the NW 13 miles in 24 houres. I have the Pink in a towe at my sterne, I feare I should lose her Company in the shoures of raine and foggs if I let her goe. I spoke to Capt*ain* Flem*m*ing to fill all his empty Casks with raine water, & to serve his men a dram of Brandy now & then, and set it of [off] in their allowance of Brandy Laid in for drinking.
I cannot gett neither amplitude nor azimuth the clouds are so thick, and dirty wet foggs, neither can I perceive any variation, when I set the Sun on a point according to the houre of the day.[3]

Fryday the 26th, rainy cloudy weather, winds variable between the ESE and the South, litle winds and turnadoes. Course made this Last 24 houres, for I allow drift to the NW:ward, the Sea coming altogether out of the South. Course is NBW. Distance drove 8 miles. Departure West 1·6 miles. Difference of Longitude West is 00°01′·8. Diff*erence* of Lat*itude* 00°08′. Lat*itude* by account 04°51′N.
Meridian distance from the Lizard West 272 leag*ues* 0·9 mil*es*.
Longitude from the Lizard West 17°02′·9.
This evening I tooke the ☼'s amplitude but found no variation at all.

Saturday the 27th faire weather, wind at South in the morning calme all day after. I judge I drove to the NW this 24 houres eight miles. Departure 5·7 miles. Diff*erence* of Longit*ude* West 00°06′. Diff*erence* of Lat*itude* N by account 00°05′·7. Latitude by account 04°57′. Lat by good obs*ervation* of ☼ on the meridian is 04°56′.
Meridian distance from the Lizard West 274 leag*ues* 0·6 mil*es*.
Longitude from the Lizard West 17°06′·9.
I tooke an amplitude at Sun Setting, and had 15° variation, westerly. [*right margin:* Variation 15° westerly] magnetic bearing agreed with the bearing to be expected from the time of day.

Sunday the 28th, faire weather, and Smooth water, wind at SEBE and at SSE at 2 of clock this morning I tacked and stood to the Eastward. Course made true from Saturday noone till to day noone is ESE 09°40′ easterly. Distance Sailed 11 miles. Departure East 10·7 miles. Diff*erence* of Longitude East 00°10′·8. Diff*erence* of Lat*itude* 00°02′·5. Lat*itude* by obs*ervation* of ☼ 04°54′N. I tooke an azimuth in the afternoone, but found no variation. [*right margin:* no variation].

[1] See above, p. 167, n. 2.
[2] Likely to cause a fever.
[3] The sun's magnetic bearing agreed with the bearing to be expected from the time of day.

[18] **November 1669. The *Sweepstakes* at Sea in the Lat*itude* of 4° &c[a] N.**
Meridian Distance from the Lizard West 270 Leag*ues* 01·9 mile.
Longitude from the Lizard West 16°58′·1.
Foure Bonnetos taken to day, faire weather, wind variable, Sometimes at South and Sometimes at South East. I stood to the Eastward with all Saile I could, judging it my best course, for in Standing to the Westward I should not bee able to weather the Shoalds of Brazill.[1]

Munday the 29th, faire weather, wind variable between the South East and SBE a small gale, I stood to the Eastwards. After divers courses, I make the true course to bee North 74°30′ East. Distance Sailed 46 miles. Depart*ure* East 44·3 miles. Diff*erence* of Lat*itude* 00°12′. Diff*erence* of Longitude East 00°46′. Latitude by observation of ☼ 05°06′.
Meridian distance from the Lizard West 255 leag*ues* 2·6 miles.
Longitude from the Lizard West 16°12′.

Tuesday the 30th, faire weather, wind between the SSE and the E a Small gale vearing to and fro, after several courses I makes my true course to bee north, 61°30′ easterly. Distance Sailed 20 miles. Departure East 00°17′·6 mil*es*.[2] Diff*erence* of Longit*ude* 00°18′. Diff*erence* of Lat*itude* 00°09′·5 by account. Latitude by observation of ☼ 05°15′N.
Meridian distance from the Lizard West 250 leagues.
Longitude from the Lizard West 15°54′.
[*margin:* a Currant.] I could never have an observation of the starrs, they being clouded. I allow eight miles in 24 houres for a Currant Setting to the NNE:ward, for I tryed it with my boate as formerly. I judge the Currant Setts to the NNW at the moons encrease and to the NNE at the moons decrease.
No fish seene about the Shipp, some fowles flying to and fro, as big as Sea mews of a black colour.[3] The Skie is all over cast. My men in indifferent good health, & so are Capt*ain* Flem*m*ings. I use all endeavours to get to the Southward, but cannot, except I would run my Selfe on the Coast of Brazil, which would bee to the losse of my passage. This day I caused an inspection to bee made into our stores of Liquour, and find beere & water enough for better then foure months to come, and so is the Pink stored also. And thus ends the month of November.

Wednesday the first of December 1669. Rainy weather and Calme. After several courses made, and what Current sett mee to the NNE I make my true Course to bee West. Distance Sailed 5·2 miles. Departure West 5·2 miles. Differ*ence* of Longit*ude* 5·3 mil*es*.[4] Lat*itude* by account at noone is 05°15′N. It being calme I tryed the Currant & find it to set to the NNE in the running of halfe a minute glasse 3 faddom.[5]
Meridian Distance from the Lizard West 251 leag*ues* 2·2 mil*es*.
Longitude from the Lizard West 15°59′·3.

[1] These are the Arquipélago dos Abrolhos. See above, p. 372.
[2] This is an error and should be '17·6 miles'.
[3] Sea mew was a term used for a sea gull. The only largely black or dark brown gull-like birds likely to have been seen in this area are the black noddy or the brown noddy.
[4] This is an error for '5′·3.'
[5] This works out at 720 yards in an hour or nearly 3 miles in a day.

Wee Caught Some Bonnetos, & Shark fishes, which are much like the dogfishes[1] so called in England, but Larger. The wind coming to the north, I steered SSE by the Compasse.

[19] **December 1669. The *Sweepstakes* at Sea in the lat*itude* of 05°15′ &c.N.**

Thursday the second day, rainy weather, wind at north, till it came to the SSE in a turnado. Course made true this last 24 houres is South 16°34′ East. Distance Sailed 38·4 miles. Departure East 11 miles. Diff*erence* of Longitude East 11′·3. Diff*erence* of Lat*itude* 00°37′. Latit*ude* by account at noon 04°38′N.
Meridian distance from the Lizard West 248 leag*ues* 0·2 mil*es*.
Longitude from the Lizard to day at noone is West 15°48′·0.

Fryday the 3^{d}, faire weather, wind at SSE, and came to the SEBE Small gale I tacked to & fro. Course made good, allowing 8 miles for the Current to Sett to the NNE. Course NNE. Distance Sailed 24 miles. Departure East 9 miles. Diff*erence* of Longit*ude* East 9°. Diff*erence* of Latit*ude* 00°22′. Latitude by observation of ☼ at noone, is 05°00′ North.
I find by my observation I Sett to the Northward when it is Calme.
Meridian Distance from the Lizard West 245 leag*ues* 0·2 mil*es*.
Longitude from the Lizard to day at noone 15°39′.
Litle wind this afternoone, At SE. I stood to the South westward, rain to night.

Saturday the 4th, faire weather, wind variable between the ESE and South small gales and hot weather. Course made this 24 houres is west, allowing for the Current 8 miles in 24 houres to set mee to the NNE. Distance Sailed 6 miles. Departure 6 miles. Diff*erence* of Longit*ude* 00°06′·3 west. Diff*erence* of Latitude 00°00′. Latitude by observation of ☼ 05°00′.
Meridian distance from the Lizard West 247 leag*ues* 0·2 mil*es*.
Longitude from the Lizard at noone West 15°45′·3.
Many flying fishes[2] seene to day, & bonnetos & shark fishes & allbycores,[3] a fish larger then a bonneto, but of that shape and diet, and live upon the flying fish as the bonneto doth. Some of these albecors wee Caught with hookes, & one sharke, our men eat them both, and account the Sharke a good fish. Faire weather and litle wind at SBE and SSE. I stood to & fro in the faire way, for in standing to the Eastward I lost my Latitude, And in Standing to the westward I put my Selfe too fast to Leeward on the Coast of Brasile.

Sunday the 5th faire weather, wind at ESE and SE and S, Smooth water and litle wind. After many Courses I make my true Course NEBN. Distance Sailed and drove 19·2 miles. Departure East 10·7 miles. Difference of Longit*ude* 00°10′·8. Differ*ence* of Latitude 00°16′. Latitude by good observation of ☼ at noone 05°16′ North.
Meridian distance from the Lizard West 243 leag*ues* 1·5 mile.
Longitude from the Lizard West at noone 15°34′·5.
I tryed the Currant it beeing Calme with a great Log[4] as wee call it fitt for that office, after the same manner as our small Logs aboard are fitted with Socket & peg, to save the Straine

[1] Dog-fish was a name commonly given to several small species of the shark family. See above, p. 170, n. 3.
[2] See above, ibid.
[3] Albacore; see above, p. 170, n. 2.
[4] This is a reference to the ship's log and line used to determine the ship's speed through the water.

of the Line in halling up, for with a sudden snatch the peg comes out, and the Log comes up much easier then a basket, which serves the same office as the basket does to try the Currant. I found the Currant Sett to the North East 14 miles in 24 houres which I found

[20] **December 1669. The *Sweepstakes* at Sea in Lat*itude* of 05°12′N.**
by my observations which I have made these two dayes, that I drove to the northward, 16 miles this 24 houres more than what I could make by my traverse, for I should have made an East southerly way according to judgment.

Munday the 6th, faire weather, litle wind at South, and smooth water, I stood to the Eastward as neare as I could with all the Saile I could make, haveing the Pink in a towe. Course made true from Sunday noone till to day noone is East B*y* South. Distance Sailed 22 miles. Departure 21·5 miles. Difference of Longit*ude* East 22′. Diff*erence* of Latit*ude* 00°04′·3. Lat*itude* by acc*ount* 05°12′N.
Meridian distance from the Lizard West 236 Leag*ues* 01 mile.
Longitude from the Lizard to day West 15°12′·5.
I allow ten miles for the Current to set, northerly in 24 houres.

Tuesday the 7th, faire & Calme, litle wind at South, I stood to the Eastward, after divers courses, the true Course is South 60° East. Distance Sailed 32 miles. Departure East 27·7 miles. Diff*erence* of Longit*ude* East 28′. Differ*ence* of Latit*ude* S. 00°16′. Latit*ude* by good obs*ervation* of ☼ upon the meridian 04°56′N.
Meridian distance from the Lizard West 227 Leag*ues* 0·3 mil*es*.
Longitude from the Lizard to day West 14°44′·5.
This day wee all began to drink water, altogether, my Selfe being served with no better allowance either for meat or drink then the worst of my men, all being Served out by a man blinded with a cloth;[1] this I did to prevent differences about Diet &c.

Wednesday the 8th, faire weather, wind variable from the South to the SW. I stood to the South-East ward, after divers Courses I make the Course to bee SE. Distance Sailed 5·6 miles. Departure East 4 miles. Difference of Longit*ude* 00°04′. Diff*erence* of Latit*ude* 00°04′. Latit*ude* by obs*ervation* ☼ 04°52′.
Meridian distance from the Lizard West 226 Leag*ues* 2·3 miles.
Longitude from the Lizard West 14°40′·5.

Thursday the 9th, blowing gusty weather, wind variable betweene the SE and SW with raine, after divers courses made this 24 houres I make the true course to bee South 74° East. Distance Sailed 28 m*iles*. Departure East 27 miles. Diff*erence* of Longit*ude* 00°27′. Diff*erence* of Latit*ude* 00°08′. Latitude by account at noone 04°44′N.
Meridian distance from the Lizard West 217 leagues 2·3 miles.
Longitude from the Lizard at noone West 14°13′·5.

[1] This was presumably a variation on the method used by Captain Bligh in the launch of the *Bounty*, in 1789, whereby the food was divided into portions and then one man turned his back while another pointed to each portion in turn saying 'Who shall have this?' to which the first man answered by calling a name. Rutter, *Log of the Bounty*, II, pp. 175, 257.

Fryday the 10th, rainy and calme, at 8 the wind came to the SW a fine gale, and So to the west. I steered South. After many Courses this 24 houres, I make my true course to bee South-South-East. Distance Sailed 22 miles. Departure East 8·4 miles. Differ*ence* of Latit*ude* at noone 00°20′·2. Difference of Longit*ude* East 00°08′·5. Latitude by account 04°24′N.
Meridian Distance from the Lizard West 215 leag*ues* 2·9 miles.
Longitude from the Lizard West 14°05′.

Saturday the 11, winds variable round the Compasse, and raine, I stand to

[21] **December 1669. The *Sweepstakes* at Sea in the Latitude of 03°00′N.**
the Southward what I can, and after severall Courses this 24 houres I make the true Course South-South-East. Distance Sailed 29 miles. Departure East 11 miles. Difference of Longitude 00°11′·2. Diff*erence* of Latit*ude* 00°26′·8. Latitude by account at noone is 03°57′N.
Meridian distance from the Lizard West 211 leagues 0·8 mile*s*.
Longitude from the Lizard West 13°53′·8.

Sunday the 12, faire weather, wind between the South West and the South, a fine gale. After divers courses I make the true Course to bee, SBE. Distance Sailed 38 miles. Departure East 7·4 m*iles*. Difference of Longit*ude* 00°07′·4. Differ*ence* of Latit*ude* 00°37′. Latit*ude* by the ☼ 03°20′N.
Meridian distance from the Lizard West 208 leag*ues* 2·4 mil*es*.
Longitude from the Lizard West 13°46′·4.
I observed the ☼s amplitude at Setting but found no variation. [*right margin:* no variation.]

Munday the 13th, wind variable between the SWBS and the SE. After several courses I make my true course S 53°18′ East. Distance Sailed 33·2 m*iles*. Departure 27 miles East. Differ*ence* of Longit*ude* 00°27′·2 East. Diff*erence* of Latit*ude* 00°20′. Latit*ude* by account at noone 03°N.
Meridian Distance from the Lizard West 199 leag*ues* 2·4 miles.
Longitude from the Lizard West 13°19′·2.

Tuesday the 14th, wind at S and SBE and SSE, small winds, after several courses I make my true Course South 54°40′ westerly. Distance Sailed 22·5 miles. Departure West 18·4 miles. Differ*ence* of Longit*ude* 18′·5W. Diff*erence* of Latit*ude* 00°13′. Lat*itude* by acc*ount* 02°50′. Latit*ude* by obs*ervation* ☼ 02°47′N.
Meridian distance from the Lizard West 205 leag*ues* 2·8 miles.
Longitude from the Lizard West 13°37′·8.
I find the Currant to set to the northward 10 or 12 miles in 24 houres, by my observation, for I should have been so much more southerly according to my Courses and distance Sailed this 24 houres. The occasion of this Currant in my opinion is, by reason of the winds hanging so much southerly, Drives the South Ocean into this Gulfe, which causeth this Currant,[1] for at other times when the winds hang easterly, the Currant is hardly taken notice of, as I have observed in two voyages this way five yeares before.

[1] Narbrough was quite correct that persistent winds cause surface currents in the oceans.

Wednesday the 15th, faire weather wind at SSE and at S. After divers courses I make my true course to bee South 32°58′W. Distance Sailed 17·9 miles. Departure West 9·7 miles. Diff*erence* of Longit*ude* West 00°09′·7. Diff*erence* of Lat*itude* 00°15′. Latitude by obs*ervation* of ☼ at noon 02°32′N.
Meridian distance from the Lizard West 209 leag*ues* 0·5 mil*es*.
Longitude from the Lizard West 13°47′·4.

[22] **December 1669. The *Sweepstakes* at Sea in the Lat*itude* of 02° &c[a] N.**
Thursday the 16, fair weather wind at SSE and at S small gales. Course made true is South West 00°10′ westerly. Distance Sailed 11·3 miles. Departure West 8 miles. Diff*erence* of Longit*ude* West 08′·2. Differ*ence* [*margin:* caught many Bonnetos] of Latit*ude* 00°08′. Latitude by the ☼ 02°24′.
Meridian distance from the Lizard West 211 leag*ues* 2·5 miles.
Longitude from the Lizard West 13°55′·6.

[*margin:* I towe Pink.] **Fryday the 17th**, faire weather, wind variable between the SW and the SBE to day. Course made South 58°42′ west. Distance Sailed 52 miles. Departure West 44·3 miles. Diff*erence* of Longit*ude* 00°44′. Diff*erence* of Lat*itude* 00°27′. Latitude by observation of ☼ 01°57′N.
Meridian distance from the Lizard West 226 leag*ues* 2·8 miles.
Longitude from the Lizard West 14°39′·9.

Saturday the 18th, faire weather, wind variable between the SBE and the SE a fresh gale I Steered by the Compasse SWBS and SW from fryday at noone till today at noone I make my true Course to bee SW 3°15′ westerly allowing all faults, as I have done before.[1] Distance Sailed 54 miles. Departure West 40·4 miles. Diff*erence* of Longit*ude* West 00°40′·4. Diff*erence* of Latit*ude* 00°36′. Latitude to day at noone by observation of the Sun 01°21′N.
Meridian distance from the Lizard West 240 leag*ues* 1·2 mile.
Longitude from the Lizard West 15°20′·3.
All the Shipps Company are in good health praised bee god for it. Most of them have beene blooded Since I crossed the tropick of Cancer & none of them troubled with the Calenture in this voyage.[2]

Sunday the 19th, faire weather, wind at SEBS and SSE and at SE a fresh gale. I made all the Saile I could, and steered by the Compasse SWBS & SW and SSW as the winds veared to and fro. Course made true from yesterday noone till today noone is SW 05°22′ westerly. Distance Sailed 58 miles. Departure West 44·7 miles. Diff*erence* of Longit*ude* 00°44′·7W. Diff*erence* of Latit*ude* 00°37′ S Latit*ude* by obs*ervation* of the ☼ 00°44′ North.
Meridian distance from the Lizard West 255 Leag*ues* 0·9 m*iles*.
Longitude to day at noone from the Lizard West 16°05′.
I do not perceive any Currant to set northerly as before, it being now in the first quarter, and then it was about a full moone, which may bee a great cause of the current, as it is in

[1] Making allowance for current, leeway etc.
[2] See above, p. 368, n. 1.

the Gulfe of Florida, and in most parts of the West Indies for on the full moones the Current runs quickest.
The men catched above 40 olbecors [albacores] to day with hookes and lines. A fine gale at SEBE this afternoone Course by the Compasse SSW and SW. No variation when the ☼ was on the meridian by the Compasse.

[23] **December 1669. The *Sweepstakes* at Sea in the Lat*itude* of 00°17′ South.**
Munday the 20th day faire weather, wind at SEBS and SSE a fresh gale and smooth water. Course made, allowing all faults, is South West B*y* west. Distance Sailed 63 miles. Departure West 52·6 miles. Diff*erence* of Longitude 00°52′·6. Diff*erence* of Latit*ude* 00°35′. Latit*ude* by ☼ on the meridian is 00°09′ North Equ*inoctial.*
Meridian distance from the Lizard West 272 leag*ues* 2·6 mil*es*.
Longitude to day from the Lizard West 16°57′·6.
Winds at SSE and South this afternoone I stood to the South West ward, Close haled, Cleare Skie and smooth water, weather not very hot, but Coole & temperate as hot as in England in the Summer. This afternoone at 6 of the Clock I crossed [*right margin:* crossed the equinoctial,] the Equinoctial, in,
Meridian distance West of the Lizard 276 leag*ues* 0·3.
Longitude West of the Lizard 17°8′·1.
Longitude East from Port Praya 00°13′·1.
Meridian distance East from Port Praya 2 leag*ues* 2 miles.
This morning I tooke the ☼s amplitude and found 00°27′ variation East.

Tuesday the 21,[1] hazy cloudy weather, wind at SEBS and at SSE and South, I stood close haled to the SW:ward. I make my true Course to bee South west. Distance Sailed 36·7 miles. Departure West 26 miles. Diff*erence* of Longit*ude* 00°26′. Diff*erence* of Latit*ude* 00°26′. Latit*ude* by obs*ervation* of ☼ 00°17′ S.
Meridian distance from the Lizard West 281 leag*ues* 1·5 mil*es*.
Longitude at noone from the Lizard West 17°23′·6.This afternoone at 6 of clock I tacked and stood to the Eastward, the wind came SBW. At 12 of clock at night the wind came to the SE. I tacked and stood to the South-west:ward, the Pink in a tow at my Sterne. Several sea-fowles flying to & fro, the water Smooth, my men in good health, being in number 86 men & boyes, all which came out of England.

Wednesday the 22d, wind at SBE and SSE a fine fresh gale. After divers courses this 24 houres, I make my true Course allowing all faults to bee S 21°22′ west. Distance Sailed 24·7 miles. Departure West 9 miles. Diff*erence* of Longit*ude* West 00°09′. Diff*erence* of Latit*ude* 00°22′. Latit*ude* by ☼ 00°40′ S.
Meridian Distance from the Lizard West 284 Leag*ues* 1·5 mil*es*.
Longitude from the Lizard West 17°32′·6.

Thursday the 23d, fair weather, wind at SE and SSE. I make my true course to bee SWBW. Distance Sailed 43·2 miles. Departure West 24·2 miles. Diff*erence* of Longit*ude* 00°24′. Diff*erence* of Latit*ude* 00°36′ S. Latitude by observation of the ☼ 01°16′ S.

[1] 'Monday' struck through.

Meridian distance from the Lizard West 292 leag*ues* 1·7 mil*es*.
Longitude to day at noone from the Lizard West 17°56′·8.

Fryday the 24th, faire weather, wind at SSE and at SEBE and at ESE

[24] **December 1669. The *Sweepstakes* at sea in the Latit*ude* of 02°00′ S.**
After divers courses this 24 houres, I make my true Course to bee SWBS. Distance Sailed 54 miles. Departure West 30 miles. Diff*erence* of Longitude 30′. Diff*erence* of Lat*itude* 00°45′. Latit*ude* by observat*ion* of ☼ 02°01′ S.
Meridian distance from the Lizard West 302 leag*ues* 1·7 mile.
Longitude at noone from the Lizard West 18°26′·8.
I find a great difference within this 48 houres between my dead account as we call it,[1] which is kept by the Log, and my observation, which [*margin:* no variation] I have had these two dayes very good, when the Sun hath been on the meridian. I find I have gone more southerly by twelve miles then the log will allow, I cannot perceive any variation, and I find the Log well kept, and the halfe minute glasse good.[2] I judge a Current Setts to the Southward, Now the winds are in the East, and the moone neare the full.

Saturday the 25th. Cloudy weather, wind at SEBE a Stiffe gale. Course by the Compasse SBW. Course made true SBW. Distance Sailed 75·5 miles. Departure West is 13·8 miles. Diff*erence* of Longit*ude* 00°13′·9. Difference of Latit*ude* 01°08′ South. Latit*ude* by observation 03°09′ South.
Meridian distance from the Lizard West 307 leag*ues* 0·6 mil*es*.
Longitude at noone from the Lizard West 18°40′·7
I find the Same difference Still or more, for by the Log the Ship has run but 54 miles in all this 24 houres, and by my observation of the ☼ at noone I have differed in Latitude 68 miles, which must be a Currant Sett to the Southward neare 14 miles in 24 houres, for my steerage was good. I have the Pink in a tow, and their account is neare as I find.

Sunday the 26th, faire weather, wind at SEBS, a fresh gale. True course is SSW. Distance Sailed 62·5 miles. Departure West 24. Diff*erence* Longit*ude* 24′. Diff*erence* Lat*itude* 00°58′. Lat*itude* by observation of ☼ 04°07′ S.
Meridian distance from the Lizard West 315 leag*ues* 0·6 mil*es*.
Longitude from the Lizard West 19°04′·7.

Munday the 27th, faire weather, wind at ESE a Stiffe gale. Course by Compasse South, westerly, I make my true Course South B*y* West. Distance Sailed 80 miles. Departure West 15·6 m*iles*. Diff*erence* of Long*itude*, West 00°15′·6. Diff*erence* of Latit*ude* 00°18′. Latit*ude* by ☼ 05°25′ S.
Meridian distance from the Lizard West 320 Leag*ues* 1·2 mil*es*.
Longitude at noone from the Lizard West 19°20′·3

[1] 'and' struck through.

[2] The method used for checking the half-minute glass is set out in Seller, *Practical Navigation*, p. 226. A weight hung on a cord with exactly 38½ inches between the pivot and the centre of gravity of the weight, will swing in exactly one second of time, thus 30 swings will define the correct running of the glass.

[*margin:* variation 3° East] Variation of the Compasse is 3° easterly, by an amplitude taken in the West horison, that is the North point inclines easterly so much and all other points Consequently.

Tuesday the 28th, hazy weather, wind at East, & East South-East, a Stiffe

[25] **December 1669. The *Sweepstakes* at Sea, in the latitude of 9° S**
gale, and something of a rough sea, Course by Compasse South easterly. But my true course I make South. Distance Sailed by my Log but 86 miles, But by Obs*ervation* at noone 95 miles. I have differed in Latit*ude* 01°35′ S. Latit*ude* at noone by observation of ☼ on the meridian 07°00′ S. I conclude that a Current Setts to the Southward. Some fish, & small sea fowle seene flying.
Meridian distance from the Lizard West 320 leag*ues* 1·2 mil*es*.
Longitude at noone from the Lizard West 19°22′·7.
Variation 5° easterly. Faire temperate weather, coole in the evenings. [right margin: Variation 5°E.

Wednesday the 29th, wind at East South East, and at East. Course by the Compasse South B*y* East and South. Course made true this 24 houres is South 6° westerly. Distance Sailed 91 miles. Departure West 9·5 miles. Differ*ence* of Longit*ude* 00°09′·7. Diff*erence* of Latit*ude* 01°30′. Latit*ude* at noone by account 08°30′ S.
Meridian distance from the Lizard West 323 leag*ues* 1·7 mil*es*.
Longitude at noone from the Lizard West 19°30′.

Thursday the 30th, hazy weather, wind at ESE and E a Stiffe gale. Course by Compasse SBE and S and S½E. I make my true Course to bee South 15° westerly. Distance Sailed 72·5 miles. Departure West 18·8 m*iles*. Diff*erence* of Longit*ude* West 00°19′. Diff*erence* of Latit*ude* 01°10′ S. Latitude by observation of the ☼ 09°40′ S.
Meridian distance from the Lizard West 329 leag*ues* 2·5 mil*es*.
Longitude at noone from the Lizard West 19°49′.
This afternoone I tooke an azimuth and find 6°10′, variation [*right margin:* Variation 6°10′ East.] easterly. My observation being a good one.
Faire weather to night. At 9 of clock nebulus major[1] was very apparent in the heaven, and shews as if it were a peece of the milky way brake from it. The Southern Constellations appears, which are neare the Pole Antarctick, the Camelion,[2] the bird of paradice,[3] the taile of litle Hydra,[4] and the water Snake.[5] These are all small starrs of the 5th or 6th

[1] See above, p. 178, n. 2.

[2] This is the constellation Chamaeleon the brightest star of which, α Chamaeleontis, is fourth magnitude and about 13° from the Antarctic pole.

[3] This is the constellation Apus the brightest star of which, α Apodis, is magnitude 3·8 and about 11° from the Antarctic pole.

[4] This is probably the constellation Hydrus, the Lesser Water Snake, the brightest stars of which are β and α, Hydri, with magnitudes of 2·8, the former, the tail, about 13° and the latter about 28° from the Antarctic pole.

[5] The Water Snake is another name for the constellation Hydra. There are a large number of stars in this constellation none of which is particularly near the Antarctic pole. Of the stars with magnitudes less than 5 the closest is about 56° from the pole.

magnitudes. No Pole-starre to bee seene, nor any starre fitt for observation within 15° of the Pole. The Crosers[1] are good starrs for observation, of the first and 2[d] magnitude, and are in this forme, when thay are on the Meridian above the Pole. [*no drawing provided*]

Fryday the 31th, faire weather wind at EBS and ESE a fine gaile. Course by the Compasse SBE and SS. I make my true Course to bee SSW. Distance Sailed 77·5 miles. Departure West 15·2 m*iles*. Latit*ude* by obs*ervation* of ☼ 10°56′ South. Diff*erence* of Longit*ude* 00°16′·7. Diff*erence* of Latitude 01°16′ S.
Meridian distance from the Lizard West 334 leag*ues* 2·7 mil*es*.
Longitude at noone from the Lizard West 20°05′·7.

[26] **January 1669.**[2] **The Sweepstakes at Sea Latit*ude* 11° &c**[a]**. S.**
[*margin:* variation 04°45′E] Variation by an amplitude taken both at sun riseing & setting 04°45′ East.

Saturday faire weather, wind at SE and SEBE and ESE a fine gale. I steered by my Compasse SSW and S as neere the wind as I could. Course made true this 24 houres is SBW. Distance Sailed 53·2 miles. Departure West 10·4 miles. Diff*erence* of Longit*ude* West 00°11′·6. Difference of Latit*ude* 00°52′. Latit*ude* by observation of the Sun 11°48′ S.
Meridian Distance from the Lizard West 338 leag*ues* 1·1 mil*es*.
Longitude at noone from the Lizard West 20°17′·3.
A Current setts to the Southward. Variation 5° East.

Sunday the 2[d] of January 1669, wind at E. Course by the Compasse SBE allowing for variation and Current. I make my true Course to bee South. Distance Sailed 74 miles. Diff*erence* of Latit*ude* 01°14′. Latit*ude* by the ☼ 13°02′.
Variation observed to bee 05°40′E and a Strong Current.
Meridian distance from the Lizard West 338 leag*ues* 1·1 mil*es*.
Longitude at noone from the Lizard West 20°18′·2.
[*margin:* sea fowles] Some sea fowles flying to & fro, a kind of Sea gull and gannet,[3] and a black sea fowle as big as a pidgeon,[4] and some large ones; Tropick birds, which are of a gray Colour, as big as pidgeons, with a long spired taile.[5]
Some bonnetos taken today, a great broad flat fish much like a Skeat follows the Ship, called by the Sea men a Sting ray,[6] for it hath a long taile and a sharpe bone in the end. If

[1] These are the stars of the Southern Cross, principally α and γ Crusis. See above, pp. 70–71.

[2] 1669/70.

[3] Gannets are not normally found in this area. These may have been boobies which are of the same family. The masked booby, the red-footed booby, and the brown booby are all found in this part of the Atlantic; see above, p. 185, n. 2.

[4] Possibly Bulwer's petrel (*Bulweria bulweria*), which might be found in this area, is slightly smaller than a pigeon, up to about 10 in (26 cm) long with a wingspan up to 27½ in (70 cm) and almost wholly of a dark sooty-brown colour. Harrison, *Seabirds*, pp. 253–4.

[5] The red-billed tropic bird and the white-tailed tropic bird are found in this area. See above, pp. 330, n. 1; 337, n. 1.

[6] Probably the pelagic stingray (*Pteroplatytrygon violacea*), which is common in tropical and sub-temperate waters of all oceans and the Mediterranean Sea. Pepperell, *Fishes*, p. 219.

it pricks[1] a man it puts him to much pain. Some call these cloake fishes, the lesser Sort are good to eat.

Munday the 3^{d}, faire weather, wind at ESE a fine gale. Course by the Compasse is SBE. My true Course SBW by reason of my tow at my Stern, and [*margin:* variation 6°E.] the variation 6° East . Distance Sailed 79·7 miles. Departure West 13·6 miles. Diff*erence* of Longit*ude* 00°14′. Diff*erence* of Latit*ude* 01°08′. Latitude by observation of ☼ 14°10′ S.
Meridian distance from the Lizard West 342 leag*ues* 2·7 miles.
Longitude from the Lizard at noone West 20°32′·3.

Tuesday the 4th, faire weather, wind at SEBE and E a fine gale. Course by Compasse SBE. But my true Course is South, allowing for the variation and Current. Distance Sailed by the Log 76 miles. But by my observation I have sailed 83 miles South. Latit*ude* by good observation of ☼ 15°33′ S.
Meridian distance from the Lizard West 342 leag*ues* 2·7 mil*es*.
Longitude to day noone from the Lizard West 20°32′·3.
At twelve of clock I steered South by Compasse, wind at East . Many flying fishes seene.
Variation of the Compasse by an amplitude at Sunset 06°25′ East.

Wednesday the fifth, faire weather, wind at EBN a fine gale and Smooth sea. Course by Compasse South, but my true course allowing all faults is South and by west. Distance Sailed 85 miles by observation and course, By Log but 74 miles which difference must bee Caused by [*margin:* Currant to South.] a Currant Setting southerly. Departure West 16·7 miles. Diff*erence* of Longit*ude* West 17′·2. Diff*erence* of Latit*ude* 01°23′. Latit*ude* by observation of ☼ 16°56′ S.

[27] **January 1669. The *Sweepstakes* at Sea, in the Latit*ude* of 15° &c^{a}. S.**
Meridian Distance from the Lizard West 348 leag*ues* 1·4 m*iles*.
Longitude from the Lizard at noon West 20°49′·5
Variation of the Compasse by an amplit*ude* in the morning 06°46′E.
This afternoone I brought the Shipp to, and sounded at 184 faddom right downe,[2] and had no ground, I being thwart of the Shoalds of Brazil caused mee to Sound, and in my thoughts the sea Looked whiter then usuall. [*right margin:* sound. no ground. at 184 fadom]
Variation at Sunset by observation 06°48′E. Some fowles seene, which wee call men of warre,[3] they live on the prey of flying fishes.

Thursday the 6th, faire weather, wind at ENE and NE a Stiffe gale. Course by Compasse is South, halfe a point easterly; allowing all faults, my true course is South 8° W. Distance

[1] 'sting' struck through.

[2] In order to get the lead line vertical in the water to take a deep sounding the ship has to be stationary, hence the requirement to lie to.

[3] Either the magnificent frigate bird or the Ascencion frigate bird, both of which might be found in this area. See above, p. 171, n. 1.

Sailed 67. Departure West 9·3 miles. Diff*erence* of Longit*ude* 00°10′ west. Diff*erence* of Latit*ude* 00°06′.[1] Latitude by observation 18°02′ S.
Meridian distance from the Lizard West 351 leag*ues* 1·7 mil*es*.
Longitude at noone from the Lizard West 20°59′·5.
The wind came to the North East this forenoone. This afternoone I caused the deep sea lead to bee hove with 190 faddom, & found no ground. [*right margin:* no ground]

Fryday the 7th, faire weather, wind at NNE, severall sea fowles seene. I am neare the latitude of the Island of Aseneam,[2] and not farre from it according to my draught and receing [reckoning] kept, but I shall pass to the West of it.
Variation is E 07°48′ by amplit*ude* taken at Sun riseing. Course made [*right margin:* variation 7°48′ East.] true, that is (when I write true) with allowance for all faults, and so my true Course this 24 houres is South, 10° west. Distance Sailed 49 miles. Departure West 8·4 miles. Diff*erence* of Longit*ude* West 00°09′. Diff*erence* of Latit*ude* 00°48′ S. Latitude by observation of the ☼ on the meridian 18°50′ South.
Meridian Distance from the Lizard West 354 leag*ues* 1·1 mil*es*.
Longitude from the Lizard West 21°08′·5.
Variation by an ampli*ude* taken this evening is 08°06′ East.
I sounded at 6 of clock & no ground at 140 faddom. Many sea fowles about the Shipp. The Island of Aseneam is in the Latit*ude* of 19°10′ S[3] in which I believe I shall bee by 10 of clock at night. I keep good watch to night, faire weather, wind at NE. Much fish about the ship but can take none, they are Seldome caught in the night. All my men are in good health.

Saturday the 8th, wind at ENE. Course by Compasse SBW. But my true course this last 24 houres is South 19°35′ west. Distance Sailed 61·3 miles. Departure West 20·6 miles. Diff*erence* of Longit*ude* 00°21′·7. Difference of Latit*ude* 00°58′ S. Latit*ude* by account at noone 19°48′ S.
Meridian distance from the Lizard West 361 leag*ues* 0·7 mil*es*.
Longitude at noone from the Lizard West 21°30′·2.
Variation by an amplitude at Sun Rise is 08°40′ East. sounded but found no ground at 150 faddom. Variat*ion* by ampl*itude* at ☼ Set is 10°06′ East. Latitude when I tooke the amplit*ude* of the ☼ was 20°00′ South.

[28] **January 1669. The *Sweepstakes* at Sea in Latit*ude* of 21° S**
Latitude by observation of the ☆ of the great beares back[4] is 20°28′S at 2 of clock on Sunday morning.

Sunday the 9th, fair weather, wind at NBE. Course by my Compasse is SSW. I tooke the ☼s amplitude in the East Horizon, and find the variation to bee 11°08′E. True Course

[1] This should be '01°06′.'

[2] These are Trindade and Martin Vaz Islands, which lie in 20°30′S, 29°19′W and 20°28′S, 28°51′W respectively. See above, p. 37, n. 2.

[3] This is the latitude given in Tapp, *Sea-Mans Kalender*, p. 178, for Trindade.

[4] Great Bear's back: Dubhe, α Ursæ Majoris. But see above, p. 181, n. 2, where this observation is said to have been to the Great Bear's side, Merak, β Ursæ Majoris.

South 30°30′ west. Distance Sailed 56·7 m*iles*. Departure West 28·9 miles. Diff*erence* of Longit*ude* 31′·2. Difference of Latitude 00°49′. Latit*ude* by account at noone is 20°27′ S.
Meridian distance from the Lizard West 370 leag*ues* 2·6 mil*es*.
Longitude from the Lizard West 22°01′·4.
The ☼ was neare my Zenith to day I could not observe it. At 2½ of clock this morning I observed the ☆ at the foot of the Crosers on the meridian,[1] and find my Selfe to bee in the Lat*itude* of 20°19′ S. At better then halfe an houre past 2 this morning, I observed the ☆ at the head of the Crosers[2] on the meridian, above the Pole as before, and find my Selfe to bee in the Latitude 20°20′ S.
The declination of the ☆ at the head of the Crosers 55°10′.[3]

The declination of the ☆ at the foot of the Crosers 61°16′.
Nebulus negro.

Munday the 10th, faire weather, wind at ENE. Course by my Compasse SSW, true Course is SWBS. Distance Sailed 80·5 miles. Departure West 44·8 miles. Diff*erence* of Longit*ude* West 00°47′·5. Diff*erence* of Lat*itude* S 01°07′. Lat*itude* by account at noone is 21°44′ S.
Meridian distance from the Lizard West 385 leag*ues* 2·4 miles.
Longitude at noone from the Lizard West 22°48′·9.
Variation by amplit*ude* at ☼ rising 11°25′E in the Latit*ude* 21°27′ S.
Variation by amplit*ude* at ☼ setting 11°52′E in the Latit*ude* 22°10′ S.

Tuesday the 11th, faire weather, temperate and healthy, wind at north. Course made true is SWBS. Distance Sailed 90 miles. Departure W 50 miles. Diff*erence* of Longit*ude* 54′·5. Diff*erence* of Latit*ude* 01°15′. Latitude by account at noone is 22°59′.
Variation of the Compasse is 11°58′E.
Meridian distance from the Lizard West 402 leag*ues* 1·4 mil*es*.
Longitude at noone from the Lizard West 23°43′·4.

Wednesday the 12, faire weather, wind came to the NNW a Stiffe gale. Course by the Compasse this 24 houres, is SSW. Course made true is SWBS. Distance Sailed 132 miles. Departure West 73·4 miles. Difference of Longit*ude* 01°20′·3W. Diff*erence* of Latit*ude* 01°50′. Latit*ude* by account at noone is 24°49′ S.
Meridian Distance from the Lizard West 426 Leag*ues* 2′· mil*es*.
Longitude from the Lizard West 25°03′·7.

[29] **January 1669. The *Sweepstakes* at Sea in Latit*ude* of 25° S.**
This afternoone wee had a Stout gale at west, and much raine. Course by the compasse SWBS.

Thursday the 13th, cloudy weather, wind at NNE, Course by Compasse, South West and by South, my true course SW. Distance Sailed 69·5 miles. Depart*ure* West 49 miles.

[1] This is α Crucis.

[2] This is γ Crucis.

[3] See above, pp. 70–71, for remarks on the declination of these stars. It must have given Narbrough confidence in his values for their declination that the latitudes fitted so well with his other observations and dead reckoning.

Diff*erence* of Longit*ude* 00°54′ west. Diff*erence* of Latit*ude* 00°49′. Latitude by account at noone 25°38′.
Meridian distance from the Lizard West 443 leag*ues* 0·8 mil*es*.
Longitude at noone from the Lizard West 25°57′·7.
Variation of the Compasse is 13°04′E. [*right margin:* variation is 13°04′ East.]

Fryday the 14th. Cloudy gusty rainy weather, wind at NNW, a great rowling Sea Comes out of the South. Course by compasse SWBS. My true course SW 7° westerly. Distance Sailed 101 miles. Departure West 79·4 miles. Diff*erence* of Longit*ude* West 01°27′·8. Diff*erence* of Latit*ude* 01°02′. Latitude by observation of the Sun 26°40′ S.
Meridian distance from the Lizard West 469 leag*ues* 2·2 mil*es*.
Longitude at noone from the Lizard West 27°25′·5.
Variation is 13°51′E.
Few fish seene, only small bonnetos taken now & then, sea fowles called[1] Black Nodis, & Curlews[2] seen flying Eastwards.

Saturday the 15th, cloudy rainy weather, wind at NNW, a gale, severall Claps of thunder and Lightening in the SSE. Course by the Compasse SWBS true course this 24 houres is SW 5°10′ westerly. Distance Sailed 81 miles. Departure West 62·4 miles. Diff*erence* of Longit*ude* 01°09′·5. Diff*erence* of Latit*ude* 00°52′. Latit*ude* at noone by account 27°32′.
Meridian distance from the Lizard West 490 leag*ues* 1·6.
Longitude from the Lizard West 28°25′.

Sunday the 16th. Cloudy, Wind at NNW in gusts, and much raine, our course by the Compasse SWBS. True course this 24 houres SW. Distance Sailed 124 miles. Departure West 88 miles. Diff*erence* of Longit*ude* 01°39′·7. Diff*erence* of Latit*ude* 01°28′ S. Latit*ude* by account at noone 29°00′ S.
Meridian distance from the Lizard West 519 leag*ues* 2·6 mil*es*.
Longitude at noone from the Lizard West 30°14′·7.
Variation is 14°E. I sounded but found no ground at 130 faddom.

Munday the 17th, wind at NNW till 6 of clock, Course by Compasse SWBS, the wind came to the SSW a fresh gale, I plyed to the Southward. Course made true this 24 houres is SW 5° southerly. Distance Sailed 89 miles. Dep*arture* West 57 m*iles*. Diff*erence* of Longit*ude* West 01°05′·5. Diff*erence* of Latit*ude* 01°08′ S.
Latitude to day at noone by observation of the ☼ 30°08′ S.
Meridian distance from the Lizard, West 538 leag*ues* 2·6 m*iles*.

[30] **January 1669. The *Sweepstakes* at Sea in the Latit*ude* of 30° S.**
Longitude from the Lizard West at noone 31°20′·2.
Variation of the Compasse is 14°14′E.

Tuesday the 18. Cloudy, winds variable, between the SSW and the SSE a fresh gale and raine, I stood to the westwards. After several Courses I make my true course to bee South

[1] 'No' struck through.
[2] See above, pp. 185, n. 3; 208, n. 7.

71° west. Distance Sailed 43 miles. Departure West 40·8 miles. Diff*erence* of Longit*ude* 00°46′·8. Diff*erence* of Latit*ude* 00°14′. Latit*ude* at noone by account 30°22′ S.
Meridian distance from the Lizard West 552 leag*ues* 1·4 mile*s*.
Longitude at noone from the Lizard West 32°07′.
Dirty rainy weather to night, wind at South East, a Stoute gale, I stood to the westward, a great Sea comes out of the South East.
Some Small sea fowles seene, but no fish. The Pink in Company with mee.

Wednesday the 19th. Cloudy gusty weather, wind at SE this 24 houres. Course by Compasse SWBS, true course is South 60° west. Distance Sailed 92 miles. Departure West 79·2 mile*s*. Diff*erence* of Longit*ude* 01°32′·5. Diff*erence* of Latit*ude* 00°46′. Latit*ude* by account at noone 31°08′.
Meridian Distance from the Lizard West 578 leag*ues* 2·6 mile*s*.
Longitude at noone from the Lizard West 33°39′·5.
This day I caused new sailes to bee brought to the yards, Doubting fowle weather,[1] for the heavens had an ill Aspect. [*margin:* variation 15° East.] Variation is 15° East. Wind blew hard at East I steered SWBS.

Thursday the 20th, faire weather, wind at ESE a Stout gale. Course by Compasse SWBS. My true Course is South 60° west. Distance Sailed 108 miles. Departure West 93·5 miles. Diff*erence* of Longit*ude* 01°49′·9. Diff*erence* of Latit*ude* 00°54′ S. Latit*ude* by obs*ervation* ☼ at noone 32°02′ S.
Meridian distance from the Lizard West 610 leag*ues* 0·1 mile*s*.
Longitude at noone from the Lizard West 35°29′.

Fryday the 21, faire weather, wind at SE and SSE, a fine gale, Smooth water, Course by Compasse SWBS. My true Course South 60° west. Distance Sailed 74·5 miles. Departure West 64·5 miles. Diff*erence* of Longit*ude* 01°16′·8. Diff*erence* of Latit*ude* 00°48′. Latit*ude* by obs*ervation* ☼ 32°50′.
Meridian Distance from the Lizard West 631 leag*ues* 1·6 mile*s*.
Longitude at noone from the Lizard West 36°45′·8.
Variation observed to bee East 18°27′.

Saturday the 22d, faire weather & Calme. I drove to the northwards this 24 houres 6 miles. Diff*erence* of Latit*ude* 00°06′. Latit*ude* by obs*ervation* ☼ 32°44′ S.
Meridian distance from the Lizard West 631 leag*ues* 1·6 mile*s*.
Longitude at noone from the Lizard West 36°45′·8.
Now temperate weather, smooth water, and a good healthy aire.

[31] **January 1669. The *Sweepstakes* at Sea in the Latit*ude* of 33° S.**
This afternoone I saw severall Small whales,[2] and sea fowles flying to and fro. I sounded but found no ground at 140 faddom.

[1] Expecting foul weather.
[2] See above, p. 187, n. 4.

An amplitude taken of the Sun in the West horizon this evening, Latitude 32°46′. South declination of the Sun 16°47′ South.

The operation as followeth

As the complement Sine of the Lat*itude* A	32°46′ South Comp*lement*	57°14′	9924
is to the Sine of the Radius	90°00′	90°00′	10000
So is the Sine of the ☼'s declination B	16°00′ South	16°47′	9460
to the Sine of the ☼'s amplitude C	20°06′ South		9536
Magnetic amplitude of ☼ is	38°30′ South		
My Compasse hath	18°24′ Variation easterly.		

[*blank space*][1]

Faire weather to night a fine gale, wind at NE. Course by Compasse SWBS. This evening neare eight of clock I observed the ☆ at the foot of the ✠[2] and am in latitude 32°50′ S.

Sunday the 23th. Wind at NE. Course by compasse this 24 houres is SWBW, but my true Course is SWBW.[3] Distance Sailed 61 miles. Departure West 50·8 miles. Diff*erence* of Longit*ude* 01°01′. Diff*erence* of Latit*ude* 00°34′. Lat*itude* by observation of the ☼ 33°18′ S.
Meridian distance from the Lizard West 648 leag*ues* 1·4 mile*s*.
Longitude at noone from the Lizard West 37°46′·8.
Wind at NE. This evening by an amplitude I find the variation to bee 18°04′E. Hazy weather to night, course by the Compasse SWBS.

Munday the 24th, hazy weather, wind at NE a fine gale. Course by the Compasse SWBS but by reason of variation I find the true course for this 24 houres to bee SW. Distance Sailed 90·5 miles. Departure West 64 miles. Diff*erence* of Longit*ude* West 01°17′. Diff*erence* of Latit*ude* 01°04′ S. Latit*ude* by observat*ion* of ☼ 34°22′ S.
Meridian distance from the Lizard West 669 leag*ues* 2·4 mile*s*.

[32] **January 1669 The *Sweepstakes* at Sea in the Latit*ude* of 33° S.**
Longitude at noone from the Lizard West 39°03′·8.
I judge a Current Setts out of the river of Plate, for I find my Selfe more to the Southward by nine miles then I did expect, I have been carefull of my Course and variation, which I find to bee but 18°20′E by amplitude taken to night. I am open of the mouth of the river of Plate.[4] I sounded to night but no ground at 145 fatham. Wind at NBE all night & close weather. I steered SWBS by my compasse.

[1] The blank space approximates to 10 lines of text.

[2] This is α Crusis.

[3] There is an error here. The true course of SWBW and distance run give the differences of Latitude and Departure recorded. The correction to the course steered to allow for leeway, current etc. is unlikely to have cancelled out the variation of about 18°E exactly, so the course steered by the compass is likely to be the one in error.

[4] Abreast the mouth of Río de la Plata.

Tuesday the 25th. Wind at NNE and N and NNW a fresh gale, and a light moon in hand neare her full. Course by my Compasse SWBS but allowing for [*margin:* variation 18°40′] the Current which setts out of the river of Plate to the SE:ward and the variation 18°40′, I make my true course as I find by my observation, to bee South West. Distance Sailed 120 miles. Departure West 85 miles. Diff*erence* of Longit*ude* 01°43′·7. Diff*erence* of Latit*ude* 01°25′. Latit*ude* by good observat*ion* of the ☼ 35°47′ S.
Meridian distance from the Lizard West 698 leag*ues* 0·4 mile*s*.
Longitude at noone from the Lizard West 40°47′·1.
A stoute gale of wind at West all night, one of my fore shrouds broke.

Wednesday the 26th. Wind at SE and SSE a stout gale, this morning it veared about from the West to the South, and to the SE. I layed a try two houres till the gust was over. After severall courses I make my true Course to bee South 61°20′ west. Distance Sailed 90 miles. Departure West 78·6 miles. Difference of Longitude West 01°37′. Diff*erence* of Latit*ude* 00°43′. Latit*ude* by obs*ervation* ☼ 36°30′.
Meridian distance from the Lizard West 724 leag*ues* 1 mile.
Longitude at noone from the Lizard West 42°24′·1.
Wind at South, and SBW to night good weather. I stood to the westward, the Pink in company with mee.

Thursday the 27th. Fair, wind at SBW. Course by Compasse SWBW and WSW and W. After several courses, I make my true Course to bee North 70° west. Distance Sailed 52·6 miles. Departure West 49·6 miles. Diff*erence* of Longitude 01°00′·6. Diff*erence* of Lat*itude* N 00°18′. Latit*ude* by good obs*ervation* of ☼ 36°12′ S.
Meridian distance from the Lizard West 740 leag*ues* 2·6 mil*es*.
Longitude at noone from the Lizard West 43°24′·7.
Variation at Sun Set is by an amplit*ude* 19°59′ East.
Magnetic amplitude was 38°11′ South.
True amplitude was 18°12′ South.

Fryday the 28th. Fair. This morning the wind came to the E and to the NE a fine gale & smooth sea , Course by the Compasse SW and W and SWBW. After several courses I make my true course to bee North 75° west. Distance Sailed 35 miles. Departure West 33·8 miles. Diff*erence* of Longitude 00°43′.

[33] **January the 29th 1669. The *Sweepstakes* at Sea in Latit*ude* of 37° S**
Difference of Latit*ude* 00°09′N. Latit*ude* by ☼ 36°03′ S.
Meridian distance from the Lizard West 752 leag*ues* 0·4 mil*es*.
Longitude at noone from the Lizard West 44°07′·7.
Course by Compasse SW, wind at NW.

Saturday 29, wind at N and NW a stiff gale all this 24 houres, Course by the compasse SW. True Course SWBW. Distance Sailed 140 miles. Departure West 117 miles. Diff*erence* of Longit*ude* 02°25′. Diff*erence* of Latit*ude* 01°18′ S. Latit*ude* by observat*ion* of ☼ 37°21′. I judge a current Setts out of the river of Plate which sets mee to the South

eastward 6 miles in 24 houres, I find I am more southerly by my observation then by my Logg account.
Meridian distance from the Lizard West 791 leag*ues* 0·4 mil*es*.
Longitude at noone from the Lizard West 46°32′·7.
Variation of the Compasse by ☼ˢ amplit*ude* in the East 19°10′ East. [*right margin:* variation 19° East.]
Foggy weather this evening with some raine, the wind came to the WSW a Stiffe gale; this night at 8 of clock I sounded but no ground at 105 faddom. It is very cold weather of a Sudden. Course by the Compasse is South.

Sunday the 30th, hazy weather, wind at South a Stiffe gale, a rowling Sea Comes out of the SE. Course by the Compasse South and SW and WSW. After several Courses I make the true Course to bee SSW. Distance Sailed 92 mil*es*. Departure West 35·4 miles. Diff*erence* of Longit*ude* 00°45′. Diff*erence* of Latit*ude* 01°25′ S. Latitude by observation of the Sun 38°46′ S.
Meridian distance from the Lizard West 802 leag*ues* 2·8 mil*es*.
Longitude at noone from the Lizard West 47°17′·7.
I find a Strong Current Setts to the Southward, neare 16 miles in 24 houres. I judge it comes out of the river of Plate, this day at 12 of clock I observed the water to bee of a whiter colour, then the usual sea water, I caused the lead to bee hove, but no ground at 100 faddom. No fish seene, Some large gray sea fowles flying to & fro. Wind came to the South this afternoone, I stood close haled to the westward.
Magnetic amplitude of ☼ in the West 37°30′ S.
True amplitude of ☼ at the Same time 18°30′ S.
Variation of the Compasse is easterly 19°00′.
Close coole weather, wind at SBE a Small gale.

Munday the 31th. Calme, at 8 this morn*ing* the wind came to the northwest a fine gale. At 11 the wind went round the Compasse to the westward, and came to the North, with much thunder and Lightening and Some rain, very dark clouds, cold hazy weather. Several Spots of sea weeds driveing in the sea , and a great many sea fowles Swimming in the sea of a browne Colour, Smooth water. Course by my Compasse is SW. Variation by an ampl*itude* at ☼ rising is 19°43′E.
All my men are in good health praised be god. I make what Saile I can to the Southward, the Pink in Company. After severall courses this 24 houres

[34] **February 1669.**[1] **The *Sweepstakes* at Sea in the Latit*ude* of 39° S.**
I make my true Course to bee South west. Distance Sailed 58 miles. Dep*arture* West 41 miles. Diff*erence* of Longit*ude* 00°52′·5 West. Diff*erence* of Latit*ude* 00°41′ S. Latitude by account at noone allowing 10 miles to Sett to the Southward by the Current, Latit*ude* 39°27′ S.
Meridian distance from the Lizard West 816 leag*ues* 1·8 mil*es*.
Longitude at noone from the Lizard West 48°10′·2.
This afternoone a fine gale at NNE. Course by the Compasse SW hazy weather, several sea fowles seene flying to & fro, and rock weeds seen also.

[*margin:* ×] [*blank space*][1]

All the Albycores, bonnetos & flying fish have quite left the Ship, not one of them to bee seene, nor any other fishes.
This evening I sounded, but no ground at 135 faddams. Wee saw severall riplins, and froath in Streames, as if there were Setts of tydes.
Cold Sharp ayre, wind at SSE. Several whales seen neare the Shipp of an ordinary bigness. Close Cloudy weather to night, no starrs to bee seene. I sounded againe at 12 of clock to night, but found no ground at 108 faddom.

Tuesday the first of February 1669. Cloudy foggy weather, and litle wind at SE. I stood to the SW:ward, this forenoone I saw abundance of sea fowles flying to and fro, Strikeing about the weeds for Small fish, several beds of sea weeds driveing past the ship, it fell Calme this forenoone, Many small Shrimps in the sea about the Shipp, 8 young Seale fishes came Close to the Shipp, they were as big as an ordinary Spaniell dog, of a black colour,[2] they went away to the westward. I sounded this forenoone but no ground at 140 faddom. No observation to day the Sun being Clouded. At 12 of clock to day wind came to the SSE. I steered SWBW by my Compasse, which is West a litle southerly, I halled in so much westerly to see the land, being to the Southward of the river of Plate. Course made true from munday noone till to day noone is WBN. Distance Sailed 61·5 miles. Departure West 60 miles. Diff*erence* of Longit*ude* 01°20′·6. Diff*erence* of Latit*ude* 00°12′ North. Latitude by account at noone is 39°15′ S.
Meridian distance from the Lizard West 836 leag*ues* 1·8 mil*es*.
Longitude at noone from the Lizard West 49°30′·8.
This afternoone a fresh gale at SSE. I steered away SWBW by my compasse, the air is mighty cold of a Sudden, as it is in England in September, these sea s are very apt to Sudden gusts, and variable winds, for the winds have beene round the Compasse two or 3 times a day for this 3 dayes. The water of the sea is whiter then usual, which makes mee believe I must bee in Soundings. Also by my account of Longitude which I have kept from the Lizard I am not

[35] **February 1669. The *Sweepstakes* at Sea, in the Latit*ude* of 39° &c[a]. S.**
above 01°28′ off the Land, by my mercators draught.[3] This evening I sounded, but had no ground at 130 faddom. Wind at S a fine gale I steered in WSW. At 10 of clock I observed the water to ripple as if it were over a Shoald. I caused the head sailes to be brased to the mast, and sounded, and had ground at 70 faddoms, fine red sand incl*ineing* to a gray. I hove the lead imediatly againe, and had 70 faddoms as before, red sand inclineing to gray. I fired a gun, and Shewed the lights for the Pink to tack. I filled my head sailes and tacked and stood to [*right margin:* ground at 70 faddam] the Eastward Close halled, the wind at S a fresh gale I called to the Pink and told Capt*ain* Flem*m*ing I had ground at 70 faddams, fine red sand, and that wee saw a Ripplin within us to the westward. I believe the Soundings rise with a sudden bank, for at 12 of clock I sounded againe, but no ground at

[1] The blank space approximates to 4 lines of text, and is marked by an x in the margin.

[2] See above, p. 191, n. 2.

[3] By Mercator's chart.

100 faddams, when I had not stood off East five miles from the place where I had 70 faddoms.
Meridian distance from the Lizard West 838 Lea*gues*.
Longit*ude* West from the Lizard to the place where I had ground at 70 fadd*oms* 49°39′.

Wednesday the 2[d], at 3 of clock this morning, I tacked and stood to the westward, wind at SBE, it came to the SBW and SW litle wind. After several courses from tuesday noone till to day noone, I make my true Course to bee west. Distance Sailed 10 miles Diff*erence* of Longit*ude* 00°12′·9. Diff*erence* of Latit*ude* 00°00′. Latitude by account and obs*ervation* of ☼ 39°15′ SS.
Meridian distance from the Lizard West 839 lea*gues* 2·8 mil*es*.
Longitude at noone from the Lizard West 49°43′·7.
Litle wind this afternoone, and fair weather, wee Lay sometimes the one way sometimes the other, wind at SWBS a small gale I hoisted out my boat, and sounded but no ground at 140 faddoms. I tryed the Current with my boate, but found very litle, or none to take notice of. The sea ripples in many places, I sounded on them but found no ground at 108 faddoms. Several beds of sea weeds driveing to & fro, in knotts, the weeds are 5 or 6 faddoms long in Strings, and broad leaves on them of a brown Colour, and a Clod or rock hangs at the root 2 or 3 pound weight. Severall sea fowles seen flying and swimming neare the Shipp. It being quite Calme, my men killed severall of them with their birding peeces,[1] for they were mighty tame, and did not move for the report of a gun, the fowles are near like a Sea gull and good meat, Some Seals and whales seene. Variation by an ampl*itude* at ☼ set is 17°05′E. A cold air this evening. I have but 3 men Sick aboard the air very Cloudy and foggy. Litle wind at SWBS to night, I stood to the South-east:ward.

Thursday the 3[d] day fair weather, wind at SWBW & S litle wind all this 24 houres. True Course is SE. Distance Sailed 9·9 miles. Depart*ure* East 7 miles. Diff*erence* of Longit*ude* 00°08′·2. Diff*erence* of Latit*ude* 00°07′ S. Latit*ude* by observation 39°22′ S.
Meridian distance from the Lizard West 837 lea*gues* 1·8 mil*es*.
Longitude at noone from the Lizard West 49°35′·2.

[36] **February 1669. the *Sweepstakes* at the Coast of America. Latit*ude* 39°22′ S.**
Variation of the Compasse is 20°30′E. Cold dewy night, no starrs seen.

Fryday the 4th, fair weather, this morning the wind came to the north, a fine gale, and warme. Course by Compasse is SWBW but my true Course from yesterday noone till to day noone is WSW. Distance sailed 62·5 miles. Departure West 58 miles. Diff*erence* of Longit*ude* West 01°17′. Diff*erence* of Lat*itude* 00°24′ S. Latit*ude* by observation of ☼ 39°46′ S.
Meridian distance from the Lizard West 856 Lea*gues* 2·8 mil*es*.
Longitude at noone from the Lizard West 50°52′·2.
Fair weather a fine gale of wind at North this afternoone. Course by my Compasse SWBS, the Pink in Company.
Variation of the Compasse by an amplit*ude* at ☼ rising 20°16′E.

[1] Fowling guns.

Variation of the Compasse by an amplit*ude* at ☼ setting 20°51′E.
I sounded this evening, but no ground at 140 faddom down.

Saturday the 5th, hazy weather, wind at N a fine gale, and smooth sea. Course by the Compasse this 24 houres is SWBS. But my true Course is SWBW. Distance sailed 101 miles. Departure West 84 miles. Diff*erence* of Longit*ude* 01°50′·4. Diff*erence* of Latit*ude* 00°56′. Latit*ude* by account 40°42′ S.
Meridian distance from the Lizard West 884 leag*ues* 2·8 mil*es*.
Longitude at noone from the Lizard West 52°42′·6.
Several beds of rock weeds seen to day, and sea fowles much like Gannets some black, some white some pied and gray,[1] severall Seale fishes Swimming in the sea, as if it were so many dogs, for their heads are much like a bull dog head, they will keep their heads above water a great while and look on the Shipp, they are very nimble in diveing, and Skipping out of the water. At 7 of clock this eveing I was in the latitude of 41° South Latitude.
Longitude West from the Lizard of England 52°50′ and in
Meridian distance West from the Lizard 895 leagues.
Meridian Distance from Port Praya 616 leagues.
Longitude from Port Praya West 35°34′.
I brought the Shipp to and sounded, and had ground at 50 faddom, the sounding fine red sand, with some black mixture of sand. I steered away from this place South and B*y* West, by my Compasse, which is SWBS for the Compasse hath 21° variation East. Wind at N a fine gale. At 12 of clock at night I sounded againe, and had ground at 70 faddom red sand as before, rather finer sand, I had then sailed from 7 of clock when I sounded and had 50 faddom to this place, five leagues SWBS & had altered my Soundings 20 faddom. I reckon my selfe to bee 20 leagues off the Land, according to the description of Mercators draughts; I steered away SWBS by my Compasse, the Pink in Company, I carry a light in the night for the Pink to keep neere mee, the wind at North a fine gale, it Looks dark & hazy to the Easter boord, and a rowling Sea comes out there.
I advised with Don Carlos to night, where it would bee best for us to

[37] **February 1669. The *Sweepstakes* on the Coast of America. Lat*itude* 41° S.**
hale in with the land, in what Latitude, or at what Cape or harbour on this Coast of America, I being now to the Southward of the river of Plate, and according to my instructions, I am come before the Coast which I am to discover, and to see for a trade with the natives. His answer was hee did not understand the Coast, nor where people Lived, but I might do what I would.
It was alwaies his discourse in the voyage that hee had been here in a gally, and that hee knew all the Coast, all along from the river of Plate to the Straits, and through the Straits all along the West coast to Baldivia and to Lemia [Lima]. Being now come here hee knows none of these places,[2] nor anything as to this concern, as I can perceive by him, hee knows nothing of a Seaman, nor anything appertaining to the sea, not so much as the Sea Compasse, nor how the Shipp is steerd, nor any thing of navigation. All that I can perceive

[1] See above, p. 194, n. 1.
[2] 'hee' struck through.

by him and of him is, hee hath lived with some West India Governour, and hath heard discourse of these parts of America from his master.
I steered SBW by my Compasse, which is neare SWBW, wind at north, at day I intend to hale in for the Land.

Sunday the 6th, hazy foggy weather, wind at N a fine gale. This morning at 6 of clock I sounded and had ground at 75 faddom, fine white sand and self greet [grit] in it. Course from 7 of clock last night till this time was South and B*y* West by my compasse, and I have sailed 14 leagues. Now I steere in South West B*y* west.
Course made true from Saturday noon till to day noone is South 48°30′ west. Distance sailed 100 miles. Departure West 74·5 miles. Diff*erence* of Longit*ude* 01°39′·3. Diff*erence* of Lati*tude* 01°06′ S. Lat*itude* by obs*ervation* ☼ 41°48′ S.
Meridian distance from the Lizard West 909 leag*ues* 2·3 miles.
Longitude at noone from the Lizard West 54°21′·9.
Very foggy weather this afternoone and litle wind at NNE. I stood in SW by my Compasse. I sounded this afternoone, no ground at 100 faddom. The Pink in company with mee, I called to her to keep neare mee, and to fire musketts now. Calm in the first of the night, but mighty thick with fogg, at 8 of clock to night the wind came up at SW a fresh gale, & extreame thick wet fogg, and Lightening round the heavens. I stood to the SE:ward, wee fired severall muskets to night to keep Company.
No amplitude nor azimuth taken to day it being foggy, I allow for the variation of the Compasse 21°E.

Munday the 7th, wind at SSW and SW very thick of fogg, and blew hard, as much as I could well Carry a pair of Courses. I stood to the SE:ward, Course by compasse SE. Allowing all faults I make my true Course South 40° East. Distance sailed 60 miles. Departure E 38·8 miles. Diff*erence* of Longit*ude* 00°51′·6. Diff*erence* of Lati*tude* 00°46′ S. Lati*tude* by account 42°34′ S.

[38] **February 1669. The *Sweepstakes* on the Coast of America. Lat*itude* 42° S.**
Meridian distance from the Lizard West 896 leag*ues* 2·5 mil*es*.
Longitude from the Lizard West 53°30′·3.
I allow for the variation E 21°00′.
Cold weather, and base wett, foggy, wind at SW. I stood off SSE to night, I carried a light for the Pink, and fired several muskets. It blew a stout gale and a short sea run. No starrs seene.

Tuesday the 8th. Cloudy hazy weather with rain, this morning at 8 of clock the wind came to the South, and veared to the West North west, a stiffe gale. I steered SSW by the Compasse. I make my true Course this last 24 houres to be South 30°11′ East. Distance sailed 40·4 miles. Departure East 20·4 miles. Diff*erence* of Lati*tude* 00°35′ South. Lati*tude* at noon by account 43°09′ South. Diff*erence* of Longit*ude* East 00°28′.
Meridian distance from the Lizard West 890 leag*ues* 0·1 mil*es*.
Longitude at noone from the Lizard West 53°02′·3.
Variation by an amplitude at ☼ rise 18°00′ East.
Variation by an amplitude at ☼ set 19°48′ E.

At 7 of clock this afternoone the wind came to the WSW a stiffe gale I stood to the Southward, much rock-weed passed by the Shipp to day & severall sea fowles seene. Very Cold aire, as to the time of yeare, it being Summer here.
Don Carlos begins to complaine of the Cold aire, and tells mee hee did not thinke wee should have gone so farre southerly, I Showed by my plats[1] how farre wee must go further, and through the Straits, and along the West coast. Hee said the Spaniards went to Chile a nearer way, I answered it was into the River of Plate, and over land, which wee could not do.[2]

Wednesday the 9th. Indifferent fair weather, this morning I took the ☼s amplitu*de* and find the variation 19°30′ E. Litle wind at SW. Course by Compasse this 24 houres is SSW and SSE sometimes. But my true Course is South 9° East. Distance sailed 66·5 miles. Departure East 10·4 miles. Diff*erence* of Long*itude* 00°14′·4. Diff*erence* of Latit*ude* 01°06′ South. Latit*ude* by account at noone 44°15′ S.
Meridian distance from the Lizard West 886 leag*ues* 1·7 mile.
Longitude at noone from the Lizard West 52°47′·9.
I am at halfe allowance of beere, the beere is excellent good, and so is the rest of the Provisions. My men are all in good health god be praised.

Thursday the 10th, hazy Cloudy cold aire, wind at SW. I stood to the SE:ward. At 11 of clock the wind came to the SBE a fresh gale; At 12 of clock I tacked and stood to the Westward, a great homeing sea comes out of the South. After several Courses last 24 houres, I make my true course to bee SW. Distance sailed 58 miles. Departure West 41. Diff*erence* of Longit*ude* 00°57′·7. Diff*erence* of Latit*ude* 00°41′ South. Latit*ude* at noone by observation of the ☼ 44°56′ South.
Meridian Distance from the Lizard West 900 leag*ues* 0·7 mil*es*.
Longitude at noone from the Lizard West 53°45′·6.

[39] **February 1669. The *Sweepstakes* in the Latitude of 44°15′ South.**
I stand to the Westward this afternoone, and to night, the wind at South, and at SSW and SBE sometimes, an ordinary gale, hazy weather.

Fryday the 11th. Cloudy hazy weather, wind at SSE and sometimes at SBW a stiffe gale. After severall courses this 24 houres, I make my true Course to bee West B*y* North 06°07′ northerly. Distance sailed 33·5 miles. Departure West 32 miles. Diff*erence* of Longit*ude* 00°46′. Diff*erence* of Latit*ude* N 00°10′. Lat*itude* by obs*ervation* ☼ 44°46′ S.
Meridian distance from the Lizard West 910 leag*ues* 2·7 miles.
Longitude at noone from the Lizard West 54°31′·6.

Saturday the 12th. Cloudy hazy weather, much wind at SW. I brought the ship to try under our main-saile & mizzen, with her head to the Northwestward. At 10 of clock I set my Courses, it being lesse wind, at SW and SWBW. I stood to the Westward to keep hold

[1] Charts.
[2] This was the route via Buenos Aires, Tucumán, Potosi, and on to Lima, first opened up by the Bishop of Tucumán, Fray Francisco de Victoria, in 1580. Israel, *Diasporas*, p. 131.

of the shore. some rain & sleety Snow to day, in gusts, a great Sea runs. After divers courses this 24 houres, my true Course is NWBN. Distance sailed 44·5 miles. Departure West 24·9 miles. Diff*erence* of Longit*ude* West 00°32′·6. Diff*erence* of Latit*ude* 00°30′ N. Latitude at noone 44°09′ South.
Meridian distance from the Lizard West 919 leag*ues* 0·6 mil*es*.
Longitude from the Lizard West 55°06′·2.
This afternoone I sounded but had no ground at 100 faddom. The wind came to the SWBW. At two of clock I tacked and stood off SE:ward, foggy.

Sunday the 13th, blowing gusty weather, wind at SW. A great sea comes out of the South, many beds of rock weeds past by the Ship to day. I sounded, but found no ground at 100 faddams. After divers courses this 24 houres, I make the true Course to bee South 75° easterly. Distance sailed and drove 42·3 miles. Departure East 41·2 miles. Diff*erence* of Longit*ude* East 00°56′·6. Diff*erence* of Latit*ude* 00°11′ S. Latit*ude* by observat*ion* of ☼ 44°20′ S.
Meridian distance from the Lizard East[1] 905 leag*ues* 1·6 mil*es*.
Longitude at noone from the Lizard E 54°09′·6.
This afternoone it proved a fine gale of wind at WNW. I stood to the SW:ward as neare as I could lye. This afternoone at Sun setting I took an amplitude of the ☼ and find the variation to bee 19°40′ E.

Munday the 14th, hazy, wind at NNW a stiffe gale. Course by Compasse SW. Courses this 24 houres were, SE 11 miles and, SW 60 miles, haveing contrary winds in the time. But I make my true Course from yesterday at noone till to day noone, to bee SWBW 01°05′ west. Distance sailed 61 miles. Departure West 51·4 miles. Diff*erence* of Longit*ude* 01°12′·6. Diff*erence* of Latitude 00°33′ S. Latit*ude* by the ☼ 44°53′ S.
Meridian Distance from the Lizard West 922 leag*ues* 2 miles.
Longitude at noone from the Lizard West 55°22′·2.
Variation by an amplitude at ☼ set 20°40′ E.

[40] **February 1669. The *Sweepstakes* at Sea in the Latit*ude* of 44°&c. S.**
This afternoone at 2 of clock the wind came to the SW and veared to the South, I stood to the SE:ward, very thick fogg.

Tuesday the 15th the wind came to the SSE this morning a fine gale, but very thick of fogg. I tacked at 4 of clock and stood to the Westwarde. After several Courses from yesterday at noone till to day at noone, I make the true Course to bee South 18°20′ west. Distance sailed 49·6 miles. Departure West 15·6 miles. Diff*erence* of Longit*ude* West 00°22′. Diff*erence* of Latit*ude* 00°47′. Latit*ude* by account at noone is 45°40′ S.
Meridian distance from the Lizard West 927 leag*ues* 2·6 mil*es*.
Longitude at noone from the Lizard West 55°44′·2.
This afternoone the wind came to the E a fine gale and Cleare weather, & a smooth Sea. I steered SW by my Compasse, which is neare West South West. The variation is 21° E. Severall Seales came swimming close to the Shipp. This evening I called to the Pink, and

[1] 'west' struck through. This and the following longitude should be West.

asked if all were well, they answered all was well, they told mee they found the Compasse vary 20° & a halfe. I called to Cap*tain* Flem*m*ing to steere in SWBW by his compasse, and I would follow close after him. I charged them to Look out well. This night at 10 of clock the wind came to the North.

Wednesday the 16th foggy weather, wind at North, a fine gale. Course by my Compasse SWBW. I sounded this morning, but no ground at 100 faddom. After some courses this 24 houres, I make my true Course to bee West 04°15′ southerly. Distance sailed 108 miles. Departure West 107 miles. Diff*erence* of Latit*ude* 00°08′ S. Diff*erence* of Longit*ude* 02°27′ W. Latitude by observation of ☼ on the meridian 45°48′ S.
Meridian distance from the Lizard West 963 leag*ues* 1·6 mil*es*.
Longitude at noon from the Lizard West 58°11′·2.
At 12 of clock to day I sounded, and had ground at 55 faddom, fine gray sand inclineing to an oase [ooze]. Wind at NNW. I steered SSW by my Compasse. At 6 of clock I sounded, and had ground at 53 faddoms fine gray Oasy sand. I ordered the Pink to keep ahead, & to have good looking out, and to keep out a light, it being dark moone. Latitude 45°52′ S. Variation by an amplit*ude* to night 19° E.

Thursday the 17th hazy weather & a small gale at NW. I steered SWBS by my compasse. At 5 and at 8 of clock in the forenoon I sounded, and had ground at 55 faddom, fine red sand inclineing to an oase, it being litle wind and smooth Sea, wee saw a dead whale floating on the sea. I hoisted out my pinnace and rowed to it, it being about a mile to the Westward of us, many sea fowles were feeding on the Stinking Carkasse, I seeing what it was went aboard againe, and caused the boate to come

[41] **February 1669. The *Sweepstakes* at Sea in Latit*ude* of 46° S.**
to a grapnell[1] to try the Current, but found litle, or none at all. After divers courses I make my true course this 24 houres to bee SWBW. Distance sailed 54 miles. Departure West 45 miles. Diff*erence* of Longit*ude* 01°06′. Diff*erence* of Latit*ude* 30° S. Latit*ude* by obs*ervation* of ☼ at noone 46°18′ South.
Meridian distance from the Lizard West 978 leag*ues* 1·7 mil*es*.
Longitude at noon from the Lizard West 59°17′·2.
This afternoone was a thick fogg. Capt*ain* Flem*m*ing came on boord of mee and had severall things hee wanted. I bad him bee Carefull to keep company whilest this fogg lasted, & when that was over, wee would hale in with the Land. At 2 of clock this afternoone the wind veared to the NE a small gale. I stood to the South Westward. Litle wind to night it veared to the E.

Fryday the 18th, very foggy weather, wind at E. This morning at 6 of clock it came to the SSE an ordinary gale, I steered SW by my Compasse. I sounded and had ground at 50 faddom, fine red sand inclining to black. [*right margin:* 50 faddom] After divers courses made from yesterday noon till to day noon, I make the true course to bee WSW. Distance sailed 44·4 miles. Departure West 41·1 mil*es*. Diff*erence* of Longitude

[1] He put a small anchor down to the seabed, thereby making the current measurement far more accurate than using the normal sea-anchor.

00°58′. Diff*erence* of Latit*ude* 00°17′ South. Latitude by account at noone 46°35′ South.
Meridian distance from the Lizard West 992 leag*ues* 0·8 mil*es*.
Longitude at noon from the Lizard West 60°15′·2.
My company are all in good health, but some of the Puny race are weakly with being so long on ship boord. I serve them vinegar every week, which is very good to prevent the Scurvey in their mouths. Also I give order that every man wash his face and hands and mouth, every morning before hee receives his allowance of bread for the day, and one man is appointed to look after them to see it performed. If neglected his dayes allowance is kept in the Stewards hand. Also every man is ordered to shift him selfe[1] every 14 dayes at the furthest, to keepe themselves cleane, and from lice. If not, hee forfeits his daye's allowance to the party which accuseth him; by this means the ship is kept sweet and Cleane.
This afternoone the wind came to the East South East, and began to rain & blow. I stood to the Southward till 2 of the clock, then tacked and stood to the NE:ward, for I was fearfull of being imbayed, in the bay of Camarones.[2] It blew very hard[3] now, and a great Sea came in. I sounded at 2 of the Clock and had ground at fifty faddom, Dark sand, with some bright sand in it. This evening the wind came to the SE with rain and blew very hard, I stood off NEBE as much as I could carry a pair of courses, the Pink in Company I carried a light all night for the Pinke much wind at SE.

[42] **February 1669. The *Sweepstakes* at Sea in Latit*ude* 46°24′ S.**
Saturday the 19th, blowing foggy weather, wind at SE the sky all overcast with dark windy like clouds. A great Sea runs, sometimes wee could Carry a pair of Courses and sometimes put to try. After severall Courses made from yesterday noone till today noone, I make the true course to bee North 30°15′ easterly. Distance sailed 12·8 miles. Departure East 6·4 miles. Diff*erence* of Longit*ude* 00°08′ E. Difference of Latit*ude* N 00°11′. Latit*ude* at noone by account 46°34′.
Meridian distance from the Lizard West 990 leag*ues* 0·4 mil*es*.
Longitude at noone from the Lizard West 60°07′·2.
I allow for the variation of the Compasse 18°00′ E.
Soundings to day several times, and had 50 and 53 faddoms, darke black sand, with some bright sand in it. And find severall beds of Rock weeds past by to day and some Seals seene, and porpoises, such as are in European seas, 3 whales seen, and many sea fowles flying to and fro. [*margin:* Pengwins] some Pengwins swim*m*ing in the sea neare the Shipp. At 2 of clock in the afternoon the wind was at EBS a stout gale and a great Sea, I stood to the Southward close haled, under my Courses, the Pinke halfe a miles to windward under his Courses, Shee sailes better then wee now it blows and puts us past our topsailes, the sea runs lofty, sometimes rain, and slatty haile, & foggy, the air temperate as to cold, but raw wett foggs and raine.
At foure of clock this afternoone the Ship fetching a sudden seele,[4] broke 3 of the weather shrouds, so that it was neare 8 at night before wee could fitt the Shipp to make saile againe,

[1] Change his clothes.
[2] This is Golfo de San Jorge (46°S, 66°W). It is not named on the Doncker chart, but Río de los Camarones is shown as running into the back of it.
[3] 'att' struck through.
[4] seeling: a sudden heeling over, and quick return.

which then wee did and stood to the Southward, the wind at EBS, a stout gale. I stood SBE having only my Courses abroade. Wee sounded at 12 of clock at night, and had 50 faddom, gray fine sand. Wee Showed our lights and the Pink answered with her lights, wind at EBS. I steered SBE by my Compasse and sailed 4 leagues in 4 houres time, scarce that. Wee saw severall white spots in the sea to night, which are small Shrimps Swimming in knotts together, which comes out of the river of Camarons as I suppose.[1]
At 12 of clock to night I reckon my selfe to bee in the Latit*ude* of 46°42′ South, when I sounded I had 50 faddom.
Longitude west, from the Lizard 60°28′.
Meridian distance from the Lizard West 994 leag*ues* 2 miles.

Sunday the 20th, hazy foggy weather, this morning at 4 of the clock I brought to and sounded, and had ground at 50 faddam fine gray sand. I could not see the lights of the Pink, wee shew our lights, sounded trumpets and fired muskets, I keepe my Course South and B*y* East, wind at E a stoute gale, at day light wee looked abroad all round but could not see her any where,

[43] **February 1669. The *Sweepstakes* at Sea in the Latit*ude* of 47° South.**
I judge shee did not make saile to keep mee company, or else shee altered her course. This forenoon I made what saile I could, steered away South B*y* East and South, wind at ENE an ordinary gale, and Continually hazy, For I had a desire to make the Land if I could before night, which I judge will bee Cape Blanco,[2] for I do reckon my selfe in the Latitude of it at 12 of clock to day, and but 20 leagues to the Eastward of it, according to Mercators Plats and the account which I have kept of the Shipps way, from the Lizard & from S[t] Iago, one of the Cape de Verde Islands, to this place.
After divers courses from yesterday at noone till to day at noone, I make the true Course to bee this 24 houres SSW. Distance run 60·5 miles. Departure West 23·3 miles. Diff*erence* of Longit*ude* 00°34′·4. Diff*erence* of Latitude 00°56′ S. Latit*ude* by account at noon is 47°20′ S. No observation by Sun nor starrs these 3 dayes, for foggs.
Meridian distance from the Lizard West 997 Leag*ues* 2·7 mil*es*.
Longitude at noon from the Lizard West 60°41′·6.
I allow for variation of the Compasse East 18°00′.
No sight of the Pinke. At 12 of clock to day I brought too and sounded, and had ground at 50 faddom, gray sand. I lay with my head sailes to the mast halfe an houre, and sent men up to the topmast heads it beeing a litle cleare but no sight of the Pink. I filled and stood away SSW by my Compasse with my top sailes set wind at EBN a fresh gale, sometimes foggy and sometimes cleare for an houre together. At one of clock the wind came to the NNE a fresh gale, I steered SW by my Compasse, and sailed 4 leagues a watch. At 4 of clock I sounded and had ground at 53 faddom, black sand and self peavell [pebble] stones, of red and black Colour, they were as bigg as pease and beanes. I hove the Lead again before I filled my sailes and had but 50 faddom water, but the same Soundings of sand and stones as before. At 4 of clock the wind came to the North a fine gale the sea pretty smooth I steered in WBN by my Compasse with a good saile, it being finely cleare.

[1] *Camarón/es* is the Spanish word for shrimp.
[2] Cabo Blanco (47°12′S, 65°45′W). See above, pp. 201, n. 4; 202, n. 2.

This wet weather and Cold Aire hath much impaired the men in their healths these 3 dayes. At 6 of clock I sounded and had ground at 50 faddom the same Soundings as before,[1] I could not see land I stood in West B*y* north, with an easy saile. At 8 of clock I sounded and had ground at 45 faddom, black sand and small peavell stones, irregular in shape, and of several Colours some gray with black spotts, some all black. At 10 of clock to night I sounded and had 38 faddom, self stones of white and black Colour as big as pease & beanes. I had sailed from 8 to ten, 8 miles WBN wind at N a fine gale but wet fog. At 10 of clock at night I lay by with my head sailes brased to the mast, with the Ships head to the WBN by my Compasse til 2 of clock in the morning, and drove 2 miles SW.

[44] **February 1669. The *Sweepstakes* off Cape Blanco. Lat*itude* 47°20′ S.**
At 2 of clock on munday morning I sounded and had 36 faddom, the same soundings as before. Then I tacked and stood off NEBN with a small saile to bring day light.

Munday the 21th. Cloudy hazy foggy weather, wind at North W a fresh gale I stood NEBN with a small saile to spend time, I dare not venture in with the shore till day light. At 4 of the clock I sounded and had ground at 42 faddoms, Large peavel stones as big as hazel nuts, some black, some whitish, I had sailed from two of clock till 4, foure miles NEBN by the compasse, the wind at NWBN. At 4 of clock this morning I tacked & stood in WBS, it being foggy wet weather and darke I lay by presently with my head to the Westward. I kept lights out all night, one in the main top, and one in the Poope hopeing the Pink would see them. At 6 of clock I filled the head sailes and stood in West by my compasse the wind at NBW a fresh gale and very foggy. I had men aloft to look out, but no Sight of the Pinke. At 7 of clock I sounded and had ground at 29 faddoms, Peavel stones but somewhat smaller then the other soundings. The wind came to the NBE a fine fresh gale. I stood in WBN. At 8 of clock this morning I sounded, & had 22 faddom self stones and some black sand, it was very hazy weather. A quarter of an houre past 8 of clock this morning I saw the Land, it bare West of mee, and was distant about 4 leagues. I sounded and had 21 faddom small stones and sand. I stood in still W by my Compasse. The land makes but of an ordinary height toward the sea side, but up in the Land it is good round high hills, and the land shows reddish, the northermost land that I could see bore NW of mee about 2 leagues, which was Cape Blanco, and the Southermost land of the face of the Cape. The land trended away to the Southward of mee Southwesterly of an ordinary height by the water side but in the Land hills table like on the tops, of no great height above the rest. The Land makes in hills and valleys all along like downes of an ordinary height. At 9 of clock this morning I braced the head sailes to the mast, and lay so halfe an houre till a fogg was over, that I might have a cleare to make the Land plaine, for I was within 5 miles of the shore side which made some what of a bay and the Sea breacked on the shore. I sounded and had 17 faddom, rough ground, but some small stones came up in the tallow of the Lead, and the lead all dinted by rocks. Between 9 & 10 of the clock there was a fine cleare, so as I could see the Land very plain. It shew reddish like seared[2] grass, no woods to bee seen in any of the hills or valleys, nor bushes, but all bare land, like grass downes in England. I dare not send my boat on shore for feare of loseing

[1] The same nature of the sea bed.

[2] Seared: Dried up, parched, withered. *NOED*.

it, being foggy, and also for sinking her at the shore the sea breaking so much on it, the wind being at NBE a fresh gale, and blows almost along the shore, and it being out but 24 houres before makes the sea run high. The land lyes by the sea side SSW and NNE

[45] **February 1669. the *Sweepstakes* off Cape Blanco. Lat*itude* 47°&c^a^. S.**
along as farre as I could see to the Southward. Wee could not see any fires or smoakes on the Land any where. The Land made in this forme when I first saw it, and was distant from it 4 leagues, by estimation.

[*blank space for view*][1]

Course made true after several courses from yesterday at noone till today at 9 of clock, when I was 3 leagues off the Land, is West 6°50′ northerly and Distance sailed 50·7 miles. Departure West 50 miles. Difference of Longitude West 01°15′. Diff*erence* of Latit*ude* N 00°06′. Latitude by account is 47°14′ S. No observation these 3 dayes it being foggy weather.
Meridian distance from the Lizard West 1014 Leag*ues* 1·7 mile.
Longitude at 9 of clock from the Lizard West 61°56′·6.
Longitude from Port Praya West 44°38′·5
Meridian Distance from Port Praya West 735 leag*ues* 1·5 mile.
Variation of the Compasse easterly 18°.
No mountains seen in the Land only table hills, and round hills of a meane height, about the height of the Land at Beachy, or at the Seaven Cliffs,[2] as the in-land is there. At ten of clock it being indifferent cleare weather, I bore away along the shore within 5 miles of it, and kept my Lead going, and had 18 and 19 faddams, sometimes small stones and sometimes rough ground. I steered along by my Compasse SSE and sometimes SBE. As I shot to the Southward I had deeper water 25 faddam shelly rocky ground. I could not see to make the Land plain for it was many times hazy and foggy, no danger as I could perceive but what showed it selfe, which were rocks neare the shore in many places, and the Sea brake on them. Sea shore is a beach steep up for foure leagues distance, and lyes North and South along. Then wee saw more to the Southward as wee sailed along, ragged rocks appeare of an indifferent height, and stood on the banks of the shore so as the sea beat against them. At 12 of clock I judge my selfe to bee in the Latitude of 47°32′ South. It being thick and hazy I could not have any observation of the Sun. My desire was to find a bay to anchor in so as I could but bring the Land in the wind of mee.[3] The wind at N a fresh gale at halfe an houre past 12 of clock I was a brest of the S craggy rocks which stand on the shoreby the sea side, and rocky Islands which are neare the shore, a litle to the Northward of the other rocks which are on the shore. These rocks on the maine stand on a point where there is a rounding in of a Bay. They make like a ragged building and a tower in it, which is a spired rock above the rest of an indifferent height and picked at his upper end.[4] The Islands showed very ragged with a low back in the midle, and shew gray, the other made black

[1] Blank space approximating to 4 lines of text.
[2] See above, pp. 251, 252, n. 1.
[3] Narbrough wished to find a bay where the land would shelter the ship from the wind.
[4] This point is identified below, on 24 Feb. as Punta de Lobos (47°58′S, 65°51′W). The bay to the south of Punta Lobos is Bahía de los Nodales.

[46] **February 1669. the *Sweepstakes* at Cape Blanco. Lat*itude* 47°&c^{a}. S.**
to our sight. I had thoughts to have anchored here, but when I edged in I saw a great deale of Broken rockes, I hove the Lead and had 22 faddom, rocky ground. I saw no safe place to anchor in. I steered away South a litle westerly, by my compasse along the shore, which makes in bayes, and broken ground Lyes before them above water. The Land is of an indifferent height neare the sea side in some rounding hills, but Larger flat topt hills into the Countrey. No trees to bee seen or any wood or bushes on the land, all grasse downes & hills

The rocks which are like a building and tower makes in this form when you are abreast of them. That is they W from you.	[*blank space for view*]

of a meane height. I steered SBW along the shore neare 8 leagues further, sailing within 5 miles of the shore side all along. The Land makes in hills & plaines with out wood, all along the sea shore in Low bayes and Beaches, and here and there some rocks stands up neare the shore or on it. I sounded all along as I sailed, and had 20 faddam and 25 faddom, sometimes rough ground and sometimes fine black sand. At 6 of clock this afternoone I brought to with my head to the Eastwards, and lay about an houre driveing, wind at NBW a fine gale. I could not see any place to anchor in with this wind, unlesse I would have stood into the bottom of the bayes, which I was unwilling to do till I saw which way the winds are enclined to blow most, and then I could better guide my selfe. The Land trends away to the South South West ward, so farre as I could see in a meane height. I sounded whilest I lay by and had 19 faddam rocky ground. I was in 5 miles of the shore. I kept men aloft to look out for the Pink. I concluded wee had shot past Port Desire Harbour, in the fogge, for the Island and rocks which wee saw were Pengwin Island, and the other Isles which lyes about it, and which Lyes to the Southward of Port Desire harbour. Many Seales seen to day, and Pengwins, and pyed Porpoises, and many sea fowles.
I took the Suns amplitude, and find 17°20′ variation East.
At 7 of clock I stood off with an easie saile, wind at NBW and blew a good fresh gale. Course NEBE by my Compasse, a pitching Sea runs in the offing. I could not observe the starrs it was over cast. I kept a light out all night in hope the Pink might see it, the aire cold to night. I have 14 men sick, which is for want of refreshing. At 12 to night the wind veared to the NNW a fresh gale, I sounded and had 38 faddom, gravell stones and fine red sand. I am now six leagues from the Land. I stood off till 3 of clock in the morning, wind at NNW, I lay up North East, and am now 8 leagues off. I sounded and had 40 faddam red sand with gravell grets [grits] in it. I tacked and stood in at 3 of clock WSW. The clouds breaks away, and a likelyhood of fine weather.

Tuesday the 22 day. Faire weather the clouds settle in the South east, wind at NWBN. At 4 of clock this morning I steered in for the Land WSW

[47] **February 1669. The *Sweepstakes* on the Coast of America Latit*ude* 48°20′ S.**
faire weather, no Sight of the Pink. I observed the Sun at noon on the meridian and found my Latitude 48°20′ South.

Litle wind this afternoone and smooth sea I hoisted out the boat and sounded, and had 27 faddom, fine black sand. I saw the Land about one of clock in the afternoone, I judge my selfe 5 leagues from the Land. It makes in large Downes and round hills, neare the water side. The Land is of a fair height. I caused the boate to ride at a grapnell[1] and try the tide or Current which way it sett. Wee found the tyde to set to the North B*y* east, an easie tyde, after the rate of a mile a watch.[2] The gale freshing I stood in with the shore, and sounded all along as I made way to the shore, and shoaldened the water by litle and Little,[3] sandy ground. In one league off the Land I had 17 faddom, Oazy sand. This evening about 6 of clock I got into the shore within two miles of it, and had 20 faddom water sandy ground, the wind at NW a fine gale, and fair weather the wind 3 points off the Land I anchored with my best Bower Anchor. It makes a self rounding Bay.[4] I found the flood to come from the Southward, [*right margin: anchor symbol*] I had no great tyde. I rode here all night, wind at NW a fresh gale. At my Anchoring I went ashore with my boat with ten men, wee were all [*right margin:* Land] provided with arms in Case of opposition. The shore side is steep up in a beach of small stones, and the water ebbs and flowes upward of 3 faddom up and downe, which wee saw by the Last full-sea marke, the water rise in the time wee were ashore. Wee went up a litle way into the Land, but saw no people, nor any animal. There went a path along the top of the Beach, frequented either by men or Beasts. The Land is dry, Sun scorched, and the grasse seared like dry hay, on the hills, no weeds nor so much as a bush to bee seen, nor fresh water. The Land is in rounding hills. No stones in the Land so farre as I went, which was not halfe a mile. So wee could see but litle of the shore, and night comeing on wee returned to the boate. I Caused my men to gather grasse and dry Sea-weeds, which lay at high water mark and make a fire that if the Pink should come along shee might see it, so wee made a great fire that burned till 12 of clock to night. This Bay wee called [Looke out Bay] and the Point on the North part [Look out Point][5] for I kept lights out all night, and men to Look out for the Pink if they could see her lights at any time in the night. Cold air to night and dark weather, yet the moon neare her full. It is 109 dayes since wee came from Port Praya, in the Island of St Iago, to this day being so long since any man was on Land till now.
By ten of clock to night I came aboard the Shipp, I sounded with my Lead all the way as I came from the shore to the Shipp, and had very good Sounding 11 faddom in 2 Cables length off the shore, gravelly ground, and so deepned by litle and Little, as I went off. I could not observe the exact time of ebbing & flowing, for in the Bay runs Counter tydes. But as neare as I could observe

[48] **February 1669. The *Sweepstakes* on the Coast of America. Lat*itude* 48° S.**
It is a high water on the full and Change day of the moone, at 11 of clock, it rises about 3 faddom perpendicular, and the flood tyde comes along the Coast from the Southward, and setts to the Northward. The ebb tyde comes from the Northward and setts to the

[1] A small anchor.

[2] A mile in 4 hours.

[3] I made my way to the shore, the water gradually shallower, sandy ground.

[4] The anchorage appears, from the subsequent description of the coast, to have been SW of Punta Mercedes (48°24′S, 66°30′W), although there is no significant 'rounding bay' in the area. See above, pp. 215, n. 1; 456.

[5] The square brackets are in the original. From the subsequent description of the coast Look out Point appears to be Punta Mercedes.

Southward. The tyde runs here at the strongest at the rate of 5 miles in 6 houres time. As for making of the Land & draughting it out, I have omitted as yet by reason I could not see it perfectly, it being foggy and hazy on the Land all along as I sailed. But I find I am more to the Southward by foure leagues, then the place where I stood off from on munday at 7 of clock. I rode fast all night, a self Shower of raine about 12 of clock to night. No sight of any lights but our own.

The Land makes thus at the Bay of Cape Lookout, where I first Anchored on this coast, when you are in two Leagues of the Bay.	[*blank space for views*]
Look out Bay in the Coast of Patagonea. Latit*ude* 48°26′ S.	

Wednesday being the 23[d] day, wind at NW a fresh gale, and a cold Aire and cloudy weather. This morning at 7 of clock I weighed and stood to the Northward along the shore to see for the Pink, for I could not judge otherwise of her, but Shee must bee in under the shore, or into the harbour of Port Desire. I went in my boat close under the shoreas the Shipp sailed along without, wee crossed over the Bay of S[t] Disues[1] which is neare 2 leagues over, there lyes a great deale of Broken rocky ground before it. It is the next bay to the Northward of Looke out Bay.[2] This Bay hath at the North point of it an Island[3] which shews copling up like a hay cock, and is whitish red. It is a rock where many sea fowles breeds, and there is innumerable quantities of Seals lyes on it. This Island lyes within halfe a Cables length of the point of the main Land:[4] a great tyde runs between it and the point. I went ashore on it and killed some Seales, and some fowles, and went off and Landed on the point of the maine. The tyde had neare sunk our boat it run so strong. I went on land here but could not go farre, For the tyde was up, and made this Point into 3 Isles. Here I saw where men had made a fire, and roasted Mussles and Limpits, and fowles bones, but no people to bee seene, nor any wild beast, excepting a hare which run out of the Long grasse. Here is prickly bushes much like Barberry bushes, no woods nor trees to bee seen. The land is grassy land of a gravell soyle, and plains, and large table hills in the Countrey, and round hills toward the water side. The sea shore is sandy Beaches, and rises in Cliffs in some places, as it does in Sole Bay in England.[5] some rocks lye Scattering about the shores.

[49] **February 1669. The *Sweepstakes* on the Coast of America.**
In a days times ten men would kill Seales and sea fowles enough to Lade a vessel of 50 tunns on this Island, for they lye as thick as sheep in Smithfield pens. Up in this Bay is a

[1] This appears to be Bahía Laura (48°24′S, 66°25′W). See above, p. 211, n. 1.
[2] The name is in large square brackets in original.
[3] Isla Rasa Chica.
[4] Cabo Guardián.
[5] Sole Bay or Southwold Bay (59°19′N, 1°40′E), between Lowestoft and Harwich off the Suffolk coast, was an open road used as a fleet anchorage during the Anglo-Dutch wars.

self river called St Doioves,[1] I did not go to it. This Island I called Seale Island. It is round and about a Cables length Diameter. It is about 2 leagues from Cape Look out NNE. There is to the seaboord of this Isle a ledge of rocks[2] which the sea Breakes on, which Lyes neare five miles off, [*right margin:* Rocks] EBS from the Island. You must go without them for there is foule ground within them. And 4 leagues from this Island into the sea E lyes a rock like the Eadeston [Edystone],[3] just dipping at the waters edge. The Shipp passed between the Rock and the ledge of rocks in a mile of the Eady Stone rock, and had 18 faddom water,

The Eady Stone lyes in the Latitude of 48°20′ S. rocky ground. They aboard saw the sea break much over, but could not see past a Spoot [spout or outcrop] of the rock as big as a boate. It Lyes dangerously in the fair way as a man sailes along the Coast. I make it to lye in the Latitude of 48°20′ S. The land in the Countrey that is anything remarkable is a sadle flat hill, which bears neare WNW from it. But there is no Certainty to bee observed by marks of that nature, for the shore is alike a long way and hath many Such hills. I put away from Seales Island, and rowed along to the Northward, in halfe a mile of the shore, wind at NW a fine gale. The Shipp was standing along to the N:ward about 2 leagues off the shore. The coast lyes from point to NNE and SSW by the Compasse, the seashore is in Beachey bayes and rocks. About 4 of the clock I put off the shore and went aboard, at 5 I got aboard and had the Seales and fowles handed in and Divided among the men, for fresh provisions, which they were very glad of. Many Seales and Penguins Swim*m*ing to and fro in this Bay. I stood as neare in to the shore as I could get, and anchored in 25 faddom, Oasy ground, about 5 miles from the shore, it was about 6 of clock and neare night. Very litle tyde runs here. I called this Seales Bay.[4] I was got about 8 leagues to the Northward of Look out Bay, here abouts is very good Soundings, 20 faddom, sandy ground, 4 miles off the shore; 15 faddom fine black sand, a league off the shore, 8 and 9 faddom faire by the shore, sandy oaze. Here is no rideing but only to stop a tyde or so, for the sea is open halfe the Compasse.

This evening it Looked very windy, the wind veared to the west. At 11 of clock it blew so much wind at west, and hailed, and Slatty Snow I was fearefull wee should have been blown off the shore. I ordered the Master to Lower the main yard and foreyard, a Porte Longs.[5] It continued till 4 of clock the next morning and held West all the time.[6]

[50] **February 1669. The *Sweepstakes* on the Coast of Patagonea. Lat*itude* 48° S.**

[*blank space for plan*] [7]

Thursday the 24th, hazy weather, wind at WNW a fresh gale. I had men up to the top mast head to Look abroad this morning, but no sight of the Pink. I judge Shee must be

[1] See above, pp. 210; 211, n. 1.

[2] Arrecife Guardián.

[3] Roca Bellaco (48°30′S, 66°11′W). See above, p. 210, n. 7.

[4] This is the bay SW of Punta Medanosa Latitude (48°06′S, 65°55′W).

[5] Down to the gunwale.

[6] 'Seales Bay' is the catch-word at the bottom of this page, which presumably refers to a plan which it was intended to insert in the blank space on the following page.

[7] The blank space approximates to 9 lines of text below the header.

in Port desire. I weighed about 8 of clock this morning and stood to the Northward with the Shipp. I went in my pinnace close along the shore as the Shipp sailed in the offing about 2 leagues off the shore. The shore side is in Beaches, and scattered rocks in many places. The Tyde of flood was with us. At the North end of Seales Bay there lyes a small rocky Island Coppling up like a hay Cock.[1] It is gray in Colour with fowles dung. Here runs a very strong tyde between this Isle and the maine. It lyes better then a Cables length from the Point of the maine. Here lyes a great many broken rocks about it. The main land is Low here by the sea syde, and sandy ground, But up in the Countrey it's Large Downes and hills. No woods nor trees to bee seen, nor fresh water any where, here is great numbers of Seales, and sea fowles on this Island. Wee called this Tom*m*a Hauke Island, for here was an [*margin:* Tomma Hauke Island] Indian club lost, which is called a Tomma Hawke by the Caribbi Indians at Suranam. This Island is all Craggy rock, and a litle bigger then Seale Island. This Island of Tomma hauke is 8 leagues to the NNE from Seales Island. There is to the northwest of this Island a deep rounding bay [*margin:* Spirings Bay] which is called Spirings bay[2] in the Charts. In this Bay lies 3 self Islands of an indifferent height. The Land in the Countrey over this Bay is Large high hills. Here is rocks lyes in the North part of this Bay. I crossed over this Bay in the Pinnace, and sounded as I went, and had 21 faddom, rough ground, in the midway. This Bay is 7 miles broad, and neare 3 leagues deepe. It rounds with a turning up to the North, Northwestward, behind a Point further than I saw. On this North part of this bay, on this rounding point stands the black rocks which makes like a ragged building, and a tower in it, which I writ of before at my comeing in with the Land.[3] I sailed close under this shore with my Boate. The shore is steep black rocks and Low bayes with Peavel stones, and sandy beaches, the grasse green on the hills. No woods nor trees nor fresh water seen. At the North East point of Spirings bay, the Land makes out full Like a foreland, and is faire high Land in Large plain hills, with sandy self Bayes.

[51] **February 1669. the *Sweepstakes* on the Coast of Patagonea Latit*ude* 48° S.**

And at the face of this foreland Lyes 6 rocky Islands. One is musket shott off the maine or nearer, the other is further of [off], the outermost is the biggest, which is in the Latitude of 47°55′ S. And is a mile from the point of the maine. This biggest Island is called Pengwin Island.[4] It [*right margin:* Pengwin Island] is indifferent high at the ends and Low in the midle. It is neare ¾ of a mile Long, NNE and SSW and neare halfe a mile broad E and W. It is all craggy rocks except in the Low of the midle, that is gravell, and in the Sum*m*er time a litle green grasse. The great black gannets lay their eggs there, and the Pengwins[5] layes all over the Isle, on the rocks and under the rocks in holes; The Seales lyes

[1] There are a number of islands off Punta Medanosa. This is probably Isla Liebres, the largest, and closest to the point, which is about 1 cable off shore.

[2] Bahía de Nodales (48°00′S, 65°52′W). It is shown as Spiering Bay on the Doncker chart, Plate 2. See above, p. 210, n. 3.

[3] Punta Lobos, described in *South America Pilot*, II, para. 3.70, as 'composed of remarkable pillars of rock, the highest of which appears to be formed of large superimposed blocks'.

[4] Isla Pingüino (47°55′S, 65°43′W).

[5] Magellanic penguins. See above, p. 276, n. 4.

all about the sides of the Island. So many Seales[1] Pengwins, and sea fowles are on these Islands, the report will bee thought incredible by them that have not seen them, the quantity of each Creatures are numberlesse that are there dayly. All these 6 Islands are full of Seales, But the Penguins frequents the greater Island most. I put ashore at one of these Isles at this time, and took in 3 hundred Pengwins in lesse then half an houres time into my Boate. I could have taken three thousand in the time if my Boate would have carried them, for it is driveing whole flocks to the boats side as shee lyes by the shore and 2 or 3 men with short truncheons knock them on the head, and the rest heave them into the boate. The Seales will run over a man if hee do not stand out of their way. The shipp was standing to the Northward about 2 leagues off. Here is many broken rocks and foule ground lyes in amongst these Islands. The tydes run very strong here, between these Islands, and without the point of the outermost it makes a great riplin, which is the strength of the tydes reverse off from the Islands against the other tyde. To the Northward of these Islands there is a Bay of 4 leagues Long, and a league and halfe deepe. In the northwest therof is the harbour of [*right margin:* Port Desire] Port Desire which wee could see from Pengwin Isle, it bore NW from Pengwin Isle, and was Distant about 3 leagues. In this bay about in the midle of it, there is steepe white Cliffs about two miles long, the upper part of the Cliffe is black in strakes downe a fourth part, which is occasioned by the water's drayneing [draining] downe on it. The Land is plaine on the topp of these Cliffes, But further into the Countrey it is high rounding hills and downes, and towards the water side Low, and at the South part of this Bay it is Craggy rocks, on the maine like walls of great houses, neare the sea. There is a sandy Cove to hale a boat up in fowle weather, if [*right margin:* sandy Cove] occasion require.[2] The Cove is just under these wall-like rocks, and lies in the Latitude of 47°54′ S by my obs*ervation* of ☼.
About 6 of clock this afternoon the Shipp stood into the Bay. I went aboard and had good Soundings as I came off, 14, and 16, and 17, faddom black sand, a league off the shore, in the midle of the Bay. When I was aboard the Shipp and had got in the Pengwins, I plyed into the Bay. At 7 of clock I anchored in

[52] **February 1669. The *Sweepstakes* in the Bay of Port Desire.**
sixteen faddom fine oazy sand, about a league off the maine. The white Cliffes bore WBS of mee, and Pengwin Island bore SE of mee, and the harbours mouth bore NW of mee by the Compasse, and was distant about 5 miles. Wind at West a fine gale wee saw a Peeked rock, stand up like a watch tower on the plaine Land of the South side of the harbour.[3] It is halfe a mile from the sea side, and stands singly by it selfe, as if it were purposely built for a mark to know the harbour, for it may bee seen in cleer weather two leagues, if it bee not shut in against other hills which are up in the Countrey.[4] But as you come from the Northward you will see it very plaine at that distance; Over the harbours mouth North West into the Land there is high round topped hills, which shew white in two spotts, as big as a top gallant saile. And on the North side of the harbour's mouth (a

[1] Probably either the South American sea lion, or South American fur seal. See above, pp. 191, n. 2; 208, n. 12; 217, n. 1.

[2] It is not possible to be sure which sandy cove Narbrough is referring to: it could be the cove close North of Punta Norte, 2 miles West of Isla Pingüino.

[3] El Torreón. See above, p. 204, n. 6.

[4] If it is not obscured by the background hills.

litle within) the Land is of a good height, in Copleing hills, and on the South side of the harbours mouth the land is but of a mean height and plain. Neare two miles to the Southward this watch tower stands on the plaine land. It is but a quarter of a mile from the water of the harbours mouth to this watch tower, which I shall speak more of herafter. I found but an easy tyde run here, and the flood comes from the Southward. The tyde did rise 2 faddom and a halfe where the Ship rode. It is a high water here in the Bay at two of clock on the full & change dayes of the moone. Many Seales swim*m*ing about the Shipp.

This morning one man of my Company dyed, diseased of the Scurvy. Humph Smith by name, hee had lived in Bucklers bury[1] London. This is the Second man of my company deceased since I came out of the Downs. I kept a light out all night.

Fryday the 25th, faire weather, wind at West a fine gale. This morning I went away with my Boate into the harbour, and sounded it, and went on Land to see if wee could discover any People, and fresh water. I put up a flagg on a staffe and stuck it on a hill, there left it, and Came away. Wee found a small pond of good fresh water, neare the river side. In a rocky valley on the North side wee saw where people and dogs had been not Long before. Wee saw a grave on the top of a hill, which was covered over with peeces of rocks, wee saw the bones of the dead. It being neare a low water I rowed in my boate from place to place in the river and sounded, and viewed the rocks which lay most dangerous, and so came Sounding the harbour, all the way out to the Shipp, the Shipp being come nearer to the harbour's mouth. I could not see any signe of the Pink's being here, which make mee judge it would not bee long before Shee would come here, or else wee should have sight of her as Shee passed by, for I believe Shee cannot bee shot past mee to the Southward but wee must have seen her. I found 5 faddom & a halfe, and six faddom water, no lesse water all along the harbour at a Low water, till I came to the Shipp, which rode in six faddom, in the entrance of the harbours mouth it was a deade Low water and Spring tydes. The Channell is of a good breadth.

[53] **February 1669. The *Sweepstakes* off of Port Desire.**

And just before you come at the narrowest part, which is at the Chaps[2] of the two points of the Land, a Cables length without the point, on the North side, there Lyes two rocks in the Channel,[3] which are as big as two small boats, and they are dry by halfe ebb, and under water by halfe flood. They Lye on the North side of the Channell, and in the Streame of one another, about 20 paces distant from one another. There is 5 faddom water at a low water, close to them on the South side, and gravelly ground; and on the North side 3 faddom water peavell stones, and a stones Cast above them to the west, there is 8 and 9 faddam water, it makes something of a bitt, these rocks have a small Ledge runs from one to the other which lyes under water, 2 faddom at a Low water. The best going in is to keep the South side, and you will have 7 faddom water, till you come within the two rocks, which lyes in the Channell. Then keepe in the midle and you will have no danger, for you will soone bee shott within the narrow where you may ride safe, being abreast of the Cliffy rocks on the South side,[4] and on the North side you will have a beach bay, which wee

1 Bucklersbury, London, EC4.

2 Chop or chapp. The entrance of a channel.

3 Rocas de la Guardia.

4 This would appear to be Punta Lista, 33 ft. (10 m).

called Copers bay.[1] It is to the Westward of a ridge of bluff rocks which are on the rivers edge[2] where some fowles do breed on them. There I rode in the midle of the river, in 6 faddom water at a low water, oazy ground, and flat rocky Isles two Cables length above mee on the North side, which the tyde Covers towards a high water those next to mee. And in the midle of the Channel there lyes a round rock, which is covered by halfe flood or before.[3] It lyes neare 3 Cables length above where I rode, on the South side, for there runs up the Channel of which I shall[4] speak more and draught it out better to bee understood. The river or harbours mouth lyes in directly west, as I said before in Comeing in you had best keep the South side and take your Soundings off there, for one [on] the North side it is broken sunken rocks[5] which you will see very well come off from a small rocky Island,[6] which lyes on the North side a mile without the harbour and a steep Cliffe rock on the maine. The sea makes a breach on [breaks over] them, or you may see growing rockweed which is good notice of shoale water. Now for the South side at the goeing in there you will see at a low water a long ledge of rocks,[7] which comes from the South point of the Land of the harbours mouth,[8] which is an Island at halfe flood, (for the tyde hath a passage between) these ledge of rocks are flat, and run out with a point, a mile SEBE into the Sea. These rocks I called mussel bank, for there is many mussels and Limpits on it. At your comeing in you may bee bold to borrow[9] neare the mussel Bank, and take your shoaldings 3,4,5, or 6 faddom sandy Chingly ground, off it also you may come to an Anchor if occasioned, you will see growing weeds neare the edge of it in two faddom water. You may saile in up to the narrow all along according to these directions, along by the South side. Over on the North side of the channel at the point of the mussel banke you will have deeper water 12 and 14 faddam foule ground.[10]

[54] February 1669. The *Sweepstakes* off of Port Desire.

You must also have that care as you come out of the sea to goe for the harbour, that you do not run up on the backside of the mussel bank, that is to say on the South side of the mussel banke, for up there, there is a ham or round bay, and you will imbay your selfe there, and bee in danger, for there is shoale water. There is passage into the harbour that way for boats towards a high water, wee called these the old haven.

As you come out of the sea to go in for the harbour, and you have sight of the watch tower rock edge [*blank*][11] to the Northward till you see the harbour open, and keep your lead going, and you will have 10, 9, 8, and 7 faddam water, gravely sand, then you will see the mussel-bank, and the seabreak on it, as you saile up along the North side of it, and you will bring the harbour open. You will see the 2 Diamond rocks[12] which lyes

[1] This is the area where the town of Puerto Deseado now stands.

[2] Punta Cascajo.

[3] Roca Magallanes.

[4] 'I shall' repeated and struck through.

[5] Restinga Foca.

[6] This is the island at the extremity of Península Foca.

[7] Restinga Chaffers.

[8] Isla Chaffers.

[9] To approach close to or hug.

[10] Unsuitable for anchoring.

[11] The missing word is probably 'keep'.

[12] These are Rocas de la Guardia which are shown on Narbrough's plan of Port Dissier (Plate 1), as Diamond. The Rocas dos Hermanas lie on the rocks fringing the shore on the North side a little further up the channel.

without the narrow. On the South side, opposite to the Diamond are black steep Rocks Low to the water, you may go close to that place, there is ten faddom at a Low water, there you will see all the harbour's mouth open. The narrow is a great bow shoot over from side to side. Within It growes broader. It is above 2 Cables length over where I rode (which is a mile within the narrow. On the North side at the narrow it is a steep Beachy point and Covered with grasse, and 3 or 4 bushes growes upon it. And in the ham[1] within there are a parcell of rocks, which the tyde overflowes. I wish you to take notice of them. There is a litle Cove-bay by them. The Land on the South shore is Beach to high water marke, there the bank rises of a meane height to the Levell of the Land, within it hath grasse and bushes grows on it. At a Low water there lyes 2 rocks as big as a good boat but they are close to the shore side. They are covered by halfe flood. The river is rocky on both shores after you are within the narrow, all along excepting here & there a small Beachy Bay.

The best going in is at a Low water, and then all the danger is seene and you will see the Channel the better, and where to Anchor. It is a very fair channel, and a fair inlet, and out let. The tydes run very strong here on the Spring tydes, and rise and fall neare 4 faddom on high tydes.

Saturday the 26, fair weather, & the wind at west, a stiffe gale. I kept a light out all night, that if the Pink did come along Shee might see it. Also at the the first part of the night there was a great fire ashore in the grasse which wee made on purpose for the Pink. Cold weather this morning. At 7 of clock I manned both my boates and went into the harbour, the Shipp rode mored at the harbour mouth, within the mussel bank in 6 faddom water, at Low water. When I went into the harbour I sent men up on the hills on the North shore to looke abroad for the Pinke, and also to make a fire in the dry grasse that the Pink might see the smoake if Shee bee in sight of Land, hereabouts. But no sight could they get of her. I sounded the harbour in many places to day at a low water

[55] **February 1669. The *Sweepstakes* before Port Desire.**

And found it a very good harbour for great shipping to ride in, Provided they have good Cables and Anchors. I searched the shore about, but could not see any wood or tree in the land nor very litle fresh water. The land is hilly and large Downes, very few bushes, but dry long grasse, growing in tuffs and knots. The soyle of the earth is gravelly and dry, in some valleys a good mixture of black mold. No people to bee seen, or fire or smoake but that which wee made. I saw in several places where they had Laid behind a bush on grasse which they had pulled up, and there they had made small fires and roasted mussles and Limpits, there lay wooll and feathers and bones of beasts, and shivers of flint stones. I went to the flagg which I left on a hill yesterday, with beads at it, But no body had been at it. Wee let it stand still. No beast seen any where except 2 hares, which run over the hills this day. Wee did not go past a mile and a halfe into the Land at this time, by reason of viewing the harbour. The Land is hot amongst the hills; on the North shore in the valleys between the rocks there grows abundance of wild pease, which had green leaves and blossomes, the leaves tasted like green pease leaves in England, and the blossoms very

[1] Ham or round bay, south of Mussel Bank, See above, p. 417.

like those in England, and blewish, the leaves and blossoms grows on vines, and tangle together.[1] Also in the same valleys there grew very sweet smelling herbs, much like tares, very green, and white and yellow flowers. Also there is green herbs much like Sage, but grows in knotts, neare the ground like Lettuce,[2] these leaves are with the pease leaves very good saletting to refresh men that are enclineing to the Scurvey, as I had several men that were, for want of fresh provisions. Here is abundance of muscles and Limpits on the rocks, very good ones. Here is an Island where many Seales frequent in the river,[3] and sea fowles, as pied Dyvers as bigg as ducks, and gray Dyvers,[4] and black Shaggs[5] and ducks and other sea fowle breeds on them amongst the rocks and bushes. I went on land to day upon one of these and got as many young black Shaggs in their nests, as laded the Pinnace. As for all the particulars of the fowles and other things seen here, I will mention herafter, when I have better discovered; Night comeing on, and it began to blow hard, I went aboard, with herbs and fowles, and such things as I had got to day. I divided all things equally to the whole Company. The boy had his Dividend as large as my own or any mans else. Partiality was Laid aside this voyage.

It blew hard this evening at west, and looked very black in the SW, an ordinary gale. I kept out a light all night in the Poop, for the Pink. This day all the Company eat of the young Seales and Pengwins, and Com*m*ends them for very good food. I judged this a very Convenient harbour to fit the Shipp, for the main mast must be unrigged, and shrowds fitted, and ballast must bee

[56] **February 1669. The *Sweepstakes* at Port Desire harbour.**
had. Also I saw it a good place for refreshment and fresh water to bee had, and it might bee a meanes to fall with the Pinke, for wee could see a great way into the sea, from the Tops of the hills, that if Shee came neare the Coast wee must needs see her.

Sunday the 27th, wind at West a fresh gale, fair weather. This morning I weighed at young flood, and turned up to the narrow, then kedged up with my top sailes and mizzon, to the place where I anchored and mored, with my best Bower to the Westward and the small Bower to the Eastward, both Laid in 6 faddom at a low water. At a high water, 9 faddom and a quarter. The westerly winds are the worst winds here, for they are most frequent, and given to hard gusts downe the river, and that Lies open.

[1] This would appear to be a variety of *Lathyrus*, either *L. nervosus*, or *L. magellanicus*. I am grateful to the Natural History Museum, London, for this identification.

[2] It has not been possible to suggest a positive identification these herbs. The plant like a tare might be *Vicia magellanica*, Moore *Flora*, pp. 145–7. It might likewise be *Anarthrophyllum desideratum*, ibid., pp. 145–6, a shrubby ground-cover plant which grows in the area, and has many pea-like varieties. There are many possibilities for the sage-like plant. *Chenopodium antarcticum*, ibid., pp. 89–91, has the most lettuce-like base but it might equally well be one of the varieties of *Atriplex*, ibid., pp. 91–4, or *Gamochaeta americana*, ibid., pp 232, 238.

[3] This is presumably the Seal Island shown on Narbrough's plan of 'Port Dissier' (Plate 1), now known as Isla de los Leones.

[4] Divers are not found in this part of the world. These may be grebes, which are similar birds, possibly the great grebe (*Podiceps major*), the silvery grebe (*P. occipitalis*), or the white-tufted grebe (*P. Rolland*), all of which are found in the coastal waters of Patagonia. Harris, *Guide*, pp. 35–6.

[5] See above, p. 216, n. 5.

Munday the 28th, fair weather, wind at NW a fresh gale. This morning I unbent my sailes, and made a tent ashore against the Shipp,[1] and put the sailes ashore that had need of mending, and set the saile makers to worke to mend them and others to unrigg the mast & put up a new sett of shrowds assoon as possible might bee. I went ashore on the North side and set a watch on the topp of the hill to Look out to seaboord for the Pinke.

I went with ten men along the shore to Look for fresh water, wee found two springs of fresh water, one in a valley Close by the water side, in a gully above the Shipp, up the river, halfe a mile. The other up a valley between the rocks just abreast where the Shipp rode, about half a mile from the rivers side, right up from Coppers Bay in the same valley.[2] These Springs are but small and the water is a litle Bracky or saltish, for the earth is naturally saltish. The dry valleys, the ground and rocks have a white rime of saltpeter hang on it. I went into the Land two miles NW and saw the Countrey hilly and dry Land without wood or water, some Craggy rocks and valleys Low, but dry, of a salt peter nature. Here and there some bushes of prickly branches & leaves Like white thorne Bushes in England. These lesser bushes have self dry Gals grows on them, and a litle dry hot seed in the mouth, of a savour like weake pepper. Not a tree seen any where. The Land is of a gravelly sandy soile generally and tuffs of seared dry grasse grows on it. I digged in several places, But saw nothing but gravelly sand and Rocks, no manner of mettall or minerall I Looked also among the broken rocks for mettles but saw no signe of any. On the topps of the hills I could see a great way into the Land, and all hills and Downs as is in Cornwal, wearisome travelling for those that are not much used to it. I could travel as farre in an houre as many of my men Could do in two.

To day we say [saw] 9 beasts feeding on the grasse, which were much

[57] **March 1669. The *Sweepstakes* in Port Desire Harbour.**

Like Deere but Larger, and Longer necks a good matter, and without hornes, they were redish of colour aloft and white under their bellies and up their flanks.[3] When wee came within a furlong of them they Looked very earnestly on us, and fell a neighing like young horses, a good while one answered the other and then ran away.

Tuesday the first of March 166$^{9}/_{70}$, fair weather wind at North and a fine gale and Cold air. I went and filled the water out of the spring into Casque and digged the spring deeper. I put a white cloth on a long Pole, and went and put it up on a hill neare a mile into the Land, where it might best bee seene to the in habitants. I left Beads, a looking glasse, a knife, a hooke, and a hatchet, in a box by it, to try if the people of the Countrey would show themselves unto us.

This afternoone I went about the hills but could not see any people, or fire or smoake, I saw 3 Estridges, but could not get neare them to have a shoot [shot]. They were feeding on grasse, but soon espied us. I had a greyhound with mee which I let slip at the Ostridges, and had a long Chase after one of them, at last gave her a turn, But Shee recovered the hills and ran away; they run a mighty pace.[4] They are gray in Colour and larger then a great

[1] From the entry on 11 March this would appear to have been on the north shore.

[2] Coopers Bay is not shown on the Narbrough's plan of 'Port Dissier' (Plate 1), but the spring is shown, located within the north shore slightly less than a mile inside Punta Cascajo, the northern entrance point.

[3] Guanaco. See above, p. 214, n. 2.

[4] Darwin's rhea; see above, pp. 207, n. 4; 214, n. 4. They are capable of bursts of speed over 30 mph (50 kph). Harris, *Guide*, p. 23.

turky cock in England. They cannot fly, they have long legs and trust to their run*n*ing. I saw two handfulls of wooll amongst the grasse where the natives had made a fire. This wooll is much like the Spanish red wooll which they bring out of India. It is very fine, and of the Colour of a red hatt, I brought it away. I saw three of the great beasts like deere. I set the greyhound at them but Shee could not come neare them, they run so swift. They have feet cloven like Deere.[1] Night coming on I returned aboard. At 7 of clock this night the wind came to the North a fresh gale & hazy weather. No sight of the Pink to day. I could see a great way from the hills. At 10 of clock to night it rained, the wind came to the East.

Wednesday the 2^d^. Cloudy rainy weather, wind at SE and blows hard wee mored the Shipp better to passe. The tyde ran very strong both ebb and flood these Spring tydes. The tydes run as strong as the tyde at gravesend.[2] It is high water in the harbour at halfe an houre past eleaven of clock on the full and Change days of the moone. The flood tyde rises 3 faddom & halfe.

Thursday the 3^d^, blowing rainy weather, wind at SE and veared to the SSE, no stirring to day this evening the wind Came to the E and blew a fine gale all night.

Fryday the 4, faire weather wind at E a fine gale. This morning I went on shore and filled fresh water, the rest of the Sea men fitted rigging. This day at 12 of clock I went with both boats, and 40 men, to Seale Island[3]

[58] **March 1669. The *Sweepstakes* in Port Desire Harbour.**

In the Harbour, every man his staffe and Clubb. Wee landed and drove the Seales up together, and besett them round, and in halfe an houres time wee had killed above foure hundred Seals young and old. Strikeing them on the head kills them presently, assoon as wee had knock'd them down wee cut their throats that they might bleed well whilest they were hott. Then I laded bothe the boates with them, and Carried them to the Bay where the tent was, and landed them & layd them upon the rocks. So the Boats fetched them all down to night.

The great Seals are as big as Colts, and much like Lyons all the fore parts, shaggy haire on their necks, and their head and face and mouths do much resemble a Lyon, also they roare like a Lyon. The female Seales are like Lionesses afore,[4] only they are hairy all over their skin as a horse is smooth and sleek haire, and the male Seale is smooth haire all over his hind parts. Their shape is very deformed for their hinder parts points away smaller and smaller till it comes to a Period. There grows out two finns or feet. They can go on land a great pace, and Clamber upon high rocks, and on good high hills, they delight to Lye & sleepe ashore much. some are very large upwards of eighteen foot long, and bigger about then a Butt is in the Bilge, and extream fatt, there are thousands fowerteen foot

[1] Guanaco.

[2] Today the tide at Gravesend runs at up to 2·7 knots at Spring tides. The rate was probably similar at this time.

[3] Narbrough's plan of 'Port Dissier' (Plate 1) indicates this is now Isla de los Leones.

[4] i.e. at the forward end.

Long. The common sort are about five foot Long, all mighty fatt.[1] The[y] will gape at you when you come to them as if they would devour you presently, two men will have Labour enough to kill one of the great ones with handspikes[2] which is the best weapon to kill them with.

[*blank space*] [3]

Saturday the 5th, fair weather wind at SW a fine gale. This morning wee went ashore and fleaed [flayed] the Seales and cut the bodies out in good handsome peeces and salted it well in bulke on deal boards ashore that the blood may drayne from it, the meat looks as well and as white as any Lamb, and it is now very good victuals, but when it is a litle salt it will eat much better. These are all young Seales that wee dresse for they suck'd of their dams. The old female Seale comes ashore and falls a bleating, Imediatly her young ones comes bleating like Lambs about her, and fall to Sucking. One old one will suckle foure or five which wee have seen, and shee beats away other young ones that comes neare her, which gives mee to believe they have 4 or 5 at a time. These young are as big as a midleing dog which wee kill[e]d to eate

[59] **March 1669. The *Sweepstakes* in Port Desire Harbour.**
And the great ones wee cut off the fatt and made oyle [oil] of it for the Lamps and other uses in the Shipp. The oyle of the young ones wee eat in frying provisions with it. It is very sweet and good to fry any food with, our men say it is as good as olive oyle. Most of my men to day gathered of these green pease leaves, and other herbs for Sallets [salads], some eat them raw, some boyles it. It is good refreshing for their bodies. Fair weather to night, the wind came to the West and towards morning blew hard.

Sunday the 6th, blowing weather wind at West. This day after prayers I went ashore on the South side of the river, and travelled 8[4] miles into the land SWBW having twelve armed men with mee, my Lieutenant went up the river in the boat 9 or ten miles to see for People that way, my other Lieuten*an*t went on the North side with ten armed men, to see for people and to view the Land. I found in my travels one of the great beasts like Deere, dead, and was whole, the vermine had not touched him. All his back was pretty Long wooll of the Colour of dryed roses, leaves, and down his sides. His belly was white wooll. Hee was as big as a small Colt. Hee had a long neck and a head like a sheep, and mouth and ears like a sheep, mighty Long legs and Cloven footed like a deer, a short bushy hairy tayle of a redish Colour, no horns, nor never had any. It was male. I believe these beasts are the Peruvian vianacos. I caused his paunch to bee opened & searched for the Bezoar stone[5] in it, and in the Pipe to the stomach. I turned them inside out, but could not find

[1] The South American sea lion. See above, pp. 208, n. 12; 217, n. 1.

[2] Handspike: a stave of tough ash used to turn the windless to raise the anchor.

[3] The space approximates to 6 lines of text.

[4] The figure '6' struck through.

[5] Bezoar stone, believed to be a counter poison or antidote. The stone was a calculus or concretion found in the stomach or intestine of some animals, chiefly ruminants, formed of concentric layers of animal matter deposited round some foreign substance, which serves as a nucleus. In South America they were found in sea mammals like manatees, as well as ruminants like llamas. *NOED*.

any. I have heard the West Indian Spaniards say that they take the Bezoar Stone out of Guinacos which caused mee to search this beast, which I believe is a Guianaco. In travelling to day I saw several Companies of Guianacos, some ten, some 30, some 40 in a Company. I could not come neer any of them to have a shoot. They neigh like so many young horses and so wander away. I saw 9 ostridges in a Company, but they would not suffer us to come in shoot of them. I put my greyhound at them but they out run her up the hill. Wee saw a fox,[1] and a wild Dog, and 5 or 6 hares, the greyhound killed one, they are larger then English hares, and much of the Shape of our hares, only they have a litle stubbe instead of a tayle, about an inch long, no hair on it.[2] These hares holes in the ground like Coneys. No woods nor tree seen in the Land, some bushes like thornes, the land is Dry of a gravelly sandy soyle, In large rounding hills not very high but in Downs and valleys, nothing growing on them but grasse. I saw here & there fresh water in Gullies in the valleys, which is made in the winter when the snow dissolves. I saw several places of saltwater in the Land, which is occasioned by the natural saltnesse of the Earth. No kind of fruit seen or herbe.

[60] **March 1669. The *Sweepstakes* in Port Desire Harbour.**

When I was at the furthest and on a hill, I could not see any signe of people nor woods, but still hills and valleys so farre as I could descrye. No fowles seene but kites[3] which are like those in Europe, and small birds like Sparrows[4] and Linnets, some flies and humble bees seen, here wee saw some small animals run*n*ing on the grasse with four feete, they are speckled gray in shape like a small Creature in England called an effet.[5] No venemous Creature seen in the Land, nor Adder nor snake. Cattle would live here very well as Cowes and horses and sheepe, goats &c[a]. Evening growing on I returned to the Shipp, it being within night before wee got aboard of our Boate. At ten of clock at night I got aboard of the Shipp. My Lieutenant which went up the river was aboard, but they which went on the North side were not come. Up the river they saw five small Islands which had sea fowles on them; and bushes, which will serve for fuell. The river grows broad upwards, and hath severall rocks in it. They saw on the shore Guianacos, Ostridges, and hares. No people, nor fire, nor smoake. They saw where people had been and made fires, and rosted mussles and Limpits. No fresh water, nor wood, nor any kind of mettall or mineral. The Land hilly, grasse growing on them.

At 12 of clock to night they that went on the North shore came aboard. They had been about eight miles into the Land, NW, saw no people. They saw where people had made fires in the grasse, and where they had layd grasse to the bushes to set on fire. They saw several places where people had Lay'd on open places, and layd bushes in halfe moones to shelter the wind & weather off them. On the top of a hill in the Land our men made a fire

[1] The culpeo fox and the Argentine grey fox are both found in this area. See above, p. 208, n. 2.

[2] Mara or Patagonian hare. See above, p. 207, n. 5.

[3] The only members of the kite family (Accipitridae) found in this area are the cinereous harrier and long-winged harrier. See above, p. 208, n. 4.

[4] The house sparrow (*Passer domesticus*) is now a common resident having been introduced from Europe. The rufous-collared sparrow (*Zonotrichia (Junco) capensis*) is described as 'sparrow-like' and a very common breeding resident in Tierra del Fuego and all South America, so these were probably the latter. Harris, *Guide*, pp. 117–18.

[5] Effet, old form of eft, a small lizard or lizard-like animal; the name is now chiefly applied to the greater water newt. *NOED*.

with grasse, to see if any[1] would answer them. They sate down by it, but could not see any fire any where all the day but their owne. The Land is in rounding Large hills, not very high, but like downes, as the Land is on the Coast of Yorkshire about Burlington. No woods nor trees seen nor fresh water – here and there a bush growing in a valley, indifferent good grasse. The Land of a Dry sandy gravelly soile, and some ridges of rock. They saw Guiancos, & Ostridges, and hares, and kites. No kind of Fruit or berry. Several litle Creatures like effets. No mineral or mettal. I charged them to bee mindfull as they travelled in any Gullies where water had run, to see if they Could find any grains of Gold, or any mettal &c[a]. for gold is found in grains in such Gullies, and much gold is found on this Land, on the other side, which is not two hundred leagues to it from us. They tell me the Land is very dry, and much salt peter hangs on the Earth, in a kind of floure, where water hath beene, the Swashes of water which they saw, were as salt as brine, which the earth made so.

[61] **March 1669. The *Sweepstakes* in Port Desire harbour.**
Munday the 7th. Cloudy rain-like weather, wind at West and veared to the South and SE and came to the East and NE towards noone, and blew a stout gale all day. This morning some hands went on shore and made a Pickle, and salted the Seales flesh into Caske, and pickled it up full. Wee had five punchions and foure hogsheads full, all sweet and good meate and looked very well as any Porke. Wee eat it aboard instead of beefe. The men aboard fitt the rigging. Wind at E all night; filled water, and trimmed Casque &c[a]. till fryday.

Fryday the 11th, wind at West a fresh gale I went ashore and filled eight hogs heads of fresh water, wee let the Cask lye at the well. The boats fetched ballast. The Coopers and saile makers at work ashore, on the North side right against the Shipp and in Call of the Shipp. I picked out a Crew of men which did least, and went on the North side and went northwesterly into the land five or 6 miles wee being ten in Company armed. The land inward is hills and vallies, grasse land and dry, no woods nor tree; litle scrabby [scrubby] bushes, here and there. Very weary some travelling, and scarce of fresh water. The soyle is rocky and dry sandy Earth with gravell stones. No people to bee seen. Several places where they had burned the grasse. There wee saw a great plaine from off the hills which might bee ten or 12 miles from the tent, where our Coopers were at worke. In this plaine I saw above a hundred Guianacos in a Company. some small bushes in it. This plain lies East and West. One part goes down to the sea, the other part runs into the Countrey up to rounding hills. Wee saw Ostridges to day, and hares, wee sprung a brace of partridges, as wee were travelling. They were bigger then English partidges and grayer, they fly much alike and make a blurring with their wings.[2] Wee saw a small flock of Stares[3] much like those of England. Wee saw several Snipes[4] to day, I shot 3 of them. Several kites[5] soaring

[1] 'body' struck through.

[2] This might be the Patagonian tinamou. See above, p. 208, n. 5.

[3] Stare: A bird of the genus *Sturnus*. Starling. *NOED*. Starlings are not found in Patagonia, and it is not certain that Narbrough was indeed referring to starlings.

[4] The common snipe (*Gallinago (Capella) gallinago paraguaiae*), is found throughout this area. Harris, *Guide*, p. 81.

[5] The kites, hawks and harriers found in this area are the white-tailed kite, red-backed hawk, and the cinereus harrier and long-winged harrier. See above, p. 208, n. 4.

over our heads one of our Company shot one of them. Wee saw 3 foxes, and one dog, which would not come neare us, neither did hee run away. I judge him to bee an Indians dog, & would not let our people shoot him, nor set our dogs on him but let him goe his way. I observed which way hee went, thinking hee would go to his master. But hee went snushing[1] sometimes one way and sometimes another way, and at last went away amongst the hills further then wee could go. So returned to the Shipp wee got down by 7 of clock at night very weary.

Saturay the 12th, blowing weather wind between the West and the West and the Northwest. Wee filled what fresh water wee could, and fetched Ballast. Our men gathered very good mussles and Limpits. I have seene very good fish in the harbour but cannot take any with hookes, and here

[62] **March 1669. The *Sweepstakes* in Port Desire Harbour.**
is never a good place to hale the Saine[2] on shore, also wee haveing plenty of Seale and Pengwins wee never tryed to shoot the net. I saw mighty large Smelts of 18 inches long lye dead on the shore. I could never as yet see any oysters or shells any where, or Crawfishes, or Lobsters, or Crabs, yet the place is very likely to have all these. I saw one fish which the Seales chased on shore, the time wee were standing by the water side, which fish was as large as a good mackrel, and much like a mullet, one of the men tooke it up and dressed it when wee came on board. It was a mighty good fish. Here must bee great quantities of fish for to maintain all these Seales, and fowles which live altogether on fish, and nothing else, and they are all mighty fatt. I have seen the Seales swimming with their heads above water, with large fish in their mouths, in this harbour. And fowles as Pengwins, Divers, and Shaggs are innumerable on this Coast, and all fish eaters, besides other Creatures which wee have not seen as yet, which live wholly on fish.

Sunday the 13th, wind at west, the air Cold. This morning I went up the river with my boat in Company with 14 men, all of us having arms. I went past the Island[3] where the brushy bushes are, where wee had the young Shaggs. The river grows broad, neare a mile from the North shore, Crosse the river to the South, and Continues that breadth foure miles. It lies up West B*y* South, then it grows narrower, and turns away SW. At this turning there is an Island[4] which is of a mean height and rocky. some small bushes and grasse grows on it. I went ashore on this Island I saw a post set up on end out of the ground neare five foot. It had been the timber of a shipp. There was a peece of board about a foot square nailed to it. I looking about, one of my men saw a square peece of sheet lead at the foot of the Post, hee took it up and gave it to mee. It had this super scription graved on it as followeth in the Dutch Language.

[1] Snush: To snuff, snuff up (tobacco); to take as snuff. *NOED*. Narbrough would appear to be using this word to mean snuffling or sniffing around sometimes one way and sometimes another.

[2] Haul the seine fishing net.

[3] This was probably the island called Shag Island on the Narbrough's plan of 'Port Dissier' (Plate 1) now known as Isla de los Pájaros.

[4] Isla del Rey. Shown on Narbrough's plan of 'Port Dissier' (Plate 1) as Le mars Ile.

MDCXV
EEN SCHIPENDE EEN IACHT GENAEMT EENDRACHT EN
HOORN GEARRIVEERT DEN VIII DECEMBER VERTROCKEN
MET EEN SCHIP D EENDRACHT DEN X IANVARY MDCXVI
C.IACQVES LE MAIRE
S.WILLEM CORNS SCHOVTS
ARES CLAESSEN
IAN CORNS SCHOVTS
CLAES IANSSEN BAN

There was a sheet of Paper written but it was not to bee read, for it was put in a Latten or tin Case, and the rust of the Case had eaten the paper all a peeces.

[63] **March 1669. The *Sweepstakes* in Port Desire Harbour.**

Excepting here and there a bitt. This I found in a hole of the Post, and a Long plugg in it, which Shewed where the box Lay. With my knife I did engrave the Shipp's name, and the date of the yeare and day of the month. I saw on this Island several pieces of boards of the wrack of some Shipp, which had been burned. These boards were drove up here by the tyde.[1] The people of the Countrey Cannot get on to this Island. I nailed the board (which I engraved) to the Post. My men brought the Lead away. This Island may Contain neare 12 acres of Land, I named this Le Maire's Isle. I went from hence on the North shore of the river and went two miles into the Land. No woods nor tree to bee seen, but many Guianacos, and Ostridges seen. The Land is of a good kind of Marly[2] soyle in many places. The hills not very high but Large downes and Plaine, with grasse growing all over. I digged in two or 3 places to see the soile. It is sandy dry ground neare a foot, then marle. In my opinion it might bee made excellent good corn ground, for it is ready to till, the Land is much like the Land on new market heath [Newmarket heath]. I could not see any people. I searched the gullies and broken rocks for grains of gold or minerall but could find neither there. I returned to the boat again and rowed further under the shore, and Landed and went up a high rocky hill[3] to see into the Countrey. On the top of the hill there grows some small bushes, I could see the river run up a great way, and I could see in the Land hill over hill all grasse land, here and there a white spot of marle, on the side of a hill. No signe

[1] This was the *Horne* which was lost as recounted by Schouten: 'The 17 [December, 1615]. We layd our shippe [*Unitie*] within the *Kings Island* on the wall, with a high water, to make it cleane, where it was drie that wee might goe round about it drie foot. The 18 the *Horne* was also layd on shore about 2 musket shot from our ship, to make it cleane. The 19 as we were busie about both the ships to make them cleane, and burnt reeds under the *Horne*, the flame of the fire sodainly got into the ship, and presently tooke such hold thereof that in the twinckling of an eye, it was so great that wee could by no means quench it, by reason it lay 50 foot drie from the water side, and by that means we were constrained to stand still, and see it burne before our eyes, not able to doe any thing to save it. The 20 at a high water we lancht the *Unitie*, into the water againe, and went to the *Horne* & quencht the fire, but the ship was burnt cleane downe to the water. The next day when we had cast the water out of that part of it that was left, we saved all the wood, iron worke, anchors, ordinance, and what else that was to be gotten and put it in our ship.' Schouten, *Relation*, pp. 18–19.

[2] Marl: A kind of soil consisting principally of clay mixed with carbonate of lime, forming a loose unconsolidated mass, valuable as a fertilizer. Marly: Resembling or partaking of the qualities of marl. *NOED*.

[3] Probably Cerro Van Noort, 177 ft (54m).

of people or of boats in this river, I came down to the boat. Here runs several Creeks a mile or two miles into the Land. I went over the river to the SE shore, there wee Laid the boat into a Creek in a[1] valley, and made her fast, and went all hands up the Land 3 miles. Wee saw many Guianacos and ostridges but could not come neare to shoot at them. I saw the footing of five men in the oaze as they had gone along, I measured the feeting by my foot, and found my foot to bee Larger and Longer by halfe an inch then any of those footsteps. Wee could not see any people. It being neare night wee went and pulled up grasse and laid it to the best advantage for shelter. Here wee Lay all night keeping two and two Centinels. Cold aire to night, the wind at West a fresh gale.
The *Sweepstakes* name I engraved on a board at Le Maire's Isle.

Munday the 14th, fair weather, but cold aire. This morning at day light wee turned out and marched into the Land SWBS about foure miles. Wee could not find any fresh water, wee made a fire in the grasse, but could not see any signe of mankind in the Land. Wee saw vinacos, hares,[2] & foxes, a wild dogg of a good bigness, and a gray Cat like an English Cat runing up on the hills. This day wee Caught an Armadillo,[3] the dogs put her to ground. They have holes like Coneys, wee soon digged her out. It was as big as a good great hedghogg

[64] **March 1669. The *Sweepstakes* in Port Desire Harbour.**
And not much unlike one, only the Armadillo is cased over his body with a shell, which shut one under another, Like shells of Armour. Our dogs could not hurt it. Wee saw Rats[4] in many places, and a kind of Polecat,[5] with 2 white strakes down his back, all the rest black. Our dogs killed two of those Polecats, they bite and stink much. Several Ostridges seene, some partridges and many kites. The Land is in fair hills without wood or fresh water. The soile of a sandy gravell, and grasse growing all over, no mineral or mettal seene. This afternoone wee returned to our boat, and went through a Creek of two miles Long which is dry at a Low water, it is not past 30 foot broade. This Creek makes a fair Island of a mean height, all plaine aloft, and grasse growing all over it.[6] No wood nor water on it. It is of a sandy marly soile in most parts of it. It is two miles long and halfe a mile broad. The greyhound killed two hares on it presently. Wee saw above 20 hares on it. I called this hare Isle. It is adjacent on the South shore, eight miles up the river from the Narrow. I went down the river, and went aboard this evening. I cannot perceive the Indians to have Canoas here, or any kind of boats in this part of the Land.

Thursday the 17th, fair weather. My men are in as good health and as lusty as when they came out of England. The Seals flesh is mighty hearty food, and so is the Pengwins, they both eat a litle strong of fish, but it agrees mighty well with every mans body. Here may bee had this sort of food having salt to preserve it, enough to victual a navy, here is such numbers of both.

[1] 'the' struck through.
[2] This was probably the mara or Patagonian hare. See above, p. 207, n. 5.
[3] The Larger Hairy Armadillo, is a common resident. See above, p. 207, n. 8.
[4] See above, p. 207, n. 9.
[5] This is the Patagonian skunk. See above, p. 207, n. 11.
[6] This is Península Viedma, shown on Narbrough's plan of 'Port Dissier' (Plate 1) as Hare Ile.

A Pengwin is a good fowle and as large as an ordinary goose. I weighed several of them, and their weight is seaven pounds and a halfe, or eight pounds, you may take the Seales of any bignesse as you please. Their skins are of a fine smooth haire, and of a gray silver-hair colour. some are as big as large horses. The hares & Armadillos are very good meat.

Sunday the 20th. I went ashore with twenty armed men on the South side, and travelled into the Land near ten miles SSW but could not see any people. Wee saw their foot steps in two places, by a salt water pond side in the Clay, they were not as large as mine. some steps were made by bare feet, others have something about their feet. Wee saw where they had Laid in many places, and had split stones in many peeces, which I judge is for arrow heads. Wee fell with a small spring of fresh water. It is two miles SBW from the watch tower rock. The Indians have made small stands with bushes at this spring to Lye behind, and shoot at Ostridges that comes to drink at this spring. They have sticked many Ostridges feathers in the bushes of their barricados. This spring is a mile and a halfe from the sea side west, up the first broad valley, in the side of a small hill, on the North side of the valley. It does not run past two bowshoot for the ground doth drink it in. I cannot give any other direction to find it, for here

[65] **March 1669. The *Sweepstakes* in Port Desire Harbour.**
is no remarkable place; when I went at the furthest into the Land, I could see one hill top over an other, as farr as wee could descry fair round hills & downs as the rest of the Land, no wood or tree to bee seen. Wee saw Guinacos and Ostridges and hares, Partridges kites and small birds. Wee not discovering any liklyhood of people, returned to our boate, wee got aboard next morning. Fair weather, wind at west.

Munday the 21 & Tuesday the 22d. I sent all my Scorbutick men ashore to gather herbs, the rest got ballast and water aboard.

Wednesday the 23d. I fitted my boat and went up the river, having 13 armed men with mee, as also Lieu*tenan*t Pecket and Mr John Wood. I draughted out the river as I rowed up, and sounded it all along. It hath several Islands and rocks in it, and the bank sides are steep rocks in some places, and in some places white marle cliffs, and Low sandy shores. Seales are on the rocks a great way up in many places. It hath 8, 9, 10, 8, 7 faddam a great way up, neare 15 miles from the mouth, Then it grows narrower and shoalder upwards. I went up with the boat about 22 miles, there it grew so narrow and shoald that I could go no higher up the river with my boate. Wee landed and some of us travelled up further a mile or better. The Land all hilly so as wee could go no further, and Cliffe rocks with veines of red flint, and white flint, and straked Coloured flints. Wee could not see any kind of mineral or any shew of mettal but Craggy broken rocks, all about the river, and Oazy sand. It is not a stones-Cast broad at a high water, and at a Low water it is dry over in oaze and sand. It was no safe staying here for us, For the Cliffs that were by the river or Creeks side were steep up, That stones and rocks being tumbled downe would stave the boat.[1] Wee launched her afloat and went Lower downe, and Landed and Looked to &

[1] Break a hole in the boat.

fro the Land But saw nothing, but two great fowles like Eagles.[1] Also wee found one deade much like an Eagle, but not so bigg. No signe of people or fire had been made hereabouts. Wee made a great smoak with grasse on the side of a hill, But no answer could wee see. I saw the river quite dry all above where wee had been. The land here by the river is of a rocky soile, But a mile in Land is Large Downs and gravelly soile, all grasse land, No woods, nor tree, nor fresh water. Here and there a small bush, no kind of fruit or herb. The river ends in a muddy sandy Lake in rocks and Craggy hills, it is all salt water, And it is about 23 miles Long from the narrow, at the Comeing in, It runs up neare twelve miles at the first West. There lyes Le Maires Isle, A high rocky Isle. Then the

[66] **March 1669. The *Sweepstakes* in Port Desire Harbour.**
river turns away SWBW and is a mile broad, and hath 8 faddam, oazy sand, for three miles. There lyes a rock above water, a good height, Copling up, sea fowles breeds on it, wee call this Bell rock, then the river turns up WSW and comes narrower, and shoale, to five faddom, Then shoalds of sands. The tyde runs but weak here, there is Creeks and Lakes in many places. As wee went up wee sounded a Trumpet several times in hopes to see people. There is more sign of people at the rivers mouth then up aloft a great deale, and of Guinacos and Ostridges wee could see none here of either. About 12 of clock at night when the tyde served I came down again. These people bury their dead on the topps of the rocky Cliffes by the river side. They Lay them on their backs, and their heads to the west, and Cover them with stones.[2] They are of a mean stature, and cut black haire. I opened a grave to Look in it, & saw the Corps.

Thursday the 24th. Wee fetched all our things off the shore, and had the Shipp in a readynesse to saile. I went ashore on the South side to the Picked rock, and saw it was a natural rock, stood on a small round hill as if it had beene builded there by man. It hath a Cliffe on the topp. It is as bigg in Circumference as a butt, and it [is] neare 50 foot high above the hill it stands on, which is as much more above the Superficies[3] of the other Land. There Lyes Lumps of rocks about it. I saw here nothing worth noting. I returned to the Shipp. The biggest stick growing neare this harbour, or any where in the Countrey so farre as I went, (which was twenty miles in Land) will not make a helve for a hatchet, Yet there is bush wood, which will serve for fireing to Carry to sea. Before night I had all things aboard and the Shipp fitted, I intend to saile the next morning and Look along the Coast for the Pinke, before I Look into St Julians harbour. Fresh water is scarce in PORT DESIRE in the Summer time. Those places which I had fresh water from, are small springs on the North side, out of which I filled neare fourty tuns of fresh water. The first spring which is on the N side as you come in, It is in a valley halfe a mile in a gully of rocks. This well beares NNW from the tower rock; Peckets well (as wee called it,) is[4] more up the river a mile, but within a bow shoot of the salt water. It is in a gully, the Land in these valleys are very green and sweet grasse. Here grows abundance of wild pease, here

[1] The only eagle found in this area is the black-chested buzzard-eagle (*Geranoaetus melanoleucus*), a large stocky bird, 24 in (60cm), with the female slightly larger. Harris, *Guide*, p. 66.

[2] See above, p. 207, n. 1.

[3] Superfice: The surface of a body or object. *NOED*. The hill stood 50 ft above the level of the surrounding land.

[4] This word is repeated.

are small Nutgales[1] growing on the bushes, but no great quantities, but few bushes of that nature. Salt may bee made here, for here in the shore side and on the rocks, I gathered severall handfulls of good salt. The picked rock on the South shore bare SBE of mee

[67] **March 1670. The *Sweepstakes* in Port Desire harbour.**
where I mored in the river, and it was touching with a split Cliffe rock on the South banke[2] where the Shipp was swinged up flood, and when Shee rid Ebb, the tower-rock was shutt in with the Cliffe rocks.[3] The flood runs 6 houres, and Ebb runs 6 houres, and both shores are shut one with the other at the narrow, so as you ride Land Lockt from the sea and safe,[4] with a sea-wind or out-wind. The West winds blow hardest, and are the worst winds for to ride with a shipp in the harbour, for they blow right down the river, so if any of the Ebb Cables &c[a] should give way it is dangerous on the tyde of Ebb, for the tydes run very strong on the Springs, and the shore sides are rocky.

Fryday the 25th of March 1670,[5] wind at NW a stiffe gale. I had the Shipp unmored. This morning I[6] went ashore on the North side on the Land, And pitched his Ma*jes*ties Colours, the Union flagg, on the Land, and took possession of all the Land for his Ma*jes*ties use, and his heires, and sounded the trumpet, and opened the ground and planted acorns and pease. I allso put Mustard seed into the ground in token of possession.[7]

I went over to the South shore and pitched up the union flag, and tooke possession for the use of his Ma*jes*tie and his heires in the hearing of both my Lieutenants, and M[r] John Wood, and John Fostien[8] and all the Company. Then I returned aboard it being 8 of clock in the morning. I called all hands aft and drank to his Ma*jes*ties health, and bad them to take notice that I had this day taken posession of this whole Land for the use of his Ma*jes*tie our Soveraigne Lord and Master and his heires, as also of this harbour, which words were as followeth.

Gentlemen, you are by mee desired to take notice, that this day I take possession of this Harbour and river of Port Desire, and of all the Land in this Countrey, On both shores, for the use of his Ma*jes*tie King Charles the Second of great Brittain and his heires. So god Save our King. And fired three peeces of ordinance in Honour of his Ma*jes*tie &c[a].

I engraved a board with the day of my arrival here, and the day of my departure and of my intent to call in at Port San Julian and to expect the Pink to come to mee there. This board I caused to bee put on a Post, on the South point, at the mouth of the harbour,

[1] Nutgall: A gall (an excrescence produced on trees by the action of insects) produced on the dyers oak (*Quercus infectoria*) used especially as a dye-stuff. *NOED.*

[2] This was probably the cliff now called Punta Lista, 33 ft (10m).

[3] Where the ship was secured, on the flood tide the tower rock was in line with the edge of a split cliff on the south bank and on the ebb the tower rock was in line with the cliff rocks.

[4] There is no direct line of sight out to sea so that the ship was sheltered from sea winds.

[5] The date of the change of year in the Julian calendar in use in England.

[6] The word 'had' struck through.

[7] In order to establish possession of land it was considered necessary to make full use of it by growing and harvesting crops, hence the token breaking and planting of seeds.

[8] Probably John Fortescue. The two lieutenants and Mr John Wood and Mr John Fortescue would represent the principal witnesses and hence are mentioned by name.

which might bee seen by any that should come there. At ten of clock, it being neare halfe flood, I sailed and was cleare into sea before twelve. Wind at West a stout gale I stood to the Northward to see if the Pink should bee on the Coast thereabout in any of the Bayes. This afternoone it blew a hard gale at WNW. I split my main saile thwart and came to an anchor in 12 faddom water gravelly ground about 4 leagues to the Northward of the Ledge of rocks which lies to the Northward of Port Desire[1] I was about 8 miles from the shore. I brought a new saile to the yard and rode here till ten of clock at night, the flood comeing I weighed and stood to the Northward wind at WNW.

Saturday the 26, wind at West, I stood to the Northward. This morning at 6 of clock when the Sun appeared above the East horizon the moon set in the West horizon. It being eclipsed at 11 of clock 10 min*utes*, in the forenoon at London. But here it was eclipsed at 6 of clock and 30 minutes past, which gives foure houres

[68] **March 1670. The *Sweepstakes* off of Port Desire.**
And 40 minutes difference of time between the Meridian of London, And the meridian of Cape Blanco, which cape Lies in the Latitude of 47°20′ South and on the South East Coast of America which was the place where I saw part of this Eclipse, which is 70° in Longitude to the Westward of the Meridian of London by this observation. But I could not see the whole Eclipse the heavens being Clouded.[2]
I find Cape Blanco by my account of sailing to Lye in the Longitude of 69°16′ to the Westward of the Meridian of London. If the moon had not been Clouded I might have been exact as to the Longitude But I dare presume my account is not much out which I have kept of the Shipp's way from England hither.[3]
I stood up to Cape San George, alias Cape Blanc*c*o. At two of clock this afternoon the pitch of the Cape bore NWBW from mee, distant 5 miles. It makes Like a round Copling Rocky Island with single picked rocks neare it. And to the Northwestward the Land threnis away in white Cliffs of a fair height and plain grasse Land aloft but hilly in the Countrey. No woods as I could see. To the Southward of the Cape the Land by the sea side is a steep beach with a small Cliffe at the grasse bank, which Looks reddish. It continues a beach for neare 8 leagues till you see port desire. The Land lies neare straight along from the Cape to Port Desire Bay, SBW½W all along a beach till you see the ledge of rocks to the N:ward of Port Desire, which lies a league off the maine, and neare 7 leagues from the Cape. This ledge of rocks show themselves, they are[4] about the length of two shipps, and Lye Low by the water, do not goe between them,[5] but keep a mile without them and you will have fifteen faddam gravelly sand. The Land is plain neare the sea all the way from the Cape till you see Port Desire, But in land hilly and grasse, no woods, nor trees, but some bushes. There is a plain valley about 4 leagues to the Southward of the Cape which runs up West into the Land, the Land is Low by the sea side at the valley. The Soundings of[f] the Cape when it beares NWBW from you, five miles, is ten faddom, small peavell stones.

[1] Roca Sorrell (47°23′S, 65°48′W).

[2] See above, pp. 209, n. 10; 222.

[3] Cabo Blanco lies in 47°12′S, 65°45′W from Greenwich. By his account Narbrough had made the Cape to lie 61°56′W from the Lizard of England, which is 67°08′W from Greenwich.

[4] Roca Sorrell.

[5] Presumably this means between them and the shore.

There is banks lies off the pittch of the Cape, the tide makes a ripling over them. They are a league off and better, there is ten faddom on them, small pibble stones. And so as you saile along to the Southwards in two leagues of the shore, you will have 18 & 19 faddom water gravelly red sand, more without and shoalder within. You may saile in a mile of the shore and have 14 faddom. No danger till you see the ledge of rocks and the Picked tower come open of Port Desire. You will see Pengwin Island before you, show ragged;[1] It will beare SBE of you. Before the bay of Port Desire you will have seventeen & 18 faddom water, sandy ground, and some Casts rough ground, all good anchoring with a westerly wind. No sign of the Pink. I tacked and stood to the Southward at 6 of clock this afternoon the wind came to the South West, and Cloudy weather, I anchored in Port Desire Bay, in seventeen faddom, black oasy sand, The picked tower bare West of mee. some rain in the night with a southerly wind.

[69] **March 1670. The *Sweepstakes* at anchor before Port Desire.**

Cape Blanco makes thus when you are three leagues ESE from it in faire weather I have Set down the faddoms of water to the Southward of it along the Coast to Port Desire and the bank on the face of the Cape.	Latit*ude* 47°20′

[*blank space for view*] [2]

Sunday the 27th, cloudy hazy cold weather wind at SSW a hard gale so as I could not get to the Southward I rode fast. This day at noon I observed the Sun on the meridian with my quadrant, and found the Latitude to bee 47°49′ S.

Munday the 28. Calme, this morning. I sent the boats to Pengwins Island, It being about two leagues off mee, to fetch fresh Pengwins. This forenoon the wind came to the WNW, I weighed and stood to the Southward, my boats came aboard laden with Pengwins by ten of clock, having about sixteen hundred in both boats, and their heads cut of [off]. At 3 of clock this afternoon the wind came to the South and blew hard, a great Sea came out of the SE and like to blow. This evening I bore back again and anchored in Port Desire Bay in 16 faddom Oazy sand. The Harbours mouth bore WNW of mee, distant about 2 leagues. You may ride in this road with a SSE wind very well, for you may bring Pengwin Island ESE of you. If you ride up in the South part of the Bay there is 12 faddom water fine white sand above a mile off the shore.
Cape Blanco lies in the Latitude of 47°20′ South.
And in Longitude from the Lizard of England West 61°56′.
And in Meridian Distance from the Lizard West 1014 leag*ues* 1·6 mil*es*.

Port Desire in America Lies in the Latitude of 47°48′ South.
And in Longitude from the Lizard of England West 62°00′.
Meridian Distance from the Lizard West 1015 leag*ues* 2·6 miles.

[1] Penguin Island will show a ragged outline.
[2] The blank space approximates to 7 lines of text.

Pengwin Isle or the Plentyfull Isle lies in the Latit*ude* of 47°55′ South.
Longitude from the Lizard West 61°57′.[1]
Meridian Distance from the Lizard West 1014 leag*ues* 2 miles.
Variation of the Compasse here is easterly 17°30′.

[70] **March 1670. The *Sweepstakes* at anchor in Port Desire Bay.**
Wednesday the 30th, hazy weather and Calm, this morning, towards noone the wind veared round the Compasse. I weighed but could not get to the Southward I anchored again, at 12 of clock to night the wind came to the NW, a fine gale, I weighed and stood to the Southward, and passed by Pengwin Island before day.

Thursday the 31, wind at WBN a fine gale, this forenoon I steered away SSW by my compasse with all the saile I could make. At 12 of clock I was in Lat*itude* 48°04′ South, by good observation of the Sun, and thwart of tome hauke Isle[2] at the North end of Seales bay. At one of clock it proved Calm, and the tyde of flood being come, I anchored in 27 faddom water, gretty black sand, I was about 5 leagues off the Land. At 6 of the clock this evening I weighed the flood being done, and Plyed to the Southward, wind at SE a fine gale, the wind veared about easterly to the north.

Fryday the first of April. 1670, wind at north, I steered SSW by Compasse, I was 4 leagues off the shore of the midle of Seales Bay at 7 of clock this morning I had 21 faddom water black sand, a many Seales in the sea, litle air, I galed ahead.[3] No observation to day. At 6 this afternoon I saw the Eady Stone rock which lies in the Latit*ude* of 48°20′ South.[4] It did but just shew it selfe at the wash of the sea it being now a high water. It does but just make a breach at the waters edge. I went a mile within it to the Westward, and had 26 faddom rocky ground when it bare East of mee a mile distant. I had the wind at NW a fine gale. I steered away SSW from it till 12 of clock at night, Then I braced my head sailes to the mast, there lay with my head to the Westward till morning. I sounded and had 29 faddom sandy ground all along as I drove, which was not much, for the tyde of flood was come and set to windward, cold Sharp air to night wind at NW a fresh gale.

Saturday the 2d of april, wind at NNW a fine gale, I filled at day light and steered away SSW and SBW by my Compasse, as the coast lyeth, I sailed along in 20 faddom water black sand, distance off the shore near 3 leagues. Here this forenoon at 9 of the clock I saw a small flat Island to the Westward of mee, it is about a league off the Land, It lies in the Latitude of 48°40′ S.[5] The Land against it is good high land in Large hills, and some round Copling top, two leagues to the Southward the Land is Low in a great plain and a beach by the seaside, but the shore against this Island is rocky. I was two leagues East from the flat Island and had 23 faddom black sand. I haled close in for the shore and sailed in 5 miles of the shore all along from this Island to Port St Julian. I sounded as I sailed along,

[1] Isla Pingüino lies in 47°55′S and 65°43′W from Greenwich or 60°31′W from the Lizard.
[2] See below, p. 580, n. 4.
[3] To gale away is to sail free, i.e. with the wind astern.
[4] Roca Bellaco (48°30′S, 66°11′W). See above, p. 210, n. 7.
[5] Islote Chato (48°45′S, 67°03′W). See above, p. 211, n. 2.

and had 18 & 20 faddom black sand, the Land is low in a valley, the seashore is beach here & there a rock. It is a long

[71] **April 1670. The *Sweepstakes* on the Coast of Patagonea.**[1]
beach, for 4 Leagues, after you are one league to the Southward of the flat Isle the shore lies SSW and NNE. At the South end of this beach in land is high round-topped hills, but at the sea side it is steep white Cliffe of an indifferent height, with a black Strake in it, over the Cliff the hill rounds up to a topp, having some small black bushes growing on the side, no wood nor tree seen. This white Cliffe is a League Long from the beach to the Southward, there it comes to a point,[2] with falls on it like stepps, up at the face of this point, below, lies a shoald point of rocks SE a mile out, they shew themselves at a Low water. The Cliff rounds about this point to the Westward and hath broken rocks at the foot of it, here is a fine round bay and low beach at the seaside, and white steep cliffs of a fair height, on the South side of this bay, plain aloft, and broken rocks at the foot, and at the East point[3] two single round rocks lies better than a mile off, they are dry at a Low water. In this bay at the Comeing in is thirteen & 12 faddom water, fine black sand, in the midle the bay flats as you go in. In this bay is Port St Julian. The harbours mouth is in the midle of the bay, But you cannot see it without, for one point shuts in with the other, you must send a boat in to discover the harbour at a Low water and the barre without, for it is a barred harbour. The Land in the Countrey over Port St Julian on the West side of the Port is high copling round hills like blunt Sugar Loaves on the tops.[4] It is the highest land I saw in all the Countrey, there is no such hills on the coast else, the Land is plain to the South without any hill further then wee could see at this time. This afternoon[5] it proved Calme, I anchored in the bay before St Julian in twelve faddom water, black oazy sand, the harbours mouth bore WSW of mee, about two leagues of[f] it. I sent in my boat to discover the harbour, and to see if the Pink were there. At 6 of clock to night the boat came aboard again my Lieutenant told mee there was a safe harbour, and water enough for a bigger Shipp then this, but no sign of the Pink here, or having been here. Now I despaired of ever seeing her more, for here Lay my hopes of her, Neverthelesse I did not question the proceeding of my voyage, yet the company doubted it would bee dangerous wee being a lone-ship, and had a stormy Countrey to saile in, and an unknown coast to search out, also if it should happen so as to run aground any where, wee could not expect any relief. These thoughts of theirs I put out of their heads telling them of the great riches of the Land, and how Captaine Drake went round the world having but one Shipp, and in those days were but ordinary navigators, and should wee doubt any thing now knowing that which they knew, and our own experience besides, yeelded us to bee much better Sea-men.

[72] **April 1670. The *Sweepstakes* before Port San Julian.**
If wee would put our selves in action, neither should I expose any man to more danger then my selfe in any service or action of this voyage.

[1] 'the *Sweepstakes*' is repeated and struck through.
[2] Cabo Curioso (49°11′S, 67°37′W).
[3] Punta Desengaño. The rocks are presumably the four rocks which dry 5 ft (1·5 m) 6½ cables NNE of the point. Rocks which dry 13ft (4 m) lie closer to the point.
[4] Monte Wood and Monte Sholl.
[5] 'fore' struck through and replaced with 'after'.

Calm to night, I rode fast, a small tyde runs where I rode, the water Ebbd neare three faddom perpendicular. It is neare nine leagues from the flat Island to S[t] Julian South South West and North North East, and the shore lyes so.
The mouth of Port S[t] Julian is in the Latitude 49°10′ S.
Longitude from the Lizard West 63°10′.[1]
Meridian Distance from the Lizard West 1030 leag*ues*.
Variation of the Compasse here, by an amplitude is 16°10′ East.

Sunday the 3[d] being Easter day and Calm. I went into the harbour with my boat, and rowed up a league in it to an Island,[2] but could not see any signe of the Pink. I stayed in the harbour one Low water, and saw it was a good safe harbour to ride in 3 faddom and a halfe at a Low water up at the Island, and it flows here neare four faddom. It is a high water on the full and Change of the moon at half an houre past eleaven of the Clock, but on the barr without the mouth at 11 of clock. Here is but five foot water on the barr at a Low water. This evening I came aboard, calme all night.

Munday the 4th, litle wind, at north. I weighed and stood to the Southward this morning, within two leagues of the shore I had 25 faddom, black oazy sand all along. This day at noon I was in the Latitude of 49°23′ by good obs*ervation* of the ☼. I steered along by my Compasse SBW for so the shore lyes. The [*margin:* Variat of the Compasse 16° East.] Compasse hath 16° variation easterly so the coast lieth, SSW near halfe a point wester. The sea shore is steep white Cliffes of a fair height, and plain grasse land aloft, all along to the Southward of S[t] Julian, but at the first 4 leagues it is a sandy shore, and rocks in the water, and a riseing grasse bank, with here and there a bush, then comes the Cliffe, and it shows ragged as you come from the Northward, but as you come neare it makes plain. The Cliffs continue along thus further then I could see. This night at 6 of Clock, it being cloudy weather and dark, I brought to and Lay by all night with her head to the Eastward. I am now in the Latitude of 49°50′ and about 3 leagues off the shore. I sounded and had 27 faddom, fine black sand, litle wind to night, and some rain, towards morning it proved Calme. No fish will take a hook here, for severall men have tryed but cannot take one.

Tuesday the 5th Cloudy hazy weather, wind came to the SBE. I made saile

[73] **April 1670. The *Sweepstakes* before Port San Julian.**
and plyed to the Southward. At 8 of clock it blew hard and proved hazy & foggy weather. I stood in to the shore. I sounded and had 30 faddom black oazy sand neare two leagues off the shore. I reckoned my selfe to bee in the Latitude of fifty[3] degrees at 9 of clock this forenoon. The cliff is steep up by the seaside, and of a good height all along, and plain grasse land aloft, not a hill to bee seene no wood or trees in the Land hereabouts. I tacked and stood off E the wind at SBE a fresh gale, and rain, a great Sea begins to make, I could not get to the Southward, I was forced to hand my topsailes. It looked very black in the southerboard and lightned. I advised with both my Lieutenants and master what course

[1] The mouth of Puerto San Julián lies in 49°15′S, 67°39′W from Greenwich or 62°27′W from the Lizard.
[2] This will have been either Islas Cormorán or Islas Justicia, which lie 2 miles within the entrance of the harbour.
[3] 'fifty' inserted above an illegible strike-out.

would bee best. I thought it best to stand off and get searoom. They judged it more safe to beare for Port San Julian, and harbour there till wee see what the weather would prove, For if it should blow a storm and wee at sea it would endanger to force the Shipp off the coast, also our boats are not fit to Cruise in the Straits afore the Shipp till a strake is raised on them. Also St Julian is the place appointed for meeting, and wee may happily fall with the Pink. I considering the great want I should have of the Pink I bore for St Julian. Cold weather, rain, & wind at SW.

Wednesday wind at WSW. I stood into the shore and Anchored in 8 faddom water, before the harbour, wee buoyed the barr at the going in of the best of the channel.

Thursday the 7th, wind at NBW very cold & a frost. I weighed at halfe flood and stood in for the harbour. I went over the barr at ¾ flood, and had 20 foot water on it. I went within the narrow two miles up, and mored in the midle of the Channel and had foure faddom at a Low water, oazy gravelly ground. I rode in a good birth having room enough. Much wind at NE.
The going in to Port St Julian as you ride in the Bay in ten faddom water you may see the Land fall away from the hills in the SW part of the Bay. There goes in the mouth of the harbour. It is at the narrow at the first going in, a Cables length and a halfe broad, and steep shores on both sides. The East point[1] is a beach and plain. The West point[2] is rocks steep up like a wall, and hills inland fourteen faddom water in the narrow, twelve faddom to the rock side. The tyde runs strong here. The barr lies two miles without the narrow NE. A beach point runs from the rocks of the West point at the mouth to the barr, and the Channel lies along by it. This beach is dry at a low water, as you ride in the bay you must send a boat and discover the barr, for a stranger will not hit the Chan*n*el before hee have discovered it. The Channel lies straight in over the barr SW all along the side of this beach to the narrow, and the best going in is to keep the West side.

[74] **April 1670. The *Sweepstakes* in Port San Julian.**
There is a Channel on the East side, and midle grounds[3] which are dry at a Low water. At halfe tyde on the barr there is sixteen foot water, and between the barr and the narrow is 4, 5, 6, 7, 8, 9, 10 faddom water. As you come in Borrow on the western side, you will see two or 3 broken rocks above water on the Eastern side, which comes from the beach point.[4] Up in the Bay to the West it is flat and shoald, and on the shore by the sea side there is a white hill, Cliffy down the side, and some small bushes grow on it.[5]
The Barre is Beach stones like deal beach,[6] and in foule weather it alters something [somewhat]. From the narrow the harbour goes in SSW and grows broader, you may anchor when you are two miles within and ride safe, till you see better, you may ride close to the Island you will see which hath small bushes growing on it, seaven faddom in the Channel there at a high water, and at a low water neare four faddom. The tyde runs strong

[1] Punta Guijarro.
[2] Punta Peña.
[3] The middle ground is Banco Ferreyra which dries in places.
[4] This is Restinga Braida.
[5] This might be Punta Sholl, which is the first headland within the narrows on the West side.
[6] Water-rounded stones like those on the beach at Deal.

as at Portsmouth in England. A mile within the harbour on the East side of the Channel lies a rock under water, which wee called the mussel bank.[1] It is dry but on Spring tydes, at the low water time, and it lyes at the mouth of a branch which goes up up in the oase to the East side. This rock lies opposite to a beach Island which is on the West side of the Channel.[2] The Stream of the channell is gravelly oase. This is a good safe harbour to ride in, and no danger, for it is flat oase in most places.

Fryday the 8th. This forenoon wind at N. I went up the harbour in my boate. It runs up but seaven miles from the mouth and there ends, in broad swashy oase and shoald water, and dry when the tyde is down, the land is white cliff like fullers earth, steep up and hilly aloft, in round Copling tops and dry grasse land, no woods nor tree to bee seen. some small prickly bushes, no fresh water, but what is in rainy Swashes. I went up the hills but could not see any people, wee saw a fox.[3] My men Shot a many Curlew[4] which were very fat, they killed 18 & 20 at a shoot. This evening I went aboard, very cold and snowed to-night.

Saturday the 9th, blowing weather wind at SW and extream cold, the land all covered with snow. I went ashore on the West side to see for people, but could not see any, wee saw where they had been, and layd behind bushes and made small fires. I saw their footstepps in the oase, where seaven of them had gone, some steps were barefooted, others had something on their feet, my bare foot was larger then any of those steps. The land is in plains and hills with dry grasse. The Land is of a sandy gravelly soile, and of a salt peter nature, for in the Low valleys the ground is dry and white with peter, no wood nor a tree to bee seen, some bushes near the river side which will make good fireing.

[75] **April 1670. The *Sweepstakes* in PORT St Julian.**
No fresh water but what is in Swashes. The river is all salt water, and muddy oase by the shore side in most places. In land is hills and high large downes, plain on the sides and tops, and short grasse growing on them, No manner of fruit, berry, or flower to bee seen, excepting smal gales[5] which grows on the bushes. I went aboard to night, it blowed hard at SSW and snowed. Very cold as winter in England.

Tuesday the 12th, wind at WSW a hard gale. This day I went ashore with 16 men on the northwesterly side up the river 4 miles. Wee find a Swash of rain and snow water near the river side, it is upon flat rocky ground, very good water. The place will hold 4 or 5 tuns, it is hard by a steep rock to land the boat at, and in a good place to get the Cask into the boat. No people could wee see, wee saw many Guianacos feeding on the hills, and Estridges, and two hares, wee saw where people had set the grasse a fire, and had roasted[6] Limpits and mussels. I put up a stick with a white handkercher on it, and a small box of

[1] Piedras Rodríguez.

[2] This is a small un-named island off Punta Tumba.

[3] The culpeo fox or Argentine gray fox. See above, p. 207, n. 2.

[4] See above, p. 208, n. 7.

[5] Gale is a name used for bog-myrtle (*Myricas gale*). *NOED*. However, these sound like the nutgalls seen in Port Desire; see above, p. 430, n. 1.

[6] There is an illegible word struck through here.

beads and a Looking glasse, two knifes, and scissers and a hatchet, on a hill, that if the people should come in our absence they might see wee intended to traffick with them, and also to invite them to come to us. Wee set these things in a place where it might bee best seen, and where the people had made fires. This evening wee went aboard litle wind, & frost.

Wednesday the 13th, fair weather & frost, wind at W. No sign of the Pink I went ashore and haled the Saine on the East side, at the first of the flood. Wee caught five hundred brave fish as big as large mullets and much like a mullet, gray and full of scales, some of these fish were as big as a mans leg. Wee caught all these fish in 4 houres time, so returned aboard & divided the fish amongst the whole ships company, every man and boy a share alike. These fish eat mighty well and is an excellent fish. Here is very good Mussels on the rocks. Many oyster shells by the shore side, and growing in vaines in the rocks but no meat is in them. Wind at W to night a gale.

Thursday the 14th, wind at W. and blow hard, this morning. The men caught two hundred and fifty fish to day, and filled some fresh water.

Fryday the 15th, cloudy blowing weather, wind at WSW. lesse wind at daylight, very cold and frost. This forenoon ten men went on the East side, but saw no people. They saw a pond of good fresh water a quarter of a mile from the river in the plain-land. There was many Ducks,[1] and brant geese,[2] and Teale in it. They got a young Guianaco with the Greyhound, and saw many Guianacos. At night they came aboard.

Saturday the 16th and Sunday the 17th, variety of weather, extream cold rains, snow, wind, frost &ca.

[76] **April 1670. The *Sweepstakes* in Port St Julian.**

Munday the 18th, wind at SW a stiff gale, & snow. The winter is come here strong and much given to Storms, so as it will bee impossible to hold the Coast to get into the Straits, for the wind blows altogether from the West or west-southerly, and in such gusts as will force a man off the Coast. This day I ordered my Purser to serve the company brandy wine for their allowance at [*margin:* Mr John Wood saw 7 Indian men] a quart a week for a man. I got a boats lading of wood of the Countrey aboard for fireing. All the Company eat salt Seale and Pengwins for their allowance and it is sweet and very good meat and keeps well in salt. It may be kept long.

Tuesday the 19th, wind at WSW, and blows hard. I went ashore on the Land to the North-Westward, without the harbours mouth, and on the beach a litle up the shore grows very good wood for fireing, it is crooked like thorn in England, here is 3 boats loads. I saw Vianacos. No people. I returned aboard, a frost to night.

[1] See above, p. 208, n. 6.

[2] These were probably upland geese or possibly kelp geese but these are normally found further south. See above, p. 233, n. 3.

Wednesday the 20th, blowing weather, wind at WSW. This morning Lieut*enant* Pecket went ashore on the NW side into the Land eight miles, saw the land all grasse land, no woods nor trees, very few bushes. The Land hilly and valley, no people to bee seen, many places where they had been, they found two arrows headed with flint-stones very artificially,[1] and feathered. The arrows are made of wood and are but small, and about two foot 4 inches Long. They are 3 peeces of sticks put into a hole at the ends of each other, and fastened with a small green gut, and so the heads of stone are put on. My Lieut*enant* and his company fell with a great salt pond, like the salt pond at the Isle of May but this being 6 times as big. Here he saw abundance of good white salt, they brought some aboard to shew mee, they saw the footsteps of people in the clay at the Pond. They saw hundreds of Guianacos in Companies. This pond is six miles from the harbours mouth NWBN into the Land, and it is in the great plain which lies between the flat Isle and Port St Julian. It is about two miles into the Land from the sea side, three leagues to the N:ward of Port St Julian. They saw several Estridges, and some hares, and some partridges, at night came aboard. This afternoon I searched all the harbour over in my boate, and found it a safe harbour for many shipps to ride in, or to hale ashore. Foure faddom at a Low water oazy sand, and two Cables length broad. Five mile up, it dryes in flatts oaze and sand at a Low water, some places rocks and Long rock weeds growing on them which shews where rocks lye. You ride Land Lock'd, no sea goes, nor winds can hurt you, if your ground tackling[2] bee good. I saw many Ducks[3] in the water and white bellied Dyvers,[4] which are a good fowle bigger then a duck, and many Sea gulls, and Sea Peckis,[5] both black and pied, many ox birds,[6] some Teale. A salt marshy ground aloft in

[77] **April 1670. The *Sweepstakes* In Port San Julian.**

the river, and it is neare round above at a high water, and about two miles Diameter, all shoald but in the Channell. The Channell runs up from the narrow to the head SSW two miles, then it is shoald and a middle ground dry, then it runs up SSW southerly foure miles, and ends to Creek and oaze. And on the West side of the Harbour, a mile within, there is two Islands which a channell goes round between them and the maine. They have bushes and grasse grows on them. They are Low Islands. The westermost is the biggest and that wee called [*margin:* Hogg Isle.] hogg Isle.[7] The other next to the Ship wee called the Island [*margin:* Justice Isle.] of justice.[8] At a Low water a man can wade from these Islands to the maine. These Islands are good for nothing. Here is a great deale of flat oaze at a Low water, and a beach Island on the East side of the Channell, over against Justice Isle, a musket [*margin:* Beach Isle.] shot from one to the other. Wee called this Beach Island.[9]

[1] Skilfully, cleverly. *NOED*.

[2] Anchors and cables.

[3] See above, p. 208, n. 6.

[4] From subsequent remarks it is possible these were rock shag, or imperial shag, see above, p. 216, n. 5. For remarks on divers, see above, p. 419, n. 4.

[5] Sea pies or oystercatchers. See above, p. 208, n. 8.

[6] See below, p. 455, n. 1.

[7] This island is shown on Narbrough's plan of 'Port San Julyan' (Plate 3), and is now part of Islas Cormorán.

[8] This island is shown on Narbrough's Narbrough's plan of 'Port San Julyan' (Plate 3), and is now the easternmost island of Islas Cormorán.

[9] This island is shown on Narbrough's plan of 'Port San Julyan' (Plate 3), and is now Isla Justicia.

Here lies a great deale of flat oaze between beach Isle and the East shore, and a small Channell or Creek runs close all along under the Beach of the East shore rounding down by the point at the East side of the Harbour's mouth. The land on the East side of the Harbour is beach, at the water side, But it is a mean raise, and all plain aloft to the East to the seaside, and some Bushes, and on the rise from the water side great bushes grow there like white thorn in England, and Crooked, good hard wood for fireing, but good for nothing else; here is enough to wood 4 good shipps, growing about the shore side. The Land to the Southward is dry gravelly soile, and grasse, but all plaine without ever a hill. On the Southwest part of the harbour, and on the West and NW part up Seaven or 8 miles in the land is high rounding hills, and round topps, like hay cocks, no such land on all the Coast as I have seen yet.

Thursday the 21 day, wind at West a stiffe gale, it freezed hard.

Fryday the 22[d], wind at SW a stiffe gale and Cold aire. This morning I went ashore on the NW side, and twenty men with mee, wee went to the salt pond. I saw salt lye like pavement, all over the pond, two inches thick for two miles along, and very white and good, here is salt enough to lade a thousand shipps in February month. Wee filled some bags of salt, and laid up neare two tuns of it, out of the water, (for there was water over the salt) and the salt began to decay with the rain and weather beating on it. At night I came aboard, wee brought as much salt aboard as filled a punchion; very good white Stone salt, whiter then French salt, and of a very pleasant smell. I saw some Guianacos and Estridges. The hills and vallies dry earth and grasse on them. On the higher hills snow lies. No people, but many places where they have made fires, And laid under a bush for shelter. No signe of mineral or mettal, or tree or fruit.

Thursday the 28th, wind at WBS a fine gale, cold frosty weather. Wee unrigg'd the Shipp, and made all snugg, for here in this harbour I intend to winter, for I see it is no passing in the Straits the winds are so stormy, and generally out of the Wester quarter, and also the nights are long and Cold that wee cannot expect to passe

[78] **April 1670. The *Sweepstakes* in Port S**[t] **Julian.**

this winter. I seeing this port safe to ride in, and good refreshing to bee had of fowles, as ducks, Picks, and Dyvers &c[a]. In the Spring I may bee ready to saile to the Southward, and wee shall have the yeare before us, and the Sun will bee in the Souther signs, which will give Long dayes & short nights and temperate weather. Wind at NNE this evening and rained, it blew a great Storm, the boat sunk at the Ships stern & lost the oares.

Munday the 2[d] of May, wind at N a fresh gale Cloudy cold weather, the boates fetched wood to burne. some men went ashore and killed foure and 5 ducks a man, with their fowling guns. They saw a great many brant geese and some Swans,[1] but could not kill any wind at W to night.

[1] Probably the coscoroba swan (*Coscoroba coscoroba*), which is largely white, like the swans found in England. The only other swan found in this area is the black-necked swan (*Cygnus melancoryphus*). Narbrough might have been expected to comment on a swan with a black neck. Harris, *Guide*, pp. 56–7.

Tuesday the 3[d], fair weather, wind at SW. I observed the Suns meridian altitude today with an Astrolabe,[1] and find this harbour to lie in the Latitude of 49°08′ South. Good weather to night, overcast.

Thursday the 5th, fair weather. I went ashore on the East side & travelled the land, but saw no people. I saw severall places which they have made with bushes like two hedges to convey the vianacos between, and there they lye and shoot them. At night I went aboard.

Fryday the 6th, wind at WNW. I went ashore on the NW side, and thirty men with mee, and travelled seaven or 8 miles up the hills. saw no people. The Land is great grasse downs in most places, and on the tops of the hills is Oyster shells very large, and in the ground is oyster shells, they lie in veins in the Earth in many places, and in the firm rock is veins of them on the sides of the hills in the Countrey, they are the biggest oyster shells that ever I saw, many shells are six and seaven inches broad. Here is not one oyster to found in the harbour, assuredly these shells were when the earth was formed. No sign of mine or mettal. No woods or tree. Wee found a good spring of fresh water up in the hills. It drayns into a salt water Swash. We saw severall salt water ponds 6 miles in land. The salt nature of the earth makes it salt. I saw Estridges and Guianacos, and a fox. I made a fire on the top of the highest hill, but could see no answer. I returned aboard, my company weary. some of my men fetched salt today.

Saturday the 7th, fair weather. My gunner[2] saw two of the Countrey people [*margin:* 2 Indians seen] today at a distance, being only himselfe, they stood and looked on him, but would not come neare him, they stayd a litle time, and went into the Land on the West side towards the hills.

Fryday the 13th. A gentleman of my Company M[r] John Wood, walking on the Island of justice found 3 small peeces of gold wire in two mussle shells which shells were made together with a green gut string, the gold was to the value of two Shillings English. It had been hammerd. The wire was as bigg as great pinns.

[79] **May 1670. The *Sweepstakes* In Port San Julian.**

Saturday the 14th. Wee fetched fresh water. I went ashore and killed 2 hares one with my gun, the other with my greyhound. I saw where the indians had been lately, but could not see any. I went ten or 12 miles about the hills to day.

Sunday the 22[d]. This forenoon I called in my lieutenants and Master, and asked their opinions if it would bee best to ride here this winter, or to go to Port Desire, there being great store of provision, wee having salt enough to preserve it. They concluded that it was more safe to ride in this place then at Port Desire for this is a much safer harbour, and here is refreshing of fowles good store, as Ducks, Picks &c[a]. Also wee should bee in danger to bee put off the Coast in going to Port Desire, if a gusty night should happen as wee find

[1] Observation with the astrolabe does not require a sea horizon. See above, p. 65.

[2] Phill White. TNA, ADM 39/2510.

are generall. I concluded to winter here. Our provisions is salt Seale and Pengwins as to flesh, and is very good food.

Thursday the 26th. I had a tent built ashore on justice Isle, for my Coopers to work in.

Munday the 30th, much frost and snow on the ground. This day I unrigged my topmast and laid the rigging drie between decks. The rats do mee much mischiefe in the bread and sailes. This day I had the boate raised part of a Strake on her side, my Carpenters are at work upon her.

Tuesday the 31. Good store of wood was brought aboard for fireing, my men killed store of wild fowles. The fowles are as shie as fowles are in England.

Wednesday the first of June 1670. I had the Shipp carried a mile higher up, and mored between the Island of Justice and the Beach Isle, in a good berth – twenty foot water at the low water of Spring tydes. Gravelly oazy ground, in the channell, and oaze and beach ashore. The Shipp draws fourteen foot water abaft, and thirteen foot foure inches afore.

Munday the 6th. Cloudy cold weather. This day I went ashore and sixteene men, wee travelled ten miles West into the land, the hills there are covered with snow, it is very cold, wee could not go any farther at this time of yeare, for snow, and the air so cold wee cannot endure to lie on the ground. On the hill that I was on wee could see nothing but hill beyond hill, all into the land. No woods, nor tree, nor bush, all grasse downs. The land is flat aloft. On the topps of the hills fresh water runs down in several places, which melts from the snow, now, and when the water leaves there is no snow. I saw many Guianacos, some Esteridges, no people or sign of people, in land, towards the water side wee saw many places where they have laid, in the open hills, in the snow. Wee saw some places where they had killed Guianacos and Estridges and had eat them. They make but small fires, with litle sticks. I do not find that they use the fire for roasting their flesh, for wee see raw flesh hang to the bones, and how they have gnawed it with their teeth, the fire is only to warm their children's fingers as wee imagin. I gathered some handfulls of Guianacos wooll, which lay at these places, these people must see us as wee travell to and fro, every day, but they will not come neare us, or

[80] **June 1670 The *Sweepstakes* at Port St Julian.**
Or bee seen by us. They live as a wild beast or worse, for they must bee at sometimes in great want of food, here is neither fruit, root, or herb for food. The Land is dry gravelly soile, with sand, and in many hills[1] a Marle, two foot below the surface. The grasse grows in knotts not very long, but thick, it is a dry grasse, in the valleys the earth is of a Petery nature. Many Estridges seen. No sign of mineral or mettal. I and my company have looked in most places where wee have travelled for it. To night wee got down but very weary.[2]

[1] 'places' struck through in the original.
[2] Following words 'It was neare tuesday' struck through.

Tuesday the 7th, new moon to day, fine weather but Coole, the starrs neare the Pole Antarctick are very visible. Some of the small starrs in the Constellation of litle Hydra are neare the Pole. Here are many good starrs neare the Pole for observation of the first and 2d magnitude. The ☆ at the South end of Aridanes [Eridanus],[1] ☆ hydras head,[2] the ☆ in the peacock's eye,[3] and ☆☆ in Tucan's bill. ☆☆ in Tucans thigh and back,[4] the ☆☆ in Grurs [Grus] head, and wing, and body.[5] But the brightest starrs are the two ☆☆ in the former foot of Centaurus[6] and the Crosers;[7] the other starrs are of the 3d and fourth, & 5th magnitude, the two Clouds[8] are seen very plainly, and a small black cloud[9] which the foot of the Crose is in is alwaies very visible when the Crosers are above the horizon, as they are alwayes here in these Latitudes. The heavens in this S. hemisphere are as the heavens in the North hemisphere, but no starrs in 18° of the Pole fitt for observation. No Pole starre as the ☆ in the taile of the litle beare is in the North.[10] The air is cold, but very healthy for stirring men. I have not had my finger ached as yet. A man has an excellent stomach here, I can eat foxes and kites as savourily as if it were mutton. Every fox and kite that wee kill, wee eat. Nothing comes amiss to our stomacks. Not one man Complains of cold in his head or of Coughs, Young men well grown and of good shape are most fitt for this Countrey, It being a dry and hungry air, and provisions to bee got with pains.

Sunday the 12th, wind at WNW. This day I killed two hares with my greyhound.[11] If I had brought two brace of greyhounds, I could Kill Guianaco's, Ostridges, and hares enough to feed the whole Company, and have provision to salt up. Here is hundreds of Guianacos in Companies, now the snow hath Covered the inlands: twenty Estridges in a Company together. The Land is so plain that a man cannot come to a shott of them; but they will stand Looking till a dog come neare them. This greyhound bitch that I have hath no heels to run, shee is but the race of a mungrel, the other dogs which the company have are water Spaniels, and two mungrel Currs, good for nothing at all but to eat, if wee should want provisions when wee are travelling in the Land. When any man comes into these Countries I do advise him to bring good store of salt, and fowling peeces, and hail-shot and 3 or 4 brace of good greyhounds.

[81] **June 1670. The *Sweepstakes* in Port San Julian.**

And two or 3 couple of Beagles, and a water dog or two, and hee will never want flesh if hee stay there seaven yeares. Shoes wears away fast in this Countrey, spades and pickaxes

[1] This is probably α Eridani (Achernar), magnitude 0·6.

[2] This is probably β Hydri, magnitude 2·9, which is relatively near the South Pole, however it might be α Hydræ (Alphard), magnitude 2·2, which is an equatorial star with declination about 8½°S.

[3] This is probably α Pavonis (Peacock), magnitude 2·1.

[4] It is not clear which these stars are; the brightest star in Tucan is α Tucanæ, magnitude 2·9.

[5] The stars in Grus are α Gruis (Al Na'ir), magnitude 2·2, β Gruis, magnitude 2·2, and γ Gruis.

[6] These are α Centauri (Rigil Kentaurus) and β Centauri (Hadar), magnitudes 0·1, and 0·9 respectively, which are quite near the Southern Cross.

[7] These are the stars of the Southern Cross the brightest of which are α Crusis (Acrux), magnitude 1·1, γ Crusis (Gacrux), magnitude 1·6, and β Crusis, magnitude 1·5.

[8] These are the larger and smaller Magellanic Clouds, which look like detached bits of the Milky Way.

[9] This is Nebulus Negro, or the Coalsack a very prominent dark nebula, resembling a large hole in the glow of the Milky Way, at the foot of the Southern Cross.

[10] Pole star, α Ursæ Minoris (Polaris).

[11] Originally in the plural but the final 's' deleted.

are good to dig the hares out of their holes, for they hole when Chased. Here is as good hunting as can bee in any part of the world. I am Confident the greyhounds will Kill Guianacos, Estridges, and hares every time they run. And the beagles will shew where the game is killed, if you should not see it. The land is clear as new market [Newmarket] heath, in rounding hills and dales, but the grasse here is a litle longer and more seared and dry. Nets for fishing, as Saines, will bee very serviceable, while the weather is warm to take fish, for here is fish enough at that time, and a man can endure the water to fish. As for salt, here is enough at this Harbour for fetching from the Salt Pond, which I spoke of before, if a man bee here in the time of the yeare, which is in the Sum*m*er months here, that is, in December, January, february, March and the first part of April. In these times here is thousands of tunns, of as good salt as any is in France. But what salt is in other parts of the Land I know not. This I know, an industrious man can make salt in most parts of the Land, by the sea side.

Wednesday the 15th. Wee fetched salt, I had all hands went with mee, excepting eight men to look after the Shipp. I cause all hands to fetch salt, to walk the men to stretch their legs, it keeps the Lazie fellows from the Scurvie, and their bodies in health. All the salt which was in the pond at our first finding it, is all dissolved into Pickle, Not one grain left, but what wee laded on the dry shore that lies as I left it. Some men killed ducks as wee went to the salt pond. Thanks bee to gods wee do not want one mouth-full of victuals, and wee eat nothing of the Ship's allowance but bread. salt seale, & pengwins is our food, and ducks and wild fowle, every day for them that will go agunning. Some men I am forced to make go a guning for themselves, they are so lazy that they will not stirre because the weather is sharp and Cold, and they favouring themselves begin to grow stiffe in their Limbs, these people are the Stewards and Chirugeons, and such kind of fellows as are from action. The young men that are alwayes in action are as healthy as any men Can bee. The Country is healthy for Europeans that are stirring. The air is much as the air in England in the dead of winter, or rather colder, and sharper. The snow does not lye long on these Lands next the sea, but on the inner hills it lies all the winter, as I have seen hitherto.

Munday the 20th. This day I took twelve men with mee, and went ashore West into the land to see for Indians, neare eight miles, but could not see any. I went to the place where I put up my Cloth, but could not perceive that any man had been there, for every thing was as I left it.

[82] **June 1670. The *Sweepstakes* in Port San Julian.**

I went to and fro in the land, and saw where the Indians had been and made small fires, and Laid behind a bush lately, but could not tell where to find them. I would willingly have had free Conference with them, to have known what the Countrey affoords in land. Their liveing is miserable for they lie on the ground like beasts, and their food as I perceive hard to come by. No wood nor tree to bee seen, many Guianacos and Estridges, some hares and foxes; my greyhound killed today two Estridges and one hare. I had the Estridge weighed, and one weighed forty nine pound. The hare weighed fourteen pound, the Estridges are nothing as big as the Estridges in Barbary nor of the colour nor feather.[1]

[1] Darwin's rhea. See above, pp. 207, n. 4; 214, n. 4.

These are grey on the back, and shaggy feathers good for nothing, and the feathers on their bellies are white, they have long legs and small wings, they cannot fly. They have a long neck, and a small head & beaked near like a goose. They are much like a great turkey cock, and good lean, dry meat, and sweet. I came aboard at night.

[*blank space*][1]

Wednesday the 22ᵈ. This day I went ashore on the East side, saw no people. This day Mʳ John Wood went ashore on the West side and three men with him, they were armed, they travelled into the Land West and B*y* North about foure miles. There they saw seaven people of the Countrey, on a hill making a noise, and wafting them to the Shipp our men went up to the rise of the hill to them. Three of the Indian men came to Mʳ Wood with their bows & arrows in their hands, and a loose skin about their bodies and a furre skin about their heads and peeces of skins about their feet, and all other parts of their bodies naked. They were painted red and white on their faces, they would not come so neare us as to let our people touch them but stepped back as you moved forward, they Continueing their noise, and wafting with their hand towards the Shipp, and kept talking, but no man could understand them, they repeated ozse, ozse, very often. They have a harsh speech, and speak in the throat. They received any thing that you cast to them on the ground. Mʳ Wood gave them a knife, a sash, a neck-cloth, and a bottle of brandy they would not drink. Mʳ Wood could not perceive any bracelets they had, or any thing about them save their skin. They are a people of a middle stature, and well shaped, tawny olive Coloured, black haire not very Long, they seem to bee of a rude behaviour, for they returned nothing for what they received, Nor took no notice of any thing. The rest of

[83] **June 1670. The *Sweepstakes* in PORT Sᵗ Julian.**

their companie staid on the hill. They can endure much cold, for their leggs, arse, and lower parts are naked. Mʳ Wood was taller then any of them, and hee judged the eldest of the three to bee upwards of fourty years old, the other thirty. They seemed to bee very fearfull, they saw their own time, and away they went into the Land. Mʳ Wood returned aboard and acquainted mee what hee had seen.[2] This night wee saw a fire in the hills, they have small dogs with them, they would not come neare our people if they had not fallen accidentally in the hills and valleys with them. I have thoughts that they have heard of the cruell dealings of the Spaniards, and dare not trust us.

[*blank space*][3]

Thursday the 23ᵈ. I went ashore this morning on the West side, with ten men, to look for the Indians. I went all over the hills where they saw them, but I could not see any signe of them. So I returned.

Fryday the first day of July 1670. Gusty Stormy weather, wind at WNW.

[1] Blank space approximating to 6 lines of text.

[2] See above, p. 235, n. 3, for Wood's account of this incident.

[3] Blank space approximating to 10 lines of text.

Saturday the 2[d]. I went ashore on the East side, wee killed a great Guianaco, with the greyhound. I looked in his paunch for the bezoar stone, but found nothing of it. I travelled to and fro but saw no people. I saw where people had made earthen pots, and had glazed them, for there lay some of their stuffe run together. At night I went aboard, wind SW. The Guianaco weighed cleare in the quarters two hundred and fifty pounds neat. Hee served all the Company for a day's flesh, and is good meat.

Tuesday the 12th. I went up to the head of the harbour, but saw no people, there is in the fullers earth Cliffs at the head of the harbour a vein of trade like rotten Ising-glasse.[1] I took some out but cannot find it good for anything. [*right margin:* calke] I digged in the Cliffs but saw nothing to bee taken notice of. I saw in two places peeces of floor timbers of a shipp, they have laid a long time a rotting. Wee saw that the biggest of the bushes have been cut by some Christian people. I saw wooden Cleets,[2] and a peece of Corke, and a peece of an old oare. Some Christian shipp hath been here formerly. I layd ashore to night.

Thursday the 14th. This day I caused all the sailes to bee haled up out of the

[84] **July 1670. The *Sweepstakes* in PORT San Julian.**
Store room, wee found the rats and mice have eaten them much. I had them ashore on justice Island, and put the saile makers to work to mend them.

Fryday the 15th. My Carpenter is at work on the long boat, and hath almost done her. I cannot build a Shallop for here is no timber to work upon, neither have I plank to work, for the Pink hath ninety of my Deale boords in her.[3] If Shee do not come to mee, I cannot build any Shallop, though I have all Iron work sufficient for it.

Munday the 18th. This morning William Christian dyed of the Scurvey, aged fourty years, and upwards, lived in Wapping[4] an able Seaman and a trumpeter.

[*blank space*][5]

Sunday the 31th, the weather is as cold now, as it is in England in the heigth of winter, and the air rather sharper and dryer. I have now 12 men lame with the Cold, and their legs and thighs are turned as black as a black hat, in spots, the Cold hath Chilled the blood that they use bathing &c[a]. to those places and all they can do to prevent it, but it rather encreases on them then otherwise. These are such people as I could not make stirre by any meanes. Those that stirre are as well as any men in the world can bee.

[1] Isinglas, a kind of gelatin derived from fish or, alternatively, mica. *NOED*. It is not clear what Narbrough means here.

[2] Cleets, cleats: Pieces of wood of different shapes and sizes used to fasten ropes upon.

[3] The material to build the shallop had been embarked in the *Batchelour*. The deal boards would have been used for the planks of the hull.

[4] Wapping, now London E1.

[5] Blank space approximating to 9 lines of text.

Tuesday the 2d of August 1670. Wee follow fitting of our rigging and getting the Ship fitt. Here are hundreds of Guianacos in Companies neare to the water side. My greyhound is lame so as I cannot make her run, also here are many Estridges. Here are now many green Plover[1] come down, to the water side, & some Swans, but not full so large as ours, they are white, save a black head, and half the neck, and legs black.[2] Here are some white geese as big as European geese; the brant geese are some white, some black and gray;[3] the mallard and Duck are gray;[4] the Teal are gray.[5]

Munday the 8th I haled[6] [heeled] the Shipp and washed her under water, and lay on stuffe. This day John Riquer[7] died of a flux, aged twenty five years, hee lived at Woolwich,[8] an able Seaman.

Thursday the 11th. Edward Web died to day of the Scurvey, aged about thirty years, hee had been a Lieutenant in the navy.[9] This day I had the sailes brought to the yards.

[85] **August 1670. The *Sweepstakes* at PORT San Julian.**

Tuesday the 16th. I sent the boat for water to a swash on the East side, two of my men saw two people of the Countrey, behind a bush, my men went towards them, they went away, and left a bundle of skins under the bush, my men [*margin:* Indians seene] made sign to speak with them, but they would not stay. My men did not go after them but sate down, they would not stay, they were but of a midle stature. My men brought the bundle aboard to show it to mee, and two mungrel dogs which were coupled together. I opened the bundle and it was several bags of skins with red earth, and white earth, and swoot[10] in a bag, this is their trade they paint themselves with, they had flint stones and arrow heads in the bundle. I searched the bundle all over to see for grains of gold, but could not find any, there was bracelets of shells and bitts of sticks, and braided thongs & arrows, and mussle shells, and Armadillo shells, and a smal point of a naile in a stick for a bodkin. Their skins were peeces of seale skins, and peeces of Guianacos skins, sewed together with small gutts, all very old and full of holes, & smelt of greese. There was peeces of flints made fast with a green gut, in the split of a Stick, which they hold fast to knock their arrow heads into shape, also there was peeces of sticks to get fire with. This was all that was in the bundle, it was made fast with Leather thongs, braided round like a whipp-lash,

[1] See above, p. 213, n. 12.

[2] Black-necked swan, up to 4 ft (122 cm) in length and common throughout Patagonia and southern South America. The feet are actually pale pink. See above, p. 440, n. 1. Peña, *Birds*, plate 15.5.

[3] The brant/brent goose is not found in this area. See above, p. 233, n. 3.

[4] See above, p. 208, n. 6.

[5] See above, ibid. Possibly the silver teal which is common in this area and might pass for grey. It has a blackish top to its head, throat and neck creamy, back blackish, rump and tail very finely barred black and white, looking silver, likewise lower body parts which are paler, while the flanks are more boldly barred black and white. See above, ibid. Peña, *Birds*, plate 17.6.

[6] 'healded' is struck through and 'haled' inserted in the margin in lieu.

[7] The name is given as John Rigman in the Muster List, TNA, ADM 29/2510, and John Rigner in BL, Add MS 88980 A; see above, p. 240.

[8] Woolwich, London, SE 18.

[9] Lieutenant Edward Webb was appointed to the *Revenge*, 1666, and to the *Anne* 1668. Tanner, *Catalogue*, I, p. 421.

[10] Swoot: old form of soot. *NOED*.

and the dogs were coupled with such strings, the mussle shells are their knives. I put all things up in the bag and made it fast. Their dogs are much of the race of Spanish dogs, a good large mungrel Curre, but very tame, any man might handle them, they were gray in Colour, and painted red in spots, they were very leane. There was two great staves of foure foot Long, which was a tough cane in short joints.[1] I carried them ashore next day.

Wednesday the 17th. This forenoone I went ashore, and carried the bundle and the staves and doggs, all as it was found to the same place where it was found, there I left it; and the staves I set up an end, and tyed a white cloth to it. I left there a bill and a hatchet, a knife and nailes for bodkins, and a needle and thread, peeces of Iron hoops, beads and a looking glasse; And about the dog's necks I made fast strings of beads, strung with wire for preventing breaking. I left all these things together, and turned the dogs loose, they went away into the Land. I went about a mile from it, and sate down on a hill for two hours time to see if I could speak with the people, for I would very gladly have seen them. I seeing no body comeing in this time, came away and left all the things there, that the Indians may see wee intend them no harm, for they are very fearfull, for they must needs heare of the Cruell dealings of the Spaniards, from one another, from the river of Plate. I am in great hopes to have Conference with them yet before wee depart this Port. My men could have made the Indians come with them, But I had given order to the whole Company at first Coming in the Land, that no man should use any violence to the people of the Countrey. But Shew them all the Civilitie

[86] **August 1670. The *Sweepstakes* in Port San Julian.**

that might bee, to gain their good wills, wherby wee might have Conference with them, to know the state of the Land which was the businesse wee came for. At night I came aboard saw no people.

Thursday the 18th. I am ready to saile with the first wind, being wooded and watered well for two months time.

Fryday the 19th. The master of the Shipp buoyed the barre at the going out with two Can buoys and two grapnells to ride them.[2]

Saturday the 20th. Wind at NE and blew a Storm, a great Sea ran on the barre which will endanger the Staveing of our buoys.[3] John Stanton died to day of the Scurvey.

Sunday the 21 day, wind at South a small gale, I made ready to saile but could not, the wind fluttering. I sent the boats for water and a sudden Storm rose at West and sunk the boats on the shore, and lost some arms & oars, this night they got them aboard, and had but litle harm done them.

Munday the 22d, wind at North a fine gale. My Master went to the barre in the boat but could not see the buoys they were both sunk or broke away.

[1] This sounds like bamboo, possibly *Chusquea culeou* which is found in the southern Argentine.

[2] Two small anchors to secure them.

[3] Will damage the buoys.

Tuesday the 23^{d}. I went to the barre in the boats and the master with mee wee sweeped[1] for the grapnels but could not find them. The one was laid in two faddom, the other in five faddom at a low water. The tyde being come strong I could not sweep any more. I went aboard.

Wednesday the 24. I went to sweep for the buoys but could not find them. I judge the barre hath covered them for wee have swept all over the Chanell, here is foure foot water on the barre at a Low water. I took marks in Land to saile out in the best of the Channell, for I would not have it buoyed any more for feare of Loseing the grapnells, for I have lost three in this harbour.

Thursday the 25. I went to the barre again and had 3 very fair sweeps but could not find the grapnells. I observed the marks for the barre, and they lieing in and out in the best of the Channell from the narrow, out NE and SW out and in from the narrow to the barre, and the mark is a bluffe point on the West side in the harbour,[2] and a white spot on a hill in the Countrey, keep them touching one with the other and that mark Carries you out in the best of the Channell, and over the barre, as the Channell is now. It alters with out winds, therfore these marks cannot serve for a stranger. I went ashore on the East side to see for Indians, and went to the place where I left their things, there had been no body at them, the dogs were gone. I came away and left all the things as they were. I could not see any body, or signe of people more than what was usual. I came aboard at night.

Fryday the 26. I could not saile to day. I went ashore on the West side & took possession of this land and harbour, for the use of our Soveraigne Lord King Charles the Second and his heires.

[87] **August 1670. The *Sweepstakes* in Port San Julian.**
This day my men killed a great Estridge which weighed sixty eight pounds, no people to bee seen, many Guianacos, and hares, the night comeing on I went aboard. I found at an Indian fire a peece of Christall rock as it grew, two inches Long.

Saturday the 27. So much wind that I could not saile.

Sunday the 28. This morning, the Sun shineing, I weighed and stood down a mile below where I rode. It proved so much wind at West, I anchored and mored, the southerly winds makes the highest tydes on this Coast. There wanted water on the barre, these neap tydes.

Munday the 29. I went into the Countrey due WNW with twelve armed men with mee. I lodged in a valley to night ten miles within the Land, no signe of people lately, wee lay quiet all night.

Tuesday the 30th. This morning wee travelled away West into the Land, ten or 12 miles, the land is all dry with grasse, and bushes in some places, like thorns, the hills high and

[1] For the method of sweeping, see above, p. 242, n. 3.

[2] This point is marked on the plan in Wood's Journal (BL, Sloane MS 3833, p. 22) and lies in the vicinity of Punta Sholl.

many, and snow on the topps, no woods nor tree to bee seen, fresh water comes runing out of the hills in a fine rivulet, no fruit, many Segey [Sedgy] bushes grows on the brink, and brave green grasse, and a green herb, of a pretty strong hot tast, some teal in the water and water birds, this is all I saw about the rivulet. Many large ponds in the Countrey but salt water, in the ponds we saw fowels like herons, but all red;[1] wee saw hundreds of Guianacos in a Company, & twenty Estridges, some hares, and some partridges, grayer and bigger then ours, some Snipes, and small birds, several genne wrens,[2] wee saw several Kites, and small hawks and owles,[3] wee caught two armadillos. I saw two foxes and a wild dogg, many brant geese. The land is in hills and valleys as farre as wee could see, and bad travelling on foot, the soile is gravelly and dry sand, of a salt peter nature, the grasse in some places long and dry, and in some places short & dry, the hills are rounding, aloft like large downes. Wee saw red earth in some places, such as the Indians use, wee saw the footsteps of people in many places, in the Clay, and places where they had been and killed Guianacos, and made fire, there I gathered Guianacos wooll; and Estridge feathers were scattered about the place, and bones, there lay the sculls of three people, no flesh on them, they were very cleane, and no larger then the sculls of European men, smooth and even, teeth Close set, one of the skulls was broke in the upper part, whether these people bee man-eaters or not I cannot tell. I judge they have warrs one with another, by reason here is so few people in this great land, and food enough to live on, and the land all cleare and good for pasturage, for Cattell. No mountains in all the Land, it is plains and grasse, here wants only woods to build with, if that were here it would bee as good a land as any part

[88] **September 1670. The *Sweepstakes* in PORT San Julian.**
of america, for the Countrey is very healthy. This afternoon it rained and was very thick of fogg, so as wee could not tell which way to go, though wee had a Compasse with us, for it is no going into the land without one, for a man will mistake his way the Countrey is so open, in great plains and downs. Wee were very much wet and Cold, wee got to bushes and there made a fire and dryed our selves, wee stayed here all night, wee neither heard nor saw any thing to night more then our own Company.

Wednesday the 31. This morning wee turned out, and read prayers, & breakfasted, and walked about the bushes but saw nothing except here and there a handfull of fine wooll, wee went to the River of fresh water, I viewed the gravell which Lay[4] in it, but could not see any grains of gold. This river is very good water, and runs strong enough to turn any over-shot mill.[5] It empties it selfe into the West end of the great Salt Pond, where wee had the salt out. No signe of any mettall or mineral droves of Guianacos feeding on the downs, and some Estridges. I being loath to hinder time in staying longer with the Shipp here if a fair wind should present, to saile, and seeing what the Countrey is, wee returned aboard

[1] Probably the Chilean flamingo. See above, p. 243, n. 4.

[2] The wrens found in this area are the grass wren (*Cistothorus platensis*) and the house wren (*Troglodytes aedon*). Harris, *Guide*, p. 111.

[3] The owls found in this area are the great horned owl (*Bubo virginianus*), the burrowing owl (*Athene (Speotyto) cunicularia*), and the short-eared owl (*Asio flammeus*). Harris, *Guide*, pp. 95–6.

[4] This word is superimposed over an illegible deleted word.

[5] Over-shot: Driven by water shot over from above, *NOED*. Hence a mill driven by a waterwheel with the water passing over it from above.

at evening. I saw more signs of people neare the water side, then up in the Land, and Sets which they make to shoot Guianacos in that passe or Estridges for there is bushes they lye behind, and have holes to put their arrows through and shoot them. To night I was down at the boat, and went aboard the Shipp. This day Policarpus Ingiham died of Scurvey, aged thirty years, Chirurgions mate, hee lived in the town of Sandwich.

Thursday the first of September, 1670, wind at North a small gale so that I could not saile, this day wee tryed for fish but Caught none, the water is too Cold.[1] I was in the land when I was at the furthest, five and twenty miles, WNW from the harbours mouth, and all things that I saw I have mentioned, excepting some small Creatures, like Effets[2] which runs in the grasse, no manner of snake or venemous creature have I seen in this Countrey, here are some earth worms and Catterpillers, and other buggs, but few in number, no wild beasts of prey or any thing to annoy the inhabitants, but cold and hunger. Here lyes a large Countrey open to receive any inhabitants from forreign parts, the Land would produce european grain if planted, and breed Cattel. This day Christopher Tuck died, Steward of the Shipp, of Scurvey. I caused his corps to bee buried, with the rest, in the Island of justice.

Sunday the fourth, this morning I got under saile, it proved Calm on the flood, I anchored again.

Munday the 5th. This forenoon the wind came to the NW and blows a mighty

[89] **September 1670. The *Sweepstakes* in PORT St Julian.**
Storme. I had the yards and topmast down. It continued stormy all night and base wet weather.

Wednesday the 7th. It blew a mighty storm I caused the sheat Anchor to bee let go. I was in danger of driveing ashore, it blows so vehemently in gusts.

Saturday the 10th. Nathaniel Nash a seaman died of the Scurvy.

Thursday the 15th. I weighed on the flood, but could not Stemm the tyde.[3] I anchored again against a place wee called fishers nose, which are a point of Rocks which lye on the West side.[4] This evening Zekias Bynon died of the Scurvey, a Seaman aged thirty five yeares Lived at Swanzey in wales.

Fryday the 16. Wind at WBS a fresh gale, this morning I weighed and got out to sea. I had on the barre a quarter lesse foure faddom,[5] It was neare a high water, the Channel lies in South West and by South by the Compasse, over the Barre and into the narrow, till

[1] Presumably this means the water was too cold for the sailors to wade in and use the seine net.

[2] See above, p. 423, n. 5.

[3] Could not make headway against the tide.

[4] This point is not named on Narbrough's plan of 'Port Dissier'; however, an anchor is shown in the channel abreast Punta Sholl which is fringed with rocks on the plan, so it may be a point in this vicinity. See Plate 1.

[5] 22 ft of water.

you bring the harbour open, Then it lies in SSW till you are past fishers nose. There you may Anchor, but have a care of a sunken rock which lies on the East side thereabouts.[1]

The channel is now neare two Cables length broad on the barre, the midle grounds[2] are beach stones and Covered at half flood, & so is the beach on the West side, which you must borrow nearer then on the East side. It is a full Sea on the barre at half an houre past eleaven of the clock on the Change day of the moon, the tyde rises neare three faddom & a halfe, and runs as strong as the tyde in the hope.[3]

This forenoon the wind came to the South West and blew a fresh gale. I could not hold the shore aboard. I considering my men being very weak, I thought it most fitt to go for Port Desire and there to refresh the men, for there I could have what Pengwins and seales I would have, which are good Provision. Also I do intend to salt up a quantity of each to Carry to sea with mee, to Lengthen my Provisions. This forenoon I steered from St Julian NNE and made what saile I could to get to Port Desire. This night it was a small gale and veared to the West South West, I judge it best to make an easie saile in the night for feare of runing up with the Eadystone Rock before day Light.

Saturday the 17th, wind at West South West a fresh gale, this morning I was thwart of the Eadystone rock, the wind came to the South a fresh gale. I steered NBE for three Leagues, then North, Westesterly [Westeasterly], to hale into the bay of Port Desire. It blew a hard gale to day and Split the fore top saile. At twelve of clock to day I anchored in the Bay of Port Desire in twelve faddom

[90] **September 1670. The *Sweepstakes* in Port Desire.**
water, neare two miles off the shore in the midle of the Bay. I could not send to Pengwins Island it blew so fresh, and a great Sea.

Sunday the 18, gusty weather, snow and haile. I weighed and stood in before the Port's mouth and turned into the narrow, and fell up into the birth where I rode when I was here before, I anchored and mored. There was a partile [partial] eclipse of the moon neare eight of the Clock this night. I could not see the time of begining nor ending the moon was Clouded.

Munday the 19th wind variable and foggy, wee got fresh water aboard. Here is a great deale of fresh water in the valley where I digged a well before, it is snow water and very good.

Tuesday the 20th. Wee went to Seale Island[4] in the harbour and killed some Seales, there was not many, this afternoon wee skinned them & every man dressed and eat what hee would, they are good food. This evening I went with the boats to Pengwin Island[5] and lay there all night on the Island, there were millions of Pengwins and Seales, there were abundance of Pengwins eggs. It is now the time of their begining to Lay.

[1] Piedras Rodríguez.

[2] Banco Ferreyra.

[3] The Hope anchorage in the River Thames, see above, p. 358, n. 4.

[4] Shown on Narbrough's plan of 'Port Dissier' (Plate 1), now Isla de los Leones.

[5] Isla Pingüino.

Wednesday the 21. This morning I had both the boats Laden with Seales, and Pengwins, and eggs. Ten men may kill ten thousand Pengwins in lesse then an houre's time, the Seales and Pengwins are numberlesse, a man cannot passe on the Island for them.

Thursday the 22[d], fair weather. I divided the eggs among the men. Wee skinned the Seales and the Pengwins, and salted the flesh in Bulk on the rock, and covered it to keep the wind from it. Good weather and litle wind to night.

Fryday the 23[d], fair weather. I went to Pengwin's Island, and Laded both the boats with Pengwins and eggs. The eggs lay so thick on the Island that a man may Lade Barks with them very speedily. These eggs are bigger and better then a Duck's egge in England. The Pengwins are so many as they Cover the Island over.

Saturday the 24th. Wee skinned the Pengwins, and salted the flesh in Bulk. My men begin now to get upon their Legs and grow hearty. These eggs are excellent refreshment, and the fowles are very good food.

Sunday the 25, foggy & rain, wind came to the North, and blows hard. I had severall men on the North shore to day, but could not see any body.

Munday the 26th wind at North West. Wee salted up our Seale's flesh and Pengwins in Cask and put Pickle to them. The Seale is very sweete and Looks very well, I have severall men on shore looking to & fro to see

[91] **September 1670. The *Sweepstakes* in Port DESIRE harbour.**
for people, but cannot see any. Wee find several places where they have laid Lately, but they will not come neare us, nor bee seen of us, by any meanes. I have beades and knives hung on a Pole upon the hill, and they come not neare it.

Fryday the 30th, wind at North. I went up the river about ten miles, And Don Carolus & ten men with mee to see for people. Wee Lay out all night on the South side, saw no people. This night the people of the Countrey came to our litle well, which is up in the valley, and stole an Iron pot and 3 Suits of clothes of the men's which were layd there a drying, with some other Linnen, but did not medle with the beads which were hung up on a pole. The people of the Countrey have made in a valley the form of the shipp, in Earth and Bushes, and stuck up peeces of sticks for masts, and redded the Bushes all over with red earth. This Model I imagin is to record our Ship, for they Cannot have any records but by imitation. This fancy wee let alone untouched of any, I laid a String or two of beads on it, and Came away. Close weather to night.

These people must Certainly have received some injury in former times from some people that have been here in shipping, otherwise they would come in sight of us. Or else they have heard of the Cruell dealings of the Spaniards towards the Indians. I have used all faire meanes possible to have a Conferrence with them, but all is in vain, they dare not trust us. They must see us walk to and fro every day. I have seen in many places as I walked the Land where they had newly been, and gone away when they saw us first appeare on the hills. This Countrey is given much to westerly winds and stout gales.

Saturday being the first of October, 1670, wind at South, & some thunder. I was up in the Land, but no people to bee seen.

Sunday the 2^{d}. I went to Pengwin's Island with both boats. This evening it thundered & lightened much & rained, much wind at West in gusts. I lay at the Island all night, the boats rode in a small Bay in the North West part of the Island, which is the best place to land on. There runs a great sea commonly on the rocks all about the Island, and make it a bad place to Land on. The whole Island is but a rock of it selfe. The tydes run very strong about these Islands, and between the Islands and the maine extreame swift, and makes great ripplens on rocks that Lyes between the Islands. A man must bee very Carefull or else hee will Lose his boate, for this place is dangerous, only the great plenty of provisions on them gives the occasion of people's coming to them, here are so many eggs as a man cannot set his feete cleere of them. Very cold to night wind at WSW.

[92] **October 1670. The *Sweepstakes* in PORT DESIRE.**
Munday the 3^{d}, wind at NW a stout gale. I left eight men on the Island to kill seales and Cut off the fat to make oyle [oil] for Lamps. To day I came aboard with the boat's lading of Seales and Pengwins.

Tuesday the 11th, wind at WSW very cold haile and slatty snow [sleety]. My men are all in good health and are Lusty and fatt. Those which had the Scurvy are got Lusty and well with eating of fresh meat and such green herbs as they can pick up on shore, as green pease leaves and such like. They mince it and fry it with eggs and seale oyle, And it hath raised every man in as good health as they were at our coming out of England. Wee fare well, and have great plenty of good provisions of Seales and Pengwins. I can Confidently say that on the Island of Pengwins there is more Seales & Pengwins at this present then three hundred tunns of Cask can hold when dressed and salted, besides what are going off & comeing on. If any have occasion for provisions of flesh, if they have salt, here they may furnish themselves with what quantity they will have, and I can assure them it will last foure months sweet if not Longer, if care bee taken in blooding and dressing, and salting as I have prescribed before. The salt may bee also had at St Julian's salt pond if in Sum*m*er time. Also I believe that salt may bee made at Port Desire, in the Summer, for here is some dryed salt in the holes in the Rocks. Here are several flats where a man may make pitts and let in water, and so make salt, as I have seen in other places.
The Pengwin is a fowle that lives by Catching and eating of fish, which hee dyves for, and is very nimble in the water, hee is as big as a brant goose, and weighs neare about 8 pounds. They have no wings but flat stumps like finns, their Coat is a downy stumped feather, they are blackish gray on their backs and heads, and white about their necks and down their bellies, they are short legged like a goose, and they stand upright like litle Children in white aprons, in companies together, they are full necked & headed and beaked like a Crow, only the point of the bill turns down a litle, they will bite hard, they are a full trussed bird, they are very tame and will drive in heards to your boat's side like sheep, and there you may knock them on the head all one after another, they will not make any great hast away.[1] Here are a great many Sea Picks,

[1] See above, p. 208, n. 13.

Ducks, Oxbirds, gulls, Sea-mews, white sea pidgeons, white breasted Dyvers and Dabchicks.[1]

[93] **October 1670. The *Sweepstakes* in Port Desire.**

Wednesday the 12th, cleare weather, wind at West. This day I got all things off the Shore, I have 12 hogsheads full of Seale, salted and pickled, And six punchions of pengwins salted. I wait the first opportunity to saile for the Straits of Magellan, and for the Coast of Chili &ca.

Fryday the 14th, fair weather, wind at West, a stiff[2] gale. At 6 of clock [*margin:* weighed] this morning the tyde of flood served, I weighed and made what saile I could, by eight of clock I was out and at sea, at ten of clock the wind came to the South South West, a fresh gale, I stood to the Southward. I saw I lost ground, the tyde of ebb being done I bore into Port Desire Bay, & [*margin:* Anchored againe] anchored in fourteen faddam water, oasy sand, I rode fast, wind at South.

Saturday the 15th. This morning the wind came to the North a fresh gale, I weighed at three of clock and stood out of the Bay, at 7 of clock I passed by Pengwin's Island, from Pengwin's Island I steered SSW. This afternoone I passed by the Eadystone rock In halfe a mile to the Eastward of it, I sounded and had ground at 21 faddom, rocky ground; the rock bore West B*y* North of mee, the sea broke upon it, It was but dipping with the water's edge, and no bigger then a Boate. The Sadle table hill on the Land bears WNW from mee. This rock lyes good five leagues off the shore. Litle wind to night at WBN I steered SSW.

Sunday the 16th, wind at NNW. I steered SWBS by my Compasse which is SW westerly. To day at noon I observed the Sun on the meridian, And found my Latitude to bee 49°08′ South, but could not see the Shore. The wind came to the East, I steered SWBS till 6 of clock, then I sounded and had ten faddam, black oasy sand, a very thick fogge. I haled off SE, at 12 of clock at night I had 40 faddom. I kept heaving the Lead as I sailed from ten faddom, and had all along deeper water every Cast, black fine sand. I reckon I am seaven Leagues off the shore, and two Leagues to the Southward of Port San Julian. Very foggy weather and wet much, the winds came to the North a fresh gale, I handed my topsailes and stood off EBS, a great Sea comes out of the NE.

[1] A sea pick is probably a sea pie or oystercatcher. See above, p. 208, n. 8. Oxbird is used for the ringed plover, sanderling and common sandpiper, *NOED*. See above, p. 213, n. 12. Sea pigeon is a name given to rock doves, black guillemots and grey kittiwakes, *NOED*. The former are not white and the latter two are northern hemisphere birds. These might have been snowy sheathbills (*Chionis alba*), which are white and not unlike pigeons. Peña, *Birds*, plate 37.1. Divers are not found in this area. However, divers also have a superficial resemblance to cormorants and shags. *Book of British Birds*, p. 206. The name 'white breast' is used elsewhere to refer to shag, so these might have been either rock shag, or imperial shag, both of which have white breasts and are common in this area. See above, p. 308, n. 7; below, p. 493, n. 2. Dabchick is a name given to the lesser grebe (*Podiceps minor*), *NOED*. The grebes found at sea in this area are the white-tufted grebe (*P. rolland*), the silvery grebe, (*P. occipitalis*), and the great grebe, (*P. major*). Peña, *Birds*, plates 4.2, 4.3, 4.4, 4.6; Harris, *Guide*, pp. 35–7.

[2] 'fine' crossed through in the original.

Munday the 17th, wind at NNE a fresh gale, and a mighty thick fogg, a great [*right margin:* N.N.E.] Sea runs. I lay by with the Shipps head to the Eastward till ten of the clock then I hove the lead and had fourty five faddom, fine black sand. I stood of[f] East South East. Very foggy I could not see the Land. I reckon my selfe twelve leagues off at 2 of the clock, and the Latitude to bee 49°40′ S. I lay off and on all night, between thirty faddams and fifty faddoms water, fine black sandy oaze. The fog is so thick that I dare not venture to saile.

Tuesday the 18th. this forenoon the wind came to the South B*y* East, and

[94] **October 1670. The *Sweepstakes* off the Coast of Patagonea.**

blew hard, at six this Afternoon it cleared and I saw the land, I was about 7 leagues off it. I sound and had 36 faddom, black sand, I reckon my selfe in the Latitude of 49°50′. The land is all plain aloft so farre as I could see, both to the northward and to the Southward, and steep white Cliffs to the sea side of a good height with black Strakes down them. This evening it proved very thick of fogg, and a great Sea, the wind at South-South-East and blows hard. I stood off to the Eastward to night with an Easie saile.

Wednesday the 19th, foggy wet weather, wind at South East a stout gale. I tacked and layd the Ship's head to the Southward. At 4 of Clock this morning I sound and had fifty six faddom. I am ten leagues off the Land. The wind came to the North a fresh gale I steered in West South West. At 8 of clock it cleared up I saw the Land, it bore West of mee, I was five leagues off it, I had thirty two fad*dom* black sand. I stood in foure leagues of the shore and had thirty faddom, black sand. The Land Lyes along by the true Compasse South W bee [by] South, And North East and be North. In the Latitude of fifty [*margin:* Lat by obs. ☼ 50°20′S] degrees the Land is low to the sea side; and is Cliffs to the northward of this low land, and the Land makes along low bay to the Southward. I steered along SWBS. At the South part of this Low land or Bay, the land rises of a good height, with steep white Cliffs to the sea-ward, And it makes a Cape as I come from the Northward. This Cape I called Beachy head. It sheweth like Beachy in England.[1] The land is high in Land in a Large Hill with a flat table aloft, and a round Coppling hill at the North end of the table land, and is as high as the table land. This is Called in the Charts, the Hill of St Ives.[2] There are round Copling hills neare the sea side to the Southward of St Ives about three miles. I had a good observation today of the Sun, and find my latitude to bee [*margin:* by obs*ervation* ☼ 50°20′S*outh*.] fifty degrees twenty minutes South. The shore side white Cliffs. The head land which I called Beachy is in the Latitude of 50°10′ and the hill of St Ives in the Lat*itude* of 50°18′ S. I have 25 faddom, and am about three leagues off the shore, the Sounding is fine black sand, very fair Soundings all along this Coast. No woods to bee seen, all grasse downes. I steer along SWBS as the land lies. It makes here & there a litle in Bayes, but pretty plain aloft. This land of St Ives is the highest land I have seen on the Coast. It is indifferent plain land to the Southward of it, rounding in some places, with Copling hills and downs. The Land is plain from Port San

[1] Probably Punta Norte (50°06′S, 68°09′W), at the entrance to Puerto Santa Cruz, or a position slightly further north. See above, p. 252, n. 1.

[2] See above, p. 252, nn. 1, 2, 3, for remarks on the location of these features.

Julian to the hill of St Ives, without ever a hill to bee seen, as you saile along from one to the other, white Cliffs face the sea shore of a good height most part of the way between them. This afternoon the wind came to the South and blew hard. I handed my topsailes and stood off to the Eastward all night, a great Sea comes out of the South East. I am put

[95] **October 1670. The *Sweepstakes* off the Coast of Patagonea Latit*ude* 50°33′ S.**
to try under my main saile to night at ten of clock, it blows so hard.

Thursday the 20th, fair weather. At 5 of clock this morning the wind veared about to the North a fine gale, I set the topsailes, and stood in for the shore SW. At two this morning I sounded and had 40 faddom, black sand. I was 9 leagues off the shore. I sounded several times to night, and had 38, 36, & 35 faddoms fine black sand.[1] And as I stood in I had fair Soundings. At 7 of clock this forenoon I was in three leagues of the shore, I had 19 faddoms, black oazy sand. The sea side is white steep Cliffs, and grasse downs aloft, in rounding hills inland of an indifferent height. No woods to be seen. The Land here makes in a Bay, where the river of Saint Cruz goes in. At the North point of the river of St Cruz there lies rocks, 3 leagues off in the sea, I saw the breach. St Cruz lies in the Latitude of 50°37′ South.[2]
The Land here lies South West and North East, for some leagues. The Compas hath variation – 16°37′ easterly. I, having a fine gale at North, steered all along the shore in lesse then three leagues of it, SW and SWBS. I have fair soundings at 19 faddom, black oazy sand. This day at noon I had a good observation and was in the Latit*ude* of – 50°33′. The shore is steep white Cliffs an indifferent height, and dawakes[3] down in some places, grasse land aloft, no woods nor tree nor bush to bee seen. I steered SWBS all night, and had a fine small gale at North. I had twenty faddom water I was foure leagues off the shore, and when I found the water to shoald, I edged off to keep my Depth – but I did not see any danger.

Fryday the 21, fair weather wind at NBE a small gale. This morning I was in foure leagues of the shore, I steere SSW as the land lyes. I had 19 faddoms oazy black sand. The land is white Cliffs steep up and Dawks in many places by the sea shore, aloft plain downs and grasse land, the Cliffs have spoots grays in many places. I cannot see any smoake in the land any where. The Land shows much like the Land at St Julians. To day at noon I was in the Latitude of 51°21′S and sailing in three leagues of the shore side, a fair Coast along. I had 19 faddoms black oazy sand. I see several whales in these seas and some Porposes no small fish, some Seale & some Pengwins, Sea mues, Sea gulls and small Peterels. The land is of a good height here and in Cliffs to the sea white.

[1] 'sand' is written over an illegible deleted word.

[2] This reference to the river of St Cruz is not in BL, Add MS 88980 A. The entrance to Río Santa Cruz lies in 50°08′S and has no rocks 3 leagues off it. This might be Ría Coig, but this lies in 50°57′S and again has no rocks 3 leagues off it. Narbrough may have inserted this based on remarks in Hakluyt, *Principal Navigations*, III, p. 725: 'From the hill of S. Yves to Rio de Cruz are 8 leagues, Northeast and Southwest: and on the North side of the river it hath a very high land, and in the toppe it is plaine and lyeth two leagues broad, layd out along North and South, and the downefall on both sides hath as it were saddles. This Cape hath many points of rocks lying 4 leagues into the sea.'

[3] This is probably a variant on 'doke, dawk' meaning dips in the coastline.

In the Latitude of fifty one deg*rees* and thirty minutes there is a steep up Cape which I called Cape fair weather,[1] by reason of a fair day. I was abreast of this Cape at 2 of clock afternoon. Southward of Cape fair-weather a mile, runs up a bay trenting to the Southwestward, and Low land. Here goes in the river of Gallegos. The Land makes low, and turns away, South for three leagues, then more easterly. From Cape fair weather I steered away SSE. About 4 leagues SSE from the Cape there is but ten faddom water, sandy ground. For four miles running the land makes low, and shows seven or 8 litle hillocks by the sea shore

[96] **October 1670. The *Sweepstakes* before the river of Gallegos.**
as if they were islands.[2] There is shoald water a great way off the shore at least foure leagues, for I saw severall riplings of the tyde, and one breach, this shoald ground lies in the Latitude of 51°38′, And runs to the Latitude of 51°46′. This is a shoale bay all over, and the Land is Low land. It was as much as I could see the Land that was West of mee, seaven or 8 litle hills apears on this low shore, the tyde runs strong here, I had my boat brought to her Grapnel to try the tyde, the Ebb Sett to the SE.[3] I made what saile I could to the Southward. This evening it proved calm, I found the flood tyde come and set to the North Westward. At 8 of clock I anchored in eight and twenty faddam water, fine black oazy sand. I was five leagues off the shore low land, the Copling hills bare West and B*y* South of mee. Latit*ude* 51°40′. The tyde of flood Sett NW of an indifferent strength. It is a high water here at ten of the Clock on the Change day of the moon. I tryed for fish, but Could not hook any. I find the Compasse to have Variation 17° easterly. Fair weather all night, the heavens very cleare. I observed the Crosers,[4] and find my Latit*ude* 51°42′ S. The tydes rise about three faddoms here, as I observed.

Saturday the 22, fair weather, the wind at North & litle. At one of clock this morning I weighed and stood SEBS. At 8 of clock I anchored in thirty four faddom, black sand it was Calm. I was about foure leagues off the shore, the land is plain aloft & grasse, no woods. The sea shore is steep white Cliffs of a mean height. The Coast lies South South east, and North North West, from the Latitude of 51°45′ S to the Southward for 14 leagues til it comes to Cape Virgin Mary,[5] at the Entrance of the Straits of Magellan, and is steep white Cliffs all along. I had a good observat*ion* of the Sun to day on the Meridian, and find my latitude to bee 51°48′ S.
At one of clock I weighed and steered SE and SSE and had 30 faddom all along, in foure leagues of the shore, sandy ground, the wind was at NNE a fine gale & sea smooth. This evening at 7 of clock I anchored [*margin:* Cape Virg: Mary.] in twenty six faddom water black sand. Cape Virgin Mary beares West South West of mee, half a point westerly, about foure leagues of[f] mee where I rode. The Cape is whitish gray Cliffe, steep upp, like Cape S[t] Vincent, in Portugal, and to the northward of the Cape the shore side is white Cliffs, steep up, of a mean height, and the sea beats against the foot of it. The shore is bold too,[6]

[1] This is Cabo Buen Tiempo (51°33′S, 68°57′W).
[2] These are probably Colinas Los Frailes (51°50′S, 69°10′W).
[3] The boat was anchored to measure the tidal stream.
[4] The stars of the Southern Cross.
[5] Now known as Cabo Vírgenes (52°20′S, 68°21′W). See above, p. 255, nn. 3, 4.
[6] A shore which rose steeply from deep water, permitting the near approach of shipping without danger.

and cleare ground, to the northward of the Cape. There is good rideing on that Coast if the wind blow between the NW and SW and the Western quarter. You may anchor in sandy ground in a league or two off the shore, and have twenty faddom, the land is plain grasse land above the white Cliffs, a litle swelling and riseing, here and there hillocks. The Cape is somewhat higher land then any of that shore for five leagues, here is here and there a black strake on the Cliffs, a cables length to the North ward of the Cape. Here is not

[97] **October 1670. The *Sweepstakes* in the Latit*ude* of 51°48′ South.**
any woods, or trees, or bushes to bee seen here, or on any part of the land, but all grasse downes and Plains. As I came from the Northwards, I saw the West land appeare out of the Cape, which runs up to the Westward like a round Copling hill, then the Cape bore W a litle northerly, off mee. At the foot of the Cape on the South part of it there begins a low[1] beach, which goes from the Cape to the SW:ward a league or four miles, then it turns up to the West, as the land lies up the Streights. This beach hath shoalds lies from it East South East, from the pitch of the Cape, a league off and better. Give them a league burth for they show themselves at a low water.[2] There grows some bushes on this beach at the point of it, bee carefull of these shoalds, and here is no other danger, for you will see the turning up of the Straits open like a [*margin:* the Strait is 9. leagues broad at the entrance; but narrower upward.] large deep bay, for the land on the South side is nine leagues off, so broad is the Strait South from the Cape to the South shore Called tierra del fuego. The land I saw plaine, it trents away to the South eastward. It is white Cliffs to the sea side, and good high land into the land.
Cape Virgin Mary at the North entrance of the Straits Lyes in the Lat*itude* 52°26′ S.
And in Longitude from the Lizard of England West 65°42′.
Meridian distance from the Lizard in Leagues, West 1062.
Variation of the Compasse here I find to bee. easterly 17°00′.
Fair weather all night and smooth water, the wind at North a small gale. The tyde runs of an indifferent Strength; the flood sets to the NW and the Ebb to the SE. The tydes rise about three faddom, and it is a high water on the Change day at nine of the Clock. I judge this is the Coast tyde where I ride now, and not the tyde in the Straits. A great whale was seen neare the Shipp to night, my men try to catch fish, but cannot. I would willingly give a better description of the Cape, but here is no remarkable Land the shore is so alike. But to fall with this Cape and to know it will bee by seeing the Straits open, like a bay, and the Land run from the Cape straight West for nine Leagues, of a mean height, and a Cliffe all along, to point Possession.[3] Also you will see the Low Beach at the foot of the Cape. But your Latitude will give you the best directions, and the Broadnesse of the Strait.

Sunday the 23[d], fair weather, wind at N a fine gale. At four of clock in the morning I weghed [weighed] and stood away SSW and then SW. I had the Cape WNW of mee, I kept my Lead going and had twenty faddoms, black sand, I saw a ripling ahead of mee, but my boat went and sound it and had seaven and eight faddams on it, and eighteen, and

[1] The following word 'cape' deleted.
[2] This is the start of Banco Sarmiento. See above, p. 255, n. 7.
[3] Cabo Posesión (52°18′S, 68°58′W). See above, p. 256, n. 6.

twenty faddoms, just by it. It is a [*margin:* a sand bank.] sand bank[1] I went over the top of it with the Shipp. It lyes East South East from the pitch of the Cape neare foure leagues. From this sand bank I steered WSW

[98] **October 1670. The *Sweepstakes* in the Strait of Magellan.**
til I brought the Cape North of mee, then I steered in West. I sounded and had fourty faddoms black sand. I was three leagues off the Cape. I steered in West B*y* North till I came in two leagues of the shore, so I saile into the Straits in that distance[2] off the North shore, West a litle northerly by the true Compasse. I have fair Soundings all along, 38 and fourty faddoms, fine black sand, there is no sign of danger in the fair way. There is a low land which comes from the Cape and the low beach, and runs up about five leagues West, under the Cliffe land, that comes from the Cape and runs straight West a litle northerly, nine leagues. There are steep Cliffs of a mean height and shew ragged, this place is Called point Possession. Now my water shoaldens to twenty eight faddoms, fair Shoaldings and Soundings, sandy ground, at point Possession the Straits is but six leagues broad to the South shore, and that Land is low by the water side, and high land in the Countrey, in a large grasse downe, no wood to bee seen in all the Land of terra del fogo hereabouts. The South Land rounds up to the North West wards that it comes so neare the point of Low Land of the North side, that it makes the first narrow of the Straite to bee but two miles broad, and neare nine miles Long, which makes this East side seem to bee but a deep bay till I came neare the narrow. From the point possession the land on the North side falls Low in a rounding bay to the North Westward, and rounds to the West and SW:ward, til it comes to the narrow. This bay is flat at the head of it near the narrow in Rocks, and Shoale points, lyes out. And on the rise of the Hill on the NW land of the Bay [*margin:* Black rocks] there stands foure Picked upp rocks Black neare together, they are like asses ears.[3] They are a good height on the Downe, and over against Point Possession on the South side of the Channel there lyes three or 4 sands which are neare dry at a low water. I called them the Brases,[4] they run up towards the narrow, therfore keep fair steerage by the North side, and till you come abreast of the Cliffs of Possession, then steer West South West three Leagues and then South West, and that will Carry you directly with the mouth of the narrow, which you will see come open. It shows like a Cliffe of a mean height and a gut runs into it, the land is but of a meane height on both side of this Narrow all about for nine or ten miles on both shores, into the Lands, and here and there a litle rounding hill, and it is plain land in a manner all grasse, not a tree to bee seen on either side. The sea shore is low and flat on the North side of the narrow up in the Bay, and there appeares two or three round Copling hills, that maketh like Islands as wee come sailing up, there lies shoalds off from that NNW

[99] **October 1670. The *Sweepstakes* in the Strait of Magellan.**
part of the Bay.[5] I sound all over with my Boat and had eight and 7 & 5 & 4 faddoms, small pible stones and gravel, as I sounded neare the shore also where there is shoale water there

[1] This is Banco Sarmiento.

[2] 'in that distance' is repeated here.

[3] Now called Orejas de Burro (Ass's Ears). See above, p. 256, n. 8.

[4] These are the shoals at the northern end of Banco Orange, shown on the 'Royal Map' and 'Sloane Map' (Foldout, Plate 5) as 'The Brackes'.

[5] The NE entrance point of Primera Angostura (First Narrow) is Punta Delgada. See above, p. 256, n. 9.

grows long rockweeds which [*margin:* warnings] are good [whishings][1] to take care. Keep your lead sounding alwayes as you saile here, for you will not have above twenty five faddoms in the fair way, oazy sand and small stones, till you come neare the mouth of the narrow at the entering between the flats that lyes on both sides before you Come to bee between the Chapps [chops] of the Lands, above a league. The flatts are dry at a low water. In the Channel there in the fair way is thirty faddoms pible stones, my draft will show you all the danger as I saw. From the Cliffs of Possession to the narrow is about six leagues distance, and it bears South West from possession. Here is anchoring all about this part of the Strait, in the fair way from Cape Virgin Mary till you Come into the narrow. I did not find much tyde any where hereabouts, But in the narrow, And there the tyde runs stronger then it does in the Hope[2] a good matter. The flood tyde setts into the Strait, and the ebb sets out. It keepeth it's Course as on other Coasts. It is 6 houres flood and 6 houres Ebb. It rises & falls neare four faddoms perpendicular. It is a high water here on the Change day of the moon at eleaven of the Clock, as I perceived. Many beds of rock-weeds are driveing to and fro here. This day at two of the clock I was a breast of point possession, I steered from thence West North West, about two leagues, and then West, and West South West, and South West B*y* South, rounding by the North Shore. As I shoalded my Soundings I had 22, 18, 16, 12 & 9 faddoms water, sandy & sometimes gravelly ground, and pible stones. I sailed rounding the shore being unacquainted and Could not tell Certainly where the narrow lay, for it was shut one land with the other so as I could not see the opening, I had the wind at NNE a fine gale. At five of clock I was open of the narrow and steered in SWBS into the Chaps of it. But [*margin:* Enter the narrow.] could not get past a league into it, the tyde being bent out and run so strong as I could not stem it.[3] I was in danger of run*n*ing the Ship against steep rocks which lye on the North side Shee taking a sheere with the tyde, and the wind was a fresh gale at NNE. There grows long rock-weeds on the rocks. I went and sounded over them, and had five foot water on them and fourteen faddom by the side of them next the channel, they come trenting from the point of the narrow of the North shore a mile off.

At 6 of the Clock the wind came to the north, at 8 of clock to the Northwest, [*margin:* put out off the narrow] it fell very dark and rained much, I was forced to fall back again out of the narrow as well as I could, the shore I could not see it was so dark. It fell flatt

[100] **The *Sweepstakes* Entering the first narrow of the Straits of Magellan.**

calm. I finding 25 faddoms water Pible stones and oasy ground I anchored and rode all night, litle wind at Southwest and Dark.

Munday the 24th, fair weather & litle wind at South South West. I saw I rode in the fair way in the Channel, the narrow bore South South West from mee three leagues, the asses ears bore North West of mee, the tyde here runs but of a mean strength. Several whales seen here. I weighed this forenoon & new birthed. I anchored again in nineteen faddoms oazy ground and small stones. I rode now more over on the North side the wind at SW a

[1] The word 'whishings' inserted in square brackets in a different hand, perhaps indicating that a space was originally left blank and the word inserted later, with 'warnings' in the margin as a possible alternative.

[2] See above, p. 358, n. 4.

[3] The tide was so strong Narbrough could not make headway against it.

fresh gale. This afternoon I sent my boat and sound, all about, and found fair Soundings 10, 12, 16 faddoms, gravell ground.

Tuesday the 25th very foggy weather this forenoon the wind came to the NE a fine gale I weighed and stood into the narrow, having a tyde of flood, I steered in SWBS. It fell Calm just as I entered, and so thick of fogg as I could not see the shore I was forced to Anchor in the narrow in fourty faddom water, and ride til the fog was over. I had rough ground which made dints in the tallow of the Lead, the tyde run very strong here, I rode about two houres and the fogg Cleared. I weighed at 10 of the Clock the wind at NE a fine gale, I steered through the narrow South West and by South a litle westerly the first two leagues, then South West nearest a litle southerly. The Strait in this narrow is near two miles broad, and nine miles long, it holds much of one breadth all the way of this nine miles, and neare Straight. From one end to the other it doth alter a point of the Compasse, and no more, in the nine miles. It is steep up banks or small Cliffs on both sides all the way through of a meane height, and at the foot a beach sand and great stones that the tyde flowes over, a stone's cast from the foot of the Cliffe to the Low water mark, or more in some places, on both sides. In the narrowest place I was in the midst of the Channel, I shot off a Saker[1] but it would not throw a shot ashore by a Cables length. The Land on both sides of this narrow is grasse land and of a meane height for 9 or 10 miles inland, and in a manner plaine saveing here and there a litle round Copling hill. Not so much as one tree to bee seen.
I saw a smoak on the South shore eight[2] miles from the narrow into the Land SE. Some Guianacos I saw feeding on the North shore. At the West point of this narrow on the North side or shore there lyes a ledge of rocks from the point a mile off WSW into the sea, they show their heads at a low water, and weeds grow on them. There is a small shoald lies from the point on the South shore, here the Strait grows broad like a sea, as much as a man Can see the shore from one side to the other. It rounds from the narrow both wayes like a bay in low land, by the water side both on the North and South Shore,

[101] **October 1670. The *Sweepstakes* in the Strait of Magellan.**
And high large Downes in land. From this first narrow I steered for the Second narrow,[3] West & by South, and West South West. I sounded as I sailed from one narrow to the other and had 25 faddom and 22 and twenty faddoms black sand for many Casts of the lead. This broad reach a man may anchor all the way from one narrow to the other, and all over on the North shore, for there I sounded; there is eight & 9 faddom halfe a mile off the shore, sandy ground. In this broad reach the shores trents rounding to the Westwards on both sides, til they come so neare as to make the Second narrow, which is neare three leagues Long, and five miles broad, steep up on both sides of an indifferent

[1] The range of a saker was 1,700 ft and random firing 8,500 ft according to Oppenheim, *Naval Tracts* pp. 39–40. Nye, *The Art of Gunnery*, ch. 38, p. 8, records that by experiment with an 8 ft saker loaded with 3 lb of powder, he obtained the following ranges: at 1° elevation 375 yd (343 m), at 5°/693 yd (634 m), at 7°/842 yd (770 m), at 10°/1,050 yd (960 m). The first of these is appreciably less than the point-blank range given by Monson (567 yd). Assuming that Narbrough's saker was elevated about 10°, the range of his gun would probably have been of the order of half a mile.

[2] '8' struck through in the original.

[3] Now Segunda Angostura. See above, pp. 257, n. 5; 258, n. 8.

height, and plain grasse land aloft without trees. It is eight leagues from the first narrow to the second, and something better. The course from one to the other is West and by South, and East and by North. [*blank*] This reach between the first & second narrow is seaven Leagues broad nearest, from the North shore to the South shore. It shows like a litle sea, when one comes into it, for wee Could not see to the Second narrow til I had sailed therin three Leagues or more. At the point of the second narrow on the North shore up to the northeastward a mile or two, there is a Bay on the North shore, and a white Cliffe of an ordinary height which is Called Cape St Gregory.[1] In this Bay you may ride in eight faddom water fine clean sandy ground, and a good half mile off the shore; This is a good road if the wind bee between the NE and the South West to the Westwards, the winds are given to blow most on the Western quarter. As I sailed through the second narrow I sounded in the fair way and had twenty eight and 30 faddoms, small stones. The North shore of this narrow makes in a Bay at the East point and is white Cliffs all the way through. This narrow lies through West South West, and ENE, and at the West end of this narrow the Land is steep up, in white Cliffs, and the South part rounds away short in a foreland which I called Sweepstakes foreland.[2] The South shore rounds away South East from this foreland, and then it trents away to the Southwards in Low land. The North shore of this Strait[3] or narrow rounds up to the northwards in white Cliffs and falls into Low shores. There goes in a harbour which hath four faddom in the Channel at the highwater. It is a flat round harbour within & oazy, I called this Oaze harbour.[4] When you are at the West part of this narrow you will see three Islands, come open, which show to bee steep up Cliffs, they lie triangle-wise one off another. They are foure leagues distance from the narrow, West South West. The smallest and eastermost Isle is Called St Bartholomewes. The biggest and westermost Isle is called Elizabeth. The midlemost and southermost Isle is called St Georges, and by some Pengwins Isle.[5]

[102] October 1670. The *Sweepstakes* in the Strait of Magellan

Here are many Pengwins on it. This evening I got up to Elizabeth Isle and anchored in eight faddoms and a halfe fine black sand two miles off the Isle. The East point beares South by East of mee, fair weather all night the wind SBW.

Wednesday the 26, hazy Cold Cloudy weather, wind SBW a fresh gale I rode fast the winds Contrary to saile. The Strait runs away South in this reach, and is about eight leagues broad from side to side. This morning I went on shore on Elizabeth Island, and at my Landing nineteen of the people of the Countrey came off the hills unto mee.[6] I had Conference with them and exchanged knives and beads for such things as they had, which

[1] Now known as Bahía Gregorio, and the cape Cabo Gregorio.

[2] Not mentioned in BL, Add MS 88980 A, but shown on both the 'Royal Map' and the 'Sloane Map' (Foldout, Plate 5) and now called Cabo San Vicente (52°47′S, 70°26′W). Promontorio Sweepstakes is the name given to the prominent headland 2 miles ENE of Cabo San Vicente.

[3] 'Cliff' struck through.

[4] This harbour is named Crabb Lake in BL, Add MS 88980 A, entry for 12 Feb 1670/71. It was apparently not discovered until then as it is not mentioned on the passage out. It is shown on the 'Royal Map' and the 'Sloane Map' (Foldout, Plate 5) as Oase Harbour and is now called Ensenada Oazy.

[5] These islands are now Isla Marta, Isla Isabel and Isla Magdalena respectively. See above, pp. 259, nn. 1–4.

[6] For information on the indigenous inhabitants of this area, see above, pp. 40–48.

was bowes and arrows, and their skin Coats which are made of young Guianacos skins, I gave them a hatchet and knives and Beades and Jews trumps &c^{a}. they seemed to bee well pleased. I shewed them gold which they would have had, I made signs to them if they had any I would give them knives and beads &c^{a} for it, or if any were in the Land. I layd gold and bright Copper into the ground and made as if I found it there, and I looked to & fro on the earth as if I looked for such things, they Looked one upon another and spoke to each other some words, But I could not perceive that they understood what I meant nor that they knew gold or any other mettall; they would gladly have had every thing they saw. They tryed to break the boat's Iron Grapnel with stones, and would have Carried it away. I let them alone and observed their actions & behaviour, which was very bruitish, they Catched at every thing they could reach although I caused some of them to sit down and I put strings of beads about their necks still they desired more. My Lieutenant Pecket danced with them hand in hand, and several of my men did dance with them and made what shew of friendshipp was possible, my lieutenant Changed his Coat for one of theirs, for they desired it because it was red, which Colour they much esteem. I was in great hopes I might find gold amongst them, I gave them all the Courteous respect I could. After two houres Conferrence with them I made signs I would go and get some more things and Come again, to them, they went and would have us land again under a Cliffe which I judge was their design to heave stones into the Boate and sink her, for the place was very Convenient for such a purpose. They set themselves down on the grasse and immediatly set fire on the grasse on the side of the bank, by what meanes they got fire so suddenly I could not understand. I went and sounded the Channel between Elizabeth's Ile and St Bartholomews Island,[1] & found it a fair Channel to saile through of a mile broad nearest, and deep water in the midle thirty eight faddoms, and nine and ten faddoms neare the shore side, gravelly sand; I saw here is a good Channel to saile

[103] **October 1670. The *Sweepstakes* in the Straits of Magellan.**

through, and to keep along the South side of Elizabeth Island, a faire birth off it[2] til you come up to the West end of the Island. Then you may saile away to the Southward all along the West shore fair by it and there is good anchoring all along in seaventeen faddoms good sandy ground. But half a mile into the Channell there is above a hundred faddom, I could not get ground neither could I perceive much tyde to run hereabout; But between the Islands of St Bartholomew, and Elizabeth, and St Georges, The tydes run strong Ebb and flood as in the Downs,[3] the water rises here ten foot perpendicular and no more on the Spring tydes. There is a Channel between the main and the West end of Elizabeth's Island my boat went through it but could not sound it all over It blew hard, I believe it may bee passable for shipps. It is a mile broad and a good tyde runs in it; off from the West end of St George island neare two Leagues, all the way from the Island there lies a shoald of four faddoms water on it,[4] I sounded over it, there grow weeds all over it which

[1] This is the north-east end of Paso Reina which passes between Isla Isabel on the north-west, and Isla Marta and Isla Magdalena on the south-east.

[2] 'it' repeated in the original.

[3] See above, p. 133, n. 3. The tidal streams in Paso Reina run at 2–3 knots between Isla Marta and Isla Isabel and 3–5 knots west of Isla Magdalena. Argentine Chart 62.

[4] This is Banco Walker which lies 4½ miles WSW from Isla Magdalena, but is not connected to it. On both the 'Royal Map' and the 'Sloane Map' (Foldout, Plate 5), Narbrough shows the bank extending from the island.

you may see when you are neare it. It lies out West nearest from the Island. There is good rideing all that bay over, on the North side of Elizabeths Isle between that and the North maine. It is a large roade and good sandy ground, ten & eleaven & nine faddoms water, and but litle tyde. There is Anchoring all the way through the Second narrow, and there is but twenty eight and thirty faddoms, gravelly ground a good handsome tyde runs here, Ebb and flood.[1] I anchored up two miles to the Westward of this narrow, in twenty two faddoms sandy ground. It was Calm, I weighed again presently and stood up to Elizabeth Isle, and there achored in nine faddoms black sand two miles off the Island.
This afternoon I went aboard the Shipp and took in some knives and beads and glasses, and armes and twenty men, and went ashore on Elizabeth Island. At my landing the same people that were with mee in the morning came to us and brought with them more people to the number of thirty foure in all, men, women, and Children. There was five women of about twenty yeares of age, they had small Children wrapt in skins and hanged at their backs, there were some very sprightly young youths, and well shaped in their Limbs, and well featured in their faces. I gave to every one a string of beades and to the women a looking glasse, and beads for their litle ones. They wondred much at the Glasse, and every one came and Looked in it, and Laughed to see their faces. I caused them all to sit downe and gave them Brandy wine, but they would not drink any. I seeing them all desirous still of more things, I made shew of exchanging of knives, scissers beads and hatchets for gold, I shewed them a bright peece of Copper barre,

[104] **October 1670. The *Sweepstakes* in the Straits of Magellan.**
they all looked on it and spake to one another, but I could not perceive they knew gold. They gave mee their bracelets which were small glittering shells tyed together on a string, and the women wears them about their necks bracelet-fashion, and braided thongs like Laces about their arms and wast[e]s. I could not observe any other wealth they had, for I looked on all their necklaces & bracelets and all things they had about them, in hopes to have seen some grains of gold. If any gold bee in this part of the Land I judge the women might wear it in Bracelets, I could not observe any they had or knew. I made signs to them to go aboard the Ship with mee, but they would not, they ever pointed into the Land with their hands, and spake much, night growing neare I made signs I would sleep, and come again with the Sun. They spake one to the other but their meaning I could not understand. They understood mee at first that I would exchange such things as I had for such things as they had, for they brought their old Bowes and Arrows with them and old Coats spare to exchange with mee for beads, and they would pick out their old broken headed arrows and proffer them in exchange, which I received and gave them beads for them, a string of beads for an arrow. I did this in hopes of haveing future Commerce with them, And that they might understand I came to trade with them and not to hurt them, which I think they did not feare, for they were very Confident with us, and would eat bread and Cheese and drink water with us, but no brandy or wine, they would take the Cup and keep it when I proffered it to them. They were very desirous of Iron trade and very Covetous, and showed one another aside to come at mee for a knife, which I gave to them. Every one kept what I gave them to themselves, they were very orderly now except one old man, and hee would run about us and snatch at anything hee Could, and if wee did not let it goe, hee would take up

[1] The tidal stream in Segunda Angostura runs at 3–6 knots. Argentine Chart 62.

a stone and threaten to strike us with it. I showed the others what hee did but they took no notice of it, for every one did what seemed best to himselfe, and were in no obedience one of the other. I had given them what I had, and it beeing neare night I went into the boate and made way to put off from the shore, the old man would willingly have kept the Grapnell, hee tryed to break the flookes off with his hands, and knocked it with stones. I lay still to observe his actions, and when hee saw hee could not break it hee went up the bank and threatned us with stones, But did not heave any at us, the rest went away danceing and makeing a noise. I made signs I would sleep and come again tomorrow so I left them and went aboard, the Ship, and they went up the hills. One man went and took up a great staffe which hee had laid in the grasse, and his bow and Arrows, hee held up the staffe and shaked it at us and hollowed & went after his Consorts.

[105] **October 1670. The *Sweepstakes* in the Straits of Magellan.**
These people are of a midle stature both men and women, & well limb'd and bodied, roundish faced and well shaped, Low foreheaded, their noses of the mean size, their eyes of the mean and black, they are smooth and even toothed, close sett and very white, small ears, their hair is smooth flag haire & very black and harsh, cut on the fore part even and round, the Locks of a mean Length, both men and women alike, they are full breasted, they are tawny olive Coloured, and reded all over their bodies with red earth, and greace, their faces dawbed in spotts down their Cheeks with white clay, and [*margin:* ×] some black Strakes [streaks] with sm*oak in no method, their arms and feet with the Like, they are small handed and Short fingers, they are active in body & nimble in going or running. Their clothing is peeces of skins of Seales & Guianacos, and Otter skins sewed together, and tewed soft, their garments is in forme of a Carpet of about five foot square, or according to the Largenesse of the person, this they wrap about their body as a Scotchman does his pladding, they have a Cap of skins of fowles with feathers on, they have about their feet peeces of skins tyed to keep their feet from the ground. They are very hardy people to endure Cold, for they seldome wear this loose skin when they are stirring, but are all naked of body from head to foot, and do not shrink for the weather, for it was very cold when I saw them, and the hills all Covered with snow. They have no haire on their bodies nor faces, nor anything to cover their privy parts excepting some of the women which had a skinn before them otherwise the men and women are Clothed alike, only the men have Caps, the women none. The women weare bracelets of shells about their necks, the men none. The men are somewhat Larger then the women in stature, & more fuller faced, the men have a harsh Language and speak rattleing in the throat, and grosse, the women shriller & Lower. They pronounce the word *ursah* often, but what it meant I could not understand, nor one word they spake. If they did not like any thing they would rattle in their throats and cry *ur urah*. Their food is what they Can gett either of fish or flesh by industry, they are under no government, but every man does as hee seem fitt, for they had no respect to any one, nor under any obedience to any body in this Company, Neither did they make any shew of worshipping any thing, either sun or moon, but came directly to us at our first going on Land, makeing a noise, and every man his bow ready strung and two arrows a man in their hands. Their bowes are about an ell Long, and their arrows near eighteen inches Long, and neatly made of wood, and headed with peeces of flint stones, neatly made broad arrow fashion and well fastened to the arrow, the other end is feathered with two feathers,

[106] **October 1670. The *Sweepstakes* in the Straits of Magellan.**
and tied on with a gutt of some beast, when it is green and moist, the bow-string is a twisted gutt. These people have very Large mungrel dogs, much like the race of Spanish dogs, and are of several Colours. I did not see any other Domestick creature they have, Neither Could I at this time see their Boats, for they Lay at the other end of the Island next the main, they waited on this Island for an opportunity of faire weather, to go to the other Isles for Pengwins, there being great numbers of those birds in the Southermost of the three Islands, and a many of white breasted dyvers.[1]

[*margin:* Natives of Mag*ellan* Straits as they appeared in Eliz. Isle.]	[*blank space for a drawing*][2]
[*margin:* their boates are made of bark of trees sewed together with guts of beasts. they are 16 foot long & some 20.	[*blank space for a drawing*]
[*margin:* their houses are made with sticks like Arbours, and covered with green boughes and grasse to keep out rain and snow.]	[*blank space for a drawing*]

Thursday the 27th, the wind at SW a fresh gale, I rode fast. This morning I sent my boat to the West end of Elizabeth Isle and sound that Channel between the Island and the main and found it a good Channel and four faddom water in it. There is a ledge of rocks in it which are seen at a Low water. My Lieutenant and men went ashore on the West end of Elizabeth's Isle, and travelled all about that part to see for the natives, and to look what was on the Island, the natives were gone off the Isle, and no sign of them any where. The Island is a grassy land and greene some bushes grows on it, but no timber trees. It is a good soile of black earth & sandy earth

[107] **October 1670. The *Sweepstakes* in Magellan Straits.**
and white cliffs to the water side in some[3] places, of a mean height, the Land is champion all over, the Island is about eight miles Long, and neare three miles broad. They could not find any kind of mettal on it, nor beast. The Channel between it and the main is about a mile broad. The main land against the Island is good plain Land, by the water side and grasse downes, But the In land is high rocky mountains and snow lyes Continually on their topps. My boat went from Elizabeth Island to St Georges Isle, and got two hundred Pengwins. These Pengwins make holes in the ground like Conies seaven or eight foot Long, they run into these holes to secure themselves, for the natives do come to those Islands and kill many of them, for at this time there lay about a hundred in a heap

[1] See p. 455, n. 1.

[2] Each of the 3 following blank spaces approximates to 7 lines of text and was presumably intended for an illustration of the indigenous people encountered, and their boats and dwellings.

[3] 'many' struck through.

dead which the natives had left. These Pengwins must be pulled [*margin:* *] out of their holes with ga*fes, they will run and bite Cruelly, they cannot fly for their wings are small like a fishes finn, and no feathers on it, but black like a peece of leather, they swim very fast and dyve much. These are very good meat and weigh neare ten pounds a peece, ten men will kill three or 4 thousand in a day, there is such plenty of them. This Isle is steep up the sides of a fair height and plain grasse land aloft, and full of holes & paths like a Cony warren, there is no wood nor fresh water on it, nor bush; it is neare a mile Long, and halfe a mile broad. A Ship may anchor on the South side or North side of it, in eight or nine faddom water good oazy sand, fair by the Island. There is severall riplings of tydes about it, a man must have a care hee do not sink his boate in those riplings for the tyde runs strong,[1] there lyes shoalds off the East and West points, there grows long rockweeds on all [*margin:* ×] the shoalds, which is very good wis*hing[2] where shoalds are. From this Isle my boat came to St Bartholomews Isle, which is the Eastermost Isle and smallest. It is three miles NBE from St Georges Isle, 'tis grasse land aloft, and many white breast dyvers breeds on it, & some Pengwins. It is cliffy on the South side and have shoalds lies from the points; And from the NE point there is a shoald lyes from it halfe a mile. This Island is a mile from Elizabeth Island, East South East, here are riplings of the tyde on the East side of this Island. My boat came aboard to night. It blew hard at SW. I rode fast.

Fryday the 28th, wind at SW & blew hard all day and some small raine, I rode fast. I could not send my boats any whither to day. Several fires seen to day on both the shores made by the natives, and very great ones on the South side. It was so much wind as I could not go to them. Here where I ride runs an indifferent tyde Ebb & flood, and it rises about two faddom. It is a high water about ten of clock on the Change day, and the flood tydes come from the Eastward, this is as neare as I could perceive. Here I saw several whales, I have tryed to Catch fish with hooks, but Cannot Catch any except one small speckled Conger. Lesse wind to night at WSW.

Saturday the 29th, hazy Cold weather, wind at West & B*y* South a fresh gale.

[108] **October 1670. The *Sweepstakes* in Magellan Straits.**
I weighed this morning and stood in between Elizabeths Isle and St Bartholomews Isle, having a tyde of flood, I plyed up all along on the South side of Elizabeth's Isle, in a mile of the shore in a fair Channel which lyes up West South West between Elizabeths Isle and the shoald which comes from St Georges Isle, and runs up to the Westwards.[3] I had fourty & 50 faddom water in this Channel, and a good tyde runs in it. I had my boat sounding on the shoald and had four faddom water on it at half tyde.[4] This evening at 5 of clock I got up close under the West shore of the maine in a bay at the South Westerly part of Elizabeths Isle. I anchored in this Bay in fifteen faddom water, clayie sand a mile off the shore, litle tyde runs here, smooth water, St Georges Isle bore EBN off mee. This Bay I called *Sweepstakes* Bay.[5] It is to the Southward of white cliffs which are on the main shore,

[1] For tidal streams in this area, see above, p. 260, n. 8.
[2] Presumably meant to be 'warning'; see above, pp. 261, n. 3; 464, n. 4.
[3] This is now called Passo Reina.
[4] This shoal is Banco Walker. See above, p. 262, n. 4.
[5] This bay is shown on the 'Royal Map' (Foldout) and is now called Bahía Laredó.

at the West South West end of Elizabeth's Isle, on these white cliffs rounding into the Bay it grows all thick with bushes, this is a low shore in the Bay and brave grasse land, and greene, here grows fine groves of green trees, which is the first beginning of the woods. Here is fresh water in Rivulets, which run into the salt water, the Inland is high snow hills. Now the Strait lies North and South nearest, all this reach along the water is very deep in the Channel, here three hundred faddom cannot get ground, but here is good Anchoring all along by this shore, with westerly winds.

Sunday the 30th, hazy foggy weather, wind at West a fine gale. This morning I weighed and stood to the Southward close along the shore, I had fourty faddom water in half a mile of the shore, But, out, no ground in the main Channel at three hundred faddoms. It proved very gusty weather today; the northwesterly shore is all thick woods and green, down to the water side, the Land trents up in high hills and woody, but all covered with snow on the topps. The Straits is about seaven leagues broad here. It is like a litle sea, tonight I anchored in a small Bay in eleaven faddom water [*margin:* *] gravelly ground half a mile off the shore, No tyde runs here as to th*arte[1] up a shipp, the water rises and falls perpendicular ten foot. This Bay hath two Rivulets of fresh water in it and good timber trees of eighteen inches through, and neare fourty foot long, the wood is much like beech. Here are wild Curran trees and many such like bushes, the woods are very thick and green, and much old wood lyes on the ground so as here is no travelling in the woods. I was ashore looking to and fro here three houres. I called this freshwater Bay.[2] This is neare nine leagues to the Southward of Sweepstakes bay. Sand point, so called by mee, is foure leagues to the Southward of Sweepstakes Bay.[3] Sand point is a mean low point, lyes out more[4] then the other points of the shore, and few trees grows on it. It is grasse land, but sand at the water side fair soundings of thirty faddoms half a mile off, there is good [anchoring] in many places on this shore, between Sweepstakes Bay and freshwater bay sandy ground. A man must bee bold on this shore for generally the winds blow off it. Here is good sweet fresh water runs down in many places, the Conveniency to wood and water here is Extraordinary, the woods smell very sweet, a man may travell all along this shore by the water side for here is a

[109] **October 1670. The *Sweepstakes* in Magellan Straits at Port Famin.**
beaten path which is made by the natives, they have burned the woods in many places, here is many Arbours or houses of the natives on this shore, and drift wood. The South shore overagainst [*sic*] freshwater bay is of a mean height, towards the water side and grasse land, But inland large high downes, and all covered with snow at this time. The Strait here is neare six[5] leagues broad, E and W from shore side to shore side. This land is of a good sandy Earthy soyle, and no doubt but it would produce our English graine, if the winter bee not too cold, and too much snow. Fair weather, I rode fast, wind at West a fine gale to night.

[1] Probably derived from 'thwart' meaning across and hence meaning that the tide is insufficient to turn the vessel across the wind.

[2] Now Bahía Agua Fresca.

[3] This is probably Punta Arenosa, 2 miles north of the modern port of Punta Arenas.

[4] The word 'further' struck through.

[5] The figure '6' crossed through. The Strait is 18–20 miles wide in this area.

Munday the 31, fair weather, wind at West a fine gale I weighed with the Shipp and stood to the Southward, fair along this shore, in halfe a mile of it, the water fine and smooth, but very deep, no ground[1] at a hundred faddoms halfe a mile off the shore side. The shore lies South along here for four leagues to a litle bay, which I called Canoa Bay.[2] I saw people here and two Canoas, at the point of this Bay there is a shoald of rocks lies out, neare a quarter of a mile dry at a low water; to the Southward of this Bay this shore trents a litle to the Westward of the South, and makes two litle Bayes or Coves, then a long point of a good height lyes from the rise of the hill with trees growing on it. Just about this point on the West side of it is a fair low sandy Bay, which is Called PORT Famin,[3] here is good Anchoring in ten, or nine faddom water, in the midle of it, and fine cleane oazy sand, litle tyde runs in the Bay. It is six leagues from fresh water Bay to Port famin,[4] South & North from the one to the point of the other, nearest. Port FAMIN cannot be seen as you come from the northward, til you come to bring the Point St Anne[5] up on the NW of you, for the Bay lyes up in a litle hooke North West. And the land on the West side of the Bay is low in a Point, and sandy, and some grasse grows on it, and much drift wood lyes on it like a Carpenter's yard. A litle Inland from the salt water side grows brave green woods and up in the valleys large timber trees two foot through, and some upwards of fourty foot Long, much like our Beech timber in England. The leaves of the trees are like green Bi*rch[6] leaves and sweet, the woods shews [*right margin:* birch] in many places as if these were Plantations, for there is several Cleare places in the woods, and grasse growing on it like fenced fields in England, the woods being so even by the sides of it, and on Point St Anne as you come sailing from the northward you will see good bushy topped trees grows on the very point of it. This point is rocky on the shore side but no danger lies off it, you may bee bold on it to get into Port famin Bay.

As wee came sailing from the northward the Strait made as if to shut up, for the South land is high mountainous hills and much snow lies on them, and the Land rounds away to the Westward, so as it shutts in against the North Land till you shoot along and bring it open. The Strait over against Point St Anne East is about six leagues broad, and there is a great Channel lies open which runs into the South East.[7] I saw several fires to day on the South East land,

[110] **October 1670. The *Sweepstakes* in the Straits of Magellan.**

which were made by the natives in the grasse. It blew so hard I durst not goe to them, that side being a Lee Shore, the wind was at West and very gusty weather. At two of clock this Afternoon I anchored with the Ship in Port Famin Bay, in eleaven faddom water sandy ground, Point St Anne bore NE of mee a mile off. I rode in the midst of the Bay, and moored with my Bowers, my inward Anchor Lay in nine faddom water, to the northward of mee sandy ground, the Bay is neare two miles deep and flat oazy sand, in the head of

[1] The word 'ground' replaces an illegible word, possibly 'water', struck through.

[2] Now Bahía Carreras.

[3] Now Puerto San Juan de la Posesión, or Puerto del Hambre (53°38′S, 70°56′W). See above, p. 262, n. 4.

[4] The distance is nearly 20 miles.

[5] Now Punta Santa Ana.

[6] BL, Add MS 88980 A, refers to beech trees (see above, pp. 264, n. 1; 305, n. 2), probably *Nothofagus pumilo* or *N. Antarctica*.

[7] This is probably Paso Boquerón, leading to Canal Whiteside, which opens on the east side of the channel between Bahía Agua Fresca (Freshwater Bay) and Punta Santa Ana.

the bay, and deep a great way at the low water. The tyde rises here about ten foot perpendicular, and it is a high water on the Change day of the moon at twelve of the clock, the flood tyde comes from the northward. Here is good anchoring in this Bay, when you are shot into it, But out in the main Channel no ground. The wind from the South to East blows right into this Bay, but a South-South-East wind is the worst wind for it comes downe the reach, and brings a popling[1] Sea with it. The general winds that blows here are at West or on that quarter. There is a flat sand lyes above a Cables length off from the point of the West side of the Bay. It lies South of the Point. There is a small river of fresh water comes running out of that point which maketh the salt water change red a mile into the Strait, as if it were shoale sand, a boat can go five miles up this river in the woods. Here is many drift trees in this river or rivulet,[2] here is good wooding & watering, and good Catching of fish with the Saine. I haled above five hundred large fish ashore at one hale, much like unto mullets all scaly fish, here are many large smelts of twenty inches Long, and many Anchoves, and some small maid Skats, here is great plenty of fish, so much as wee feed wholly on it, and salt up much of the mullets and Anchoves.

Here grows many trees of good large tall timber fourteen inches through the Leaves are green and large much like Bay tree leaves in England, and the rind is gray on the out side and pretty thick rinded.[3] This rind or bark of these trees if you chew it in your mouth, it is hotter then pepper and more quick, it is of a spicy smell when it is dry. I cut of the bark and made use of it in my pease and other provisions instead of spice & found it very wholsome and good. Wee steeped it in our water and drank it. It gave the water a pretty Flavour. Here grows of these trees in the woods in many places in the Straits on both shores. I saw the natives in Canoa Bay and their Canoas. This afternoon I went ashore to them and held up my hand kercher [handkerchief], they came out of the woods to mee, and sate down, after I had given them some beads, there was fourteen of them in all men women and Children, they were of a midle Stature, and tawny Coloured & reded with red earth and greace, black hair on their heads and flaggy not very Long, but Cut round below their ears men and women alike, the women had bracelets of shells about their necks. I saw they were very kind and familiar with us. I went to the hutt or arbour and viewed their bundle but could not see any grains of gold or other mettal, they had a fire and were rosting of mussles & sea-eggs.

[111] **November 1670. The *Sweepstakes* at Port Famin in Magellan Straits.**

They gave mee sea eggs to eat, and fetched their paile of fresh water for us to drink and seemed to bee a very Civil people. I looked on their two Canoas & saw they were made of the rind of the trees, and sewed together and splinted with sticks split on the inside they were doubled with peeces of rind, and ballast lay in their bottoms. These Boats were built very well, and much like the Canoas in New England, peeked up at each end like a norway yaule [yawl],[4] they have small padles to padle them, these boats would Carry eight or ten people in each, they were eighteen foot Long and neare four foot broad, and thirty inches deep. I gave the people knives and beads, and made signs to them to come to the

[1] See above, p. 162, n. 1.

[2] Río San Juan, called by Narbrough River Sedger after the ship's carpenter. See below, p. 588, n. 7.

[3] The Winter's bark tree, see above, p. 268, n. 2.

[4] Norway yawl: British term for an open boat that resembled some of the small Norwegian fishing craft. Mariners' Museum, *Dictionary of the World's Watercraft*, p. 412.

Ship, it being neare night I went aboard. Fair weather to night litle wind at West I rode fast.
Port famin lies in the Latitude, of fifty three degrees, & thirty five minutes South.
And in Longitude, West from the Lizard, sixty eight degrees, nine minutes.[1]
Meridian distance, one thousand, ninety and two leagues West.
As my account is in my sailing this voyage, I give not Credit to the plain sailing therefore this meridian distance signifies very litle as to navigation.

Tuesday the first of November 1670, the wind at South and blew a fresh fine gale with some showers of raine. This morning I went ashore, wee Cut wood and filled water, and Cut an Anchor stock and a main topsaile yard. I travelled in the woods in many places, but could not see any fruit trees or oaks or Ashes, or hazel, or any timber like ours in England. Here is but two sorts of timber in all these woods, and one is the Pepper-rind tree, which is indifferent wood, and the other is the timber much like beech,[2] here are the best and biggest trees in all the Straits, here are trees of two foot and a half through, & between thirty and fourty foot Long. There may be good plank cut out of them.
I could not see any graines of mettal or mineral in any place and I looked very carefully in gullies and places where water had guttered. Here are some herbs to bee picked up that wee boyled for Salletting, and green grasse with it which relished pretty well. The Land in the woods is dry and of a gravelly sandy soyle and some places good brown earth. It is bad travelling in the woods, for old trees and underwood, the woods trents all up the sides of the hills. The land all about on the NW and West of Port famin trents up to very high hills, and the Inland is very high hills, for wee can see the tops of them all barren and ragged, peeping over those mountains next to the shore side, much snow lies Continually on them. The Land on the South shore is very high and peeked broken Land, inland; & much fogg hangs on their tops in rainy weather &c[a].

To day at one of the clock the natives of the Land that were with mee yesterday came to the shore side and Wafted with their skin-coats. I went to them and ten men with mee, wee Carried some boyled Seale's flesh with us. I gave them Seale which they Eat very heartily, and eat bread and Cheese with mee, there was seaven of them, four men and three youths. I gave them hatchets and knives, they gave

[112] **November 1670. The *Sweepstakes* in the Straits of MAGELLAN.**
mee Bows and arrows, and their skin Coats made of the skins of Guianacos and one of the Coats was made of Bever skins which I have. The people were very Civil and tractable, for I desired them to shoot with an arrow which they did, and shot very well at one of my mens hats. Three or foure shot neare twenty yards distance, they did not hit the hat one shot. I desired them to sling stones with a hand sling of their own, which they did very actively. I could not understand one word what they spake, nor they mee, but what wee desired was by signs one to the other. I signed them to go aboard but they would not. I showed them gold in a ring and made signs to give them knives and hatchets, for some if they had any, they did not understand mee. Night being neare they went away to their

[1] Puerto San Juan de la Posesión lies in 53°38′S, 70°56′W from Greenwich or 65°44′ W from the Lizard.
[2] Probably *Nothofagus pumelo*. See above, p. 305, n. 2.

boats which Lay in another bay about the point St Ann to the northward.[1] At evening I went aboard. Calm to night and dark weather, I rode fast. Many ducks and brant geese and teale on the shores sides and in the fresh waters, some whales spouting in the maine Channel to night.

Wednesday the 2^{d}, calm. This forenoon we fetched wood & fresh water, I ordered the Carpenter to Cut a fish[2] for the mast which hee did. This forenoon the Indians came to us as wee were Cutting wood, and helped us to draw the sawe. I sent for meat ashore and gave it to them which they did Eat very freely I proffered them brandy but they did not care for drinking it. I saw them so familiar I was in great hopes to have found a trade amongst them. I brought brasse Counters and farthings ashore with mee they being punched with holes to put Strings through, I put about every one of their necks a Counter or farthing and beads. I shewed them my gold ring and a peece of bright Copper barre, and made signs by Laying it in the ground, and looking about on the ground to find such things, & that I would have such like of them, and I would give them knives for it. I gave to one of them my gold ring to Look on, and hee thought hee might have kept it, I gave him a knife and hee returned mee my ring againe and was thankfull for the knife. I still made signs to them for gold, at last they understood my meaning and spake very earnestly one to the other a small time, and them spoke to mee, and pointed to my ring several times, and weafed [waved] his hand up on the mountains which lies North over Port famin, and are high Craggy tops & barren with snow on them. They Lye on the back of these hills which are next to the water side and are growne all over with woods very thick.

I was in hopes now to find some grains of gold amongst them if opportunity would permit, by reason they understood my meaning and that I desired such things in exchange for hatchets and knives. I made signs to them to look for such as they wafted was in the hills and bring it to mee. They spake one to the other, but what they said or intended I cannot tell. I signed for them to go aboard with mee which one of the oldest men did, and stayed aboard the Ship two houres. I shewed him hatchets & knives and glasses and Jews trumps &c^{a}. I made him a red Cap and put a red sash of cloth about his wast, and gave him a knife and a Comb & a pair of Scissers

[113] **November 1670. The *Sweepstakes* in the Straits of Magellan.**

and a glasse, and auls to sew withall, and filled his belly. Hee was mightyly pleased with all his new things, and desired to go ashore again, hee greazed himselfe all over with stinking Lamp oyle. Aboard the Ship hee took very litle notice of any thing but his new estate which over joyed him that hee could not mind any thing else. I set him ashore to his Consorts, and Carried them a platter of boyled Seale, and a Bucket of oyle, and peeces of painted Linnen[3] for flaps for to cover the women's nakednesse, for wee saw they were ashamed of their nakednesse before us. The women and men which were a shore made signs of gladnesse to see the man come ashore, and were very full of Laughter to see him in his new dresse. Here was in all this company ten, four men of about fourty years of age, two young men of about eighteen years of age, one young Lad of ten years, and three

[1] Probably Bahía Carreras, shown on the 'Royal Map' (Foldout) as Canoa Bay.
[2] See above p. 173, n. 1.
[3] The word 'Linnen' substituted for an illegible word crossed through in the original.

young women of seaventeen or eighteen years old. They were now wholly naked, but wee put Linnen aprons before them, which pleased them much. They were well featured and shaped, they were very merry, and much given to Laughter more then the men, they would often repeat words after us and Laugh. *Uzah* is much repeated by them but what it means I could not understand, nor one word of their Language nor they ours. Wee spake Spanish to them but they could not understand one word of it. They had four mungrel dogs with them much like the race of Spanish dogs. These people might be taught in a short time to understand tradeing, and if they have gold in the land to gather it, & make exchange of it for hatchets, knives &c[a]. with European people.

I do verily believe that in these mountains there is some mettal either gold or Copper, for the man that went aboard pointed up to the mountains, and spake to mee when I shewed him my ring. These people eat up the provisions which was Carried to them, and greased themselves all over with the oyle, and greased their skin Coats with it. I made signs to them to go and get some gold & bring it to mee. Some of them went away to their boats, the rest sate still, on the grasse talking one to the other and pointing to the Ship. Their Language is much in the throat, and not very fluent but uttered with good deliberation. I could not perceive they had any government, but only that the younger were obedient to the elder, and that the women were in obedience to the men, for I took the mens Coats and put about the women, but the men would not suffer them to keep the Coats Long, and themselves to bee naked, but took the Coats from the women, and put them about themselves. I proffered them to exchange one of my Lads for one of theirs and they Laughed, But the Indian Lad would not go with mee, but hung back. I gave to the men knives and fish hooks, and to the Lads Jews trumps & pipes, and to the women Looking glasses and beads. I did this to gaine their loves, and in hopes to have tradeing with them for the future.

[114] **November 1670. The *Sweepstakes* in the Straits of Magellan.**
Night being neare I went aboard the Shipp, and the Indians went to the Bay where their Canoas were laid. It being my intent next morning if the winds held contrary, to go with some of my Company with the Indians up to the mountains, so farre as I could to see if it were possible to find of that mettal which they made signs of. Calm to night I rode fast.

Thursday the 3[d], calme, at four of clock this morning the wind came to the North North West a fine gale. I weighed and steered South & B*y* East by my Compasse five leagues, so the Strait Lyes in this reach to point Low,[1] which is a point on the North shore which is seen as you ride in Port famin.
[*margin:* Var of comp.16°] The Compasse hath sixteen degrees variation here, easterly, so that my South B*y* East is South four degrees forty five minutes westerly by the true compasse. The Strait here at Port famin is neare five leagues broad to the South east, and at point Low about four leagues broad, the South land rounds up to the Westward, and shuts in with the North Land at the end of every reach, so as if there [were] no passage. But as you saile along it opens more and more unto you. The Land is of a great height on both sides rounding up the sides of the hills & woods growing green on them, but snow

[1] Cabo San Isidro (53°47′S, 70°58′W). Shown on the 'Royal Map' (Foldout) as P[t] Low.

lyes on the tops. The Channel is very deep water and no ground at two hundred faddom, but under the North shore there is anchoring in the Low Bayes.
This morning when I weighed out of Port famin the natives were come on the hill and wafted their Coates, but I could not go to them, the wind being faire to saile I was Loath to Lose the opportunity of it for feare I should lose my passage in getting through the Straite. It being for an uncertainty although I was unwilling to part from these people without further discovery of the Land, and of what they signed unto mee having such acquaintance with them as I had. The wind blowing fresh I proceeded on my Course to Cape Froward[1] which lies neare foure Leagues South West from point Low. Here at Cape Froward the Strait rounds away to the West inclining a litle to the north, the South shore over against Cape Froward is very high and craggy rocky peeked mountains all over that Land, so farr as I could see, and much snow lying on them. There runs into the Land two Sounds of a fair breadth, but how farr I cannot tell whether they run quite through the Land or bee only Sounds.[2]
Cape Froward is the Southermost Land of America, and it is very high Land on the back of it, the face of the Cape is steep up of a Cliff of rocks, and it is blackish gray of a good height and deep water close to it. I sounded with my boate close to it and had fourty faddom, a man may Lay a Ship's side to the face of the Cape for there is water enough, there is no ground in the Channel at two hundred faddoms, and but litle tyde nor any riplins as I saw, but a fair Channel to saile through of three leagues broad from the North shore to the South shore. It is best for a Ship to keep nearer the North shore then the South for the winds are more

[115] **November 1670. The *Sweepstakes* in the Straits of MAGELLAN.**
general off the Wester quarter. I sailed fair along in the midle of the Straits. In these reaches the wind being at NNE a fine gale, carried mee to the Westward of Cape Froward about three leagues by five of the clock this afternoon, then the wind came to the West a fresh gale and Cloudy, I plyed here from side to side all night and had several gusts of wind at West, with rain and haile. The Strait here rounds up West and B*y* North, and it is neare foure Leagues broad from the North shore to the South shore, and no danger but the shore sides and they are steep too & rocky & high land. It is neare nine Leagues from Port Famin to the pitch of Cape Froward, in two Courses. From Port famin to a point on the North shore which I called point Low, It is five leagues South halfe a point westerly, and from point Low to the Pitch of the Cape four Leagues SW. There are some small Coves and Bayes on the North shore, and some Islands adjacent between point Low and Cape Froward. There are Islands lye in several places close to the South shore all hereabouts.
Gusty weather to night the wind at West I plyed from side to side the moon but two dayes old, dark nights but short ones, not four houres Long. I split my topsailes to night in tacking the ship but got them mended again presently, my men were very forward to have them set again. I being resolved to ply here this night to try what Currant or tyde runs here, in this part of the Straite, this being the greatest elbow or turning in all the Straits, and former writers have given strange reports of this navigation and Currant, which

[1] Cabo Froward (53°54′S, 71°18′W). See above, p. 265, n. 7.
[2] These could be Seno Magdalena and Canal Acwalisnan both of which lead through the islands and eventually to the ocean, but Narbrough might equally well be referring to the entrances to the bays opposite Cabo Froward. See above, p. 265, n. 8.

seemeth to mee as yet to bee as ordinary as the Navigation in other parts of the world, & no Currant but tydes both ebb and flood as ordinary as on other Coasts, six houres one way and six the other way, but of a mean strength, and the flood comes from the North sea, and the tydes rise and fall perpendicular by the shore about ten foot or twelve and not more. And it is a high water about eleaven of the clock on the full and Change dayes of the moon, as I could perceive at Cape Froward. I conclude the Evil reports of this navigation come from the Spaniards. They being unwilling that the South Sea should bee known by an other nation but themselves.
Cape Froward in Magellan Straits lyes in the Latitude of 33°52′ S.[1]
And in Longitude West from the Lizard in England 68°40′W.
And meridian distance in Leagues 1099 and two miles West.
The Compasse hath sixteen degrees variation easterly at Cape Froward.
As to the Inclineing point I cannot say any thing I wanted a needle.[2]

Fryday the 4th, it proved Calm. At day light this morning I was in a mile of Cape froward to the Westward of it eight miles was all I drove this night, having tacked

[116] **November 1670. The *Sweepstakes* in the Straits of Magellan.**
eleaven times in the night from side to side and had several gusts of wind that caused mee to hand my topsailes, which if any Currant or tyde had runn here as is reported it would have set mee a great deale further either easterly or westerly. I lay becalmed till two of the Clock this afternoon and did drive a mile to the Westward in all this time. Neither could I perceive any tyde or Currant to run or ripple all this day.

Several whales seen to day, and beds of drift rockweeds, no ground at two hundred faddoms. This afternoon I had a small gale of wind at East. I steered[3] West a litle northerly as this reach lyeth. I sent my boat unto the North shore to sound three leagues to the Westward of Cape froward into a small sandy Bay, which the Land trents low to it, but it was deep water all along close to the shore, from Cape froward to that Bay, and a small Island lyes close under the shore, two leagues to the Westward of the Cape.[4] In the small sandy Bay there was fifteen faddom water, but it was close to the shore. I called this Wood's Bay by my mate's name that was in the Boate.[5] I keep the Ship fair by the North shore all this night and had very litle wind to night. I got about a league to the Westward, tonight it being so litle wind the water as smooth as in the river of Thames. I had my Boat towing ahead of the Ship all night to keep her right an End with the reach,[6] for I could see the North shore very plain all night by the snow that Lyes on the mountains the Land being high Close to the water side.

[1] Narbrough's latitude is an error for 53°52′S, which is the figure given in Narborough, 'Voyage to the South-Sea', p. 71, and BL, Add MS 88980 A, see above, p. 265. Cabo Froward lies in 53°54′S, 71°18′W from Greenwich or 66°06′ W from the Lizard.

[2] This is a reference to the vertical component of the earth's magnetic field, which is measured with a dip circle (a divided circle with a magnetic needle mounted vertically on a horizontal pivot).

[3] The words 'I steered' repeated and struck through.

[4] Bahía Snug with Islote Lambert off it lies 6 miles from Cabo Froward.

[5] Giles Wood, Master's mate. There is some confusion here. In BL, Add MS 88980 A. Narbrough states the sandy bay was 4 leagues west of Cape Froward, see above, p. 266. This bay is named Woods B. on the 'Royal Map' and 'Sloane Map' (Foldout, Plate 5) and is now Bahía Wood. It is 13 miles from Cabo Froward.

[6] The boat was pulling the ship's head round to keep her pointing down the reach.

Saturday the fifth day, a fine gale at East. This morning I steered West & B*y* north, as this reach lyeth, in the midle of the reach. At six of clock this morning I was abreast of Cape Holland which is on the North shore about six leagues to the Westward of Cape Froward. This Cape Holland is a face of steep black rocky Cliffs, the Strait is here three Leagues broad from side to side, and on the South side there is severall Islands close to the shore all along this reach. And several Sounds and openings into the high land, and I believe may bee good Harbours for Ships if they bee discovered, If all the South land bee not divided into Isles by these inlets. I could not search that shore by reason of my dispatch through the Straite, for I ever kept the North shore aboard all along as yet.
A league and a halfe to the Westward of Cape Holland on the faces of the Cliffs is a point which I called Cape Coventry,[1] this Point is steep up. A litle to the Westward of Cape Coventry is a sandy gravelly small Bay which I called Andrew Bay.[2] Here is anchoring in it in nine ten or fifteen faddom, fair by the shore. The ground is pible stones and some weeds grow here, the water is very deep at the bank. I sounded this Bay with my Boate, here is a rivulet of fresh water, here is also wood. From Andrew Bay along to the Westward on the North shore there is a Bay and two or three Spoots or litle Isles in it, and a Brook or Rivulet of fresh water

[117] **November 1670. The *Sweepstakes* in the Straits of Magellan.**
and wood grows here. The wood on the shore between these two Bays is dry & seary. This Bay is called Cordis Bay.[3] Three leagues to the Westward of Andrew Bay on the North shore there is a Bay which I called Fortiscues Bay;[4] in this Bay there is a hook runs into it which rounds to the Westwards which makes a very brave small harbour for shipping three faddom in it at a Low water sandy Oazy ground. No tyde runs in it the water rises in it ten foot. It is high water on the Change day of the moon at twelve of the Clock. This is a safe harbour to Lay a shipp a shore in it. By the shore side there grows woods and fresh water runs into it in two rivulets, it is environed with Large high mountains. This harbour I called Port Gallant,[5] for it's nearnesse to Cape gallant.[6] This afternoon the wind came to the Northwest and flew in flaws, I plyed to the Westward between Cape Coventry and Fortiscues Bay, the Strait being here between three and foure Leagues broad from the North side to the South side. But a brest of Cordis Bay in the midle of the Strait there are several Islands. Some have small wood growing on them, some grasse, some are rocks, there is broken ground amongst them at the East part of them; and also between them and the South shore; but there is no danger, for the Strait Lies fair in sailing between the Islands and the North shore. It is two leagues broad and mighty deep water.

[1] This is shown on the 'Royal Map' and 'Sloane Map' (Foldout, Plate 5) and is now the north-west end of Cabo Holland (53°47′S, 71°41′W), which is a remarkable bold ridge of precipitous cliffs and densely wooded ledges, 4 miles in length, lying along the NE shore of the Strait. It was probably named for Sir William Coventry (1627–86) secretary to the Lord High Admiral, James Duke of York, 1660–67, Navy Board Commissioner 1662–67, Privy Councillor 1665 and MP for Great Yarmouth 1661–79. Lee, 'Coventry, Sir William', *ODNB*.

[2] Now Bahía Andrés.

[3] Now Bahía Cordes.

[4] Now Bahía Fortescue. The name is not given on either the 'Royal Map' or 'Sloane Map' (Foldout, Plate 5).

[5] Now Puerto Gallant.

[6] Cabo Gallant (53°42′S, 72°02′W).

This afternoon at five of the Clock I anchored in Fortiscues bay in nine faddom water, sandy ground half a mile off the shore right before the mouth of Port Gallant. In the mouth of Port gallant it is rock on the shore side. This going into Port gallant cannot bee seen till one is in it, for it is not a Cable's length broad, and it rounds up at once. Indifferent weather the wind at West North West to night I rode fast, I had the wind off the shore & smooth water. No tyde runs here.
A breast of this Bay two leagues off is the Island which I called Charles Island and Monmouth Isle, more to the Westward is James Island and Ruperts Island and the Lord Arlingtons Island and the Earl of Sandwich's Island, And Secretary Wren's Isles.[1] This Reach I called English reach.[2] A league more to the Westward of Fortiscues bay is Cape gallant.

Sunday the 6th. Calm, I rode fast. This morning I went in my boat and ten men with mee over to Charles Island to discover it. This morning my Lieutenant & Mr Wood & eight men with them went up on the mountains by Port gallant to discover that Land. On Charles Island there grows good Large trees of such timber as is in the other part of the Straits. This Island is high land, and steep up Cliffs on the South side. It is a mile Broad and five miles Long, there was two Indian Arbours on it. It is rocky by the shore side, I could not see any kind of mettal or mineral on the Island, wee all Looked very diligently for it. James's Island lyes at the West end of Charles's Island, close to it. It is not so big as Charles's Island nor so wooddy. I named these Islands in honour of his Ma*jes*tie and Royal High*ne*sse and the Royal family and the rest of the nobility.

[118] **November 1670. The *Sweepstakes* in the Straits of Magellan.**
The Straits shews now as if there were no further passage to the Westward for the South land rounds up so much to the North West, that is shuts against the North Land to a mans sight at this distance. I saw two large openings into the South Land. One oposite [*sic*] to Charles's Island,[3] the other more to the [*margin:* *] Westward up of the round South Bite*, there I saw many whales spouting that place I called Whales Bay.[4] I saw several Brant geese and Ducks here. I left the Indians houses Beades, and a knife in hopes of future Com*m*erce. I saw on the South side a fire made by the natives in the grasse and bushes. At ten of clock the wind Came to the East a fine gale, I went aboard the Ship and weighed, my Lieutenant was come a board but could not discover any thing of mettal, the mountains runs up into peeked ragged rocky topps in [*margin:* *] a mere Chaios*[5] and all full of snow. Into the Land to the Northward, all the Land is high here and ragged on both shores, and nothing so much wood as about Port Famin. At two of Clock I was a weigh, I stood out into the Channel & stood West and by North to Cape Gallant; from Cape Gallant the next reach rounds away West North West, and Northwest and by West,

[1] These islands are all identified on the 'Royal Map' and 'Sloane Map' (Foldout, Plate 5). See above, pp. 302–3, for present identification.

[2] Now Paso Inglés.

[3] Shown on the 'Royal Map' (Foldout) as Broad Sound and now called Canal Bárbara.

[4] This is shown on the 'Royal Map' and 'Sloane Map' (Foldout, Plate 5) as Whales Bay leading to Whale Sound, the latter of which is now known as Seno Ballena. The southern entrance to Canal David, which passes SW of Isla Carlos III, leads out of Seno Ballena.

[5] Presumably the word is 'chaos'.

and Northwest. This reach is in all but four leagues long, then you come into another reach which is somewhat broader then this, and it Lies away more to the Westward again so as the Lands seem to close. From the pitch of Cape Froward to the pitch of Cape Holland, the Strait lyes in the Channel West and by North, nearest; and is distant full five Leagues; And, from the pitch of Cape Holland to the pitch of Cape Gallant the Strait Lyes in the Channel West and by North a litle northerly and is distant eight Leagues. From the pitch of Cape Gallant to a Low point three Leagues to the Westward[1] the Strait Lyes in the Channel, North-West and by West a litle northerly.

This reach is not more then two miles broad from the North shore to the Islands which I called the Royal Isles, when I was a brest of the Westernmost Island which I called Rupert's Island, I being in the midle of the Channel with the ship shot off one of my Sakers with a shott and the shot Lodged Close to the Island's side.[2] This Low point abreast of Rupert's Island on the North shore I called Point Passage. This evening at 6 of clock I was shot past point passage halfe a mile to the Westward of it having a fine easterly gale, but it Looked very Cloudy and dark to the Westward. I haled into the Bay on the North shore to the North West of Point passage just about the point, and Anchored in twelve faddom water black sand in three Cables length of the shore and lesse, there being no ground at fifty faddom half a Cables length further out. I mored presently with my smal Anchor to the shore. The wind came about to the West with much raine and Some Lightening. This is a fine sandy bay & good anchoring in it, in shoalder water if one please. On the West part of the Bay near the shore lies a rock, but it is seen by the waters edge at a high water, and the southeast point of this Bay is the point I call point Passage. It is Low & rocky

[119] **November 1670 The *Sweepstakes* in the Straits of Magellan.**

with weeds growing on them. This Bay is called Elizabeth's Bay[3] it is Low & sandy on the wash of the shore, and bushes and green trees grow on the land the land is mountainous inland, here is a rivulet of fresh water. I haled the Saine here this Evening and Caught but one fish. Calm to night I rode fast. The winds which come off the mountains are Cold by reason of snow.

Munday the Seaventh Cloudy gusty foggy weather, the wind at West and sometimes at Northwest, I rode fast all day Close aboard the Shore. This afternoon I went in my boat over to the South side opposite to Elizabeth's Bay at a point called whale point,[4] for the many whales spouting therby. I travelled up the hills two miles but could not see any gold or mettall, the land very irregular and rocky with mossy kind of grasse growing on it, and very boggy and rotten, for I thrust down a Lance of sixteen foot Long down into the ground with one hand very easyly. Here grow many Juniper trees[5] some of a foot through, the wood not very sweet. Here I saw many brant geese and ducks, much snow on the inland mountains, so as I could not travell any further. I returned down to the boat again. I saw where the natives had been by the burning of the grasse, but I could not have sight

[1] Called Point Passage by Narbrough below. See above, p. 302, n. 4.

[2] See above, p. 462, n. 1, for Saker's range.

[3] Shown on the 'Royal Map' and 'Sloane Map' (Foldout, Plate 5), and now Bahía Isabel. See above, p. 267, n. 10.

[4] Shown on the 'Royal Map' (Foldout), and now Punta Ballena at the SE end of Isla Carlos III.

[5] See above, p. 302, n. 1.

of any. Here are many good mussles on the rocks of five inches Long, and good fish in them, and many seed pearle in every mussel, here are Large Limpits and sea eggs amongst the rocks. This evening I got aboard the Shipp the wind at West, and at West North West, all night a stout gale. I rode fast but on a Lee shore and very neare it, But it cannot bee otherwise in most of these roads if the wind shift. No anchoring can bee had in the Channel.

Tuesday the 8th wind at West North West, & blew and rained much, most part of this day, this being the worst wind that could bee for this road, it coming right down the reach & making a short Sea, and wee rideing so neare the shore is dangerous. I had both my Bowers laid out to the best advantage I could to ride it out, for I could not by any means get out of this Bay as Long as the wind blows on these points. Much rain & slatty snow in gusts to night. I rode fast.

Thursday the 10th, rainy base weather the wind came to the West and blew very hard. I let fall the Sheat Anchor and rode by all three Anchors, much wind in gusts and haile and snow. I rode with my stern in lesse then the Shipps length of the shore, I had six faddom water astern at the Low water, the tydes rise and fall here on the Spring tides about ten foot perpendicular, And it is a high water on the full and Change dayes of the moon about ten of the Clock the tyde runs pretty strong here, and the flood Comes from the Westwards. In the Channel there is rippling of the tydes abreast of point passage which may bee occasioned by the meeting of the tydes which come from the North Sea, and from the West or South Sea, For at this point it is most probable for them to meet, And

[120] **November 1670. The *Sweepstakes* in the Straits of Magellan.**

It is the most crookedest part in all the Strait. I went with my boat & sounded on this rippling but had no ground at fifty faddom. It makes an eddy in one place when the tyde runs strong as if there were a rock Lay under water, But I could not get ground on the same place at twelve faddom all this rippling is not worth the taking notice of for it is but an hours time on both tydes Ebb and flood when the tydes run very strong, neither are the tydes anything prejudicial to the navigation of the Straite, but rather advantagious, to help to turn from roade to roade, either way; for I have had a benefit of them in plying from place to place. The weather indifferent this afternoon I went ashore after I had done sounding, but saw no people nor any kind of mettal. The woods very thick and several trees of the hot bark, the other trees much like beech timber, some ducks & brant geese seen on the shore side. At night I went aboard, much rain & slatty snow to night the wind at West & blew hard I rode fast.

Fryday the 11th, wind between SW and NW & blew hard I weighed the Sheat Anchor much raine to night & slatty snow.

Sunday the 13th, the wind at South a small gale. I ordered my lieutenant to weigh with the Shipp assoon as the wind served and come away to the Westward for I went away with my Boat to discover the Strait, for the West end of this reach the Strait Shutts in one land with the other as if there were no further passage. This reach lyes WNW from Elizabeths Bay foure leagues, to Saint Jorem's Channel,[1] which is a Channel or river of two miles broad, which runs into the North Land, between very high mountains winding to the North-North-Eastward farther then I could see. The North Land here inland is mighty high peeked and ragged mountains covered on the West sides with snow. This S[t] Jorem's Channel is deep water, and shews at a distance as if it were the passage of the Strait.

The Strait in this reach between Elizabeth's Bay and S[t] Jorem's river is about two leagues broad, and high land on the South side, And a Bay on the South side which hath several brave Coves in it Like the wet dock at Deptford and safe to Lay Ships in them, from either much wind or any Sea. This Bay I called Mussle Bay[2] for in it there is great plenty of good Mussles. The shore sides are rocky steep to in most places, no ground at a hundred faddom in the main Channel, also in the Bays on the South side it is deep water, and small Islands Lyes in the Bayes, and close along the South shore Lyes small Islands. Here are many whales, and I saw many Pengwins and some Seales. The shores are woody on both sides, but ragged timber and boggy ground, the topps of the hill bare rocks[3] and irregular. Several streames of snow water runs downe in the Cliffs of the hills two leagues to the Westwards of Elizabeth Bay; On the North shore the Land is Low & wooddy neare the water side and up of a valley, in this

[121] **November 1670. The *Sweepstakes* in the Straits of Magellan.**

Low land there runs a fresh water river. I went into it with my boat. It is but shallow at the Low water, hardly water enough for my Boat, here I saw several arbours of the Indians making, but no people. This river is a very convenient place to Lay Shallops or such like small vessels in, they may go into it at a high water, the tyde rises here eight or nine foot. This river I called Batchellours river.[4] Before the mouth of the river in the Straits there is good anchoring, in nine, ten, or twelve faddoms, sandy ground, a fair birth off the shore, the tyde runs but ordinarily, and the flood comes from the West, and the tyde that comes out of S[t] Jorem's Channel makes a rippling with the tyde that comes along the Stream of the Straits. I called this Road that is before Batchellour's river York Road.[5] This is a good place to ride in with westerly winds, for here cannot go any great Sea, neither shall a man bee imbayed that if a cable give way hee hath the Straits open to Carry it away, for the westerly winds are the greatest that blows here, by the trees, for they all stoop to those winds and Leane to the Eastwards, and the West side of all the trees that stand open are made flat with the winds. The tops of the mountains looks to the Eastwards. The easterly winds seldome blows strong here as to what I have observed by the shore side which lyes open to the East, the grasse grows down to the water mark & they are greener shores and the trees are straight and tall on the East sides of the Hills. But on the West shores the grasse & trees are much weather beaten and Crippled, and the shore side much tewed with the surge of the waters. The Channel or river of Saint Jorems is two leagues to the WNW of Batchellours river.

[1] Shown on the 'Royal Map' and 'Sloane Map' (Foldout, Plate 5), as San Jeroms R., now Canal Jerónimo (53°33′S, 72°23′W).

[2] Now Bahía Mussel. This bay was visited on the return voyage.

[3] The repetition of this word is struck through.

[4] Shown on the 'Royal Map' and 'Sloane Map' (Foldout, Plate 5), as Batcheller R. and now Río Batchelor. The river was visited on the return passage. See above, pp. 301; 308, n. 8.

[5] Now Rada York.

At seaven of clock this morning the Ship weighed out of Elizabeths Bay and came to the Westwards the wind was at South East a small gale. At ten of clock I went aboard of her, Shee was before St Jorems river in the midle of the Straite. This reach lies West and B*y* South two leagues, & then[1] West four miles to Cape Quad.[2] At Cape Quad the land Shutts one with the other as if there were no further passage, But as you make nearer to it you will see the opening more and more, as the Straits rounds there more to the Northward again. Cape Quad is on the North shore and it is a steep up Cape of a rocky grayish face of a good height. Before one come at it, It shews like a great building of an old Castle, for it points off with a rise*[3] from [*right margin:* raise] the other mountains so much into the Channel of the Strait, that it makes shutting in against the South land, and maketh an Elbow in the Straite. The Straits is not past four miles broad here, from shore to shore, and the Land is steepe too on both sides and rocky, the mountains high on both shores, and Craggy barren rocks, some trees and bushes growing here and there, much snow on the mountains on both sides.

[122] **November 1670. The *Sweepstakes* in the Straits of Magellan.**

Opposite to Cape de Quad on the South side is a fine large Bay, which is called Riders Bay,[4] I did not go into it, if there bee anchoring in it, it is a fair road for any winds. The water is very deep here in the main Channell, no ground at a hundred faddoms, this part of the Strait from point Passage on to Cape de Quad is the most Crooked part of all the Straits, therfore I called this Crooked Reach.[5]

Here are two small Islands on the North shore to the Eastward of Cape quad,[6] at four of the clock to day I was abreast of Cape Quad. I had the wind at East a small gale the water very smooth. I perceive but very litle tyde to run here as I have sailed either with mee or against mee, The Compasse hath sixteen [*margin:*Var. Comp. East 16. degrees] degrees variation easterly here now. Assoon as I was to the westward of of Cape Quad in the midle of the Strait or Channel, I steered away North West, half a point westerly, as the midle of the Strait lyes in this reach by the true Compas.

Just on the westward of Cape de Quad there lies on the North side two [*margin:**] small Isles,[7] and up on the Bi*tt[8] on the North shore there is a Bay or Cove under the high Land, but there is small Isles and rocks lyes before it & in it.[9] I sent my Boat under the North shore to search for a place to anchor in with the Ship, if in Case the wind should prove Contrary, they went into a Sound on the North shore three Leagues to the westward of Cape Quad, but could not see any place to Anchor in. This Sound run into

[1] 'and then' repeated.

[2] Cabo Quod (53°32′S, 72°33′W). See above, p. 270, n. 6.

[3] The word 'rise' is written over a deleted illegible word.

[4] Shown as Ridder Bay on the Doncker chart (Plate 2), now Bahía Butler. It affords relatively sheltered anchorage for small vessels.

[5] Now Paso Tortuoso.

[6] These are Isla Borja Grande and Islote Borja Chica. A further group of small islands, Islas Ortiz, lie between these islands and the shore.

[7] This is probably Islote Beware, 3 cables West of Cabo Quod.

[8] Bitt normally means one of a pair of stout posts used for securing the cable or other lines onboard ship. In this case it is probably a misprint for Bite, Bight, meaning a large bay, coastal indentation or rounding of the coastline.

[9] This is Bahía Barceló (53°31′ S, 72°33′ W).

the North land further then they could see it is not a quarter of a mile Broad, but no ground at sixty faddom. I called this Narrow Sound.[1] Here I ordered my Cables & Cutt off what was worn & not to bee relyed on.

I fired a gun at 6 of clock this evening to call my boat aboard for I was resolved to saile all night seeing the reach lying neare straight along and the wind freshning in at South East, the straits being here about five miles broad and high Land on both sides & steep to the shore side no danger of rocks or shoalds in the midle of the main Channel. I judged I could not run more then I could see at night before day light next morning, and the nights being light for the moon is eleaven dayes old. At 8 of clock to night I was foure Leagues to the westward of Cape de Quad. The wind at South East a fine gale I steered North West B*y* West by the true Compasse in the midle of the Channel, I saw the Land all night on both shores, and several openings and Sounds on both shores run into the Land at every mile or two miles distance. At twelve of clock at night I was about eight Leagues to the westward of Cape Quad, the Land very high on the South side and ragged rocky mountains, and much Snow Lyeing on them, the North shore is high Craggy rocky Land, no travelling on either shoars, the shores sides rocky and steep too. The Strait here is about six miles broad from shore side to shore side, and mighty deep water. Fair close

[123] **November 1670. The Sweepstake in the Straits of Magellan.**
weather to night wind at South East, my Course northwest and B*y* west, so the Strait lyes, here.

Munday the 14th, fair weather, wind at South East and B*y* East, a fine fresh gale, I steered North West and B*y* West and NW as the Strait lyes. At five of clock this morning I was abreast of Cape Munday,[2] so I called it, It being a Cape on the South side and is distant from Cape de Quad about 13 [thirteen] leagues, the Strait is here about foure miles broad, and the North shore makes into the Land with great Sounds & broken Islands.[3] The Land on both shores is high rocky hills and Barren, very litle woods or grasse growing on them. Here at Cape Munday the Straits grow broader and broader, to the westwards, but keep all one Course, NWBW to Cape Upright,[4] which is a steep upright Cliffe on the South side and it is distant from Cape Munday four Leagues, here the Straits inclines to the Westwards, near half a point. The Straits Lye from Cape Munday West North West half a point northerly, right out into the South Sea if you bee in the midle of the Channel or near the North shore.

I find litle or no tyde to run here or Currant. No ground in the Chan*n*el at two hundred fathom, in a musket Shot of the shore on either side. Here runs into the South shore many Sounds and Coves. I have sailed fair[5] along by the South shore all this day, for the North shore makes in broken Islands, and Sounds. Here lies all along the South shore several small Islands, but no danger for they are all steep to, the Straits is a very fair Channel to saile through. This day at noon I was abreast of an Island, which lyes on the North side

[1] This is probably Seno del Léon, which lies 5 miles West of Cabo Quado; it is about 1 cable wide and extends 2½ miles into the land.

[2] Now Cabo Monday (53°11′S, 73°24′W). See above, p. 271, n. 6.

[3] Golfo Xaultegua lies opposite Cabo Monday on the north shore with Grupo Santa Ana in its entrance.

[4] Now Cabo Upright.

[5] Originally 'fair all', but 'all' is struck through.

of the Straits, I called it Westminster Island, there lies a great many Islands between that and the North shore, and to the Eastwards and Westwards of it, and also some broken ground and rocks lies about it. These Islands I called the Loẙers.[1] This Island which I called Westminster Isle is a high rocky [*right margin:* Lawẙers] Isle, and it shews like Westminster Hall,[2] the Strait is five leagues Broade between Westminster Island and the South shore, But between that and the North shore there is many rocky Islands, and broken ground. I had a fine gale this afternoon at East, I steered West North West fair along by the South shore, and at 7 of clock this evening Cape Desiade[3] bore South Southwest from mee and was distant about five miles. It fell calm to night I Lay in the midle of the mouth of the Straits, all night becalmed, and much rain, the water indifferent smooth I saw the South Sea open. Here runs but very litle tyde as I can perceive, for I find that the Ship drives but very litle, and that is to the northwestward. I sounded but could not get ground at one hundred & forty faddoms, when Cape Desseade bare SSW of mee, and Distant two leagues off. The Straits mouth here is about six leagues broad from Cape Dessiade to the Islands, that lies on the North side, which I called the Loẙers Islands. But from Cape Dessiade

[124] **November 1670. The *Sweepstakes* in Magellans Straits off of Cape Dessiade.** to the North shore the Strait is nine or ten leagues broad, there lies many rocky Islands and broken ground on that shore, and it is dangerous to come on that side with a shipp.

The Strait lies from Cape Munday to Cape Dessiade, West North West and East South East half a point northerly & southerly nearest, and they are distant one from the other near fifteen Leagues. From Cape Quad to Cape Dessiade it is about eight and twenty Leagues, and the Strait Lies neare North West & B*y* West from Cape Quad into the South Sea, and near in one Reach which I called Long Reach, some of my Company Called it Long Lane.[4] This part may bee properly called the Straits, for it is high land all the way on both shores, and Barren rocks, with snow on them from Cape Quad into the South Sea. This land I called South Desolation, it being so desolate a Land to behold.

Cape Dessiade is on the South land on the West end of Magellan Straits, it is the westermost point of that Land, it faces to the West Ocean. It is high Craggy rocky land, and maketh irregular in Peeked topps aloft, at the foot of it there lyes broken rocks, and foule ground near two leagues from it West into the sea. I saw some rocks above water, and some that the sea broke much upon, these rocks I called the Judges,[5] they are very dangerous rocks to fall amongst with a ship in the night or foule weather. The Land trents away to the southward of Cape Dessiade South East. As one comes sailing out of the Straits fair by the South shore, hee will see a steep up pitch of Land before hee can see Cape Dessiade. This pitch of Land is the point at the End of the Strait. There stands up

[1] From Narbrough's the 'Royal Map' and 'Sloane Map' (Foldout, Plate 5), these islands are now known as Grupo Westminster and Grupo Narborough further west. Isla Westminster Hall, 1,122 ft (442 m), (52°37′S, 74°22′W), and Islas Lawyers are part of Grupo Westminster.

[2] 'Isla Westminster Hall, a precipitous granite island ... has a remarkable appearance from all directions.' *South America Pilot,* II, para. 7.514.

[3] Cabo Deseado (52°45′S, 74°43′W). See above, p. 274.

[4] Today this area is divided into Paso Largo which leads from the west end of Paso Tortuoso, about 5 miles west of Cabo Quod, to the vicinity of Cabo Monday, and then continues as Paso del Mar to Cabo Pilar.

[5] Now Rocas Apóstoles.

a high peeked pillar in the sea Close by it, which is distant from the shore side a shipp's length and there is two rocks Close by it, just above water. There stands another peeked pillar on the shore side near the other Pillar just at the Corner of the Land or Cape. This Cape I called Cape Pillar.[1] The land trents rounding from Cape Pillar South West, to Cape Desiade, and is distant neare two Leagues, the Land is a face of high land between them and is steep to. It makes in a Bay a litle between the two Capes, and some rocks lies neare the shore, all that part of Land Looks very Ragged and Desolate.
Cape Desiade lies in the Latitude of fifty three degrees & ten minutes South.
Longitude West from the Lizard of England, seaventy two degrees forty six Min*utes*.[2]
Meridian Distance, one thousand one hundred & fourty Nine Leagues.
The Compasse hath fourteen degrees ten minutes, variation here, easterly.
I make the whole length of the Straits of Magellan, from Cape Virgin Mary, to Cape Dessiade with every Reach and turning to bee one hundred and sixteen Leagues, And so much I sailed from the one sea to the other according to my Estimation.[3]

[125] **November 1670. The *Sweepstakes* Entering the South Sea.**

The mouth of Magellan's Straits on the West end next the South Sea lies in the Latitude of fifty three degrees South,[4] as I observed by the Quadrant of Mr John Davises invention,[5] and the mouth is seaven Leagues broad from the South shore to the Islands on the North shore. But from CAPE Desseade to Cape Victory,[6] it is eleaven Leagues, Cape Victory is the Cape on the North shore opposite to Cape Dessiade. The best Landfall in my opinion is to make the face of Cape Dessiade, if one come out of the South Sea to go into the Strait of Magellan. The Straits lies in East and west, at the first till you come abreast of Cape Pillar then the Course is South East and by East, nearest; Be carefull to keep the South shore in fair view, for the North shore is broken Islands and Sounds, that a man may mistake the right Channel, or Strait; and steer up in one of them, as hee comes out from the South Sea, if hee lose sight of the South shore.

Here lies foure small Islands at the North part of the mouth of the Strait in the South Sea, they lye pretty neare together, the Eastermost stands singly by himselfe, and is round Coppling up, of a fair height like a hay cock or Sugar-Loafe the other three are flattish aloft, the westermost makes with a Dawke in it. They lye from Cape Pillar North North West, by the true Compasse, six Leagues off, they are distant from Cape Victory near foure leagues, SW. I Called them the Islands of Directions,[7] they are a good wishing to fall with the mouth of the Straits.

Tuesday the 15th, it proved very foggy and rained much. This morning at day light the wind blew fresh at Northwest, and it Looked very dirtyly on the wester board. I sett Cape

[1] Now Cabo Pilar (52°44′S, 74°40′W).
[2] Cabo Deseado lies in 52°45′S, 74°43′W of Greenwich or 69°31′W of the Lizard. BL, Add 88980A puts the cape in 53°05′S. See above, p. 274.
[3] A modern estimate would be about 104 leagues between the two capes.
[4] The western mouth of the Strait lies in about 52°40′S and it is hard to see how Narbrough can have been so much in error.
[5] The back-staff.
[6] Cabo Victoria (52°17′S, 74°55′W).
[7] Now Islotes (Grupo) Evangelistas (52°45′S, 75°06′W) See above, p. 273, n. 6.

Pillar it bore South-South-West of mee, and was distant three Leagues off. At four of clock this morning I stood to & fro, Crosse the mouth of the Straits til eight of the clock in hopes the wind might favour mee, to carry it into the sea, for I saw the South Sea open. I could not observe any tyde or Currant to[1] run here worth observing. I sounded several times but could not get ground at sixty faddoms. When I stood over to the North side toward the Lawyers Isles I saw the sea break on foule ground amongst those Islands. I tacked and stood over to Cape Dessiade. I seeing I could not get into the sea nor carry it Clear of the North Land to the northward the wind begining to blow at West North West, and rain much, and the sea begining to make; I bore up under the South shore, and anchored in a small open bay two Leagues to the Eastward of Cape Pillar, on the South shore. I anchored in ten faddom water sandy ground, in a Cables length of the shore, I mored with my small Bower in this Bay. On the South West Corner there is a fine small Cove which is Land-locked, I called this Sleepers Cove, and they Bay where I rode I called Tuesday Bay.[2] On the West side of this bay there lyes three Islands[3] which makes this a Bay, these Islands are rocky, and all the shore is rocky,

[126] **November 1670. The *Sweepstakes* in Magellan's Straits.**
and very high and steep to, here grows a Crabbed wood which serves for fuell and here runs down fresh water in many places the tops of the Craggy hills are all Covered with snow, here is no Earth on the shore, for all the mountains are a meer rock and mossy grasse growing on them, in some places. Here is no travelling on any part of this Land, all along from opposite to Cape Froward to Cape dessiade, but the Land is all rocks and peeked spires runs up like Piramids. It is all a meer Desolation, and the North shore is the same in fo*rm [*right margin:* Chajos*] and meer Chaos, all along from Cape Quad to Cape Victory, the tops of the peeks are high, and the foggy Clouds hang generally on them. I rode fast.

Wednesday the 16th, very foggy & rain, much wind I rode fast. I find the tyde to rise here about eight foot and to run but very litle, and the flood to come out of the South Sea. It is a high water here on full & Change day of the moon at twelve of the Clock. Here is good Soundings all over this Bay, ten and fifteen faddoms, and 17 faddoms, good fine white sand, in most places of the Bay, and many beds of Long rockweeds grow here.

Thursday the 17th, foggy rainy weather, & wind Contrary I rode fast all day and night.

Fryday the 18. I rode fast. John Richardson died of the Scurvey.

Saturday the 19th, wind at North a small gale. I got up my Sheat Anchor, and had the Ship unmored, I went ashore but saw nothing worth observation. The land is steep to the Sea and rocky in the Bay. The shore is very high with a steep rocky Cliffe, I could not travel a bow-shot any way. I saw a place where fire had been made, and mussle & limpit shells lay, in heeps by it, which had been rosted there. I saw peeces of sticks made sharp at

[1] 'Sett' struck through.

[2] Tusday (Teuesday) Bay is shown on the 'Royal Map' and 'Sloane Map' (Foldout, Plate 5). See above, p. 272, n. 8.

[3] There are in fact more than 3 islands here, the largest of which is now called Islote Observación.

one end and knocked down the sides with stops.[1] I judge them to bee instruments to strike fish with, which the natives use. I could not see any of the Natives here I saw a smoak of the natives making, on the ragged land of the North shore. I sent my boats aboard Laden with wood and fresh water, I saw some brant geese and Ducks here, & some broods of young Brant geese. I searched about the rocks for minerals but found none, the rocks are black hard rocks, much like the Rocks in Norway. I saw several good mussles and Limpitts grow on the rocks, but never could see one oyster in all the Strait. The worst winds for this road are from the North North West to the North East, For they blow right in. At twelve of clock I went aboard, the wind came to the East a fine gale. I weighed and stood out very neare the Islands which bee on the West side of the Bay. I went through the growing weeds & had five faddom water, I was almost doubtful I should have been put upon them before I could get the Ship under way. I was forced to run hard adventures with the Ship, or otherwise I should lose the opportunities of sailing as well at other times as now. At three of Clock afternoon I was abreast of Cape Pillar; I Lay to and got in my Boats, and made them fast & stowed my

[127] **November 1670. The *Sweepstakes* Entering the South Sea.**
Anchors,[2] for without there run a great swelling Sea, which comes out of the South West, the wind being on that quarter of the Compasse the day before, at sea and blew hard. At five of Clock I made what saile I could, and I steered West North West, to run into the sea, the Pitch of Cape Pillar bore South of mee, and was distant one League off. The wind was at East North East, a fine gale I left the land astern a good pace, between five and six of clock I saw the four small Islands, which I called the Isles of Directions they bore northwest of mee, and I judged them neare five leagues from mee, I steered at 6 of clock North West and B*y* West, by the true Compasse. I saw the sea break to the southwards of mee, on the rocks off of Cape Desseade, which I called the Judges. I reckon these Isles of Directions to bee about seaven leagues from the judges, North and by West. At 8 of clock to night the Isles of Directions bore North and B*y* west, off mee; neare three leagues distant. It being litle wind I sounded and had thirty eight faddoms, rocky ground, For the tallow of the lead came up all dinted and some Crumms of rock in it, two Cast following.[3] I could not see Cape Victory, for much fog hung on the Land, as I sailed out, But I saw the Land over Cape Pillar and Cape Dessiada and the face of the Land between the two Capes. It makes a high bluffe Land, and ragged aloft, the North part of it is highest, and makes in two peaks, and the southermost peek is the highest. The Land is steepe on the North side of these Peeks, which is the point of Cape Pillar at the entrance into the Strait.

This face of land which is between the two Capes lyes near SW & NE and is in length near two leagues, the southermost part of it is the Lowest and Craggy & much irregular aloft, the whole land is a meer rock, and the colour is blackish gray, the fog hangs much on it. This is all I can give as to the knowledge of the Land, For my better understanding to know the Straits again. If I can make the Islands of Directions they may bee the better known, by the Sugar loafe Isle which is the easter Island of the foure.

[1] Notched down the side to form barbs.

[2] See above, pp. 145, n. 11; 302, n. 6, on Boat hoisting and Catting and stowing the anchor.

[3] Two subsequent casts of the lead gave the same nature of the seabed.

The safest way to fall with the mouth of the Straits will bee to bee carefull to keep in the Latitude of it which is fifty three degrees South, of the Equinoctial line, the midle of the West mouth.[1] At ten of clock to night it began to blow, the wind came to the North-North East, and to the North, and blew very hard and rained much, I handed the topsailes there run*n*ing a base hollow Sea that came out of the South West. I stood of[f] to the westward what I could all night having the main topsaile set againe.
[*margin:* var. Comp. 14° E] The variation of the Compasse here, is fourteen degrees Easterly.4

Sunday the 20th, much rain & foggy this forenoon the wind came to the South West and blew very hard, I tacked and stood to the North West:ward having only my Courses set. A very great western Sea runs here, which

[128] **November 1670. The *Sweepstakes* in the South Sea, Lat*itude* 52°51′ S.**
Causeth the Shipp to Labour very much, I cannot see any Land to day. I reckon I have made my way West from Cape Pillar, twelve leagues, At eight of clock this morning when I tacked.
No observation to bee taken to day of the Sun it being Clouded. After several courses from Saturday at 5 of clock afternoon til to day at twelve of clock I make my true Course to bee West twenty one degrees fourty six northerly and my distance sailed 37·6 miles. Departure 35·4 miles west. Diff*erence* of Longitude 01°00′·7 west. Difference of Lat*itude* from Cape Pillar North 00°14′. Lat*itude* by account is 52°51′ S.
Meridian Distance from Cape Pillar West 11 leagues 2·4 miles.
Longitude at noon from Cape Pillar West 01°00′·7
Longitude at noone from the Lizard West 73°52′·0
Meridian Distance from the Lizard West 1160 leagues 2·4 miles.
A very loft Sea this afternoon, the wind at South West and blew hard. I kept my Course to the Northwestward, what I could; No land to be seen, this evening several sea fowles seen as gannets and sea gulls, some whales seen. Towards twelve of Clock to night the wind veared to the SW&BW and was lesse wind and left raining. I set my topsailes and steered NW&BN all the rest of the night.

Munday the 21th. Indifferent fair weather, wind at WSW a fresh gale Course North-North West, the water reasonably smooth, the sea of a dark blew colour. I sounded but no ground at 97 faddoms. No land to bee seen This morning; several beds of Drift rockweeds seen. After several courses I make my true Course from yesterday noon till to day noon to bee North & B*y* west. Distance sailed 60 miles. Depart*ure* West 11·7 miles. Diff*erence* of Longit*ude* 00°19′·2. Diff*erence* of Lat*itude* 00°59′N. Latitude by observation of ☼ 51°52′ S.
Meridian Distance from Cape Pillar West 15 leag*ues* 2·1 miles.
Longitude from Cape Pillar West 01°19′·9.
Longitude from the Lizard West 74°11′·2.
Meridian Distance from the Lizard West 1164 leag*ues* 2·4 miles.

[1] The middle of the west mouth of the Strait is in about 52°40′S.

At one of clock this afternoon I saw the Land, it bare East and B*y* North of mee. It was distant neare nine leagues from mee. It made in severall hills, with snow on the tops. It is high land and it makes like islands, at this distance; It made ragged on the North part of it, and rounded off at the North end like a head land. It shews to mee to bee about five leagues in length stretching North and South. I held it not safe for mee to beare any nearer it, the wind being at West which made it a lee shore, also I was not acquainted how the wind blows as yet on this Coast. I steered North this afternoon the wind at West a fresh gale, the sea indifferent smooth, I sounded but could not get ground at seaventy faddoms, when the Land bore easterly

[129] **November 1670. The *Sweepstakes* in the South Sea. Latit*ude* 49°00′ S.**
and distance off by my Estimation, eight leagues in the Latitude of 51°46′ South. I saw several whales to day and sea fowles, and some Pengwins. At four of clock I was out of sight of Land. This lyeth to the westward of the meridian of Cape Dessiada, near eight leagues by my account. This Cape is called in the Draughts Cape de Santa Catalina.[1] Fair weather to night and Calm, I could not observe the ✠ [2] for Clouds.

Tuesday the 22[d] day, some rain and the air Cold and sharp. This forenoon the wind came to the South a fine gale, I steered northwest to gett an offing. I sounded but could not get ground at eighty faddoms, no sight of Land; I now want a small vessell to Coast in with the shore to discover it. I dare not bee too bold with the Land in these Latitudes, having but one shipp to trust to until I better know the temper of the weather, and how the winds do generally blow, and what points they bee inclined to most.

My Course made true from yesterday noon til to day noon is North. Distance sailed fifty two miles. Diff*erence* of Latit*ude* 00°52′ N. Latitude at noon by good observation of the ☼ is 51°00′ South.

Meridian Distance at noon from Cape Pillar West is 15 leag*ues* 2·1 mil*es*.

Longitude at noon from Cape Pillar West is 01°19′·9.

Longitude at noon from the Lizard West is 74°11′·2.

Meridian Distance at noon from the Lizard West is 1164 leag*ues* 2·4 mil*es*.

This afternoon the wind came to the South West a fresh gale I steered NWBW. At one of clock this afternoon I sent for Don Carlos into the great Cabbin to advise with him what hee understood of the Countrey, and where hee judged it most fit to Land on the Coast, and what Port hee thought best to go to here abouts. I Laid a draught on the table before him, and shewed him all the Coast along from the Straits mouth to Baldivia, my Lieutenants and the Master of the Ship being at the Consultation with mee. I shewed him by the draught where abouts I was on the Coast, and that I could go to any part of Chili between this and Baldivia where wee might with most probabilty endeavour a Conference with the natives, to effect the design wee are engaged upon or to do the utmost of our Endeavours towards the performance of it, for it is a considerable Charge his Ma*jes*tie hath been at in setting us forth, and wee have exposed our selves to many dangers and a great deale of hardship to get hither which god hath been pleased to permit

[1] This is at the SW extremity of Isla Diego de Almagro and is shown on the Doncker chart (Plate 2). It is now named Cabo Santa Lucia (51°36′S, 75°19W′).

[2] This symbol represents the Southern Cross; see above, pp. 70–71; see also Figure 8.

us, with very litle losse as yet of our Ship's furniture, or any thing to prejudice our Concern, wee being now in this Sea & having the Summer before us. And if any businesse bee to bee done with the Boats I will go in them my selfe, as it is well known I have performed that point all along hitherto, having the Ship in any security wherby I may absent my selfe from her.

[130] **November 1670. The *Sweepstakes* in the South Sea, Lat*itude* 49° South.**
I declared my Instructions which I had from his Royall Highnesse, to act in this voyage, and how farre I was to saile on this Coast, And that I was not to medle with any Spaniards either at sea or ashore, And that I am to take Don Carlos his advice in Landing &c[a].

Sir I desire you will bee pleased to signifie the place unto mee you judge will bee most fitt for our purpose to have Conferrence with the Natives, and with gods leave I will go directly unto it.

Hee would have mee to hale into the Land at the Island which is called in the draughts I. de Nuestra Señora del Socorro, which lies in about the Latitude of fourty five degrees South. I desired of him if there were no harbours on this Coast between that place and this Latitude, that I was now in. His answer was that hee knew none but the Harbour of St Domingo, which lay against the Isle of Soccorro,[1] which hee advised[2] to go to. I desired my officers to take notice of the place, which D*on* Carlos Concluded to go to, wherby that wee might give an account of what was acted when it should bee demanded of them. I ordered the Master to steer North at eight of clock to night. I had the wind at South West a fresh gale all night, hazy weather I could not have any observation of the starrs.

I am very doubtful[3] D*on* Carlos never was in these parts of America, for I cannot understand by his discourse that hee hath knowledge of any one place or people, or can speak one word of the Natives Language for all the time that I was in the Straits of Magellan hee never would look out of his Cabbin, or speak one word to any of my officers, for feare of questions being asked him touching the navigation through the Straits, for hee ever reported hee had been at Port Desire, and at Port S[t] Julian, and that hee had passed through the Straits of Magellan, and when wee Came to any of these places hee knew nothing of them; and I am doubtfull hee knows no better on this Coast.

Hee is no Seaman for hee doth not know the sea Compasse nor anything that pertaineth to a shipp or navigation, Neither can hee stand on his feet aboard a Ship at sea, but is very sea-sick.

Hee is no Soldier for hee doth not know the use of arms. I am of opinion hee is of the race of the Jews, & hath been some gentleman's man in Spaine that hath lived in the West Indies, and hath heard the Relation of that Countrey; hee hath told mee several times hee was in England seaven yeares agone and waited on the Spanish Embassador, hee speaks as good English as I can speak, and hee could read & write English very well, hee could speak and read French, hee could tell mee more of the Nobility of England then

[1] The Doncker chart (Plate 2) shows I. de Nuestra Señora del Socorro in approximate 45°S with P[o] de S. Domingo in an estuary to the east of it. See above, pp. 278, nn. 4, 6; 380, n. 1.

[2] Here 'advised' is written above 'desired' which is struck through.

[3] Narbrough's sentence construction seems to contradict his point. Here Narbrough uses 'doubt, doubtful' in the alternative sense of 'suspect, suspicious'. He suspects that Don Carlos had never been in those parts, and that he knew no more about the coast of southern Chile than he did about that of Patagonia and the Strait.

[131] **November 1670. The *Sweepstakes* in the South Sea. Lat*itude* 46°11′.**
then I ever knew, hee hath related several times hee hath travelled most parts of Europe, & knew the temper of most Nations.

Wednesday the 23d, wind at Southwest a fresh gale, I steered North by my Compasse, that is North and by East. The Compasse hath twelve degrees variation here easterly. Towards noon the gale freshing in at SW and very hazy. I saile after the rate of nine leagues in four houres time. No observation of the Sun to day it being Clouded. After some courses from yesterday noon til to day noon I make my true course to bee North, twenty five deg*ree*s westerly. Distance sailed 140 miles. Depart*ure* West 59 miles. Difference of Longitude West 01°31′. Differ*ence* of Lat*itude* North by account 02°06′. Latitude by account 48°54′ South.
Meridian distance at noon from Cape Pillar West 35 leag*ues* 1·1 mil*es*.
Longitude at noon from Cape Pillar West 02°51′.
Longitude at noon from the Lizard West 75°42′.
Meridian distance at noon from the Lizard West 1184 leag*ues* 1·4 mile.
This afternoon the wind came to the West South West, and blew hard and rained. I steered North and by East a great Sea run here. I cannot perceive any Currant to run[1] in this sea. some whales seen to day and sea fowles. Cold airy weather to night & some rain and slatty snow the wind at WSW all night.

Thursay the 24th, hazy cold weather wind at Southwest, a stout gale my Course is North B*y* East. At 7 of clock the wind came to the South-South West and blew hard & rained in gusts, the sea run lofty. Course made true from yesterday noon til to day noon is North 15° easterly. Distance sailed 170 miles. Departure East 44 miles. Difference of Longitude East 01°05′. Diff*erence* of Latit*ude* 02°43′ North. No observ*ation* to day the ☼ being clouded. Latitude by account is 46°11′ S.
Meridian Distance from Cape Pillar West 20 leag*ues* 2·1 mil*es*.
Longitude at noon from Cape Pillar West 01°46′.
Longitude at noon from the Lizard West 74°37′.
Meridian Distance from the Lizard West 1169 leag*ues* 2·4 mil*es*.
To day at twelve of clock I steered NNE, the wind at SSW a stoute gale. I dare not hale in with the Land till now, the winds blowing so generally out of the sea, and Stormy with rain and thick weather, and the sea running lofty make mee doubtfull of my main mast, for it is defective at the partners. I have a fish on it now. Cold weather to night and wett wind at South West, a hard gale; my Course is NNE.

Fryday the 25th, hazy foggy & small rain, wind at South West and blew hard. I altered my Course this morning at three of clock and steered

[132] **November 1670. The *Sweepstakes* in the South Sea off of the Isle Socorro.**
in for the Land, East North East. After several courses from yesterday noon till to day noon, I make my true Course to bee North East & B*y* East 3°45′ easterly. Distance sailed

[1] 'here' struck through.

80 miles. Depart*ure* East 69·5 miles. Diff*erence* of Longit*ude* East 01°39′. Diff*erence* of Latit*ude* 00°40′ N. Latitude by observation of the Sun at noon, 45°31′ S.
Meridian Distance from Cape Pillar East 2 leagues 1·4 mil*es*.
Longitude at noon from Cape Pillar West 00°07′.
Longitude at noon from the Lizard West 72°58′.
Meridian Distance from the Lizard West 1146 leag*ues* 1·9. mil*es*.
Hazy weather this afternoon I steer in at 12 of clock EBN to make the Land. I judge the Compasse hath a point variation easterly. This afternoon at seaven of clock I saw the land. It bore NE of mee, by estimation five leagues off. It made in rounding hills of a good height, and trented away to the Northwards, and the southermost part trented to the Eastwards, as if it were a Bay at 9 of clock I brought to & sounded, but could not get ground at 80 faddom. I stood off[1] and in all night, the wind at South West a fresh gale and hazy weather.

[*blank space for drawing*][2]

Saturday the 26th, hazy cloudy weather & cold, wind at South West and B*y* South, a stout gale. At day light I steered in with the Land NE for so it bore off mee this morning. The Land makes in Islands lying neare the maine. The main land is high and large hills inland which stretch N and South some snow lying on the tops of the higher hills. At 8 of clock I made the Island of Nuestra Señora del Socorro,[3] in the Spanish tongue. It is called the Island of our Lady of Succour. I steered with it NEBE. It made rounding up at the eastermost End and Lower in the midle then at either end. It maketh with a ridge running from one End to the other and trees growing on it. The shore side is rocky on the South side of the Island, and some broken rocks lies near the shore side, and at the South East end of the Island[4] there stands two peeked Copling rocks close to the shore, they are white on the tops with fowles dung, the sea beats much on them. I haled in fair by the South West part of the Island, and saile all along the West part of the Island in lesse then a mile of the shore, and saw no danger,

[133] **November 1670. The *Sweepstakes* at Anchor at the Island of Socorro.**
I kept sounding as I came in with the Island but could not get ground til I came in a mile of the shore, then I had twenty nine faddoms rough ground, as I came nearer I had shoalder water, I sailed along in sixteen faddom rough ground til I came near the point of the North West part of the Island, Then my sounding was gravelly black sand. This point lyes off half a mile from the shore side and hath but three faddom water on it sandy ground, the sea rippled on it. I edged off and kept in ten faddom giving the point a quarter of a mile birth, assoon as I was about the point I luffed up and sailed fair along by the North side of the Island in three quarters of a mile of the shore, I had ten faddom water sandy ground. I had brought the wind off the shore, and had fine smooth water, I stood along the Island [un]til I saw the East end of it, and the sea came rowling about the South-East point. I tacked and stood along to the westward under the Island in half a mile of the

[1] 'I stood off' is repeated and struck through.
[2] The blank space approximates to 7 lines of text.
[3] This is now Isla Guamblín (44°51′S, 75°05′W). See above, p. 278, n. 4.
[4] Punta Edwards, which is charted with rocks off it.

shore side in fair Soundings nine and ten faddoms fine black sand. The shore side is low to the sea and sandy in most places, and great clay clods, and some places rocks. The Island is of a fine height and all woody the trees grow down to the water side on the North side of the Island, and fresh water runs down in five or 6 gullies the woods are all green and very thick. I anchored about 12 of clock to day on the North side of the Island in ten faddom water black oazy sand, near a mile off the shore side, very litle tyde runs here. The westermost part of the Island bare North West & B*y* West of mee distant neare a league, and the Easter point bore SE of mee distant about two miles, the body of the Isle bore SSW of mee. This side of the Island maketh some what a Bay if one bee near the shore.[1]
After several courses from yesterday at noon til to day at noon, that then the Island of Socorro bare South of mee, I make my true Course to bee NEBE 02°25′ Easter. Distance sailed 61·2 miles. Departure East 52 miles. Diff*erence* of Longit*ude* 01°16′ East. Differ*ence* of Latitude 00°31′ North. Latit*ude* by account 45° S.
Meridian Distance at noon from Cape Pillar East 20 leag*ues* 00·4 mil*es*.
Longitude at noon from Cape Pillar East 01°19′.
Longitude at noon from the Lizard West 71°42′.
Meridian Distance from the Lizard West 1128 leag*ues* 2·9 mil*es*.
The Island of Nuestra Señora del Socorro lies in the Latitude of 45° South. [*margin:* var. Comp. E. 11°] The Compasse hath 11° variation here – easterly.

This afternoon I sent my Lieutenant ashore and ten men with him on the Island of Socorro and right against the Shipp to discover the Land, and to sound the depth of water all the way to the shore. At 6 of clock this afternoon my Lieutenant came aboard and acquainted mee of his discovery, that the Soundings was very fair all the way from the Ship to the shore, and the water shoaldened

[134] **November 1670. The *Sweepstakes* at the Island of Socorro.**
by litle and litle, and the ground is fine black sand to the shore side, the shore was gravelly sand at the place where hee landed the water fine & smooth and good Landing now the wind being at SW. The Isle is all wooddy indifferent Large timber, of such as is in the Strait of Magellan, and the trees with the strong-tasted bark, some trees of good sound heavy wood no fruit to bee seen nor herbs very litle grasse, fresh water running in several places into the sea, no sign of beast, Several brant geese & Ducks seen, no people to bee seen, nor any kind of mettal or mineral. Night coming on Caused him to come off, hee brought 200 young white breast Shaggs[2] with him aboard, those fowles breads [breeds] there on a point of Clayie earth that lyes of[f] from the shore. Rainy weather to night, wind at SW & blew hard.

Sunday the 27th. Cloudy hazy weather wind at WSW a stout gale much rain most part of this day, and foggy. I asked Don Carlos this morning if hee would go ashore, hee told mee hee was not well and durst not venture into the Cold. I went ashore with both my boats for fresh water, here is enough and very good. I searched the shore what I could I saw an old hutt or Arbour of the Indians making and several sticks that were Cut but all

[1] Narbrough would appear to have been anchored in the bay on the north-east side of the island between Punta Norte and Punta Arena.

[2] These were probably rock shag, or imperial shag; see above, p. 308, n. 7.

old done, I could not see any sign of people on the Island now. I believe the people come rambleing from the main in the best Season of the year to get young fowles, in this Island, for I do not see any thing else on the Island for the sustenance of man's life. I could not see any kind of mineral or mettal, the soile is sandy black earth, and some banks of rocks, the Island is irregular and grown all over with impenetrable thick wood, so as I could not see the Inward part of it, the woods are ordinary timber none that I see is fitt to make plank of, the nature of the wood is much like Beech and birch, and a sort of heavy wood But good for litle but for the fire, It is white. No fruit or herbs very litle grasse, the woods are so thick. Much kind of Long sedgy grasse. No wild beast to bee seen, several small birds in the woods like Sparrows &c. and other great ones like kites, Several black and white brant geese on the shores & some Ducks and Sea peeks,[1] and Sea mews, & black & Pied Shaggs[2] and other such sea fowles, what else the Island affoords I cannot tell. I made a fire on the shore in hopes to have answer of it on the main, but had not. At noon I went aboard, I sent my boats ashore again for more water and wood whilest the weather permitted Landing.

Don Carlos this afternoon desired mee to have Consultation with my selfe & officers. I sent for my Lieutenants and Master into the great Cabbin presently. When wee were together hee desired to speak. Hee declared thus, That he thought it most requisite to saile directly for Baldivia for there hee should speak with the people, of the Countrey and know whether his friends were living or not, and if the Spaniards had Conquered all the Countrey of Chilie or no, which if they had his businesse was done, for hee could not tell where to find his friends, for

[135] **November 1670. The *Sweepstakes* at Anchor at the Island of Socorro.**

they lived up in the frontiers and in the mountains when hee came from thence, which was in the year 1665, and hee had not heard from them since, thus hee concluded.

I answered thus. Gentlemen you know our Last resolution was to see for people here and on the main opposite to this place which you see is within four leagues of us, and to see for the Port of St Domingo for I must discover all the Coast along to Baldivia, and see what harbours there are on the Coast, and what the Countrey doth affoord, for I know where the Spaniards are planted there is nothing for us. Our businesse is to discover the Land and to have Conferrence with the natives, and assoon as weather permitted I would go over to the main with the Ship and see what can bee done there. It cannot bee expected wee should meet with with people here, neither will one day or two procure acquaintance. For in the Straits at Port Famin I slipped one opportunity of discovering the Countrey by coming away from the natives so suddenly, I hope it will not bee so any more, for now wee may take our time. Thus wee concluded to discover on the main over against the Island assoon as the weather would permit. Rainy foggy weather all night, & blew hard, wind at WSW.

Munday the 28th. I could not weigh, I caused my Lieutenant to go ashore and search[3] the Island as farr as hee could travell. I ordered the Purser to get up all the Bread out of the

[1] These are probably sea pies, oystercatchers. The Magellanic oystercatcher (*Haematopus leucopodus*) and the blackish oystercatcher (*H. ater*) are found in this area. Peña, *Birds*, plates 33.2, 33.3.

[2] The black shag would be the olivaceous cormorant (*Phalacrocorax olivaceus*), which is found throughout the area. For the pied shag, see above, p. 308, n. 7. Peña, *Birds*, plate 12.1.

[3] 'search' is written above 'discover' which is struck through.

bread-roome, that I might know how much bread wee had in the Shipp. Wee found that the rats had made great spoile in the bread for they had Eaten several great holes in the bottom of the Room clean through the seeling of the Ship. I found but four dayes bread for the whole Company, But I had beefe, pease, and salted Seale's flesh for five months. It blew hard & rained much this afternoon. My Lieut*enant* came aboard but saw nothing more then was seen formerly. I rode fast to night. It is convenient to have the bread-room Plated.

Tuesday the 29th, foggy weather, wind contrary I could not saile. I sent my boat ashore for wood. This afternoon Don Carlos would have mee Land him ashore at Cape de Piedras which is in about the Latitude of 43° South,[1] and hee would travel to Baldivia which is distant above sixty leagues through the woods and over the mountains, a way that never was travelled by man. I desired of him how hee would get through the woods and over the mountains, so great a distance as that was, his answer was hee would have a hatchet and Cut his way through. I really believed the gentleman is distracted by his discourse, and his being so uncertain of his resolutions. I desired hee would have patience and wait the almighty's pleasure for wind and weather, and then I would go to any place hee desired, Lying within the extent of my Com*m*ands. Lesse wind I rode fast all night.

Wednesday the 30th, fair weather, and wind at North West a small gale I weighed and stood over to the main opposite to the Island. I had very fair Soundings all the way between the Isle & the main 12 faddom & 14, 16, 18, 20 and 25 faddom was

[136] **November 1670. The *Sweepstakes* at the Island of Socorro.**

the most that was in the midle, then it shoaldened from thence to the main very fairly, all fine black sand was the ground. At ten of clock this forenoon I was over on the main side, the Ship lay off & in, I went ashore with my Boate on an Island which lyeth adjacent to the main,[2] there was a Channel between that and the main and many rocks lyes in it and foule ground so as I dare not venture the Ship into it. This Island showed as if it had been the main til I went to it with my Boat. This Island is about four leagues Long, from the North point to the South point, and in some places a league broad, and in some places two leagues broad, the Island is of a mean height and grown all over with green woods very thick, the timber is such as it is on the Island of Socorro, I could not see any mineral or mettal on it. The shore side sandy in some places, and rocky in others, the earth on the Island is of a sandy black soile, but very wett with the continued rains that are here. Not finding this Island named in the draughts I called it after my own name Narbrough's Island. I took possession of it for the use of his Ma*jes*tie and his heires and then put off from it.

[1] Cape de Piedras is not shown on the Doncker chart (Plate 2), or Narbrough's published chart (Plate 9), nor is there any point of this name in this vicinity on modern charts. The position, 43°S, is on the west coast of Isla Chiloé.

[2] This appears to be Isla Ipun (44°37′S, 74°42′W), which lies about 15 miles ENE of Isla Guamblín, adjacent to the main line of islands which form the Archipiélago de los Chonos. It is about 8 miles long from north to south and 3–4 miles wide, and is separated from its nearest neighbour to the east by a narrow passage with rocks in it. Narbrough's published chart (Plate 9), has the name adjacent to a group of islands which includes I. De Nuestra Señora del Socorro (Isla Guamblín), although the latter is not named.

I could not see people or any sign of them here; the place where I landed on it was on the East part, and on the East South East part of the Island there is good anchoring in ten or 12 faddom fine black sand half a mile off the shore and good rideing with Northerly, Northwest & West North West winds. The worst winds are SW and S & SE & East. On the South side of this Island there lies a ledge of rocks a quarter of a mile off the shore, and at the SSE point there are rocks which are of a mean height and Sea fowles breeds on them the ledge of rocks lies low by the water. I went from this Island over to the main, but could not Land on the main the sea running so much, on the shore I was in danger of sinking my Boat, the shore side is all rocky. The main is high land, and many Large hills and much wood growing on them. This Island lies about a mile and halfe off the main, and between it and the main there lies 3 or four small Isles and rocks, one Rock where several Sea-fowles breed on it, this rock is round Copling up like a sugar loafe. Here runs out a strong tyde which I judge comes out from some Inland Channels, that are further then I could see, between the Island and the main. I could not see any sign of people on the main, either by fires or appearance, the woods were all green. SE from Narbroughs Isle on the main distant about three[1] leagues there runs into the Land a river or Sound.[2] The shore sides is rocky and some broken ground lies before it, the hills are high in the Land on both sides of it. This opening lies in East and West, I take it for the place which is in the draughts called St Domingo. This place lyeth in the latitude [*margin:* St Domingo lies in 44°50′ S.] of in the Latitude of fourty foure degrees, fifty minutes South. More to the southwards of this place there lies several round Copling high Islands, grown over with woods all along the Coast as farr as I could see there lies Islands adjacent to the main and they are of a great height.

[137] **December 1670. The *Sweepstakes* at the Island of Socorro.**
Gusty stormy weather comeing I went aboard the Ship at 5 of clock and stood over to the Island of Socorro to get Anchoring there, for I could not stay any Longer discovering of the main, the wind blowing at West South West so hard and rain and foggy and a Lee shore to deale with, I dare not stay any Longer for fear of miscarriage in the night in case it should over blow. At seaven of clock to night I was got over to the Island of Socorro. I anchored at the East end of the Island in eight faddom water, fine black sand, about a mile off the shore. It blew hard at NW to night and much rain I rode fast all night.

Thursday the first of December 1670. Rainy weather wind at NWBN a hard gale all this forenoon, this afternoon the wind came to the SW a small gale but very foggy. I weighed and stood a league off the Island towards the main. It fell calm. I anchored at 8 of clock in thirteen faddom water sandy ground. Litle or no tide runs here as I could perceive, the water rises and falls perpendicular by the shore side eight foot on the Spring tydes, And it is a high water on the Change day of the moon at nine of the clock at the Island of Socorro, that tyde that runs is but small, the flood comes from the southwards. Calm and rainy weather to night I rode fast.

[1] The figure 3 is struck through here.

[2] This could be the channel between Isla Rowlett and Isla Williams which has a number of small islands in the entrance and leads to Canal Bynon. Its entrance is about 15 miles SE from Isla Ipun and is in 44°50′ S. There is also an entrance between Isla Stokes and Isla Rowlett which also has islands in its entrance and is 7 miles SE from Isla Ipun, which leads to Canal Memory and thence south to Canal Bynon.

Fryday the 2^d^, fair weather the wind at West a fine gale. This forenoon I weighed and stood to the northward. At twelve of clock I observed the Sun on the meridian and was in the Latitude of fourty four degrees & thirty four minutes. At one of the clock the wind came to the North West & blew hard & rained, I could not carry it off the Coast to the Northwards, I being in two leagues of the shore. I sounded and had thirty two faddom, fine black sand, I tacked and stood to the southward. It blew so hard in gusts as forced me to hand my top sailes, and the sea ran high. I bore away to the East end of the Island of Socorro, and anchored in a sandy bay in nine faddom water, oazy sand about a mile off the shore side. It blew hard to night at NW. I rode fast all night.

Saturday the 3^d^, very base weather in gusts and haile and rain, the wind at North West, a great Sea comes rowleing in about the point of the Island. I ride a hard Road Stead. On the South East point of the Island there lyes a shoald pointing off SE at least a miles and half from the Island, the sea breaks much upon the shoald. The East end of the Island makes in a Bay, and it is neare a League Long from the North East point to the South East point.[1] The shore side of the Bay is Low and sandy the woods grow down to the sand, the Island is indifferent even in this End of it. The North-East point lyes shoald off neare half a mile. This Island of Socorro lies about four or five leagues off the main, And I believe a ship may saile round between it and the main keeping in the midle. As I ride at the East end of the Island I can see the high round Islands that lyeth near the main. They bear NEBE of mee, and some bear East and some South East of mee.

[138] **December 1670. The *Sweepstakes* at the Island of Socorro.**
The Land is very high on the main against them and snow lyeth on the topps of the hills. I can see as I ride here the opening of that place which I take for St Domingo it bears neare North East of mee. I cannot discover that place nor any other hereabouts except I had another vessel of lesse draught of water then this Shipp, and then I could with the Almighty's leave discover all this Coast. This day all the bread in the Ship is expended, all the Company of the Shipp my self as well as any other eat Ple*ase[2] in lieu of bread. My Company are all of indifferent good health I thank god for it, being seaventy two in Company. No fish to bee taken with hooks, many porposes seen and some whales, several sea fowles seen swimming to day much wind to night at NW. I ride fast But doubtfull of my Cable.

Munday the fifth rainy & cloudy, much fogg hanging on the Land, litle wind at South. I weighed at 8 of clock this morning and stood to the northward, at ten of clock the wind veared round the Compasse, I plyed off into the sea. At 8 of clock this evening the West part of the Isle of Socorro bore South of mee distant about five leagues. I stood off North West the wind at West South West a hard gale, a great Sea comes out of the Southwest. At 12 of clock to night the wind came out at North West I stood to the North-North East ward.

Tuesday the 6th, fair weather this forenoon the wind at NW a fresh gale I stood to the northward. At seaven of clock I saw Land out of the North and B*y* East. I stood with it,

[1] This would appear to be the bay between Punta Arena and Punta Edwards which is 3 miles long.
[2] The asterisk presumably marks the mispelling of 'peas'.

at 12 of clock I was close aboard of it, on the South side. I observed the Sun to day on the Meridian, I find my Latitude to bee [*margin:* Lat. 43°47′ South.] 43°47′ South. I make this to bee an Island[1] for I stood to the East part of it and saw[2] it all a steep shore of rocks, and at the East end a ledge of rocks lies halfe a mile off from the point of the Island a litle above water. I could not get ground any where on this side of the Island in a quarter of a mile of the shore at sixty faddom. I could see the main all along for seaven leagues distance. It is high land in many Large hills, this Island is five leagues off the maine, and the shore side is all rocky on the East part, South part, & West Part. The North part &c[a]. I did not see. The Land is high and all grown over with woods. I sent my Lieu*tenan*t and ten men with my boat to the shore to see for people and what else they could discover, they came aboard at night and told mee they could not by any meanes possibly Land on the shore without Loseing the boat the sea run so high on the shore. I stood to & fro close under the shore all the time in sight of them. They could not discern any thing on the shore but trees and rocks, and sea fowles & seales on the Rocks. The wind was at North West all this time, and blew hard I intend to Lye on the South side of the Island all night off and in to keep in smooth water, and on the morning to discover the shore, and the maine, for I know here must bee store of people, for the main land appeareth in high large hills nothing so irregular as at the river of S[t] Domingo, and the Air is not so cold as it is to the southwards. I called this place No Mans Island, by reason my

[139] **December 1670. The *Sweepstakes* off No Mans Island.**

men could not get on the Land. After several Courses made from Munday at eight of clock at night when the Island of Socorro bore South of mee till to day at 12 of clock that I was at No Man's Island I make my true Course to bee from the one Island to the other the westermost parts of both, North 6°15′ East. Distance 73·5 miles. Departure East 8 miles. Difference of Longit*ude* 00°10′·1. Difference of Latitude 01°13′. Latitude by good observation of the Sun 43°47′.

No mans Island lyes in the Latit*ude* of 43°47′ S.
Longit*ude* West from the Lizard of England 71°32′.
Meridian Distance from the Lizard of England 1126 leagues 00·9 miles.
Meridian Dist*ance* from Cape Pillar East 22 leagues 02·4 mil*es*.
Longitude from Cape Pillar East 01°29′·1
Variation of the Compasse is 10° easterly here.

The South part of No mans Island is about two Leagues Long from the West point to the East point, but how farr it is from the North part to the South part I cannot tell, for I could not see it a storm prevented my discovery further here. This Island is that which the draughts make to Lye at the South end of Castro, at the going in of that Channel.[3] The Draughts are false in Laying down of this Coast, the Latitudes of most places are very neare but the coast is Layd out false; here are many islands adjacent on the Coast and none Layd down in the Draughts.

[1] From Narbrough's description and the position of this island as shown on Narbrough's published chart (Plate 9), it is Isla Guafo (43°37′S, 74°44′W). The south point of the island is in 43°41′S, which agrees reasonably well with the noon position. See above, p. 282, n. 2.

[2] Here 'make' is struck through and replaced by 'saw'.

[3] This is Boca del Guafo leading to Golfo Corcovado.

This night at 8 of clock it blew much wind at NW. I stood off West South West, it rained much & the sea run high, at ten of clock I handed my topsails it was so much wind I dare not venture in with the shore for feare of the wind coming out, for it Lightened much on the wester board and Looked very dark and windy. I stood off with my Courses.

I perceive but Litle tyde or Currant to run in these Seas, the winds are much on the wester quarter of the Compasse, and blows hard, but they are variable from the South-Southwest to the NNW so as a Ship may sail either to the northwards or southwards, making use of the winds when they best serve. I find it more hard to get to the northward then to get to the Southward here.

Wednesday the 7th, very stormy weather wind at WNW and sometimes at NNW with rain and haile, a great Sea runs I stood to the southwest-ward. The Ship maketh water at her hoodings[1] and Labours very much. No observation to day, I saw the Land this morning to Leeward of mee. Course made true from No man's Island til today at noon is SW. Distance sailed 40 miles. Departure West 28·4 miles. Difference of Longitude 00°39′·3. Differ*ence* of Latit*ude* 00°28′·4. Latitude by account at noon 44°15′ South.

[140] **December 1670. The *Sweepstakes* in the South Sea. Latit*ude* 44°15′ S.**
Meridian Distance at[2] noon from Cape Pillar East 13 Leagues 01 mile.
Longitude at noon from Cape Pillar East 00°49′·8.
Longitude at noon from the Lizard West 72°11′·3.
Meridian Distance from the Lizard West 1135 leagues 2·3. miles.
Very stormy weather the wind at West North West, this afternoon, and much rain. I stood to the Southwestwards under my Courses scarce able to Carry them for wind. I reckon my self eight Leagues off the Land, very thick weather I could not see it.

Thursday the 8th, cloudy gusty weather this morning wind at West and B*y* South at 4 of clock I tacked and stood to the Northward, the weather cleared up towards noon. I observed the Sun on the Meridian and found my Latitude to bee 44°38′. After several Courses from yesterday at noon til to day noon I make my true Course to bee South 35°19′ westerly. Distance sailed 28·1 miles. Departure West 16·3 miles. Difference of Longit*ude* West 00°22′·7. Difference of Latitude South 00°23′.
Latitude by good Observation of the Sun on the Meridian is 44°38′ S.
Meridian Distance from Cape Pillar East 7 leagues 2·7 miles.
Longitude at noon from Cape Pillar East 00°27′·1.
Longitude from the Lizard West 72°34′.
Meridian distance from the Lizard West 1141 leagues 00·6 mil*es*.
This afternoon it blew hard and rained and slatty Snow, I stood to the Northward the wind at West South West. At 9 of clock the wind came to the North-West I tacked and stood to the Westward, very dirty weather. At 12 of clock the wind came to the SWBW, I tacked and stood to the Northward.

[1] Hooding, whooding. See above, p. 282, n. 1.
[2] 'at' is repeated and struck through.

Fryday the 9th. Wind at West South West, and blew very hard I plyed what I could to the Northward. After several courses from yesterday till to day noon I make my true course to bee Northwest. Distance sailed 11·3 miles. Depart*ure* West 8 miles. Differ*ence* of Longit*ude* 00°11′. Diff*erence* of Latitude 00°08′ N.
Latitude by account 44°30′ S.
Meridian Distance at noon from Cape Pillar East 5 leagues 00·7 mil*es*.
Longitude from Cape Pillar East 00°16′·1.
Longitude from the Lizard West 72°44′.
Meridian distance from the Lizard West 1143 leagues 2·6 mil*es*.
Blustering weather this afternoon, the wind sometimes at West & NW. I stand sometimes the one way sometimes the other way to keep off the shore till the weather is settled, for I have a desire to see in at the Island of Castro[1] at the first fair weather. The sails & rigging tows [tews] very much I am forced to Cut up several new ropes, & use much of the new Canvas. Blowing rainy weather to night wind at WSW.

[141] **December 1670. *Sweepstakes* in the South Sea. Latit*ude* 44°30′ S.**
Saturday the 10th, the wind vearing between the NW and the WSW gusty stormy weather, and a great Sea, my main-mast decayes at the partners and opens more and more every storm. The winds in the nights vear to the Northwards, and in the days to the southwards, I ply off the shore what I can. After several courses from yesterday noon til to day at noon, I make my true course to bee NNW. Distance sailed 10·8 miles. Departure West 4·1 miles. Differ*ence* of Longit*ude* West 00°06′·3. Differ*ence* of Latit*ude* 00°10′ N. Latitude by account at noon is 44°20′ South.
Meridian Distance at noon from Cape Pillar East 3 leagues 2·6 mil*es*.
Longitude from Cape Pillar East 00°09′·8.
Longitude from the Lizard West 72°50′·3.
Meridian distance from the Lizard West 1145 leagues 00·7 mil*es*.
I stood to and fro this afternoon sometimes the top sailes set and sometimes the courses, the wind vearing from the West to the North West, hard gales to night and much rain, the Ship Labours much, the seas run very Lofty, the main top sail split in handing, I brought a new one to the yard. I stood to the Northward all night.

Sunday the 11th, rainy gusty weather, the wind at NW, at 11 of clock the wind veared to the NBW and blew hard. I tacked and stood to the Westward a great Lofty Sea runs here as it doth on the West Coast of Ireland. I do find any Current or tyde to run in this sea in the offing, and but very litle when I was near the shore. Course made true from yesterday at noon til to day noon is North. Distance sailed 70 miles. Differ*ence* of Lat*itude* North 01°10′. Latitude by account is 43°10′ S.
Meridian Distance at noon from Cape Pillar East is 3 leagues 2·6 mil*es*.
Longitude at noon from Cape Pillar East 00°09′·8.
Longitude at noon from the Lizard West 72°50′·3.
Meridian distance from the Lizard West 1145 leagues 00·7 mil*es*.
This afternoon the wind veared to the westwards & blew very hard to night and rained much. Vile & base weather.

[1] Isla Chiloé is shown on Narbrough's published chart (Plate 9) named Castro: on the Doncker chart (Plate 2) it is named C.astro [*sic*].

Munday the 12th, much wind at two of clock at Northwest and hail & rain I could not carry my Courses. I handed the foresail and tryed with the main sail & mizzen. I laid the Ship's head to the Southwestward. The Sea is very Lofty and runs mighty hollow, which causeth the Ship to Labour very much and make water. I am now very doubtfull of my main mast the Ship rowleth so extreamly. Shee makes much water abaft so as wee are forced to bale it out as well as pump, the Ship worketh so much that I have not one dry place in her from Stem to Stern, but every place is extreamly wet, the sea breaks over all many times. The Ship is well conditioned as for the sea but shee wants to bee Iron bound better aloft,[1] for her upper works open and work much. Course made true from yesterday at noon til to day

[142] **December 1670. The *Sweepstakes* in the South Sea. Lat*itude* 43° &c^a^ S.**
at noon is SSW. Distance sailed and drove 47 miles. Departure West 18 miles. Diff*erence* of Long*itude* West 00°24′·8. Diff*erence* of Lat*itude* 00°43′ S. Latitude by account at noon 43°53′ South.
Meridian Distance at noon from Cape Pillar West 02 leag*ues* 00·4 mil*es*.
Longitude from Cape Pillar West 00°15′.
Longitude from Cape Lizard West 73°15′·1.
Meridian distance at noon from the Lizard West 1151 leagues 00·7 mil*es*.
Much wind this afternoon at North West the main sail split, I had it unbent and a new one brought to the yard. The mizzen split, I had another brought to. At 2 of Clock this afternoon the wind veared to the South West, I brought the Ship on the other tack and tryed to the northward.

Tuesday the 13th. some rain this morning at 2 of clock the storm Ceased. I made saile and steered North West to get off til I saw the weather Settled. I am Cautions of being near the shore in foule weather, for my main-mast is [*margin:* *] sprung and I cannot bear a pres* sail[2] on it to beat it off of a Lee shore, for fear of Loseing it. I have three good fishes on it now. Course made true from yesterday noon til to day noon is North. Distance sailed 51 miles. Difference of Latit*ude* 00°51′. Latitude by observation 43°02′ South.
Meridian distance at noon from Cape Pillar West 2 leag*ues* 00·4 mil*es*.
Longit*ude* from Cape Pillar West 00°15′.
Longitude from the Lizard West 73°15′·1.
Meridian distance from the Lizard West 1151 Leagues 00·7 mil*es*.
This day at 12 of clock I steered NBE the wind at WSW a stout gale, a great Sea runs. This afternoon I put a fish on the main-mast. I caused 8 faddoms of the Sheat Cable to bee Cut off, next the Anchor, it was half stranded, I had four faddom of the best Bower Cable Cut off next the Anchor, it being much worne. Indifferent fair weather to night wind at West South West a fresh gale, course NBE.

Wednesday the 14th, fair weather, the wind South West a fine gale, I steered North-East for to make the Land. Course made true from yesterday noon til to day at noon is North

[1] This refers to the upper deck and the part of the hull above the waterline.
[2] Press of sail: As much sail as the strength of the wind will allow the ship to carry.

and B*y* East. Distance sailed 68 miles. Departure East 13·4 miles. Diff*erence* of Longitude East 00°18′. Differ*ence* of Lat*itude* 01°07′. Latitude by observation 41°55′ S.
Meridian distance from Cape Pillar East 2 leag*ues* 01 mil*e*.
Longitude at noon from Cape Pillar East 00°03′.
Longitude at noon from the Lizard West 72°57′·1.
Meridian distance from the Lizard West 1146 leag*ues* 2·3 mil*es*.
Fair weather this afternoon and to night wind at SW. I steer in East North-East to make the Land. Don Carolus came to mee this Evening & told mee that if I would Land him at Baldivia hee could soon speak with the Indians

[143] **December 1670. The *Sweepstakes* in the South Sea Latit*ude* 40° &ca.**
and Spaniards and have a trade with them for gold, and what I would desire. I told Him I must discover the Coast all along and so come to Baldivia. And Castro would bee a place which I hoped would produce a trade. Hee answered mee that Castro was a shoald place, and if I had not a care I might Lose the Ship there.[1] I desired of him if hee had been there hee told mee no, But hee had heard of it several times by Spanish Pilots. I told him I had a great desire to see it if wind and weather permits. Hee asked mee if I had no Commission to take Spaniards, I told him I had none: But my businesse is to discover the Countrey, and to have Conferrence with the natives wherby wee might settle a trade, as you acquainted his Ma*jes*tie you Could do, which was the occasion of our Comeing here. His answer was that hee thought I would take Spaniards or else hee would not have come this way. I sent for my Lieutenants and Master and acquainted them that Don Carlos would bee Landed at Baldivia, and that hee could procure a trade there with the natives and Spaniards, and that hee was not acquainted at Castro, and that Castro hee said was a shoald place. Also I signified to my officers that I would gladly see the Coast all along to Baldivia, and discover it so as to have Conference with the natives, wherby I may return with an account of it. I desired their advice what they thought might bee best. They Concluded it would bee best to goe for Baldivia by Reason D*on* Carlos was acquainted there, I answered I would see the coast all along if wind & weather permitted. So wee departed at this time; I ordered the Master to keep in East North East all night & til further order from mee. I verily believe Don Carlos is fearfull of being drowned, since hee hath seen this stormy weather, my men are much tewed out with this foule weather and baleing.[2]

I will not complain of the generality of our English Seamen as to their Endurance of weather or diet, But I find I can worst all the Company at either, and reckon it matter of no great hardship. I have the same allowance of provision as other men have, and not a mouthfull more, I am very well satisfied with it, and for duty in Looking out, or labour in tending the sails, or in boats at all times, I do much more than any one. I believe they are out of heart in being so farre from home, or otherwise in Being so Long in a Strange Countrey they are doubtfull they shall never see their own. The best men I have in the Ship are the youths, and young men; for they are desirous of seeing new Countreys and are well satisfied, and those that have any practice will bee beneficial for the future, and

[1] Depths in the approach now are 30–36 ft (9–11 m) between the entrance points, shoaling to 18 ft (5·5 m) 2 cables within.

[2] See above, p. 499.

can give directions in these wayes hereafter. But married men are ever Lingering home and learn litle and take notice of lesse, for their fortunes are past and their honour and desires are to live with their wives though with Labour they are forced to maintain them. Young men of knowledge and honour without wives are fittest for these voyages. If I might have my choice I would not have one old or married man in the Ship

[144] **December 1670. The *Sweepstakes* in the South Sea Lat*itude* 40° &c[a].**
with mee in such a voiage as this is; Men of twenty years of age & well grown are best in health in all Climats, and most serviceable.

Thursday the 15th, fair weather, the wind SW a stout gale. This morning I saw the Land it Bore East of mee about six leagues distant, I am now in the Latitude of 40°50′. I sounded but could not have ground at seaventy faddoms, I stood in with the Land in a League of the shore I sounded there but could not get ground at 63 faddom. I could not see any place to stand into to Anchor or Bay to send my boat in to Land in it. The shore side is rocky and steep too as what I could see of it. The Land is of a good height in Large hills lying North and South, trenting meanly from their tops towards the sea side. The Land is wooded all over and green, it shews to bee a fair good land. I got out my boat this morning and made account to send her ashore but I could not it was so much wind at SSW. I bore alongst the shore to the northward to see to find a Bay to Anchor in. The Coast lyeth nearest NNE and SSW and it is a fair coast to saile by and free from rocks or shoalds, except what lies on the edge of the shore. Several whales and porpoises seen to day and sea fowls and some kites; In the Latitude of 40°30′ I saw a rivulet of fresh water run down the mountain to the sea, and a peeked rock like a Sugar loafe stand neare the Edge of the shore in the sea.[1] It blew so hard as I could not send my boat ashore, and a great Sea breached against the shore side. I steered North & B*y* East, and North-North east, fair by the shore side, as the Coast lyeth. I observe but very litle tyde or Current to run in this sea, and the winds are vearable to saile either to the North or Southward, as to what I see as yet, and the sea is as our European sea in the same Latitudes, beeing of[f] the shore. Today at 12 of clock I was in the Latitude of 40°23′ South, by good observation of the Sun, on the meridian, and within four miles of the shore side, the Land is a good height and all wooddy, the shore side rocky and of a mean height, the sea deep, I could not get ground at sixty faddoms. After several Courses made from yesterday noon til to day noone I make my true Course to bee NE 5° easterly. Distance sailed 143 miles. Departure East 109·4 miles. Difference of Longitude 02°26′·6. Differ*ence* of Latitude 01°32′. Latitude by account & obs*ervation* 40°23′ S.
Meridian Distance at noon from Cape Pillar East 38 leag*ues* 2·4 miles.
Longitude from Cape Pillar East 02°29′·6.
Longitude at Noone from the Lizard West 70°30′·5.
Meridian distance from the Lizard West 1110 Leag*ues* 0·9 mil*es*.
A hard gale this afternoon at SWBS and Clear weather. I sailed all along the shore in a league of it, Course NBE and NNE, the Coast lyeth so, It maketh a litle in Bays and bluffe heads, on the edge of the shore. At two of clock this afternoon I was abreast a sandy Bay which hath a low point

[1] Possibly El Farallón (40°20′S 73°49′W). See above, p. 285, n. 1.

[145] **December 1670. The *Sweepstakes* on the Coast of CHILIE.**
of Land on the South part of it, and rocky on the face of the shore.[1] The Land is Low and sandy in this Bay on the sea shore, But it riseth in land to Large high hills, and all grown over with woods, the Land maketh very fair over this Bay. Here is a Large vally runs Inland from this Bay all wooddy. I stood into the Bay in a mile of the shore and sounded, I had thirty eight faddom sandy ground. I could not Anchor nor send my boat ashore it blew so much wind and alongst the shore, I sailed along the shore to the Northward. I could not see any sign of people on the shore all along [*margin:* * Baldivia] as I sailed. At four of clock this afternoon I was abrest of Baldivia. I could not make the harbour til I came right before it, then it Bore SEBE. I saw it open, it made in a Bay,[2] I stood in with it, when I brought it open wee saw a Smoak rise, like the Smoak of a gun in the midle of the opening. I stood directly in with it, I kept sounding, I had sixty faddom sandy ground about two miles off the point on the South side of the Bay, as I stood in I shoaldened the water. When the point or Cape bare South South West of mee I had thirty faddom black sand; when it bore SWBS I had twenty five faddoms black sand, I was distant from the South point Called point Galere[3] a mile or more, And from the mouth of the harbour two miles. It bare SE of mee. I saw that it was Baldivia, and that I had run my extent in Latitude, for I reckoned my selfe in the Latitude of 40°. It proved lesse wind, I laid my head sails to the mast and drove. I sent for my officers and Don Carlos into the great Cabbin.

My Lieu*tenant*s and Master being present with mee and Don Carlos, I am now before Baldivia, and Don Carlos hath a desire to bee landed ashore to night within the point, hee sayes hee will speak with the natives, and inform himself how matters stand as to his businesse and hee will come to the same place again to night and make a fire, and hee would have the boat come to him to the fire, and hee will give mee an account of his proceedings. I desired Don Carlos to appoint the time when hee would bee set on shore, and the place. Hee shewed mee the place, and hee would have mee set him ashore presently. I ordered Lieu*tenant* Picket [Peckett] to have the pinnace well man'd and fitted and to wait on Don Carlos and set him ashore at the place appointed, and return aboard again when hee shall give you order for it.

At 6 of clock this afternoon Don Carlos went from aboard the *Sweepstakes* in my pinnace with my Lieutenant Nathanael Picket having the Charge of the boat, and to see him safe set ashore in the Bay at the place hee desired.[4] Don Carlos carried with him a sword & Case of Pistols, His best apparel, a bag with beads & knives, Scissers looking glasses, Combs, rings, Pipes, Jews harps, Bells and tobacco &c[a].

[146] **December 1670. The *Sweepstakes* at BALDIVIA.**
all which things hee had of mee to give the natives. At Seaven of clock Señor Carlos was set on shore, on the South side of the harbour of Baldivia without the mouth of it a mile, in a small sandy Bay about two miles within the Point Gallere between the point and the mouth of the harbour. When he was ashore hee took his leave of my Lieutenant, and bid him go aboard and look out for his fire in the night, hee went from the boat alongst the sea side in a path towards the harbour's mouth, the men in the boat saw him go along for

[1] This bay might be Caleta Chaihuín which lies about 10 miles WSW from the entrance to Bahía Corral.

[2] Bahía Corral (39°49′S, 73°27′W).

[3] This is the point under Morro Gonzalo (39°51′S, 73°28′W). See above, p. 284, n. 3.

[4] Caleta San Carlos, a little over one mile east of Morro Gonzalo.

a quarter of a miles distance till hee turned behind a point of rocks out of sight. The shore side is low & sandy and some scattered rocks lyes on it, the land riseth trenting inland to large hills. The Land is all woody and very thick that there is no travelling but by the water side, my Lieutenant went ashore to the edge of the woods and gathered several green apples off of the trees, for there grows apple-trees on the shore side, much like our European winter fruit, the apples were bigger then walnuts with their shells on, whether these trees were planted by the Spaniards or grow naturally in the Countrey I cannot tell;[1] a rivulet of good fresh water came running Down the side of the[2] hill, where hee was landed, it run into the Sea. There grows many long Canes where the fresh water runs, the Canes are knotty jointed like a bastard Japan,[3] and tough, they run up the trees like wood bines.[4] My Lieut*enan*t staid at the shore side neare an houre, in expectation of seeing some people, but could not, hee came aboard and acquainted mee what was done, and what D*on* Carlos ordered him to doe, which was to look out for his fire at night.

I Lay off and on all this time with the Ship before the mouth of Baldivia about 2[5] miles off I had 28 & 30 faddoms water, the ground fine black sand the sea fine and smooth, now the wind came to the South a fine gale, I found the Current to set out of the harbour. At seaven of clock this evening there came a Canoa out of the harbour, and came aboard the Shipp. Shee was rowed by six indian men, there was one Spaniard in her which sate abaft, they took hold of the wast rope[6] but would not come into the Ship for the Spaniard saw that wee were not his Countreymen, put off again and went away. I spoke to him in Spanish and desired him to come on board, and that wee were his friends and that hee should bee welcome, hee would not answer one word but went away with all the speed hee could. I let him go as peaceably as hee came, I perceive hee did not know what Ship wee were til hee came at us, but took us for one of his own nation, they being litle acquainted with shipping, I haveing no colours Spread at this time, but kept them close for feare of giveing mistrust.

This evening I stood West South West into the sea, the wind at South & B*y* West a fine gale, I plyed off and on all night before the Harbour of Baldivia, in a League

[147] **December 1670. The *Sweepstakes* at Baldivia in Chili.**

and two leagues of the shore alwayes looking out for the fires ashore which Don Carlos promised to make, at the place where hee Landed. I kept fair before that all night, but could not see any sign of fire. I kept my Lead sounding and had 40 faddom water sandy ground a league off the shore, But further off no ground at seaventy faddom; I observed the Suns amplitude at setting, and found the variation of the Compasse to bee Eight

[1] The apple, genus *Malus*, is found in Asiatic-European areas, naturally occurring in northern temperate climates only, and so these apple trees must have been imported.

[2] 'the' substituted for 'a'.

[3] Among the meanings of Japan in *NOED* is 'a black varnished cane'. Bastard (again among other meanings): Having the appearance of, somewhat resembling; an inferior or less-proper kind of; esp. in scientific nomenclature applied to things resembling but not identical with, the species which legitimately bears the name. *NOED*. It would appear therefore that the meaning of this is resembling a black varnished cane. These would appear to be bamboos. For the forms growing in Chile, see above, p. 290, n. 2.

[4] Woodbines: a name in early use for climbing plants, such as ivy and convolvulus.

[5] The word 'two' was struck through in the original and the figure substituted.

[6] Waist rope: a rope hanging from the waist (that part of the ship between the main mast and the forecastle) to enable boats to remain alongside the gangway.

degrees easterly, and no more; Latitude 40°00′ South, and near the Port of Baldivia. Good weather all night and a temperate air, and not very cold. A fine dew falls to-night.

I do not find any Current or tyde to set on this Coast that is any way prejudicial to Navigation, neither do I find the winds to blow trade,[1] but they are vearable, and are given to blow hard, on the western quarter, & rain much.

The mouth of the Harbour of Baldivia on the Coast of Chili in the South Sea Lieth in the Latitude of 39°56′ South.
Longitude West from the Lizard of England 70°19′.
Meridian Distance from Cape Pillar East 41 Leagues 2·1 miles.
Longitude from Cape Pillar East 02°41′·1.[2]
This account I make of my sailing from the Meridian of the Lizard, according to my dayly account of the Ship's way. I do not make any account of plain sailing to bee fit for Seamen to observe, But the best navigation is by Mercator's sailing according to the Circle of the Globe, which I ever sail by, and keep my account of Easting and Westing by Longitude, which is the best & most [*margin:* *] certain sailing to give the true descr*iption of the Globe. I have noted down the meridian distance I made dayly, wherby such Navigators and Sea men as know no better may have that to give them knowledge of the Distance of places according to their understanding. Most of out Navigators in this age sail by the plain Chart, and keep their accounts of the Ships way accordingly, although they sail neare the Poles, which is the greatest errour that can bee com*m*itted, for they Cannot tell how to find the way home again by reason of their mistake, as I have some in the Ship with mee now, that is in the same errour for want of understanding the true difference of the meridians according to their miles of Longitude in the several Latitudes. I could wish all Sea men would give over sailing by the false plain Chart, and saile by Mercators Chart, which is according to the truth of Navigation, But it is a hard matter to Convince any of the old Navigators from their method of sailing by the plain Chart, Shew most of them the globes yet they will walk in their wonted road.

Fryday the 16th, fair weather, wind at South-South West a stout gale. I stood in this morning before Baldivia, and sent my boat ashore with my Lieutenant Nathanael Picket in her and twelve men, being armed with small shot. I ordered

[148] **December 1670. The *Sweepstakes* at Baldivia in Chili.**
my Lieu*tenan*t to row in to the shore and Look for Don Carlos, at the place where hee Landed him, and if hee bee not there to row all along the shore on the South side that way as Don Carlos went, into the Port, and see for him; and also see what people Live in the Port, and how farre hee could go that way, & to observe the manner of the Lyeing of the Port, so as I may make a draught of it, & to observe the depth of water, & what ground, the sett of the tydes the ebbing & flowing, and the riseing, And to observe the shore, and give mee an account of the soile, and what grows on it, and if possible to speak with the natives of the Countrey, and treat them Courteously so as to have their friendship and Love, wherby wee may have commerce with them. I also gave my Lieu*tenan*t Hatchets,

[1] Constantly from one direction like the trade winds.
[2] The entrance to the mouth of the harbour of Valdivia lies in 39°50′S, 73°26′W from Greenwich or 68°14′W from the Lizard, or 1°14′E from Cabo Pilar.

beads, knives &c^{a}. along with him to give to the Natives, and if hee saw any Spaniards to bee kind and repective[1] to them, and to have a care and not do them any Injury, But endeavour to understand of what force they are, what their trade is and their manner of liveing. At 8 of clock in the forenoon my boat put from mee, and rowed within point Galere, to the place where D*on* Carlos was Landed. I Lay off and on with the Ship before the Port, the boat rowed all along the shore by the place where D*on* Carlos was landed, and alongst the shore into the harbour.

At the point on the South side of the harbour stands a small fort, of seaven guns called St James's Fort,[2] my boat came suddenly upon it before they perceived it to bee a Fort, they were in Shot of it. The Spaniards stood on the shore & weafted with a white flagg,[3] and Called to them, my Lieu*tenan*t Rowed to them and asked them of what Countrey they were, they answered of Spain. They asked my Lieu*tenan*t of what Countrey hee was, Hee answered of England, they asked him to come ashore which hee did, in hope to have seen Don Carlos there, for the path that D*on* Carlos went in when hee was Landed, went directly to this Fort by the sea side, and it was not a mile to the Fort from the place where hee was Landed, so as hee must go to this Fort, and bee upon it before hee was aware of it, unlesse hee knew it before, the path went all along between the woods and the sea. In the woods there is no travelling they are so thick, and grow on the side of a hill. The Fort stands just by the woods side on a rise of a bank of five yards ascent from the sea, with a bank of Earth Cast up before the ordinance, and Slight palisados placed in a half moon, four yards distance from the guns to the Southwards, which palisados are to keep the Natives from running violently on the Ordinance. So these Spaniards guard themselves with long lances against the natives. In the fort the Spaniards have match-Lock musketons,[4] but they are very ordinary ones, and they are as silly[5] in useing them.
The great guns are demi-Culvering, and Saker, of brasse, they stand open Looking over the bank, they are now mounted on old field Carriages. A file of

[149] **December 1670. The *Sweepstakes* at Baldivia.**

resolved men would run down all the Palissados before them and take possession of the Fort, the fortification is so slight, and the Spaniards but few, and those but ordinary soldiers, for they do not understand what it is to bee opposed with fire arms, and men of courage, their fighting is with naked Indians which have no other weapons then Bows & arrows, and Lances and Staves. And these people maintain a warre against the Spaniards, and do them much spoile every yeare and kill many of them.

At my Lieutenant's Landing about twenty Spaniards and Indians came to the water side in arms and received him & his Company ashore, & carried him some twenty yards from the water side, up the rise of the bank under a great tree, where the Captain of the Fort and

[1] Narbrough appears to misspell and misuse 'respective' here, but this word also had the meaning 'cautious, careful', still found in 18th-century dictionaries. He means 'respectful'.

[2] This fort was situated on the lower slopes of Punta Amargos, (39°52′S, 73°25′W). It is shown on Narbrough's plan of the 'Port oF Baldavia' (Plate 4), where the name is spelled F^{t}. S. IAGUA.

[3] Waved, or signalled, to them with a white flag.

[4] Matchlock musket, a musket fired by match on the cock opening the firing pan, as opposed to flintlock which fired by a flint striking a spark which was directed into the firing pan. The latter was invented at the start of the 17th century and was in common use by the middle of it, so that by this time matchlocks were old fashioned.

[5] In this case 'silly' is probably being used to mean untrained, or ignorant, rather than foolish. *NOED*.

two other Spanish gentlemen received him under the shade with great Courtesie after the Spanish Ceremony, they sate them on Chairs and benches placed about a table under the Shade, for the sun shined very warm, it being a very fair day. The Spanish Captain called for wine which was brought him in a great Silver bowle. Hee drank to my Lieu*tenan*t and bad him wellcome ashore, and Caused five of his ordinance to bee fired being glad to see English men in this place, and told him that this was Baldivia, speaking very kindly, & how welcome they were to him. After every one had drunk and my Lieu*tenan*t had thanked him for his Entertainment, hee desired my Gentlemen to sit down, and hee discoursed with them and asked from whence hee came, and which way hee came into this sea, and what the Captain's name was, and if there were warrs in England. My Lieu*tenan*t answered him to his demands, and asked him if they were in peace with the Indians, hee answered that they were at warrs with them round about, weafting his hand round the harbour and that they were valliant people & very barbarous, and fought on horsback, and did them much spoile, and that two dayes before the Indians came out of the woods and killed a Captain as hee stood at his duty, by the side of the Fort, and Cut off his head & carried it away, sticking on their Lance. Hee shewed my Lieu*tenan*t the place where the Indians came out of the woods, and the place where the man was killed. They seem to bee very fearfull of the Indians, for they will not stirre any way but they will have their peece or their Lance also this is a signe that they are much affraid of the Indians, for they have no more ground then the Fort, nor do not cleare any part of the woods on this side of the harbour, nor walk a musket shot distance from the Pallisados alongst the woods sides. They say the Indians have much gold, and that their armour for their breast is gold. In the afternoon a dinner was brought out of the Fort to the tent where they were and placed on the table; the first course was Soupes, then Ollas,[1] then pullets, then fresh fish, all dressed with hot sauce and very good diet it was; the last course was sweetmeats, every Course was served in silver dishes, and all the plaites were silver, and the potts & Stuepans

[150] **December 1670. The *Sweepstakes* at BALDIVIA.**

and all the utensils belonging to the dressing of the provisions were all silver, and a large vessel which held fresh water was silver, and the bason which they brought water in to wash their hands was very large of silver, and the hilts of the soldiers swords was silver, and the hilts of the Officers swords were gold of good value, and the Plate at the butt end of the stock of their musketoons was silver, and the pipes that the rod runs in was silver, and the tip of the gun-stick, their tobacco boxes & snuff boxes silver, their staves which they walk with were headed and verrelled[2] with silver, and verrelled on the joints with silver. They are masters of much silver and gold, and it is but of litle esteem with them, their boasting was, *plata no valle nada, mucho oro en tierra*.[3]

After they had dined the Captain told my Lieutenant and gentlemen they were welcome, hee drank the King of Englands health and fired seaven peeces of ordinance and caused it to bee drank by the whole Company, with their heads uncovered, their drink was the wine of Chili, much Like the worser sort of Madera wine, and strong and heady drink, they drank it out of a great silver bowle to the quantity of a pint at a time, after

[1] Stew of meat and vegetables.

[2] Ferruled, fitted with a cap at the end to prevent wear and a band to secure and strengthen the joints of their sticks.

[3] 'Silver costs nothing, much gold in the earth.'

this health passed round & ended at my Lieu*tenan*t hee drank the King of Spain's health, the Captain Commanded seaven guns to bee fired and the health to go round, then the Captain drank his Royall highnesse the Duke of York's health, and fired five guns, and caused it to bee drunk round, my Lieu*tenan*t drank the queen of Spain's health the Captain fired five guns and had the health drunk round.[1]

The Captain Caused his servants to give my Seamen wine and bread that were in my boat. After these healths were ended the Captain desired the Company to sit down, and began his discourse with my Lieutenant and the other gentlemen [*margin:* *] with him, their discourse was* of the news in Europe, which my Lieu*tenan*t satisfied him was all peace when hee came from thence, Excepting the Turks at the Island of Candia,[2] which was in wars with the Venetians at that time. Many various discourses hee had Concerning the French nation and the Spaniards, And whether they were in peace or warrs. My Lieu*tenan*t answered that at our Comeing away the French had invaded Flan*ders, and it was thought that the French the next Summer would bee master of all that Countrey, if they continue their design and make a warre.[3]

After this discourse was ended my Lieu*tenan*t asked the Captain if wee could have wood and water here and some refreshing for our men and hee should have what satisfaction hee would, either in money or goods, the Captain told him hee should have what the Countrey affoorded. It being about five of clock in the afternoon and the wind began to blow fresh at Southwest, my Lieu*tenan*t desired leave of the Capt*ain* hee might depart for night grew neare, and the Ship under saile a great way off, the Capt*ain* very Civilly bid him take his own time, so my Lieu*tenan*t and Company took their Leaves of the Spanish Captain and his Gentlemen

[151] **December 1670. The *Sweepstakes* at Baldivia in Chili.**

and came to the pinnace and the Spaniards with them to the water side discoursing of many Circumstances not worthy of relation. When they came to take boat four Spanish gentlemen desired to go aboard with my Lieu*tenan*t and see the Shipp, and Pilot her into the harbour if I would come in, which they did not question but I would as I understood afterwards by a Spaniard that came aboard to mee, which told mee their whole design how they intended to surprise the Ship which I ever took care to prevent, giving them no opportunity, for it hath been a general practice with the Spaniards in America to betray all forraign interests in those parts, as I had read of their treacherous dealings with Capt*ain* Hawkins at S[t] Juan de Ulua.[4]

[1] The king of Spain at this time was Carlos II and the queen was his mother, the Queen Regent Mariana of Austria, widow of Philip IV. See further below, p. 515, n. 2. For gun salutes with toasts, see above, p. 132, n. 1.

[2] The Duchy of Candia was the official name of Crete while it was under Venetian control. The Cretan war (1645–69), between the Ottoman Empire and the Venetian Republic, was fought mainly in Crete and in various naval engagements. It culminated in the two-year siege of Candia (modern Heraklyon). When the fortress surrendered Crete was lost to the Republic.

[3] This would appear to be a reference to the French attack on the Spanish Netherlands in 1667, which was brought to a halt the next year by the diplomatic intervention of the Triple Alliance,of England, Sweden and the Dutch Republic. See below, p. 662, n. 1.

[4] This refers to the outcome of the 3rd expedition led by Sir John Hawkins to the Caribbean, (1567–8). After a year of privateering and slave trading his fleet of 5 ships was virtually annihilated off San Juan d'Uloa (now Veracruz,) when the Spanish fleet, carrying the new Viceroy of Mexico entered harbour and attacked his vessels, disregarding an agreed truce. See, Kelsey, *Sir John Hawkins*, pp. 70–93; Morgan, 'Hawkins, Sir John', *ODNB*.

At my Lieu*tenan*ts comeing off from the shore four Spaniards came aboard with him of good quality, one was a Captain, the other Ensigns & a Serjeant, men of good deportments and well apparelled, born in old Spain, but had lived in those parts upwards of ten years. When my boat put from the shore and my Lieutenant took leave of the Captain of the Fort, hee caused five guns to bee fired and bid him farewell. My Lieu*tenan*t saluted him again with a volley of small shott fired by his boats Crew, and three hollows,[1] and then came aboard the Ship. At evening my Lieu*tenan*t came aboard the *Sweepstakes*, and the whole crew as went with him and the four Spanish Gentlemen, which I received at the side, and Carried them aft into the great Cabbin, and desired them to sit down at my table, and had a glasse of good wines for them, and I caused my interpreter to tell them they were wellcome aboard the King of England's Ship, and fired five peeces of Ordinance, my trumpets sounded and musick played which pleased them much. They being a litle Sea Sick with the motion of the Ship and wet in comeing off in my boat, I had them shifted with my Linnen and Cloths,[2] and burned a glasse of wine for them, seeing they were but fresh water Seamen. I caused a good peece of English Beef & a pudding to bee brought to the table, But they had but small Stomacks to eat. I lodged them in my bed and on Carpets and quilts in the great Cabbin for this night, and stood off and on with the Shipp before the harbour. Fair weather all night and a fine fresh gale at South West, and at South sometimes, the heavens cleare & fine temperate weather, neither too hot nor too Cold, but a good health Climate. My men I praise god are all in good health and Lusty, as men can bee, being seaventy three in number men and Boyes. After I had the Spaniards to bed I discoursed with my Lieu*tenan*t concerning their day's passing ashore, the matters were as what is related in the former leaves, But no news of Don Carlos; But hee believes hee must bee with the Spaniards, for hee could not go any other way but to the Fort which is Called Fort St Iago.[3]

Saturday the 17th, flattering hazy foggy weather, wind at Southwest a stout

[152] **December 1670. The *Sweepstakes* at Baldivia in Chili.**

gale towards the midle of the day and a swelling Sea came along with it. I stood in to the shore with intent to Anchor before the harbour of Baldivia, between Cape galere[4] and the harbour's mouth under that shore. I kept sounding as I stood in but could not get ground at eighty faddoms two Leagues off the Land about a league off I had sixty five faddoms fine black sand, and as I stood in I shoaldened my water to thirty faddom, then Cape Gallere bare South of mee half a mile distance. I find but litle Current or tyde to set any way but what sets out of the Harbour, which is of a mean strength, and it is occasioned by the fresh waters which comes out of the rivers that runs into the Land.

This day I saw a great ring like a rainbow round about the Sun here, two degrees distance from the Sun and very ap*p*arent, I do not remember I ever saw the like in any part of the world before this time, it was in the same manner as the rings are many times about the moon, against foule weather, this was at one of Clock in the afternoon. I stood into the bay before Baldivia Harbour, and anchored in fourteen faddom water fine black sand, half a mile off the shore side near a mile within Cape

[1] Presumably 3 cheers or halloos.

[2] Changed into his linen and clothes.

[3] Fort St James, see above, p. 507, n. 2.

[4] This is the headland under Morro Gonzal.

Gallere.[1] The Cape bare West South West of mee, the harbours mouth half open about a mile & half from mee. I saluted the Castle with seaven guns, they answered mee five, I fired three, they answered one. I had all my Colours flying, Jack, Ensign, & Pendants at every mast head and my wast clothes[2] stretched fore and Aft, and the Ship clear, and the guns out abaft the mast, and on the upper deck. The Spaniards expected I would have gone within the Com*m*and of their guns into the harbour. When they saw mee bring the Ship round to, and com*m*and the master to Let go the Anchor which was done accordingly, They asked mee if I would not go into the harbour. I answered them that I found shoald water, & that I dare not venture the Ship any further til I had sounded the depths of water all the way in, for the Ship was of great draught of water, and if Shee Should come on ground Shee would oversett, And Shee was a very rich Ship of goods so as I dare not venture in for feare of danger. They said it was a good harbour and that there was no lesse then six faddom water in it where I should Ride and that they came aboard to carry the Ship in. I gave them many thanks but desired of them to be excused til I had seen the Commodiousnesse of it, they answered I might do what I pleased. I caused the Ship to bee mored with the Stream anchor & cable, for I had but litle wind at [and] that was at South West off the shore 2 points.

I had much discourse with the Spanish Gentlemen this day Concerning Baldivia and Chili; they tell mee they have much gold here at Baldivia, but the natives do much hinder their getting of it, for they are at Cruell warrs with them, and will not permit them to plant any thing near hereabouts nor at Baldivia, but they Come

[153] **December 1670. The *Sweepstakes* at Baldivia in Chili.**

and destroy it with fire, and they are very Cruel and barbarous. If they take any Spaniard they Cut off his head and Carry it away on their Lance. They tell mee they Live as the Spaniards do at Mam*m*ora in Barbary[3] with their enemies round about them. They say the Indians are mighty valliant men, and fight on horsback eight and ten thousand in Battallia,[4] and that they have much gold and have armour of gold, & their weapons are Long Lances, Bows & arrows, swords and some muskets which they have taken from the Spaniards, and know how to use them in service, taking also ammunition &c[a]. The Indians are very populous in the Land about Baldivia and at Osorno[5] and Castro, and in Chilue,[6] and they have much gold, as the people say.

[1] The anchorage is shown on Narbrough's plan of 'Port oF Baldavia' (Plate 4) off Caleta San Carlos.

[2] Wast clothes: today this would be called 'Dressed overall'. The wast clothes are 'A long red cloth about three quarters of a yard broad, edged on each side with Calico or linnen cloth, that goeth round about the ship on the out sides of all her upper works fore and aft, and before the cubbridge heads {the bulkheads of the forecastle and half decks]; ... as for the countenance and grace of the ship as to cover the men for being seene.' Smith, *Sea Grammar*, p. 77.

[3] La Mámora was the Spanish name for Mehdia in Morocco, on the west bank of Sebou River at its mouth. It was under Spanish rule from 1641 until 1681.

[4] *Batalla*, battle.

[5] Osorno is shown on the Doncker chart (Plate 2) on the NE shore of Golfo de Ancud, east of Chiloé (C.astro). Heylyn described it in 1662 as '*sorno*, on the banks of the Bay of *Chilve*, (or *Ancud* as the *Salvages* call it) situate in a barren soyl, but well stored with Gold, and thought to be more populous than *Valdivia* it self', in *Cosmographie*, p. 1074. The city, which is not in Golfo de Ancud or indeed on the coast, was founded in 1558 and destroyed by the Araucanian Indians a number of times. It is shown on chart 101 in Basil Ringrose's *South Sea Waggoner*, in an estuary about 50 miles south of Punta Galera. The position of the present town is 40°35′S, 73°09′W. Howes, *Buccaneers Atlas*, p. 247.

[6] Castro, see p. 280, n. 3. Chilue is probably Chiloé.

This Captain tells mee they have six great Ships goes yearly from Peru to mannillos,[1] and they do sail in the month of January from Calleo,[2] & their passage is but litle more then two months to the City of the Manillos, And they come from thence to the Port of Aquatulco,[3] which is on the West Coast of New Spain, and from thence to Panama,[4] and then to the Port of Lima.[5] They have a great trade from Japan and China, by way of the Mannillos. The Captain demanded of mee whither I was Bound, I answered I was bound for China, And that I had rich lading for that Countrey, and that I only touched in at this place knowing here were settlements of the King of Spain's subjects, hopeing here to have wood and fresh water, and refreshing for my men, wherby I might the better proceed on my voyage. Hee said I should have what the Countrey would affoord, and that the Captain of the Fort had sent for provisions for mee, and that I might have water on the shore, and said it was [*Equa dle Oro*][6] the water of Gold. His [*right margin:* del] saying this caused mee to Laugh, then hee said that it came running from the hills where they find gold, and that there is some gold in that Rivulet. I asked him how they gett the gold. Hee said they wash the earth which is in the mountains and find the gold in the Bowle or tray when the earth is washed out, and they Buy much gold of the Indians which they gather in the hills which is washed into the gullies, by the rains & snow from the higher mountains, which they say are very high and barren rocks thirty Leagues in land from the sea shore. The Land between those barren mountains (which they Call the Andes) and the sea, is mighty good Land, and the Countrey very fruitfull and many plains and much Cattel that the Indians have as horses and Cowes, goates and sheep which they have taken from the Spaniards since they came into this Countrey. They said that those mountains run all along the Land to terra firma in a row, to Sta Martha,[7] but the most gold is in Chili, and at Castro. But they have but litle knowledge of the Land all along from Baldivia to the Straits mouth, as what I can understand by them, except at the Island of Castero [*sic*] they have a settlement, and

[154] **December 1670. The *Sweepstakes* at Baldivia in Chili.**

on the main against Castero at a place called Orsono, But not any further southerly then Castero. They are but meanly peopled at Orsono, and at Castro And there are many Indians, and they have much gold, they are very valliant people in Chile. The Captain that was aboard of mee his name was Pedro Martens,[8] hee said that the Indians would defie the Spaniards in the plaines and stand and dare them spreading abroad their armes and showing their brest to them, and would have them shoot at them. But if they misse the Indian runs in upon him with his Lance and kills him and Cuts off his head and Carries it away with him. And hee said that they are of such Gyantly Stature that on

[1] Manila, in the Philippines.

[2] Callao (12°04′S, 77°08′W).

[3] Acapulco (16°55′N, 99°52′W).

[4] Panamá (8°56′N, 79°36′W).

[5] Lima (12°04′S, 77°03′W).

[6] The square brackets are in the original. 'dle' is corrected to 'del' in the margin. '*Aqua DL Oro*' is marked, in the back of Caleta San Carlos, on Narbrough's plan of the 'Port oF Baldavia' (Plate 4).

[7] It is not clear what these limits signify. It might be from Tierra del Fuego in the south to Santa Marta (11°16′N, 74°12′W), on the north coast of Colombia, in the north, which would not be an unreasonable description.

[8] Probably Martines. It has not been possible to find out anything about this officer.

horsback they will take a Spaniard by the hair of his head, and ride clear away with him hanging in his hand. The Captain spoke this openly on the quarter deck before mee and my officers, any man may believe it that will.

Here was one Spanish shipp rideing in the Port of one hundred & twenty tuns or thereabouts. Shee had no guns, but her built was much after the old Spanish fashion. Shee rode with her yards across and her flag and Ensign & Jack flying of white and the Laurel garland in it. Shee rode Land-Locked up in the South part of the harbour in a Bay Close by the shore, about two miles from the harbours mouth.[1] In the Bay where Shee rode there is a small sconce of three guns.[2] I suppose it is to keep the natives from Comeing down off that South river, the Spaniards said Shee rid in five faddom water, and it was fresh water. This Ship came from Lima five and fourty dayes before. Shee came all along the Coast, the general passage from Lima to Baldivia as they say is between thirty and 40 dayes. But from Baldivia to Lima is eighteen or 20 dayes, For the winds are much at South, more northerly on the height of the day,[3] But in the night off the shore. This ship brought from Lima provisions for Baldivia and the forts, as Cloths, ammunition, tobacco, wine of Chili, sugar &c. And Shee Carries away gold, Bezoar Stone, vianaco's wooll &c[a]. and Indian Slaves that they take in these parts. They carry them to Peru and make perpetual Slaves of them there, and the Peruvian Indians they bring hither and make soldiers of them against the Chili Indians, which are many hereabouts, which my men saw when they were at the fort. There might bee about 30 indians and *muzteses*[4] Souldiers, there were not above sixteen white men they being officers, also the Spaniards make up of these Indians to trade with the Chili Indians for gold, for they of Chili without doubt are desirous of trade, wherby they may furnish themselves of knives scissors Combs &c. which is wanting amongst them, and arms many times are sold to them by stealth, although they bee prohibited, traders will bee dealing so as they Can get benefit. They do not Consider future danger, by it's [its] meanes, so

[155] **December 1670. The *Sweepstakes* at Baldivia.**
as it misse them at that time.

Now I shall relate the succeeding discourse I had with the Spanish Capt*ain* and Gentlemen aboard the *Sweepstakes*, this day being 17th Dec*ember* 1670. This forenoon when they were got up and dressed themselves, I went into the great Cabbin to visit them, for I lay all the night before on the quarter deck, I lodged them in the great Cabbin. At my visit they seemed to bee very merry and Inclineing to drink, they were much delighted with Madera wine and com*m*ended it to bee better farr then any wine that grows in Chili. They say much grapes grows in Arauco, which is a Province in Chili.[5] They asked me if I had any Cakes [casks] of this wine to sell, they would give two hundred peeces of eight[6]

[1] Shown on Narbrough's plan of the 'Port oF Baldavia' (Plate 4) lying in what is now Puerto Corral (39°53′S, 73°25′W).

[2] Shown as F. S. Andrew on Narbrough's plan of the 'Port oF Baldavia' (Plate 4), probably on Punta Chorocamayo.

[3] In the middle of the day.

[4] *Mestizo*, a person of mixed Spanish and Indigenous descent. *Mulatto*, a person of mixed Spanish and African descent.

[5] This area now approximates to the province of Araucanía.

[6] See above, p. xx.

for a Pipe[1] of it. I answered I had none to sell, mine was to be given some here & at other parts where I should come, and that my master the king Laid into all his ships great store of wines for the accommodating of gentlemen that should come aboard, and brandy wines great store was laid in by the king for the Seamen, at this measure a day for a man, for two years, the measure which I shewed them would Contain a quarter of a pint. I signified also unto them that every man had for his allowance for every day a pound of bread & two pound of beef or halfe a pound of Cheese and a quarter of a pound of butter, and a great bason of pease. They said it was great allowance. I told them that I had for ten months at that allowance aboard which would Carry mee to England, without recruiting any where, but for water & wood and a litle refreshing as I wanted now. They said they would furnish mee with anything the Countrey doth affoord. I asked them if they had Corn growing here they answered mee that the Indians burned it here, But in the province of Arauco there was much wheat and Cattle. They said they had Cattel at Baldivia Cows and Bulls, hogs, Sheep & goats, And that they had sent for some, which I did not believe one word they said as to that matter.

I Carried them fore and Aft and shewed them the Ship aloft and between the decks and the Hatchwayes in the hold, and the gun roome which they admired to see so many Arms and so much munition for warr. They said the Shipp was like a Pallace, and they thought it impossible Shee could have Carried so many great guns &c[a]. if they had not seen it, for Shee showed but a small shipp to us when wee were ashore.

I had provided wine and Brandy for their morning's draught which they took very cheerfully. I had my noise of trumpets sounded all the morning, I had them up on the quarter deck that they might view our Colours for I had them a flying abroad. They Com*m*ended the Ship much and said they believed it was the handsomest ship in the world. I told them that the King of England had two hundred shipps of his own much better then this that did nothing but saile

[156] **December 1670. The *Sweepstakes* at Baldivia.**

to and fro the Seas at his pleasure, to cause all the Nations of the world to Strike their flags and sails at the Sight of them, in hommage to his Soveraignty which all Ships do immediately, otherwise they are to sinke them, or never to return to England, for the better Confirmation of my discourse I shewed them Instructions in print for the same which every Captain had. And also that all the Kings and Princes in Europe, that had any maritime Concerns had agreed upon Articles to strike their flags and sailes if themselves were in their Ships, to the worst Ship the King of England had. And that all the Kings and Princes in Europe were in Amity with the King of England, for the English are masters of the Seas,[2] and have ships sent this yeare to all parts of the world to see how they are peopled, and how the Countreys lye, and what trade they afford, and the State their

[1] A large cask or barrel for wine, holding approximately 125 gallons.

[2] See above, p. 132, n. 1, for details of salutes by foreign vessels. These extravagant remarks seem to echo John Selden's on the two ways foreign nations recognize the King of England's dominion over the sea: 'The one is the usual striking of the Top-sails, by every ship of any Forein Nation whatsoever, if they sail near the King's Navie or any Ship belonging to the same Navie in the Sea. The other is a *Libel* published of old, or a *Bill of complaint* instituted, wherein very many forein Nations heretofore, in the time of *Edward* the First, did all together, and by common consent with the *English*, acknowledge the Dominum of the Kings of *England* by Sea.' Seldon, *Of the Dominum or ownership of the Sea*, p. 398.

Princes & governours live in, and many words of the like discourse passed between us, which would bee too tedious to write here, being matters of no Consequence to a future Concerne.

Before I desist I will relate some passage of the discourse which was as followeth. The Capt*ain* asked mee where the king my Master kept his Court. Speaking very Confidently, I told him at London when I came from thence, But hee had many spacious Pallaces, in many parts of his kingdome, builded by the most Ingenious Architects in Europe. And they were adorned accordingly with the most Heroick king & Nobles & good guards of well disciplind soldiers which had been lately exercised against the French, Hollanders & Danes, to their great proof of valour. I do not hear of any Comparative in the world as yet with the Court of my king, which if there bee any such wee will soon search them out.

Now with this discourse the Capt*ain* smiled and said wee had a good Countrey & good soldiers. I answered him wee have a good king and a great soldier, and the Kingdome of England is all a garrison, well fortified with all munition of warre, and people innumerable. The Captain sate silent at this discourse, and Looked on mee and my Interpreter. At last hee said hee had not been in Europe this fifteen years, hee was born in Spain, but his father had lived in London, hee said they had news from Spain but of six months date, and that came by the way of the river of Plate, But there were letters which came in the Galleons to Port Bel,[1] and they came after by Land by the way of Panama, & to Lima by shipping, and so into these parts of Chili. I asked him how the King of Spain did, hee said hee was very well. I told him hee formerly was troubled with much sicknesse. Hee answered mee hee was but young then, But now hee had out-grown it, and was a hopefull Prince.[2]

I caused a glasse of wine to bee given mee and I drank the king of Spain's

[157] **December 1670. The *Sweepstakes* at Baldivia.**

health, and fired 7 guns and had the health passed round, it ended at the Spanish Captain hee drank the King of England's health, I fired seaven guns and had the health passed round. I drank the Queen of Spain's[3] health & fired five guns, and had the health passed round. It ended at the Spanish Capt*ain* But hee would not drink more healths at this time desiring hee might go ashore. I caused my boat to bee manned with the best men, apparelled accordingly with the best ap*p*arell they had, which was very good as most men Carry to sea. I had this done whereby the Spaniards ashore might see that I had men of good presence & well apparelld which I judged would honour the English nation in their appearance & behaviour, for they were all young and Comely proper men and well demeanourd, all with Lofty Spirits, and ambitious of honourable acts, and seeing new places, were all willing to go ashore, and as many more as I had occasion for at that time attended the motion of my Command.

[1] Portobelo (9°32′N, 79°41′W), on the north coast of Panama.

[2] Carlos II (1661–1700), the son of Philip IV and his second Queen Mariana of Austria, came to the throne at the age of 4 in 1665, with his mother acting as Regent. He was born with both physical and mental disabilities. He married Marie Louise d'Orléans, a niece of Louis XIV of France in 1679, who died in 1689. He married Maria Anna of Neuberg, daughter of the Elector of the Palatinate, in 1690. He had no children and his death brought to an end to the line of the Spanish house of Hapsburg.

[3] This was the Regent, Queen Mariana, widow of Philip IV.

I had my boat well fitted with Arms, as swords quarter pikes, and every man his fusee[1] and some Pistols. But I had given my Lieu*tenan*t such Charge not to molest any man upon any occasion whatsoever as hee would answer it at his peril, but to defend himself against opposition, and so make his retreat aboard the Ship to mee. The occasion why I caused my men to go well armed is, that through Carelessenesse there have proved the greatest miscarriages, which generally English men are addicted to, Contemning other men & trusting too much upon their own strength, especially being often succesfull gives a great occasion of negligence. And the Spaniards in this part of the world, or in any part of America are not to bee trusted, Example Sr John Hawkins at St Juan de Ulua in the Bay of Mexico.[2]

These gentlemen had a great desire to buy my fowling peeces, they proffered mee fourty peeces of eight for a fowling peece, which stood mee but in three pounds in London. They made Choice of most of the fowling peeces I had, and desired I would save them for them till to morrow, and not let any other have them, for then they would come & bring money enough to pay for them and many other things which they saw in the Ship, for my man had shewed them a box of Linnen and some Cases of knives, and some searges [serges], all which they bought afterwards. Also my man told them that I had many Chests of silks, and silk Stockings, & fine broad Cloths, and good fowling guns & powder. All these things the Spaniards had a great desire to buy, but they had not so much money about them as would pay for the guns which they desired might bee kept for them till they brought money. I told them they might have any thing as I had in the Ship ashore along with them if they pleased for I had no need of money. I Shewed them two hundred pounds in new Crown peeces of his Ma*jes*tie's coine.[3] They looked on the make of the Coin, and said it was very fair plate [*plata*], and that they had much plate on shore. I asked them if they had silver mines here, they answered no, but much gold, and that the

[158] **December 1670. The *Sweepstakes* at Baldivia.**

Plate came from Potose,[4] where there was much.

I shewed them fifty new peeces of his Ma*jes*tie's coin in gold, and some peeces of old gold, they looked on them, and valued the new peeces of gold which wee call Ginnys [Guineas] but at three peeces of eight a peece, and the other peeces which wee call Jacobuses[5] at 3 peeces of eight and half the peeces, they set but Low value on money it being plentifull with them. I asked them how farr it was to Baldivia they told mee three leagues, and that boats could go up to it, and that it was scituated by the side of the river and the plain, and that there was five great ordinance in a fort to Com*m*and the Citty, and that there were a thousand inhabitants in the Citty of all sorts, men women & Children. I asked them if there were passage by land from Baldivia to other parts of Chili, they said there was, and they sent every week, but they went with good guards to go secure from the Indians. I asked them if the build shipping here, they said no, at Valperrazco[6] they did

[1] Lighted match for igniting powder.

[2] See above, p. 509, n. 4.

[3] See above, p. xx. Crowns were silver coins.

[4] Potosi (19°36′S, 65°47′W); variants, Potossi, Pottossi. The mountain of silver was first discovered in 1545.

[5] See above, p. xx.

[6] Puerto de Valparaíso (33°02′S, 71°38′W.); variants, Valparaiso, Valperazso, Valperrazco.

build great Ships. I asked them who lived on the Island of Mocha.[1] They said Indians, many men and women, and that they were *poco megos* [*amigos*] to them, in English they are but small friends to the Spaniards, there is many sheep goats & hogs & hens, which the Indians will sell for hatchets, knives, beads; And the Island of Santa Mariea,[2] the Spaniards are masters of it, and have a fort on it with five guns, but few Spaniards live there. It is plentiful of provisions as hogs, sheep, corn, Potatos &c[a].

They say there is some gold that the Indians have on the Island of Mocha but they will not part from it. The Spaniards did not care for answering mee to those things I would gladly have heard of those parts, for I laid the draught of [*margin:* *] all that Coast on the table before them, and asked who lived at this Port, and w*ho lived at that, some places they would say the Spaniards lived there and some the Indians, but they did not care to Answer my desires but would frame other discourses to wave [waive] mine.

I find they are but litle acquainted on the Coast to the southward of Baldivia. They say they have Spaniards live on the Island of Castro, and that there is much Corn grows there, European wheat, and that on the main they have Spaniards live at a place called Osorno which is against Castro, and there they have Gold, and there are many Indians. I asked them if ships could go in between Castro and the main, they Could not tell mee, or would not, they said small ships went thither which came from Lima with furniture for the people.

The Anchoring at the Island of Mocha is on the North North East part of it in a sandy Bay in Eight faddom water, near the shore, a North East wind is the worst wind for the Road. On the South side of Mocha there lyes a ledge of Rocks, and some broken rocks on that part of the Island, scattered from the shore.

The Anchoring at the Island of S[ta] Maria is on the North side in a fair

[159] **December 1670. The *Sweepstakes* at Baldivia.**

sandy Bay in eight, 9, or ten faddom, a fair birth from the shore, the North North West wind is the worst wind for that Road, there is wood & fresh water on both the Islands as the Spaniards report. The Tydes are but mean on this Coast, & the flood Comes from the Southwards and rise about 8 or nine foot water.

The Island of Mocha lyes in the Latitude of 38°30′ South.

The Island of S[t] Mary lies in the Latitude of 37°14′ South.

These gentlemen I perceived lived in this Countrey as Garrison soldiers, and Could not tell when they should be relieved. On this part of Chili they are forced to maintain good guards and keep out the natives from pressing into the planted Countreys to the northwards, and from destroying the Corn & provisions & vines which they have in the Province of Arauco, and their fruits which are of the European plants which grows mighty well there. They have apples plums pears olives Apricots peaches quinces Oranges Lem*m*ons mushmellons watermellons &c[a]. and many other fruits that I cannot remember.

They report it to bee the finest Countrey in the whole world, and the people live with the greatest Luxury of any on Earth. They enjoy their health with so much delight and have so much wealth and pleasure so as they Compare it to a paradise abounding above other Countreys. I saw a good testimony of the healthfullnesse of the Countrey, for these

[1] Isla Mocha (38°22′S, 73°55′W).

[2] Isla Santa Maria (36°59′S, 73°32′W), in the entrance to Golfo Arauco.

4 men as are aboard, are as well-complexiond men as ever I saw in my dayes, and several men and women ashore which my people saw there are mighty well favourd of a ruddy healthy Complexion, and some of the men are very Corpulent, and look is if they came from a plentifull part of the world where there was no want of provisions.

Spice of the East Indies is not over plentifull here, for the Captain asked mee for some, which I did give to Each man, near half a pound of Nutmegs which was all the spice I had. I sent a pound of Nutmegs ashore to the Capt*ain* of the Fort S[t] Iago and a Chesshire Cheese, a dozen quart bottles of Madera wine, half a dozen of Large drinking glasses, and 6 dozen of tobacco pipes. Also I gave the Capt*ain* which was aboard 6 dozen of tobacco pipes, for hee much desired them, there was not one pipe to smoak in a shore, they smoaked their tobacco in paper, they said a pipe was worth a Royal of plate ashore, and a nutmeg was worth a Royal of plate. But what quantity would have sold at that price I know [not].

I am of Opinion that in the remotest part of the earth from Europe and the alteration of Climates will not alter the Spaniards humours, for that which any man have least of, that thing hee do want most, as I have seen many times in Spaine they have been very inquisitive to know what goods a man have, and that thing as you have least of, that hee pretends to have most occasion for, when hee have no need of it, their humours are such in Spain as they are not to bee forgot here.

This afternoon after a sea dinner on a long voyage of good English Pork & pease which the Captain and the others eat very heartily of, and said that they

[160] **December 1670. The *Sweepstakes* at Baldivia.**

had rather have it then the best fresh meat whatsoever, by reason it came out of Europe, they desired to take leave and go ashore. My Lieu*tenan*t Nathanael Picket had the boat ready mand, with this order as followeth from mee.

Lieutenant you are to take Care and set these 4 gentlemen ashore at the place where you received them in, And present my respects to the Governour of the Fort, and deliver to him these things as I send, which is a Chesshire Cheese, bottles of wine, spice &c[a]. and desire of him if I shall send for water this evening or tomorrow morning, and take his Answer and return aboard assoone as you Can with Conveniency. But bee mindfull to observe their actions, and if you can discover whether Don Carlos bee there or not, and use your endeavours to have Conference with the natives, if it can bee done without disobligeing the Spaniards, as you shall see the means how it may bee when you are there, take beads &c[a]. along with you to give to the natives, and bee Carefull of your selves, and also have a Care that none of your Company give any occasion of difference, but to bee ever respective & Courteous whereby wee may obtaine reputation and effect the design wee come on, which will bee if wee can have Conference with the natives, and use them kindly and gain their loves, for you see the great hatred they have to the Spaniards, and how Cruel the Spaniards are to them, which will bee to our advantage, and our design must bee by going into the harbour for water & wood, as what I can observe as yet, the care of these your proceeding order to your best discretion as you shall find most convenient when you are in the Harbour, according as I have given you directions, So god prosper you.
December the 17th 1670. John Narbrough

This afternoon being the 17th December, at two of clock I set the four Spanish gentlemen which came aboard the *Sweepstakes* ashore at the fort, where my boat took them in.[1] At their going away I fired seaven guns, & desired the Capt*ain* hee would assist mee in getting fresh water which is very Easie to bee had here, the Capt*ain* promised mee hee would, So wee parted at the Ships side with the guns fired and three hollows, the Spaniards all of them had a shift of my Linnen and Cloths which they Carried ashore with them, their own being wet in comeing aboard the *Sweepstakes*.

There went ashore in this Boat eighteen of my best men I had in the Ship, and men of good observations to inspect in matters of Concernment, which I had acquainted them with, as touching the manner of the Harbour, and the fortifications they had, and the disposition of the people, and that it was my whole desire to have Conference with the Natives of the Countrey that are at warrs with the Spaniards, if by any means possible it may bee obtained. For it is my whole desire to Lay the foundation of[2] a trade for the English Nation for the future

[161] **December 1670. The *Sweepstakes* at Baldivia.**
for I see plainly the Countrey is lost for want of knowledge of it. But I hope wee shall give a good account of it to his Majestie, which will bee by the meanes of your observations in this proceeding therfore bee mindfull of what I signifie unto you, and let no opportunity slip wherby you may gain information, for it will bee much for the honour of our action to understand really the State of these parts. And whosoever it bee amongst you that shall find or recover any gold by trade[3] shall have it for his pains, let the value of it bee litle or much. And I will also give him encouragement for his discovery, and acquaint his Royall high*ne*sses Secretary of the Care pains and vigilance of the person.

At three of clock in the afternoon my boat set the four Spaniards safe ashore at the Fort St Iago, where they were received with many welcomes ashore by their Companions, they com*m*ending the great Civilities that they received aboard the Ship, and that their entertainment was fit for men of honour. And that they had seen the finest ship in the world, And that Shee had in her much Silks and many other rich com*m*odities, & that the Ship & men were the king of Englands, and were friends to the Spanish Nation &ca.

My L*ieutenan*t presented the Capt*ain* of the Fort the presents which I sent him with my respects, and desired leave of him to fill fresh water, hee answered him it should bee graunted. My Lieu*tenan*t desired to take leave of him at present & to go aboard and get Cask to fill water. The gouvernour of Capt*ain* of the place said that the Capt*ain* of St Peter's Fort[4] had sent to speak with him, and that the Capt*ain* would go along with him to St Peters Fort. My Lieu*tenan*t caused the boat to bee manned & hee went over to him, there went also the Spanish Captain and a Fryer of the order of St Francis in my boat and a Spanish gentleman. After my Lieu*tenan*t was landed on the Island, and the fryer had acquainted the Capt*ain* of my Lieu*tenan*ts being there, it was near an houre before the Capt*ain* came to him. At his comeing my Lieu*tenan*t presented my respects to him, and

[1] Fort St James.

[2] 'for' crossed through in the original and 'of' inserted above.

[3] 'Or otherwise' struck through in the original.

[4] On Isla Mancera, (39°53′S, 73°24′W). Shown on Narbrough's plan of the 'Port oF Baldavia' (Plate 4) as S. Peter F.

acquainted him what wee were, and that I desired leave to fill fresh water, and to wood, and to buy refreshing for my men, and that I would give satisfaction for it in money or goods to the utmost. The Capt*ain* answered I should have any thing the Countrey did affoord assoon as possibly hee could get it, for hee had sent to Baldivia for things for mee, and that tomorrow if I would send in the Boat hee would Send soldiers to guard my men from the Indians, for they are very Barbarous. Hee asked my Lieu*tenan*t whither wee were bound &c[a]. My Lieu*tenan*t answered for China to trade there. My Lieu*tenan*t took his leave of him and Came away, the Captain Drank the King of Englands health and bid my L*ieutenan*t go aboard, and not to go to the other Fort. My L*ieutenan*t answered he had left two men there, and that hee would take them in and go aboard. The Capt*ain* told him then hee might go thither. Hee desired my Lieu*tenan*t to spare him some english butter for his wife, Shee was sick at the Citty of Baldivia. This governour of S[t] Peter's Fort is a man of about fifty years of age, of a midle Stature and somewhat Corpulent

[162] **December 1670. The *Sweepstakes* at Baldivia.**

but much of the Spanish gravity, hee was born in old Spain, hee had been governour of the Island of Madera, when the Spaniards had it, his name is as followeth: *Diego de Earais Codox yes lo var.*[1]

My Lieu*tenan*t caused the interpreter to tell him that any thing that was in the Ship was at his service, and so hee took his leave of him and went over to fort S[t] Iago. As hee went over hee rowed neare the Spanish Ship & viewed her,[2] the master would have had him come aboard her, which my L*ieutenan*t would have done But a Spanish fryer that was in his Boat had no desire to it, and night being near hee passed by her and went to the Fort. My men [in] the boat observed the Harbour and the fortifications, and tooke good notice of the people. The Spaniards bought several things of my boat's crew, and paid for what they bought in good pillar peeces of eight.[3] They would not part from any gold although my men desired to have some rather then silver for their goods, neither would they part from any bread in payment pretending that they should have bread come tomorrow from Baldivia. The things which they bought of my men at this time was two fowling peeces which cost in England about twenty shillings a peece, and the Spaniards give sixteen peeces of eight a peece for them, and Cases of knives of three shillings a peece in England, the Spaniards gave five peeces of eight a peece for them, & for single ten-penny knives they give a peece of eight for them, a peece; And for ordinary leather gloves of ten pence a pair they give a peece of eight a pair, And for broad Cloth Coats of the Seamen's which cost 16 shillings in England they give nine peeces of eight for a Coat. They were very desirous to buy cloakes, and peeces of bays & Cloths &c[a].[4]

The men were very gallant in apparel in their Plush Coats, & under garments of silk and silver wrought together, and good linnen and good flanders laces and broad about the

[1] This was Diego de Lara Escobar, Knight of the order of St James. He was born in Santiago de Chile and is recorded as a soldier in 1652. He was transferred to the garrison at Valdivia in 1663, as comisario general in the cavalry. In 1670 he was serving as Governor of St Peter's Fort, Mancera and later became interim governor of Valdivia and then corregidor of the town of Ica. He died on 28 July 1681. Guarda, *La Sociedad*, No. 117, p. 103; Roa y Ursúa, *El Reyno*, No. 2714, pp. 694–5; Valdivia, *Arte*, p. iii.

[2] This was the vessel at anchor in what is now Puerto Corral, see above, p. 513. The vessel is shown on Narbrough's plan of the 'Port oF Baldavia' (Plate 4), as 'A Spanish Ship'.

[3] See above, p. xx.

[4] Baize, coarse cloth of a russet colour.

Crown of their hatts, in fashion of a hatband, and a great silk scarfe with gold lace at the ends of it that was Crosse [*margin:* *] over their Shoulders as a b*elt. A short Cravat of Linnen about their necks and a Cane in their hands headed with silver their shoes & stockings & breeches after the Spanish fashion. They were very kind to my Lieu*tenan*t and men, and treated them very Courteously, they were not permitted to go into the fort but were Entertained in a Tent, by the Fort; four of the Spaniards wives would needs go into the English boat & sit downe on the Benches, to say they had been in a boat which came from Europe. These were very proper white women born in the kingdome of Peru of Spanish Parents, they never had been in Europe. The Spaniards had some Indian women to their wives, the women were all well apparelled in silks after the Spanish fashion, and about their necks great gold Chaines and Pendents at their Ears.

The Capt*ain* of St Iago fort is a man of about fourty years of age of a good Stature and deportment, hee was born in old Spain and hath lived

[163] **December 1670. The *Sweepstakes* at Baldivia.**

in these Countreys upwards of twelve years, his name is as followeth.

Simon Dias Deaillon[1]

The Governour's name of Baldivia and Capt*ain* General of Chili

Don pi de Montoya. Hee is a knight of St James.[2]

This evening my Lieu*tenan*t came on board and brought all his men with him that hee Carried ashore, and a present from the Capt*ain* of St Iago Fort to mee, two jarrs of Chili wine, twenty *monocos* of Peruan tobacco and a dozen Loaves of white bread made of the flower of wheat very good. The wine was much like the Madera wine, but thicker, and it have a tast like to mum, But it is very strong and will make men drunk presently. I gave it to the Sea-men and it caused some of them to Stare with the litle portion they had of it.

The Capt*ain* and the other three which were aboard with mee sent mee some tobacco, and a thousand thanks for their entertainment, they sent mee all my Linnen and cloths which they had to shift themselves with, & also that they would bee aboard with mee in the morning, and that the Capt*ain* of the fort of St Iago, would come aboard to see mee tomorrow. The Captain presented my Lieu*tenan*t with a silver tobacco box, a silver headed Cane, & a Plume of Estridges feathers, which hee wore on his hat at the same time. The feather of the Plume is but small, nothing so good as the Barbary feather, this feather was of red & white & blew dyed in that Countrey. But I saw another Plume which was given to a gentleman of mine, by a Spanish gentleman, which was black & large and very good, made of the Estridges feather of the Countrey, there is many Estridges in the plain lands, and guianacos, which are the beast that the red wooll comes off of, and they have much of it in Chili.

My people could not by any meanes come to Converse with the natives which are at wars with the Spaniards and have the gold, without violating the Spaniards power, for one [on] the shore within the harbour the Indians made a fire, by the woods side, and

[1] This was Simón Diaz de Ayllón. He was a captain in Valdivia's first army company from 1658 before being appointed fort warden in 1673. Roa y Ursúa, *El Reyno*, No. 2408, p. 62.

[2] Pedro Ruiz de Montoya, Knight of the Order of St. James, was born in Baeza, Andalucia. He is recorded as living in Peru in 1643. He was appointed corregidor of Arica in 1655 and was Governor of Túcuman Province 1660–64. The Conde de Lemos, who described him as 'one of the best soldiers he could have', sent him to Valdivia as Governor in 1670.

hung out a white flag on a long Pole, and kept weafting of it a long time. My Lieu*tenan*t would have gone to them but the Spaniards would not permit him, and said that they were their own people which lived there. Hee having orders to bee respective, and not to violate any power, dare not presume without leave, being in the harbour, But was in hopes wee might obtain Conferrence with them by our meanes of going for water or wood, hee saw several of the Natives which the Spaniards had as slaves, they are a proper well made people, of a tawny Complexion, & seeme to bee very active, they were sensible that wee were not Spaniards, my men gave some of them beads and knives as they had opportunities to do it out of sight of the Spaniards, in hopes they would acquaint the other Indians with

[164] **December 1670. The *Sweepstakes* at Baldivia.**
it, so as they might bee sensible wee would bee kind to them. It was fair weather this night the wind at South a small gale, I set a good watch all night and rode fast.

Sunday the 18th, fair weather, Wind at South West, a fine gale. This morning at 6 of clock I caused my long boat to bee fitted with water Casks and made ready to go for water. I had a Choice crew of Sea-men in her, and well armed, I put in some beads, knives and bells for trade for the Indians, if they should fall with them; I also had my pinnace mannd and armed well to go along with the Long boat, to guard her, for I ever was jealous of the Spaniards, that they would betray mee when they could get an opportunity to their advantage, and also I could not bee satisfied in my thoughts of Don Carlos, what should become of him, whether hee might bee taken by the Indians and killed, or run to the Spaniards, and so design to betray the Ship or men. Sometimes I was in one mind & sometimes in another what should bee become of him, I rideing within call of the same place where hee was Landed, and had not heard nor seen any people or sign of people there, and I saw that hee could not go any other way then to the fort, and that being not a mile from the place, gave mee the greater cause to believe that hee must bee with the Spaniards, and not with the Indians. For if the Indians had fallen with him they would have been about the shore, so as I should have heard or seen them. And one cause gave mee to doubt that hee had no intent to come to mee again, for I looked into his Cabbin to inspect what things hee had left, and I found nothing there but an old bed and rug and pillow, and some old rags and blotted papers, and an old trunk empty. Hee Carried away two shifts[1] of Linnen, and two suits of apparel on his back, and all things hee had which was not much at the first. Hee carried away with him four great seales of four several Coats of arms, which hee had Cut in England, [*margin:* the seals were engraved in silver, and Ivory heads to them.] they were as large as a twelve penny peece. I saw them once in the voyage but what use hee intended them for I could never understand, they were fairly cut, and the Coat was some forraign arms, which I never had seen before to my knowledge.

I thought it not convenient to send my boats directly for water in case I might offend the Spaniards in comeing so Early in the morning and not acquaint them with it. I caused my boats to lye by the side and have all their businesse ready. I sent for my Lieu*tenan*ts and advised with them as to the sending for water, or to send in my small boat first to the Capt*ain* of the Forts, and give him notice of my intentions, and ask his leave and at what

[1] Changes of clothing.

place wee should go to. My Lieu*tenan*ts Concluded it to bee the safest way & means to prevent disgust.

I being intended to send my trumpeter with a flag of truce, my Lieu*tenan*t Thomas Armiger desired mee that hee might bee sent on the message, which

[165] **December 1670. The *Sweepstakes* at Baldivia in Chili.**

I granted hee should go, and John Fortiscue, and Hugh Cooe Master Trumpeter and Thomas highway interpreter, and two Sea-men to row the boat, and that they should Carry a white flag on a Pike flying for truce, and the Trumpeter to sound when hee came near in shot of the Fort, whereby they might take notice of the comeing of my boat. I was mighty doubtfall that the Spaniards would detain my boat, and people; For I acquainted Lieu*tenan*t Armiger that my mind was that they would bee detained by the Spaniards, and that it would bee safer to send some other person. It being a matter of small Concernment, my Lieu*tenan*t earnestly desired that hee might proceed on the message. I ordered my Lieu*tenan*t to go to the forts with a flag of truce flying & trumpet sounding, and to deliver the governour of S[t] Iago fort an Eastland Case of bottles, and present my respects to him, & thank him for his kindnesse to mee and my people, and desire of him if there bee order for my Boats to fetch water, if there bee send mee notice of it. If not go to S[t] Peter's Fort and present my respects to that governour, and present him these things as followeth. A Chesshire Cheese, half a dozen bottles of wine, six drinking glasses a pott of butter, a pound of Nutmegs, and a basket of tobacco-pipes. And acquaint him that you come from mee to desire to know if I shall send my boats for water to day, and that they lye ready with Cask in them expecting his order therin &c[a]. And if hee grant order for them, desire him to fire a gun to give mee notice, and send my boat off to mee with his answer assoon as possibly you can, for I have a great desire to have them at the watering place and there I am in hopes to have Conferrence with my golden friends &c[a].

This morning between six and seaven of clock my lieu*tenan*t put from the Shipp with the boat & the men & the things as is mentioned before, with a flag of truce flying & trumpet sounding. Hee rowed directly into the Harbour towards S[t] Iago Fort, And there Landed with the flag of truce flying, and the trumpet sounding. I and my Company aboard the Ship saw a white flag put out at the fort, S[t] Peters in answer to my flag that wee might observe they saw my Boat which was the sign the day before that there was admittance to come ashore. For when the Spaniards the day before saw my boat[1] Comeing towards them, they put out a white flag, and kept it out all the time my boat was ashore, and when my boat came away they took it in. I waited all this forenoon in expectation of the gun firing or boat. At two of clock this afternoon my boat came aboard with only three of my Seamen,[2] and two Indians to help to row aboard which the Spaniards put into the Boat, they being slaves to the Spaniards.

My Seamen which came aboard in my boat came to mee and told mee that the Lieu*tenen*t had been at the Fort S[t] Iago & had delivered my message, there to the Capt*ain* but hee had no order for my fetching of water, and wished my Lieu*tenan*t to go to Fort S[t] Peters, which hee did, and a fryer and two Spaniards went over with

[1] 'people' struck through and 'boat' substituted.

[2] There is a discrepancy here. Narbrough stated above that there were only two seamen to row the boat in addition to the four who were detained.

[166] **December 1670. The *Sweepstakes* at Baldivia.**

him in the boat, the flag of truce was flying in the boat and the Trumpet sounding according to my order all the time till they landed at the Fort. And at their Landing the Lieu*tenan*t was received very Courteously by several Spanish Gentlemen, and desired to walk up to the Governour which my Lieu*tenan*t did to a tent, which was near by, where the governour was. The governour received him with much respect and desired him to sit down, my Lieu*tenan*t presented my Respects to him & delivered him the Cheese & butter & all the things that I sent him, and acquainted him that I sent him to desire to know if hee would bee pleased to permit my sending for water to day, for my boats were ready and had the Cask in them and waited his Answer. The Governour caused my Lieu*tenan*t and M[r] Fortescue to sit down, and drank to them in a silver bowle with Chili wine, and gave no answer to my Lieu*tenan*t at present, but sent an officer & soldiers and seized on my boat. My Lieu*tenan*t desired to know what the meaning was that possession was taken of the boat. The Governour answered hee had order from Don Pedro dẽ Montais[1] Capt*ain* General of Chili to keep them til the Ship was brought into the Harbour, under the Com*m*and of the Castles, and hee was Sorry that hee had no more officers of the Shipps in Possession. My Lieu*tenan*t spake to him that hee had best to have a Care what hee did in detaining any comission officers of the king of England's, and that hee came ashore with a flag of truce & a trumpeter, and was received with licence by him according to the manner of soldiers, and that it was ever allowed for truce to return, if wee had been enemies to each other. My Lieu*tenan*t showed his Com*m*ission which was from his Royal Highnesse, and that hee would Certainly suffer for what wrong hee did to the king of England's servants & Subjects. His answer was hee did not Care &c[a].

The other Spaniards that stood by and heard the discourse talked to the governour, and said it was dishonourable to keep a flag of truce, and that the Spanish nation would suffer much for it, For all the princes in the world would Condemn the action, and that they had great Civilities shewn to them aboard the Ship, and that wee were in Amity with them, and like discourse they had in[2] very Loft Language to each other, my people being under the Charge of a guard of soldiers, expecting to bee carried away to Prison.

But the Governour Considering a time sent the three Seamen into my boat and ordered them to tell mee, that if I would bring the Ship into the harbour I should have my men and any thing that the Countrey affoorded, and bid them begone & present his respects to the Capt*ain* and present him those things as I ordered to bee put into the boat, which was two Jarrs of Chili wine, and two Canesters of bread, having one hundred and twenty loaves of bread in them, about the bignesse of a penny wheaten loafe in England, and they are made of good wheat-flower. My men could not row the boat aboard it blew fresh. A Captain that was

[167] **December 1670. The *Sweepstakes* at Baldivia in Chili.**

there, caused two Indians to go into the Boat and help to row her aboard, so they came away and brought this letter as followeth from my Lieu*tenan*t which hee wrote the time

[1] Guarda, *La Sociedad*, No. 273, p. 117. Pedro Ruiz de Montoya was subsequently dismissed from his post in 1671, being held responsible for the arrest of Narbrough's men who had landed under a flag of truce, which Lemos feared would give the English an excuse to continue their depredations in the area. AGI, Lima 72, Conde de Lemos to the Queen Regent, Lima, 15 May 1672.

[2] 'a' follows struck through.

the things were putting into the boat, being troubled to get Ink or paper, being scarce there.

A Letter from Lieu*tenan*t Armiger to Capt*ain* John Narbrough.

S*ir*,

My self and M[r] Fortiscue are kept here as Prisoners, but for what Cause I cannot tell, but they still pretend much friendship, and sayes that if you will bring the Ship into the harbour you shall have all the accommodation that may bee. S*ir* I need not advise you farther I am &c[a].

December the 18th 1670. Thomas Armiger. John Fortiscue.

I examined my Seamen which came in my boat from the Lieu*tenan*t & they related to mee the whole matter, and they believed that the Spaniards had a design to betray the Ship, but they could not agree amongst themselves. I talked with the 2 Indians which came aboard, they could speak the Spanish tongue indifferent well. They told mee that I was a friend to the Indians of the mountains, and that I was no Spaniard they would needs know of mee where my Countrey was, and if I would Come againe. I made him answer that my Countrey was a litle way off on the other side of the sea, and that I would come again and bring knives, hatchets, beads & glasses &c[a], & live in the Countrey with them. And that they should see my Countrey, and that my king would give them many things, and they should live with us, and that my king is the greatest king in the world, and Commands all other kings, & that our name is English. The Indian laughed & seemed to bee very glad, I bid the Indians acquaint the Indians of the In-lands, that I came to speak with them, And that I was their friend and would give them many hatchets & knives & swords &c[a]. if they would come to mee, and that I came purposely to speak with them, And that my Master the great king of England have sent them many things & would willingly see them.

After these people heard all that I said unto them they sate a time mute, And considering of the kindnesse they received from mee and my Company, and that they must go ashore again under the Com*m*and of the Cruell Spaniards, they weeped extreamly and uttered these words, [*humbra Spainalos mucheo Deoblo.*] which is in the English[1] tongue, the Spanish men are much devils. I verily believe these poor innocent creatures speak truth, for they are great devils in abuseing these poor Soules so unmercifully as they do. In the sight of my men the Spaniards with a great staffe would strike an Indian on the head as hee talked with him, and beat him all along for no Cause at all. But this they do to shew their greatnesse and imperiousnesse, the best name they can affoord to call them by is dog & devil, and such like names. These Indians said that there is much gold, and that the Indians and Spaniards have much *oroe* [gold]. I give each of the Indians a knife and

[168] **December 1670. The *Sweepstakes* at Baldivia.**

a small looking glasse and some beads, they were very thankfull. I bid them speak to the Indians of the Mountains that I would give them knives & glases if they would come to mee. I was in great hopes all this time I should have the opportunity to speak

[1] The square brackets are in the original. 'Spanish' struck through and 'English' substituted.

with my golden friends, by the means of these people for they were very glad to have the message.

These people are of a mildle stature, strongly set & well fleshed, they are tawny Coloured and long black flagg hair, they have small Caps on their heads like *mountero's*, their garments is a square peece of Woollen cloth like a mantle, of their own weaveing of the wooll of Guianacos, they cut a hole in the midle of it and there hee puts his head through, and it hangs on his shoulders and Covers his whole body like a Cloake, some have their garment so side as it reacheth down to their midleg, some to their knees,[1] they wear half stockings on their legs, but no shoes nor shirts, some have breeches close knee'd.

[*margin:* the natives of Baldivia] [*blank space for drawing*][2]

This afternoon being the 18th I Sent my three Seamen and[3] two Indians ashore in my boat, to the Fort St Peter, with one letter to the Spanish governour, and one letter to Lieu*tenan*t Armiger. The Seaman that I entrusted my letters with his name was John Wilkings[4] a Carefull fellow and stout, hee was very willing to go ashore on the message, although most of my officers were doubtfull they would bee detained. I ordered this John Wilkings to make hast aboard again, assoon as hee had delivered the Letters and received an answer.

The Letters were as followeth.

S*i*r – I desire that my Lieu*tenan*t and the rest of my men as are detained by y*ou*r Com*m*and may bee permitted to come aboard his Ma*jes*ties Ship the *Sweepstakes*, hoping they have not given any occasion whereby they should bee detained in your garrison.
I am here Capt*ain* of one of his Ma*jes*ties Ships of England desiring leave to water & wood which was granted mee, not doubting of y*ou*r Civility herein, And should bee very unwilling to Act anything as should disoblige any of his Ma*jes*ties Subjects of Spain;
S^r^ I desire your answer assoon as may bee with Conveniency by the hands of one of your gentlemen, whom I shall give satisfaction to, of what I am as farre as honour will permit, also I engage the honour of a soldier for his safety ashore again. Kissing your hands I rest
Dec*ember* 18. 1670
S*i*r. your humble Servant
John Narbrough

For the Hon*oura*ble the Governour of the
Forts of Baldivia these present.

[169] **December 1670. The *Sweepstakes* at Baldivia.**

My Letter to Lieutenant Armiger

Lieutenant Armiger, I have received your letter of the 18th date, wherin I understand that your selfe and Mr Fortescue, Thomas Highway & Hugh Coe are detained in St Peter's fort by the Governours order, also you write that it is the Governours' desire that I should bring the Shipp into the harbour. Present my respects to the Governour and acquaint him

[1] A poncho.

[2] The blank space approximates to 7 lines of text, intended for drawings of the indigenous peoples encountered at Valdivia.

[3] 'my' crossed through here in the original.

[4] John Wilkins is listed on the Muster List, TNA, ADM 39/2510.

that the Ship is his *Majes*ties of England, and is in a safe roade, where there is no danger of her miscarriage by foule weather, the time I expect to stay on this Coast. I hope hee will not detaine you Long because it will be prejudicial to his *Majes*tie's Ship & voyage, it must bee expected there will bee an account given to his *Majes*tie where satisfaction will bee had. Acquaint the governour that if hee will bee pleased to send any gentleman off to mee, I will show him my Commission, or what in honour can bee demanded of mee, for his better satisfaction that I am a servant of his *Majes*tie's of England. And that I do engage the honour of a soldier, and promise to set the gentleman safe ashore again when hee shall desire it. I have sent the Governour a Letter which you must cause Thomas Highway to interpret as you read it to him. I shall wait here to night and tomorrow to know his answer, and in expectation of *you*r comeing aboard, Not else but I wish you bee of good Cheer, with my hearty love to you all I rest Your Loving friend and Captain
For L*ieutenan*t Armiger in S[t] Peters Fort in Baldivia. John Narbrough

A Note which I sent to my L*ieutenan*t enclosed in his Letter.
Lieutenant, take what notice you can of the fortification of the Fort, and what strength they have of people in it, and whether they are able to with stand a Ship, what quantity of provisions they have in it and whether Don Carlos bee there. Send mee an account of this by John Wilkins. I will use all endeavours to have you off when I understand the strength of the place,
I remain &c[a]. John Narbr*ough*.

This Evening my boat and three Seamen came aboard againe which I sent to S[t] Peters fort with Letters to the Governour, and to my L*ieutenan*t Tho*mas* Armiger. The Sea man which I sent the letters by, named John Wilkins, came to mee and acquainted mee that hee had done my message and delivered my Letters to the Lieu*tenan*t and governour, and stayd till the Letters were read & took his answer, which was this: That if the Capt*ain* would bring the Ship under the Com*m*and of the Castle hee should have water & provisions. If not hee looked upon us as Pirats, and that if I sent ashore either for wood or fresh water, hee would kill the men, and for those men as hee had in Custody they should bee sent for Spain, and hee was sorry hee had no more officers from the Ship. Hee turned his back and bid my Sea-man beegone aboard, and so concluded his discourse at that time with my men.

My Lieu*tenan*t and the rest were very well but melancholly, they desired to bee remembred to all aboard. My Lieu*tenan*t told this John Wilkins that he understood that

[170] **December 1670. The *Sweepstakes* at Baldivia.**
there was nine Cannon which I believe are Culvering,[1] and that there were a hundred Spaniards and many Indian soldiers, and that they had sent for more forces to Baldivia, But provisions hee knew not what they had, and that they expected the Ship would fight them, and they provided for it. Hee was very well treated hitherto, hee could not understand any thing of Don Carlos, whether hee was there or not, hee would use his endeavours to satisfie my desires. Hee desired I would send him his Cloths ashore in the morning, so hee caused my boat to make hast aboard it being neare night, and gave John

[1] See below, p. 507; and above, p. 550, n. 2.

Wilkins a note for mee, which was as much as hee could write at that time. They were in a tent by the bank of the Fort without side, and a guard of soldiers of twelve men, some matchlock muskets, and some were Lances. So they came away and left them there, under guard of the Spaniards in the manner as aforesaid.

A brief note from Lieutenant Armiger.

S*ir*. I received yours and am glad to heare you are well. I thank you for your kindnesse in sending to mee, and for what you desire I will endeavour to perform but I cannot heare anything of Don Carlos. I desire S*ir* our cloths may bee sent to us, wee are well used here hitherto, in hast I rest &c[a]. Tho*mas* Arm*iger*.

After I had done talking with John Wilkins concerning the Fort and the Spaniards, I spake with the two Indians which came aboard the second time in my boat, from the Fort. They were two other Indians, for those which went ashore went away, these Indians said that the Indians of the Countrey have much gold, and they sell it the Spaniards for knives, hatchets, beads, glasses &c[a]. They say that the Indians of the Countrey fight with the Spaniards and kill them, and cut off their heads, and that they burn the Spaniards houses and Corn, and get their horses and ride on them, and fight on horsback [*sic*]. I gave these Indians wine and victuals for their suppers, and ordered a lodging for them to sleep in to night in the old sailes.

I caused a good watch to bee set and Carefull officers on the guard to night on the fore castle. I lay myselfe on the quarter deck, and I had my boat manned and Shee lay within the Ship and the shore to look out if any boats or Barks passed to or[1] fro, for I could not Certainly tell whether they had more vessels then the one in the river, or not, for wee did not see what was up the rivers although wee saw what was in the first part of the harbour I did not value all the force they could have there abouts, yet it is no part of discretion to bee too confident, of ones self, and so bee negilgent. After the watch was set and all things in order, those that were not on duty went to sleep. Fair weather to night the wind at South East a fine Brize out of the harbour. The Ship rode fast in smooth water, and a small tyde or Current set out of the harbour.

[171 **December 1670. The *Sweepstakes* at Baldivia.**

A fine fragrant smell came from the green woods as the breezes blew. I caused the Bell to be strooke every half houre, and to bee rung at every two houres, I did not see any boates stirring all night, nor heard any thing except the bleating of seale fishes, for there are a many about the rocks by Cape galere, and very large ones. I saw lights several times in the night at S[t] Peters Fort, and in other places on the shores within the Harbour, which I believe might bee indians fires. The air fair & temperate all night & fine pleasant dews fell.

This evening I took the Sun's amplitude with my azimuth compasse, & had a good observation, I find the variation of the Compasse to bee eight degrees ten minutes easterly.

I do much reason with my self as to the variation that it differs so much in the same Latitude between the East & West side of the Land of America, for on the East side as I sailed in the Latitude of fourty degrees I found the Compasse to have twenty degrees variation easterly, by several good observations which I took with the same Instrument as

[1] 'and' struck through and replaced by 'or.'

I now do use, & here I find but 8 degrees and ten minutes, and it is but eight degrees of Longitude more westerly in the same paralel. I find the land to bee but one hundred & twenty five leagues broad from the East side to the West side, in the Latitude of fourty degrees South. Certainly the Attractive quality of the magnet must be very powerfull in the eastern part of the Land, more then in the western, which causeth the difference. Yet I admire being on both sides of the Land the Compasse should have alwayes the same variation easterly. I was of the opinion that the variation would have been westerly on the West side, it being easterly on the East side. But I find it the contrary by Experience, therfore I believe that the attractive quality is not much in this part of the Land of America, But in some other part more to the Eastward then I was, for if the attractive quality had been in this Land and I sailing on both sides of it the variation must have been easterly on the one side and westerly on the other side. This discourse I shall leave to a better understanding, for I am not as yet satisfied what occasioneth the variation, and the great difference of it, although I have been on several voyages, and have made great benefit of the understanding of the variation of the Compasse, in directing of the true Course &c[a].

Munday the 19th, fair weather, this morning the wind came to the South West a fine gale. At five of clock I discharged the watch with a great gun and a volley of small shott, as is the usual manner aboard of his M*aj*es*tie's Ships of warr. This morning I discoursed with my Sea men concerning the attacquing the forts, and whether they were willing to fight the Spaniards, their answer was in general with all their hearts, if I thought it fit for they were sure to get gold and silver enough, and there was no question but to bee masters of all the forts & countrey before dinner time, for

[172] **December 1670. The *Sweepstakes* at Baldivia.**
they were confident the Spaniards would not stand one broadside, and if I would but give order they were all ready to fall on.

This discourse put them in great hopes I would have gone in, and I was much satisfied with their couragious answers, although I was grieved that I had not com*m*ission to take satisfaction for the wrong the Spaniards had done mee in detaining my officers, but my Commission charged mee not to molest any Spaniards at sea or on land, so I durst not proceed in any hostile manner against them but according to the tenour of my Instructions, which was ever my resolution to perform, as I would advise all persons to do the same.

My temptations were great, for here was much wealth and easily to bee recovered, their force being weak and ill soldiers, mine being good soldiers and couragious, and wanted wealth, which tempted us much and the desire to revenge our wrongs[1] against so perfidious a people as the Spaniards are, and so imperious as to offer so base an act in detaining an officer, a flag of truce, and a trumpeter, judging themselves safe by being remote from Europe. But I hope to see the time when these base inhumane fellows shall not have a house to put their heads in, For what nation soever come into this part of the world with four saile of Ships and five hundred men with power to take, will make themselves masters of all this Countrey of Chili a pleasure,[2] and bee well paid with gold

[1] 'selves' struck through and 'wrongs' inserted above.

[2] At their pleasure.

& silver for their pains. And also enjoy the fountains of gold & silver which the whole world thirst after, for the Indians will bee their friends and help them to destroy the Spaniards through the whole land.

I ordered my officers to see my Lieutenant's cloths and the others cloths which were with him ashore, to bee packt up & put into the boat. Also I caused an invoyce to bee taken of all their things which were to bee sent to them, and of what remained in the Custody of their Consorts, wherby their relations might receive them, when it please god the Ship ariveth [*sic*] in England.

I ordered my lieutenant Picket to man the boate and see them well armed, and take a flag of truce with him and row into the mouth of the Harbour, and there lye upon a parly to deliver the cloths and the letters which I sent by him, to any boat as shall come to him bringing a note from Lieu*tenan*t Armiger signifying the delivery, but do not molest the boat by any meanes neither would I have you go ashore by any meanes among the Spaniards, or trust them as to any promise they shall make you. I would have you to bee very observant in every respect, and not to do any injury to any person, but use your endeavour to gain what knowledge you can of the place, and of D*on* Carlos, and to come aboard again before night.

At 8 of clock this morning my Lieu*tenan*t Picket put from the Ship with the boate and went to the mouth of the Harbour, and there Layd at his grapnel in 8 faddom water, fine black sandy ground, with his flag of truce flying, all the day, but no boat would come neare him. I rode fast without having all the Colours flying aboard the

[173] **December 1670. The *Sweepstakes* at Baldivia.**
Ship, and the wast cloths[1] spread fore and aft. At ten of the clock to day I went ashore at the place where Don Carlos was set ashore, I walked on the shore side both waies a quarter of a mile, for there is the Fort St Iago within half a mile of the place into the Harbourward. Here lies many scattered rocks by the shore side and some places of the shore are rocks, and some small sandy bayes. I saw good store of fish amongst the rocks but what sort of fish they were I know not, for I caught none of them. The Land is riseing in hills and all grown over with woods of a good large timber tree, much like beech and like maple, on the shore side adjacent to the woods there grows several apple trees which were full of good apples, as big as tennis balls, and some lesse, the fruit thrives well here, and it is much like our european winter fruit, there grows many apple trees on most places of the shore side, whether they bee natural to the Countrey or planted by the Spaniards I know not.[2] Also here grows many Canes which runs amongst the trees like vines, very thick and Long, these canes are a firm stick and strong, much like a bastard Japan Cane,[3] my men cut several of them and some long[4] ones for Angleing rods. The Spaniards and Indians make their long Lance staves of them they are so strong, and here is such plenty of them that one may Cut five or six hundred of them in a day. The woods are all green and very thick that there is no passing in them for old wood, and shrubby under wood. The earth is a fat black mould, and moist. Here grows a great deal of mints and spear mint, and wild

[1] See above, p. 511, n. 2.
[2] See above, p. 505, n. 1.
[3] See above, p. 505, n. 3.
[4] 'long' substituted for 'large' struck through.

mustard, and many flowers very pleasant, my men gathered several herbs and flowers Such as they found, and many green apples which they codled[1] and were very good refreshing.

Here runs out of the woods several rivulets of pure fresh water into the sea the slatty [slatey] stones that lye in the rivulets of watter, glitter like gold, but I could not see any gold here, for I and my Company looked in the Rivulets and in the Land but all was In vain. I rowed under the shore side to Cape Galere and went sounding off from the shore aboard the Ship. I had fair Soundings from the shore side deeping my water by litle and litle to fourteen faddom where the Ship rode, the ground was fine black sand most part of the way, from the Ship to the shore, but near the shore about halfe a Cable's length is rocky in some places, & three & four faddom water.

The Cape Galere is a gray steep up rock, to the sea of a good height, and bare aloft, and it rounds in a bluffe head,[2] there lies rocks scattering near the foot of it on both sides. And on the East side of it towards the Harbour, about a Cables length or more from it, there lies a rock as big as a boat, just by the Surface of the water, this rock lies about a Cables length from the shore, you may see it as you stand in it shews like a Canoa afishing.[3] It lyes single by it selfe, But it is best to give the Cape halfe a mile birth, as one stands in for the harbour, & then there is no danger, as I saw, and there is good Soundings at thirty faddoms.

[174] **December 1670. The *Sweepstakes* at Baldivia.**

And as one stands nearer the harbour's mouth hee will find shoalder water, and good anchoring, with the wind at South-East, or at South, or at South West, for one may bring the Cape to beare West South West of him, and the sea will bee indifferent smooth if the wind bee not to the westwards of[4] the South West.

There is anchoring right before the mouth of the Harbour in twelve faddom water fine black sandy ground, and one rides out of shot of the forts, and the water will bee as smooth as may bee if the wind bee to the Southward of the South-West, all the danger is if the wind come out at West, or at North West & blow, then the sea comes wholly in, and there is no carrying it off shore,[5] So a man must ride it out, or bee forced into the Harbour.

The Harbour is a fair Port, and a ship may ride Land-locked up in the southern arm or Bay[6] in five faddom water as the Spaniards tell mee and have sandy ground. No winds can hurt them if they have good ground tackling.[7] There rode a Spanish Ship in that south Bay or Arme, of one hundred & twenty[8] tuns,[9] and I could not see her at the Harbour's mouth, the point of Land was shutt against her.[10] It is fresh water within where the Ship rid, which

[1] Codlings were a variety of apple sold roasted on the streets of London and referred to as hot-codlings. *NOED*. Presumably these were roasted on board.

[2] Shown as Point Gally on Narbrough's plan of the 'Port oF Baldavia' (Plate 4). The cape Narbrough refers to rises to Morro Gonzalo.

[3] Roca Peña Sola.

[4] 'of' repeated.

[5] A ship cannot get out of the anchorage to sea.

[6] Ensenada San Juan.

[7] Sound anchors and cables.

[8] 'forty' struck through and 'twenty' substituted.

[9] This was the vessel in what is now Puerto Corral (see above, p. 513), shown on Narbrough's plan of the 'Port oF Baldavia' (Plate 4).

[10] She was behind the point of land.

is occasioned by the fresh waters which come out of the Countrey in three rivers. It causeth the Streame to set Constantly out of a mean strength about 4 miles an houre.[1] The tydes rise and fall about eight foot or there abouts perpendicular,[2] And it is a high water at the mouth of the Port at nine of clock on the full & Change day of the moon, as I observed, but there is never lesse then six faddom water at all times at the going into the Port, a good way up above a mile from mouth.[3] After one is within the mouth hee must hale up to the southwards – that is the best part to ride in. The North point at the entrance[4] is shoald & broken ground half a Cable's length off of it or more, the mouth of the harbour is above a mile broad[5] from the North point to the South point and it lies in South East & *By* East, at the first entrance, then it rounds in a Bay up to the Southwards. It is so faire a Port that a man may Anchor where hee pleaseth, if hee have occasion by the shift of winds or Calm, as to what I saw of it. It is best to keep more neare the South shore then the North, at the going in, on the point of the South side of the entrance, there lies a rock as bigg as a boat.[6] It is above water, & lies neare a Stones throw off the shore. A Ship may saile fair by it and have seaven faddom water. There is some rocks within the Harbour which lyes under water near the shore, on the South side between the point of the entrance and the Fort S[t] Iago. What rocks or shoalds there are else in the Port that are dangerous I have not knowledge of them, therfore whose fortune it is to come here must bee mindfull to discover the rest. Right before the mouth of the Harbour on the East side there is the Fort of S[t] Peter, on an Island adjacent to the main,[7] and very neare the maine, I am not certain whether there bee a Channel between the Island and the East shore for boats to pass. This Island is

[175] **December 1670. The *Sweepstakes* at Baldivia.**

much about the biggnesse of S[t] Francis Island[8] which lieth in Plimouth Sound, but is somewhat higher on the South East part,[9] and steep up on the West side, and scattering rocks lies on the shore side, the landing place now is on the Northeast end of it, about the point to the Eastwards. There is the gate or door of the Fort about a bow shott from the water side, the Fort is only a work cast up of earth and kept up with Pallisados from shooting down, and thus it ranges in a good part of the top of the North part of the Island, like a wall or instead of a wall, for the town is built within it, the houses are low, and built like barnes with wooden sides and thatched. The tops are seene above the range of the fort

[1] The in-going tidal stream usually has a rate of 2 knots in the narrows ESE of Morro Gonzalo. In winter, during westerly winds, the in-going tidal stream is frequently hardly noticeable, but the out-going tidal stream, augmented by the outflow from the rivers reaches 3–4 knots and may be as much as 5 or 6 knots off Morro. Gonzalo, *South America Pilot*, III, para. 7.66.

[2] The Mean Higher High Water level today is 4 ft (1·2 m).

[3] 'Port' struck through here and replaced by 'mouth'.

[4] Punta Piojo (39°52′S, 73°34′W). Rocks extend about one cable's length from the point and the 3 fathom (5·5 m) line extends south nearly 4 cables from it.

[5] It is 8½ cables between Punta Amargos and the coast by Morro Niebla.

[6] Roca Peña Sola. See above, p. 531.

[7] The fort is shown on Narbrough's plan of the 'Port oF Baldavia' (Plate 4) as 'S. Peter F'. It is on Isla Mancera: the channel between the island and the main land is 3½ cables wide with depths of less than 2 fathoms (3·6 m) in it. There are patches of rocks south of the island.

[8] The island in Plymouth Sound is now known as Drake's Island.

[9] Isla Mancera is 292 ft (89 m) high.

a good height, the town cannot bee above 30 or fourty houses at most. The Spaniards would not permit any of my men to go into it, the guns are planted about it, five are on the West side on the top of the Island in Platformes a good height from the water. They have a small rise of a bank of earth for a breastwork before them, but very slight, these five guns look towards the Harbour's mouth, and into the Harbour, the other guns are placed about the town to secure that against the Indians.

The Magazin for all the Harbour and the Citty of Baldivia is in this towne in storehouses, for here they keep it safe from the Indians as they judge, And in other places they are doubtfull of the Indians destroying of it by fire, as they have done formerly. Here was boats unlading of goods & provisions, & jarrs of wine which came in the Spanish Ship from Peru. And here were boates taking in of goods and provisions & wine to Carry to Baldivia.

They look upon this Island of S[t] Peters to bee the safest place of all the Harbour, for here they keep the gold till the vessels take it in and carry it away for Lima. This vessel that was here was taking in gold, & bezoar stones, & red wooll, and so to saile along the Coast and make up her fraight with druggs, and silver &c. and saile to the Port of Lima and unlade, and other Shipps and vessells take in the goods at Lima and Carry it for Panama. The navigation from Baldivia to Lima is about twenty dayes time in sailing, the winds are given much to bee at Southwest, all along the Coast and at South, and off the shore in the nights. It is for the most part of the year fair weather, the distance from Baldivia to Lima is about five hundred and seaventy leagues, and from Lima to Panama it is about four hundred and sixty leagues. It is good sailing all along that Coast.

In the Port of Baldivia there is three fair rivers which comes out of the countrey, which empty themselves into Port with a brisk streame of fresh waters. One river runs up in the South East part of the Harbour, another runs up to the East into the Countrey on the back of S[t] Peter's Fort, And the third runs up about the North point of the Harbours mouth, between the point and the North end of S[t] Peter's Island.[1] It runs up to the northeastward, and nine or ten miles up in

[176] **December 1670. The *Sweepstakes* at Baldivia.**

this river from the Harbour's mouth is the Citty of Baldivia, scituated on the bank of the river.[2] I judge this Baldivia is but a small place, and kept only as a garrison and a place for trade with the Indians for gold &c[a]. for the Spaniards said there is but five guns in it, and three hundred men, I know they speak of the most in those matters.

I judge these rivers may run into the Countrey a long way, and the Spaniards to have but litle knowledge in the inward parts of them, for the Indians will not suffer them to search up in the inlands. I believe these rivers are not navigable for Shipping for if they were the Bark which was there would Certainly have gone up to the Citty of Baldivia, and unlivered[3] her goods there, and troubled themselve to carry the goods up in boates and small flat bottom barges, which they have there for the purposes. The Barges are built much like our West Countrey Barges, But smaller. They will carry about ten or twelve

[1] The southern arm is Ensenada San Juan. Río Torna Galeones runs SE and Río Valdivia NE.

[2] Ciudad de Valdivia lies 9 miles up Río Valdivia on the South bank. The river above Valdivia is now known as Río Calle-Calle.

[3] A combination of 'unloaded' and 'delivered', not found in *NOED*.

tuns, they steer with a rudder, and have one mast and saile as our Barges have, the saile is made of Cotton cloth. The ropes are made of the rind of Mangrove trees, and instead of Anchors they have woodden kellakes.[1] Anchors ropes and sailes are scarce in these Countreys, & good masts for their Ships, for they are in great want of masts, which are good. The masts for their Ships are made of white Cedar and such like wood, for there is no firre trees growing in the Countrey, also good workmen are very scarce in these parts. The smaller boats which they have here are Canoas, they are cut out of the body of a large tree, and shaped somewhat like a boat at the ends, some are near thirty foot long, and built up with one strake on a side higher,[2] they will carry neare twenty men in a canoa, some are lesse, some they row with oares some with paddles, those which are wa*lt, they have a great Bam*e made fast, on each side without board which lyeth fore and aft, like a wale to keep them from oversetting,[3] they are very ill built. The Indians are their Slaves to row them to & fro and to do all matters of Labour, for the Spaniards will not lay their hands to any thing in that nature, accounting it beneath them to fowle their fingers with work, for they scorne to bee servants one to another, let the one bee never so Potent and the other not worth the Cloths that hee weareth, yet he scorns to bee a servant.

[*blank space for drawing*][4]

The Land about the harbour of Baldivia is of a good height, and in land it riseth in Large hills, and the whole Countrey is grown over with green woods, so as there is no travelling as I could perceive from one place to another.

[177] **December 1670. The *Sweepstakes* at Baldivia.**

The Indians live in the woods, for I saw severall smoakes rise out of the woods in the day times, and fires in the night, the Indians have Canoas but they keep them up in the rivers, for the Spaniards have small forts or sconces of two and three guns in each, at the point of the rivers mouths,[5] to keep the Indians from comeing into the harbour to do mischief to their boats.

The Harbour is neare a mile and a half broad, the guns cannot Com*m*and from one side to the other. St Peters Fort is neare two miles from the Harbour's mouth, any ship may come in & beat them from their guns at St Iago's Fort,[6] and St Andrews Sconce, which are on the West side of the harbour after you are in, And St Peters fort can do very litle or no hurt at all, to the ships. The Spaniards have no plantation on this side, but only keep the

[1] 'Kellagh' is the Erse term for a wooden anchor with a stone in it. The term 'killick, killock' is used today for a small anchor.

[2] The canoe was dug out of the trunk of a tree, shaped at the ends like a boat, some 30 ft long, with the sides raised by one plank on each side.

[3] For Walt read Wale: Of a ship, unsteady, crank. *NOED*. Bame: beam. Wales: strong planks extending all along the outward timbers of a ships side a little above the water line. Thus the canoes had a beam secured on either side along the full length of the boat to give it stability.

[4] The blank space approximates to 5 lines of text.

[5] Two such forts are shown on Narbrough's plan of the 'Port oF Baldavia' (Plate 4), Fort St Andrew (F. S. Andrew), on the west side of Ensenada San Juan, and Fort St John (F. S. John), on the west side of Río Torna Galeones at its entrance into the harbour.

[6] The distance between St Peter's Fort and St Jago's Fort is about 1½ miles, but the range was still too great for the guns at St Peter's Fort to engage a vessel attacking the latter.

forts for possession, that no forreign Ship may come & have the Port free to ride in, and trade with the natives. This harbour is like a Sound after one is within the mouth of it.

Before the Harbour without in the Bay there is very good sandy ground all over from Cape Galere to the North shore, and very fair Soundings of thirty faddoms and twenty six faddoms and 24, 22, 18, 16, 14, 12, 8, faddoms, & without, sixty & 50 & 40 &c[a]. about 3 miles off sandy ground. The land lies away to the northward of the Harbour's mouth, North & B*y* East for 3 leagues to a point[1] which was as farre as I could see that way, for there the Coast falls in a Bay, to the eastwards, the shore side is small sandy Bayes in some places, and some places rocks, the point is steep rocks. The land is all wooddy and of a good height, fresh water runs down into the sea in every valley and Gully. The shore is bold to, a great surge of a Sea Runs on the shore, on all parts of the Coast, so that it is bad to Land with a boat any where, except it bee in Bays where one can bring a point to take off the swell of the sea. It is the same all along the Coast to the southward of Cape Gallere, but the Land there is higher, for four leagues to the southward there is a Low valley, but it is all wooddy, and a round hill stands in the valley, all grown over with woods, and against this valley is a fair sandy bay above a mile long, and flat on the sea shore. Here is anchoring at twenty faddom and sandy ground a mile off the shore.[2] Here is fresh water runs into the sea, here is wood to bee had and Canes grows here. On the South side of this sandy bay the shore is all rocky by the sea side, and many Seales lyes on the rocks. A ship may ride in this Bay with the wind as farr to the westward as the South West & B*y* South, for the point bears Southwest from the Bay.[3] This point is neare 3 leagues from the bay, there lies some rocks scattering about the point, the land is but of a mean height on the point, and also a league to the southward of it, there grows shrubby bushes on the Land over the Point, for a mile distance both wayes, and

[178] **December 1670. The *Sweepstakes* at Baldivia.**

all about on the Land the woods grow very thick on the hills, the trees all stoop to the eastwards, being pressed down with the burden of the westerly winds, which blows much on this Coast.

Here is no Soundings on this Coast two leagues off, there is sixty and seaventy faddom in lesse then a mile of the shore, except in Bayes. I kept my Lead going ever as I sailed on the Coast, but could not get ground at ninety and a hundred faddom, until I came neare the shore side. If the weather bee fair the Land may bee seen nine or ten leagues off, at sea, for it is of a good height in Land, and large hills lying along North & South nearest, as the coast lieth. The Coast is very fair to sail by, and bold to deale with all, as what I see of it.

Now I will relate the succeeding part of mundayes proceedings after my comeing aboard from the shore by Cape Galere, which was about four of clock in the afternoon, and not seeing any people ashore or sign of any thereaboutes but my own men. I made a weaft[4] for my pinnace to come aboard, which was sent with the Cloths, which came immediately to mee, and acquainted mee that they could not speak with any body, that

[1] Punta Rocura (39°41′S, 73°24′W).

[2] This is Caleta Chaihuín, see p. 292, n. 1.

[3] Punta Galera (39°59′S, 73°43′W), which is prominent, low and wooded, lies 7 miles SW of the bay with Punta Falsa Galera, also low and wooded with dangers extending half a mile from it, 3 miles NE of it.

[4] Waft: Any item, flag, gown etc. hoisted in different parts of the ship with a specific meaning as arranged by the Captain. In this case the meaning is 'I made a signal to recall the pinnace'.

would come & receive the Cloths, of them; But some Spaniards called from the shore to have them come to the shore but finding it not safe they did not go to them. They let go the grapnel at the very mouth of the Harbour, and had eight faddom water, the ground fine black sand, the Streame set out, the water was drinkable for it had but a small touch of saltnesse, the place where they lay at their grapnel was neare in the midle of the mouth of the harbour, somewhat nearer the South side then the North.

I disco*ursed with the Indians which were aboard of mee. They said the Indians of the Land had much gold, pointing their hands to the shore right within the harbour on the East side. I gave these two Indians knives, beads, scissers &c[a]. which things they had rather have then so much gold, for they were mightily pleased with what I gave to them. I bad them tell the Indians of the Land that if they would come aboard I would give them the like, and that wee were English men, and did not know the Spaniards, and that wee were sent to speak with them, and to give them things and to live with them, and to help them to get their whole Countrey againe from the Spaniards, and would show them how to shoot guns, &c[a]. and such like discourse as this I used with them, in hopes they would acquaint the inland Indians with it, wherby I might gain a Correspondency with them, & trade for some of their gold. After these two Indians had eat & drunk I set them ashore at the place where Don Carlos was Landed,[1] with two letters, one to my Lieutenant Thomas Armiger, and the other for the governour of S[t] Peters Fort. The letters were as followeth: my boat rowed all along the shore to see the way as they went till they came to S[t] Iago's Fort, which was In lesse then three quarters of an houre's time, after

[179] **December 1670. The *Sweepstakes* at Baldivia in Chili.**

they were landed, they went the same way by the water side in the path as Don Carlos did, when hee was set on shore. This passage of the Indians going so directly to the Fort gives mee to believe Don Carlos must bee with the Spaniards and in no other hands, for hee went directly to them, as the path leads to the Fort.

A note I sent to Lieutenant Armiger enclosed in the letter
which the Indians Carried to him.

Lieutenant. I hope you and M[r] Fortescue and the rest are in good health and Cheerfull. I sent your cloths & things as you desired in my boate into the Harbour but could not have any one to come neare my men to receive them for you. I advise you to speak to the Governour that a boat may come for them, and I will see the things safely delivered, and I promise upon honour to set them safe into the Harbour againe, and not to molest them except it bee with Civility, not else. I desire to bee remembered to you all, I am,

Decemb*er* 19. 1670 Your Loveing friend
John Narbrough

My Letter to Lieutenant Armiger which
I sent by the Indians.

Lieutenant Armiger, I having an opportunity to write to you by these 2 Indians which I have set on shore, I hope you & the rest are well in health. Acquaint the Governour that if hee will send any man off to mee, I will engage my honour to see him set safe ashore

[1] See above, p. 286.

againe when it shall bee desired of him, also acquaint him that I do not come on this coast to do any prejudice to any man of his nation but only to fill fresh water with his leave, and to buy refreshing for my men, And so to proceed on my voyage to the English factories in the East Indies, as our nation do yearly trade into those parts, with shipping. And that if hee do not send you and the rest off to mee hee will over throw my voyage, which will bee two hundred thousand pounds loss to his M*ajes*tie of England, which summe will bee required of him or the Spanish nation where satisfaction must bee made to the uttermost Royal.[1] I would have you send mee word of the state of the Countrey as what you understand as to the fortifications, and what riches the Indians have, and if you heare of D*on* Carlos. Do not beare up to them more then honour & Civility allow. If I had no more concern then you in the service of his M*ajes*tie in this voyage, I would bee glad to bee in your place to learn the tongue, and see the Countrey all along to Lima, and to the West indies or elsewhere, which will not bee past a yeare before you are in England, for they dare not detain you in this land alwaies. I have demanded you of the governour in his letter, and if hee keep you to give you repect as persons of quality, in your voyage for Europe. Also send mee word why Thomas Highway spake to my men when they came away to have a care of the Shipp, and to bee gone. I know there is no danger of any Shipping to come to surprise mee, this two months, If I would let them do it then. Not else but my

[180] **December 1670. The *Sweepstakes* at Anchor before Baldivia.**

Love to you and all the rest, wishing you much happynesse I rest,
aboard the *Sweepstakes* Dec*ember* 19 1670. Your Loving Captain
John Narbrough

My letter to the Governour of the Fort
which I sent by the Indians.

Sir. This is the second time of my sending unto you as concerning the returning of my Lieutenant and the other men, which are by you discourteously kept, as prisoners contrary to the accustomed manner of soldiers and Christians, they being sent to you with a flag of truce and a Trumpeter sounding, in the boate, to desire license in sending for water which was your promise the day before to mee, that I should be supplyed with any thing the Countrey affoorded. S*i*r now I demand them of you. If there bee warrs between the two Crowns, with England & Spain, I desire to understand it. S*i*r these actions of yours will bee given to my Prince where satisfaction will bee had. If I had Com*m*ission now to require it I could speedily take satisfaction. S*i*r I shall stay here this night in expectation of their comeing off to mee, or your answer. If neither I desire you will bee so honourable as to order them entertainment as persons of quality, and Commission officers of his M*ajes*ties of England, for their voyage for Europe. S*i*r I kiss your hands and am
Dec*ember* 19 1670. Sr Your humble Servant
John Narbrough.

After my boat came onboard which set the Indians ashore it grew neare night I caused all the Company to bee called aft to prayers, which was performed accordingly as is usually

[1] *Real*, see above p. xx.

aboard of Ships. After prayers I saw the watch set, and the boate at her station towards the Harbour's mouth as was the night before. Fair weather all night and litle wind at South, the moon being about a quarter old wee had some light of it, the nights being but short so our watching was no great trouble to us, also wee rode quietly without being in any wayes disturbed. I saw lights at St Peters fort several times to night, and on the Land on the East side of the Harbour within, which I suppose might bee Indians fires, for their being is in the woods as I understand by the Spaniards.

Tuesday the 20th. Indifferent fair weather, the wind came to day to the Southwest & B*y* West and blew a stout gale. I rode fast all day. This day I sent my Boat ashore at the place where Don Carlos Landed, to see for him. There they filled some fresh water in Barrells, and returned aboard againe, without any news or sign of him or any else.

This afternoon at one of the clock a Spaniard came aboard of the *Sweepstakes* in a Canoa from Fort St Peters. six Indians rowed him aboard which are servants to the Spaniards, this man's name was Don Juan de Bueltron y Murica,[1] what it is in English I know not, hee said that hee came from the Governour, and that hee had a letter for mee, which came from my Lieutenant

[181] **December 1670. The *Sweepstakes* at Anchor before Baldivia.**
which was delivered to mee which is as followeth.

This man said that the Governour spake to him to tell mee, that if I would come into the Harbour with the Shipp I should have any thing that the Countrey afforded, If I would not, I should not have neither wood nor fresh water, And that hee would send the men to the Vice Roy of Peru, which is at Lima. Also hee said my Lieu*tenan*t was well & desired to bee remembered to mee, and that hee came for his cloths as the letter mentioned. I desired this gentleman to sit downe & I made him wellcome with wine and provisions such as I had, which was English beefe & pease. This man said hee was a Sergeant in the Fort, and had lived in these parts fifteen years, hee was born in Galliçia, hee was a proper man of stature, and well Complexioned, of a ruddy Colour, hee was well apparelld after the Spanish fashion with stuffs and woolsted stockings, and a sword by his side, hee was very full of talke, hee brought a great bag of peeces of eight aboard, to buy linnen and other things, which I and my Company sold to him, & received his money for the goods.

The letter which my Lieutenant sent mee by the Spaniard.

S*i*r Yours I received by the Indians, and am glad to heare from you. I pray send our Cloths by this bearer and use him well, for wee are very respectively used hitherto and promised the like for the future. S*i*r I pray send us some of the king's goods as large black beads,

[1] This is Don Juan de Buitrón y Múgica (b. 1649), obtained a post as an infantry soldier in the Chilean Army in 1652. He was posted to Valdiva in 1668 as an ayudante reformado and promoted to infantry captain in charge of mulatto troops. In 1684, he obtained a licence to transfer to Peru where he served in the South Seas Navy. In 1688, he was proposed by the *Junta de Guerra de Indias* for the post of engineer-in-chief at Valdivia, but rejected by Carlos II, despite his experience in the construction of St James' (Amargos) Fort, the dock at Valdivia and the rampart at Pura y Limpia Concepción de Lemos (Niebla) castle. He was married twice, first to Beatriz de Salas and then to Isabel María del Castillo with whom he had a son who subsequently became an official of the Inquisition. Guarda, *La Sociedad*, No. 271, pp. 116–17; Roa y Ursúa, *El Reyno*, No. 3020, p.768.

linnen cloth & knives, or otherwise furnish us with money. I pray put mee up two books, Fullers holy State, and his holy warr.[1] I pray let both our cases bee filled with wine and brandy and send them to us, and so depart this day for England, for here is nothing to bee done by fair or by foule meanes, and god blesse you all.
Baldivia the 20th Dec*ember* Thomas Armiger.

S*ir* here are some people that bring meale and other things for to exchange for commodities, I pray use them well for our sakes. If you love your selfe begone with the Shipp. I pray send a peece of striped linnen for to make our selves cloths.

This afternoon I shewed the Spaniard my Commission. That the Ship was one of his Ma*jes*ties ships of England, and that I was bound for the kingdome of China, with goods of his Ma*jes*ties to the value of two hundred thousand pounds Sterling, and if the governour kept my officers from mee, I should not bee able to perform the voyage without them, which would bee so much loss to the king of England besides the Charges hee was at already in fitting the Ship out, which is very Considerable, and the hinderance of his Ma*jes*ties designe will bee a breach of the Articles between the two Crowns of England & Spain.

I desire that you will bee pleased to acquaint the governor of what you have seen and heard, and that hee had best to advise himselfe what hee doth in detaining the king of England's servants. And that I charge the whole losse to him which will bee required of the Spanish nation, and satisfaction will bee had to the uttermost royal.[2] I shall stay here this night and to morrow in Expectation that the

[182] **December 1670. The *Sweepstakes* at Anchor before Baldivia.**
Governour will send my Lieutenant and the other gentlemen off to mee, and give mee satisfaction of the wrong hee hath done mee, in hindering my time.

The Spaniard said hee would tell the Governour what I sayd to him, And that hee would come again tomorrow, if hee might have leave, and give mee an account of what the Governour said to it. Hee confessed himself that it was a very ill act of the Governour to detaine a flag of truce and a trumpeter, & that all the gentlemen ashore were much troubled at the matter, for they did intend to come aboard and buy goods.

I shewed this Spaniard the Ship fore and aft, and the hold, and Cask of provisions, and the Chists [chests], and told him that those Chists were full of Linnen and fine Cloths, and Laces and silks &c[a]. Hee said if the governour would give[3] leave the gentlemen that were ashore would bring off money and buy them all of mee. The things which this man now bought were peeces of Callicos, cases of knives, silk Shashes[4] two watches, leather gloves, thread gloves, and some Serges &c. Callicos which cost mee ten shillings the peece in the City of London I had ten, & twelve peeces of eight for the peece. And for Cases of knives which cost three shillings a case in London, I had five & 6 peeces of 8 for a case here. For an East India Sash I had three peeces of eight and for the watches wee had fourty peeces of eight a peece for them, one watch Cost three pounds in London, and the other

[1] Thomas Fuller (1607/8–61). The works which Armiger had taken to sea with him were, *The Historie of the Holy Warre*, Cambridge, 1639, and *The Holy State*, London, 1642.

[2] See above, p. xx.

[3] 'him' scored out.

[4] 'Shash', later 'Sash', is an Indian word, its use here reflecting the impact of the extensive import of Indian textiles into England in the 17th century.

Cost four pounds five shillings. I had a peece of eight a pair for leather gloves, which cost twelve pence the pair in London; And for thread gloves I had three peeces of eight a pair for them which cost four shillings the pair in London. The peeces of Serge were sold for three times as much as they Cost in London.

This man gave his own price for hee knew what advantage hee could make of them ashore, I believe if I had asked more for the goods hee would have given it mee, for it was worth a great deale more ashore. All com*m*odities which come from Europe are very deare here, and scarce, for they have none brought them but by the way of Panama, and by the river of Plate, which comes through several merchant's hands before it comes into these parts, and the transport from place to place is very Chargeable.

Also money is but of litle esteeme, here being such plenty of it. Fine hollands silks, flanders laces, silk stockings, ribbi*ning,[1] french linnen, looking glasses &c. were much enquired for here, and would have sold at great price. And gunpowder for fowling is worth a peece of eight a pound, and bird-shott is two royals a pound, and a royal & a half a pound. All commodities of European workmanship is of great worth here as I understand, and I believe more northerly on the Coast of Chili about Valperazso, & Coquimbo, & Arica[2] where there are more inhabitants Commodities would beare a greater price, and vent greater quantities, for silver is more plentifull in those parts by much then at Baldivia, they being nearer the mines of Potossi,[3] for the silver of Pottossi comes down to the Port

[183] **December 1670. The *Sweepstakes* at Anchor before Baldivia.**

of Arica, and from thence it is carried to Lima by sea. I am of the opinion that the most advantagious trade in the world might bee made in these parts, if it were but followed, and that Liberty were graunted by the king of Spain for the English nation to trade freely on all parts of that coast, and in these Ports, for the people which are livers [residents] there are very desirous of a trade, but the governours durst not suffer any such thing without orders from the king of Spaine, unlesse such ships of force were to go into these parts and trade with the common people, in despight of their governours, which might bee easily performed by four ships of twenty and thirty guns in a Ship. And also I believe the Natives in these Southern parts of Chili, about the Islands of Castro, and Osorno,[4] and at Baldivia would easily bee brought to trade with us when once they grew acquainted with those as should bee employed upon the designe, And they do but use them Civilly at the first and gaine their loves, which will bee by giveing them knives, scissers, looking glasses, beads, combs, hatchets, and such like commodities, and they will return for these things Gold, Bezoar stones, and red wooll &c[a].

For what I can understand by the Indians which were aboard of mee they are masters of the golden part of the Countrey, and that they have much gold, and would bee glad to bee acquainted with any nation, except the Spaniards, but them they cannot endure, for the Spaniards have been so cruell to them when they have had conference with Each other, so that it is a hard matter now for the Spanish nation to gain their favour, they being so much incensed against the name of a Spaniard.

[1] Ribbaning, Ribanding: Ribbons and ribbon work. *NOED*.

[2] Valparaíso (33°03′S, 71°36′W), Coquimbo (29°58′S, 71°20′W), Arica (18°29′S, 70°20′W).

[3] For the silver mines of Potosi, see above, p. 515, n. 4.

[4] Osorno (40°35′S, 73°09′W).

Therfore I would not advise any man that should desire to have Conference with these Indians to speak one word of the Spanish tongue. But get some Indians which have lived with the Spaniards, & can speak Spanish and the Indian Language also, and employ such people in the businesse first, that the Indians may know that you are not Spanish, and that you are English & would desire to trade with them, and supply them with such things as they have occasion for. There are enough of these Indians to bee found for Interpreters at any of the Spanish settlements which would bee glad of the Employment, for I had two such fellows came aboard of mee while I rode before Baldivia. One of the two was an Indian of the Island of Mocha[1] taken by the Spaniards in a Canoa when hee was a lad, hee is now a slave to one of the Captains in the Forts. This Indian desired mee to go to the Island of Mocha, and told mee that there I might have what fresh provisions I would, for knives, beads, hatchets, scissers, looking glasses, Jews trumps &c., hee said I might have a great hog there for a knife, and a sheep for a knife, & hens for beads & glasses.

This fellow says they are all Indians which live on the Island of Mocha and there are many people, and that they will not suffer the Spaniard to live amongst them, and that they kill Spaniards they can come at, and

[184] **December 1670. The *Sweepstakes* at Anchor before Baldivia.**

cut off their heads and put them on poles. They have gold on the Island, But they will not sell any to the Spaniards, hee said that I might have gold for hatchets and swords, for they much esteem such things or any Iron for to make weapons. Hee says that the Island hath much wood on it, and that it is*greene, and there are many townes of Indians, and they have great plenty of provisions, much Indian Corn and Potatoes, wheat, beanes, and much other grain, many fowles, and sheep, hogs, goats, and the like.

The Indians there wear cloths which they make of the wooll of their sheep, their garment is a long Coat loose, and some of them weare loose Jackets and britches, stockings & caps. There are several governours amongst them which are as Captains in their villages. They have bezoar stone there which they have out of the Guianacos, and they have much red wooll.

This Indian man I verily believe would have been very faithfull to mee and would have used his best skill to have brought mee acquainted with the natives of Mocha, if I would have gone thither with him. It was a fair opportunity for mee to have had Conference with those Mochians, this fellow being one of the Island, and his Relations lived on it then.

I would have gone to the Island willingly, but my Instructions obliged mee to proceed no further northerly then Baldivia, on that coast unlesse in Case of necessity, which I blesse god I have not now any such Case, And I dare not attempt any such matter contrary to order, which is the occasion I did not make use of this Indian. Hee was very sorry I did not goe, & Cryed with grief. I gave him a knife, a small looking glasse, and some beads to satisfie him, and told him I would come again and bring more things and go with him. These sayings did please him, but hee was more willing to stay aboard the Ship and go any where with mee, then to go ashore again to the Spanish Forts, but I would not Condescend hee should stay with mee by reason of my promise to the Governour that I would not carry a man of his away.

[1] Isla Mocha (38°11′S, 73°31′W).

The Spanish gentleman aboard the Ship hath a great desire to stay in the Ship and go for England with mee or any where else. I asked him his reason why hee desired to stay, hee said hee was weary in being so long in these garrisons, and that hee would gladly see his native Countrey and relations. I answered him I would not carry away any[1] man that came aboard with[2] flag of truce or otherwise that was a subject to the king of Spaine. But if hee had a desire to go ashore my boat should bee fitted to sett him ashore immediatly, his answer was hee would stay till it was nearer night.

I did not know whether hee was reall in what hee said therfore I would not discourse more of that Concerne with him. I thanked him for all his kindnesse in comeing aboard of mee, and bringing the letter from my Lieutenant. I presented him a pound of Nutmegs, a pair of new Cordevant gloves, an East-India walking cane, half a dozen of Ivory Combs, two dozen of tobacco pipes

[185] **December 1670. The *Sweepstakes* at anchor before Baldivia.**

and half a dozen of knives. For these things hee gave mee many thanks and promised mee that hee would serve mee to the uttermost of his power, in any thing I should desire him to do, and whatever I sent to the gentlemen ashore hee would see it safe delivered to them, and that hee had a real affection to my Lieutenant and to Englishmen that hee came off to mee, and that hee heard the Gentlemen which had been aboard applaud the Civility that they received aboard the Shipp from strangers, which was so extraordinary, that I have gained the Love of most of the people ashore, and most of them were desirous to come off to see mee and the Ship and to buy goods if the governour would give a graunt to them. And that for his own part hee never desired a meals meat so much as hee did to come off to the Ship, for Shee looked so bravely when hee saw her come in to Anchor, and such like discourse as this hee held till towards night. All which hee said would bee too tedious to relate here, it being of no consequence.

This man did not know that the Mocha Indian had said any thing to mee, So I asked him what people lived on the Island of Mocha, hee told mee that they were all Indians, and that there were many people, and that they were but *Poco megos* to the Spaniards, the English is they were but litle friends to the Spaniards. Hee says that they have much provisions there, And that if I can but trade with them, I might buy hogs, goats, sheep, & hens, what I would have for knives, scissers, and beads. But I must have a care that they do not betray my boats, for they are very valliant men and barbarous. They have some gold there, which hee thinks they have from the maine, of the Indians there, for they will not part from it.

I asked him what people lived on the Island of Castro,[3] Shewing him the draught of all the Coast of America,[4] and pointing from one place to another. Hee said some few Spaniards lived on Castro and at Osorno, but they were not relieved with recruits not in a Long time, and that they had but few Cloths to wear, and that the women had not smocks to put on their backs, when the last boat came from them, they have fortifications in both places, but hee knows not the number of ordinance nor the strength of the places. Hee sayes there are many Indians on the Island of Castro, and on the main by Osorno, And that they have much gold, and that the Spaniards trade with them for gold, and bezoar stones and wooll.

[1] 'any' substituted for 'a' struck through.

[2] Illegible word scored out.

[3] See above, p. 280, n, 3,

[4] This could be the Doncker chart (Plate 2), which shows Isla Chiloé as C.astro.

Hee says that the Spaniards are a leaving their settlement at Osorno, for the Indians are at warrs with them, and do them much spoile &c. I asked him what provisions the Spaniards have on the Island of Castro, hee said that they have good European wheat, and beanes grow there and other graine, and they have cows, horses, hogs, sheep and goats, and fowles all as

[186] **December 1670. The *Sweepstakes* at Baldivia.**
good as any are in Spain. I asked him what manner of harbour it is for entertaining of shipping, hee could not tell mee any thing of it for hee never had been there, but the vessels that used there were Barks of about fourty or fifty tuns apeece, these barks carry recruits thither & bring from thence gold & bezoar stones and red wooll, and Carry it to Lima.

I asked him if any Spaniards lived on the Coast anywhere to the southwards of Castro towards the Strait of Magellan hee said that hee never did heare of any that lived thereabouts, or any man that knew that part of the Countrey to the southward of Castro.

I asked him what manner of people the Indians were in the land here at Baldivia. Hee said they were men of great stature of Nine or ten foot high, and very valliant Cruel and barbarous, and hold warrs with the Spaniards, and were in Armies of eight thousand men together that used to come down and burn the standing corn, and do great spoile to the Spaniards, and that they have many horses and fight on horsback, & have much provision. The countrey hee sayes is very fertile, and much grapes grows in the Land. And that the mountains of snow which they call the Andes are about thirty Leagues from the sea side, and that the Indians have much gold, and that their armour and all their utensils are[1] made of gold, for iron is wanting much amongst them, and other mettals. Hee said that some of the Indians which live neare the forts trade with the Spaniards and give them gold for their Com*m*odities which they buy of them.

Hee said that the Spaniards which are ashore would willingly come aboard to buy Linnens, silks, and flanders laces, if the governour would not hinder them, for they want these commodities which I have much. But the Governour will not permitt any of them to come off upon their perills, without I had brought the king of Spain's Order. And that the Com*m*on people of Baldivia are much vexed with him by reason they cannot trade.

Linnens, silks, good flanders laces, woollen Cloth, and all manner of European Com*m*odities are much wanted here.

This man Sayes that their Governours come into this Countrey but for three years time to get themselves Estates, and then they are gone from them, so they care not what becomes of the Inhabitants.

I asked him the vice Roy's name of Peru hee said his name is.

Don Francisco antoneoa Dariex Counte de Lima.[2]

[1] 'is' struck through and 'are' substituted.

[2] The Viceroy of Peru was Pedro Antonio Fernández de Castro de Andrade y Portugal (1632–72), 10th Conde de Lemos, 7th Marquis of Sarría and Duke of Taurisano, the son of Francisco Fernández de Castro (1613–62) who had been Viceroy of Arragon (1649–53) and Sardinia (1653–7). He was born in Monforte de Lemos 20 Oct. 1632, and appointed Viceroy of Peru, President of the Audiencia de Lima and Captain General of the Provinces of Peru, by the Council of the Indies, on 21 Oct. 1666. He arrived in Callao 9 Nov. 1667 and took office on 21 Nov. the same year. He died in office in Lima, 6 Dec. 1672. Following his death his wife and five children returned to Spain in June 1675. Lohmann, *El Conde*, pp. 6, 31, 373–4.

Some of my men which were ashore heard the Spaniard say that the vice roy's name of Peru is Don Pedro de Castro, Counte de Lima &c.

[187] **December 1670. The *Sweepstakes* at Anchor before Baldivia.**

The Captain Generall of Chili and Governour of *Baldivia &c[a].

Don PE. de Montoya, a knight of S[t] Iago &c.

The Governours name of S[t] Peter's Fort which is the Chief Magazin.

Diego de Earais Codex yes lo var &c.

The governours name of S[t] Iago's Fort which is on the South point at the going in of the Harbours mouth is Simon dies deaillon.[1]

What I understand by the gentlemen which came aboard of mee at the first, and by this Gentleman, and by the people ashore, that every body in the whole Countrey are mighty desirous to trade, for they have great plenty of silver, and gold, and are much Inclined to bee gallant in their apparell, but cannot gett commodities for their moneys without great trouble. I am of the opinion that there might bee great gain made by Cargos of goods from Europe. That if 3 or four good ships of force laden with Commodities suitable for the countrey which would bee fine Hollands, and french Linnen, silks, flanders laces, cloths, stuffs,[2] great Looking-glasses, with all manner of such Commodities as are to bee bought in England at all times would bee sold here, and on the Coast of Chili to the Spaniards at great gaines. And if ever if happen that the natives once come to trade with them, then the benefits would bee exceeding greater then can bee now immagined. For the Spaniards live partly by tradeing with the natives, and get great quantities of gold of them, which wee might receive for Iron and Weapons, and woollen cloth &c[a]. as well as they.

This evening at six of clock the Spanish gentleman went from the Shipp and Carried my Lieutenants Cloths and things which hee sent for, in his Canoa with himselfe. This man promised mee hee would acquaint the Governour what I said to him as concerning the sending my men aboard, and that I desired only to recruit my self with water and wood and a litle refreshing & so to bee gone, for the kingdome of China, and that the Ship is his M*ajes*ties of England and on his M*ajes*ties employment, and that I will not do any injury to any of the king of Spain's subjects, neither would I bring the Ship into Harbour.

This man would fain have had mee kept him aboard, but I would not in the Least condescend to his request, but told him, Wheras hee came aboard with a flag of truce, I would see him and those which came with him set safe ashore, as I had given my promise I would, and that I scorned to break my word. Hee said hee would come off to mee in the night if possible hee could, and bring money with him, and stay with mee and go for England, and that there was more men ashore would come off with him, hee desired that hee might leave mee a note for memorandum, that I might not fire at him in the night, but examin him by the note when hee came neare mee to know that hee was the man his note is as followeth as hee writ it himself. – *A qui vine al nairo con el mentagid Ingobix naden unatural dib y eia uamaie* – Don Juan de Buittron y manuaxil D.[3]

[1] See above, p. 521, n. 1.

[2] Woollen fabric.

[3] Narbrough may have retained a copy of the note, or this is his garbled memory of the Spanish now conveyed to the clerk. While it is impossible to translate accurately it was intended to convey to whomever was on watch, that the bearer was D. Juan de Buittron y Manuaxil, and that he was a friend, as Narbrough explains below, when he writes about setting the evening watch.

[188] **December 1670. The *Sweepstakes* at Baldivia.**
After hee writ this note hee took his Leave of mee, but very unwillingly, hee went over the Ship side into his Boat, the poor Indians which rowed his boat Cryed when they were to go away from my men, for I had given them beads, knives and glasses to encourage them to bring off any thing that the Countrey affoorded, if they could, and also to gain their affections, and that they might know that wee were not Spaniards, but wee were English men and desired to bee their friends, in case any ships should have occasion to come on this Coast to look for a trade, as I hope there will bee some hereafter, when once they understand what tradeing is to be had in these parts.

I gave the gentleman two letters to Carry ashore, one was for L*ieutenan*t Armiger the other was for the Governour of St Peter's fort, hee promised mee hee would deliver them, and so took leave of mee very Gravely, & put off from the Ship. At his putting off I caused five guns to bee fired and took my Leave of him. I sent my L*ieutenan*t Picket in my Pinnace to tow his boat in, and to see him safe ashore, for his boat was deep laden with goods, and the tyde run out a fine Stream alwayes. After my L*ieutenan*t has seen the Canoa safe into the harbour hee came aboard again and acquainted mee that the Canoa was safe in the Harbour.

I sent my boat ashore this Evening at the place where Don Carlos was Landed to see for him. Shee returned aboard again after one houre's time staying ashore, but could not see him, or hear any thing of him, or any else in that place or thereabouts.

After prayers this Evening, I set the watch, and charged my officers that they should not permit any boat to come near the Ship without my knowledge, although the Spaniard have left a note wherby hee might bee examined, Yet I could not tell but hee designed to come and do mee prejudice, which I was ever wary of.

Fair weather to night, the wind came off of the shore, at South a fine gale. I rode fast and quietly, for no boats came near mee all night, neither could wee see any fires in the wood, or hear any noise of man or beast.

The air healthy and temperate for heat or Cold, a fine dew fell towards morning, and a pleasant smell came from the green woods. No fish could wee take with our hookes, for some of my Company ever were a trying, but never could have a bite. Many white Squabs or Jelly fish seen swim*m*ing by the side.

My Letter to L*ieutenan*t Armiger, I sent to him by the Spanish Gentleman.
Lieutenant Yours I received by this bearer, and I am glad to heare that you are all in good health and Cheerfull, as wee are god bee praised, and I hope hee will Continue it with us both as wee trust in him. I have treated the bearer and the Indians which came with him with all Civility, and hee promised mee hee

[189] **December 1670. The *Sweepstakes* at anchor before Baldivia.**
would tell the governour what I desired him to do, concerning the sending you off to mee. I have sent your Cloths and Chist [chest] and what else you desired, and your man hath sent you a note of the particulars, And I have sent Mr Fortescues things and a gown to wear in the Cold mornings. I advise you all to bee of good courage,[1] for you need not question your usage, and you may bee in Europe before mee which if you bee present my most

[1] 'Courage' substituted for 'Cheer' struck through.

humble duty to his Ma*jes*tie and Royal Highnesse, and Certifie my proceedings hitherto. I will wait here some time til I have an answer of these letters, and then I will bee gone. When you write to mee I pray let bee more at Large. If you read the letter which I send to the Governour cause Thomas Highway to make good interpretation of it to the Governour, And not bee affraid to speak to him, what I have writ: for they dare not do any of you the Least harme that is, you being detained with a flag of truce, and went to them upon an honourable message. The Articles between the two Crowns allow of being supplied with wood and fresh water, or any recruits otherwise that is wanting. I wish you all much health and prosperity and a good passage for Europe I rest,

Dec*ember* 20. 1670. Your Loving friend
John Narbrough.

My letter to the Governour of S[t] Peter's Fort.

S*i*r. This is the 3[d] time of my sending unto you concerning the returning of my Lieu*tenan*t and the other three men which are by you discourteously kept as Prisoners, Contrary to the accustomed manner of soldiers and Christians, they being sent to you with a flag of truce and a Trumpeter in the boat, to desire leave in sending for water, which was your promise the day before to mee, that I should have wood, fresh water, and any thing that the Countrey affoorded.

S*i*r Now I demand them of you. If there bee warrs beetween the two Crowns with England and Spain I desire to understand it. Sir these actions of your will bee made known to my prince, and satisfaction will bee had. Sir if I had Commission to require it I could speedily take satisfaction here.

Sir, I Shall stay here this night in Expectation of their comeing off to mee, or your answer to the Contrary. If neither I desire you to bee so honourable as to order them Entertainment as persons of quality, & commission officers of his Ma*jes*ties of England, for their voyage to Europe &c[a].

Sir I set your two Indians ashore yesterday with a letter to you, and by your gentleman I hear they are safe at the Fort, But I have no answer of the Letter whether it bee delivered to you or not which cause I write this, Sir I kisse your hands and am,

from on board &c[a]. Dec*ember* 20. 1670 Sir your humble Servant
John Narbrough.

[190] **December 1670. The *Sweepstakes* at anchor before Baldivia.**

Wednesday the 21, hazy weather the wind at South Southwest a fine gale but towards twelve of clock the wind came to the West South West and blew a stout gale. It looked very Cloudy to seaward, and made shew of foule weather, for the sea came rowling into the Bay.

This morning I sent my Long boat and pinnace ashore right against the Ship, at the place where Don Carlos landed at the first, there I filled about twenty hogsheads of pure fresh water, which came runing down the hill out if the woods, in a fine rivulet into the sea, this water the Spaniards call *aqua del oro*,[1] the Spaniards said it comes runing [*sic*] out of the hills from the gold. Here is very good filling of fresh water in many[2] rivulets between Cape Gallery and the point of the Harbour's mouth, and no suff [surf] of the sea

[1] Shown on Narbrough's plan of the 'Port oF Baldavia' (Plate 4) as '*Aqua DL ORO*'.
[2] 'rivulets' substituted for 'places' struck through.

runs on the shore, unlesse the wind bee out and blow on the western quarter of the Compasse, or northerly, then the sea comes rowling into the bay. My men and my self looked in all those rivulets where the water had washed the sand down for gold, and also alongst the shore side but wee could never find one grain of mettal.

Here is very good wooding, and good gravelly sand in some places on the shore for Ballast. But here are many rocks lies in the sea, but close to the shore side, except one rock which lies just within the Pitch of the Cape to the northwards a Cables length off the shore or there about. It is as big as a boat, and above the surface of the water.

Here grows many Canes on the shore, such as are worn in England for walking staves and are called Bamboas. They grow amongst the woods like vines, and run up about the boughs of the trees above twenty foot long, they are a good stiff and strong stick and firm, and none of them hollow. My men Cut some of them and brought aboard of the Ship, there are of all sizes. These sticks are jointed after a knotty manner, and about five or six inches assunder.[1] The Spaniards and Indians make their lance staves of them, of twenty foot Long and more, and they are very stiff and stronge and not haevie.[2] In the woods my men saw many wood pigeons & doves, and other small birds like Sparrows and some Kites, and other great fowls like a kite, which is called a Stinking Carrion Crow.[3]

In the sea by the shore side there they saw many white and gray Sea mues and some black Cormorants, and Sea dyvers, and some Curlews & small teal, and ducks and widgeon, and brant geese such as are in England. No sign of wild beast in the woods &c[a]. The trees are somewhat like beech trees & maples and alders, they grow very thick that there is no travelling in the woods, many apple trees grows by the wood sides, which were full of green apples, my men gathered some bags full & codled them aboard.[4]

[191] **December 1670. The *Sweepstakes* at anchor before Baldivia.**
This forenoon the same Spaniard that was yesterday aboard, came again in his Canoa, and six Indians rowed him, hee had a flag of truce in his boate flying, as hee came neare mee hee called to us to give him a rope.

He was very gallant in his apparel to what hee was the day before, hee had a good black hat on his head broad Crownd & flat after the Spanish mode, and a great plume of Estridge feathers on it white. Hee had a loose Jacket over a Satten wastcoat. His Jacket was of China Silk with Silver waft[5] in it. His breeches were fine broad cloth of a lemmon Colour, made straite after the Spanish fashion, his stockings silk, his shoes were made of goats Leather, and pinked[6] his Linnen on his back was french Cloth, hee had a long broad Rapier by his side, the guard was a large Shell [guard] of Steele after the Spanish fashion.

When I received him over the side I carried him aft into the great Cabbin, where hee delivered his message, which is this as followeth as hee told it to my Interpreters, and they to mee; for I cannot speak Spanish, yet I understand many words of the tongue.

[1] Between the knots.
[2] *Chusquea quilla*; see above, p. 291, n. 2.
[3] See above, p. 292, n. 3.
[4] See above, p. 531, n. 1.
[5] Waft: An old form of weft, the threads that go from side to side in weaving. *NOED.*
[6] Possibly a pattern made by pricking or puncturing the leather, or perhaps decorated with leather cut at the edges in zig-zag form, as if by pinking shears.

Thus hee related, that the Governour and all the Spanish gentlemen ashore desired to bee remembered to mee, and that Don Pedro de Montoyes the General of Chili was at the fort, and sent him off to mee, which was the Cause of his comeing now, and his Com*m*and was this, that if I would bring the Shipp into the Harbour within Com*m*and of their Forts I should have all the accommodation that the Land would affoord, But otherwise I should not have any thing off from them, and hee would keep those men hee had in Posession and send them to the Vice-Roy at Lima.

This man brought off in his boat some small Loaves of wheat bread to sell, and some wheat flower, and some green beanes, and ten Jarrs of wine of Chili, as they Call it, and some Sallads which was Lettice & purslane. And hee brought of peeces of eight in two great baggs, to the number of two or three hundred peeces in a bag or thereabouts, to buy commodities with, which hee did before hee went from on board.

I would not suffer one drop of the wine to come into the Ship, for feare it should be adulterated, neither would I permit any of my men to go into his boat, to prevent them from drinking of the wine, being also doubtfull it would put them into fluxes, their bodies not being accustomed to strong wines, as that was, and some of their wine hath Syrup of Sugar put into it, which is bad for fluxes.

The bread and the other things I permitted my men to buy, which they gaves knives, linnen and stockings for it, for hee would not take money for

[192] **December 1670. The *Sweepstakes* before BALDIVIA.**

any thing hee had, but goods; for money hee said there was enough ashore, the bread hee sold as Cheap as it could have been bought in England, but the wine hee valued at the rate of a peece of eight a gallon, and some Jarrs hold about six gallons. Tobacco hee rated at a peece of eight the pound. It is very excellent tobacco.[1] It grows in the kingdome of Peru. My men made the Indians very welcome. I ordered them provisions for their dinners, and wine to drink.

After this man had delivered his message and Laid out his moneys in commodities with my men, I had him to dinner with mee and the drinking of a bottle or two of wine, hee was very merry and full of discourse declaring the plentifullnesse of provisions in Chili, in the province of Arauco, hee said it was the best Countrey in the world, it might bee compared to Paradice, for the delights in it, for there was all thing fit for man in it &c[a].

There are many fine beautifull women both whites and Indians, great store of silver and gold and other riches, many rare fruits, & pleasant herbs and flowers, and the like which I cannot relate all here for it would bee too tedious.

But said hee if you will carry mee for England I will leave this land for I have a desire to see my native Countrey, and relations, and then I will come againe and settle in these parts, hee would have sent the Canoa ashore and stayed himself aboard. I answered him that I had engaged the honour of a soldier to the governour to set him safe ashore againe, And that I scorned to break my promise for all the wealth in the kingdome of Chili, neither would I carry any of the king of Spain's subjects out of this Land hee said that hee was sorry for it.

I asked him why hee did not bring off more things in his boat, knowing hee might buy goods of my men, hee said that the Governour Charged him not to carry anything off to

[1] A word deleted here.

the English Shipp. But when hee came away the people put these things into her, to buy them Commodities unknown to the Governour, But if they could have leave they would bring off a great many things, and money enough to Lade the boats for to buy Commodities, and that the Captain of the Spanish ship would willingly come aboard to buy sailes and ropes &c.

I asked him why hee did not come off to mee last night as hee said hee would, his answer was that all the boats were secured by the guards, And that it was impossible for him to get off but the guards would know it and secure him. Hee said that hee acquainted the Governour with every particular as what I said to him, and that I shewed my Commission, and

[193] **December 1670. The *Sweepstakes* before BALDIVIA.**

that the Ship was the king of England's but the Governour made slight of it. I asked him how my officers did, hee said they were well, and that hee*had letters for mee from them, But the Governour would not write to mee knowing I could not understand Spanish writeing.

I asked him what hee thought the Governour intended with my Lieu*tenan*t and the other three men, hee said they would doubtlesse bee sent to Lima to the vice roy, and so sent to Spain next yeare, for the vice roy have but one yeare to stay in Peru, and then hee goes for Spaine, which every man in this Countrey is glad of, for hee is a Cruel severe man and covetous, so that no man loves him.

I finding this gentleman so free in discourse, I asked him what hee thought the Governour would do If I should go into the Harbour with the Shipp. Hee said the Governour would keep mee there till hee sent to the vice roy, and have orders from him again, for the Governour believes that I come to take Spaniards, and that there will come more ships after mee suddenly as hee*heares by my men, and that I stay here for them, and to get provisions, for I have neither water nor provisions in the Shipp, but only Seals flesh to eat, as hee hears. I heartily thanked the Gentleman for his Information. I presented him a peece of Callico and a Case of knives, for these things hee gave mee many thanks, and would have given mee his Plume of Estridges feathers off of his hat, but I excused his good will, and would not receive any thing from him as guift.

I asked him how many great guns there is in the Forts in this Harbour, naming each particular Fort. Hee said that in all the forts here and at Baldivia there were twenty six in all, as followeth.

In the Fort St Iago there are seaven guns of copper, whole Cul*verin*g, & D*emi* C*ulvering*.

In St Peters Fort are nine guns, some Copper, whole Cul*vering* & D*emi* C*ulvering*.

In St Johns Fort are two guns, not so big as the other.

In St Andrews Fort are three guns, I judge may bee Sakers.

In the Citty of Baldivia are five guns, Demi Cul*vering* or of that Na*ture*.

These are all the Ordinance that are now in this Harbour and rivers, But what the natures of them bee I am not Certain, but as near as I can understand by him they are whole Culvering & Demiculvering and Saker.[1]

[1] Types of ordnance in use in the 17th century included: Culverin, bore 5½ in; weight 4,500 lb, range, point blank 2,000 ft, random 12,500 ft; Demiculverin, bore 4½ in, weight 3,400 lb, range, point blank 2,000 ft, random 12,500 ft : Saker ordinary, bore 3½ in, weight 1,400 lb, range 1,700 ft, random 8,500 feet. Oppenheim, *Naval tracts*, pp. 39–40.

This man is not acquainted with great guns nor fire locks,[1] Neither is there one man in fourty amongst them that can tell how to use a firelock for theirs are all match locks. The Spanish Captains which were aboard of mee Could not tell when the peeces were whole bent or half bent.[2] This man said hee was bred a souldier, and hee understood Fortifications and

[194] **December 1670. The *Sweepstakes* before Baldivia.**
the like in Architecture. Hee showed mee a draught which hee had in his Pocket drawn on paper. It was a draught of a work which was intended at Baldivia to secure the land side of the Citty, But his draught was such as I could not understand any thing of it. I asked him how many soldiers there might bee in all these Foorts and at the Citty of de Baldivia, hee said in all about one thousand, But there was but three hundred Spaniards, the rest were Indians & Musteses & Mulatos.[3]

I could not understand by him what manner of Citty Baldivia is, hee said it was but small. It have no walls, and that there are not above two hundred houses in all. Hee said it is settled on the side of the river which runs up to the Northeastward, nine miles from St Peters Fort, and that the boats which wee called barges go up to it. I saw the boats sailing up and down that river every day as wee were aboard of the Ship, for they have a fair wind to saile up the river in the midle of the day, and a small wind & the fresh[4] to bring them down in the mornings, the tyde never runs in with any Streame, for the fresh alwaies have a fine Stream out, running after the rate of four miles in an houre, I tryed it with my Log. But the flood rises & falls within the Harbour about seaven or eight foot perpendicular, and that is the most, And it is a high water in the Harbour about nine of the Clock on the full and change dayes of the moon, and at the going in at the mouth of the Harbour, there is seaven faddom water sandy ground. And in the harbour there is six five and four faddom, the shore sides within the Harbour are rocky in some places, and sandy Bayes in other places with glittering stones like gold, which lyes in the sand. These observations wee made of the tydes rideing here ourselves.

I cannot give much Credit to all that this man relates, by reason hee speaks to the disliking of the Governour, and to strangers, which it seems to mee somewhat a Romance. I find that hee hath no affection for the governour, which gives mee to believe hee hath transgressed formerly, and the Governour hath punished him, which causeth this ill will, or hee is some troublesome fellow and the Governour doth not Care for him, hee said at his taking leave of the Governour hee bade him farewell, for hee would see England. Hee said that he is serjeant of a Company which is in St Peter's fort now, and most of all the

[1] Firelock: a gun-lock in which sparks were produced (either by friction or percussion) to ignite the priming. *NOED.*

[2] At this time ordnance was described by Seller, *The Sea-Gunner*, pp. 142–3, as having differing levels of fortification, referring to the thickness of the metal at the touch-hole, trunnions and muzzle in proportion to the bore. There were three levels: Legitimate Pieces which were the standard proportion, lesser pieces called Bastard Pieces (these might also be shorter then normal), and extraordinary pieces which were Double Fortified. The meanings of 'bent' include: degree of endurance, capacity for taking in or receiving, limit of capacity etc. *NOED.* From which, 'whole bent' and 'half bent' would appear to be a reference to the amount of powder with which a gun could be charged depending on the thickness of the barrel, and hence Narbrough was apparently asking if the great guns were 'legitimate ' or 'bastard' pieces.

[3] See above, p. 513, n. 4.

[4] This is the fresh water outflow from the river.

soldiers are drawn down to these Forts by reason of my being here, And that they are to stay in the forts as long as the Ship is on the Coast &c[a].

Last night the Governour Caused all the soldiers to bee in arms And to bee in readynesse to fight mee if that I had come in as the governour did expect I would. When I fired the gun in the Evening hee thought that I had cleared

[195] **December 1670. The *Sweepstakes* before Baldivia.**
my guns then to fight him, which was when I set the watch the gun was fired. I asked him if they had any great ships in this Countrey. Hee said that there was seaven or 8 great ships at Lima that Carried fifty & sixty guns in a ship, But they never come this way. Some of them carry the silver and gold from Lima to Panama, And some of them trade to the Phillipine Islands and China, and to the Moluccas, and so for New Spain. There are hundreds of other ships and Barks of merchants, which have no guns, that saile to & fro on all these Coasts of Chili & Peru, & to Panama New Spain &c[a]. I asked if the [they] traded much to the Phillipine Islands, hee said the ships of New Spaine did trade much to the Island Lucon,[1] & to the haven of Manhelas,[2] and to China and other places.

This man Says that Chili runs no further southerly then the Island of Castro and Osorno, and the Countrey southward to Magelan Straits is called Patagona. I asked him the reason why it was called the Land of Patagona, hee sayd that there is men of great stature in the Land. I asked him how the ammunition is brought into those parts hee said by shiping [*sic*] alongst the Coast from Lima, and that it cannot bee brought by land well for mountains which lye between Peru and Chili, and that the Indians will take it if they meet with it.

I find that these Spaniards are ready to Rebell in case any opportunity should present by an Enemie that should take any of the Ports in Chili and possesse it (which might bee easily performed) and treat the Common sort of people kindly so as they may have hopes of Living more freely then now they do under their own Governours, and have the Liberty to trade, they would bee easily induced to come wholly in, and bring in with them all the trade of Chili, which would bee very rich, and in time the whole trade in that part of the world, in spight of all the Spanish force.

This man says that the fortifications are but ordinary on all the Coast of Chili, and that there are but few guns mounted in any of their forts, alongst the Coast. Hee says the Spaniards have a small Fort on the Island of S[t] Marys[3] and at Valparaiso.

I am Confident that the Natives would second any nation that should come into these parts against the Spaniards, and assist them much in beating of the Spaniards out of any of their Holds, which would soon bee done when once it were attempted, for the Spaniards will not fight against any people that use fire arms, for they cannot endure that sport, neither do they understand it, for the Indians here worst them if they meet them out of their Forts, they said so themselves to mee.

[196] **December 1670. The *Sweepstakes* before Baldivia.**
These people are too wealthy to fight being they have room enough to run away. And here is encouragement to make the greatest Coward on the earth to fight valiantly, for

[1] Luzon in the Philippines.
[2] Manila (14°34′N, 120°59′E), Luzon.
[3] Isla Santa Maria, in Golfo de Aruco (36°59′S, 73°32′W).

when hee wins the field his reward will bee gold and silver plentifull, and a pleasant and rich Countrey to bee Master of.

I asked the Indians which came aboard with the Spaniard this time how many Spaniards there were at Baldivia, they said no more then two hundred, and those were down at the Forts save only some to keep guard there.

I asked them if they had any gold seeing them have gold wyre in their eares, they said that they were servants to the Spaniards and had nothing, but the Indians in the Land have gold enough, and they are my friends, and the Indians ashore say so, and that wee are good men and give them things. I gave these poor Souls knives, scissers, beads, Jues trumps, and a small Looking glasse, they were very thankfull for them. I bad them tell the Indians of the

Land that I have many knives and glasses to give them. And that I will come again and Live with them, and that I am their friend. some of these Indians that I gave these things to were not Slaves to the Spaniards [*margin:* *] but lived near the Spaniard's Forts and their Caseque [cacique] make them Serve the Spaniards Sometimes a week and Sometimes a fortnight at a time, and then they go home again to their own dwellings. These Indians said that they would tell the Indians of the Land what I said, these Indians spake so much Spanish as my interpreters could tell what they said. None of us could speak their natural Language, or understand one word, they have a harsh Language and pronounce it in the throat as a Moor doth in Barbary.

These poor people live a miserable life under these Cruell Spaniards, for they have many blows with a Cudgell and but litle foode, they would willingly have stayed with mee and come for England but I could not consent that they should stay, by reason they were servants & subjects to the Spaniards. If they had been otherwise I would gladly have given them Entertainment.

— In a peaceable way of tradeing. —

I am of the opinion that English ships which are of force that need not feare the being surprised by Spanish ships, which might bee fitted out from Lima against them, might make great advantages in tradeing, all along the Coast of Chili from Castro til they come to Arica, with Cargos of such Commodities as would vend here, which will bee fine Linnens & silks, stokings [*sic*], Ribbons, laces, spice, woollen cloth, Looking glasses, Clocks and watches, Armes and all manner of commodities as are sold in London to Adorn houses, would bee sold here to the

[197] **December 1670. The *Sweepstakes* before Baldivia.**

Spaniards and Indians for ready gold and silver, for the Com*m*on people would trade in spight of their Governours, as what I perceive by them here, that if I had any Cargo of such Commodities and three or four ships that had been of some force, I might have sold the goods at what rates I would, alongst the Coast in several places to the Spaniards. And if I should but once have brought the Indians to understand, and to have commerce with them, without doubt I might have what quantity of gold I would in reason receive for all such goods as they would have a desire for, which would bee chiefly, arms, woollen cloth, and Iron tools as I suppose.

In case the English Nation should ever desire to send peaceably into this part of the world to Create a trade with the Natives and Spaniards It would bee convenient to send four ships. One of about thirty guns, one of twenty guns, one of sixteen guns and one pink of six guns, burden of ninety or a hundred tuns. Shee will bee a fitt vessel to discover the Coast and to ride in the day time near the shore and trade.

These vessels ought to bee firm and well fitted, well manned and provided with good boats and materials to build boats in the Countreys where they shall arrive at, once they come into the fair weather, which will bee when they are as farre as the Island of Mocha or St Marys. But to the southwards of these Latitudes the Countrey is stormy as it is in England, and the sea runs Lofty, So that it would not bee safe to have more boats thereabouts then what can bee stowed on the Decks.

I cannot tell but the natives in Magellan Straits may have gold great plenty when once they bee acquainted what it is good for, and that it will purchase them hatchets, knives, and the like. I can bee confident that there is either gold or Copper in the mountains about Port Famine, for two Indians made signs to my gold ring on my finger and pointed to the Inland hills, many times speaking and pointing. I would have had them gone with mee to have got some of the mettal, but they would not go with mee at this time, by reason they would try their knives and hatchets how they would Cutt sticks, being overjoyed with such Convenient instruments for their use in Cutting sticks, and to make bows & Arrows &c^a^. Also these ships might Cruse the South Land of Magellan Straits and discover what those people are, there are many people on that South land at the first narrow by the many fires and smoaks that I saw on the sides of the hills in the grasse, as you may see in my Large draught of the Straits of Magellan and in my Journal in passing it.

After those Ships have passed through the Straits into the South Sea, it will

[198] **December 1670. The *Sweepstakes* before Baldivia.**

bee best for to get twenty leagues off from the shore assoon as they can for the winds are much given to blow hard on the West quarter, and a great Sea comes with it, so having an offing it will bee convenient to hale in with the Land again, in the Latitude of fourty eight or thereabouts, if weather presents, And it is possible there may bee good harbours found on that coast for Entertaining of shiping, and the people there may have gold. There lies some Islands adjacent to the shore in the Latitude of 45°½ and the land is woody and high in the Latitude of 45°.

The Island of Socorro lies in about four Leagues from[1] the maine, And on the maine against the Island of Socorro there is the harbour of St Domingo.[2] It seems to be a good Port. It goes in between two high lands, and some rocks lies on the shore side at the mouth of it. And the land that lies on the West side of the Entrance is of a fair height and some woods growing on it. There is good Anchoring on the North East side of Socorro, in nine faddom and good Soundings between that and the main, and there is wood and fresh water on the Isle, and under the South East point of Narbrough Isle, which is about three leagues from St Domingo, to the westwards, there is good anchoring in twelve faddom for northerly & westerly winds there is much wood and some fresh water, this Isle is close to the maine. I would have discovered St Domingo but strong winds prevented mee, I was just before it in my boate and forced away.

[1] 'from' substituted for 'of' struck through.

[2] See above, pp. 494, n. 6; 615.

From St Domingo the shore may bee Coasted to the Island of Castro, And there lives both Spaniards and Indians, and they have much gold, And at Osorno, there they may bee sure to trade, And all along the Coast of Chili to Arica, and on the Coast of Peru. And from thence to the Coast of Nova hispania[1] and from thence to the northern parts of the kingdome of China or the Island of Japan, And so by Bantam,[2] they may return home to England. All this may bee performed in two year's time And the Peeces of eight which they receive of the Spaniards on the Coast of America will buy goods in those Eastern parts of China, Japan, Bantam, or in other places. These shipps ought to bee well furnished with netts for to take fish, and fowling peeces and haile shott, and good store of salt, whereby they may save Provisions, And they being industrious will never bee in any great want of foode, for on the Coast of Chili and Peru they will bee supplied with beefe and swine and flower good store, they having salt may provide for the future.

Also there is great plenty of fish to bee got with the Saine in Magellan Strait at Port Famine &c. and many sea fowles in most parts which are very good for refreshment for men, and they may bee salted up in Cask for

[199] **December 1670. The *Sweepstakes* before Baldivia.**

future provisions as I did at Port Desire[3] with seals flesh and Pengwins, which is good victuals salted for four or five months time, taking care to renew it sometimes with fresh Pickle, but more properly to bee Called new pickle. I would willingly bee one to bee employed in this designe, for I am Confident the Profits would bee great, which would bee made upon all com*m*odities with the Indians and Spaniards, And if a letter were procured from the king of Spaine to shew to his Governours in America to permit English ships to wood and water in these parts, it would bee a pleasurable voiage, for under the pretence of watering wee might see most parts of the Coast, and dispose of our goods at the better price, and sooner by much then otherwise, and bee in nothing so much danger.

It will bee best to saile out of England in the latter end of the month of May, or in the begining of June, and so touch at the Island of Maderas[4] and there take in wines &c^a^. for refreshment for the men. And from thence to the Isle of May and take in salt, but it is a bad time of the year for salt there. It would bee better to have that supplied in England. But however it will bee convenient to touch at the Island of St Iago, at Port Praya[5] and there to fill all their Cask with fresh water, and buy Cattel & oats for to eat at sea, as they have occasion to spend provisions they may kill them. A good bullock may bee bought for six peeces of eight at St Iago, and grasse to feed them, water may bee very conveniently filled at Praya. It is not safe for any European people to lye ashore at this Island, for it throws them into violent fevers and Calentures,[6] and so will the fruit of the Countrey if

[1] New Spain (Nueva España).

[2] Now Banten, Indonesia (6°01′S, 106°08′E), at the eastern entrance to Selat Sunda between Sumatera and Jawa.

[3] Puerto Deseado.

[4] Ilha da Madeira.

[5] São Tiago, Porto Praia.

[6] See above, p. 368, n. 1.

much of it bee eaten, prove dangerous to those that eat it, as it hath been experienced by the lives of many.

It will bee convenient to carry from hence Goats, Swine & Conies, male & female to put on shore in the South parts of the world to breed, which in time might prove very numerous, and bee mighty assistant towards that Navigation in the supplying of at Port San Julian,[1] and at Elizabeths Island[2] in Magellan Straits seeing the land is all grassy and fitt for such animals to live on, and without doubt would thrive well there or on any other Islands if not too rocky so there bee but food for them.

It will bee a very good seasonable time of the yeare to arrive on the Coast of America at Port Desire in the month of September or in the begining [*sic*] of October, for then the first of the Summer and Spring comes in there, and the weather is fair and warme, and the winds Inclinable to bee easterly and northerly, so as it will bee good passing the Straits, or to go to the

[200] **December 1670. The *Sweepstakes* before Baldivia.**

Southward, about all the South Land through Straits Lemair,[3] and so into the South and West Sea, which I believe is as good or a better passage into the South Sea then through Magellan Straits.

Also in the latter end of September and in October there is very good refreshment for men at Pengwin Islands by Port Desire with Pengwins eggs, and sea fowls eggs, very good at their first of laying which is at that time, but after that they are sate on & nought, also the Pengwins are at the best then. It will bee good to bee in the Straits in October.

A letter which I received from Lieu*tenan*t Armiger
which the Spanish Gentleman brought off to mee
the Last time hee came aboard the Shipp.

Sir,

You are desirous that I shall write more at Large but I find the inconvenience of it, for if I write much they make stop of the letters, for I know one that was never sent you, but there was nothing in it that I value who see it. As to what you desired of mee I know no more then you, But the reason why I am so desirous of your being gone off the coast is, I understand they have writ for ships to surprise you, and for our parts wee are very well satisfied with our Conditions, by reason it is upon so honourable an account. And do not doubt that ever wee will do any thing that shall bee dishonourable to our king or Countrey, And I pray take care to secure his Ma*jes*ties Shipp.

Wee are hitherto treated very Civilly, and are promised the like so long as wee are in their Custodyes, wee have found them very treacherous in doing that I think never Christians or Turks was ever guilty of. But let our Conditions bee what it can happen wee are well satisfied in suffering upon so honourable an account. I pray if you bee in England before us present our dutyes to our king and the Duke of York, and acquaint him with our Condition, So with our service and love to all our friends I rest,

St Peters fort December 21, 1670.

Yours to Command
Thomas Armiger.

[1] Puerto San Julián. [2] Isla Isabel. [3] Estrecho de Le Maire.

I pray do mee that honour as to send mee twenty dollars by this bearer, that wee may have money in our Pockets, I will see you satisfied, wee have received our Cloths and Chists and the things you were pleased to send to us.

A letter which I received from Mr Fortescue which was brought off by the Spanish Gentleman the second time hee came aboard:

[201] **December 1670. The *Sweepstakes* before Baldivia.**
Sir, These are to acquaint you that wee have received our things you sent us, and I thank you for my Gown and all your kindnesse shewed to mee this voyage. The governour of Baldivia desires you to spare him your small Pinnace for his use, and what the Carpenter will have for her my father[1] shall pay him in England. If hee do question that I pray pay him your self, and bee satisfied out of my wages that is due to mee. I Suppose Mr Wood will see him paid, which I desire him to do, for wee are both engaged to the Governour that you will send him the boat, if you do not go away before that the boat come ashore to us, and a boat can bee sent to you again. Wee will send you off what you demand either in moneys or wine of Chili, or honey or Tobacco. I pray send her, for it is for our goods. The Captain of the place hath a great desire for a Bulldog. I pray Sr send the dog ashore and I will send off any thing for him. This Capt*ain* have sent you a dish of green beanes. I pray Sir bee kind to him for hee is the man which have charge of us, & have been very kind to us. I pray send four or five dozen of tobacco pipes to us to give to the Governour of Baldivia and the Captain of this place, for they want them to smoak in for here is none to bee had.

Sir. you have gained the Love of all the Gentlemen here ashore for your noble use of them aboard the ship, which is for the honour of our king, & countrey. S*i*r you were pleased in your letter to desire mee not to bear up to the Spaniards one inch. S*i*r I thank you for your advice and love to mee, I scorn to do any thing that is dishonourable and beneath a gentleman, and a souldier, to gain my Liberty or all the riches that ever Baldivia did affoord for I value death no more then I do a pipe of tobacco, which is as plentifull here as dirt. Sir could I give you an account of what you desired in your last letter I would do it in spight of all the devills in hell. I pray desire Mr Wood to send mee his Razor, his case and all in it, to trim our selvs [*sic*] with and to send mee a cheese and my Case of Bottles & Brandy. Desire Capt*ain* Witson[2] to send the razor hee promised the fryer, So wishing you a straight return into England and my love to all my friends I remain,
[St Peters fort Baldivia.][3]

Sir your humble Servant
John Fortescue.

A note in Mr Fortiscues letter which hee sent to mee.
My duty to the king and the Duke of York &ca. If you do not make the best of your way off this Coast you will repent it for they have sent for ships to surprise you besides your

[1] It is possible his father was Captain John Fortescue who served in command of the *Colchester*, 1661; *Hind* see *Hound*, 1662; *Loyal Subject*, 1665; *Charles V*, 1667; *French Victory*, 1668, and was dead by 1688. Tanner, *Catalogue*, I, p. 351.

[2] It is not clear to whom this refers. There was no Captain Witson on board. It might possibly be a reference to John Wilkins who was in a position to have promised to send the friar a razor.

[3] The square brackets are in the original.

staying here signifieth nothing. I pray write us word if the Letters bee broke up or not, So god prosper you. John Fortiscue.

[202] **December 1670. The *Sweepstakes* before Baldivia.**
I had viewed the Letters when I received the gentleman, as I had before taken notice of the other letters, but I could not perceive that any of them had ever been broken open.

This Spaniard in his discourse asked mee if I did not set a Jew ashore at my first comeing in, when I sent the boat ashore in the Bay where the fresh water is. I told him I did not set any body ashore, I only sent in my boat to see if any people inhabited there. His answer was to mee yes you did set a Jew ashore, I asked him where the Jew was then, hee said hee could not tell, but hee heard say a Jew was set on shore.

I thought it not convenient to say any thing more concerning this matter for I do believe that hee had heard some talk of Don Carlos, and they take him for a Jew, for hee do much resemble a Jew in his Countenance.

The afternoon spent away and the evening coming on, it looked very cloudy to the sea board, and the wind blew fresh at West, I was doubtfull it would bee foule weather to night. I told the Spaniard I would make way to saile presently, and bee gone. I desired him that hee would get his goods which hee had bought of us into his boate, in a readinesse, and that I would put in all the things which I intended to send to my officers, I wrote these letters as followeth, to send by him to Lieu*tenan*t Armiger & M[r] Fortiscue.

A letter I sent to Lieutenant Armiger.

Lieutenant Armiger.
Your letter I received this day of the Spanish gentleman which I had with mee yesterday. I am glad to heare you are all in good health. I have sent you twenty peeces of eight and a peece of Linnen Cloth, and six dozen of tobacco pipes and the rest of your things you sent for, And I will give order that care bee taken of what is here, of yours. I pray acquaint the Governour that I charge the Losse of my voyage to him, to the value of two hundred thousand pounds, which the king of England will bee damnified[1] by his detaining of you and the rest, If it bee not the whole losse which will bee much more, And that I cannot stay here any longer, for it is like to bee Stormy weather to night, and I am now a weighing my Anchor to bee gone for England, without proceeding any further as towards China. I wish you much health and prosperity and a happy meeting again. It is possible you may bee in Europe before mee for your journey will bee nothing to mine. I hope you will ever containe honourable principles as you have done hitherto, I leave you to the protection of the Almighty and remain.
Your Loving friend John Narbrough.
Dec*ember* 21. 1670 aboard
the *Sweepstakes*.

[203] **December 1670. The *Sweepstakes* before Baldivia.**

A letter to M[r] John Fortiscue when I sailed.

Sir. I received your letter of this day's date and I am glad to heare from you and that you are in good health and I hope god will continue it with you. I have sent you five dozen of

[1] Damnify: to cause injury or loss, to wrong. *NOED*.

tobacco pipes, which is all I can spare, and I have sent you half a pound of Nutmegs, and I present the Captain which sent mee the beanes with a pound of Nutmegs, they are put in your case. I have sent you all the things you write for excepting the boat and the dog, and those things I cannot part from without great prejudice to my self, for in case I lose the boat I have no other to trust to, and the dog is the only thing wee have to kill us wild game in places where wee shall fall with it, for wee have a great many places to go to before wee shall arrive in Europe. If the Governour or Capt*ain* have such a desire for a Bulldog they should have sent off a Bull or two for fresh meat, and then wee should not have needed the dog hereafter. I pray present my respects to all the Spanish Gentlemen ashore, and especially to those four Captains which were with mee, and I thank Capt*ain* Mertenes[1] for the sugar & other things hee sent mee. I have sent him a paper of Nutmegs by this bearer for his Lady. I am at this instant a weighing my Anchor with intention to bee gone for Europe. I shall not medle with any Spaniard I meet with to do them any prejudice. So you may bee assuredly satisfied in that matter, that if the vice roy should Charge you with any hostility Com*m*itted by mee, it is false. I pray bee honourable in all your actions, and I do not question but to see you with Joy in England. I have sent Lieu*tenan*t Armiger and your self twenty peeces of eight by this bearer, who promises to bee civil to you. My hearty love to you and all the rest, with desires of all your healths, I leave you all to the protection of the Lord & rest.

Dec*ember* 21. 1670.

Your assured friend
John Narbrough.

I delivered these letters to this Spanish Gentleman which came aboard, who promised mee to deliver them and all the things I sent by him to my officers. I desired him that hee would acquaint the Governour that I charged two hundred thousand pounds Sterling to him for dammage in detaining my men, which would bee the cause of loseing my voyage, and that it would Certainly bee had of the king of Spaine in very short time after I shall arrive in Europe. And that it is not convenient for mee to waite here any Longer, in expectation of my men, for it is like to bee bad weather to night, and I shall endanger the Ship if I stay. This afternoon at four of clock my boat came from the shore where Don Carlos was landed, my men having been there all this day filling fresh water, and looking to & fro in the skirt of the wood & the shore, but no sign of D*on* Carlos or any body else.

[204] **December 1670 The *Sweepstakes* before Baldivia.**

Between four and five of clock this afternoon the Spanish Gentleman got all his things into the Canoa and his Indians, hee would willingly have stayed with mee, and so would the Indians also for the Spaniards are so Cruel to them.

At five of clock this man put off and rowed into the harbour, at his going from the ship I caused five guns to bee fired and I took leave of him desiring him to remember mee to my officers &c[a].

I sent my Lieu*tenan*t in my boat to tow the Canoa into the harbour's mouth, Shee being deep laden with the Jarrs of wine which I would not permit to come into the Ship,

[1] Captain Pedro Martens [Martines], the captain who came on board when the ship first arrived. See above, p. 512.

and also with goods which hee bought, And things hee carried to Lieu*tenan*t Armiger. My Lieu*tenan*t saw him safe in the harbour, tooke leave of him and came aboard & acquainted mee with it. My Lieu*tenan*t told mee that the time hee was towing in of the Canoa the Spaniards beat the poor Indians with a big staffe, most inhumanly, as it grieved him to behold it for hee would strike them on the head and beat them down, and call them all the evil names hee could expresse, with threatenings, And they took it patiently and said not one word but cryed when hee came away from them. I stayed before the Harbour til I saw the white flag which was out at the fort taken in, for then I perceived the Canoa was ashore or neare it.

About six of the clock I came away out of the Bay and plyed to windward to get out into the sea, the wind being at West and B*y* South, a fine fresh [*margin:* came away from Baldivia] gale. When I came away I fired five guns to take leave of my officers which I left, and of the forts. I had all the Colours flying, and the wast cloths[1] spread from stem to sterne, and the trumpets sounding. I caused the whole Company to give three shouts as is usual at sea, which might bee very well heard ashore and so I left the place.

I could not perceive ever a gun to bee fired in either of the forts in answer when I stood off. In S[t] Peters fort wee saw the flag flying but nothing in any other place.

The ground which I rode in was very good for Anchoring, it is a stiff blew clay under the sand which came up on the Anchor flooke,[2] neither could I perceive the least rub in my Cable. I got out of the Bay presently, for the Streame which alwaies sets out of the harbour helped mee off into the sea. I stood off to the Northwestward this first part of the night till I found how the weather would prove, for it looked very black and streaming to the Westward and some small rain fell, and the sea began to bee smoother, which is a sign of fair weather. My intent being if the winds permit mee, to sail along the Coast from Baldivia to the Southwards, and to go in at Castro and search that place to see for tradeing either with the Spaniards or the natives and from thence to

[205] **December 1670. The *Sweepstakes* under saile from Baldivia.**

discover along the Coast til I come to the Straits mouth at Cape Desiada, and so to passe through the Straits into the North Sea. I am in great hope I shall meet with the Indians in some parts of the coast and trade with them for gold, and at the Island of Castro I do not doubt but to trade with the Spaniards and at Orsorno, and to understand that part of the Countrey, And whether they live accordingly as the Spaniards informed mee here, which is that they have great want of Linnen &c[a].

Fair weather to night at ten of the clock and the Clouds brake away to the northwards the wind at West a fine Gale, the night coole & Star light, the moon near twenty dayes old so as the light was not much. At this time the mouth of Baldivia bare near SE&BS of mee three leagues off. No sign of any fire on the shore, for I ordered men to Look out all night for fires, in Case that Don Carlos should come to the place appointed, for sometimes hee would bee fresh in my thoughts, Yet I concluded while I was at anchor that hee could not bee any where but with the Spanish Governour. At 12 of clock tonight it rained and the wind came to the South West, a fine gale I plyed what I could

[1] See above, p. 511, n. 2.

[2] Anchor fluke.

to the Southwards, the sea finely smooth, no Soundings three leagues off the shore at seaventy faddom deep.

The names of the four men of my Company which the Spaniards detained at Baldivia, and I left them there.

Thomas Armiger. Lieutenant. aged near 40 years born in Norfolk.

John Fortiscue. Gent*leman*: aged near twenty seaven years. born in Kent.

Hugh Cooe. M*aste*r Trum[p]eter. aged near 28 years. born in Wapping.

Thomas Highway. Linguist. aged near 35 years. born in Barbary.

This Thomas Highway was born of Moor's Parents in Barbary, and is of a tawney countenance, hee speaks the Spanish tongue very clear, hee had lived with a Spanish Merchant at Cales,[1] But hee hath lived these ten years in England and is a Christian, and hath a dwelling house in London.

All these foure men were very healthy and sound and of a good presence and spirit which gives mee great hopes they will live to come into England and give an account of that Countrey, and of their travells.

Don Carlos the Spanish Gentleman which went out of England with mee stayd here at Baldivia. I cannot tell where hee was born nor Certainly what countreyman hee was but by his own report hee said hee was a Spaniard but hee looked like a Jew, hee was about 40. years of age, hee spake the Spanish & French tongues, and the English tongue, and did write them all very well, hee said hee had seen most parts of the world, and that hee had lived formerly in Chili. I could not understand what hee was, for hee knew

[206] **December 1670. The *Sweepstakes* under saile from Baldivia.**

nothing at all of a Sea man, or a Mathematician, or a souldier for hee could not manage a fowling peece, or any arms neither had hee any Religion, hee took but litle notice of any thing except for his victuals, all the time hee was along with mee in the voyage.

Cape Gallery which is at the outermost point towards the sea on the South side of the Harbour's mouth of Baldivia in Chili lieth in the Latitude of 39°57′ South of the Equinoctial.

And in the Longitude to the Westward of the Meridian of the Lizard in England seaventy degrees twenty minutes, according to my account which I kept of my sailing by Mercator's rules.

And Meridian distance to the Westward of the Lizard in England, one thousand, one hundred and eight Leagues, according to the plain C[h]art, which is false without the Ship saile exactly in the same course & traverses back again as Shee came out.

And in Longitude East from Cape Pillar at the West end of the Magellan Strait, two degrees & fourty minutes.

And in Meridian Distance East from Cape Pillar fourty two leagues nearest according to the plain Chart.[2]

[1] Probably Cádiz.

[2] Narbrough's Cape Gallery is actually Morro Gonzalo 39°51′S, 73°28′W from Greenwich, 68°16′W from the Lizard, or 1°12′E from Cabo Pilar.

Thursday the 22th day, this morning it proved very fair weather at day light, the wind being at Southwest a fresh gale the sea indifferent smooth I plyed to Windward alongst the Coast. I was about three leagues off the shore, somewhat to the Southward of Cape Gallery, out of sight of the people of Baldivia for the Cape I had shut in with the Land to[1] the Northward of the Harbour. At 12 of clock I had a good observation of the Sun with my Quadrant, and I found my self in the Latitude of 40°3′ South. As I estimated, I was within 3 or 4 leagues of the land, and sounded but could not have ground at 80 faddom. I was to the Southward of Cape Gallery. I stood in towards the shore, this afternoon I fetched in with the shore, by five of the Clock, I got ground at 60 faddom black sandy ground then fifty five faddom sandy ground about a mile off the shore. The shore side is rocky and some small sandy spots amongst the rocks, the land fair and high in large hills the green trees growing of a fine height downe the sides of the hills to the sea side.

I could not find a place to Anchor in. I stood off again and Plyed to windward, the wind being at South West a fine gale to night, the weather fair & temperate and a very healthy Aire. The Inland hills are of a good height & large, lying near North & South, along as the Coast lyeth, they are all grown over with woods as I perceive at a distance by my prospective glasse,[2] the land

[207] **December 1670. The *Sweepstakes* under saile from Baldivia.**

may bee seen ten Leagues if not more, in fair weather, from the top of the Ship[3] or on the quarter deck.

This evening I took the Sun's amplitude and I find the Compasse to have eight degrees ten minutes variation easterly and no more. I [*margin:* variat:East 08°10′.] stood off and in all night as I found the winds to favour mee, which were sometimes at SW and at SSW fine gales. I could not see any fires to night on the shore, or any sign of people to live hereabouts in this wooddy Land.

Fryday the 23^d^, fair weather this forenoon, but after it proved hazy and foggy, the wind was at West South West, a fresh gale. I stood in for the shore and had Soundings sandy ground at sixty faddom a mile off. I stood in still and shoaldened my water, I anchored in twenty faddom water, black sandy ground, in half a mile of the shore side, in a sandy Bay, Low to the sea side.[4] This Bay is about 4 Leagues to the Southward of Cape Gallery, to the Northward of this Bay the shore side is rocky, in most places, And there is no Anchoring between this Bay and Cape Gallery, And to the Southward of this Bay the shore side is all rocky for 3 leagues distance to a Low rocky point which I called hope point.[5] This sandy Bay is about a mile Long from one end to the other. The land is all grown over with woods, and the hills in the Land are of a fair good height. Against this sandy Bay the Land is indifferent Low in a valley, But all grown over with trees. There is a round Copling hill in the midle of the valley, about two miles from the sea side and that is also grown over with green trees. The countrey shows very fair to the view, as one sails along by it, But

[1] 'to' substituted for 'in' struck through.

[2] Telescope or spy-glass. The first known working telescope was invented in 1608.

[3] This probably refers to the main top, at the head of the main mast.

[4] Caleta Chaihuín (39°55′S, 73°36′W). See above, p. 292, n. 1.

[5] This is probably the point now known as Punta Galera. See above, p. 292, nn. 1, 2.

here is not many remarkable places, wherby a man may give particular directions to know this place. But the Latitudes of most places on this Coast is sufficient to direct to the place intended to, for the Coast lyeth nearest North & B*y* East, and South and B*y* West, inclining to the East and West.

I sent my Boat about this Bay and sounded, there is very good Soundings near the shore, 16, 14, & 13 faddoms, and so shoalden to eight, 6 and 5 faddom, fine red sand, about a Cables length off the shore. I do not find any tyde run in this Bay, to bee taken notice of, either ebb or flood. The tyde rises and falls perpendicular by the shore about 8 foot, and the flood comes from the Southwards. Where I rode the Southermost point of this Bay which I called Hope point Bore South West & B*y* South of mee, distant somewhat above two leagues.

I sent my Boat ashore with my Lieu*tenan*t in her to see if posssible hee could speak with any people, or discover whether any people lived here, my boat Landed on the South side of the sandy Bay, at a point behind the rocks where the least Suff [surf]

[208] **December 1670. The *Sweepstakes* at anchor in a sandy Bay.**

of the sea ran, for on all the coast the sea runs with a great Suff on the shore, so as it maketh bad landing for Boats on most places of this coast. After my Lieu*tenan*t and men got ashore, being sixteen in sumber, two Looked to the boate, and the rest travelled alongst the shore, into the sandy Bay and sometimes in the woods and other places to and fro where they could perceive any thing to appeare like habitations, or otherwise, so as it might bee worth their discovering.

Their Relation of this Place.

The shore side is rocky by the sea where the boat Landed, but a litle distance up the bank it is good black soile of Earth and all the sides of the hills are good earth, But grown all over with timber trees of an indifferent bignesse and height, some are a foot & half through their bodies, and about thirty foot Long and large spread tops. The major part of the trees are like Beech in the woods, and some like Maples, neither Oake nor Ash to bee seen, the brush woods prickly like Barberry bushes, the trees lean to the Eastward, being constantly Pressed with westerly winds, which blows hard out of the sea. I believe further into the Land the trees are larger and better, my men could not get into the woods a musket shot distance from the water side, the trees are so thick, & so much old wood under foot & shrubs which hindred them, they saw but the out skirts of the woods.

There is not a path to bee seen anywhere about this Bay or in the woods here grow several apple trees by the woods sides, & many green apples were hanging on the trees, near half ripe, the fruit is much like our winter fruit in England, the trees are not very Large but broad tops they seem as if they were planted there for in the woods there are no apple trees to bee seen.

Here grow many Long Canes such as are at Baldivia, here are three rivulets of fresh water, on the South end of the sandy Bay which run into the sea. My people made a fire by the woods side in the sandy Bay in hopes to have seen some answer of it by Indians, But none was made, for wee could not discern any fire or smoake to bee in the woods or hills all the day Long. But the smoake which my people made might bee seen eight or ten miles distance.

[1] The sea shore is normally the worst part of the country.

I suppose the natives cannot live here in these thick woods but more into the Land behind the hills the Countrey may bee Clear and a pleasant land to live in, for it lies in a fine Latitude for health, and it showeth to bee a pleasant Countrey in Land, by the fair appearance of the sea Coast, which is the worst ever.[1] On the rocks by the sea side there were many great Seales and sea fowles as gray gulls and Sea mews and Sea dyvers. No fish to bee Caught with hooks or any to bee seen neare the shore side amongst the rocks.

[209] **December 1670. The *Sweepstakes* under saile in the South Sea.**
No wild beasts seen or heard in the woods, some small birds like linnets in the woods, and some wood pidgeons, some gray doves and kites. No signe of mineral or mettal to bee seen on the shore, or any thing worth observation more then is related.

Night comeing on my boat came aboard I made way to get up my Anchor, the wind at South West and by South, a stout gale and some small raine. It was very foggy to seaward, & like to bee bad weather, and the wind to bee out of the sea.
This sandy Bay lieth in the latitude of 40°06′ S.
And in the Longitude from the Lizard in England 70°22′ West.
And in Meridian distance from the Lizard West 1108 leagues 1·6 mil*es*.
And in Longitude from Cape Pillar East 02°37′·8
And in Merid*ian* distance from Cape Pillar East 41 leag*ues* 1·4 mil*es*.

This evening near 6 of clock I weighed and stood off to sea the wind at South and B*y* West a fresh gale and thick fog and small drisling rain. I got in my boat and all things fitted in Case of foule weather. I kept up to the Southward what I could with intent to see in at the Island of Castro. At 12 of Clock to night it blew hard the wind came to the Southwest, I caused the topsails to bee handed, I stood off into the sea.

Saturday the 24th. This morning at one of the clock I stood off under my Courses the wind at SW and sometimes at SSW and blew hard and rained and thick foggy weather, the sea began to make lofty. I reckon my self three leagues North West from hope point at one of the clock. I sounded but could not get ground at seaventy faddom deep. At day light I looked out for land but could not see it the weather being foggy & small drisly raine. No observation to day of ☼.

From last night that I weighed my Anchor out of Sandy Bay til to day at 12 of the clock I make my true course to bee West and By North. Distance sailed 46 miles. Departure West 45 miles. Difference of Longitude 01°00′. Differ*ence* of Lat*itude* 00°09′. Latitude at noon by account is 39°57′ South.
Meridian distance from Cape Gallery West 15 leagues 1·6 mil*es*.
Longitude at noon from Cape Gallery West 01°02′·2.
Longitude at noon from the Lizard West 71°22′·2.
Meridian distance from the Lizard West 1123 leagues 1·6 mile.

Very foggy weather this afternoon and all night, this evening the wind veared to the West and blew hard. I tacked at five of clock and stood to the Southwards, under my Courses, a great Sea comes out of the Wester board. No fish or fowle to bee seen, no observations to bee had of the ☆ to night.

[210] **December 1670. The *Sweepstakes* in the South Sea Lat*itude* 40°45′ S.**

Sunday the 25th, hazy Gusty weather, the wind at WNW and rained much, I stood to the Southwards, sometimes my topsails set, and sometimes under my Courses. After divers courses made from Saturday Noon till to day noon I make my true Course to bee South and B*y* West 06°45′ westerly. Distance sailed 50·4 miles. Departure West 15·6 miles. Difference of Longitude West 00°20′·5. Diff*erence* of Lat*itude* 00°48′. Lat*itude* by acc*ount* 40°45′.
Meridian distance from Cape Gallery West 20 leagues 2·2 miles.
Longitude at noon from Cape Gallery West 01°22′·7.
Longitude at noon from the Lizard West 71°42′·7.
Meridian Distance from the Lizard West 1128 leagues 2·2 miles.
This afternoon the wind veared to the NorthWest & blew hard, I steered South-South West with an easie saile. I caused several running ropes[1] to bee taken downe, which were old and worne, and new ones to bee put up in their places. This evening one of the main shrowds broke at the head of the mast, which I caused to bee mended presently, the Ship rowles much the Sea comeing out of the West. I cannot deale with the land the weather is so Stormy, and the winds are so generally out of the sea. At nine of clock to night the wind shifted with raine & hail from the North West, to the South East, and it came to the South and blew hard, and rained I tacked and stood off West South West into the sea, with my Courses to get off the shore. Base rainy gusty cold weather all night.

Munday the 26th, hazy foggy Cloudy weather and rain the wind at South a stout gale a great Sea runs here which comes out of the South West I stood off WSW. After several courses made from Sunday at Noon til to day noon I make my true Course to bee South West & B*y* West 25° Westerly. Distance sailed sixty miles. Departure West 50 miles. Differ*ence* of Longitude West 01°07′. Diff*erence* of Latitude 00°33′. Lat*itude* by account at noon 41°18′ South.
Meridian distance from Cape Gallery West 37 leagues 1·2 mile.
Longitude at Noon from Cape Gallery West 72°49′·7.
Longitude at Noon from the Lizard West 02°29′·7.[2]
Meridian distance from the Lizard West 1145 leagues 1·2 mile.

Gusty dark weather this afternoon and rain and hail, the wind sometimes veared to the South West in showers and then came to the South againe. I stood off to the Westwards, being doubtfull of bad weather and of being imbayed on the shore, if it should overblow,[3] for I much feared my main mast. It being sprung in the partners, so much as I dare not Carry any stiff saile on it, and I had secured it what I could by fishing of it.

[211] **December 1670. The *Sweepstakes* sailing in the South Sea. Lat*itude* 41° &c[a].**
At ten of clock to night the wind came to the West, I tacked and stood to the Southwards, I stemmed SSW it blew hard.

[1] Running ropes are those ropes which run through blocks. These were presumably the ropes that were used to control the set of the sails.

[2] These two Longitudes have been transposed.

[3] 'It over blowes when we can beare no top-sailes', Goell, *A Sea Grammar*, p. 59. Thus Narbrough feared the wind would be so strong that he could not beat to windward off the coast.

[4] Gannets are not found in this area. These may have been Peruvian boobies (*Sula variegata*), which are the only boobies likely to be found in this area. Harris, *Seabirds*, p. 290.

Tuesday the 27th, rainy base weather the wind at West North West and blew stiffly, I stood to the SSW under a pair of courses, and sometimes a topsaile set. No fish or fowle to bee seen in the sea excepting some petterells and gray Gannets.[4] After several courses made from munday at noone till today noone, I make my true Course to bee South 41°15′ Westerly. Dist*ance* sailed 40 miles. Departure West 26·3 miles. Diff*erence* of Longit*ude* West 00°34′·5. Diff*erence* of Lat*itude* 00°30′. Latitude by account at noon is 41°48′ South.
Meridian distance from Cape Gallery West 46 leagues 0·5 mile.
Longitude at noon from Cape Gallery West 03°04′·7.
Longitude at noon from the Lizard West 73°24′·7.
Meridian distance from the Lizard West 1154 leag*ues* 0·5 mil*e*.This afternoon it blew hard at West, I stood to the Southwards with my Courses, and sometimes my topsailes set, as I could Carry them for wind. This afternoon at 5 of clock my main mast sprung in the partners of the gun-deck I was doubtfull that the mast would go by the board, and that I should bee in a bad Condition with the Ship, upon a Lee shore and not acquainted with the Coast, whereby I might put in for a harbour. All our desires were for fair weather and NE winds so that I might deale with the Coast, at Castro, for it grieved mee at my heart to think that I should lose the opportunity of discovering in at the Island of Castro & Orsorno when the weather prove fair, after all the care and troubles I have had in the voyage to get hither, for at Castro and at other places on the Coast of Chili, I do not question but to have Conferrence with the natives, and trade with them for gold. If it please god to send fair weather so as I can discover but a harbour to ride safe in with the Ship, for it is my earnest desire to discover this Coast, according to my Instructions, Wherby I may give his Ma*jes*tie and Royal highnesse satisfaction, and for the good of our nation hereafter, and that wee may live with reputation in the world. I caused the mast to bee well woulded[1] and shrouded with preventer shrouds,[2] & fished with an Anchor Stock, and so Secured as well as I could, and it seemed to bee indifferent firm, so as I may have some hopes when this weather breaks up. This night it blew hard & rained the wind came to the WNW. I stood to the Southward, I was forced to Carry what saile I could conveniently to keep off the Coast, for I do not reckon my self to bee above thirty five Leagues off of the Land. Base raw cold gusty weather all this Night.

[212] **December 1670. The *Sweepstakes* in the South Sea. Lat*itude* 43° &c[a].**

Wednesday the 28th, cloudy hazy weather the wind at West a stout gale I steer sometimes South and by West, and South South West, a great Sea comes out of the South West. My course made true from Tuesday noone til to day noon is S&BW. Distance sailed 106 miles. Departure West 20·7 miles. Diff*erence* of Longitude West 00°28′. Diff*erence* of Lat*itude* 01°43′ S. Latitude at noon by observation of ☼ 43°31′ S.
Meridian distance from Gape Gallery West 53 leagues 0·2 mil*e*.
Longitude at noon from Cape Gallery West 03°32′·7.
Longitude at noon from the Lizard West 73°52′·7.
Meridian distance from the Lizard West 1161 leagues 0·2 mil*e*.

[1] Woulded, see above, p. 173, n. 1.
[2] Preventer shrouds are additional shrouds to support those already in place.

Cloudy rainy weather this afternoon the wind at West I stood to the Southwards, sometimes my foretopsaile set and sometimes under my Courses, for I stretched along to the Southwards, that in case the mast should give way I might reach the Straits mouth, for I saw that it would bee no dealing with the coast with these winds if the mast were sound, rainy gusty weather tonight and some haile in showers. At ten of clock tonight it blew hard at WNW. I caused the head sailes to bee handed and the Ship to bee brought to try under her main saile and Mizzen, a great Sea came out of the South West, the Ship Labours very much, so as I was doubtfull the main mast would go by the board, for it cracked in the step, and fetched way, and broke the shrowds. I did what I could to prevent it with lashings and shores[1] between decks, and in the hould. I saw that I could not deale with the Land, and that lying a try would prove dangerous, I set the head sails and stood away to the Southward. At twelve of clock it blew hard.

Thursday the 29th, cloudy weather the wind at West sometimes and at WNW a stout gale, I stood to the Southwards, a great Sea came out of the South West. I saw three great Whales this Morning and five seales several Sea mues flying to & fro & petterells. After several Courses made from Wednesday noon till today noon I make my true Course to bee South. Distance sailed 73 miles. Diff*erence* of Latitude 01°13′. Latitude by obs*ervation* of the Sun 44°44′ South.
Meridian distance from Cape Gallery West 53 leagues 0·2 mil*e*.
Longitude at noon from Cape Gallery West 03°32′·7.
Longitude at noon from the Lizard West 73°52′·7.
Meridian distance from the Lizard West 1161 leagues 0·2 mil*e*.
Gusty rainy weather this afternoon and Cold, the wind veared this evening to the North West. I haled off South-South West by my Compasse.

[213] **December 1670. The *Sweepstakes* sailing in the South Sea.**

Fryday the 30th day Stormy weather with rain and hail the wind veared to the NNW and blew much wind, and a lofty Sea run. I brought the Ship to try under her main sail low set, & mizzen. I laid her head to the Westwards, I was in hopes it would prove fair weather, the wind vearing Northerly and that I might get an opportunity to deale with the shore, for I was shot to the Southwards of Castro, above sixty leagues by my account much rain and hail this forenoon. The Ship lies very easy in the sea now, for the rowling Sea comes right a head, so as Shee play[2] at it. No observation to day of the Sun.

After several courses from Thursday noon til to day noon I make my true course to bee South-South West. Distance sailed 100 miles. Departure West 38 miles. Diff*erence* of Longitude West 00°53′·3. Difference of Latit*ude* 01°32′ South. Latitude by account 46°16′ South.
Meridian distance from Cape Gallery West 65 leag*ues* 2·2 mil*es*.

[1] Shores (wooden props), in this case between firm parts of the vessel and the mast, to support it and prevent it moving between decks and in the hold.

[2] 'Play' normally refers to motion in the frame or planks. This could be a reference to the ship riding smoothly over the waves with a head sea and not rolling, since the mast could be well supported in a fore and aft direction, and the danger of losing it was consequently reduced.

Longitude at noon from Cape Gallery West 04°26′.
Longitude at noon from the Lizard West 74°46′.
Meridian distance from the Lizard West 1173 leag*ues* 2·2 mil*es*.
At 12 of clock to day the wind came to the West South West it being a hard gale, I weared[1] the Ship and Laid her a try with her head to the Northward. I reckon myself to bee about thirty eight leagues off the land.

This afternoon the master Carpenter of the Ship William Sedger by name came to mee into my Cabbin, and acquainted mee that the Main Mast cracked in the partners, on the gun deck, and that hee was doubtfull it would fall by the board. I went immediately & searched the mast in the well and about the partners where the old Crack was, And I found the mast broke short below the partners on the gun deck, and fetched such way at every rowle that I thought it would have gone over board and have torn up the decks. I forthwith caused all things as did any service in Gyeing of it to bee set toate,[2] and the Carpenter to get a fish on to it forthwith, which hee did. And with plank and Iron Crows,[3] wee made it as secure as wee could, hopeing it would stand to Carry the Ship into the Straits of Magellan, where I knew I might get strong fishes at Port Famin to secure it firmly, for I saw that I could not deale with the Coast in the Condition I was in, in any fair weather with any safety, where I was not acquainted, And to fall with the Straits mouth I do not question it with god's permission. My men are all in good health I prayse god for it, although our diet is but litle, for wee have not one mouthfull of bread in the Ship, Wee

[214] **December 1670. The *Sweepstakes* in the South Sea. Lat*itude* 47° S.**
have three ounces of flower for a man a day, and Seales flesh in lieu of Beef & pork, which is healthy food.

This afternoon at 7 of clock I had the mast made as secure as possible wee could, and all things in their places again, and the Ship pumped, which held very tight.[4] I caused all my men to bee Called aft to prayers. After wee had given the lord prayse for his great mercy in preserving us and humbly beseeched his protection & blessing to continue with us, I set the watch. Gusty rainy weather to night and some haile, the air cold, the wind at West-South West, & sometimes at West. I lay atry with the Ships head to the Northward, til towards morning, then the wind vearing northerly I laid the Ships head to the South Westward and tryed all night, towards morning it rained much and sometime hailed, the sea running lofty.

Saturday the 31th day, Cold rayny gusty weather the wind at WSW and at West sometimes in showers of haile. At 5 of clock this morning the wind came to the WNW. I caused the lead to bee hove to sound but could not get ground at eighty two faddom deep. I finding the wind inclineing Northerly I advised with my officers what they thought of the main mast, whether I might venture to deale with the shore, to discover some

[1] 'To wear' is to alter course away from the wind, which puts less strain on the masts and sails than tacking which is altering course into the wind.

[2] Caused anything that did service as a guy rope to be set taut.

[3] Crowbars.

[4] Did not leak.

harbour, wherby I might secure the Ship in it, and find out some means to supply our wants, and have Conferrence with the Natives, & trade with them for gold &c[a].

Their answer was, that I might do what I pleased, but there was no safety in the mast, and that they looked every rowle of the Ship it would fall over board, which would bee very dangerous, and especially if near the shore, with outerly winds,[1] and there is no Anchoring on the Coast, And that I knew the Condition of every thing better then them selves, and that it would bee safe to keep an offing whilest I had it, whereby I might recover the Straits, and not bee put upon the Coast with westerly winds, and have a Lee shore to deale with in this Condition. I considered that it would bee very dangerous for to bee taken with a Storm out of the sea, and lose the mast as I was sensible I should in any extremity of weather, for I haveing done all I could to preserve it I saw it was but slight to carry a saile on it, in Case I should bee forced so to do.

This morning the wind came to the NorthWest a stout gale. I caused the Ship to bee weared and set the foresaile and steered South West B*y* South for the Straits mouth, and to make the best of these northerly winds to gain

[215] **December 1670. The *Sweepstakes* in the South Sea. Lat*itude* 47° S.**
the passage before any bad weather should overtake mee. I was very much dissatisfied to leave this Countrey undiscovered, having taken so much pains to get to it, and the desire I ever have had to see it troubled mee much to part thus from it, and not perform my Instructions which I have from his Royal highnesse to discover the land in these parts of Chili. But I saw it could not bee done at this time, the Lord being pleased to ordain it otherwise for us, which wee hope is for our goods, and some other time more convenient to discover the Countrey then now which the Lord will appoint &c[a].

The wind blowing hard at NW I steered South-South West, I having made much Leeward way by driveing this last night. After severall courses made from fryday noon til to day noon, I make my true Course to bee South East 17°00′ easterly. Distance sailed 19·2 miles. Departure East 17 miles. Diff*erence* of Longit*ude* 00°22′ East. Differ*ence* of Latitude 00°09′. Latitude by account 46°25′.
Meridian distance from Cape Gallery West at noon 60 leagues 0·2 mil*e*.
Longitude at noon from Cape Gallery West 04°04′.
Longitude at noon from the Lizard West 74°24′.
Meridian distance from the Lizard West 1168 leagues 0·2 mil*e*.
This afternoon it blew hard at North West, and rained. I steered South West and by South, by my Compasse this afternoon & to night.

Here are several sorts of Porpose fish in these seas, some like ours in Europe and some Pied white and black, and some gray, and large ones. Rainy weather to night, no observation to bee made of the starrs.

Sunday being the first day **of January 167$^{0}/_{1}$.** Raw cold cloudy weather and rain and some haile, the wind at North West a stout gale and a great Sea. I was much afraid I should lose my Mainmast, it fetched such way, and broke the spikes, that fastened the fishes with working. I steered SSW to ease the Ship from rowling what I could. After several courses made from yesterday noon til to day noon I make my true course to

[1] Winds blowing from out to sea.

bee South 39°00′ westerly. distance sailed 105 miles. Departure West 66 miles. Differ*ence* of Longitude 01°37′·4. Diff*erence* of Lat*itude* 01°22′ S. Lat*itude* by acc*oun*t 47°47′ S.
Meridian distance from Cape Gallery West 82 leagues 0·2 mil*e*.
Longitude at Noon from Cape Gallery West 05°41′·4.
Longitude at Noon from the Lizard West 76°01′·4.
Meridian distance from the Lizard West 1190 leagues 0·2 mil*e*.
This afternoon the wind veared to the North and blew hard and rained. I

[216] **January 167⁰/₁. The *Sweepstakes* sailing in the South Sea.**
steered away South and B*y* East by my Compasse which is but South allowing the variation. This evening one of my Company named Richard Earle a Sea man fell off of the main shrowds in to the Sea And was drowned, hee was born in Woollwich, aged 28 years, a waterman by profession. Much wind at North, I steered South all night having only the foresaile low sett, to ease the Ship.

Munday the 2[d] day, very Stormy weather the wind came from the North to the West, and to the South West, and blowed so hard as it forced mee to hand the foresaile, and bring the Ship to try under my mizzen and staysaile, with her head to the Southward. In rowling one of the main shrowds broke, and the main mast fetched much way, did I what I could to prevent it. Course made true from Sunday noon til to day noon is South. Distance sailed 88 miles. Diff*erence* of Lat*itude* 01°28′ S. Latit*ude* by acc*oun*t 49°15′ S.
Meridian distance from point Gallery West 82 leagues 0·2 mil*e*.
Longitude at noon from point Gallery West 05°41′·4.
Longitude at noon from the Lizard West 76°01′·4.
Meridian distance from the Lizard West 1190 leagues 0·2 mil*e*.
Stormy weather this afternoon, the tiller broke short off in the rudder head. I caused a new one to bee fitted which I had spare by mee. It blew hard all night, I lay a try with the Ship's head to the Southward.

Tuesday the 3[d] day rainy gusty weather the wind West South West I set my courses this morning at day light and steered away South-South East, two of my main shrowds broke, I shipped much water over the wast, which filled my boats, and forced the planks from the timbers, the foresail split, I caused the other to bee brought to the yard. The standing rigging and running, tows and wears much, the ship work much in all her upper work, great showres of haile today. After driveing and sailing from munday noon til to day noon, I make my true course to bee SE&BS and my distance run 62·3 miles. Departure East 34·7 miles. Differ*ence* of Longitude East 00°53′. Differ*ence* of Lat*itude* 00°52′ S. Latitude to day by observation of the Sun 50°07′ South.
Meridian distance from Cape Gallery West 70 leagues 1·5 mil*es*.
Longitude at noon from Cape Gallery West 04°48′·4.
Longitude at noon from the Lizard West 75°08′·4.
Meridian distance from the Lizard West 1178 leagues 1·5 mil*es*.
This afternoon I steered away South, the wind at West and sometimes at West-South West, a great Sea runs in hillocks breaking as if a Current

[217] **January 167$^{0}/_{1}$. The *Sweepstakes* in the South Sea Lat*itude* 50° &c[a].**
or tyde set to windward, which I have not found in this sea by any of my observations. This evening the wind came to the West North West a fresh gale, and so continued all night. I kept my course to the Southward, SBE by my Compas.

Wednesday the 4th day, indifferent fair weather, the wind at North West, and sometimes WNW a fine gale, I kept my Course South. some porpose fish seen to day, and some whales, and sea fowles, many litle petterells. This morning I took the Sun's amplitude, and find the Compasse to have 10°28′ variation easterly.

My Course made true from tuesday noon til to day noon is South. Distance sailed 84 miles. Difference of Lat*itude* 01°24′ South. Latitude by good observation of ☼ on the meridian 51°31′ South.
Meridian distance from point Gallery West 70 leagues 1·5 mil*es*.
Longitude at Noon from point Gallery West 04°48′·4.
Longitude at Noon from the Lizard West 75°08′·4.
Meridian distance from the Lizard West 1178 leagues 1·5 mil*es*.

This afternoon the wind came to the West South West, I kept my Course South and B*y* East by my Compasse. This night it fell foggy and some small rain, the wind at WSW and at West, a fresh gale, a great rowling Sea comes out of the South West. I reckon my self to night at twelve of clock to bee in the Latitude of 52°15′ S And about eighteen leagues off the land. I brought to and sounded but could not get ground at 78 faddom. I filled the sailes and kept on my Course SBE by my Compas, and good looking out &c[a].

Thursday the 5th, foggy weather and small rain, the wind at WSW a stout gale sometimes, I steered my Course SSE by my Compasse, til 8 of the clock this morning, then it proved very thick weather and rained. I caused the Ship to bee layd by with her head to the Southward, til the weather cleared up, for I reckoned my self to bee in the Latitude of the Straits mouth, and about twenty five leagues to the Westward of it. If neither Current or tydes have put mee out of my reckoning, which I have not perceived either Current or tyde to bee prejudicial in these seas to Navigation. The weather being dirty and foggy I am unwilling to beare away til it prove clearer, so as I may see before mee. No observation to day of the Sun.

[218] **January 167$^{0}/_{1}$. The *Sweepstakes* in the SSeas. Lat*itude* 52° S.**
my Course made true from wednesday noon til to day noon is South & B*y* East. Distance sailed 82 miles. Departure East 16 miles. Difference of Longitude East 00°25′·7. Diff*erence* of Lat*itude* 01°20′. Latitude by account at noon 52°51′ South.
Meridian distance from point Gallery West 65 leag*ues* 0·5 mil*e*.
Longitude at Noon from point Gallery West 04°22′·7.
Longitude at Noon from the Lizard West 1173 leag*ues* 0·5 mil*e*.[1]

At twelve of Clock today it Cleared up So as I could see 3 or 4 leagues the wind at West and B*y* South a fresh gale. I sounded but could not get ground at sixty faddom. I caused the head sailes to bee filled and steered away for Cape pillar East and B*y* North, by my Compasse. At 6 of clock it proved foggy and thick, I brought the Ship to, and lay driveing

[1] This is an error. The Longitude difference has been omitted and the meridian distance inserted in its place.

in expectation of clear weather to beare in with the Land. I sailed this afternoon from 12 of clock til 6 of clock seaven leagues East.

The first part of the night it rained, the wind at WBS a fresh gale, the swell of the sea comes out of the South West. At ten of clock I caused the mates to sound, but Could not have ground at sixty five faddom. It Cleared up I filled the head sailes, and bore in with the Land, E&BN half a point northerly, to make Cape Pillar or Cape Desiada, the wind at West South West, a good gale. At twelve of clock to night I judged my self in the Latitude of 52°56′S and near 14 leagues from *Cape* Pillar.

Fryday the 6th day, hazy foggy weather this morning, the wind at West-South West a stout gale. I stood in for to make the 4 Islands which I called the Isles of direction, or to make Cape Desiada, my Course was ENE by my Compasse. The nights being but short & light, for the moon being near the full I could see at some clears a league before us.

At 4 of clock this morning it being fair day light I caused the lead to bee hove, but could not get ground at eighty faddom. I reckoned my selfe about ten leagues from Cape Dessiada, and in the Latitude of 52°53′ S.

A litle past 4 of clock it cleared up in the East horizon, wee looked well abroad and saw the four Isles called the Directions, which lieth at the mouth of the Straits, NNW from Cape Dessiada, distant from it about eight leagues.

These Islands make in 4 Homm*accos like haycocks when I first saw them, they bore NE. of mee Distant about 4 leagues. They lye in the

[219] **January 167$^{0}/_{1}$. The *Sweepstakes* Entering the Straits of Magellan.**
Latitude of 52°42′ S.[1]
[*margin:* 3*] At five of clock the Islands bare North of mee, distance 3* leagues off, I sounded but could not get ground at seaventy faddoms. I saw Cape Desseada. It cleared up for the fog was much on the hills, the Cape bare East South East of mee, Distant neare 8 leagues, the tops of the ragged hills or rocky Spiers were Clouded, with the flying fog, so as I could not see the Cape sooner, for in clear weather the land at Cape Pillar & Cape Desseada may bee seen fifteen or sixteen leagues it is so high and ragged.

I steered for Cape Piller East & B*y* South, the wind at WSW a fresh gale, a great homeing Sea[2] runs here, which came out of the SW. I saw the sea break upon broken ground which lieth at least foure leagues from the point of Cape Dessiada, West into the sea, and much sunken[3] rocks and points of rocks above water, which the sea breaketh terribly on, these lyeth off of Cape Desseada about two leagues, and a league and some not half a mile off, very dangerous.[4]

As I came nearer the Straits mouth I raised the Land, on the North side by Cape Victory, and the broken Islands within the Straits, which I called Westminster Isles and

[1] The Islotes Evangelistas lie in 52°24′S. See above, p. 273, n. 6.

[2] See above, pp. 335, n. 2; 376, n. 1.

[3] 'broken' struck through and replaced by 'sunken'.

[4] These are now known as Rocas Apóstoles, named 'Judges Rocks' on the 'Royal Map' and 'Sloane Map' (Foldout, Plate 5).

[5] These are now known as Roquerío Buena Esperanza, fringing Grupo Narborough to the westward of Grupo Westminster and Islas Lawyers.

the Lawyers Isles, they make ragged in hillocks at the first sight.[5] At 9 of clock Cape Pillar bare South of mee distant about a mile and a half from mee. I saw the land on the N side of the Straits it made like Islands very ragged and high in Peeked tops, and white with snow, here was much snow on the tops of the ragged mountains, on the South side. The 4 Islands were out of my sight by 7 of clock this morning, for I made fresh way in it, being a brisk gale of wind at WSW and no tyde or Current as I could perceive set either in or out of the Straits, so as to prejudice Navigation.

After several courses made from thursday noon till to day[1] at Nine of the Clock, Then Cape Pillar at the entering bare South of mee, Distance near a mile and a half, I make my true course to bee East. Distance sailed 60 miles. Differ*ence* of Longit*ude* East 01°39′·4.
Latitude by my account now is but 52°51′ South.
And formerly my account of the Latitude of this place was 52°58′ South.
Meridian distance at 9 of clock from Point gallery W 35 leag*ues* 0·5 mil*e*.
Longitude from Point Gallery West 02°43′·3.
Longitude at 9 of clock from the Lizard West 73°03′·3.
Merid*ian* Distance from the Lizard West 1153 leag*ues* 0·5 m*ile*.
I find but very litle tyde or Current in this sea of *Mare del Zur*, for I am but three minutes of Longitude out of my account in sailing between Cape Gallery and Cape Pillar forwards & backwards.[2]

[220] **January 167$^{0}/_{1}$. The *Sweepstakes* in the W end of Mag*ellan* Straits.**

[*blank space*][3]

At any time if thou hast a desire to enter the Straits of Magellan at the West mouth It will be safest in my opinion to beare in for the land in the Latitude of 52°50′ South,[4] and then thou will see the 4 Isles of Direction, which lye before the mouth of the Straits somewhat towards the North side, they lye North North West from Cape Pillar neare 8 leagues Distance. These Islands may bee known for there is but foure of them, and they bee but of an Indifferent height, and but small, and bare irregular rocks, and they bee near together, the easternmost Isle is near a mile distant from the other three, And it is peeked up like a Sugar loafe,[5] the sea breaks much on these Isles, with westerly winds. &c[a].

Cape Pillar is the steep point of rocks on the South side of the Straits mouth, at the entering of the Straits. Cape Desseada is the westerly point, for it falleth off from Cape Pillar wear South West and it is distante about two leagues one from the other which is the fall of the land between these two Capes. For at the point of Cape Desseada the land at the South side of the Cape trents off to the South-South Eastwards, all high ragged rocky mountains what I saw of it. At the Pitch of Cape Desseada there lyeth many scattered rocks, which are above water, and sheweth like the

[1] 'noon' struck through.
[2] Cape Gallery, which lies 2°40′ east from Cape Pillar.
[3] The blank space approximates to 19 lines of text.
[4] This is too far south, since the Islands of Direction (Islotes Evangelistas) lie in 52°24′S.
[5] Now Islote Pan de Azúcar.

[221] **January 167$^{0}/_{1}$. The *Sweepstakes* in the W. end of Magellan Straits.**
ruins of old houses, and there are ledges of sunken rocks which lyeth neare four leagues off the Cape West, the sea breaks much on them, they are dangerous, they lie in the Latitude of 53°10′ S by my reckoning.

I called these rocks the Judges[1] they are neare ten leagues distance S&BW from the Isles of Direction, so broad is the first opening of the Straits, for when thou canst but once see the Land to make it there is no danger. But a stranger that shall passe out of the South Sea, and had not passed the Straits before, will find it very difficult to passe the Straits from the West to the East. For at the first entrance into it out of the South Sea as wee Call it, there are many openings and sounds on the North side, which seem fairer for a passage then the Straits it selfe doth, therefore it is best to keep the South side fair aboard all along from Cape Pillar, which is the point at the entrance. The Course will bee East & by South, for a mile or two, and then ESE and SEBE, so the channel lyeth to Cape Quade, which Cape is on the North shore, distant from Cape Pillar near thirty leagues. All the Straits from Cape Pillar to Cape Quade there is no ground to bee got in the Channel, at two hundred faddom deep, and the shore is steep to the rocks sides. There lieth many small Isles and rocks close by the shore on the South side, and there is many Sounds, Coves, and harbours[2] on the South side of the Straits between Cape Pillar and Cape Quad, and the land is very high & irregular in peeked rocks all along. I cannot say but all the South side may bee Islands, and these as I take for Sounds may bee passages between them. The South land is all a desolate mountainous rocky Countrey, from Cape Desseada to the Eastward, until it come opposite to Port Famine, and much snow lieth on the mountains. Here is wood growing in many places on the Lower parts of the hills, and much fresh water runs into the sea, in the Sounds; and many mussels grow to the rocks which may bee gathered at a low water.

The North side of the Straits from Cape Victory all along to the Eastwards to Cape Froward is all ragged rocky mountainous desolate Countrey, many high rocky Islands, and small rocks, and sunken rocks lieth on the North side of the Straits at the coming in out of Mar del Zur; Fifteen leagues in distance into the Straits to the Eastward, there runs great Sounds and waters into the north land which shew like a passage more then the Strait doth, there is no safety for a Ship to keep the North shore aboard in

[222] **January 1670/1. The *Sweepstakes* Entering the W End of Mag*ellan* Straits.**
this part[3] for here lieth so many Islands and rocks, and if the weather prove foggy and thick, a man may mistake the right Channel, and steer in amongst the broken Islands, & rocks, so farre as to endanger his Ship, if the wind bee westerly as it is for the most part of the Winter there, and very foggy and thick.[4]

[1] See above, pp. 274, n. 5; 571, n. 4.

[2] Illegible word deleted.

[3] 'of the Strait' struck through.

[4] This is probably a reference to the entrance to Canal Smyth and Bahía Beaufort (52°50′S, 73°55′W), which lie north of Isla Tamar in the middle of the channel. The channel passes south of Isla Tamar and reduces in width from about 14 to 7 miles. A vessel following the north shore might easily pass north of Isla Tamar and end up among islands and rocks, out of the Strait itself, in a very dangerous position and unable to make her way back against a Westerly wind.

Here are many Sounds & Coves on the North side between Cape Victory and Cape Quade, but how farr they run into the land I know not. I wanted a sloope or some other small vessel to discover these Sounds, and many other places in the Straits which I would gladly have seene. The North land is very ragged and bare rocks, and but small store of wood growing on it, from Cape Victory to Cape Quad. And from Cape Quad to Cape Froward there grows a great deale of wood, on the sides of the hills, and very thick in many places and indifferent large timber like beech, & some Juniper trees, and the trees which have the strong barke, good fresh water in many places, but litle other sustenance. My Large draught sheweth the whole Course of the Straits.[1]

At nine of clock this morning I entered the Straits, for then Cape Pillar being South of mee I could not get ground at seaventy faddom, the water being indifferent smooth I brought the Ship to and hoisted out the boats the wind being at West a stout gale, the land very foggy & much snow lying on the tops of the peeked mountains. It rained much this forenoon & very cold more then it is at Sea, for the Cold* comes off of the snowy hills which causeth the Straits to bee so cold in this West part more then the East part, there being no snow but in winter time, the land being grasse land & dry.

At 12 of clock to day I was shot near four leagues within the Straits, I kept fair by the South side in half a mile of it, I found very litle tyde or Current to set into the Strait. My Course being East & B*y* South I passed by Tuesday Bay, which is on the South side two leagues within Cape Pillar, Eastward.[2] I went along the shore side in my Boat to see how the shore lay. I passed by a Sound which lyeth about three leagues to the Eastward of Tuesday Bay.[3] I would have put into it with the Shipp & anchored, but could not, the wind blew right out of it, and it was mighty deep water at the mouth, for I could not get ground.

It proved very foggy this afternoon and rained, I stood close under the shore with the Ship, and got into an open Bay, and plyed to & fro in it til I found a place to Anchor in, which was but a small spot that I

[223] **January $167^0/_1$. The *Sweepstakes* Entering the W. end of Mag*ellan* Straits.**
found just within the point. I anchored in fourteen faddom water, sandy gravelly ground, close to beds of Rock weeds, I was not above a Cables length and a half from the West shore.[4] In this Bay the point is a high rocky hill, and then Low to the other land, if it bee not an Island. This Bay have four or five rocky Islands in it, some have green bushes growing on them, this Bay have three rounding Coves in the South West Co*rner of it, and in the South part of it there runs up a Sound half a mile broade and mighty deep water, but how farre I know not. It is likely it run through the land into the sea, & so do many more. The land here is all rocky and mountainous, the shore side is steep to, like wharfs, all rocky, and a swelling Suff [surf] runs against it. These places are dangerous for Ships to ride in til a man get acquainted with the anchoring places, for the water is very deep, and the wind blows Cruelly in Gusts sufficient to oversett a ship, which doth

[1] Probably either the 'Sloane Map' or the 'Royal Map' (Plate 5, Foldout).

[2] Now Puerto Misericordia, lying 4½ miles east of Cabo Pilar. See above, p. 272, n. 8.

[3] Now Bahía Trujillo, leading to Bahía Tuesday.

[4] This anchorage is in Bahía Valentina (52°56′S, 74°15′W), close east of Cabo Valentina, and is shown on the 'Royal Map' and 'Sloane Map' (Foldout, Plate 5) named Island Bay. Only the 'Royal Map' has an anchor symbol.

endanger the breaking loose of a ship; and to drive ashore, if shee bee cast the Contrary way. Yet here is very safe rideing in many places and good ground.

The water rises and falls about eight foot perpendicular, the tydes soaketh in and out but slowly. This afternoon I went ashore in the Bay but could go but a litle way, the land being so irregular and rocky, and steep cliffs, the whole Land is a meer rock of a kind of hard gray marble, and some peeces of White marble. No mettal or mineral to bee seen by us, or any thing else of worth. This Bay I called Island bay, for the Island which lyeth in it. This Bay is on the South side of the Straits about 7 leagues to the Eastward of Cape Pillar, into the Straite. Between Cape Pillar and this place there is Tuesday bay, and next a Strait Sound, and next the Sound a small Bay, and then this Island bay,[1] just about a steepe high bluff point. On the face of this is a hollow place like a porch of a great church &c^{a}. in the rock, and the rock over hangs aloft. In the hollow place of this point many sea fowles as dyvers and Shags have their nests, and breed there, so it may bee knowne.

Here grow thick shrubby bushes on the Lower land, which have many berrys like whorts growing on them. These bushes grow on a mossy loose earth which lyeth four or 5 foot thick on the rock, these bushes will serve for fewell. Here grows also long sedgy grasse very thick, many geese & ducks do make their nests and breed in it, and other sea fowle, here are ducks and white & Pied brant geese, and many gray gulls, and Sea mews, and sea dyvers,

[224] **January 167^{0}/$_{1}$. The *Sweepstakes* in Magellan Straits.**
And Pengwins in the water. I could not see any people now, but people have been here, for I saw where they had made fires, and made an Arbour, here are Mussels & limpits on the rocks, as for fish I saw none. I rowed two miles up the Sound, and would have gone further but it rained so much & blew so hard as I dare not bee absent from the Shipp. The water is mighty deep up in the Sound. At night I got aboard my Sea men were joyfull to see mee, for they were afraid that the Ship would have broke lose, in the time of my Absence. Much rain to night, & foggs, the wind at WSW a stout gale all night I rode fast in smooth water, having the point in the North West of mee.

Here is a great deale of fresh water Comes running down the sides of the bare rocky mountains, into the salt water. Many whales spouting to and fro in these bays and Sounds, and some Seales on the rocks. This part is very desolate and a meer Chaos, &c^{a}.

Saturday the 7th day, Cloudy foggy weather and small raine, the wind at West a stout gale, the Air cold and the wind sharp. At four of the clock this morning I caused the master to weigh the Anchor, which was immediatly performed, and I stood out of the Bay into the Straits, for where I rode a musket [shot] to the Eastward was a ledge of rocks, and a spot where rock-weed grow, but there is five faddom water[2] on it at a low water. It is gravelly ground. When I was out of the Channel of the Strait I steered away East and B*y* South, by my Compasse, which is near ESE by the true Compasse, for the Compasse varieth here ten degrees easterly if not more.

[1] See above, p. 300, n. 5.
[2] The word 'water' is repeated in the original.
[3] Now Paso Largo.

Very foggy weather most part of this day and the wind at West a fine gale. I steered all along in a mile of the South shore, for Cape Munday. At ten of clock I came into the narrow reach of this West part of the Strait, which I call long reach.[3] It lieth North West & By West and South East and By East nearest, for twelve leagues distance. The Land is high and rocky on both sides and Barren the hills having much snow on them. Some shrubby bushes growing green amongst the lower rocks. The Strait in this reach is not above five miles broad from side to side, No ground to bee got in the Channel, the water is mighty deep and the shore side is steep to. But here is many small Islands lieth close to the shore, on both sides. Here is no danger but what lyeth above water, and neare the shore on all this part of the Straits. Here are many Sounds & harbours

[225] **January 167⁰/₁. The *Sweepstakes* at Anchor In Island Bay.**

and Bays and Coves, on both sides, but most are on the South side, for there are Sounds, and Bayes & Coves &c[a]. at every mile or two mile's distance, or a league's distance, all the way from Cape Pillar til one come opposite to Cape Froward. I believe many of them many bee secure roads for Shiping [*sic*]. I would have sent my boat into them to have discovered what they were, but it was such thick weather that I was unwilling to bee without her, so I have but litle knowledge of them more then seeing the mouths as I sailed by them. At 6 of clock this afternoon I passed by Cape Quad. Here the Strait sheweth as if there were no passage, for the Cape shutteth in with the other Land, which is on the South side.

At eight of clock this evening I anchored before the place called Batchellours river,[1] in nine faddom water cleare sandy ground, two Cable's length from the shore. Here is very good Cleane sandy ground before this River, and good Anchoring in six, 7, 8, or 9, or 10, or 11 faddom, a fine birth from the shore, and good rideing with Westerly winds and Northerly winds the worst wind is a South wind for it blows right on the shore. But there cannot go much Sea here for the Strait in this reach is but two leagues broad.

This Batchellours river is near five leagues to the Eastward of Cape Quade, and two leagues to the Eastward of S[t] Jerom's Channel on the North side. The tyde runs of an indifferent strength in this place, both ebb and flood. It sets in and out of S[t] Jorem's Channel. It rises and falls about eight or nine foot perpendicular. Here is not above ten foot water at a high water at the going in of Batchellours river. This river is a good harbour for Barks & Sloops or the like. This river lieth in a valley and a fine grove of green trees grows on the West point at the entrance, here is very good fresh water, and a good place to wood at, the Indian people or Natives frequent this place often, for here are many Arbours which are their houses. Calm weather to night and foggy, I rode fast the Ship being mored.

Sunday the 8th day Calm weather, and a fair sunshine and warme. This morning at day light I went into Batchellours river with my boate and twenty men with mee I rowed up the Creek or River four miles which was the furthest wee could get the boat, and it being a high water, the river ends in a small Creeke which comes out of a Lake of standing fresh water, in a

[1] This is Rada York (53°34′S, 72°19′W), where Río Batchelor flows into the Strait. It is named 'York Road' on the 'Royal Map' and 'Sloane Map' (Foldout, Plate 5).

[226] **January 167$^{0}/_{1}$. The *Sweepstakes* before Batchellors River at Anchor.**
valley amongst the hills. I made the boat fast and wee all marched into the land five or six miles, which was the farthest wee could get for the hills, riseing very steep and mountainous and the woods impenetrable. Wee made several fires but could not see any people, or any signe of them so farre in land. No beast or any Creature to bee seen, many small streams of fresh water comes running from the snowy mountains, with great falls from the steep rocks. Wee did look in many places of the Earth, and in the streams where the water ran downe for gold, &c[a]. but could never see any or any kind of mettal or mineral. Here are many small red berryes, much like whorts growing on the bushes, very good to eat.[1] The grasse land is very loose and boggy, the Rocks are a kind of white Marble, the trees are such as grow at Port Famin, here are small Juniper trees.[2] To night I got aboard, calm weather, I rode fast with the Ship.

Munday the 9th day, litle wind this morning at East and foggy. I manned my boat, and went to over to the South side into a Bay which is neare six leagues from Cape Quad, to the Eastward, it is almost opposite Batchelours river, but somewhat easterly. I called this Bay Whales bay,[3] for here were many whales spouting to and fro in it. I found it a deep water bay for I could not get ground at eighty faddom in the Bay, but there are many close Coves and places like docks safe for Ships to lye in, and to more [moor] to the trees between foure. These Coves are on the East side of the Bay, also in this Bay there are four or five small rocky Islands. Here are many good mussles in these Coves, of five and six inches long & well meated and much pearle in them, the mussles are to bee got at a low water. I laded my boate with these mussles and found them to bee good food. The water Rises & falls here about eight foot. It raineth much here, for the mountains are high on this part of the Straits, and generally Covered with snow, fresh water runs down in many places, on the sides of the hills; much wood groweth here, the trees are much like beech and Bay trees, and here grow many large Juniper trees, for the earth is poor and boggy and rotten which lyeth above the rocks. Many Indians or Natives of the Countrey frequents this Bay.[4]

[1] *Empetrum rubrum*; see above, p. 264, n. 4.

[2] Probably *Pilgerodendron uviferum*; see above, p. 264, n. 4.

[3] Whales Bay is shown on the 'Royal Map' and 'Sloane Map' (Foldout, Plate 5) to the east of Isla Carlos III. In his Journal, BL, Add MS 88980 A, Narbrough states that the bay visited here was Bahía Mussel. See above, p. 481, n. 2.

[4] The text ends here and the remaining pages of the book are blank and unnumbered.

PART III

The Records of Nathaniel Peckett, Richard Williams and William Chambers

a:
[f.1r] **The Voyage of the King's Shipp Called the *Sweepstakes* to Baldavia.**[1] **Annoq*ue* Domini**[2] **1669. By Nathanyell Peckett, L*ieutenan*t.**

[f. 2r] **King's Shipp *Sweepstakes* Anno Domini 1669. A J*our*nal of the S*ai*d Shipps Voyage for the Streight of *Magil*aine and into the South Seas & so to Baldavia, & also** of our **Return to England in the Yeare 1671, kept by me Nath*anyell* Peckett L*ieutenan*t of the S*ai*d Shipp Capt*ain* Jo*h*n Narbrow Comander.**

Septemb*er* 26th Anno 1669 being Saturday fair weather and the wind at NE. This morning at 9 of the Clocke we Sett Saile out of the Downs haveing the *Batcheller* Pinke Capt*ain* Humphry Flemminge Comand*er* to be our Consort.

Septemb*er* 29th being Wednesday fair Weather and the Wind NNW. I this day tooke my Departure from the Lizard in England, & at 12 of the Clocke I was in the Latitude by Observation 49°39′ Northerne Latitude, at which time the Lizard bore of me N by E distance about 9 Leagues, and directed our Course to the Southwards.

Octob*er* 13th being Wednesday fair Weather, and the Wind at NNE. This day at 12 of the Clocke the Island of Porto Sancto[3] we had Sight of it bore S by E of me Distance about 10 Leagues; and we made all the Saile we could for the Maderas[4] and in the Seeing of it the SE end of the Maderas bore S of me distance about 4 Leagues & we laid Short all the Night following.[5]

The 14th Day **being Thursday** fair weather and the wind at NNW. This after noon at 2 of the Clock we Anchor'd in 40 fath*om* water in Fantiall[6] Bay at Maderas Island.

The 17th Day being Sunday fair Weather and the Wind at NW. This morning at 2 of the Clocke we Sett Saile from the Maderas Island directing our Course S intending for St Iago.

[1] BL, Sloane 819, 23 folios. See above, p. 12. The folios are numbered in pencil by a curator.
[2] Meaning 'and year of the Lord', normally used when a regnal year is followed by a calendar year.
[3] Ilha do Port Santo.
[4] Arquipélago da Madeira.
[5] With shortened or reduced sail to slow the ship down.
[6] Funchal on Isla de Madeira (39°29′N, 16°54′W).

The 27th being Wednesday fair Weather and a fresh gale of Wind at NE. This morning at 9 of the Clock we Saw the Island of Saull,[1] it bore W by N, distance 5 Leagues, & then we directed our Course South by W. At 2 of the Clock we Saw Bona Vist,[2] it bore S of me distance about 5 Leagues, and in the evening we pass by it, & Stood to the Southward and Sometimes Lay by the Lee.[3]

[f. 2v] **October 28th** being Thursday fair Weather and the Wind at ENE. This morning we Saw the Island of May,[4] it bore S by W of me and we haled in for the Road and there Anchor'd in 11 fath*o*m water Sandy Ground, this Island of May affords neither wood nor fresh Water.

The 29th day being Friday fair Weather and the Wind at NE. This [day] at 12 of the Clock we Sett Saile for St Iago.[5] This Island of St Iago affords plenty of good fresh Water and fresh provisions but wood is Scarce, and deare.

The 30th day. At 12 of the Clock we Anchor'd in 10 fath*o*m water at Port praym[6] at St Iago.

Novemb*er* 5th being friday fair weather, & the Wind at ENE, a fresh gale. This day at 4 of the Clock in the Afternoon, we Sett Saile for[7] Port Pray directing our Course S for Cape Blanco,[8] or Cape St Georges, on the Coast of America in the Latitude 47°S Latitude.

Feb*ruary* 20th 1669[9] it was hazy foggy weather the wind at NE. This last night past we lost our Consort Capt*ain* Humphry Flemming in the *Batcheller* Pink. This day at 12 of the Clock I was in the Latitude of 17°22′S Latitude, Longitude from St Iago [*blank space*][10]

Feb*ruary* 21st *being Monday*. It was hazy foggy weather, and a fresh gale of wind at N by E. This morning at 8 of the Clock it Clear'd up & we Saw the Land, it bore off me distance about 4 Leagues. The Land we first Saw was Pengwin Island,[11] but we being unacquainted with the Land and haveing no observation, made Pengwin Island for[12] the Cape Called Cape Blanco. This Island makes with 2 round Hamocks. We not knowing this Island but Supposing to be the Cape we then Stood to the Southward and expected to fall with Port Desir.[13] We went with in 2 or 3 Leagues of the Shore, in 25 Fath*om* Water and finding not

[1] Ilha Sal, Cape Verde (16°49′N, 22°53′W); variants Sale, Sall, Saull.

[2] Ilha Boa Vista (16°05′N, 22°50′W).

[3] The corner of the original page is torn, but this word appears to be 'Lee'. To lay a ship by the lee is to let her run until the wind is brought on the lee-quarter, so that all her sails lie flat against the masts and shrouds. Smyth, *Sailor's Wordbook*, p. 437.

[4] Ilha Maio (15°04′N, 23°12′W); variants, May.

[5] Ilha São Tiago (15°05′N, 23°35′W).

[6] Praia (14°55′N, 23°31′W).

[7] Peckett uses the form 'for' when he departs from a port.

[8] Cabo Blanco (47°12′S, 65°45′W).

[9] 1669/70.

[10] 43°23′·5 in Narbrough's journal; see above, p. 201.

[11] Isla Pengüino (47°55′S, 65°43′W).

[12] 'for' repeated.

[13] Puerto Deseado (47°45′S, 65°53′W).

Port Desire, at night we brought too and lay of[f] and on all the night following.[1] I make my Difference of Longitud from St Iago to Pengwin Island, to be 46°38′, and my Meridian Distance to be 23° 21·1miles[2] westing from St Iago, Pengwin Island lying So farr to the Westward of St Iago.

Feb*ruary* 22 1669/70 being Tuesday fair and the Wind at NW. This morning we Stood in for the Shoare and at 12 of the Clock we had a very good Observation, [f. 3r] and I was in the Latitude of 48°20′ South Latitude, and by our observation we found our Selves to be to the Southward of Port Desire, and in the evening we came to an Anchor in 20 fath*om* Water in a fair Sandy Bay, which I tooke for Seales Bay.[3] It is in the Latitude of 48°15′ South Latitude, at the North end of this Bay is a Rocky Island full of Seales therefore we called it Seales Bay.

The 23rd day being Wednesday fair weather and the Wind at NW. This morning we weighed and Stood to the Northward, to Looke for the Port Desire, and I went a long the Shoare in our pinnace and went close along a great Bay, at the South end of this Bay is Seale Island and at the North end of the Island before Mentioned is this deepe Bay, and at the North end of the Bay is a Small Rocky Island, whereon this Island is plenty of Seales, and the fowles here are not affraid of us, which Rocky Island we called Tonine Hooke.[4] We knockt the fowles downe with Stickes, here are fowles bigger than our English Ducks, their backs are black, their brests are White, and their bills are round we called them White Brests.[5] In the evening we went aboard of our Shipp againe, and came to an Anchor in 25 fath*om* Water Ozey ground, we ridd about Six miles off the Shoare.

The 24th being Thursday fair Weather and the wind at West NW: we wayed and Stood to the Northward with our Shipp and I went alongst the Shoare with our Pinnace and Crost over a great deepe Bay, Called Spirings Bay,[6] there lye 3 Rocky Islands with in this Bay as in Pengwin Island,[7] which have Severall Small Rocks about it, and 5 or 6 Small Rocky Islands within itt, it Lyes about on [one] Mile & a halfe from the Maine. As Soon as we landed upon Pengwin Island we Sett a Tarr Barr*ell* on fire to give Notice on Board that it was the Island we looked for, and all we had to know it By was the Pengwins, they are so thicke its impossible to Numb*er* them. We drave them downe with Stickes, they are about the biggniss of a Goose they cannot flee nor go very fast, they have no wings but small Stumps

[1] Sailing in and out off the land to remain in one place, relative to the land, throughout the hours of darkness.

[2] Since the initial figure is given as 23^d^ (23°), the remainder of the figure clearly should not be read as miles, as can be seen below in the Table of the Daily Account (p. 610), where the figure is 23°21′·7.

[3] From Narbrough's account the anchorage would appear to have been SW of Punta Mercedes (48°24′S, 66°14′W). Seal Island appears to have been Isla Rasa Chica, and Seal Bay was Bahía Desvelos (48°18′S, 66°17′W), north-eastwards to Punta Medanosa. See above, p. 215.

[4] Narbrough's account states 'we gave it the name of *Tomahauke* Island, from an *Indian* Club lost here, called by the *Carribbe-Indians* at *Surinam* a *Tomahauke*, 'tis all a craggy Rock, a little bigger than *Seal-Island*'. This is probably Isla Libres, off Punta Medanosa (48°06′S, 65°55′W).

[5] These were probably imperial cormorants. Narbrough states that Peckett brought 200 young white breast shags aboard on 26 Nov. at Isla Guamblín. See above, p. 493.

[6] Bahía de los Nodales (48°00′S, 65°52′W).

[7] Isla Pingüino (47°55′S, 65°43′W).

[f. 3v] They Swimme with, they gett their food out of the Sea. This night wee went on board of the Shipp, and we Anchor'd in the Bay of Port Desire in 16 fath*o*m Water.

Feb*ruary* 25th being Friday fair weather and a fresh Gale of wind at West. This morning we wayed and went farther into the Bay of Port Desire, and there Anchor'd, where we Ridd we had 6 fath*om* Water at low water, the flood came from the Southward.

Feb*ruary* 27th being Sunday fair weather and a fresh gale of wind at W. This morning we wayed and went in with our Shipp into Port Desire Harbour.

Feb*ruary* 28th 1669/70 *Sweepstakes* in Port Desire Harbour. This Port Desire Lyeth in the Latitude of 47°30′ South Lat*itude*.[1] A Shipp may go into Port Desire at any time of the Tyde if the wind be fair for there is Water enough at Low water, and at 3 q*uarter* Ebb you may See all the Dangers going in or a q*uarter* flood, and I would not advise any man to go in with his Shipp till he has View'd the Harbour at a Low water for then he will see the Danger very Plaine, and then you may have marke upon the Land to go in.[2]

Directions how to know Desire Port.
As you come from the Northward from Cape Blanco alongst the Shoare to the Northward of Port Desire Bay there Lyeth a Ledge of Rocks which Shoot themselves a good hight above water, and are about a League from the Shoare and Severall Breaches more, and on the South Side of this Bay is Pengwin Island and 5 or 6 Small Islands in the North part of this Bay is Port Desire Harbour which hath on the Entrance of it a Spired Rock,[3] on the South Side much Like a Steple or Watch Tower; which is a very good marke for the Harbour. It Stands on the South Side goeing in, about halfe a mile from the Sea Side, and much about the Same Distance from the River Side. When we Ridd in Port Desire the Spire Rock bore SE of me and it was Shutt in with a parcell of Bluf Rocks,[4] [f. 4r] Rocks which lay Close by the water Side & there is on the North Side two Small Springs of water, the[y] Rise in the Valies. The westermost Spring is not a bow Shott[5] from the water Side, and the eastmost is above a q*uarter* of a mile, and where we Ridd the westermost bore NW by W of me and the eastermost bore NNE of me, or the Shipp. Here are Severall Small Islands in the Harbour, on each Side of the River. This River runns up about 25 or 30 Miles. Wee went up as high as we could with our Pinnace, and we Saw it dry from Side to Side, we were above 20 Miles up and could not gett no higher with our boate & we put a Shoare, and went up by Land but we saw no Signe of people nor any thing worth observation but a barren Land, which affordeth but very little wood or fresh Water for it is Scarce to gett.

SWEEPSTAKES IN PORT DESIRE

Annoq*ues* 1669/70. Now I will give an Acco*unt* of the Ebbing & frowing of the Tide, and what the Harbour affords. Within this Harbour of Port Desire it is high water at 12

[1] The actual position is (47°45′S, 65°53′W).
[2] Can identify marks on the shore to lead into the harbour.
[3] This is El Torreón; see above, p. 204, n. 6.
[4] The Spire Rock was in line with the bluff rocks.
[5] Probably about 300 yards. See above, p. xix.

a Clocke upon the full of the Moon and at Change day, and at Spring Tides it Ebbs and flows about 3 fath*o*m right up and Downe, and the Tide runneth very Strong. The Harbours mouth is but narrow at the entrance it is not much above Musquit Shott[1] from Side to Side. This Harbour affords but little Wood or water. The Land is dry and Barren but here is plenty of winnackoes or Spanish Sheep;[2] they are as Large as our English Deere, here is great Store of them but wild and here is good plenty of Hares; and Ostridges which are very Shye, here is plenty of fowles as Duck & Pickes and Curlews, Black Shaggs, white brests & great blew Ducks as bigg as geese, and many other good fowles, and we feed more upon those fowles and other fresh food, During the time of our Continuance in this Harbour. Blew fowles are not very Shye, here is also great Store of Seales upon one of the Islands, in this Port [f. 4v] we killed and Salted up a good quantity of them for food, which was indefferent food, here is also upon ever[y] Rocke great Store of Large Mussells and Limpertts, you may Load and boate in a Small time. The Harbour hath been a place of good refreshing to our men. The time we lay here upon an Island in this Harbour, we found a piece of Sheete Lead, whereon was ingraven in Dutch, and Left by Capt*ain* Jaques Le Marie[3] as followeth

MDCXV
EEN SHIPENDE EEN IACHT GENAMT
EENIDRACHT HORN GEARRIVEERT DEN
VIII DECEMBER VERTROCKEN MET EEN
DACHTDEN X IANVARY MDCXVI C IACOVLE
MARIR S WILLIAM CORNS SCHOVTS
ARES CLAREESSEN IAN CORNS COVTS
CLAES IANSSEN BAN.

March 25 1670. We sett saile for[4] Port Desire intending to go for Port S[t] Julian,[5] the wind being at WNW a fresh Gale.

April 2[d] being Saterday fair weather and the wind at N by W. This afternoon we fell with a great Deepe Bay, in the Latitude of 49°00′ South Latitude, and I went in with our Pinnace to see for S[t] Julian, and I found it in the South part of this Bay, and I went on shoare and made two fires, which was the Signall Ord*ere*d to make the Capt*ain* answered me againe by hoysting up our Ensigne, and then I went and Sounded the Harbour and Came a Board againe, and we Anchor'd in 9 fath*o*m water in the Bay of Porte S[t] Julian and there we Rodd all night.

April 3[d] being Sunday fair Weather and little wind. This morning the Capt*ain* and I went a Shoare with our Pinnace to view the Harbour, and there Staid untill Low water and Sounded going in and Coming out. [f. 5r] When we had don we came on Board againe.

[1] Musket shot, about 400 yards. Smyth, *Sailor's Word-Book*, p. 489.
[2] Guanaco.
[3] Le Maire, see above, pp. 218–19, 425–6.
[4] See above, p. 579, n. 7.
[5] Puerto San Julián (49°19′S, 67°43′W).

April 4th being Munday fair weather, and little wind Northerly. This morning at 6 of the Clocke we wayed and Stood to the Southward. We went with in 6 miles of the Shoare, and had not less then 25 fath*om* water, all a long untill wee were in the Latitude 49°55′ South Latitude, and then we return'd againe for St Julian, by reason we did not Like the weather.

April 6th being Wednesday fair weather and the wind at SSW. This morning we Stood into the Bay or Port St Julian, and came to an Anchor in eight fath*om* Water, and I went into Port St Julian, and the Mas*te*r a long with me to Bouye the Harbour, & came a board againe.

April 7th being Thursday Cloudy weather and the wind at N by W. This morning wee wayed and went in with the Shipp and anchor'd about a mile with in the Narrow, in 9 fath*om* water at a high water, and at Low water we had but 4½ [fathom] water. Within this Harbour we wintered with our Shipp.

April 20th being Wednesday fair weather. This day I went a Shoare (with 10 of our men along with me) to See if I could meete with any Indians but we could not see any, and about 9 Miles West[1] from the Harbours mouth I fell with a Salt Pann of very good Salt,[2] which was made by the heate of the Sunn. This pond was about 3 Miles Long and a Mile broad. The next day our men went to this pond, with Baggs and brought as much as they could away with them; we had as much Salt as we desired, at times about 5 Tunns which Salt did us a great deale of good.
Directions to find Port St Julian, and how the Harbour Lyeth in the Latitude of 49°00′ South Latitude & Longitude westing from St Iago, meridian Distance from St Iago.[3] This Port hath to the Northward of it high Land, and to the Westward round Copling hills and to the Southward it is [f. 5v] very plaine Levell Land, and Steepe Cliffs from St Julian to the hill of St Ives. The best of the Chanell going into St Julian Lyeth SW & NE and when you are in the Harbour it Lyeth SSW & NNE. If you Should go into the Harbour with a Shipp, it is good to Bouye it first, it is a Broad place, at Low water there is not above 4 foot water upon the Barr. It is high water here about halfe an hour past 11 of the Clock upon the full of the Moon; or Change day; the water waxeth here about four fath*om* and a halfe. In the Harbour there are Severall Islands, there are 3 Islands on the West Side, which lye very high & nigh one to another, so that at Low water you may go from one to another, or from them to the Maine, on the West Side there is a Polasse[4] Point of Rocks, and just above those Rocks is a Chingley Beach.[5] At this Beach we Landed our Caske to fill with fresh water. Here are two pounds with in Bow Shott of the water Side, the first where of is Salt water, but the next is very good fresh water; and on the East Side is greate Pond of fresh water but that is not so good. Here is fresh water and wood for fuell, but not over plenty. Here is one Island on the East Side of the Chanell, which we called Beach Island,[6] where great Store of white Brests Lodge. We Rad [road] betwixt this and the Island of true

[1] Wood states that the salt pan was north from Monte Wood. BL, MS 46A., p. 147.
[2] There is a large salt pan shown on the modern chart about 5 miles NW of the harbour entrance.
[3] No figures are given in Narbrough's journal.
[4] The meaning of this word is not clear.
[5] Shingle beach.
[6] This island is shown on Narbrough's plan of 'Port San Julyan' (Plate 3), and is now in the Islas Justicia.

Justice,[1] and one of the three. The Harbour affords greate Store of White Brests and other fowles, as Ducks & Geese & Teele & Black Shaggs Curlews Plover, greate Blew Ducks, and a greate many other good fowles & good fish as our English Mullett, also the Island Winnackoes Ostidges and Such good food the Winnackoes we called Deere.

April the 10th 1670. Mr Jo*hn* Wood saw 5 or 6 Indians, but they were a good way off and he being alone thought it not Convenient to go to them.

[f. 6r] **June 22th** day. Mr Jo*h*n Wood & 3 of our Company more being a Shoare, Saw 7 Indians & Spake with them, but could not understand each other, but by Signs the[y] understood that the Indians would have them be gon. These Indians had Nothing worth observation, their Clotheing were Skinns of wild Beasts as Winnackeoes or Such as they could gett, it was made of fashon of a Blankett, and so they throw it on their Shoulders, Mr Wood gave them a knife and other things & so came away.

August 16th beinge Wednesday Close weather wind at SW. This day 2 of our men Saw 2 Indians, they being a Shoare, and the Indians runn away and left their Baggs which were made of Skinns behind them, & their 2 Doges, being fast togather in a String and our men brought both the baggs & the Doges on Board with them, but the Capt*ain* Sent the Baggs & the Doggs on Shoare againe with the men that brought them to Leave them againe where they found them, and there was Set with their Baggs some Beades and Knives & other things for them. There was in the Baggs nothing but a little redd[2] painte and pieces of flint Stones which flint Stones I Suppose they Carryed with them to make heads for their arrows. We could not perceive them to have any thing of value. This St Julian is Barrin Land like Port Desire. Here is great Store of Mussllells and Limperts, and nothing more but what I have given you acco*unt* of, also duering the time of our wintering here in the Port of St Julian, which was from April to Septemb*er* we[3] found the Season of the Yeare to be very cold with great Store of frost & Snow and accompanied with high westerly winds.

Septemb*er* 16th. Being fair weather & the wind at West by S. This day we Sett Saile from Port St Julian to go to Port Desire.

[f. 6v] **Septemb*er* 18th** being Sunday fair weather. This day we Anchor'd in Port Desire Harbour, and we found that in our absence from this Port, Some Indians have been downe near the water Side, by a parsell of earth flung up together and Sticks placed in it and coloured over with redd Oker made in the Imitation of a Shipp as well as they could form it, we concluded they had Seen us though we never Saw them whiles wee were in the Port. And in this Port we Salted up a greate quantity of Seales and Pengwins for food which we kill'd and brought in our boate from Pengwin Island, and here we fitted our Ship for the Sea.

Octob*er* 14th being fair weather & the wind westerly. We Sett Saile from Port Desire, to go for the Streights of *Magil*aine, Southward.

[1] Now in the Islas Cormorán.
[2] Struck through in the original.
[3] Word repeated at the start of a new line.

December[1] **19th 1670**, being Wednesday. This day we fell with a fair white Cape which Lyes in the Latitude of 50°00′ South Latitude & our Capt*ain* named it Beach[y] Head, and we saw the hill of St Ives[2] in Latitude 50°00′ which maketh a flatt Table Land aloft, and there Stand a round Cobling Hill att the North end of it which is just even with it in hight, & there are Some round Cobling hills to the South of it. Still directing out Course to the Streights of *Magil*laine.

Octob*er* the 21st. Fair Weather and the wind at N by E. This day we fell with a fair white Cape, which our Capt*ain* named Cape Faire[3] by reason it was a very fair day. This Cape Lyeth in the Latitude of 50°16′ South Latitude by good observation.

Octob*er* 22th being Saturday fair weather and Little wind, Northerly. This day at 12 of the Clocke I was by Observation in Latitude 51°50′ South Latitude, We Still Standing to the Southward. In the evening we Saw Cape Virgin Mary,[4] which is at the enterance of the Streights of *Magil*laine & we Anchor'd in 26 fath*om* Water black Owsy Sand and the Cape bore W by S distance 4 Leagues and about 4 Leagues to the North of this Cape it is all white [f. 7r] Cliffes, and Steepe up the Cape being the higher Land, and about a Cables Length to the North of the Cape, there is a blacke Spott in the Cliffe over which Spott there is a fall from the Plaine, it being plaine aloft, and from the Pitch of this Cape SW there lyeth a Beachy Point about a League Long into the Sea. There are Little Bushes growing on the Topp of the Beach. This Cape Lyeth in the Latitude of 52°15′ South Latitude. The Land from Cape Blanco to Cape Virgin Mary Seemeth to be barren Land and there is not any Signe of Wood to be Seene. What Course the Tyde keepeth here I know not, nor which way the Flood Setts, for we Ride the Wind with our Shipp,[5] and it was then but little Wind.

Octob*er* 23th being Sunday, and the wind Northerly. This morning we waied, and Stood to the Southward till Cape Virgin Mary bore WNW of us and then wee altered our Course and Steer'd SW, and we fell with a Sand Shoall where we had about 7 fath*om* water, but close aboard of it we had 8 fath*om* & 20 fath*om* water, but we saw Severall Riplings to the Southward of it and the Cape bore N of us, we Steer'd away W by N, & W, & W by S untill we came thwart[6] of Point Possession,[7] which is with in the Cape about 8 Leagues, it is on the North side. We came a long with in two Leagues of the North Shoare, and the first time we Strooke ground[8] we had 36 fath*om* Water black Ousey Sand, and the Water Shoulled to 34 fath*om* and so to 30 & 28, 24, 20, 19 & in 20 fath*om* is the Faire[way], and saileing a long the Shoare to Cape Oringe[9] there is 20 & 25 fath*om* Water

[1] Error for Oct.

[2] For identification of Beachy Head and the Hill of St Ives, see above, p. 252, nn. 1, 2, 3.

[3] Narbrough named it Cape Fair Weather, probably Cabo Buen Tiempo (51°33′S, 68°57′W). See above, p. 253, n. 2.

[4] Cabo Vírgenes (52°20′S, 68°21′W). See above, p. 255, nn. 3, 4.

[5] The ship lay to the wind.

[6] Abreast.

[7] Cabo Posesión (52°18′S, 68°58′W).

[8] The first sounding obtained.

[9] Cabo Orange (52°28′S, 69°23′W).

in the Faire Way. About 4 Leagues SW of Point Possession we haled in West by N to gett the N Shoare aboard,[1] and we fell with Shoale Water. At once we had but 5 fath*om* Water, and then Cape Oringe bore SSW of us distance two Leagues. It is good to give this Shoale a Burth, we bore off SE againe and had 19 fath*o*m Water. Imediatly we Steered away S which was with the first Narrow,[2] expecting to gett through, but night Coming on, and the Tide against us, we bore out againe and came to an Anchor in 25 fath*om* Water among greate Piblle stones[3] & ouse and there we Ridd all night. It is hight water here at 8 of the Clocke upon the full of the Moon or at Change day.

[f.7v] **Octob*er*** being the 25th fair Weather and the wind NE a fair Gale. This morning at 4 of the Clocke we wayed, intending to go through the first Narrow but when we were about 2 miles with in the Narrow it was thick weather, that we could not See the Land, and wee Anchor'd againe in 38 fath*om* Water and at 8 of the Clock it Cleered up. Againe we wayed and runn through the first Narrow by 12 of the Clock we were on the South Shoare. The Land on both Sides is of indifferent hight towards the water Side, but inland it is higher. Now we being Cleer of the first Narrow, we Stood away Southwest, & SW by W and we Sounded & had 25 & 24 fath*om* Water in Middway Ouse ground with Small Pebbles Stones and Sheeles [shells]. Before you come to the Second Narrow,[4] On the North Side there is Cape Called Cape Gregory[5] and severall white Cliffes, this is very nigh the entrance of the Second Narrow. This afternoon at 4 of the Clock wee entred the Second Narrow with a fresh Gale of wind at NE. The Land on the South Side of this Narrow is of an indifferent hight, and Steepe white Cliffes but the Land on the North Side is not So high. The Narrow lyeth SW westerly and NE easterly, and is in Length about 3 Leagues and in Breadth about 4 or 5 Miles. If you Saile throw this Narrow it is good to keepe the Middway, and after you be through have a care of Coming to [too] nigh the South Shoare, for there is a Shoale Lyeth off SW about a League of the West End of the Narrow. Both these points at the SW end of the Narrow are Steepe up white Cliffes. This evening at 7 of the Clock wee Anchor'd at 8 fath*om* Water, black Sand and Shells under Queene Elizabeths Island,[6] it bore SW by S of me distance 3 Miles and St Georges Island[7] bore SSE distance 9 Miles & St Bartholomeus Island[8] bore SE of me distance 5 Miles and the South point of the Second Narrow bore NE by E of me distance 6 Miles. Before you be throw this Narrow these Islands will be Open. The Largest of the Islands is Elizabeths and the lest [least] is St Bartholomeus. [f. 8r] The Land in the Country on the North Side is high Land and Covered with Snow. This Land Seemeth to be Barren Land & affords neither wood nor fresh Water & the Aire is very Cold.

Octob*er* the 26th being Wednesday faire Weather and the Wind S. This morning our Capt*ain* and I went a Shoare with our Pinnace to Queene Elizabeths Island, and there

[1] To get close to the north shore.

[2] Primera Angostura (52°30′S, 69°35′W).

[3] Pebble stones, water-rounded stones. Normally the lead would only bring up small pebbles, but, since the ship anchored, it can be presumed that large pebbles were brought up on the anchor stuck in the soft mud.

[4] Segunda Angostura (52°43′S, 70°20′W).

[5] Cabo Gregorio (52°40′S, 70°13′W).

[6] Isla Isabel (52°53′S, 70°44′W). See above, p. 259, nn. 1, 4.

[7] Now Isla Magdalena (52°55′S, 70°35′W).

[8] Now Isla Marta (52°51′S, 70°35′W).

we fell with some Indians and we gave them Beades & knives for Bowes & arrows & Winnakoes Skinns, which is all the Clothing they have. As for any sort of Minerall I cannot perceive they have any. There women ware brassletts made of Small Sheeles [shells] about their Necks, Which they String on the Sinnues of Some Beast they gett. These Indians are of meane Stature and there was in a Company about 30 men & women of them. We went with our Boats from Queene Elizabeths Island to S[t] Bartholomeus Island and Sound with our Lead and had 30 fathom water betwixt the Islands. Then we return'd a Board againe.

Octob*er* 27th being Thursday fair Weather and the Wind at NW. This morning I went about Queene Elizabeths Island with the Pinnace to See for the Indians Cannow, but it was gon. There is a passage betweene the Island and the North Shoare, but it is dangerous by reason of the fowle Ground. After I had been round this Island, I went to S[t] Georges Island and tooke in Pengwins. We were forced to hale them out of their hooles in the Ground like Conneys Burrows with a gaffe & our boate hooke, and when I had don I came a board againe. From Elizabeths Island to S[t] Georges is 7 miles SSE & Elizabeths to S[t] Bartholomeus is 2 Miles E by N, from S[t] Bertholo*meus* to the South part of the Second Narrow it is 5 Miles. Queene Elizabeths Island & S[t] Georges Island Lye in the Latitude 52°45′ South Latitude, & S[t] Barthol*meus* in Latitude 52°40′ South Latitude. Betwixt Elizabeths and S[t] Georges Island there is a Ledge of Rocks[1] ranckes [f. 8v] to the Westward of S[t] Georges Island 2 or 3 Miles, & the beast [best] passage is betweene Elizabeths Island and the Redge of Rocks. They are under water, but by the weed you may know when you come neare them for there is weed all over them, & when You See weed have a care.

Octob*er* the 28th. We Ridd fast under Queene Elizabeths Island. We have Seene Severall fires on the South Side, as we came along, and this day we saw two greate fires on the South Side.

Octob*er* 29th being Saturday fair weather and the Wind at West by S. This day we wayed & went betweene Elizabeths & S[t] Bartho*lomeus* Island, & turned up to the Maine of [off] the North Shoare, at the SW end of Elizabeths Island, and there Anchor'd in 15 fatho*m* water black Sand, and about one Mile & a half from the Shoare, in a little Bay that is a little to the Southward of a Steepe White Cliffe, which is on the Maine, att the South end of the Passage between Elizabeths Island & the Maine.[2] Where we Ridd S[t] Georges Island bore NE off here runneth little or no Tide.

Octob*er* the 30 it was hazy weather & fogy & the wind westerly. This morning we wayed & stood to the Southward, faire by the Shoare. Here the Land lyeth N & S, & the hills are of a good hight, but trend downe Low to the Water Side, & are full of green bushes, very thick and the hills are Covered with Snow. This wood[3] is indefferent good but not very tall of gro*w*th, it groweth much like Elmes, Ellder & Bayes. We made the best of our way

[1] This bank is made up of a number of shoal patches extending from Isla Marta (St Bartholomeus Island) terminating in Banco Walker at its southern end.

[2] This bay is Bahía Laredo (52°58′S, 70°48′W), the steep white cliff is Cabo Porpesse, and the passage Paso Pelícano.

[3] 'This wood' repeated in the original.

to the Southward, the Wind being at SW and some gusts off the hills & night Coming on, wee Anchor'd in 11 fath*om* Water, gravilly Sand. In this Bay we found two Rivelletts of fresh water where you may row your Boate & fill your Caske in the Boate, wood and water is plenty here, & easie to come. Here are Brand Geesse & Ducks plenty, here are Trees much like Currant Trees. [f. 9r] This Bay our Capt*ain* named fresh Water Bay.[1] The Streights is here about 5 Leagues Broad from Side, to Side. This Bay is on the West Side & it is about 9 Leages to the Southward of Elizabeths Island.

October 31th being Wednesday fair weather & the wind westerly. This morning we wayed and Stood to the Southward; and we had much wind & gusty at WNW. The Capt*ain* and I went a long the Shoare in the Pinnace and about 2 Leagues & a ½ to the Southward of freshwater Bay, we fell with a Small Sandy Bay;[2] at the NE end of this Bay there lyeth Rocks and Shoale Water; about 2 Cables Length off. In this Bay we saw two Indian Cannows & went a Shoare, & Spoke with the Indians and they Seemed to be very quiett people, and were Suddainely familiar[3] with us – both men & women were much delighted to have beads & redd ribbons tyed about their necks & arms, as we did, & we gave them Severall things. They esteemed any thing that was read either lynning or wolling[4] they gave us in liew of our things Bows and there Skinn Coats, which are Deere Skinns & severall other Skinns Sowed together with Thonges cutt out of Seales Skinns. Here is very good fresh water & good plenty in this Bay. Our Shipp being gon before me I made all the hast I could after her, and found her at an Anchor at Port Famine.[5] This Port Famine is a fine Port, & you may ridd there in 8 or 9 Fath*om* Water, a good birth from the Shoare, a SE wind is the worst wind cann blow here. It flows about 10 fath*om*[6] Water, and it is high water about 12 of the Clock at full moon, or Change day. In the S part of the Bay is a River of water, and great Store of Drift Timber, on Both Sides of this River, the Capt*ain* named it Sedgares River.[7] [f. 9v] Here we wooded & watered & fitted our Shipp So well as we could. Here is good store of ducks & Geesse and other Willde fowles & fresh fish which we caught with our Seanes.[8] Here is good Anchoring all the way from Elizabeths Island to Port Famine, you will find 14 15 & 16 fath*om* Water with in halfe a mile of the Shoare, on the West Side, but if you go one League of [off] you cannot gett ground with a hundred fath*om* Line. The Point before you come to Port Famine[9] is of indefferent hight, and not much wood on it, Trees grows here and there a Single Tree on the Top of the Hill by it selfe,[10] which you may See after you come about the Point. Here the hill begineth to be very high and Covered with Snow but the Land Treads Lowe to the Water

[1] Bahía Agua Fresca (53°23′S, 70°58′W).

[2] This bay must be Bahía Carreras (53°36′S, 70°55′W), which is 7 leagues from Bahía Agua Fresca, and is described by Narbrough in similar terms; see above, p. 262, n. 6.

[3] Familiar meaning, courteous, friendly, sociable. *NOED*.

[4] Anything that was red, either linen or woollen.

[5] Now known as Puerto San Juan de la Posesíon or Puerto del Hambre (53°38′S, 70°56′W).

[6] Presumably this is an error for 'feet'.

[7] Segars River in Narbrough, 'Voyage to the South-Sea', p. 122. The river was called after the ship's carpenter, William Sedger. TNA, ADM 39/2510.

[8] Seine fishing net. The net is laid out in a circular fashion and then the ends hauled together to pull in the fish contained inside the net. It can either be hauled from a boat or hauled ashore.

[9] Punta Santa Ana.

[10] There is a single tree at the top of the Point.

Side, and full of good & Large Timber for many uses. Here are Small Berries which Grow on little Bushes much Like Bill Berries, here are Currant Trees and Severall other Trees. The Streight is [*blank space*] Leagues broad from Side to Side.

November 2[d] fair Weather & the wind variable. This day the Indians that we Saw before came against the Shipp, and we Seeing them, went a Shoare, and one of them came off a board with us & we gave him Victualls & Severall Small things of Little value, and Sett him a Shoare againe. I cannot perceive any signe of Minerall in the Land, or about the People. The women ware Small glistering Shells, about their necks & wee carri'd a Shoare a little Seale[1] & they Oyled their bodies al over with it.

November 3[d] **1670** being Tuesday fair weather & little wind at WNW. This morning we weighed & Stood to the Southward, Correcting our Course S by E & SSE by our Compass about 5 Leagues to a point we named Shutt up point,[2] here the Streights are about five Leagues broad, & high Craggy Rocks on both Sides & Steepe too. From this Point the Streights round to the Westward, & we Steer'd from this point to Cape Froward,[3] SW by W about 3 Leagues. [f.10r] Here at Cape Froward the Straights is 3 Leagues Broad, & the Straight rounds away to the Westward Still. This Cape is a high hill, Steepe up and we could not Strike ground in the Channell. Both these Shoares are Steepe too,[4] and the Land in Craggy Rocks and hills whos Topps are Covered with Snow. There [are] Coves for Shipps, if they were we discovered on both Shoares, here is a Cove on the South Side over against Cape Froward Somewhat to the S W ward. There Lyes Islands fair by the S Shoare,[5] and to the Westward of Cape Froward, the Land is very Craggy Rocky Land, and little or no wood to what the other Part affords. The weather being very gusty with Foggs we haveing no place [to] Anchor in, Lay plying too & Frow in the Streights all night, about 3 or 4 Leagues to the Westward of Cape Froward.

November 4th being Friday fair weather & Calme all the afternoon. We Lay driving to & frow [fro] a little to the Westward of Cape Froward, and could not find no [any] Anchoring place, by 12 of the Clock we were backe to Cape Froward. From Cape Froward to Cape Holland,[6] the Course is W by N distance about 5 Leagues, and a little to the E:ward of Cape Holland is a Sandy Bay, our Capt*ain* Called it Woods Bay,[7] where you may Ride in 18 or 20 Fath*om* water a good Birth of[f] the Shoare but we could not gett into it. This evening at 6 of the Clock Cape Froward bore E & N of me, distance 3 Leagues

[1] Seal flesh.

[2] Cabo San Isidro (53°47′S, 70°58′W).

[3] Cabo Froward (53°54′S, 71°18′W).

[4] Normally 'steep to' means that there is deep water close to the shore, but in this case it probably means that the shores themselves rise steeply, since, not having sounded close inshore on both sides of the channel, they cannot have known what the depth of water was.

[5] These are probably Islotes Dos Hermanos, described as two prominent islets lying in the mouth of Seno Lyell. *South America Pilot*, II, para. 7.354.

[6] Cabo Holland (53°47′S, 71°41′W).

[7] Bahía Wood (53°49′S, 71°37′W). Narbrough, 'Voyage to the South-Sea', p. 71, states 'November 4. 1670. I was in *Wood's Bay*, called by my Mate's Name.' John Wood's journal (see above, p. 266, n. 5) states that Giles Wood (who appears in the Muster List, TNA, ADM 39/2510) was the Master's mate. The bay would therefore appear to be named after him.

and we plying to & fro all the night following, with the wind at W by S & Some times being calme being fair all night.

Novemb*er* 5th being fair weather & little wind at E by N. This morning at 7 of the Clocke we were short of Cape Holland & we Steerd a way WNW to gitt the N Shoare a Board, for on the S Side is Small Islands & Craggy Rocks & Severall Coves. Saileing we saw a fire to the S side. A little Westward of the Cape Holland is a Sandy Bay[1] where you may ridd in 8, 9 or 10 fath*om* water 4 or 5 Cables Length from the Shoare this is on the N Side. This afternoon the wind coming [10v] about to the NW and blowing hard in flawes[2] and night coming on, we came to an Anchor in 9 fath*om* Water in a Sandy Bay on the N Side but halfe a mile from the Shoare. This Bay is to the E:ward of Cape Gallant,[3] this Bay we called Forstcues Bay.[4] With in this Bay is a fair Sandy Cove for Small Shipps, and there is 3 fath*om* Water. The Water Riseth here 10 foote and it is high water here at 10 of the Clocke upon the full of the moon or Changes day. This Cove our Capt*ain* Called Port Gallant,[5] with in this Port is two Rivaletts of fresh water and good wood plenty. The Land tread Low to the water Side. To the E:ward of this Port, and there is a Bay about 2 Miles Long, in which there is a Little Island and Some Rocks. This Bay is Called Corders Bay,[6] and the Land to the W:ward of Port Gallant is very high Land, whos topps are Covered with Snow. Here the Streights is 4 Leagues Broad, and there lyeth 2 or 3 Islands in the Midway S & W one from another, and 2 of them are good Large Islands,[7] full of Timb*er* and there are Severall Small Rocky Islands about them, they Lye Short of Cape Gallant. Here the Streights round to the NW and as it were Shutt up.

Novemb*er* 6th being Sunday. This afternoon we Sett Saile from Fostcues Bay, with the Wind at SE, a fine Gale and we Steer'd a way W and then NW by our Compas, and night Coming on, we gott into a fair Sandy Bay, Called Elizabeths Bay,[8] & there we Anchor'd in 12 fath*om* Water. This Bay is on the N Shoare at the begining of the NW Beach. As we Compassed Cape Gallant, we Saw Severall Islands of[f] the South Shoare, and there is little or no wood on the South Side.[9] Here the Tide Runneth indifferent Stronge, and the water riseth about 2 fath*om*, and it is high water about a 11 of the Clock upon the full moon, or Change day and the flood Cometh from the Westward, and Riding in this Bay Called Elizabeth Bay, the Streights make as if they were Shutt up [f.11r] and there were no passage. Here the Streights is about 3 Leagues Broad, and two Leagues to the Westward of this Bay, is a fresh water River, our Capt*ain* named it Batchellers River.[10] Here is good Anchoring in the Bay, off either Side of this River you may Ridd in eight or 10 fath*om*

1 Bahía Andrés lies close West of Cabo Holland.

2 Sudden gusts of wind blowing with great violence.

3 Cabo Gallant (53°42′S, 72°02′W).

4 Bahía Fortescue (53°42′S, 72°00′W).

5 Puerto Gallant.

6 Bahía Cordes (53°43′S, 71°55′W), named after Simon de Cordes who sailed with Jacob Mahu in 5 ships from Rotterdam in 1598. The latter died and Cordes took over the command. They entered the Strait of Magellan in April 1599 and wintered in this bay until August, during which time they buried above 120 men.

7 Islas Charles (53°44′S, 72°06′W).

8 Bahía Isabel (53°37′S, 72°12′W).

9 For details of the islands in this part of the Strait, see above, pp. 302–3.

10 Río Batchelor (53°34′S, 72°19′W).

Water, above a quart*er* of a mile of [off] the Shoare. Our Pinnace went into the River, but it is Shoald, and about a bow Shott from Side to Side; here the water riseth about 8 fath*om*[1] in Batchellers Bay.

Novemb*er* 7th Cloudy gusty weather and the wind at NW. This day our boate went over to the South Shoare, but Saw not any thing worth the observation for the Land is Irregular with hills Covered with Snow on the Topes of them, and of a boggy mossie Quality with Small Trees and Rushey Grass. There are Some Junippers Trees[2] and other trees which bare Leaves like Bay Leaves, or Leaves of Lemmon Trees, whos barke is very hott like Ginger, in a mans mouth.[3] Here is greate Store of those Trees on the North Side.

Novemb*er* 13th being Sunday fair weather and little wind at SE. This morning at 6 of the Clock we Sett Saile out of Elizabeths Bay, and at 12 of the Clock we were thwart St Jerom's Channell,[4] and at 2 of the Clock we were thwart of Cape Quad,[5] and we made the best use of our time we could to gett to the Westward of Cape Quad. We went along the Shoare to the North with our Pinnace to See for an Anchoring place, but could find none, and we Stood to the W ward, & at 8 of the Clock at night Cape Quad bore of Me E by N & E, distance 4 Leagues and we Steer'd away West by N ½ N all night with the wind at SSE & S by E a fine Gale.

Novemb*er* 14 being Munday – fair weather and the wind at ESE. This morning we made all the Saile to the Westward and at 6 of the Clocke were thwart a point of Land on the South Side which was more out than the other Land [f. 11v] to the North beareth, and our Capt*ain* named this Cape Moonday.[6] This Cape is distant from Cape Quad about 13 Leagues, and the Course from Cape Quad to it is W by N ½ N. Here is 16 or 17 degrees to the Eastward of this true place, the variation from the N point is so many degrees to the E:ward of its true Place, and so it is all the Streights over. Here at Cape Moonday the Streights are 4 Leagues Broad, and the Land is all high Craggy Rocks on Both Sides, and Snow on the topps, from Cape Froward to Cape disado,[7] but there is many good Anchoring places betwixt them. As we came Sailing from Cape Quad we saw many Harbours Rivers & Sounds on the South running a great way into the Land, with many turnings & windings every way, and I know nothing to the Contrary but that they may be all Islands, for we had no time to Discover them.

This day the wind being Easterly, we made all the saile we could directing our Course to the Westward, of the South Sea, and we kept all a long with in 2 Leagues of South Shoare, which is the boldest Shoare, for on the N Shoare at the entrance of the South Sea it is all Islands, and which is the Cape they call Cape Victory[8] I know not, for it maks like high

1 Presumably this should be 'feet', bearing in mind the tidal range in 'Forstcues Bay' is given as 10 ft.

2 See above for *Pilgerodendron uviferum*, the only member of the family *Cupressaceae*, to which junipers belong, that grows in this area.

3 Winter's bark trees.

4 Canal Jerónimo (53°33′S, 72°23′W).

5 Cabo Quod (53°32′S, 72°33′W).

6 Cabo Monday (53°11′S, 73°24′W).

7 Cabo Deseado (52°45′S, 74°43′W).

8 Cabo Victoria (52°16′S, 74°53′W).

Rocky Islands. This morning Cape Disado [bore] SW ½ a point westerly of me by our Compasse, Distant 3 Leagues. From Cape Moonday to Cape Disado, the Course is West by N by our Compasse, and they are distant one from another 13 Leagues. Cape disado WSW from you makes much like the Needles going into the Isle of White, but bigger and not of that Colour, and as you come from the Eastward, Saileing a long the Westwards with in 2 or 3 Leagues of the South Shoare you will open 2 Small Rocks, and when the Cape beareth SW of you, you open the Low Land to the S:ward of the Cape. This night we Layd Plying to the Westward open of the Streights mouth, the wind at NW but not much wind, but much Raine.

Novemb*er* 15th 1670 being Tuesday. It was thick hazy foggy weather, and the wind at NW. This morning at 4 of the Clocke Cape Disado bore SSW of me distance about 12 Leagues, [f. 12r] the weather being thick and durty, and like to blow, So we bore into the Streights againe to looke for a place to Anchor in to Secure our Shipp haveing information of a Cove about 3 Leagues with in the Streights,[1] and lookeing for this Cove, we fell with a Small Bay, about 3 Leagues with in the Cape where we Anchor'd in 13 fath*om* Water, Sandy Ground. At the W end of this Bay, lyeth 5 or 6 Small Rocky Islands; they Shew not themselves when you are a Mile from them, then they Shew as if they joyned to the Maine. Here is 2 or 3 Bedds of Weeds goeing to the Bay, but there is water enough over them. In this Bay you may Ride in what Depth of Water you please, from 7 Fath*om* to 13. The E part of the Bay is Shoaldish; but it is all good ground, and at the W end of this Bay there is a Small Cove, the water is very deepe, but [you] may Ride in what Depth of water you will from 10 to 3 fath*om*, the ground is Sandy, no wind can hurt you. We ridd halfe a Mile from the Maine, & the Cove is a good Birth from the Islands, they were open of the Maine.
This day our Capt*ain* named it Teusday Bay.[2] Here is Wood and water plenty, here are Wild Geesse & Ducks & other Wild fowles, as all the Streights over.

Novemb*er* 19th being Saturday, it was hazy Rainy weather and the Wind variable. This afternoon at one of the Clocke we Sett Saile out of Tuesday Bay, with the wind ESE to gon from[3] Baldavia and at 4 of the Clocke the Cape bore S of me distance about 3 Leagues, and we Steer'd away NNW, and at 8 of the Clock Cape Disado bore ESE of me distance 5 Leagues, & we saw 4 Small Islands which bore NNW about 2 Leagues,[4] and we heaved our Lead & had 35 fath*om* Water, Rocky Ground.

Novemb*er* 25th being Friday indifferent fair weather and a fresh gale of Wind SSW. This afternoon we Shorten'd our Saile and Lay with our head to the South E*ast*ward, and So lay too & fro [f. 12v] and at 7 of the Clock we Saw the Land, but night coming on we lay still.

[1] Presumably Puerto Misericordia, known to the English as the Harbour of Mercy, which lies 5 miles within the Strait.

[2] This is Puerto Misericordia (52°47′S, 74°35′W), not the bay now known as Bahía Tuesday (52°51′S, 74°25′W). See above, p. 272, n. 8.

[3] To sail to Valdivia. The river is entered through Bahía Corral 39°49′S, 73°27′W.

[4] Now Islotes Evangelistas: Narbrough names them the Norris Islands in his journal, but in his published 'Voyage to the South-Sea', p. 79, and on the 'Royal Map' and 'Sloane Map' (Foldout and Plate 5) refers to them as the Islands of Direction (52°24′S, 75°06′W).

Plate 1. A DRAUGHT OF PORT DISSIER HARBOWER (BL, Add MS 88980C). Courtesy of the Trustees of the British Library.

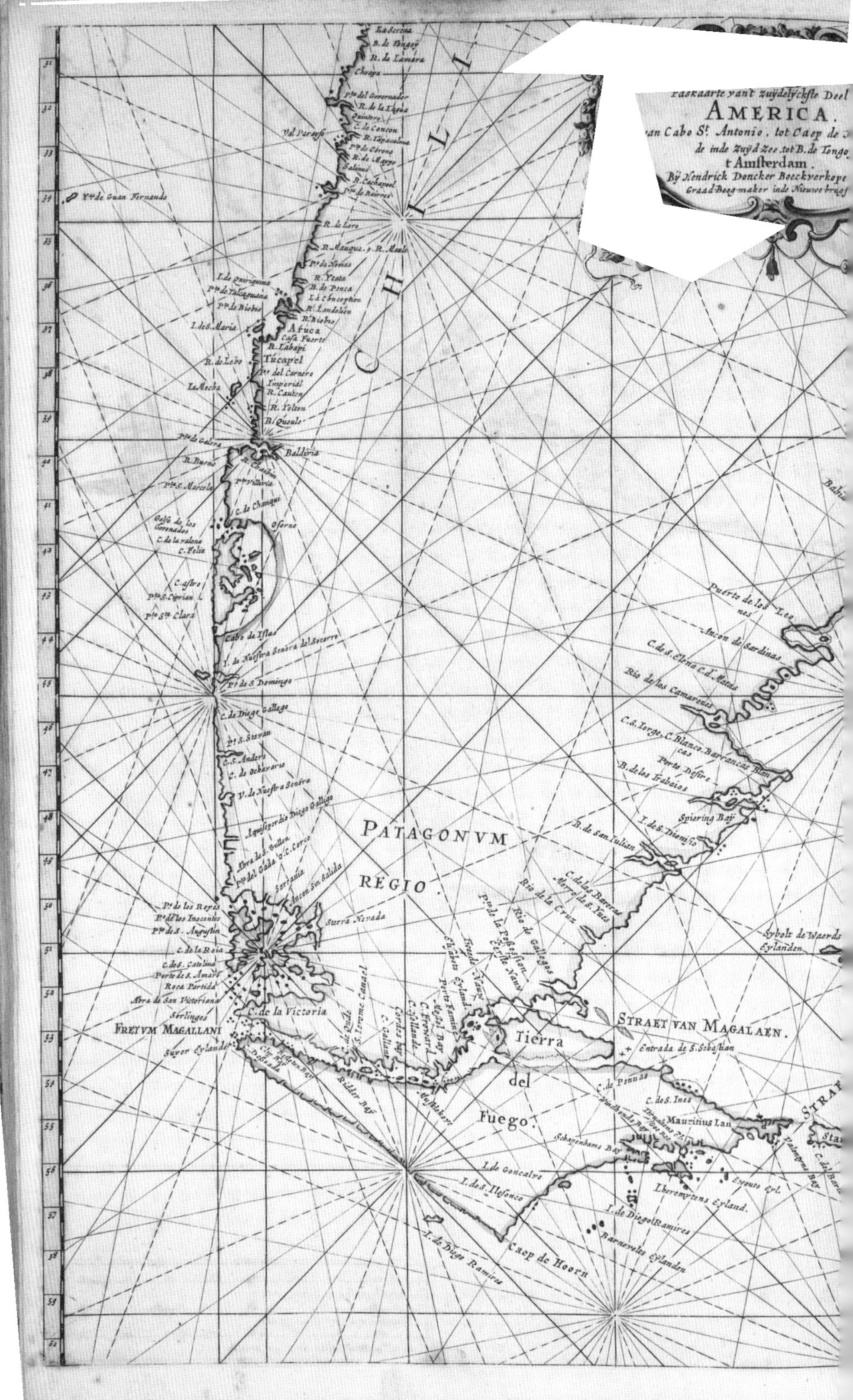

Paskaarte van't Zuydelyckste Deel
AMERICA.
van Cabo St. Antonio, tot Caep de
de inde Zuyd Zee tot B. de Tongo
t Amsterdam.
By Hendrick Doncker Boeckverkoper
Graad-Boog-maker inde Nieuwe brugs
CHILI
La Serena
B. de Tongoy
R. de Lamara
Choapa
Pto del Governador
R. de la Ligua
Quintero
C. de Concon
Val Parayso
R. Topocalma
Pto de Corona
R. de Maypo
Salinas
R. Cachapool
Pto de Bairres
Y. de Guan Fernando
R. de Loro
R. Mauque
R. Maule
Pto de Nonas
R. Ytata
B. de Penca
I. de Quiriquina
Pto de Talcaguana
Pto de Biobio
La Conception
R. Biobio
I. de S. Maria
Aruca
Casa Fuerte
R. Labapi
R. de Lobo
Tucapel
Pto del Carnero
Imperial
La Mocha
R. Cauten
R. Tolten
B. Queule
Pto de Galera
Baldivia
R. Bueno
Pto Villaria
Pto S. Marcela
C. de Changue
Golfo de los Govenados
Osorno
C. de la valena
C. Felix
C. astro
Pto S. Ciprian
Pto Sta Clara
Cabo de Islas
I. de Nuestra Senora del Socorro
Pto de S. Domingo
C. de Diego Gallego
Pto S. Stevan
C. S. Andres
C. de Ochavario
V. de Nuestra Senora
Aguas segur dis Diego Galligo
Abra de S. Guillen
Pto del Gada
Serrania
Ancon Sin Salida
Pto de los Reyes
Pto de los Inocentes
Pto de S. Augustin
Sierra Nevada
C. de la Roia
C. de S. Catelina
Porto de S. Amaro
Roca Partida
Abra de San Victoriana
Sorlinges
FRETVM MAGALLANI
C. de la Victoria
Suyer Eylanden
S. Jerome Canael
C. Gallant
C. Hollande
C. Froward
Porto Famine
Ridder Bay
PATAGONVM
REGIO
Rio de la Cruz
Rio de Gallegos
Puerto de los Leones
Ancon de Sardinas
C. de S. Elena
Rio de los Camarones
C. S. Iorge
C. Blanco
Barrancas Blancas
Porto Desire
B. de los Trabajos
Spiering Bay
I. de S. Dionysio
B. de San Iulian
Sybolt de Waerds Eylanden
STRAET VAN MAGALAEN.
Entrada de S. Sebastian
Tierra
del
Fuego.
C. de Pinnas
C. de S. Ines
Mauritius Lan
Schapenhams Bay
I. de Goncalvo
I. de S. Ilefonso
Lheremyten Eyland.
I. de Diego Ramires
Barnevelts Eylanden
Caep de Hoorn
I. de Diego Ramires

Plate 2. Paskaarte van't zuÿdelÿckste Deel ven AMERICA van Cabo St. Antonio, tot Caep de Hoorn, Amsterdam, Bÿ Hendrick Doncker [1663]. Courtesy of the Trustees of the British Library.

Plate 3. A DRAUGHT OF PORTE SAN JULYAN in THE South EAST COAST OF AMARICA CALLEd PATAGONA. (BL, Add MS 88980C) Courtesy of the Trustees of the British Library.

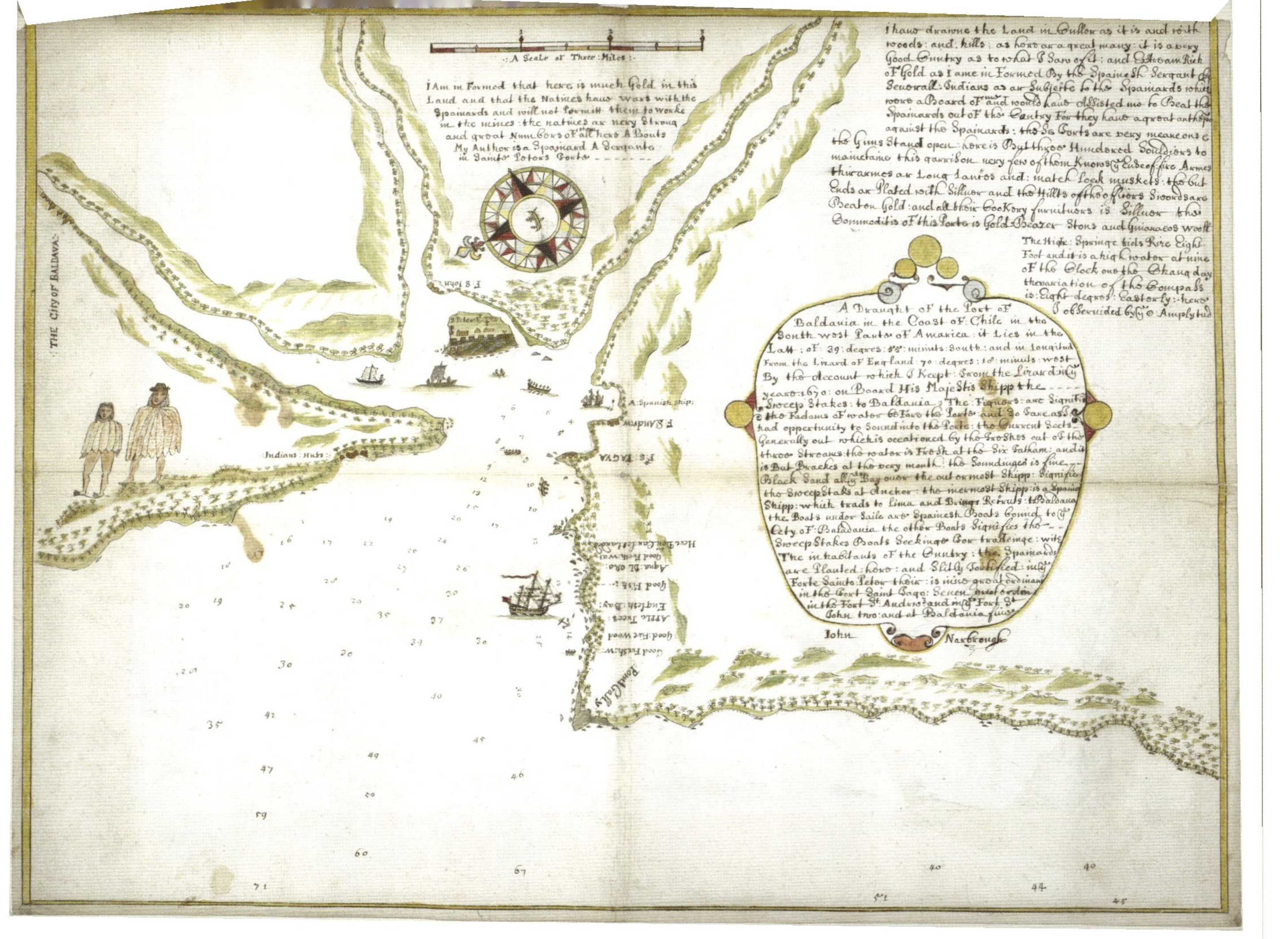

Plate 4. A Draught of the Port oF Baldavia (BL, Add.MS 88980D). Courtesy of the Trustees of the British Library.

Plate 5 A Mapp of the Streights of Magelan drawn by Captn John Narbrough &c. (BL, Maps, Add MS 5414,29), the 'Sloane Map'.

Plate 6. Chart of Patagonia Regio Inscribed to the R. Hon.Robert Earl of Oxford and Manchester &c. (Bl, Add. MS 88980E). Courtesy of the Trustees of the British Library.

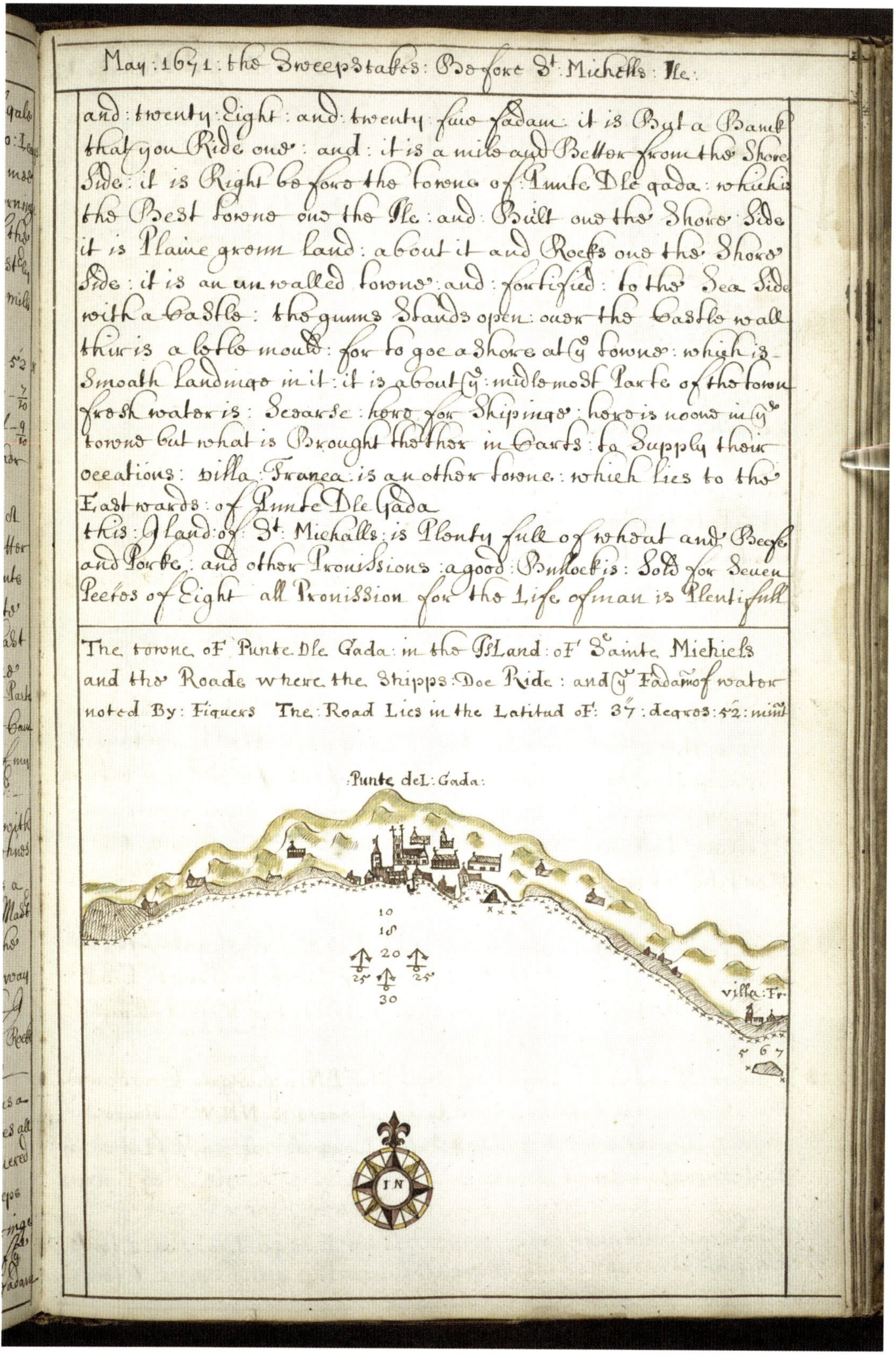

May: 1671: the Sweepstakes: Before St. Michells: Ile:

and: twenty: Eight: and: twenty five fadam: it is By a Bank
that you Ride one: and: it is a mile and Better from the Shore
Side: it is Right before the towne of: Punte Dle gada: which is
the Best towne one the Ile: and: Built one the Shore Side
it is Plaine growne land: about it and Rocks one the Shore
Side: it is an unwalled towne: and: fortified: to the Sea Side
with a Castle: the gunns Stands open: over the Castle wall
thir is a little mould: for to goe a Shore at ye towne: which is-
Smoath landinge in it: it is about ye midlemost Parte of the town
fresh water is: Scarse: here for Shippinge: here is noone in ye
towne but what is Brought thether in Carts: to Supply their
occations: villa: Franca is another towne: which lies to the
Eastwards: of Punte Dle Gada
this: Iland: of: St. Michalls: is Plenty full of wheat and Beefe
and Porke: and other Provissions: a good: Bullock is: Sold for Seven
Peeces of Eight all Provission for the Life of man is Plentifull

The towne oF Punte Dle Gada: in the Island: oF Sainte Michiels
and the Roade where the Shipps: Doe Ride: and ye Fadam of water
noted By: Figuers The: Road Lies in the Latitud oF: 37: degrees: 52: minit

Plate 7. The towne oF Punte Dle Gada in the Island oF Sainte Michiels (BL, Add MS 88980A), p. 216. Courtesy of the Trustees of the British Library.

Plate 8. The City and Castle: and Roade of Angria: in the Iland of Trecera. (BL, Add MS 88980A), p. 219. Courtesy of the Trustees of the British Library.

Plate 9. A New Mapp of MAGELLANS STRAIGHTS Discovered by Capt: John Narbro

ʟe and sold by John Thornton 1673. Courtesy of the Trustees of the British Library.

Sr: John Narbroughs
Island
A Scale of sixteen English miles
4
8
12
16
20
30
70
70
19

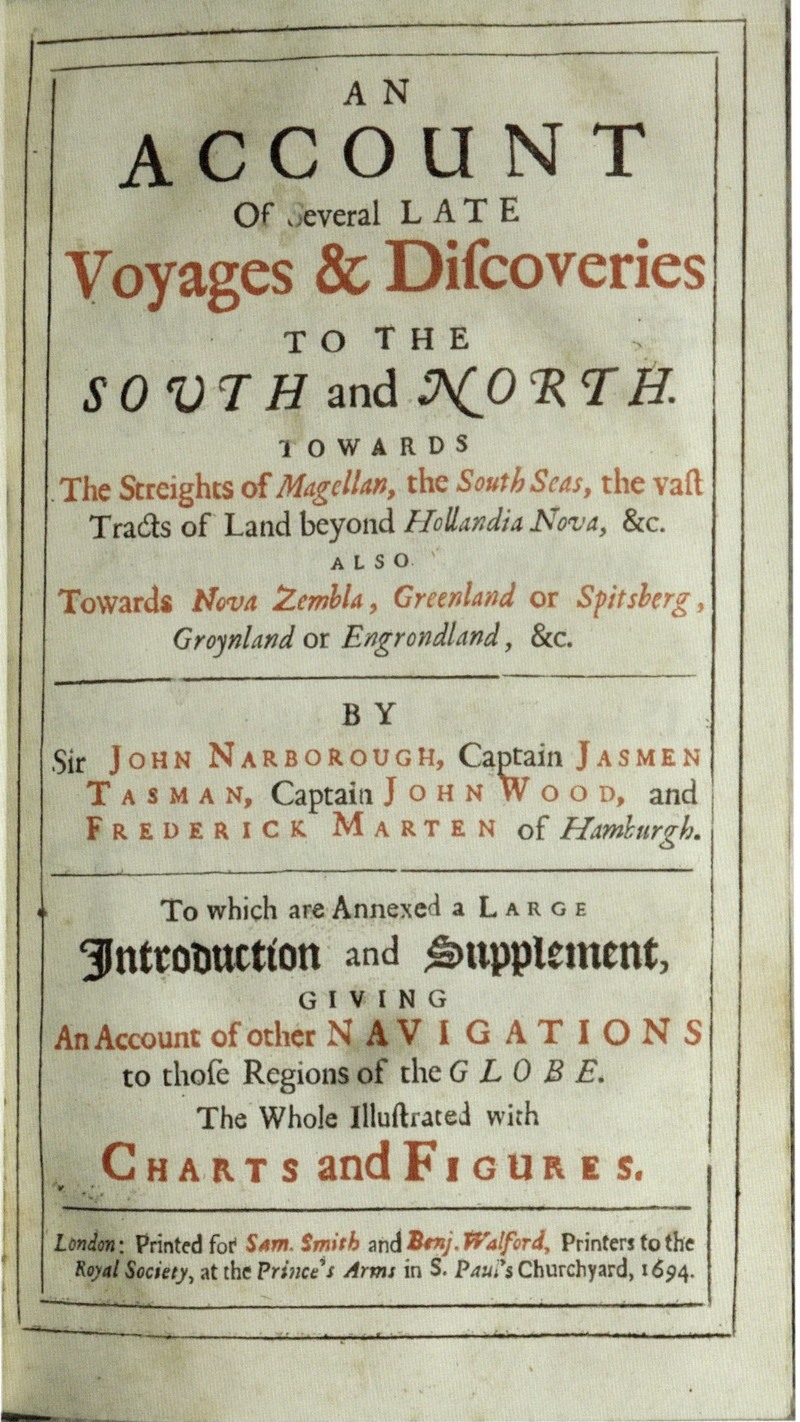

AN

ACCOUNT

Of Several LATE

Voyages & Discoveries

TO THE

SOUTH and *NORTH*.

TOWARDS

The Streights of *Magellan*, the *South Seas*, the vast Tracts of Land beyond *Hollandia Nova*, &c.

ALSO

Towards *Nova Zembla*, *Greenland* or *Spitsberg*, *Groynland* or *Engrondland*, &c.

BY

Sir JOHN NARBOROUGH, Captain JASMEN TASMAN, Captain JOHN WOOD, and FREDERICK MARTEN of *Hamburgh*.

To which are Annexed a LARGE

Introduction and Supplement,

GIVING

An Account of other NAVIGATIONS to those Regions of the *GLOBE*.

The Whole Illustrated with

CHARTS and FIGURES.

London: Printed for *Sam. Smith* and *Benj. Walford*, Printers to the *Royal Society*, at the *Prince's Arms* in S. *Paul's* Churchyard, 1694.

Plate 11. The title page of Smith and Walford's 1694 edition of *An account of several Late Voyages & Discoveries* containing Sir John Narbrough's Voyage to the Streights of Magellan. Photograph courtesy of Richard J. Campbell.

AN

ACCOUNT

Of ſeveral LATE

Voyages and *Diſcoveries:*

I. Sir *John Narbrough's* Voyage

TO THE

SOUTH-SEA

By the Command of King *Charles the Second:* And his Inſtructions for Setling a *Commerce* in thoſe Parts. With a Deſcription of the Capes, Harbours, Rivers, Cuſtom of the Inhabitants, and Commodities in which they Trade.

II. Captain *J. Taſman's* Diſcoveries on the Coaſt of the South *Terra Incognita.*

III. Captain *J. Wood's* Attempt to Diſcover a North-Eaſt Paſſage to *CHINA.*

IV. *F. Marten's* Obſervations made in *Greenland*, and other Northern Countries.

To which are Added, a LARGE INTRODUCTION and SUPPLEMENT, CONTAINING Short Abſtracts of other Voyages into thoſe Parts, and Brief Deſcriptions of them.

The Whole Illuſtrated with Exact CHARTS, and Curious FIGURES.

LONDON, Printed for *D. Brown* without *Temple-Bar*, *J. Round* in *Exchange-Ally*, *W. Innys* in St. *Paul's* Church-yard, and *T. Ward* in the *Temple-Lane.* 1711.

Plate 12. The title page of the 1711 republication of *An account of several Late Voyages & Discoveries*. Photograph courtesy of Richard J. Campbell.

Plate 13. Sir John Narbrough's tomb in St Clement's Church, Knowlton, Kent. Photograph courtesy of Richard J.Campbell.

Plate 14. The monument to Sir John Narbrough's sons, Sir John and Mr James, opposite Narbrough's chest tomb in St Clement's Church, Knowlton, Kent but often mistaken for his tomb. Photograph courtesy of Richard J. Campbell.

Novemb*er* the 26th being Saturday, it was hazy Drisly weather & a fresh Gale of wind SSW. This morning at day light we Stood into the Shoare, and at 6 of the Clocke we Saw the Island Called NESTRIA SENIORA DEL SACORA,[1] and at one of the Clocke we came to an Anchor in 10 fath*om* Water in a fair Sandy Bay, on the E Side of the Island.[2] I find the Course from Cape Disado to this Island to be N and the distance to be 159 Leagues by my Acco*unt*. One point of Island where we ridd bore NW by W of me distance 5 Miles and we ridd about one Mile & a halfe from any part of the Island. We were no Sooner at Anchor but the Capt*ain* Ordered me a Shoare to See for Indians, and See what the Island afforded, which is wood and fresh water plenty, but I Saw no Indians. I Saw indeed an Indians house much like our Arbours under the Side of a Rocke, on the which Rock there Sate greate Store of white Brests, being fowles of the Same Sort we Saw before in the N Sea,[3] and I went and killed about 2 or 300 of them and brought them on board with me, we knocked them down with Sticks, they being young and Could not Flee. Here are Brand Geese and Ducks & Peecks, good Store & divers other Wild fowles.

Novemb*er* 30th being Wednesday – fair weather and the wind Southerly. This morning at Six of the Clocke we wayed & went [to] looke for a Harbour to Secure our Shipp in NW from the place we Ridd. We Saw an Opening which we Supposed to be Santo Domingo, and we Stand over to view it saw Severall openings like Harbours, or Sounds and it maketh all like Islands.[4] I went into one of those openings, with our Pinnace expecting it had been a good Harbour, but it was not for it was an Island. I Saw the Sea Open to the E:*ward* of it, and there ly [lie] Rocks in the Middway, betwixt the Maine and it, & Shoal Water from Side, to Side,[5] [f.13r] We had but 4 fath*om* Water, and a great Sea. Here are Small Sandy Bays, you may Ridd in with a NW wind, but there is no getting out with a S wind. The wind being now at West NW we returned back againe to the Island of Succor & are Anchor'd in 7 fath*om* Water & there ridd for a wind.[6]

Decemb*er* 5th being Monday. This day we Sett Saile from the Island of Succor, to go to Castro, the wind being at SW by W. This eveing at 8 of the Clocke the Island of Succor bore S by E of me distance 5 Leagues.

Decemb*er* 6th being Tuesday fair weather and the Wind westerly a Fresh Gale. This day at 12 of the Clocke we Saw the Island of Castro,[7] it bore WNW of me distance 4 Miles, and we Stood Close a board the Shoare, and runn Downe NNW until the E most part of the Island bore NW of us, and betwixt the N & the NW it is all open, and we could [not] See any Land but only the Island & the Maine Land, to the E:ward of us, & we

[1] Isla Guamblín (44°51′S, 75°05′W).

[2] This was probably the bay between Punta Arena and Punta Edwards at the SE end of the island.

[3] See above, p. 580.

[4] The coast east of Isla Guamblín is all islands, Isla Ipun, Isla Stokes, Isla Rowlett, Isla Williams with Isla Paz and Isla Liebre to the West of it, Isla James, Isla Kent and Isla Lemu. They have channels between them, any one of which might have looked like the entrance to Santo Domingo.

[5] This might be the channel between Isla Ipun and Isla Stokes, which agrees reasonably well with the description.

[6] To wait for a favourable wind.

[7] This was probably Isla Guafo (43°37′S, 74°44′W), lying off Boca del Corcovado, the channel south of Isla Chiloé, on the east side of which Ciudad de Castro is situated.

Tackt & ply'd close under the Island, and our Capt*ain* ord*ered* me to take the Pinnace, & Sett Senior Carolus a Shoare, to See for Indians & to Trade with them, and there went So much Sea that I could not Land him So return'd a board againe, and we Stood Off to Sea all night, intending for Baldavia.[1] We had much wind at NW to night.

Decemb*er* 15th 1670 being Thursday – fair Weather and the wind Southerly. This afternoon at 5 of the Clocke we fell with the River Baldavia, and the Spaniards at St Peters discovered our Shipp; fired a gunn. We Stood in with our Shipp as farr as we thought fitt. I find the Course to be N 6°45′ Easterly from Cape Disado to this River of Baldivia, distance 262 Leagues. This morning the Capt*ain* Order'd me to Land Senior Carolus, which I did According to Ord*er*. There [came] two Cannows of[f] but would not come a Board, but one of them came to the Ships Side, [f. 13v] but imediatly he put away againe, discovering us to be Strangers, the other Cannow would not come near, but imediatly put back againe, and we Stood off & on all night following.

Decemb*er* 16th. This morning we Stood in for Baldavia, to See for Senior Carolus, but did not see him no nor Signe of him, & the Capt*ain* Sent me in with a flagg of Truce, to know if we might have the Liberty to Wood & Water, which they granted us, and they Sent of [off] a Pilot to Carry the Shipp in, and it was night before I gott a board, for our Shipp was Drove a great way and we Keep plying to Windward all night.

Decemb*er* 17th being Saturday – fair weather and the wind Westerly. We Stood in for Baldavia & at 12 of the Clocke we Anchor'd in 15 fath*om* Water black Sandy [ground] open with the River of Baldavia, and where we Ridd, Point Gallera[2] on the S Side of the River bore W by S of us distance about a Mile, and St Peters fort, which Stands in the Midle of the River, bore SE by E of us distance about 4 Miles.
This afternoon our Capt*ain* Sent me in with our Pinnace to Sett the Pylott a Shoare, and Landed him at the Same Fort he belonged unto, which was a Small Fort going in on the S Side, and I was no Sooner a Shoare but the Governer of St Peters Fort Sent for me & I went over to him, and I found he was [wanted] to know what we were and where we were bound, and from thence I returned a board againe. I heard nothing of Senior Carolus.

Decemb*er* 18th. This day the Governer of St Peters Fort Stopped 4 of our men a Shoare, but for what I know not. With in the River there are 3 Forts 2 of them Stand on the S Side going in and the other Stands on an Island in the Middle of the River, that is Called St Peters Fort. I Suppose there is 8 Gunns in it, and there was a Small vessell in the River about 30 Tunns, & Shee rod [f. 14r] under the South Shoare, in Command of the Small Forts.[3] I saw not any boats they had but great open boats which they have to Transport Goods & Soldiers, & ill Shaped Cannows.

[1] Puerto de Valdivia is 8 miles up the Río Valdivia which flows into Bahía Corral (39°49′S, 73°27′W). Fort St Peter is situated deeper into Bahía Corral on Isla Mancera (39°53′S, 73°24′W). Narbrough does not mention the firing of a gun from that fort on his arrival.

[2] This is the point under Morro Gonzal (39°51′S, 73°28′W). Punta Galera lies in 39°59′S, 73°43′W, 15 miles SW of Morro Gonzalo.

[3] In a position commanded by the guns of the forts.

Decemb*er* 19th. I was Sent with a Flagg of Truce to Parlie with them at a distance, but they would not come off to answer our expectation, So I returned a board againe. This morning I Sett two Indians a Shoare by ord*er* of the Capt*ain*, and one of them Carry'd a letter with him for the Governer which our Capt*ain* Sent to demand the Reason why he kept our men.

Decemb*er* 20th. This day the Governer Sent off a Cannow to fetch the Clothes a Shoare which belonged to our men, whom they had detained and it being the Mens desire the Capt*ain* Sent the Clothes and a letter to the Governer to know if he would Send his men off, if not to know the reason why he detained them.

Decemb*er* 21th being Wednesday. This day came a Cannow from St Fort off with a Flagg of Truce, and brought word that the Govern*er* would not Send of[f] the men – So return'd againe, and we Sett Saile and Stood off to Sea, the wind being Easterly.

December 22th being Thursday faire weather & the wind variable. This day at 12 of the Clocke point Gallera bore NE by E distance about 3 Leagues, & at 8 a Clock at night point Gallera bore E of me distance 5 Leagues, & we Stood off with the wind S & by W.

Decemb*er* 23rd being Friday fair weather, & the wind Southerly. This day we Stood in with the Shoare againe, & at 11 of the Clocke we came to an Anchor in 15 Fath*om* Water, in a Sandy Bay,[1] about 9 Miles from Baldavia, to the Southward of it & the Capt*ain* Sent me a Shoare, to See for Indians & to Trade with them, and there was very bad Landing, but I went a Shoare and made a fire, this is a very Woody Country, but could See noe Signe of people, and So I came a board againe & wee wayed & Stood off to Sea, the wind being Southerly and made the best of our way for the Streights of *Magil*lane.

[f. 14v] **January 6th 1670/71**. This morning at 4 of the Clock we Saw 4 Islands[2] which lye NNW from Cape Disado about 7 Leagues. When we first Saw the Islands, they bore NE by N of us distance 4 Leagues, and then we altered our Course & Steered E and E by S & at 6 of the Clocke we Saw Cape Disado, it bore E by S of us distance about 4 Leagues, and at 10 of the Clocke we were entered into the Streights of *Magil*laine, and at 4 of the Clocke in the afternoon we Anchor'd in a Bay 7 Leagues with in the Streights, in 14 fath*om* Water.[3]

January 7th being Saturday it was cloudy Rainny & hazy weather and a Fresh Gale of Wind at W. This morning at 4 of the Clocke we Sett Saile to the Eastward, & at 8 of the Clock at night, we Anchor'd in 8 fath*om* Water, in a fair Sandy Bay,[4] at the mouth of Batchellers River which is about 2 Leagues to the W:ward of Elizabeths Bay to the N Side.

[1] Probably Caleta Chaihuín (39°55′S, 73°36′W).

[2] Islotes (Grupo) Evangelistas, see above, pp. 273, n. 6; 592, n. 4.

[3] This anchorage is shown on the 'Royal Map' (Foldout) and is close east of Cabo Valentina (52°55′S, 74°17′W).

[4] Rada York (53°34′S, 72°19′W).

January 8th being Sunday fair weather & the Wind variable, round the Compass. This day the Capt*ain* and I went up Batcheller*s* River 4 or 5 Miles, which was as high as we could gett with a boate, and we Saw the end of the River, it runn up about 8 or 9 Miles. We went to See for Indians but we could not See any nor no Signe of Indians, & we came a board againe.

January 9th being Monday, it was Rainy foggy Weather and little Wind round the Compass. This day the Capt*ain* & I went to the S Side to See for Indians, but could See None, but they had been there very Latley, and we came a board againe.

January the 10th being Tuesday – hazy Foggy weather & the wind at W. This morning we Sett Saile with the *Sweepstakes* out of Batchellers Bay to go for Port Famine, and at 10 of the Clocke we were thwart Cape Froward.[1] It being little wind & calme all the Night following, & we Lay driving too & Fro in the Streights.

January 11th being Wednesday fair Weather, & the wind variable from the SE to the SW. This morning we made the best of our way to gett into Port Famine[2] & at 12 of the Clocke we Anchord at 9 fath*om* in the Bay of Port Famine. Here we had fishes from the Shoare to Fish our Maine Mast [f. 15r] and those we Wanted, and the place affords very good and Large Trees for fishes, and good water & good Wildfowles, also fish much like unto Mulletts, large Smelts. Here we fitted our Shipps mast and Rigging, as well as we Could and Carreen'd her,[3] & filled all our Caske with fresh Water, & tooke as much a board as we thought fitt.

January 16th *Sweepstakes* at Port Famine, in the Streights. This day being Monday fair Weather and little Wind, westerly. The Capt*ain* ord*ered* me to goe up with the boate into Sedgers River,[4] as farr as I could with Conveniencie to See for Indians, & I went up about 9 Miles but Could not gett higher, with the Boate by reason of the sunk Timber & Shoale Water. I therefore Landed & went up 2 Miles by Land to See for Indians, but could [not] See any or any thing Worth Observation, and how farr the River runneth up I know not for I could not See the End of it so I Return'd.

January 29th being Sunday fair weather & little wind at SW. This morning the Capt*ain* went over to the S Shoare to See for Indians with the Pinnace, and if there was ever a Harbour thwart of Port Famine for Shipping. This day came an Indian to the Point of Port Famine, and made a Fire & I went a Shoare to See what he had. And he had neither bow nor Arrow nor any thing to the value of a Farthing. I would have had him come a board with me, but he would not. As farr as I could understand by his Signs, that he made to me, that he had been a Slave to Some other Indians & had runn away from them and was Travelling home.

[1] Cabo Froward (53°54′S, 71°18′W).

[2] Puerto San Juan de la Posesíon or Puerto del Hambre (53°38′S, 70°56′W).

[3] To careen a ship she is heaved her down on one side and then the other, by shifting ballast and by applying purchase to the masts, to raise first one side then the other above the water level, so that they can be cleaned and repaired.

[4] Río San Juan.

January 31th fair weather and the Wind variable. This evening the Capt*ain* came a board, and haveing been over on the South Shoare to See for Harbour but could Find none.

Feb*ruary* 4th being Saturday — fair weather & the wind at W by N. This morning at 4 of the Clocke we Sett Saile for Port Famine, and by 11 we were thwart fresh Water Bay,[1] and at 6 of the Clock in the evening we Anchor'd in 12 fath*om* water in a fine Sandy Bay about 5 Leagues to the N:ward of fresh Water Bay.[2]

[f. 15v] **Feb*ruary* 5** being Sunday fair weather but very much wind at SW & WSW. This morning the Capt*ain* Sent me to fresh Water Bay to See for Indians but I saw none, So I returned a board againe.

Feb*ruary* 7th being Tuesday, fair weather and the wind Northerly. This morning the Capt*ain* ord*ered* me to take the Pinnace and goe a long the N Shoare, between Elizabeths Island and the Shoare to See for Indians, & in the afternoon it blew hard Northerly, that we could not row a head, and I put backe into a Sandy Bay & went a Shoare, and Stayed there all night, and in this Bay we haled a Seane,[3] and gott a great many good and Large Fish, which were Smelts of 20 inches Long and 8 inches Broad.

Feb*ruary* 8th being Wednesday – fair Weather and Wind at W by W.[4] This morning at 4 of the Clocke I runn downe the Streights with the Pinnace keeping the N Shoare a board, & runn betwixt it and Elizabeths Island, and Saw no Indians, but I Saw Severall places where the [they] had been very Lately, & where they had built their Cannows. From Cape Disado to Elizabeths Island there is Wood and fresh Water plenty, & from Elizabeths Island to Cape Virgin Mary Wood & Fresh Water is Scarce to come by. This afternoon at 3 of the Clocke I gott a board againe, and at 4 of the Clocke we came to an Anchor in 8 fath*om* Water black Sand. We ridd with in a Mile of the N Shoare of St Gregerys[5] & St Bartholomews Island, they where both Shutt in one,[6] & they bore SSE of me & Elizabeths Island bore S by E, & here we ridd with the Shipp all night.[7]

Feb*ruary* 9th being Thursday – fair Weather & the [wind] westerly. This morning the Capt*ain* Sent me to See for Indians, but I could See none, but I fell with a good harbour for Small Vessells on the N Side, and at the South end of the Great Deepe Bay, thwart of Elizabeths Island.[8] At the enterance of this Harbour it is not a bow Shott from Side to Side, & I Sounded it & there was 12 foote Water at a Low Water. From the entrance of this Harbour to the upper end of it is about 7 Miles. In this Harbour there is great Store

[1] Bahía Agua Fresca (53°23′S Longitude 70°58′W).

[2] This would put the bay in the vicinity of the modern port of Punta Arenas; however, Narbrough says this anchorage was 2 leagues to the north of Freshwater Bay; see above, p. 310.

[3] Hauled the seine net.

[4] Narbrough's journal has 'wind at West a fine gale' for this day.

[5] This was St Georges Island.

[6] In line one with the other.

[7] This anchorage was in Bahía Whitsand (52°44′S, 70°36′W).

[8] This is shown on the 'Royal Map' and 'Sloane Map' (Foldout and Plate 5), as Peckits Harbour. It is now called Puerto Zenteno (52°46′S, 70°44′W). The mouth is well over a bow shot across, but the configuration of the land and the islets at the entrance make the identification certain.

of Geese & Ducks [f. 16r] & a Shoare there is great Store of heath Berries & hurts[1] & Small Black Berryes, very good & well tasted, but I saw no Indians, So I return'd againe aboard. The Capt*ain* went into an other Harbour, a Mile to the S:ward of the Second Narrow on the N Shoare & Sounded, & had 4 fath*om* Water in it. It is very broad within, & there is great Store of Sea Crabbs in it.[2]

Feb*ruary* 11th. Fair Weather, & the wind variable. This day the Capt*ain* ord*ered* me to go with the Pinnace & discover the N Shoare, & if I could with Convenience discover Some part of the South Land, & to go to the first Narrow & there to Stay for the Shipp. So I went through the Second Narrow & Land on the South Side, in a fine Sandy Bay, or Cove, expecting to fall with some Indians, for I Saw many fires upon the Land, and I went up about 5 or 6 Miles up into the Country, but could See no Indians, and night Coming on I returned backe againe, & we picted [pitched] at Tent to Ly in & there we Lay all night, and it being high water I Sett a Seane thwart a pond of water,[3] & there it Stood till it was day, and then I hall'd all over the Pond, at once & hall'd a Shoare about 700 good & Large fish like Mulletts.[4] The Land is very dry Barren Land and nothing to be seen on it worth observation.

Feb*ruary* 12 being Sunday fair weather & wind Northerly. This morning I went over to the N Shoare, & there I fell with a fair Sandy Bay, I Sounded & it had 6, 7, 8, 9, 10, 11 fath*om* Water, about halfe a Mile from the Shoare. This Bay is betwixt the 2d Narrow and Cape Gregory,[5] Close under Cape Gregory. This Cape is about 5 or 6 Miles to the Eastward of the Second Narrow. Here I Landed the wind being Easterly a fresh Gale, & haled the Boate up dry, and went up into the Country to See for Indians, but Saw none and I returned to our Boate againe, where we Pitched our Tent & there Laid all night.

Feb*ruary* 13th being Monday, fair weather and a fresh Gale of Wind Westerly. This morning I rune all along the N Shoare, from Cape Gregory to the first Narrow, But Seeing 3 Anchors that lay up above high water marke in a Small Sandy Cove,[6] [f. 16v] I there Landed & haled up the Boate, and Searching about to See if we Could fall with any Gunns, or other Trade, one of our men found an Iron Commander[7] for Small Shipps Toppe. One of those Anchors was 12 foot in the Shanke[8] & the other 2 were[9] foot apeece,

[1] Peckett refers here to hurtleberries otherwise known as whortleberies; see above, pp. 260, n. 3; 577.

[2] Ensenada Oazy (52°42′S, 70°33′W). It is shown on the 'Royal Map' and 'Sloane Map' (Foldout and Plate 5) as Oase Harbour.

[3] Set the seine fishing net across the pond and hauled it in the morning.

[4] Possibly John Wood accompanied this party. In BL, MS 46A, p. 162, he notes that 'The Land from the South Side to the Second Narrow to the Southward of these Isleands is high Land and by the many fires we saw I doe really beleive it to be well peopled. It is a Sandy shore and shold off: within the narrow on the South Side is a little Cove where at high water is abundance of Fishes like Mulletts: wee catcht at one hall in our seane 700 of them the best being as bigg as a Mackerell.'

[5] Cabo Gregorio (52°40′S, 70°13′W). The bay is not named on modern charts.

[6] The anchors are shown on the 'Royal Map' and 'Sloane Map' (Foldout and Plate 5) lying on the north shore of the First Narrow (Primera Angostura).

[7] See above, p. 314, n. 5.

[8] This is the main vertical piece of the anchor.

[9] Blank Space. Narbrough's journal has 11 ft, for 14 Feb. 1670; see above, p. 314.

they were all Spanish Anchors. The Land here is Barren dry Land, and affords neither wood nor fresh water, and for the Space of 5 or 6 Miles the Land is full of Ratts, who have holes in the ground like Coney Boroughs, there food I Suppose to be Limppetts for there is a great Store of Limppett Shells lying near there holes. I Saw no Indians here nor anything worth observation, and it being night here we Pitched our Tent & Lay here all night. Here are very good Sandy Bayes, in the N Side, betwixt the first and Second Narrow, for I Sounded all a long as I came downe in the boate, I had 10 & 12 fath*om* water a great birth from the Shoare.

Feb*ruary* 14th being Tuesday Close hazy weather with some Raine & very much wind Westerly. This morning I Saw the Shipp coming downe the Streights and after Shee was through the Narrow, she bore too[1] & I gott a board, and we made all the Saile we could and by night we gott Cleare of the Streights, into the North Sea, and at 8 of the Clock Cape Virgin Mary[2] bore NW half a point westerly, distance 4 Leagues.

Feb*ruary* 23th being Thursday, fair weather & the Wind variable from the NNW to the WNW. This evening we Came to an Anchor in 22 fath*om*, Sandy ground, on the N part of America, in the Latitude 47°15′ South Latitude; and then Cape Blanco bore NNW distance about 6 Leagues.

Feb*ruary* 24th being Friday – fair weather and little wind Northerly. This morning we weighed to go for Port desire Bay, in the evening at 6 of the Clocke we Anchor'd in the Bay in 14 fath*om* Water.

Feb*ruary* 25th being Saturday, fair weather and the wind easterly a fresh Gale. This day the Long boate went into Port Desire[3] for fresh Water, but could not gett above 5 or 6 Puncheons full, for there was no more to be had, and [f. 17r] what was Brought a Board was Brackish. Fair weather tonight.

Feb*ruary* 26th being Sunday – fair weather and a fresh gale a wind at SSW. This morning we Sett Saile from Port Desire to go for England, and at 12 of the Clocke we were in Latitude 47°10′ S Latit*ude*, and then Cape Blanco bore NW of me but not by the Campass, for here is a point & a ½ variation Easterly,[4] & at 4 of the Clocke Cape Blanco bore NNW off by the Compass, distance 9 Miles, and then we had 20 fath*om* water, and when it bore WNW from us & but 8 Miles off we had but 10 fath*om* Water. Here is very good Sounding all the Coast along, from this Cape to Cape Virgin Mary, which lyeth in Latitude 52°15′ S Lat*itude*,[5] within 5 Leagues of[f] the Maine you will have 25 or 30 fath*om*, & 10 Leagues of you will have 50 or 55 fath*om* Water, it is Black ousey Sand.

[1] Hove to, or lay to, by adjusting the sails to counteract each other and hence take the way off the ship.

[2] Cabo Vírgenes.

[3] Puerto Deseado (47°45′S, 65°53′W).

[4] 16°52′·5.

[5] Cabo Vírgenes (52°20′S, 68°21′W).

May the 17th. Fair Weather. This morning we Saw the Island of St Maryes,[1] one of the Isles of Azores. It bore ENE distance about 16 Leagues, by Estimation, it being fair weather & the wind SE.

May 19th being Friday fair weather & the wind easterly. This morning at 7 of the Clocke the Towne of Pantelege[2] upon the Island of St Micheals one of the Isles of Azores, bore N of me distance about 2 Leagues and my Lat*itu*de difference from Cape Blanco to this Towne is, [*blank space*] Meridian distance from Cape Blanco to this Town is Longitude [*blank space*] Miles towards the E. This Towne Lyeth so far to the E:ward of the Cape. This day the Capt*ain* Sent me a Shoare to enquire News from England, and whether we had warr or peace with any other Nation or not. I was informed by Mr Rich*ard* Hutchinson, Consull, that we had Warr with none but the Algereens.[3] So I returned a board againe & we made all the Saile we Could for England.

May 23th 1671 being Tuesday – fair weather & much Wind at NE, & our Provisions all most done & but little water in the Shipp we bore up to go for Tecsera.[4]

May the 24th being Wednesday Close hazy weather & a fresh gale of wind at NE by E. This afternoon we Anchor'd in Angrea Roade[5] in 16 fath*om* Water.

May the 26 being Friday fair weather & Little wind at NE. This afternoon we Sett Saile out of Angrea Roade to go for England.

[1] Santa Maria (37°N, 25°W).

[2] Ponta Delgada (37°45′N, 25°40′W), on the island of São Miguel.

[3] Algerians. This refers to the continual conflict with the Algerian pirates in the Mediterranean.

[4] Terceira (38°39′N, 27°14′W).

[5] Angra do Heroismo (38°39′N, 27°14′W).

[f. 18r][1] A daily accompt of the Sweepstakes way, kept by me Nathaniell Peckett Lieutenant from the Lizard in England to the Maderas. Septemb*er* 29th the Lizard bore N by E distance 9 Leagues. Anno 1669.

Anno 1669 Month	Day	Latitude by Observation or accompt	What Latitude I am in	Difference Of Latitude	Longitude from the Lizard	Difference of Longitude	Distance run	Easting	Westing	Northing	Southing	Course Made Good	How we Had the wind	Variation
Septem.	29	By accompt	49°38′	0°32′	0°09′	0°09′	33	–	6	–	–	–		
	30	By accompt	49°24′	0°14′	0°47′	0°38′	29	–	5·3	–	14	S61°20′W		
Octob.	1	By observation	49°23′	0°01′	0°38′	0°51′	36·1	–	36	–	1	S88°25′W		
	2	By accompt	49°26′	0°03′	2°51′	1°13′	50	–	49·8	3	–	N86°30′W		
	3	By observation	49°07′	0°19′	3°20′	0°29′	27	–	19	–	19	S45°00′W		
	4	By accompt	48°35′	0°32′	3°50′	0°30′	35	–	12·3	–	32	S21°50′W		
	5	By accompt	47°54′	0°41′	3°56′	0°06′	42	–	4	–	41	S5°27′W		
	6	By accompt	47°46′	0°08′	4°05′	0°09′	11·4	–	7·1	–	8	S38°50′W		
	7	By observation	46°30′	1°16′	5°02′	0°57′	85	–	38	–	76	S26°40′W		
	8	By accompt	45°10′	1°20′	6°35′	1°35′	102	–	64·4	–	80	S39°00′W		
	9	By accompt	42°50′	2°22′	7°36′	1°1′	146	–	43·4	–	140	S17°15′W		
	10	By accompt	40°33′	2°17′	8°13′	0°37′	140	–	27·2	–	137	S11°15′W		
	11	By accompt	38°11′	2°22′	8°49′	0°36′	145	–	29·1	–	142	S11°15′W		
	12	By observation	33°48′[2]	2°23′	9°36′	0°47′	144	–	36	–	143	S14°35′W		
	13	By observation	33°40′	2°08′	9°53′	0°17′	129	–	11·3	–	128	S5°00′W		
	14	By accompt	33°19′	0°21′	10°18′	0°25′	30	–	21·2	–	21	S45°00′W		

Anno 1669. Octob*er* 13th being Wednesday fair weather this day at 12 of the clocke we saw the Island of Port Sancto it bore S by W of me distance about 10 Leagues, and we made all the Saile we could for the Maderas, in the evening the South end of the Maderas bore S of me distance about 4 Leagues. Now my Latitude[3] difference is 10°18′and west from the Lizard in England , my Meridian distance 143 Leagues 1·8 from the Lizard.

[1] In the following table the number of minutes are normally given by Peckett without an initial zero, however to make it easier to follow this has been inserted, e.g. 2°04′ and not 2°4′.

[2] This should be 35°48′.

[3] This should be Longitude.

[f. 18v] A daily accompt of the Ship's way kept by me Nath*aniell* Peckett L*ieutenan*t from the Island of Madera to the Island Cape de Verde. This morning at 2 of the Clocke being the 17th of Octob*er* we sett Saile out of the Bay of Fanshawll at the Madera Island and at 12 of the Clock the Island bore NE of mee Distance 9 Leagues.

1669 Month	Day	Latitude by Observation & accompt	What Latitude I am in	Difference Of Latitude	Latitude[1] From the Maderas	Difference Of Longitude	Distance run	Easting	Westing	Northing	Southing	Course Made good	How we had the wind	Variation
Octob.	17	By accompt	31°57′	0°19′	0°23′	–	37	–	19	–	19	S45°00′W		
	18	By observation	31°22′	0°35′	0°23′	–	35	–	–	–	35	S	WSW	
	19	By accompt	29°12′	1°40′	1°11′	0°48′	102	–	38·5	–	100	S22°30′W	Variable	
	20	By observation	27°51′	1°51′	2°04′	0°53′	120	–	46	–	111	S22°30′W	N by E	
	21	By accompt	26°02′	1°49′	2°28′	0°24′	112	–	21·8	–	109	S11°15′W	N by E	
	22	By observation	24°29′	1°33′	2°49′	0°21′	85	–	18·1	–	93	S11°15W	NE by N	
	23	By observation	23°04′	1°25′	3°11′	0°22′	87	–	17	–	85	S11°15′W	NNE	
	24	By accompt	21°13′	1°51′	3°24′	0°17′	113	–	13·6	–	111	S5°00′W	NE by N	
	25	By observation	18°50′	2°23′	4°06′	0°38′	149	–	36·6	–	143	S14°15′W	NE by N	
	26	By observation	16°38′	2°12′	4°57′	0°51′	141	–	48	–	132	S15°50′W	NNE	
	27	By accompt	16°34′	0°00′	6°09′	0°12′	70	–	70	–	–	West	NE	
					6°09′				331		938			

Octob*er* 21, 1669 being Wednesday, fair weather & the wind at NE. This Morning at Nine of the Clocke wee Saw the Island of Saull when wee saw the Island first it bore W by N of me distance about 5 Leagues. Now my Madera Distance is about 331 Miles westing, and in Difference of Longitude from the Madera Island is 6°09′. Sall Island being to the Westward.

[1] This should be Longitude.

[f. 19r] Novemb*er* 5th 1669. This afternoon at 4 of the Clocke we Sett Saile for Port Bray at St Jago one of the Islands of Cape de Verde, for Cape Blanco or Cape St George, upon the Coast of America. This evening at 8 of the Clocke the Island of St Iago bore NNE of me distance 6 miles.

1669 Month	Day	Latitude by Observation & accompt	What Latitude I am in	Difference of Latitude	Latitude[1] from the Maderas	Difference of Longitude	Distance run	Easting	Westing	Northing	Southing	Course made good	How we had the wind	Variation
Novemb.	6	By accompt	13°19′	1°05′	1°10′	0°10′	66	9·6	–	–	65	S8°24′E	ENE	
	7	By accompt	11°31′	1°48′	0°19′	0°09′	110	8·3	–	–	108	S5°00′E	ENE	
	8	By accompt	10°22′	1°09′	0°13′	0°06′	69	–	5·7	–	69	S4°45′W	ENE	
	9	By observation	10°00′	0°27′	0°04′	0°09′	25	–	9·5	–	22	S22°30′W	Easterly	
	10	By observation	8°43′	1°17′	0°28′	0°32′	48[2]	–	32	–	77	S22°30′W	E by N	
	11	By accompt	7°41′	1°02′	0°28′	0°00′	62	–	–	–	62	S	E by S	
	12	By accompt	7°07′	0°34′	1°02′	0°34′	47	–	34	–	34	S45°00′W	ESE	
	13	By observation	6°12′	0°05′	1°02′	0°00′	55	–	–	–	55	S	E by N	
	14	By accompt	5°04′	1°08′	1°02′	0°00′	68	–	–	–	68	S	E by N	
	15	By observation	4°00′	1°04′	1°56′	0°54′	84	–	54	–	64	S40°00′W	SE	
	16	By Observation	3°13′	0°47′	2°14′	0°20′	51	–	19·5	–	47	S11°15′W	SE	
	17	By accompt	3°51′	0°38′	1°23′	0°51′	63	50	–	38	–	N52°50′E	SE	
	18	By accompt	4°15′	0°24′	0°21′	0°58′	62	57	–	24		N61°30′W	SSE	

[1] This should be Longitude.
[2] To match the differences in Westing and Southing this should be 84.

[f. 19v]

1669 Month	Day	Latitude by Observation & accompt	What Latitude I am in	Difference of Latitude	Longitude from St Iago	Difference of Longitude	Distance run	Easting	Westing	Northing	Southing	Course made good	How we had the wind	Variation
Novemb.	19	By accompt	4°25′	0°10′	0°04′	0°21′	23	21	–	10	–	N64°30′E	Variable	
	20	By accompt	4°16′	0°09′	0°08′	0°04′	10		3·8	–	9	S22°30′W	Variable	
	21	By observation	5°25′	1°08′	0°08′	0°00′	68	–	–	68	–	N	Variable	
	22	By accompt	5°10′	0°15′	0°23′	0°15′	21	–	4·8[1]	–	15	S45°00′W	Variable	
	23	By accompt	4°56′	0°14′	0°03′	0°20′	24	20	–	–	14	S56°15′E	Variable	
	24	By accompt	4°53′	0°03′	0°06′	0°03′	4	–	2·3	–	3	S35°40′W	ESE	
	25	By accompt	4°50′	0°03′	0°24′	0°18′	18·4	–	18	–	3	S82°27′W	Variable	
	26	By accompt	4°44′	0°06′	0°18′	0°06′	9	6	–	–	6	S45°00′E	Variable	
	27	By accompt	4°50′	0°06′	0°24′	0°06′	9	–	6	6	–	N45°00′W	SE	
	28	By observation	4°46′	0°04′	0°21′	0°03′	5	3	–	–	4	S23°45′E	SE by E	
	29	By observation	5°30′	0°17′	0°22′	0°43′	46	43.4	–	17	0	N19°10′E	SE	
	30	By observation	5°15′	0°12′	0°37′	0°15′	19	14·7	–	12	–	N00°40′E[2]	Variable	
Decemb.	1	By accompt	5°07′	0°08′	0°34′	0°03′	8·5	–	3·3	–	8	S22°30′W	Easterly	
	2	By accompt	4°39′	0°28′	1°02′	0°28′	40	28	–	–	28	S45°00′E	Variable	

[1] From the course and distance run this should be 15.

[2] From the distance run and easting and northing this should be N50°40′E.

[f. 20r]

Month	Day	Latitude by Observation & accompt	What Latitude I am in	Difference of Latitude	Longitude from St Iago	Difference of Longitude	Distance run	Easting	Westing	Northing	Southing	Course made good	How we had the wind	Variation
Decemb.	3	By accompt	4°59′	0°29′	1°04′	0°02′	36[1]	30	–	20	–	N56°15′E	SSE	
	4	By accompt	5°17′[2]	0°02′	1°00′	0°04′	4·5	–	4	–	2	S67°30′W	SSE	
	5	By observation	5°16′	0°19′	1°19′	0°19′	27	19	–	19	–	N45°00′E	Southerly	
	6	By observation	5°13′	0°03′	1°42′	0°23′	23·2	23	–	–	3	S82°30′E	Southerly	
	7	By observation	5°08′	0°12′	2°11′	0°29′	3·4[3]	29	–	–	12	S67°30′E	Variable	
	8	By accompt	8°55′[4]	0°06′	2°00′	0°09′	10·8	9	–	–	6	S59°00′E	Variable	
	9	By accompt	4°49′	0°06′	2°47′	0°27′	28	27·6	–	–	6	S78°15′E	Southerly	
	10	By accompt	4°27′	0°22′	2°52′	0°05′	23	4·8	–	–	22	S11°15′E	Variable	
	11	By accompt	4°00′	0°27′	3°12′	0°20′	34	20·5	–	–	27	S37°15′E	Variable	
	12	By observation	3°18′	0°42′	3°40′	0°28′	50·5	28	–	–	42	S33°45′E	Southerly	
	13	By observation	3°02′	0°16′	4°06′	0°26′	30·5	26	–	–	16	S58°45′E	Easterly	
	14	By observation	2°46′	0°16′	3°40′	0°16′	22·5		16	–	16	S45°00′W	Southerly	
	15	By observation	2°37′	0°09′	3°27′	0°17′	19	–	17	–	9	S62°30′W	SSE	
	16	By observation	2°24′	0°13′	2°39′	0°48′[5]	40	–	38	–	13	S71°15′W	Southerly	
	17	By observation	1°55′	0°29′	3°24′	0°45′	54	–	45·5	–	29	S57°30′W	SSE	
	18	By observation	1°21′	0°34′	2°42′	0°42′	54	–	42	–	34	S51°00′W	S by E	

[1] There appears to be an error here. The course and differences would give a distance run of 32 miles.
[2] This should be 4°57′
[3] This is given in the original as 3·4.
[4] This should be 4°55′.
[5] This is an error. The longitude from St Jago has been corrected on the next line.

[f. 20v]

1669 Month	Day	Latitude by Observation & accompt	What Latitude I am in	Difference of Latitude	Longitude from St Iago	Difference of Longitude	Distance run	Easting	Westing	Northing	Southing	Course made Good	How we had the wind	Variation
Decemb.	19	By observation	0°44′	0°37′	1°58′	0°44′	56·5	–	43	–	37	S47°20′E	SE	
	20	By observation	0°00′[1]	0°37′	1°02′	0°56′	67	–	56	–	37	S56°15′W	SE	
	21	By observation	South Lat 0°17′	0°24′	0°03′	0°28′	28[2]		29·5		24	S51°00′W	SE by S	
	22	By observation	0°40′	0°23′	0°15′	0°17′	28	–	27	–	23	S37°00′W	SE	
	23	By observation	1°16′	0°36′	0°39′	0°24′	43	–	24	–	36	S33°45′W	SE	
	24	By observation	2°03′	0°47′	1°04′	0°25′	54	–	26	–	47	S29°00′W	SSW	
	25	By observation	3°09′	1°06′	1°26′	0°22′	65·5	–	21·4	–	66	S18°00′W	SE by E	
	26	By observation	4°08′	0°59′	1°56′	0°30′	66	–	30	–	59	S27°00′W	SE	
	27	By observation	5°30′	1°30′	1°56′	0°00′	90	–	–	–	90	South	Easterly	
	28	By accompt	7°07′	1°29′	1°56′	0°00′	89	–	–	–	89	South	E by S	
	29	By accompt	8°36′	1°29′	1°56′	0°00′	90	–	–	–	90	South	E by S	
	30	By accompt	9°48′	1°11′	1°56′	0°00′	71	–	–	–	71	South	E by S	
	31	By accompt	10°56′	1°08′	2°30′	0°34′	76	–	34	–	68	S26°30′W	ESE	07°28′
January	1	By observation	11°48′	0°52′	2°48′	0°14′	54·5	–	14	–	52	S16°52′W	SE	
	2	By observation	12°56′	1°08′	3°04′	0°00′[3]	71	–	20	–	68	S16°52′W	E by S	37°15′[4]
	3	By observation	14°16′	1°20′	3°20′	0°16′	82	–	16	–	*80*	S11°15′W	E by S	7°37′

[1] This would appear to be put on the equator on purpose as the latitude has been corrected on the next line.

[2] This should be 38 to match the course and difference of westing and southing.

[3] This is an error. The difference is 16′ but the westing of 20 miles gives 20′·5 in this latitude.

[4] This should presumably be 7°15′.

[f. 21r]

1669/70 Month	Day	Latitude by observation & accompt	What Latitude I am in	Difference of Latitude	Longitude from St Iago	Difference of Longitude	Distance run	Easting	Westing	Northing	Southing	Course made Good	How we had the wind	Variation
January	4	By observation	15°32′	1°16′	3°35′	0°15′	78	–	15	–	76	S11°15′W	S by E	6°04′
	5	By observation	17°04′	1°22′	3°36′	0°11′	82·4	–	16·9	–	82	S7°34′W	Easterly	7°04′
	6	By observation	18°07′	1°03′	3°38′	0°32′[1]	63·4	–	7·7	–	6[2]	S7°00′W	Easterly	7°34′
	7	By accompt	18°56′	0°49′	4°08′	0°10′	50	–	9·7	–	49	S11°15′W	Variable	7°45′
	8	By accompt	19°44′	0°58′	4°37′	0°29′	60	–	27·5	–	52	S23°17′W	ENE	8°47′
	9	By accompt	20°38′	0°50′	5°19′	0°36′	60	–	33·2	–	50	S33°45′W	Northerly	10°40′
	10	By accompt	21°43′	1°05′	5°59′	0°46′	70	–	39	–	65	S33°45′W	NNE	11°26′
	11	By accompt	22°58′	1°15′	6°14′	0°55′	90	–	50	–	75	S33°45′W	Northerly	11°46′
	12	By accompt	24°40′	1°42′	8°14′	1°20′	122	–	68	–	102	S33°45′W	Northerly	11°41′
	13	By observation	25°34′	0°51′	9°14′	1°00′	76	–	53·5	–	54	S45°00′W	Variable	
	14	By observation	26°35′	1°01′	10°38′	1°24′	96	–	74	–	61	S51°00′W	Variable	13°16′
	15	By accompt	27°30′	0°55′	11°45′	1°07′	82	–	60	–	55	S47°21′W	NNW	
	16	By acompt	28°51′	1°21′	13°25′	1°40′	120	–	87·5	–	81	S47°21′W	NNW	
	17	By observation	30°04′	1°13′	14°38′	1°23′	103	–	73	–	73	S45°00′W	Variable	
	18	By observation	30°23′	0°19′	15°39′	0°51′	50	–	46	–	19	S67°30′W	SE	
	19	By accompt	31°22′	0°59′	17°06′	1°27′	95	–	75	–	59	S51°47′W	SE	

[1] This is either a serious error in calcualtion or a mistake in entry.
[2] This should be 63.

[f. 21v]

1669/70 Month	Day	Latitude by Observation & accompt	What Latitude I am in	Difference of Latitude	Longitude from St Iago	Difference of Longitude	Distance run	Easting	Westing	Northing	Southing	Course made Good	How we had the wind	Variation
Jan.	20	By accompt	32°20′	0°58′	18°29′	1°23′	100	–	81	–	58	S54°30′W	ESE	
	21	By accompt	33°06′	0°46′	19°39′	1°08′	74	–	57·1	–	46	S51°00′W	SE	
	22	By accompt	33°06′	0°00′	19°48′	0°11′	9	-	9	–	–	W	Calme	
	23	By accompt	33°36′[1]	0°32′	20°45′	0°57′	58	–	48	–	92[2]	S56°15′W	NE	
	24	By accompt	34°31′	0°53′	22°04′	1°19′	84	–	65	–	53	S51°00′W	E by S	
	25	By observation	35°37′	1°06′	22°04′[3]	2°00′	119	–	98·5	–	66	S56°14′W	Easterly	
	26	By observation	36°29′	0°52′	25°04′	1°37′	94	–	97·5	–	52	S56°15′W	SE by E	
	27	By accompt	36°19′	0°10′	27°31′	1°05′	51	–	50	10	–	N78°45′W	Southerly	20°56′
	28	By accompt	36°19′	0°00′	28°45′	0°44′	35	–	35	–	–	W	Variable	
	29	By observation	38°18′[4]	0°59′	30°20′	2°25′	130	–	115	–	59	S63°00′W	Vari*able*	
	30	By observation	38°43′	1°26′	31°25′	0°45′	92	–	35	–	86	S22°30′W	Vari*able*	
	31	By accompt	38°52′	0°09′	32°15′	0°50′	46	–	45	–	9	S78°45′W	NW	
Febr.	1	By accompt	39°00′	0°08′	33°11′	0°56′	42	–	41	–	8	S78°45′W	Vari*able*	
	2	By observation	39°11′	0°11′	33°35′	0°24′	22	–	19·3	–	11	S60°40′W	Vari*able*	
	3	By observation	39°22′	0°11′	33°35′	0°00′	11	–	–	–	11	S		

[1] This is an error of transcription for 33°38′ since the correct figure appears in the next line.
[2] This should be 32.
[3] This should be 24°04′.
[4] This should be 37°18′.

[f. 22r]

1669 Month	Day	Latitude by observation & Accompt	What Latitude I am in	Difference of Latitude	Longitude from St Iago	Difference of Longitude	Distance run	Easting	Westing	Northing	Southing	Course made Good	How we had the Wind	Variation
Febr.	4	By observation	39°48′	0°26′	34°42′	1°07′	58	–	51·5	–	26	S63°20′W	N by E	
	5	By accompt	40°44′	0°56′	36°32′	1°50′	100	–	84	–	56	S56°15′W	NW by N	
	6	By accompt	41°57′	1°13′	37°34′	1°02′	95	–	60·4	–	73	S39°50′W	NNW	
	7	By accompt	42°49′	0°52′	37°55′	0°21′[1]	56	16.4	–	–	52	S16°52′E	Southerly	
	8	By account	43°25′	0°36′	37°39′	0°16′	37	12·3	–	–	36	S18°55′E	WNW	18°05′
	9	By accompt	44°25′	1°00′	37°39′	0°00′	60	–	–	–	60	S	Variable	19°00′
	10	By observation	44°57′	0°32′	38°19′	0°40′	42·1	–	27·9	–	32	S40°45′W	Variable	
	11	By observation	44°47′	0°10′	39°07′	0°48′	35		33·5	10	–	N73°45′W	Southerly	
	12	By observation	44°17′	0°07′	39°45′	0°38′	48	–	36·7[2]	7	–	N83°45′W	Southerly	19°42′
	13	By observation	44°20′	0°13′	39°27′	0°18′	18·3	13	–	–	13	S45°00′E	SW	20°47′
	14	By observation	44°53′	0°33′	40°29′	1°02′	55	–	44	–	33	S53°30′W	Variable	
	15	By accompt	45°33′	0°40′	41°02′	0°33′	47	–	22·5	–	40	S30°00′W	ESE	24°42′

[1] This difference of longitude appears to have been applied in the wrong direction.
[2] The course made good gives a figure of 47·7.

[f. 22v]

1669/70 Month	Day	Latitude by Observation & accompt	What Latitude I am in	Difference of Latitude	Longitude from St Iago	Difference of Longitude	Distance run	Easting	Westing	Northing	Southing	Course made Good	How we had the Wind	Variation
Febr.	16	By accompt	45°54′	0°21′	43°33′	2°31′	107	–	105	–	21	S78°45′W	Northerly	
	17	By observation	46°15′	0°21′	44°43′	1°10′	54	–	45	–	21	NE by N[1]		
	18	By accompt	46°35′	0°20′	45°40′	0°57′	44	–	39·6	–	20	S63°15′W	ESE	
	19	By accompt	46°29′	0°06′	45°16′	0°04′	17·1	16·1	–	6	–	N69°40′E	E by S	
	20	By accompt	47°22′	0°53′	45°43′	0°27′	58	–	22·3	–	53	S22°30′W	NE	
	21	By accompt	47°43′	0°21′	46°38′	0°55′	43	–	37	–	21	S60°30′W	NE	

Feb*ruary* 21st being monday it was Cloudy hazy foggy Weather & the Wind at N by E. This morning at 8 of the Clock it Clear'd up & we saw Penguin Island, it bore W of me Distance about 4 Leagues now my Meridian distance is 23°21′·7. Westing from Port Bray in St Jago one of the Islands of Cape Verde, & my Difference of Longitude 46°38′ – it being so farr to the Westward of St Jago.

[1] This would appear to be the wind in the wrong column and the course has been omitted.

[f. 23r] **The Course of the South part of America from Cape Blanco to Cape Virgin Mary, & through the Streights of Magillane to Cape Disado and from thence to Baldavia in the South Sea.**

		Leagues
From Cape Blanco to Cape Desire	S by W	10
From Cape Desire to Pengwin Island	SSE	04
From Pengwin Island to Edestone Rock	S by W	12
From Edistone Rock to Port S[t] Julian	SW	21
From Port S[t] Julian to the Hill of S[t] Ives	SW	32
From the Hill of S[t] Ives to River de Cruce	SW	11
From River de Cruce to River de Gallogue	SW by S	19
From River de Gallogue to Cape Virgin Mary	SSE	20
From Cape Virgin Mary to Cape Oringe	W	15
From Cape Oringe to the S end of the first Narrow	SW by S	03
From the S end of the first Narrow to the N end of the 2[d] Narrow	SW by W	09
From the N end of the second Narrow to the S end	SW	03
From the S end of the second Narrow to Elizab*eth* Island	SSW	02
From NE end of Eliz*abeth* Island to the S end	SW	05
From Port Famine to Shutt up Point		
From S end of Eliz*abeth* Island to fresh Water Bay	SSW	10
From fresh Water Bay to Port Famine	S by W	05
From Port Famine to Shutt up Point	S	05
From Shutt up Point to Cape Froward	SW by W	03
From Cape Froward to Cape Holland	NNW	05
From Cape Holland to Cape Gallant	WNW	06
From Cape Gallant to Elizabeths Bay	NW	04
From Elizabeths Bay to S[t] Jerom's Channell	SE by E	04
From S[t] Jerom's Channell to Cape Quad	WSW	02
From Cape Quad to Cape Moonday	NW by W	13
From Cape Moonday to Cape disado	NW by N	13
From Cape Disado to the Island Called in Spanish NESTRIA SENIORA SARRACO	N	[*blank*]
From Cape Disado to Baldavia	W 6°45′Easterly	162

FINIS

b. Richard Williams's 'short accompt'[1]

Cap[t] Narbrow Commander — A Voyage of the Sweepstake to the Straits of Magallan

Aug*ust* 9 1669. We wai'd from Long Reach[2] and sailed to the Downes,[3] where we staid till the **26** September, for a Spaniard,[4] that pretended to have been this voyage before, that we were now bound upon.

Sept*ember* 26 1669. We wai'd from the Downes, having the *Batchelour* Pinke 40 accompany us; we steered for the Madera's,[5] and arrived there **Oct*ober* 14**. Here we took in some wine, and for the easement of our ship struck 11 guns into the hold.

Oct*ober* 16. We wai'd at night and steered for the Island of Cape Deverd,[6] and the **25**[th] we arrived at the Isle of Mayo, where we bought some cattle for a refreshment for our men. The **29**[th] wee saw the Brazill-fleet bound for S[t] Iagoe;[7] we wai'd at night, and the next day came to Anchor at Port Priam,[8] where they rid at Anchor, consisting of 30 saile, and one of them an English ship called the *Jerusalem*, Cap*tain* Wilshire commander: Here wee filled with water we wanted, and got such other necessaryes as wee lacked.

Nov*ember* 5th **1669.** We wai'd from hence, and made saile in pursuance of our voyage, and had indifferent weather, till we came to 46° South-latitude, where we had a storme of weather. **Febr*uary* 19**[th] that splitt our main course, and broake 3 of our maine shrouds, and separated us and the pink that we never saw here since.

Febr*uary* 21. We made Cape Blanco,[9] which stands in 47° South lat*itude* on the Coast of Patagonia on the main of America; wee being unacquainted with the Coast, and a single ship, made us more fearefull to venture neare the shore so that we over shot our port that night, & by the next day at noon the tide had set us so far to the South, that we were certain by our observation, we were pas't our port; the Spaniard, that was called Signo*r* Carollus, who had pretended to his Ma*jes*tie that he had been this voyage before, & whom we expected to be some assistance to us, kept his cabin close, and would not be seen on

[1] Royal Society CI.P/7i/32.

[2] Long Reach, in the River Thames, extends from Crayford Ness (51°28′·9N, 0°12′·8E) to Greenhithe (51°7′N, 0°7′E).

[3] The anchorage off Deal (51°13′N, 1°27′E).

[4] Don Carlos.

[5] Ilha da Madeira (32°45′N, 17°00′W).

[6] Ilhas do Cabo Verde (16°S, 24°W).

[7] São Tiago (15°05′N, 23°35′W).

[8] Praia (14°55′N, 23°31′W).

[9] Cabo Blanco (47°12′S, 65°45′W).

deck, but when we enquired of him concerning any of those places, where we were bound to, his reply would be, that when he was that way before, he kept his chamber; therefore we came to Anchor that night in a Bay, that our Cap*tain* called the Bay of Reception.[1]

Febr*uary* 23 1669/70. We way'd from the Bay of Reception, and turned to windward; our Cap*tain* himselfe being very diligent in his pinnace,[2] a head of the ship, searching of all creeks and bays for a harbour. The **24**th we found it, and having well sounded it the **27.** we went in with our ship: It was named by S*i*r Francis Drake the Port of desire.[3] Whilest we begin here to fit our ship, we searched the countrey very diligently for inhabitants, but could find none; all the land here abouts is very dry and barren, not affording as much as wood and fresh water; but as the snow dissolves in some season of the yeare, and runneth into holes in the ground, which serveth the heards of this countrey to drink. They are those that Heylin[4] in his little description of the great world calleth Wyanacoes, that breed the Besoa Stone;[5] the Spaniards make use of them, as horses to carry burdens, and call them sheep; they are of the bigness of our English Staggs; their wool is of an extraordinary finenesse, their flesh but course [coarse] food. Here are allso great store of Eastridges,[6] and upon Islands of rocks such an innumerable store of seales[7] that it is beyond belief. We killed in 4 houres 2000, some of them we salted, and of the fat of others we made oyle: there are allso the like store of birds, which are called pengwins,[8] and are about the bigness of a goose, they have instead of feathers a kind of matted downe, and short pinions, so that they can not fly, and are very helplesse onshore, but so swift in the water that no fish can be swifter; of these wee killed, in lesse than an houres time, 1400; having salted of them (as farre as our salt would go, which was about 3 months provision,)[9] of both; and having got our ship new rigged, we took possession in his[10] Ma*jes*ties name of all the land from the River of Platte to the Straits of[11] Magellan.

March 25. 1670. We wai'd from Port desire and made saile in search of a harbour, called Port St Julian,[12] that stood in 49°, there we intended to winter; the winter coming on as the Sun hath his declination to the Tropick of Cancer.

Apr*il* 7th Wee fell with Port St Julian, which proved a very good harbor: the **9**th of this month the Hills were all covered with snow, we made shift to get snow-water and a little

[1] This bay is not named by Narbrough but see p. 203, n. 4 and from the description in Peckett's journal (see above, pp. 215, 580) would appear to be Bahía Desvelos (48°18′S, 66°17′W).

[2] Two illegible words struck through .

[3] Puerto Deseado (47°45′S, 65°53′W).

[4] Peter Heylyn (1599–1662) makes no mention of Wyanacoes in *Microcosmos: a Little Description of the Great World*, Oxford, 1621, 8th edn published in 1639. His *Cosmographie*, 1652, a popular expansion of the *Microcosmos*, ran into numerous editions. The 'Huanacu', appear on p. 1063 of the 3rd edn, published 1666.

[5] Bezoar stone, see above, p. 422, n. 5.

[6] See above, p. 207, n. 4.

[7] See above, pp. 192, n. 2; 208, n. 12.

[8] See above, p. 208, n. 13.

[9] 'Provision' repeated and struck through.

[10] 'Their' crossed through with 'his' written above it.

[11] This word is repeated .

[12] Puerto San Julián (49°19′S, 67°43′W).

brushy wood to serve us all the winter, and in our travells in the countrey, we found a very large brave salt-pond, 10 miles from the water side, and as the weather permitted, we went thither for salt; our Cap*tain* himselfe, to encourage the rest of his company, would carry a burden, as well as the meanest man there, & through his endeavour and encouragem*ent* we made a shift to get 6 tuns on board; we found also here a kind of minerall, that looks much like Isinglasse, but very ponderus,[1] I have a little of it. Wee buried of our company whilst we stai'd here 8; and 2 before.

Sept*ember* 16. We wai'd from Port St Julian after a long and hard winter, & made saile for Port Desire for more seale and pengwins; we arrived there the **17th** at night; The next day we sent our boats to those Islands for seals and pengwins, but they found there such plenty of Eggs, that they loaded the boat with nothing else, which was a great refreshing to our men that were well and a great helpe to recover others that were downe; wee salted 3 months provision of pengwins and seales.

Oct*ober* 15th We wai'd the second time from Port Desire and made saile in pursuance of our voyage: [*margin:* Oct. 23.] the **23rd** we entered the Straits mouth, which stands in 52° South-lat*itude* and came to Anchor by the first narrow,[2] which is 14 leagues within the straits; [*margin:* Oct 24.] the **24th** was calme; the **25** wee wayed, and sayled through the first and second Narrow,[3] which is distant one from the other 8 leagues, and came to Anchor that night under Queen Elizab*eth* Island;[4] there are 2 Islands more in sight, standing in triangle-wise,[5] the one is called St Bartholomew,[6] and the other St George:[7] the narrowest place of all the Straits is good a[8] league broad and very navigable, when once discovered; our Cap*tain* going on shoare on Queen Eliz*abeth* Island met with 30 Indians that came to him and his company, jumping and dancing all the way; they had a very big voyce in the throat, their garments were the skins of those beasts afore named about their shoulders, but their owne skin was so thick painted with okor [ochre], that the pores of the body needed no greater resistance against the cold; their arms were bows and arrows, which were very artificially made, and headed with flint-stones; they made an exchange of them with our men for knifes and sheares. Our Cap*tain*, after 2 days time here, saw that there was nothing else to be had here of them, gave them some bills and Axes, and to try their courage fir'd of[f] his gun, but they no sooner heard the report but all went away and would not be entreated to tarry any longer; our boats having discovered our way, wee wai'd the **29th October** [*margin:* Oct 29.] and sailed between the Islands keeping close under Queen Eliz*abeth* Island, by reason of a ledge of Rocks that came from St George Island: The **31** we came to anchor at port Famin[9] [*margin:* Oct 31] so named by the Spaniards here, when King Philip's towne was built, but all the

[1] Possibly mica, see above, p. 446, n. 1. *NOED*.

[2] Primera Angostura (52°30′S, 69°35′W).

[3] Segunda Angostura (52°43′S, 70°20′W).

[4] Isla Isabel (52°53′S, 70°44′W).

[5] 'manner' struck through and 'wise' written over it.

[6] Isla Marta, 52°51′S, 70°35′W.

[7] Isla Magdalena, 52°55′S, 70°35′W.

[8] Originally written 'a good league' and then amended to 'good a league'.

[9] See above, p. 262, n. 4. It is now Puerto San Juan de la Posesíon or Puerto del Hambre, (53°38′S, 70°56′W).

Spaniards[1] starved; and now hath no signe of any house that was ever there built; the countrey hereabouts is all woody, and hath fine fresh-water Rivers running down into the Straits in severall places. Whilst we staid here to wood and water, there came some Indians to us; they had canoes, that were made of the barke of trees, and sewed together with thongs of Seal skins; they had no other trade, but such as the first had, and loth to part with any of that, but willing to receive all that we would give them; one of them came on board with our Cap*tain*, and to encourage others he gave him a bill & an Axe, and some knifes and sheares, and a cap and some beads, and put him on shore, but there came no more neare us whilst we stayed.

Nov*ember* 3d. We wai'd from Port Famin, & made saile in search of our passage, which we could not espy by reason of the great many windings and turnings, and the great height of those hills that over-topp[2] one the other, and are continually covered with snow; at last we doubled Cape Froward,[3] which indeed is not misnamed; it stands in 54° *South* Lat*itude*; [*margin:* 6.] & the **6th** we got to Anchor in Queen Eliza*beth* Bay.[4] Crosse wind staid us here a week; in that time we found some trees,[5] the barke of which being chewed in ones mouth, had as hot a taste as pepper; I have some sample of it.

Nov*ember* 13th. We wai'd from *Queen* Eliz*abeth* bay, and sailed till the **15th**; the wind turning upon us forced us to come to Anchor in a cove, 3 leagues within Cape Desire[6] and Cape Victory,[7] which make the entrance into the South-Sea; the Straits is about 100 leagues through.

Nov*ember* 19. We wai'd from this cove and made saile for the South Sea; & the next day, to wellcome us, we had a mighty storm [*margin:* Nov 25.] the **25th** we stood into the land, & the **26.** we came to Anchor under an Island called the Island of Succour[8] in 45°, this Island is all woody and hath no Inhabitants; here we got more wood and water a board; and the **30th** we wai'd and stood over to the maine in search of a harbour, called St Domingoe,[9] but wee could not find it, we came to anchor again under the same Island; we had the wind at N till [*margin:* 5.] **Dec*ember* 5th** then we sailed from the Island of Succour, and the **6th** wee made an Island in the lat*itude* of 44° which lyeth of[f] off [of] Castoe,[10] the southerne-most part that is inhabited by the Spaniards; this Island was also all woody and without inhabitants; the Spaniard would have gone ashore here, but there ran such stuff,[11] that we could not land him: dirty weather was coming on, then wee stood

[1] 'was' struck through.

[2] Written 'toppth' with the last two letters struck through.

[3] Cabo Froward (53°54′S, 71°18′W). 'Froward', meaning difficult to deal with or contrary, which Williams felt accurately described the conditions off that cape. *NOED*.

[4] Bahía Isabel (53°37′S, 72°12′W).

[5] 'that' crossed through.

[6] Cabo Deseado (52°45′S, 74°43′W).

[7] Cabo Victoria (52°17′S, 74°55′W).

[8] Isla Guamblín (44°51′S, 75°05′W).

[9] Probably Puerto Santo Domingo (43°58′S, 73°06′W); see above, pp. 280, n. 1; 496–7.

[10] Probably Isla Guafo. See above, pp. 282, n. 2; 498, n. 1; 593, n. 7.

[11] Two attempts to spell this word, one being 'stuffe' struck through, the other also struck through and illegible. By 'stuff', Williams presumably meant 'surf'.

to sea; [*margin:* 9.] the **9**th wee had a great storme of [*margin:* 15.] weather, and we sprung a leake into our beefe room; this storme continued till the **13**th; the **15**th we made the land again, and by 4 of the clock wee saw the fort of Baldivia:[1] wee sent our pinace to land Signo*r* Carrolus a league and a ½ short of the fort; he promised to our Cap*tain* to be downe at the water side within a day or 2 at the furthest with some Chilians along with him, and that he would make a signe with fire where we should send our boats to take them in: the Spaniards at the fort seeing a ship without, sent a Canoe with 4 Indians, and one Spaniard in her, to see who wee were, which came close aboard, & askt if that we were from old Spain; our men being busy about tacking of our ship & talking English to one another did so scare the Spaniard that he padled for the shore with all the speed hee could; that night wee kept under saile, and the next morning wee stood in, and the Cap*tain* Sent one of our Lif*tenan*ts[2] and my selfe with a trumpeter and a flagg of truce, to know if we might have leave without offence to come into their harbour to wood and water, we being bound to the East Indies, and standing in need of such necessaryes; they courteously entertained us, and sent a pilot to pilote the ship in, and 3 Gentlemen more came off with us with a present from the Governour for the Cap*tain*, of 4 Jarrs of wine a bagg of new bread, and a goate, with a complement that wee should bee furnished with all things[3] wee stood in need off, they assuring us, that they had received orders from the Queen of Spain, that if any of the King of England's ships should chance to touch in any of those parts, that they should let them want for nothing[4] they had to serve them withall. Our Cap*tain* mistrusting their complem*ent* only to be a wheedle to get the ship under command,[5] allthough wee needed not feare the force they had there, whilst wee kept without command, they having but a briganteen, and 2 barks of longgoe,[6] 16 guns mounted ashore, and about 200 men, which, though not of force to fight us at Sea, yet, could they get us in, might either fitt[7] those to burne us, or else spoyle our masts and yards from their forts, which in all were 3; therefore wee came to anchor a league without command, and saluted their fort with 9 guns; they thanked us with 7. Wee sent the Gentlemen shore and the Pilote, whom our Cap*tain* civilly treated whilst they were aboard, and sent the same Lift*enant* that had been ashore before, with one of the Duke of Yorks Gentlemen, that was a Reformado[8] aboard of us, to Accompany them with a present for the Governour, this day they were civilly entertained, & presented with plumes of feathers, & the Governour promised them that he would be aboard the next day; but our Cap*tain* sent in the morning our Cheife Lift*enant* and one Mr Fortescue with the Trumpeter, and an interpreter with the flagge of truce, and 2 hands more [*margin:* Dec 18 1670.][9] to know,

[1] This is probably Fort St Peter on Isla Mancera (39°53′S, 73°24′W), in Bahía de Corral; see above, pp. 285, n. 4; 532, n. 7; 594, n. 1.

[2] Lieutenant Peckett.

[3] 'that' crossed through.

[4] 'that' crossed through.

[5] Within the range of the guns in the forts and hence under their control.

[6] By '*longgoe*', Williams most likely refers to oared longboats.

[7] The word 'fight' crossed through and 'fitt' substituted. The meaning is presumably that the two barks could be fitted as fireships to burn the *Sweepstakes*.

[8] Reformades. The sons of the nobility and gentry who served in the navy under letters from Charles II, and were allowed table-money and other encouragements to raise the character of the service. Smyth, *Sailor's Word-book*, p. 566. This might be a reference to John Wood.

[9] 'in the gale' struck through .

if[1] without offence he might send his boats to fetch some wood and water, our desires being to give them no cause of suspition, but to hold faire correspondence with them, whilst wee migh heare from Signo*r* Carollus: And they on the otherside seeing they could not worke their owne desires on us, stopt our Lift*enant*,[2] Mr Fortescue, the Trumpeter, and the Lingester [linguist], and sent 2 Indians to helpe the other 2 men to row the boat a board to fetch their cloths, and a letter to the Cap*tain* that they must send them to the Vice-Roy at Lima, for for ought they knew, wee might be Pirats, because wee kept without command. Our Cap*tain* taking it into consideration that night what he had best to do, allthough we were of a sufficient force to master that place, & that it seemed to be a mighty rich place, all their slaves armor being of beaten silver, and most of the Spaniards, that were of any fashion, having the hilts of their swords of beaten gold; yet our Cap*tain*, having a strict order not to molest them, we were forced to let this opportunity slip; thus having come to the well-head, wee must returne home empty. In the morning the Cap*tain* sent mee with their cloths and the 2 Indians, with a flagg of truce, within shot, and to wave them off with a boat to meet us on the water, but they would not venture, allthough wee were under command of their owne guns. But a little before night they came abreast of us by land with about 50 small-shott men, and asked our demands, which we told them was that they would send off a boat to take the Gentlemen's cloths, and their Indians a shore. They told us, that they had nere a boat at the fort, for all we saw to the contrary; & desired us to land them there, but wee being too lately deceived to trust them again so soon, & strictly commanded by the Cap*ain* not to come neare the shore, I returned with them aboard that night, & the next morning wee put the Indians ashore a breast of our ship. Our Lift*enan*t that was in their hands engaged on his life that if[3] they would send off a boat a board for their cloths, that it should not be stopt or molested: the next day they sent off a boat with one Spaniard & 4 Indians with a letter from the Lift*enant* for their cloths. The Cap*tain*[4] treated the Spaniard very civilly, & he would faine have the Cap*tain* to detaine him, or if the Cap*tain* would promise him entertainm*ent* he would steale aboard in the night, & he would engage his life that he would carry us to an Island 2° to the N, called by the Spaniards mochoe,[5] and a kind of store room for them, being only inhabited by Indians, where wee should for a few beads have as much provision as wee stood in need off [of]. But our Cap*tain* looking on a Spaniard's promise but only as a complement, told him that he was not come there to do the King of Spain the least injury in the world; for had hee so intended, he had had opportunity sufficient since he arrived there, neither could he answer the transporting of any of his subjects, when it should please God to send him home to his M*ajest*y the King of England. The Spaniard after a kind entertainm*ent* went ashore, & the next day came aboard again with 100 dollars to buy watches, & such like toyes that he had seen the day before, & a letter from our Lift*enant* that desired us[6] by all meanes to weigh & begone to sea, for there was some designe in hand to destroy us very speedily; but[7] how, that he could not understand.

[1] 'that' struck through .
[2] Lieutenant Armiger.
[3] 'they would send, that if' struck through.
[4] Word struck through.
[5] Isla Mocha (38°22′S, 73°55′W), see above, pp. 517, 541.
[6] Word repeated and scratched out.
[7] Illegible word scratched out.

About 4 of the clock the Spaniard went ashore, & at night we wai'd, & stood to sea, not going any further to the N, because our order was to the contrary; we stai'ed at Baldivia 6 days & could not heare any news from Sign*or* Carollus nor see any signe according to his promise, which made us judge he was among the Spaniards, & that he only wanted a passage to the S*outh* Sea, & was got to his wisht port. 2 days after wee came to anchor in a bay 3 leagues to the S of Baldivia,[1] & sent our boat ashore to see if they could meet with any Indians, or see any signe of Sign*or* Carollus, but we found the shore here so naturally fortifyed with great Rocks & intermingled weeds, that it was impossible for a dog, much less a man, to enter them, & so is the coast all along except those Inletts, which the Spaniards have hold of,[2] and fortifyed. So that we saw plainly, there was but little hopes for us to have any treaty with they Chilians, or for any others that shall ever endeavour it hereafter, without they make warre with the Spaniard and so force their way to the Chilians, which the Spaniards with their great guns keep up in the inland; but they[3] are people, by the Spaniard's owne confesion, that never lett them rest in quiet, nor will they agree any condition of peace, bringing their wives into the feild to fight with them, telling them that they hate the Spaniards Tyranny & defy their yoake.

Dec*ember* 23. 1670. At night we wai'd, & directed our course for the straits again, when we came to the Lat*itude* 50°, we had as bad weather, as we had before we broake one of[4] our main shrouds, & our tiller in the rudder-head. In the afternoon the fury of it was over, so that we got a new tiller fitted, & our rigging mended, and **Jan*uary* 6th** we made the Straits mouth, & at night came to anchor 7 leagues within the Straites in a cove.[5] The next day we wayed, & sailed by judgm*en*t of a draught[6] that our Cap*tain* had drawne going through before the weather being very thick & foggy, so that we could not see a ships length ahead. The **11th** of this month we got to anchor at port Famin; here wee unrigged our ship, & found our main mast broke a foot & a ½ above the step; wee fitted a paire of sheeres & wayed it & sawd it off 2 foot shorter;[7] & **Feb*uary* 3d** we had made an end of rigging our ship, & fixed our masts & bolt spit [bowsprit], & got wood and water aboard, & got some fresh fish with our saine, which was a great refreshm*ent* to our men.

Feb*uary* 4th. we waid and sent our pinace a long the shore before us to see if they could meet with any Indians; for wee saw severall fires on both sides [of] the straits, & none would come neare us, & as the boat went [to] come neare the fire, still the Indians would be gone from it. The last day, which was the **14th**, our boat-crew found 3 anchors in the wash of the water,[8] & about 100 acres of land full of ratts, & just like a cony-burrow, which made us judge that some ship had been lost there some years since: this day we got clear of the Straits & made saile for Port Desire,[9] thinking we might fill what casks we should

[1] Probably Caleta Chaihuín (39°55′S, 73°36′W).

[2] 'holed up' crossed through.

[3] 'yet' struck through.

[4] 'of' struck through.

[5] This anchorage is shown on the 'Royal Map' (Foldout), close east of Cabo Valentina (52°55′S, Longitude74°17′W).

[6] 'draft' crossed through.

[7] See above, pp. 306, n. 4; 307; Figure 7, for details of this operation.

[8] At the high-water line.

[9] Puerto Deseado (47°45′S, 65°53′W).

empty, by that time that we should get so farre, with water: wee arrived there the **24**th & found no water but such as was too brakish to drink: the 26th we wai'd from port Desire & directed our course for England & [*margin:* April 12.] **April 12** we crossed the Equinoctiall, and **May** 7th we met a Dutch ship in the Lat*itude* of 27 N that was bound to the Barbados to fish for plate out of the 3 Spanish galloons, that hath been ther lost, they having Engineers to blow them to peices; they had the Duke of York's commission, and allso one English man aboard, that was to take an account of what they should get, and in the Dukes behalfe to look after his share. They informed us that there was great apprehension[1] of warre between the Dutch & the French, & that the English had war with the Turks;[2] the next day wee got our guns mounted that was in the hold, and fitted our ship if we should have occasion to fight. The **12**th wee met with a Pink of London, that had been at the Canaryes[3] with corne, and was bound to New England: [*margin:* May 17.] wee made to the Island of St Marys,[4] which is one of the westerne Islands, and the **19**th sent our pinace a shore on St Michaels[5] for some garden herbs for our men, but the wind being at NE, the **23**th we were forced to beare up for Terceris[6] to get some bread & water, our store being but very small: the **26**th we wayed from Tercera's, and this morning arrived in the Downs. Thus have I endeavoured to give your Hon*oure*s a short accompt of our two years proceedings.

Your Hon*ou*rs humble Servant
Richard Williams.

From aboard their
Ma*jes*ties Sweepstakes
June 13. 1671
in the Downs.

[1] 'apprehension' is substituted for a word scratched out and now illegible.

[2] Williams refers to Barbary pirates. Numerous English naval expeditions were directed against Barbary raiders in the reign of Charles II. Narbrough was to lead a conclusive assault on Tunis in 1676.

[3] Islas Canarias (28°N, 16°W).

[4] Santa Maria (36°58′N, 25°06′W).

[5] São Miguel (37°45′N, 25°30′W).

[6] Terceira (38°39′N, 27°14′W).

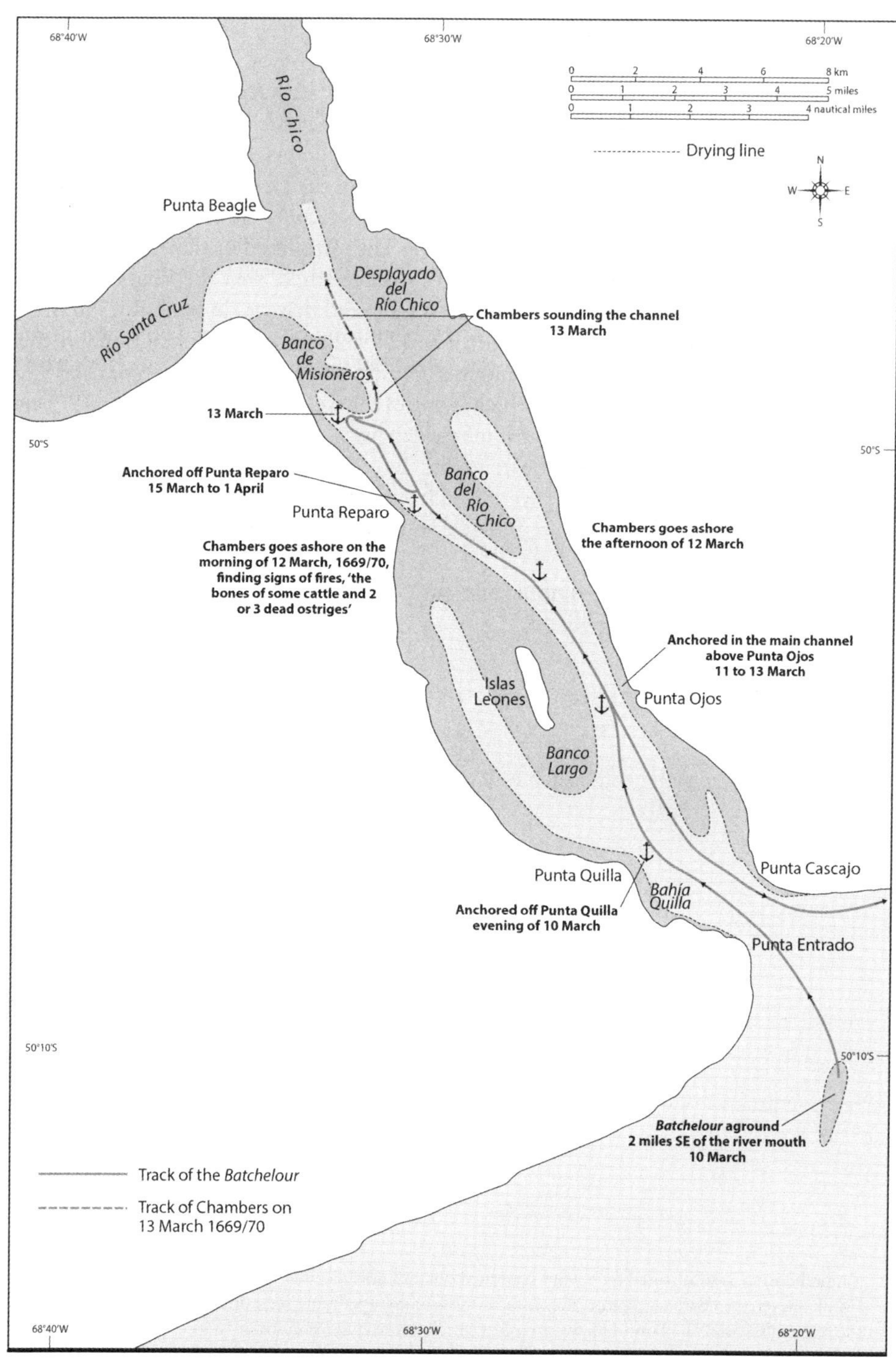
68°40'W
68°30'W
68°20'W
0 2 4 6 8 km
0 1 2 3 4 5 miles
0 1 2 3 4 nautical miles
Drying line
N
W
E
S
Rio Chico
Punta Beagle
Rio Santa Cruz
Desplayado del Río Chico
Chambers sounding the channel 13 March
Banco de Misioneros
13 March
50°S
Anchored off Punta Reparo 15 March to 1 April
Banco del Río Chico
Punta Reparo
Chambers goes ashore the afternoon of 12 March
Chambers goes ashore on the morning of 12 March, 1669/70, finding signs of fires, 'the bones of some cattle and 2 or 3 dead ostriges'
Anchored in the main channel above Punta Ojos 11 to 13 March
Islas Leones
Punta Ojos
Banco Largo
Punta Cascajo
Punta Quilla
Bahía Quilla
Anchored off Punta Quilla evening of 10 March
Punta Entrado
50°10'S
Batchelour aground 2 miles SE of the river mouth 10 March
Track of the Batchelour
Track of Chambers on 13 March 1669/70

Map 11. The *Batchelour* at Puerto Santa Cruz, 10 March 1669/70 to 2 April 1670.

c: The Journal of William Chambers[1]

This is a journall of a master of a ~~shipp~~ Pinke that sailed from England in Company of another Shipp bound for the Straights of Magellan with a Spaniard aboard her to make discovery of advantages to be gotten in Trade or otherwise There.
They went out of the river of Thames in the beginning of Octob*er* 1669. and in my Journall of 19th of octob*er* 1669 mention is made of This designe: mention also is made Thereoff in my journall July 21 1669.[2]

Novemb*er* 1669. *Batchlor* of London for St Julian.
At St Iago.[3]

2. Being Tuesday the Adm*ira*ll of the Portugaller fleet went away & some of his fleet with him for Brazeele they weighed about one of the Clock att Noone.

3. Being Wednesday the vice Adm*ira*ll of the fleet went away and all the fleet with him for Brazeel, our Cargoe on board the Admirall.[4]

4. Being Thursday the *Sweepstakes* Boat went to the Town of St Iago,[5] with 6 of our men, & the Jew, & came aboard again about 10 a clock at Night.

5. Being fryday wee weighed about 5 of the Clock [*margin:* This day wee put 3 hogsh. of salt on board the *Sweepstakes.*] in the morning, & drove a little further out, & cam to an anchor the sam day, wee weighed about 3 a Clock in the Afternoon bound for St Julian's that lies in the 49°20′ S Lat*itude*.

6. From yesterday till this day noon being Saturday wee are by observac*io*n 70 miles distance SSE from our departur from

Novemb*er* 1669. *Bachelor* of London for St Julian.[6]
St Iago and it beares off us NNW no observac*io*n the wind at East.

7. From yesterday noon till this day noon, being Sabath day wee have stear'd away [*margin:* latt 11°50′: Long. 0°32′ By Estimac*io*n.][7] by Compasse SBE distance run 108 miles, South

[1] Beinecke Library, Osborn b394. None of the folios are numbered. With the exception of the note, written on the verso of the front flyleaf, all the following diary entries are written on the rectos of the volume with the versos left blank.
[2] The flyleaf note is in the hand of Edward Montagu, 1st Earl of Sandwich. For the references in his journal, see above, p. 13.
[3] São Tiago, in the Cape Verde Islands.
[4] This refers to the *Sweepstakes.*
[5] The two ships were anchored off Praia (14°55′N, 23°31′W).
[6] Final 's' on Julian crossed through.
[7] Chambers's marginalia run as a series of discrete observations in the left margin down the side of the discrete daily entries. To avoid clutter they have been grouped together in one square bracket within the text of an entry

106 miles, Easting 20 miles, by wind at EBN. Some raine hazy weather, & a fine easy gale, the same day the *Sweepstakes* took us in a Tow. No observac*i*on.

8. From yesterday noon till this day noon being monday, wee have steared between SBE & SBW, & I find by Judgm*ent* that wee [*margin:* 10°28′: 00°32′ by Estimac*i*on][1] have made our way good S dist*ance* run 72 miles, the Wind at EBN, & SE, little wind Cloudy dark weather, some showers of Raine, and Lightning the moon being in his last quart*er*.

9. From yesterday noon till this day noon being Tuesday wee have had cross winds from the [*margin:*10°18′: 01°01′] EBN to the SE Cloudy weather & Raine, with gusts of wind and some Lightning.

10. From Yesterday noon till this day noon being Wednesday wee have steered by Compass SSE, but by observac*i*on I find that wee have

Novem*ber* ***Bachelor*** **bound for Sr Julians Lat. 47°20′ S Lat. 1669.**
[*margin:* Lat. 09°00′: Long 01°38′ Good observac*i*on. This day a Mizen made of our foresayle.] made our way SSE 2° Easterly distance run 88 miles, southing 88 miles,[2] Easting 37 miles the wind at ENE & E & EBS, very darke Cloudy weather, especially in the night with some raine. No observac*i*on, the moon in the last Quarter.

11. From yesterday noon till this day noon being Thursday, wee have steered by the Compass [*margin:* 07°57′: 01°52′ by esteemac*i*on. This day wee made a maine Stay Sayle.] between SSE, the SBE, & the SSW, but by esteemac*i*on wee have made our way good SBE ¼ Easterly distance run 65 Miles S 63 miles, E*ast* 14 miles, the wind at E & SE little wind with some showers of rain & Lightning & thunder, & a great swelling Sea comeing out of the SE board, the which has been seen by mee from the seaventh of this Instant till this day. No Observac*i*on by reason of Clouds

12. From yesterday noon till this day noon being saturday wee have steered by the Compass SBE & SSW, but by worke I find that wee have made our way good SBW ½ Easterly[3] dist*ance* run 50 miles South

Novemb*er*. ***Bachelor*** **bound for Sr Julians Lat. 47°20′ S. Lat. 1669.**
Westing 13 miles, wee haveing the winds [*margin:* 07°28′: 1°40′ Good observac*i*on.] at EBS & SE, very little wind with some rain. Now by dead reckoning I should be in the Lat*itude* of 7°9′, but by observac*i*on I find my selfe to be in the Lat*itude* of 7°28′ the which is 19 miles more Northerly.

---

at the point where they begin. Some marginalia have been placed in the footnotes where they reflect a calculation running down several lines.

[1] Chambers appears to be giving his longitudes from Praia; however, his mathematics was not very good and the figures do not always agree with the given courses and distances run. See above, pp. 73–4, on Chambers's navigation.

[2] This is an error. Narbrough has 85 miles for the distance run, so that accepting 88 miles, as given here as correct, on this course the southing should be 78 miles.

[3] Presumably this should be 'westerly'. Narbrough made the course SW.

13. From yesterday noon till this day noon being saturday wee have steered by the [*margin:* 06°36′: 1°53′ Good observac*io*n.] Compass SBE & SSE dist*ance* by the logg 20 Leagues or 60 miles, but by observac*io*n I find that wee have made our way good SSE distance run 63 south 58 m*iles* E*ast* 13 with the wind at E, & EBN, & ENE, little wind in the nights, much lightning good observac*io*ns by the new moon.

14. From Yesterday noon till this day noon being Sabath day wee have steered by compasse SSE & S but by observac*io*n I find that wee have made our way SSE ½ a poynt So*uther*ly, dist*ance* run 65 miles S*outhin*g 62 mil*es* E*astin*g 20 m*iles* the wind at E & EBN. Good weather & good observac*io*n very little wind. The same day at 7 in the morning the *Sweepstakes* take us in a tow.

November. *Bachelor* bound for St Julians. 1669.

15. From yesterday noon till this day noon being [*margin:* 04°12′: 01°17′ Good Observac*io*n.][1] moonday, wee have steer'd by the Compasse from the SBW to the SWBW, but by observac*io*n I find that wee have made our way good SW 2° E*aster*ly distanc*e* run 84 miles, Southing 62 miles, Westing 56 miles, the wind at E & ESE with Turnathoes [tornados], much Raine. The same day at noon wee went about with the wind at SE & wee stood ENE, till 4 of the clock in the afternoon, & then the wind came up at NE, in a gust of Raine, & wee tack'd againe standing to the south*wa*rd the same tim*e* about 5 a Clock, it proved a little wind & great sea, insomuch that it was convenient to be cast loose fro*m* being tow'd, & it was so done.

16. From yesterday noon till this day noon [*margin:* 03°31′: 01°03′ Good Observac*io*n.] Tuesday wee have made our way by Compas upon sev'all [several] poynts, fro*m* S to SBW, but by observac*io*n I find that wee have made our way good SBW 7° W*ester*ly, southing 43 miles, Westing 14 miles, the Wind at NE & SE with much raine & a great swelling SEBE Sea, a fresh gale, this day at noon we*e* tack'd with the wind at SEBE, stem*m*ing[2] away NEBE.

November *Bachelor* bound for St Julians. 1669.

17. From yesterday noon till this day noon being [*margin:* 04°09′: 1°43′ Good observac*io*n. The moon in her first quarter.] Wednesday, wee have steerd by the compass sev'all courses from the NEBE to the EBN with cross winds, but by observac*io*n I find that wee have made our way good NE ½ a point North*er*ly distance Run, 63 miles, North*in*g 48 miles Easting 45 miles, the wind from the ESE to the EBS with many darke Clouds & gusts of Wind & rain very uncertaine weather. Good observac*io*n.

18. From yesterday noon till this day noon being Thursday wee [*margin:* 04°40′: 2°15′ by Esteemac*io*n.] have had cross winds, but I find by Judgm*en*t that wee hav*e* made our way good NE, distance run 46 miles, northing 32 miles East 32 miles, the wind from the SSE to the E very unconstant weather very dark, cloudy weather, with much raine. No Observac*io*n.

[1] The change in here is far greater than the 62 miles 'Southing' quoted in the text. Presumably it was adjusted to agree with the observed value.

[2] 'Stemming' indicates the direction of the ship's head or stem.

19. From yesterday noon till this day noon being fryday, I have made our way good by Observac*i*on [*margin:* 04°54′: 02°52′ A Portuguess Ship Good Observac*i*on.] ENE distance run 40 miles North*er*ly 15 miles Easterly 37, the Crosse [wind] from the EBN to the SSE. Very bad weather & some rain good observac*i*on, the Sky very dark & Cloudy, the same day wee spy'd a shipp very dark and cloudy.

Novemb*er*　　*Bachelor* bound for St Julians Lat. 48°20′. 1669.

20. From yesterday noon till this day noon being [*margin:* 04°03′: 02°02′[1] Good observac*i*on Shipp in Sight.] Saturday, wee hav*e* had little wind, and very much raine, & I find that wee have made our way good S distance run 50 miles Good observac*i*on, the wind at ESE & EBN, the same day about 1 of the Clock in the morning wee left the *Sweepstakes*.

21. From yesterday noon till this day noon being Sabboth day we have Steered upon sev'all Courses from the N to the SW, distance run by Logg 56 miles, but by observac*i*on I find that wee have made our way good N*orth* distance run 70 miles, the which is by reason of a Northern Current that has set us to the N*orthwar*d 15 miles more than the Logg. The same day wee cam foule of a great part of the Brazeele fleet. The Saturday night wee mett with the *Sweepstakes*, about 11 of the Clock wee stand to the N*orthwar*d the wind at ESE & South.

22. From yesterday noon till this day noon being Monday wee have steered severall Corses from the NNE to the SW*es*t, but dead reckoning I find that wee have made our way good SSE 3° E*aster*ly distance run 33 miles Southing 29 miles Easting 14 miles,

Novemb*er*　　*Bachelor* bound for St Julian. 1669.
[*margin:* 04°51′: 03°06′ No Observac*i*on.] the wind variable from the ESE to the SE, sometimes little wind & sometimes much wind with much raine & Cloudy Darke weather, this same day wee splitt our fore top sayle.

23. From yesterday noon till this day noon being Tuesday wee have made [*margin:* 04°13′: 3°21′] our way good by Judgm*ent* SEBE Distance runn 46 mile southing 38 miles Easting 25 mile the wind variable between the ESE & the NNW^t^ sometime Calme sometimes wind in gusts and much raine when we had a fair*e* wind wee steer'd away SSE. No observac*i*on by reason of rainy Cloudy weather.

24. From yesterday noon till this day noon being Wednesday, wee have made our way upon sev'all Courses from the NE to the SSW, but by esteemac*i*on I have made our way good South 30 miles and wee have had

Novemb*er*　　*Bachelor* bound for D° Lat*itude* D°.[2]
[*margin:* 04°43′: 23°21′[3]] our wind at ESE and SE with much wind sometimes in gusts & much raine & sometimes no wind, uncertain Weather.

[1] The longitude here should be 02°52′.
[2] The same place, the same latitude.
[3] The longitude here should be 03°21′.

25. From yesterday noon till this day noon being Thursday wee have made our way [*margin:* 04°06′: 03°10′] up on sev'all points from the NE to the EBN, sometimes wind & sometimes none with much raine, but I find by observac*i*on that wee have made our way SSW distance run 3 miles[1] Southing 87 miles Westing 11 miles the wind variable from the So*uth* to the ESE. The same day I was aboard the admirall, the same day they tryed the Current, & they found it to sett NW 20 miles in 24 houres but before that I had found from the 20th day a Northerne Current. The same day our Master, and our Merchant[2] was on board the Admirall.

Novemb*er*. *Bachelor* bound for D° Lat*itude* D°. 1669.

26. From Yesterday noon till this day noon being fryday wee have steered upon sev'all poynts from the SSE to the SW, but by esteemac*i*on I find that wee have made our way good South, distance runn 10 miles the wind variable from the E to the SSE, fickle weather with very much raine no observac*i*on.

27. From yesterday noon till this day [*margin:* Lat. by observac*i*on 04°55′ Lat. by ded[3] 05°22′.] noon being Saturday, wee have been becalmed, but wee allow her 20 miles NWt by reason the Current setts NWt & by dead reckoning I should be in the Latitud of [*blank*] but this day I haveing a good observac*i*on, I find that I am in the latitud of 4°55′ which is 70 miles more Northerly then I am by dead reckoning, the distance westing shall be expressed.[4]

Novemb*er*. *Bachelor* bound for St Julians. 1669.

28. From Yesterday noon till this day noon [*margin:* 04°55′: 02°46′ good observac*i*on.] being Sabboth day, wee have steered by the Compasse from the So*uth* to the ENE but by observac*i*on I find that Wee have made our way good East 23 miles, Wee haveing the Wind from the ESE to the SE, easy gale & good Weather, the moon being at the full good observac*i*on.

29. From yesterday noon till this day noon being Monday wee have steered from [*margin:* '05°02′: 03°33′ good Observac*i*on.] the SBW to the EBN, distanc run*n* 46 miles, but by observac*i*on I find that wee have made our way good East distance runn 23 miles wee haveing the wind from the SEBE, to the SSE, easy gale & good weather, Northing 9 Easting 47 miles.

30. From yesterday noon till this day noon being Tuesday, wee have had very little or no wind, lying with her Stem [*margin:* 05°27′: 03°33′ good Observac*i*on] E & ENE, distance

[1] This must be an error. It looks as though this should be 30 miles and the southing 27 miles, which would agree with the course and the easting. The difference in the distance run from the previous day is 37′ which might be accounted for by the fact that the second is based on observation. Narbrough has a distance run for this day of 14·1 miles.

[2] Solomon Franco.

[3] Dead reckoning.

[4] How the distance was to be expressed is not given. There is an error here since the difference between the two latitudes is nothing like 70 miles, furthermore the observed (which agrees almost perfectly with Narbrough's latitude) is south of that by dead reckoning.

run 30 miles, but by observac*i*on I find that wee have made our way good N*orth* 25 miles by reason of a NW Current, the wind that was, was at SSE, very Clear weather with Calmes, the moon being in her third quarter and a good observac*i*on.

Decemb*er*. *Bachelor* bound for St Julians. 1669.

1. From yesterday noon till this day noon [*margin:* 05°38′: 3°37′.] being Wednesday, wee had Calm. The same day our Master & I went on board the admirall, the same day wee tryed the Current, & found it to sett 20 miles in 24 hour's, the same day wee had the wind come up at NNW^t^, little wind no observac*i*on but according to Judgm*ent* of the Current I allow her A NNE Course distance run*n* 12 mile Easting 04·05 Northing 11 miles.

2. From yesterday noon till this day noon being [*margin:* 04°59′: 03°04′. Ded reckoning No observac*i*on 69.] Thursday wee have had the Wind Variable & with all unsettled, but I find by Judgm*ent* that I have found our way good SBE distance 40 miles South 39 m*iles* East 7 m*iles,* no observac*i*on, Rain shift[1] of Wind.

Decemb*er*. Ditto[2]

3. From yesterday noon till this day noon being [*margin:* 05°00′: 03°19′ good Observac*i*on.] fryday wee have steered upon sev'all Courses from the ENE to the SW, sometimes little wind, sometimes Calme Weather, much rain in the Night but by observac*i*on I find that wee have [*margin:* lat. Meridd.] made our way good East distance run 15 miles, the winds variable between the SE and the SEBS. Good observac*i*on.

4. From yesterday noon till this day noon [*margin:* 04°51′: 03°04′ good Observac*i*on.] being Saturday, wee have had very little wind and some p*ar*te of the time Stark Calme, & I find that wee have made our way good by observac*i*on, that I have made WSW 2[3] Distance Run 18 miles, Southing 9 miles Westing 15 miles. the winds round the Compass good observa*cion*.

5. From yesterday noon till this day noon being Sabboth day, wee have had very little wind & Calme but I find by observac*i*on that wee have made our way good

Decem*ber*. Ditto

NE, distance runn 24 miles East 14 [*margin:* 05°18′: 03°21′ good Observac*i*on. Current tryed NE 17 miles in 24 hours.] miles North 17 miles, the wind that was at S & SBW & wee lay with our Stem **B**E & EBS but by reason of a Northern Current that setts NE 17

[1] Repetition of 'shift' struck through.

[2] Chamber's headers for each recto up to 1 Dec.1669 follow the form '*Bachelor* bound for St Julians', sometimes with and sometimes without the presumed latitude of the latter. From Dec. 1669 onwards many of the recto headers are reduced to the month and 'D/ditto'. The presumed latitude of Puerto San Julián changes, given as 47°20′S, 48°20′S, 48°40′S, 49°20′S and 49°40′S.

[3] Presumably this means 2° off WSW, but the direction is not stated. From the westing and southing the course should be 240°. WSW is 247½°, so there is also an error here.

miles in 24 hour's, our Shipp is to the Nor*th*ward of my last observac*i*on, the which other wise would have been to the Southward. The same day wee tryed the Current with our boat.

6. From yesterday noon till this day noon being Monday wee have had little or [*margin:* 05°13′: 03°50′ good Observac*i*on: this day we haled our Mast after.][1] no wind, & wee have lain with our Stem EBS & ESE & SEBE, dist*ance* run 30 miles, but by observac*i*on I find that wee have made our way good East 8° Southerly East 29 miles, Southerly 05 miles, the wind that was between the SBE and the SSW. Good Observac*i*on still wee find a Northern Current.

Decem*ber*.   *Bachelor* bound for St Julians. 1669.

7. From yesterday noon till this day noon being Tuesday wee have made our way by dead [*margin:* 04°48′: 04°20′ good Observac*i*on: this last 24 hours I find a South Current by Observac*i*on] reckoning SEBE, dist*ance* runn 40 miles but by Observac*i*on I find that wee have made our way good SE 6° Easterly Dist*ance* 40 miles Easting 30 miles Southing 27 miles, the wind variable between the South & B West, & the NNW little wind. This day at 8 a clock in the morning we tacked haveing the wind at NE a fresh gale but away againe in an hours time good weather & a good Observac*i*on.

8. From yesterday noon till this day noon [*margin:* 04°52′: 04°31′ good Observac*i*on North Current Lat Meridd.] being Wednesday wee have had little or no wind, but the wind that was, was all round the Compasse. Dist*ance* runn by the logg 8 mile East & EBS, but I find by observac*i*on that wee have made our way good ENE, dist*ance* run 12 miles Easting 11 miles Northing 4·5 m*iles* good weather, and a good observac*i*on.

Decem*ber*.   Ditto

9. From yesterday noon till this day noon [*margin:* 05°00′: 04°37′ no Observac*i*on.] being thursday wee have had little or no wind, sometime lying with our head to the Eastward, & sometime lying with our head to the Southward, & wee had no observac*i*on by reason of Cloudy weather, but by esteemac*i*on I find that wee are in the Lat*itude* of 5°00′. Distance runn 08 NE North 6 East 6.

10. From yesterday noon till this day noon [*margin:* 04°42′: 04°37′ no Observac*i*on.] being fryday wee had no observac*i*on, but by dead Reckoning, I find that wee have made our way good South dist*ance* run 18 miles the winds variable, some raine very little wind.

11. From yesterday noon till this day noon being saturday, wee had no observac*i*on [*margin:* 04°14′: 04°37′ No Observac*i*on.] but by dead reckoning, I find that wee have made our way good South distance run*n* 28 miles, wee haveing the wind variable, but very little of it with some raine.

[1] They raked the mast aft, to shift the centre of pressure of the sails aft and thus decrease the amount of helm the ship had to carry to maintain her course and so improve her speed.

Decem*ber*. Ditto

12. From yesterday noon till this day noon [*margin:* 03°12′: 05°03′ good Observac*i*on New Moon.] being Sabboth day I find by dead reckoning that I should be in the Lat*itude* of 3°38′ but by observac*i*on I find that I am in the Lat*itude* of 3°12′ distanc*e* run*n* this last 24 hours 37 miles SE. South 26 m*iles* Easting 26 miles the wind variable, between the South, & the SW. Little wind, the distance between by Observac*i*on and my dead reckoning is 26 miles that I am Southerly.

13. From yesterday noon till this day [*margin:* '03°00′: 05°41′. good observac*i*on.] noon being Monday, wee steered by Compasse E & ESE and SEBE, but by Observac*i*on I find that wee have made good ESE 4° eas*terly* distance runn 40 miles south 12 miles East 38 miles the Wind upon the South quarter. Terrible raine a good Observac*i*on.

Decem*ber*. Ditto

14. From yesterday noon till this day noon [*margin:* 02°42′: 05°15′. Good Observac*i*on Moon in the first quarter.] being Tuesday I have made our way by Compass SW 6° W*este*rly & wee have lain with our head upon sev'all Courses from the EBW[1] to the WSW but I find by observac*i*on that I have made our way good SW 9° W*este*rly, distance runn 33 miles Southing 19 miles, westing 26 miles the wind from the south to the SBE, a fine fresh gale & a good Observac*i*on some raine wee standing to the Eastward.[2]
This day being the 14th of Decemb*er* is 30 day's that wee have had the Wind between the East & the SSW, from Lat*itude* 4°12′ North to Lat*itude* 2°42′ North the wind like to hold still, in that time wee had some.[3]

15. From yesterday noon till this day noon [*margin:* 02°35′: 05°06′ No Observac*i*on: Water Cask from the admirall to fill to Make our shipp Stiff.[4]] being Wednesday I had no Observac*i*on, but wee have layne with our stem to the southward the wind being at South and SSE, an Easy gale and good Weather little raine.

Decem*ber*. *Bachelor* bound for St Julians Lat*itude* 48°20′ S.. 1669.

16. From yesterday noon till this day noon [*margin:* '02°27′: 04°49′. Good Observacion. Tow. Lat. Meridd.] being thursday wee have layne with our head to the south Westward, & wee have runn 20 miles the wind at SBE, a fine easy gale & good weather & a good Observac*i*on, the same day the *Sweepstakes* took us in a Tow about 4 a Clock in the afternoon Steering away SW, the wind at SSE.

17. From yesterday noon till this day none [*margin:* 01°57′: 04°15′. Dead reckoning. Tow.] being fryday Wee had no Observac*i*on but wee standing to the southward, haveing

[1] It is not clear what this should be, but bearing in mind the course made good it is probably SBW.
[2] Presumably this should be 'westward.'
[3] The line ends with a full stop. The missing word might be 'raine'.
[4] To lower the centre of gravity and make the ship less liable to heel over to the wind or sea and thus sail faster by presenting a greater sail area to the wind.

the wind at SSE a fresh gale dist*ance* run*n* 55 miles WSW South 35 miles, West 51 miles with the wind at SSE Cloudy Weather.

18. From yesterday noon till this day noon being Saturday wee have made our way [*margin:* Tow.] good SWBW 3° Westerly dist*ance* runn 55 miles South 27 west 48 miles with the wind at SSE & SE a fresh gale but a great SE Sea good Observac*i*on.

Decemb*er*. Ditto.

19. From yesterday noon till this day noon [*margin:* 00°49′: 02°41′. Good observac*i*on the Moon a q*uar*ter old. Tow.] being Sabboth day wee have laine with our stem SSW and SW but by observac*i*on I find that wee have made our way SWBW 3° So*uther*ly, dist*ance* runn 58 miles South 34 miles west 47. The wind at SSE and SE a fresh gale cloudy weather but a good Observac*i*on.

20. From yesterday noon till this day [*margin:* 00°05′: 01°53′. Good observac*i*on North Lat. Æquin*octia*ll crossed. Tow. Wee crossed the Æquinoctiall line in 11°46′ true long from the Lizard, or haveing made thier 220 leagues west from the Lizard.][1] noon being Monday, wee have stem*m*ed away SSW & SWBS & SW, but by observac*i*on I find that wee have made our way good SWBW dist*ance* runn 59 miles Southing 34 westing 48 the wind at SSE & SEBS & SE a fresh gale & Cloudy Weather, but a good Observac*i*on, like to be good Weather.

Decemb*er*. Ditto.

21. This day wee crossed the Equin*octia*ll Lyne. [*margin:* The *Sweepstakes* had her water & half her deales[2] & wee had 11 empty Casks to fill in the leiu of them punchions & hogsheads.] [*blank space*][3]

22. From Monday noon till Wednesday noon [*margin:* 00°32′: 00°37′ South Lat. Good observac*i*on. Tow.] we have lain with our stem SSW and SWBS & 4 hou*rs* EBS but by Observac*i*on & distance runn I find that I have made our way good WSW half W*ester*ly, westing 86 miles South 27[4] the wind at SEBS and SSE a very fresh gale.

23. From yesterday noon till this day noon being thursday wee have layn with our stem SSW & SWBS, but by observac*i*on I find that wee have made our way good SBW 25 ho[r5] 43 miles but by the logg I find that wee have runn but 40 miles & my difference of Lat*itude* is 42 miles, that is 2 miles more than my logg gives but I judg it is by reason

Decem*ber*. Ditto.

[1] It is not clear how this longitude was calculated; 220 leagues would give 11° according to a reckoning by plain sailing. Narbrough gives 17°08′·1 west from the Lizard.

[2] Deales are the planks for building the shallop.

[3] The blank space is equivalent to the marginal note which is written in 6 lines in the margin.

[4] These figures correspond to a distance run of 90 miles.

[5] The meaning of this is obscure but it may mean that the run was over a period of 25 hours.

[*margin:* 01′14′: 00°29′. South Lat. Good Observac*i*on. South Current. Tow. Lat Merid] of a Southern Current my westing though [through] 24h is 8 miles, the wind being at SE & SEBS, a fine fresh gale, & good weather and a good observac*i*on. The same day our Master went on board the *Sweepstakes*.

24. From yesterday noon till this day noon [*margin:* '02°03′: 00°29′ South Southern Current good Observac*i*on Tow.'] being fryday wee have layne with our Stem to the South & SBW & SSW for the most p*ar*t dist*ance* runn by the logg 42 miles, but by observac*i*on I find that wee have differ'd our Lat*itude* 49 miles the which is by a great Southerne Current that has set us 7 miles more to S*outhwar*d then she has runn by the logg, So I conclude that wee have made our way good S dist*ance* run 49 miles the wind being at EBS & South E a fine fresh gale & good observac*i*on.

25. From yesterday noon till this day [*margin:* '03°07′: 00°29′ S. Lat. S. Current. Christs Nativity. Tow.] noon being Saturday wee have runn by the logg 54 miles SBW & SSW but by Observac*i*on I find I have diff*er*'d my Lat*itude* 64 miles therefore I conclude that I have made my way good.

Decemb*er*. *Bachelor* bound for St Julians Lat*itude* 48°20′ S. 1669.
South distance run 64 miles by reason of a Southern Current the wind being then at SEBE & SE a fresh gale, & good weather, flocks of birds seen to flock on the water.

26. From yesterday noon till this day noon [*margin:* 04°01′[1]: 00°29′ South Lat. South Current not so strong as it was. Tow.] being Saboth day wee steered by the Compass S & SBW & SSW 64 miles but by observac*i*on I find that I have differ'd my Lat*itude* 64 miles the which is by the s*outhwar*d Current, therefore I conclude that I have made my way good S distance runn 64 miles. Good weather & good observac*i*on, the wind at ESE & SEBE, a fine fresh gale.

27. From yesterday noon till this day noon being moonday wee have steer'd by the [*margin:* 05°38′: 00°29′ South Lat. South Current little. Tow.] Compasse SBW and S for the most part, but by Observac*i*on I find that wee have made our way good S dist*ance* runn 81 miles, difference of Lat*itude* 81 miles therefore I grant that the Current was still to the S but not so strong as it did bifor. Wee haveing the wind at ESE, a fresh gale and good observac*i*on.

Decemb*er*. *Bachelor* bound for Do. S. Lat*itude* 48°30′. 1669.

28. From yesterday noon till this day noon being Tuesday, wee have [*margin:* '07°10′: 00°29′. Good observac*i*on. S Current abated. Tow.] layn with our stem S & SBW and SBE with the wind at ESE & SEBE & EBS a fresh gale, but by observac*i*on I find that wee have made our way good South dist*ance* run*n* by the logg 88 miles but by difference of Lat*itude* 92 miles the which is 4 miles more then the Logg. Good weather but Cloudy good observac*i*on.

[1] The latitude should be 04°11′.

29. From yesterday noon till this day noon [*margin:* '08°25': 00°29': No observacion to loose our shipp the worse for Towing Leakey. Merid.] being Wednesday wee have steered away by the Compasse S & SBW & SSE but by Judgm*ent* I find my selfe to be in the Lat*itude* of 8°25'. No Observac*i*on. The wind at E & EBN and EBS a fresh gale, good weather but Cloudy dist*ance* runn by the Log 80 miles. The same day about 4 in the morning

Decem*ber* *Bachelor* bound for D°. S L*atitude* 48°30'. 1669.

our Cable broak that wee were towed with at noon, hee[1] spoke with us & desired us to sterre away SBE.

30. From yesterday noon till this day noon being [m*argin:* 09°43': 00°29'. Good Observac*i*on. Variac*i*on 7° from the S.W[ly] and from the N. E[ly]. Tow'd again.] thursday wee have steered by the Compasse S & SBE dist*ance* runn 72 miles, but by observac*i*on I find that I have made our way good S dist*ance* runn 78 miles the wind at E & bS & ESE fresh gale. The same day the *Sweepstakes* took us in a Tow with his own Stream Cable, Good weather and a good observac*i*on, but Cloudy.[2]

31. From yesterday noon till this day noon being [*margin:* 10°59': 00°22'. Light south Current good Observac*i*on. Tow.] fryday wee have steered by the Compasse SBE & SSE & SBW but by observac*i*on, I find that wee have made our way good SBW dist*ance* run*n* by the logg 72 miles, but by observac*i*on distance runn is 76 miles, S 75·8, westing 6·6 miles, good weather and a good Observac*i*on. The wind at East and EBS & ESE a fine fresh gale.

January. Anno 1669.[3]

1. From yesterday noon till this day noon being [*margin:* 11°51': 00°23'. Variac*i*on 5° from the North E[ly] and from the South W[ly]. Tow.] Saturday wee have Steered by the Compasse S & SBE and SBW but by Observation I find that wee have made our way good S dist*ance* runn by the Logg 50 miles but by Observac*i*on 52 miles the wind at ESE and EBS a fresh gale and good Observac*i*on. The same day I was on board the Admirall and wee tooke an Azimuth and an Amplitude in the afternoon and found the Variac*i*on to be as in the Margent.

2. From yesterday noon till this day noon being Saboth day wee have steered by the Compass S and SBE dist*ance* runn by the logg 67 miles,

Jan*uary*. *Bachelor* bound for S[t] Julians L*atitude* 48°3' S.

[*margin:* 12°55': 00°22'. Good observac*i*on. Magil Clouds. Tow.] but by observac*i*on I find that wee have made our way good S E*aster*ly dist*ance* 66 miles S the wind at ESE &

[1] Captain Narbrough in *Sweepstakes*.

[2] Chambers has assumed that his course has been South for the last 7 days and that therefore there has been no westing. Over this period Narbrough records a westing of 111·3 miles, and his Longitude is 2°33'·3 west of Praia.

[3] Chambers uses the English Julian calendar, and does not note the beginning of the New Year in the Gregorian calendar.

EBS a fresh gale, and good weather, the same night I beheld the Magilmian Clouds[1] two in number.

3. From yesterday noon till this day noon being Monday wee have made our way [*margin:* 14°14′: 00°17′. South Lat. By observac*io*n I find a S Str*ong* Current. Variac*io*n as before. Tow.] good by Compass & Logg S 5° W*ester*ly dist*ance* runn 68 miles but by observac*io*n I find that wee have made our way good S 5° W*ester*ly dist*ance* runn 75 miles and 5[2] Southing 79 miles west 7 miles. The wind at ESE and EBS a fine fresh gale and Exceeding good weather, good observac*io*n. These 24 houres I find the shipp to have out runn the logg 11 miles,[3] sometimes more sometimes less.

January. Ditto.

4. From yesterday noon till this day noon [*margin:* 15°36′: 00°15′. S Lat.. A small S Current. Variac*io*n 6° W^ly^.[4] Tow. Merid.] being Tuesday wee have steered away S and SBE by the Compasse & distane runn by the Logg 72 miles, but by observac*io*n I find that wee have made our way good S distan[c]e Runn 82 miles good weather, & the wind at EBS a fine fresh gale. The same day at Sun riseing I observe the sun Cutt a Merid*dian* Compasse,[5] & found it to rise EBS ½ S the which is 16° from true E, but I find the true ampliyude to be ESE the which is 22°20′.[6] Therefore I conclude that the Variac*io*n of the Compass to be 6° from the N Merid*dian* to the E*astwar*d and from the S merid*dian* Westward.

5. From yesterday noon till this day noon being wednesday wee have made our way good by the logg & Compasse SBW 5° W*este*rly but by distance run & difference of Lat*itude* I find that I have made our way good

January. Ditto.
[*margin:* 17°02′: 00°15′ S Lat. Same Variac*io*n. Tow. *Sweepstakes* sounded but had no ground.] S*outher*ly, distance run by the Log 73 miles S*outher*ly 86 miles or differ of Lat*itude*[7] the wind at E & EBS and ESE, & wee steering away S ½ W*ester*ly. Very good weather, and a good Observac*io*n considering the ☼ to be with in 4° of our Zenith in that Lat*itude*.

6. From yesterday noon till this day noon [*margin:* 18°15′: 00°01′ S Lat. Merid E. Twelveth day. *Sweepstak*'s sounded, but no Ground. Tow.] being Thursday wee steered

[1] Magellanic clouds: Two large globular cloudy spots formed of vast numbers of nebulae and clusters of stars, visible in the Southern Hemisphere. *NOED*.

[2] This could mean 80 or 75·5 miles, but 80 miles agrees with 79 miles south and 7 miles west and the distance of 79 miles south agrees with the difference between the two noon latitudes.

[3] The actual distance run was greater than that recorded by the log by 11 miles.

[4] Westerly refers to the south point of the compass; see below, p. 658, for Chambers's remark at the end of the journal. Narbrough has the variation 6°25′ East on this day.

[5] The meridian compass has a sighting vane standing up at the side, and this means that either the observer watched it cast a shadow across the compass or he used it to obtain the magnetic bearing of the sun at sun rise.

[6] This should be 22°30′.

[7] The log gave a distance run of 73 miles but the distance between the noon sights gave 86 miles, which is the figure used to calculate the new Latitude.

away by the Compasse S & SBE dist*ance* Runn 58 miles but by Observac*i*on I find that wee have made our way good SBW allowing for a SSW Current & ½ a poynt for west Variac*i*on dist*ance* runn 75 miles, S 73 miles W*est* 16. Exceeding good weather & a fine fresh gale of wind at EBN & ENE the sun being then with in two degrees of Our Zenith.

7. From yesterday noon till this day noon [*margin:* 18°54′: 00°17′ South Lat. Tow loose at Six a Clock. SSW Current. Variac*i*on W*ester*ly ½ a poynt.][1] being fryday wee have steered by the Compass S & SBW, & dist*ance* run by the Logg 32 miles, but by Observac*i*on I find that wee have made our way good S & SW dist*ance* runn 42 miles, Southing 39 Westing 16 exceeding good weather

Jan*uary* 1669. B*achelor* bound for St Julians Lat*itude* 48°30′ S.

& little easy gale of wind at NNE good observac*i*on, Wee have out runn the Logg 7 miles Sun ine our Zenith.

8. From yesterday noon till this day noon [*margin:* 20°00′: 00°43′ South Lat. Merid dist. W*est*. Variac*i*on 9° W^ly^. Took us in a Tow about 7 of the Clock in the morning with his own stream Cable.] being Saturday, wee have steered by the logg & Compasse SBW dist*ance* runne 54 miles but by Judgm*en*t I find allowing for West Variac*i*on 9°, & for a SSW Current that wee have made our way good SSW distance runn 71 miles, S*outhing* 66 miles Westing 26 miles with the wind at NBE & NNE a fine fresh gale, the *Sweepstakes* keeping her selfe some 3 leagues to the westward of us to see if wee see the Islands that Lye in the Lat*itude* of 19°00′ & 20°00′[2] but wee did not see them. No Observac*i*on by reason the Sunn [in] our Zenith very hott, the same time wee saw severall fowle some white like a duck in the head but their wings long and sharpe at the end, & some grey & some black flying low on the water and Swiming,[3] exceeding good weather.

Jan*uary*. *Bachelor* bound for St Julians. Lat*itude* 48°30′ S.

9. From yesterday noon till this day noon being Sunday wee have steered by the Compasse [*margin:* 22°01′: 02°23′ South Lat.[4] W^ly^. ten degrees West Variac*i*on. Lat. Merid.] SSW and distance runn by the logg 72 miles, but by Judgm*en*t I find her to make SWBS way by reason of almost a whole poynt Variac*i*on W, Southing 61 miles W*esting* 40 miles with the wind at NNE a fine fresh gale and Exceeding good weather. No observac*i*on the Sunn Zeneth.

10. From yesterday noon till this day noon [*margin:* 22°05′: 02°04′ S Westing. 10° W Variac*i*on. Towed still.] being monday wee have steered by the Compass SSW & distance

[1] Presumably this means that the compass varied ½ a point (5°37′·5) west of south. Chambers continues to record the variation as westerly from south rather than using the normal convention, followed by Narbrough, of easterly.

[2] Trindade (20°30′S, 29°19′W) and Martin Vaz Islands (20°28′S, 28°51′W). See above, pp. 37, n. 4; 181, n. 2.

[3] This sounds like an albatross, possibly the wandering albatross (*Diomedia exulans*), of which the older birds are largely white (the upper wing has black primaries and a narrow margin along secondaries), while the younger ones tend to have more brown and black markings. Harrison, *Seabirds*, pp. 222–4.

[4] The longitude here should be 01°23′.

run by the Logg 72 miles, but by Judgm*en*t I make my selfe to be in the Lat*itude* of 22°5′ dist*ance* runn 76 miles, South 64 west 41, Course SWbS, exceeding good Weather with the wind at NNE a fine fresh gale, still white fowle seen. No Observac*i*on by reason the Sun Neere our Zenith.

Jan*uary* 1669. *Bachelor* bound for St Julians Lat*itude* 49°40′ S.

11. From yesterday noon till this day noon being [*margin:* 23°12′: 02°48′ South Latitude, by dead reckoning W Variac*i*on. Trop Capricorn. Tow.] Tuesday, wee steered by the Compass SSW but allowing a point W Variac*i*on I grant that wee have made our way good SWBS, distance Run 80 miles, S 67 W 44 exceeding good weather, with the wind at NNE & NNW a fine fresh gale no oberva*t*ion Sunne in the Zenith.

12. From yesterday noon till this day noon [*margin:* 24°50′: 04°03′ South Variac*i*on W 11° dead Reckoning. Tow Still. Lat. Merid.] being Wednesday wee have steered by the Compass SSW & SWBS dist*ance* runn 122 miles, & I make her to be in the Lat*itude* of 24°50′ S and Course that 24 hours allowing a poynt Variac*i*on SWBS five degrees W*ester*ly, S 98 miles W75 miles, with the wind at NNW & NW a fresh gale. Wee had a Tornado out of the Westward board about 12 a Clock at Noone, it lasted about 3 hour's, very much Wind & raine. No Observac*i*on.

Jan*uary* 1669 *Batchelor* bound for St Julians Lat*itude* 49°40′ S.

13. From yesterday noon till this day noon [*margin:* 25°30′: 04°40′. Dead reckoning Corrected. Good observac*i*on. Tow Loose.] being thursday, Wee have had the Winds Very Variable, Sometimes Wind and sometimes Calme, but we Steering away SSW & SWBS, dist*ance* runn 62 miles. I find by my dead reckoning that I should be in the lat*itude* of 25°39′ but this day I haveing Clear and good Observac*i*on, I find that I am in the Lat*itude* of 25°30′, that is 9 miles distance, that is to say I am further N*orther*ly by my Observac*i*on, then by my dead reckoning SWBS.

14. From yesterday [*margin:* 26°25′: 05°49′.[1] Variac*i*on 11° West. Loose. W Longit. from St Iago 6°1′.] noon till this day noon being fryday, wee have steered by the Compasse SWBS, but by Observac*i*on I find that wee have made our way good SW dist*ance* runn 98 miles, Southing 65 westing 65 the winds Variable from the NE to the NW, much Wind and raine and darke Cloudy weather with some thunder and lightening but I find no Current.

Jan*uary* 1669. *Bachelor* bound for St Julians. Lat*itude* 49°40′ S.

15. From yesterday noon till this day noon [*margin:* 27°26′: 06°40′. dead reckoning. Variac*i*on W 13°. Loose.] being Saturday wee have steered by the Compass SWBS dist*ance* run*n* 72 miles, but by observac*i*on I allow her a SW way southing 51 m*iles* W*est* 51 miles, the wind at N & NBE & NEBN according to the Compass, but I find the

[1] The latitude should be 26°35′ to agree with difference in text.

Compasse to Vary 13° W. Gusty weather & raine The moon being in her first quarter. No observac*i*on.

16. From yesterday noon till this day [*margin*: 28°52′: 08°06′. dead reckoning. Variac*i*on 13° W. The Sunn haveing S declina*t*ion decreasing. Loose.] noon being Sabath day, wee have steered by the Compasse SWBS, but by observac*i*on. I find that she has made her way SW dist*ance* runn 122 miles, S 86, W 86, with the wind at N & NNE & NBW. Much wind & raine, thick cloudy weather with some thunder & lightning. No observac*i*on, the moon in her first quarter. I find by an amplitude taken by a Merid*dian* Compasse at sun setting the Variac*i*on to be 13° W that is from N Merid*dian* E*aster*ly, and from the South Merid*dian* W*ester*ly.

Jan*uary* 1669. Ditto bound for D°. Lat*itude* 49°20′ S.

17. From yesterday noon till this day noon [*margin:* 30°05′: 08°43′. Corrected by Observac*i*on. Variac*i*on 13° W. Loose. Lat. Merid.] being monday wee have steered by the Compass SWBS & 6 houres WSW, the wind being for the most part at N & NNW & NW and at Six of the Clock in the morning the wind cam up at SSW & S, & wee tacked & wee stood into the Westward distance runn this 24 hour's 80 miles SW, Southing 57, W*estin*g 57 so that by dead reckoning, I should be in the Lat*itude* of 29°49′, but this day I haveing a good observac*i*on, I find that I am in the Lat*itude* of 30°09′ so that I am further S*outhwar*d by my Observac*i*on then by my dead reckoning 20 miles, hazy weather great swelling sea N.

18. From yesterday noon till this day noon being [*margin:* 30°23′: 09°16′. By observac*i*on. Loose.] Tuesday wee have steered by Contrary winds SWBW & SW & SWBS, but by Observac*i*on I find that wee have made our way good WSW dist*ance* runn 36 miles, Westing 33 miles S*outhing* 14, the winds between the SSE[1] a fresh gale and a great swelling sea, coole weather and dry.

Ditto. Ditto bound for D°. Lat*itude* 49°20′ S.

19. From yesterday noon till this day noon [*margin:*31°03′: 10°21′. Dead reckoning. Sails bent new] being Wednesday, wee have steered by the Compass SWBS, dist*ance* run*n* 85 miles but by esteemac*i*on I find that wee have made our way good SWBW halfe a point W*ester*ly, S*outhin*g 40 W*estin*g 75 miles with the wind at SEBE & ESE & SE a very stiff gale, & a great sea, new Sails brought too.

20. From yesterday noon [*margin:* 32°00′: 11°55′. Good observac*i*on.] till this day noon being Thursday, wee have steered by the Compass SWBS, but by Observac*i*on I find that wee have made our way good SWBW two degrees W*ester*ly, distance Runn 110 miles S*outhin*g 57 miles W*estin*g 94 miles, the wind at ESE & SEBE a Stiff gale, coole & clear weather.

[1] There would appear to be a second direction left out here.

21. From yesterday noon till this day [*margin:* '32°45': 13°07'. Good Observac*i*on.] noon being fryday, wee have steered by the Compasse SWBS, dist*ance* runn 85 miles but by Observac*i*on I find that wee have made our way good SWBW 1° W*este*rly, S*outhin*g 45 miles Westing 72 miles with the wind

Jan*uary* 1669. Ditto.

[*margin:* Variac*i*on 18° W.] at E & EBS a fine easy gale, calme, Sometime Coole weather & good weather.

22. From yesterday noon till this day [*margin:* 32°47': 13°8'. Dead reckoning. Variac*i*on 18° W. Scrapd and washd our shipps bottom.] noon, being Saturday it has been very calme for the most part, & very smooth water, wee had no observac*i*on the same day, I tryed the Current & I found none at all that I could disserne, the same day our boat went aboard the *Sweepstakes*, & wee cleaned our shipp.

23. From yesterday noon till this day noon [*margin:* 33°04': 14°4'. Good observac*i*on. Variac*i*on 17°15' W. Heere I am 180 leagues off the land by the book. Lat. Merid.] being Sabboth day wee have steered by the Compass SWBS, but by Observac*i*on I find that I have made our way good WSW 2° W*este*rly dist*ance* runn 58 miles S*outhin*g 18 miles, W*estin*g 56 miles, with the wind at NEBN a fine gentle gale, & exceeding good cleare weather and very smooth water. Good Observac*i*on.

Jan*ua*ry 1669. Ditto.

24. From yesterday noon till this day [*margin:* 34°26': 15°26'. Good observac*i*on. A great south Current. Variac*i*on W17°48'. Merid.] noon being Monday wee have steered by the Compasse SWBS, dist*ance* runn by the logg 89 miles but by Observac*i*on I find that wee alter'd our latitude 82 miles the which as I judg by reason of a S*outhe*rn Current, therefore I conclude that I have made our way good SW, distance runn 116 miles S*outhin*g 82 miles W*estin*g 82, with the wind at NEBN a very fine easy gale & exceeding good weather, & smooth Water the moon being neere the full. The same day at 6 of the Clock in the morning I took an Azimuth the sunn being 5° above the horizon and I found 17°42' W Variation.

Jan*ua*ry 1669. Ditto.

25. From yesterday noon till this day [*margin:* 35°37': 17°10' Good Observac*i*on. No Current. A Turtle seen. Variac*i*on W.] noon being Tuesday wee have steered by the Compass SWBS, & dist*ance* run by the logg 123 miles, but by observac*i*on I find that wee have made our way good SWBW 1° W*este*rly, dist*ance* 123 miles S*outhin*g 71 W*esting* 104 with the wind at NNE & NEBN, a fresh gale & smooth water. The moon at the full. In the Nights a great dew falls. In the Evenings Hazy. Wee Judg by Lat*itude* to be open with the mouth of Rio de la Platto but the water is not changed at all in colour nor in tast. I Judg my selfe to be by the Waggoner[1] [*blank*] leagues off shoar.

[1] A Waggoner is an atlas of charts, so called after the atlases published by Lucas Janszoon Waghenaer van Enckhuysen from 1584.

26. From yesterday noon till this day noon being [*margin:* 36°20′: 18°42′. Variac*i*on West no Current.] Wednesday, wee have steered by the Compass for the most p*ar*t SWBS & SWBS Ry:[1] 2 hours WSW way, but by Observac*i*on I

Jan*uary* 1669. Ditto.

find that wee have made our way good SWBW 8° W*ester*ly dist*ance* run 102 miles S*outhin*g 43 miles W*estin*g 92 miles the Wind for the most at N & NEBN, a fresh gale till 4 of the Clock this morning & then the wind came up at SW & went round to the SE & proved a storme for the time it held, with much raine. It held some 3 hours; the same time a full moon, this day the water seemed somewhat greener [*margin:* Lat Merid.] then before.

27. From yesterday noon till this day [*margin:* 35°36′[2]: 19°33′. Variac*i*on W. No Current.] noon being Thursday, wee haveing Contrary winds have steered by the Compasse SW & SWBW & WSW & WBS and W & WBW[3] dist*ance* runn 56 miles but by Observac*i*on I find that wee have made our way good WNW 2° N*orther*ly, dist*ance* runn 56 miles N*orthin*g 24 W*estin*g 51, the wind from the SSE to the SWBS, a fine easy gale and smooth water.

Jan*uary* 1669. *Bachelor* bound for St Julians. L*atitude* 49°20′ S.

28. From yesterday noon till this day noon [*margin:* 35°57′: 20°12′. Variac*i*on W 18°. Our boat went on board the Admirall.] being fryday, wee steered upon severall courses between the SW & the West distance Runn 39 miles, but by observac*i*on I find that wee have made our way good W*estwa*rd S*outher*ly, Southing 1 mile W*estin*g 39, very little wind, that which was, was at N & NW. Very good weather.

29. From yesterday noon till this day noon [*margin:* 37°10′: 21°53′. Variac*i*on 18° W. No Current. Longit 23° from St Iago.] being Saturday, wee have Steered by the Compasse SW & SWBS, but by observac*i*on I find that wee have made our way good SWBW, dist*ance* runn 125 miles S*outhin*g 74 W*estin*g 101. The wind from the NE to the NW, a very fresh gale but clear weather & good.

30. From yesterday noon till this day noon [*margin:* 38°44′: 23°03′. Variac*i*on 18° W. Great S Current that set out of Rio De la platto.] being Sabboth day, wee have steered upon Sev'all Courses, by reason of Contrary winds between the W & S. Dist*ance* runn by the logg 73 miles, but by Observac*i*on I find that wee have made our way good SWBS, dist*ance* runn 112 miles

Jan*uary* 1669. Ditto.

S*outhin*g 94 miles W*estin*g 70 miles, fickle weather at 12 of the Clock at Noon the water looked white, but wee sounded no ground.

[1] It is not clear what this means: possibly it indicates a modification in the course.

[2] This should be 35°56′ to agree with difference in text.

[3] This is, of course, an incorrect direction.

31. From yesterday noon till this day noon being [*margin:* 39°29′: 24°09′. Dead reckoning. Variac*io*n W.] Monday Wee have had the Wind Variable round the Compasse, sometimes much wind & raine with lightning & Thunder in so much that wee lower'd our low yards, but gon pr*es*ently over, and sometimes no wind Our Course was SW. I had no Observac*io*n by reason of thick weather, but by Judgm*ent* I find her to make SW&BW way dist*ance* runn 80 miles, S 45 miles W*estin*g 66 miles the most Wind at NW & N. The water looking green & very smooth with riplings and aboundance of Sea fowle swimming on the water like Ducks with white Necks.

Ditto.
February 1669.

1. [*margin:* 39°29′: 25°14′. dead reckoning. The same day our boat was on board the *Sweepstakes*. Variac*io*n W.] From yesterday noon till this day noon being Tuesday, Wee had contrary winds & wee have made our way good by Judgm*ent* W*ester*ly dist*ance* runn 65 miles. The wind at SSE & S & SBE sometimes Calme, the same day wee tryed the Current & wee found it to sett WNW 15 miles in 24 hours. The same day the *Sweepstakes* sounded & had 70 fathoms of water, small black sand at 10 of the Clock in the Night & tack'd & stood to Eastward the wind at SSE & S very little wind, & exceeding smooth water, before wee had ground wee saw two Seales.[1]

February. 1669. Ditto.

2. [*margin:* 39°14′: 25°53′. Good Observac*io*n. Variac*io*n W 18°.] From yesterday noon till this day noon being Wednesday wee have had very little wind at S & SSW, & wee have made our way [by] Compasse ESE but by Observac*io*n I find that wee have made Our way good WNW dist*ance* run*n* 43 miles, N*orthin*g 15 miles, W*estin*g 39. The same morning wee sounded with an hundred fathome of line but had no ground.

3. From yesterday noon till this day noon [*margin:* '39°20′: 26°26′. No Observac*io*n. Variac*io*n W.] being thursday, Wee have made our way by Judgm*en*t WSW dist*ance* runn 35 miles. The winds Very Variable round the Compasse, & exceeding good weather, & smooth Water with many fowle, The moon being in his last quarter. The same day the *Sweepstakes* boat was on board our shipp, many Ripplings on the water, which in the Night make a great Noyse like some breach.[2]

Feb*ruary* 1669. *Bachelor* bound for St Julians Lat*itude* 49°20′ S.

4. From yesterday noon till this day noon [*margin:* '39°34′: 26°47′. Good Observac*io*n a little N Current. Variac*io*n W 15°. Lat. Merid.] being fryday wee have steered by the Compasse SSW, & SWBS, the Wind Very Variable round the Compasse but for the most p*ar*te at SE & NNE little wind but by Observac*io*n I find that wee have made our way good SWBW dist*ance* runn 25 miles S*outhin*g 14 miles W*estin*g 21. Good Weather & Exceeding Smooth Water with ripplings & birds.

[1] A 4-line entry for 2 Feb. follows here, which is crossed out.

[2] Like waves breaking on a beach.

5. From yesterday noon till this day noon [*margin:* 40°42′: 27°36′. Good Observac*i*on. No Current. Sounded at 6 clock at night 50 fathom Water fine red sand the Water very green. Variac*i*on W15°.] being Saturday wee have steered by the Compasse SWBS, but by Observac*i*on I find that wee have made our way good SWBW dist*ance* run*n* 119 miles S 68 miles, W*esting* 49 miles, with the wind at NEBN & NNE, a good fresh gale, and good weather, but foggy, these winds cause an extream dew to fall in the night, & very Cold, Some Rockweed is seen they are of a very dark green, the same day wee stayed our maine mast forward,[1] to make our shipp saile better.

Feb*ruary* 1669. **Ditto.**

6. From yesterday noon till this day noon [*margin:* 41°58′: 28°31′. No Observac*i*on. Variac*i*on W 15°. Soundings 75 fathome.] being Sabboth day, wee have steered by the Compasse SBW, but by Judgm*ent* I make her way SWBS a quarter of a point W*ester*ly, S*outhin*g 76 miles, W*estin*g 55 miles the Wind at N & NBE, a fine fresh gale but very foggy & hazy, in so much that wee could have no Observac*i*on. In the night very much lightning, & thunder, but it produced no bad weather. Wee sounded at 12 a Clock at Night, & had no ground, but wee sounded at 8 a Clock this morning & had 75 fathome water, Very fine sand of a yellowish Colour with black pepery specks, then still steering away as before. Wee sounded at 5 a Clock in the afternoon, & had no ground, wee find the land to trench away more S*outher*ly by a poynt and a halfe then the book specifieth. Here I reckon my selfe to be 190 leagues off Cap blanco,[2] bearing off mee SW, according to Sounding.

Ditto.

[*margin:* Lat. Merid.][3]

7. From yesterday noon till this day noon [*margin:* 42°53′[4]: 27°56′. Dead reckoning. No Observac*i*on. Variac*i*on West. Lat. Merid] being Monday, by[5] Contrary Winds wee have steered by the Compasse SBW & SE & ESE, with the winds at N & S & SSW, sometimes Calme with very thick foggs, but by Judgm*ent* I make her way good, SEBS dist*ance* run*n* 65 miles, S*outhin*g 45 miles W*esting*[6] 35 miles this day very much wind at SSW & a great Sea Wee standing away to the Eastward, many rock weeds seene & small birds like swallows.

8. From yesterday noon till this day noon being Tuesday wee have steered by the [*margin:* 43°28′: 27°21′.[7] Dead reckoning. No Observac*i*on. Var W18° by the Amplitude.] Compasse E&BS & ESE & South&BW, with the wind at SBE & NW indifferent weather, but by Judgm*ent* I find that wee have made our way good SE, distance run*n* 50 miles, S*outhin*g 35 E*astin*g 35. No setled Weather, the moon at the least, Very Coole.

[1] See above, p. 627, n. 1, where the mast was raked aft.

[2] Cabo Blanco (47°12′S, 65°45′W).

[3] This refers to the entry of the previous day.

[4] Should be 42°43′ to agree with difference in text.

[5] Possibly 'reason of' has been omitted here.

[6] This should be 'easting'.

[7] The position, as originally written, has been struck through, and replaced as above.

Ditto.

9. From yesterday noon till this day noon [*margin:* Merid. 44°18′: 26°48′. Dead reckoning. No Observ*acion*. Var W 18°.] being Wednesday wee have steered by the Compasse from the SSW to the SE, with the winds at N & SSW, a good stiff gale, but by Judgm*ent* I find that wee have made our way good SEBS, dist*ance* runn 60 miles S*outhin*g 50 miles Westing[1] 33 miles. This day a new moon, fickle weather but Cold, I find neere the Shore the lesse Variac*i*on.

10. From yesterday noon till this day noon being [*margin:* 44°57′: 26°50′. Good Observac*i*on. Dead reckoning Corrected. Var W.] thursday wee have steered upon sev'all Courses, by reason of Contrary Winds, Wee have steered from the SW to the SEBE & SSE with the winds at NW & SBE, a stif gale dist*ance* runn by the Logg, 76 miles. So that by dead reckoning I should be this day in the Lat*itude* of 45°5′, but haveing a good Observac*i*on I find that I am in the Lat*itude* of 44°57′ so the difference is 8 miles that I am further N*orther*ly then I expected. Att 10 of the clock this morning wee Tack'd and stood to the westward with the wind off SBE

Feb*ruary* 1669. ***Bachelor* bound for St Julians L*atitude* 49°20′ S.**
much wind & very Cold.

11. From yesterday noon till this day [*margin:* 44°38′: 26°22′. Good Observac*i*on. Var W. The moon 3 dayes old.] noon being fryday, wee have steered by the Compasse WBS to the EBS sometimes one way, sometimes another, by reason of the Wind from the SSE to the SSW, much wind with some raine, but by Observac*i*on, I find that wee have made our way good NNE dist*ance* 34 miles N*orthin*g 19 miles, very bad weather, & Very Cold & a great Sea, East 28 m*iles*.

12. From yesterday noon till this day [*margin:* 44°00′: 26°22′. Good Observac*i*on. Var W. Try Sometimes.] noon being Saturday wee have steered by the Compass W & EBS. Tryed under a main Course sometimes with the wind at SSE & SSW, very much wind and some raine, but by Observac*i*on I find that I have made our way good N*orther*ly dist*ance* Runn & difference of Lat*itude* 38 miles. Bad weather and very Cold, with a very great Swelling Sea, but the next fair wind is Ours.

Ditto.

13. From yesterday noon till this day noon [*margin:* Merid. 44°00′: 26°04′. Dead reckoning. Varia W 17°30′ by an Amplitude.] being Saboth day wee have lain with our stem to the SEBS & ESE, very much wind at SWBS & S Very cold and a great sea, but by esteemac*i*on I find that wee have made our way good E dist*ance* runn 18 miles. Wee find it as Cold here now as it is England in November.

[1] This should be 'easting'.

14. From yesterday noon till this day noon [*margin:* 45°00′: 26°04′. Good Observac*i*on. Var W. Fickle weather.] being Monday, wee have steered by the Compasse from the ESE to the WSW, with the wind from the South to the NWBN, a fresh gale, but I conclude by Observac*i*on that wee have made our way good S*outher*ly, distan run 60 miles Very Cleare coole weather. The same day wee see a Seale about 9 a clock in the morning. Att that time I Judged my selfe to be 90 leagues off shore, and the Cape Blanco to bear off me WSW dist*ance* of 190 leagues.

Ditto.

15. From yesterday noon till this day noon [*margin:* 45°59′: 26°16′. Dead reckoning. Vari W. Many Rock weeds seen very Large.] being Tuesday wee have steered by the compass from the SSE to the SSW, but by Judgm*en*t I find that I have made my way good SBW dist*ance* run 60 miles, S*outhin*g 59 W*estin*g 11, with the wind from the SW to the SE, sometimes a very fresh gale, and sometimes little misty foggs. No Observac*i*on, mild weather, not cold.
Here I reckon my selfe to be by the book 190 Leagues off Cape blanco bearing off mee WSW half a point W*ester*ly.

16. From yesterday noon till this day [*margin:* 45°40′ [1]: 28°58′. Good Observac*i*on. Varia W. North Current. Soundings at 12 a Clock 55 fatham the same like ground as before.] noon being Wednesday, wee have steered by the Compasse SW and SWBW, dist*ance* runn by the logg 117 miles, so that by dead reckoning I should be in the Latt*itude* of 46°22′, but haveing a good Observac*i*on I find that I am not so farr S by 22 miles the which is by reason of a N Current.

Ditto.
Wee have had the wind these 24 hour's at NNE & NE, so I conclude that I have made our way good from the last observac*i*on WBS 2° S, dist*ance* run*n* 177 miles S 40 miles W 174 miles, very good mild weather, but hazy fresh gales. The same day the *Sweepstakes* sounded, & had 55 fatham water, the ground much like to the last soundings but a little more oosy, at 12 a clock at Noon the same time wee alter'd our course from SWBW to SSW.

17. From yesterday noon till this day noon [*margin:* 46°12′: 29°49′. Good observac*i*on. Variac*i*on W. Sounding 55, 53 & 50 fatham. No Current. Boat aboard of the Admirall.] being Thursday wee have steered by the Compasse SW & SWBS, but by Observac*i*on I find that wee have made our way good SWBW two degrees W*estin*g, distance run 60 miles S*outhin*g 32 miles, W*estin*g 51 miles the wind at N & NE, a fine easy gale with very much lightning and some Thunder. The same day a dead Whale seen in length about 30 foot. Wee have sounded sev'all times and wee have found always 55 & 53.

Ditto.
fathome, the ground much alike as before fine browne sand with black specks very little Osie.

[1] The latitude appears to be wrong here. According to the text they ought to be 46°00′; however, the next difference of 40′ does not agree with this value either.

18. [*margin:* '46°38′: 30°26′. Dead reckoning. Sounding as bifore, the same depth & ground.] From yesterday noon till this day noon being fryday wee have steered by the Compasse SW & SWBS & SSW, with the wind at NW & E & SEBE, sometimes little wind and some times much wind, but by Judgm*ent* I find that wee have made our way good SWBW½W*ester*ly, dist*ance* run 40 miles, S 26 mile West 37 mile very thick weather and wett foggs many Rock weeds seen, they drive in great beds Closse Compacted together.

19. From yesterday noon till this day noon [*margin:* 46°49′: 30°43′. Dead reckoning. Wee sounded many times but had no ground with 60 fathom of line. *Sweepstakes* still in Company with good Care.] being Saturday wee have steered by the Compasse from the SW to the NEBE, the wind being at SSE & SE and SEBE very much wind & thick Weather and Wett, but by Judgm*ent* I find, that wee have made our way Good SWBS,

Ditto.

distance run 20 miles S 11 miles W 17 miles. Sometimes wee lost the *Sweepstakes* by reason of barring of Sayle, for by reason of the wind & sea Wee were put from our top sayles to a pair of Sayles, & so to a maine Course still remaining[1] pin = game Seene.[2]

20. [*margin:* Lat. Merid. 47°35′: 30°53′. dead reckoning. *Sweepstakes* lost Company.] From yesterday noon till this day noon being Saboth day, wee have stered by the Compasse S & SBE and SSE & SEBE & WSW but by Judgm*ent* I find that wee have made our way good SBW distance run 47 miles S 46 miles W 10 miles the wind being at ESE & SE & ENE, very thick & hazy with wett foggs. this Morning between 7 & 8 of the Clock wee had sight of the *Sweepstakes* bearing off us SEBS the which was on our weather bow dist*ance* from us some three miles, they might have bore to us but wee could not gett to him[3] & it being thick wee lost sight of him

Feb*ruary* 1669. *Bachelor* bound for St Julians. L*atitude* 49°20′ S.

then wee being neer our Lat*itude* of Cape Blanco, wee sounded at 8 a clock in the morning, & had 49 fathome Water still steering away SSE 7 miles more, the ground was sand & little red stones and white shells as broad as a penny still being hazy: then wee sounded at 10 a Clock the same morning & had 50 fathom Water fine browne sand with black specks. Then wee finding our selves to be in the Lat*itude* of Cape blanco, Wee steered away WSW by the Compass to keepe our Lat*itude*, then steering that Course wee sounded againe at 2 a clock in the afternoon & found 53 fathome water the ground being very grosse browne sand[4] with little small red stones, & some shells, then it being very thick and foggy Wee haled off E & ESE, fireing of Gunns peradventure hee[5] might heare us.

[1] The *Sweepstakes* could carry more sail than the *Bachelor*. The pinke was reducing her sails, being forced to furl first her top sails, leaving two courses, and then furl another, leaving only the main sail.

[2] This appears to be Chambers's spelling for penguin.

[3] The *Sweepstakes* could have run down wind to the *Bachelor* but the latter could not make it up wind to the *Sweepstakes*.

[4] Coarse brown sand.

[5] *Sweepstakes*.

Ditto.

21. This day being Monday about one a Clock [*margin:* Lat. Merid. 47°35′: 31°29′. Longit by Judgmt.] in the morning wee laid our head to the W*estwa*rd still lying by it being very thick and foggy Wee keeping good looking out if wee could see her but could not, and sounding every two houres, or every houre according as need required & found little or no altera*t*ion of ground or depth, which was 50, 52, 53 fathome browne Sand but fine sometimes one or 2 little red stones, would come up on the lead. Then about 6 a Clock in the morning wee made sayle steering away SW & SWBW, the which made us WSW way & WBS, steering that course till 8 a Clock the which was two houres & then wee sounded & had 45 fathome water very little sand but many stones of a red Colour about the bignesse of the biggest sort of Pease, only one stone of a white colour as wee call a fire stone[1] as

Ditto.

21. as bigg as an[2] acorne with mosse growing on it. Then Wee haled up WSW & WBS, the Wind still at NW & NWBW, hazy thick weather but not so thick as it was, wee makeing all the sayle wee could. Judging my selfe to be in the Lat*itude* of 48°, or thereabout, then wee sounded againe at 10 of the Clock in [*margin:* I have made from the Lizard to Cape blanco 44°10′ merid distance, or 883 leagues.] the forenoon & had 30 fathoms beachy stones[3] about the biggness of a french beane, then wee had sayled from our last soundings some 5 leagues WSW & WBS the Colour of the stones of our last soundings were black & red, so that in two houres time wee alter'd our depth 15 fathome, still steering away WSW, Judging it to make a West Way, by reason of Varia*cion*. Then at 12 a Clock at noon wee sounded, haveing sayled some 6 miles on the Course & had 15 fathom the same like ground as before, beachy Shinglstoane, with beds of Rock weeds seen, & the water much changed,

Ditto.

to a whey Colour,[4] still wee kept on not altering our course, haveing a bold wind, wee keept the lead going immagining wee should see some Land, or should then after that wee had runn about one league wee had 13 fathome still stones much like the [*margin:* Land made Cape blanco.] former & immediately wee espyed the land in a small cleare of the fogg right ahead bearing off Us WSW halfe S*outher*ly, dist*ance* from us some 4 miles lying neerest NBE and SBW. Still wee run in with an Easy gale keeping off the lead going the very next cast after that wee had 13 fathome, wee had 25 fathome. [*margin:* merid. 48°20′: 32°30′. Long. by Judgmt.] The land is not low nor very high but of a good height. The ground that wee had in 25 fathome water was stiff clay in so much that the lead stuck fast being hard to hale out, left the Tallow behind it but some of the clay stuck

Ditto.

fast to the lead, the which satisfyd us that it was clay ground, then wee Judged our selves to be some three miles off shore still running in W with a Couple of Courses. Wee

[1] Fire stone: A popular name for iron pyrites, or flint. *NOED*.

[2] This word is repeated and crossed through.

[3] Water-rounded stones, pebbles.

[4] Whey colour: A reference to the pale colour of whey. *NOED*.

sounded & had 30 fathom beaches stones, & at the same time wee did see the Surff of the shore, & a ledg of broaken[1] ground that lyes some 1½ miles off shore, about 1½ miles in length bearing off us WBS, distance from Us about a league not more. Then wee Tack'd, lay'd our stem NE With the wind at NNW a fresh gale with a Couple of Courses, then after wee had stood that way some 3 miles wee sounded & had the same depth as befor, that is to say 13 & 14 & 17 fathome so I Judg that it is a banke that lyes E some 4 miles off shore,[2] that's to say off the Cape blanco, the land make some 5 leagues of [off] baring of WNW almost like 3 Islands, the Cape it selfe, & it is whiteish

Ditto.

whiteish Clifts, and it is some 4 leagues in length along shore. Then at 12 clock at Night wee tack'd and stood in for the shore, & when wee tack'd wee sounded and had no ground.

Thursday 22. With 60 fathome of line then wee stood in W & WBS, 2 houres about some 2 leagues & sounded again & had 37 fathome, stoney ground, & wee keept still sounding & wee had 30 & 29 fathome Scuruy[3] stoney ground, then wee were about some 6 leagues off shore that is to say off from the Sothermost part of the Cape, then still steering in WSW & WBS you shall have 30 & 29 fathome, darke Osie [oozy] sand, & then you are some five miles off the Island that lies to the S quart*er* of the Cape & the first little Islands that you will see are two together, & off of the No[r]thermost Island there lyes a ledg of broaken ground about a mile off Shore, & about a league long it is

Ditto.

it is[4] all sunke under water, but the sea break's on it, & when wee brought it WSW off us wee sounded, & had no ground with 30 fathome of line still running along SBW & SSW & S & as wee pas'd one Rock wee came to another, some high Rocks, & some just of [off] the waters edg, all on the Starboard side, still sounding and had no ground with 20 fathome of line, then at last wee cast the deep sea lead & had 34 fathome rockey ground still running in. It being a very fair day & cleare sun shine with the wind at NNE, a fresh gale. I observed & found that wee were [*margin:* 47°54′ by Observac*i*on, the Lat. of Port Desire.] in the Latit*ude* of 47°54′ a very good Observac*i*on.[5] Then wee were assur'd by latitude that wee were thwart of Port desire.[6] Then by Seyn*o*r Frakos[7] Order wee haled off, for he would not that wee should endeavour to goe in to port desire, but to make the best of our way to

Ditto.

St Julians,[8] then wee steered away SBE & S & SW & SWBW, & made the maine land that trenches away to the S off Port desire but wee tooke it to be Islands, but it proved the

[1] Final letter 'g' struck through.

[2] There are a number of banks off Cabo Blanco. Banco Byron lies between 4 and 6 miles east of Cabo Blanco, with depths of ½ to 10 fathoms on it, with Banco Ana SSE of it.

[3] Probably 'scurvy' in the sense of poor, worthless.

[4] The catchwords from the previous recto 'it is' are repeated here.

[5] Puerto Deseado (47°45′S, 65°53′W).

[6] Thwart: abreast of, in the same latitude as Port Desire.

[7] Solomon Franco.

[8] Puerto San Julián (49°19′S, 67°43′W).

maine land. It makes pretty low & levell & it lies along SSW half W*ester*ly & NNE half E*aster*ly & wee steering away SSW & SWBS along the shore with in 3 and 2½ miles of the land, & sounded & had 35 & 30 & 24 fathom Rockey ground, & close aboard the shore there lies little black rocks above the [*margin:* That low land lyes along SWBS. NEBN.] water a matter of halfe a mile the shoar about a mile a sunder Some more some lesse & the further you run along the shore the land makes to the S*outhwa*rd a matter of 6 or 7 leagues, together along the shore. Judging our selves to be then in the Lat*itude* of 48°24′S, then night approaching wee haled off into the Sea SE & ESE

Ditto.

[*margin:* 48°24′ but the draught make it to ly SW½ Wly & NE½Ely.] till 12 a clock at Night, & then wee lay by with our head to the E*astwa*r*d* til 4 a Clock in the morning, **Wednesday 23**. then wee made all the sayle wee could in for the shore Judging our selves to be some 26 leagues WSW S*outher*ly from S[t] Julians, if it doth lye as the draught showeth, then about 6 a clock in the morning the wind came up fresh at W & continued till 10 of the Clock at Noon & then it fell calme, then wee sounded and had 60 fathome water the ground was very dark brown sand with bitts of hard red clay like bitts of brick. Then were wee by observac*i*on in the Lat*itude* of 48°54′ Judging our selves to be some 19 leagues distant from S[t] Julians bearing off us WBS S*outher*ly then steering in WSW, with the wind at NNE some 3 leagues, wee sounded & had 55 fathome water, the sand more blacker and Courser then before

Ditto.

with 3 or 4 little stones about the biggness of a great pinns head of Sev'all Colours still wee steered in WSW, looking out for a sunken rock that the draught specifies to lye in the Lat*itude* of 49°10′ some 6 leagues off shore,[1] but could not see it. Then all that night we passed looking out if peradventure wee might see the *Sweepstakes*, or some danger that might befall us being in Untrodden wayes, but did not **Thursday 24** see none the wind at W & WNW wee makeing all the way wee could to endeavo*ur* to fall in with the land that wee last parted from, that wee might see & discover what wee might with Convenience. This day at noon I am by Judgm*en*t some 30 leagues WSW from S[t] Julians. Wee being then in the lat*itude* of 48°44′ by Judgm*en*t, the winds being Variable from the W to the N

Ditto.

sometimes blowing very hard at W, & sometimes calme with some raine, very fickle weather. Wee sometimes stood to the S*outhwa*rd & sometim's to the N*orthwa*rd takeing all advantages to the N*orthwa*rd all night, & at 12 a clock at night wee sounded & had no ground with 55 fathome of Lyne still standing WNW & NW, wee sounded at 4 a clock in the morning & had 42 fathome water Course sand and of a grey colour, then wee were about 6 leagues off the maine shore that lyes to the S*outhwa*rd of Spearrings Bay, otherwise called Seale bay[2] bearing off Us **Fryday 25.** NWBN. And at 5 a Clock this Morning wee

[1] Roca Bellaco (48°30′S, 66°11′W). See above, p. 210, n. 7.

[2] This bay, identified from Narbrough's description (see above, pp. 210–11), is now know as Bahía de los Nodales (48°00′S, 65°52′W).

did see the land a little after daylight, bearing off WNW N^{ly}, it makes low, then wee sounded & had 35 fathome water, Scraffy ground[1] & soft like Chaff almost, still running on

Ditto.

NWBN. Wee did see one little Rock above water, & a great deal of broaken ground or Suncken rocks all round it, but most in length both without & within the dry rock, & it bore off us SSW. The furthermost Suncken rocks that wee could see Easterly doe lye about 7 leagues at the least off shore, and all the rocks together [*margin:* Sunken Rocks discove*r*d.][2] but there is between the shore & that breaches, & 2 or 3 little high dry rocks & breaches. So the wind being WSW wee stood with ¾ of a mile off the Sunken rocks & sounded & had 25 fathome water Rockey ground; & with all finding a Tyde to sett us at that time SW the which did sett us wholly on to the rocks then Wee tack'd and stood in NW, into the shore to see what wee could discover, & wee did see more broken ground that did

Feb*ruary* 1669. Ditto.

did beare from the maine Sunken Rocks NWBW;[3] & they lye some 3 miles off shore, when wee did see them, some of them bore off us N*orth*, & some bearing off NWBW, then at that time the body of the first bore off us SSE. Then Wee sounded & found 20 fathome water with in 4 miles or thereabouts off the shore,[4] Rocky ground being with in a mile of those innermost Rocks; then wee tack'd, & stood right off into the Sea E & EBS. Then it p*ro*ved Calme & then wee could not gett out but as it pleased God the other Tyde which I Judg was the Tyde of Ebb, did sett us off NNE from the rocks. Then at noon wee observed and found them Suncken rocks to lye exactly in the Lat*itude* of 48°31′ the which the draught makes lye in the Lat*itude* of 49°10′[5] Soe that

[1] The meaning of this is not clear, but possibly it should be 'scrappy ground' in the sense of rough, made up of odds and ends.

[2] Roca Bellaco, about 4 or 5 leagues in length

[3] Arrecife Guardián which extends 4½ miles SE from Cabo Guardián (48°21′S, 66°21′W).

[4] At this point a series of calculations were entered taking up the rest of the margin on this recto.

Zenith	43°22′
☼ declin*ation*	04 57
	48 19
	00 12
	48 31

This 12 miles is the dist*ance* South.'
The true Lat. of the suncken rocks found to be 48°31′.
'Example
The ☼ Zenith distance that day was 43°22′ & the ☼

Declin*ation* was	4°57′
so decrease	44°12′
	04°57′
	09′.

The actual Latitude is 40°30′S, so this is a very accurate value.

[5] This rock is not shown on the Doncker chart (Plate 2) so Chambers must have had another chart on board as well.

Feb*ruary* 1669. Ditto.
So that the difference is 39 miles that they doe lye more N*orther*ly than the Draught specify's which is a great Err*or*: the Rock it selfe when you see it makes like a boat under Sayle but black. Then about 2 a clock the wind came up NEBN, a fine gentle gale and wee steered off SE, & sounded & had 42 fathome rockey ground. Wee kept in that Course till 4 a clock in the afternoon, & then wee sounded and had 54 fathome water, sand & ston's with bitts of green Clay, then the high rock at that time did beare off us WNW some 9 leagues off then wee steered away SSE, till 6 a clock in the Evening & sounded & found 54 fathome water grey sand and many stones; then Wee did see the high Rock at Topp mast head bearing off Us NWBW some 10 miles off us then wee steered away

Feb*ruary* 1669. *Bachelor* bound for St Julians L*atitude* 49°20′ S.
by the mas*te*rs Order SWBS, with the wind at NE&BN, & SW&BS & WSW for the most pte [part], wee sounding every 2 hour's according as occasion required, & found about 50 fathome water about 9 leagues off the maine at 12 a Clock at night to the S*outhwa*rd of the Suncken rocks, **Saturday 26.** the ground was very dark brown sand but very fine. Then wee still steered in WSW, wee had sometime 38 & 35 fathome water, sandy ground as before, but in 35 fathome the Sand was Course, then wee were a matter of 4 leagues the most, off the land at 4 a clock in the morning, for I did see it by the moon light. It maks broaken at first table land as in the Margent sheweth, [*margin: drawing of view and note* 'No double land but as you see. Lat. 48°47′.] but the neerer in it makes all in one. This is in the Lat*itude* 48°7′ neerest the shore it is bold too, & also when you are fair in with the shore, you shall see sev'all

Feb*ruary* 1669. Ditto.
severall white spotts in the Land like white houses. Still wee looking out for St Julians but could not see that nor any harbo*ur* or bay, or river, the wind being at NW wee could not stem in with the land, but stood in WSW as neere as wee could lye, with very little wind. Wee espyed a little low flatt Island, or rock lyeing about a League or 4 miles off shore,[1] & it is not above a quarter of a mile long, and it is very low & flatt; [*margin:* 48°49′ by observac*i*on.] when wee did see it first it made like a boat under the shore bearing off Us WbN, but as wee run further into the shore wee brought it open to the Sea,[2] bold and no danger as wee did see, 30, 40 fathome. The same time at noon I observed & found my selfe to be in the Lat*itude* of 48°49′ exactly then the low flatt Island bearing off us at that time N*orth* dist*ance* some 6 miles off

Feb*ruary* 1669. Ditto.
For wee did see it, so I Judge that Island to lye exactly in the Latitude of 48°43′[3] in this Lat*itude* & some two miles off shore, you shall [have] 38 and 37 fathome, soft Oz [ooze] & stiff the lead sticking in it, then to the S*outhwa*rd of this the Land did seem to Us as if there had been a going in of some harbo*ur*. Then wee Judging it to be St Julians, wee steered in SW & SW & SWBW with the wind at NW, a fine easy gale, wee running along with in two

[1] Islote Chato (48°45′S, 67°03′W); see above, p. 211, n. 2.
[2] They could see the island clear of the land, and could see exactly what it was.
[3] Compared with the actual latitude, 48°45′S, this is remarkably accurate.

miles of the shore, wee did see land on our larbord bow, & right at head we did see as if it had been a going in with land marke like a flatt Island in the midle still wee run in

Feb*rua*ry 1669. Ditto.
it proved a bay where wee Anchor'd in the very Codd of it[1] with in a mile of the shore, but all the way running in wee kept the lead going, sometimes 20 fathome rockey ground, and sometimes sandy, & sometimes no ground, but where wee anchor'd wee had 10 fathome small shingle ston's but firme clay underneath as the Anchor brought up:[2] wee rid there all night, [*margin:* Batchellors Bay.] wee did see but little Wood wee had the sea open from the NBE to the S. That night wee had bad Weather, wind and rain at W & SW & SSE, much wind. This bay which I call Batchellors bay[3] lyes [*margin:* Lat. 49°.] neerest in the Lat*itude* of 49°00′.

Feb*rua*ry 1669. Ditto.

Sabboth day 27. This day at 7 a clock in the morning, wee weighed with the wind at SW, a fine gale & good weather standing off to Sea in the pursute of S[t] Julians: & when wee came in the Latitud of 49°5′ wee sounded & had 26 fathome water & 36 fathome water, some 3 leagues off shore [*margin:* This high land lyes directly in 49°23′, by Observac*i*on.] Ozy land, & when wee were 4 leagues off shore wee had 35 fathome the same ground as before the land very high and rugged but little of it,[4] there is no such land all along the coast as that is from the Lat*itude*

Feb*ruary* 1669. Ditto.
Lat*itude* of 47°40′ to the Lat*itude* of 50°5′ & there is almost such at the going in of Rio de Crews. This land that I expresse in the Lat*itude* of 48°50′ to the Lat*itude* of 49°15′ lyes along SBW & NBE directly.

Monday 28. This day wee Judging our selves to be to the N*orth*wa*r*d of S[t] Julians wee made our way to the S*outhwa*rd with in two miles of the shore & 4 miles the furthest, with a bold wind at N & NE a fresh gale, still expecting every poynt that wee did see to be the going in of S[t] Julians, but the land is Very bold all along I beleive steep too, & it lyes nearest SSW & NE which the draught makes to lye SW halfe W*ester*ly & NE halfe E*aster*ly, a grosse error. From the Lat*itude* of 49° to the Lat*itude* of

Feb*rua*ry 1669. Ditto.
of 49°40′ no S[t] Julian to be seen,[5] nor any other bay or harbo*ur* or River, the least water you will have is 13 fathome, with in two miles of the Shore dark osy ground, the land is

[1] In the bottom of the bay.

[2] The lead can only tell what lies on the surface of the seabed, while the flukes of the anchor dig into the bottom and then, when the anchor is weighed, the deeper sediment may be brought up on them.

[3] This would appear to be the slight coastal indentation between Cabo Dañoso (48°50′S, 67°13′W) and Cabo Curioso (49°11′S, 67°37′W), 25 miles SW. The latter is the northern entrance point to Puerto San Julián.

[4] This is the high land, Monte Wood and Monte Sholl, that Narbrough describes as 'the only Marke to Know the Harbower of St Julyan'. See above, p. 211, n. 5.

[4] The entrance to Puerto San Julián lies in 49°13′, so they had now sailed past it, without sighting it.

very much like the land of Fair Lee with Archicall white Cliffts but no so high;[1] on the topp green grasse but no Wood to be seen at all. There is no such land all along the Coast [*margin:* 49°50′.] as that is, for it is white Cliff land and levell a topp, then when you are pas'd the Archicall Clifft, you must hale up SWS & SW, then the land is all in one Cliff. Then the first high land that you see is the S side, the S poynt of the going of Rio de Crews,[2] the which I find to lye in the Lat*itude* of 50°05′ wee running still along the shore in the pursute of St Julians, wee came so neere

Feb*ruary* 1669. **Ditto.**

this River that wee dissern'd it to be a harbo*ur*, & were intended God willing to have gone in for beleife of wood and water,[3] & the least water wee found was 6½ fathome & 7 fathom, & wee did see no danger, the wind then chop'd up at W & did blow very fresh, & at that time there came a perfect white Dew aboard of us. Then by reason wee could not gett in, wee went about and stood to the N*orthwa*rd again With the Wind at W & NW, about 6 a clock in the Evening still in pursute of St Julians Wee steering away NE and NEBN all night with the Wind WNE a fresh gale.

March 1669. **Ditto.**

Tuesday 1. Tuesday this day I observed & found my selfe to be in the Lat*itude* of 49°23′ being at that time some 5 leagues,[4] soundings at that time is 30 fathome, Osy ground; all this night wee lay off & untill day light because wee would[5] not over shoot it in the night, and about mid-night the wind came at SE & SEBS, & wee being close in with the land, wee did make the best of our way off to Sea, for it was very bad like weather with raine and wind; wee Judg our selves [*margin:* 48°40′.] to be in the Lat*itude* of 48°40′.

Wednesday 2. This morning at 7 a clock wee being with in 4 leagues of the shore stem*m*ing away EBN & ENE till 4 of the Clock in the afternoon,

March 1669. **Ditto.**

with very much wind SE, a dead wind it put us to a payre [pair] of Sayles, thick weather. Wee tacked steming off S & SBW being with in 3 leagues of the shore, wee found that we Sagd;[6] finding that wee sagd, wholy in upon the shore We tack'd again steming away ENE with the tyde of Ebb, which doe sett to the S*outh*wa*r*d, still a pair of Courses by reason of wind & raine & sea; wee were forced to stand that way keeping the lead going to see what danger might befall us, but this wee knew, that would be a very hard matter to

[1] This is probably a reference to Fairlight cliffs east of Hastings on the coast of Kent. 'The coast E of Hastings rises in steep cliffs of a yellow-brown colour to Fairlight Down; these cliffs are broken at intervals by grassy slopes.' Fairlight Down (50°52′N, 0°39′E), rises to 565 ft (172 m). *Dover Strait Pilot*, paras. 3.130–31. Archical: Of the nature of a first principle, primordial. *NOED*.

[2] Punta Entrada, (50°08′S, 68°21′W). The point itself is low, but 7 cables within the point the land rises to Monte Entrada, 433 ft (132 m), and from thence to south-westward the coast is backed by Barrancas de Santa Cruz, cliffs rising to 515 ft (157 m).

[3] In the belief that wood and water would be available.

[4] Presumably this means 5 leagues offshore.

[5] 'could' struck through and 'would' substituted.

[6] 'Saged' means being forced away to leeward of the course steered.

weather the Suncken rocks,[1] & to stand the other way wee run wholy on the shore. So wee trusted to Gods mercy, using our endeavour*s* wee weather'd them in the night but how wee scaped them it is beyond any mans thoughts.

March 1669. **Ditto.**

Thursday 3. Still wee stood off all this day ENE & EBN & E very bad Weather, with gusts of raine and Hailey. No observac*i*on but by Judgm*en*t I am in the lat*itude* of 48°10′ the wind dullers now at 6 a Clock in the Evening, for wee lay by till this time, about which time the wind that was, was at NNE & NE and

Fryday 4. towards morning it freshned on & wee sounded & had 50 and 60 fathome water sandy ground, Wee being then by Judgm*en*t in the Lat*itude* of 48°00′ some 12 leagues off shore wee stealing away South, & when wee Judged ourselves to be in the latit*ude* of the rock wee sounded and had 54 fathome, Sand and bitts of hard Clay at 10 a Clock at noon. The same noone wee observed & I found we were in Lat*itude*

March 1669. **Ditto**

of 48°39′ directly, wee then steering W*est* for the shore supposeing that [we] were some 8 leagurs off shore. At the same time the wind cam up at SBW, a fine easy gale, still wee steering in W& steering a way W & WBS, still sounding at 4 a Clock at the Evening, & had 38 fathome water rockey ground, **Saturday 5**. then at that time the rock[2] bore off us NNW dist*ance* from us some 3 leagues & the main land bore off us at that time W distance some 7 leagues makeing like Islands seeming low. All this night being Saturday night wee lay off and on the shore with the wind at S & SBE, little wind and good weather, still sounding every two houres and sometimes every houre or glasse,[3] according as Occasion requires.

March 1669. **Ditto.**

Sabboth day 6. This day at 7 a clock in the morning wee were with in 4 miles of the maine land that wee had not discovered before, then those suncken rocks bore off us NE & at that time wee did see broken ground with in ½ a mile of the shore, aright in the Wake of the Sunken rocks, still looking out for S[t] Julians, but could not see it but wee did see as the draught makes, a small going in as it were right[4] in, over the broken ground.[5] It is so dangerous, that wee could not gett in still the wind being at S & SBE wee could not get to the *Southwa*rd but were forced to stand off to Sea again, till wee could gett an oportunity

March 1669. **Ditto.**

to discover the land from this Lat*itude* 48°35′ to the Lat*itude* 48°45′; for from the Lat*itude* 50° with in 2 or 3 miles of the shore to the Lat*itude* of 48°45′ wee cannot disserne any such

[1] Roca Bellaco.

[2] Roca Bellaco.

[3] The hourglass would normally be turned every half-hour, so this means every hour or half-hour.

[4] 'going' struck through.

[5] This would appear to be Bahía Laura (48°24′S, 66°25′W). See above, p. 211, n. 5.

harbour as St Julians, nor any other small nor great, but that which lyes directly in the lat*itude* of 50° or thereabouts, the which I Judg to be rio de Crewes that the draught makes to lye in the lat*itude* of 50°55′ or thereabouts being distant from the suncken rocks about 30 leagues, but by the draught makes it 40 leagues, & I find that land to lye along SSW almost, & the draught maks it to lye along SWBW almost. Now at 5 a Clock have a little gale at N, Wee steering in W for to

March 1669. **Ditto.**

gett in close to the shore, that wee might be sure not to slipp by it & when wee were with in 4 miles of the shore, wee sounded & had 26 fathome with in 4 miles of the suncken Rocks,[1] bearing off us N Rockey ground, but if you are to the N*orthwa*rd of the suncken Rocks so that they beare S of you one mile from them you shall have 25 fathome water Rockey ground. All this night wee stood off, & on close aboard of the Suncken Rocks, sometimes 25 & 28 & 38 fathom Rockey ground, the wind being at N and wee to the S*outhwa*rd of them.

March 1669. **Ditto.**

Monday 7. Towards morning the wind blows very fresh, in so much that it putts us some matter of two Leagues to Leeward of that land wee did intend to steere in with, but nevertheless we could see it, but no S[t] Julians,[2] nor *Sweepstakes*, the more was my greife by reason that wee were very well assured that it was not between the Lat*itude* of 48°00′ & the Lat*itude* of 50°05′. Then wee being in great scearsity of wood and water, wee are constreined and with all resolved to seeke for some Harbour for some releife, haveing not above 8 or 9 days wood in the shipp nor above a fortnights water at a quart a day for each man

March 1669. **Ditto.**

nor know not where to gett more but trusty providence. Wee made our way to the S*outhwa*rd, to that place wee Judged to be Rio de Crewes, wee being when wee bore up the helm in the Lat*itude* of 48°40′ by Judgm*en*t some 4 or 5 miles off the shore, seeing at the same time the little low flatt Island[3] distant from us some 8 miles, and bearing off us SWBW, all this night wee steering away S. It proved much wind & bad weather, the wind at NNW & W in so much that wee lay by under a maine Course with our head to the W*estwa*rd for feare wee should overshoot our Port.

Tuesday 8. about 3 a Clock in the morning and at 6 a Clock wee made

March 1669. **Ditto.**

sayle, stem*m*ing away SSW with the wind at W, wee being then by Judgm*en*t 12 leagues from our intended Port, & about 8 a clock wee were some 5 leagues off the Shore. The same day I observed my selfe to be in the Lat*itude* of 49°33′ it being little wind now, & wee takeing all advantages to gett to our Port & great [*margin:* Lat. 49°33′ by

[1] Roca Bellaco.

[2] Norie, *Piloting Directions*, p. 6, says of this port that 'its entrance is somewhat difficult to discover, on account of its outer jutting point'.

[3] Islote Chato.

observac*i*on.] need. Now all this night it proved little wind at SW & W and NW, wee standing off & on according as Occasion requires.

Wednesday 9. All this day following wee had little or no wind; very good and Cleare weather and many Pinguins and Seales. Wee were most part of this day with in

March 1669. **Ditto.**

Thursday 10. with in 2 leagues of the shore & had 50 fathom water in the Lat*itude* of 49°33′ and also in the Lat*itude* of 49°40′ wee had 46 fathome water, Course sand and red stones, still wee makeing the best of our way, with sad hearts for that harbour, now all this night wee had little or no wind.

Thursday 10. This morning the wind cam up at N & NNE an easy gale at first but as the Sun rose it freshned, wee steering away SW and SWBW. Then it pleased God about 4 a Clock in the afternoon wee gott neere to the Rivers mouth, & it was at that time about a low water so that the flood, was Just made & wee going with in a mile of the shore keeping the Lead going

March 1669. **Ditto.**

and had 4 and 5 and 3 and ½ fathome[1] water till wee came with in 2 miles of the Rivers mouth and there wee ran fast a ground on a barr of sand, that lyes from the shore SE of some 2 miles long I judg it is all dry at low water. Wee lay aground a Matter of one houre beating sev'all knochs, but the flood being made strong and the wind being at NW, the which was off land wee gott an anch*o*r out of sterne & stop'd her till she floated,[2] the which she did with out makeing any water more than she did before [*margin:* Lat 50°5′.] & then wee Judging it to be half flood wee weighed and gott well into an anchor about 7 a clock

March 1669. **Ditto.**

in the Evening in 13 fathom water some three miles from the River,[3] where there run an extream Tyde, it being Spring Tyde it flows there some 7 fathome[4] and at the Rivers mouth it floats at full and chang NEBN and SWBS the which is neere upon 10 a clock.[5] So wee moored with two bowers water shott,[6] and it proved very much wind, in so much that wee drove in the night and brought both our anchors ahead,[7] the wind being at NW and WNW.[8]

[1] Presumably these are not separate soundings and this is 3½ fathoms.

[2] Carried an anchor out astern to prevent the ship driving farther on the bank while they waited for the tide to rise and float the vessel.

[3] This would appear to mean in the river, within the river's mouth. The anchorage used was probably off Punta Quilla, on the SW side 2½–3 miles above, Punta Entrada (an anchorage still in use today).

[4] Rises some 7 fathom.

[5] The tidal stream flows into the harbour at spring tides at a rate of 5 knots and out at 6 knots. The height of Mean High Water Spring Tide is 35 ft (10·8 m).

[6] Water-shot is a kind of mooring with the anchors laid not across, nor right up and down tide, but quartering between the two.

[7] The ship dragged both her anchors so that they came together ahead of the ship.

[8] Straight down the harbour.

Fryday 11. This day all day it proved a storme of wind at WNW and W in so much that with the Leeward Tyde[1] it was almost

March 1669. **Ditto.**
impossible that anchors & Cables should hold. Then it pleased God that Evening it proved little wind and good weather, so wee weighed and gott up with the Tyde of flood some 4 miles higher up and Anchored by reason it was dark, and wee unacquainted in 6 fathome water it being then about half flood;[2] so wee moor'd again and at low water I tasted the water, yett not with standing it was so neer the sea the water is but little brackish the which gave us no small Joy for then wee were assured of Water which wee did Want very much.

March 1669. **Ditto.**[3]
Saturday 12. This morning I went with the boat to sound, & I found deep water on the S side 10 and 12 fathome water at half flood.[4] The same day before I went aboard I went a shore on the south side, to see if wee could discover any fresh water, but wee did see no Water but sev'all places where there had been fires and the bones of some Cattle,[5] and 2 or 3 dead ostriges[6] and a great deale of crusty wood close to the rivers side, and where the wood grows it's very low land a matter of a mile up from the Waters side to the foot

March 1669. ***Bachelor* bound for Rio de Crews Lat*itude* 50°5′ S.**
foot of the hills,[7] and on them hills there is not any wood at all, but the topps of them are very flatt and levell only some grasse and between the high land and the River side wee did see the dung of Severall Creaturs, and the footing of Cattle & espeecially of Deere; then the Ebb being come we returned aboard the same afternoon, Went a shore on the North side the which shore is very low, with a steep stoney Beech, & there wee see many Deere Very large and Very Wild insomuch that wee could not come with in shott of them.[8] The same Evening

[1] With wind and tide driving in the same direction.

[2] Today, and most probably in the 17th century since Chambers's description fits reasonably well, the harbour above Punta Quilla divides, with the main channel following the north-eastern shore. In the middle lies Islas Leones from the northern end of which is a bank which dries and extends to the western shore. The new anchorage appears to have been, in or adjacent to the main channel, NE of Islas Leones, probably above Punta Ojos, which lies on the eastern shore.

[3] This is the last 'ditto' referring back to the header stating that the *Bachelor* was 'bound for St Julyans', although the search for the latter had been given up on 7 March in favour of making for Puerto Santa Cruz, and the pink had arrived off the harbour on 10 March.

[4] Today the channel leads NW, with depths of 4–7 fathoms at low water (7–10 fathoms at half-flood spring tide), north of Islas Leones, across the river to the south side at Punta Reparo (where the town of Santa Cruz now stands) whence the main channel proceeds NNW before ending in shallows where Río Santa Cruz and Río Chico flow into the estuary.

[5] These may have been guanaco bones. See above, p. 207, n. 3.

[6] Darwin's rhea. See above, pp. 207, n. 4; 214, n. 4.

[7] The only place on the south-western side of the estuary where the hills are a mile from the foreshore is in the vicinity of Punta Reparo. The hills are generally flat on top with heights up to about 400 ft (121 m).

[8] The tracks and the animals were probably guanacoes.

March 1669. **Ditto.**

before wee gott aboard wee did see a great smoak by the sea side wee Judged it to be about 2 miles from us; the same time wee lost one of our doggs wee know not how.

Sabboth day 13. This day about 7 a clock in the morning wee weighed and drove up close along the S side, for there is the deepest water 10 & 7 & 4 fathome Water,[1] at a q*uarte*r flood wee not dreaming a shole that lyes from the S river quite over to the N*orth* side and a matter of 2 miles ½ in length, and above 2 mile broad so wee

March 1669. **Lat*itude* 50°5′**

finding the water shole so fast wee anchor'd in 4½ fathome & it was then about ½ floud. Then I went in the boat to sound & found 6½ fathome still, wee driveing up sounding with the boat found all one depth and discovered a river [*margin:* A ground in the River.] running up SW, neerest some two miles broad,[2] and before wee came on board again the which was the same ebb, they had weighed with the shipp and drove a little higher upp and at low water wee were dry a ground. This same S river is some 13 miles from the entrance of the main rivers mouth. I sounded from side to side

March 1669. *Bachelor* bound for Rio de Crews Lat*itude* 50°5′ S.

at the mouth of the S river & I found 9 & 8 & 7 & 6 fathome water at the very topp of high Water a matter of halfe a mile with in the said river,[3] & wee did see pritty store of wood on both sides, but most on the East side. Wee grounded our shipp three times p[er] force the first time wee cleaned her[4] and after that **Monday** [**14**]. wee would have gone higher up but the weather was so bad that wee durst not venture with out a good boat or sloop to fors*ee* the danger. Then it being dangerous lying where wee are, we used

March 1669. **Ditto.**

all the meanes wee could to fall downe into deepe water, and did a little, but the wind blowing very hard at S & SSE and SW that wee came a ground two houres before low water the ground is fine sand and very levell & not very hard. Then our shipp being on ground she made a dock.[5] Wee filled about 1½ Tun of good drinking Water which was but very little brackish, it was so at that time because that the *Southerl*y winds blow so hard that forced the freshes[6] downe out of the S river, where without doubt is many fish, for wee found sev'all on the sands dead that came downe in the fresh

[1] Today, above Punta Reparo the main channel leads in the middle of the estuary, while an arm, which ends in Banco Misioneros, follows the south-western shore. From Chambers's description it is possible that in the 17th century the southern arm was the main, and possibly the only channel leading north. Since the flats all dry and would have been visible at low water, it would seem likely that the ship took the main channel and ended up on the flats in which the channel terminates.

[2] The boat must have been sounding in the main channel, which, today, after a patch of less than 3 fathoms (5·5 m) at its southern end has depths of 6–7 fathoms (11–13 m) to its northern end where the estuary terminates in sand and mud flats off Punta Beagle, 13 miles from the entrance. At this point Río Santa Cruz leads off WSW and Río Chico continues NNW.

[3] Today, depths in the entrance (which is 1½ miles wide) vary between 2 and 10 feet (0·6 and 3 m) between drying flats, at low water.

[4] Cleaned the ship's bottom, scraping off the weed etc.

[5] The ship sank in the sand and made quite an appreciable hole, resembling a dock.

[6] Freshets, small floods flowing down to the sea.

March 1669. Ditto.
as big as a larg salmon but not like a salmon but exceeding good.
[*margin:* This day our boat sunck by our side with the force of the tyde but wee saved her.]
This shole that I expresse lye fro*m* side to side of the maine River so that you may goe from Land to land on the sand at low water for I beleive that the Deere doe goe over it. It is about 3 miles long and so broad that it almost fills up, only between the S main and that there is a small Channell, you shall have at low water on this shole[1] at high water 6, 5, 4½ fathome water all over it.[2] This Night wee weighed about one of the clock it being then at high water and fell downe at a deep water.[3]

Tuesday 15. The same Night, wee did see a fire on shore on the N side,

March 1669. Ditto.
wee Judg it to be much about the Place where wee did see it before. Heere wee rid now in 10 foot water at low water & 8 fathom at high still very bad weather & much wind, in so much that wee could neither gett wood or water the Wind at SW & W, the feircest Winds that blow in this part of the world. Wee fitting our rigging. This same day I went in our boat to sound, close over to the beach on the S side, the which I call beche point[4] in my draught of the said river,[5] and I found 6 fathom water at low water, with in a Cables length of the shore the wind being then at E & ESE. Little wind with some raine all this night.

March 1669. *Bachelor* bound for Rio de Crews Lat*itude* 50°5′ S.

Wednesday 16. This day wee weighed to gett into deep water,[6] for where wee rid wee had not above halfe a foot water more then wee did draw. The same day wee went a shore to see if wee could find any fresh water but could not find any but one little pond some ¾ of a mile from the river side, where wee did see the footing of many deere[7] & I doe Judg by the ground that in time of raine, all this land is overflown with the waters that come down from the high land.

Thursday 17. Now the moone being a qu*arte*r old wee have good setled weather and warme, for allways 3 or 4 days before or after full and change is extreame bad turbulent weather the wind at SW & W & NW. This night

March 1669. Ditto.
our boat went up to the S river for water and brought 6 quarter Casks full aboard, so wee lost no time some fetching water and some fitting our ligging [rigging] still good weather.

[1] No depth is given.

[2] This shoal is Banco Misioneros on the west side of the channel and Desplayado del Río Chico on the east side. It dries up to 17 feet (5 m) in places on both sides.

[3] The new anchorage was in the vicinity of Punta Reparo, probably slightly above it. See below.

[4] This is probably Punta Reparo, which matches the description with deep water close alongside.

[5] There is no plan (draught) with this journal.

[6] This move would be to the deep-water anchorage off Punta Reparo, named Beche, Beech, Beachy Point by Chambers.

[7] Probably guanacos.

Fryday 18. This day wee filled as good water by the side at low water as could be dranck for a matter of an hour's time. The same day wee gott some wood aboard, the Carpenter Callkin [caulking] our shipp bowes.

Saturday 19. This day wee filled most of our water and fitted the most part still every man Imployed.

Sabboth day 20. This Sabboth day wee rested.

Monday 21. This day wee filled all our water only 2 qu*arte*r Cask the wind at S & SW blowing fresh. This night wee fired 2 gunns, by reason wee thought wee heard gunns fir'd at sea but it was nothing but thunder as wee Judg. Carp*ente*r & boatswain still imploy'd.

March 1669. **Ditto.**

Tuesday 22. This day wee filled up our Caske that was leaked out, for our Casks were very bad, & wee had no Cooper to trim them. The Carpenter and boatswaine still imploy'd.

Wednesday 23. This day wee went a shore to cut wood and haled the saine at a low water at Beech poynt, & made 3 hales and gott as many fish as did serve all our men two dayes, exceeding good fish, some weighing 18 or 20 pound, some much like Trouts in Scale and tast, but all in generall very good.

Thursday 24. This day wee gott two boat load of wood, & I and another killed at two shott about 3 dozen of fowle, Very much like Snipes[1]

March 1670.[2] **Ditto.**

and very fatt insomuch that if they be roasted they bast themselves. These fowles are in great flocks on the shore side, and they are not fishey.

Fryday 25. This day being neerer the full moon it blows very hard at W & SW in so much that our boate cannot goe a shore for wood.

Saturday 26. This day in the morning wee went on shore for wood or ballast, which wee could best, but when wee were gott a shore it blew a frett[3] of wind SW in so much that wee could not gett a board all day till night for then most com*m*only in the night it is little wind.

Sabboth day 27. This day being Sabboth day wee rested it being indifferent good weather, & the wind at SW & W.

[1] Probably the common snipe which is found in this area. Harris, *Guide*, p. 81.

[2] 1669 struck through and replaced by 1670. In the Julian calendar the New Year began on 25 March.

[3] Fret: A sudden disturbance of weather; a gust, squall of wind. *NOED*.

March 1670. Ditto.
Monday 28. This day wee got an ancho*r* aboard intending to sail if wind & weather permit us. The Tyde it being high water about 12 a Clock at noon flowing there where wee [*margin:* NNE ½ an houre past 10 NEBN 3 qu*arte*rs past 9 a clock.] Rid at beechy poynt NNE and SSW full and change, but with out at the Rivers mouth NEBN & SWBS. Now it blowing very hard at SW wee did not think it convenient to weigh this tyde but rid single.[1]

Tuesday 29. This day wee went a shore, & gott mor wood, & at the Evening we haled the saine and gott plenty of fish and amongst the fish wee haled 1 smelt, the which was in length by the rule 13½ Inches and 5½ about, with out doubt there is store of smelts and other good fish in this River.

March 1670. *Bachelor*[2] in Rio de Crews Lat*itude* 50°05′ S.
This same day wee weighed & went neere to the shore, because of getting aboard some ballast.

Wednesday 30. This day wee gott some 3 Tunn of ballist aboard and some wood riding still at beachy poynt very neer the shore water enough.[3] It is steep too, at high Tyde.

Thursday 31. This day the wind at E and ESE very little wind and very good weather till the afternoon and then it blew fresh at SW insomuch that the boat could not bring any ballist aboard.

Aprill 1. Fryday. This day wee weighed from beachy poynt about 7 a clock in the morning and fell down some two miles, the which was just below a land that I call middle ground.[4]

Aprill 1670. Ditto.
It is dry about 3 hours every low water. Wee anchored with in half a Cables length off it to the S off [of] it in 5 fathome Water at low water, and on the South side there lyes a great shole adjoyning to the maine land, so that at high water it [is] but Just Covered[5] this middle-ground, it [is] distance from it some ¾ of a mile.[6] The great shole I call in my draught Steepe shole.

[1] Remained at a single anchor.

[2] 'bound' struck through.

[3] The water was deep enough for the ship to lie close to the beach.

[4] A bank with channels round it is normally referred to as a middle ground. This would appear to be Banco del Río Chico which, today, extends from the southern end of Desplayado del Río Chico (NE of Punta Reparo) about 3 miles, to a position north of Islas Leones, lying along the north-eastern side of the main channel and with a channel between it and the eastern shore which terminates in a flat drying 3 ft (1 m) reconnecting it to the main channel of Punta Reparo. This bank dries 10–14 ft (3–4 m) so it would cover at half-tide.

[5] This is the shoal, which extends from the western side of the estuary at Punta Reparo along the west side of the main channel, and on which Islas Leones lies today.

[6] The great shoal lies ¾ mile from the middle ground. Today the width of the channel between the shoals is 4 cables at its narrowest point, opening out to a mile off Punta Reparo.

Saturday 2. This day about 7 a clock in the morning wee weighed and fell lower downe, as low as the Ebb would Carry us, and stopp [for] the flood and at high water wee weighed and gott out of the River and the least water that wee had on the barr was ¼ less 4 fathoms.

Aprill 1670. **Ditto.**

As for the Varia*ci*on that here in my Journall I give the Term of West Varia*ci*on, is to say that the Compasse Varies from the North Meridian E*aster*ly and from the South Meridian W*ester*ly that is to say the whole Compasse swerves about to the right hand.[1]

Wm Chambers.[2]

[1] In Chambers's journal, the term 'west variation' means that the compass, magnetic north, is to the east of true north, and to the west of south, or the magnetic compass is rotated clockwise with respect to the true compass.

[2] 31 blank leaves follow.

PART IV

A Declaration made by one Charles Henrique Clerck off the Proposalls made by the Royall Comp*ani*a for trade, to his Ma*jes*tie Anno 1663 – dated in Baldiuia 28 January 1671 a Towne or Citty in Westindia, & directed to the Governor of those Teritories.[1]

[f. 2r] General Information respecting the Propositions made to Charles II King of Great Britain in the year 1663 by the Solicitors and Commissioners of the Royal Company of General Trade of the Kingdoms of England to the manifest harm and prejudice of his Catholic Majesty and of his kingdoms of America in the manner which Carlos Enrique Clerque states below and reports to Your Excellency as prince, governor and lieutenant general for the most high and most mighty and catholic monarch, king of the Spains.

He entreats that Your Excellency[2] may be pleased to accept his good intentions [which are] pure and directed to no end other than the aim of serving God and his church without hopes of or pretentions to rewards or worldly approval since he has in free will renounced and abandoned those which he possessed and those which he expected going forward in [terms of] honour and esteem on his return to England, all to prevent the damage which may result to this empire because there are some powers in Europe which, being envious of the military power and riches spread among the rest of the world, try to disturb the peace and tranquility which is enjoyed[.] As, it is given to understand, are the preparations which are being put in place in England under different pretexts in appearance of peace and friendship to shatter this uneasy time with invasion and hostilities in these peaceful seas. I trust in the Spirit of Almighty God in order to assist Your Excellency to impart to you the enlightenment necessary to understand the risk and having [f. 2v] understood it to take preventions to remedy what is lacking in these parts through [present] neglect, by

[1] Translated and contributed by Joyce Lorimer. BL, Add 21539, ff. 16r–23v, acquired from the library of the Earl of Melfort, contains several State Papers relating to Spanish settlements in Panama, Peru and Chile originally held by John Drummond (1649–1714), second son of the 3rd Earl of Perth, who was created Earl of Melfort, Viscount of Forth, Lord Drummond of Rickerstoun, Castlemains, and Gilstoun, 12 Aug. 1686. He was one of the principal Secretaries of State for Scotland under James II and VII (r. 1684–8). He accompanied James II into exile in 1689. The title is taken from the endorsement of the document, which according to the curator, was written by James, Duke of York. The document is written on Spanish sealed paper in Don Carlos's hand and with his signature, and appears to be the original copy received from an informant in Spain. Another copy of this document, written in a different hand, on ordinary paper and with no endorsements, is to be found in BL, Add 28457, ff. 2r–22r. It may well be a fair, legible copy made from BL, Add MS 21539 after it was received in England, since the the latter is barely legible in parts where the ink bled through the paper. This transcription and translation follows BL, Add 28457 version which differs slightly, largely because it cuts down some of the extended sentences and exaggerated statements made by Don Carlos. Any significant differences with BL, Add 21539, ff. 16r– 23v have been noted.

[2] The letter is addressed to Pedro Antonio Fernández de Castro, 10th Conde de Lemos, Viceroy of Peru 1667–72. See above, p. 543, n. 2.

which the coasts of the Tierra Firme and Yslas de Barlobento[1] have suffered so many and so continuous calamities by devastation and sack, with notable decrease to the authority and detriment of the Royal Treasury of His Catholic Majesty and great bankrupting of his royal commerce. Furthermore they will be able to probe the coasts and waters of the South Sea if Your Excellency does not attend promptly to the correction of that which the necessity of the occasion requires. May Your Excellency with zeal prudence and effort, assisted by your power, authority and nobility, dispose what may be seen to be suitable to the royal service of His Majesty. And because I am about to depart for the Ciudad de los Reyes[2] and find myself in poor health, and the roads from here to Balparaiso according to what I am told are difficult with few comforts and many [f. 3r] dangers from enemies, I have not wished to take my leave without writing these warnings in the form of a testament in case I actually find myself (*in articulo mortis*)[3] as may occur naturally or by other accidents which by Divine disposition may overcome me and, by warning of future eventualities as is my duty, so that Your Excellency and these kingdoms may be assured of the veracity [of what I report] of which were it to be unknown for the lack of my writings, everything will remain in the same [state of] confusion, ignorance and risk as it was before my arrival at this port without any understanding of the mystery of why I was sent to these waters. For which, trusting in the wisdom, loyalty and discretion of Don Pedro de Montoya, the Governor of this place, I have beseeched him to remit these writings to your court, on the first occasion for dispatch which offers, all of which I relate to Your Excellency are the experiences and certain information acquired over seventeen years and more that I have served the British Crown in continuous occupations in which the said King[4] was pleased to place me at sea or on land within or outside his realms attending at diverse times in Councils of State and War, as well in particular commissions with ambassadors. [f. 3v] I omit relation of the circumstances of my birth and upbringing because it is not important or relevant. It is more than enough for me to make clear to Your Excellency that by birth I am from Alsazia[5] in Germany and in inclination and religion I am Spanish. From tender infancy up to sixteen years of age I was continuously under the protection of the Queen Mother of England,[6] and from sixteen to twenty-two years of age I was wandering through various kingdoms and provinces to see and reflect on the world and acquire the knowledge that is needed in youth. Since 22 years up to my present age[7] I was occuppied in the duties referred to above and, to get to what matters, in the year 1663[8] as aforesaid, the Royal Company presented a memorial to the

[1] Windward Islands.

[2] Lima.

[3] A legal term meaning 'at the point of death'.

[4] It is not clear whether Don Carlos is counting backwards from the beginning of Narbrough's venture in 1669 or 1671. In either case, since Charles II did not assume the English Crown until 1660, Don Carlos seems to be claiming service in exile. Charles II counted his regnal years from the death of his father in 1649.

[5] Alsace.

[6] Queen Henrietta Maria (1602–69), daughter of Henri IV of France, widow of Charles I. A devout Catholic she had gone into exile in France in 1642, returning for a short period in 1644 and again, after the Restoration, in 1660–65. She died in France. See, Hibbard, 'Henrietta Maria', *ODNB*. His claim to have been brought up in her household reflects Don Carlos's new pretensions to be the illegitimate son of Prince Rupert as his fellow detainees were to report; see above, p. 49.

[7] This would suggest that Don Carlos was born c. 1630 and was about 40 years of age at this time.

[8] BL, Add 28457, f. 3v, miscopies this date as 1600.

King[1] by their commissioners and general attorneys in which they gave information on the following matters the import of which, translated from the English language into Castilian is as follows.

The said [gentle]men propose in their memorial, informing that King of the harm and loss which the said trade has suffered on a daily basis in its factories and voyages not only in Assia[2] but also in those in Africa in [f. 4r] parts of Guinea caused by the Dutch who being very powerful in those said parts intentionally disrupt the trade with pretexts and unjust searches, with great disrespect and contempt for his British Majesty. And should war break out between the two powers if the said Dutch should not have moved to give them satisfaction for these insults in good faith without breaking the peace treaties, then those of the said Company doubted that they would be able to avoid bankruptcy and the peril of losing all that which up to now they had held in Assia and Africa at the cost of immeasurable treasure seeing the said Dutch becoming lords of the better part of the Yndia,[3] predominating over all in those parts as much by sea as land and being absolute in the passage and strait of Batabia[4] where 36 armed frigates of notable strength cross continually and guard and defend it, by which they disrupt with malicious blockades trade with China and the Islands of Japon[5] on which depends our greatest interests that trade being the largest and richest of all Assia. [f. 4v] And all that was caused by the neglect of the Council of State during his Majesty's absence from his realms, which could have prevented these these accidents, by [taking] the political positions to the Dutch either that there be equal participation in these conquests or by sequestering [their ships] by embargo, and by complaining to Portugal about the advantages which might have followed under the pretext of mediation or specific assistence.[6] By these means they might have [averted] so many inconveniences keeping Holland always in need of English patronage and protection for its safety from that which might threaten it without her. Now Spain is about to find that doors which were previously closed are now open to the riches of these said conquests. They will find [the Dutch] arrogantly and haughtily to have the means to bring the French and Germans to their aid and win the good will of Sweden and Denmark, in case of need, in an offensive or defensive league while otherwise preserving their neutrality [f. 5r] and they will make such deep roots in in the parts of Assia America and Africa that it could, if Your Majesty should delay remedying it, without doubt bring about the the

[1] Don Carlos's contacts within the Jewish community may have made him aware of the proposal, made to Oliver Cromwell by one Simón de Cáceres in 1655, for an expedition via Cape Horn to assault Valdivia in order to establish a base from which to attack shipping in the Pacific. See, Bradley, 'Narbrough's Don Carlos', pp, 471–3. Don Carlos may have used that knowledge to construct this version of his story.

[2] Asia.

[3] The context indicates that this refers to India and the Far East.

[4] Batavia, the fort and settlement founded by the Dutch in 1619 on the ruins of the Javanese port of Jakarta, on the strait of Selat Sunda (6°00′S, 105°30′E).

[5] Japan.

[6] This is a difficult shorthand sentence. If it refers to the period of the Protectorate when the Council of State assisted Cromwell from late 1653, then it relates to treaties which Oliver Cromwell made with the Dutch and the Portuguese in 1654. In the case of the Dutch, Cromwell would have liked, but did not achieve, a division of colonial spheres of interest and nothing was done to lessen commercial rivalry between the two powers. The treaty with Portugal gave the English right of trade in Portuguese colonies. See, Howat, *Stuart and Cromwellian*, pp. 69–94.

general ruin of Your Royal Commerce on which depends the principal strength of all the realm.[1]

These propositions having been heard by the King[2] who finding himself with these same concerns and other greater ones to attend to first responded that he would look into it and consult with his Council; moreover since there were various problems occurring daily and the matter touching this negotiation could not be resolved at that time and postponing it to a more suitable occasion,which the said gentlemen of the Royal Company found to be after seeing the peace was settled between the Crown of England and the States of Holland with all the rest of the Princes their allies, they returned a second time to beseech His Majesty that he might be pleased to attend to the aforesaid business and proposal touching the well-being and growth of his Crown and preservation of his royal commerce. His Majesty and his royal Council resolved and concluded the business in the year 1669 and he was pleased to send a frigate for me with orders [f. 5v] that I should quickly embark without delay and take passage to London in his royal service leaving affairs in the state in which they were in the City of [Stockholm].[3] I did so and after I having arrived at London and kissed his hand and given an account of the state of the affairs with which I had been charged, he gave me a summary of all that the Royal Company was claiming with order that I should give him my opinion in writing of the form of what must be considered in the execution of it with such advice as occurred to me according to my experience and knowledge which I did making the points which follow.

That diligent efforts should be made to reconnoiter the coast which runs and extends from Cauo [Cabo] de San Antonio[4] situated south of the Rio de la Platta to the Estrecho de Magallanes, endeavouring to pass through it and enter the South Sea and from there they should continue as far as the Californias to look for the Strait of Anian[5] in order to verify and assure the said passages, for even though they have been discovered and navigated by different people there has been none of the notice or attention given which

[1] Don Carlos's complaints suggest that he did not have access to any of the foreign policy discussions of Charles II's inner ministers after his arrival in London in the Summer of 1669. His representation of the concerns of the so-called 'Royal Company', supposedly first delivered to Charles II in 1663, possibly reflects that he had some knowledge of considerations of the Board of Trade or ongoing discussion in the London merchant community. In the next paragraph he appears to set the second approach by the so-called 'Royal Company' in or about 1668. The Triple Alliance between England, Holland and Sweden was concluded in early 1668. The terms of the alliance preshadowed the terms by which peace might be made between France and Spain, which was achieved shortly thereafter by the Treaty of Aix-la- Chapelle and which established the temporary line of the frontier between France and the Netherlands. Holland was, however, England's long-established commercial rival. From the midsummer of 1668, complex covert and overt negotiations were underway which ultimately established the public and secret terms of the Treaty of Dover between Charles II and Louis XIV in 1670. Ibid., pp. 95–126.

[2] Charles II.

[3] It is difficult to establish the name of the city in which Don Carlos claimed to be at the time that he was summoned to the court of Charles II. BL, Add MS 21539 reads 'escodme' and BL, Add 28457, 'Lito colme'. It appears to have been Stockholm. See Bradley, 'Narbrough's Don Carlos', p. 467.

[4] See above, p. 189, n. 1.

[5] The Strait of Anian first appears on a map by Giacomo Gastaldi of 1562 as a strait lying between Asia and North America. Subsequent opinion reduced it to a strait across the North American continent running west from the vicinity of Hudson Bay. It was reputed to have been discovered by Juan de Fucca in 1592 in the vicinity of 47°–48°N on the Pacific coast of North America, and was subsequently searched for by numerous navigators until the 18th century. See, Purchas, *His Pilgrims*, III, iv, pp. 849–51; Gough, Historica CANADA, thecanadianencyclopedia.ca.

is required [f. 6r] to ensure that trading vessels can go out and return from the parts in safety as necessary.

Regarding the discoverers who have passed through the said straits, although their reports are very certain, the Spaniards have falsified them so that foreigners might not be certain about them and thus would desist from from navigating them, and even if the English, French and Dutch have not left off passing through that of Magallanes many times since they did so for the specific purpose of privateering they hastened their passages without taking the time to acquire the information necessary; there has been no effort to discover that of Anian from the south [sea] side which is said to be easy, although it has been done from the North as will be discussed further.

The said Company should be asked to reconnoitre the ports which exist on one and the other side within the confines and the surrounding areas of the said straits [which are] safe for vessels and suitable to settle and fortify and easy to defend where outward bound and returning particular fleets that they have sent out to the South Sea, [f. 6v] the Salamon Islands and those of Japon and New Guinea, the coasts of China and other parts of the Indies which are to the North of the Strait of Batauia, may make stop-overs in the new settlements which will have been established in order to refresh and ready themselves for whatever incidents may occur in times of peace or war.[1]

The gentlemen of the Company assure Your Majesty that they have seen the journals of captains and pilots of nine English vessels which passed through to the Mar del Sur[2] on different occasions since Francisco Draque who was the first who went around the world with such fortune, the reknown of which is published in histories – some of these provide that the said strait is good to pass at [all] times in the year and not perilous there being throughout every two or [three] leagues more or less, good ports and roads to anchor in and many large rivers and wood and that by the strait they they will make safer and shorter voyages to the East Indies the winds being usually south and southwest and north and northeast the one and the other favourable for the outward and return voyage. [f. 7r] Other English captains and some Dutch report, without contradicting each other, by which it may be believed, a discovery which was made in the said strait of Magallanes a little more or less than 30 leagues to the east of Cauo [Cabo]de la Vitoria[3] in a channel which is called San Geronimo[4] which they entered with launches leaving their ships at the mouth of the channel. And having gone more than twenty leagues up they found themselves in very pleasant populated plains up to which it was possible to bring up vessels of more than one thousand *toneladas*[5] even with the rise and fall of the tide. A river which is abundant with different sorts of fish empties into the channel. They say that they disembarked at one of the native villages on the river where they conversed and traded

[1] The Spanish word for war, 'Guerra', found in BL, Add 21539, was misread as 'Guinea' by the copyist here.

[2] The Pacific Ocean.

[3] Cabo Victoria, (52°16′S, 74°53′W).

[4] Canal Jerónimo (53°33′S, 72°23′W), entered between Punta San Jerónimo and Punta San Jorge. Also known as Jorem's Channel. See above, p. 189, n. 1.

[5] Don Carlos uses the Spanish measurement here. The *tonelada* was a measure of cargo capacity (*tonelada de arquero*) or displacement (*tonelada de desplazamiento*). In 1552 the *tonelada* was described as two *pipas* (barrels) of 27·5 *arrobas* (11·5 kg), i.e. of about 632.5 kg or 0·6225 tons. At this time ship's tonnages in England were calculated from their dimensions. Tons Burden = (k × b × ½b) ÷ 94, where k = Keel length and b = Beam inside the wales. See, Winfield, *British Warships*, p. xlix.

with the natives for smelted gold of more than 21 carats[1] in small two to three ounce pieces, copper [bars] and some suckling pigs, hens, maize and beans and chickpeas all in exchange for bells, corals and false pearls and glass beads.

They say that they saw in [f.7v] different parts of the said village crosses made like those of Spain, the which emblem might come from to the observance of some form of religion. They state that they had heard at intervals the distinct sound of church bells, the echo of which seemed to come from the air some two leagues or a little less away. Also they say that their houses were very well made and roofed with tiles and in some of those which they entered they saw antequated firearms hung up on the walls and swords, iron pots and clay dishes [decorated] like those of Seville. The people have a very agreeable language even if it could not be understood, a gentle disposition and comely countenances, their colour between white and pallid tending towards hazel – they are very docile and friendly. The things they use ordinarily are made of copper and bronze seeing which it can understood that they have quantities of copper, tin and lead in minerals as well as mines and gold-panning sites.The reason for their[2] not staying any longer amongst them, which was no more than three hours, was because of a crowd of piraguas full of armed people [f.8r] coming down the river and also many other squads by land with spears, bows and arrows which forced them to embark and return to their ships for fear of what might occur.[3] They say it is certain that the said settlements are those to which the Spaniards who abandoned the [towns]of San Phelipe and Jesus[4] retreated, the which were settled and fortified by General Pedro Sarmiento in the said Estrecho de Magellanes by order of King Phelipe the second – the which were [in number] 6 priests 400 men and 33 women[5] of which [some] died before abandoning the said parts or cities and excepting 23 which Thomas Condic found alive on [his] first voyage which did not wish to embark with him.[6] And six years afterwards returning for a second time to the Mar del sur he found only one person in the city of San Phelipe and Jesus[7] who had lived alone for some three years the which he carried off too and disembarked at Balparayso[8] where he left him, carrying four bronze pieces to England which he had found buried in one of the bastions

[1] The Spanish reads '*quilates del ley*', meaning carats.

[2] The visiting party from the ship.

[3] This tale appears to be reworking of the legend of *Ciudad de los Césares*. Francisco César sailed on Sebastian Cabot's voyage to the Río de la Plata (1526–30) and after a land expedition to the westwards reported finding a fabulously rich city, which could not subsequently be found again. This story later became conflated with the legend of the survivors of Alonso de Camargo's expedition of 1539–40 (more commonly known as the Bishop of Plascencia's expedition), who were reported to the Viceroy of Peru in 1587 to be in Patagonia. The myth of lost Spanish settlements in Patagonia grew in due course to include the supposed survivors of Pedro Sarmiento de Gamboa's two settlements left in the Strait in Feb. 1584. See, Howgego, *Encyclopedia*, pp. 181, 208.

[4] Sarmiento named his settlements Ciudad del Rey Filipe and Ciudad del Nombre de Jesus.

[5] Many of the settlers originally bound for the Strait were lost to shipwreck and sickness. Sarmiento founded his colony in 1584 with 338 people, including settlers, craftsmen and soldiers; Phillips, *Struggle*, p. 51.

[6] Thomas Cavendish; variants Candish, Candisich, Canduiq, Condic. On his first voyage Cavendish picked up only one survivor, and has been subsequently criticized by historians for abandoning the remaining 23. See, Hakluyt, *Principal Navigations*, III, p. 806; Markham, *Voyages of Pedro Sarmiento de Gamboa*, pp. 352–75; Maxwell, 'Cavendish, Thomas', *ODNB*.

[7] This man was picked up by John Chidley in the *Delight* of Bristol. See, Hakluyt, *Principal Navigations*, III, p. 839.

[8] Valparaiso.

of the said city of Jesus[1] whose settlers joined with the peoples of the said parts [f. 8v] having procreated and multiplied between them a great number [of people].

Also the gentlemen of the said Company signified to His Majesty the advantages which would flow to his crown in the event it was possible to discover the said settlements winning the good will of their inhabitants settlers and also referred to the certain news which they had of the Salomon Islands and New Guinea and of their great riches.

And the said Company told His Majesty of the report which the General Francisco Draque[2] made to the Queen Dona Yzabel[3] on his arrival at London on his return from his voyage in the Mar del sur by the East Indies, in which he tells how he arrived at New Alblon[4] needing to careen his ship of 150 *toneladas*, with 10 pieces of artillery and 120 men and carrying the treasure which he had taken from the Spaniards which he seized in those seas, the which treasure amounted to more than four million, in gold, jewels and silver in bullion and coin.

He entered a harbour on that coast which is said to one of the largest in the Mar del Sur and found there a settlement of more than twenty thousand Indians whose houses were spread along the bank [f. 9r] of a river which came down into the harbour.On the news of his arrival the king of that land came attended by more than two thousand armed men as his guard who seemingly maintained his court some 15 to 20 leagues away from the sea which accordingly delayed his arrival. The said King and all of his vassals were very affable and friendly with el Draque[5] and his company the King visiting him in person going and coming with much confidence and without any distrust on board his ship and permitting him to build a small stockade ashore to protect the said treasure, arms, munitions and gear while he careened his vessel. And after having finished everything and ready to continue his voyage on taking leave of the said Prince he was moved by his many demonstrations of sadness that he [Drake] should be going away giving him many things among them wonderful feathers and rare cloths and some pieces of gold and valuable stones.[6]

From the said harbour he followed his course towards the Strait of Anian entering it with the resolve to pass through it. Having reached what would be a matter of 20 [f. 9v] leagues within he encountered problems not having nautical charts which marked the said strait or even information from those who had approached from the north [Atlantic] side and lacking the oared boats necessary for such work he turned back to the sea returning to England by the Yndia Oriental[7] – the said Francisco Draque says in his journal (assuring the Queen) that the discovery of the said strait to be easier than what Hernando Magallanes faced in discovering that named after him. – He explains that if he had not found himself with the said treasure and without another vessel for company he would have passed through and reached England very shortly and he concludes asserting

[1] The cannon were recovered from Ciudad del Rey Filipe. Hakluyt, *Principal Navigations*, III, p. 806.

[2] Francis Drake; variants, Francisco; Draq, Draque.

[3] Queen Elizabeth I; variants, Isauel, Izabel, Ysaul, Yzabela.

[4] A miscopy for Albion.

[5] The common Spanish name for Francis Drake.

[6] The visit of Drake to *New Albion* is recorded in Hakluyt, *Principal Navigations*, III, pp.737–9, and in Drake, *World Encompassed*, pp. 67–81.

[7] Drake searched as far north as 48°N and found no passage round North America prior to his time at New Albion, whence he sailed directly across the Pacific Ocean; *World Encompassed*, pp. 67, 82.

that the said strait is easier to discover by approaches from the Mar del Sur, it having been impossible to achieve this by efforts which had been made from the north divers times which the kings of England, France, Sweden, Denmark and Holland have attempted sending vessels, the which returned with great loss [f.10r] of people who perished from the cold or hardship having got themselves into inlets and rivers from which it it had been very difficult to get out. And according to their journals they found it impossible to discover the said strait by the north [sea] because there are so many entrances that one does not know which to attempt and the winter is extremely cold and windy with infinite ice and snow.

The Company further states, in order to draw and persuade the King to make the said discovery, that in the year 1609 a Spanish ship of more than 200 *toneladas* built in the Mar del Sur reached and achored in Dociblin in France[1] the which [ship] had left the port of Acapulco in New Spain and having left the said port a storm forced them to enter the said strait they judging it to be a place where they could make anchor until the storm ceased the which kept going until they found themselves in the Mares del Norte. The captain and master were Portuguese by nation as was their pilot, all men of great experience and reputed to be good cosmographers whom it is judged had made [f. 10v] the said voyage on purpose to get to Europe with the riches that they carried without paying taxes to the King [of Spain] first, and in hopes of rewards for having discovered the said passage by necessity. Being too damaged to make for Spain they arrived in the said port in Ireland according to their report and records where they [remained] for less than two months under the pretext of needing supplies which were given to them. They then made sail and went to Lisbon where having arrived they presented their journals to the Casa de la Yndia and the report of the reasons obliging them to come by the said route, notice of which was given to the Lord King Phelipe the third who ordered that the papers books and nautical charts should be quickly collected and burned and the confiscating all the goods and the vessel so that they should learn their lesson and the said passage remain unknown as before and not come to the knowledge of the Princes of the North whose subjects would infest the said strait with invasions of the *Mares del sur*;[2] the captains who have been in the said sea believe that voyages to Yndia could be made from [f. 11r] the estrecho de Aniam[3] in less than 40 days and less than thirty to Panama and down to Baldivia in less than fifty days. By which information and without more of less importance the King was persuaded to settle the said business having consulted, and my opinion[4] having been seen in his Consejo de Estado and Juntas de mar, concluding with the summary of the orders which were to be observed in this voyage with the utmost dilgence as will be said later.

[1] Clearly meant to be Dublin, Ireland, as seen by what follows.

[2] The Casa da India, Lisbon, managed all Portuguese trade with the kingdom's overseas territories. It has not been possible to find any information on a voyage of this nature and date. The accounts of the apocryphal voyages of Lorenzo Ferrer Maldonado (1588) and Bartolomé de Fonte (1640) were first published in 1708 and 1810 respectively and so are unlikely to have been known to Don Carlos. This may, therefore, be a voyage originating from his own imagination.

[3] Mispelled by the copyist.

[4] Don Carlos uses the word '*parecer*' meaning in Spanish governance, an opinion formally given and minuted of consideration in a Council or Committee or other consultative group.

The King attended by his brother the Duke of Yorque and Prince Roberto his first cousin[1] and the Duke of Boquingar the Duke of Abel Male and he who temporarily holds and exercises the office of the Lord Chancellor he having withdrawn to France[2] and the Secretary of State Merladinton[3] all [at a] private meeting which was held in the Royal Chamber of His Majesty where I was summoned to be given the Regulations and Orders which were to be observed in the voyage which I have copied here which contained the following articles.

Signor Carlos Henrique, being aware of your [f. 11v] religion, trustworthiness and loyalty by the experiences which I have had and have of your honorable proceedings as well as of the parts and offices which you have performed in my Royal service in the north and south of both poles in occasions where you have shown the experience which you have as a seaman and soldier, today I am offered an undertaking in which it is necessary to employ you with the post of Director General to govern at your will with appropriate actions as in your opinion conform with my instructions. For which I give you my Royal word that should God bring you back into my presence giving me news of that with which I have entrusted you in the matter of establishing new colonies in the parts of America and Assia, I give and concede to you from now and forever to you and to all your successors the proprietary title charge and exercise of the said colonies the which you will settle and fortify and preserve with Catholic families which you will take out from my kingdoms under the the Divine and human laws which are observed by those who through the design of the King my father went out to settle the coasts and ports [f.12r] of Marilano[4] which today exist in the new kingdom of England.[5] I accepted the honours and favours which it pleased his Majesty give me with such tokens of good will for which I thanked him kissing his royal hand with the gratitude and humility my obedience owed to him, making a vow of homage to observe and keep with all fidelity and secrecy whatever his Majesty was pleased to order me in his royal instructions. This *auto*[6] being concluded I was given sealed documents one to open as soon as I reached my lodgings and the other after passing the Islands of Cauoberde, and having taken leave of His Majesty and the rest of the Princes of the committee I left London for Grabesin[7] in the company of the three comissary generals charged with the preparation and despatch of His Majesty's fleets and squadrons who carried orders to assist and provide me with the following as seen in the first orders.

[1] Prince Rupert. See above, pp. 20; 138, n. 2.

[2] Edward Hyde, Earl of Clarendon, who had fled to France to avoid impeachment for treason over his conduct of the Second Anglo-Dutch War.

[3] The Duke of York, Prince Rupert, the Duke of Buckingham, the Duke of Albemarle and Lord Arlington were all members of the Council of Trade, having been appointed in Oct. 1668 and re-appointed in April 1669. Sir Henry Bennet (created Lord Arlington in 1665, and Earl of Arlington in 1672) held the office of Secretary of State (South), 1662–74. See, Andrews, *British Committees*, p. 93; Sainty, *Officials of the Boards of Trade*, pp. 18, 19; Sainty, *Officials of the Secretaries of State*, p. 65.

[4] George Calvert,1st Lord Baltimore was granted proprietary rights to territory east of the Potomac river in 1632, which was subsequently named Maryland after Queen Henrietta Maria. After his death in the same year, the proprietorship passed to his son Cecilius who founded the colony in 1634 as a refuge for Catholics.

[5] New England.

[6] The Spanish term for an official statement of an act to be undertaken after consultation.

[7] Gravesend; see above, p. 140.

[*margin:* Orders] Carlos Henrrique – You will depart from the Port of las Duenas[1] at the first opportunity enter the Channel southward following your course for the island of the Madera and we order you that before leaving the said Port of las Duenas that you should make known and have made known on sea and land that that you are making [f. 12v] a voyage to the Windward Islands, Surunam and the Rio de las Amaçonas.[2] We charge you that the company that you take on board be chosen to your satisfaction in no case carrying any volunteers or reformers so as to avoid the upsets and mutinies which tend to occur in long and extended voyages. Also we excuse you from carrying any passengers. You will be delivered ten thousand pesos in Spanish *reales de a ocho* and *doblones*[3] in order to supply what is necessary in victuals or other needs in whatever Ports where you may make a stopover for which you will give a receipt to my Comissary Generals.

Also you will take on board the quantity of merchandise on which you have advised me as presents and gifts to those with whom you make contact in your voyage and discoveries. carrying also the goods which were requested of me for the relief and assistance of your sea men in the quantity which you deem to be advisable that you should distribute in need and payment of their wages such as tobacco, pipes, ready made clothes, bedding, shoes, stockings and soap and other trifles and victuals for the period [f. 13r] of twenty months on quarter rations as is common in long voyages for which reason they are given on return four and a half shillings each month as recompense for the short rations on top of their wages.

Item: For the sick you will carry, in addition to the ordinary,[4] some quantity of sugar, kinds of sweet wine, white bread raisins and almonds and for when the beer is finished you will load thirty barrels of french brandy which you will share out to each one as is the custom in norwegian voyages .

You will carry the things necessary you deem to be convenient in arms munitions and equipment for war having it embarked with all speed and without loss of time. I did everything which His Majesty ordered in less than four days and on the 26 of September of the year 1669 left las Dunas with a royal frigate and a Pink and in a few days I arrived at the Isla de la Madera where I had orders to go to receive from the Consul of that nation [English Consul] some sweet wine and fruits for the entertainment of the Council[5] and other personages who might come on board in some [f. 13r] parts of the said island. I was ordered in the said instructions to go to the Isla de Santiago de Cabo Verde where I should refresh the company and take on water and firewood and having done the said task I was to set sail and losing sight of land to call together the captains of both vessels in whose presence I should open His Majesty's documents which contained the following articles.

[1] The Downs; see above, p. 135, n. 3.

[2] The Windward Isles are Guadeloupe, Dominica, Martinique, St Lucia, St Vincent, the Grenadines, Grenada and Barbados. Narbrough's expedition was originally intended to go to the West Indies, with no apparent mention of Suriname or the River Amazon. Here Don Carlos presents the orders given to Narbrough as if they had been given to himself.

[3] See above, p. xx.

[4] Usual common diet.

[5] Madeira wine fell increasingly under the control of English merchants as Portugal became closely associated with England in the second half of the 17th century. The Spanish word is 'Camara', having the political sense of Chamber or House. After the restoration of the Portuguese monarchy in 1640 Madeira was governed by a Captain General residing in Funchal.

You will steer [set your course] to reconnoitre the coasts of Brasil to the windward of the Cauo de Fernambuco[1] without coming very close to the said coast or entering any port or anchoring on the coast taking all care not to be seen from the land. When you have passed the Rio de la Plata you should approach as far as possible the Cauo de San Antt*oni*o[2] which is to the south of the said river from whence you will sail along as close as you can to the coast as far as the estrecho de Magallanes and reconnoitring and surveying the land and if it has ports inlets rivers and coves, sounding at the and rise and fall and observing the course of the tides, the winds climate and herbs plants flowers fruits birds fish and animals, minerals [f. 14r] and gold panning sites and all the rest of the things which may be worth report. And above all we charge you to seek to communicate and converse with the natives of the said coasts and moreover, if you succeed and are able to come across them, to endeavour to get interpreters of the Indian language from among the Spaniards by any means by which may prudently achieve it giving them the recompense which they merit without giving insult to any living person whether Spaniard or whatsoever other. And in particular with great caution you will try to find and meet the malcontents of the Provinces of Paraguay Tucuman and Chille[3] which with gifts and presents you should try to draw to friendship with you informing them of my power and authority over land and sea and taking note of their leanings ceremonies and political and military dispositions the trade and the goods that they value, and you should take a good record of all to inform me on your return of the benefits which may come to my Crown in time of peace as well as war. And in order that you will be better able to achieve all the above you will have built a pinnace of fifteen to twenty [f. 14v] *toneladas* with deck, oars and artillery as appropriate in a port which you may find suitable and safe in which the two large vessels can anchor safely while you undertake the said tasks with the men necessary. You should observe with great attention the entrances and exits of the ports and their tides, noting the ports where it might be possible to occupy and fortify for the security guard and defence of the said settlements, and at the places where you should come in close and make tests with eight pounder artillery what the batteries might be able to do. Having done the said tasks, if able, you will go through into the Mar del Sur by the estrecho de Magallanes in which you will make effort to see if you can discover the settlements previously discussed[4] and the ports and places which Pedro Sarmiento settled and fortified leaving Spaniards to guard the said strait.

When you have entered the Mar del Sur follow the shoreline carefully [f. 15r]
up to the altitude of forty degrees south of the Equator where the city of Baldiuia is situated, from whence if you find yourself with a healthy company and sufficient provisions you should try to cross to the other coast of Acapulco reconnoitring the Californias and the rest of the coastline as far as the estrecho de Anian; the which, should your men be reluctant to enter the same because of the delay [time it would take] and the risk, you should guarantee and promise them rewards in addition to their wages when you see that it is finished with all secure after you have arrived in my realms. And if in the said latitude of Baldivia you find it impossible to go through the said regions you should

[1] Pernambuco (8°02′S, 34°48′W).

[2] Cabo San Antonio is the southern entrance point of Río de la Plata.

[3] See above, pp. 89–91, 95–6.

[4] See above, pp. 663–4.

return to England by Magallanes touching at the Isla de Santa Elena[1] where you should refresh your men and get necessary provisions without touching in Brasil or any other part until arriving directly in my realms, and if you should get to the coast of Acapulco and cannot find the estrecho de Anian you will return by Yndia[2] visiting my factories and providing yourself with what is needed. I also order you [f. 15v] that should you encounter any vessels on the coasts and waters of Brasil and other parts of America belonging to the Crown of Portugal or of Spain you should not engage with them removing yourself from any opportunity to molest or be molested by them, but if by some accident they seek to offend you will rebuke them according to the peace and friendship which we maintain [with them] and if they persist in their intention you will defend yourself as soldier and my vassal according at all times to the military [conventions] observed under English laws.

All the above was contained in the written instructions apart from other less important advice – and in full by word in discussion together they directed me to seek to find out, very cautiously and where I could in conversation, what type of fortifications, artillery, munitions, garrisons and inhabitants there are in Baldiuia, Callao, Panama and the port of Acapulco, and the kind and number of warships and merchant vessels in each port of the Mar del Sur.

[f. 16r] This Your Excellency is the greater part of what was contained in the public and secret, written and spoken orders of the King and I assure you in all truthfulness that the King and the rest of the princes have been forced into it more because the state of his kingdoms so obliges them, than a will to disturb the peace which he wishes to preserve and maintain as a benign and peace-loving Prince, and all those of his Royal family not being able either to prevent things much against his will, toning them down as much as they can. The course of this voyage has been conducted with such diplomacy and form as to my position that I am able to swear as a Christian that if the frigate in which I came to these waters returns to England it will be something,[3] and that if it should arrive it will be with such horror and fatigue bringing as tidings miserable news [of] disasters and calamities representing no greater threat [to Spain] than the exploration of the ports of which paintings are carried in the frigate. The which exploration I could not avoid because of circumstances which obliged me to undertake it having in the same exposed myself to great hazard of my honour and life all to avoid risk [f. 16v] and harm to this monarchy.[4] One of the said ports is situated at 45 degrees of latitude south of the Rio de la Plata which is called Rio de Camarones.[5] The second is situated in forty five and a half degrees south of the other which is has the name Puerto Deseado,[6] that of the Camarones is only for

[1] Saint Helena (15°56′S, 05°43′W).

[2] Presumably he means that he was ordered to return by crossing the Pacific. His inventiveness did not extend to explaining which specific factories he was allegedly directed to visit.

[3] In other words, more than might be reasonably expected.

[4] This passage is as convoluted as the writer's intentions. Don Carlos is clearly faced with the dilemma of maintaining his claims to have been leader of the expedition and, at the same time, separating himself from his fellow detainees and the company of the *Sweepstakes* which had by then left for England. He therefore claims that he had carried out his mission carefully and diplomatically, and that Narbrough, if he made it back at all, would not carry back to England anything more significant than the 'pinturas', presumably the maps, made of the coast. It appears as if Don Carlos may be claiming to have made them himself.

[5] Bahía Camarones (44°40′S, 64°50′W).

[6] Puerto Deseado (47°45′S, 65°53′W).

small vessels up to sixty *toneladas*, Deseado is one of the best ports which can be had to enter and depart and for safety or as many kinds of vessels in number and weight as may be desired.

At the mouth of the said port there is a small island which nature created for its defence that with a small fort that may be built on it [whomever it may be] can defend the entrance against the greatest seagoing armada. There are many advantages to settling and fortifying the said ports, the one situated where it is possible to go to and from Buenos Aires in whatever weather in less than a month, and to and from the Estrecho de Magallanes in ten or twelve days the coastline being clean, well known and sounded, with prevailing [f. 17r] north, northeast and east winds all the year. By land [there are] good tracks by which it is possible to go from some places to others easily for the countryside is flat with no mountains, few rivers and good grassland. One can come overland to La Concepcion in less than twenty days. The said coast abounds with fish in season and inland [there is] good hunting for animals and fowl and some gold-pans and many wild Indians. If the foreigners are given time to settle these ports I have no doubt that in time it will cause significant disturbance in the mares del sur [if they] maintain privateering vessels in them which may enter and exit the mares del sur[1] very easily and assault Buenos Ayres should wars break out. I cannot cease to express to Your Excellency the major objectives and reasons of state, intention and aspirations and direction with which and for which this voyage has been made, the Royal Company having persuaded the King and obliged him to make it against his will and about which he has dealt and conversed many [f. 17v] times with the said gentlemen about matters concerning the said business and in other particulars and generalities with the Lords Councillors of State. [I being] solely moved by my conscience and religion which I profess as a Christian, for the observance and greater security of which I have been obliged to flee and separate myself from the perils which could occur by remaining under obedience to a monarch whose crown survives only as long as the tyranny and perilous condition of his subjects allows, and is disturbed by the multitude of arrows which the Devil places each day in his subjects and all in opposition to his authority and the Catholics of his realms. For which causes and by reason that God permits, by the incomprehensible and just judgement of his Divine Majesty, the said infidels to predominate over the true Church of England, even though the King might grant me on my return from this voyage to England that I might transport Catholic families to settle the many ports which I can discover in these parts, that is insufficient [f. 18r] to prevent heretics gaining a foothold in the said ports from whence they might infest America to the notable prejudice and diminution of the Catholic faith which has spread within it to such honour and glory of God. For which [reason] I have much preferred to live with sorrows and afflictions exposed to the vituperation of slanderers who might brand me as disloyal to my worldly Prince[2] than remain with pleasures and honours among those who might force me to be an instrument for the persecution of the Holy Church under the shadow of piety and loyalty to the Princes whom I have served with all love, in all that has not done detriment to my conscience, as has been the case up to now in England. That which is being discussed in the said realm in meetings and secret

[1] Here he refers to the Pacific in the plural, presumably because he refers to the threat to Asian as well as American waters.

[2] This may well be a reference to his fellow detainees from the *Sweepstakes*.

conversations of Lords councillors and ambassadors all of which is [about] how to make themselves lords of the Mar del Sur, and they find no other means to do so than to explore the two straits and settle and fortify the ports which they may find most suitable in them or the surrounding areas by which efforts they might open and close the doors to the said seas and their trade as they desire [f. 18v] being able with the same diligence to win the good will of the Indians and slaves and malcontents of the America and dominate the kingdoms subject to His Catholic Majesty. The said lords facilitating it, know by experience that the English accommodate themselves to whatever others, and even more so to the Indians, as is known from the experience of Virginea and New England and other parts where there are Indians and they are all one in superstitions and drunkeness and lechery[1] and other vices because they attract all those who love the life of maximum liberty above restraint of persons marrying Indian women[2] and giving them the same status as themselves without differentiating the ones from the others between them in [terms of] freedom, by which [means] they get on in all peace and security. And the hopes by which the said gentlemen in England think and live is that by following the same plan it will be very easy to win and hold the port of Baldiuia it being the biggest in the south and situated [f. 19r] at the most advantageous place which might be desired for giving a hand in need, by sea or land, to the ports which are to be settled east of the estrecho de Magallanes.

Also they are planning to sack and destroy the port of Callao,[3] knowing it is the stronghold in those waters in which there is greatest confidence for the security of the Imperial court [of the viceroyalty of Peru] and the shelter of the vessels of war and trade commerce from all the said kingdom to Panama. To win and fortify it will ensure passage for the relief to be sent to them from England or the Islas de Barlouento by Portvelo or Cruzes[4] and maintain trade from one place to others. The Queen lady Ysauel intended to execute [the same] making Francisco Draq, after his return to England from the Mar del Sur, General of an armada composed of 36 frigates not counting the pataches with the order to sack and ruin the coasts of Tierra Firme and its presidios amongst which were Portouelo, Nombre de Dios and Cartagena. [f. 19v] Thomas Canduiq[5] general of another squadron composed of nine sails [ships] was to pass through the estrecho de Magallanes to attack Panama and that pass being cleared would be advantageous for other larger parties. They attempted this then without the power men ships or territory which they are seen to have at present so close to the Tierra firme, as is known by the offences which her coasts experience daily caused by the said neighbours and knowing that Spain may flourish with greater power than that which it has now in soldiers, treasure and the ships which are the most powerful in Europa, Africa and Assia. The port of Acapulco is among the number of those which they talk about holding in the case that the estrecho de Anian is discovered from which [port] they may disturb and molest the kingdoms of New Spain

[1] In BL, Add 21539, the word used is 'lujo' meaning 'luxury'. BL Add 28457 has 'lujaria' meaning 'lechery'. Since the word 'luxury' can have the meaning of carnal indulgence it has been translated as 'lechery' here.

[2] This represents a radical revision of the statements made to Charles II about Don Carlos's own familial associations with indigenous women.

[3] See above, p. 512, n. 2.

[4] This refers to the Casa or Venta de Cruces, a depot on the Río Chagre, on the very difficult portage route across the isthmus from Panama city to Nombre de Dios.

[5] Cavendish, spelled Candisich in BL, Add MS 21539, f. 22r.

and maintain commerce with the rest of the coasts from the Islas de Salamon to Japon and China and they might cross to Baldivia for trade in negros which from the Port of Baldiuia will [f.20r] lead to Angola and Guinea. As in many cases these things are very secret in England and very unknown in Spain and they are being arranged with such order and certainty that with whatever settlement they may make, close to whichever of the two straits, an infinite number of people of all nations who join with the English will pass through in little time, the poor in their countries will look for a similar chance, the more so when moved to avarice by the fame of the riches said to be carried on these waters. And if modesty permits me to say what I feel, speaking with the due respect required by my affection for his Catholic Majesty into whose royal protection I was received in the castle of San Luis situated at the mouth of this port of Baldiuia,[1] the first refuge and relief which I found among the Catholic vassals of His Majesty in his realms, I say that Spain may still remain confident by understanding its peril and knowing the great general opposition [caused by] [f. 20v] the natural antipathy of all who under white flags[2] fire off arrows. Some under the veil of friendship rob her by carrying off her treasure in trade for goods of no value being able to replace them with better ones if their idleness did not prevent it. Others under pretence of neutrality divert her in order the more to deceive her and take the opportunity to extract the price taking her gold and silver through the *asientos* to which they have bound her, others in the name of peace put her to sleep with the intention they may cautiously get better themselves by pinching at her to draw blood for what ails them, all trusting to benefit in the inheritance. The one says I will send forces by sea, others I will close the ports by land, others I will waste its treasures with hopes and promises. England is seeking the ports in which it can maintain its fleets, France is sending innumerable soldiers every day to its [f. 21r] frontiers as may be seen in the Yslas de Barlobento and the north coast of the Ysla de S*an*to Domingo, neutral Holland through Curazao, in return for *negros* spews out goods which ruin her trade and, finally, the Princes of Italy behind masks hide their hands and throw stone[s]. The [Holy Roman] emperor and the electors are unable to assist her before being assisted themselves. Sueçia and Dignamarca[3] [are] in a secret offensive and defensive league with England and everywhere there are preparations by sea and land each one procuring their [reserves] and preserving their authority, not letting their attention stray by constant vigilance.

Only Spain which trusts in its riches expects to prevail always and neither takes care nor wishes to associate itself with the clamour of arms by land even less place itself in danger on the seas, for which shortcoming and omission her opponents gain courage like sparrow hawks which finding the eagle sleeping steal her feathers each one enriching itself and leaving [f. 21v] [the eagle] naked and unable to revenge the injury received from those,

[1] Narbrough names the forts in Bahía Corral, San Andreas, San Iago, San Juan, and San Pedro. See above, pp. 290, 507, 534, 540, Map 7 and Narbrough's plan of the 'Port oF Baldavia' (Plate 4). Don Carlos claims to have surrendered himself at fort San Luís. A fort named San Luís de Alba sited on a crag on Punta de Amargos was begun in 1658 but not completed until the early 1670s. Narbrough's description of the fort of San Iagua (for San Iago) or St James, states that it stood 'just by the woods side on a rise of a bank of five yards ascent from the sea', close to where he set Don Carlos ashore. See above, pp. 289, 504–5. It was clearly a small fort lower on the point. Don Carlos's letter to the Conde de Lemos was written 28 Jan. 1671. He may well have confused the name of the fort at which he surrendered if the completion of San Luis was then under discussion.

[2] Don Carlos's remark here is clearly intended to support the detention of Armiger and his party in violation of the conditions of a flag of truce, on the grounds that the English had hostile intentions.

[3] Sweden and Denmark. Presumably a reference to the Triple Alliance; see above, p. 662, n. 1.

who although they know her to be superior and their Queen[1] who holds power over them, dare to lose the respect and duty which they owe her.[2]

I beg Your Excellency to excuse my boldness and ignorance and ill manners, stating in conclusion that I will be able to supply [the information] which I have from overseas and that Your Noble Excellency may be pleased to forgive the pain and hurt of a loving heart which, zealous of the well-being of this eagle, dares to overcome the limitations of time while it might still do good considering that in the midst of dangers one must try to awaken her.

May your all powerful Excellency be the first who with wisdom and loyal zeal advises and reminds and is the means by which she [the eagle] opens her eyes and gathers strength. Then she still may with a little effort restore herself punishing [f. 22r] the inattentiveness and insolence of those who aspire to disturb the peace and tranquillity she enjoys and on the preservation of which depends and [rests] the greater safety of the Catholic faith.

Of the rest which has happened and occurred since the day that I arrived with the frigate at this port, Governor Don Pedro de Montoya[3] will bring you up to date. Regarding which gentleman, so as not to fall short [in courtesy], permit me to mention to Your Excellency his merits, parts and many gifts and, since Your Excellency knows them, you will be pleased to thank him for the favours which I have received from his honour as a guest, even as I received them knowing Your Excellency to be the principal instrument in providing them. May his Divine Majesty increase your life by many years for the comfort peace and preservation of such extended realms

Baldiuia January 28 1671,

Your Excellency's most faithful servant who kisses your hand

Carlos Henriques Clerque[4]

[*Endorsements:*][5]

A Declaration made by one Charles Henrique Clerck off the Proposalls made by the Royall Comp*ani*a for trade, to his Ma*jes*tie Anno 1663 — dated in Baldiuia 28 January 1671 a Towne or Citty in Westindia, & directed to the Gouernor of those Teritories. Baldivia 28 Jan*uary* <u>1671</u>.[6]

Declaration of the English Director given in the port of Valdiuia[7]

[1] Mariana of Austria, widow of Philip IV (1621–65), acting as regent for their son Carlos II (1665–1700) who was a minor.

[2] Don Carlos's extended metaphor is difficult to follow. Eagle is a female-gendered noun. Don Carlos's sentences switch between masculine and feminine usage. The translation retains the feminine gender given his reference to 'the Queen', presumably a studied allusion to the Queen Regent.

[3] The Governor of Baldivia, see above, pp. 521, n. 2; 524, n. 1.

[4] Don Carlos signs himself as Carlos Enrique Clerque in BL, Add 21539, f. 23v. In BL, Add 28457, the name is given as Carlos Henrriques Clerque.

[5] BL, Add 28457 has no endorsements. The endorsements on BL, Add 21539, f. 23v follow here.

[6] In English, see above, pp. 98–111.

[7] In Spanish, see above, p. 22, n. 4.

APPENDIX 1

The Legends on the Charts Drawn by John Narbrough

BL, Add MS88980C [Plate 1]
'A DRAUGHT OF PORT DISSIER HARBOWER: Latitud 48" = 7'S'

BL, Add MS88980C [Plate 3]
'A DRAUGHT OF PORTE SAN JULYAN in THE South EAST COAST OF AMARICA CALLEd PATAGONA.'

C: JONN NARBROGH FECIT: ANNO: 1670

THE NATIVES OF this land as they Apeered to us: June 22 Anno 1670

Here I Wintered: Anno 1670: And KiLLed many Ducks & Geese & Hars & osterages &c.
Here are Many Good Fowles in the winter.

Here are Good Store oF Mullets in Sumer And very Good Salt in A Pond: Seven mils NNW From Rock Point in Land.

The DrauGht oF Port S. Julyan in Patagonia in the South East Coast oF Amarica: it Lies in the Latitud oF 49 degres 08 minuts South. And in Longitud 63 degrs 10 minuts West From the Lizard oF England: the Compas Have 16^{d} 30^{m} variation Easterly: The Figuers Signifie Fathams oF water.

The Tide Rise Nere Fower Fathams one [on] the Springs: & Run Stronge it is A High Water at HalFe An Houer Past A Eleven oF the Clock one [on] the Change Day oF the Moone this is A Bard Harbower.'

BL, Add MS88980D [Plate 4]
A Draught oF the Port oF Baldavia in the Coast oF Chile in the South west Parte of Amarica: it lies in the Latt: oF 39 degres 55 minuts South: and in the Longitud From the Lizard oF England 70 degres 18 minuts west By the Account which I Keept From the Lizard in the yeare 1670: on Board His Majestis Shipp the Sweepstakes to Baldavia. The Figuers are Signifiing the Fadams oF water beFore the Porte: and So fare as I had oppertunity to Sound into the Porte: the Current Seets Generally out which is occationed by the Freshes out of the three Streams: the water is Fresh at the Six Fatham: and it is But Brackes [brackish] at the very mouth: the Soundinges is fine Black Sand all the Bay over

the outermost Shipp Signifie the Sweepstaks at Anchor: the inermost Shipp is a Spainesh Shipp which trads to Lima and Brings Recruts to Baldava: the boats under Saile are Spainesh Boats bound to the City oF Baldavia the other Boats Signifies the Sweepstakes Boats Seekinge for tradeinge with The inhabitants oF the Cuntry: the Spainards are Planted here and Slitly Fortified: in the Forte Sainte Peter there is nine great ordinance in the Fort Saint Iago Seven Great ordinance in the Fort S[t] Andrew and in the Fort S[t] John two: and at Baldavia five.
John Narbrough.

I Am in Formed that here is much Gold in this Land and that the Natives have wars with the Spainards and will not Permitt them to worke in the mines: the natives ar very Strong and great Numbers oF them all here A Bouts. My Auther is a Spainard A Sergante in Sainte Peters Forte.

I have drawne the Land in Culler as it is and with woods and hills: as here ar a great many: it is a very Good Cuntry as to what I saw of it: and Extream Rich oF Gold as I ame in Formed By the Spainesh Sergant and by Severall Indians as ar Subjecte to the Spainards which were aBoard oF me and would have Assisted me to Beat the Spainards out oF the Cuntry For they have a great anthopethy [antipathy] against the Spainards: these Forts are very meane ons and the Guns Stand open: here is But three Hundered Souldiers to mainetaine this garrison very few of them Knows the Euse [use] of fire Armes: their armes ar Long Lances and match lock muskets: the but Ends ar Plated with Sillver and the Hillts of the officers Swords are Beaten Gold: and all their CooKery furnituers is Sillver: the Commoditis oF this Porte is Gold Beazer Stons and Guianacos wooll.

The Highe Springe tids Rize Eight Foot and it is a high water at nine oF the Clock one [on] the Chang[e] day: the variation of the compass is Eight degrees Easterly: here I observided by the ☼ Amplytud.

BL Add MS5414,29, The 'Sloane Map' [Plate 5]
'A Mapp of the Streights of Magelan drawn by Capt*ai*n John Narbrough who Commanded his M*aj*e*s*ties Shipp the Sweepstakes through the Said Streights and Coasted the Shoare in Boates in Anno 1670 for Discovery there of.'

BL Maps K Top 124.84, The 'Royal Map' [Foldout]
THE LAND OF PATAGONA &C.THE DRAUGhT OF MAGELLAN STRAITS DRAWEN BY CAPTAIN JOHN NARBROUgh: ANN° 1670 ON BOARD HIS MAJESTIS ShIPP SWEEPSTAKS AS I PASED AND REPASED THE STRAITS

The Natives oF this Land as they Apeared unto me: Some oF them haveing Loose Garments of Beasts Skines Sewed to Gethers: others Naked; ther Weapons ar Bows & Arrows they are oF a Medle Stature, noe taler then Generally Englesh men are; they ar Tawny Coloured as the Natives in New England be; and they Daweb them Selves all over their Bodies with Greas & Red Earth; they are not obedient to any Supremecy, But Every one doth as it Seme Best to him Selve as I Could Perceive by them: the orniments these People have is Small Glistering Shells which the women have A bout their Necks: For Breaslets & Mussell Shells: I Saw Severall men & women & Children: But never Could

Perceive that they have Any thing of Vallew Amongst them, they were very Farmiliar with us the time I Staied with them which was three days: they Ar very Desierus to have Nives & hatchets & Nails & Fish hookes & Such Like trade: But they have nothinge to Return you for them but bows & Arrows & their Loose Garments: They made Singes to mee that their is Gold in the Mountaines over Porte Famin: But I Could never finde any: These People have a harse Language & Pronounce it much in the Throate they often Repeate ozse: what they mean by it I Could not Understand nor one word they Said: they are very intelledgable one to the other & talke much, they live like Beasts wanderinge to & frow from Place to Place to Git food, they have noe Settled habitation, neither do they Plant any or keepe any domistick Creatuer But doggs, which they many of them of A Mungerall Raze. These People would Easely be Brought to Under Standing & Knowledge with Cevill Useage: here are many People in the Straits one [on] Boath Sids, I Saw many firs &Smoaks one [on] the South Land at the Comeinge In which I Call South Ulster: they Goe from one Side to the other in their Cannoas: which is made of the Barke of trees & will Carry tenn or twelfe People in one of them, they Keepe much one [on] the South Side in the Summer time; the Land is of a Good Soile one [on] the East Parte of the Straits: one [on] Boath Sids: forom Cape Vergen Mary to Porte Famin Here is no wood one [on] either Sid till one Come up to Sweepstaks Bay: there the Woods Begin & Grows very thick: At Port Famin the Barke oF Some trees is Strong like Pepper & Ceniment.

In the West Parte of the Straits & in the South Sea: there is Very Lettle tide or Current Run Either way Soe As to hinder Navigation. The tide Rise & Fall a Bout Eight foote all the west parte of the Straits: It is much better to Come out of the South Sea & Soe Pase the Straits to the Eastwards into the north Sea: then it is to Pass the Straits, to the westward into the South Sea, For the wind is much westerly & Blow hard.

The Tide of Flod Comes from the South wards and Sets Strong into the Straits at the First Narrow: it keeps it Course as one [on] other Coasts, and Sets in Six houres & the Ebb Set out Six houres: The Flood Rise Perpendiculer in the first Narrow Better then three Fatham: & It is A high water In the Narrow at Eleven oF the Clock one [on] the Change day of the Moone: as I observed. the Tide Run boath Ebb & Flood Stronger then at Gravesend: But after it is Past the Narrow it is nothinge Soe Strong, at the Second Narrow the tide Rise about tenn foot & Runn of a meane Strength: & between Elezebeths Iland & the other Ile the tide Runn IndiferentStronge, But after it is past those Ilands it is but ordinary: and in all the west Parte of the Straits the tids are nothinge. Here is Noe Current in all the Straits: It is Tids which Set in & out according to the Moone: And if a man be Acquainted in the Straits: he may Ply tidworke as well as in the Chanell of England: It is much better to Come from the westward: then to Goe to the westward for the winds ar Much Given to Blow westerly: and that is the Caues the Navigation is dificult: other wise It would be as Easey Pased as through a River.
The Figuers in the Straits Signifieth the Fathams of water & the Anchors the Places I Anchored In: The Red Pricked line Sheweth the Track the Ship Sailed Through.

APPENDIX 2

Place-Names Given by Narbrough Still in Use Today

The majority of Narbrough's names have been translated into Spanish and some of them have been moved and no longer apply to the same features to which he gave them. In general the spelling of Narbrough's names has been taken from the 'Royal Map' (BL Maps K. Top 124.84). Those marked * are taken from the 'Sloane Map' (BL Add MS 5414,29), while those marked ** are not named on either and are taken from statements in the text. It should also be noted that not all the names given are recorded in the voyage texts as having been assigned by Narbrough.

Narbrough's name	*Modern name*	*Lat. South*	*Long. West*
Queen Katherine's Foreland*	Punta Catalina	52°32′	68°46′
Rocks Like Asses Ears*	Orejas de Burro	52°08′	69°32′
Sweepstaks Foreland	Sweepstakes Promontario	52°46′	70°24′
Oase Harbour	Ensenada Oazy	52°42′	70°33′
Sand Pointe	Punta Arenosa	53°08′	70°51′
Fresh water Bay	Bahía Agua Fresca	53°23′	70°58′
C. Monmouth	Cabo Monmouth	53°22′	70°27′
Woods Bay	Bahía Wood	53°49′	71°37′
Andrew Bay	Bahía Andrés	53°46′	71°45′
C. Coventry	Cabo Coventry	53°45′	71°51′
Port Gallant	Caleta (Puerto) Gallant	53°41′	72°00′
Fortescue Bay**	Bahía Fortescue	53°42′	72°00′
Secretary Wrenns Ile	Islote Wren	53°46′	72°05′
Charless Ile	Islas Charles	53°44′	72°06′
Jamess Ile	Isla James	53°42′	72°13′
Ruperts Ile	Isla Rupert	53°39′	71°12′
Monmouths Ile	Isla Monmouth	53°42′	72°11′
English Reach**	Paso Inglés	53°42′	72°07′
Whales P.	Punta Ballena	53°40′	72°15′
Whales Bay	Seno Ballena	53°40′	72°20′
C. Midleton*	Cabo Middleton	53°37′	72°16′
Passage Point**	Punta Pasaje	53°38′	72°12′
York Road	Rada York	53°34′	72°19′
Batcheller R.	Río Batchelor	53°33′	72°18′
Mussell Bay*	Bahía Mussel	53°37′	72°17′
Crooked Reach**	Paso Tortuoso	53°33′	72°30′

C. Munday	Cabo Monday	53°11′	73°24′
C. Up Right	Cabo Upright	53°05′	73°36′
Tusday Bay	Bahía Tuesday	52°51′	74°27′
Westminster Iles	Grupo Westminster	52°36′	74°26′
Westminster Hall**	Isla Westminster Hall	52°37′	74°22′
The Lawyers Iles	Islas Lawyers	52°36′	74°20′
South Desolation	Isla Desolación	53°05′	74°00′
Cape Piller	Cabo Pilar	52°44′	74°40′
Suger Loofe I.	Islote Pan de Azúcar	52°25	75°04′

APPENDIX 3

Personnel: Recruitment and Pay

Recruitment

The Captains and Lieutenants in the fleet held their authority by virtue of commissions from the Lord High Admiral, who appointed them to a specific ship for as long as that ship remained in service. The master, boatswain, gunner, carpenter, purser, cook, chaplain and surgeon were appointed by warrant. Of these the master, chaplain and surgeon served only for the period of active service of the ship. The remainder, formed the basis of the reserve crew who maintained the ship 'in ordinary' while laid up and not in service. Below the warrant officers came the petty officers, the master's, boatswain's, gunner's and carpenter's mates, the midshipmen, quartermasters, coxswain and the swabber, who were appointed on an internal basis by the captain in consultation with his officers.[1]

The normal method of entry for the commissioned officers was either as a boy or as volunteer 'per order', although officers might also be appointed directly without going through either of these routes. Boys started as a captain's or other officer's servant at the age of 9 or 10, rising through the various ranks.[2] This system was regularized in 1662–3 to make them apprentices, indentured for seven years. The 'volunteer' system was instituted in 1661 and was originally intended to get young gentlemen to learn navigation and seamanship to qualify them for a commission. It entailed service on several voyages by authority of a royal letter to the ship's captain, at a midshipman's rate of pay. List-books were kept with certificates and recommendations for both commissioned and warrant posts, and when vacancies occurred the position was filled by appointment from them.[3]

In peacetime there were generally enough volunteers to man the fleet. Crews were recruited by the ship's captain to serve in a specific ship for a specific voyage, frequently from his home area, where seamen were generally willing to serve under a well-known and respected captain. In wartime it was necessary to resort to compulsion, and men were pressed into service. Chartered companies of watermen and fishermen were supposed to supply quotas, counties and cities were also assessed for quotas according to the size of their seafaring communities, returning merchantmen were a prime target for the press gang, and small numbers of foreigners were also pressed.[4]

[1] Davies, *Gentlemen*, p. 11.

[2] This would appear to have been the method by which Narbrough joined, serving as a cabin-boy under his kinsman Christopher Myngs, and probably following him from ship to ship. Dyer, *Life*, p. 8.

[3] Davies, *Gentlemen*, pp. 16–17. The examination for Lieutenant was not introduced until 1677, as a result of complaints from Narbrough (then commanding in the Mediterranean) of the 'defectiveness' of his lieutenants 'in their seamanship'. Tanner, *Catalogue*, I, pp. 202–5.

[4] Davies, *Gentlemen*, pp. 69–77.

Pay

The wages paid to seamen had been set under the Commonwealth in 1653. At the Restoration, on 28 September 1660, the Duke of York informed the Principal Officers, 'I have thought fit to direct that you continue to allow all Wages and Sallaries, according to later Practice, until farther Consideration be had thereof, and you receive Order to the Contrary.'[1]

The Scale of wages per 28-day month for a fourth rate included: Captain £10 10s 0d, Lieutenant £3 10s 0d, Master £4 6s 2d, Master's Mate £2 7s 10d, Boatswain £2 2s 0d, Carpenter £2 10s 0d, Gunner £2 10s 0d, Purser £2 10s 0d, Midshipman £1 13s 9d, Quartermaster £1 10s 0d, Able Seaman £1 4s 0d, Ordinary Seaman £0 19s 0d, and Boy £0 9s 6d.[2] Rates of pay in the Merchant Navy were similar, but generally greater in time of war,[3] These compare with average daily wages ashore of Carpenter 1s 8d, Mason 1s 6d, Tiler 1s 6½d, Labourer to artisan 1s 0d, and Farm labourer 10½d. London rates were higher, Carpenter 3s 6d and Mason 3s 0d.[4] Allowing 6 working days per week the comparable 4-weekly wages are: Carpenter £2 0s 0d, Mason £1 16s 0d, Tiler £1 17s 0d, Labourer to artisan £1 4s 0d, Farm labourer £1 1s 0d, London Carpenter £4 4s 0d and London Mason £3 12s 0d. Comparing these rates it must be born in mind that the sailor was fed (at 6d per day in harbour and 8d per day at sea, 8¾d per day for ships going 27° southward[5]) and did not pay rent for his lodging, while the worker ashore paid both these and was also liable to periods of unemployment. There were also possibilities for prize money and bounties, which did not arise on Narbrough's voyage.[6]

Ships' Companies were generally paid at the end of a commission,[7] normally in cash in peacetime, but in wartime usually by ticket, which could be redeemed for cash at the Ticket Office.[8] This was a certificate signed by the officers of the ship, which, when countersigned by the navy board was the sailor's warrant for payment from the treasury office. The original purpose was to obviate the requirement to have large sums of money available wherever a ship might be paid off. The system was in use in early Stuart times and throughout the Commonwealth period. Tickets were printed with counterfoils as early as August 1654, but manuscript tickets were not abandoned until 1657.[9] The chronic

[1] James, *Memoirs*, p. 3.

[2] This scale (or part of it) is given in: Powell and Timings, *Rupert and Monck*, pp. 178–9; Rodger, *Command*, p. 619; Davies, *Pepys's Navy*, pp. 103, 122; Davies, *Gentlemen*, pp, 51, 79; Oppenheim, *History*, pp. 314, 360; Fox, *Four Days' Battle*, pp. 32–3. Oppenheim and Fox give the Captain's pay as £10 0s 0d.

[3] See Davis, *Rise of the English Shipping*, pp. 133–6.

[4] Thorold Rogers, *History*, pp. 668–9: Clark, 'Farm Wages', p. 502.

[5] Tanner, *Catalogue*, I, p. 155.

[6] The principle of prize money was long-standing, see Twiss, *Black Book*, I, pp. 21–3, 135, 145–7. For details, see Davies, *Gentlemen*, pp. 55–6, 80–81; Davies, *Pepys's Navy*, pp. 104–5, 112–13.

[7] Barlow while serving in the frigate *Monke*, 58, Captain Thomas Penrose, having been pressed, records that the Commissioners boarded the ships anchored in the Hope before the Four Days' Battle in 1666 and paying eight or nine months' wages, and 'keeping nine more in hand for fear of our running away from the ship'. Again while riding at the Nore Buoy he received a years pay in 1666. Lubbock, *Barlow's Journal*, pp. 93, 115, 130.

[8] This was a major cause of resentment among seamen, since going to London to exchange their tickets for cash was an expensive and time-consuming activity. The result was tickets were frequently sold to ticket-brokers at considerable loss to the sailor. Davies, *Gentlemen*, p. 82. See also Tanner, *Administration*, pp. 42–3, n. 196, for a detailed description of the system.

[9] Tanner, *Administration*, pp. 42–3, n. 196. See also Davies, *Pepys's Navy*, pp. 122–3.

shortage of cash resulted in ships being kept in commission since there was no money to pay their people, and wages being in arrears for years with consequent hardship for the sailors and causing discontent, rioting and mutiny.[1] When a ship was paid the Comptroller or one of the other Principal Officers was required to attend, a rule that was relaxed by the Duke of York on 13 June 1672.[2] Prompt payment was a matter for comment, for example in 1628 when the fleet returned from La Rochelle 'the men were surprised and delighted to find they were to be paid. "The seamen are much joyed with the Lord Treasurer's care to pay them so suddenly".'[3]

The Duke of York ordered an additional payment to be made to the Ship's Company for short allowance of victuals.[4] Narbrough records that his company went onto 'six men to fower mens alowance all Sorts of Provissions' on 27 September 1669 and returned to full allowance on 14 March 1670/71, for which they were each paid £5 9s 6d.[5]

[1] Tanner, *Catalogue*, I, pp. 140–44; Oppenheimer, *Administration*, pp. 187n, 286–8, 316, 320, 369; Davies, *Pepys's Navy*, pp. 122–3.

[2] James, *Memoirs*, p. 247.

[3] Oppenheim, *Administration*, p. 235, quoting State Papers.

[4] James, *Memoirs*, pp. 15–16. James, Duke of York to Sir John Lawson, 21 Feb. 1660/61. Oppenhheim, *Administration*, p. 326, notes that, in 1653, 2d per day was allowed when the sailors had to drink water instead of beer 'to reconcile them to the change'.

[5] See above, p. 364.

APPENDIX 4

Subsequent Publications Containing Narbrough's 'The Voyage to the South-Sea', 1694.

English

1. *Navigantium atque itinerantium bibliotheca, or, A Compleat Collection of Voyages and Travels &c*, vol. II, pp. 801–15, published by John Harris, London, 1705.

This follows the original 1694 edition quite closely, but has been rewritten in some places and contains a number of errors. This version was relied on by Thomas Lediard in *The Naval History of England &c.*, London, 1735, vol. II, pp. 593–4 which contains a brief précis ending 'The Journal of this Voyage, which we have in *Harris*, being a meer Seaman's Journal, containing little more than the Winds, Soundings, Distances and Bearings of Places, but being very barren of Adventures and Action, I have for Brevity's sake contracted it within this narrow Compass.'

2. John Callander, *Terra Australis Cognita or Voyages to the Terra Australis or Southern Hemisphere &c.*, Edinburgh, 1768, vol. II, pp. 422–518.
This contains an almost verbatim reprint with a few minor typographic changes and the exclusion of the diagram 'The *Crosers Stars*' found on p. 15 of the original. On pp. 518–19 Callander remarks 'This Journal has always been reckoned the best drawn up, and the most useful of any wrote by the navigators to *Magellanica*, and accordingly we find it often appealed to by *Frezier, Anson* and other seamen in their accounts of those coasts.'[1]

3. James Burney, *A Chronological History of the Voyages and Discoveries in the South Sea or Pacific Ocean, Part III*, London 1813, pp. 316–76, with remarks on the Charts of the Strait of Magellan, pp. 376–82.
This contains extracts from the 1694 edition with additions from Captain John Wood's published account and Lieutenant Nathaniel Peckett's MS journal. In his introduction to the voyage Burney states that Smith and Walford 'received the original Journal of Captain Narbrough from the then Secretary of the Admiralty, the Hon. Samuel Pepys. Some want of skill in drawing up the abridgement has occasioned breaks in the narrative; but the

[1] I have been unable to find any mention of it in Frézier, *Voyage to the South Sea*. There is a reference to 'gathering Memoirs for drawing of the chart [of the Strait of Magellan]' on p. 285 but this, while showing a number of tracks of French vessels starting in 1706, has no reference to Narbrough, nor indeed would his chart appear to have contributed to its production. He does mention that Monsieur de Lisle showed him '*English* Memoirs', p. 287, which might be a reference to Narbrough's account. For Commodore Anson's use of Narbrough, see above, p. 82. Walter, *Anson's Voyage*, pp. 58, 61, 64, 65, 88–90 and 92. See above and pp. 79–82, for other users of Narbrough's account.

parts deficient can be supplied from other sources, of which the principal is the manuscript journal of one of Narbrough's Lieutenants, Nathaniel Pecket, which has been preserved in the British Museum.'[1]

4. John Narborough, *An Account of Several Voyages to the South and North*, facsimile of the first edition by Nico Israel, Amsterdam, Da Capo Press New York, 1969.

French

5. *Voyages de François Coreal aux Indes Occidentales contenant ce qu'il y a vû de plus remarquable pendant son séjour depuis 1666 jusqu'en 1679 ... & le voyage de Narborough à la Mer du Sud par le détroit de Magellan, etc.*, Paris 1722.
The French translation of Narbrough's voyage is found in vol. II, pp. 139–318, and is preceded by a track chart. An edition was also published in Amsterdam, 1722, and although Narborough's voyage is included in the title it is not normally present in this edition.

German

6. Johann Joachim Schwabe, *Allgemeine historie der Reisenzu Wasser und zu Lande &c*, vol. 12, Leipzig, 1754, pp. 29–49.
The German version, entitled 'Reise des Ritters Johann Narborough', covers the period from arrival on the South American coast and passage through the Strait of Magellan in detail, but the outward and return passages and sojourn in Valdivia are much abbreviated.

Subsequent Eighteenth-Century Publications Containing William Hack(e)'s *John Wood's* Voyage through the Streights of Magellan

English

1. *Captain William Dampier's Voyages around the World*, James Knapton, London 1729.
Knapton republished Hack(e)'s publication of *John Wood's Voyage thro' the Streights of Magellan* as volume IV of the above. Dampier's Voyages, together with *A Voyage Round the World containing an Account of Captain Dampier's Expedition into the South Seas in the Ship George, In the Years 1703 and 1704 &c. together with the Author's Voyage from Amapalla on the West Coast of Mexico to EAST-INDIA*, by William Funnell, originally published by Knapton, London, 1707.

[1] Now the British Library.

Burney, Vol. 3, states, on p. 316, that 'The Captain Wood whose name is prefixed to this second narrative [Hack(e)'s *Collection*], was a Mr. John Wood, who sailed with Captain Narbrough to the South Sea as Master's mate.' This statement is incorrect in that Mr John Wood was not the Master's mate, a position held by Mr Giles Wood, but was apparently a gentleman volunteer.

French

2. *Voyage de Guillaume Dampier aux Terres aux Terres Australes, A la Nouvelle Hollande, &c. Ou l'on a joint: I. Le Voyage du Capitaine Wood traverse le Detroit de Magellan &c.* Tome Cinquiéme, A Amsterdam chez la Veuve de Paul Marret, 1712.

BIBLIOGRAPHY

PRIMARY SOURCES

Manuscript Sources

London, The British Library

Additional MS

Add MS 17938 A, C.
Add MS 21536.
Add MS 21539.
Add MS 28457.
Add MS 5414,29.
Add MS 88980 A, B, C, D, E.

Sloane MS

Sloane MS 46 A, B.
Sloane MS 86.
Sloane MS 819.
Sloane MS 3833.

Maps

Maps K Top 124.84.
Maps 7 Tab. 122

London, The National Archives, Kew

Admiralty Records

ADM 33/113.
ADM 33/121.
ADM 39/2510.
ADM 106/2908.

Colonial Office

CO 1/15.
CO 1/29.
CO 1/33.

Probate

PROB 11/370, 385.
PROB 11/414/93.
PROB 11/483/275.
PROB 11/488/196.

State Papers

SP 89/10.
SP 94/54.
SP 94/55.

Treasury Solicitor
TS 21/3.

London, The Royal Society, Carlton House Terrace
CI.P/7i/32.

Oxford, Bodleian Libraries, University of Oxford
Rawlinson MS
Rawl. A. 318.

Cambridge, Pepys Library, Magdelen College, University of Cambridge
Pepys MS 2555.

Mapperton, Dorset, Archive of the Earls of Sandwich
Journal of the First Earl of Sandwich, vols 9, 10.

Taunton, United Kingdom Hydrographic Office
A List c.80.

New Haven, USA, Beinecke Rare Book and Manuscript Library, Yale University
The James Marshall and Marie-Louise Osborn Collection
Osborn b394.

Paris, France, Bibliothèque Nationale de France
BN Mélange Colbert 31, 5260557.

Madrid, Spain, Archivo Histórico Nacional
Diversos, Cartas de Indias 392.

Madrid, Spain, Biblioteca Nacional de España
BNE, MS 18719[28].
BNE, MS 18719[29].
BNE, MS 2341.

Sevilla, Spain, Archivo General de Indias
Audiencia de Lima, leg. 72, 73, 74.

Lima, Peru, Biblioteca Nacional
Lima MS F 160.
Lima MS B 283.

Printed Primary Sources

Anderson, R. C., *Journals and Narratives of the Third Dutch War*, Navy Records Society, vol. 86, 1946.
Armitage, Sir George R, *Middlesex Pedigrees as collected by Richard Munday in Harleian Manuscript No. 1551*, Harleian Society, vol. 65, London, 1914.
Ayala, Guaman Poma de, *The First New Chronicle and Good Government, 1615–16*, trans. and ed., David Frye, Indianopolis, 2006.
Bayer, Johann, *Uranometria, omnium asterismorum continens schemata, nova methodo delineata, aereis laminis expressa*, Berlin, 1661.

Beaglehole, J. C., ed. *The Endeavour Journal of Joseph Banks, 1768–1771*, Sydney, 1962.

Beer, E. S. de, ed., *The Diary of John Evelyn*, Oxford, 1959.

Benton, Lauren and Benjamin Straumann, 'Acquiring Empire by Law. Doctrine to Early Modern Practice', *Law and History Review*, 28, no.1, 2010, pp. 1–38.

Binning, Thomas, *A light to the Art of Gunnery &c.*, London 1689.

Black, Jeannette D. *The Blathwayt Atlas*, 2 vols, Providence, 1970, 1975.

Blanckley, Thomas Riley, *A Naval Expositor &c.*, London, 1750; reprinted Rochester, 1988.

Bougainville, Louis de, *A Voyage Round the World*, London, 1772, trans. John Reinhold Foster, Amsterdam, New York, 1969.

Bulkeley, John and John Cummins, *A Voyage to the South Seas by His Majesty's Ship the Wager in the years 1740–1741*, London, 1743; 2nd edn Philadelphia 1757; 3rd edn London 1927.

Campbell, R. J., ed., 'The Journal of HMS *BEAGLE* in the Strait of Magellan by Pringle Stokes, Commander RN 1827', in Herbert K. Beals et al., *Four Travel Journals: The Americas, Antarctica, and Africa, 1775–1874*, Hakluyt Society, 3rd ser., 18, London, 2007, pp. 141–251.

Carrington, Hugh, ed., *The Discovery of Tahiti: A Journal of the Second Voyage of the H.M.S. Dolphin round the World ,under the Command of Captain Wallis, R.N., in the Years 1766, 1767, and 1768, Written by her Master, George Robertson*, Hakluyt Society, 2nd ser., 98, London, 1948.

Coreal, François, *Voyages de François Coreal aux Indies Occidentales contenant ce qu'il y a vû de plus remarquable pendant son séjour depuis 1666 jusqu'en 1679 ... & le voyage de Narborough à la Mer du Sud par le détroit de Magellan, etc.*, Paris, 1722.

Dampier, William, *A New Voyage Round the World, describing particularly, the Isthmus of America, several coasts and islands in the West Indies ...*, London 1697[–1698].

—. *Voyage de Guillaume Dampier aux Terres Australes &c.* Tome Cinquiéme, Amsterdam, 1712.

Doncker, Henry, *The Sea Atlas or the Watter World, shewing all the Sea Coasts of ye known parts of y earth with a generall description of the same*, Amsterdam, 1663.

Drake, Sir Francis, *The World Encompassed,* London, 1628; facs. edn, Cleveland, 1966.

Dunmore, John, ed. *The Pacific Journal of Louis-Antoine de Bougainville 1767–1768*, Hakluyt Society, 3rd ser., 9, London, 2002.

Frézier, Amédée François, *A Voyage to the South Sea and along the Coasts of Chili and Peru in the years 1712, 1713 and 1714, [Translated from the French]*, ... London, 1717.

Gallagher. Robert E., *Byron's Journal of his Circumnavigation 1764–1766*, Hakluyt Society, 2nd ser., 122, Cambridge, 1964.

Gellibrand, Henry, *A Discourse Mathematical on the Variation of the Magneticall Needle together with its admirable diminution lately discovered*, London 1635.

Gentili, Alberico, *De Jure Belli Libri Tres*, 1612, trans. John C. Rolfe, vol. 2, Oxford, 1933.

Glenn, J. Ames, ed., *En Nome de Deus: The Journal of the First Voyage of Vasco da Gama to India, 1497–1499*, Leiden, 2009.

Goell, Kermit, ed., *A Sea Grammar: with plaine exposition of Smiths accidence for young sea-men, enlarged*, London 1970.

Hacke, William, *A collection of original voyages: containing, I. Capt. Cowley's Voyage round the globe. II. Capt. Sharp's Journey over the Isthmus of Darien. III. Capt. Wood's Voyage thro' the Streights of Magellan. IV. Mr. Roberts's Adventures among the Corsairs of the Levant, etc. ... With ... maps and draughts. Published by Capt. W. H.*, London, 1699.

Hakluyt, Richard, *A Particuler Discourse Concerning the Greate Necessitie and manifold Commodyties that are like to Growe to this realm of Englande by the Westerne Discoueries lately Attempted. Written in the Yere 1584. By Richarde Hackluyt of Oxforde Known as Discourse of Western Planting*, ed. David B. Quinn and Alison M. Quinn, Hakluyt Society, extra ser., 45, London, 1993.

—, *The Principall Navigations Voiages and Discoveries of the English Nation*, London, 1589; facs. edn, Hakluyt Society, extra ser., xxxix, 2 vols, Cambridge, 1965.

—. *The Principal Navigations, Voiages, Traffiques and Discoveries of the English Nation*, 3 vols, London, 1598–1600.

Hartgill, George, *Astronomical tables shewing the declinations, right ascentions, and aspects of three hundred sixty five of the most principall fixed stars ... First invented by George Hartgill ... And now reduced to this our age by John and Timothy Gadbury*, London, 1656.

Heylyn, Peter, *Cosmographie in four books containing the Chorographie and History of the World*, bk 4, 3rd edn, London, 1665.

Houtman, Frederick de, *Spraek ende Woordboeck, in de Maleysche ende Madagaskarsche*, Amsterdam, 1603.

Howes, Derek and Norman J. W. Thrower, eds, *A Buccaneer's Atlas: Basil Ringrose's South Sea Waggoner*, Berkeley, Los Angeles, Oxford, 1992.

Ingram, Bruce S., ed., *Three Sea Journals of Stuart Times*, London, 1936.

James, Captain Thomas, *The Dangerous Voyage of Capt. Thomas James in his intended Discovery of the North West Passage*, 1633; 2nd edn, London, 1740.

James, Duke of York, *Memoirs of English Affairs, Chiefly Naval, 1660 to 1673*, London, 1729.

Kepler, Johannes, *Tabulæ Rudolphinæ*, Ulm, 1627.

King, Captain P. Parker, and Captain Robert Fitz-Roy, *Narrative of the Surveying Voyages of His Majesty's Ships Adventure and Beagle Between the years 1826 and 1836 describing their Examination of the Southern Shores of South America and the Beagle's circumnavigation of the globe*, 3 vols, London, 1839.

Knighton, C. S., and D. M. Loades, eds, *The Anthony Roll of Henry VIII's Navy*, Navy Records Society, Occasional Publications, vol. 12, Cambridge, 2000.

Latham, Robert and William Matthews, eds, *The Diary of Samuel Pepys*, vols IX, X, London, 1983.

— and Charles Knighton, transcr., *Samuel Pepys and the Second Dutch War*, Navy Records Society, vol. 133, Aldershot, 1995.

Lavery, Brian, ed., *Deane's Doctrine of Naval Architecture*, 1670, London, 1981.

Lightbody, James, *The Mariners Jewel*, London, 1695.

Locke John, *Two Treatises of Government*, London, 1689.

López, J. L., *Decission de la Real Audiencia de Los Reyes en Favour de la Regalia, i Real jurisdicion, sobre el Articulo dos vezes remetido, en la causa de OLIBEROS BELIN llamado comunmente DON CARLOS CLERQUE*, Lima, 1682.

Manwayring, Sir Henry, *The Seaman's Dictionary &c.*, London 1644, facs. reprint, Menston, 1972.

Markham, Albert Hastings, *The Voyages and Works of John Davis the Navigator*, Hakluyt Society, 1st ser., 69, London, 1880.

McCarl, Clayton, ed., *Francisco de Seyxas y Lovera, Piratas y contrabandistsas de ambas Indias y estado presente de ellas* (1693), Coruña, 2011.

Milet-Mureau, L. A., ed., *A Voyage Round the World performed in the Years 1785, 1786, 1787 and 1788 by the Boussole and Astrolabe Under the Command of J. F. G. de la Pérouse ... Translated from the French*, London, 1799; reprint Amsterdam, 1968.

Mugaburu, F., *Chronicle of Colonial Lima 1640–97*, ed. R. R. Miller, Norman, OK, 1975.

Narborough, John, 'The voyage to the South-Sea', in *An Account of Several Late Voyages & Discoveries to the South and North &c.*, London 1694.

Nye, Nathaniel, *The Art of Gunnery. Wherein is described the true way to make all sorts of gunpowder ... To make divers sorts of artificiall fire-works, etc.*, London, 1647.

Oppenheim, M., ed., *The Naval Tracts of Sir William Monson*, Navy Records Society, vols 22, 23, 42, 45, 47, London, 1902–14.

Perrin, W. G., ed., *Boteler's Dialogues*, Navy Records Society, vol. 65, Colchester, London and Eton, 1929.

Phillips, Carla Rahn, ed., *The Struggle for the South Atlantic: The Armada of the Strait, 1581–1584*, Hakluyt Society, 3rd ser., 31, London, 2016.

Phipps, Constantine John, *A Voyage towards the North Pole undertaken at His Majesty's Command, 1773*, London, 1774.

Powell, The Rev. J. R. and E. K. Timings, eds, *The Rupert and Monck Letter Book 1666*, Navy Records Society, vol. 112, London and Colchester, 1969.

Purchas, Samuel, *Purchas his Pilgrimage or Relations of the World and the Religions Observed*, London, 1613.

Rale[i]gh, Sir Walter, 'A Discourse of the first Invention of Shipping', in *Judicious and Select Essays and Observations*, London, 1650, pp. 1–42.

Rowse, A. L. and Robert O. Dougan, eds, *The World Encompassed of Sir Francis Drake, 1628 and The Relation of a Wonderfull Voiage by William Cornelison Schouten, 1619*, Cleveland, 1966.

Rutter, Owen, ed., *The Log of the Bounty: being Lieutenant William Bligh's log of the proceedings of His Majesty's armed vessel Bounty in a voyage to the South Seas,* London, 1937.

Sarmiento de Gambóa, Pedro de, *Viage al Estrecho de Magellanes por P. Sarmiento de Gamboa en los años de 1579 y 1580, y noticia de la expedicion que despues hizo para poblarle*, Madrid, 1768.

Schouten, Cornelison, *The Relation of a Wonderfull Voiage made by William Cornelison Schouten*, London 1619; facs. reprint, Cleveland, 1966.

Scott, James Brown, ed., Ralph van Deman Magoffin, trans., *The Freedom of the Sea; or, the right which belongs to the Dutch to take part in the East Indian trade. A dissertation by Hugo Grotius. (Mare Liberum, etc.) Translated, with a revision of the Latin text of 1633*, New York, 1916.

Seldon, John, *Of the Dominion, or, Ownership of the Sea two books ... Written at first in Latin, and entituled, Mare Clausum ... Translated ... with som additional evidences and discourses by Marchamont Nedham*, London, 1652.

Seller, John, *The English Pilot, the First Book describing the sea-coasts... in the whole Northern Navigation*, London, 1671.

—, *Practical Navigation: or, An introduction to that whole art. Containing I. Several definitions in geometry, astronomy, geography, and navigation. 2. A new and exact kalender, etc.*, 4th edn, London, 1680; reprint. New York, 1993.

—, *The Sea-Gunner: shewing the practical part of Gunnery as it is used at Sea ... To which is added an appendix, shewing the use of a proportional scale, etc.*, London, 1691.

S[harpe], E., *Britains Busse or A Computation as well of the Charge of a Busse or Herring-Fishing Ship. As also of the gaine and profit thereby. &c.* London, 1615; reprinted in John B. Hattendorf, introduction, *Englands way to win wealth, and Employ Ships and Marriners* (1614) *&c.*, New York, 1992.

Skelton, R. A., trans. and ed., *Magellan's Voyage: A Narrative Account of the First Circumnavigation by Antonio Pigafetta*, 2 vols, New Haven and London, 1969.

Smith, John. *A Sea Grammar with the plaine exposition of Smiths Accidence for young sea-men, enlarged. Diuided into fifteene chapters: what they are you may partly conceiue by the contents. Written by Captaine John Smith, sometimes gouernour of Virginia*, London, 1627.

Sturmy, Captain Samuel, *The Mariners Magazine; or, Sturmy's Mathematical and practical arts* ..., 3rd edn, London 1684.

Tanner, J. R., *Samuel Pepys's Naval Minutes*, Navy Record Society, vol. 20, 1926.

Tapp, John, *The Sea-Mans Kalender or an Ephimerides of the Sun, Moon and certain of the most notable fixed Stars &c., Newly calculated and corrected by Henry Phillippes*, London, 1669.

Taylor, E. G. R., ed., *The Original Writings & Correspondence of the two Richard Hakluyts*, Hakluyt Society, 2nd ser., 76, 77, London, 1935.

—, *A Regiment for the Sea*, Hakluyt Society, 2nd ser., 121, Cambridge, 1963.

Vargas y Ponce, Josef de, *Relacion del último viage al Estrecho de Magallanes de la Fregata de S.M.* María de la Cabeza *en los años 1785 y 1786*, Madrid, 1788.

—, *Apéndice a la Relacion ... que contiene el Paquebotes* Santa Casilda *y de* Santa Eulalia *para completar el reconocimiento del Estrecho en los años 1788 y 1789*, Madrid, 1793.

Vea, A. de, 'Relación diaria del viaje marítimo y descripción de las costas Sur', *Anuario Hidrográfico de le Marina de Chile*, XI, BN (Santiago de Chile), 1886, pp. 540–96.

Vitoria, Francisco de, *Political Writings*, ed. Anthony Pagden and Jeremy Lawrance, Cambridge, 1991.

Wallis, Helen, ed., *Carteret's Voyage Round the World*, Hakluyt Society, 2nd. ser., 124, 125, Cambridge, 1965.

Warner, Sir George, ed., *The Libelle of Englyshe Polycye A Poem on the use of Sea-Power, 1436*, Oxford, 1926.

Watson, Alan, trans. and ed., *Digest of Justinian*, 2 vols, Philadelphia, 1985.

Williamson, James A., ed., *The Observations of Sir Richard Hawkins, from the text of 1622, with introduction, notes and appendices*, London, 1933.

Wright, Edward, *Certain Errors in Navigation Detected and Corrected by Edw. Wright. With Additions that were not in the former Editions*, London 1657.

Wood, John , 'Capt. Wood's Voyage thro' the Streights of Magellan', in William Hacke, *A collection of original voyages*, London 1699.

—, *Le Voyage du Capitaine Wood a travers le Detroit de Magellan, &c.* in *Dampier*, Guillaume, *Voyage de Guillaume Dampier aux Terres Australes &c.* vol. V, Amsterdam, 1712.

SECONDARY SOURCES

Printed Works

Albion, Robert G., 'The Problem of Timber in the Royal Navy', *The Mariner's Mirror*, 38, 1952, pp. 4–22.

Andrews, Charles M., *British Committees, Commissions, and Councils of Trade and Plantations 1622–1675*, Baltimore, 1908.

Andrews, William J. H., *The Quest for Longitude*, Cambridge, MA, 1996.

Arbell, Mordecai, *Spanish and Portuguese Jews in the Caribbean and the Guianas: A Bibliography*, Providence, RI, 1999.

Baigent, Elizabeth, 'Collins, Greenvile', *Oxford Dictionary of National Biography*, Oxford, 2004; online edn September 2010 [http://www.oxforddnb.com.libproxy.wlu.ca/view/article/5938, accessed 7 March 2017] .

Barlow, Peter, *Essay on the Strength of Timber*, 3rd edn, London, 1826.

Barras Arana, Diego, *Historia General de Chile*, vols IV, V, 2nd edn, Santiago de Chile, 1999–2000.

Beckles, Willson, *The Great Company (1667–1871): Being a History of the Honourable Company of Merchants-Adventurers Trading into Hudson's Bay*, Toronto, 1899.

Bennett, J. A., *The Divided Circle: A History of Instruments for Astronomy, Navigation and Surveying*, Oxford, 1987.

Benton, Lauren and Benjamin Straumann, 'Acquiring Empire by Law: From Roman Doctrine to Early Modern European Practice', *Law and History Review*, 28, no. 1, pp. 1–38, 2010.

Bernard, Toby, 'Southwell, Sir Robert (1635–1688)', *Oxford Dictionary of National Biography*, Oxford, 2004 [http://www.oxforddnb.com/view/article/26066, accessed 19 December 2016].

Berry, William, *Encyclopædia Heraldica, or Complete Dictionary of Heraldry*, 4 vols, London, n.d. [1828].

Boccara, G., 'Poder colonial e etnicidade no Chile: territorialização e reestruturação entre os Mapuche da época colonial', *The Hispanic American Historical Review*, 79, no. 3, 1999, pp. 425–61.

Book of British Birds, London, 1969.

Borrero, L. A., 'The Origins of Ethnographic Subsistence Patterns in Fuego-Patagonia', in C. McEwan, L. A., Borrero and A. Prieto, eds, *Patagonia: Natural History, Prehistory, and Ethnography at the Uttermost End of the Earth*, Princeton Legacy Library, London. 1997, pp. 60–61.

Boxer, C. R., *The Portuguese Seaborne Empire*, London, 1969; reprinted Lisbon, 1997.

Bradley, Peter T., 'Narborough's Don Carlos', *The Mariner's Mirror*, 72, London, 1986, pp. 465–75.

—, *The Lure of Peru*, Basingstoke, 1989.

—, *Pirates on the Coast of Peru, 1598–1701*, Raleigh NC, lulu.com, 2008.

—, *Spain and the Defence of Peru, 1579–1700: Royal Reluctance and Colonial Self-Reliance*, Raleigh NC, lulu.com, 2011.

—, *The Last Buccaneers in the South Sea 1686–95*, Raleigh, NC, 2015.

Bridges, E. Lucas, *Uttermost Parts of the Earth*, London, 1948.

Burke's Peerage and Baronetage, 107th edn, Wilmington, DE, 2003.

Burney, J., *A Chronological History of the Voyages and Discoveries in the South Sea or Pacific Ocean*, 5 vols, London, 1803–17; reprint. Amsterdam and New York 1967.

Burney, William, *A New and Universal Dictionary of the Marine being a copious explanation of the technical terms and phrases usually employed in the construction, equipment, machinery, movements and military as well as naval operations of ships: with such parts of astronomy and navigation, as will be found useful to Practical Navigators*, London, 1830.

Callandar, John, *Terra Australis Cognita or Voyages to the Terra Australis &c.* Edinburgh, 3 vols, 1766–8; reprint. Amsterdam, 1967.

Campbell, John, *The Lives of the Admirals and Other Eminent British Seamen &c.*, 4 vols, London, 1742–4.

Carpenter, Kenneth J., *The History of Scurvey and Vitamin C*, Cambridge, 1986.

Chacon, R. J. and R. G. Mendoza, *Latin American Indigenous Warfare and Ritual Violence*, Tucson, AZ,, 2007.

Chapman, Anne, *European Encounters with the Yamana People of Cape Horn before Darwin*, Cambridge, 2010.

Charnock, John, *Biographia Navalis*, 6 vols, London 1794; reprint. Milton Keynes, 2009.

Clark, Gregory, 'Farm Wages and Living Standards in the Industrial Revolution: England, 1670–1869', *Economic History Review*, 54, no. 3, 2001, pp. 477–505.

Collinge, J. M., *Navy Board Officials 1660–1832*, London, 1978.

Collins, Greenvile, *Great-Britain's Coasting Pilot*, London 1753.

Cortesão, A. and A. Teixeira da Mota, *Portugaliae Monumenta Cartographica*, 5 vols, Lisbon 1960; reprint. Lisbon 1987.

Cunningham, Robert O., *Notes on the Natural History of the Strait of Magellan and West Coast of Patagonia*, Edinburgh, 1871.

Davies, J. D., *Gentlemen and Tarpaulins*, Oxford, 1991.

—, '"*A Lover of the Sea, and Skillful in Shipping*"; King Charles II and his Navy', The Royal Stuart Society, paper no. 42, 1992.

—, *Pepys's Navy, Ships, Men and Warfare, 1649–1689*, Barnsley, 2008.

—, 'Butler, Thomas, Sixth Earl of Ossary (1634–1680)', *Oxford Dictionary of National Biography*, Oxford, 2004; online edn, May 2010. [http://www.oxforddnb.com/view/article/4210, accessed 19 December 2016].

—, 'Montagu, Edward, First Earl of Sandwich (1625–1672)', *Oxford Dictionary of National Biography*, Oxford, 2004; online edn, May 2010 [http://www.oxforddnb.com/view/article/19010, accessed 19 December 2016].

—, 'Narbrough, Sir John (*bap.* 1640, *d.* 1688)', *Oxford Dictionary of National Biography*, Oxford, 2004; online edn, January 2008 [http://www.oxforddnb.com/view/article/19776, accessed 19 December 2016].

Davis, Ralph, *The Rise of the English Shipping Industry in the 17th and 18th Centuries*, Newton Abbot, 1962.

—. 'English Foreign Trade, 1660–1700', in W. E. Minchinton, ed., *The Growth of English Overseas Trade in the Seventeenth and Eighteenth Centuries*, London, 1969, pp. 78–98.

Diamond, Master A. S., 'The Cemetery of the Resettlement', *Transactions of the Jewish Historical Society of England*, vol. XIX, London, 1960, pp. 163–90.

Duarte, Enrique Barbudo, *Diccionario Maritimo*, Cadiz, 1965.

Dyer, Florence E., *The Life of Admiral Sir John Narbrough*, London, 1931.

Earle, Peter, *The Wreck of the Almiranta*, London, 1979.

Elliott, J. H., *Empires of the Atlantic World: Britain and Spain in America 1492–1830*, New Haven and London, 2006.

Espinosa, Juan José Martínez, *Diccionario Marino*, Madrid, 1849.

Falconer, William, *An Universal Marine Dictionary*, London 1769.

Farina, L. F. and C. K. Zacher, eds, *The Genoese Cartographic Tradition and Christopher Columbus*, Rome, 1996.

Farrington, Anthony, *A Biographical Index of East India Company Maritime Service Officers 1600–1834*, London, 1999.

Ferris, John, 'Littleton, Sir Thomas, Second Baronet (1619/20?–1681)', *Oxford Dictionary of National Biography*, Oxford, 2004; online edn, January 2008 [http://www.oxforddnb.com/view/article/58142, accessed 19 December 2016].

Fox, Frank L., *The Four Days' Battle of 1666: The Greatest Sea Fight of the Age of Sail*, Barnsley, 2009.

Fraser, Antonia, 'Cromwell, Charles II and the Jews', *European Judaism*, 14, no. 2, 1980, pp. 19–24.

Goicovich, F. S., 'On the Mechanisms of Power in the Southern Forests of the Kingdom of Chile in the "Transition Stage" (1598–1683)', *Student Journal of Latin American Studies*, 1, Austin, TX, 2009, pp. 76–99.

Guarda, Gabriel, *La Sociedad en Chile austral antes de la Colonización Alemana: Valdivia, Osorno, Río Bueno, La Unión 1645–1850*, Santiago, Chile, 2006.

Halley, Edmond, 'Some Remarks on the Variations of the Magnetical Compas &c. made by E Halley; as also concerning the true Longitude of the Magellan Streights', *Philosophical Transactions of the Royal Society*, 29, 1714, pp. 165–8.

Handley, Stuart, 'Wren, Matthew (1629–1672)', *Oxford Dictionary of National Biography*, Oxford, 2004; online edn, January 2008 [http://www.oxforddnb.com/view/article/30022, accessed 19 December 2016].

Hanke, L., ed., *Los virreyes españoles en América durante el gobierno de la Casa de Austria*, Ser. Biblioteca de autores españoles, vols 273, 280–86, Madrid, 1976, 1978–80.

Harland, John, *Seamanship in the Age of Sail*, London, 1984.

Harper, Lawrence A., *The English Navigation Laws*, New York, 1973.

Harris, Graham, *A Guide to the Birds and Mammals of Coastal Patagonia*, Princeton, 1998.

Harris, John, *Navigantium atque Itinerantium Bibliotecha or a Compleat Collection of Voyages and Travels*, 2 vols, London, 1705.

Harris, Simon, *Sir Cloudesley Shovel: Stuart Admiral*, Staplehurst, 2001.

Harrison, Peter, *Seabirds: An Identification Guide*, Beckenham, 1983.

Hatfield, Commander H. R., *Admiralty Manual of Hydrographic Surveying*, vol. I, London, 1965.

Hernandez, M., C. García-Moro and C. Lalueza-Fox, 'Brief Communication: Stature Estimation in Extinct Aónikenk and the Myth of Patagonian Gigantism', *American Journal of Physical Anthropology*, 10, 1998, pp. 545–51.

Hilster, Nicolàs de, 'Observational Methods and Procedures for the Mariner's Astrolabe', *The Mariner's Mirror*, 100, no. 3, 2014, pp. 261–81.

Hoberman, Michael, *New Israel/New England*, Amherst, MA, 2011.

Howgego, Raymond John, *Encyclopedia of Exploration to 1800*, Potts Point, 2011.

Hutton, Ronald, 'Digby, George, Second Earl of Bristol (1612–1677)', *Oxford Dictionary of National Biography,* 2004; online edn, May 2009 [http://www.oxforddnb.com/view/article/7627, accessed 19 December 2016].

Hyamson, Albert, M., *The Sephardim of England: A History of the Spanish and Portuguese Jewish Community 1492–1951*, London, 1951.

Israel, Jonathan, *Diasporas within a Diaspora*, Leiden, 2002.

Jaramillo, Alvaro, *Birds of Chile*, London, 2003.

Jones, J. R., *Charles II, Royal Politician*, London, 1987.

Jones, K. L., 'Warfare, Reorganization, and Readaptation at the Margins of Spanish Rule: The Southern Margin (1573–1882)', in F. Salomon and S. Schwartz, eds, *South America*, Pt 2, The Cambridge History of the Native Peoples of the Americas, 1999, pp. 138–87.

Kaplan, Yoseph, *An Alternative Path to Modernity*, Leiden, 2000.

Keevil, J. J., *Medicine and the Navy 1200–1900*, vol. II, *1649–1714*, Edinburgh and London, 1958.

Kelly, James Williams, 'Hack, William (*fl.* 1671–1702)', *Oxford Dictionary of National Biography*, 2004; online edn [http://www.oxforddnb.com/view/article/56995, accessed 19 December 2016].

Kingsbury, Benedict and Benjamin Straumann, *The Roman Foundations of the Law of Nations: Alberico Gentili and the Justice of Empire*, Oxford, 2010.

Klooster, Wim, *Illicit Riches: Dutch Trade in the Caribbean, 1648–1795*, Leiden, 1998.

Knighton, C. S., 'Middleton, Thomas (*d.* 1672)', *Oxford Dictionary of National Biography,* Oxford, 2004; online edn, January 2008 [http://www.oxforddnb.com/view/article/66463, accessed 19 December 2016].

—. 'Smith, Sir Jeremiah (*d.* 1675)', *Oxford Dictionary of National Biography*, Oxford, 2004; online edn, January 2008 [http://www.oxforddnb.com/view/article/25828, accessed 19 December 2016].

Knox-Johnston, R. 'Practical Assessment of the Accuracy of the Astrolabe', *The Mariner's Mirror*, 99, no. 1, 2013, pp. 67–71.

Köberer, Wolfgang, 'On the Attempts to Assess the Accuracy of the Astrolabe', *The Mariner's Mirror*, 100, no. 2, 2014, pp. 198–203.

LaCombe, Michael A., 'Willoughby, Francis Fifth Baron Willoughby of Parham (*bap* 1614, *d.* 1666))', *Oxford Dictionary of National Biography*, Oxford, 2004; [http://www.oxforddnb.com/view/article 29597, accessed 12 January 2017].

Lee, Sidney, 'Coventry, Sir William (*bap.* 1627, *d.* 1686)', *Oxford Dictionary of National Biography*, Oxford, 2004; online edn, January 2008 [http://www.oxforddnb.com/view/article/6485, accessed 19 December 2016].

Lees, James, *The Masting and Rigging of English Ships of War 1625–1860*, London, 1979.

Lohmann Villena, Guillermo, *El Conde de Lemos Virrey del Perú*, Madrid, 1946.

—, *Los Americanos en las Ordénes Nobiliarias*, 2 vols, Madrid, 1993.

Lorandi, Ana María, *Spanish King of the Incas The Epic Life of Pedro Bohorques*, Pittsburgh, 2005.

Lord, Rexford D., *Mammals of South America*, Baltimore, 2007.

Lyon, David, *The Sailing Navy List: All the Ships of the Royal Navy: Built, Purchased and Captured 1688–1860*, London, 1993.

Maclean, Gordon Lindsay, *Roberts' Birds of Southern Africa*, 5th edn, Cape Town, 1985.

MacGregor, Arthur, 'Sloane, Sir Hans, baronet (1660–1753)', *Oxford Dictionary of National Biography*, Oxford, 2004 [http://www.oxforddnb.com/view/article/25730, accessed 19 December 2016].

Mariners' Museum, The, *A Dictionary of the World's Watercraft*, London, 2000.

Markham, Clements R., ed., *Narratives of the Voyages of Pedro Sarmiento de Gamboa to the Straits of Magellan,* Hakluyt Society, 1st ser., 91, London 1895.

—, *The Threshold of the Unknown Region*, 4th edn, London, 1876.

Marsden, Peter, ed. *Mary Rose: Your Noblest Shippe: Anatomy of a Tudor Warship*, 2 vols, Portsmouth, 2009.

Marshall, Alan, 'Bennet, Henry, First Earl of Arlington (*bap.* 1618, *d.* 1685)', *Oxford Dictionary of National Biography*, Oxford, 2004; online edn, January 2008 [http://www.oxforddnb.com/view/article/2104, accessed 19 December 2016].

—, 'Williamson, Sir Joseph (1633–1701)', *Oxford Dictionary of National Biography*, Oxford, 2004; online edn, January 2008 [http://www.oxforddnb.com/view/article/29571, accessed 19 December 2016].

Martinic Beros, M., 'The Meeting of Two Cultures: Indians and Colonists in the Magellan Region', in C. McEwan, L. A. Borrero and A. Prieto, eds, *Patagonia: Natural History, Prehistory, and Ethnography at the Uttermost End of the Earth*, Princeton Legacy Library, London, 1997, pp. 110–26.

McCarl, Clayton, 'Carlos Enriques Clerque as Crypto-Jewish Confidence Man in Francisco de Seyxas y Lovera's Piratas y contrabandistas (1693)', *Colonial Latin American Review*, 24, no. 3, 2015, pp. 406–20.

McConnell, Anita, 'Houghton, Sir John (1645–1705)', *Oxford Dictionary of National Biography*, Oxford, 2004 [http://www.oxforddnb.com/view/article/13868 accessed 20 December 2016].

McCusker, John J., *Money and Exchange in Europe and America 1600–1775: A Handbook*, Williamsburg, VA, 1978.

McEwan, C., L. A. Borrero and A. Prieto, eds, *Patagonia: Natural History, Prehistory, and Ethnography at the Uttermost end of the Earth*, Princeton Legacy Library, London, 1997.

McIntyre, G. S., 'Brouncker, William, Second Viscount Brouncker of Lyons (1620–1684)', *Oxford Dictionary of National Biography*, Oxford, 2004; online edn, January 2011 [http://www.oxforddnb.com/view/article/3597, accessed 1 January, 2017].

Miller, Robert Ryal, 'The Fake Inca of Tucuman: Don Pedro de Bohorques', *The Americas*, 32, no. 2, 1975, pp. 196–210.

Moore, David M., *Flora of Tierra del Fuego*, Oswestry, 1983.

Morgan, Basil, 'Hawkins, Sir John (1532–1596)', *Oxford Dictionary of National Biography*, Oxford, 2004; online edn, October 2007 [http://www.oxforddnb.com/view/article/12672, accessed 19 December 2016].

Norie, J. W., *Directions for Sailing to and from the Coast of Brazil &c.*, London, 1819.

—, *Piloting Directions for the East and West Coasts of South America &c.*, London 1825.

Norwood, Richard, *The Seaman's Practice containing a Fundamental Problem in Navigation experimentally verified*, 10th edn, London, 1732.

Oppenheim, M., *A History of the Administration of the Royal Navy and of Merchant Shipping in Relation to the Navy*, London, 1896.

O'Scanlon, Timoteo, *Diccionario Marítimo Español*, Madrid, 1831.

Pagden, Anthony, 'The Struggle for Legitimacy', in Nicholas Canny, ed., *The Origins of Empire: British Overseas Enterprise to the Close of the Seventeenth Century*, Oxford, 1988, pp. 34–54.

Peña, Martín R. de la, and Maurice Rumboll, *Birds of Southern South America and Antarctica*, Princetown, 1998.

Peñazola, F., 'The Ethnographic Imagination and the Tehuelches', *STAR (Scotland's Transatlantic Relations) Project Archive*, www.star.ac.uk April 2004.

Penrose, R. A. F., 'The Gold Regions of the Strait of Magellan and Tierra del Fuego', *Journal of Geology*, 16, no. 8, 1908, pp. 683–97.

Pepperell, Julian, *Fishes of the Open Ocean: A Natural History and Illustrated Guide*, Chicago and London, 2010.

Pinches, J. H. and R. V. Pinches, *The Royal Heraldry of England*, London, 1974.

Piponnier, Françoise, 'Cloth Merchants' Inventories in Dijon in the Fourteenth and Fifteenth Centuries', in N. B. Harte and K. G. Ponting, eds, *Cloth and Clothing in Medieval Europe: Essays in Memory of Professor E. M. Carus Wilson*, London, 1983, pp. 230–47.

Rich, Edwin Earnest, *The History of the Hudson's Bay Company*, Hudson's Bay Record Society, London 1958.

Rodger, N. A. M., *Articles of War*, Havant, 1982.

—. *The Safeguard of the Sea, a Naval History of Britain 660–1649*, London 1997.

—. *The Command of the Ocean, A Naval History of Britain, 1649–1815*, London 2004.

—. 'Anson, George, Baron Anson (1697–1762)', *Oxford Dictionary of National Biography*, Oxford, 2004; online edn, May 2008 [http://www.oxforddnb.com/view/article/574, accessed 19 December 2016].

Roa y Ursúa, Louis de, *El Reyno de Chile 1535–1810*, Valladolid, 1945.

Roy, Ian, 'Rupert, Prince and Count Palatine of the Rhine and Duke of Cumberland (1619–1682)', *Oxford Dictionary of National Biography*, Oxford, 2004; online edn, May 2011 [http://www.oxforddnb.com/view/article/24281, accessed 19 December 2016].

Ross, J. M., 'Naturalisation of Jews in England', *Transactions of the Jewish Historical Society of England*, vol. XXIV, London, 1975, pp. 59–72.

Roth, Cecil, 'The Resettlement of the Jews in England', in V. D. Lipman, ed., *Three Centuries of Anglo-Jewish History*, Cambridge, 1961, pp. 1–25.

Rye, Walter, *A Glossary of Words used in East Anglia*, London, 1895.

Sainty, J. C., *Admiralty Officials*, London, 1975.

Samuel, E. R. 'Portuguese Jews in Jacobean London', *Transactions of the Jewish Historical Society of England*, vol. XVIII, London, 1958, pp. 171–230.

Samuel, Edgar, 'The readmission of the Jews to England in 1656', *Transactions of the Jewish Historical Society of England*, vol. XXXI, Torquay, 1990, pp. 153–69.

Samuel, W.S., 'A List of Jewish Persons Endenizened and Naturalised 1609–1799', *Transactions of the Jewish Historical Society of England*, vol. XXII, London, 1970, pp. 111–44.

San Pio, Pilar Aladren and Carmen Moreno Zamaron, *Catálogo de la Colección de Vargas Ponce que posee el Museo Naval*, vol. I, Madrid, 1979.

Sandahl, Bertil, *Middle English Sea Terms*, 3 vols, Uppsala, 1951, 1958 and 1982.

Sarna, Jonathan D., Ellen Smith and Scott-Martin Kosofsky, eds, *The Jews of Boston*, New Haven, 2005.

Sauer, J. J., *The Archaeology and Ethnohistory of Araucanian Resilience*, Springer, 2014.

Schuchard, Marsha Keith, *Restoring the Temple of Vision: Cabalistic Freemasonry and Stuart Culture*, Leiden, 2002.

Seed, Patricia, *Ceremonies of Possession in Europe's Conquest of the New World 1492–1640*, Cambridge, 1995.

Shirihai, Hadoram, *A Complete Guide to Antarctic Wildlife: The Birds and Marine Mammals of the Antarctic Continent and the Southern Ocean*, 2nd edn, London, 2007.

Smith, Ellen, 'Strangers and Sojourners: The Jews of Colonial Boston', in Jonathan D. Sarna, Ellen Smith and Scott-Martin Kosofsky, eds, *The Jews of Boston*, New Haven, 2005, pp. 21–4.

Smith, J. R., *From Plane to Spheroid*, Rancho Cordova, CA, 1986.

Smith, Thomas R., 'Manuscript and Printed Sea Charts in Seventeenth Century London: The Case for the Thames School', in Norman J. W. Thrower, ed., *The Compleat Plattmaker*, Berkeley, 1978, pp. 45–100.

Smyth, Admiral W. H., *The Sailor's Word Book*, London 1867.

Smolenaars, Marja and Ann Veenhoff, 'Smith, Samuel (*bap.* 1658, *d.* 1707', *Oxford Dictionary of National Biography*, Oxford, 2004; online edn, January 2008 [http://www.oxforddnb.com/view/article/63289, accessed 19 December 2016].

South America Pilot, Vol II, Taunton, 1993, Vol III, Taunton, 1987.

Speck, W. A., 'James II and VII (1633–1701)', *Oxford Dictionary of National Biography*, Oxford, 2004; online edn, October 2009 [http://www.oxforddnb.com/view/article/14593, accessed 19 December 2016].

Strickland, Matthew and Robert Hardy, *The Great Warbow*, Sparkford, 2005.

Tanner, J. R., 'The Administration of the Navy from the Restoration to the Revolution, part I', *English Historical Review*, 12, 1897, pp. 16–66.

—, *A Descriptive Catalogue of the Naval Manuscripts in the Pepysian Library &c.*, vol. 1, Navy Records Society, vol 26; 1903.

Taylor, E. G. R., *The Mathematical Practitioners of Tudor and Stuart England*, vol. I, Cambridge, 1954.

Tedder, Arthur William, *The Navy of the Restoration: From the Death of Cromwell to the Treaty of Breda: Its Work, Growth and Influence,* Cambridge, 1916.

Thirsk, Joan, ed., *The Agrarian History of England and Wales*, vol. V, *1640–1750*, pt II, *Agrarian Change*, Cambridge, 1985.

Thorold Rogers, James, E., *A History of Agriculture and Prices in England*, vol. V, *1583–1702*, Oxford, 1887; reprint. 2011.

Troide, Lars, 'Burney, James (1750–1821)', *Oxford Dictionary of National Biography*, Oxford, 2004; online edn, September 2016 [http://www.oxforddnb.com/view/article/4080, accessed 19 December 2016].

Twiss, Sir Travers, *The Black Book of the Admiralty*, 4 vols, London, 1871.

Tyacke, Sarah, *London Map-Sellers 1660–1720*, Tring, 1978.

Unger, Richard W., *Shipping and Economic Growth 1350–1850*, Leiden, 2011.

Urbina, Maria Ximena. 'El chono Cristóbal Talcapillán y su información sobre colonias inglesas en la Patagonia Insular, 1674', *Boletín de la Academia de Historia Naval y Marítima de Chile*, 19, 2005, pp. 27–44.

—, 'La sospecha de Ingleses en el Extremo Sur de Chile, 1669–1683; Actitudes Imperiales y Locales como consucuencia de la Expedición de John Narborough', *Magallania* (Chile), 44, no. 1, 2016, pp. 15–40.

Vea, A. de, 'Relación diaria del viaje marítimo y descripción de las costas Sur', *Anuario Hidrográfico de le Marina de Chile*, XI, BN (Santiago de Chile), 1886, pp. 540–96.

Venning, Timothy, 'Werden, Sir John first baronet (1640–1716)', *Oxford Dictionary of National Biography*, Oxford, 2004; online edn, January 2008 [http://www.oxforddnb.com/view/article/29063, accessed 19 December 2016].

Williams, Glyndwr, *The Great South Sea*, New Haven and London, 1997.

Williamson, James A., *The Observations of Sir Richard Hawkins*, London, 1933.

Witsen, Nicolaes, *Nord en Oost Tartarye ... &c.*, 2 vols in 1, Amsterdam, 1705.

Wolf, Lucien, 'The Jewry of the Restoration, 1660–1664', *Transactions of the Jewish Historical Society of England*, vol. V, Edinburgh and London, 1908, pp. 5–33.

Woolf, Maurice, 'Foreign Trade of London Jews in the Seventeenth Century', *Transactions of the Jewish Historical Society of England*, vol. XXIV, London, 1975, pp. 38–58.

Charts Consulted

Servicio Hidrografía Naval de la Armada Argentina

19	Cabo Tres Puntas a Bahía Laura	1926
48	Bahía de los Nodales	1926
62	De Cabo Vírgenes a Cabo Peñas Estrecho de Magallanes	1937
H 317	De Faro Cabo Blanco a Puerto San Julián	2009
H 360	Rada Puerto Deseado	1973
H 361	Ría Deseado	1973

H 364	Puerto San Julián	1992
H 367	Puerto Santa Cruz	1981
H 413	De Puerto San Julián a Río Gallegos	2009
H 424	Estrecho de Magallen De Cabo Vírgenes a Bahía San Sebastián	1984
H 451A	Puerto Río Gallegos (Barra Exterior)	2000
H 452	Puerto Río Gallegos	1964

Servicio Higrográfico y Oceanográfico de la Armada de Chile

6241	Bahía y Puerto Corral	1989
11115	Puertos en el Estrecho de Magallanes	1958
11300	Estrecho de Magallanes Cabo Froward to Paso Tortuoso	1993
11312	Fondeaderos en el Estrecho de Magallanes	1963
11432	Bahías en el Estrecho de Magallanes	2001

United Kingdom Hydrographic Office

366	Arquipélago de Cabo Verde	1989
1692	Cabo Vírgenes to Primera Angostura	1986
1693	Primera Angostura to Segunda Angostura	1991
1694	Segunda Angostura to Punta Arenas	2000
1950	Arquipélago dos Açores	1994
3107	Puerto San Julián to Estrecho de Magallanes	1964
4245	Golfo de Arruco to Bahía Corral	2008
4250	Bahía Corral to Isla Guafo	2008
4255	Isla Guafo to Golfo de Penas	2008
4258	Golfo de Penas to Golfo Trinidad	2008
4259	Estrecho de Magallanes to Canal Trinidad	2008
4262	Paso Tortuoso to Canal Jerónimo	2006
4264	Paso del Mar to Islotes Evangelistas	2005
4265	Paso Tortuoso to Paso del Mar	2005
4266	Paso del Hambre to Paso Tortuoso	2005
4267	Paso Nuevo to Paso del Hambre	2005
4609	Valparaíso to Islas Diego Ramírez	2010

INDEX